USED $ 72.10

W9-CLP-765

R-12314

microeconomics

Paul Krugman

Princeton University

Robin Wells

Princeton University

WORTH PUBLISHERS

To beginning students everywhere, which we all were at one time.

Publisher: Catherine Woods
Executive Editor: Craig Bleyer
Acquisitions Editor: Charlie Van Wagner
Executive Development Editor: Sharon Balbos
Development Editors: Marilyn Freedman, Becky Kohn
Consultant: Andreas Bentz
Director of Market Development: Steven Rigolosi
Senior Marketing Manager: Jeffrey Rucker
Associate Managing Editor: Tracey Kuehn
Art Director, Cover Designer: Babs Reingold
Interior Designer: Babs Reingold
Layout Designer: Lee Ann Mahler
Illustrations: TSI Graphics, Paul Lacy
Photo Research Manager: Patricia Marx
Photo Editor: Ted Szczepanski
Photo Researcher: Julie Tesser
Production Manager: Barbara Anne Seixas
Composition: TSI Graphics
Printing and Binding: R. R. Donnelley and Sons

ISBN: 0-7167-5229-8 (EAN: 9780716752295)

Library of Congress Control Number: 2004113015

Printed in the United States of America

First printing 2004

Text and photo credits appear on page xxiv, which constitutes a continuation of the copyright page.

Worth Publishers
41 Madison Avenue
New York, NY 10010

www.worthpublishers.com

About the Authors

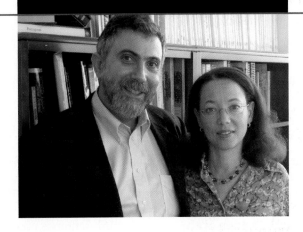

Paul Krugman is Professor of Economics at Princeton University, where he regularly teaches the principles course. He received his BA from Yale and his PhD from MIT. Prior to his current position, he taught at Yale, Stanford, and MIT. He also spent a year on the staff of the Council of Economic Advisers in 1982–1983. His research is mainly in the area of international trade, where he is one of the founders of the "new trade theory," which focuses on increasing returns and imperfect competition. He also works in international finance, with a concentration in currency crises. In 1991, Krugman received the American Economic Association's John Bates Clark medal. In addition to his teaching and academic research, Krugman writes extensively for nontechnical audiences. Krugman is a regular op-ed columnist for the *New York Times*. His latest trade book is a best-selling collection of his *Times* articles entitled *The Great Unraveling: Losing Our Way in the New Century.* His earlier books, *Peddling Prosperity* and *The Age of Diminished Expectations,* have become modern classics.

Robin Wells is Researcher in Economics at Princeton University, where she regularly teaches undergraduate courses. She received her BA from the University of Chicago and her PhD from the University of California at Berkeley; she then did postdoctoral work at MIT. She has taught at the University of Michigan, the University of Southampton (United Kingdom), Stanford, and MIT. Her teaching and research focus on the theory of organizations and incentives. She writes regularly for academic journals.

Preface

FROM PAUL

Robin and I like to think that we wrote this book with a similar principle in mind. We wanted to write a different sort of book, one in which making sure the student understands how the models apply to the real world is given as much attention as the models themselves. We wanted to adapt Orwell's principle to the writing of an economics textbook: to let the purpose of economics—to achieve a deeper understanding of the world—rather than the mechanics of economics dictate the writing.

We believe that writing in this style reflects a commitment to the reader—a commitment to approach the material from a beginner's point of view, to make the material entertaining and accessible, to make discovery a joy. That's the fun part. But we also believe that there is another, equally compelling obligation on the part of an author of a principles of economics text. Economics is an extremely powerful tool. Many of us who are economists originally started in other disciplines (I started in history, Robin in chemistry). And we fell in love with economics because we believed it offers what most other disciplines don't—a coherent worldview that offers real guidelines to making the world a better place. (Yes, most economists are idealists at heart.) But like any powerful tool, economics should be treated with great care. For us, this obligation became a commitment that students would learn the appropriate use of the models—understand their assumptions and know their limitations as well as their positive uses. Why do we care about this? Because we don't live in a "one model of the economy fits all" world. To achieve deeper levels of understanding of the real world through economics, students must learn to appreciate the kinds of trade-offs and ambiguities that economists and policy makers face when applying their models to real-world problems. We hope this approach will make students more insightful and more effective participants in our common economic, social, and political lives.

To those familiar with my academic work, this perspective will probably look familiar. There I tried to make the problem to be solved the focus, and to avoid unnecessary technique. I tried to simplify. And I tried to choose topics that had important real-world implications. Writing for a large, nontechnical audience has only reinforced and expanded these tendencies. I had to begin with the working assumption that readers initially have no reason to care about what I am writing about—that it is my responsibility to show them why they should care. So the beginning of each chapter of this book is written according to the dictum: "If you haven't hooked them by the third sentence, then you've lost them." I've also learned that about all you can take for granted in writing for a lay audience is basic numeracy—addition and subtraction, but no more than that. Concepts must be fully explained; likely confusions must be anticipated and headed off. And most of all, you must be judicious in choosing the content and pacing of the writing—don't overwhelm your reader.

FROM ROBIN

Like Paul, I wanted to write a book that appeals to students without unduly sacrificing an instructor's obligation to teach economics well. I arrived at a similar perspective on how this book should be written, but by a different path. It came from my experiences teaching economics in a business school for a few years. Facing students who were typically impatient with abstraction and often altogether unhappy to be taking economics (and who would often exact bloody revenge in teaching evaluations), I learned how important it is to "hook" the students into the subject matter. Teaching with case studies, I found that concepts had been truly learned only when students could successfully apply them. And one of the most important lessons I learned was not to patronize. We—economists, that is—often assume that people who aren't familiar with conceptual thinking aren't smart and capable. Teaching in a business school showed me otherwise. The majority of my students were smart and capable, and many had shouldered a lot of responsibility in their working lives. Although adept at solving practical problems, they weren't trained to think conceptually. I had to learn to acknowledge the practical skills that they did have, but also show them the importance of the conceptual skills they didn't have. Although I eventually returned to an economics department, the lessons I learned about teaching economics in a business school stayed with me and, I believe, have been crucial ingredients in writing this textbook.

Advantages of This Book

Despite our fine words, why should any instructor use our text? We believe our book distinguishes itself in several ways that will make your introductory economics course an easier and more successful undertaking for the following reasons:

- **Chapters build intuition through realistic examples.** In every chapter, we use real-world examples, stories, applications, and case studies to teach the core concepts and motivate student learning. We believe that the best way to introduce concepts and reinforce them is through real-world examples; students simply relate more easily to them.

- **Pedagogical features reinforce learning.** We've worked hard to craft a set of features that will be genuinely helpful to students. We describe these features in the next section, "Tools for Learning."

- **Chapters have been written to be accessible and entertaining.** We have used a fluid and friendly writing style that makes the concepts accessible. And we have tried whenever possible to use examples that are familiar to students: for example, choosing which course to take, buying a used textbook, or deciding where to eat at the food court at the local shopping mall.

- **Although easy to understand, the book also prepares students for further coursework.** Too often, instructors find that selecting a textbook means choosing between two unappealing alternatives: a textbook that is "easy to teach" but leaves major gaps in students' understanding, or a textbook that is "hard to teach" but adequately prepares students for future coursework. We have worked very hard to create an easy-to-understand textbook that offers the best of both worlds.

- **The book permits flexible yet conceptually structured use of chapters.** We recognize that many instructors will prefer to teach the chapters in a sequence different from the one found in the book. Chapters were written with this in mind. Instructors can use the chapters in any order they wish. Our overarching goal was flexibility of organization for everyone. For a detailed look at the organization of chapters and ways to use them, see pages ix through xiv of this preface.

Tools for Learning

We have structured each of the chapters around a common set of features. The following features are intended to help students learn better while also keeping them engaged.

"What You Will Learn in This Chapter"

To help readers get oriented, the first page of each chapter contains a preview of the chapter's contents, in an easy-to-review bulleted list format, that alerts students to the critical concepts and details the objectives of the chapter.

Opening Story

In contrast to other books in which each chapter begins with a recitation of some aspect of economics, we open each chapter with a compelling story that often extends through the entire chapter. Stories were chosen to accomplish two things: to illustrate important concepts in the chapter and then to encourage students to want to read on to learn more.

As we've mentioned, one of our main goals is to build intuition with realistic examples. Because each chapter is introduced with a real-world story, students will relate more easily to the material. For example, Chapter 3 teaches supply and demand in the context of a market for scalped tickets to a sports event (our opening story on page 56 is "Gretzky's Last Game"). A complete list of our opening stories appears on the inside front cover.

"Economics in Action" Case Studies

In addition to introducing chapters with vivid stories, we conclude virtually every major text section with still more examples: a real-world case study called "Economics in Action." This feature provides a short but compelling application of the major concept just covered in that section. Students will experience an immediate payoff from being able to apply the concepts they've just read about to real phenomena. For example, in Chapter 6 we use the case of eBay, the online auctioneer, to communicate the concept of efficiency (see the "Economics in Action" entitled "eBay and Efficiency" on page 151). For a complete list of all the "Economics in Action" cases in the text, see the page facing the inside front cover and also our table of contents.

Unique End-of-Section Review: "Quick Review" and "Check Your Understanding" Questions

In contrast to most other textbooks, which offer a review of concepts only at the end of each chapter, we include review material at the end of each major section within a chapter.

Economics contains a lot of jargon and abstract concepts that can quickly overwhelm the principles student. So we provide **Quick Reviews,** short bulleted summaries of concepts at the end of each major section. This review helps ensure that students understand what they have just read.

The **Check Your Understanding** feature, which appears along with every "Quick Review," consists of a short set of review questions; solutions to these questions appear at the back of the book in the section set off with a burgundy tab at the edge of each page. These questions and solutions allow students to immediately test their understanding of the section just read. If they're not getting the questions right, it's a clear signal for them to go back and reread before moving on.

The "Economics in Action" cases, followed by the "Quick Reviews" and "Check Your Understanding" questions comprise our unique end-of-section pedagogical set that encourages students to apply what they've learned (via the "Economics in Action") and then review it (with the "Quick Reviews" and "Check Your Understanding" questions). Our hope is that students will be more successful in the course if they make use of this carefully constructed set of study aids.

"For Inquiring Minds" Boxes

To further our goal of helping students build intuition with real-world examples, each chapter contains one or more "For Inquiring Minds" boxes, in which concepts are applied to real-world events in unexpected and sometimes surprising ways, generating a sense of the power and breadth of economics. These boxes help impress on students that economics can be fun despite being labeled "the dismal science."

In a Chapter 10 box, for example, students learn how prices in a budget line serve the same function as the number of points assigned to a particular food in a Weight Watchers' diet plan (see the "For Inquiring Minds" entitled "Food for Thought on Budget Constraints," on page 240.) For a list of all "For Inquiring Minds" boxes, see the page facing the inside front cover and our table of contents.

"Pitfalls" Boxes

Certain concepts are prone to be misunderstood when students are beginning their study of economics. We have tried to alert students to these mistakes in the "Pitfalls" boxes. Here common misunderstandings are spelled out and corrected—for example, the difference between increasing total cost and increasing marginal cost (see the "Pitfalls" box on this topic on page 167). For a list of all the "Pitfalls" boxes in chapters, see the table of contents.

Student-Friendly Graphs

Comprehending graphs is often one of the biggest hurdles for principles students. To help alleviate that problem, this book has been designed so that figures are large, clear, and easy for students to follow. Many contain helpful annotations—in an easy-to-see balloon label format—that link to concepts within the text. Figure captions have been written to complement the text discussion of figures and to help students more readily grasp what they're seeing.

We've worked hard to make these graphs student-friendly. For example, to help students navigate one of the stickier thickets—the distinction between a shifting curve and movement along a curve—we encourage students to see this difference by using two types of arrows: a shift arrow (⟶) and what we call a "movement-along" arrow (⟶). You can see these arrows at work in Figures 3-12 and 3-13 on pages 73 and 74.

In addition, several graphs in each chapter are accompanied by the icon **>web...**, which indicates that these graphs are available online as simulations (the graphs are animated in a Flash format and can be manipulated). Every interactive graph is accompanied by a quiz on key concepts to further help students in their work with graphs.

Helpful Graphing Appendix For students who would benefit from an explanation of how graphs are constructed, interpreted, and used in economics, we've included a detailed graphing appendix after Chapter 2 on page 41. This appendix is more comprehensive than most because we know that some students need this helpful background, and we didn't want to breeze through the material. Our hope is that this comprehensive graphing appendix will better prepare students to use and interpret the graphs in this textbook and then out in the real world (in newspapers, magazines, and elsewhere).

Definitions of Key Terms

Every key term, in addition to being defined in the text, is also placed and defined in the margin to make it easier for students to study and review.

A Look Ahead

The text of each chapter ends with an "A Look Ahead" section, a short overview of what lies ahead in upcoming chapters. This concluding section provides students with a sense of continuity among chapters.

End-of-Chapter Review

In addition to the "Quick Review" at the end of each major section, each chapter ends with a complete but brief **Summary** of the key terms and concepts. In addition, a list of the **Key Terms** is placed at the end of each chapter along with page references.

Finally, we have created for each chapter a comprehensive set of **End-of-Chapter Problems**—problems that test intuition as well as the ability to calculate important variables. Much care and attention have been devoted to the creation of these problems so that instructors can be assured that they provide a true test of students' learning.

Upcoming Variations of This Book

The text you are now holding is our introduction to microeconomics, intended for the one-semester principles course in microeconomics.

Here is an overview of other textbooks in this series:

- ➤ *Economics:* The complete version of this textbook, containing all microeconomics chapters plus the full complement of macroeconomics chapters, is intended for the two-semester principles course.

- ➤ *Macroeconomics:* The complete introduction to macroeconomics is intended for a one-semester principles course in macroeconomics.

The Organization of This Book and How to Use It

This book is organized as a series of building blocks in which conceptual material learned at one stage is clearly built upon and then integrated into the conceptual material covered in the next stage. These building blocks correspond to the ten parts into which the chapters are divided. It's equally important to remember that an instructor need not teach these parts in the same sequence as they are found in the book. We recognize that a number of chapters will be considered optional and that many instructors will prefer to teach the chapters using a different order. Chapters and sections have been written to incorporate a degree of flexibility in the sequence in which they are taught, without sacrificing conceptual continuity. So an instructor can achieve some course customization through the choice of which chapters to cover and in which order to cover them. We will give a brief overview of each part and chapter, followed by a discussion of the various ways in which an instructor can tailor this book to meet his or her needs.

Part 1: What Is Economics?

In the **Introduction, "The Ordinary Business of Life,"** students are initiated into the study of economics in the context of a shopping trip on any given Sunday in everyday America. It provides students with basic definitions of terms such as *economics*, the *invisible hand*, and *market structure*. In addition it serves as a "tour d'horizon" of economics, explaining the difference between microeconomics and macroeconomics.

In **Chapter 1, "First Principles,"** nine principles are presented and explained: four principles of individual choice, covering concepts such as opportunity cost, marginal analysis, and incentives; and five principles of interaction between individuals, covering concepts such as gains from trade, market efficiency, and market failure. In later chapters, we build intuition by frequently referring to these principles in the explanation of specific models. Students learn that these nine principles form a cohesive conceptual foundation for all of economics.

Chapter 2, "Economic Models: Trade-offs and Trade," shows students how to think like economists by using three models—the production possibility frontier, comparative advantage and trade, and the circular-flow diagram—to analyze the world around them. It gives students an early introduction to gains from trade and to international comparisons. The **Chapter 2 appendix** contains a comprehensive math and graphing review for those students and instructors who wish to cover this material.

Part 2: Supply and Demand

Chapter 3, "Supply and Demand," covers the standard material in a fresh and compelling way: supply and demand, market equilibrium, and surplus and shortage are all illustrated using an example of the market for scalped tickets to a sports event. Students learn how the demand and supply curves of scalped tickets shift in response to the announcements of a star player's impending retirement.

Chapter 4, "The Market Strikes Back," covers various types of market interventions and their consequences: price and quantity controls, inefficiency and deadweight loss, and excise taxes. Through tangible examples such as New York City rent control regulations and New York City taxi licenses, the costs generated by attempts to control markets are made real to students.

In **Chapter 5, "Elasticity,"** the actions of OPEC and their consequences for the world market for oil taken together are the real-world motivating example in our discussion of the price elasticity of demand. In this chapter, we introduce the various elasticity measures and show how elasticities are used to evaluate the incidence of an excise tax.

Part 3: Individuals and Markets

Through examples such as a market for used textbooks and eBay, students learn how markets increase welfare in **Chapter 6, "Consumer and Producer Surplus."** Although the concepts of market efficiency and deadweight loss are strongly emphasized, we also preview the ways in which a market can fail.

Chapter 7, "Making Decisions," is a unique chapter. Microeconomics is fundamentally a science of how to make decisions. But that aspect is rarely highlighted in introductory microeconomics. Rather, other textbooks place much of the emphasis on comprehending the consequences of decision making instead of on developing an understanding of how decisions should be made in any context. For example, due to the almost exclusive emphasis that economics textbooks place on marginal analysis, we believe that students are often unable to distinguish between what is and what isn't a marginal decision. To remedy this, we have included an entire section on "either-or" versus "how much" decisions—a distinction that is particularly useful in later chapters where we compare a firm's output decision to its entry/exit decision. In addition, in Chapter 7 we reprise the concept of opportunity cost; present a thorough treatment of marginal analysis; explain the concept of sunk cost; and, for instructors who wish to teach it, cover present discounted value. Full coverage of sunk cost at this point will help students later in understanding the irrelevance of fixed cost in the firm's short-run output decision. We think this chapter will be an important teaching aid because it helps students develop a deeper intuition about the common conceptual foundations of microeconomic models.

What Comes Next: The Firm or the Consumer? You may have noticed that we have placed the chapters covering the producer before the chapters covering the consumer. Why have we done this? Because we believe that it is a more natural conceptual progression to cover the producer after Chapter 7, "Making Decisions," than it is to cover the consumer. Since students have just studied opportunity cost, economic profit versus accounting profit, marginal benefit and marginal cost, and sunk cost, we think examining the firm's cost curves, its output decision, and its entry/exit decision is an easier next step for them to undertake.

We are aware that some instructors are likely to be skeptical of this approach. We have often heard instructors say that the consumer should be studied before the producer because students can relate to being a consumer but not to being the owner of a firm. We hope, however, to change that viewpoint because what we really want students to do is not just relate to being a consumer but *think like a rational consumer—a consumer who maximizes utility subject to scarce resources.* And we believe that it is easier for students to understand utility maximization (utility being an inherently slippery concept) after they have come to understand profit maximization.

Nonetheless, we want to strongly emphasize that it is very easy for instructors who wish to follow a traditional chapter sequence—with the consumer before the firm—to do just that. We wrote the chapters so that there is no loss whatsoever if an instructor follows Chapter 7 with Chapter 10, "The Rational Consumer," and Chapter 11, "Consumer Preferences and Consumer Choice" (an optional chapter).

Part 4: The Producer

In Chapter 8, "Behind the Supply Curve: Inputs and Costs," we develop the production function and the various cost measures of the firm. There is an extensive discussion of the difference between average cost and marginal cost, illustrated by examples such as a student's grade point average. **Chapter 9, "Perfect Competition and the Supply Curve,"** explains the output decision of the perfectly competitive firm, its entry/exit decision, the industry supply curve, and the equilibrium of a perfectly competitive market. We draw on examples such as generic pharmaceuticals and the California energy crisis of 2000–2001 to contrast the behavior of oligopolists and monopolists.

Part 5: The Consumer

Chapter 10, "The Rational Consumer," provides a complete treatment of consumer behavior for instructors who don't cover indifference curves. There is a simple, intuitive exposition of the budget line, the optimal consumption choice, diminishing marginal utility, and income and substitution effects and their relationship to market demand. Students learn, for example, that a budget line constructed using prices is much like a Weight Watchers' diet plan constructed using a "point" system. **Chapter 11, "Consumer Preferences and Consumer Choice,"** offers a more detailed treatment for those who wish to cover indifference curves. It contains an analysis of the optimal consumption choice using the marginal rate of substitution as well as income and substitution effects.

What Comes Next: Markets and Efficiency or Market Structure? Many instructors are likely to consider the next two chapters—Chapter 12, "Factor Markets and the Distribution of Income," and Chapter 13 "Efficiency and Equity"—optional. For those who wish to skip them, the next topic area will be market structure beyond perfect competition: monopoly, oligopoly, and monopolistic competition. Chapters 12 and 13 are likely to be used by instructors who want more in-depth coverage of microeconomics, as well as those who wish to emphasize labor markets, welfare, and public policy issues.

Instructors who prefer a traditional sequence of topics may wish to go from Part 5 ("The Consumer") to Part 4 ("The Producer") to Part 7 ("Market Structure: Beyond Perfect Competition"), bypassing Part 6 ("Markets and Efficiency") altogether or covering it later. This is a good choice for those who wish to contrast the difference between the perfectly competitive firm's output decision and the monopolist's output decision. But, those who follow the existing chapter sequence—"The Producer" followed by "The Consumer" followed by "Market Structure: Beyond Perfect Competition"—will be able to draw a tighter connection among consumer behavior, monopoly pricing, price discrimination, product differentiation, and monopolistic competition. We have written the chapters so that either sequence works equally well.

Part 6: Markets and Efficiency

Chapter 12, "Factor Markets and the Distribution of Income," covers the competitive factor market model and the factor distribution of income. It also contains modifications and alternative interpretations of the labor market: the efficiency-wage model of the labor market is discussed, and the influences of education, discrimination, and market power are also addressed. It presents, we hope, a balanced and well-rounded view of the strengths and limitations of the competitive market model of labor markets and leads to a greater appreciation of the issues of efficiency and equity discussed in the next chapter. For instructors who covered indifference curves in Chapter 11, the **Chapter 12 appendix** offers a detailed examination of the labor-leisure trade-off and the backward-bending labor supply curve.

In **Chapter 13, "Efficiency and Equity,"** after recapping efficiency in a single market, we compare and contrast this to what it means to have efficiency in a market economy as a whole. Some may wonder why it is useful to draw the distinction between partial equilibrium and general equilibrium in a principles course. We believe that doing so gives students a deeper understanding of the often-conflicting objectives of efficiency and equity—something that really can't be fully explored in a partial equilibrium setting. As a real-world example, we discuss the reunification of West and East Germany in terms of the trade-offs faced by German policy makers, who sacrificed some efficiency-enhancing measures in order to reduce the income differences between East and West Germans. Students should come away from this chapter with a fuller appreciation of the complexity of real-world economic policy making—that is, how democracies may sometimes choose to sacrifice some efficiency for equity purposes.

Part 7: Market Structure: Beyond Perfect Competition

Chapter 14, "Monopoly," is a full treatment of monopoly, including topics such as price discrimination and the welfare effects of monopoly. We provide an array of compelling examples, such as De Beers Diamonds, price manipulation by California power companies, and airline ticket–pricing. In **Chapter 15, "Oligopoly,"** we present basic game theory in both a one-shot and repeated-game context, as well as an integrated treatment of the kinked demand curve model. The models are applied to a wide set of actual examples, such as Archer Daniels Midland, a European vitamin cartel, OPEC, and airline ticket–pricing wars. In **Chapter 16, "Monopolistic Competition and Product Differentiation,"** students are brought face to face early on with an example of monopolistic competition that is a familiar feature of their lives: the food court at the local mall. We go on to cover entry and exit, efficiency considerations, and advertising in monopolistic competition.

What Comes Next: Extending Market Boundaries or Microeconomics and Public Policy? The next section of the book, "Extending Market Boundaries," is devoted to applications and extensions of the competitive market model: Chapter 17, "International Trade," and Chapter 18, "Uncertainty, Risk, and Private Information." Both of these chapters are entirely optional. Instructors who prefer to skip one or both of these chapters can proceed to the following section, "Microeconomics and Public Policy."

Part 8: Extending Market Boundaries

In Chapter 2, we presented a full exposition of gains from trade and the difference between comparative and absolute advantage, illustrated with an international example (trade between high-wage and low-wage countries). **Chapter 17, "International Trade,"** builds on that material. It contains a recap of comparative advantage, traces the sources of comparative advantage, considers tariffs and quotas, and explores the politics of trade protection. In response to current events, we give in-depth coverage to the controversy over imports from low-wage countries.

The inclusion in a principles text of **Chapter 18, "Uncertainty, Risk, and Private Information,"** may come as a surprise to some—a common reaction being "Isn't this material too hard for principles students?" We believe that, with our treatment, the answer is "no" for many more students than is typically expected. In this chapter we explain attitudes toward risk in a careful and methodical way, grounded in the basic concept of diminishing marginal utility. This allows us to analyze a simple competitive insurance market, and to examine the benefits and limits of diversification. Next comes an easily comprehensible and intuitive presentation of private information in the context of adverse selection and moral hazard, with illustrations drawn from the market for lemons (used cars) and franchising. We believe that instructors will be surprised by how easy it is to teach this material and how much it will enlighten students about the relevance of economics to their everyday lives.

Part 9: Microeconomics and Public Policy

Chapter 19, "Externalities," covers negative externalities and solutions such as Coasian private trades, emissions taxes, and a system of tradable permits. We also examine positive externalities, technological spillovers, and the resulting arguments for industrial policy. Chapter 20, "Public Goods and Common Resources," makes an immediate impression by opening with the story of how "The Great Stink of 1858" compelled Londoners to build a public sewer system. Students learn how to classify goods into four categories (private goods, common resources, public goods, and artificially scarce goods) based on two dimensions: excludability and rivalry in consumption. With this system, they can develop an intuitive understanding of why some goods but not others can be efficiently managed by markets.

Chapter 21, "Taxes, Social Insurance, and Income Distribution," begins with a review of the burden of taxation and considerations of equity versus efficiency. Next, it examines the structure of taxes, current tax policy, and public spending in the United States. This is followed by an investigation into the sources of poverty and their implications for government tax and transfer policies. From this chapter, students can gain an appreciation of the difficult questions policy makers face in addressing issues of economic efficiency and welfare.

Part 10: New Directions for Markets

The final section of the book contains one chapter, Chapter 22, "Technology, Information Goods, and Network Externalities."

We believe that Chapter 22, even though providing real economic models and relevant cases, will be enjoyable for both instructors and students. Starting with the example of sharing music files over the Internet, it introduces the concept of information goods and network externalities and analyzes the problems they cause for efficient pricing. We discuss the implications for standard-setting and the ambiguities that network externalities present for regulatory policy. Students will see how these issues affect their

daily lives through references to Kazaa, Apple Computers, and Microsoft.

What's Core, What's Optional?

As noted earlier, we realize that some of our chapters will be considered optional. On the facing page is a listing of what we view as core chapters and those that could be considered optional. We've annotated the list of optional chapters to indicate what they cover should you wish to consider incorporating them into your course.

A Selection of Possible Outlines

To illustrate how instructors can use this book to meet their specific goals, we've constructed a selection of three possible outlines (see page xiv). By no means exclusive, these outlines reflect a likely range of different ways in which this book could be used:

➤ **Traditional Outline** (consumer first, producer second)
➤ **Public Policy and Welfare Outline** (includes factor markets and efficiency)
➤ **Applied Microeconomics Outline** (includes international trade and uncertainty, risk, and private information)

Although we don't outline it here, we also offer a Decision-Based Outline. The choice between a Traditional Outline and the Decision-Based Outline is primarily a choice about the sequencing of Parts 4 and 5. An instructor who prefers to cover "The Consumer" before "The Producer" will choose the Traditional Outline. An instructor who wants to emphasize decision making should instead cover "The Producer" before "The Consumer," just covering Parts 4 and 5 as ordered.

At this point, instructors can skip immediately to Part 7, to cover monopoly, oligopoly, and monopolistic competition. However, instructors who wish to focus more intensely on international economics, tools of microeconomics, or public policy (the Applied Microeconomics Outline or the Public Policy and Welfare Outline) may choose to teach Part 6, which addresses factor markets and economy-wide efficiency, before moving on to Part 7. After Part 7, instructors who have adopted an applied microeconomics or public policy focus may wish to cover some or all of Part 8, which contains a chapter on international trade and a chapter on risk and private information. Others, however, will prefer to skip to Part 9, which covers externalities, public goods, common resources, and tax policy. Finally, Part 10, consisting solely of Chapter 22 on the network economy, is a suitable choice for any of these outlines. But it will be a particularly good chapter for those who wish to focus on public policy.

WHAT'S CORE, WHAT'S OPTIONAL: AN OVERVIEW

Core

1. **First Principles**
2. **Economic Models: Trade-offs and Trade**

3. **Supply and Demand**
4. **The Market Strikes Back**
5. **Elasticity**
6. **Consumer and Producer Surplus**

8. **Behind the Supply Curve: Inputs and Costs**
9. **Perfect Competition and the Supply Curve**
10. **The Rational Consumer**

14. **Monopoly**
15. **Oligopoly**
16. **Monopolistic Competition and Product Differentiation**

19. **Externalities**
20. **Public Goods and Common Resources**
21. **Taxes, Social Insurance, and Income Distribution**

Optional

Introduction: The Ordinary Business of Life

Appendix: Graphs in Economics
A comprehensive review of graphing and math for students who would find such a refresher helpful.

7. **Making Decisions**
A unique chapter aimed at helping students understand how decisions should be made in any context. Includes coverage of marginal analysis and cost-benefit analysis. Pairs well with Chapter 6. Prepares students for coverage of models in upcoming chapters.

11. **Consumer Preferences and Consumer Choice**
This chapter offers a more detailed treatment of consumer behavior for instructors who wish to cover indifference curves.

12. **Factor Markets and the Distribution of Income Plus Appendix: Indifference Curve Analysis of Labor Supply**
For instructors who want to go more in depth, this chapter covers the efficiency-wage model of the labor market as well as the influences of education, discrimination, and market power. The appendix examines the labor-leisure trade-off and the backward-bending labor supply curve.

13. **Efficiency and Equity**
A unique chapter that explores what it means to have efficiency in a market economy as a whole. Gives students a deeper understanding of the often-conflicting objectives of efficiency and equity. Intended for instructors who emphasize welfare and public policy issues.

17. **International Trade**
This chapter recaps comparative advantage, considers tariffs and quotas, and explores the politics of trade protection. Coverage here links back to the international coverage in Chapter 2.

18. **Uncertainty, Risk, and Private Information**
A unique, applied chapter that explains attitudes toward risk, examines the benefits and limits of diversification, and considers private information in the context of adverse selection and moral hazard.

22. **Technology, Information Goods, and Network Externalities**
A unique chapter that shows students how to use economic models to analyze information goods. A nice treat for students and instructors!

THREE POSSIBLE OUTLINES

Traditional	Public Policy and Welfare	Applied Microeconomics

Traditional

Part 1
1. First Principles
2. Economic Models: Trade-offs and Trade

   Appendix: Graphs in Economics

Part 2
3. Supply and Demand
4. The Market Strikes Back
5. Elasticity

Part 3
6. Consumer and Producer Surplus
7. Making Decisions

Part 5*
10. The Rational Consumer
11. Consumer Preferences and Consumer Choice

Part 4*
8. Behind the Supply Curve: Inputs and Costs
9. Perfect Competition and the Supply Curve

Part 7
14. Monopoly
15. Oligopoly
16. Monopolistic Competition and Product Differentiation

Part 9
19. Externalities
20. Public Goods and Common Resources
21. Taxes, Social Insurance, and Income Distribution

Public Policy and Welfare

Part 1
1. First Principles
2. Economic Models: Trade-offs and Trade

   Appendix: Graphs in Economics

Part 2
3. Supply and Demand
4. The Market Strikes Back
5. Elasticity

Part 3
6. Consumer and Producer Surplus
7. Making Decisions

Either **Part 4, then 5** Or, **Part 5, then Part 4**

Part 6
12. Factor Markets and the Distribution of Income

   Appendix: Indifference Curve Analysis of Labor Supply
13. Efficiency and Equity

Part 7
14. Monopoly
15. Oligopoly
16. Monopolistic Competition and Product Differentiation

Part 8
17. International Trade
18. Uncertainty, Risk, and Private Information

Part 9
19. Externalities
20. Public Goods and Common Resources
21. Taxes, Social Insurance, and Income Distribution

Part 10
22. Technology, Information Goods, and Network Externalities

Applied Microeconomics

Part 1
1. First Principles
2. Economic Models: Trade-offs and Trade

   Appendix: Graphs in Economics

Part 2
3. Supply and Demand
4. The Market Strikes Back
5. Elasticity

Part 3
6. Consumer and Producer Surplus
7. Making Decisions

Either **Part 4, then 5** Or, **Part 5, then Part 4**

Part 6
12. Factor Markets and the Distribution of Income

   Appendix: Indifference Curve Analysis of Labor Supply
13. Efficiency and Equity

Part 7
14. Monopoly
15. Oligopoly
16. Monopolistic Competition and Product Differentiation

Part 8
17. International Trade
18. Uncertainty, Risk, and Private Information

Part 9
19. Externalities
20. Public Goods and Common Resources
21. Taxes, Social Insurance, and Income Distribution

*Instructors who wish to follow a decision-based sequence should use the parts of this text as we've ordered them: Part 4, "The Producer," followed by Part 5, "The Consumer."

Supplements and Media

Worth Publishers is pleased to offer an exciting and useful supplements and media package to accompany this textbook. The package has been crafted to help instructors teach their principles course and to help students grasp concepts more readily.

The entire package has been coordinated by Martha Olney, University of California-Berkeley, to provide consistency in level and quality. Rosemary Cunningham, Agnes Scott College, has coordinated all of the quizzing materials in the Study Guide, Test Bank, and all the online materials to guarantee uniformity.

Since accuracy is so critically important, all the supplements have been scrutinized and double-checked by members of the supplements team, reviewers, and a team of additional accuracy checkers. The time and care that have been put into the supplements and media ensure a seamless package.

Companion Website for Students and Instructors

econ X change

(www.worthpublishers.com/krugmanwells)
The companion website for the Krugman/Wells text offers valuable tools for both the instructor and students.

For instructors, this completely customized website offers many opportunities for quizzing and, most important, powerful grading tools. The site gives you the ability to track students' interaction with the Homework Advantage Center, the Practice Quizzing Center, and the Graphing Center by accessing separate online gradebooks for each category.

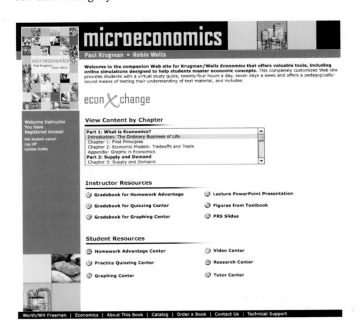

For students, the site offers many opportunities to practice, practice, practice. On the site, students can find online simulations, practice quizzes, video resources, graphing tutorials, and links to many other resources designed to help them master economic concepts. In essence, this site provides students with a virtual study guide, twenty-four hours a day, seven days a week by offering a pedagogically sound means of testing their understanding of text material.

This helpful, powerful site contains the following:

Homework Advantage Center This section of the site offers a secure, interactive, online environment. It allows you to create customized homework assignments, quizzes, or tests.

Selected end-of-chapter questions from the textbook have been incorporated into an online quizzing engine that allows the variables of each question to be algorithmically generated. Questions from the textbook's Test Bank are also incorporated into this engine with the same algorithmic generation capabilities. You can add your own questions or edit the questions provided by Worth.

The Homework Advantage Center enables you to create a customized test for each and every student. Although each student will be asked the same question, the values of those questions will be completely different. Using the Homework Advantage Center, you can easily create and assign tests for automatic grading. You can also use the Homework Advantage Center to allow students to test their own skills and diagnose their understanding of the material.

All the student responses are stored in an electronic gradebook so that you can easily grade exams and generate reports. The gradebook has the following features that allow for flexibility in assessing students' abilities.

- Grades can be organized into as many as 25 related categories (tests, papers, homework, etc.).

- Assignments can be independently weighted.

- Letter grade cutoffs can be adjusted, and custom grading created ("Fair," "Good," "Excellent," and so on).

- Assignment scores and category averages can be entered or displayed as percentages, points, letter grades, or according to your own customized grading scheme.

- Gradebooks can be set up to report final averages as points earned across all categories.

- Student properties can include ID number, password (for online testing), e-mail address, and status (active, withdraw, incomplete).

- Grades can be dropped manually or automatically.

- Assignment, category, and final scores can be curved.

> Numerous reports can be customized and printed with an interactive print preview.

> Results can be merged from TheTestingCenter.Com.

> Student rosters can be imported and exported.

Practice Quizzing Center Developed by Debbie Mullin, University of Colorado-Colorado Springs, this quizzing engine provides 20 multiple-choice questions per chapter with appropriate feedback and page references to the textbook. The questions as well as the answer choices are randomized to give students a different quiz with every refresh of the screen. All student answers are saved in an online database that can be accessed by instructors.

Graphing Center Developed by Cadre LLC in conjunction with Debbie Mullin, University of Colorado-Colorado Springs, the Graphing Center includes selected graphs from the textbook that have been animated in a Flash format, allowing students to manipulate curves and plot data points when appropriate. Approximately five graphs from each chapter have been animated and are identified in the textbook by a web icon **>web...** within the appropriate figure. Having the ability to manipulate graphs and observe the results of the manipulation provides students with a keen understanding of the effects of the shifts and movements of the curves. Every interactive graph is accompanied by questions that quiz students on key concepts from the textbook and provide instructors with feedback on student progress. Student responses and interactions are tracked and stored in an online database that can be accessed by the instructor.

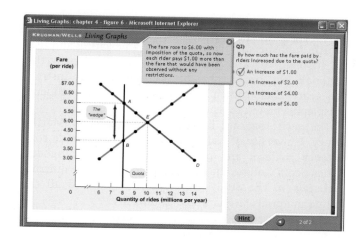

Research Center Created and continually updated by Jules Kaplan, University of Colorado-Boulder, the Research Center allows students to easily and effectively locate outside resources and readings that relate to topics covered in the textbook. It lists web addresses that hotlink to relevant websites; each URL is accompanied by a detailed description of the site and its relevance to each chapter, allowing students to conduct research and explore related readings on specific topics with ease. Also hotlinked are relevant articles by Paul Krugman and other leading economists.

Video Center In video interviews, the text's authors, Paul Krugman and Robin Wells, comment on specific aspects of each chapter and their relevance to students' lives. Each video is embedded in a Flash format with other pedagogical features and a running transcript of the authors' remarks. Videos can be presented in class to generate discussion or assigned as homework to give students a deeper understanding of key topics in the textbook.

Tutor Center Created by Can Erbil, Brandeis University, this PowerPoint presentation is ideal for students who need extra help in understanding the concepts in each chapter. The PowerPoint presentations for each chapter come complete with animations, notes, summaries, and graphics. This tool enables students to review and practice and helps them to more readily grasp economic concepts. The Tutor Center nicely complements the already extensive learning apparatus within the text itself.

Additional Student Supplements

Student CD-ROM This CD-ROM contains all of the multimedia content found on the Krugman/Wells Companion website, including the practice quizzes, interactive graphs, Krugman/Wells videos, and the student PowerPoint slides. This CD-ROM is ideal for students with limited web access or for use in a lab setting. Available upon request, this CD can be packaged with the textbook at no additional cost to the student.

Study Guide Prepared by Rosemary Cunningham, Agnes Scott College, and Elizabeth Sawyer-Kelley, University of Wisconsin-Madison, and coordinated by Martha Olney, University of California-Berkeley, the Study Guide reinforces the topics and key concepts covered in the text. For each chapter, the Study Guide provides an introduction, fill-in-the-blank chapter review, learning tips with graphical analysis, four or five comprehensive problems and exercises, 20 multiple-choice questions, and solutions to all fill-in-the-blank reviews, problems, exercises, and quizzes found within the Study Guide.

Additional Instructor Supplements

Instructor's Resource Manual The Instructor's Resource Manual written by Diane Keenan, Cerritos Community College, and coordinated by Martha Olney, University of California-Berkeley, is an ideal resource for instructors teaching principles of economics. The manual includes:

➤ Chapter-by-chapter learning objectives

➤ Chapter outlines

➤ Teaching tips and ideas

➤ Hints on how to create student interest

➤ Common misunderstandings that are typical among students

➤ Activities that can be conducted in or out of the classroom

➤ Detailed solutions to every end-of-chapter problem from the textbook

Printed Test Bank The Test Bank, coordinated by Rosemary Cunningham, Agnes Scott College, with contributing authors Jack Chambless, Valencia Community College; Ardeshir Dalal, Northern Illinois University; Mark Funk, University of Arkansas-Little Rock; Lynn Gillette, University of Kentucky; Gus W. Herring, Brookhaven College; and Ranita Wyatt, Dallas Community College District, provides a wide range of creative and versatile questions ranging in levels of difficulty. Selected questions are paired with original graphs and graphs from the textbook to reinforce comprehension. Totaling over 2,500 questions, the Test Bank offers 60 multiple-choice questions and 20 true/false questions per chapter assessing comprehension, interpretation, analysis, and synthesis. Each question is conveniently cross referenced to the page number in the text where the appropriate topic is discussed. Questions have been checked by the entire supplements team, reviewed extensively, and checked again for accuracy.

Diploma 6.3 Computerized Test Bank The Krugman/Wells printed Test Bank is also available in CD-ROM format, powered by Brownstone, for both Windows and Macintosh users. With Diploma, you can easily create tests, write and edit questions, and create study sessions for students. You can add an unlimited number of questions, scramble questions, and include pictures, equations, and multimedia links. Tests can be printed in a wide range of formats or administered to students with Brownstone's network or Internet testing software. The software's unique synthesis of flexible word-processing and database features creates a program that is extremely intuitive and capable. With the new Diploma 6.3, you can:

➤ Work with complete word processing functions (including creating tables).

➤ Work with myriad question formats, including multiple choice, true/false, short answer, matching, fill in the blank, and essay.

➤ Attach feedback (rationales) to questions (or answers).

➤ Create, install, and use an unlimited number of question banks.

➤ Incorporate references (including tables, figures, and case studies).

➤ Attach customized instructions.

➤ Use multiple graphic formats (BMP, DIB, RLE, DXF, EPS, FPX, GIF, IMG, JPG, PCD, PCX, DCX, PNG, TGA, TIF, WMF, and WPG).

➤ Take advantage of a powerful algorithm engine for complex, dynamic question types and dynamic equations.

➤ Export self-grading tests (in HTML formats) for use with web browsers.

➤ Export test files in Rich Text File format for use with any word-processing program.

➤ Export test files to EDU, WebCT, and Blackboard course management systems.

➤ Preview and re-format tests before printing them.

➤ Include custom splash screens that feature graphics or images.

➤ Post tests to Diploma's online testing site, TheTestingCenter.com.

This computerized Test Bank is accompanied by a gradebook that enables you to record students' grades throughout a course; it also includes the capacity to track student records and view detailed analyses of test items, curve tests, generate reports, add weights to grades, and allows you to:

- Organize grades into as many as 25 related categories.
- Adjust letter grade cutoffs and create customized grading.
- Enter/display assignment scores and category averages as percentages, points, letter grades, or according to your own customized grading scheme.
- Report final averages as points earned across all categories.
- Customize student properties (including ID number, password, e-mail address, and status).
- Drop grades either manually or automatically.
- Import and export student rosters.

Diploma Online Testing at www.brownstone.net is another useful tool within the Brownstone software that allows instructors to provide online exams for students using Test Bank questions. With Diploma, you can easily create and administer secure exams over a network and over the Internet, with questions that incorporate multimedia and interactive exercises. The program allows you to restrict tests to specific computers or time blocks, and it includes an impressive suite of gradebook and result-analysis features.

PowerPoint Slides Created by Can Erbil, Brandeis University, the enhanced PowerPoint presentation slides are designed to assist you with lecture preparation and presentation by providing original animations, graphs from the textbook, data tables, and bulleted lists of key concepts suitable for large lecture presentation. Although the slides are organized by topic from the text's table of contents, you can customize these slides to suit your individual needs by adding your own data, questions, and lecture notes. You can access these files on the instructor's side of the website or on the Instructor's Resource CD-ROM.

Instructor's Resource CD-ROM Using the Instructor's Resource CD-ROM, you can easily build classroom presentations around a variety of still and moving images—from the Krugman/Wells text, from your own sources, and even from the web. This customized presentation CD-ROM contains all text figures (in JPEG and GIF formats), video clips of interviews with Paul Krugman and Robin Wells, animated graphs, and enhanced PowerPoint slides. All of these resources are compatible with Microsoft PowerPoint software but can also be used independently to create a classroom presentation providing an unbeatable combination of convenience and power. This CD allows you to combine all of the publisher-provided instructor materials with your own materials into a customized presentation suitable for all lecture needs.

Overhead Transparencies Worth is also happy to provide you with more than 200 vivid color acetates of text figures designed for superior projection quality.

Web-CT E-pack The Krugman/Wells WebCT E-Packs enable you to create a thorough, interactive, and pedagogically sound online course or course website. The Krugman/Wells E-Pack provides you with cutting-edge online materials that facilitate critical thinking and learning, including course outlines, preprogrammed quizzes, links, activities, threaded discussion topics, animated graphs, and a whole array of other materials. Best of all, this material is pre-programmed and fully functional in the WebCT environment. Prebuilt materials eliminate hours of course-preparation work and offer significant support as you develop your online course. You can also obtain a WebCT-formatted version of the text's test bank.

Blackboard The Krugman/Wells Blackboard Course Cartridge allows you to combine Blackboard's popular tools and easy-to-use interface with the Krugman/Wells' text-specific, rich web content, including course outlines, preprogrammed quizzes, links, activities, interactive graphs, and a whole array of other materials. The result: an interactive, comprehensive online course that allow for effortless implementation, management, and use. The Worth electronic files are organized and prebuilt to work within the Blackboard software and can be easily downloaded from the Blackboard content showcases directly onto your department server. You can also obtain a Blackboard-formatted version of the book's test bank.

Aplia Aplia, founded by Paul Romer, Stanford University, is the first web-based company to integrate pedagogical features from a textbook with interactive media. Specifically designed for use with the Krugman/Wells text, the figures, end-of-chapter problems, boxes, text, and other pedagogical resources have been combined with Aplia's interactive media to save time for professors and encourage students to exert more effort in their learning.

The integrated online version of the Aplia media and the Krugman/Wells text includes:

- Extra problem sets suitable for homework and keyed to specific topics from each chapter
- Regularly updated news analyses
- Real-time online simulations of market interactions
- Interactive tutorials to assist with math
- Graphs and statistics
- Instant online reports that allow instructors to target student trouble areas more efficiently

With Aplia, you retain complete control and flexibility for your course. You choose the topics you want students to cover, and you decide how to organize it. You decide whether online activities are practice (ungraded or graded). You can even edit the Aplia content—making cuts or addtions as you see fit for your course.

For a preview of Aplia materials and to learn more, visit http://www.aplia.com.

Dallas TeleLearning videos The Krugman/Wells text was chosen to accompany the economics telecourse developed by the Dallas Community College District (DCCCD). For use in class, instructors have access to videos produced by the DCCCD, the nation's leading developer of distance-learning materials. These videos dramatize key economic concepts and can be used in a classroom setting.

EduCue Personal Response System (PRS)—"Clickers"
Instructors can create a dynamic, interactive classroom environment with a personal response system, powered by EduCue. This wireless remote system allows you to ask your students questions, record their responses, and calculate grades instantly during lectures. Students use a hand-held wireless device (about the size of a television remote control) to transmit immediate feedback to a lecture hall receiver.

Wall Street Journal Edition For adopters of the Krugman/Wells text, Worth Publishers and the *Wall Street Journal* are offering a ten-week subscription to students at a tremendous savings. Professors also receive their own free *Wall Street Journal* subscription plus additional instructor supplements created exclusively by the *Wall Street Journal*. Please contact your local sales rep for more information or go to the *Wall Street Journal* online at www.wsj.com.

Financial Times Edition For adopters of the Krugman/Wells text, Worth Publishers and the *Financial Times* are offering a fifteen-week subscription to students at a tremendous savings. Professors also receive their own free *Financial Times* subscription for one year. Students and professors may access research and archived information at www.ft.com.

Acknowledgments

Writing a textbook is a team effort and we could never have reached this point without all of the talented and thoughtful consultants, reviewers, focus-group participants, class testers, and others who have been so generous with their insights on our work.

We are indebted to the following reviewers and other consultants for their suggestions and advice on portions of our manuscript:

Lee Adkins, *Oklahoma State University*
Elena Alvarez, *State University of New York, Albany*
David A. Anderson, *Centre College*
Sheryl Ball, *Virginia Polytechnic Institute and State University*
Charles L. Ballard, *Michigan State University*
Richard Barrett, *University of Montana*
Daniel Barszcz, *College of DuPage*
Charles A. Bennett, *Gannon University*
Andreas Bentz, *Dartmouth College*
Harmanna Bloemen, *Houston Community College*
Michael Bordo, *Rutgers University, NBER*
James Bradley, Jr., *University of South Carolina*
William Branch, *University of Oregon*
Michael Brandl, *University of Texas, Austin*
Charles Callahan, III, *State University of New York, College at Brockport*
Leonard A. Carlson, *Emory University*
Shirley Cassing, *University of Pittsburgh*
Jim Cobbe, *Florida State University*
Eleanor D. Craig, *University of Delaware*
Rosemary Thomas Cunningham, *Agnes Scott College*
James Cypher, *California State University, Fresno*
Susan Dadres, *Southern Methodist University*
Ardeshir Dalal, *Northern Illinois University*
A. Edward Day, *University of Texas, Dallas*
Stephen J. DeCanio, *University of California, Santa Barbara*
J. Bradford DeLong, *University of California, Berkeley*
Jim Eden, *Portland Community College*
Can Erbil, *Brandeis University*
Joe Essuman, *University of Wisconsin, Waukesha*
David W. Findlay, *Colby College*
Oliver Franke, *Athabasca University*
Rhona Free, *Eastern Connecticut State University*
Susan Gale, *New York University*
J. Robert Gillette, *University of Kentucky*
Lynn G. Gillette, *University of Kentucky*
James N. Giordano, *Villanova University*
Robert Godby, *University of Wyoming*
David Goodwin, *University of New Brunswick*
Lisa Grobar, *California State University, Long Beach*
Philip Grossman, *St. Cloud State University*
Wayne Grove, *Syracuse University*
Jang-Ting Guo, *University of California, Riverside*
Jonathan Hamilton, *University of Florida*
Julie Heath, *University of Memphis*
Jill M. Hendrickson, *University of the South*
David Horlacher, *Middlebury College*
Robert Horn, *James Madison University*
Scott Houser, *California State University, Fresno*
Patrik T. Hultberg, *University of Wyoming*
Nancy Jianakoplos, *Colorado State University*

Donn Johnson, *Quinnipiac University*

Bruce Johnson, *Centre College*

James Jozefowicz, *Indiana University of Pennsylvania*

Matthew Kahn, *Columbia University*

Barry Keating, *University of Notre Dame*

Diane Keenan, *Cerritos College*

Bill Kerby, *California State University, Sacramento*

Kyoo Kim, *Bowling Green University*

Philip King, *San Francisco State University*

Sharmila King, *University of the Pacific*

Kala Krishna, *Penn State University, NBER*

Tom Larson, *California State University, Los Angeles*

Susan K. Laury, *Georgia State University*

Jim Lee, *Texas A&M University—Corpus Christi*

Tony Lima, *California State University, Hayward*

Rachel McCulloch, *Brandeis University*

Diego Mendez-Carbajo, *Illinois Wesleyan University*

Juan Mendoza, *State University of New York at Buffalo*

Jeffrey Michael, *Towson University*

Jenny Minier, *University of Miami*

Ida A. Mirzaie, *John Carroll University*

Kristen Monaco, *California State University, Long Beach*

W. Douglas Morgan, *University of California, Santa Barbara*

Peter B. Morgan, *University of Michigan*

John A. Neri, *University of Maryland*

Seamus O'Cleireacain, *Columbia University / State University of New York, Purchase*

Martha Olney, *University of California, Berkeley*

Chris Papageorgiou, *Louisiana State University*

John Pharr, *Dallas County Community College*

Raymond E. Polchow, *Zane State College*

Jeffrey Racine, *University of South Florida*

Matthew Rafferty, *Quinnipiac University*

Dixie Watts Reaves, *Virginia Polytechnic Institute and State University*

Siobhán Reilly, *Mills College*

Thomas Rhoads, *Towson University*

Libby Rittenberg, *Colorado College*

Michael Rolleigh, *Williams College*

Christina Romer, *University of California, Berkeley*

Patricia Rottschaefer, *California State University, Fullerton*

Jeff Rubin, *Rutgers University*

Henry D. Ryder, *Gloucester Community College*

Allen Sanderson, *University of Chicago*

Rolando Santos, *Lakeland Community College*

Christine Sauer, *University of New Mexico*

Elizabeth Sawyer-Kelly, *University of Wisconsin, Madison*

Edward Sayre, *Agnes Scott College*

Robert Schwab, *University of Maryland*

Stanley Sedo, *University of Maryland*

Eugene Silberberg, *University of Washington*

Bill Smith, *University of Memphis*

Marcia S. Snyder, *College of Charleston*

John Solow, *University of Iowa*

David E. Spencer, *Brigham Young University*

Denise Stanley, *California State University, Fullerton*

Martha A. Starr, *American University*

Richard Startz, *University of Washington*

Jill Stowe, *Texas A&M University, Austin*

Rodney Swanson, *University of California, Los Angeles*

Jason Taylor, *University of Virginia*

Mark Thoma, *University of California, San Diego*

Karen Travis, *Pacific Lutheran University*

Arienne Turner, *Fullerton College*

Abu Wahid, *Tennessee State University*

Stephan Weiler, *Colorado State University*

Robert Whaples, *Wake Forest University*

Jonathan B. Wight, *University of Richmond*

Mark Wohar, *University of Nebraska, Omaha*

Cemile Yavas, *Pennsylvania State University*

We must also thank the following graduate student reviewers for their assistance: Casey Rothschild, Massachusetts Institute of Technology; Naomi E. Feldman, University of Michigan, Ann Arbor; and, Malte Loos, Massachusetts Institute of Techology.

And there are undergraduate student reviewers to thank—students at Princeton taking our principles course who used and reviewed early drafts of chapters. We'd like to thank these following former students for their suggestions and honest criticisms (both on paper and in person): Todd Beattie, Maura Bolger, James Brandt, Allison Bryan, Jenness I. Crawford, Adam Dressner, Catherine Farmer, Liz Federowicz, Katherine Griswold, Elizabeth S. Irwin, Crystal Jiang, Caitlin Loomis, Akshay Mahajan, Veronika Musilova, Brendon O'Donnell Carrington, Kaitlyn Parlin, Darlyn Pirakitikulr, Lisa A. Pugh, Sasha S. Rao, Robert Richardson, Dena Rachel Schlamowitz, Emily Scott, Samuel Spector, Suzanne Sprague, Michael Tibbetts, Joseph Tursi, Fei Wang, and Julie Zankel.

Thanks, too, to the following students who reviewed the design for our book: Devin Cohen at New York University; Vishal Dave at the University of Calfornia, Berkeley; Melissa Duelks at Rutgers; Chloe Gale at Cambridge University; Mike Geier at New York University; Jaret Gronczewski at Rutgers; and Becky Zissel at University of California, Berkeley.

During the course of drafting our manuscript, we met with instructors of principles courses for face-to-face focus-group sessions that afforded us invaluable input. We appreciate the forthright advice and suggestions from these colleagues:

Michael Bordo, *Rutgers University*

Jim Cobbe, *Florida State University*

Tom Creahan, *Morehead State University*

Stephen DeCanio, *University of California, Santa Barbara*

Jim Eden, *Portland Community College, Sylvania*

David Flath, *North Carolina State University*

Rhona Free, *Eastern Connecticut State University*
Rick Godby, *University of Wyoming*
Wayne Grove, *Syracuse University*
Jonathan Hamilton, *University of Florida*
Robert Horn, *James Madison University*
Patrik Hultberg, *University of Wyoming*
Bruce Johnson, *Centre College*
Jim Jozefowicz, *Indiana University of Pennsylvania*
Jim Lee, *Texas A&M University, Corpus Christi*
Rachel McCulloch, *Brandeis University*
Ida Mirzaie, *John Carroll University*
Henry Ryder, *Gloucester Community College*
Marcia Snyder, *College of Charleston*
Brian Trinque, *University of Texas, Austin*
William C. Wood, *James Madison University*

Many thanks to the class testers who took the time to use early drafts of our chapters in their classrooms. The following instructors should know that we made use of their helpful suggestions. We also extend special thanks to so many of your students who filled out user surveys about our chapters. This student input inspired us.

Ashley Abramson, *Barstow College*
Terry Alexander, *Iowa State University*
Leon Battista, *Bronx Community College*
Richard Beil, *Auburn University*
Charles Bennett, *Gannon University*
Andreas Bentz, *Dartmouth College*
John Bockino, *Suffolk County Community College*
Ellen Bowen, *Fisher College, New Bedford*
Anne Bresnock, *University of California, Los Angeles*
Bruce Brown, *California State Polytechnic University, Pomona*
John Buck, *Jacksonville University*
Raymonda Burgman, *University of Southern Florida*
William Carlisle, *University of Utah*
Kevin Carlson, *University of Massachusetts, Boston*
Fred Carstensen, *University of Connecticut*
Shirley Cassing, *University of Pittsburgh*
Ramon Castillo-Ponce, *California State University, Los Angeles*
Emily Chamlee-Wright, *Beloit College*
Anthony Chan, *Santa Monica College*
Yuna Chen, *South Georgia College*
Maryanne Clifford, *Eastern Connecticut State University*
Gregory Colman, *Pace University*
Sarah Culver, *University of Alabama*
Rosa Lea Danielson, *College of DuPage*
Stephen Davis, *University of Minnesota, Crookston*
Tom DelGiudice, *Hofstra University*
Arna Desser, *United States Naval Academy*
Dorsey Dyer, *Davidson County Community College*
Mary Edwards, *St. Cloud State Univesity*
Fritz Efaw, *University of Tennessee at Chattanooga*

Herb Elliot, *Alan Hancock College*
Can Erbil, *Brandeis University*
Yee Tien Fu, *Stanford University*
Yoram Gelman, *Lehman College, The City University of New York*
E.B. Gendel, *Woodbury College*
Doug Gentry, *St. Mary's College*
Satyajit Ghosh, *University of Scranton*
Richard Gosselin, *Houston Community College, Central*
Patricia Graham, *University of Northern Colorado*
Kathleen Greer Rossman, *Birmingham Southern College*
Wayne Grove, *Syracuse University*
Eleanor Gubins, *Rosemont College*
Alan Haight, *State University of New York, Cortland*
Gautam Hazarika, *University of Texas, Brownsville*
Tom Head, *George Fox University*
Susan Helper, *Case Western Reserve University*
Paul Hettler, *Duquesne University*
Roger Hewett, *Drake University*
Jill Holman, *University of Wisconsin, Milwaukee*
Scott Houser, *California State University, Fresno*
Ray Hubbard, *Central Georgia Technical College*
Murat Iyigun, *University of Colorado*
Habib Jam, *Rowan University*
Louis Johnston, *College of St. Benedict/St. John's University*
Jack Julian, *Indiana University of Pennsylvania*
Soheila Kahkashan, *Towson University*
Charles Kaplan, *St. Joseph's College*
Bentzil Kasper, *Broome Community College*
Sinan Koont, *Dickinson College*
Kenneth Kriz, *University of Nebraska, Omaha*
Tom Larson, *California State University, Los Angeles*
Delores Linton, *Tarrant County College, Northwest*
Rolf Lokke, *Albuquerque Academy*
Ellen Magenheim, *Swarthmore College*
Diana McCoy, *Truckee Meadows Community College*
Garrett Milam, *Ryerson University*
Robert Miller, *Fisher College, New Bedford Campus*
Michael Milligan, *Front Range Community College*
Larry Miners, *Fairfield University*
Cathy Miners, *Fairfield University*
Kristen Monaco, *California State University, Long Beach*
Marie Mora, *University of Texas, Pan American*
James Mueller, *Alma College*
Ranganath Murthy, *Bucknell University*
Gerardo Nebbia, *Glendale College*
Anthony Negbenebor, *Gardner-Webb University*
Joseph Nowakowski, *Muskingum College*
Kimberley Ott, *Kent State University, Salem Campus*
Philip Packard, *St. Mary's College*
Jamie Pelley, *Mary Baldwin College*
Mary K. Perkins, *Howard University*

John Pharr, *Dallas Community College, Cedar Valley*

Ray Polchow, *Muskingum Area Technical College*

Ernest Poole, *Fashion Institute of Technology*

Reza Ramazani, *St. Michael's College*

Charles Reichheld, *Cuyahoga Community College*

Siobhan Reilly, *Mills College*

Malcolm Robinson, *Thomas More College*

Charles Rock, *Rollins College*

Richard Romano, *Broome Community College*

Jeff Romine, *University of Colorado, Denver*

Bernie Rose, *Rocky Mountain College*

Dan Rubenson, *Southern Oregon University*

Jeff Rubin, *Rutgers University*

Lynda Rush, *California State Polytechnic University, Pomona*

Martin Sabo, *Community College of Denver*

Sara Saderion, *Houston Community College, Southwest*

George Sawdy, *Providence College*

Ted Scheinman, *Mt. Hood Community College*

Russell Settle, *University of Delaware*

Anna Shostya, *Pace University*

John Somers, *Portland Community College*

Jim Spellicy, *Lowell High School*

Kurt Stephenson, *Virginia Tech*

Charles Stull, *Kalamazoo College*

Laddie Sula, *Loras College*

David Switzer, *University of Northern Michigan*

Deborah Thorsen, *Palm Beach Community College*

Andrew Toole, *Cook College/Rutgers University*

Arienne Turner, *Fullerton College*

Anthony Uremovic, *Joliet Junior College*

Jane Wallace, *University of Pittsburgh*

Tom Watkins, *Eastern Kentucky University*

Larry Wolfenbarger, *Macon State College*

James Woods, *Portland State University*

Mickey Wu, *Coe College*

Lou Zaera, *Fashion Institute of Technology*

Andrea Zanter, *Hillsborough Community College, Dale Mabry Campus*

We also appreciate the contributions of our Two-Year/ Community College Advisory Panel:

Kathleen Bromley, *Monroe Community College*

Barbara Connolly, *Westchester Community College*

Will Cummings, *Grossmont College*

Richard Gosselin, *Houston Community College, Central Campus*

Gus Herring, *Brookhaven College*

Charles Okeke, *Community College of Southern Nevada*

Charles Reichheld, *Cuyahoga Community College*

Sara Saderion, *Houston Community College, Southwest*

Ted Scheinman, *Mt. Hood Community College*

J. Ross Thomas, *Albuquerque Technical Vocational Institute*

Deborah Thorsen, *Palm Beach Community College*

Ranita Wyatt, *Dallas Community College*

We must thank the following instructors whose creativity and contributions helped to make the card deck—a lovely, thoughtful marketing piece—what it is:

Charles Antholt, *Western Washington University*

Richard Ball, *Haverford University*

Edward Blomdahl, *Bridgewater State College*

Michael Brace, *Jamestown Community College*

Tom Cooper, *Georgetown College*

James Craven, *Clark College*

Asif Dowla, *St. Mary's College of Maryland*

James Dulgeroff, *San Bernardino Valley Community College*

Tom Duston, *Keene State College*

Debra Dwyer, *State University of New York, Stony Brook*

Michael Ellis, *New Mexico State University*

Can Erbil, *Brandeis University*

Chuck Fischer, *Pittsburg State University*

Eric Fisher, *The Ohio State University*

Pat Graham, *University of Northern Colorado*

Hart Hodges, *Western Washington University*

Yu Hsing, *Southeastern Louisiana University*

Elia Kacapyr, *Ithaca College*

Farida Khan, *University of Wisconsin, Parkside*

Kent Klitgaard, *Wells College*

Margaret Landman, *Bridgewater State College*

Bill Lee, *St. Mary's College*

Nelson Nagai, *San Joaquin Delta College*

William O'Dea, *State University of New York, Oneonta*

Douglas Orr, *Eastern Washington University*

Brian Peterson, *Central College*

Kevin Quinn, *Bowling Green State University*

Richard Schatz, *Whitworth College*

Kathleen Segerson, *University of Connecticut*

Millicent Sites, *Carson-Newman College*

Herrick Smith, *Nease High School*

Maurice Weinrobe, *Clark University*

Gary Wolfram, *Hillsdale College*

Paul Zak, *Claremont Graduate University*

We would also like to thank the hundreds of instructors who took the time to offer their useful feedback to online marketing surveys about our project. There are nearly 800 of you out there. We only wish we had enough room in this small space to thank each and every one of you individually for your input and ideas. Please accept our deep gratitude for your role in our project.

The following key people critically read every page in virtually every chapter from many of our drafts and offered us so much: Andreas Bentz, Dartmouth College, oversaw accuracy checking, but his role turned into much more than that—a constant, tireless adviser who clarified our work at every step. It is extremely rare to find someone as faithful as Andreas has been to this project, and we are immensely grateful to him. Martha Olney, University of California, Berkeley, provided insightful input throughout—we had a number of moments when we realized that her advice saved us from a serious pedagogical misstep. Our deepest thanks also go to Martha. Development editor Marilyn Freedman helped us in shaping a book that instructors can really use and injected much-needed doses of common sense at crucial moments. We've even relied upon her to sort out pedagogical differences between the two of us. Elizabeth Sawyer-Kelly, University of Wisconsin, Madison, has played, and continues to play, an invaluable role as a close reader of our chapters. Her detailed and wise input is enormously helpful to us. Special thanks go to Malte Loos for his assistance in the page-proof stage. Thanks also to Becky Kohn, development editor in the early stages, who turned a rough idea into the beginnings of an actual book.

We've already thanked Rhona Free for her contributions as a reviewer and a focus-group participant. But, we must also thank her for the essential role she played in the development of our graphing appendix. We must also extend special thanks to Rosemary Cunningham for her many contributions to this text and its supplements.

We'd like to thank the current and former Worth people who made this project possible. Paul Shensa and Bob Worth suggested that we write this book. Alan McClare led us through the difficult transition from a vague intent into an actual writing process. Craig Bleyer, executive editor, kept that process moving, with just the right mix of patience and whip-cracking. Craig's able leadership and patience has helped us get this book finished.

Elizabeth Widdicombe, president of Freeman and Worth, and Catherine Woods, publisher at Worth, urged us on and kept faith with what must have been a very exasperating project at times.

We have had an incredible production and design team on this book. Tracey Kuehn, our associate managing editor, has worked tirelessly and with great skill to turn our rough manuscript into this beautiful textbook—and on a very tight schedule. Thank you, Tracey. Karen Osborne, our copyeditor, did a fine job helping us streamline and refine our writing. Babs Reingold created the spectacular cover for this book and came up with a design for the book that awed us each time we saw a new chapter in page proof. All we can say is "wow" and thanks.

And, we would not have been so awed with the look of each and every spread, without the page-layout magic that Lee Mahler worked for us. Thanks, too, to Barbara Seixas, for her work on the manufacturing end. We've heard about some of the miracles you've worked for us, Barbara, and we appreciate all you've done. The lovely photos you see in this book come to us courtesy of Julie Tesser, our photo researcher. Thanks too, to Patricia Marx and Ted Szczepanski for their assistance with photos. And for all of her help, thanks to Sarah Fleischman, editorial assistant.

Many thanks to Charlie Van Wagner, acquisitions editor, for devising and coordinating the impressive collection of media and supplements that accompany our book. And, many thanks to the incredible team of supplements writers and coordinators who worked with Charlie to make the supplements and media package so strong.

Thanks to Steve Rigolosi, director of market development, and Jeffrey Rucker, senior marketing manager, for their energetic and creative work in marketing this book. Thanks to Tom Kling, national economics consultant, for his critical role in helping to seed business for this text. We would also like to thank the Sales Representative Advisory Board at Worth for their efforts. We met with this wonderful group of salespeople at critical points during our project's development and our heartfelt thanks go to Janet Alexander, Kevin Carlson, Greg David, Joe Diggins, Karita dos Santos, Kate Geraghty, Michael Krotine, Charles Linsmeier, Nikkole Meimbresse, Michelle Merlo, Tara Reifenheiser, Kimberly Smith, Chris Spavins, Bill Soeltz, Ed Tiefenthaler, Maureen Tomlin, and Mark Weber. And, thank you Barbara Monteiro of Monteiro and Company; as well as John Murphy and Dori Weintraub of St. Martin's Press for your help with publicity for the book.

And most of all, special thanks to Sharon Balbos, executive development editor on this project, who must have been as stressed out as we were—but kept her cool throughout many years of tough slogging. We hope that this book lives up to the level of dedication and professionalism that she put into this project.

Paul Krugman   Robin Wells

Credits

Photo Credits

Grateful acknowledgment is given for permission to reprint the following cover photos:

Front Cover

Row 1 (left to right): Fresh vegetables, Photodisc; Seagulls and cooling tower, EyeWire; Buying shoes, Photodisc; **Row 2 (left to right):** Electronic components assembly, Photodisc; Meeting with laptop, Photodisc; Happy graduates, ©image 100 Ltd.; Tractor hauling haybales, Stockbyte; **Row 3 (left to right):** Bar-B-Q Sign, Photodisc; Empty shopping cart, Photodisc; Man checking classified ads, Photodisc; Male college student pumping gas, Alden Pellet/ The Image Works; **Row 4:** Hip kids sharing headphones, ©image100 Ltd./Veer; **Row 5:** New York Stock Exchange interior, Image Source/Veer; **Row 6 (left to right):** Father carrying his baby boy on his shoulders, Photodisc; Business man on cell phone in front of Petronas Towers, Kuala Lumpur, Malaysia, ©image100 Ltd./Veer; Food stand, Photodisc; Oil-pumping rig, EyeWire; **Row 7 (left to right):** Big Ben and Commonwealth of Flags, Photodisc; Postal worker dropping letter in mail slot, Photodisc; Indian woman on cell phone and computer, Thinkstock/Getty Images; **Row 8 (left to right):** Satellite dish, Stockbyte; Couple crossing street with sales signs in background, Image Source/Picture Quest; Father kissing baby, Photodisc; Busy Hong Kong intersection, Photodisc; **Row 9 (left to right):** Portrait of a young woman, Photodisc; Office building under construction, EyeWire; Businesspeople paying taxi fare, Photodisc; Used car lot, Photodisc

Back Cover

Row 1 (left to right): Wood frame building under construction, EyeWire; Market fruit stand, Photodisc; Vancouver skyline, Photodisc; Nuclear plant cooling tower with steam, EyeWire; **Row 2 (left to right):** East River tugboat, EyeWire; Man making pizza at a pizza stand, Photodisc; Shoe repair window, Photodisc; **Row 3 (left to right):** Refinery, EyeWire; Plumber working, Photodisc; St. Louis Arch at sunset, Photodisc; Making cappuccino, Photodisc; **Row 4:** Bunches of asparagus, Photodisc; **Row 5:** Manhattan, Photodisc; **Row 6:** Fresh fish, Photodisc; **Row 7 (left to right):** European hotel, Photodisc; Sign for drive-up bank, Photodisc; Trishaw, Phnom Penh, Cambodia, Photodisc; **Row 8 (left to right):** Window display in men's shop, Photodisc; Logging truck, EyeWire; Chemical plant, EyeWire; **Row 9 (left to right):** Antique store, Photodisc; Dark meeting with laptop and videoconference, Photodisc; Woman holding bicycle on assembly line, EyeWire

Author photo

page iii: Ted Szczepanski

Text Credits

Chapter 5

Source information for Table 5-1, page 113:

Eggs, beef: Kuo S. Huang and Biing-Hwan Lin, Estimation of Food Demand and Nutrient Elasticities from Household Survey Data, United States Department of Agriculture Economic Research Service Technical Bulletin, No. 1887 (Washington, DC: U.S. Department of Agriculture, 2000);

Stationery, gasoline, airline travel, foreign travel: H. S. Houthakker and Lester D. Taylor, *Consumer Demand in the United States, 1929-1970: Analyses and Projections* (Cambridge, MA: Harvard University Press, 1966);

Housing, restaurant meals: H. S. Houthakker and Lester D. Taylor, *Consumer Demand in the United States: Analyses and Projections,* 2nd ed. (Cambridge, MA: Harvard University Press, 1970).

Chapter 12

Source article of "For Inquiring Minds" box on page 300:

C. Camerer et al., Labor Supply of New York City Cab Drivers: One Day at a Time. *Quarterly Journal of Economics, 112,* 407–471.

Chapter 19

Source article of "Economics in Action" on page 461:
M. Gross, J.L. Sindelar, J. Mullahy, and R. Anderson, Policy Watch: Alcohol and Cigarette Taxes, *Journal of Economic Perspectives, 7,* 211–222, 1993.

BRIEF CONTENTS

CONTENTS

Part 3 Individuals and Markets

>>Introduction: The Ordinary Business of Life

ANY GIVEN SUNDAY

IT'S SUNDAY AFTERNOON IN THE SUMMER of 2003, and Route 1 in central New Jersey is a busy place. Thousands of people crowd the shopping malls that line the road for 20 miles, all the way from Trenton to New Brunswick. Most of the shoppers are cheerful—and why not? The stores in those malls offer an extraordinary range of choice; you can buy everything from sophisticated electronic equipment to fashionable clothes to organic carrots. There are probably 100,000 distinct items available

The scene along Route 1 that summer day was, of course, perfectly ordinary—very much like the scene along hundreds of other stretches of road, all across America, that same afternoon. But the discipline of economics is mainly concerned with ordinary things. As the great nineteenth-century economist Alfred Marshall put it, economics is "a study of mankind in the ordinary business of life."

What can economics say about this "ordinary business"? Quite a lot, it turns

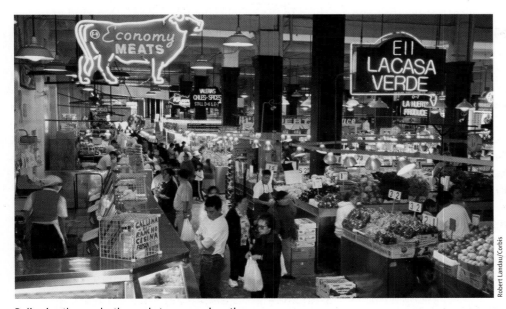

Delivering the goods: the market economy in action

along that stretch of road. And most of these items are not luxury goods that only the rich can afford; they are products that millions of Americans can and do purchase every day.

out. What we'll see in this book is that even familiar scenes of economic life pose some very important questions—questions that economics can help answer. Among these questions are:

- How does our economic system work? That is, how does it manage to deliver the goods?

- When and why does our economic system go astray, leading people into counterproductive behavior?

- Why are there ups and downs in the economy? That is, why does the economy sometimes have a "bad year"?

- Finally, why is the long run mainly a story of ups rather than downs? That is, why has America, along with other advanced nations, become so much richer over time?

Let's take a look at these questions and offer a brief preview of what you will learn in this book.

The Invisible Hand

That ordinary scene in central New Jersey would not have looked at all ordinary to an American from colonial times—say, one of the patriots who helped George Washington win the battle of Trenton in 1776. (At the time, Trenton was a small village with not a shopping mall in sight, and farms lined the unpaved road that would eventually become Route 1.)

Imagine that you could transport an American from the colonial period forward in time to our own era. (Isn't that the plot of a movie? Several, actually.) What would this time-traveler find amazing?

Surely the most amazing thing would be the sheer prosperity of modern America—the range of goods and services that ordinary families can afford. Looking at all that wealth, our transplanted colonial would wonder, "How can I get some of that?" Or perhaps he would ask himself, "How can my society get some of that?"

The answer is that to get this kind of prosperity, you need a well-functioning system for coordinating productive activities—the activities that create the goods and services people want and get them to the people who want them. That kind of system is what we mean when we talk about the **economy**. And **economics** is the study of economies, at the level both of individuals and of society as a whole.

An economy succeeds to the extent that it, literally, delivers the goods. A time-traveler from the eighteenth century—or even from 1950—would be amazed at how many goods and services the modern American economy delivers and at how many people can afford them. Compared with any past economy and with all but a few other countries today, America has an incredibly high standard of living.

So our economy must be doing something right, and the time-traveler might want to compliment the person in charge. But guess what? There isn't anyone in charge. The United States has a **market economy**, in which production and consumption are the result of decentralized decisions by many firms and individuals. There is no central authority telling people what to produce or where to ship it. Each individual producer makes what he or she thinks will be most profitable; each consumer buys what he or she chooses.

The alternative to a market economy is a *command economy,* in which there *is* a central authority making decisions about production and consumption. Command economies have been tried, most notably in the Soviet Union between 1917 and 1991. But they didn't work very well. Producers in the Soviet Union routinely found themselves unable to produce because they did not have crucial raw materials, or they succeeded in producing but then found that nobody wanted their products. Consumers were often unable to find necessary items—command economies are famous for long lines at shops.

Market economies, however, are able to coordinate even highly complex activities and to reliably provide consumers with the goods and services they want. Indeed, people quite casually trust their lives to the market system: residents of any major city

An **economy** is a system for coordinating society's productive activities.

Economics is the study of economies, at the level both of individuals and of society as a whole.

A **market economy** is an economy in which decisions about production and consumption are made by individual producers and consumers.

would starve in days if the unplanned yet somehow orderly actions of thousands of businesses did not deliver a steady supply of food. Surprisingly, the unplanned "chaos" of a market economy turns out to be far more orderly than the "planning" of a command economy.

In 1776, in a famous passage in his book *The Wealth of Nations*, the pioneering Scottish economist Adam Smith wrote about how individuals, in pursuing their own interests, often end up serving the interests of society as a whole. Of a businessman whose pursuit of profit makes the nation wealthier, Smith wrote: "[H]e intends only his own gain, and he is in this, as in many other cases, led by an invisible hand to promote an end which was no part of his intention." Ever since, economists have used the term **invisible hand** to refer to the way a market economy manages to harness the power of self-interest for the good of society.

The study of how individuals make decisions and how these decisions interact is called **microeconomics**. One of the key themes in microeconomics is the validity of Adam Smith's insight: Individuals pursuing their own interests often do promote the interests of society as a whole.

So part of the answer to our time-traveler's question—"How can my society achieve the kind of prosperity you take for granted?"—is that his society should learn to appreciate the virtues of a market economy and the power of the invisible hand.

But the invisible hand isn't always our friend. It's also important to understand when and why the individual pursuit of self-interest can lead to counterproductive behavior.

The **invisible hand** refers to the way in which the individual pursuit of self-interest can lead to good results for society as a whole.

Microeconomics is the branch of economics that studies how people make decisions and how these decisions interact.

My Benefit, Your Cost

One thing that our time-traveler would not admire about modern Route 1 is the traffic. In fact, although most things have gotten better in America over time, traffic congestion has gotten a lot worse.

When traffic is congested, each driver is imposing a cost on all the other drivers on the road—he is literally getting in their way (and they are getting in his way). This cost can be substantial: in major metropolitan areas, each time someone drives to work, as opposed to taking public transportation or working at home, he can easily impose $15 or more in hidden costs on other drivers. Yet when deciding whether or not to drive, commuters have no incentive to take the costs they impose on others into account.

Traffic congestion is a familiar example of a much broader problem: sometimes the individual pursuit of one's own interest, instead of promoting the interests of society as a whole, can actually make society worse off. When this happens, it is known as **market failure**. Other important examples of market failure involve air and water pollution as well as the overexploitation of natural resources such as fish and forests.

The good news, as you will learn as you use this book to study microeconomics, is that economic analysis can be used to diagnose cases of market failure. And often, economic analysis can also be used to devise solutions for the problem.

When the individual pursuit of self-interest leads to bad results for society as a whole, there is **market failure**.

ECONOMICS THROUGH THE AGES

BARTER: "I'LL SPLIT MY NEXT MAMMOTH WITH YOU IF I CAN CRASH IN YOUR CAVE." "ARE YOU **NUTS**? I'M STUPID BUT I'M NOT DUMB!"

CASH: "LET ME TELL YOU AGAIN: I GIVE YOU A PIECE OF PAPER PRINTED BY A GROUP OF PEOPLE WHO PROMISE TO GIVE YOU STUFF, AND YOU GIVE ME STUFF IN EXCHANGE." "I DUNNO."

CREDIT: "I KNOW IT'S WEIRD, BUT THE TINT OF THE PLASTIC DETERMINES WHETHER OR NOT I'M TREATED WITH RESPECT." "AND THEY TRUST YOU TO PAY 'WHENEVER'?"

NEW ECONOMY: "I'LL GIVE YOU A BANNER AD IF I CAN CO-BRAND YOUR E-COMMERCE SEGMENT." "SOUNDS TASTY TO ME!"

8-3-00-C

Good Times, Bad Times

Route 1 was bustling on that summer day in 2003—but it wasn't bustling quite as much as merchants would have liked, because in mid-2003 the U.S. economy wasn't doing all that well. The main problem was jobs: in early 2001, businesses began laying off workers in large numbers, and as of June 2003, employment had not yet started to recover.

Such troubled periods are a regular feature of modern economies. The fact is that the economy does not always run smoothly: it experiences *fluctuations,* a series of ups and downs. By middle age, a typical American will have experienced three or four downs, known as **recessions**. (The U.S. economy experienced serious recessions beginning in 1973, 1981, 1990, and 2001.) During a severe recession, millions of workers may be laid off.

Like market failure, recessions are a fact of life; but also like market failure, they are a problem to which economic analysis offers some solutions. Recessions are one of the main concerns of the branch of economics known as **macroeconomics**, which is concerned with the overall ups and downs of the economy. If you study macroeconomics, you will learn how economists explain recessions and how government policies can be used to minimize the damage from economic fluctuations.

Despite the occasional recession, however, over the long run the story of the U.S. economy contains many more ups than downs. And that long-run ascent is the subject of our final question.

A **recession** is a downturn in the economy.

Macroeconomics is the branch of economics that is concerned with overall ups and downs in the economy.

Onward and Upward

At the beginning of the twentieth century, most Americans lived under conditions that we would now think of as extreme poverty. Only 10 percent of homes had flush toilets, only 8 percent had central heating, only 2 percent had electricity, and almost nobody had a car, let alone a washing machine or air conditioning.

Such comparisons are a stark reminder of how much our lives have been changed by **economic growth**, the growing ability of the economy to produce goods and services.

Why does the economy grow over time? And why does economic growth occur faster in some times and places than in others? These are key questions for economics because economic growth is a good thing, as those shoppers on Route 1 can attest, and most of us want more of it.

Economic growth is the growing ability of the economy to produce goods and services.

An Engine for Discovery

We hope we have convinced you that the "ordinary business of life" is really quite extraordinary, if you stop to think about it, and that it can lead us to ask some very interesting and important questions.

In this book, we will describe the answers economists have given to these questions. But this book, like economics as a whole, isn't a list of answers: it's an introduction to a discipline, a way to address questions like those we have just asked. Or as Alfred Marshall, who described economics as a study of the "ordinary business of life," put it: "Economics . . . is not a body of concrete truth, but an engine for the discovery of concrete truth."

So let's turn the key in the ignition.

KEY TERMS

Economy, p. 2
Economics, p. 2
Market economy, p. 2
Invisible hand, p. 3
Microeconomics, p. 3
Market failure, p. 3
Recession, p. 4
Macroeconomics, p. 4
Economic growth, p. 4

>>First Principles

COMMON GROUND

THE ANNUAL MEETING OF THE AMERICAN Economic Association draws thousands of economists, young and old, famous and obscure. There are booksellers, business meetings, and quite a few job interviews. But mainly the economists gather to talk and listen. During the busiest times, 60 or more presentations may be taking place simultaneously, on questions that range from the future of the stock market to who does the cooking in two-earner families.

What do these people have in common? An expert on the stock market probably knows very little about the economics of housework, and vice versa. Yet an economist who wanders into the wrong seminar and ends up listening to presentations on some unfamiliar topic is nonetheless likely to hear much that is familiar. The reason is that all economic analysis is based on a set of common principles that apply to many different issues.

Some of these principles involve *individual choice*—for economics is, first of all, about the choices that individuals make. Do you choose to work over the summer or take a backpacking trip? Do you buy a new CD or go to a movie? These decisions involve *making a choice* among a limited number of alternatives—limited because no one can have everything that he or she wants. Every question in economics at its most basic level involves individuals making choices.

But to understand how an economy works, you need to understand more than how individuals make choices. None of us are Robinson Crusoe, alone on an island—we must make decisions in an environment that is shaped by the decisions of others. Indeed, in a modern economy even the simplest decisions you

One must choose.

Richard Hamilton Smith/Corbis

make—say, what to have for breakfast—are shaped by the decisions of thousands of other people, from the banana grower in Costa Rica who decided to grow the fruit you eat to the farmer in Iowa who provided the corn in your cornflakes. And because each of us in a market economy depends on

What you will learn in this chapter:

➤ A set of principles for understanding the economics of how individuals make choices

➤ A set of principles for understanding how individual choices interact so many others—and they, in turn, depend on us—our choices interact. So although all economics at a basic level is about individual choice, in order to understand how market economies behave we must also understand economy-wide *interaction*—how my choices affect your choices, and vice versa.

In this chapter, we will look at nine basic principles of economics—four principles involving individual choice and five involving the way individual choices interact.

Individual Choice: The Core of Economics

Every economic issue involves, at its most basic level, **individual choice**—decisions by an individual about what to do and what *not* to do. In fact, you might say that it isn't economics if it isn't about choice.

Step into a big store like a Wal-Mart or Home Depot. There are thousands of different products available, and it is extremely unlikely that you—or anyone else—could afford to buy everything you might want to have. And anyway, there's only so much space in your dorm room or apartment. So will you buy another bookcase or a mini-refrigerator? Given limitations on your budget and your living space, you must choose which products to buy and which to leave on the shelf.

The fact that those products are on the shelf in the first place involves choice—the store manager chose to put them there, and the manufacturers of the products chose to produce them. All economic activities involve individual choice.

Four economic principles underlie the economics of individual choice, as shown in Table 1-1. We'll now examine each of these principles in more detail.

Resources Are Scarce

You can't always get what you want. Everyone would like to have a beautiful house in a great location (and help with the housecleaning), two or three luxury cars, and frequent vacations in fancy hotels. But even in a rich country like the United States, not many families can afford all that. So they must make choices—whether to go to Disney World this year or buy a better car, whether to make do with a small backyard or accept a longer commute in order to live where land is cheaper.

Limited income isn't the only thing that keeps people from having everything they want. Time is also in limited supply: there are only 24 hours in a day. And because the time we have is limited, choosing to spend time on one activity also means choosing not to spend time on a different activity—spending time studying for an exam means forgoing a night at the movies. Indeed, many people are so limited by the number of hours in the day that they are willing to trade money for time. For example, convenience stores normally charge higher prices than a regular supermarket. But they fulfill a valuable role by catering to time-pressured customers who would rather pay more than travel farther to the supermarket.

Why do individuals have to make choices? The ultimate reason is that *resources are scarce*. A **resource** is anything that can be used to produce something else. Lists of the economy's resources usually begin with land, labor (the available time of workers), capital (machinery, buildings, and other man-made productive assets), and human capital (the educational achievements and skills of workers). A resource is **scarce** when the quantity of the resource available isn't large enough to satisfy all productive uses. There are many scarce resources. These include natural resources—resources that come from the physical environment, such as minerals, lumber, and petroleum. There is also a limited quantity of human resources—labor, skill, and intelligence. And in a growing world economy with a rapidly increasing human population, even clean air and water have become scarce resources.

Individual choice is the decision by an individual of what to do, which necessarily involves a decision of what not to do.

TABLE 1-1

Principles That Underlie the Economics of Individual Choice

1. Resources are scarce.
   ← *opportunity cost*
2. The real cost of something is what you must give up to get it.

3. "How much?" is a decision at the margin.

4. People usually exploit opportunities to make themselves better off.

A **resource** is anything that can be used to produce something else.

Resources are **scarce**—the quantity available isn't large enough to satisfy all productive uses.

Just as individuals must make choices, the scarcity of resources means that society as a whole must make choices. One way for a society to make choices is simply to allow them to emerge as the result of many individual choices, which is what usually happens in a market economy. For example, Americans as a group have only so many hours in a week: how many of those hours will they spend going to supermarkets to get lower prices, rather than saving time by shopping at convenience stores? The answer is the sum of individual decisions: each of the millions of individuals in the economy makes his or her own choice about where to shop, and the overall choice is simply the sum of those individual decisions.

But for various reasons, there are some decisions that a society decides are best not left to individual choice. For example, the authors live in an area that until recently was mainly farmland but is now being rapidly built up. Most local residents feel that the community would be a more pleasant place to live if some of the land were left undeveloped. But no individual has an incentive to keep his or her land as open space, rather than selling it to a developer. So a trend has emerged in many communities across the United States of local governments purchasing undeveloped land and preserving it as open space. We'll see in later chapters why decisions about how to use scarce resources are often best left to individuals but sometimes should be made at a higher, community-wide, level.

Opportunity Cost: The Real Cost of Something Is What You Must Give Up to Get It

It is the last term before you graduate, and your class schedule allows you to take only one elective. There are two, however, that you would really like to take: History of Jazz and Beginning Tennis.

Suppose you decide to take the History of Jazz course. What's the cost of that decision? It is the fact that you can't take Beginning Tennis. Economists call that kind of cost—what you must forgo in order to get something you want—the **opportunity cost** of that item. So the opportunity cost of the History of Jazz class is the enjoyment you would have derived from the Beginning Tennis class.

The concept of opportunity cost is crucial to understanding individual choice because, in the end, all costs are opportunity costs. Sometimes critics claim that economists are concerned only with costs and benefits that can be measured in dollars and cents. But that is not true. Much economic analysis involves cases like our elective course example, where it costs no extra tuition to take one elective course—that is, there is no direct monetary cost. Nonetheless, the elective you choose has an opportunity cost—the other desirable elective course that you must forgo because your limited time permits taking only one.

You might think that opportunity cost is an add-on—that is, something *additional* to the monetary cost of an item. Suppose that an elective class costs additional tuition of $750; now there is a monetary cost to taking History of Jazz. Is the opportunity cost of taking that course something separate from that monetary cost?

Well, consider two cases. First, suppose that taking Beginning Tennis also costs $750. In this case, you would have to spend that $750 no matter which class you take. So what you give up to take the History of Jazz class is still the Beginning Tennis class, period—you would have to spend that $750 either way. But suppose there isn't any fee for the tennis class. In that case, what you give up to take the jazz class is the tennis class *plus* whatever you would have bought with the $750.

Either way, the cost of taking your preferred class is what you must give up to get it. *All* costs are ultimately opportunity costs.

Sometimes the money you have to pay for something is a good indication of its opportunity cost. But many times it is not. One very important example of how poorly monetary cost can indicate opportunity cost is the cost of attending college.

The real cost of an item is its **opportunity cost**: what you must give up in order to get it.

At many cash registers—for example, the one in our college cafeteria—there is a little basket full of pennies. People are encouraged to use the basket to round their purchases up or down: if it costs $5.02, you give the cashier $5 and take two pennies from the basket; if it costs $4.99, you pay $5 and the cashier throws in a penny. It makes everyone's life a bit easier. Of course, it would be easier still if we just abolished the penny, a step that some economists have urged.

But then why do we have pennies in the first place? If it's too small a sum to worry about, why calculate prices that exactly?

The answer is that a penny wasn't always such a negligible sum: the purchasing power of a penny has been greatly reduced by inflation. Forty years ago, a penny had more purchasing power than a nickel does today.

Why does this matter? Well, remember the saying: "A penny saved is a penny earned." But there are other ways to earn money, so you must decide whether saving a penny is a productive use of your time. Could you earn more by devoting that time to other uses?

Forty years ago, the average wage was about $2 an hour. A penny was equivalent to 18 seconds' worth of work—it was worth saving a penny if doing so took less than 18 seconds. But wages have risen along with overall prices, so that the average worker is now paid more than $17 per hour. A penny is therefore equivalent to just over 2 seconds of work—and so it's not worth the opportunity cost of the time it takes to worry about a penny more or less.

In short, the rising opportunity cost of time in terms of money has turned a penny from a useful coin into a nuisance.

AP/Wide World Photos

Tiger Woods understood the concept of opportunity cost. The rest is history.

Tuition and housing are major monetary expenses for most students; but even if these things were free, attending college would still be an expensive proposition because most college students, if they were not in college, would have a job. That is, by going to college, students *forgo* the income they could have made if they had worked instead. This means that the opportunity cost of attending college is what you pay for tuition and housing *plus* the forgone income you would have earned in a job.

It's easy to see that the opportunity cost of going to college is especially high for people who could be earning a lot during what would otherwise have been their college years. That is why star athletes often skip college or, like Tiger Woods, leave before graduating.

"How Much?" Is a Decision at the Margin

Some important decisions involve an "either-or" choice—for example, you decide either to go to college or to begin working; you decide either to take economics or to take something else. But other important decisions involve "how much" choices—for example, if you are taking both economics and chemistry this semester, you must decide how much time to spend studying for each. When it comes to understanding "how much" decisions, economics has an important insight to offer: "how much" is a decision made *at the margin*.

Suppose you are taking both economics and chemistry. And suppose you are a pre-med student, so that your grade in chemistry matters more to you than your grade in economics. Does that therefore imply that you should spend *all* your study time on chemistry and wing it on the economics exam? Probably not; even if you think your chemistry grade is more important, you should put some effort into studying for economics.

Spending more time studying for economics involves a benefit (a higher expected grade in that course) and a cost (you could have spent that time doing something else, such as studying to get a higher grade in chemistry). That is, your decision involves a **trade-off**—a comparison of costs and benefits.

How do you decide this kind of "how much" question? The typical answer is that you make the decision a bit at a time, by asking how you should spend the next hour.

You make a **trade-off** when you compare the costs with the benefits of doing something.

Say both exams are on the same day, and the night before you spend time reviewing your notes for both courses. At 6:00 P.M., you decide that it's a good idea to spend at least an hour on each course. At 8:00 P.M., you decide you'd better spend another hour on each course. At 10:00 P.M., you are getting tired and figure you have one more hour to study before bed—chemistry or economics? If you are pre-med, it's likely to be chemistry; if you are pre-MBA, it's likely to be economics.

Note how you've made the decision to allocate your time: at each point the question is whether or not to spend *one more hour* on either course. And in deciding whether to spend another hour studying for chemistry, you weigh the costs (an hour forgone of studying for economics or an hour forgone of sleeping) versus the benefits (a likely increase in your chemistry grade). As long as the benefit of studying one more hour for chemistry outweighs the cost, you should choose to study for that additional hour.

Decisions of this type—what to do with your next hour, what to do with your next dollar, and so on—are **marginal decisions**. They involve making trade-offs *at the margin*: comparing the costs and benefits of doing a little bit more of an activity versus doing a little bit less. The study of such decisions is known as **marginal analysis**.

Many of the questions that we face in economics—as well as in real life—involve marginal analysis: How many workers should I hire in my shop? At what mileage should I change the oil in my car? What is an acceptable rate of negative side effects from a new medicine? Marginal analysis plays a central role in economics because it is the key to deciding "how much" of an activity to do.

People Usually Exploit Opportunities to Make Themselves Better Off

One day, while listening to the morning financial news, the authors heard a great tip about how to park cheaply in Manhattan. Garages in the Wall Street area charge as much as $30 per day. But according to the newscaster, some people had found a better way: instead of parking in a garage, they had their oil changed at the Manhattan Jiffy Lube, where it costs $19.95 to change your oil—and they keep your car all day!

It's a great story, but unfortunately it turned out not to be true—in fact, there is no Jiffy Lube in Manhattan. But if there were, you can be sure there would be a lot of oil changes there. Why? Because when people are offered opportunities to make themselves better off, they normally take them—and if they could find a way to park their car all day for $19.95 rather than $30, they would.

When you try to predict how individuals will behave in an economic situation, it is a very good bet that they will exploit opportunities to make themselves better off. Furthermore, individuals will *continue* to exploit these opportunities until they have been fully exhausted—that is, people will exploit opportunities until those opportunities have been fully taken.

If there really was a Manhattan Jiffy Lube and an oil change really was a cheap way to park your car, we can safely predict that before long the waiting list for oil changes would be weeks, if not months.

In fact, the principle that people will exploit opportunities to make themselves better off is the basis of *all* predictions by economists about individual behavior. If the earnings of those who get MBAs soar while the earnings of those who get law degrees decline, we can expect more students to go to business school and fewer to go to law school. If the price of gasoline rises and stays high for an extended period of time, we can expect people to buy smaller cars with higher gas mileage—making themselves better off in the presence of higher gas prices by driving more fuel-efficient cars.

When changes in the available opportunities offer rewards to those who change their behavior, we say that people face new **incentives**. If the price of parking in Manhattan rises, those who can find alternative ways to get to their Wall Street jobs

Decisions about whether to do a bit more or a bit less of an activity are **marginal decisions**. The study of such decisions is known as **marginal analysis**.

An **incentive** is anything that offers rewards to people who change their behavior.

The true reward for learning is, of course, the learning itself. But teachers and schools often feel that it's worth throwing in a few extras. Elementary school students who do well get gold stars; at higher levels, students who score well on tests may receive trophies, plaques, or even gift certificates.

But what about cash?

A few years ago, some Florida schools stirred widespread debate by offering actual cash bonuses to students who scored high on the state's standardized exams. At Parrott Middle School, which offered the highest amounts, an eighth-grader with a top score on an exam received a $50 savings bond.

Many people questioned the monetary awards. In fact, the great majority of teachers feel that cash rewards for learning are a bad idea—the dollar amounts can't be made large enough to give students a real sense of how important their education is, and they make learning seem like work-for-pay. So why did the schools engage in the practice?

The answer, it turns out, is that the previous year the state government had introduced a pay-for-performance scheme for schools: schools whose students earned high marks on the state exams received extra state funds. The problem arose of how to motivate the students to take the exams as seriously as the school administrators

did. Parrott's principal defended the pay-for-grades practice by pointing out that good students would often "Christmas tree" their exams—ignore the questions and fill out the bubble sheets in the shape of Christmas trees. With large sums of money for the school at stake, he decided to set aside his misgivings and pay students to do well on the exams.

Does paying students for grades lead to higher grades? Interviews with students suggest that it does spur at least some students to try harder on state exams. And some Florida schools that have introduced rewards for good grades on state exams report substantial improvements in student performance.

will save money by doing so—and so we can expect fewer people to drive to work.

One last point: economists tend to be skeptical of any attempt to change people's behavior that *doesn't* change their incentives. For example, a plan that calls on manufacturers to reduce pollution voluntarily probably won't be effective; a plan that gives them a financial incentive to reduce pollution is a lot more likely to work.

Individual Choice: Summing It Up

We have just seen that there are four basic principles of individual choice:

- *Resources are scarce.* It is always necessary to make choices.
- *The real cost of something is what you must give up to get it.* All costs are opportunity costs.
- *"How much?" is a decision at the margin.* Usually the question is not "whether," but "how much." And that is a question whose answer hinges on the costs and benefits of doing a bit more.
- *People usually exploit opportunities to make themselves better off.* As a result, people will respond to incentives.

So are we ready to do economics? Not yet—because most of the interesting things that happen in the economy are the result not merely of individual choices but of the way in which individual choices *interact*.

economics in action

A Woman's Work

One of the great social transformations of the twentieth century was the change in the nature of women's work. In 1900, only 6 percent of married women worked for pay outside the home. By the early twenty-first century, the number was about 60 percent.

What caused this transformation? Changing attitudes toward work outside the home certainly played a role: in the first half of the twentieth century, it was often considered improper for a married woman to work outside the home if she could afford not to, whereas today it is considered normal. But an important driving force was the invention and growing availability of home appliances, especially washing machines. Before these appliances became available, housework was an extremely laborious task—much more so than a full-time job. In 1945, government researchers clocked a farm wife as she did the weekly wash by hand; she spent 4 hours washing clothes and 4½ hours ironing, and she walked more than a mile. Then she was equipped with a washing machine; the same wash took 41 minutes, ironing was reduced to 1¾ hours, and the distance walked was reduced by 90 percent.

The point is that in pre-appliance days, the opportunity cost of working outside the home was very high: it was something women typically did only in the face of dire financial necessity. With modern appliances, the opportunities available to women changed—and the rest is history. ■

> > > > > > > > > > > > > > > > > > > >

>>CHECK YOUR UNDERSTANDING 1-1

1. Explain how each of the following situations illustrates one of the four principles of individual choice.
   a. You are on your third trip to a restaurant's all-you-can-eat dessert buffet and are feeling very full. Although it would cost you no additional money, you forgo another slice of coconut cream pie but have a slice of chocolate cake.
   b. Even if there were more resources in the world, there would still be scarcity.
   c. Different teaching assistants teach several Economics 101 tutorials. Those taught by the teaching assistants with the best reputations fill up quickly, with spaces left unfilled in the ones taught by assistants with poor reputations.
   d. To decide how many hours per week to exercise, you compare the health benefits of one more hour of exercise to the effect on your grades of one less hour spent studying.

2. You make $45,000 per year at your current job with Whiz Kids Consultants. You are considering a job offer from Brainiacs, Inc., which will pay you $50,000 per year. Which of the following are elements of the opportunity cost of accepting the new job at Brainiacs, Inc.?
   a. The increased time spent commuting to your new job
   b. The $45,000 salary from your old job
   c. The more spacious office at your new job

Solutions appear at back of book.

Interaction: How Economies Work

As we learned in the Introduction, an economy is a system for coordinating the productive activities of many people. In a market economy, such as the one we live in, that coordination takes place without any coordinator: each individual makes his or her own choices. Yet those choices are by no means independent of each other: each individual's opportunities, and hence choices, depend to a large extent on the choices made by other people. So to understand how a market economy behaves, we have to examine this **interaction** in which my choices affect your choices, and vice versa.

When studying economic interaction, we quickly learn that the end result of individual choices may be quite different from what any one individual intends.

For example, over the past century farmers in the United States have eagerly adopted new farming techniques and crop strains that have reduced their costs and increased their yields. Clearly, it's in the interest of each farmer to keep up with the latest farming techniques. But the end result of each farmer trying to increase his or her own income has actually been to drive many farmers out of business. Because American farmers have been so successful at producing larger yields, agricultural

Interaction of choices—my choices affect your choices, and vice versa—is a feature of most economic situations. The results of this interaction are often quite different from what the individuals intend.

TABLE 1-2

Principles That Underlie the Interaction of Individual Choices

1. There are gains from trade.

2. Markets move toward equilibrium.

3. Resources should be used as efficiently as possible to achieve society's goals.

4. Markets usually lead to efficiency.

5. When markets don't achieve efficiency, government intervention can improve society's welfare.

In a market economy, individuals engage in **trade**: They provide goods and services to others and receive goods and services in return.

There are **gains from trade**: people can get more of what they want through trade than they could if they tried to be self-sufficient. This increase in output is due to **specialization**: each person specializes in the task that he or she is good at performing.

---

prices have steadily fallen. These falling prices have reduced the incomes of many farmers, and as a result fewer and fewer people find farming worth doing. That is, an individual farmer who plants a better variety of corn is better off; but when many farmers plant a better variety of corn, the result may be to make farmers as a group worse off.

A farmer who plants a new, more productive corn variety doesn't just grow more corn. Such a farmer also affects the market for corn through the increased yields attained, with consequences that will be felt by other farmers, consumers, and beyond.

Just as there are four economic principles that fall under the theme of choice, there are five principles that fall under the theme of interaction. These five principles are summarized in Table 1-2. We will now examine each of these principles more closely.

There Are Gains from Trade

Why do the choices I make interact with the choices you make? A family could try to take care of all its own needs—growing its own food, sewing its own clothing, providing itself with entertainment, writing its own economics textbooks. But trying to live that way would be very hard. The key to a much better standard of living for everyone is **trade**, in which people divide tasks among themselves and each person provides a good or service that other people want in return for different goods and services that he or she wants.

The reason we have an economy, not many self-sufficient individuals, is that there are **gains from trade**: by dividing tasks and trading, two people (or 6 billion people) can each get more of what they each want than they could get by being self-sufficient. Gains from trade arise, in particular, from this division of tasks, which economists call **specialization**—a situation in which different people each engage in a different task.

The advantages of specialization, and the resulting gains from trade, were the starting point for Adam Smith's 1776 book *The Wealth of Nations*, which many regard as the beginning of economics as a discipline. Smith's book begins with a description of an eighteenth-century pin factory where, rather than each of the 10 workers making a pin from start to finish, each worker specialized in one of the many steps in pin-making:

> One man draws out the wire, another straights it, a third cuts it, a fourth points it, a fifth grinds it at the top for receiving the head; to make the head requires two or three distinct operations; to put it on, is a particular business, to whiten the pins is another; it is even a trade by itself to put them into the paper; and the important business of making a pin is, in this manner, divided into about eighteen distinct operations . . . Those ten persons, therefore, could make among them upwards of forty-eight thousand pins in a day. But if they had all wrought separately and independently, and without any of them having been educated to this particular business, they certainly could not each of them have made twenty, perhaps not one pin a day. . . .

The same principle applies when we look at how people divide tasks among themselves and trade in an economy. *The economy, as a whole, can produce more when each person specializes in a task and trades with others.*

The benefits of specialization are the reason a person typically chooses only one career. It takes many years of study and experience to become a doctor; it also takes many years of study and experience to become a commercial airline pilot. Many doctors might well have had the potential to become excellent pilots, and vice versa;

"I hunt and she gathers—otherwise we couldn't make ends meet."

but it is very unlikely that anyone who decided to pursue both careers would be as good a pilot or as good a doctor as someone who decided at the beginning to specialize in that field. So it is to everyone's advantage that individuals specialize in their career choices.

Markets are what allow a doctor and a pilot to specialize in their own fields. Because markets for commercial flights and for doctors' services exist, a doctor is assured that she can find a flight and a pilot is assured that he can find a doctor. As long as individuals know that they can find the goods and services that they want in the market, they are willing to forgo self-sufficiency and are willing to specialize. But what assures people that markets will deliver what they want? The answer to that question leads us to our second principle of economy-wide interaction.

Markets Move Toward Equilibrium

It's a busy afternoon at the supermarket; there are long lines at the checkout counters. Then one of the previously closed cash registers opens. What happens?

The first thing that happens, of course, is a rush to that register. After a couple of minutes, however, things will have settled down; shoppers will have rearranged themselves so that the line at the newly opened register is about the same length as the lines at all the other registers.

How do we know that? We know from our fourth principle of individual choice that people will exploit opportunities to make themselves better off. This means that people will rush to the newly opened register in order to save time standing in line. And things will settle down when shoppers can no longer improve their position by switching lines—that is, when the opportunities to make themselves better off have all been exploited.

A story about supermarket checkout lines may seem to have little to do with economy-wide interactions, but in fact it illustrates an important principle. A situation in which individuals cannot make themselves better off by doing something different—the situation in which all the checkout lines are the same length—is what economists call an **equilibrium**. An economic situation is in equilibrium when no individual would be better off doing something different.

Recall the story about the mythical Jiffy Lube, where it was supposedly cheaper to leave your car for an oil change than to pay for parking. If that opportunity had

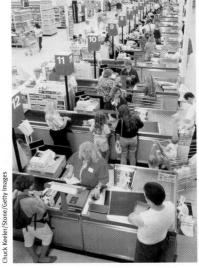

Chuck Keeler/Stone/Getty Images

Witness equilibrium in action at the checkout lines in your neighborhood supermarket.

An economic situation is in **equilibrium** when no individual would be better off doing something different.

FOR INQUIRING MINDS

CHOOSING SIDES

Why do people in America drive on the right side of the road? Of course, it's the law. But long before it was the law, it was an equilibrium.

Before there were formal traffic laws, there were informal "rules of the road," practices that everyone expected everyone else to follow. These rules included an understanding that people would normally keep to one side of the road. In some places, such as England, the rule was to keep to the left; in others, such as France, it was to keep to the right.

Why would some places choose the right and others, the left? That's not completely

clear, although it may have depended on the dominant form of traffic. Men riding horses and carrying swords on their left hip preferred to ride on the left (think about getting on or off the horse, and you'll see why). On the other hand, right-handed people walking but leading horses apparently preferred to walk on the right.

In any case, once a rule of the road was established, there were strong incentives for each individual to stay on the "usual" side of the road: those who didn't would keep colliding with oncoming traffic. So once established, the rule of the road would be self-enforcing—that is, it would

be an equilibrium. Nowadays, of course, which side you drive on is determined by law; some countries have even changed sides (Sweden went from left to right in 1967). But what about pedestrians? There are no laws—but there are informal rules. In the United States, urban pedestrians normally keep to the right. But if you should happen to visit Japan, watch out: the Japanese, who drive on the left, also typically walk on the left. So when in Japan, do as the Japanese do. You won't be arrested if you walk on the right, but you will be worse off than if you accept the equilibrium and walk on the left.

really existed and people were still paying $30 to park in garages, the situation would *not* have been an equilibrium.

And that should have been a giveaway that the story couldn't be true. In reality, people would have seized an opportunity to park cheaply, just as they seize opportunities to save time at the checkout line. And in so doing they would have eliminated the opportunity! Either it would have become very hard to get an appointment for an oil change or the price of a lube job would have increased to the point that it was no longer an attractive option (unless you really needed a lube job).

As we will see, markets usually reach equilibrium via changes in prices, which rise or fall until no opportunities for individuals to make themselves better off remain.

The concept of equilibrium is extremely helpful in understanding economic interactions because it provides a way of cutting through the sometimes complex details of those interactions. To understand what happens when a new line is opened at a supermarket, you don't need to worry about exactly how shoppers rearrange themselves, who moves ahead of whom, which register just opened, and so on. What you need to know is that any time there is a change, the situation will move to an equilibrium.

The fact that markets move toward equilibrium is why we can depend on them to work in a predictable way. In fact, we can trust markets to supply us with the essentials of life. For example, people who live in big cities can be sure that the supermarket shelves will always be fully stocked. Why? Because if some merchants who distribute food *didn't* make deliveries, a big profit opportunity would be created for any merchant who did—and there would be a rush to supply food, just like the rush to a newly opened cash register. So the market ensures that food will always be available for city dwellers. And, returning to our previous principle, this allows city dwellers to be city dwellers—to specialize in doing city jobs rather than living on farms and growing their own food.

A market economy also allows people to achieve gains from trade. But how do we know how well such an economy is doing? The next principle gives us a standard to use in evaluating an economy's performance.

Resources Should Be Used as Efficiently as Possible to Achieve Society's Goals

Suppose you are taking a course in which the classroom is too small for the number of students—many people are forced to stand or sit on the floor—despite the fact that large, empty classrooms are available nearby. You would say, correctly, that this is no way to run a college. Economists would call this an *inefficient* use of resources.

But if an inefficient use of resources is undesirable, just what does it mean to use resources *efficiently?* You might imagine that the efficient use of resources has something to do with money, maybe that it is measured in dollars-and-cents terms. But in economics, as in life, money is only a means to other ends. The measure that economists really care about is not money but people's happiness or welfare. Economists say that *an economy's resources are used efficiently when they are used in a way that has fully exploited all opportunities to make everyone better off.* To put it another way, an economy is **efficient** if it takes all opportunities to make some people better off without making other people worse off.

In our classroom example, there clearly was a way to make everyone better off—moving the class to a larger room would make people in the class better off without hurting anyone else in the college. Assigning the course to the smaller classroom was an inefficient use of the college's resources, while assigning the course to the larger classroom would have been an efficient use of the college's resources.

When an economy is efficient, it is producing the maximum gains from trade possible given the resources available. Why? Because there is no way to rearrange how resources are used in a way that can make everyone better off. When an economy is efficient, one person can be made better off by rearranging how resources are used *only*

An economy is **efficient** if it takes all opportunities to make some people better off without making other people worse off.

by making someone else worse off. In our classroom example, if all larger classrooms were already occupied, the college would have been run in an efficient way: your class could be made better off by moving to a larger classroom only by making people in the larger classroom worse off by making them move to a smaller classroom.

Should economic policy makers always strive to achieve economic efficiency? Well, not quite, because efficiency is not the only criterion by which to evaluate an economy. People also care about issues of fairness or **equity**. And there is typically a trade-off between equity and efficiency: policies that promote equity often come at a cost of decreased efficiency in the economy, and vice versa.

To see this, consider the case of disabled-designated parking spaces in public parking lots. Many people have great difficulty walking due to age or disability, so it seems only fair to assign closer parking spaces specifically for their use. You may have noticed, however, that a certain amount of inefficiency is involved. To make sure that there is always an appropriate space available should a disabled person want one, there are typically quite a number of disabled-designated spaces. So at any one time there are typically more such spaces available than there are disabled people who want one. As a result, desirable parking spaces are unused. (And the temptation for non-disabled people to use them is so great that we must be dissuaded by fear of getting a ticket.) So, short of hiring parking valets to allocate spaces, there is a conflict between *equity*, making life "fairer" for disabled people, and *efficiency*, making sure that all opportunities to make people better off have been fully exploited by never letting close-in parking spaces go unused.

Exactly how far policy makers should go in promoting equity over efficiency is a very difficult question that goes to the heart of the political process. As such, it is not a question that economists can answer. What is important for economists, however, is to always seek to use the economy's resources as efficiently as possible in the pursuit of society's goals, whatever those goals may be.

> **Equity** means that everyone gets his or her fair share. Since people can disagree about what's "fair," equity isn't as well-defined a concept as efficiency.

Markets Usually Lead to Efficiency

No branch of the U.S. government is entrusted with ensuring the general economic efficiency of our market economy—we don't have agents who go around making sure that brain surgeons aren't plowing fields, that Minnesota farmers aren't trying to grow oranges, that prime beachfront property isn't taken up by used-car dealerships, that colleges aren't wasting valuable classroom space. The government doesn't need to enforce efficiency because in most cases the invisible hand does the job.

In other words, the incentives built into a market economy already ensure that resources are usually put to good use, that opportunities to make people better off are not wasted. If a college were known for its habit of crowding students into small classrooms while large classrooms go unused, it would soon find its enrollment dropping, putting the jobs of its administrators at risk. The "market" for college students would respond in a way that induces administrators to run the college efficiently.

A detailed explanation of why markets are usually very good at making sure that resources are used well will have to wait until we have studied how markets actually work. But the most basic reason is that in a market economy, in which individuals are free to choose what to consume and what to produce, opportunities for mutual gain are normally taken. If there is a way in which some people can be made better off, people will usually be able to take advantage of that opportunity. And that is exactly what defines efficiency: all the opportunities to make everyone better off have been exploited.

As we learned in the Introduction, however, there are exceptions to this principle that markets are generally efficient. In cases of *market failure*, the individual pursuit of self-interest found in markets makes society worse off—that is, the market outcome is inefficient. And, as we will see in examining the next principle, when markets fail, government intervention can help. But short of instances of market failure, the general rule is that markets are a remarkably good way of organizing an economy.

When Markets Don't Achieve Efficiency, Government Intervention Can Improve Society's Welfare

Let's recall from the Introduction the nature of the market failure caused by traffic congestion—a commuter driving to work has no incentive to take into account the cost that his or her action inflicts on other drivers in the form of increased traffic congestion. There are several possible remedies to this situation; examples include charging road tolls, subsidizing the cost of public transportation, or taxing sales of gasoline to individual drivers. All these remedies work by changing the incentives of would-be drivers—motivating them to drive less and use alternative transportation. But they also share another feature: each relies on government intervention in the market.

This brings us to our fifth and last principle of interaction: *When markets don't achieve efficiency, government intervention can improve society's welfare.* That is, when markets go wrong, an appropriately designed government policy can sometimes move society closer to an efficient outcome by changing how society's resources are used.

A very important branch of economics is devoted to studying why markets fail and what policies should be adopted to improve social welfare. We will study these problems and their remedies in depth in later chapters, but here we give a brief overview of why markets fail. They fail for three principal reasons:

- Individual actions have *side effects* that are not properly taken into account by the market.

- One party prevents mutually beneficial trades from occurring in the attempt to capture a greater share of resources for itself.

- Some goods, by their very nature, are unsuited for efficient management by markets.

An important part of your education in economics is learning to identify not just when markets work but also when they don't work—and to judge what government policies are appropriate in each situation.

economics in action

Restoring Equilibrium on the Freeways

In 1994 a powerful earthquake struck the Los Angeles area, causing several freeway bridges to collapse and thereby disrupting the normal commuting routes of hundreds of thousands of drivers. The events that followed offer a particularly clear example of interdependent decision making—in this case, the decisions of commuters about how to get to work.

In the immediate aftermath of the earthquake, there was great concern about the impact on traffic, since motorists would now have to crowd onto alternative routes or detour around the blockages by using city streets. Public officials and news programs warned commuters to expect massive delays and urged them to avoid unnecessary travel, reschedule their work to commute before or after the rush, or use mass transit. These warnings were unexpectedly effective. In fact, so many people heeded them that in the first few days following the quake, those who maintained their regular commuting routine actually found the drive to and from work faster than before.

Of course, this situation could not last. As word spread that traffic was actually not bad at all, people abandoned their less convenient new commuting methods and reverted to their cars—and traffic got steadily worse. Within a few weeks after the quake, serious traffic jams had appeared. After a few more weeks, however, the situation stabilized: the reality of worse-than-usual congestion discouraged enough drivers to prevent the nightmare of citywide gridlock from materializing. Los Angeles traffic, in short, had settled into a new equilibrium, in which each commuter was making the best choice he or she could, given what everyone else was doing.

This was not, by the way, the end of the story: fears that the city would strangle on traffic led local authorities to repair the roads with record speed. Within only 18 months after the quake, all the freeways were back to normal, ready for the next one. ∎

> > > > > > > > > > > > > > > > > > > >

>>CHECK YOUR UNDERSTANDING 1-2

1. Explain how each of the following situations illustrates one of the five principles of interaction.
   a. Using the college website, any student who wants to sell a used textbook for at least $X is able to sell it to another who is willing to pay $X.
   b. At a college tutoring co-op, students can arrange to provide tutoring in subjects they are good in (like economics) in return for receiving tutoring in subjects they are poor in (like philosophy).
   c. The local municipality imposes a law that requires bars and nightclubs near residential areas to keep their noise levels below a certain threshold.
   d. To provide better care for low-income patients, the city of Tampa has decided to close some underutilized neighborhood clinics and shift funds to the main hospital.
   e. On the college website, books of a given title with approximately the same level of wear and tear sell for about the same price.

2. Which of the following describes an equilibrium situation? Which does not? Explain your answer.
   a. The restaurants across the street from the university dining hall serve better-tasting and cheaper meals than those served at the university dining hall. The vast majority of students continue to eat at the dining hall.
   b. You currently take the subway to work. Although taking the bus is cheaper, the ride takes longer. So you are willing to pay the higher subway fare in order to save time.

Solutions appear at back of book.

>>QUICK REVIEW

➤ A feature of most economic situations is the *interaction* of choices made by individuals, the end result of which may be quite different than what was intended. In a market economy, this takes the form of *trade* between individuals.
➤ Individuals interact because there are *gains from trade*. Gains from trade arise from *specialization*.
➤ Economic situations normally move toward *equilibrium*.
➤ As far as possible, there should be an *efficient* use of resources to achieve society's goals. But efficiency is not the only way to evaluate an economy; *equity* may also be desirable, and there is often a trade-off between equity and efficiency.
➤ Markets normally *are* efficient, except for certain well-defined exceptions.
➤ When markets fail to achieve efficiency, government intervention can improve society's welfare.

• A LOOK AHEAD •

The nine basic principles we have described lie behind almost all economic analysis. Although they can be immediately helpful in understanding many situations, they are usually not enough. Applying the principles to real economic issues takes one more step.

That step is the creation of *models*—simplified representations of economic situations. Models must be realistic enough to provide real-world guidance but simple enough that they allow us to see clearly the implications of the principles described in this chapter. So our next step is to show how models are used to actually do economic analysis.

SUMMARY

1. All economic analysis is based on a short list of basic principles. These principles apply to two levels of economic understanding. First, we must understand how individuals make choices; second, we must understand how these choices interact.

2. Everyone has to make choices about what to do and what *not* to do. **Individual choice** is the basis of economics—if it doesn't involve choice, it isn't economics.

3. The reason choices must be made is that **resources**—anything that can be used to produce something else—are **scarce.** Individuals are limited in their choices by money and time; economies are limited by their supplies of human and natural resources.

4. Because you must choose among limited alternatives, the true cost of anything is what you must give up to get it—all costs are **opportunity costs.**

5. Many economic decisions involve questions not of "whether" but of "how much"—how much to spend on some good, how much to produce, and so on. Such decisions must be taken by performing a **trade-off** *at the margin*—by comparing the costs and benefits of doing a bit more or a bit less. Decisions of this type are called **marginal decisions,** and the study of them, **marginal analysis,** plays a central role in economics.

6. The study of how people *should* make decisions is also a good way to understand actual behavior. Individuals usually exploit opportunities to make themselves better off. If opportunities change, so does behavior: people respond to **incentives.**

7. **Interaction**—my choices depend on your choices, and vice versa—adds another level to economic understanding.

When individuals interact, the end result may be different from what anyone intends.

8. The reason for interaction is that there are **gains from trade:** by engaging in the **trade** of goods and services with one another, the members of an economy can all be made better off. Underlying gains from trade are the advantages of **specialization,** of having individuals specialize in the tasks they are good at.

9. Economies normally move toward **equilibrium**—a situation in which no individual can make himself or herself better off by taking a different action.

10. An economy is **efficient** if all opportunities to make someone better off without making others worse off are taken. Resources should be used as efficiently as possible to achieve society's goals. But efficiency is not the sole way to evaluate an economy: **equity,** or fairness, is also desirable, and there is often a trade-off between equity and efficiency.

11. Markets usually lead to efficiency, with some well-defined exceptions.

12. When markets fail and do not achieve efficiency, government intervention can improve society's welfare.

KEY TERMS

Individual choice, p. 6
Resource, p. 6
Scarce, p. 6
Opportunity cost, p. 7
Trade-off, p. 8

Marginal decisions, p. 9
Marginal analysis, p. 9
Incentive, p. 9
Interaction, p. 11
Trade, p. 12

Gains from trade, p. 12
Specialization, p. 12
Equilibrium, p. 13
Efficient, p. 14
Equity, p. 15

PROBLEMS

1. In each of the following situations, identify which of the nine principles is at work.

   a. You choose to shop at the local discount store rather than paying a higher price for the same merchandise at the local department store.

   b. On your spring vacation trip, your budget is limited to $35 a day.

   c. The student union provides a website on which departing students can sell items such as used books, appliances, and furniture rather than giving them away to their roommates as they formerly did.

   d. You decide how many cups of coffee to have when studying the night before an exam by considering how much more work you can do by having another cup versus how jittery it will make you feel.

   e. There is limited lab space available to do the project required in Chemistry 101. The lab supervisor assigns lab time to each student based on when that student is able to come.

   f. You realize that you can graduate a semester early by forgoing a semester of study abroad.

   g. At the student union, there is a bulletin board on which people advertise used items for sale, such as bicycles. Once you have adjusted for differences in quality, all the bikes sell for about the same price.

   h. You are better at performing lab experiments, and your lab partner is better at writing lab reports. So the two of you agree that you will do all the experiments, and she will write up all the reports.

   i. State governments mandate that it is illegal to drive without passing a driving exam.

2. Describe some of the opportunity costs when you decide to do the following.

   a. Attend college instead of taking a job

   b. Watch a movie instead of studying for an exam

   c. Ride the bus instead of driving your car

3. Liza needs to buy a textbook for the next economics class. The price at the college bookstore is $65. One online site offers it for $55 and another site for $57. All prices include sales tax. The accompanying table indicates the typical shipping and handling charges for the textbook ordered online.

   a. What is the opportunity cost of buying online?

   b. Show the relevant choices for this student. What determines which of these options the student will choose?

Shipping method	Delivery time	Charge
Standard shipping	3–7 days	$3.99
Second-day air	2 business days	$8.98
Next-day air	1 business day	$13.98

4. Use the concept of opportunity cost to explain the following.

   a. More people choose to get graduate degrees when the job market is poor.

   b. More people choose to do their own home repairs when the economy is slow.

   c. There are more parks in suburban areas than in urban areas.

d. Convenience stores, which have higher prices than supermarkets, cater to busy people.

e. Fewer students enroll in classes that meet before 10:00 A.M.

5. In the following examples, state how you would use the principle of marginal analysis to make a decision.

a. Deciding how many days to wait before doing your laundry

b. Deciding how much library research to do before writing your term paper

c. Deciding how many bags of chips to eat

d. Deciding how many lectures of a class to skip

6. This morning you made the following individual choices: you bought a bagel and coffee at the local café, you drove to school in your car during rush hour, and you typed your roommate's term paper because you are a fast typist—in return for which she will do your laundry for a month. In each of these actions, describe how your individual choices interacted with the individual choices made by others. Were other people left better off or worse off by your choices in each case?

7. On the east side of the Hatatoochie River lives the Hatfield family, while the McCoy family lives on the west side. Each family's diet consists of fried chicken and corn-on-the-cob, and each is self-sufficient, raising their own chickens and growing their own corn. Explain the conditions under which each of the following would be true.

a. The two families are made better off when the Hatfields specialize in raising chickens, the McCoys specialize in raising corn, and the two families trade.

b. The two families are made better off when the McCoys specialize in raising chickens, the Hatfields specialize in raising corn, and the two families trade.

8. Which of the following situations describes an equilibrium? Which does not? If the situation does not describe an equilibrium, what would an equilibrium look like?

a. Many people regularly commute from the suburbs to downtown Pleasantville. Due to traffic congestion, the trip takes 30 minutes when you travel by highway, but only 15 minutes when you go by side streets.

b. At the intersection of Main and Broadway are two gas stations. One station charges $3.00 per gallon for regular gas and the other charges $2.85 per gallon. Customers can get service immediately at the first station, but must wait in a long line at the second.

c. Every student enrolled in Economics 101 must also attend a weekly tutorial. This year there are two sections offered: section A and section B, which meet at the same time in adjoining classrooms and are taught by equally competent instructors. Section A is overcrowded, with people sitting on the floor and often unable to see the chalkboard. Section B has many empty seats.

9. In each of the following cases, explain whether you think the situation is efficient or not. If it is not efficient, why not? What actions would make the situation efficient?

a. Electricity is included in the rent at your dorm. Some residents in your dorm leave lights, computers, and appliances on when they are not in their rooms.

b. Although they cost the same amount to prepare, the cafeteria in your dorm consistently provides too many dishes that diners don't like, such as tofu casserole, and too few dishes that diners do like, such as roast turkey with dressing.

c. The enrollment for a particular course exceeds the spaces available. Some students who need to take this course to complete their major are unable to get a space while others who are taking it as an elective do get a space.

10. Discuss the efficiency and equity implications of each of the following policies. How would you go about balancing the concerns of equity and efficiency in these areas?

a. The government pays the full tuition for every college student to study whatever subject he or she wishes.

b. When people lose their jobs, the government provides unemployment benefits until they find new ones.

11. Governments often adopt certain policies in order to promote desired behavior among their citizens. For each of the following policies, determine what the incentive is and what behavior the government wishes to promote. In each case, why do you think that the government might wish to change people's behavior, rather than allow their actions to be solely determined by individual choice?

a. A tax of $5 per pack is imposed on cigarettes.

b. The government pays parents $100 when their child is vaccinated for measles.

c. The government pays college students to tutor children from low-income families.

d. The government imposes a tax on the amount of air pollution that a company discharges.

12. In each of the following situations, explain how government intervention could improve society's welfare by changing people's incentives. In what sense is the market going wrong?

a. Pollution from auto emissions has reached unhealthy levels.

b. Everyone in Woodville would be better off if streetlights were installed in the town. But no individual resident is willing to pay for installation of a streetlight in front of his or her house because it is impossible to recoup the cost by charging other residents for the benefit they receive from it.

>web... To continue your study and review of concepts in this chapter, please visit the Krugman/Wells website for quizzes, animated graph tutorials, web links to helpful resources, and more.

www.worthpublishers.com/krugmanwells

>>Economic Models: Trade-offs and Trade

TUNNEL VISION

IN 1901 WILBUR AND ORVILLE WRIGHT built something that would change the world. No, not the airplane—their successful flight at Kitty Hawk would come two years later. What made the Wright brothers true visionaries was their wind tunnel, an apparatus that let them experiment with many different designs for wings and control surfaces. These experiments gave them the knowledge that would make heavier-than-air flight possible.

A miniature airplane sitting motionless in a wind tunnel isn't the same thing as an actual aircraft in flight. But it is a very useful model of a flying plane—a simplified representation of the real thing that can be used to answer crucial questions, such as how much lift a given wing shape will generate at a given airspeed.

Needless to say, testing an airplane design in a wind tunnel is cheaper and safer than building a full-scale version and hoping it will fly. More generally, models play a crucial role in almost all scientific research—economics very much included.

In fact, you could say that economic theory consists mainly of a collection of models, a series of simplified representations of economic reality that allow us to understand a variety of economic issues.

Clearly, the Wright brothers believed in their model.

Landov Photos

In this chapter, we will look at three economic models that are crucially important in their own right and also illustrate why such models are so useful. We'll conclude with a look at how economists actually use models in their work.

Models in Economics: Some Important Examples

A **model** is any simplified representation of reality that is used to better understand real-life situations. But how do we create a simplified representation of an economic situation?

One possibility—an economist's equivalent of a wind tunnel—is to find or create a real but simplified economy. For example, economists interested in the economic role of money have studied the system of exchange that developed in World War II prison camps, in which cigarettes became a universally accepted form of payment even among prisoners who didn't smoke.

Another possibility is to simulate the workings of the economy on a computer. For example, when changes in tax law are proposed, government officials use *tax models*—large computer programs—to assess how the proposed changes would affect different types of people.

The importance of models is that they allow economists to focus on the effects of only one change at a time. That is, they allow us to hold everything else constant and study how one change affects the overall economic outcome. So the **other things equal assumption**, which means that all other relevant factors remain unchanged, is an important assumption when building economic models.

A **model** is a simplified representation of a real situation that is used to better understand real-life situations.

The **other things equal assumption** means that all other relevant factors remain unchanged.

FOR INQUIRING MINDS

MODELS FOR MONEY

What's an economic model worth, anyway? In some cases, quite a lot of money.

Although many economic models are developed for purely scientific purposes, others are developed to help governments make economic policies. And there is a growing business in developing economic models to help corporations make decisions.

Who models for money? There are dozens of consulting firms that use models to predict future trends, offer advice based on their models, or develop custom models for business and government clients. A notable example is Global Insight, the world's biggest economic consulting firm. It was created by a merger between Data Resources, Inc., founded by professors from Harvard and MIT, and Wharton Economic Forecasting Associates, founded by professors at the University of Pennsylvania.

One particularly lucrative branch of economics is finance theory, which helps investors figure out what assets, such as shares in a company, are worth. Finance theorists often become highly paid "rocket scientists" at big Wall Street firms because financial models demand a high level of technical expertise.

Unfortunately, the most famous business application of finance theory came spectacularly to grief. In 1994 a group of Wall Street traders teamed up with famous finance theorists—including two Nobel Prize winners—to form Long-Term Capital Management (LTCM), a fund that used sophisticated financial models to invest the money of wealthy clients. At first, the fund did very well. But in 1998 bad news from all over the world—with countries as disparate as Russia, Japan, and Brazil in trouble at the same time—inflicted huge losses on LTCM's investments. For a few anxious days, many people feared not only that the fund would collapse but also that it would bring many other companies down with it. Thanks in part to a rescue operation organized by government officials, this did not happen; but LTCM was closed a few months later, with some of its investors losing most of the money they had put in.

What went wrong? Partly it was bad luck. But experienced hands also faulted the economists at LTCM for taking too many risks. Their models said that a run of bad news like the one that actually happened was extremely unlikely—but a sensible economist knows that sometimes even the best model misses important possibilities.

But you can't always find or create a small-scale version of the whole economy, and a computer program is only as good as the data it uses. (Programmers have a saying: garbage in, garbage out.) For many purposes, the most effective form of economic modeling is the construction of "thought experiments": simplified, hypothetical versions of real-life situations.

In Chapter 1 we illustrated the concept of equilibrium with the example of how customers at a supermarket would rearrange themselves when a new cash register opens. Though we didn't say it, this was an example of a simple model—an imaginary supermarket, in which many details were ignored (what are the customers buying? never mind), that could be used to answer a "what if" question: what if another cash register were opened?

As the cash register story showed, it is often possible to describe and analyze a useful economic model in plain English. However, because much of economics involves changes in quantities—in the price of a product, the number of units produced, or the number of workers employed in its production—economists often find that using some mathematics helps clarify an issue. In particular, a numerical example, a simple equation, or—especially—a graph can be key to understanding an economic concept.

Whatever form it takes, a good economic model can be a tremendous aid to understanding. The best way to make this point is to consider some simple but important economic models and what they tell us. First, we will look at the *production possibility frontier*, a model that helps economists think about the trade-offs every economy faces. Then we will turn to *comparative advantage*, a model that clarifies the principle of gains from trade—trade both between individuals and between countries. Finally, we'll examine the *circular-flow model*, which helps economists analyze the monetary transactions taking place in the economy as a whole.

In discussing these models, we make considerable use of graphs to represent mathematical relationships. Such graphs will play an important role throughout this book. If you are already familiar with the use of graphs, the material that follows should not present any problem. If you are not, this would be a good time to turn to the appendix of this chapter, which provides a brief introduction to the use of graphs in economics.

Trade-offs: The Production Possibility Frontier

The hit movie *Cast Away*, starring Tom Hanks, was an update of the classic story of Robinson Crusoe, the hero of Daniel Defoe's eighteenth-century novel. Hanks played the sole survivor of a plane crash, stranded on a remote island. As in the original story of Robinson Crusoe, the character played by Hanks had limited resources: the natural resources of the island, a few items he managed to salvage from the plane, and, of course, his own time and effort. With only these resources, he had to make a life. In effect, he became a one-man economy.

The first principle of economics we introduced in Chapter 1 was that resources are scarce and that, as a result, any economy—whether it contains one person or millions of people—faces trade-offs. For example, if a castaway devotes resources to catching fish, he cannot use those same resources to gather coconuts.

To think about the trade-offs that face any economy, economists often use the model known as the **production possibility frontier**. The idea behind this model is to improve our understanding of trade-offs by considering a simplified economy that produces only two goods. This simplification enables us to show the trade-off graphically.

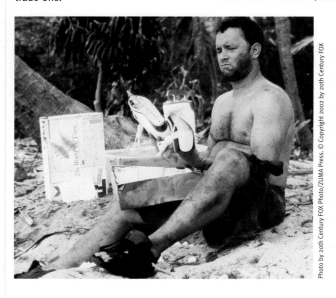

What to do? Even a castaway faces trade-offs.

Photo by 20th Century FOX Photo/ZUMA Press. © Copyright 2002 by 20th Century FOX

Figure 2-1 shows a hypothetical production possibility frontier for Tom, a castaway alone on an island, who must make a trade-off between production of fish and production of coconuts. The frontier—the curve in the diagram—shows the maximum number of fish Tom can catch during a week *given* the quantity of coconuts he gathers, and vice versa. That is, it answers questions of the form, "What is the maximum number of fish Tom can catch if he also gathers 20 (or 25, or 30) coconuts?" (We'll explain the bowed-out shape of the curve in Figure 2-1 shortly, after we've seen how to interpret the production possibility frontier.)

There is a crucial distinction between points *inside* or *on* the curve (the shaded area) and *outside* the curve. If a production point lies inside or on the frontier—like the point labeled *C*, at which Tom catches 20 fish and gathers 20 coconuts—it is feasible. After all, the frontier tells us that if Tom catches 20 fish, he could also gather a maximum of 25 coconuts, so he could certainly gather 20 coconuts. On the other hand, a production point that lies outside the frontier—such as the hypothetical production point shown in the figure as point *D*, where Tom catches 40 fish and gathers 30 coconuts—isn't feasible. (In this case, Tom could catch 40 fish and gather no coconuts *or* he could gather 30 coconuts and catch no fish, but he can't do both.)

In Figure 2-1 the production possibility frontier intersects the horizontal axis at 40 fish. This means that if Tom devoted all his resources to catching fish, he would catch 40 fish per week but would have no resources left over to gather coconuts. The production possibility frontier intersects the vertical axis at 30 coconuts; this means that if Tom devoted all his resources to gathering coconuts, he could gather 30 coconuts per week but would have no resources left over to catch fish.

The figure also shows less extreme trade-offs. For example, if Tom decides to catch 20 fish, he is able to gather 25 coconuts; this production choice is illustrated by point *A*. If Tom decides to catch 30 fish, he can gather at most only 20 coconuts, as shown by point *B*.

Thinking in terms of a production possibility frontier simplifies the complexities of reality. The real-world economy produces millions of different goods. Even a castaway on an island would produce more than two different items (for example, he would need clothing and housing as well as food). But in this model we imagine an economy that produces only two goods.

If we simplify reality, however, the production possibility frontier helps us understand some aspects of the real economy better than we could without the model.

> The **production possibility frontier** illustrates the trade-offs facing an economy that produces only two goods. It shows the maximum quantity of one good that can be produced for any given quantity produced of the other.

Figure 2-1

The Production Possibility Frontier

The production possibility frontier illustrates the trade-offs facing an economy that produces two goods. It shows the maximum quantity of one good that can be produced given the quantity of the other good produced. Here, the maximum number of coconuts that Tom can gather depends on the number of fish he catches, and vice versa. His feasible production is shown by the area *inside* or *on* the curve. Production at point *C* is feasible but not efficient. Points *A* and *B* are feasible and efficient, but point *D* is not feasible. **>web...**

>web... Throughout our book, this icon will be used to indicate which graphs are available in an interactive format on our text's website. You can work with these interactive graph tutorials and find additional learning resources if you go to www.worthpublishers.com/krugmanwells.

First of all, the production possibility frontier is a good way to illustrate the general economic concept of *efficiency*. Recall from Chapter 1 that an economy is efficient if there are no missed opportunities—there is no way to make some people better off without making other people worse off. A key element of efficiency is that there are no missed opportunities in production—there is no way to produce more of one good without producing less of other goods.

As long as Tom is on the production possibility frontier, his production is efficient. At point *A*, the 25 coconuts he gathers are the maximum number he can get *given* that he has chosen to catch 20 fish; at point *B*, the 20 coconuts he gathers are the maximum he can get *given* his choice to catch 30 fish; and so on.

But suppose that for some reason Tom was at point *C*, producing 20 fish and 20 coconuts. Then this one-person economy would definitely be *inefficient*: it could be producing more of both goods.

The production possibility frontier is also useful as a reminder of the fundamental point that the true cost of any good is not just the amount of money it costs to buy, but everything else in addition to money that must be given up in order to get that good—the *opportunity cost*. If Tom were to catch 30 fish instead of 20, he would be able to gather only 20 coconuts instead of 25. So the opportunity cost of those 10 extra fish is the 5 coconuts not gathered. And if 10 extra fish have an opportunity cost of 5 coconuts, each 1 fish has an opportunity cost of $5/10 = 0.5$ coconuts.

We can now explain the bowed-out shape of the production possibility frontier we saw in Figure 2-1: it reflects an assumption about how opportunity costs change as the mix of output changes. Figure 2-2 shows the same production possibility frontier as Figure 2-1. The arrows in Figure 2-2 illustrate the fact that with this bowed-out production possibility frontier, Tom faces *increasing opportunity cost*: the more fish he catches, the more coconuts he has to give up to catch an additional fish, and vice versa. For example, to go from producing zero fish to producing 20 fish, he has to give up 5 coconuts. That is, the opportunity cost of those 20 fish is 5 coconuts. But to increase his fish production to 40—that is, to produce an additional 20 fish—he must give up 25 more coconuts, a much higher opportunity cost.

Economists believe that opportunity costs are usually increasing. The reason is that when only a small amount of a good is produced, the economy can use

Figure 2-2

Increasing Opportunity Cost

The bowed-out shape of the production possibility frontier reflects increasing opportunity cost. In this example, to produce the first 20 fish, Tom must give up 5 coconuts. But to produce an additional 20 fish, he must give up 25 more coconuts. **>web...**

Producing the first 20 fish . . . . . . requires giving up 5 coconuts.

But producing 20 more fish . . . . . . requires giving up 25 more coconuts.

PPF

resources that are especially well suited for that production. For example, if an economy grows only a small amount of corn, that corn can be grown in places where the soil and climate are perfect for corn-growing but less suitable for growing anything else, like wheat. So growing that corn involves giving up only a small amount of potential wheat production. If the economy grows a lot of corn, however, land that isn't so great for corn and would have been well suited for wheat must be pressed into service, so the additional corn production will involve sacrificing considerably more wheat production.

Finally, the production possibility frontier helps us understand what it means to talk about *economic growth*. We introduced the concept of economic growth in the Introduction, defining it as *the growing ability of the economy to produce goods and services*. As we saw, economic growth is one of the fundamental features of the real economy. But are we really justified in saying that the economy has grown? After all, although the U.S. economy produces more of many things than it did a century ago, it produces less of other things—for example, horse-drawn carriages. Production of many goods, in other words, is actually down. So how can we say for sure that the economy as a whole has grown?

The answer, illustrated in Figure 2-3, is that economic growth means an *expansion of the economy's production possibilities*: the economy *can* produce more of everything. For example, if Tom's production is initially at point *A* (20 fish and 25 coconuts), economic growth means that he could move to point *E* (25 fish and 30 coconuts). *E* lies outside the original frontier; so in the production possibility frontier model, growth is shown as an outward shift of the frontier.

What the economy actually produces depends on the choices people make. After his production possibilities expand, Tom might not actually choose to produce both more fish and more coconuts—he might choose to increase production of only one good, or he might even choose to produce less of one good. But even if, for some reason, he chooses to produce either fewer coconuts or fewer fish than before, we would still say that his economy has grown—because he *could* have produced more of everything.

The production possibility frontier is a very simplified model of an economy. Yet it teaches us important lessons about real-life economies. It gives us our first clear sense of a key element of economic efficiency, it illustrates the concept of opportunity cost, and it makes clear what economic growth is all about.

Figure 2-3

Economic Growth

Economic growth results in an *outward shift* of the production possibility frontier because production possibilities are expanded. The economy can now produce more of everything. For example, if production is initially at point *A* (20 fish and 25 coconuts), it could move to point *E* (25 fish and 30 coconuts).

Comparative Advantage and Gains from Trade

Among the nine principles of economics described in Chapter 1 was that of *gains from trade*—the mutual gains that individuals can achieve by specializing in doing different things and trading with one another. Our second illustration of an economic model is a particularly useful model of gains from trade—trade based on *comparative advantage*.

Let's stick with Tom stranded on his island, but now let's suppose that a second castaway, who just happens to be named Hank, is washed ashore. Can they benefit from trading with each other?

It's obvious that there will be potential gains from trade if the two castaways do different things particularly well. For example, if Tom is a skilled fisherman and Hank is very good at climbing trees, clearly it makes sense for Tom to catch fish and Hank to gather coconuts—and for the two men to trade the products of their efforts.

But one of the most important insights in all of economics is that there are gains from trade even if one of the trading parties isn't especially good at anything. Suppose, for example, that Hank is less well suited to primitive life than Tom; he's not nearly as good at catching fish, and compared to Tom even his coconut-gathering leaves something to be desired. Nonetheless, what we'll see is that both Tom and Hank can live better by trading with each other than either could alone.

For the purposes of this example, let's slightly redraw Tom's production possibilities represented by the production possibility frontier in panel (a) of Figure 2-4. According to this diagram, Tom could catch at most 40 fish, but only if he gathered no coconuts, and could gather 30 coconuts, but only if he caught no fish, as before.

In Figure 2-4, we have replaced the curved production possibility frontier of Figure 2-1 with a straight line. Why do this, when we've already seen that economists regard a bowed-out production possibility frontier as normal? The answer is that it simplifies our discussion—and as we have explained, modeling is all about simplification. The principle of comparative advantage doesn't depend on the assumption of straight-line production possibility frontiers, but it is easier to explain with that assumption.

The straight-line production possibility frontier in panel (a) of Figure 2-4 has a *constant slope* of −¾. (The appendix to this chapter explains how to calculate the slope of a line.) That is, for every 4 additional fish that Tom chooses to catch, he

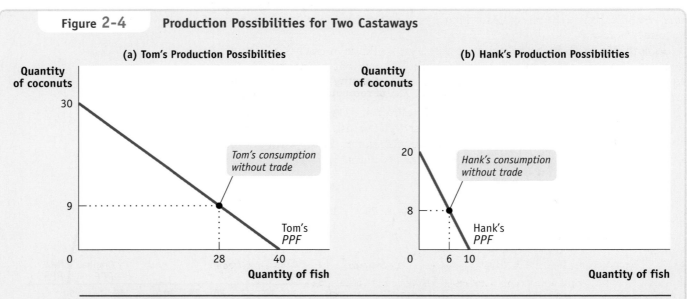

Figure 2-4   Production Possibilities for Two Castaways

Here, each of the two castaways has a constant opportunity cost of fish and a straight-line production possibility frontier: In Tom's case, each fish always has an opportunity cost of ¾ of a coconut. In Hank's case, each fish always has an opportunity cost of 2 coconuts. **>web...**

gathers 3 fewer coconuts. So Tom's opportunity cost of a fish is ¾ of a coconut regardless of how many or how few fish he catches. In contrast, a production possibility frontier is curved when the opportunity cost of a good changes according to how much of the good has already been produced. For example, you can see from Figure 2-2 that if Tom starts at the point of having caught zero fish and gathers 30 coconuts, his opportunity cost of catching 20 fish is 5 coconuts. But once he has already caught 20 fish, the opportunity cost of an additional 20 fish increases to 25 coconuts.

Panel (b) of Figure 2-4 shows Hank's production possibilities. Like Tom's, Hank's production possibility frontier is a straight line, implying a constant opportunity cost of fish in terms of coconuts. His production possibility frontier has a constant slope of −2. Hank is less productive all around: at most he can produce 10 fish or 20 coconuts. But he is particularly bad at fishing; whereas Tom sacrifices ¾ of a coconut per fish caught, for Hank the opportunity cost of a fish is 2 whole coconuts. Table 2-1 summarizes the two castaways' opportunity costs for fish and coconuts.

Now Tom and Hank could go their separate ways, each living on his own side of the island, catching his own fish and gathering his own coconuts. Let's suppose that they start out that way and make the consumption choices shown in Figure 2-4: in the absence of trade, Tom consumes 28 fish and 9 coconuts per week, while Hank consumes 6 fish and 8 coconuts.

But is this the best they can do? No, it isn't. Given that the two castaways have different opportunity costs, they can strike a deal that makes both of them better off.

Table 2-2 shows how such a deal works: Tom specializes in the production of fish, catching 40 per week, and gives 10 to Hank. Meanwhile, Hank specializes in the production of coconuts, gathering 20 per week, and gives 10 to Tom. The result is shown in Figure 2-5 on page 28. Tom now consumes more of both goods than before: instead of 28 fish and 9 coconuts, he consumes 30 fish and 10 coconuts. And Hank also consumes more, going from 6 fish and 8 coconuts to 10 fish and 10 coconuts. As Table 2-2 also shows, both Tom and Hank experience gains from trade: Tom's consumption of fish increases by two, and his consumption of coconuts increases by one. Hank's consumption of fish increases by four, and his consumption of coconuts by two.

So both castaways are better off when they each specialize in what they are good at and trade. It's a good idea for Tom to catch the fish for both of them because his opportunity cost of a fish is only ¾ of a coconut not gathered versus 2 coconuts for Hank. Correspondingly, it's a good idea for Hank to gather coconuts for the both of them.

Or we could put it the other way around: Because Tom is so good at catching fish, his opportunity cost of gathering coconuts is high: ⁴⁄₃ fish not caught for every coconut gathered. Because Hank is a pretty poor fisherman, his opportunity cost of gathering coconuts is much less, only ½ a fish per coconut.

TABLE 2-1

Tom's and Hank's Opportunity Costs of Fish and Coconuts

	Tom's Opportunity Cost	Hank's Opportunity Cost
One fish	3/4 coconut	2 coconuts
One coconut	4/3 fish	1/2 fish

TABLE 2-2

How the Castaways Gain from Trade

		Without Trade		With Trade		Gains from Trade
		Production	Consumption	Production	Consumption	
Tom	Fish	28	28	40	30	+2
	Coconuts	9	9	0	10	+1
Hank	Fish	6	6	0	10	+4
	Coconuts	8	8	20	10	+2

Figure 2-5 **Comparative Advantage and Gains From Trade**

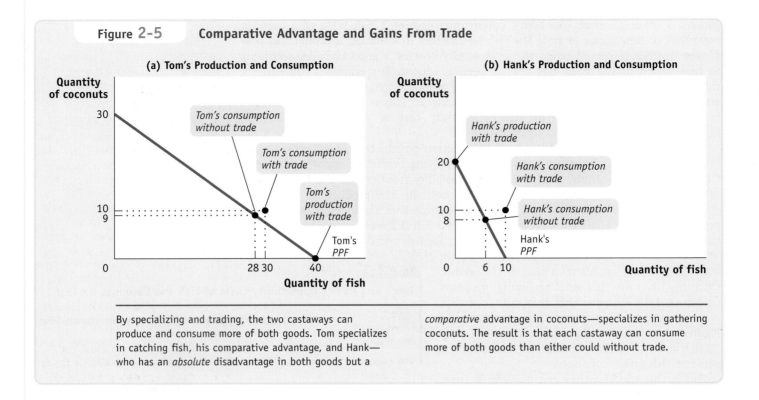

By specializing and trading, the two castaways can produce and consume more of both goods. Tom specializes in catching fish, his comparative advantage, and Hank—who has an *absolute* disadvantage in both goods but a *comparative* advantage in coconuts—specializes in gathering coconuts. The result is that each castaway can consume more of both goods than either could without trade.

An individual has a **comparative advantage** in producing a good or service if the opportunity cost of producing the good is lower for that individual than for other people.

What we would say in this case is that Tom has a **comparative advantage** in catching fish and Hank has a comparative advantage in gathering coconuts. An individual has a comparative advantage in producing something if the opportunity cost of that production is lower for that individual than for other people. In other words, Hank has a comparative advantage over Tom in producing a particular good or service if Hank's opportunity cost of producing that good or service is lower than Tom's.

The story of Tom and Hank clearly simplifies reality. Yet it teaches us some very important lessons that apply to the real economy, too.

First, the model provides a clear illustration of the gains from trade: by agreeing to specialize and provide goods to each other, Tom and Hank can produce more and therefore both be better off than if they tried to be self-sufficient.

Second, the model demonstrates a very important point that is often overlooked in real-world arguments: as long as people have different opportunity costs, *everyone has a comparative advantage in something, and everyone has a comparative disadvantage in something.*

Notice that in our example Tom is actually better than Hank at producing both goods: Tom can catch more fish in a week, and he can also gather more coconuts.

An individual has an **absolute advantage** in an activity if he or she can do it better than other people. Having an absolute advantage is not the same thing as having a comparative advantage.

That is, Tom has an **absolute advantage** in both activities: he can produce more output with a given amount of input (in this case, his time) than Hank. You might therefore be tempted to think that Tom has nothing to gain from trading with the less competent Hank.

But we've just seen that Tom can indeed benefit from a deal with Hank because *comparative*, not *absolute*, advantage is the basis for mutual gain. It doesn't matter that it takes Hank more time to gather a coconut; what matters is that for him the opportunity cost of that coconut in terms of fish is lower. So Hank, despite his absolute disadvantage, even in coconuts, has a comparative advantage in coconut-gathering. Meanwhile Tom, who can use his time better by catching fish, has a comparative *disadvantage* in coconut-gathering.

If comparative advantage were relevant only to castaways, it might not be that interesting. In fact, however, the idea of comparative advantage applies to many activities in the economy. Perhaps its most important application is to trade—not between individuals, but between countries. So let's look briefly at how the model of comparative advantage helps in understanding both the causes and the effects of international trade.

Comparative Advantage and International Trade

Look at the label on a manufactured good sold in the United States, and there's a good chance you will find that it was produced in some other country—in China, or Japan, or even in Canada, eh? On the other side, many U.S. industries sell a large fraction of their output overseas (this is particularly true of agriculture, high technology, and entertainment).

Should all this international exchange of goods and services be celebrated, or is it cause for concern? Politicians and the public often question the desirability of international trade, arguing that the nation should produce goods for itself rather than buying them from foreigners. Industries around the world demand protection from foreign competition: Japanese farmers want to keep out American rice, American steelworkers want to keep out European steel. And these demands are often supported by public opinion.

Economists, however, have a very positive view of international trade. Why? Because they view it in terms of comparative advantage.

Figure 2-6 shows, with a simple example, how international trade can be interpreted in terms of comparative advantage. Although the example as constructed is hypothetical, it is based on an actual pattern of international trade: American exports of pork to Canada and Canadian exports of aircraft to the United States. Panels (a) and (b) of Figure 2-6 illustrate hypothetical production possibility frontiers for the United States and

PITFALLS

MISUNDERSTANDING COMPARATIVE ADVANTAGE

Students do it, pundits do it, and politicians do it all the time: they confuse *comparative* advantage with *absolute* advantage. For example, back in the 1980s, when the U.S. economy seemed to be lagging behind that of Japan, one often heard commentators warn that if we didn't improve our productivity, we would soon have no comparative advantage in anything.

What those commentators meant was that we would have no *absolute* advantage in anything—that there might come a time when the Japanese were better at everything than we were. (It didn't turn out that way, but that's another story.) And they had the idea that in that case we would no longer be able to benefit from trade with Japan.

But just as Hank is able to benefit from trade with Tom (and vice versa) despite the fact that Tom is better at everything, nations can still gain from trade even if they are less productive in all industries than the countries they trade with.

| Figure 2-6 | Comparative Advantage and International Trade |

In this hypothetical example, Canada and the United States produce only two goods: pork and aircraft. Aircraft are measured on the vertical axis and pork on the horizontal axis. Panel (a) shows the U.S. production possibility frontier. It is relatively flat, implying that the United States has a comparative advantage in pork production. Panel (b) shows the Canadian production possibility frontier. It is relatively steep, implying that Canada has a comparative advantage in aircraft production. Just like two individuals, both countries gain from specialization and trade. **>web...**

Canada, with pork measured on the horizontal axis and aircraft measured on the vertical axis. The U.S. production possibility frontier is flatter than the Canadian frontier, implying that the United States has a comparative advantage in pork and Canada has a comparative advantage in aircraft.

Although the consumption points in Figure 2-6 are hypothetical, they illustrate a general principle: just like the example of Tom and Hank, the United States and Canada can both achieve mutual gains from trade. If the United States concentrates on producing pork and ships some of its output to Canada, while Canada concentrates on aircraft and ships some of its output to the United States, both countries can consume more than if they insisted on being self-sufficient.

Moreover, these mutual gains don't depend on each country being better at producing one kind of good. Even if one country has, say, higher output per person-hour in both industries—that is, even if one country has an absolute advantage in both industries—there are still mutual gains from trade.

But how does trade actually take place in market interactions? This brings us to our final model, the circular-flow diagram, which helps economists analyze the transactions that take place in a market economy.

Transactions: The Circular-Flow Diagram

The little economy created by Tom and Hank on their island lacks many features of the economy modern Americans live in. For one thing, though millions of Americans are self-employed, most workers are employed by someone else, usually a company with hundreds or thousands of employees. Also, Tom and Hank engage only in the simplest of economic transactions, **barter**, in which an individual directly trades a good or service he or she has for a good or service he or she wants. In the modern economy, simple barter is rare: usually people trade goods or services for money—pieces of colored paper with no inherent value—and then trade those pieces of colored paper for the goods or services they want. That is, they sell goods or services and buy other goods or services.

And they both sell and buy a lot of different things. The U.S. economy is a vastly complex entity, with more than a hundred million workers employed by hundreds of thousands of companies, producing millions of different goods and services. Yet you can learn some very important things about the economy by considering the simple model shown in Figure 2-7, the **circular-flow diagram.** This diagram represents the transactions that take place in an economy by two kinds of flows around a circle: flows of physical things such as goods, services, labor, or raw materials in one direction, and flows of money that pay for these physical things in the opposite direction. In this case the physical flows are shown in yellow, the money flows in green.

The simplest circular-flow diagram models an economy that contains only two kinds of "inhabitants": **households** and **firms**. A household consists of either an individual or a group of people (usually, but not necessarily, a family) that share their income. A firm is an organization (usually, but not necessarily, a corporation) that produces goods and services for sale—and that employs members of households.

As you can see in Figure 2-7, there are two kinds of markets in this model economy. On one side (here the left side) there are **markets for goods and services** in which households buy the goods and services they want from firms. This produces a flow of goods and services to households and a return flow of money to firms.

On the other side, there are **factor markets.** A **factor of production** is a resource used to produce goods and services. Economists usually use the term *factor of production* to refer to a resource that is not used up in production. For example, workers use sewing machines to convert cloth into shirts; the workers and the sewing machines are factors of production, but the cloth is not. Broadly speaking, the main factors of

Trade takes the form of **barter** when people directly exchange goods or services that they have for goods or services that they want.

The **circular-flow diagram** is a model that represents the transactions in an economy by flows around a circle.

A **household** is a person or a group of people that share their income.

A **firm** is an organization that produces goods and services for sale.

Firms sell goods and services that they produce to households in **markets for goods and services**.

Firms buy the resources they need to produce—**factors of production**—in **factor markets**.

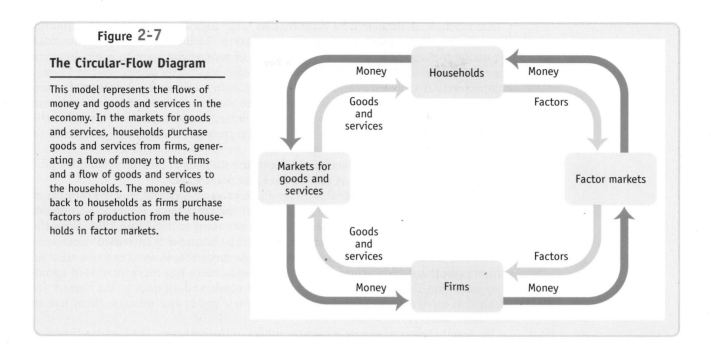

Figure 2-7

The Circular-Flow Diagram

This model represents the flows of money and goods and services in the economy. In the markets for goods and services, households purchase goods and services from firms, generating a flow of money to the firms and a flow of goods and services to the households. The money flows back to households as firms purchase factors of production from the households in factor markets.

production are labor, land, capital, and human capital. Labor is the work of human beings; land is a resource supplied by nature; capital refers to "created" resources such as machines and buildings; and human capital refers to the educational achievements and skills of the labor force, which enhance its productivity. Of course, each of these is really a category rather than a single factor: land in North Dakota is quite different from land in Florida.

The factor market most of us know best is the *labor market*, in which workers are paid for their time. Besides labor, we can think of households as owning and selling the other factors of production to firms. For example, when a corporation pays dividends to its stockholders, who are members of households, it is in effect paying them for the use of the machines and buildings that ultimately belong to those investors.

In what sense is Figure 2-7 a model? That is, in what sense is it a *simplified* representation of reality? The answer is that this picture ignores a number of real-world complications. A few examples:

- In the real world, the distinction between firms and households isn't always that clear-cut. Consider a small, family-run business—a farm, a shop, a small hotel. Is this a firm or a household? A more complete picture would include a separate box for family businesses.

- Many of the sales firms make are not to households but to other firms; for example, steel companies sell mainly to other companies such as auto manufacturers, not to households. A more complete picture would include these flows of goods and money within the business sector.

- The figure doesn't show the government, which in the real world diverts quite a lot of money out of the circular flow in the form of taxes but also injects a lot of money back into the flow in the form of spending.

Figure 2-7, in other words, is by no means a complete picture either of all the types of "inhabitants" of the real economy or of all the flows of money and physical items that take place among these inhabitants.

Despite its simplicity, the circular-flow diagram, like any good economic model, is a very useful aid to thinking about the economy.

For example, a circular-flow diagram can help us understand how the economy manages to provide jobs for a growing population. To illustrate, consider the huge expansion in the U.S. labor force—the number of people who want to work—between the early 1960s and the late 1980s. This increase was partly caused by the 15-year baby boom that followed World War II; the first baby boomers began looking for jobs in the early 1960s and the last of them went to work in the late 1980s. In addition, social changes led a much higher fraction of women to seek paid work outside the home. As a result, between 1962 and 1988 the number of Americans employed or seeking jobs increased by 71 percent.

That's a lot of new job seekers. But luckily, the number of jobs also expanded during the same period, by almost exactly the same percentage.

Or was it luck? The circular-flow diagram helps us understand why the number of jobs available grew along with the expansion of the labor force. Figure 2-8 compares the money flows around the circle for the U.S. economy in 1962 and 1988. Both the money paid to households and the money spent by households increased enormously over the period—and that was no accident. As more people went to work—that is, as more labor was sold in the factor markets—households had more income to spend. They used that increased income to buy more goods and services in the market for goods and services. And in order to produce these goods and services, firms had to hire more workers!

So, despite being an extremely simple model of the economy, the circular-flow diagram helps us to understand some important facts about the real U.S. economy. The number of jobs isn't fixed, the model tells us, because it depends on how much households spend; and the amount households spend depends on how many people are working. It is, in other words, no accident that the economy somehow creates enough jobs even when the working population grows rapidly.

| Figure **2-8** | **Growth in the U.S. Economy from 1962 to 1988** |

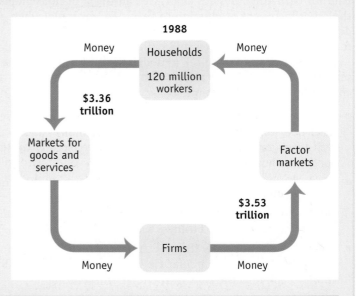

These two circular-flow diagrams—one corresponding to 1962, the other corresponding to 1988—help us understand how the U.S. economy was able to produce enough jobs for its rapidly growing labor force. A roughly twofold increase in the number of workers from 1962 to 1988 was accompanied by a ninefold increase in money flows between households and firms. As the labor force grew, money going to households increased and their spending on goods and services increased. This led firms to hire more workers to meet the increased desire for goods and services and generated more jobs for households.

economics in action

Rich Nation, Poor Nation

Try taking off your clothes—at a suitable time and in a suitable place, of course—and take a look at the labels inside that say where they were made. It's a very good bet that much, if not most, of your clothing was manufactured overseas, in a country that is much poorer than the United States—say, in El Salvador, Sri Lanka, or Bangladesh.

Why are these countries so much poorer than we are? The immediate reason is that their economies are much less *productive*—firms in these countries are just not able to produce as much from a given quantity of resources as comparable firms in the United States or other wealthy countries. Why countries differ so much in productivity is a deep question—indeed, one of the main questions that preoccupy economists. But in any case, the difference in productivity is a fact.

But if the economies of these countries are so much less productive than ours, how is it that they make so much of our clothing? Why don't we do it for ourselves?

The answer is "comparative advantage." Just about every industry in Bangladesh is much less productive than the corresponding industry in the United States. But the productivity difference between rich and poor countries varies across goods; it is very large in the production of sophisticated goods like aircraft but not that large in the production of simpler goods like clothing. So Bangladesh's position with regard to clothing production is like Hank's position with respect to coconut gathering: he's not as good at it as his fellow castaway, but it's the thing he does comparatively well.

The point is that Bangladesh, though it is at an absolute disadvantage compared with the United States in almost everything, has a comparative advantage in clothing production. This means that both the United States and Bangladesh are able to consume more because they specialize in producing different things, with Bangladesh supplying our clothing and the United States supplying Bangladesh with more sophisticated goods. ■

Although less productive than American workers, Bengali workers have a comparative advantage in clothing production.

> > > > > > > > > > > > > > > > > > > >

>>CHECK YOUR UNDERSTANDING 2-1

1. True or false? Explain your answer.
   a. An increase in the amount of resources available to Tom for use in producing coconuts and fish does not change his production possibility frontier.
   b. A technological change that allows Tom to catch more fish for any amount of coconuts gathered results in a change in his production possibility frontier.
   c. The production possibility frontier is useful because it illustrates how much of one good an economy must give up to get more of another good regardless of whether resources are being used efficiently.

2. In Italy, an automobile can be produced by 8 workers in one day and a washing machine by 3 workers in one day. In the United States, an automobile can be produced by 6 workers in one day, and a washing machine by 2 workers in one day.
   a. Which country has an absolute advantage in the production of automobiles? In washing machines?
   b. Which country has a comparative advantage in the production of washing machines? In automobiles?
   c. What pattern of specialization results in the greatest gains from trade between the two countries?

3. Use the circular-flow diagram to explain how an increase in the amount of money spent by households results in an increase in the number of jobs in the economy. Describe in words what the circular-flow model predicts.

Solutions appear at back of book.

Using Models

Economics, we have now learned, is mainly a matter of creating models that draw on a set of basic principles but add some more specific assumptions that allow the modeler to apply those principles to a particular situation. But what do economists actually *do* with their models?

Positive versus Normative Economics

Imagine that you are an economic adviser to the governor of your state. What kinds of questions might the governor ask you to answer?

Well, here are three possible questions:

1. How much revenue will the tolls on the state turnpike yield next year?

2. How much would that revenue increase if the toll were raised from $1 to $1.50?

3. Should the toll be raised, bearing in mind that a toll increase will reduce traffic and air pollution near the road but will impose some financial hardship on frequent commuters?

There is a big difference between the first two questions and the third one. The first two are questions about facts. Your forecast of next year's toll collection will be proved right or wrong when the numbers actually come in. Your estimate of the impact of a change in the toll is a little harder to check—revenue depends on other factors besides the toll, and it may be hard to disentangle the causes of any change in revenue. Still, in principle there is only one right answer.

But the question of whether tolls should be raised may not have a "right" answer—two people who agree on the effects of a higher toll could still disagree about whether raising the toll is a good idea. For example, someone who lives near the turnpike but doesn't commute on it will care a lot about noise and air pollution but not so much about commuting costs. A regular commuter who doesn't live near the turnpike will have the opposite priorities.

This example highlights a key distinction between two roles of economic analysis. Analysis that tries to answer questions about the way the world works, which have definite right and wrong answers, is known as **positive economics**. In contrast, analysis that involves saying how the world *should* work is known as **normative economics**. To put it another way, positive economics is about description, normative economics is about prescription.

Positive economics occupies most of the time and effort of the economics profession. And models play a crucial role in almost all positive economics. As we mentioned earlier, the U.S. government uses a computer model to assess proposed changes in national tax policy, and many state governments have similar models to assess the effects of their own tax policy.

It's worth noting that there is a subtle but important difference between the first and second questions we imagined the governor asking. Question 1 asked for a simple prediction about next year's revenue—a **forecast**. Question 2 was a "what if" question, asking how revenue would change if the tax law were to change. Economists are often called upon to answer both types of questions, but models are especially useful for answering "what if" questions.

The answers to such questions often serve as a guide to policy, but they are still predictions, not prescriptions. That is, they tell you what will happen if a policy is changed; they don't tell you whether that result is good or not. Suppose that your economic model tells you that the governor's proposed increase in highway tolls will raise property values in communities near the road but will hurt those people who must use the turnpike to get to work. Does that make this proposed toll increase a good idea or a bad one? It depends on whom you ask. As we've just seen, someone who is very concerned with the communities near the road will support the increase, but someone who is very concerned with the welfare of drivers will feel differently. That's a value judgment—it's not a question of economic analysis.

Positive economics is the branch of economic analysis that describes the way the economy actually works. **Normative economics** makes prescriptions about the way the economy *should* work.

A **forecast** is a simple prediction of the future.

Still, economists often do end up giving policy advice. That is, they do engage in normative economics. How can they do this when there may be no "right" answer?

One answer is that economists are also citizens, and we all have our opinions. But economic analysis can often be used to show that some policies are clearly better than others, regardless of anyone's opinions.

Suppose that policy A makes everyone better off than policy B—or at least makes some people better off without making other people worse off. Then A is clearly more efficient than B. That's not a value judgment: we're talking about how best to achieve a goal, not about the goal itself.

For example, two different policies have been used to help low-income families obtain housing: rent control, which limits the rents landlords are allowed to charge, and rent subsidies, which provide families with additional money to pay rent. Almost all economists agree that subsidies are the more efficient policy. (In Chapter 4 we'll see why this is so.) And so the great majority of economists, whatever their personal politics, favor subsidies over rent control.

When policies can be clearly ranked in this way, then economists generally agree. But it is no secret that economists sometimes disagree. Why does this happen?

When and Why Economists Disagree

Economists have a reputation for arguing with each other. Where does this reputation come from?

One important answer is that media coverage tends to exaggerate the real differences in views among economists. If nearly all economists agree on an issue—for example, the proposition that rent controls lead to housing shortages—reporters and editors are likely to conclude that there is no story worth covering, and so the professional consensus tends to go unreported. But when there is some issue on which prominent economists take opposing sides—for example, whether cutting taxes right now would help the economy—that does make a good news story. So you hear much more about the areas of disagreement within economics than you do about the large areas of agreement.

It is also worth remembering that economics is, unavoidably, often tied up in politics. On a number of issues powerful interest groups know what opinions they want to hear; they therefore have an incentive to find and promote economists who profess those opinions, giving these economists a prominence and visibility out of proportion to their support among their colleagues.

But although the appearance of disagreement among economists exceeds the reality, it remains true that economists often *do* disagree about important things. For example, some very respected economists argue vehemently that the U.S. government should replace the income tax with a *value-added tax* (a national sales tax, which is the main source of government revenue in many European countries). Other equally respected economists disagree. Why this difference of opinion?

One important source of differences is in values: as in any diverse group of individuals, reasonable people can differ. In comparison to an income tax, a value-added tax typically falls more heavily on people of modest means. So an economist who values a society with more social and income equality for its own sake will tend to oppose a value-added tax. An economist with different values will be less likely to oppose it.

A second important source of differences arises from economic modeling. Because economists base their conclusions on models, which are simplified representations of reality, two economists can legitimately disagree about which simplifications are appropriate—and therefore arrive at different conclusions.

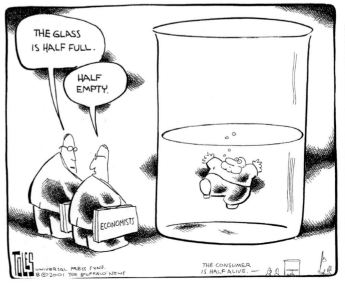

Suppose that the U.S. government were considering introducing a value-added tax. Economist A may rely on a model that focuses on the administrative costs of tax systems—that is, the costs of monitoring, processing papers, collecting the tax, and so on. This economist might then point to the well-known high costs of administering a value-added tax and argue against the change. But Economist B may think that the right way to approach the question is to ignore the administrative costs and focus on how the proposed law would change savings behavior. This economist might point to studies suggesting that value-added taxes promote higher consumer saving, a desirable result.

Because the economists have used different models—that is, made different simplifying assumptions—they arrive at different conclusions. And so the two economists may find themselves on different sides of the issue.

Most such disputes are eventually resolved by the accumulation of evidence showing which of the various models proposed by economists does a better job of fitting the facts. However, in economics as in any science, it can take a long time before research settles important disputes—decades, in some cases. And since the economy is always changing, in ways that make old models invalid or raise new policy questions, there are always new issues on which economists disagree. The policy maker must then decide which economist to believe.

The important point is that economic analysis is a method, not a set of conclusions.

economics in action

Economists in Government

Many economists are mainly engaged in teaching and research. But quite a few economists have a more direct hand in events.

As described in For Inquiring Minds on page 21, economists play a significant role in the business world, especially in the financial industry. But the most striking involvement of economists in the "real" world is their extensive participation in government.

This shouldn't be surprising: One of the most important functions of government is to make economic policy, and almost every government policy decision must take economic effects into consideration. So governments around the world employ economists in a variety of roles.

In the U.S. government, a key role is played by the Council of Economic Advisers, a branch of the Executive Office (that is, the staff of the president) whose sole purpose is to advise the White House on economic matters and to prepare the annual Economic Report of the President. Unusually for a government agency, most of the economists at the Council are not long-term civil servants; instead, they are mainly professors on leave for one or two years from their universities. Many of the nation's best-known economists have served on the Council of Economic Advisers at some point during their careers.

Economists also play an important role in many other parts of the U.S. government. Indeed, as the Bureau of Labor Statistics *Occupational Outlook Handbook* says, "Some economists work in almost every area of government." Needless to say, the Bureau of Labor Statistics is itself a major employer of economists.

It's also worth noting that economists play an especially important role in two international organizations headquartered in Washington, D.C.: the International Monetary Fund, which provides advice and loans to countries experiencing economic difficulties, and the World Bank, which provides advice and loans to promote long-term economic development.

Do all these economists in government disagree with each other all the time? Are their positions largely dictated by political affiliation? The answer to both questions is no. Although there are important disputes over economic issues in government, and politics inevitably plays some role, there is broad agreement among economists on many issues, and most economists in government try very hard to assess issues as objectively as possible. ■

> > > > > > > > > > > > > > > > > >

> Economists do mostly *positive economics*, analysis of the way the world works, in which there are definite right and wrong answers and which involve making *forecasts*. But in *normative economics*, which makes prescriptions about how things ought to be, there are often no right answers and only value judgments.
> Economists do disagree—though not as much as legend has it—for two main reasons. One, they may disagree about which simplifications to make in a model. Two, economists may disagree—like everyone else—about values.

>>CHECK YOUR UNDERSTANDING 2-2

1. Which of the following statements is a positive statement? Which is a normative statement?
   a. Society should take measures to prevent people from engaging in dangerous personal behavior.
   b. People who engage in dangerous personal behavior impose higher costs on society through higher medical costs.

2. True or false? Explain your answer.
   a. Policy choice A and policy choice B attempt to achieve the same social goal. Policy choice A, however, results in a much less efficient use of resources than policy choice B. Therefore economists are more likely to agree on choosing policy choice B.
   b. When two economists disagree on the desirability of a policy, it's typically because one of them has made a mistake.
   c. Policy makers can always use economics to figure out which goals a society should try to achieve.

Solutions appear at back of book.

• A LOOK AHEAD •

This chapter has given you a first view of what it means to do economics, starting with the general idea of models as a way to make sense of a complicated world and then moving on to three simple introductory models.

To get a real sense of how economic analysis works, however, and to show just how useful such analysis can be, we need to move on to a more powerful model. In the next two chapters we will study the quintessential economic model, one that has an amazing ability to make sense of many policy issues, predict the effects of many forces, and change the way you look at the world. That model is known as "supply and demand."

SUMMARY

1. Almost all economics is based on **models,** "thought experiments" or simplified versions of reality, many of which use mathematical tools such as graphs. An important assumption in economic models is the **other things equal assumption,** which allows analysis of the effect of a change in one factor by holding all other relevant factors unchanged.

2. One important economic model is the **production possibility frontier.** It illustrates: opportunity cost (showing how much less of one good can be produced if more of the other good is produced); efficiency (an economy is efficient if it produces on the production possibility frontier); and economic growth (an expansion of the production possibility frontier).

3. Another important model is **comparative advantage,** which explains the source of gains from trade between individuals and countries. Everyone has a comparative advantage in something—some good or service in which that person has a lower opportunity cost than everyone else. But it is often confused with **absolute advantage,** an ability to produce a particular good or service better than anyone else. This confusion leads some to erroneously conclude that there are no gains from trade between people or countries.

4. In the simplest economies people **barter**—trade goods and services for one another—rather than trade them for money, as in a modern economy. The **circular-flow diagram** is a model representing transactions within the economy as flows of goods, services, and income between **households** and **firms.** These transactions occur in **markets for goods and services** and **factor markets,** markets for **factors of production** such as labor. It is useful in understanding how spending, production, employment, income, and growth are related in the economy.

5. Economists use economic models for both **positive economics,** which describes how the economy works, and for **normative economics,** which prescribes how the economy should work. Positive economics often involves making **forecasts.** Economists can determine correct answers for positive questions, but typically not for normative questions, which involve value judgments. The exceptions are when policies designed to achieve a certain prescription can be clearly ranked in terms of efficiency.

6. There are two main reasons economists disagree. One, they may disagree about which simplifications to make in a model. Two, economists may disagree—like everyone else—about values.

KEY TERMS

Model, p. 21
Other things equal assumption, p. 21
Production possibility frontier, p. 22
Comparative advantage, p. 28
Absolute advantage, p. 28

Barter, p. 30
Circular-flow diagram, p. 30
Household, p. 30
Firm, p. 30
Markets for goods and services, p. 30

Factor markets, p. 30
Factors of production, p. 30
Positive economics, p. 34
Normative economics, p. 34
Forecast, p. 34

PROBLEMS

1. Atlantis is a small, isolated island in the South Atlantic. The inhabitants grow potatoes and catch fresh fish. The accompanying table shows the maximum annual output combinations of potatoes and fish that can be produced. Obviously, given their limited resources and available technology, as they use more of their resources for potato production, there are fewer resources available for catching fish.

Maximum annual output options	Quantity of potatoes (pounds)	Quantity of fish (pounds)
A	1,000	0
B	800	300
C	600	500
D	400	600
E	200	650
F	0	675

a. Draw a production possibility frontier with potatoes on the horizontal axis and fish on the vertical axis illustrating these options, showing points A–F.

b. Can Atlantis produce 500 pounds of fish and 800 pounds of potatoes? Explain. Where would this point lie relative to the production possibility frontier?

c. What is the opportunity cost of increasing the annual output of potatoes from 600 to 800 pounds?

d. What is the opportunity cost of increasing the annual output of potatoes from 200 to 400 pounds?

e. Can you explain why the answers to parts c and d are not the same? What does this imply about the slope of the production possibility frontier?

2. In the ancient country of Roma, only two goods, spaghetti and meatballs, are produced. There are two tribes in Roma, the Tivoli and the Frivoli. By themselves, the Tivoli each month can produce either 30 pounds of spaghetti and no meatballs,

or 50 pounds of meatballs and no spaghetti, or any combination in between. The Frivoli, by themselves, each month can produce 40 pounds of spaghetti and no meatballs, or 30 pounds of meatballs and no spaghetti, or any combination in between.

a. Assume that all production possibility frontiers are straight lines. Draw one diagram showing the monthly production possibility frontier for the Tivoli and another showing the monthly production possibility frontier for the Frivoli. Show how you calculated them.

b. Which tribe has the comparative advantage in spaghetti production? In meatball production?

In A.D. 100 the Frivoli discover a new technique for making meatballs that doubles the quantity of meatballs they can produce each month.

c. Draw the new monthly production possibility frontier for the Frivoli.

d. After the innovation, which tribe now has the absolute advantage in producing meatballs? In producing spaghetti? Which has the comparative advantage in meatball production? In spaghetti production?

3. Peter Pundit, an economics reporter, states that the European Union (EU) is increasing its productivity very rapidly in all industries. He claims that this productivity advance is so rapid that output from the EU in these industries will soon exceed that of the United States and, as a result, the United States will no longer benefit from trade with the EU.

a. Do you think Peter Pundit is correct or not? If not, what do you think is the source of his mistake?

b. If the EU and the United States continue to trade, what do you think will characterize the goods that the EU exports to the United States and the goods that the United States exports to the EU?

4. You are in charge of allocating residents to your dormitory's baseball and basketball teams. You are down to the last four people, two of whom must be allocated to baseball and two to basketball. The accompanying table gives each person's batting average and free-throw average. Explain how you would use the concept of comparative advantage to allocate the players. Begin by establishing each player's opportunity cost of free throws in terms of batting average.

Name	Batting average	Free-throw average
Kelley	70%	60%
Jackie	50%	50%
Curt	10%	30%
Gerry	80%	70%

Why is it likely that the other basketball players will be unhappy about this arrangement but the other baseball players will be satisfied? Nonetheless, why would an economist say that this is an efficient way to allocate players for your dormitory's sports teams?

5. The economy of Atlantis has developed, and the inhabitants now use money in the form of cowry shells. Draw a circular-flow diagram showing households and firms. Firms produce potatoes and fish, and households buy potatoes and fish. Households also provide the land and labor to firms. Identify where in the flows of cowry shells or physical things (goods and services, or resources) each of the following impacts would occur. Describe how this impact spreads around the circle.

a. A devastating hurricane floods many of the potato fields.

b. A very productive fishing season yields a very large number of fish caught.

c. The inhabitants of Atlantis discover the Macarena and spend several days a month at dancing festivals.

6. An economist might say that colleges and universities "produce" education, using faculty members and students as inputs. According to this line of reasoning, education is then "consumed" by households. Construct a circular-flow diagram like the one found in this chapter to represent the sector of the economy devoted to college education: colleges and universities represent firms, and households both consume education and provide faculty and students to universities. What are the relevant markets in this model? What is being bought and sold in each direction? What would happen in the model if the government decided to subsidize 50 percent of all college students' tuition?

7. Your dormitory roommate plays loud music most of the time; you, however, would prefer more peace and quiet. You suggest that she buy some earphones. She responds that although she would be happy to use earphones, she has many other things that she would prefer to spend her money on right now. You discuss this situation with a friend who is an economics major. The following exchange takes place:
He: How much would it cost to buy earphones?
You: $15.
He: How much do you value having some peace and quiet for the rest of the semester?
You: $30.
He: It is efficient for you to buy the earphones and give them to your roommate. You gain more than you lose; the benefit exceeds the cost. You should do that.
You: It just isn't fair that I have to pay for the earphones when I'm not the one making the noise.

a. Which parts of this conversation contain positive statements and which parts contain normative statements?

b. Compose an argument supporting your viewpoint that your roommate should be the one to change her behavior. Similarly, compose an argument from the viewpoint of your roommate that you should be the one to buy the earphones. If your dormitory has a policy that gives residents the unlimited right to play music, whose argument is likely to win? If your dormitory has a rule that a person must stop playing music whenever a roommate complains, whose argument is likely to win?

8. A representative of the American clothing industry recently made the following statement: "Workers in Asia often work in sweatshop conditions earning only pennies an hour. American workers are more productive and as a result earn higher wages. In order to preserve the dignity of the American workplace, the government should enact legislation banning imports of low-wage Asian clothing."

  a. Which parts of this quote are positive statements? Which parts are normative statements?

  b. Is the policy that is being advocated consistent with the preceding statements about the wages and productivities of American and Asian workers?

  c. Would such a policy make some Americans better off without making any other Americans worse off? That is, would this policy be efficient from the viewpoint of all Americans?

  d. Would low-wage Asian workers benefit from or be hurt by such a policy?

9. Are the following statements true or false? Explain your answers.

  a. "When people must pay higher taxes on their wage earnings, it reduces their incentive to work" is a positive statement.

  b. "We should lower taxes to encourage more work" is a positive statement.

  c. Economics cannot always be used to completely decide what society ought to do.

  d. "The system of public education in this country generates greater benefits to society than the cost of running the system" is a normative statement.

  e. All disagreements among economists are generated by the media.

10. Evaluate the following statement: "It is easier to build an economic model that accurately reflects events that have already occurred than to build an economic model to forecast future events." Do you think that this is true or not? Why? What does this imply about the difficulties of building good economic models?

11. Economists who work for the government are often called on to make policy recommendations. Why do you think it is important for the public to be able to differentiate normative statements from positive statements in these recommendations?

12. The mayor of Gotham City, worried about a potential epidemic of deadly influenza this winter, asks an economic adviser the following series of questions. Does each question require the economic adviser to make a positive assessment or a normative assessment?

  a. How much vaccine will be in stock in the city by the end of November?

  b. If we offer to pay 10 percent more per dose to the pharmaceutical companies providing the vaccines, will they provide additional doses?

  c. If there is a shortage of vaccine in the city, whom should we vaccinate first—the elderly or the very young? (Assume that a person from one group has an equal likelihood of dying from influenza as a person from the other group.)

  d. If the city charges $25 per shot, how many people will pay?

  e. If the city charges $25 per shot, it will make a profit of $10 per shot, money that can go to pay for inoculating poor people. Should the city engage in such a scheme?

13. Assess the following statement: "If economists just had enough data, they could solve all policy questions in a way that maximizes the social good. There would be no need for divisive political debates, such as whether the government should provide free medical care for all."

>web... To continue your study and review of concepts in this chapter, please visit the Krugman/Wells website for quizzes, animated graph tutorials, web links to helpful resources, and more.

www.worthpublishers.com/krugmanwells

>> Chapter 2 Appendix:
Graphs in Economics

Getting the Picture

Whether you're reading about economics in the *Wall Street Journal* or in your economics textbook, you will see many graphs. Visual images can make it much easier to understand verbal descriptions, numerical information, or ideas. In economics, graphs are the type of visual image used to facilitate understanding. To fully understand the ideas and information being discussed, you need to be familiar with how to interpret these visual aids. This appendix explains how graphs are constructed and interpreted and how they are used in economics.

Graphs, Variables, and Economic Models

One reason to attend college is that a bachelor's degree provides access to higher-paying jobs. Additional degrees, such as MBAs or law degrees, increase earnings even more. If you were to read an article about the relationship between educational attainment and income, you would probably see a graph showing the income levels for workers with different amounts of education. And this graph would depict the idea that, in general, more education increases income. This graph, like most of those in economics, would depict the relationship between two economic variables. A **variable** is a quantity that can take on more than one value, such as the number of years of education a person has, the price of a can of soda, or a household's income.

> A quantity that can take on more than one value is called a **variable**.

As you learned in this chapter, economic analysis relies heavily on *models*, simplified descriptions of real situations. Most economic models describe the relationship between two variables, simplified by holding constant other variables that may affect the relationship. For example, an economic model might describe the relationship between the price of a can of soda and the number of cans of soda that consumers will buy, assuming that everything else that affects consumers' purchases of soda stays constant. This type of model can be described mathematically or verbally, but illustrating the relationship in a graph makes it easier to understand. Next we show how graphs that depict economic models are constructed and interpreted.

How Graphs Work

Most graphs in economics are based on a grid built around two perpendicular lines that show the values of two variables, helping you visualize the relationship between them. So a first step in understanding the use of such graphs is to see how this system works.

Two-Variable Graphs

Figure 2A-1 on page 42 shows a typical two-variable graph. It illustrates the data in the accompanying table on outside temperature and the number of sodas a typical vendor can expect to sell at a baseball stadium during one game. The first column shows the values of outside temperature (the first variable) and the second column shows the values of the number of sodas sold (the second variable). Five combinations or pairs of the two variables are shown, each denoted by *A* through *E* in the third column.

Now let's turn to graphing the data in this table. In any two-variable graph, one variable is called the *x*-variable and the other is called the *y*-variable. Here we have made outside temperature the *x*-variable and number of sodas sold the *y*-variable. The solid

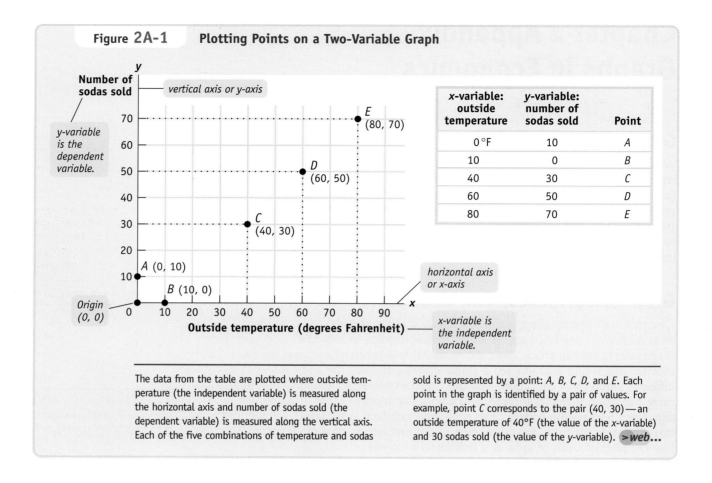

Figure 2A-1   Plotting Points on a Two-Variable Graph

x-variable: outside temperature	y-variable: number of sodas sold	Point
0°F	10	A
10	0	B
40	30	C
60	50	D
80	70	E

The data from the table are plotted where outside temperature (the independent variable) is measured along the horizontal axis and number of sodas sold (the dependent variable) is measured along the vertical axis. Each of the five combinations of temperature and sodas sold is represented by a point: A, B, C, D, and E. Each point in the graph is identified by a pair of values. For example, point C corresponds to the pair (40, 30)—an outside temperature of 40°F (the value of the x-variable) and 30 sodas sold (the value of the y-variable). >web…

The line along which values of the x-variable are measured is called the **horizontal axis or x-axis.** The line along which values of the y-variable are measured is called the **vertical axis or y-axis.** The point where the axes of a two-variable graph meet is the **origin.**

horizontal line in the graph is called the **horizontal axis or x-axis,** and values of the x-variable—outside temperature—are measured along it. Similarly, the solid vertical line in the graph is called the **vertical axis or y-axis,** and values of the y-variable—number of sodas sold—are measured along it. At the **origin,** the point where the two axes meet, each variable is equal to zero. As you move rightward from the origin along the x-axis, values of the x-variable are positive and increasing. As you move up from the origin along the y-axis, values of the y-variable are positive and increasing.

You can plot each of the five points A through E on this graph by using a pair of numbers—the values that the x-variable and the y-variable take on for a given point. In Figure 2A-1, at point C, the x-variable takes on the value 40 and the y-variable takes on the value 30. You plot point C by drawing a line straight up from 40 on the x-axis and a horizontal line across from 30 on the y-axis. We write point C as (40, 30). We write the origin as (0, 0).

Looking at point A and point B in Figure 2A-1, you can see that when one of the variables for a point has a value of zero, it will lie on one of the axes. If the value of x is zero, the point will lie on the vertical axis, like point A. If the value of y is zero, the point will lie on the horizontal axis, like point B.

A **causal relationship** exists between two variables when the value taken by one variable directly influences or determines the value taken by the other variable. In a causal relationship, the determining variable is called the **independent variable;** the variable it determines is called the **dependent variable.**

Most graphs that depict relationships between two economic variables represent a **causal relationship,** a relationship in which the value taken by one variable directly influences or determines the value taken by the other variable. In a causal relationship, the determining variable is called the **independent variable;** the variable it determines is called the **dependent variable.** In our example of soda sales, the outside temperature is the independent variable. It directly influences the number of sodas that are sold, the dependent variable in this case.

By convention, we put the independent variable on the horizontal axis and the dependent variable on the vertical axis. Figure 2A-1 is constructed consistent with this convention; the independent variable (outside temperature) is on the horizontal axis and the dependent variable (number of sodas sold) is on the vertical axis. An important exception to this convention is in graphs showing the economic relationship between the price of a product and quantity of the product: although price is generally the independent variable that determines quantity, it is always measured on the vertical axis.

Curves on a Graph

Panel (a) of Figure 2A-2 contains some of the same information as Figure 2A-1, with a line drawn through the points *B*, *C*, *D*, and *E*. Such a line on a graph is called a **curve,** regardless of whether it is a straight line or a curved line. If the curve that shows the relationship between two variables is a straight line, or linear, the variables have a **linear relationship.** When the curve is not a straight line, or nonlinear, the variables have a **nonlinear relationship.**

A point on a curve indicates the value of the *y*-variable for a specific value of the *x*-variable. For example, point *D* indicates that at a temperature of 60°F, a vendor can expect to sell 50 sodas. The shape and orientation of a curve reveal the general nature of the relationship between the two variables. The upward tilt of the curve in panel (a) of Figure 2A-2 suggests that vendors can expect to sell more sodas at higher outside temperatures.

> A **curve** is a line on a graph that depicts a relationship between two variables. It may be either a straight line or a curved line. If the curve is a straight line, the variables have a **linear relationship.** If the curve is not a straight line, the variables have a **nonlinear relationship.**

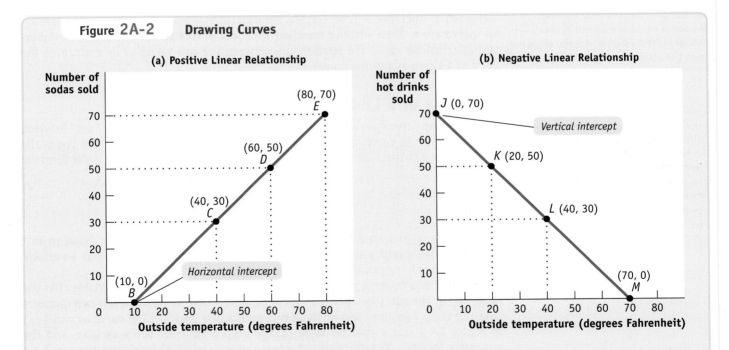

Figure 2A-2   Drawing Curves

(a) Positive Linear Relationship

(b) Negative Linear Relationship

The curve in panel (a) illustrates the relationship between the two variables, outside temperature and number of sodas sold. The two variables have a positive linear relationship: positive because the curve has an upward tilt, and linear because it is a straight line. It implies that an increase in *x* (outside temperature) leads to an increase in *y* (number of sodas sold). The curve in panel (b) is also a straight line, but it tilts downward. The two variables

here, outside temperature and number of hot drinks sold, have a negative linear relationship: an increase in *x* (outside temperature) leads to a decrease in *y* (number of hot drinks sold). The curve in panel (a) has a horizontal intercept at point *B*, where it hits the horizontal axis. The curve in panel (b) has a vertical intercept at point *J*, where it hits the vertical axis and a horizontal intercept at point *M*, where it hits the horizontal axis. **>web...**

Two variables have a **positive relationship** when an increase in the value of one variable is associated with an increase in the value of the other variable. It is illustrated by a curve that slopes upward from left to right.

Two variables have a **negative relationship** when an increase in the value of one variable is associated with a decrease in the value of the other variable. It is illustrated by a curve that slopes downward from left to right.

The **horizontal intercept** of a curve is the point at which it hits the horizontal axis; it indicates the value of the *x*-variable when the value of the *y*-variable is zero.

The **vertical intercept** of a curve is the point at which it hits the vertical axis; it shows the value of the *y*-variable when the value of the *x*-variable is zero.

The **slope** of a line or curve is a measure of how steep it is. The slope of a line is measured by "rise over run"—the change in the *y*-variable between two points on the line divided by the change in the *x*-variable between those same two points.

When variables are related this way—that is, when an increase in one variable is associated with an increase in the other variable—the variables are said to have a **positive relationship.** It is illustrated by a curve that slopes upward from left to right. Because this curve is also linear, the relationship between outside temperature and number of sodas sold illustrated by the curve in panel (a) of Figure 2A-2 is a positive linear relationship.

When an increase in one variable is associated with a decrease in the other variable, the two variables are said to have a **negative relationship.** It is illustrated by a curve that slopes downward from left to right, like the curve in panel (b) of Figure 2A-2. Because this curve is also linear, the relationship it depicts is a negative linear relationship. Two variables that might have such a relationship are the outside temperature and the number of hot drinks a vendor can expect to sell at a baseball stadium.

Return for a moment to the curve in panel (a) of Figure 2A-2 and you can see that it hits the horizontal axis at point B. This point, known as the **horizontal intercept,** shows the value of the *x*-variable when the value of the *y*-variable is zero. In panel (b) of Figure 2A-2 the curve hits the vertical axis at point J. This point, called the **vertical intercept,** indicates the value of the *y*-variable when the value of the *x*-variable is zero.

A Key Concept: The Slope of a Curve

The **slope** of a line or curve is a measure of how steep it is and indicates how sensitive the *y*-variable is to a change in the *x*-variable. In our example of outside temperature and the number of cans of soda a vendor can expect to sell, the slope of the curve would indicate how many more cans of soda the vendor could expect to sell with each 1° increase in temperature. Interpreted this way, the slope gives meaningful information. Even without numbers for *x* and *y*, it is possible to arrive at important conclusions about the relationship between the two variables by examining the slope of a curve at various points.

The Slope of a Linear Curve

Along a linear curve the slope, or steepness, is measured by dividing the "rise" between two points on the curve by the "run" between those same two points. The rise is the amount that *y* changes, and the run is the amount that *x* changes. Here is the formula:

$$\frac{\text{Change in } y}{\text{Change in } x} = \frac{\Delta y}{\Delta x} = \text{Slope}$$

In the formula, the symbol Δ (the Greek uppercase delta) stands for "change in." When a variable increases, the change in that variable is positive; when a variable decreases, the change in that variable is negative.

The slope of a curve is positive when the rise (the change in the *y*-variable) has the same sign as the run (the change in the *x*-variable). That's because when two numbers have the same sign, the ratio of those two numbers is positive. The curve in panel (a) of Figure 2A-2 has a positive slope: along the curve, both the *y*-variable and the *x*-variable increase. The slope of a curve is negative when the rise and the run have different signs. That's because when two numbers have different signs, the ratio of those two numbers is negative. The curve in panel (b) of Figure 2A-2 has a negative slope: along the curve, an increase in the *x*-variable is associated with a decrease in the *y*-variable.

Figure 2A-3 illustrates how to calculate the slope of a linear curve. Let's focus first on panel (a). From point A to point B the value of *y* changes from 25 to 20 and the value of *x* changes from 10 to 20. So the slope of the line between these two points is:

$$\frac{\text{Change in } y}{\text{Change in } x} = \frac{\Delta y}{\Delta x} = \frac{-5}{10} = -\frac{1}{2} = -0.5$$

Figure 2A-3   **Calculating the Slope**

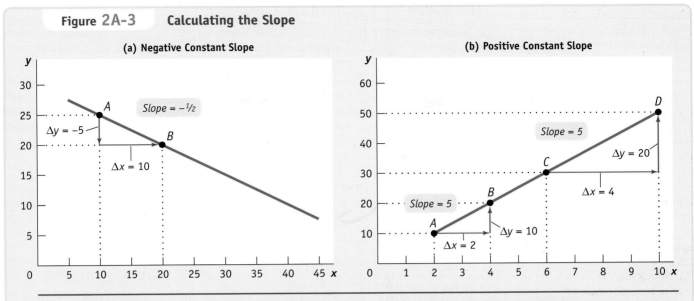

(a) Negative Constant Slope

(b) Positive Constant Slope

Panels (a) and (b) show two linear curves. Between points A and B on the curve in panel (a), the change in y (the rise) is -5 and the change in x (the run) is 10. So the slope from A to B is $\Delta y/\Delta x = -5/10 = -\frac{1}{2} = -0.5$, where the negative sign indicates that the curve is downward sloping. In panel (b), the curve has a slope from A to B of $\Delta y/\Delta x = 10/2 = 5$. The slope from C to D is $\Delta y/\Delta x = 20/4 = 5$. The slope is positive, indicating that the curve is upward sloping. Furthermore, the slope between A and B is the same as the slope between C and D, making this a linear curve. The slope of a linear curve is constant: it is the same regardless of where it is calculated along the curve. **>web...**

Because a straight line is equally steep at all points, the slope of a straight line is the same at all points. In other words, a straight line has a constant slope. You can check this by calculating the slope of the linear curve between points A and B and between points C and D in panel (b) of Figure 2A-3.

Between A and B:
$$\frac{\Delta y}{\Delta x} = \frac{10}{2} = 5$$

Between C and D:
$$\frac{\Delta y}{\Delta x} = \frac{20}{4} = 5$$

Horizontal and Vertical Curves and Their Slopes

When a curve is horizontal, the value of y along that curve never changes—it is constant. Everywhere along the curve, the change in y is zero. Now, zero divided by any number is zero. So, regardless of the value of the change in x, the slope of a horizontal curve is always zero.

If a curve is vertical, the value of x along the curve never changes—it is constant. Everywhere along the curve, the change in x is zero. This means that the slope of a vertical line is a ratio with zero in the denominator. A ratio with zero in the denominator is equal to infinity—that is, an infinitely large number. So the slope of a vertical line is equal to infinity.

A vertical or a horizontal curve has a special implication: it means that the x-variable and the y-variable are unrelated. Two variables are unrelated when a change in one of the variables (the independent variable) has no effect on the other variable (the dependent variable). Or to put it a slightly different way, two variables are unrelated when the dependent variable is constant regardless of the value of the independent variable. If, as is usual, the y-variable is the dependent variable, the curve is horizontal. If the dependent variable is the x-variable, the curve is vertical.

The Slope of a Nonlinear Curve

A **nonlinear curve** is one in which the slope changes as you move along it. Panels (a), (b), (c), and (d) of Figure 2A-4 show various nonlinear curves. Panels (a) and (b) show nonlinear curves whose slopes change as you move along them, but the slopes always remain positive. Although both curves tilt upward, the curve in panel (a) gets steeper as you move from left to right in contrast to the curve in panel (b), which gets flatter. A curve that is upward sloping and gets steeper, as in panel (a), is said to have *positive increasing* slope. A curve that is upward sloping but gets flatter, as in panel (b), is said to have *positive decreasing* slope.

Figure 2A-4   Nonlinear Curves

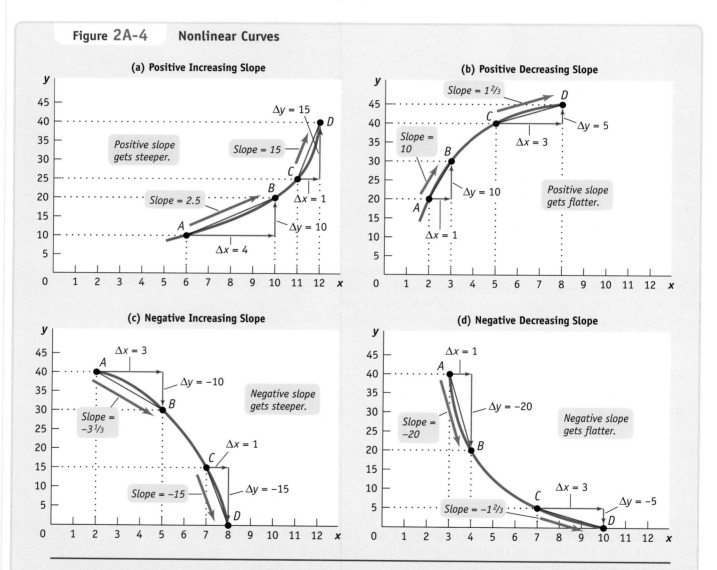

In panel (a) the slope of the curve from A to B is $\Delta y/\Delta x = 10/4$ = 2.5, and from C to D it is $\Delta y/\Delta x = 15/1 = 15$. The slope is positive and increasing; it gets steeper as you move to the right. In panel (b) the slope of the curve slope from A to B is $\Delta y/\Delta x = 10/1 = 10$, and from C to D it is $\Delta y/\Delta x = 5/3 = 1\,2/3$. The slope is positive and decreasing; it gets flatter as you move to the right. In panel (c) the slope from A to B is $\Delta y/\Delta x = -10/3 = -3\,1/3$, and from C to D it is $\Delta y/\Delta x = -15/1 = -15$. The slope is negative and increasing; it gets steeper as you move to the

right. And in panel (d) the slope from A to B is $\Delta y/\Delta x = -20/1 = -20$, and from C to D it is $\Delta y/\Delta x = -5/3 = -1\,2/3$. The slope is negative and decreasing; it gets flatter as you move to the right. The slope in each case has been calculated by using the arc method—that is, by drawing a straight line connecting two points along a curve. The average slope between those two points is equal to the slope of the straight line between those two points. **>web...**

When we calculate the slope along these nonlinear curves, we obtain different values for the slope at different points. How the slope changes along the curve determines the curve's shape. For example, in panel (a) of Figure 2A-4, the slope of the curve is a positive number that steadily increases as you move from left to right, whereas in panel (b), the slope is a positive number that steadily decreases.

The slopes of the curves in panels (c) and (d) are negative numbers. Economists often prefer to express a negative number as its **absolute value,** which is the value of the negative number without the minus sign. In general, we denote the absolute value of a number by two parallel bars around the number; for example, the absolute value of −4 is written as $|-4| = 4$. In panel (c), the absolute value of the slope steadily increases as you move from left to right. The curve therefore has *negative increasing* slope. And in panel (d), the absolute value of the slope of the curve steadily decreases along the curve. This curve therefore has *negative decreasing* slope.

Calculating the Slope Along a Nonlinear Curve

We've just seen that along a nonlinear curve, the value of the slope depends on where you are on that curve. So how do you calculate the slope of a nonlinear curve? We will focus on two methods: the *arc method* and the *point method*.

The Arc Method of Calculating the Slope An arc of a curve is some piece or segment of that curve. For example, panel (a) of Figure 2A-4 shows an arc consisting of the segment of the curve between points A and B. To calculate the slope along a nonlinear curve using the arc method, you draw a straight line between the two endpoints of the arc. The slope of that straight line is a measure of the average slope of the curve between those two end-points. You can see from panel (a) of Figure 2A-4 that the straight line drawn between points A and B increases along the x-axis from 6 to 10 (so that $\Delta x = 4$) as it increases along the y-axis from 10 to 20 (so that $\Delta y = 10$). Therefore the slope of the straight line connecting points A and B is:

$$\frac{\Delta y}{\Delta x} = \frac{10}{4} = 2.5$$

This means that the average slope of the curve between points A and B is 2.5.

Now consider the arc on the same curve between points C and D. A straight line drawn through these two points increases along the x-axis from 11 to 12 ($\Delta x = 1$) as it increases along the y-axis from 25 to 40 ($\Delta y = 15$). So the average slope between points C and D is:

$$\frac{\Delta y}{\Delta x} = \frac{15}{1} = 15$$

Therefore the average slope between points C and D is larger than the average slope between points A and B. These calculations verify what we have already observed—that this upward-tilted curve gets steeper as you move from left to right and therefore has positive increasing slope.

The Point Method of Calculating the Slope The point method calculates the slope of a nonlinear curve at a specific point on that curve. Figure 2A-5 on page 48 illustrates how to calculate the slope at point B on the curve. First, we draw a straight line that just touches the curve at point B. Such a line is called a **tangent line:** the fact that it just touches the curve at point B and does not touch the curve at any other point on the curve means that the straight line is *tangent* to the curve at point B. The slope of this tangent line is equal to the slope of the nonlinear curve at point B.

Figure 2A-5

Calculating the Slope Using the Point Method

Here a tangent line has been drawn, a line that just touches the curve at point B. The slope of this line is equal to the slope of the curve at point B. The slope of the tangent line, measuring from A to C, is $\Delta y/\Delta x = {}^{15}\!/_5 = 3$. **>web...**

You can see from Figure 2A-5 how the slope of the tangent line is calculated: from point A to point C, the change in y is 15 units and the change in x is 5 units, generating a slope of:

$$\frac{\Delta y}{\Delta x} = \frac{15}{5} = 3$$

By the point method, the slope of the curve at point B is equal to 3.

A natural question to ask at this point is how to determine which method to use—the arc method or the point method—in calculating the slope of a nonlinear curve. The answer depends on the curve itself and the data used to construct it. You use the arc method when you don't have enough information to be able to draw a smooth curve. For example, suppose that in panel (a) of Figure 2A-4 you have only the data represented by points A, C, and D and don't have the data represented by point B or any of the rest of the curve. Clearly, then, you can't use the point method to calculate the slope at point B; you would have to use the arc method to approximate the slope of the curve in this area by drawing a straight line between points A and C. But if you have sufficient data to draw the smooth curve shown in panel (a) of Figure 2A-4, then you could use the point method to calculate the slope at point B—and at every other point along the curve as well.

Maximum and Minimum Points

The slope of a nonlinear curve can change from positive to negative or vice versa. When the slope of a curve changes from positive to negative, it creates what is called a *maximum* point of the curve. When the slope of a curve changes from negative to positive, it creates a *minimum* point.

Panel (a) of Figure 2A-6 illustrates a curve in which the slope changes from positive to negative as you move from left to right. When x is between 0 and 50, the slope of the curve is positive. At x equal to 50, the curve attains its highest point—the largest value of y along the curve. This point is called the **maximum** of the curve. When x exceeds 50, the slope becomes negative as the curve turns downward. Many important curves in economics, such as the curve that represents how the profit of a firm changes as it produces more output, are hill-shaped like this.

In contrast, the curve shown in panel (b) of Figure 2A-6 is U-shaped: it has a slope that changes from negative to positive. At x equal to 50, the curve reaches its lowest

A nonlinear curve may have a **maximum** point, the highest point along the curve. At the maximum, the slope of the curve changes from positive to negative.

Figure 2A-6   Maximum and Minimum Points

Panel (a) shows a curve with a maximum point, the point at which the slope changes from positive to negative. Panel (b) shows a curve with a minimum point, the point at which the slope changes from negative to positive.

point—the smallest value of *y* along the curve. This point is called the **minimum** of the curve. Various important curves in economics, such as the curve that represents how the costs of some firms change as output increases, are U-shaped like this.

> A nonlinear curve may have a **minimum** point, the lowest point along the curve. At the minimum, the slope of the curve changes from negative to positive.

Graphs That Depict Numerical Information

Graphs can also be used as a convenient way to summarize and display data without assuming some underlying causal relationship. Graphs that simply display numerical information are called *numerical graphs*. Here we will consider four types of numerical graphs: *time-series graphs*, *scatter diagrams*, *pie charts*, and *bar graphs*. These are widely used to display real, empirical data about different economic variables because they often help economists and policy makers identify patterns or trends in the economy. But as we will also see, you must be careful not to misinterpret or draw unwarranted conclusions from numerical graphs. That is, you must be aware of both the usefulness and the limitations of numerical graphs.

Types of Numerical Graphs

You have probably seen graphs in newspapers that show what has happened over time to economic variables such as the unemployment rate or stock prices. A **time-series graph** has successive dates on the horizontal axis and the values of a variable that occurred on those dates on the vertical axis. For example, Figure 2A-7 on page 50 shows the unemployment rate in the United States from 1989 to mid-2004. A line connecting the points that correspond to the unemployment rate for each year gives a clear idea of the overall trend in unemployment over these years.

> A **time-series graph** has dates on the horizontal axis and values of a variable that occurred on those dates on the vertical axis.

Figure 2A-8 on page 50 is an example of a different kind of numerical graph. It represents information from a sample of 158 countries on average life expectancy and gross national product (GNP) per capita—a rough measure of a country's standard of living. Each point here indicates an average resident's life expectancy and the log of GNP per capita for a given country. (Economists have found that the log of GNP rather than the simple level of GNP is more closely tied to average life expectancy.) The points

Figure 2A-7

Time-Series Graph

Time-series graphs show successive dates on the x-axis and values for a variable on the y-axis. This time-series graph shows the seasonally adjusted unemployment rate in the United States from 1989 to mid-2004.

Source: Bureau of Labor Statistics.

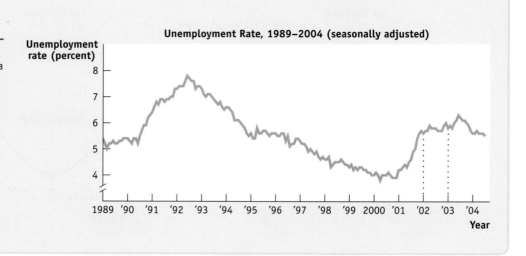

Unemployment Rate, 1989–2004 (seasonally adjusted)

lying in the upper right of the graph, which show combinations of high life expectancy and high log GNP per capita, represent economically advanced countries such as the United States. Points lying in the bottom left of the graph, which show combinations of low life expectancy and low log GNP per capita, represent economically less advanced countries such as Afghanistan and Sierra Leone. The pattern of points indicates that there is a positive relationship between life expectancy and log GNP per capita: on the whole, people live longer in countries with a higher standard of living. This type of graph is called a **scatter diagram,** a diagram in which each point corresponds to an actual observation of the x-variable and the y-variable. In scatter diagrams, a curve is typically fitted to the scatter of points; that is, a curve is drawn that approximates as closely as possible the general relationship between the variables. As you can see, the fitted curve in Figure 2A-8 is upward sloping, indicating the underlying positive relationship between the two variables. Scatter diagrams are often used to show how a general relationship can be inferred from a set of data.

A **scatter diagram** shows points that correspond to actual observations of the x- and y-variables. A curve is usually fitted to the scatter of points.

Figure 2A-8

Scatter Diagram

In a scatter diagram, each point represents the corresponding values of the x- and y-variables for a given observation. Here, each point indicates the observed average life expectancy and the log of GNP per capita of a given country for a sample of 158 countries. The upward-sloping fitted line here is the best approximation of the general relationship between the two variables.

Source: Eduard Bos et al., *Health, Nutrition, and Population Indicators: A Statistical Handbook* (Washington, DC: World Bank, 1999).

Standard of Living and Average Life Expectancy

Figure 2A-9

Pie Chart

A pie chart shows the percentages of a total amount that can be attributed to various components. This pie chart shows the percentages of total federal revenues that come from each source.

Source: Executive Office of the President, Office of Management and Budget.

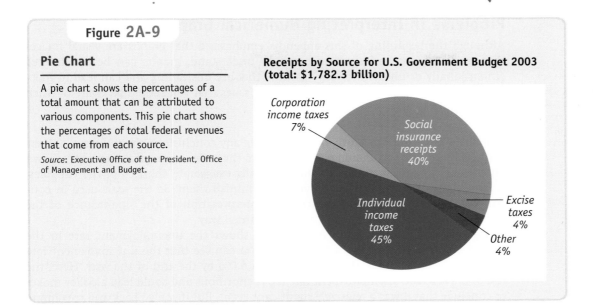

Receipts by Source for U.S. Government Budget 2003 (total: $1,782.3 billion)

A **pie chart** shows the share of a total amount that is accounted for by various components, usually expressed in percentages. For example, Figure 2A-9 is a pie chart that depicts the various sources of revenue for the U.S. government budget in 2003, expressed in percentages of the total revenue amount, $1,782.3 billion. As you can see, social insurance receipts (the revenues collected to fund Social Security, Medicare, and unemployment insurance) accounted for 40% of total government revenue and individual income tax receipts accounted for 45%.

Bar graphs use bars of various heights or lengths to indicate values of a variable. In the bar graph in Figure 2A-10, the bars show the percent change in the number of unemployed workers in the United States from 2001 to 2002, separately for White, Black or African-American, and Asian workers. Exact values of the variable that is being measured may be written at the end of the bar as in this figure. For instance, the number of unemployed Asian workers in the United States increased by 35% between 2001 and 2002. But even without the precise values, comparing the heights or lengths of the bars can give useful insight into the relative magnitudes of the different values of the variable.

> A **pie chart** shows how some total is divided among its components, usually expressed in percentages.

> A **bar graph** uses bars of varying height or length to show the comparative sizes of different observations of a variable.

Figure 2A-10

Bar Graph

A bar graph measures a variable by using bars of various heights or lengths. This bar graph shows the percent increase in the number of unemployed between 2001 and 2002, separately for White, Black or African-American, and Asian workers.

Source: Bureau of Labor Statistics.

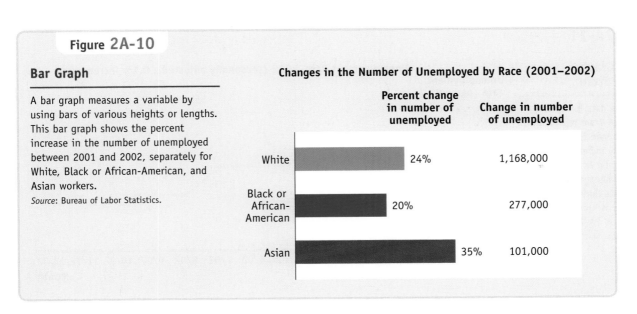

Changes in the Number of Unemployed by Race (2001–2002)

Problems in Interpreting Numerical Graphs

Although the beginning of this appendix emphasized that graphs are visual images that make ideas or information easier to understand, graphs can be constructed (intentionally or unintentionally) in ways that are misleading and can lead to inaccurate conclusions. This section raises some issues that you should be aware of when you interpret graphs.

Features of Construction Before drawing any conclusions about what a numerical graph implies, you should pay attention to the scale, or size of increments, shown on the axes. Small increments tend to visually exaggerate changes in the variables, whereas large increments tend to visually diminish them. So the scale used in construction of a graph can influence your interpretation of the significance of the changes it illustrates—perhaps in an unwarranted way.

Take, for example, Figure 2A-11, which shows the unemployment rate in the United States in 2002 using a 0.1% scale. You can see that the unemployment rate rose from 5.6% at the beginning of 2002 to 6.0% by the end of the year. Here, the rise of 0.4% in the unemployment rate looks enormous and could lead a policy maker to conclude that it was a relatively significant event. But if you go back and reexamine Figure 2A-7, which shows the unemployment rate in the United States from 1989 to 2004, you can see that this would be a misguided conclusion. Figure 2A-7 includes the same data shown in Figure 2A-11, but it is constructed with a 1% scale rather than a 0.1% scale. From it you can see that the rise of 0.4% in the unemployment rate during 2002 was, in fact, a relatively insignificant event, at least compared to the rise in unemployment during 1990 or during 2001. This comparison shows that if you are not careful to factor in the choice of scale in interpreting a graph, you can arrive at very different, and possibly misguided, conclusions.

Related to the choice of scale is the use of *truncation* in constructing a graph. An axis is **truncated** when part of the range is omitted. This is indicated by two slashes (//) in the axis near the origin. You can see that the vertical axis of Figure 2A-11 has been truncated—the range of values from 0 to 5.6 has been omitted and a // appears in the axis. Truncation saves space in the presentation of a graph and allows larger increments to be used in constructing it. As a result, changes in the variable depicted on a graph that has been truncated appear larger compared to a graph that has not been truncated and that uses smaller increments.

> An axis is **truncated** when some of the values on the axis are omitted, usually to save space.

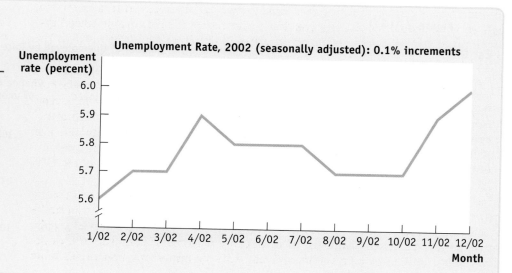

Figure 2A-11

Interpreting Graphs: The Effect of Scale

Some of the same data for 2002 used for Figure 2A-7 are represented here, except that here they are shown using 0.1% increments rather than 1% increments. As a result of this change in scale, the rise in the unemployment rate during 2002 looks much larger in this figure compared to Figure 2A-7.

Source: Bureau of Labor Statistics.

Unemployment Rate, 2002 (seasonally adjusted): 0.1% increments

Unemployment rate (percent)

You must also pay close attention to exactly what a graph is illustrating. For example, in Figure 2A-10, you should recognize that what is being shown here are percentage changes in the number of unemployed, not numerical changes. The unemployment rate for Asian workers increased by the highest percentage, 35% in this example. If you confused numerical changes with percentage changes, you would erroneously conclude that the greatest number of newly unemployed workers were Asian. But, in fact, a correct interpretation of Figure 2A-10 shows that the greatest number of newly unemployed workers were white: the total number of unemployed white workers grew by 1,168,000 workers, which is greater than the increase in the number of unemployed Asian workers, which is 101,000 in this example. Although there was a higher percentage increase in the number of unemployed Asian workers, the number of unemployed Asian workers in the United States in 2001 was much smaller than the number of unemployed white workers, leading to a smaller number of newly unemployed Asian workers than white workers.

Omitted Variables   From a scatter diagram that shows two variables moving either positively or negatively in relation to each other, it is easy to conclude that there is a causal relationship. But relationships between two variables are not always due to direct cause and effect. Quite possibly an observed relationship between two variables is due to the *unobserved* effect of a third variable on each of the other two variables. An unobserved variable that, through its influence on other variables, creates the erroneous appearance of a direct causal relationship among those variables is called an **omitted variable.** For example, in New England, a greater amount of snowfall during a given week will typically cause people to buy more snow shovels. It will also cause people to buy more de-icer fluid. But if you omitted the influence of the snowfall and simply plotted the number of snow shovels sold versus the number of bottles of de-icer fluid, you would produce a scatter diagram that showed an upward tilt in the pattern of points, indicating a positive relationship between snow shovels sold and de-icer fluid sold. To attribute a causal relationship between these two variables, however, is misguided; more snow shovels sold do not cause more de-icer fluid to be sold, or vice versa. They move together because they are both influenced by a third, determining, variable—the weekly snowfall—which is the omitted variable in this case. So before assuming that a pattern in a scatter diagram implies a cause-and-effect relationship, it is important to consider whether the pattern is instead the result of an omitted variable. Or to put it succinctly: Correlation is not causation.

> An **omitted variable** is an unobserved variable that, through its influence on other variables, creates the erroneous appearance of a direct causal relationship among those variables.

Reverse Causality   Even when you are confident that there is no omitted variable and that there is a causal relationship between two variables shown in a numerical graph, you must also be careful that you don't make the mistake of **reverse causality**—coming to an erroneous conclusion about which is the dependent and which is the independent variable by reversing the true direction of causality between the two variables. For example, imagine a scatter diagram that depicts the grade point averages (GPAs) of 20 of your classmates on one axis and the number of hours that each of them spends studying on the other. A line fitted between the points will probably have a positive slope, showing a positive relationship between GPA and hours of studying. We could reasonably infer that hours spent studying is the independent variable and that GPA is the dependent variable. But you could make the error of reverse causality: you could infer that a high GPA causes a student to study more whereas a low GPA causes a student to study less.

> The error of **reverse causality** is committed when the true direction of causality between two variables is reversed.

The significance of understanding how graphs can mislead or be incorrectly interpreted is not purely academic. Policy decisions, business decisions, and political arguments are often based on interpretation of the types of numerical graphs that we've just discussed. Problems of misleading features of construction, omitted variables, and reverse causality can lead to very important and undesirable consequences.

PROBLEMS

1. Study the four accompanying diagrams. Consider the following statements and indicate which diagram matches each statement. Which variable would appear on the horizontal and which on the vertical axis? In each of these statements, is the slope positive, negative, zero, or infinity?

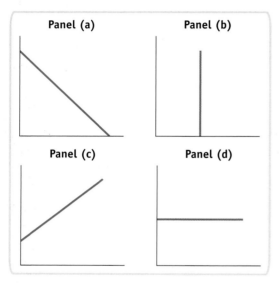

a. If the price of movies increases, fewer consumers go to see movies.

b. More experienced workers typically have higher incomes than less experienced workers.

c. Whatever the temperature outside, Americans consume the same number of hot dogs per day.

d. Consumers buy more frozen yogurt when the price of ice cream goes up.

e. Research finds no relationship between the number of diet books purchased and the number of pounds lost by the average dieter.

f. Regardless of its price, Americans buy the same quantity of salt.

2. During the Reagan administration, economist Arthur Laffer argued in favor of lowering income tax rates in order to increase tax revenues. Like most economists, he believed that at tax rates above a certain level, tax revenue would fall because high taxes would discourage some people from working and that people would refuse to work at all if they received no income after paying taxes. This relationship between tax rates and tax revenue is graphically summarized in what is widely known as the Laffer curve. Plot the Laffer curve relationship assuming that it has the shape of a nonlinear curve. The following questions will help you construct the graph.

a. Which is the independent variable? Which is the dependent variable? On which axis do you therefore measure the income tax rate? On which axis do you measure income tax revenue?

b. What would tax revenue be at a 0% income tax rate?

c. The maximum possible income tax rate is 100%. What would tax revenue be at a 100% income tax rate?

d. Estimates now show that the maximum point on the Laffer curve is (approximately) at a tax rate of 80%. For tax rates less than 80%, how would you describe the relationship between the tax rate and tax revenue, and how is this relationship reflected in the slope? For tax rates higher than 80%, how would you describe the relationship between the tax rate and tax revenue, and how is this relationship reflected in the slope?

3. In the accompanying figures, the numbers on the axes have been lost. All you know is that the units shown on the vertical axis are the same as the units on the horizontal axis.

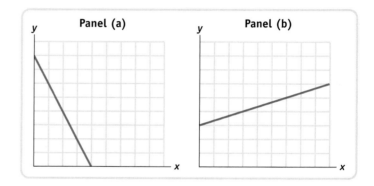

a. In panel (a), what is the slope of the line? Show that the slope is constant along the line.

b. In panel (b), what is the slope of the line? Show that the slope is constant along the line.

4. Answer each of the following questions by drawing a schematic diagram.

a. Taking measurements of the slope of a curve at three points farther and farther to the right along the horizontal axis, the slope of the curve changes from −0.3, to −0.8, to −2.5, measured by the point method. Draw a schematic diagram of this curve. How would you describe the relationship illustrated in your diagram?

b. Taking measurements of the slope of a curve at five points farther and farther to the right along the horizontal axis, the slope of the curve changes from 1.5, to 0.5, to 0, to −0.5, to −1.5, measured by the point method. Draw a schematic diagram of this curve. Does it have a maximum or a minimum?

5. The accompanying table shows the relationship between workers' hours of work per week and their hourly wage rate. Apart from the fact that they receive a different hourly wage rate and work different hours, these five workers are otherwise identical.

Name	Quantity of labor (hours per week)	Wage rate (per hour)
Athena	30	$15
Boris	35	30
Curt	37	45
Diego	36	60
Emily	32	75

a. Which variable is the independent variable? Which is the dependent variable?

b. Draw a scatter diagram illustrating this relationship. Draw a (nonlinear) curve that connects the points. Put the hourly wage rate on the vertical axis.

c. As the wage rate increases from $15 to $30, how does the number of hours worked respond according to the relationship depicted here? What is the average slope of the curve between Athena's and Boris's data points?

d. As the wage rate increases from $60 to $75, how does the number of hours worked respond according to the relationship depicted here? What is the average slope of the curve between Diego's and Emily's data points?

6. Studies have found a relationship between a country's yearly rate of economic growth and the yearly rate of increase in airborne pollutants. It is believed that a higher rate of economic growth allows a country's residents to have more cars and travel more, thereby releasing more airborne pollutants.

a. Which variable is the independent variable? Which is the dependent variable?

b. Suppose that in the country of Sudland, when the yearly rate of economic growth fell from 3.0% to 1.5%, the yearly rate of increase in airborne pollutants fell from 6% to 5%. What is the average slope of a nonlinear curve between these points using the arc method?

c. Now suppose that when the yearly rate of economic growth rose from 3.5% to 4.5%, the yearly rate of increase in airborne pollutants rose from 5.5% to 7.5%. What is the average slope of a nonlinear curve between these two points using the arc method?

d. How would you describe the relationship between the two variables here?

7. An insurance company has found that the severity of property damage in a fire is positively related to the number of firefighters arriving at the scene.

a. Draw a diagram that depicts this finding with number of firefighters on the horizontal axis and amount of property damage on the vertical axis. What is the argument made by this diagram? Suppose you reverse what is measured on the two axes. What is the argument made then?

b. In order to reduce its payouts to policyholders, should the insurance company therefore ask the city to send fewer firefighters to any fire?

8. The accompanying table illustrates annual salaries and income tax owed by five individuals. Apart from the fact that they receive different salaries and owe different amounts of income tax, these five individuals are otherwise identical.

Name	Annual salary	Annual income tax owed
Susan	$22,000	$3,304
Bill	63,000	14,317
John	3,000	454
Mary	94,000	23,927
Peter	37,000	7,020

a. If you were to plot these points on a graph, what would be the average slope of the curve between the points for Bill's and Mary's salaries and taxes using the arc method? How would you interpret this value for slope?

b. What is the average slope of the curve between the points for John's and Susan's salaries and taxes using the arc method? How would you interpret that value for slope?

c. What happens to the slope as salary increases? What does this relationship imply about how the level of income taxes affects a person's incentive to earn a higher salary?

>web... To continue your study and review of concepts in this chapter, please visit the Krugman/Wells website for quizzes, animated graph tutorials, web links to helpful resources, and more.

www.worthpublishers.com/krugmanwells

>> Supply and Demand

GRETZKY'S LAST GAME

THERE ARE SEVERAL WAYS YOU CAN GET tickets for a sporting event. You might have a season pass that gives you a seat at every home game, you could buy a ticket for a single game from the box office, or you could buy a ticket from a *scalper*. Scalpers buy tickets in advance—either from the box office or from season ticket-holders who decide to forgo the game—and then resell them shortly before the event.

Scalping is not always legal, but it is often profitable. A scalper might buy tickets at the box office and then, after the box office has sold out, resell them at a higher price to fans who have decided at the last minute to attend the event. Of course, the profits are not guaranteed. Sometimes an event is unexpectedly "hot" and scalped tickets can be sold for high prices, but sometimes an event is unexpectedly "cold" and scalpers end up selling at a loss.

Over time, however, even with some unlucky nights, scalpers can make money from eager fans.

Ticket scalpers in the Canadian city of Ottawa had a good few days in April 1999. Why? Because Wayne Gretzky, the Canadian hockey star, unexpectedly announced that he would retire from the sport and that the April 15 match between the Ottawa Senators and his team, the New York Rangers, would be his last game on Canadian soil. Many Canadian fans wanted to see the great Gretzky play one last time—and would not give up just because the box office had long since sold out.

Clearly, scalpers who had already stocked up on tickets—or who could acquire more tickets—were in for a bonanza. After the announcement, scalped tickets began selling for four or five times their face value. It was just a matter of supply and demand.

What you will learn in this chapter:

➤ What a **competitive market** is and how it is described by the **supply and demand model**

➤ What the **demand curve** is and what the **supply curve** is

➤ The difference between **movements along a curve** and **shifts of a curve**

➤ How the supply and demand curves determine a market's **equilibrium price** and **equilibrium quantity**

➤ In the case of a **shortage** or **surplus,** how price moves the market back to equilibrium

Shelly Castellanos/Zuma

AFB/Corbis

Ronal Siemonet/Corbis

Fans paid hundreds, even thousands, of dollars to see Wayne Gretzky and Michael Jordan play their last games. How much would you pay to see a music star, such as Jennifer Lopez, one last time? What about your favorite athlete?

But what do we mean by that? Many people use *supply and demand* as a sort of catchphrase to mean "the laws of the marketplace at work." To economists, however, the concept of supply and demand has a precise meaning: it is a *model of how a market behaves* that is extremely useful for understanding many—but not all—markets.

In this chapter, we lay out the pieces that make up the supply and demand model, put them together, and show how this model can be used to understand how many—but not all—markets behave.

Supply and Demand: A Model of a Competitive Market

Ticket scalpers and their customers constitute a market—a group of sellers and buyers. More than that, they constitute a particular type of market, known as a competitive market. Roughly, a **competitive market** is a market in which there are many buyers and sellers of the same good or service. More precisely, the key feature of a competitive market is that no individual's actions have a noticeable effect on the price at which the good or service is sold.

A **competitive market** is a market in which there are many buyers and sellers of the same good or service.

It's a little hard to explain why competitive markets are different from other markets until we've seen how a competitive market works. So let's take a rain check—we'll return to that issue at the end of this chapter. For now, let's just say that it's easier to model competitive markets than other markets. When taking an exam, it's always a good strategy to begin by answering the easier questions. In this book, we're going to do the same thing. So we will start with competitive markets.

When a market is competitive, its behavior is well described by a model known as the **supply and demand model**. And because many markets *are* competitive, the supply and demand model is a very useful one indeed.

The **supply and demand model** is a model of how a competitive market works.

There are five key elements in this model:

- The *demand curve*
- The *supply curve*
- The set of factors that cause the demand curve to shift, and the set of factors that cause the supply curve to shift
- The *equilibrium price*
- The way the equilibrium price changes when the supply or demand curves shift

To understand the supply and demand model, we will examine each of these elements.

The Demand Curve

How many people wanted to buy scalped tickets to see the New York Rangers and the Ottawa Senators play that April night? You might at first think the answer was: every hockey fan in Ontario who didn't already have a ticket. But although every hockey fan wanted to see Wayne Gretzky play one last time, most fans weren't willing to pay four or five times the normal ticket price. In general, the number of people who want to buy a hockey ticket, or any other good, depends on the price. The higher the price, the fewer people who want to buy the good; the lower the price, the more people who want to buy the good.

So the answer to the question "How many people will want to buy a ticket to Gretzky's last game?" depends on the price of a ticket. If you don't yet know what the price will be, you can start by making a table of how many tickets people would want to buy at a number of different prices. Such a table is known as a *demand schedule.* This, in turn, can be used to draw a *demand curve,* which is one of the key elements of the supply and demand model.

The Demand Schedule and the Demand Curve

A **demand schedule** shows how much of a good or service consumers will want to buy at different prices.

A **demand curve** is a graphical representation of the demand schedule. It shows how much of a good or service consumers want to buy at any given price.

The **quantity demanded** is the actual amount consumers are willing to buy at some specific price.

A **demand schedule** is a table showing how much of a good or service consumers will want to buy at different prices. At the right of Figure 3-1, we show a hypothetical demand schedule for tickets to a hockey game.

According to the table, if scalped tickets are available at $100 each (roughly their face value), 20,000 people are willing to buy them; at $150, some fans will decide this price is too high, and only 15,000 are willing to buy. At $200, even fewer people want tickets, and so on. So the higher the price, the fewer the tickets people want to purchase. In other words, as the price rises, the quantity of tickets demanded falls.

The graph in Figure 3-1 is a visual representation of the information in the table. (You might want to review the discussion of graphs in economics in the appendix to Chapter 2.) The vertical axis shows the price of a ticket, and the horizontal axis shows the quantity of tickets. Each point on the graph corresponds to one of the entries in the table. The curve that connects these points is a **demand curve.** A demand curve is a graphical representation of the demand schedule, another way of showing how much of a good or service consumers want to buy at any given price.

Suppose scalpers are charging $250 per ticket. We can see from Figure 3-1 that 8,000 fans are willing to pay that price; that is, 8,000 is the **quantity demanded** at a price of $250.

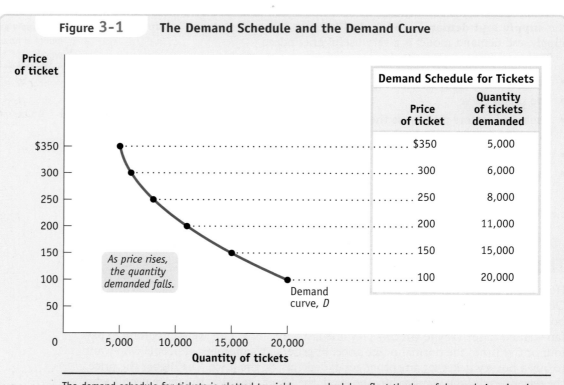

Figure 3-1   The Demand Schedule and the Demand Curve

As price rises, the quantity demanded falls.

Demand curve, D

Demand Schedule for Tickets	
Price of ticket	Quantity of tickets demanded
$350	5,000
300	6,000
250	8,000
200	11,000
150	15,000
100	20,000

The demand schedule for tickets is plotted to yield the corresponding demand curve, which shows how much of a good consumers want to buy at any given price. The demand curve and the demand schedule reflect the law of demand: As price rises, the quantity demanded falls. Similarly, a decrease in price raises the quantity demanded. As a result, the demand curve is downward sloping.

Note that the demand curve shown in Figure 3-1 slopes downward. This reflects the general proposition that a higher price reduces the number of people willing to buy a good. In this case, many people who would lay out $100 to see the great Gretzky aren't willing to pay $350. In the real world, demand curves almost always, with some very specific exceptions, *do* slope downward. The exceptions are goods called "Giffen goods," but economists think these are so rare that for practical purposes we can ignore them. Generally, the proposition that a higher price for a good, *other things equal*, leads people to demand a smaller quantity of that good is so reliable that economists are willing to call it a "law"—the **law of demand.**

The **law of demand** says that a higher price for a good, other things equal, leads people to demand a smaller quantity of the good.

Shifts of the Demand Curve

When Gretzky's retirement was announced, the immediate effect was that more people were willing to buy tickets for that April 15 game at any given price. That is, at every price the quantity demanded rose as a consequence of the announcement. Figure 3-2 illustrates this phenomenon in terms of the demand schedule and the demand curve for scalped tickets.

The table in Figure 3-2 shows two demand schedules. The second one shows the demand schedule after the announcement, the same one shown in Figure 3-1. But the first demand schedule shows the demand for scalped tickets *before* Gretzky announced his retirement. As you can see, after the announcement the number of people willing to pay $350 for a ticket increased, the number willing to pay $300 increased, and so on. So at each price, the second schedule—the schedule after the announcement—shows a larger quantity demanded. For example, at $200, the quantity of tickets fans were willing to buy increased from 5,500 to 11,000.

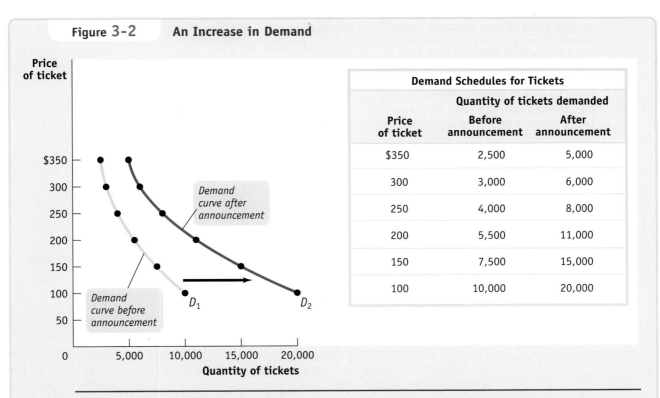

Figure 3-2   An Increase in Demand

Demand Schedules for Tickets		
	Quantity of tickets demanded	
Price of ticket	Before announcement	After announcement
$350	2,500	5,000
300	3,000	6,000
250	4,000	8,000
200	5,500	11,000
150	7,500	15,000
100	10,000	20,000

Announcement of Gretzky's retirement generates an increase in demand—a rise in the quantity demanded at any given price. This event is represented by the two demand schedules—one showing demand before the announcement, the other showing demand after the announcement—and their corresponding demand curves. The increase in demand shifts the demand curve to the right. **>web...**

The announcement of Gretzky's retirement generated a *new* demand schedule, one in which the quantity demanded is greater at any given price than in the original demand schedule. The two curves in Figure 3-2 show the same information graphically. As you can see, the new demand schedule after the announcement corresponds to a new demand curve, D_2, that is to the right of the demand curve before the announcement, D_1. This **shift of the demand curve** shows the change in the quantity demanded at any given price, represented by the change in position of the original demand curve D_1 to its new location at D_2.

It's crucial to make the distinction between such shifts of the demand curve and **movements along the demand curve**, changes in the quantity demanded of a good that result from a change in that good's price. Figure 3-3 illustrates the difference.

The movement from point *A* to point *B* is a movement along the demand curve: the quantity demanded rises due to a fall in price as you move down D_1. Here, a fall in price from \$350 to \$215 generates a rise in the quantity demanded from 2,500 to 5,000 tickets. But the quantity demanded can also rise when the price is unchanged if there is an increase in demand—a rightward shift of the demand curve. This is illustrated in Figure 3-3 by the shift of the demand curve from D_1 to D_2. Holding price constant at \$350, the quantity demanded rises from 2,500 tickets at point *A* on D_1 to 5,000 tickets at point *C* on D_2.

When economists say "the demand for *X* increased" or "the demand for *Y* decreased," they mean that the demand curve for *X* or *Y* shifted—*not* that the quantity demanded rose or fell because of a change in the price.

A **shift of the demand curve** is a change in the quantity demanded at any given price, represented by the change of the original demand curve to a new position, denoted by a new demand curve.

A **movement along the demand curve** is a change in the quantity demanded of a good that is the result of a change in that good's price.

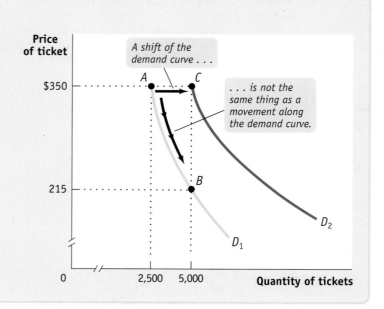

Figure 3-3

Movement Along the Demand Curve Versus Shift of the Demand Curve

The rise in quantity demanded when going from point *A* to point *B* reflects a movement along the demand curve: it is the result of a fall in the price of the good. The rise in quantity demanded when going from point *A* to point *C* reflects a shift of the demand curve: it is the result of a rise in the quantity demanded at any given price.

Understanding Shifts of the Demand Curve

Figure 3-4 illustrates the two basic ways in which demand curves can shift. When economists talk about an "increase in demand," they mean a *rightward* shift of the demand curve: at any given price, consumers demand a larger quantity of the good than before. This is shown in Figure 3-4 by the rightward shift of the original demand curve D_1 to D_2. And when economists talk about a "decrease in demand," they mean a *leftward* shift of the demand curve: at any given price, consumers demand a smaller quantity of the good than before. This is shown in Figure 3-4 by the leftward shift of the original demand curve D_1 to D_3.

Figure 3-4

Shifts of the Demand Curve

Any event that increases demand shifts the demand curve to the right, reflecting a rise in the quantity demanded at any given price. Any event that decreases demand shifts the demand curve to the left, reflecting a fall in the quantity demanded at any given price.

But what causes a demand curve to shift? In our example, the event that shifts the demand curve for tickets is the announcement of Gretzky's imminent retirement. But if you think about it, you can come up with other things that would be likely to shift the demand curve for those tickets. For example, suppose there is a music concert the same evening as the hockey game, and the band announces that it will sell tickets at half-price. This is likely to cause a decrease in demand for hockey tickets: hockey fans who also like music will prefer to purchase half-price concert tickets rather than hockey game tickets.

Economists believe that there are four principal factors that shift the demand curve for a good:

- Changes in the prices of related goods
- Changes in income
- Changes in tastes
- Changes in expectations

Although this is not an exhaustive list, it contains the four most important factors that can shift demand curves. When we said before that the quantity of a good demanded falls as its price rises, *other things equal,* we were referring to the factors that shift demand as remaining unchanged.

Changes in the Prices of Related Goods If you want to have a good night out but aren't too particular about what you do, a music concert is an alternative to the hockey game—it is what economists call a *substitute* for the hockey game. A pair of goods are **substitutes** if a fall in the price of one good (music concerts) makes consumers less willing to buy the other good (hockey games). Substitutes are usually goods that in some way serve a similar function: concerts and hockey games, muffins and doughnuts, trains and buses. A fall in the price of the alternative good induces some consumers to purchase it *instead of* the original good, shifting the demand for the original good to the left.

But sometimes a fall in the price of one good makes consumers *more* willing to buy another good. Such pairs of goods are known as **complements**. Complements are usually goods that in some sense are consumed together: sports tickets and parking at the stadium garage, hamburgers and buns, cars and gasoline. If the garage next to the hockey arena offered free parking, more people would be willing to buy tickets to see

Two goods are **substitutes** if a fall in the price of one of the goods makes consumers less willing to buy the other good.

Two goods are **complements** if a fall in the price of one good makes people more willing to buy the other good.

the game at any given price because the cost of the "package"—game plus parking—would have fallen. When the price of a complement falls, the quantity of the original good demanded at any given price rises; so the demand curve shifts to the right.

Changes in Income　When individuals have more income, they are normally more likely to purchase a good at any given price. For example, if a family's income rises, it is more likely to take that summer trip to Disney World—and therefore also more likely to buy plane tickets. So a rise in consumer incomes will cause the demand curves for most goods to shift to the right.

Why do we say "most goods," not "all goods"? Most goods are **normal goods**—the demand for them increases when consumer income rises. However, the demand for some products falls when income rises—people with high incomes are less likely to take buses than people with lower incomes. Goods for which the demand decreases when income rises are known as **inferior goods**. When a good is inferior, a rise in income shifts the demand curve to the left.

Changes in Tastes　Why do people want what they want? Fortunately, we don't need to answer that question—we just need to acknowledge that people have certain preferences, or tastes, that determine what they choose to consume and that these tastes can change. Economists usually lump together changes in demand due to fads, beliefs, cultural shifts, and so on under the heading of changes in *tastes* or *preferences*.

For example, once upon a time men wore hats. Up until around World War II, a respectable man wasn't fully dressed unless he wore a dignified hat along with his suit. But the returning GIs adopted a more informal style, perhaps due to the rigors of the war. And, President Eisenhower, who had been supreme commander of Allied Forces, often went hatless. The demand curve for hats had shifted leftward, reflecting a decline in the demand for hats.

The main distinguishing feature of changes in tastes is that economists have little to say about them and usually take them as given. When tastes change in favor of a good, more people want to buy it at any given price, so the demand curve shifts to the right. When tastes change against a good, fewer people want to buy it at any given price, so the demand curve shifts to the left.

Changes in Expectations　You could say that the increase in demand for tickets to the April 15 hockey game was the result of a change in expectations: fans no longer expected to have future opportunities to see Gretzky in action, so they became more eager to see him while they could.

Depending on the specifics of the case, changes in expectations can either decrease or increase the demand for a good. For example, savvy shoppers often wait for seasonal sales—say, buying holiday gifts during the post-holiday markdowns. In this case, expectations of a future drop in price lead to a decrease in demand today. Alternatively, expectations of a future rise in price are likely to cause an increase in demand today.

Expected changes in future income can also lead to changes in demand: if you expect your income to rise in the future, you will typically borrow today and increase your demand for certain goods; and if you expect your income to fall in the future, you are likely to save today and reduce your demand for some goods.

economics in action

Beating the Traffic

All big cities have traffic problems, and many local authorities try to discourage driving in the crowded city center. If we think of an auto trip to the city center as a good that people consume, we can use the economics of demand to analyze anti-traffic policies.

When a rise in income increases the demand for a good—the normal case—we say that the good is a **normal good**.

When a rise in income decreases the demand for a good, it is an **inferior good**.

One common strategy of local governments is to reduce the demand for auto trips by lowering the prices of substitutes. Many metropolitan areas subsidize bus and rail service, hoping to lure commuters out of their cars.

An alternative strategy is raising the price of complements: several major U.S. cities impose high taxes on commercial parking garages, both to raise revenue and to discourage people from driving into the city. (Short time limits on parking meters, combined with vigilant parking enforcement, is a related tactic.)

However, few cities have been willing to adopt the politically controversial direct approach: reducing congestion by raising the price of driving. So it was a shock when, in 2003, London imposed a "congestion charge" of £5 (about $9) on all cars entering the city center during business hours.

Compliance is monitored with automatic cameras that photograph license plates. People can either pay the charge in advance or pay it by midnight of the day they have driven. If they don't pay and are caught, a fine of £100 (about $180) is imposed for each transgression. (A full description of the rules can be found at www.cclondon.com.)

Not surprisingly, the result of the new policy confirms the law of demand: according to an August 2003 news report, traffic into central London had fallen 32 percent and cars were traveling more than a third faster as a result of the congestion charge. ■

>>CHECK YOUR UNDERSTANDING 3-1

1. Explain whether each of the following events represents (i) a *shift of* the demand curve or (ii) a *movement along* the demand curve.
   a. A store owner finds that customers are willing to pay more for umbrellas on rainy days.
   b. When XYZ Telecom, a long-distance telephone service provider, offered reduced rates on weekends, the volume of weekend calling increased sharply.
   c. People buy more long-stem roses the week of Valentine's Day, even though the prices are higher than at other times during the year.
   d. The sharp rise in the price of gasoline leads many commuters to join carpools in order to reduce their gasoline purchases.

Solutions appear at back of book.

The Supply Curve

Ticket scalpers have to acquire the tickets they sell, and many of them do so from ticket-holders who decide to sell. The decision of whether to sell your own ticket to a scalper depends in part on the price offered: the higher the price offered, the more likely that you will be willing to sell.

So just as the quantity of tickets that people are willing to buy depends on the price they have to pay, the quantity that people are willing to sell—the **quantity supplied**—depends on the price they are offered. (Notice that this is the supply of tickets *to the market in scalped tickets*. The number of seats in the stadium is whatever it is, regardless of the price—but that's not the quantity we're concerned with here.)

The Supply Schedule and the Supply Curve

The table in Figure 3-5 on page 64 shows how the quantity of tickets made available varies with the price—that is, it shows a hypothetical **supply schedule** for tickets to Gretzky's last game.

A supply schedule works the same way as the demand schedule shown in Figure 3-1: in this case, the table shows the quantity of tickets season subscribers are willing to sell at different prices. At a price of $100, only 2,000 people are willing to part with their tickets. At $150, some more people decide that it is worth passing up the game in order to have more money for something else, increasing the quantity of tickets available to 5,000. At $200, the quantity of tickets supplied rises to 7,000, and so on.

The **quantity supplied** is the actual amount of a good or service people are willing to sell at some specific price.

A **supply schedule** shows how much of a good or service would be supplied at different prices.

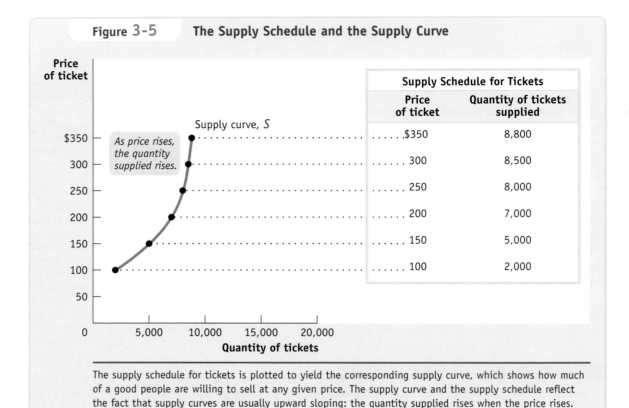

Figure 3-5   The Supply Schedule and the Supply Curve

Supply Schedule for Tickets	
Price of ticket	Quantity of tickets supplied
$350	8,800
300	8,500
250	8,000
200	7,000
150	5,000
100	2,000

The supply schedule for tickets is plotted to yield the corresponding supply curve, which shows how much of a good people are willing to sell at any given price. The supply curve and the supply schedule reflect the fact that supply curves are usually upward sloping: the quantity supplied rises when the price rises.

A **supply curve** shows graphically how much of a good or service people are willing to sell at any given price.

In the same way that a demand schedule can be represented graphically by a demand curve, a supply schedule can be represented by a **supply curve,** as shown in Figure 3-5. Each point on the curve represents an entry from the table.

Suppose that the price scalpers offer rises from $200 to $250; we can see from Figure 3-5 that the quantity of tickets sold to them rises from 7,000 to 8,000. This is the normal situation for a supply curve, reflecting the general proposition that a higher price leads to a higher quantity supplied. So just as demand curves normally slope downward, supply curves normally slope upward: the higher the price being offered, the more hockey tickets people will be willing to part with—the more of any good they will be willing to sell.

Shifts of the Supply Curve

When Gretzky's retirement was announced, the immediate effect was that people who already had tickets for the April 15 game became less willing to sell those tickets to scalpers at any given price. So the quantity of tickets supplied at any given price fell: the number of tickets people were willing to sell at $350 fell, the number they were willing to sell at $300 fell, and so on. Figure 3-6 shows us how to illustrate this event in terms of the supply schedule and the supply curve for tickets.

The table in Figure 3-6 shows two supply schedules; the schedule after the announcement is the same one as in Figure 3-5. The first supply schedule shows the supply of scalped tickets *before* Gretzky announced his retirement. And just as a change in demand schedules leads to a shift of the demand curve, a change in supply schedules leads to a **shift of the supply curve**—a change in the quantity supplied at any given price. This is shown in Figure 3-6 by the shift of the supply curve before the announcement, S_1, to its new position after the announcement, S_2. Notice that S_2 lies to the left of S_1, a reflection of the fact that quantity supplied decreased at any given price in the aftermath of Gretzky's announcement.

A **shift of the supply curve** is a change in the quantity supplied of a good or service at any given price. It is represented by the change of the original supply curve to a new position, denoted by a new supply curve.

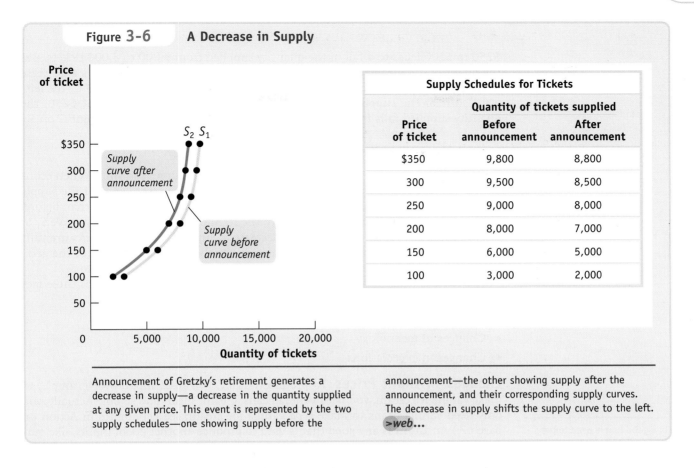

Figure 3-6   **A Decrease in Supply**

Supply Schedules for Tickets		
	Quantity of tickets supplied	
Price of ticket	Before announcement	After announcement
$350	9,800	8,800
300	9,500	8,500
250	9,000	8,000
200	8,000	7,000
150	6,000	5,000
100	3,000	2,000

Announcement of Gretzky's retirement generates a decrease in supply—a decrease in the quantity supplied at any given price. This event is represented by the two supply schedules—one showing supply before the announcement—the other showing supply after the announcement, and their corresponding supply curves. The decrease in supply shifts the supply curve to the left. >web...

As in the analysis of demand, it's crucial to draw a distinction between such shifts of the supply curve and **movements along the supply curve**—changes in the quantity supplied that result from a change in price. We can see this difference in Figure 3-7. The movement from point *A* to point *B* is a movement along the supply curve: the quantity supplied falls along S_1 due to a fall in price. Here, a fall in price from

> A **movement along the supply curve** is a change in the quantity supplied of a good that is the result of a change in that good's price.

Figure 3-7

Movement Along the Supply Curve Versus Shift of the Supply Curve

The fall in quantity supplied when going from point *A* to point *B* reflects a movement along the supply curve: it is the result of a fall in the price of the good. The fall in quantity supplied when going from point *A* to point *C* reflects a shift of the supply curve: it is the result of a fall in the quantity supplied at any given price.

$250 to $200 leads to a fall in the quantity supplied from 9,000 to 8,000 tickets. But the quantity supplied can also fall when the price is unchanged if there is a decrease in supply—a leftward shift of the supply curve. This is shown in Figure 3-7 by the leftward shift of the supply curve from S_1 to S_2. Holding price constant at $250, the quantity supplied falls from 9,000 tickets at point A on S_1 to 8,000 at point C on S_2.

Understanding Shifts of the Supply Curve

Figure 3-8 illustrates the two basic ways in which supply curves can shift. When economists talk about an "increase in supply," they mean a *rightward* shift of the supply curve: at any given price, people will supply a larger quantity of the good than before. This is shown in Figure 3-8 by the shift to the right of the original supply curve S_1 to S_2. And when economists talk about a "decrease in supply," they mean a *leftward* shift of the supply curve: at any given price, people supply a smaller quantity of the good than before. This is represented in Figure 3-8 by the leftward shift of S_1 to S_3.

Economists believe that shifts of supply curves are mainly the result of three factors (though, as in the case of demand, there are other possible causes):

- Changes in input prices
- Changes in technology
- Changes in expectations

Changes in Input Prices   To produce output, you need inputs—for example, to make vanilla ice cream, you need vanilla beans, cream, sugar, and so on. (Actually, you only need vanilla beans to make *good* vanilla ice cream; see Economics in Action on page 67.) An **input** is any good that is used to produce another good. Inputs, like output, have prices. And an increase in the price of an input makes the production of the final good more costly for those who produce and sell the good. So sellers are less willing to supply the good at any given price, and the supply curve shifts to the left. For example, newspaper publishers buy large quantities of newsprint (the paper on which newspapers are printed). When newsprint prices rose sharply in 1994–1995, the supply of newspapers fell: several newspapers went out of business and a number of new publishing ventures were canceled. Similarly, a fall in the price of an input makes the production of the final good less costly for sellers. They are more willing to supply the good at any given price, and the supply curve shifts to the right.

An **input** is a good that is used to produce another good.

Figure 3-8

Shifts of the Supply Curve

Any event that increases supply shifts the supply curve to the right, reflecting a rise in the quantity supplied at any given price. Any event that decreases supply shifts the supply curve to the left, reflecting a fall in the quantity supplied at any given price.

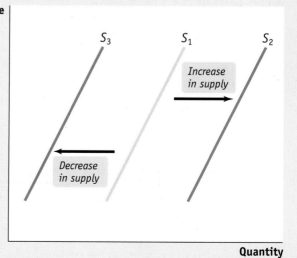

Changes in Technology When economists talk about "technology," they don't necessarily mean high technology—they mean all the ways in which people can turn inputs into useful goods. The whole complex set of activities that turn corn from an Iowa farm into cornflakes on your breakfast table is technology in this sense. And when a better technology becomes available, reducing the cost of production—that is, letting a producer spend less on inputs yet produce the same output—supply increases, and the supply curve shifts to the right. For example, an improved strain of corn that is more resistant to disease makes farmers willing to supply more corn at any given price.

Changes in Expectations Imagine that you had a ticket for the April 15 game but couldn't go. You'd want to sell the ticket to a scalper. But if you heard a credible rumor about Gretzky's imminent retirement, you would know that the ticket would soon sky-rocket in value. So you'd hold off on selling the ticket until his decision to retire was made public. This illustrates how expectations can alter supply: an expectation that the price of a good will be higher in the future causes supply to decrease today, but an expectation that the price of a good will be lower in the future causes supply to increase today.

economics in action

Down (and Up) on the Farm

Many countries have designed farm policies based on the belief—or maybe the hope—that producers *won't* respond much to changes in the price of their product. But they have found out, to their dismay, that the price does indeed matter.

Advanced countries (including the United States) have historically tried to legislate farm prices *up*. (Chapter 4 describes how such price floors work in practice.) The point was to raise farmers' incomes, not to increase production—but production nonetheless did go up. Until the nations of the European Union began guaranteeing farmers high prices in the 1960s, they had limited agricultural production and imported much of their food. Once price supports were in place, production expanded rapidly, and European farmers began growing more grains and producing more dairy products than consumers wanted to buy.

In poorer countries, especially in Africa, governments have often sought to keep farm prices *down*. The typical strategy was to require farmers to sell their produce to a "marketing board," which then resold it to urban consumers or overseas buyers. A famous example is Ghana, once the world's main supplier of cocoa, the principal ingredient in chocolate. From 1965 until the 1980s, farmers were required to sell their cocoa beans to the government at prices that lagged steadily behind those chocolate manufacturers were paying elsewhere. The Ghanaian government hoped that cocoa production would be little affected by this policy and that it could profit by buying low and selling high. In fact, production fell sharply. By 1980, Ghana's share of the world market was down to 12 percent, while other cocoa-exporting countries that did not follow the same policy—including its African neighbors—were steadily increasing their sales.

Today Europe is trying to reform its agricultural policy, and most developing countries have abandoned their efforts to hold farm prices down. Governments seem finally to have learned that supply curves really do slope upward after all. ■

> > > > > > > > > > > > > > > > > > >

continued

>>CHECK YOUR UNDERSTANDING 3-2

1. Explain whether each of the following events represents (i) a *shift of* the supply curve or (ii) a *movement along* the supply curve.
   a. More homeowners put their houses up for sale during a real estate boom that causes house prices to rise.
   b. Many strawberry farmers open temporary roadside stands during harvest season, even though prices are usually low at that time.

>>QUICK REVIEW

- The *supply schedule* shows how the *quantity supplied* depends on the price. The relationship between the two is illustrated by the *supply curve*.
- Supply curves are normally upward sloping: at a higher price, people are willing to supply more of the good.
- A change in price results in a *movement along the supply curve* and a change in the quantity supplied.
- As with demand, when economists talk of increases or decreases in supply, they mean *shifts of the supply curve*, not changes in the quantity supplied. An increase in supply is a rightward shift: the quantity supplied rises for any given price. A decrease in supply is a leftward shift: the quantity supplied falls for any given price.
- The three main factors that can shift the supply curve are changes in (1) input prices, (2) technology, and (3) expectations.

continued

    c. Immediately after the school year begins, fast-food chains must raise wages to attract workers.

    d. Many construction workers temporarily move to areas that have suffered hurricane damage, lured by higher wages which represent the price of labor.

    e. Since new technologies have made it possible to build larger cruise ships (which are cheaper to run per passenger), Caribbean cruise lines have offered more cabins, at lower prices, than before.

Solutions appear at back of book.

Supply, Demand, and Equilibrium

A competitive market is in equilibrium when price has moved to a level at which the quantity demanded of a good equals the quantity supplied of that good. The price at which this takes place is the **equilibrium price**, also referred to as the **market-clearing price**. The quantity of the good bought and sold at that price is the **equilibrium quantity**.

We have now covered the first three key elements in the supply and demand model: the supply curve, the demand curve, and the set of factors that shift each curve. The next step is to put these elements together to show how they can be used to predict the actual price at which a good will be bought and sold.

What determines the price at which a good is bought and sold? In Chapter 1 we learned the general principle that *markets move toward equilibrium*, a situation in which no individual would be better off taking a different action. In the case of a competitive market, we can be more specific: a competitive market is in equilibrium when the price has moved to a level at which the quantity demanded of a good equals the quantity supplied of that good. At that price, no individual seller could make herself better off by offering to sell either more or less of the good and no individual buyer could make himself better off by offering to buy more or less of the good.

The price that matches the quantity supplied and the quantity demanded is the **equilibrium price;** the quantity bought and sold at that price is the **equilibrium quantity.** The equilibrium price is also known as the **market-clearing price:** it is the price that "clears the market" by ensuring that every buyer willing to pay that price finds a seller willing to sell at that price, and vice versa.

You may notice from this point on that we will no longer focus on middlemen such as scalpers but focus directly on the market price and quantity. Why? Because the function of a middleman is to bring buyers and sellers together to trade. But what makes buyers and sellers willing to trade is in reality not the middleman, but the price they agree upon—the equilibrium price. By going deeper and examining how price functions within a market, we can safely assume that the middlemen are doing their job and leave them in the background.

So, how do we find the equilibrium price and quantity?

PITFALLS

BOUGHT *AND* SOLD?
We have been talking about the price at which a good is bought *and* sold, as if the two were the same. But shouldn't we make a distinction between the price received by sellers and that paid by buyers? In principle, yes; but it is helpful at this point to sacrifice a bit of realism in the interests of simplicity—by assuming away the difference between the prices received by sellers and those paid by buyers. In reality, people who sell hockey tickets to scalpers, although they sometimes receive high prices, generally receive less than those who eventually buy these tickets pay. No mystery there: that difference is how a scalper or any other "middleman"—someone who brings buyers and sellers together—makes a living. In many markets, however, the difference between the buying and selling price is quite small. It is therefore not a bad approximation to think of the price paid by buyers as being the *same* as the price received by sellers. And that is what we will assume in the remainder of this chapter.

Finding the Equilibrium Price and Quantity

The easiest way to determine the equilibrium price and quantity in a market is by putting the supply curve and the demand curve on the same diagram. Since the supply curve shows the quantity supplied at any given price and the demand curve shows the quantity demanded at any given price, the price at which the two curves cross is the equilibrium price: the price at which quantity supplied equals quantity demanded.

Figure 3-9 combines the demand curve from Figure 3-1 and the supply curve from Figure 3-5. They *intersect* at point *E*, which is the equilibrium of this market; that is, $250 is the equilibrium price and 8,000 tickets is the equilibrium quantity.

Let's confirm that point *E* fits our definition of equilibrium. At a price of $250 per ticket, 8,000 ticket-holders are willing to resell their tickets and 8,000 people who do not have tickets are willing to buy. So at the price of $250 the quantity of tickets supplied equals the quantity demanded. Notice that at any other price the market would not clear: every willing buyer would not be able to find a willing seller, or vice versa. In other words, if the price were more than $250, the quantity supplied would exceed the quantity demanded; if the price were less than $250, the quantity demanded would exceed the quantity supplied.

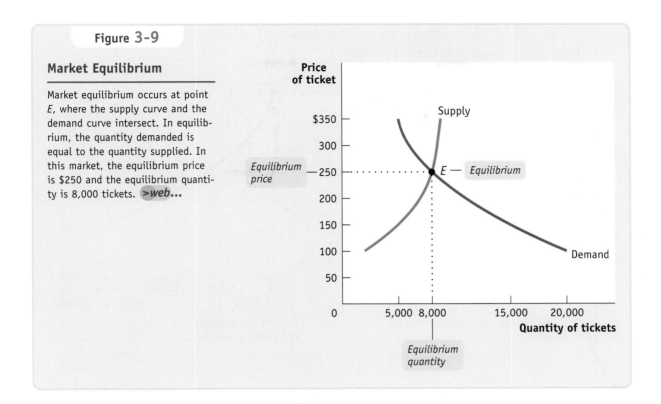

Figure 3-9

Market Equilibrium

Market equilibrium occurs at point E, where the supply curve and the demand curve intersect. In equilibrium, the quantity demanded is equal to the quantity supplied. In this market, the equilibrium price is $250 and the equilibrium quantity is 8,000 tickets. >web...

The model of supply and demand, then, predicts that given the demand and supply curves shown in Figure 3-9, 8,000 tickets would change hands at a price of $250 each.

But how can we be sure that the market will arrive at the equilibrium price? We begin by answering three simpler questions:

1. Why do all sales and purchases in a market take place at the same price?
2. Why does the market price fall if it is above the equilibrium price?
3. Why does the market price rise if it is below the equilibrium price?

Why Do All Sales and Purchases in a Market Take Place at the Same Price?

There are some markets where the same good can sell for many different prices, depending on who is selling or who is buying. For example, have you ever bought a souvenir in a "tourist trap" and then seen the same item on sale somewhere else (perhaps even in the next store) for a lower price? Because tourists don't know which shops offer the best deals and don't have time for comparison shopping, sellers in tourist areas can charge different prices for the same good.

But in any market where the buyers and sellers have both been around for some time, sales and purchases tend to converge at a generally uniform price, so that we can safely talk about *the* market price. It's easy to see why. Suppose a seller offered a potential buyer a price noticeably above what the buyer knew other people to be paying. The buyer would clearly be better off shopping elsewhere—unless the seller was prepared to offer a better deal. Conversely, a seller would not be willing to sell for significantly less than the amount he knew most buyers were paying; he would be better off waiting to get a more reasonable customer. So in any well-established, ongoing market, all sellers receive and all buyers pay approximately the same price. This is what we call the *market price*.

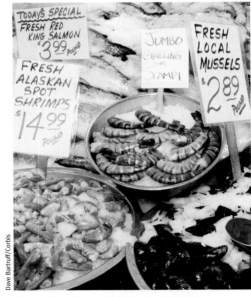

The market price is the same for everyone.

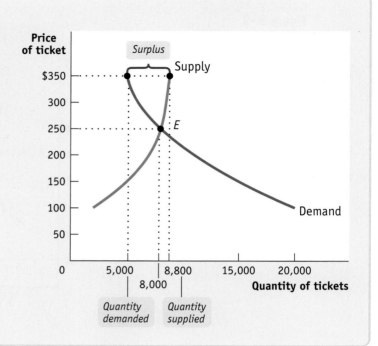

Figure 3-10

Price Above Its Equilibrium Level Creates a Surplus

The market price of $350 is above the equilibrium price of $250. This creates a surplus: at $350 per ticket, suppliers would like to sell 8,800 tickets but fans are willing to purchase only 5,000, so there is a surplus of 3,800 tickets. This surplus will push the price down until it reaches the equilibrium price of $250. **>web...**

Why Does the Market Price Fall If It Is Above the Equilibrium Price?

Suppose the supply and demand curves are as shown in Figure 3-9, but the market price is above the equilibrium level of $250—say, $350. This situation is illustrated in Figure 3-10. Why can't the price stay there?

As the figure shows, at a price of $350 there would be more tickets available than hockey fans wanted to buy: 8,800 versus 5,000. The difference of 3,800 is the **surplus**—also known as the *excess supply*—of tickets at $350.

This surplus means that some would-be sellers are being frustrated: they cannot find anyone to buy what they want to sell. So the surplus offers an incentive for those 3,800 would-be sellers to offer a lower price in order to poach business from other sellers. It also offers an incentive for would-be buyers to seek a bargain by offering a lower price. Sellers who reject the lower price will fail to find buyers, and the result of this price cutting will be to push the prevailing price down until it reaches the equilibrium price. So, the price of a good will fall whenever there is a surplus—that is, whenever the price is above its equilibrium level.

> There is a **surplus** of a good when the quantity supplied exceeds the quantity demanded. Surpluses occur when the price is above its equilibrium level.
>
> There is a **shortage** of a good when the quantity demanded exceeds the quantity supplied. Shortages occur when the price is below its equilibrium level.

Why Does the Market Price Rise If It Is Below the Equilibrium Price?

Now suppose the price is below its equilibrium level—say, at $150 per ticket, as shown in Figure 3-11. In this case, the quantity demanded (15,000 tickets) exceeds the quantity supplied (5,000 tickets), implying that there are 10,000 would-be buyers who cannot find tickets: there is a **shortage**, also known as an *excess demand*, of 10,000 tickets.

When there is a shortage, there are frustrated would-be buyers—people who want to purchase tickets but cannot find willing sellers at the current price. In this situation, either buyers will offer more than the prevailing price or sellers will realize that they can charge higher prices. Either way, the result is to drive up the prevailing price. This bidding up of prices happens whenever there are shortages—and there will be shortages whenever the price is below its equilibrium level. So the price will always rise if it is below the equilibrium level.

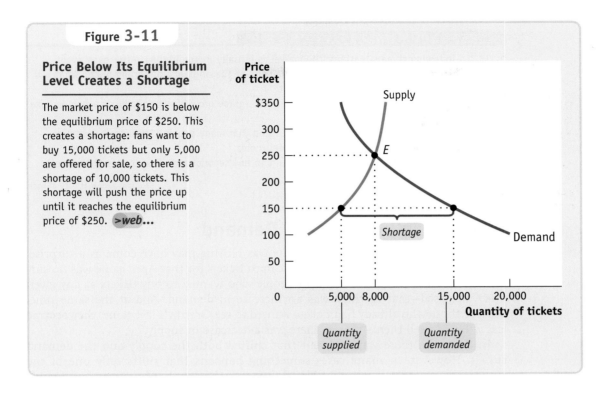

Figure 3-11

Price Below Its Equilibrium Level Creates a Shortage

The market price of $150 is below the equilibrium price of $250. This creates a shortage: fans want to buy 15,000 tickets but only 5,000 are offered for sale, so there is a shortage of 10,000 tickets. This shortage will push the price up until it reaches the equilibrium price of $250. **>web...**

Using Equilibrium to Describe Markets

We have now seen that a market tends to have a single price; that the market price falls if it is above the equilibrium level but rises if it is below that level. So the market price always *moves toward* the equilibrium price, the price at which there is neither surplus nor shortage.

economics in action

A Fish Story

In market equilibrium, something remarkable supposedly happens: everyone who wants to sell a good finds a willing buyer, and everyone who wants to buy that good finds a willing seller. It's a beautiful theory—but is it realistic?

In New York City the answer can be seen every day, just before dawn, at the famous Fulton Fish Market, which has operated since 1835 (though it has moved from its original Fulton Street location). There, every morning, fishermen bring their catch and haggle over prices with restaurant owners, shopkeepers, and a variety of middlemen and brokers.

The stakes are high. Restaurant owners who can't provide their customers with the fresh fish they expect stand to lose a lot of business, so it's important that would-be buyers find willing sellers. It's even more important for fishermen to make a sale: unsold fish loses much, if not all, of its value. But the market does reach equilibrium: just about every would-be buyer finds a willing seller, and vice versa. The reason is that every day the price of each type of fish quickly converges to a level that matches the quantity supplied and the quantity demanded.

So the tendency of markets to reach equilibrium isn't just theoretical speculation. You can see (and smell) it happening, early every morning. ■

> > > > > > > > > > > > > > > > > > > >

>> **QUICK REVIEW**

➤ Price in a competitive market moves to the *equilibrium price*, or *market-clearing price*, where the quantity supplied is equal to the quantity demanded. This quantity is the *equilibrium quantity*.

➤ All sales and purchases in a market take place at the same price. If the price is above its equilibrium level, there is a *surplus* that drives the price down. If the price is below its equilibrium level, there is a *shortage* that drives the price up.

>>CHECK YOUR UNDERSTANDING 3-3

1. In the following three situations, the market is initially in equilibrium. After each event described below, does a surplus or shortage exist at the original equilibrium price? What will happen to the equilibrium price as a result?
   a. 1997 was a very good year for California wine-grape growers, who produced a bumper-size crop.
   b. After a hurricane, Florida hoteliers often find that many people cancel their upcoming vacations, leaving them with empty hotel rooms.
   c. After a heavy snowfall, many people want to buy secondhand snowblowers at the local tool shop.

Solutions appear at back of book.

Changes in Supply and Demand

Wayne Gretzky's announcement that he was retiring may have come as a surprise, but the subsequent rise in the price of scalped tickets for that April game was no surprise at all. Suddenly the number of people who wanted to buy tickets at any given price increased—that is, there was an increase in demand. And at the same time, because those who already had tickets wanted to see Gretzky's last game, they became less willing to sell them—that is, there was a decrease in supply.

In this case, there was an event that shifted both the supply and the demand curves. However, in many cases something happens that shifts only one of the curves. For example, a freeze in Florida reduces the supply of oranges but doesn't change the demand. A medical report that eggs are bad for your health reduces the demand for eggs but does not affect the supply. That is, events often shift either the supply curve or the demand curve, but not both; it is therefore useful to ask what happens in each case.

We have seen that when a curve shifts, the equilibrium price and quantity change. We will now concentrate on exactly how the shift of a curve alters the equilibrium price and quantity.

What Happens When the Demand Curve Shifts

Coffee and tea are substitutes: if the price of tea rises, the demand for coffee will increase, and if the price of tea falls, the demand for coffee will decrease. But how does the price of tea affect the *market* for coffee?

Figure 3-12 shows the effect of a rise in the price of tea on the market for coffee. The rise in the price of tea increases the demand for coffee. Point E_1 shows the equilibrium corresponding to the original demand curve, with P_1 the equilibrium price and Q_1 the equilibrium quantity bought and sold.

An increase in demand is indicated by a *rightward* shift of the demand curve from D_1 to D_2. At the original market price P_1, this market is no longer in equilibrium: a shortage occurs because the quantity demanded exceeds the quantity supplied. So the price of coffee rises and generates an increase in the quantity supplied, an upward *movement along the supply curve*. A new equilibrium is established at point E_2, with a higher equilibrium price P_2 and higher equilibrium quantity Q_2. This sequence of events reflects a general principle: *When demand for a good increases, the equilibrium price and the equilibrium quantity of the good both rise.*

And what would happen in the reverse case, a fall in the price of tea? A fall in the price of tea decreases the demand for coffee, shifting the demand curve to the *left*. At the original price, a surplus occurs as quantity supplied exceeds quantity demanded. The price falls and leads to a decrease in the quantity supplied, with a lower equilibrium price and a lower equilibrium quantity. This illustrates another general principle: *When demand for a good decreases, the equilibrium price of the good and the equilibrium quantity of the good both fall.*

Equilibrium and Shifts of the Demand Curve

The original equilibrium in the market for coffee is at E_1, at the intersection of the supply curve and the original demand curve D_1. A rise in the price of tea, a substitute, shifts the demand curve rightward to D_2. A shortage exists at the original price P_1, so both price and the quantity supplied rise, a movement along the supply curve. A new equilibrium is reached at E_2, with a higher equilibrium price P_2 and a higher equilibrium quantity Q_2. *When demand for a good increases, the equilibrium price and the equilibrium quantity of the good both rise.* **>web...**

To summarize how a market responds to a change in demand: *An increase in demand leads to a rise in both the equilibrium price and the equilibrium quantity. A decrease in demand leads to a fall in both the equilibrium price and the equilibrium quantity.*

What Happens When the Supply Curve Shifts

In the real world, it is a bit easier to predict changes in supply than changes in demand. Physical factors that affect supply, like the availability of inputs, are easier to get a handle on than the fickle tastes that affect demand. Still, with supply as with demand, what we really know are the *effects* of shifts of the supply curve.

A spectacular example of a change in technology increasing supply occurred in the manufacture of semiconductors—the silicon chips that are the core of computers, video games, and many other devices. In the early 1970s, engineers learned how to use a process known as photolithography to put microscopic electronic components onto a silicon chip; subsequent progress in the technique has allowed ever more components to be put on each chip. Figure 3-13 (page 74) shows the effect of such an innovation on the market for silicon chips. The demand curve does not change. The original equilibrium is at E_1, the point of intersection of the original supply curve S_1 and the demand curve, with equilibrium price P_1 and equilibrium quantity Q_1. As a result of the technological change, supply increases and S_1 shifts *rightward* to S_2. At the original price P_1, a surplus of chips now exists and the market is no longer in equilibrium. The surplus causes a fall in price and a rise in quantity demanded, a downward movement along the demand curve. The new equilibrium is at E_2, with an equilibrium price P_2 and an equilibrium quantity Q_2. In the new equilibrium E_2, the price is lower and the equilibrium quantity higher than before. This may be stated as a general principle: *An increase in supply leads to a fall in the equilibrium price and a rise in the equilibrium quantity.*

What happens to the market when supply decreases? A decrease in supply leads to a *leftward* shift of the supply curve. At the original price, a shortage now exists; as a result, the equilibrium price rises and the quantity demanded falls. This describes the sequence of events in the newspaper market in 1994–1995, which we

Figure 3-13

Equilibrium and Shifts of the Supply Curve

The original equilibrium in the market for silicon chips is at E_1, at the intersection of the demand curve and the original supply curve S_1. After a technological change increases the supply of silicon chips, the supply curve shifts rightward to S_2. A surplus exists at the original price P_1, so price falls and the quantity demanded rises, a movement along the demand curve. A new equilibrium is reached at E_2, with a lower equilibrium price P_2 and a higher equilibrium quantity Q_2. *When supply of a good increases, the equilibrium price of the good falls and the equilibrium quantity rises.* **>web...**

discussed earlier: a decrease in the supply of newsprint led to a rise in the price and the closure of many newspapers. We can formulate a general principle: *A decrease in supply leads to a rise in the equilibrium price and a fall in the equilibrium quantity.*

To summarize how a market responds to a change in supply: *An increase in supply leads to a fall in the equilibrium price and a rise in the equilibrium quantity. A decrease in supply leads to a rise in the equilibrium price and a fall in the equilibrium quantity.*

Simultaneous Shifts in Supply and Demand

Finally, it sometimes happens that events shift *both* the demand and supply curves. In fact, this chapter began with an example of such a simultaneous shift. Wayne Gretzky's announcement that he was retiring increased the demand for scalped tickets because more people wanted to see him play one last time; but it also decreased the supply because those who already had tickets became less willing to part with them.

Figure 3-14 illustrates what happened. In both panels we show an increase in demand—that is, a rightward shift of the demand curve, from D_1 to D_2. Notice that the rightward shift in panel (a) is relatively larger than the one in panel (b). Both panels also show a decrease in supply—that is, a leftward shift of the supply curve, from S_1 to S_2. Notice that the leftward shift in panel (b) is relatively larger than the one in panel (a).

In both cases, the equilibrium price rises, from P_1 to P_2, as the equilibrium moves from E_1 to E_2. But what happens to the equilibrium quantity, the quantity of scalped tickets bought and sold? In panel (a) the increase in demand is large relative to the decrease in supply, and the equilibrium quantity rises as a result. In panel (b) the decrease in supply is large relative to the increase in demand, and the equilibrium quantity falls as a result. That is, when demand increases and

PITFALLS

WHICH CURVE IS IT, ANYWAY?
When the price of some good changes, in general we can say that this reflects a change in either supply or demand. But it is easy to get confused about which one. A helpful clue is the direction of change in the quantity. If the quantity sold changes in the *same* direction as the price—for example, if both the price and the quantity rise—this suggests that the demand curve has shifted. If the price and the quantity move in *opposite* directions, the likely cause is a shift in the supply curve.

Figure 3-14   Simultaneous Shifts of the Demand and Supply Curves

(a) One Possible Outcome:
Price Rises, Quantity Rises

(b) Another Possible Outcome:
Price Rises, Quantity Falls

In panel (a) there is a simultaneous rightward shift of the demand curve and leftward shift of the supply curve. Here the increase in demand is relatively larger than the decrease in supply, so the equilibrium price and equilibrium quantity both rise.

In panel (b) there is also a simultaneous rightward shift of the demand curve and leftward shift of the supply curve. Here the decrease in supply is relatively larger than the increase in demand, so the equilibrium price rises and the equilibrium quantity falls.

supply decreases, the actual quantity bought and sold can go either way, depending on *how much* the demand and supply curves have shifted.

In general, when supply and demand shift in opposite directions, we can't predict what the ultimate effect will be on the quantity bought and sold. What we can say is that a curve that shifts a disproportionately greater distance than the other curve will have a disproportionately greater effect on the quantity bought and sold. That said, we can make the following prediction about the outcome when the supply and demand curves shift in opposite directions:

- When demand increases and supply decreases, the price rises but the change in the quantity is ambiguous.

- When demand decreases and supply increases, the price falls but the change in the quantity is ambiguous.

But suppose that the demand and supply curves shift in the same direction. Can we safely make any predictions about the changes in price and quantity? In this situation, the change in quantity bought and sold can be predicted but the change in price is ambiguous. The two possible outcomes when the supply and demand curves shift in the same direction (which you should check for yourself) are as follows:

- When both demand and supply increase, the quantity increases but the change in price is ambiguous.

- When both demand and supply decrease, the quantity decreases but the change in price is ambiguous.

SUPPLY, DEMAND, AND CONTROLLED SUBSTANCES

The big "issue" movie of the year 2000 was *Traffic*, a panoramic treatment of the drug trade. The movie was loosely based on the 1989 British TV miniseries *Traffik*. Despite the lapse of 11 years, the basic outlines of the situation—in which the drug trade flourishes despite laws that are supposed to prevent it—had not changed. Not only has the so-called war on drugs by law enforcement officials not succeeded in eliminating the trade in illegal drugs; according to most assessments, it has not even done much to reduce consumption.

The failure of the war on drugs has a historical precedent: during Prohibition, from 1920 to 1933, the sale and consumption of alcohol was illegal in the United States. But liquor, produced and distributed by "bootleggers," nonetheless remained widely available. In fact, by 1929 per capita consumption of alcohol was higher than it had been a decade earlier. As with illegal drugs today, the production and distribution of the banned substance became a large enterprise that flourished despite its illegality.

Why is it so hard to choke off markets in alcohol and drugs? Think of the war on drugs as a policy that shifts the supply curve but has not done much to shift the demand curve.

Although it is illegal to use drugs such as cocaine, just as it was once illegal to drink alcohol, in practice the war on drugs focuses mainly on the suppliers. As a result, the cost of supplying drugs includes the risk of being caught and sent to jail, perhaps even of being executed. This undoubtedly reduces the quantity of drugs supplied *at any given price*, in effect shifting the supply curve for drugs to the left. In Figure 3-15, this is shown as a shift in the supply curve from S_1

to S_2. If the war on drugs had no effect on the price of drugs, and the price remained at P_1, this leftward shift would reflect a reduction in the quantity of drugs supplied equal in magnitude to the leftward shift of supply.

But as we have seen, when the supply curve for a good shifts to the left, the effect is to raise the market price of that good. In Figure 3-15 the effect of the war on drugs would be to move the equilibrium from E_1 to E_2, and to raise the price of drugs from P_1 to P_2, a movement along the demand curve. Because the market price rises, the actual decline in the quantity of drugs supplied is less than the decline in the quantity that would have been supplied at the original price.

The crucial reason Prohibition was so ineffective was that as the market price of alcohol rose, consumers trimmed back only

slightly on their consumption—yet the higher prices were enough to induce many potential suppliers to take the risk of jail time. So while Prohibition raised the price of alcohol, it did not do much to reduce consumption. Unfortunately, the same seems to be true of current drug policy. The policy raises the price of drugs to those who use them, but this does not do much to discourage consumption. Meanwhile, the higher prices are enough to induce suppliers to provide drugs despite the penalties.

What is the answer? Some argue that the policy should be refocused on the demand side—more antidrug education, more counseling, and so on. If these policies worked, they would shift demand to the left. Others argue that drugs, like alcohol, should be made legal but heavily taxed. While the debate goes on, so does the war on drugs.

Figure 3-15

Effects of the War on Drugs

The war on drugs shifts the supply curve to the left. However, we can see by comparing the original equilibrium E_1 with the new equilibrium E_2 that the actual reduction in the quantity of drugs supplied is much smaller than the shift of the supply curve. The equilibrium price rises from P_1 to P_2—a movement along the demand curve. This leads suppliers to provide drugs despite the risks.

economics in action

Plain Vanilla Gets Fancy

Vanilla doesn't get any respect. It's such a common flavoring that "plain vanilla" has become a generic term for ordinary, unembellished products. But between 2000 and 2003, plain vanilla got quite fancy—at least if you looked at the price. At the supermarket, the price of a small bottle of vanilla extract rose from about $5 to about $15. The wholesale price of vanilla beans rose 400 percent.

The cause of the price spike was bad weather—not here, but in the Indian Ocean. Most of the world's vanilla comes from Madagascar, an island nation off Africa's southeast coast. A huge cyclone struck there in 2000, and a combination of colder-than-normal weather and excessive rain impeded recovery.

The higher price of vanilla led to a fall in the quantity demanded: worldwide consumption of vanilla fell about 35 percent from 2000 to 2003. Consumers didn't stop eating vanilla-flavored products; instead, they switched (often without realizing it) to ice cream and other products flavored with synthetic vanillin, which is a by-product of wood pulp and petroleum production.

Notice that there was never a shortage of vanilla: you could always find it in the store if you were willing to pay the price. That is, the vanilla market remained in equilibrium. ■

1. In each of the following examples, determine (i) the market in question; (ii) whether a shift in demand or supply occurred, the direction of the shift, and what induced the shift; and (iii) the effect of the shift on the equilibrium price and the equilibrium quantity.
   a. As the price of gasoline fell in the United States during the 1990s, more people bought large cars.
   b. As technological innovation has lowered the cost of recycling used paper, fresh paper made from recycled stock is used more frequently.
   c. As a local cable company offers cheaper pay-per-view films, local movie theaters have more unfilled seats.

2. Periodically, a computer chip maker like Intel introduces a new chip that is faster than the previous one. In response, demand for computers using the earlier chip decreases as customers put off purchases in anticipation of machines containing the new chip. Simultaneously, computer makers increase their production of computers containing the earlier chip in order to clear out their stocks of those chips.

   Draw two diagrams of the market for computers containing the earlier chip: (a) one in which the equilibrium quantity falls in response to these events and (b) one in which the equilibrium quantity rises. What happens to the equilibrium price in each diagram?

   Solutions appear at back of book.

>> QUICK REVIEW

➤ Changes in the equilibrium price and quantity in a market result from shifts in the supply curve, the demand curve, or both.
➤ An increase in demand—a rightward shift of the demand curve—increases both the equilibrium price and the equilibrium quantity. A decrease in demand—a leftward shift of the demand curve—pushes down both the equilibrium price and the equilibrium quantity.
➤ An increase in supply drives the equilibrium price down but increases the equilibrium quantity. A decrease in supply raises the equilibrium price but reduces the equilibrium quantity.
➤ Often the fluctuations in markets involve shifts of both the supply and demand curves. When they shift in the same direction, the change in quantity is predictable but the change in price is not. When they move in opposite directions, the change in price is predictable but the change in quantity is not. When there are simultaneous shifts of the demand and supply curves, the curve that shifts the greater distance has a greater effect on the change in price and quantity.

Competitive Markets—And Others

Early in this chapter, we defined a competitive market and explained that the supply and demand framework is a model of competitive markets. But we took a rain check on the question of why it matters whether or not a market is competitive. Now that we've seen how the supply and demand model works, we can offer some explanation.

To understand why competitive markets are different from other markets, compare the problems facing two individuals: a wheat farmer who must decide whether to grow more wheat, and the president of a giant aluminum company—say, Alcoa—who must decide whether to produce more aluminum.

For the wheat farmer, the question is simply whether the extra wheat can be sold at a price high enough to justify the extra production cost. The farmer need not worry about whether producing more wheat will affect the price of the wheat he or she was already planning to grow. That's because the wheat market is competitive. There are thousands of wheat farmers, and no one farmer's decision will have much impact on the market price.

For the Alcoa executive, things are not that simple because the aluminum market is *not* competitive. There are only a few big players, including Alcoa, and each of them is well aware that its actions *do* have a noticeable impact on the market price. This adds a whole new level of complexity to the decisions producers have to make. Alcoa can't decide whether or not to produce more aluminum just by asking whether the additional product will sell for more than it costs to make. The company also has to ask whether producing more aluminum will drive down the market price and reduce its profit.

When a market is competitive, individuals can base decisions on less complicated analyses than those used in a noncompetitive market. This in turn means that it's easier for economists to build a model of a competitive market than of a noncompetitive market.

Don't take this to mean that economic analysis has nothing to say about noncompetitive markets. On the contrary, economists can offer some very important insights into how other kinds of markets work. But those insights require other models. In the next chapter, we will focus on what we can learn about competitive markets from the very useful model we have just developed: supply and demand.

• A LOOK AHEAD •

We've now developed a model that explains how markets arrive at prices and why markets "work" in the sense that buyers can almost always find sellers, and vice versa. But this model could use a little more clarification.

But, nothing demonstrates a principle quite as well as what happens when people try to defy it. And governments do, fairly often, try to defy the principles of supply and demand. In the next chapter we consider what happens when they do—the revenge of the market.

SUMMARY

1. The **supply and demand model** illustrates how a **competitive market**, one with many buyers and sellers, works.

2. The **demand schedule** shows the **quantity demanded** at each price and is represented graphically by a **demand curve**. The **law of demand** says that demand curves slope downward.

3. A **movement along the demand curve** occurs when the price changes and causes a change in the quantity demanded. When economists talk of increasing or decreasing demand, they mean **shifts of the demand curve**—a change in the quantity demanded at any given price. An increase in demand causes a rightward shift of the demand curve. A decrease in demand causes a leftward shift.

4. There are four main factors that shift the demand curve:
   - A change in the prices of related goods, such as **substitutes** or **complements**
   - A change in income: when income rises, the demand for **normal goods** increases and the demand for **inferior goods** decreases.
   - A change in tastes
   - A change in expectations

5. The **supply schedule** shows the **quantity supplied** at each price and is represented graphically by a **supply curve**. Supply curves usually slope upward.

6. A **movement along the supply curve** occurs when the price changes and causes a change in the quantity supplied. When economists talk of increasing or decreasing supply, they mean **shifts of the supply curve**—a change in the quantity supplied at any given price. An increase in supply causes a rightward shift of the supply curve. A decrease in supply causes a leftward shift.

7. There are three main factors that shift the supply curve:
   - A change in **input** prices
   - A change in technology
   - A change in expectations

8. The supply and demand model is based on the principle that the price in a market moves to its **equilibrium price, or market-clearing price,** the price at which the quantity demanded is equal to the quantity supplied. This quantity is the **equilibrium quantity**. When the price is above its market-clearing level, there is a **surplus** that pushes the price down. When the price is below its market-clearing level, there is a **shortage** that pushes the price up.

9. An increase in demand increases both the equilibrium price and the equilibrium quantity; a decrease in demand has the opposite effect. An increase in supply reduces the equilibrium price and increases the equilibrium quantity; a decrease in supply has the opposite effect.

10. Shifts of the demand curve and the supply curve can happen simultaneously. When they shift in opposite directions, the change in price is predictable but the change in quantity is not. When they shift in the same direction, the change in quantity is predictable but the change in price is not. In general, the curve that shifts the greater distance has a greater effect on the changes in price and quantity.

KEY TERMS

Competitive market, p. 57
Supply and demand model, p. 57
Demand schedule, p. 58
Demand curve, p. 58
Quantity demanded, p. 58
Law of demand, p. 59
Shift of the demand curve, p. 60
Movement along the demand curve, p. 60

Substitutes, p. 61
Complements, p. 61
Normal good, p. 62
Inferior good, p. 62
Quantity supplied, p. 63
Supply schedule, p. 63
Supply curve, p. 64
Shift of the supply curve, p. 64

Movement along the supply curve, p. 65
Input, p. 66
Equilibrium price, p. 68
Equilibrium quantity, p. 68
Market-clearing price, p. 68
Surplus, p. 70
Shortage, p. 70

PROBLEMS

1. A survey indicated that chocolate ice cream is America's favorite ice-cream flavor. For each of the following, indicate the possible effects on demand and/or supply and equilibrium price and quantity of chocolate ice cream.

  a. A severe drought in the Midwest causes dairy farmers to reduce the number of milk-producing cattle in their herds by a third. These dairy farmers supply cream that is used to manufacture chocolate ice cream.

  b. A new report by the American Medical Association reveals that chocolate does, in fact, have significant health benefits.

  c. The discovery of cheaper synthetic vanilla flavoring lowers the price of vanilla ice cream.

  d. New technology for mixing and freezing ice cream lowers manufacturers' costs of producing chocolate ice cream.

2. In a supply and demand diagram, draw the shift in demand for hamburgers in your hometown due to the following events. In each case show the effect on equilibrium price and quantity.

  a. The price of tacos increases.

  b. All hamburger sellers raise the price of their french fries.

  c. Income falls in town. Assume that hamburgers are a normal good for most people.

  d. Income falls in town. Assume that hamburgers are an inferior good for most people.

  e. Hot dog stands cut the price of hot dogs.

3. The market for many goods changes in predictable ways according to the time of year, in response to events such as holidays, vacation times, seasonal changes in production, and so on. Using supply and demand, explain the change in price in each of the following cases. Note that supply and demand may shift simultaneously.

  a. Lobster prices usually fall during the summer peak harvest season, despite the fact that people like to eat lobster during the summer months more than during any other time of year.

  b. The price of a Christmas tree is lower after Christmas than before and fewer trees are sold.

  c. The price of a round-trip ticket to Paris on Air France falls by more than $200 after the end of school vacation in September. This happens despite the fact that generally worsening weather increases the cost of operating flights to Paris, and Air France therefore reduces the number of flights to Paris at any given price.

4. Show in a diagram the effect on the demand curve, the supply curve, the equilibrium price, and the equilibrium quantity of each of the following events.

  a. The market for newspapers in your town.

   Case 1:   The salaries of journalists go up.
   Case 2:   There is a big news event in your town, which is reported in the newspapers.

  b. The market for St. Louis Rams cotton T-shirts.

   Case 1:   The Rams win the national championship.
   Case 2:   The price of cotton increases.

  c. The market for bagels.

   Case 1:   People realize how fattening bagels are.
   Case 2:   People have less time to make themselves a cooked breakfast.

  d. The market for the Krugman and Wells economics textbook.

   Case 1:   Your professor makes it required reading for all of his or her students.
   Case 2:   Printing costs for textbooks are lowered by the use of synthetic paper.

5. Suppose that the supply schedule of Maine lobsters is as follows:

Price of lobster (per pound)	Quantity of lobster supplied (pounds)
$25	800
20	700
15	600
10	500
5	400

Suppose that Maine lobsters can be sold only in the United States. The U.S. demand schedule for Maine lobsters is as follows:

Price of lobster (per pound)	Quantity of lobster demanded (pounds)
$25	200
20	400
15	600
10	800
5	1,000

a. Draw the demand curve and the supply curve for Maine lobsters. What is the equilibrium price and quantity of lobsters?

Now suppose that Maine lobsters can be sold in France. The French demand schedule for Maine lobsters is as follows:

Price of lobster (per pound)	Quantity of lobster demanded (pounds)
$25	100
20	300
15	500
10	700
5	900

b. What is the demand schedule for Maine lobsters now that French consumers can also buy them? Draw a supply and demand diagram that illustrates the new equilibrium price and quantity of lobsters. What will happen to the price at which fishermen can sell lobster? What will happen to the price paid by U.S. consumers? What will happen to the quantity consumed by U.S. consumers?

6. Find the flaws in reasoning in the following statements, paying particular attention to the distinction between shifts of and movements along the supply and demand curves. Draw a diagram to illustrate what actually happens in each situation.

a. "A technological innovation that lowers the cost of producing a good might seem at first to result in a reduction in the price of the good to consumers. But a fall in price will increase demand for the good, and higher demand will send the price up again. It is not certain, therefore, that an innovation will really reduce price in the end."

b. "A study shows that eating a clove of garlic a day can help prevent heart disease, causing many consumers to demand more garlic. This increase in demand results in a rise in the price of garlic. Consumers, seeing that the price of garlic has gone up, reduce their demand for garlic. This causes the demand for garlic to decrease and the price of garlic to fall. Therefore, the ultimate effect of the study on the price of garlic is uncertain."

7. Some points on a demand curve for a normal good are given here:

Price	Quantity demanded
$23	70
21	90
19	110
17	130

Do you think that the increase in quantity demanded (from 90 to 110 in the table) when price decreases (from 21 to 19) is due to a rise in consumers' income? Explain clearly (and briefly) why or why not.

8. Aaron Hank is a star hitter for the Bay City baseball team. He is close to breaking the major league record for home runs hit during one season, and it is widely anticipated that in the next game he will break that record. As a result, tickets for the team's next game have been a hot commodity. But today it is announced that, due to a knee injury, he will not in fact play in the team's next game. Assume that season ticket-holders are able to resell their tickets if they wish. Use supply and demand diagrams to explain the following.

a. Show the case in which this announcement results in a lower equilibrium price and a lower equilibrium quantity than before the announcement.

b. Show the case in which this announcement results in a lower equilibrium price and a higher equilibrium quantity than before the announcement.

c. What accounts for whether case a or case b occurs?

d. Suppose that a scalper had secretly learned before the announcement that Aaron Hank would not play in the next game. What actions do you think he would take?

9. In *Rolling Stone* magazine, several fans and rock stars, including Pearl Jam, were bemoaning the high price of concert tickets. One superstar argued, "It just isn't worth $75 to see me play. No one should have to pay that much to go to a concert." Assume this star sold out arenas around the country at an average ticket price of $75.

a. How would you evaluate the arguments that ticket prices are too high?

b. Suppose that due to this star's protests, ticket prices were lowered to $50. In what sense is this price too low? Draw a diagram using supply and demand curves to support your argument.

c. Suppose Pearl Jam really wanted to bring down ticket prices. Since the band controls the supply of its services, what do you recommend they do? Explain using a supply and demand diagram.

d. Suppose the band's next CD was a total dud. Do you think they would still have to worry about ticket prices being too high? Why or why not? Draw a supply and demand diagram to support your argument.

e. Suppose the group announced their next tour was going to be their last. What effect would this likely have on the demand for and price of tickets? Illustrate with a supply and demand diagram.

10. The accompanying table gives the annual U.S. demand and supply schedules for pickup trucks.

Price of truck	Quantity of trucks demanded (millions)	Quantity of trucks supplied (millions)
$20,000	20	14
25,000	18	15
30,000	16	16
35,000	14	17
40,000	12	18

a. Plot the demand and supply curves using these schedules. Indicate the equilibrium price and quantity on your diagram.

b. Suppose the tires used on pickup trucks are found to be defective. What would you expect to happen in the market for pickup trucks? Show this on your diagram.

c. Suppose that the U.S. Department of Transportation imposes costly regulations on manufacturers that cause them to reduce supply by one-third at any given price. Calculate and plot the new supply schedule and indicate the new equilibrium price and quantity on your diagram.

11. After several years of decline, the market for handmade acoustic guitars is making a comeback. These guitars are usually made in small workshops employing relatively few highly skilled luthiers. Assess the impact on the equilibrium price and quantity of handmade acoustic guitars as a result of each of the following events. In your answers indicate which curve(s) shift(s) and in which direction.

a. Environmentalists succeed in having the use of Brazilian rosewood banned in the United States, forcing luthiers to seek out alternative, more costly woods.

b. A foreign producer reengineers the guitar-making process and floods the market with identical guitars.

c. Music featuring handmade acoustic guitars makes a comeback as audiences tire of heavy metal and grunge music.

d. The country goes into a deep recession and the income of the average American falls sharply.

12. *Demand twisters*: Sketch and explain the demand relationship in each of the following statements.

a. I would never buy a Britney Spears CD! You couldn't even give me one for nothing.

b. I generally buy a bit more coffee as the price falls. But once the price falls to $2 per pound, I'll buy out the entire stock of the supermarket.

c. I spend more on orange juice even as the price rises. (Does this mean that I must be violating the law of demand?)

d. Due to a tuition rise, most students at a college find themselves with lower disposable income. Almost all of them eat more frequently at the school cafeteria and less often at restaurants, even though prices at the cafeteria have risen too. (This one requires that you draw both the demand and the supply curves for dormitory cafeteria meals.)

13. Will Shakespeare is a struggling playwright in sixteenth-century London. As the price he receives for writing a play increases, he is willing to write more plays. For the following situations, use a diagram to illustrate how each event affects the equilibrium price and quantity in the market for Shakespeare's plays.

a. The playwright Christopher Marlowe, Shakespeare's chief rival, is killed in a bar brawl.

b. The bubonic plague, a deadly infectious disease, breaks out in London.

c. To celebrate the defeat of the Spanish Armada, Queen Elizabeth declares several weeks of festivities, which involves commissioning new plays.

14. The small town of Middling experiences a sudden doubling of the birth rate. After three years, the birth rate returns to normal. Use a diagram to illustrate the effect of these events on the following.

a. The market for an hour of babysitting services in Middling today

b. The market for an hour of babysitting services 14 years into the future, after the birth rate has returned to normal, by which time children born today are old enough to work as babysitters

c. The market for an hour of babysitting services 30 years into the future, when children born today are likely to be having children of their own

15. Use a diagram to illustrate how each of the following events affects the equilibrium price and quantity of pizza.

a. The price of mozzarella cheese rises.

b. The health hazards of hamburgers are widely publicized.

c. The price of tomato sauce falls.

d. The incomes of consumers rise and pizza is an inferior good.

e. Consumers expect the price of pizza to fall next week.

16. Although he was a prolific artist, Pablo Picasso painted only 1,000 canvases during his "Blue Period." Picasso is now dead, and all of his Blue Period works are currently on display in museums and private galleries throughout Europe and the United States.

   a. Draw a supply curve for Picasso Blue Period works. Why is this supply curve different from ones you have seen?

   b. Given the supply curve from part a, the price of a Picasso Blue Period work will be entirely dependent on what factor(s)? Draw a diagram showing how the equilibrium price of such a work is determined.

   c. Suppose that rich art collectors decide that it is essential to acquire Picasso Blue Period art for their collections. Show the impact of this on the market for these paintings.

17. Draw the appropriate curve in each of the following cases. Is it like or unlike the curves you have seen so far? Explain.

   a. The demand for cardiac bypass surgery, given that the government pays the full cost for any patient

   b. The demand for elective cosmetic plastic surgery, given that the patient pays the full cost

   c. The supply of Rembrandt paintings

   d. The supply of reproductions of Rembrandt paintings

>web... To continue your study and review of concepts in this chapter, please visit the Krugman/Wells website for quizzes, animated graph tutorials, web links to helpful resources, and more.

www.worthpublishers.com/krugmanwells

>>The Market Strikes Back

BIG CITY, NOT-SO-BRIGHT IDEAS

NEW YORK CITY IS A PLACE WHERE YOU can find almost anything—that is, almost anything, except a taxicab when you need one or a decent apartment at a rent you can afford. You might think that New York's notorious shortages of cabs and apartments are the inevitable price of big-city living. However, they are largely the product of government policies—specifically, of government policies that have, one way or another, tried to prevail over the market forces of supply and demand.

In the previous chapter, we learned the principle that a market moves to equilibrium—that the market price rises or falls to the level at which the quantity of a good that people are willing to supply is equal to the quantity that other people want to demand. But sometimes governments try to defy that principle. When they do, the market strikes back in predictable ways. And our ability to predict what will happen when governments try to defy supply and demand shows the power and usefulness of supply and demand analysis itself.

The shortages of apartments and taxicabs in New York are particular examples that illuminate what happens when the logic of the market is defied. New York's housing shortage is the result of *rent control,* a law that prevents landlords from raising rents except when specifically given permission. Rent control was introduced during World War II to protect the interests of tenants, and it still remains in force. Many other American cities have had rent control at one time or another, but with the notable exceptions of New York and San Francisco, these controls have largely been done away with. Similarly, New York's limited supply of taxis is the result of a licensing system introduced in the 1930s. New York taxi licenses are known as "medallions," and only taxis with medallions are allowed to pick up passengers. And although this

New York City: An empty taxi is hard to find.

PNI Ltd./Picture Quest

system was originally intended to protect the interests of both drivers and customers, it has generated a shortage of taxis in the city. The number of medallions remained fixed from 1937 until 1995, and only a handful of additional licenses have been issued since then.

What you will learn in this chapter:

➤ The meaning of **price controls** and **quantity controls,** two kinds of government intervention in markets

➤ How price and quantity controls create problems and make a market **inefficient**

➤ Why economists are often deeply skeptical of attempts to intervene in markets

➤ Who benefits and who loses from market interventions, and why they are used despite their well-known problems

➤ What an **excise tax** is and why its effect is similar to a quantity control

➤ Why the **deadweight loss** of a tax means that its true cost is more than the amount of tax revenue collected

In this chapter, we begin by examining what happens when governments try to control prices in a competitive market, keeping the price in a market either below its equilibrium level—a *price ceiling* such as rent control—or above it—a *price floor*. We then turn to schemes such as taxi medallions that attempt to dictate the quantity of a good bought and sold. Finally, we consider the effects of taxes on sales or purchases.

Why Governments Control Prices

You learned in Chapter 3 that a market moves to equilibrium—that is, the market price moves to the level at which the quantity supplied equals the quantity demanded. But this equilibrium price does not necessarily please either buyers or sellers.

After all, buyers would always like to pay less if they could, and sometimes they can make a strong moral or political case that they should pay lower prices. For example, what if the equilibrium between supply and demand for apartments in a major city leads to rental rates that an average working person can't afford? In that case, a government might well be under pressure to impose limits on the rents landlords can charge.

Sellers, however, would always like to get more money for what they sell, and sometimes they can make a strong moral or political case that they should receive higher prices. For example, consider the labor market: the price for an hour of a worker's time is the wage rate. What if the equilibrium between supply and demand for less-skilled workers leads to wage rates that are below the poverty level? In that case, a government might well find itself pressured to require employers to pay a rate no lower than some specified minimum wage.

In other words, there is often a strong political demand for governments to intervene in markets. When a government intervenes to regulate prices, we say that it imposes **price controls**. These controls typically take the form either of an upper limit, a **price ceiling**, or a lower limit, a **price floor**.

Unfortunately, it's not that easy to tell a market what to do. As we will now see, when a government tries to legislate prices—whether it legislates them *down* by imposing a price ceiling or *up* by imposing a price floor—there are certain predictable and unpleasant side effects.

We should note an important caveat here: our analysis in this chapter considers only what happens when price controls are imposed on *competitive markets*, which, as you should recall from Chapter 3, are markets with many buyers and sellers in which no buyer or seller can have any influence on the price. When markets are *not* competitive—as in a monopoly, where there is only one seller—price controls don't necessarily cause the same problems. In practice, however, price controls often *are* imposed on competitive markets—like the New York apartment market. And so the analysis in this chapter applies to many important real-world situations.

Price controls are legal restrictions on how high or low a market price may go. They can take two forms: a **price ceiling**, a maximum price sellers are allowed to charge for a good, or a **price floor**, a minimum price buyers are required to pay for a good.

Price Ceilings

Aside from rent control, there are not many price ceilings in the United States today. But at times they have been widespread. Price ceilings are typically imposed during crises—wars, harvest failures, natural disasters—because these events often lead to sudden price increases that hurt many people but produce big gains for a lucky few. The U.S. government imposed ceilings on many prices during World War II: the war sharply increased demand for raw materials, such as aluminum and steel, and price controls prevented those with access to these raw materials from earning huge profits. Price controls on oil were imposed in 1973, when an embargo by Arab oil-exporting countries seemed likely to generate huge profits for U.S. oil companies. (See

Economics in Action on page 89.) Price controls were imposed on California's whole-sale electricity market in 2001, when a shortage was creating big profits for a few power-generating companies but leading to higher bills for consumers.

Rent control in New York is, believe it or not, a legacy of World War II: it was imposed because the war produced an economic boom, which increased demand for apartments at a time when the labor and raw materials that might have been used to build them were being used to win the war instead. Although most price controls were removed soon after the war ended, New York's rent limits were retained and gradually extended to buildings not previously covered, leading to some very strange situations.

You can rent a one-bedroom apartment in Manhattan on fairly short notice—if you are able and willing to pay about $1,700 a month and live in a less-than-desirable area. Yet some people pay only a small fraction of this for comparable apartments and others pay hardly more for bigger apartments in better locations.

Aside from producing great deals for some renters, however, what are the broader consequences of New York's rent control system? To answer this question, we turn to the model we developed in Chapter 3: the supply and demand model.

Modeling a Price Ceiling

To see what can go wrong when a government imposes a price ceiling on a competitive market, consider Figure 4-1, which shows a simplified model of the market for apartments in New York. For the sake of simplicity, we imagine that all apartments are exactly the same and would therefore rent for the same price in an uncontrolled market. The table in the figure shows the demand and supply schedules; the implied demand and supply curves are shown on the left of the figure. We show the quantity of apartments on the horizontal axis and the monthly rent per apartment on the vertical axis. You can see that in an unregulated market the equilibrium would be at point *E*: 2 million apartments would be rented for $1,000 each per month.

Figure 4-1   **The Market for Apartments in the Absence of Government Controls**

Monthly rent (per apartment)	Quantity of apartments (millions)	
	Quantity demanded	Quantity supplied
$1,400	1.6	2.4
1,300	1.7	2.3
1,200	1.8	2.2
1,100	1.9	2.1
1,000	2.0	2.0
900	2.1	1.9
800	2.2	1.8
700	2.3	1.7
600	2.4	1.6

Without government intervention, the market for apartments reaches equilibrium at point *E* with a market rent of $1,000 per month and 2 million apartments rented. **>web...**

Now suppose that the government imposes a price ceiling, limiting rents to a price below the equilibrium price—say no more than $800.

Figure 4-2 shows the effect of the price ceiling, represented by the line at $800. At the enforced rental rate of $800, landlords will have less incentive to offer apartments, so they won't be willing to supply as many as they would at the equilibrium rate of $1,000. So they will choose point *A* on the supply curve, offering only 1.8 million apartments for rent, 200,000 fewer than in the free-market situation. At the same time, more people will want to rent apartments at a price of $800 than at the equilibrium price of $1,000; as shown at point *B* on the demand curve, at a monthly rent of $800 the quantity of apartments demanded rises to 2.2 million, 200,000 more than in the free-market situation and 400,000 more than are actually available at the price of $800. So there is now a persistent shortage of rental housing: at that price, 400,000 more people want to rent than are able to find apartments.

Do price ceilings always cause shortages? No. If a price ceiling is set above the equilibrium price, it won't have any effect. Suppose that the equilibrium rental rate on apartments is $1,000 per month and the city government sets a ceiling of $1,200. Who cares? In this case, the price ceiling won't be binding—it won't actually constrain market behavior—and it will have no effect.

Why a Price Ceiling Causes Inefficiency

The housing shortage shown in Figure 4-2 is not merely annoying: like any shortage induced by price controls, it can be seriously harmful because it leads to *inefficiency*. We introduced the concept of *efficiency* back in Chapter 1, where we learned that an economy is efficient if there is no way to make some people better off without making others worse off. We also learned the basic principle that a market economy, left to itself, is usually efficient.

A market or an economy becomes **inefficient** when there are missed opportunities—ways in which production or consumption could be rearranged that would make some people better off without making other people worse off.

A market or an economy is **inefficient** if there are missed opportunities: some people could be made better off without making other people worse off.

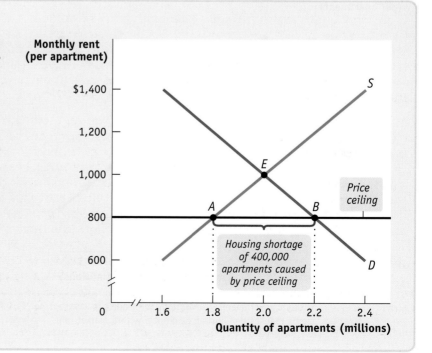

Figure 4-2

The Effects of a Price Ceiling

The dark horizontal line represents the government-imposed price ceiling on rents of $800 per month. This price ceiling reduces the quantity of apartments supplied to 1.8 million, point *A*, and increases the quantity demanded to 2.2 million, point *B*. This creates a persistent shortage of 400,000 units: 400,000 people who want apartments at the legal rent of $800 but cannot get them.

Rent control, like all price ceilings, creates inefficiency in at least three distinct ways: in the allocation of apartments to renters, in the time wasted searching for apartments, and in the inefficiently low quality or condition in which landlords maintain apartments. In addition to inefficiency, price ceilings give rise to illegal behavior as people try to circumvent them.

Inefficient Allocation to Consumers In the case shown in Figure 4-2, 2.2 million people would like to rent an apartment at $800 per month, but only 1.8 million apartments are available. Of those 2.2 million who are seeking an apartment, some want an apartment badly and are willing to pay a high price to get one. Others have a less urgent need and are only willing to pay a low price, perhaps because they have alternative housing. An efficient allocation of apartments would reflect these differences: people who really want an apartment will get one and people who aren't all that anxious to find an apartment won't. In an inefficient distribution of apartments, the opposite will happen: some people who are not especially anxious to find an apartment will get one but others who are very anxious to find an apartment won't. And because under rent control people usually get apartments through luck or personal connections, rent control generally results in an **inefficient allocation to consumers** of the few apartments available.

To see the inefficiency involved, consider the plight of the Lees, a family with young children who have no alternative housing and would be willing to pay up to $1,500 for an apartment—but are unable to find one. Also consider George, a retiree who lives most of the year in Florida but still has a lease on the New York apartment he moved into 40 years ago. George pays $800 per month for this apartment, but if the rent were even slightly more—say, $850—he would give it up and stay with his children when he is in New York.

This allocation of apartments—George has one and the Lees do not—is a missed opportunity: there is a way to make the Lees and George both better off at no additional cost. The Lees would be happy to pay George, say, $1,200 a month to sublet his apartment, which he would happily accept since the apartment is worth no more than $850 a month to him. George would prefer the money he gets from the Lees to keeping his apartment; the Lees would prefer to have the apartment rather than the money. So both would be made better off by this transaction—and nobody else would be hurt.

Generally, if people who really want apartments could sublet them from people who are less eager to stay in them, both those who gain apartments and those who trade their leases for more money would be better off. However, subletting is illegal under rent control because it would occur at prices above the price ceiling. But just because subletting is illegal doesn't mean it never happens; in fact, it does occur in New York, although not on a scale that would undo the effects of rent control. This illegal subletting is a kind of *black market activity*, which we will discuss shortly.

> Price ceilings often lead to inefficiency in the form of **inefficient allocation to consumers**: people who want the good badly and are willing to pay a high price don't get it, and those who care relatively little about the good and are only willing to pay a low price do get it.

Wasted Resources A second reason a price ceiling causes inefficiency is that it leads to **wasted resources**. The Economics in Action on page 89 describes the gasoline shortages of 1979, when millions of Americans spent hours each week waiting in lines at gas stations. The *opportunity cost* of the time spent in gas lines—the wages not earned, the leisure time not enjoyed—constituted wasted resources from the point of view of consumers and of the economy as a whole. Because of rent control, the Lees will spend all their spare time for several months searching for an apartment, time they would rather have spent working or in family activities. That is, there is an opportunity cost to the Lees' prolonged search for an apartment—the leisure or income they had to forgo. If the market for apartments worked freely, the Lees would quickly find an apartment at the equilibrium rent of $1,000 and have time to earn more or to enjoy themselves—an outcome that would make them better off without making anyone else worse off. Again, rent control creates missed opportunities.

> Price ceilings typically lead to inefficiency in the form of **wasted resources**: people spend money and expend effort in order to deal with the shortages caused by the price ceiling.

Inefficiently Low Quality A third way a price ceiling causes inefficiency is by causing goods to be of **inefficiently low quality**.

> Price ceilings often lead to inefficiency in that the goods being offered are of **inefficiently low quality**: sellers offer low-quality goods at a low price even though buyers would prefer a higher quality at a higher price.

FOR INQUIRING MINDS

THE RENT CONTROL ARISTOCRACY

One of the ironies of New York's rent-control system is that some of the biggest beneficiaries are not the working-class families the system was intended to help but affluent tenants whose families have lived for many decades in choice apartments that would now command very high rents.

One well-known example: the 1986 movie *Hannah and Her Sisters* took place mainly in the real-life home of actress Mia Farrow, a spectacular 11-room apartment overlooking Central Park. Ms. Farrow "inherited" this apartment from her mother, the actress Maureen O'Sullivan. A few years after the movie came out, a study found that Ms. Farrow was paying less than $2,300 a month—about what a 2-bedroom apartment in a far less desirable location would have cost on the uncontrolled market.

Again, consider rent control. Landlords have no incentive to provide better conditions because they cannot raise rents to cover their repair costs but are still able to find tenants easily. In many cases tenants would be willing to pay much more for improved conditions than it would cost for the landlord to provide them—for example, the upgrade of an antiquated electrical system that cannot safely run air conditioners or computers. But any additional payment for such improvements would be legally considered a rent increase, which is prohibited. Indeed, rent-controlled apartments are notoriously badly maintained, rarely painted, subject to frequent electrical and plumbing problems, sometimes even hazardous to inhabit. As one former manager of Manhattan buildings described his job: "At unregulated apartments we'd do most things that the tenants requested. But on the rent-regulated units, we did absolutely only what the law required. . . . We had a perverse incentive to make those tenants unhappy. With regulated apartments, the ultimate objective is to get people out of the building."

This whole situation is a missed opportunity—some tenants would be happy to pay for better conditions, and landlords would be happy to provide them for payment. But such an exchange would occur only if the market were allowed to operate freely.

Black Markets And that leads us to a last aspect of price ceilings: the incentive they provide for *illegal activities*, specifically the emergence of **black markets**. We have already described one kind of black market activity—illegal subletting by tenants. But it does not stop there. Clearly, there is a temptation for a landlord to say to a potential tenant, "Look, you can have the place if you slip me an extra few hundred in cash each month"—and for the tenant to agree, if he or she is one of those people who would be willing to pay much more than the maximum legal rent.

What's wrong with black markets? In general, it's a bad thing if people break *any* law, because it encourages disrespect for the law in general. Worse yet, in this case illegal activity worsens the position of those who try to be honest. If the Lees are scrupulous about not breaking the rent control law but others—who may need an apartment less than the Lees do—are willing to bribe landlords, the Lees may *never* find an apartment.

A **black market** is a market in which goods or services are bought and sold illegally—either because it is illegal to sell them at all or because the prices charged are legally prohibited by a price ceiling.

So Why Are There Price Ceilings?

We have seen three common results of price ceilings:

- A persistent shortage of the good
- Inefficiency arising from this persistent shortage in the form of inefficient allocation of the good to consumers, resources wasted in searching for the good, and the inefficiently low quality of the good offered for sale
- The emergence of illegal, black market activity

Given these unpleasant consequences, why do governments still sometimes impose price ceilings—and why does rent control, in particular, persist in New York?

One answer is that although price ceilings may have adverse effects, they do benefit some people. In practice, New York's rent control rules—which are more complex than our simple model—hurt most residents but give a small minority of renters much cheaper housing than they would get in an unregulated market. And those who benefit from the controls are typically better organized and more vocal than those who are harmed by them.

Also, when price ceilings have been in effect for a long time, buyers may not have a realistic idea of what would happen without them. In our previous example, the rental rate in an uncontrolled market (Figure 4-1) would be only 25 percent higher than in the controlled market (Figure 4-2)—$1,000 instead of $800. But how would renters know that? Indeed, they might have heard about black market transactions at much higher prices—the Lees or some other family paying George $1,200 or more—and would not realize that these black market prices are much higher than the price that would prevail in a fully free market.

A last answer is that government officials often do not understand supply and demand analysis! It is a great mistake to suppose that economic policies in the real world are always sensible or well informed.

economics in action

Oil Shortages in the 1970s

In 1979 a revolution overthrew the government of Iran, one of the world's major petroleum-exporting countries. The political chaos in Iran disrupted oil production there, and the sudden fall in world supply caused the price of crude oil to shoot up by 300 percent.

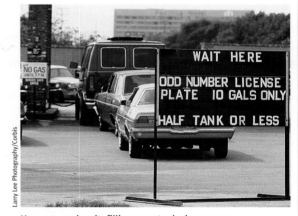

Hurry up and wait: filling your tank circa 1979.

In most of the world this price increase made gasoline more expensive at the pump but did not lead to shortages. In the United States, however, gasoline was subject to a price ceiling, imposed six years earlier during an oil crisis sparked by the Arab–Israeli war of 1973. The main purpose of those price controls was to prevent U.S. oil producers from reaping large profits as a result of temporary disruptions of supply.

As we learned in Chapter 3, a fall in supply generally raises prices. But here, because the price of gasoline at the pump couldn't rise, the reduction in supply showed up as shortages. As it turned out, these shortages became much worse because of panic: drivers who weren't sure when they would next be able to get gas rushed to fill up even if they still had plenty in their tanks. This produced a temporary surge in demand and long lines at gas stations.

For a few months the gasoline shortage dominated the national scene. Hours were wasted sitting in gasoline lines; families canceled vacations for fear of being stranded. Eventually, higher production began to work its way through the refineries, increasing supply. And the end of the summer driving season reduced demand. Both together led to a fall in price.

In 1981 price controls on gasoline, now discredited as a policy, were abolished. But the uncontrolled gasoline market faced a major test in the spring of 2000. Oil-producing nations restricted their output in order to drive up prices and achieved unexpected success, more than doubling world prices over a period of a few months. Prices at the pump rose sharply—many people altered their driving plans and some felt distinctly poorer as a result of the higher prices. But there were no shortages and life continued in the United States without nearly as much disruption as price controls had generated in the 1970s.

Interestingly, however, the oil price shock of 2000 *did* cause serious disruptions in some European countries—because truck drivers and farmers, protesting the high price of fuel, blocked deliveries. This protest was an extreme illustration of the reasons why governments sometimes try to control prices despite the known problems with price controls! ■

> > > > > > > > > > > > > > > > > > >

1. Homeowners near Middletown University's stadium used to rent parking spaces in their driveways to fans at a going rate of $11. A new town ordinance now sets a maximum parking fee of $7. Use the accompanying supply and demand diagram to explain how each of the following corresponds to a price-ceiling concept.

   a. Some homeowners now think it's not worth the hassle to rent out spaces.
   b. Some fans who used to carpool to the game now drive alone.
   c. Some fans can't find parking and leave without seeing the game.

   Explain how each of the following arises from the price ceiling.

   d. Some fans now arrive several hours early to find parking.
   e. Friends of homeowners near the stadium regularly attend games, even if they aren't big fans. But some serious fans have given up because of the parking situation.
   f. Some homeowners rent spaces for more than $7 but pretend that the buyers are non-paying friends or family.

2. True or false? Explain your answer. Compared to a free market, price ceilings at a price below the equilibrium price do the following:
   a. Increase quantity supplied
   b. Make some people who want to consume the good worse off
   c. Make all producers worse off

Solutions appear at back of book.

Price Floors

Sometimes governments intervene to push market prices up instead of down. *Price floors* have been widely legislated for agricultural products, such as wheat and milk, as a way to support the incomes of farmers. Historically, there were also price floors on such services as trucking and air travel, although these were phased out by the United States in the 1970s. If you have ever worked in a fast-food restaurant, you are likely to have encountered a price floor: the United States and many other countries maintain a lower limit on the hourly wage rate of a worker's labor—that is, a floor on the price of labor, called the **minimum wage**.

The **minimum wage** is a legal floor on the wage rate, which is the market price of labor.

Just like price ceilings, price floors are intended to help some people but generate predictable and undesirable side effects. Figure 4-3 shows hypothetical supply and demand curves for butter. Left to itself, the market would move to equilibrium at point E, with 10 million pounds of butter bought and sold at a price of $1 per pound.

But now suppose that the government, in order to help dairy farmers, imposes a price floor on butter of $1.20 per pound. Its effects are shown in Figure 4-4, where the line at $1.20 represents the price floor. At a price of $1.20 per pound, producers would want to supply 12 million pounds (point B on the supply curve) but consumers would want to buy only 9 million pounds (point A on the demand curve). There would therefore be a persistent surplus of 3 million pounds of butter.

Does a price floor always lead to an unwanted surplus? No. Just as in the case of a price ceiling, the floor may not be binding—that is, it may be irrelevant. If the equilibrium price of butter is $1 per pound but the floor is set at only $0.80, the floor has no effect.

But suppose that a price floor is binding: what happens to the unwanted surplus? The answer depends on government policy. In the case of agricultural price floors, governments buy up unwanted surplus. Therefore the U.S. government has at times found itself warehousing thousands of tons of butter, cheese, and other farm products. (The European Commission, which administers price floors for a number of European countries, once found itself the owner of a so-called butter mountain, equal in weight to the entire population of Austria.) The government then has to find a way to dispose of these unwanted goods.

Some countries pay exporters to sell products at a loss overseas; this is standard procedure for the European Union. (See For Inquiring Minds on page 92.) At one point the United States tried giving away surplus cheese to the poor. In some cases, governments have actually destroyed the surplus production. To avoid the problem of

Figure 4-3   The Market for Butter in the Absence of Government Controls

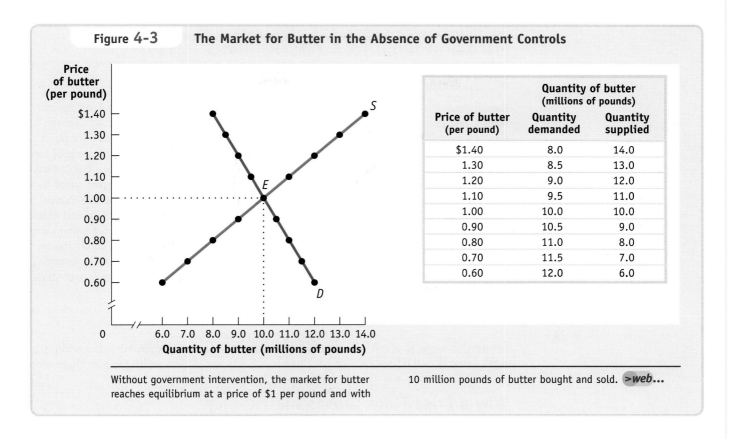

Price of butter (per pound)	Quantity of butter (millions of pounds)	
	Quantity demanded	Quantity supplied
$1.40	8.0	14.0
1.30	8.5	13.0
1.20	9.0	12.0
1.10	9.5	11.0
1.00	10.0	10.0
0.90	10.5	9.0
0.80	11.0	8.0
0.70	11.5	7.0
0.60	12.0	6.0

Without government intervention, the market for butter reaches equilibrium at a price of $1 per pound and with 10 million pounds of butter bought and sold. **>web...**

dealing with the unwanted supplies, the U.S. government typically pays farmers not to produce the products at all.

When the government is not prepared to purchase the unwanted surplus, a price floor means that would-be sellers cannot find buyers. This is what happens when there is a price floor on the wage rate paid for an hour of labor, the *minimum wage*: when the

Figure 4-4

The Effects of a Price Floor

The dark horizontal line represents the government-imposed price floor of $1.20 per pound of butter. The quantity of butter demanded falls to 9 million pounds while the quantity supplied rises to 12 million pounds, generating a persistent surplus of 3 million pounds of butter. **>web...**

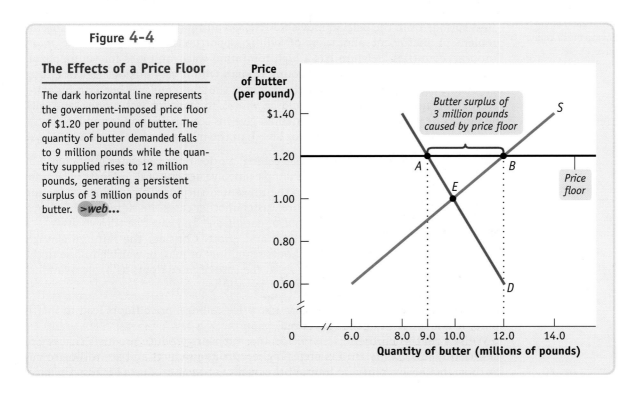

PRICE FLOORS AND BUTTER COOKIES

Wander down the cookie aisle of your super-market, and you will probably find a large section of imported cookies, especially "butter cookies"—cookies containing lots of butter—from Denmark and other countries. Why does the United States—with a pretty strong cookie-baking tradition of its own—import cookies from overseas? Part of the answer lies in European price floors.

Twenty-five European countries are currently members of the European Union, an organization that coordinates their policies on foreign trade, regulations, and other matters. The

European Union also sets price floors for agricultural goods, under the so-called Common Agricultural Policy, or CAP. These price floors have led to large surpluses, particularly of butter. To cope with these surpluses, the CAP pays a subsidy to companies that export goods such as butter—that is, sell them outside Europe.

And guess what: butter contained in a cookie sold in America counts as exported butter—and receives a subsidy. As a result, butter cookies from Europe are artificially cheap in America. So now you know why your supermarket stocks them. *Bon appetit!*

minimum wage is above the equilibrium wage rate, some people who are willing to work—that is, sell labor—cannot find buyers—that is, employers willing to give them jobs.

Why a Price Floor Causes Inefficiency

The persistent surplus that results from a price floor creates missed opportunities—inefficiencies—that resemble those created by the shortage that results from a price ceiling. These include inefficient allocation of sales among sellers, wasted resources, inefficiently high quality, and the temptation to break the law by selling below the legal price.

Inefficient Allocation of Sales Among Sellers Like a price ceiling, a price floor can lead to *inefficient allocation*—but in this case **inefficient allocation of sales among sellers** rather than inefficient allocation to consumers.

An episode from the Belgian movie *Rosetta*, a realistic fictional story, illustrates the problem of inefficient allocation of selling opportunities quite well. Like many European countries, Belgium has a high minimum wage, and jobs for young people are scarce. At one point Rosetta, a young woman who is very anxious to work, loses her job at a fast-food stand because the owner of the stand replaces her with his son—a very reluctant worker. Rosetta would be willing to work for less money, and with the money he would save, the owner could give his son an allowance and let him do something else. But to hire Rosetta for less than the minimum wage would be illegal.

Wasted Resources Also like a price ceiling, a price floor generates inefficiency by *wasting resources*. The most graphic examples involve agricultural products with price floors when the government buys up the unwanted surplus. The surplus production is sometimes destroyed, which is a pure waste; in other cases the stored produce goes, as officials euphemistically put it, "out of condition" and must be thrown away.

Price floors also lead to wasted time and effort. Consider the minimum wage. Would-be workers who spend many hours searching for jobs, or waiting in line in the hope of getting jobs, play the same role in the case of price floors as hapless families searching for apartments in the case of price ceilings.

Inefficiently High Quality Again like price ceilings, price floors lead to inefficiency in the quality of goods produced.

We saw that when there is a price ceiling, suppliers produce products that are of inefficiently low quality: buyers prefer higher-quality products and are willing to pay for them, but sellers refuse to improve the quality of their products because the price

Price floors lead to **inefficient allocation of sales among sellers:** those who would be willing to sell the good at the lowest price are not always those who actually manage to sell it.

ceiling prevents their being compensated for doing so. This same logic applies to price floors, but in reverse: suppliers offer goods of **inefficiently high quality**.

How can this be? Isn't high quality a good thing? Yes, but only if it is worth the cost. Suppose that suppliers spend a lot to make goods of very high quality but that this quality is not worth all that much to consumers, who would rather receive the money spent on that quality in the form of a lower price. This represents a missed opportunity: suppliers and buyers could make a mutually beneficial deal in which buyers got goods of somewhat lower quality for a much lower price.

A good example of the inefficiency of excessive quality comes from the days when transatlantic airfares were set artificially high by international treaty. Forbidden to compete for customers by offering lower ticket prices, airlines instead offered expensive services, like lavish in-flight meals that went largely uneaten. At one point the regulators tried to restrict this practice by defining maximum service standards—for example, that snack service should consist of no more than a sandwich. One airline then introduced what it called a "Scandinavian Sandwich," a towering affair that forced the convening of another conference to define *sandwich*. All of this was wasteful, especially considering that what passengers really wanted was less food and lower airfares.

Since the deregulation of U.S. airlines in the 1970s, American passengers have experienced a large decrease in ticket prices accompanied by a decrease in the quality of in-flight service—smaller seats, lower-quality food, and so on. Everyone complains about the service—but thanks to lower fares, the number of people flying on U.S. carriers has grown several hundred percent since airline deregulation.

Illegal Activity   Finally, like price ceilings, price floors can provide an incentive for *illegal activity*. For example, in countries where the minimum wage is far above the equilibrium wage rate, workers desperate for jobs sometimes agree to work off the books for employers who conceal their employment from the government—or bribe the government inspectors. This practice, known in Europe as "black labor," is especially common in Southern European countries such as Italy and Spain (see Economics in Action below).

> Price floors often lead to inefficiency in that goods of **inefficiently high quality** are offered: sellers offer high-quality goods at a high price, even though buyers would prefer a lower quality at a lower price.

So Why Are There Price Floors?

To sum up, a price floor creates various negative side effects:

- A persistent surplus of the good
- Inefficiency arising from the persistent surplus in the form of inefficient allocation of sales among sellers, wasted resources, and an inefficiently high level of quality offered by suppliers
- The temptation to engage in illegal activity, particularly bribery and corruption of government officials

So why do governments impose price floors when they have so many negative side effects? The reasons are similar to those for imposing price ceilings. Government officials often disregard warnings about the consequences of price floors either because they believe that the relevant market is poorly described by the supply and demand model or, more often, because they do not understand the model. Above all, just as price ceilings are often imposed because they benefit some influential buyers of a good, price floors are often imposed because they benefit some influential *sellers*.

economics in action

"Black Labor" in Southern Europe

The best-known example of a price floor is the minimum wage. Most economists believe, however, that the minimum wage has relatively little effect on the job market in the United States, mainly because the floor is set so low. (This effectively makes the U.S. minimum wage a *nonbinding* price floor—a political symbol more than a substantive policy.) In 1968, the U.S. minimum wage was 53 percent of the average wage of blue-collar workers; by 2003, it had fallen to about 34 percent.

The situation is different, however, in many European countries, where minimum wages have been set much higher than in the United States. This has happened despite the fact that European workers are somewhat less productive than their American counterparts, which means that the equilibrium wage in Europe—the wage that would clear the labor market—is probably lower in Europe than in the United States. Moreover, European countries often require employers to pay for health and retirement benefits, which are more extensive and therefore more costly than comparable American benefits. These mandated benefits make the actual cost of hiring a European worker considerably more than the worker's paycheck.

The result is that in Europe the price floor on labor is definitely binding: the minimum wage is well above the wage rate that would make the quantity of labor supplied by workers equal to the quantity of labor demanded by employers.

The persistent surplus that results from this price floor appears in the form of high unemployment—millions of workers, especially young workers, seek jobs but cannot find them. In countries where the enforcement of labor laws is lax, however, there is a second, entirely predictable result: widespread evasion of the law. In both Italy and Spain, officials believe there are hundreds of thousands, if not millions, of workers who are employed by companies that pay them less than the legal minimum, fail to provide the required health and retirement benefits, or both. In many cases the jobs are simply unreported: Spanish economists estimate that about a third of the country's reported unemployed are in the black labor market—working at unreported jobs. In fact, Spaniards waiting to collect checks from the unemployment office have been known to complain about the long lines that keep them from getting back to work!

Employers in these countries have also found legal ways to evade the wage floor. For example, Italy's labor regulations apply only to companies with 15 or more workers. This gives a big cost advantage to small Italian firms, many of which remain small in order to avoid having to pay higher wages and benefits. And sure enough, in some Italian industries there is an astonishing proliferation of tiny companies. For example, one of Italy's most successful industries is the manufacture of fine woolen cloth, centered in the Prato region. The average textile firm in that region employs only four workers! ∎

< < < < < < < < < < < < < < < < < <

▶▶QUICK REVIEW

➤ The most familiar price floor is the *minimum wage.* Price floors are also commonly imposed on agricultural goods.
➤ A price floor above the equilibrium price benefits successful sellers but causes predictable adverse effects such as a persistent *surplus,* which leads to three kinds of inefficiencies: *inefficient allocation of sales among sellers, wasted resources,* and *inefficiently high quality.*
➤ Price floors encourage illegal activity, such as workers who work off the books, often leading to official corruption.

▶▶CHECK YOUR UNDERSTANDING 4-2

1. The state legislature mandates a price floor for gasoline of $4 per gallon. Assess the following statements and illustrate your answer using the figure provided:

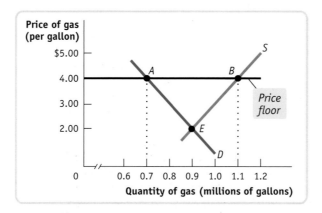

a. Proponents of the law claim it will increase the income of gas station owners. Opponents claim it will hurt gas station owners because they will lose customers.
b. Proponents claim consumers will be better off because gas stations will provide better service. Opponents claim consumers will be generally worse off because they prefer to buy gas at cheaper prices.
c. Proponents claim that they are helping gas station owners without hurting anyone else. Opponents claim that consumers are hurt and will end up doing things like buying gas in a nearby state or on the black market.

Solutions appear at back of book.

Controlling Quantities

In the 1930s, New York City instituted a system of licensing for taxicabs: only taxis with a "medallion" were allowed to pick up passengers. Because this system was intended to assure quality, medallion owners were supposed to maintain certain standards, including safety and cleanliness. A total of 11,787 medallions were issued, with taxi owners paying $10 for each medallion.

In 1995, there were still only 11,787 licensed taxicabs in New York, even though the city had meanwhile become the financial capital of the world, a place where hundreds of thousands of people in a hurry tried to hail a cab every day. (An additional 400 medallions were issued in 1995, and in 2003 plans were announced to issue 900 more over a period of three years.)

The result of this restriction on the number of taxis was that those medallions became very valuable: if you wanted to operate a New York taxi, you had to lease a medallion from someone else or buy one for a going price of about $250,000.

It turns out that the New York story is not unique; other cities introduced similar medallion systems in the 1930s and, like New York, have issued few new medallions since. In San Francisco and Boston, as in New York, taxi medallions trade for six-figure prices.

A taxi medallion system is a form of **quantity control**, or **quota**, by which the government regulates the quantity of a good that can be bought and sold rather than the price at which it is transacted. The total amount of the good that can be transacted under the quantity control is called the **quota limit**. Typically, the government limits quantity in a market by issuing **licenses;** only people with a license can legally supply the good. A taxi medallion is just such a license. The government of New York City limits the number of taxi rides that can be sold by limiting the number of taxis to only those who hold medallions. There are many other cases of quantity controls, ranging from limits on how much foreign currency (for instance, British pounds or Mexican pesos) people are allowed to buy to the quantity of clams New Jersey fishing boats are allowed to catch. Notice, by the way, that although there are price controls on both sides of the equilibrium price—price ceilings and price floors—in the real world, quantity controls always set an upper, not a lower, limit on quantities. After all, nobody can be forced to buy or sell more than they want to!

> A **quantity control**, or **quota,** is an upper limit on the quantity of some good that can be bought or sold. The total amount of the good that can be legally transacted is the **quota limit.**
>
> A **license** gives its owner the right to supply a good.

Some of these attempts to control quantities are undertaken for good economic reasons, some for bad ones. In many cases, as we will see, quantity controls introduced to address a temporary problem become politically hard to remove later because the beneficiaries don't want them abolished, even after the original reason for their existence is long gone. But whatever the reasons for such controls, they have certain predictable—and usually undesirable—economic consequences.

The Anatomy of Quantity Controls

To understand why a New York taxi medallion is worth so much money, we consider a simplified version of the market for taxi rides, shown in Figure 4-5 on page 96. Just as we assumed in the analysis of rent controls that all apartments are the same, we now suppose that all taxi rides are the same—ignoring the real-world complication that some taxi rides are longer, and thus more expensive, than others. The table in the figure shows supply and demand schedules. The equilibrium—indicated by point E in the figure and by the shaded entries in the table—is a fare of $5 per ride, with 10 million rides taken per year. (You'll see in a minute why we present the equilibrium this way.)

The New York medallion system limits the number of taxis, but each taxi driver can offer as many rides as he or she can manage. (Now you know why New York taxi drivers are so aggressive!) To simplify our analysis, however, we will assume that a medallion system limits the number of taxi rides that can legally be given to 8 million per year.

Until now, we have derived the demand curve by answering questions of the form: "How many taxi rides will passengers want to take if the price is $5 per ride?" But it is possible to reverse the question and ask instead: "At what price will consumers want to buy 10 million rides per year?" The price at which consumers want to buy a given quantity—in this case, 10 million rides at $5 per ride—is the **demand price** of that

> The **demand price** of a given quantity is the price at which consumers will demand that quantity.

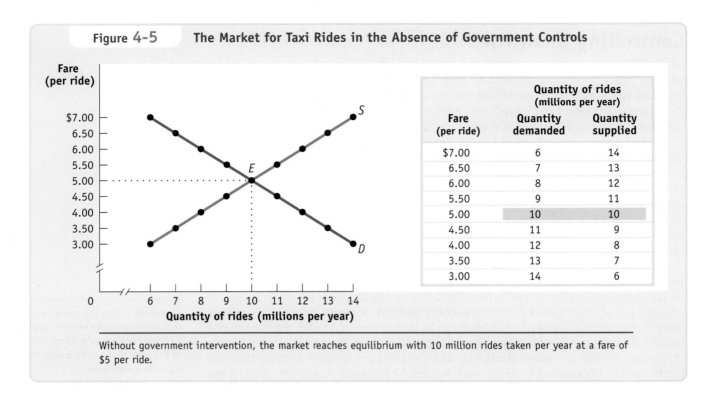

Figure 4-5	The Market for Taxi Rides in the Absence of Government Controls

Fare (per ride)	Quantity of rides (millions per year)	
	Quantity demanded	Quantity supplied
$7.00	6	14
6.50	7	13
6.00	8	12
5.50	9	11
5.00	10	10
4.50	11	9
4.00	12	8
3.50	13	7
3.00	14	6

Without government intervention, the market reaches equilibrium with 10 million rides taken per year at a fare of $5 per ride.

quantity. You can see from the demand schedule in Figure 4-5 that the demand price of 6 million rides is $7, the demand price of 7 million rides is $6.50, and so on.

Similarly, the supply curve represents the answer to questions of the form: "How many taxi rides would taxi drivers supply at a price of $5 each?" But we can also reverse this question to ask: "At what price will suppliers be willing to supply 10 million rides per year?" The price at which suppliers will supply a given quantity—in this case, 10 million rides at $5 per ride—is the **supply price** of that quantity. We can see from the supply schedule in Figure 4-5 that the supply price of 6 million rides is $3, the supply price of 7 million rides is $3.50, and so on.

> The **supply price** of a given quantity is the price at which producers will supply that quantity.

Now we are ready to analyze a quota. We have assumed that the city government limits the quantity of taxi rides to 8 million per year. Medallions, each of which carries the right to provide a certain number of taxi rides per year, are made available to selected people in such a way that a total of 8 million rides will be provided. Medallion holders may then either drive their own taxis or rent their medallions to others for a fee.

Figure 4-6 shows the resulting market for taxi rides, with the line at 8 million rides per year representing the quota limit. Because the quantity of rides is limited to 8 million, consumers must be at point *A* on the demand curve, corresponding to the shaded entry in the demand schedule: the demand price of 8 million rides is $6. Meanwhile, taxi drivers must be at point *B* on the supply curve, corresponding to the shaded entry in the supply schedule: the supply price of 8 million rides is $4.

But how can the price received by taxi drivers be $4 when the price paid by taxi riders is $6? The answer is that in addition to the market in taxi rides, there will also be a market in medallions. Medallion-holders may not always want to drive their taxis: they may be ill or on vacation. So those who do not want to drive their own taxis will sell the right to use the medallion to someone else. So we need to consider two sets of transactions here, and hence two prices: (1) the transactions in taxi rides and the price at which these will occur, and (2) the transactions in medallions and the price at which these will occur. It turns out that since we are looking at two markets, the $4 and $6 prices will both be right.

To see how this all works, consider two imaginary New York taxi drivers, Sunil and Harriet. Sunil has a medallion but can't use it because he's recovering from a severely sprained wrist. So he's looking to rent his medallion out to someone else. Harriet

Figure 4-6   Effect of a Quota on the Market for Taxi Rides

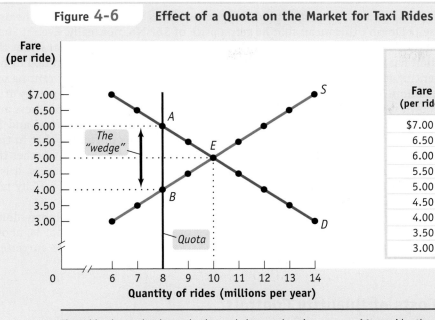

Fare (per ride)	Quantity of rides (millions per year)	
	Quantity demanded	Quantity supplied
$7.00	6	14
6.50	7	13
6.00	8	12
5.50	9	11
5.00	10	10
4.50	11	9
4.00	12	8
3.50	13	7
3.00	14	6

The table shows the demand price and the supply price corresponding to each quantity: the price at which that quantity would be demanded and supplied, respectively. The city government imposes a quota of 8 million rides by selling licenses for only 8 million rides, represented by the dark vertical line. The price paid by consumers rises to $6 per ride, the demand price of 8 million rides, shown by point *A*. The supply price of 8 million rides is only $4 per ride, shown by point *B*. The difference between these two prices is the quota rent per ride, the earnings that accrue to the owner of a license. The quota rent drives a wedge between the demand price and the supply price. **>web...**

doesn't have a medallion but would like to rent one. Furthermore, at any point in time there are many other people like Harriet who would like to rent a medallion as well as many others like Sunil who have a medallion to rent. Suppose Sunil agrees to rent his medallion to Harriet. To make things simple, assume that any driver can give only one ride per day and that Sunil is renting his medallion to Harriet for one day. What rental price will they agree on?

To answer this question, we need to look at the transactions from the viewpoints of both drivers. Once she has the medallion, Harriet knows she can make $6 per day—the demand price of a ride under the quota. And she is willing to rent the medallion only if she makes at least $4 per day—the supply price of a ride under the quota. So Sunil cannot demand a rent of more than $2—the difference between $6 and $4. And if Harriet offered Sunil less than $2—say, $1.50—there would be other eager drivers willing to offer him more, up to $2. Hence, in order to get the medallion, Harriet must offer Sunil at least $2. Therefore, since the rent can be no more than $2 and no less than $2, it must be exactly $2.

It is no coincidence that $2 is exactly the difference between $6, the demand price of 8 million rides, and $4, the supply price of 8 million rides. In every case in which the supply of a good is legally restricted, there is a **wedge** between the demand price of the quantity transacted and the supply price of the quantity transacted. This wedge, illustrated by the double-headed arrow in Figure 4-6, has a special name: the **quota rent**. It is the earnings that accrue to the license-holder from ownership of a valuable commodity, the license. In the case of Sunil and Harriet, the quota rent of $2 goes to Sunil because he owns the license, and the remaining $4 from the total fare of $6 goes to Harriet.

So Figure 4-6 also illustrates the quota rent in the market for New York taxi rides. The quota limits the quantity of rides to 8 million per year, a quantity at which the demand price of $6 exceeds the supply price of $4. The wedge between these two prices, $2, is the quota rent that results from the restrictions placed on the quantity of taxi rides in this market.

A quantity control, or quota, drives a **wedge** between the demand price and the supply price of a good; that is, the price paid by buyers ends up being higher than that received by sellers. The difference between the demand and supply price at the quota limit is the **quota rent**, the earnings that accrue to the license-holder from ownership of the right to sell the good. It is equal to the market price of the license when the licenses are traded.

But wait a second. What if Sunil doesn't rent out his medallion? What if he uses it himself? Doesn't this mean that he gets a price of $6? No, not really. Even if Sunil doesn't rent out his medallion, he could have rented it out, which means that the medallion has an *opportunity cost* of $2: if Sunil decides to drive his own taxi rather than renting it to Harriet, the $2 represents his opportunity cost of not renting out his medallion. That is, the $2 quota rent is now the rental income he forgoes by driving his own taxi. In effect, Sunil is in two businesses—the taxi-driving business and the medallion-renting business. He makes $4 per ride from driving his taxi and $2 per ride from renting out his medallion. It doesn't make any difference that in this particular case he has rented his medallion to himself! So regardless of whether the medallion owner uses the medallion himself or herself, or rents it to others, it is a valuable asset. And this is represented in the going price for a New York City taxi medallion: in 2004, it was around $250,000.

Notice, by the way, that quotas—like price ceilings and price floors—don't always have a real effect. If the quota were set at 12 million rides—that is, above the equilibrium quantity in an unregulated market—it would have no effect because it would not be binding.

The Costs of Quantity Controls

Like price controls, quantity controls can have some undesirable side effects. The first is the by-now-familiar problem of *inefficiency* due to missed opportunities: quantity controls prevent mutually beneficial transactions from occurring, transactions that would benefit both buyers and sellers. Looking back at Figure 4-6, you can see that starting at the quota limit of 8 million rides, New Yorkers would be willing to pay at least $5.50 per ride for an additional 1 million rides and that taxi drivers would be willing to provide those rides as long as they got at least $4.50 per ride. These are rides that would have taken place if there were no quota limit. The same is true for the next 1 million rides: New Yorkers would be willing to pay at least $5 per ride when the quantity of rides is increased from 9 to 10 million, and taxi drivers would be willing to provide those rides as long as they got at least $5 per ride. Again, these rides would have occurred without the quota limit. Only when the market has reached the free-market equilibrium quantity of 10 million rides are there no "missed-opportunity rides"—the quota limit of 8 million rides has caused 2 million "missed-opportunity rides." Generally, *as long as the demand price of a given quantity exceeds the supply price, there is a missed opportunity.* A buyer would be willing to buy the good at a price that the seller would be willing to accept, but such a transaction does not occur because it is forbidden by the quota.

And because there are transactions that people would like to make but are not allowed to, quantity controls generate an incentive to evade them or even to break the law. New York's taxi industry again provides clear examples. Taxi regulation applies only to those drivers who are hailed by passengers on the street. A car service that makes prearranged pickups does not need a medallion. As a result, such hired cars provide much of the service that might otherwise be provided by taxis, as in other cities. In addition, there are substantial numbers of unlicensed cabs that simply defy the law by picking up passengers without a medallion. Because these cabs are illegal, their drivers are completely unregulated, and they generate a disproportionately large share of traffic accidents in New York.

In fact, in 2004 the hardships caused by the limited number of New York taxis led city leaders to authorize an increase in the number of licensed taxis from 12,187 to a little over 13,000 by 2007—a move that certainly cheered New York riders. But those who already owned medallions were less happy with the increase; they understood that the nearly 900 new taxis would reduce or eliminate the shortage of taxis. As a result, taxi drivers might find their revenues decline as they would no longer always be assured of finding willing customers. And, in turn, the value of a medallion would fall. So to placate the medallion owners, city officials also agreed in 2004 to raise fares by 25 percent, a move that slightly diminished the newfound cheer of New York riders.

In sum, quantity controls typically create the following undesirable side effects:

- Inefficiencies, or missed opportunities, in the form of mutually beneficial transactions that don't occur
- Incentives for illegal activities

economics in action

The Clams of New Jersey

Forget the refineries along the Jersey Turnpike; one industry that New Jersey *really* dominates is clam fishing. The Garden State supplies 80 percent of the world's surf clams, whose tongues are used in fried-clam dinners, and 40 percent of the quahogs, which are used to make clam chowder.

In the 1980s, however, excessive fishing threatened to wipe out New Jersey's clam beds. To save the resource, the U.S. government introduced a clam quota, which sets an overall limit on the number of bushels of clams that may be caught and allocates licenses to owners of fishing boats based on their historical catches.

Notice, by the way, that this is an example of a quota that is probably justified by broader economic and environmental considerations—unlike the New York taxicab quota, which has long since lost any economic rationale. Still, whatever its rationale, the New Jersey clam quota works the same way as any other quota.

Once the quota system was established, many boat owners stopped fishing for clams. They realized that rather than operate a boat part time, it was more profitable to sell or rent their licenses to someone else, who could then assemble enough licenses to operate a boat full time. Today, there are about 50 boats fishing for clams; the license required to operate one is worth more than the boat itself. ∎

> > > > > > > > > > > > > > > > > > > >

>>CHECK YOUR UNDERSTANDING 4-3

1. Suppose that the supply and demand for taxi rides is given by Figure 4-5 but the quota is set at 6 million rides instead of 8 million. Find the following and indicate them on Figure 4-5.
   a. The price of a ride
   b. The quota rent
   c. Suppose the quota limit on taxi rides is increased to 9 million. What happens to the quota rent?
2. Assume that the quota limit is 8 million rides. Suppose demand decreases due to a decline in tourism. What is the smallest parallel leftward shift in demand that would result in the quota no longer having an effect on the market? Illustrate your answer using Figure 4-5.

Solutions appear at back of book.

A Surprise Parallel: Taxes

To provide the services we want, from national defense to public parks, governments must collect taxes. But taxes impose costs on the economy. Among the most important roles of economics is tax analysis: figuring out the economic costs of taxation, determining who bears those costs, and suggesting ways to change the tax system that will reduce the costs it imposes. It turns out that the same analysis we have just used to understand quotas can be used, with hardly any modification, to make a preliminary analysis of taxes, too.

Why Is a Tax Like a Quota?

Suppose that the supply and demand curves for New York taxis were exactly as shown in Figure 4-5. This means that in the absence of government action, the equilibrium price of a taxi ride will be $5 and 10 million rides will be bought and sold.

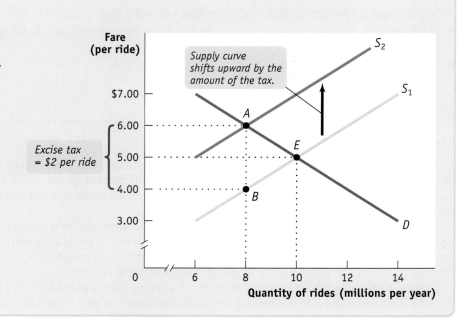

Figure 4-7

Effect of an Excise Tax Levied on Sales of Taxi Rides

S_1 is the supply curve before the tax. After the city requires drivers to pay a tax of $2 for every ride they give, the supply curve shifts upward by $2, to the new supply curve S_2. This means that the price drivers receive net of tax is $4, represented by point B on the old supply curve S_1. And the price paid by riders is $6, represented by point A on the new supply curve S_2. The tax drives a wedge between the demand price, $6, and the original supply price, $4.

An **excise tax** is a tax on sales of a good or service.

Now suppose that instead of imposing a quota on the quantity of rides, the city imposes an **excise tax**—a tax on sales. Specifically, it charges taxi drivers $2 for each ride they provide. What is the effect of the tax?

From the point of view of a taxi driver, the tax means that he or she doesn't get to keep all of the fare: if a passenger pays $5, $2 is collected as a tax, so the driver gets only $3. For any given quantity of rides supplied, the *post-tax supply price* is higher than the pre-tax supply price. For example, drivers will now require a price of $6 to supply as many rides as they would have been willing to supply at a price of $4 in the absence of the $2 tax.

So the tax on sales shifts the supply curve upward, by the amount of the tax. This is shown in Figure 4-7, where S_1 is the supply curve before the tax is imposed and S_2 is the supply curve after the tax is imposed. The market equilibrium moves from E, where the price is $5 per ride and 10 million rides are bought and sold, to A, where the price is $6 per ride and 8 million rides are bought and sold. A is, of course, on both the demand curve D and the new supply curve S_2.

But how do we know that 8 million rides will be supplied at a price of $6? Because the price *net of the tax* is $4 and the pre-tax supply price of 8 million rides is $4, as shown by point B in Figure 4-7.

Does all this look familiar? It should. The equilibrium with a $2 tax on rides, which reduces the quantity bought and sold to 8 million rides, looks just like the equilibrium with a quota of 8 million rides, which leads to a quota rent of $2 per ride. Just like a quota, the tax *drives a wedge* between the demand price and the original, pre-tax supply price.

The only difference is that instead of paying a $2 rent to the owner of a license, drivers pay a $2 tax to the city. In fact, there is a way to make an excise tax and a quota completely equivalent. Imagine that instead of issuing a limited number of licenses, the city simply sold licenses at $2 each. This $2 license fee would, for all practical purposes, be a $2 excise tax.

Finally, imagine that instead of selling licenses at a fixed price, the city were to issue 8 million licenses and auction them off—that is, sell them for whatever price the, um, traffic will bear. What would be the price of a license? Surely it would be $2—the quota rent. And so in this case the quota rent would act just like an excise tax.

Who Pays an Excise Tax?

We have just imagined a tax that must be paid by the *sellers* of a good. But what would happen if the tax were instead paid by the *buyers*—say, if you had to pay a special $2 tax to ride in a taxicab?

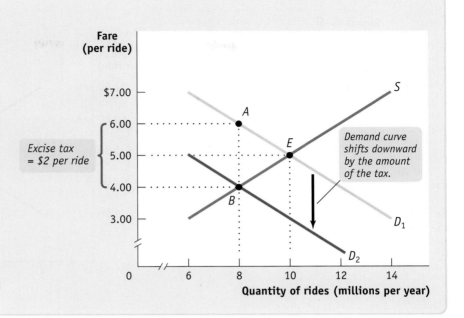

Figure 4-8

Effect of an Excise Tax Levied on Purchases of Taxi Rides

D_1 is the demand curve before the tax. After the city requires riders to pay the $2 tax per ride, the demand curve shifts down by $2 to the new demand curve D_2. Drivers again receive, net of tax, $4, represented by point B, while riders again pay a total price of $6, represented by point A. The incidence of the tax is exactly the same as in Figure 4-7. This shows that who officially pays a tax is irrelevant when answering the question of who bears the burden of the tax.

The answer is shown in Figure 4-8. If a taxi rider must pay a $2 tax on each ride, then the price riders pay must be $2 less in order for the quantity of taxi rides demanded post-tax to be the same quantity as that demanded pre-tax. So the demand curve shifts *downward*, from D_1 to D_2, by the amount of the tax. This shifts the equilibrium from E to B, where the market price is $4 per ride and 8 million rides are bought and sold. In this case, $4 is the supply price of 8 million rides and $6 is the demand price—but in effect riders do pay $6, when you include the tax. So it is just as if riders were on their original demand curve at point A.

If you compare Figures 4-7 and 4-8, you will immediately notice that they show the same price effect. In each case, buyers pay an effective price of $6, sellers receive an effective price of $4, and 8 million rides are bought and sold. *It doesn't seem to make any difference who officially pays the tax.*

This insight is a general one in analyzing taxes: the **incidence** of a tax—who really bears the burden of the tax—is often not a question you can answer by asking who actually writes the check to the government. In this particular case, a $2 tax on taxi rides is reflected in a $1 increase in the price paid by buyers and a $1 decrease in the price received by sellers; so the incidence of the tax is actually evenly split between buyers and sellers. This incidence is the same regardless of whether the check to the city government is made out by buyers or by sellers.

The incidence of an excise tax isn't always split evenly between buyers and sellers as in this example. Depending on the shapes of supply and demand curves, the incidence of an excise tax may be divided differently.

The **incidence** of a tax is a measure of who really pays it.

The Revenue from an Excise Tax

Although both buyers and sellers lose from an excise tax, the government does collect revenue—which is the whole point of the tax. How much revenue does the government collect? The revenue is equal to the area of the shaded rectangle in Figure 4-9 on the next page.

To see why this is the revenue collected by a $2 tax on taxi rides, notice that the *height* of the rectangle is $2. This is the amount of the tax per ride; it is also, as we have seen, the size of the wedge that the tax drives between the supply price and the demand price. Meanwhile, the *width* of the rectangle is 8 million rides, which is the equilibrium quantity of rides given that $2 tax.

Figure 4-9

The Revenue from an Excise Tax

The government revenue collected by this excise tax is equal to the area of the shaded rectangle. In this case it is $2 per ride × 8 million rides = $16 million.

The revenue collected by the tax is

$$Revenue = \$2 \text{ per ride} \times 8 \text{ million rides} = \$16 \text{ million}$$

But the area of the rectangle is

$$Area = height \times width = \$2 \text{ per ride} \times 8 \text{ million rides} = \$16 \text{ million}$$

This is a general principle: *The revenue collected by an excise tax is equal to the area of the rectangle whose height is the wedge that the tax drives between the supply and demand curves, and whose width is the quantity bought and sold under the tax.*

The Costs of Taxation

What is the cost of a tax? You might be inclined to answer that it is the money tax-payers pay to the government. But suppose the government used that money to provide services everyone wants or simply handed the money back to taxpayers. Would we then say that the tax didn't cost anything?

No—because a tax, like a quota, prevents mutually beneficial transactions from occurring. Consider Figure 4-9 once more. With a $2 tax on taxi rides, riders pay $6 per ride but drivers receive only $4. There are therefore some potential riders who would be willing to pay only, say, $5.50 per ride; and there are some drivers who would be willing to charge them, say, $4.50. If those drivers and riders could be brought together, this would be a mutually beneficial transaction. But such a deal would be illegal, because the $2 tax would not have been paid.

More broadly, we know that there are 2 million potential taxi rides that would have been taken in the absence of the tax, to the mutual benefit of riders and drivers, that do not take place because of that tax.

So an excise tax imposes additional costs, over and above the money actually paid in taxes, in the form of inefficiency, which occurs because the tax discourages mutually beneficial transactions. This is the **excess burden,** or **deadweight loss,** from a tax. And all real-world taxes do impose some excess burden, although badly designed taxes impose bigger excess burdens than well-thought-out ones.

Economists sometimes say that the real cost of a tax is not the taxes that people pay but the taxes that they *don't* pay. What they mean is that people change their

The **excess burden**, or **deadweight loss,** from a tax is the extra cost in the form of inefficiency that results because the tax discourages mutually beneficial transactions.

IF SELLING CIGARETTES IS A CRIME, ONLY CRIMINALS WILL SELL CIGARETTES

Cigarettes have long been subject to state excise taxes. As the antismoking movement has gained political power, many states and local governments have increased those taxes. Officials see high taxes on cigarettes as a way of doing well by doing good—raising more revenue while discouraging a bad habit. In 2002, increases at both the state and local levels raised the tax on a pack of cigarettes sold in New York City from $1.19 to $3.

But tobacco-growing states have not followed the trend. In Virginia, for example, the cigarette tax is only 2.5 cents per pack. And this divergence has created an opportunity for those who don't mind breaking the law: there is large-scale smuggling of cigarettes from low-tax tobacco-growing states to high-tax locations like New York.

Authorities believe that interstate cigarette smuggling, like alcohol smuggling during Prohibition, has largely been taken over by organized crime. But there is still room for smaller players: in July 2000, the FBI broke up a group, based in Charlotte, North Carolina, that had been funneling its profits to a foreign group that the U.S. government classifies as a terrorist organization.

behavior in order to avoid taxes—for example, by walking instead of taking a taxi—and in so doing miss opportunities for mutual benefit.

One final point: like all of the other government policies analyzed in this chapter, taxes create incentives for illegal activity. For Inquiring Minds above explains how excise taxes on cigarettes have given rise to a substantial smuggling business. And, of course, even seemingly respectable people have been known to be a bit creative with their income taxes.

economics in action

Who Pays the FICA?

Anyone who works for an employer receives a paycheck that itemizes not only the money received but also the money deducted for various taxes. One of the big items for most people is *FICA*, which stands for Federal Insurance Contributions Act. This is the money taken out of your paycheck for the Social Security and Medicare systems, which provide income and medical care to retired and disabled Americans.

As of the time of writing, most American workers paid 7.65 percent of their earnings in FICA. But this is literally only the half of it: employers are required to pay an equal amount.

So how should we think about FICA? Well, it's like an excise tax—a tax on the sale and purchase of labor. Half of it is a tax on the sellers—that is, workers. The other half is a tax on the buyers—that is, employers.

But we already know that the incidence of a tax does not really depend on who actually makes out the check. So the fact that employers nominally pay half the FICA tells us nothing about who really bears the burden.

In fact, most economists believe that the real effect of the FICA is, to a very good approximation, to reduce wages by the full amount of the combined employee and employer payments. That is, you not only pay your own share; your employer's share is reflected in a lower wage, so that you really pay that share, too. Your employer, though she pays the tax, is fully compensated by the lower wage rate. So workers, not employers, bear the burden of both halves of the tax.

The reason economists think that workers, not employers, really pay the FICA is that the supply of labor (the number of workers willing to take jobs) is much less responsive to the wage rate than is the demand for labor (the number of jobs employers are willing to offer). According to this reasoning, since workers are relatively unresponsive to decreases in the wage rate, employers can easily pass the burden of the tax on to them through lower wages. ∎

< < < < < < < < < < < < < < < < < <

>>CHECK YOUR UNDERSTANDING 4-4

1. Use Figure 4-3 to answer the following questions.
   a. What amount of excise tax generates the same level of inefficiency as a quota of 9 million pounds of butter?
   b. What quota level generates the same level of inefficiency as an excise tax of $0.60 per pound of butter?
   c. In part a, find how the burden of an excise tax is split between buyers and sellers. That is, explain how much of the tax is paid by buyers and how much by sellers in each case.

Solutions appear at back of book.

• A LOOK AHEAD •

In the last two chapters we have gotten a first taste of how economic models help us understand the real world. As we've seen, supply and demand—a simple model of how competitive markets work—can be used to understand and predict the effects of everything from bad weather to misconceived government policies.

In the chapters to come, we'll see how models—including supply and demand, but also going beyond it—can shed light on a wide variety of economic phenomena and issues.

SUMMARY

1. Governments often intervene in markets in attempts to "defy" supply and demand. Interventions can take the form of **price controls** or **quantity controls**. But they generate predictable and undesirable side effects, consisting of various forms of inefficiency and illegal activity.

2. A **price ceiling**, a maximum market price below the equilibrium price, benefits successful buyers but creates persistent shortages: Because the price is maintained below the equilibrium price, the quantity demanded is increased and the quantity supplied is decreased compared to the equilibrium quantity. This leads to predictable problems: **inefficiencies** in the form of **inefficient allocation to consumers**, **wasted resources**, and **inefficiently low quality**. It also encourages illegal activity as people turn to **black markets** to get the good. Because of these problems, price ceilings have generally lost favor as an economic policy tool. But some governments continue to impose them either because they don't understand the effects or because the price ceilings benefit some influential group.

3. A **price floor**, a minimum market price above the equilibrium price, benefits successful sellers but creates persistent surplus: because the price is maintained above the equilibrium price, the quantity demanded is decreased and the quantity supplied is increased compared to the equilibrium quantity. This leads to predictable problems: inefficiencies in the form of **inefficient allocation of sales among sellers**, **wasted resources**, and **inefficiently high quality**. It also encourages illegal activity and black markets. The most well known kind of price floor is the **minimum wage**, but price floors are also commonly applied to agricultural products.

4. **Quantity controls**, or **quotas**, limit the quantity of a good that can be bought or sold. The amount allowed for sale is the **quota limit**. The government issues **licenses** to individuals, the right to sell a given quantity of the good. The owner of a license earns a **quota rent**, earnings that accrue from ownership of the right to sell the good. It is equal to the difference between the **demand price** at the quota limit, what consumers are willing to pay for that amount, and the **supply price** at the quota limit, what suppliers are willing to accept for that amount. Economists say that a quota drives a **wedge** between the demand price and the supply price; this wedge is equal to the quota rent. Quantity controls generate inefficiency in the form of mutually beneficial transactions that don't occur in addition to encouraging illegal activity.

5. **Excise taxes**—taxes on the purchase or sale of a good—have effects similar to quotas. They raise the price paid by buyers and reduce the price received by sellers, driving a wedge between the two. The **incidence** of the tax—the division of higher prices to consumers and lower prices to sellers—does not depend on who officially pays the tax. Excise taxes cause inefficiency—called **excess burden** or **deadweight loss**—because they prevent some mutually beneficial transactions. They also encourage illegal activity in attempts to avoid the tax.

KEY TERMS

Price controls, p. 84
Price ceiling, p. 84
Price floor, p. 84
Inefficient, p. 86
Inefficient allocation to consumers, p. 87
Wasted resources, p. 87
Inefficiently low quality, p. 87
Black markets, p. 88

Minimum wage, p. 90
Inefficient allocation of sales among sellers, p. 92
Inefficiently high quality, p. 93
Quantity control, p. 95
Quota, p. 95
Quota limit, p. 95
License, p. 95

Demand price, p. 95
Supply price, p. 96
Wedge, p. 97
Quota rent, p. 97
Excise tax, p. 100
Incidence, p. 101
Excess burden, p. 102
Deadweight loss, p. 102

PROBLEMS

1. Suppose it is decided that rent control in New York City will be abolished and that market rents will now prevail. Assume that all rental units are identical and are therefore offered at the same rent. To address the plight of residents who may be unable to pay the market rent, an income supplement will be paid to all low-income households equal to the difference between the old controlled rent and the new market rent.

   a. Use a diagram to show the effect on the rental market of the elimination of rent control. What will happen to the quality and quantity of rental housing supplied?

   b. Now use a second diagram to show the additional effect of the income-supplement policy on the market. What effect does it have on the market rent and quantity of rental housing supplied in comparison to your answers to part a?

   c. Are tenants better or worse off as a result of these policies? Are landlords better or worse off?

   d. From a political standpoint, why do you think cities have been more likely to resort to rent control rather than a policy of income supplements to help low-income people pay for housing?

2. In order to ingratiate himself with voters, the mayor of Gotham City decides to lower the price of taxi rides. Assume, for simplicity, that all taxi rides are the same distance and therefore cost the same. The accompanying table shows the demand and supply schedules for taxi rides.

Fare (per ride)	Quantity of rides (millions per year)	
	Quantity demanded	Quantity supplied
$7.00	10	12
6.50	11	11
6.00	12	10
5.50	13	9
5.00	14	8
4.50	15	7

   a. Assume that there are no restrictions on the number of taxi rides that can be supplied in the city (i.e., there is no medallion system). Find the equilibrium price and quantity.

   b. Suppose that the mayor sets a price ceiling at $5.50. How large is the shortage of rides? Illustrate with a diagram. Who loses and who benefits from this policy?

   c. Suppose that the stock market crashes and, as a result, people in Gotham City are poorer. This reduces the quantity of taxi rides demanded by 6 million rides per year at any given price. What effect will the mayor's new policy have now? Illustrate with a diagram.

   d. Suppose that the stock market rises and the demand for taxi rides returns to normal (that is, returns to the demand schedule given in the table). The mayor now decides to ingratiate himself with taxi drivers. He announces a policy in which operating licenses are given to existing taxi drivers; the number of licenses is restricted such that only 10 million rides per year can be given. Illustrate the effect of this policy on the market, and indicate the resulting price and quantity transacted. What is the quota rent per ride?

3. In the late eighteenth century, the price of bread in New York City was controlled, set at a predetermined price above the market price.

   a. Draw a diagram showing the effect of the policy. Did the policy act as a price ceiling or a price floor?

   b. What kinds of inefficiencies were likely to have arisen when the controlled price of bread was above the market price? Explain in detail.

   One year during this period, a poor wheat harvest caused a leftward shift in the supply of bread and therefore an increase in its market price. New York bakers found that the controlled price of bread in New York was below the market price.

   c. Draw a diagram showing the effect of the price control on the market for bread during this one-year period. Did the policy act as a price ceiling or a price floor?

   d. What kinds of inefficiencies do you think occurred during this period? Explain in detail.

4. The accompanying table shows the demand and supply schedules for milk per year. The U.S. government decides that the incomes of dairy farmers should be maintained at a level that allows the traditional family dairy farm to survive. It therefore implements a price floor of $1 per pint by buying surplus milk until the market price is $1 per pint.

Price of milk (per pint)	Quantity of milk (millions of pints per year)	
	Quantity demanded	Quantity supplied
$1.20	550	850
1.10	600	800
1.00	650	750
0.90	700	700
0.80	750	650

   a. How much surplus milk will be produced as a result of this policy?

   b. What will be the cost to the government of this policy?

   c. Since milk is an important source of protein and calcium, the government decides to provide the surplus milk it purchases to elementary schools at a price of only $0.60 per pint. Assume that schools will buy any amount of milk available at this low price. But parents now reduce their purchases of milk at any price by 50 million pints per year because they know their children are getting milk at school. How much will the dairy program now cost the government?

   d. Give two examples of inefficiencies arising from wasted resources that are likely to result from this policy. What is the missed opportunity in each case?

5. As noted in the text, European governments tend to make greater use of price controls than does the American government. For example, the French government sets minimum starting yearly wages for new hires who have completed le bac, certification roughly equivalent to a high school diploma. The demand schedule for new hires with le bac and the supply schedule for similarly credentialed new job seekers are given in the accompanying table. The price here—given in euros, the currency used in France—is the same as the yearly wage.

Wage (per year)	Quantity demanded (new job offers per year)	Quantity supplied (new job seekers per year)
€45,000	200,000	325,000
40,000	220,000	320,000
35,000	250,000	310,000
30,000	290,000	290,000
25,000	370,000	200,000

   a. In the absence of government interference, what is the equilibrium wage and number of graduates hired per year? Illustrate with a diagram. Will there be anyone seeking a job at the equilibrium wage who is unable to find one— that is, will there be anyone who is involuntarily unemployed?

   b. Suppose the French government sets a minimum yearly wage of €35,000. Is there any involuntary unemployment at this wage? If so, how much? Illustrate with a diagram. What if the minimum wage is set at €40,000? Also illustrate with a diagram.

   c. Given your answer to part b and the information in the table, what do you think is the relationship between the level of involuntary unemployment and the level of the minimum wage? Who benefits from such a policy? Who loses? What is the missed opportunity here?

6. Until recently, the standard number of hours worked per week for a full-time job in France was 39 hours, just as in the United States. But in response to social unrest over high levels of involuntary unemployment, the French government instituted a 35-hour workweek—a worker could not work more than 35 hours per week even if both the worker and employer wanted it. The motivation behind this policy was that if current employees worked fewer hours, employers would be forced to hire more new workers. Assume that it is costly for employers to train new workers. French employers were greatly opposed to this policy and threatened to move their operations to neighboring countries that did not have such employment restrictions. Can you explain their attitude? Give an example of both an inefficiency and an illegal activity that are likely to arise from this policy.

7. For the last 70 years the U.S. government has used price supports to provide income assistance to American farmers. At times the government has used price floors, which it maintains by buying up the surplus farm products. At other times, it has used target prices, a policy by which the government gives the farmer an amount equal to the difference between the market price and the target price for each unit sold. Consider the market for corn depicted in the accompanying figure.

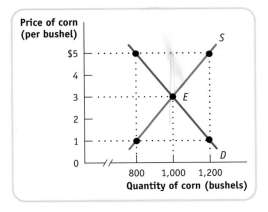

a. If the government sets a price floor of $5 per bushel, how many bushels of corn are produced? How many are purchased by consumers? By the government? How much does the program cost the government? How much revenue do corn farmers receive?

b. Suppose the government sets a target price of $5 per bushel for any quantity supplied up to 1,000 bushels. How many bushels of corn are purchased by consumers and at what price? By the government? How much does the program cost the government? How much revenue do corn farmers receive?

c. Which of these programs (in parts a and b) costs corn consumers more? Which program costs the government more? Explain.

d. What are the inefficiencies that arise in each of these cases (parts a and b)?

8. The waters off the North Atlantic coast were once teeming with fish. Now, due to overfishing by the commercial fishing industry, the stocks of fish are seriously depleted. In 1991, the National Marine Fishery Service of the U.S. government implemented a quota to allow fish stocks to recover. The quota limited the amount of swordfish caught per year by all U.S.-licensed fishing boats to 7 million pounds. As soon as the U.S. fishing fleet had met the quota limit, the swordfish catch was closed down for the rest of the year. The accompanying table gives the hypothetical demand and supply schedules for swordfish caught in the United States per year.

Price of swordfish (per pound)	Quantity of swordfish (millions of pounds per year)	
	Quantity demanded	Quantity supplied
$20	6	15
18	7	13
16	8	11
14	9	9
12	10	7

a. Use a diagram to show the effect of the quota on the market for swordfish in 1991.

b. How do you think fishermen will change how they fish in response to this policy?

c. Use your diagram from part a to show an excise tax that achieves the same reduction in the amount of pounds of swordfish caught as the quota. What is the amount of the tax per pound?

d. What kinds of activities do you think an excise tax will tempt people to engage in?

e. The excise tax is collected from the fishermen, who protest that they alone are bearing the burden of this policy. Why might this protest be misguided?

9. The U.S. government would like to help the American auto industry compete against foreign automakers that sell trucks in the United States. It can do this either by imposing a quota on the number of foreign trucks imported or by imposing an excise tax on each foreign truck sold in the United States. The hypothetical demand and supply schedules for imported trucks are given in the accompanying table.

Price of imported truck	Quantity of imported trucks (thousands)	
	Quantity demanded	Quantity supplied
$32,000	100	400
31,000	200	350
30,000	300	300
29,000	400	250
28,000	500	200
27,000	600	150

a. In the absence of government interference, what is the price of an imported truck? How many are sold in the United States? Illustrate with a diagram.

b. Suppose the government adopts a quota, allowing no more than 200,000 foreign trucks to be imported. What is the effect on the market for these trucks? Illustrate using your diagram from part a and explain.

c. Now suppose that, instead of a quota, the government imposes an excise tax of $3,000 per truck. Illustrate the effect of this excise tax in your diagram from part a. How many trucks will now be purchased and at what price? What will the foreign automaker receive per truck?

d. Calculate the government revenue raised by the excise tax in part c. Then illustrate it on your diagram from that part. Do you think the government, from a revenue standpoint, prefers an excise tax or a quota?

e. Explain how the government policy, whether it be a quota or an excise tax, benefits American automakers. Whom does it hurt? What is the missed opportunity here and how does it reflect inefficiency?

10. In Maine, you must have a license to harvest lobster commercially; these licenses are issued yearly. The state of Maine is concerned about the dwindling supplies of lobsters found off its coast. The state fishery department has decided to place a yearly quota of 80,000 pounds of lobsters harvested in all Maine waters. It has also decided to give licenses this year only to those fishermen who had licenses last year. The accompanying figure shows the demand and supply curves for Maine lobsters.

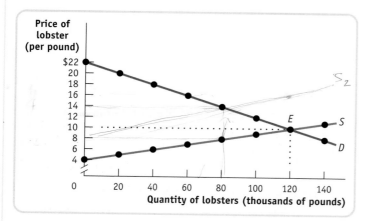

a. In the absence of government restrictions, what are the equilibrium price and quantity?

b. What is the *demand price* at which consumers wish to purchase 80,000 pounds of lobsters?

c. What is the *supply price* at which suppliers are willing to supply 80,000 pounds of lobsters?

d. What is the *quota rent* per pound of lobster when 80,000 pounds are sold?

e. Find an excise tax that achieves the same reduction in the harvest of lobsters. Show it on the figure. What is the government revenue collected from this tax?

f. Explain a transaction that benefits both buyer and seller but is prevented by the quota restriction. Explain a transaction that benefits both buyer and seller but is prevented by the excise tax.

11. In each of the following cases involving taxes, explain: (i) whether the incidence of the tax falls more heavily on consumers or producers, (ii) why government revenue raised from the tax is not a good indicator of the true cost of the tax, and (iii) what missed opportunity, or inefficiency, arises.

a. The government imposes an excise tax on the sale of all college textbooks. Before the tax was imposed, 1 million textbooks were sold every year at a price of $50. After the tax is imposed, 600,000 books are sold yearly; students pay $55 per book, $30 of which publishers receive.

b. The government imposes an excise tax on the sale of all airplane tickets. Before the tax was imposed, 3 million airline tickets were sold every year at a price of $500. After the tax is imposed, 1.5 million tickets are sold yearly; travelers pay $550 per ticket, $450 of which the airlines receive.

c. The government imposes an excise tax on the sale of all toothbrushes. Before the tax, 2 million toothbrushes were sold every year at a price of $1.50. After the tax is imposed, 800,000 toothbrushes are sold every year; consumers pay $2 per toothbrush, $1.25 of which producers receive.

>web... To continue your study and review of concepts in this chapter, please visit the Krugman/Wells website for quizzes, animated graph tutorials, web links to helpful resources, and more.

www.worthpublishers.com/krugmanwells

>> Elasticity

DRIVE WE MUST

IN EARLY 1998, LUIS TELLEZ HELD A secret meeting with his Saudi Arabian counterpart. Tellez was Mexico's oil minister, the government official who decided how many barrels of oil Mexico would produce and sell to other countries. The purpose of the secret meeting? To increase their earnings, or revenues, from selling oil by raising the world price of oil, which had fallen 50 percent over the previous two years. This low world price was creating serious problems for both governments, which depended on revenue from oil sales. But a plan to raise oil prices would not succeed unless other oil-exporting countries were also willing to commit to reductions in oil production.

Why was it necessary to reduce production? Why not just raise prices? Because by the *law of demand*, a price increase leads to a fall in the quantity demanded. So if output didn't also fall, there would soon be a surplus of oil on the market, pushing the price right back down again. To make the plan work, Tellez had to persuade his fellow oil ministers to produce less. But how much less?

If consumers responded to the price increase by using a lot less oil, output would have to fall by a large amount. And

if output fell by a large enough amount in response to the price increase, revenue would decline, not increase. The crucial question for Tellez, then, was how responsive the quantity of oil demanded was to changes in the price of oil.

But how do we define *responsiveness?* The answer, and what Tellez needed to know in this case, is a particular number: the *price elasticity of demand*. In this chapter, we will show how the price elasticity of demand is measured and why it is the best measure of how the quantity demanded

Gassing up: A hard habit to break.

responds to changes in price. We will then see that the price elasticity of demand is only one of a family of related concepts, including the *income elasticity of demand* and the *price elasticity of supply*. Finally, we will see how elasticities are used to determine who bears the greater share of the burden of a tax—producers or consumers.

What you will learn in this chapter:

➤ The definition of **elasticity**, a measure of responsiveness to changes in prices or incomes

➤ The importance of the **price elasticity of demand**, which measures the responsiveness of the quantity demanded to price

➤ The meaning and importance of the **income elasticity of demand**, a measure of the responsiveness of demand to income

➤ The significance of the **price elasticity of supply**, which measures the responsiveness of the quantity supplied to price

➤ What factors influence the size of these various elasticities

➤ How elasticity affects the incidence of a tax, the measure of who bears its burden

Defining and Measuring Elasticity

Luis Tellez, who is a trained economist, knew that to calculate the cut in oil output needed to achieve his price target, he would have to know the *price elasticity of demand* for oil.

The Price Elasticity of Demand

Figure 5-1 shows a hypothetical world demand curve for oil. At a price of $20 per barrel, world consumers would demand 10 million barrels of oil per day (point A); at a price of $21 per barrel, the quantity demanded would fall to 9.9 million barrels (point B).

Figure 5-1, then, tells us the response of the quantity demanded to a particular change in the price. But how can we turn this into a measure of price responsiveness? The answer is to calculate the *price elasticity of demand.*

The price elasticity of demand compares the *percent change in quantity demanded* to the *percent change in price* as we move along the demand curve. As we'll see later in this chapter, the reason economists use percent changes is to get a measure that doesn't depend on the units in which a good is measured (say, gallons versus barrels of oil). But before we get to that, let's look at how elasticity is calculated.

To calculate the price elasticity of demand, we first calculate the *percent change in the quantity demanded* and the corresponding *percent change in the price* as we move along the demand curve. These are defined as follows:

$$\textbf{(5-1)} \quad \% \text{ change in quantity demanded} = \frac{\text{Change in quantity demanded}}{\text{Initial quantity demanded}} \times 100$$

and

$$\textbf{(5-2)} \quad \% \text{ change in price} = \frac{\text{Change in price}}{\text{Initial price}} \times 100$$

In Figure 5-1, we see that when the price rises from $20 to $21, the quantity demanded falls from 10 million to 9.9 million barrels, yielding a change in the

---

Figure 5-1

The World Demand for Oil

At a price of $20 per barrel, the world quantity of oil demanded is 10 million barrels per day (point A). When price rises to $21 per barrel, world demand falls to 9.9 million barrels per day (point B).

quantity demanded of 0.1 million barrels. So the percent change in the quantity demanded is

$$\text{\% change in quantity demanded} = \frac{0.1 \text{ million barrels}}{10 \text{ million barrels}} \times 100 = 1\%$$

The initial price is $20 and the change in the price is $1, so the percent change in price is

$$\text{\% change in price} = \frac{\$1}{\$20} \times 100 = 5\%$$

To calculate the price elasticity of demand, we find the ratio of the percent change in the quantity demanded to the percent change in the price:

(5-3) Price elasticity of demand $= \dfrac{\text{\% change in quantity demanded}}{\text{\% change in price}}$

In Figure 5-1, the price elasticity of demand is therefore

$$\frac{1\%}{5\%} = 0.2$$

> The **price elasticity of demand** is the ratio of the percent change in the quantity demanded to the percent change in the price as we move along the demand curve.

The *law of demand* says that demand curves slope downward. This means that the price elasticity of demand is, in strictly mathematical terms, a negative number (if the price rises, which is a positive percent change, the quantity demanded falls, which is strictly speaking a *negative* percent change). However, it is a nuisance to keep writing that minus sign. So when economists talk about the price elasticity of demand, they usually drop the minus sign and report the absolute value of the elasticity. In this case, for example, economists would usually say "the price elasticity of demand is 0.2," taking it for granted that you understand they mean *minus* 0.2. As we have just done, we follow this convention and drop the minus sign when referring to the price elasticity of demand.

The larger the price elasticity of demand, the more responsive the quantity demanded is to the price. When the price elasticity of demand is large—when consumers change their quantity demanded by a large percentage compared with the percent change in the price—economists say that demand is highly elastic.

As we'll see shortly, a price elasticity of 0.2 indicates a small response of quantity demanded to price. That is, the quantity demanded will fall by a relatively small amount when price rises. This is what economists call *inelastic* demand. And inelastic demand was exactly what Tellez needed for his strategy to increase revenue by raising oil prices.

Using the Midpoint Method to Calculate Elasticities

Price elasticity of demand compares the *percent change in quantity demanded* with the *percent change in price*. When we look at some other elasticities, which we will do shortly, we'll see why it is important to focus on percent changes. But at this point we need to discuss a technical issue that arises when you calculate percent changes in variables and how economists deal with it.

The best way to understand the issue is with a real example. Suppose you were trying to estimate the price elasticity of demand for gasoline by comparing gasoline prices and consumption in different countries. Because of high taxes, gasoline usually costs about three times as much per gallon in Europe as it does in the United States. So what is the percent difference between American and European gas prices?

Well, it depends on which way you measure it. The price of gasoline in Europe is three times higher than in the United States, so it is 200 percent higher. The price of gasoline in the United States is one-third as high as in Europe, so it is 66.7 percent lower.

This is a nuisance: we'd like to have a percent measure of the difference in prices that doesn't depend on which way you measure it. A good way to avoid computing different elasticities for rising and falling prices is to use the *midpoint method*.

The **midpoint method** replaces the usual definition of the percent change in a variable, X, with a slightly different definition:

> The **midpoint method** is a technique for calculating the percent change. In this approach, we calculate changes in a variable compared with the average, or midpoint, of the starting and final values.

$$\textbf{(5-4)} \quad \% \text{ change in } X = \frac{\text{Change in } X}{\text{Average value of } X} \times 100$$

where the average value of X is defined as

$$\text{Average value of } X = \frac{\text{Starting value of } X + \text{final value of } X}{2}$$

When calculating the price elasticity of demand using the midpoint method, both the percent change in the price and the percent change in the quantity demanded are found using this method.

To see how this method works, suppose you have the following data for some good:

	Price	**Quantity demanded**
Situation A	$0.90	1,100
Situation B	$1.10	900

To calculate the percent change in quantity going from situation A to situation B, we compare the change in the quantity demanded—200 units—with the *average* of the quantity demanded in the two situations. So we calculate

$$\% \text{ change in quantity demanded} = \frac{200}{(1,100 + 900)/2} \times 100 = \frac{200}{1,000} \times 100$$

$$= 20\%$$

In the same way, we calculate

$$\% \text{ change in price} = \frac{\$0.20}{(\$0.90 + \$1.10)/2} \times 100 = \frac{\$0.20}{\$1.00} \times 100$$

$$= 20\%$$

So in this case we would calculate the price elasticity of demand to be

$$\text{Price elasticity of demand} = \frac{\% \text{ change in quantity demanded}}{\% \text{ change in price}} = \frac{20\%}{20\%} = 1$$

The important point is that we would get the same result, a price elasticity of demand of 1, whether we go up the demand curve from situation A to situation B or down from situation B to situation A.

To arrive at a more general formula for price elasticity of demand, suppose that we have data for two points on a demand curve. At point 1 the quantity demanded and price are (Q_1, P_1); at point 2 they are (Q_2, P_2). Then the formula for calculating the price elasticity of demand is:

$$(5\text{-}5) \quad \text{Price elasticity of demand} = \dfrac{\dfrac{Q_2 - Q_1}{(Q_1 + Q_2)/2}}{\dfrac{P_2 - P_1}{(P_1 + P_2)/2}}$$

As before, when reporting a price elasticity of demand calculated by the midpoint method, we usually drop the negative sign and report the absolute value.

economics in action

Estimating Elasticities

You might think it's easy to estimate price elasticities of demand from real-world data: just compare percent changes in prices with percent changes in quantities demanded. Unfortunately, it's rarely that simple because changes in price aren't the only thing affecting changes in the quantity demanded: other factors—such as changes in income, changes in population, and changes in the prices of other goods—shift the demand curve, thereby changing the quantity demanded for any given price. To estimate price elasticities of demand, economists must use careful statistical analysis to separate the influence of these different factors, holding other things equal.

The most comprehensive effort to estimate price elasticities of demand was a mammoth study by the economists Hendrik S. Houthakker and Lester D. Taylor. Some of their results are summarized in Table 5-1. These estimates show a wide range of price elasticities. There are some goods, like eggs, for which demand hardly responds at all to changes in the price; there are other goods, most notably foreign travel, where the quantity demanded is very sensitive to the price.

Notice that Table 5-1 is divided into two parts: inelastic and elastic demand. We'll explain in the next section the significance of that division. ∎

> > > > > > > > > > > > > > > > > >

>>CHECK YOUR UNDERSTANDING 5-1

1. The price of strawberries falls from $1.50 to $1.00 per carton and the quantity demanded goes from 100,000 to 200,000 cartons. Use the midpoint method to find the price elasticity of demand.

2. At the present level of consumption, 4,000 movie tickets, and at the current price, $5 per ticket, the price elasticity of demand for movie tickets is 1. Using the midpoint method, calculate the percentage by which the owners of movie theaters must reduce price in order to sell 5,000 tickets.

3. The price elasticity of demand for ice-cream sandwiches is 1.2 at the current price of $0.50 per sandwich and the current consumption level of 100,000 sandwiches. Calculate the change in the quantity demanded when price rises by $0.05. Use Equations 5-1 and 5-2 to calculate percent changes, and Equation 5-3 to relate price elasticity of demand to the percent changes.

Solutions appear at back of book.

TABLE 5-1

Some Estimated Price Elasticities of Demand

Good	Price elasticity of demand
Inelastic demand	
Eggs	0.1
Beef	0.4
Stationery	0.5
Gasoline	0.5
Elastic demand	
Housing	1.2
Restaurant meals	2.3
Airline travel	2.4
Foreign travel	4.1

Please find source information on page xxii.

>>QUICK REVIEW

> The *price elasticity of demand* is equal to the percent change in the quantity demanded divided by the percent change in the price as you move along the demand curve.
> Percent changes are best measured using the *midpoint method*, in which the percent change in each variable is calculated using the average of starting and final values.

Interpreting the Price Elasticity of Demand

Mexico and other oil-producing countries believed they could succeed in driving up oil prices with only a small decrease in the quantity sold because the price elasticity of oil demand was low. But what does that mean? How low does a price elasticity have to be for us to classify it as low? How high does it have to be for us to consider it high? And what determines whether the price elasticity of demand is high or low, anyway?

To answer these questions, we need to look more deeply at the price elasticity of demand.

How Elastic Is Elastic?

As a first step toward classifying price elasticities of demand, let's look at the extreme cases.

First, consider the demand for a good when people pay no attention to the price—say, shoelaces. Suppose that U.S. consumers will buy 1 billion pairs of shoelaces per year regardless of the price. In this case, the demand curve for shoelaces would look like the curve shown in panel (a) of Figure 5-2: it would be a vertical line at 1 billion pairs of shoelaces. Since the percent change in the quantity demanded is zero for *any* change in the price, the price elasticity of demand in this case is zero. The case of a zero price elasticity of demand is known as **perfectly inelastic demand**.

The opposite extreme occurs when even a tiny rise in the price will cause the quantity demanded to drop to zero or even a tiny fall in the price will cause the quantity demanded to get extremely large. Panel (b) of Figure 5-2 shows the case of pink tennis balls; we suppose that tennis players really don't care what color their balls are and that other colors, such as neon green and vivid yellow, are available at $5 per dozen balls. In this case, consumers will buy no pink balls if they cost more than $5 per dozen but will buy only pink balls if they cost less than $5. The demand curve will therefore be a horizontal line at a price of $5 per dozen balls. As you move back and forth along this line, there is a change in the quantity demanded but no change in the price. Roughly speaking, when you divide a number by zero, you get infinity, so a horizontal demand curve implies an infinite price elasticity of demand. When the price elasticity of demand is infinite, economists say that demand is **perfectly elastic**.

The price elasticity of demand for the vast majority of goods is somewhere between these two extreme cases. Economists use one main criterion for classifying these intermediate cases: they ask whether the price elasticity of demand is higher or lower than 1. When the price elasticity of demand is greater than 1, economists say that demand is **elastic**. When the price elasticity of demand is less than 1, they say that demand is **inelastic**. The borderline case is **unit-elastic demand**, where the price elasticity of demand is—surprise—exactly 1.

Demand is **perfectly inelastic** when the quantity demanded does not respond at all to changes in the price. When demand is perfectly inelastic, the demand curve is a vertical line.

Demand is **perfectly elastic** when any price increase will cause the quantity demanded to drop to zero. When demand is perfectly elastic, the demand curve is a horizontal line.

Demand is **elastic** if the price elasticity of demand is greater than 1, **inelastic** if the price elasticity of demand is less than 1, and **unit-elastic** if the price elasticity of demand is exactly 1.

Figure 5-2   Two Extreme Cases of Price Elasticity of Demand

Panel (a) shows a perfectly inelastic demand curve, which is a vertical line. The quantity of shoelaces demanded is always 1 billion pairs, regardless of price. As a result, the price elasticity of demand is zero—the quantity demanded is unaffected by the price. Panel (b) shows a perfectly elastic demand curve, which is a horizontal line. At a price of $5, consumers will buy any quantity of pink tennis balls, but will buy none at a price above $5. If price falls below $5, they will buy an extremely large number of pink tennis balls and none of any other color.

To see why a price elasticity of demand equal to 1 is a useful dividing line, let's consider a hypothetical example: a toll bridge operated by the state highway department. Other things equal, the number of drivers who use the bridge depends on the toll, the price the highway department charges for crossing the bridge: the higher the toll, the fewer the drivers who use the bridge.

Figure 5-3 shows three hypothetical demand curves—one in which demand is unit-elastic, one in which it is inelastic, and one in which it is elastic. In each case, point A shows the quantity demanded if the toll is $0.90 and point B shows the quantity demanded if the toll is $1.10. An increase in the toll from $0.90 to $1.10 is an increase of 20% if we use the midpoint method to calculate percent changes.

Panel (a) shows what happens when the toll is raised from $0.90 to $1.10 and the demand curve is unit-elastic. Here the 20% price rise leads to a fall in the quantity of cars using the bridge each day from 1,100 to 900, which is a 20% decline (again using the midpoint method). So the price elasticity of demand is 20%/20% = 1.

Panel (b) shows a case of inelastic demand when the toll is raised from $0.90 to $1.10. The same 20% price rise reduces the quantity demanded from 1,050 to 950. That's only a 10% decline, so in this case the price elasticity of demand is 10%/20% = 0.5.

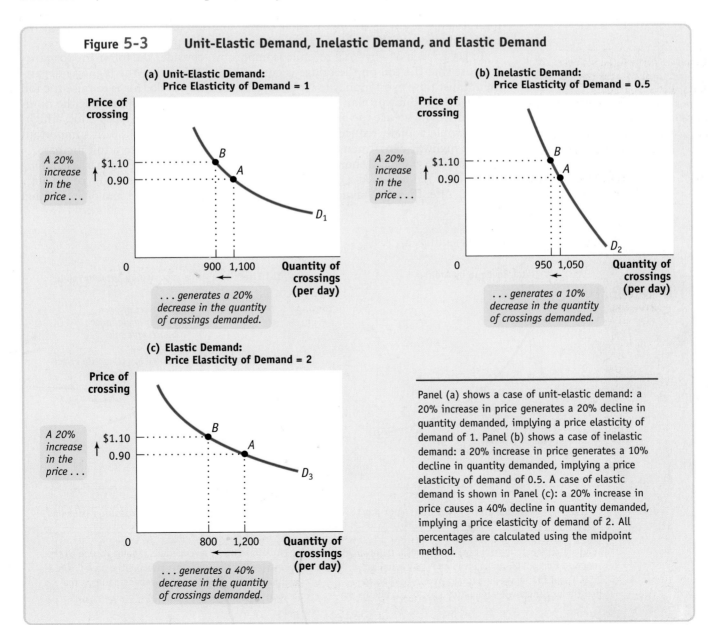

Figure 5-3   **Unit-Elastic Demand, Inelastic Demand, and Elastic Demand**

(a) Unit-Elastic Demand:
Price Elasticity of Demand = 1

A 20% increase in the price . . .

. . . generates a 20% decrease in the quantity of crossings demanded.

(b) Inelastic Demand:
Price Elasticity of Demand = 0.5

A 20% increase in the price . . .

. . . generates a 10% decrease in the quantity of crossings demanded.

(c) Elastic Demand:
Price Elasticity of Demand = 2

A 20% increase in the price . . .

. . . generates a 40% decrease in the quantity of crossings demanded.

Panel (a) shows a case of unit-elastic demand: a 20% increase in price generates a 20% decline in quantity demanded, implying a price elasticity of demand of 1. Panel (b) shows a case of inelastic demand: a 20% increase in price generates a 10% decline in quantity demanded, implying a price elasticity of demand of 0.5. A case of elastic demand is shown in Panel (c): a 20% increase in price causes a 40% decline in quantity demanded, implying a price elasticity of demand of 2. All percentages are calculated using the midpoint method.

Panel (c) shows a case of elastic demand when the toll is raised from $0.90 to $1.10. The 20% price increase causes the quantity demanded to fall from 1,200 to 800—a 40% decline, so the price elasticity of demand is 40%/20% = 2.

Why does it matter whether demand is unit-elastic, inelastic, or elastic? Because this classification predicts how changes in the price of a good will affect the *total revenue* earned by producers from the sale of that good. In many real-life situations, such as the one faced by Luis Tellez, it is crucial to know how price changes affect total revenue. **Total revenue** is defined as the total value of sales of a good or service: the price multiplied by the quantity sold.

> The **total revenue** is the total value of sales of a good or service. It is equal to the price multiplied by the quantity sold.

(5-6) Total revenue = Price × quantity sold

Total revenue has a useful graphical representation that can help us understand why knowing the price elasticity of demand is crucial when we ask whether a price rise will increase or reduce total revenue. Panel (a) of Figure 5-4 shows the same demand curve as panel (a) of Figure 5-3. We see that 1,100 drivers will use the bridge if the toll is $0.90. The total revenue at a price of $0.90 is therefore $0.90 × 1,100 = $990. This value is equal to the area of the green rectangle, which is drawn with the bottom left corner at the point (0, 0) and the top right corner at (1,100, 0.90). In general, the total revenue at any given price is equal to the area of a rectangle whose height is the price and whose width is the quantity demanded at that price.

To get an idea of why total revenue is important, consider the following scenario. Suppose that the toll on the bridge is currently $0.90 but that the highway department must raise extra money for road repairs. One way to do this is to raise the toll on the bridge. But this plan might backfire, since a higher toll will reduce the number of drivers who use the bridge. And if traffic on the bridge dropped a lot, a higher toll would actually reduce total revenue instead of increasing it. So it's important for the highway department to know how drivers will respond to a toll increase.

We can see graphically how the toll increase affects total bridge revenue by examining panel (b) of Figure 5-4. At a toll of $0.90, total revenue is given by the sum of the areas A and B. After the toll is raised to $1.10, total revenue is given by the sum of areas B and

Figure 5-4   Total Revenue

(a) Total Revenue by Area

Price of crossing

$0.90

Total revenue = price × quantity = $990

D

0   1,100
Quantity of crossings (per day)

(b) Effect of a Price Increase on Total Revenue

Price of crossing

Price effect of price increase: higher price for each unit sold

$1.10

C

0.90

Quantity effect of price increase: fewer units are sold

B   A

D

0   900 1,100
Quantity of crossings (per day)

The green rectangle in panel (a) represents total revenue generated from 1,100 drivers who each pay a toll of $0.90. Panel (b) shows how total revenue is affected when the price increases from $0.90 to $1.10. Due to the

quantity effect, total revenue falls by area A. Due to the price effect, total revenue increases by the area C. The overall effect can go either way, depending upon the price elasticity of demand.

C. So when the toll is raised, revenue represented by area A is lost but revenue represented by area C is gained. These two areas have important interpretations. Area C represents the revenue gain that comes from the additional $0.20 paid by drivers who continue to use the bridge. That is, the 900 who continue to use the bridge contribute an additional $0.20 × 900 = $180 per day to total revenue, represented by area C. On the other hand, 200 drivers who would have used the bridge at a price of $0.90 no longer do so, generating a loss to total revenue of $0.90 × 200 = $180 per day, represented by area A.

Except in the rare case of a good with perfectly elastic or perfectly inelastic demand, when a seller raises the price of a good, two countervailing effects are present:

- *A price effect.* After a price increase, each unit sold sells at a higher price, which tends to raise revenue.

- *A quantity effect.* After a price increase, fewer units are sold, which tends to lower revenue.

But then, you may ask, what is the ultimate effect on total revenue: does it go up or down? The answer is that, in general, the effect on total revenue can go either way—a price rise may increase total revenue or may lower it. If the price effect, which tends to raise total revenue, is the stronger of the two effects, then total revenue goes up. If the quantity effect, which tends to reduce total revenue, is the stronger, then total revenue goes down. And if the strengths of the two effects are exactly equal—as in our toll bridge example, where a $180 gain offsets a $180 loss—total revenue is unchanged by the price increase.

The price elasticity of demand tells us what happens to total revenue when price changes: its size determines which effect—the price effect or the quantity effect—is stronger. Specifically:

- If demand for a good is *elastic* (the price elasticity of demand is greater than 1), an increase in price reduces total revenue. In this case, the quantity effect is stronger than the price effect.

- If demand for a good is *inelastic* (the price elasticity of demand is less than 1), a higher price increases total revenue. In this case, the price effect is stronger than the quantity effect.

- If demand for a good is *unit-elastic* (the price elasticity of demand is 1), an increase in price does not change total revenue. In this case, the quantity effect and the price effect exactly offset each other.

Table 5-2 shows how the effect of a price increase on total revenue depends on the price elasticity of demand, using the same data as in Figure 5-3. An increase in the price from $0.90 to $1.10 leaves total revenue unchanged at $990 when demand is unit-elastic. When demand is inelastic, the price effect dominates the quantity effect; the same price increase leads to an increase in total revenue from $945 to $1,045. And when demand is elastic, the quantity effect dominates the price effect; the price increase leads to a decline in total revenue from $1,080 to $880.

TABLE **5-2**

Price Elasticity of Demand and Total Revenue

	Price of crossing = $0.90	Price of crossing = $1.10
Unit-elastic demand (price elasticity of demand = 1)		
Quantity demanded	1,100	900
Total revenue	$990	$990
Inelastic demand (price elasticity of demand = 0.5)		
Quantity demanded	1,050	950
Total revenue	$945	$1,045
Elastic demand (price elasticity of demand = 2)		
Quantity demanded	1,200	800
Total revenue	$1,080	$880

The price elasticity of demand also predicts the effect of a *fall* in price on total revenue. When the price falls, the same two countervailing effects are present, but they work in the opposite directions as in the case of a price rise. There is the price effect of a lower price per unit sold, which tends to lower revenue. This is countered by the quantity effect of more units sold, which tends to raise revenue. Which effect dominates depends on the price elasticity. Here is a quick summary:

- When demand is *elastic*, the quantity effect dominates the price effect; so a fall in price increases total revenue.
- When demand is *inelastic*, the price effect dominates the quantity effect; so a fall in price reduces total revenue.
- When demand is *unit-elastic*, the two effects exactly balance; so a fall in price has no effect on total revenue.

Price Elasticity Along the Demand Curve

Suppose that an economist says that "the price elasticity of demand for coffee is 0.25." What he or she means is that *at the current price* the elasticity is 0.25. In the previous discussion of the toll bridge, what we were really describing was the elasticity *at the price* of $0.90. Why this qualification? Because for the vast majority of demand curves, the price elasticity of demand at one point along the curve is different from the price elasticity of demand at other points along the same curve.

To see this, consider the table in Figure 5-5, which shows a hypothetical demand schedule. It also shows in the last column the total revenue generated at each price and quantity combination in the demand schedule. The upper panel of the graph in Figure 5-5 shows the corresponding demand curve. The lower panel illustrates the same data on total revenue: the height of a bar at each quantity demanded—which corresponds to a particular price—measures the total revenue generated at that price.

In Figure 5-5, you can see that when the price is low, raising the price increases total revenue: starting at a price of $1, raising the price to $2 increases total revenue from $9 to $16. This means that when the price is low, demand is inelastic. Moreover, you can see that demand is inelastic on the entire section of the demand curve from a price of $0 to a price of $5.

When the price is high, however, raising it further reduces total revenue: starting at a price of $8, raising the price to $9 reduces total revenue, from $16 to $9. This means that when the price is high, demand is elastic. Furthermore, you can see that demand is elastic over the section of the demand curve from a price of $5 to $10.

For the vast majority of goods, the price elasticity of demand changes along the demand curve. So whenever you measure the elasticity, you are really measuring it at a particular point or section of the demand curve.

What Factors Determine the Price Elasticity of Demand?

1998 was not the first time Americans had been subject to an attempt by oil-exporting countries to increase revenue by raising oil prices. In the 1970s, gasoline prices in the United States jumped significantly after oil exporters reduced output and raised oil prices. Americans initially reacted by changing their consumption of gasoline very little. Over time, however, they gradually adapted to the higher prices. After a few years, drivers had cut their consumption of gasoline in various ways: increased carpooling, greater use of public transportation, and, most importantly, replacement of large, gas-guzzling cars with smaller, more fuel-efficient models.

The experience of the 1970s illustrates the three main factors that determine elasticity: whether close substitutes are available, whether the good is a necessity or a luxury, and how much time has elapsed since the price change. We'll briefly examine each of these three factors.

Figure 5-5   The Price Elasticity of Demand Changes Along the Demand Curve

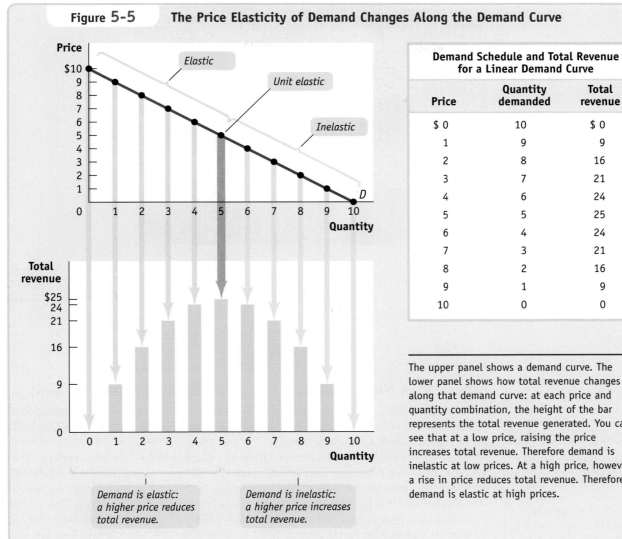

Demand Schedule and Total Revenue for a Linear Demand Curve		
Price	Quantity demanded	Total revenue
$ 0	10	$ 0
1	9	9
2	8	16
3	7	21
4	6	24
5	5	25
6	4	24
7	3	21
8	2	16
9	1	9
10	0	0

The upper panel shows a demand curve. The lower panel shows how total revenue changes along that demand curve: at each price and quantity combination, the height of the bar represents the total revenue generated. You can see that at a low price, raising the price increases total revenue. Therefore demand is inelastic at low prices. At a high price, however, a rise in price reduces total revenue. Therefore demand is elastic at high prices.

Demand is elastic: a higher price reduces total revenue.

Demand is inelastic: a higher price increases total revenue.

Whether Close Substitutes Are Available The price elasticity of demand tends to be high if there are other goods that consumers regard as similar and would be willing to consume instead. The price elasticity of demand tends to be low if there are no close substitutes.

Whether the Good Is a Necessity or a Luxury The price elasticity of demand tends to be low if a good is something you must have, like a life-saving medicine. The price elasticity of demand tends to be high if the good is a luxury—something you can easily live without.

Time In general, the price elasticity of demand tends to increase as consumers have more time to adjust to a price change. This means that the long-run price elasticity of demand is often higher than the short-run elasticity.

So when gasoline prices first increased dramatically in the United States at the end of the 1970s, consumption fell very little because there were no close substitutes for gasoline and because driving their cars was necessary for people to carry out the ordinary tasks of life. Over time, however, Americans changed their habits in ways that enabled them to gradually reduce their gasoline consumption. The result was a steady

Mike Thompson, Detroit Free Press. Reprinted by permission.

decline in gasoline consumption over the next decade, even though the price of gasoline did not continue to rise, confirming that the long-run price elasticity of demand for gasoline was indeed much larger than the short-run elasticity.

economics in action

America's a Nice Place to Live, but We Can't Afford to Visit

In 1992, 18.6 million Canadians visited the United States, but only 11.8 million U.S. residents visited Canada. By 2002, however, roles had been reversed: more U.S. residents visited Canada than vice versa.

Why did the tourist traffic reverse direction? Canada didn't get any warmer from 1992 to 2002—but it did get cheaper for Americans. The reason was a large change in the exchange rate between the two nations' currencies: in 1992 a Canadian dollar was worth $0.80, but by 2002 it had fallen in value by nearly 20 percent to about $0.65. This meant that Canadian goods and services, particularly hotel rooms and meals, were about 20 percent cheaper for Americans in 2002 compared to 1992. So Canada had become a cheap vacation destination for Americans by 2002. Things were not so rosy, however, when viewed from the other side of the border: American vacations had become 20 percent more expensive for Canadians. Canadians responded by vacationing in their own country or in other parts of the world besides the United States.

Foreign travel is an example of a good that has a high price elasticity of demand: as we saw in Table 5-1, it has been estimated at about 4.1. One reason is that foreign travel is a luxury good for most people—you may regret not going to Paris this year, but you can live without it. A second reason is that a good substitute for foreign travel typically exists—domestic travel. A Canadian who finds it too expensive to vacation in San Francisco this year is likely to find that Vancouver is a pretty good alternative. ■

< < < < < < < < < < < < < < < < <

>> CHECK YOUR UNDERSTANDING 5-2

1. For each case, choose the condition that characterizes demand: elastic demand, inelastic demand, or unit-elastic demand.
   a. Total revenue decreases when price increases. *Elastic*
   b. The additional revenue generated by an increase in quantity sold is exactly offset by revenue lost from the fall in price received per unit. *Unit*
   c. Total revenue falls when output increases. *Elastic*
   d. Producers in an industry find they can increase their total revenues by working together to reduce industry output. *Inelastic*

continued

2. For the following goods, what is the elasticity of demand? Explain. What is the shape of the demand curve?
  a. Demand by a snake-bite victim for an antidote
  b. Demand by students for green erasers

Solutions appear at back of book.

Other Demand Elasticities

The quantity of a good demanded depends not only on the price of that good but on other variables. In particular, demand curves shift because of changes in the prices of related goods and changes in consumers' incomes. It is often important to have a measure of these other effects, and the best measures are—you guessed it—elasticities. Specifically, we can best measure how the demand for a good is affected by prices of other goods using a measure called the *cross-price elasticity of demand*, and we can best measure how demand is affected by changes in income using the *income elasticity of demand*.

The Cross-Price Elasticity of Demand

In Chapter 3 you learned that the demand for a good is often affected by the prices of other, related goods—goods that are substitutes or complements. There you saw that a change in the price of a related good shifts the demand curve of the original good, reflecting a change in the quantity demanded at any given price. The strength of such a "cross" effect on demand can be measured by the **cross-price elasticity of demand**, defined as the ratio of the percent change in the quantity demanded of one good to the percent change in the price of the other.

The **cross-price elasticity of demand** between two goods measures the effect of the change in one good's price on the quantity demanded of the other good. It is equal to the percent change in the quantity demanded of one good divided by the percent change in the other good's price.

(5-7) Cross-price elasticity of demand between goods A and B

$$= \frac{\text{\% change in quantity of A demanded}}{\text{\% change in price of B}}$$

When two goods are substitutes, like hot dogs and hamburgers, the cross-price elasticity of demand is positive: a rise in the price of hot dogs increases the demand for hamburgers—that is, it causes a rightward shift of the demand curve for hamburgers. If the goods are close substitutes, the cross-price elasticity will be positive and large; if they are not close substitutes, the cross-price elasticity will be positive and small. So when the cross-price elasticity of demand is positive, it is a measure of how closely substitutable for each other two goods are.

When two goods are complements, like hot dogs and hot dog buns, the cross-price elasticity is negative: a rise in the price of hot dogs decreases the demand for hot dog buns—that is, it causes a leftward shift of the demand curve for hot dog buns. As with substitutes, the size of the cross-price elasticity of demand between two complements tells us how strongly complementary they are: if the cross-price elasticity is only slightly below zero, they are weak complements; if it is very negative, they are strong complements.

Note that in the case of the cross-price elasticity of demand, the sign (plus or minus) is very important: it tells us whether the two goods are complements or substitutes. So we cannot drop the minus sign as we did for the price elasticity of demand.

Our discussion of the cross-price elasticity of demand is a useful place to return to a point we made earlier: elasticity is a *unit-free* measure—that is, it doesn't depend on the units in which goods are measured.

To see the potential problem, suppose someone told you that "if the price of hot dog buns rises by $0.30, Americans will buy 10 million fewer hot dogs this year." If you've ever bought hot dog buns, you'll immediately wonder: is that a $0.30 increase in the price *per bun*, or is it a $0.30 increase in the price *per package* (buns are usually sold by the dozen)? It makes a big difference what units we are talking about! However, if someone says that the cross-price elasticity of demand between buns and hot dogs is −0.3, it doesn't matter whether buns are sold individually or by the package. So elasticity is defined as a ratio of percent changes, as a way of making sure that confusion over units doesn't arise.

The Income Elasticity of Demand

The **income elasticity of demand** is the percent change in the quantity of a good demanded when a consumer's income changes divided by the percent change in the consumer's income.

The **income elasticity of demand** is a measure of how much the demand for a good is affected by changes in consumers' incomes. It allows us to determine whether a good is a normal or inferior good as well as measure how intensely the demand for the good responds to changes in income.

$$\text{(5-8)} \qquad \text{Income elasticity of demand} = \frac{\% \text{ change in quantity demanded}}{\% \text{ change in income}}$$

Just as the cross-price elasticity of demand between two goods can be either positive or negative, depending on whether the goods are substitutes or complements, the income elasticity of demand for a good can also be either positive or negative. Recall from Chapter 3 that goods can be either *normal goods*, for which demand increases when income rises, or *inferior goods*, for which demand decreases when income rises. These definitions relate directly to the sign of the income elasticity of demand:

- When the income elasticity of demand is positive, the good is a normal good—that is, the quantity demanded at any given price increases as income increases.

- When the income elasticity of demand is negative, the good is an inferior good—that is, the quantity demanded at any given price decreases as income increases.

Economists often use estimates of the income elasticity of demand to predict which industries will grow most rapidly as the incomes of consumers grow over time. In doing this, they often find it useful to make a further distinction among normal goods, identifying which are *income-elastic* and which are *income-inelastic*.

The demand for a good is **income-elastic** if the income elasticity of demand for that good is greater than 1.

The demand for a good is **income-inelastic** if the income elasticity of demand for that good is positive but less than 1.

The demand for a good is **income-elastic** if the income elasticity of demand for that good is greater than 1. When income rises, the demand for income-elastic goods rises *faster* than income. Luxury goods such as second homes and international travel tend to be income-elastic. The demand for a good is **income-inelastic** if the income elasticity of demand for that good is positive but less than 1. When income rises, the demand for income-inelastic goods rises, but more slowly than income. Necessities such as food and clothing tend to be income-inelastic.

FOR INQUIRING MINDS

WHERE HAVE ALL THE FARMERS GONE?

What percentage of Americans live on farms? Sad to say, the U.S. government no longer publishes that number. In 1991 the official percentage was 1.9, but in that year the government decided it was no longer a meaningful indicator of the size of the agricultural sector because a large proportion of those who live on farms actually make their living doing something else. But in the days of the Founding Fathers, the great majority of Americans lived on farms. As recently as the 1940s, one American in six—or approximately 17%—still did.

Why do so few people now live and work on farms in the United States? There are two main reasons, both involving elasticities.

First, the income elasticity of demand for food is much less than 1—it is income-

inelastic. As consumers grow richer, other things equal, spending on food rises less than income. As a result, as the U.S. economy has grown, the share of income it spends on food—and therefore the share of total income earned by farmers—has fallen.

Second, agriculture has been a technologically progressive sector for approximately 150 years in the United States, with steadily increasing yields over time. You might think that technological progress would be good for farmers. But competition among farmers means that technological progress leads to lower food prices. Meanwhile, the demand for food is price-inelastic, so falling prices of agricultural goods, other things equal, reduce the total revenue of farmers. That's right: progress in

farming is good for consumers but bad for farmers.

The combination of these effects explains the relative decline of farming. Even if farming weren't such a technologically progressive sector, the low income elasticity of demand for food would ensure that the income of farmers grows more slowly than the economy as a whole. The combination of rapid technological progress in farming with price-inelastic demand for farm products reinforces this effect, further reducing the growth of farm income. In short, the U.S. farm sector has been a victim of success—the U.S. economy's success as a whole (which reduces the importance of spending on food) and its own success in increasing yields.

economics in action

Spending It

The U.S. Bureau of Labor Statistics carries out extensive surveys of how families spend their incomes. This is not just a matter of intellectual curiosity. Quite a few government programs involve some adjustment for changes in the cost of living; to estimate those changes, the government must know how people spend their money. But an additional payoff to these surveys is evidence on the income elasticity of demand for various goods.

What stands out from these studies? The classic result is that the income elasticity of demand for "food eaten at home" is considerably less than 1: as a family's income rises, the share of its income spent on food consumed at home falls. Correspondingly, the lower a family's income, the higher the share of income spent on food consumed at home. In poor countries, many families spend more than half their income on food consumed at home. While the income elasticity of "food eaten at home" is estimated at less than 0.5 in the United States, "food eaten away from home" (restaurant meals) is estimated to be much higher—close to 1. Families with higher incomes eat out more often and at fancier places. In 1950,

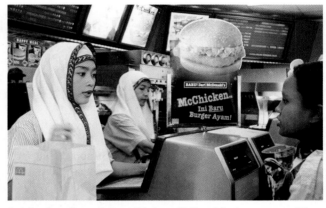

Judging from the activity at this busy McDonald's, incomes are rising in Jakarta, Indonesia.

about 19 percent of U.S. income was spent on food consumed at home, a number which has dropped to 7 percent today. But over the same time period, the share of U.S. income spent on food away from home has stayed constant at 5 percent. In fact, a sure sign of rising income levels in developing countries is the arrival of fast-food restaurants that cater to newly affluent customers. For example, McDonald's can now be found in Jakarta, Shanghai, and Bombay.

There is one clear example of an inferior good found in the surveys: rental housing. Families with higher income actually spend less on rent than families with lower income, because they are much more likely to own their own homes. And the category identified as "other housing"—which basically means second homes—is highly income-elastic. Only higher-income families can afford a vacation home at all, so "other housing" has an income elasticity of demand greater than 1. ■

> > > > > > > > > > > > > > > > > > >

>> **CHECK YOUR UNDERSTANDING 5-3**

1. After Chelsea's income increased from $12,000 to $18,000 a year, her purchases of CDs increased from 10 to 40 CDs a year. Calculate Chelsea's income elasticity of demand for CDs using the midpoint method.

2. Expensive restaurant meals are income-elastic goods for most people, including Sanjay. Suppose his income falls by 10% this year. What can you predict about the change in Sanjay's consumption of expensive restaurant meals?

3. As the price of margarine rises by 20%, a manufacturer of baked goods increases its quantity of butter demanded by 5%. Calculate the cross-price elasticity of demand between butter and margarine. Are butter and margarine substitutes or complements for this manufacturer?

Solutions appear at back of book.

The Price Elasticity of Supply

The Tellez plan to drive up the price of oil would have been much less effective if a higher price had induced large increases in output by countries that were not party to the agreement. For example, if American oil producers had responded to the higher price by significantly increasing their production, they could have pushed the price of oil back down. But they didn't—in fact, producers of oil who were not members of OPEC (Organization of Petroleum Exporting Countries) did not respond much to the higher price. This was another critical element in the success of the Tellez plan: a low responsiveness in output to a higher price of oil from other oil producers. To measure the response of producers to price changes, we need a measure parallel to the price elasticity of demand—the *price elasticity of supply*.

Measuring the Price Elasticity of Supply

The **price elasticity of supply** is a measure of the responsiveness of the quantity of a good supplied to the price of that good. It is the ratio of the percent change in the quantity supplied to the percent change in the price as we move along the supply curve.

The **price elasticity of supply** is defined the same way as the price elasticity of demand:

$$(5\text{-}9) \quad \text{Price elasticity of supply} = \frac{\%\ \text{change in quantity supplied}}{\%\ \text{change in price}}$$

The only difference is that this time we consider movements along the supply curve rather than movements along the demand curve.

Suppose that the price of tomatoes rises by 10%. If the quantity of tomatoes supplied also increases by 10% in response, the price elasticity of supply of tomatoes is 1 (10%/10%), and supply is unit-elastic. If the quantity supplied increases by 5%, the price elasticity of supply is 0.5 and supply is inelastic; if the quantity increases by 20%, the price elasticity of supply is 2 and supply is elastic.

As in the case of demand, the extreme values of the price elasticity of supply have a simple graphical representation.

Panel (a) of Figure 5-6 shows the supply of cell phone frequencies, the portion of the radio spectrum which is suitable for sending and receiving cell phone signals. Governments own the right to sell the use of this part of the radio spectrum to cell phone operators inside their borders. In Chapter 7, we will discuss how governments

Figure 5-6 **Two Extreme Cases of Price Elasticity of Supply**

Panel (a) shows a perfectly inelastic supply curve, which is a vertical line. The price elasticity of supply is zero: the quantity supplied is always the same, regardless of price. Panel (b) shows a perfectly elastic supply curve, which is a horizontal line. At a price of $12, producers will supply any quantity, but will supply none at a price below $12. If price rises above $12, they will supply an extremely large quantity.

recently sold off their cell phone frequencies to the highest bidder in an auction. But governments can't increase or decrease the number of cell phone frequencies that they have to offer—for technical reasons, the quantity of frequencies suitable for cell phone operation is a fixed quantity. So the supply curve for cell phone frequencies is a vertical line, which we have assumed is set at the quantity of 100 frequencies. As you move up and down that curve, the change in the quantity supplied by the government is zero, whatever the change in price. So panel (a) illustrates a case in which the price elasticity of supply is zero. This is a case of **perfectly inelastic supply.**

Panel (b) shows the supply curve for pizza. We suppose that it costs $12 to produce a pizza, including all opportunity costs such as the implicit cost of capital invested in pizza parlors. At any price below $12, it would be unprofitable to produce pizza and all the pizza parlors in America would go out of business. Alternatively, there are many producers who could operate pizza parlors if they were profitable. The ingredients—dough, tomatoes, cheese—are plentiful. And if necessary, more tomatoes could be grown, more milk could be produced to make mozzarella, and so on. So any price above $12 would elicit an extremely large quantity of pizzas supplied. The implied supply curve is therefore a horizontal line at $12. Since even a tiny increase in the price would lead to a huge increase in the quantity supplied, the price elasticity of supply would be more or less infinite. This is a case of **perfectly elastic supply**.

As our cell phone frequencies and pizza examples suggest, real-world instances of both perfectly inelastic and perfectly elastic supply are easy to find—much easier than their counterparts in demand.

There is **perfectly inelastic supply** when the price elasticity of supply is zero, so that changes in the price of the good have no effect on the quantity supplied. A perfectly inelastic supply curve is a vertical line.

There is **perfectly elastic supply** when even a tiny increase or reduction in the price will lead to very large changes in the quantity supplied, so that the price elasticity of supply is infinite. A perfectly elastic supply curve is a horizontal line.

What Factors Determine the Price Elasticity of Supply?

Our examples tell us the main determinant of the price elasticity of supply: the availability of inputs. In addition, as with the price elasticity of demand, time may also play a role in the price elasticity of supply. Here we briefly summarize the two factors.

The Availability of Inputs The price elasticity of supply tends to be large when inputs are easily available. It tends to be small when inputs are difficult to obtain.

Time The price elasticity of supply tends to become larger as producers have more time to respond to a price change. This means that the long-run price elasticity of supply is often higher than the short-run elasticity.

The price elasticity of pizza supply is very high because the inputs needed to expand the industry are readily available. The price elasticity of cell phone frequencies is zero because an essential input—the radio spectrum—cannot be increased at all.

Many industries are like pizza and have large price elasticities of supply: they can be readily expanded because they don't require any special or unique resources. On the other hand, the price elasticity of supply is usually substantially less than perfectly elastic for goods that involve limited natural resources: minerals like gold or copper, agricultural products like coffee that flourish only on certain types of land, renewable resources like ocean fish that can only be exploited up to a point without destroying the resource.

But given enough time, producers are often able to significantly change the amount they produce in response to a price change, even when production involves a limited natural resource. For example, consider again the effects of a surge in oil prices, but this time focus on the supply response. If oil prices were to rise to $50 per barrel and stay there for a number of years, there would almost certainly be a substantial increase in oil production. Oil companies would search for and exploit oil in inaccessible places, such as deep-sea waters; costly equipment would be put in place to squeeze still more oil out of already-exploited reservoirs; and so on. But Rome wasn't built in a day, and all these oil-production efforts can't take place in a month or even a year.

For this reason, economists often make a distinction between the short-run elasticity of supply, usually referring to a few weeks or months, and the long-run elasticity of supply, usually referring to several years. In most industries, the long-run elasticity of supply is larger than the short-run elasticity.

economics in action

European Farm Surpluses

One of the policies we analyzed in Chapter 4 was the imposition of a *price floor*, a lower limit on the price of a good. We saw that price floors are often used by governments to support the incomes of farmers but create large unwanted surpluses of farm produce. The most dramatic example of this is found in the European Union, where price floors have created a "butter mountain," a "wine lake," and so on.

Were European politicians unaware that their price floors would create huge surpluses? They probably knew that surpluses would arise, but underestimated the price elasticity of agricultural supply. In fact, when the agricultural price supports were put in place, many analysts thought they were unlikely to lead to big increases in production. After all, European countries are densely populated and there was little new land available for cultivation.

What the analysts failed to realize, however, was how much farm production could expand by adding other resources, especially fertilizer and pesticides. So although farm acreage didn't increase much, farm production did! ∎

< < < < < < < < < < < < < < < < < < < <

>>CHECK YOUR UNDERSTANDING 5-4

1. Using the midpoint method, calculate the price elasticity of supply for web-design services when the price per hour rises from $100 to $150 and the number of hours transacted increases from 300,000 hours to 500,000. Is supply elastic, inelastic, or unit-elastic?
2. True or false? If the demand for milk were to rise, then, in the long run, milk-drinkers would be better off if supply were elastic rather than inelastic.
3. True or false? Long-run price elasticities of supply are generally larger than short-run price elasticities of supply. Therefore the short-run supply curves are generally flatter than the long-run supply curves.
4. True or false? When supply is perfectly elastic, changes in demand have no effect on price.

Solutions appear at back of book.

An Elasticity Menagerie

We've just run through quite a few different elasticities. Keeping them all straight can be a problem. So in Table 5-3 we provide a summary of all the elasticities we have discussed and their implications.

Using Elasticity: The Incidence of an Excise Tax

In Chapter 4 we introduced the concept of the *incidence* of a tax—the measure of who really bears the burden of the tax. We saw in the case of an excise tax—a tax on sales or purchases of a product—that the incidence does not depend on who literally pays the money to the government. It doesn't matter, in other words, whether the tax is assessed on the sellers or the buyers. But we also noted that to determine who really pays the tax, we need the concept of elasticity.

We are now ready to see how the price elasticity of demand and the price elasticity of supply determine the incidence of an excise tax.

TABLE **5-3**

An Elasticity Menagerie

Name	Possible values	Significance
Price elasticity of demand = $\dfrac{\text{\% change in quantity demanded}}{\text{\% change in price}}$ (use absolute value)		
Perfectly inelastic demand	0	Price has no effect on quantity demanded (vertical demand curve).
Inelastic demand	Between 0 and 1	A rise in price increases total revenue.
Unit-elastic demand	Exactly 1	Changes in price have no effect on total revenue.
Elastic demand	Greater than 1, less than ∞	A rise in price reduces total revenue.
Perfectly elastic demand	∞	A rise in price causes quantity demanded to fall to 0. A fall in price leads to an infinite quantity demanded (horizontal demand curve).
Cross-price elasticity of demand = $\dfrac{\text{\% change in quantity } \textit{of one good } \text{demanded}}{\text{\% change in price } \textit{of another good}}$		
Complements	Negative	Quantity demanded of one good falls when the price of another rises.
Substitutes	Positive	Quantity demanded of one good rises when the price of another rises.
Income elasticity of demand = $\dfrac{\text{\% change in quantity demanded}}{\text{\% change in income}}$		
Inferior good	Negative	Quantity demanded falls when income rises.
Normal good, income-inelastic	Positive, less than 1	Quantity demanded rises when income rises, but not as rapidly as income.
Normal good, income-elastic	Greater than 1	Quantity demanded rises when income rises, and more rapidly than income.
Price elasticity of supply = $\dfrac{\text{\% change in quantity supplied}}{\text{\% change in price}}$		
Perfectly inelastic supply	0	Price has no effect on quantity supplied (vertical supply curve).
	Greater than 0, less than ∞	Ordinary upward-sloping supply curve.
Perfectly elastic supply	∞	Any fall in price causes quantity supplied to fall to 0. Any rise in price elicits an infinite quantity supplied (horizontal supply curve).

When an Excise Tax Is Paid Mainly by Consumers

Figure 5-7 on page 128 shows an excise tax that falls mainly on consumers: an excise tax on gasoline, which we set at $1 per gallon. (There really is a federal excise tax on gasoline, though it is actually only about $0.18 per gallon in the United States. In addition, states impose excise taxes between $0.08 and $0.30 per gallon.) According to Figure 5-7, in the absence of the tax, gasoline would sell for $1 per gallon.

Two key assumptions are reflected in the supply and demand curves. First, the price elasticity of demand for gasoline is very low, so the demand curve is relatively steep. Second, the price elasticity of supply is very high, so the supply curve is relatively flat.

We know from Chapter 4 that an excise tax drives a wedge, equal to the size of the tax, between the price paid by consumers and the price received by producers. This

Figure 5-7

An Excise Tax Paid Mainly by Consumers

The relatively steep demand curve here reflects a low price elasticity of demand for gasoline. The relatively flat supply curve reflects a high price elasticity of supply. The pre-tax price of a gallon of gas is $1.00, and a tax of $1.00 per gallon is imposed. The cost to consumers rises by $0.95 to $1.95, reflecting the fact that most of the burden of the tax falls on consumers. Only a small portion of the tax is borne by producers: the price they receive falls by only $0.05 to $0.95.

wedge drives the price paid by consumers up, and the price received by producers down. But as we can see from the figure, in this case those two effects are very unequal in size. The price received by producers falls only slightly, from $1.00 to $0.95, while the price paid by consumers rises by a lot, from $1.00 to $1.95.

This example illustrates a general principle: When the price elasticity of demand is low and the price elasticity of supply is high, the burden of an excise tax falls mainly on consumers. This is probably a good description of the main excise taxes actually collected in the United States today, such as taxes on cigarettes and alcoholic beverages.

When an Excise Tax Is Paid Mainly by Producers

Figure 5-8 shows an excise tax paid mainly by producers. In this case, we consider a $5.00 per day tax on downtown parking in a small city. In the market equilibrium, parking would cost $6.00 per day in the absence of the tax.

The price elasticity of supply is assumed to be very low because the lots used for parking have very few alternative uses. So the supply curve is relatively steep. The price elasticity of demand, however, is high: consumers can easily switch to other parking spaces a few minutes' walk from downtown. So the demand curve is relatively flat.

The tax drives a wedge between the price paid by consumers and the price received by producers. This time, however, the price to consumers rises only slightly, from $6.00 to $6.50, but the price received by producers falls a lot, from $6.00 to $1.50. So a consumer bears only $0.50 of the $5 tax, with a producer bearing the remaining $4.50.

Again, this example illustrates a general principle: When the price elasticity of demand is high and the price elasticity of supply is low, the burden of an excise tax falls mainly on producers. A real-world example is the tax on purchases of existing houses. Over the past few years, house prices in many towns in desirable locations have gone up as well-off outsiders move in, a process called gentrification. Some of these towns have imposed taxes on house sales in an effort to extract money from the new arrivals. But this ignores the fact that the elasticity of demand for houses in a particular town is often high, because buyers can choose to move to other towns. Furthermore, the elasticity of supply is probably low, because most sellers must sell their houses due to things like job transfers to other locations. So taxes on home purchases are actually paid mainly by the sellers—not, as town officials imagine, by wealthy buyers.

An Excise Tax Paid Mainly by Producers

The relatively flat demand curve here reflects a high price elasticity of demand for downtown parking, and a relatively steep supply curve results from a low price elasticity of supply. The pre-tax price of a daily parking space is $6.00 and a tax of $5.00 is imposed. The price received by producers falls a lot, to $1.50, reflecting the fact that they bear most of the burden of the tax. The price paid by consumers rises a small amount, $0.50, to $6.50, as they bear very little of the burden.

Putting It All Together

We've just seen that when the price elasticity of supply is high and the price elasticity of demand is low, an excise tax falls mainly on consumers; when the price elasticity of supply is low and the price elasticity of demand is high, an excise tax falls mainly on producers. This leads us to the general rule: When the price elasticity of demand is higher than the price elasticity of supply, an excise tax falls mainly on the producers. When the price elasticity of supply is higher than the price elasticity of demand, an excise tax falls mainly on consumers. So elasticity—not who literally pays the tax—determines the incidence of an excise tax.

economics in action

So Who Does Pay the FICA?

As we explained in Chapter 4, one of the main taxes levied by the federal government is the FICA, or payroll tax. Half of this tax is paid by workers, half by their employers. But we have learned that this tells us nothing about who *really* pays the tax, that is, about the incidence of the FICA.

So who does pay the FICA? Almost all economists who have studied the issue agree that the answer is that the FICA is a tax on workers, not on their employers.

The reason for this conclusion lies in a comparison of the price elasticities of the supply of labor by households and the demand for labor by firms. The evidence suggests that the price elasticity of demand for labor is quite high, at least 3. That is, an increase in average wages of 1 percent would lead to at least a 3 percent decline in the number of hours of work demanded. The price elasticity of supply of labor, however, is generally believed to be very low. The reason is that although a rise in the wage rate increases the incentive to work, it also makes people richer and more able to afford leisure. So the number of hours people are willing to work increases very little—if at all—when the wage per hour goes up.

Our analysis already tells us that when the price elasticity of demand is much higher than the price elasticity of supply, the burden of an excise tax falls mainly on the suppliers. So the FICA falls mainly on the suppliers of labor, that is, workers—even though on paper half the tax is paid by employers.

This conclusion tells us something important about our tax system: that the FICA, rather than the much-hated income tax, is the main tax on most families. The FICA is 15.3 percent of all wages and salaries up to more than $80,000 per year; that is, the great majority of workers in the United States pay 15.3 percent of their wages in FICA. But only a minority of American families pay more than 15 percent of their income in income tax. According to estimates by the Congressional Budget Office, the FICA is Uncle Sam's main bite out of the income of more than 70 percent of families. ■

< < < < < < < < < < < < < < < < < < <

>>CHECK YOUR UNDERSTANDING 5-5

1. The demand for economics textbooks is very inelastic, but the supply is somewhat elastic. What does this imply about the incidence of a tax? Illustrate with a diagram.

2. True or false? When a substitute for a good is readily available to consumers, but it is difficult for producers to adjust the quantity of the good produced, then the burden of a tax on the good falls more heavily on producers.

3. The supply of bottled spring water is very inelastic, but the demand for it is somewhat elastic. What does this imply about the incidence of a tax? Illustrate with a diagram.

4. True or false? Other things equal, consumers would prefer to face a less elastic supply curve when a tax is imposed.

Solutions appear at back of book.

• A LOOK AHEAD •

The concept of elasticity deepens our understanding of supply and demand, among other things helping us predict not only in which direction prices will move but also by how much. For example, we now know that supply and demand elasticities determine how the burden of a tax will be divided between producers and consumers. And, to come back to an example from very early on in this chapter, the concept of elasticity was just what Luis Tellez needed to be able to engineer a reduction in output by oil-exporting countries that led to an increase in oil prices and an increase in their total oil revenues.

But we don't yet have a way to translate the changes in prices that result from a tax, or from any other change in the situation, into a measure of gains or losses to individuals. In the next chapter, we show how to make that translation—how to use the supply and demand curves to calculate gains and losses to producers and consumers.

SUMMARY

1. Many economic questions depend on the size of consumer or producer response to changes in prices or other variables. *Elasticity* is a general measure of responsiveness that can be used to answer such questions.

2. The **price elasticity of demand**—the percent change in the quantity demanded divided by the percent change in the price (dropping the minus sign)—is a measure of the responsiveness of the quantity demanded to changes in the price. In practical calculations, it is usually best to use the **midpoint method**, which calculates percent changes in prices and quantities based on the average of starting and final values.

3. The responsiveness of the quantity demanded to price can range from **perfectly inelastic demand**, where the quantity demanded is unaffected by the price, to **perfectly elastic demand**, where there is a unique price at which consumers will buy as much or as little as they are offered. When demand is perfectly inelastic, the demand curve is a vertical line; when it is perfectly elastic, the demand curve is a horizontal line.

4. The price elasticity of demand is classified according to whether it is more or less than 1. If it is greater than 1, demand is **elastic**; if it is less than 1, demand is **inelastic**; if it is exactly 1, demand is **unit-elastic**. This classification

determines how **total revenue**, the total value of sales, changes when the price changes. If demand is elastic, total revenue falls when the price increases and rises when the price decreases. If demand is inelastic, total revenue rises when the price increases and falls when the price decreases.

5. The price elasticity of demand depends on whether there are close substitutes for the good in question, whether the good is a necessity or a luxury, and the length of time that has elapsed since the price change.

6. The **cross-price elasticity of demand** measures the effect of a change in one good's price on the quantity of another good demanded. The cross-price elasticity of demand can be positive, in which case the goods are substitutes, or negative, in which case they are complements.

7. The **income elasticity of demand** is the percent change in the quantity of a good demanded when a consumer's income changes divided by the percent change in income. The income elasticity of demand indicates how intensely the demand for a good responds to changes in income. It can be negative; in that case the good is an inferior good. Goods with positive income elasticities of demand are normal goods. If the income elasticity is greater than 1, a good is **income-elastic**; if it is positive and less than 1, the good is **income-inelastic**.

8. The **price elasticity of supply** is the percent change in the quantity of a good supplied divided by the percent change in the price. If the quantity supplied does not change at all, we have an instance of **perfectly inelastic supply**; the supply curve is a vertical line. If the quantity supplied is zero below some price but infinite above that price, we have an instance of **perfectly elastic supply**; the supply curve is a horizontal line.

9. The price elasticity of supply depends on the availability of resources to expand production and on time. It is higher when inputs are easily available and the longer the time elapsed since the price change.

10. The incidence of an excise tax depends on the price elasticities of supply and demand. If the price elasticity of demand is higher than the price elasticity of supply, the tax falls mainly on producers; if the price elasticity of supply is higher than the price elasticity of demand, the tax falls mainly on consumers.

KEY TERMS

Price elasticity of demand, p. 111
Midpoint method, p. 112
Perfectly inelastic demand, p. 114
Perfectly elastic demand, p. 114
Elastic demand, p. 114

Inelastic demand, p. 114
Unit-elastic demand, p. 114
Total revenue, p. 116
Cross-price elasticity of demand, p. 121
Income elasticity of demand, p. 122

Income-elastic demand, p. 122
Income-inelastic demand, p. 122
Price elasticity of supply, p. 124
Perfectly inelastic supply, p. 125
Perfectly elastic supply, p. 125

PROBLEMS

1. TheNile.com, the online bookseller, wants to increase its total revenue. Currently, every book it sells is priced at $10.50. One suggested strategy is to offer a discount that lowers the price of a book to $9.50, a 10% reduction in price using the midpoint method. TheNile.com knows that its customers can be divided into two distinct groups according to their likely responses to the discount. The accompanying table shows how the two groups respond to the discount.

	Group A (sales per week)	Group B (sales per week)
Volume of sales before the 10% discount	1.55 million	1.50 million
Volume of sales after the 10% discount	1.65 million	1.70 million

a. Using the midpoint method, calculate the price elasticities of demand for Group A and Group B.

b. Explain how the discount will affect total revenue from each group.

c. Suppose TheNile.com knows which group each customer belongs to when he or she logs on and can choose whether or not to offer the 10% discount. If TheNile.com wants to increase its total revenue, should discounts be offered to Group A or to Group B, to neither group, or to both groups?

2. Do you think the price elasticity of demand for Ford sport-utility vehicles (SUVs) will increase, decrease, or remain the same when each of the following events occurs? Explain your answer.

a. Other car manufacturers, such as General Motors, decide to make and sell SUVs.

b. SUVs produced in foreign countries are banned from the American market.

c. Due to ad campaigns, Americans believe that SUVs are much safer than ordinary passenger cars.

d. The time period over which you measure the elasticity lengthens. During that longer time, new models such as four-wheel-drive cargo vans appear.

3. U.S. winter wheat production increased dramatically in 1999 after a bumper harvest. The supply curve shifted rightward; as a result, the price decreased and the quantity demanded increased (a movement along the demand curve). The accompanying table describes what happened to prices and the quantity demanded of wheat.

	1998	1999
Quantity demanded (bushels)	1.74 billion	1.9 billion
Average price (per bushel)	$3.70	$2.72

a. Using the midpoint method, calculate the price elasticity of demand for winter wheat.

b. What is the total revenue for U.S. wheat farmers in 1998 and 1999?

c. Did the bumper harvest increase or decrease the total revenue of American wheat farmers? How could you have predicted this from your answer to part a?

4. The accompanying table gives part of the supply schedule for personal computers in the United States.

Price of computer	Quantity of computers supplied
$1,100	12,000
900	8,000

a. Calculate the price elasticity of supply when the price increases from $900 to $1,100 using the midpoint method.

b. Suppose firms produce 1,000 more computers at any given price due to improved technology. As price increases from $900 to $1,100, is the price elasticity of supply now greater than, less than, or the same as it was in part a?

c. Suppose a longer time period under consideration means that the quantity supplied at any given price is 20% higher than the figures given in the table. As price increases from $900 to $1,100, is the price elasticity of supply now greater than, less than, or the same as it was in part a?

5. The accompanying table lists the cross-price elasticities of demand for several goods, where the percent price change is measured for the first good of the pair, and the percent quantity change is measured for the second good.

Good	Cross-price elasticities of demand
Air-conditioning units and kilowatts of electricity	−0.34
Coke and Pepsi	+0.63
High-fuel-consuming sport-utility vehicles (SUVs) and gasoline	−0.28
McDonald's burgers and Burger King burgers	+0.82
Butter and margarine	+1.54

a. Explain the sign of each of the cross-price elasticities. What does it imply about the relationship between the two goods in question?

b. Compare the absolute values of the cross-price elasticities and explain their magnitudes. For example, why is the cross-price elasticity of McDonald's and Burger King less than the cross-elasticity of butter and margarine?

c. Use the information in the table to calculate how a 5% increase in the price of Pepsi affects the quantity of Coke demanded.

d. Use the information in the table to calculate how a 10% decrease in the price of gasoline affects the quantity of SUVs demanded.

6. What can you conclude about the price elasticity of demand in each of the following statements?

a. "The pizza delivery business in this town is very competitive. I'd lose half my customers if I raised the price by as little as 10%."

b. "I owned both of the two Jerry Garcia autographed lithographs in existence. I sold one on eBay for a high price. But when I sold the second one, the price dropped a lot."

c. "My economics professor has chosen to use the Krugman/Wells textbook for this class. I have no choice but to buy this book."

d. "I always spend a total of exactly $10 per week on coffee."

7. Take a linear demand curve like that shown in Figure 5-5, where the range of prices for which demand is elastic and inelastic is labeled. In each of the following scenarios, the supply curve shifts. Show along which portion of the demand curve (that is, the elastic or the inelastic portion) the supply curve must have shifted in order to generate the event described. In each case, show on the diagram the quantity effect and the price effect.

a. Recent attempts by the Colombian army to stop the flow of illegal drugs into the United States have actually benefited drug dealers.

b. New construction increased the number of seats in the football stadium and resulted in greater total revenue from box-office ticket sales.

c. A fall in input prices has led to higher output of Porsches. But total revenue for the Porsche Company has declined as a result.

8. The accompanying table shows the price and yearly quantity sold of souvenir T-shirts in the town of Crystal Lake according to the average income of the tourists visiting.

Price of T-shirt	Quantity of T-shirts demanded when average tourist income is $20,000	Quantity of T-shirts demanded when average tourist income is $30,000
$4	3,000	5,000
5	2,400	4,200
6	1,600	3,000
7	800	1,800

a. Using the midpoint method, calculate the price elasticity of demand when the price of a T-shirt rises from $5 to $6 when the average tourist income is $20,000. Also calculate it when the average tourist income is $30,000.

b. Using the midpoint method, calculate the income elasticity of demand when the average tourist income increases from $20,000 to $30,000 when the price of a T-shirt is $4. Also calculate it when the price is $7.

9. A recent study determined the following elasticities for Volkswagen Beetles:

Price elasticity of demand = 2
Income elasticity of demand = 1.5

The supply of Beetles is elastic. Based on this information, are the following statements true or false? Explain your reasoning.

a. A 10% increase in the price of a Beetle will reduce the quantity demanded by 20%.

b. An increase in consumer income will increase the price and quantity sold of Beetles. Since price elasticity of demand is greater than 1, total revenue will go down.

10. In each of the following cases, do you think the price elasticity of supply is (i) perfectly elastic; (ii) perfectly inelastic; (iii) elastic, but not perfectly elastic; or (iv) inelastic, but not perfectly inelastic? Explain using a diagram.

a. An increase in demand this summer for luxury cruises leads to a huge jump in the sales price of a cabin on the Queen Mary.

b. The price of a kilowatt of electricity is the same during periods of high electricity demand as during periods of low electricity demand.

c. Fewer people want to fly during February than during any other month. The airlines cancel about 10% of their flights as ticket prices fall about 20% during this month.

d. Owners of vacation homes in Maine rent them out during the summer. Due to the soft economy this year, a 30% decline in the price of a vacation rental leads more than half of homeowners to occupy their vacation homes themselves during the summer.

11. Use an elasticity concept to explain each of the following observations.

a. During economic boom times, the number of new personal care businesses, such as gyms and tanning salons, is proportionately greater than the number of other new businesses, such as grocery stores.

b. Cement is the primary building material in Mexico. After new technology makes cement cheaper to produce, the supply curve for the Mexican cement industry becomes relatively flatter.

c. Some goods that were once considered luxuries, like a telephone, are now considered virtual necessities. As a result, the demand curve for telephone services has become steeper over time.

d. Consumers in a less developed country like Guatemala spend proportionately more of their income on equipment for producing things at home, like sewing machines, than consumers in a more developed country like Canada.

12. Taiwan is a major world supplier of semiconductor chips. A recent earthquake severely damaged the production facilities of Taiwanese chip-producing companies, sharply reducing the amount of chips they could produce.

a. Assume that the total revenue of a typical non-Taiwanese chip manufacturer rises due to these events. In terms of an elasticity, what must be true for this to happen? Illustrate the change in total revenue with a diagram, indicating the price effect and the quantity effect of the Taiwan earthquake on this company's total revenue.

b. Now assume that the total revenue of a typical non-Taiwanese chip manufacturer falls due to these events. In terms of an elasticity, what must be true for this to happen? Illustrate the change in total revenue with a diagram, indicating the price effect and the quantity effect of the Taiwan earthquake on this company's total revenue.

13. There is a debate about whether sterile hypodermic needles should be passed out free of charge in cities with high drug use. Proponents argue that doing so will reduce the incidence of diseases, such as HIV/AIDS, that are often spread by needle sharing among drug users. Opponents believe that doing so will encourage more drug use by reducing the risks of this behavior. As an economist asked to assess the policy, you must know the following: (i) how responsive the spread of diseases like HIV/AIDS is to the price of sterile needles; and (ii) how responsive drug use is to the price of sterile needles. Assuming that you know these two things, use the concepts of price elasticity of demand for sterile needles and the cross-price elasticity between drugs and sterile needles to answer the following questions.

a. In what circumstances do you believe this is a beneficial policy?

b. In what circumstances do you believe this is a bad policy?

14. Suppose the government imposes an excise tax of $1 for every gallon of gas sold. Before the tax, the price of a gallon of gas is $2. Consider the following four after-tax scenarios. In each case, (i) use an elasticity concept to explain what must be true for this scenario to arise; (ii) determine who bears relatively more of the burden of the tax, producers or consumers; and (iii) illustrate your answer with a diagram.

a. The price of gasoline paid by consumers rises to $3 per gallon. Assume that the demand curve is downward sloping.

b. The price paid by consumers remains at $2 per gallon after the tax is imposed. Assume that the supply curve is upward sloping.

c. The price of gasoline paid by consumers rises to $2.75.

d. The price of gasoline paid by consumers rises to $2.25.

15. Describe how the following events will affect the incidence of taxation—that is, after the event, will the tax fall more heavily on consumers or producers in comparison to before the event? Use the concept of elasticity to explain your answer.

   a. Sales of gasoline are taxed. Ethanol, a substitute for gasoline, becomes widely available.

   b. Sales of electricity to California residents are taxed. Regulations are introduced that make it much more difficult for California utility companies to divert supplies of electricity from the California market to markets in neighboring states like Nevada.

   c. Sales of electricity to California residents are taxed. Regulations are introduced that make it much easier for California utility companies to divert supplies of electricity from the California market to markets in neighboring states like Nevada.

   d. The sale of municipally provided water is taxed. Legislation is introduced that forbids the use of private sources of water such as wells and the diversion of rivers.

16. In devising taxes, there is often a debate about (i) who bears the burden of the tax and (ii) whether the tax achieves some desirable social goal, such as discouraging undesirable behavior by making it more expensive. In the case of cigarettes, smokers tend to be highly addicted and have lower income than the average nonsmoker. Taxes on cigarettes have historically had the effect of raising the price to consumers almost one for one with the size of the tax.

   a. Why might such a tax be undesirable when considering issues of tax equity—that is, whether or not the tax burden falls more heavily on lower-income people? How do the price elasticities of supply and demand for cigarettes affect the equity of cigarette taxation?

   b. How do the price elasticities of supply and demand for cigarettes affect the effectiveness of the tax in discouraging smoking?

   c. In light of your answers to parts a and b and the historical response of price to the tax, what trade-offs must policy makers make when considering a cigarette tax?

17. Worldwide, the average coffee grower has increased the amount of acreage under cultivation over the past few years. The result has been that the average coffee plantation produces significantly more coffee than it did 10 to 20 years ago. Unfortunately for the growers, however, this has also been a period in which their total revenues have plunged. In terms of an elasticity, what must be true for these events to have occurred? Illustrate these events with a diagram, indicating the quantity effect and the price effect that gave rise to these events.

>**web**... To continue your study and review of concepts in this chapter, please visit the Krugman/Wells website for quizzes, animated graph tutorials, web links to helpful resources, and more.

www.worthpublishers.com/krugmanwells

>> Consumer and Producer Surplus

MAKING GAINS BY THE BOOK

T HERE IS A LIVELY MARKET IN SECOND-hand college textbooks. At the end of each term, some students who took a course decide that the money they can get by selling their used books is worth more to them than keeping the books. And some students who are taking the course next term prefer to buy a somewhat battered but inexpensive used textbook rather than pay the full price for a new one.

Textbook publishers and authors are not happy about these transactions, because they cut into sales of new books. But both the students who sell used books and those who buy them clearly benefit from the existence of the market. That is why many college bookstores facilitate their trade, buying used textbooks and selling them alongside the new books.

But can we put a number on what used textbook buyers and sellers gain from these transactions? Can we answer the question, "*How much* do the buyers and sellers of textbooks gain from the existence of the used-book market?"

Yes, we can. In this chapter we will see how to measure benefits, such as those to buyers of used textbooks, from being able to purchase a good—known as *consumer surplus*. And we will see that there is a corresponding measure, *producer surplus*, of the benefits sellers receive from being able to sell a good.

The concepts of consumer surplus and producer surplus are extremely useful for analyzing a wide variety of economic issues.

How much am I willing to pay for that used textbook?

They let us calculate how much benefit producers and consumers receive from the existence of a market. They also allow us to calculate how the welfare of consumers and producers is affected by changes in market

What you will learn in this chapter:

➤ The meaning of **consumer surplus** and its relationship to the demand curve

➤ The meaning of **producer surplus** and its relationship to the supply curve

➤ The meaning and importance of **total surplus** and how it can be used both to measure the gains from trade and to evaluate the efficiency of a market

➤ How to use changes in total surplus to measure the deadweight loss of taxes prices. Such calculations play a crucial role in evaluating many economic policies.

What information do we need to calculate consumer and producer surplus? The answer, surprisingly, is that all we need are the demand and supply curves for a good. That is, the supply and demand model isn't just a model of how a competitive market works—it's also a model of how much consumers and producers gain from participating in that market. So our first step will be to learn how consumer and producer surplus can be derived from the demand and supply curves. We will then see how these concepts can be applied to actual economic issues.

Consumer Surplus and the Demand Curve

The market in used textbooks is not a big business in terms of dollars and cents. But it is a convenient starting point for developing the concepts of consumer and producer surplus.

So let's look at the market for used textbooks, starting with the buyers. The key point, as we'll see in a minute, is that the demand curve is derived from their tastes or preferences—and that those same preferences also determine how much they gain from the opportunity to buy used books.

Willingness to Pay and the Demand Curve

A used book is not as good as a new book—it will be battered and coffee-stained, may include someone else's highlighting, and may not be completely up to date. How much this bothers you depends on your own preferences. Some potential buyers would prefer to buy the used book if it is only slightly cheaper than a new book, while others would buy the used book only if it is considerably cheaper. Let's define a potential buyer's **willingness to pay** as the maximum price at which he or she would buy a good, in this case a used textbook. An individual won't buy the book if it costs more than this amount but is eager to do so if it costs less. If the price is just equal to an individual's willingness to pay, he or she is indifferent between buying and not buying.

The table in Figure 6-1 shows five potential buyers of a used book that costs $100 new, listed in order of their willingness to pay. At one extreme is Aleisha, who will buy a second-hand book even if the price is as high as $59. Brad is less willing to have a used book and will buy one only if the price is $45 or less. Claudia is willing to pay only $35, Darren only $25. And Edwina, who really doesn't like the idea of a used book, will buy one only if it costs no more than $10.

How many of these five students will actually buy a used book? It depends on the price. If the price of a used book is $55, only Aleisha buys one; if the price is $40, Aleisha and Brad both buy used books, and so on. So the information in the table on willingness to pay also defines the *demand schedule* for used textbooks.

As we saw in Chapter 3, we can use this demand schedule to derive the market demand curve shown in Figure 6-1. Because we are considering only a small number of consumers, this curve doesn't look like the smooth demand curves of earlier chapters, where markets contained hundreds or thousands of consumers. This demand curve is step-shaped, with alternating horizontal and vertical segments. Each horizontal segment—each step—corresponds to one potential buyer's willingness to pay. However, we'll see shortly that for the analysis of consumer surplus it doesn't matter whether the demand curve is stepped, as in this figure, or whether there are many consumers, making the curve smooth.

A consumer's **willingness to pay** for a good is the maximum price at which he or she would buy that good.

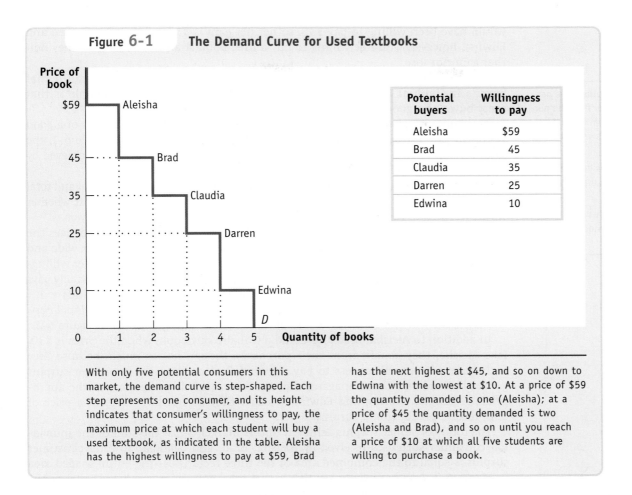

Figure 6-1   **The Demand Curve for Used Textbooks**

Potential buyers	Willingness to pay
Aleisha	$59
Brad	45
Claudia	35
Darren	25
Edwina	10

With only five potential consumers in this market, the demand curve is step-shaped. Each step represents one consumer, and its height indicates that consumer's willingness to pay, the maximum price at which each student will buy a used textbook, as indicated in the table. Aleisha has the highest willingness to pay at $59, Brad has the next highest at $45, and so on down to Edwina with the lowest at $10. At a price of $59 the quantity demanded is one (Aleisha); at a price of $45 the quantity demanded is two (Aleisha and Brad), and so on until you reach a price of $10 at which all five students are willing to purchase a book.

Willingness to Pay and Consumer Surplus

Suppose that the campus bookstore makes used textbooks available at a price of $30. In that case Aleisha, Brad, and Claudia will buy books. Do they gain from their purchases, and if so, how much?

The answer, shown in Table 6-1, is that each student who purchases a book does achieve a net gain but that the amount of the gain differs among students.

Aleisha would have been willing to pay $59, so her net gain is $59 – $30 = $29. Brad would have been willing to pay $45, so his net gain is $45 – $30 = $15. Claudia

TABLE 6-1

Consumer Surplus When the Price of a Used Textbook Is $30

Potential buyer	Willingness to pay	Price paid	Individual consumer surplus = willingness to pay – price paid
Aleisha	$59	$30	$29
Brad	45	30	15
Claudia	35	30	5
Darren	25	—	—
Edwina	10	—	—
		Total consumer surplus: $49	

would have been willing to pay $35, so her net gain is $35 − $30 = $5. Darren and Edwina, however, won't be willing to buy a used book at a price of $30, so they neither gain nor lose.

The net gain that a buyer achieves from the purchase of a good is called that buyer's **individual consumer surplus**. What we learn from this example is that every buyer of a good achieves some individual consumer surplus.

The sum of the individual consumer surpluses achieved by all the buyers of a good is known as the **total consumer surplus** achieved in the market. In Table 6-1, the total consumer surplus is the sum of the individual consumer surpluses achieved by Aleisha, Brad, and Claudia: $29 + $15 + $5 = $49.

Economists often use the term **consumer surplus** to refer to both individual and total consumer surplus. We will follow this practice; it will always be clear in context whether we are referring to the consumer surplus achieved by an individual or by all buyers.

Total consumer surplus can be represented graphically. Figure 6-2 reproduces the demand curve from Figure 6-1. Each step in that demand curve is one book wide and represents one consumer. For example, the height of Aleisha's step is $59, her willingness to pay. This step forms the top of a rectangle, with $30—the price she actually pays for a book—forming the bottom. The area of Aleisha's rectangle, ($59 − $30) × 1 = $29, is her consumer surplus from purchasing a book at $30. So the individual consumer surplus Aleisha gains is the *area of the dark blue rectangle* shown in Figure 6-2.

In addition to Aleisha, Brad and Claudia will also buy books when the price is $30. Like Aleisha, they benefit from their purchases, though not as much, because they each have a lower willingness to pay. Figure 6-2 also shows the consumer surplus gained by Brad and Claudia; again, this can be measured by the areas of the appropriate rectangles. Darren and Edwina, because they do not buy books at a price of $30, receive no consumer surplus.

The total consumer surplus achieved in this market is just the sum of the individual consumer surpluses received by Aleisha, Brad, and Claudia. So total consumer surplus is equal to the combined area of the three rectangles—the entire shaded area in Figure 6-2. Another way to say this is that total consumer surplus is equal to the area that is under the demand curve but above the price.

Individual consumer surplus is the net gain to an individual buyer from the purchase of a good. It is equal to the difference between the buyer's willingness to pay and the price paid.

Total consumer surplus is the sum of the individual consumer surpluses of all the buyers of a good.

The term **consumer surplus** is often used to refer to both individual and to total consumer surplus.

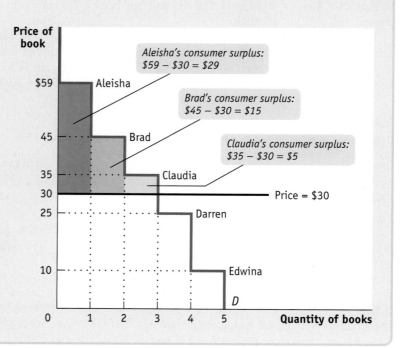

Figure 6-2

Consumer Surplus in the Used-Textbook Market

At a price of $30, Aleisha, Brad, and Claudia each buy a book but Darren and Edwina do not. Aleisha, Brad, and Claudia get individual consumer surpluses equal to the difference between their willingness to pay and the price, illustrated by the areas of the shaded rectangles. Both Darren and Edwina have a willingness to pay less than $30, so they are unwilling to buy a book in this market; they receive zero consumer surplus. The total consumer surplus is given by the entire shaded area—the sum of the individual consumer surpluses of Aleisha, Brad, and Claudia—equal to $29 + $15 + $5 = $49.

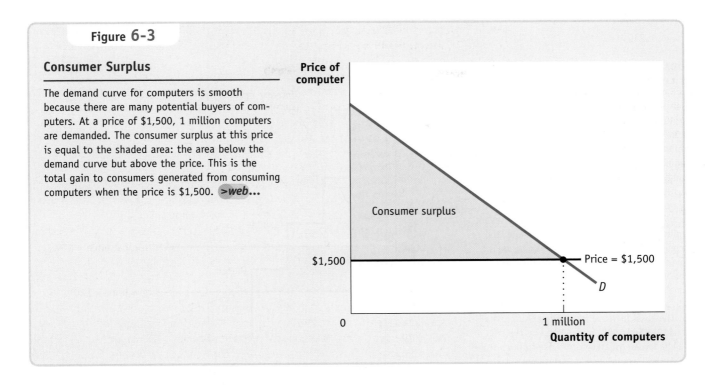

Figure 6-3

Consumer Surplus

The demand curve for computers is smooth because there are many potential buyers of computers. At a price of $1,500, 1 million computers are demanded. The consumer surplus at this price is equal to the shaded area: the area below the demand curve but above the price. This is the total gain to consumers generated from consuming computers when the price is $1,500. **>web...**

This illustrates the following general principle: *The total consumer surplus generated by purchases of a good at a given price is equal to the area below the demand curve but above that price.* The same principle applies regardless of the number of consumers.

When we consider large markets, this graphical representation becomes extremely helpful. Consider, for example, the sales of personal computers to millions of potential buyers. Each potential buyer has a maximum price that he or she is willing to pay. With so many potential buyers, the demand curve will be smooth, like the one shown in Figure 6-3.

Suppose that at a price of $1,500, a total of 1 million computers are purchased. How much do consumers gain from being able to buy those 1 million computers? We could answer that question by calculating the consumer surplus of each individual buyer and then adding these numbers up to arrive at a total. But it is much easier just to look at Figure 6-3 and use the fact that the total consumer surplus is equal to the shaded area. As in our original example, consumer surplus is equal to the area below the demand curve but above the price.

How Changing Prices Affect Consumer Surplus

It is often important to know how much consumer surplus *changes* when the price changes. For example, we may want to know how much consumers are hurt if a frost in Florida drives up orange prices or how much consumers gain if the introduction of fish farming makes salmon less expensive. The same approach we have used to derive consumer surplus can be used to answer questions about how changes in prices affect consumers.

Let's return to the example of the market for used textbooks. Suppose that the bookstore decided to sell used textbooks for $20 instead of $30. How much would this increase consumer surplus?

The answer is illustrated in Figure 6-4 on page 140. As shown in the figure, there are two parts to the increase in consumer surplus. The first part, shaded dark blue, is the gain of those who would have bought books even at the higher price. Each of the students who would have bought books at $30—Aleisha, Brad, and Claudia—pays $10 less, and therefore each gains $10 in consumer surplus from the fall in price to

Figure 6-4

Consumer Surplus and a Fall in the Price of Used Textbooks

There are two parts to the increase in consumer surplus generated by a fall in price from $30 to $20. The first is given by the dark blue rectangle: each person who would have bought at the original price of $30—Aleisha, Brad, and Claudia—receives an increase in consumer surplus equal to the total fall in price, $10. So the area of the dark blue rectangle corresponds to an amount equal to 3 × $10 = $30. The second part is given by the light blue rectangle: the increase in consumer surplus for those who would *not* have bought at the original price of $30 but who buy at the new price of $20—namely, Darren. Darren's willingness to pay is $25, so he now receives consumer surplus of $5. The total increase in consumer surplus is 3 × $10 + $5 = $35, represented by the sum of the shaded areas. Likewise, a rise in price from $20 to $30 would decrease consumer surplus by an amount equal to the sum of the shaded areas.

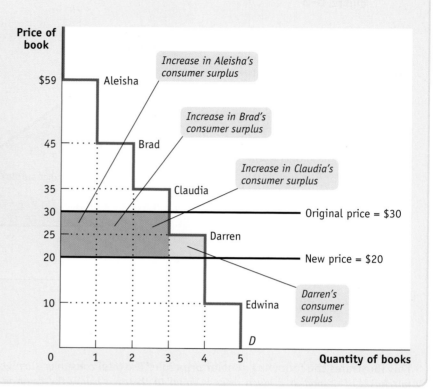

$20. So the dark blue area represents the $30 increase in consumer surplus to those three buyers. The second part, shaded light blue, is the gain to those who would not have bought a book at $30 but are willing to pay more than $20. In this case that means Darren, who would not have bought a book at $30 but does buy one at $20. He gains $5—the difference between his willingness to pay $25 and the new price of $20. So the light blue area represents a further $5 gain in consumer surplus. The total increase in consumer surplus is the sum of the shaded areas, $35. Likewise, a rise in price from $20 to $30 would decrease consumer surplus by an amount equal to the sum of the shaded areas.

Figure 6-4 illustrates that when the price of a good falls, the area under the demand curve but above the price—which we have seen is equal to the total consumer surplus—increases. Figure 6-5 shows the same result for the case of a smooth demand curve, the demand for personal computers. Here we assume that the price of computers falls from $5,000 to $1,500, leading to an increase in the quantity demanded from 200,000 to 1 million units. As in the used-textbook example, we divide the gain in consumer surplus into two parts. The dark blue rectangle in Figure 6-5 corresponds to the dark blue area in Figure 6-4: it is the gain to the 200,000 people who would have bought computers even at the higher price of $5,000. As a result of the price fall, each receives additional surplus of $3,500. The light blue triangle in Figure 6-5 corresponds to the light blue area in Figure 6-4: it is the gain to people who would not have bought the good at the higher price but are willing to do so at a price of $1,500. For example, the light blue triangle includes the gain to someone who would have been willing to pay $2,000 for a computer and therefore gains $500 in consumer surplus when he or she is able to buy a computer for only $1,500. As before, the total gain in consumer surplus is the sum of the shaded areas, the increase in the area under the demand curve but above the price.

What would happen if the price of a good were to rise instead of fall? We would do the same analysis in reverse. Suppose, for example, that for some reason the price

Figure 6-5

A Fall in the Price Increases Consumer Surplus

A fall in the price of a computer from $5,000 to $1,500 leads to an increase in the quantity demanded and an increase in consumer surplus. The change in total consumer surplus is given by the sum of the shaded areas: the total area below the demand curve but between the old and new prices. Here, the dark blue area represents the increase in consumer surplus for the 200,000 consumers who would have bought a computer at the original price of $5,000; they each receive an increase in consumer surplus of $3,500. The light blue area represents the increase in consumer surplus for those willing to buy at a price equal to or greater than $1,500 but less than $5,000. Similarly, a rise in the price of a computer from $1,500 to $5,000 generates a decrease in consumer surplus equal to the sum of the two shaded areas. **>web...**

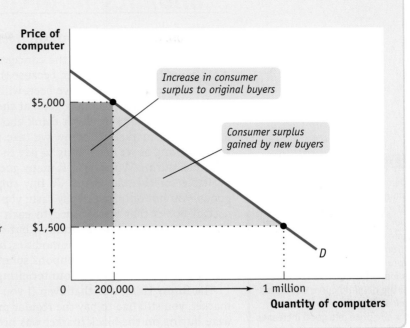

of computers rises from $1,500 to $5,000. This would lead to a fall in consumer surplus, equal to the shaded area in Figure 6-5. This loss consists of two parts. The dark blue rectangle represents the loss to consumers who would still buy a computer, even at a price of $5,000. The light blue triangle represents the loss to consumers who decide not to buy a computer at the higher price.

FOR INQUIRING MINDS

I WANT A NEW DRUG . . .

The pharmaceutical industry is constantly introducing new prescription drugs. Some of these drugs do the same thing as other, existing drugs, but a bit better—for example, pretty good allergy medicines have been around for years, but newer versions that are somewhat more effective or have fewer side effects keep emerging. Other drugs do something that was previously considered impossible—a famous example from the late 1990s was Propecia, the pill that slows and in some cases reverses hair loss.

Such innovations raise a difficult question for the people who are supposed to measure economic growth: how do you calculate the contribution of a new product to the economy?

You might at first say that it's just a matter of dollars and cents. But that could be wrong, in either direction. A new painkiller that is just slightly better than aspirin might have huge sales, because it would take over the painkiller market—but it wouldn't really add much to

consumer welfare. On the other hand, the benefits of a drug that cures the previously incurable might be much larger than the money actually spent on it—after all, people *would have been willing* to pay much more.

Consider, for example, the benefits of antibiotics. When penicillin was introduced in 1941, it transformed the treatment of infectious disease; illnesses that had previously crippled or killed millions of people were suddenly easy to treat. Presumably most people would be willing to pay a lot not to go back to the days before penicillin. Yet the average American spends only a few dollars per year on antibiotics.

The right way to measure the gains from a new drug—or any new product—is therefore to try to figure out what people would have been willing to pay for the good, and subtract what they actually pay. In other words, the gains from a new drug should be measured by calculating consumer surplus!

economics in action

When Money Isn't Enough

The key insight we get from the concept of consumer surplus is that purchases yield a net benefit to the consumer, because the consumer pays a price that is less than the amount he or she would have been willing to pay for the good. Another way to say this is that the right to buy a good at the going price is a valuable thing in itself.

Most of the time we don't think about the value associated with the right to buy a good. In a market economy, we take it for granted that we can buy whatever we want, as long as we are willing to pay the price. But that hasn't always been true. For example, during World War II many goods were rationed in order to make resources available for the war effort. To buy sugar, meat, coffee, gasoline, and many other goods, you not only had to pay cash; you also had to present stamps or coupons from special books that were issued to each family by the government. These pieces of paper, which represented nothing but the right to buy goods at the market price, quickly became valuable commodities in themselves. As a result, black markets in meat stamps and gasoline coupons sprang into existence. Moreover, criminals began stealing coupons and even counterfeiting stamps.

The funny thing was that even if you had bought a gasoline coupon on the black market, you still had to pay the regular price of gasoline to fill your tank. So what you were buying on the black market was not the good but *the right to buy the good*—that is, people who bought ration coupons on the black market were paying for the right to get some consumer surplus. ∎

< < < < < < < < < < < < < < < < < < <

>>CHECK YOUR UNDERSTANDING 6-1

1. Consider the market for cheese-stuffed jalapeno peppers. There are two consumers, Casey and Josie, and their willingness to pay for each pepper is given in the accompanying table. Use the table (i) to construct the demand schedule for peppers for prices of $0.00, $0.10, and so on, up to $0.90; and (ii) to calculate the total consumer surplus when the price of a pepper is $0.40.

Quantity of peppers	Casey's willingness to pay	Josie's willingness to pay
1st pepper	$0.90	$0.80
2nd pepper	0.70	0.60
3rd pepper	0.50	0.40
4th pepper	0.30	0.30

Solutions appear at back of book.

Producer Surplus and the Supply Curve

Just as buyers of a good would have been willing to pay more for their purchase than the price they actually pay, sellers of a good would have been willing to sell it for less than the price they actually receive. We can therefore carry out an analysis of producer surplus and the supply curve that is almost exactly parallel to that of consumer surplus and the demand curve.

Cost and Producer Surplus

Consider a group of students who are potential sellers of used textbooks. Because they have different preferences, the various potential sellers differ in the price at which they are willing to sell their books. The table in Figure 6-6 shows the prices at which several different students would be willing to sell. Andrew is willing to sell the book as long as he can get anything more than $5; Betty won't sell unless she can get at least $15; Carlos, unless he can get $25; Donna, unless she can get $35; Engelbert, unless he can get $45.

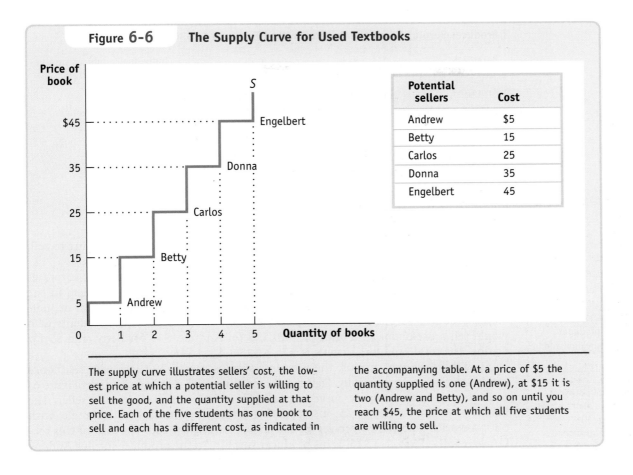

Figure 6-6   The Supply Curve for Used Textbooks

Potential sellers	Cost
Andrew	$5
Betty	15
Carlos	25
Donna	35
Engelbert	45

The supply curve illustrates sellers' cost, the lowest price at which a potential seller is willing to sell the good, and the quantity supplied at that price. Each of the five students has one book to sell and each has a different cost, as indicated in the accompanying table. At a price of $5 the quantity supplied is one (Andrew), at $15 it is two (Andrew and Betty), and so on until you reach $45, the price at which all five students are willing to sell.

The lowest price at which a potential seller is willing to sell has a special name in economics: it is called the seller's **cost**. So Andrew's cost is $5, Betty's is $15, and so on.

Using the term *cost*, which people normally associate with the monetary cost of producing a good, may sound a little strange when applied to sellers of used textbooks. The students don't have to manufacture the books, so it doesn't cost the student who sells a book anything to make that book available for sale, does it?

Yes, it does. A student who sells a book won't have it later, as part of a personal collection. So there is an *opportunity cost* to selling a textbook, even if the owner has completed the course for which it was required. And remember that one of the basic principles of economics is that the true measure of the cost of doing anything is always its opportunity cost—the real cost of something is what you must give up to get it.

So it is good economics to talk of the minimum price at which someone will sell a good as the "cost" of selling that good, even if he or she doesn't spend any money to make the good available for sale. Of course, in most real-world markets the sellers are also those who produce the good—and therefore *do* spend money to make the good available for sale. In this case the cost of making the good available for sale *includes* monetary costs—but it may also include other opportunity costs.

Getting back to the example, suppose that Andrew sells his book for $30. Clearly he has gained from the transaction: he would have been willing to sell for only $5, so he has gained $25. This gain, the difference between the price he actually gets and his cost—the minimum price at which he would have been willing to sell—is known as his **individual producer surplus.**

Just as we derived the demand curve from the willingness to pay of different consumers, we can derive the supply curve from the cost of different producers. The step-shaped curve in Figure 6-6 shows the supply curve implied by the costs shown in the

> A potential seller's **cost** is the lowest price at which he or she is willing to sell a good.

> **Individual producer surplus** is the net gain to a seller from selling a good. It is equal to the difference between the price received and the seller's cost.

TABLE 6-2

Producer Surplus When the Price of a Used Textbook Is $30

Potential seller	Cost	Price received	Individual producer surplus = price received − cost
Andrew	$5	$30	$25
Betty	15	30	15
Carlos	25	30	5
Donna	35	—	—
Engelbert	45	—	—
			Total producer surplus: $45

accompanying table. At a price less than $5, none of the students are willing to sell; at a price between $5 and $15, only Andrew is willing to sell, and so on.

As in the case of consumer surplus, we can add the individual producer surpluses of sellers to calculate the **total producer surplus**, the total gains to sellers in the market. Economists use the term **producer surplus** to refer to either total or individual producer surplus. Table 6-2 shows the net gain to each of the students who would sell a used book at a price of $30: $25 for Andrew, $15 for Betty, and $5 for Carlos. The total producer surplus is $25 + $15 + $5 = $45.

As with consumer surplus, the producer surplus gained by those who sell books can be represented graphically. Figure 6-7 reproduces the supply curve from Figure 6-6. Each step in that supply curve is one book wide and represents one seller. The height of Andrew's step is $5, his cost. This forms the bottom of a rectangle, with $30, the price he actually receives for his book, forming the top. The area of this rectangle, ($30 − $5) × 1 = $25, is his producer surplus. So the producer surplus Andrew gains from selling his book is the *area of the dark red rectangle* shown in the figure.

Let's assume that the campus bookstore is willing to buy all the used copies of this book that students are willing to sell at a price of $30. Then, in addition to Andrew, Betty and Carlos will also sell their books. They will also benefit from their sales, though not as much as Andrew, because they have higher costs. Andrew, as we have

> **Total producer surplus** in a market is the sum of the individual producer surpluses of all the sellers of a good. Economists use the term **producer surplus** to refer both to individual and to total producer surplus.

Figure 6-7

Producer Surplus in the Used-Textbook Market

At a price of $30, Andrew, Betty, and Carlos each sell a book but Donna and Engelbert do not. Andrew, Betty, and Carlos get individual producer surpluses equal to the difference between the price and their cost, illustrated here by the shaded rectangles. Donna and Engelbert each have a cost that is greater than the price of $30, so they are unwilling to sell a book and therefore receive zero producer surplus. The total producer surplus is given by the entire shaded area, the sum of the individual producer surpluses of Andrew, Betty, and Carlos, equal to $25 + $15 + $5 = $45.

Figure **6-8**

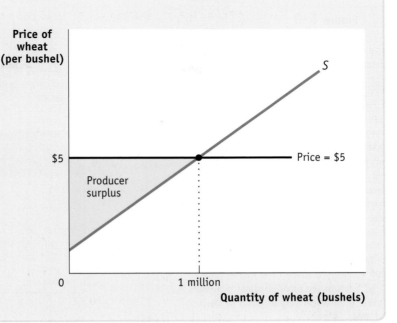

Producer Surplus

Here is the supply curve for wheat. At a price of $5 per bushel, farmers supply 1 million bushels. The producer surplus at this price is equal to the shaded area: the area above the supply curve but below the price. This is the total gain to producers—farmers in this case—from supplying their product when the price is $5. **>web...**

seen, gains $25. Betty gains a smaller amount: since her cost is $15, she gains only $15. Carlos gains even less, only $5.

Again, as with consumer surplus, we have a general rule for determining the total producer surplus from sales of a good: *The total producer surplus from sales of a good at a given price is the area above the supply curve but below that price.*

This rule applies both to examples like the one shown in Figure 6-7, where there are a small number of producers and a step-shaped supply curve, and to more realistic examples where there are many producers and the supply curve is more or less smooth.

Consider, for example, the supply of wheat. Figure 6-8 shows how producer surplus depends on the price per bushel. Suppose that, as shown in the figure, the price is $5 per bushel and farmers supply 1 million bushels. What is the benefit to the farmers from selling their wheat at a price of $5? Their producer surplus is equal to the shaded area in the figure—the area above the supply curve but below the price of $5 per bushel.

Changes in Producer Surplus

If the price of a good rises, producers of the good will experience an increase in producer surplus, though not all producers gain the same amount. Some producers would have produced the good even at the original price; they will gain the entire price increase on every unit they produce. Other producers will enter the market because of the higher price; they will gain only the difference between the new price and their cost.

Figure 6-9 on page 146 is the supply counterpart of Figure 6-5. It shows the effect on producer surplus of a rise in the price of wheat from $5 to $7 per bushel. The increase in producer surplus is the entire shaded area, which consists of two parts. First, there is a red rectangle corresponding to the gains to those farmers who would have supplied wheat even at the original $5 price. Second, there is an additional pink triangle that corresponds to the gains to those farmers who would not have supplied wheat at the original price but are drawn into the market by the higher price.

If the price were to fall from $7 to $5 per bushel, the story would run in reverse. The whole shaded area would now be the decline in producer surplus, the fall in the area above the supply curve but below the price. The loss would consist of two parts, the loss to farmers who would still grow wheat at a price of $5 (the red rectangle) and the loss to farmers who decide not to grow wheat because of the lower price (the pink triangle).

Figure 6-9

A Rise in the Price Increases Producer Surplus

A rise in the price of wheat from $5 to $7 leads to an increase in the quantity supplied and an increase in producer surplus. The change in total producer surplus is given by the sum of the shaded areas: the total area above the supply curve but between the old and new prices. The red area represents the gain to the farmers who would have supplied 1 million bushels at the original price of $5; they each receive an increase in producer surplus of $2 for each of those bushels. The triangular pink area represents the increase in producer surplus achieved by the farmers who supply the additional 500,000 bushels because of the higher price. Similarly, a fall in the price of wheat generates a decrease in producer surplus equal to the shaded areas. **>web...**

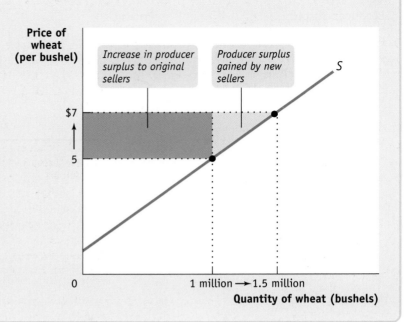

economics in action

Gaining from Disaster

In 1992 Hurricane Andrew swept through Florida, destroying thousands of homes and businesses. The state quickly began rebuilding, with the help of thousands of construction workers who moved temporarily to Florida to help out.

These construction workers were not motivated mainly by sympathy for Florida residents. They were lured by the high wages available there—and took home billions of dollars.

But how much did the temporary workers actually gain? Certainly we should not count all the money they earned in Florida as a net benefit. For one thing, most of these workers would have earned something—though not as much—if they had stayed home. In addition to this opportunity cost, the temporary move to Florida had other costs: the expense of motel rooms and of transportation, the wear and tear of being away from families and friends.

Clearly the workers viewed the benefits as being larger than the costs—otherwise they wouldn't have gone down to Florida in the first place. But the producer surplus earned by those temporary workers was much less than the money they earned. ■

< < < < < < < < < < < < < < < < < < <

>>CHECK YOUR UNDERSTANDING 6-2

1. Consider the market for cheese-stuffed jalapeno peppers. There are two producers, Cara and Jamie, and their costs of producing each pepper are given in the accompanying table. Use the table (i) to construct the supply schedule for peppers for prices of $0.00, $0.10, and so on, up to $0.90; and (ii) to calculate the total producer surplus when the price of a pepper is $0.70.

Solutions appear at back of book.

Quantity of peppers	Cara's cost	Jamie's cost
1st pepper	$0.10	$0.30
2nd pepper	0.10	0.50
3rd pepper	0.40	0.70
4th pepper	0.60	0.90

>>QUICK REVIEW

➤ The supply curve for a good is determined by the *cost* of each potential seller.

➤ The difference between the price and cost is the seller's *individual producer surplus*.

➤ The *total producer surplus* is equal to the area above the supply curve but below the price.

➤ When the price of a good rises, producer surplus increases through two channels: the gains of those who would have supplied the good even at the original, lower price and the gains of those who are induced to supply the good by the higher price. A fall in the price of a good similarly leads to a fall in producer surplus.

Consumer Surplus, Producer Surplus, and the Gains from Trade

One of the nine core principles of economics we introduced in Chapter 1 is that markets are a remarkably effective way to organize economic activity: they generally make society as well off as possible given the available resources. The concepts of consumer surplus and producer surplus can help us deepen our understanding of why this is so.

The Gains from Trade

Let's go back to the market in used textbooks but now consider a much bigger market—say, one at a large state university—where there are many potential buyers and sellers. Let's line up incoming students—who are potential buyers of the book—in order of their willingness to pay, so that the entering student with the highest willingness to pay is potential buyer number 1, the student with the next highest willingness to pay is number 2, and so on. Then we can use their willingness to pay to derive a demand curve like the one in Figure 6-10. Similarly, we can line up outgoing students, who are potential sellers of the book, in order of their cost, starting with the student with the lowest cost, then the student with the next lowest cost, and so on, to derive a supply curve like the one shown in the same figure.

As we have drawn the curves, the market reaches equilibrium at a price of $30 per book, and 1,000 books are bought and sold at that price. The two shaded triangles show the consumer surplus (blue) and the producer surplus (red) generated by this market. The sum of consumer and producer surplus is known as the **total surplus** generated in a market.

The striking thing about this picture is that both consumers and producers gain—that is, both consumers and producers are better off because there is a market in this good. But this should come as no surprise—it illustrates another core principle of economics: there are *gains from trade*. These gains from trade are the reason everyone is better off participating in a market economy than they would be if each individual tried to be self-sufficient.

But are we as well off as we could be? This brings us to the question of the efficiency of markets.

> The **total surplus** generated in a market is the total net gain to consumers and producers from trading in the market. It is the sum of the producer and the consumer surplus.

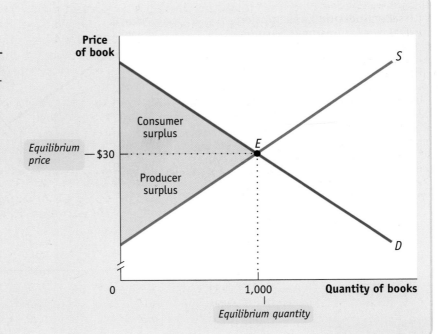

Figure 6-10

Total Surplus

In the market for used textbooks, the equilibrium price is $30 and the equilibrium quantity is 1,000 books. Consumer surplus is given by the blue area, the area below the demand curve but above the price. Producer surplus is given by the red area, the area above the supply curve but below the price. The sum of the blue and the red areas is total surplus, the total benefit to society from the production and consumption of the good. **>web...**

The Efficiency of Markets: A Preliminary View

Markets produce gains from trade, but in Chapter 1 we made a bigger claim: that markets are usually *efficient*. That is, we claimed that once the market has produced its gains from trade, there is usually no way to make some people better off without making others worse off (with some well-defined exceptions).

We're not yet ready to carry out a full discussion of the efficiency of markets—that will have to wait until we've looked in more detail at the behavior of producers and consumers. However, we can get an intuitive sense of the efficiency of markets by noticing a key feature of the market equilibrium shown in Figure 6-10: the maximum possible total surplus is achieved at market equilibrium. That is, the market equilibrium allocates the consumption of the good among potential consumers and sales of the good among potential sellers in a way that achieves the highest possible gain to society.

How do we know this? By comparing the total surplus generated by the consumption and production choices in the market equilibrium to the surplus generated by a different set of production and consumption choices. We can show that any change from the market equilibrium reduces total surplus.

Let's consider three ways in which you might try to increase the total surplus:

1. *Reallocate consumption among consumers*—take the good away from buyers who would have purchased the good in the market equilibrium, and instead give it to potential consumers who would not have bought it in equilibrium.

2. *Reallocate sales among sellers*—take sales away from sellers who would have sold the good in the market equilibrium, and instead compel potential sellers who would not have sold the good in equilibrium to sell it.

3. *Change the quantity traded*—compel consumers and producers to transact either more or less than the equilibrium quantity.

It turns out that each of these actions will not only fail to increase the total surplus; in fact, each will reduce the total surplus.

Figure 6-11 shows why reallocating consumption of the good among consumers will reduce the total surplus. Points *A* and *B* show the positions on the demand curve of two potential buyers of a used book, Ana and Bob. As we can see from the figure,

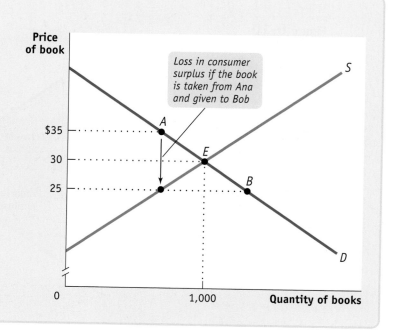

Figure 6-11

Reallocating Consumption Lowers Consumer Surplus

Ana (point *A*) has a willingness to pay of $35. Bob (point *B*) has a willingness to pay of only $25. At the market equilibrium price of $30, Ana purchases a book but Bob does not. If we rearrange consumption by taking a book from Ana and giving it to Bob, consumer surplus declines by $10 and, as a result, total surplus declines by $10. The market equilibrium generates the highest possible consumer surplus by ensuring that those who consume the good are those who value it the most. >*web*...

Ana is willing to pay $35 for a book, but Bob is willing to pay only $25. Since the equilibrium price is $30, Ana buys a book and Bob does not.

Now suppose that we try to reallocate consumption. This would mean taking a book away from somebody who *would* have bought one at the equilibrium price of $30, like Ana, and giving that book to someone who would *not* have bought at that price, like Bob. But since the book is worth $35 to Ana, but only $25 to Bob, this would *reduce total consumer surplus* by $35 − $25 = $10.

This result doesn't depend on which two students we pick. Every student who buys a book in equilibrium has a willingness to pay that is *more* than $30, and every student who doesn't buy a book has a willingness to pay that is *less* than $30. So reallocating the good among consumers always means taking a book away from a student who values it more and giving it to a student who values it less, which necessarily reduces consumer surplus.

A similar argument, illustrated by Figure 6-12, holds for producer surplus. Here points *X* and *Y* show the positions on the supply curve of Xavier, who has a cost of $25, and Yvonne, who has a cost of $35. At the equilibrium price of $30, Xavier would sell his book but Yvonne would not. If we reallocated sales, forcing Xavier to keep his book and forcing Yvonne to give up hers, total producer surplus would be reduced by $35 − $25 = $10. Again, it doesn't matter which two students we choose. Any student who sells a book in equilibrium has a lower cost than any student who does not, so reallocating sales among sellers necessarily increases total cost and reduces producer surplus. In this way the market equilibrium generates the highest possible producer surplus: it ensures that those who sell their books are those who most value the right to sell them.

Finally, changing the quantity bought and sold reduces the sum of producer and consumer surplus. Figure 6-13 on page 150 shows all four students: potential buyers Ana and Bob, and potential sellers Xavier and Yvonne. To reduce sales, we would have to prevent someone like Xavier, who would have sold the book in equilibrium, from making the sale; and the book would then not be made available to someone like Ana who would have bought it in equilibrium. As we've seen, however, Ana would be willing to pay $35, but Xavier's cost is only $25. So preventing this sale would reduce total surplus by $35 − $25 = $10. Once again, this result doesn't depend on which two students we pick: any student who would have sold the book in equilibrium has

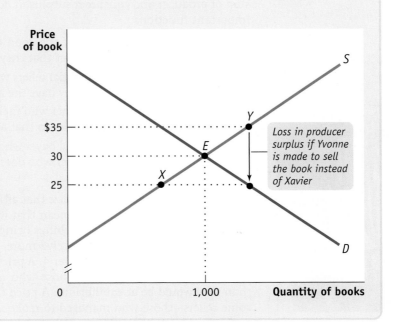

Figure 6-12

Reallocating Sales Lowers Producer Surplus

Yvonne (point *Y*) has a cost of $35, $10 more than Xavier (point *X*) who has a cost of $25. At the market equilibrium price of $30, Xavier sells a book, but Yvonne does not. If we rearrange sales by preventing Xavier from selling his book and compelling Yvonne to sell hers, producer surplus declines by $10 and, as a result, total surplus declines by $10. The market equilibrium generates the highest possible producer surplus by assuring that those who sell the good are those who value the right to sell it the most. **>web...**

Loss in producer surplus if Yvonne is made to sell the book instead of Xavier

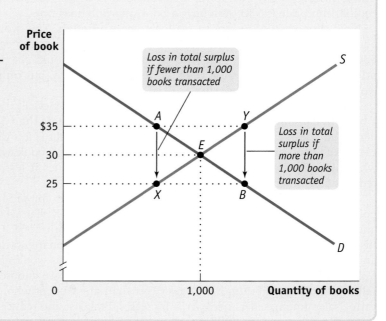

Figure 6-13

Changing the Quantity Lowers Total Surplus

If Xavier (point *X*) were prevented from selling his book to someone like Ana (point *A*), total surplus would fall by $10, the difference between Ana's willingness to pay ($35) and Xavier's cost ($25). This means that total surplus falls whenever fewer than 1,000 books— the equilibrium quantity—are transacted. Likewise, if Yvonne (point *Y*) were compelled to sell her book to someone like Bob (point *B*), total surplus would also fall by $10, the difference between Yvonne's cost ($35) and Bob's willingness to pay ($25). This means that total surplus falls whenever more than 1,000 books are transacted. These two examples show that at market equilibrium, all beneficial transactions—and only beneficial transactions—occur.

a cost of *less* than $30, and any student who would have purchased the book in equilibrium would be willing to pay *more* than $30, so preventing any sale that would have taken place in equilibrium reduces total surplus.

Finally, to increase sales would mean forcing someone like Yvonne, who would not have sold her book in equilibrium, to sell it, and giving it to someone like Bob, who would not have bought a book in equilibrium. Because Yvonne's cost is $35 but Bob is only willing to pay $25, this reduces total surplus by $10. And once again it doesn't matter which two students we pick—anyone who wouldn't have bought the book is willing to pay less than $30, and anyone who wouldn't have sold has a cost of more than $30.

What we have shown is that the market equilibrium maximizes total surplus—the sum of producer and consumer surplus. It does this because the market performs four important functions:

1. It allocates consumption of the good to the potential buyers who value it the most, as indicated by the fact that they have the highest willingness to pay.

2. It allocates sales to the potential sellers who most value the right to sell the good, as indicated by the fact that they have the lowest cost.

3. It ensures that every consumer who makes a purchase values the good more than every seller who makes a sale, so that all transactions are mutually beneficial.

4. It ensures that every potential buyer who doesn't make a purchase values the good less than every potential seller who doesn't make a sale, so that no mutually beneficial transactions are missed.

A caveat: it's important to realize that although the market equilibrium maximizes the total surplus, this does not mean that it is the best outcome for every individual consumer and producer. Other things being equal, each buyer would like to pay less and each seller would like to receive more. So some people would benefit from the price controls discussed in Chapter 4. A price ceiling that held down the market price would leave some consumers—those who managed to make a purchase—better off than they would be at equilibrium. A price floor that kept the price up would benefit some sellers—those who managed to make a sale.

But in the market equilibrium there is no way to make some people better off without making others worse off—and that's the definition of efficiency.

Maximizing total surplus at your local hardware store.

A Few Words of Caution

Markets are an amazingly effective way to organize economic activity; we've just demonstrated that, under certain conditions, a market is actually efficient—there is literally no way to make some people better off without making others worse off.

But how secure is this result? Are markets really that good?

The answer is "not always." As we discussed briefly in Chapter 1 in our ninth and final principle of economics (*when markets don't achieve efficiency, government intervention can improve society's welfare*), markets can fail to be efficient for a number of reasons. When a market is not efficient, we have what is known as a case of **market failure**. We will examine various causes of *market failure* in depth in later chapters; for now, let's review the three main reasons why markets sometimes fall short of efficiency in reality.

First, markets can fail when, in an attempt to capture more resources, one party prevents mutually beneficial trades from occurring. This situation arises, for instance, when a market contains only a single seller of a good, known as a *monopolist*. In this case, the assumption we have relied on in supply and demand analysis—that no individual buyer and seller can have a noticeable effect on the market price—is no longer valid; the monopolist can determine the market price. As we'll see in Chapter 14, this gives rise to inefficiency as a monopolist manipulates the market price in order to increase profits, thereby preventing mutually beneficial trades from occurring.

Second, actions of individuals sometimes have *side effects* on the welfare of other individuals that markets don't take into account. The best-known example of such an *externality* is pollution. We'll see in Chapter 19 that pollution and other externalities also give rise to inefficiency.

Third, markets for some goods can fail because these goods, by their very nature, are unsuited for efficient management by markets. In Chapter 18 we will analyze goods that fall into this category because of problems of *private information*—information about a good that some people possess but others don't. In Chapter 20, we will encounter other types of goods that fall into this category—*public goods*, *common resources*, and *artificially scarce goods*. These are goods for which markets fail because of problems in limiting people's access to and consumption of the good. And in Chapter 22 we will learn about *information goods:* goods like a downloaded tune, that are costly to create but, once created, cost nothing to consume.

But even with these caveats, it's remarkable how well markets work at maximizing the gains from trade.

> **Market failure** occurs when a market fails to be efficient.

economics in action

eBay and Efficiency

Garage sales are an old American tradition: they are a way for families to sell items they don't want to other families that have some use for them, to the benefit of both parties. But many potentially beneficial trades were missed. For all Mr. Smith knew, there was someone 1,000 miles away who would really have loved that 1930s gramophone he had in the basement; for all Ms. Jones knew, there was someone 1,000 miles away who had that 1930s gramophone she had always wanted. But there was no way for Mr. Smith and Ms. Jones to find each other.

Enter eBay, the online auction service. eBay was founded in 1995 by Pierre Omidyar, a programmer whose fiancée was a collector of Pez candy dispensers and wanted a way to find potential sellers. The company, which says that its mission is "to help practically anyone trade practically anything on earth," provides a way for would-be buyers and would-be sellers of unique or used items to find each other, even if they don't live in the same neighborhood or even the same city.

"I got it from eBay"

The potential gains from trade were evidently large: in 2003, 95 million people were registered by eBay, and in the same year almost $24 billion in goods were bought and sold using the service. The Omidyars now possess a large collection of Pez dispensers. They are also billionaires. ■

< < < < < < < < < < < < < < < < < < <

>>CHECK YOUR UNDERSTANDING 6-3

1. Using the tables in Check Your Understanding 6-1 and 6-2, find the equilibrium price and quantity in the market for cheese-stuffed jalapeno peppers. What is total surplus in the equilibrium in this market, and who receives it?

2. Show how each of the following three actions reduces total surplus:
   a. Having Josie consume one less pepper, and Casey one more pepper, than in the market equilibrium
   b. Having Cara produce one less pepper, and Jamie one more pepper, than in the market equilibrium
   c. Having Josie consume one less pepper, and Cara produce one less pepper, than in the market equilibrium

Solutions appear at back of book.

Applying Consumer and Producer Surplus: The Efficiency Costs of a Tax

The concepts of consumer and producer surplus are extremely useful in many economic applications. Among the most important of these is assessing the efficiency cost of taxation.

In Chapter 4 we introduced the concept of an *excise tax*, a tax on the purchase or sale of a good. We saw that such a tax drives a *wedge* between the price paid by consumers and that received by producers: the price paid by consumers rises, and the price received by producers falls, with the difference equal to the tax per unit. The *incidence* of the tax—how much of the burden falls on consumers, how much on producers—does not depend on who actually writes the check to the government. Instead, as we saw in Chapter 5, the burden of the tax depends on the price elasticities of supply and demand: the higher the price elasticity of demand, the greater the burden on producers; the higher the price elasticity of supply, the greater the burden on consumers.

We also learned that there is an additional cost of a tax, over and above the money actually paid to the government. A tax causes a *deadweight loss* to society, because less of the good is produced and consumed than in the absence of the tax. As a result, some mutually beneficial trades between producers and consumers do not take place.

Now we can complete the picture, because the concepts of consumer and producer surplus are what we need to pin down precisely the deadweight loss that an excise tax imposes.

Figure 6-14 shows the effects of an excise tax on consumer and producer surplus. In the absence of the tax, the equilibrium is at E, and the equilibrium price and quantity are P_E and Q_E, respectively. An excise tax drives a wedge equal to the amount of the tax between the price received by producers and the price paid by consumers, reducing the quantity bought and sold. In this case, where the tax is T dollars per unit, the quantity bought and sold falls to Q_T. The price paid by consumers rises to P_C, the demand price of the reduced quantity, Q_T, and the price received by producers falls to P_P, the supply price of that quantity. The difference between these prices, $P_C - P_P$, is equal to the excise tax, T.

What we can now do, using the concepts of producer and consumer surplus, is show exactly how much surplus producers and consumers lose as a result of the tax.

We saw earlier, in Figure 6-5, that a fall in the price of a good generates a gain in consumer surplus that is equal to the sum of the areas of a rectangle and a triangle. A price increase causes a loss to consumers that looks exactly the same. In the case of an excise tax, the rise in the price paid by consumers causes a loss equal to the sum

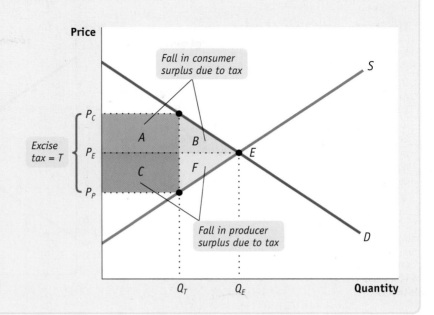

Figure 6-14

A Tax Reduces Consumer and Producer Surplus

Before the tax, the equilibrium price and quantity are P_E and Q_E, respectively. After an excise tax of T per unit is imposed, the price to consumers rises to P_C and consumer surplus falls by the sum of the dark blue rectangle, labeled A, and the light blue triangle, labeled B. The tax also causes the price to producers to fall to P_P; producer surplus falls by the sum of the red rectangle, labeled C, and the pink triangle, labeled F. The government receives revenue from the tax, $Q_T \times T$, which is given by the sum of the areas A and C. Areas B and F represent the losses to consumer and producer surplus that are not collected by the government as revenue; they are the deadweight loss to society of the tax. **>web...**

of the area of the dark blue rectangle labeled A and the area of the light blue triangle labeled B in Figure 6-14.

Meanwhile, the fall in the price received by producers causes a fall in producer surplus. This, too, is the sum of the areas of a rectangle and a triangle. The loss in producer surplus is the sum of the areas of the red rectangle labeled C and the pink triangle labeled F in Figure 6-14.

Of course, although consumers and producers are hurt by the tax, the government gains revenue. The revenue the government collects is equal to the tax per unit sold, T, multiplied by the quantity sold, Q_T. This revenue is equal to the area of a rectangle Q_T wide and T high. And we already have that rectangle in the figure: it is the sum of rectangles A and C. So the government gains part of what consumers and producers lose from an excise tax.

But there is a part of the loss to producers and consumers from the tax that is not offset by a gain to the government—specifically, the two triangles B and F. The deadweight loss caused by the tax is equal to the combined area of these triangles. It represents the total surplus that would have been generated by transactions that do not take place because of the tax.

Figure 6-15 on page 154 is a version of the same picture, leaving out the shaded rectangles—which represent money shifted from consumers and producers to the government—and showing only the deadweight loss, this time as a triangle shaded yellow. The base of that triangle is the tax wedge, T; the height of the triangle is the reduction the tax causes in the quantity sold, $Q_E - Q_T$. Notice that if the excise tax *didn't* reduce the quantity bought and sold in this market—if Q_T weren't less than Q_E—the deadweight loss represented by the yellow triangle would disappear. This observation ties in with the explanation given in Chapter 4 of why an excise tax generates a deadweight loss to society: the tax causes inefficiency because it discourages mutually beneficial transactions between buyers and sellers.

The idea that deadweight loss can be measured by the area of a triangle recurs in many economic applications. Deadweight-loss triangles are produced not only by excise taxes but also by other types of taxation. They are also produced by other kinds of distortions of markets, such as monopoly. And triangles are often used to evaluate other public policies besides taxation—for example, decisions about whether to build new highways.

Figure 6-15

The Deadweight Loss of a Tax

A tax leads to a deadweight loss because it creates inefficiency: some mutually beneficial transactions never take place because of the tax, namely the transactions $Q_E - Q_T$. The yellow area here represents the value of the deadweight loss: it is the total surplus that would have been gained from the $Q_E - Q_T$ transactions. If the tax had not discouraged transactions—had the number of transactions remained at Q_E—no deadweight loss would have been incurred.

>web...

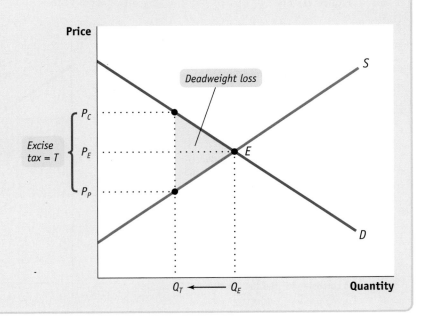

Deadweight Loss and Elasticities

The general rule for economic policy is that other things equal, you want to choose the policy that produces the smallest deadweight loss. This principle gives valuable guidance on everything from the design of the tax system to environmental policy. But how can we predict the size of the deadweight loss associated with a given policy? For the answer to that question, we return to a familiar concept: elasticity.

Deadweight Loss and Elasticities

The deadweight loss from an excise tax arises because it prevents some mutually beneficial transactions from occurring. In particular, the producer and consumer surplus that is forgone from these missing transactions is equal to the size of the deadweight loss itself. This means that the larger the number of transactions that are impeded by the tax, the larger the deadweight loss.

This gives us an important clue in understanding the relationship between elasticity and the size of the deadweight loss from a tax. Recall that when demand or supply is elastic, it means that the quantity demanded or the quantity supplied is relatively responsive to price. So a tax imposed on a good for which either demand or supply, or both, is elastic will cause a relatively large decrease in the quantity bought and sold and a large deadweight loss. And when we say that demand or supply is inelastic, we mean that the quantity demanded or the quantity supplied is relatively unresponsive to price. As a result, a tax imposed when demand or supply, or both, is inelastic will cause a relatively small decrease in the quantity bought and sold and a small deadweight loss.

The four panels of Figure 6-16 illustrate the positive relationship between price elasticity of either demand or supply and the deadweight loss of taxation. In each panel, the size of the deadweight loss is given by the area of the shaded triangle. In panel (a), the deadweight-loss triangle is large because demand is relatively elastic—a large number of transactions fail to occur because of the tax. In panel (b), the same supply curve is drawn as in panel (a), but demand is now relatively inelastic; as a result, the triangle is small because only a small number of transactions are forgone. Likewise, panels (c) and (d) contain the same demand curve but different supply curves. In panel (c), an elastic supply curve gives rise to a large deadweight-loss triangle, but in panel (d) an inelastic supply curve gives rise to a small deadweight-loss triangle.

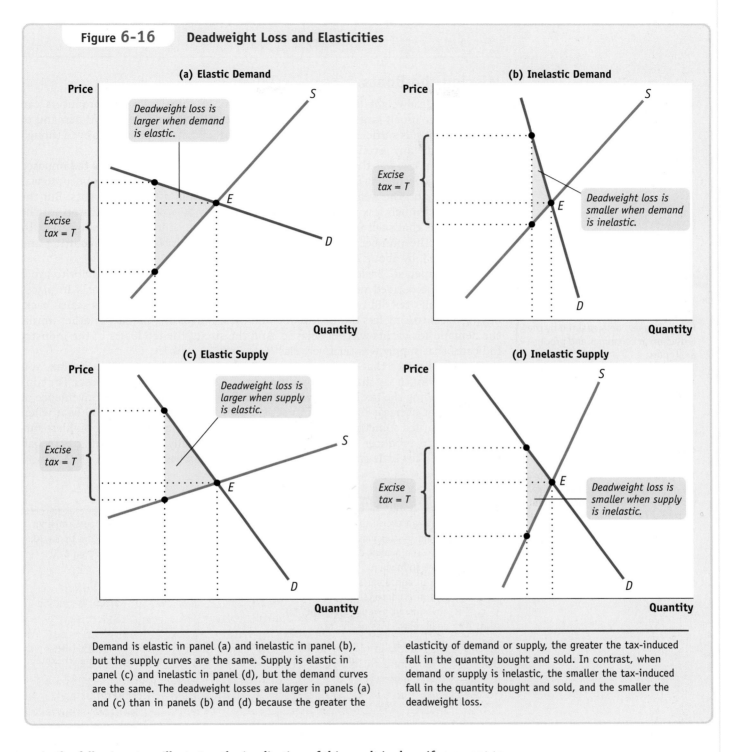

Figure 6-16   Deadweight Loss and Elasticities

Demand is elastic in panel (a) and inelastic in panel (b), but the supply curves are the same. Supply is elastic in panel (c) and inelastic in panel (d), but the demand curves are the same. The deadweight losses are larger in panels (a) and (c) than in panels (b) and (d) because the greater the elasticity of demand or supply, the greater the tax-induced fall in the quantity bought and sold. In contrast, when demand or supply is inelastic, the smaller the tax-induced fall in the quantity bought and sold, and the smaller the deadweight loss.

As the following story illustrates, the implication of this result is clear: if you want to lessen the efficiency costs of taxation, you should devise taxes to fall on goods for which either demand or supply, or both, is relatively inelastic. And this lesson carries a flip-side: using a tax to purposely decrease the amount of a harmful activity, such as underage drinking, will have the most impact when that activity is elastically demanded or supplied. In the extreme case in which demand is perfectly inelastic (a vertical demand curve), the quantity demanded is unchanged by the imposition of the tax. As a result, the tax imposes no deadweight loss. Similarly, if supply is perfectly inelastic (a vertical supply curve), the quantity supplied is unchanged by the tax and there is also no deadweight loss.

economics in action

Missing the Boats

Because of deadweight losses, the costs of a tax to consumers and producers can sometimes be much larger than the actual value of taxes paid. In fact, if demand or supply, or both, is sufficiently elastic, a tax can inflict considerable losses even though it raises hardly any revenue.

A case in point was the infamous "yacht tax" of 1990, a special sales tax imposed by the U.S. government on yachts whose price exceeded $100,000. The purpose was to raise taxes on the wealthy, the only people who could afford such boats. But the tax generated much less revenue than expected, only $7 million. The reason for the low yield was that sales of $100,000-plus yachts in the United States fell sharply, by 71 percent. The number of jobs in the yacht industry, in both manufacturing and sales, also fell, by about 25 percent.

What happened? Basically, potential yacht buyers changed their behavior to avoid the tax. Some decided not to buy yachts at all; others bought their boats in places where the sales tax did not apply, such as the Bahamas; and still others scaled back, buying boats costing less than $100,000 and thereby avoiding the tax. In other words, the demand for yachts was very elastic. And the size of the job losses in the industry indicates that supply was relatively elastic as well.

Despite the fact that few potential yacht buyers ended up paying the tax, you would not want to say that it imposed no costs on consumers and producers. For consumers, avoiding the tax had its own costs, such as the expense and inconvenience of buying a boat overseas or the loss in satisfaction from buying a $99,000 boat when you really wanted something fancier. Moreover, the sales force and boat builders suffered a loss in producer surplus. Policy makers eventually concluded that pain had been inflicted for little gain in tax revenue, and the tax was repealed in 1993. ■

< < < < < < < < < < < < < < < < < <

>>QUICK REVIEW

> The losses suffered by producers and consumers when an excise tax is imposed can be measured by the reduction in consumer and producer surplus.

> The government gains revenue from an excise tax, but this government revenue is less than the loss in total surplus.

> The difference between the government revenue from an excise tax and the reduction in total surplus is the deadweight loss from the tax.

> The greater the elasticities of supply or demand, or both, the larger the number of transactions prevented by a tax and the larger the deadweight loss.

>>CHECK YOUR UNDERSTANDING 6-4

1. Suppose that an excise tax of $0.40 is imposed on cheese-stuffed jalapeno peppers, raising the price paid by consumers to $0.70 and lowering the price received by producers to $0.30. Compared to the market equilibrium without the tax from Check Your Understanding 6-3, calculate the following:
   a. The loss in consumer surplus and who loses consumer surplus
   b. The loss in producer surplus and who loses producer surplus
   c. The government revenue from this tax
   d. The deadweight loss of the tax

2. In each of the following cases, focus on the elasticity of demand and use a diagram to illustrate the likely size—small or large—of the deadweight loss resulting from a tax. Explain your reasoning.
   a. Gasoline
   b. Milk chocolate bars

Solutions appear at back of book.

• A LOOK AHEAD •

We have now almost completed our tour of the supply and demand model. But there is one more topic we need to address: how do producers and consumers make decisions? Up to now we have looked at simple situations where it is immediately clear what an individual should do. For example, a consumer should buy if the price is less than his or her willingness to pay. But not all situations are that simple. In the next chapter, we take a deeper look at how producers and consumers make decisions.

SUMMARY

1. The **willingness to pay** of each individual consumer determines the demand curve. When price is less than or equal to the willingness to pay, the potential consumer purchases the good. The difference between price and willingness to pay is the net gain to the consumer, the **individual consumer surplus.**

2. The **total consumer surplus** in a market, the sum of all individual consumer surpluses in a market, is equal to the area below the demand curve but above the price. A rise in the price of a good reduces consumer surplus; a fall in the price increases consumer surplus. The term **consumer surplus** is often used to refer both to individual and to total consumer surplus.

3. The **cost** of each potential producer, the lowest price at which he or she is willing to supply a unit of that good, determines the supply curve. If the price of a good is above a producer's cost, a sale generates a net gain to the producer, known as the **individual producer surplus.**

4. The **total producer surplus,** the sum of the individual producer surpluses, is equal to the area above the supply curve but below the price. A rise in the price of a good increases producer surplus; a fall in the price reduces producer surplus. The term **producer surplus** is often used to refer both to the individual and to the total producer surplus.

5. **Total surplus,** the total gain to society from the production and consumption of a good, is the sum of consumer and producer surplus.

6. Usually, markets are efficient and achieve the maximum total surplus. Any possible rearrangement of consumption or sales, or change in the quantity bought and sold, reduces total surplus.

7. Under certain conditions, **market failure** occurs and markets fail to be efficient. This situation arises from three principal sources: attempts to capture more resources that create inefficiencies, side effects of some transactions, and problems in the nature of the good.

8. Economic policies can be evaluated by their effect on total surplus. For example, an excise tax generates revenue for the government but lowers total surplus. The loss in total surplus exceeds the tax revenue, resulting in a deadweight loss to society. The value of this deadweight loss is shown by the triangle that represents the value of the transactions discouraged by the tax. The greater the elasticity of demand or supply, or both, the larger the deadweight loss of a tax.

KEY TERMS

Willingness to pay, p. 136
Individual consumer surplus, p. 138
Total consumer surplus, p. 138
Consumer surplus, p. 138

Cost, p. 143
Individual producer surplus, p. 143
Total producer surplus, p. 144

Producer surplus, p. 144
Total surplus, p. 147
Market failure, p. 151

PROBLEMS

1. Determine the amount of consumer surplus generated in each of the following situations.

   a. Paul goes to the clothing store to buy a new T-shirt, for which he is willing to pay up to $10. He picks out one he likes with a price tag of exactly $10. At the cash register, he is told that his T-shirt is on sale for half the posted price.

   b. Robin goes to the CD store hoping to find a used copy of the *Eagles Greatest Hits* for up to $10. The store has one copy selling for $10.

   c. After soccer practice, Phil is willing to pay $2 for a bottle of mineral water. The 7-Eleven sells mineral water for $2.25 per bottle.

2. Determine the amount of producer surplus generated in each of the following situations.

   a. Bob lists his old Lionel electric trains on eBay. He sets a minimum acceptable price, known as his *reserve price*, of $75. After five days of bidding, the final high bid is exactly $75.

   b. Jenny advertises her car for sale in the used-car section of the student newspaper for $2,000, but she is willing to sell the car for any price higher than $1,500. The best offer she gets is $1,200.

   c. Sanjay likes his job so much that he would be willing to do it for free. However, his annual salary is $80,000.

3. Hollywood writers negotiate a new agreement with movie producers that they will receive 10 percent of the revenue from every video rental of a movie they worked on. They have no such agreement for movies shown on pay-per-view television.

   a. When the new writers' agreement comes into effect, what will happen in the market for video rentals—that is, will supply or demand shift, and how? As a result, how will consumer surplus in the market for video rentals change? Illustrate with a diagram. Do you think the writers' agreement will be popular with consumers who rent videos?

   b. Consumers consider video rentals and pay-per-view movies substitutable to some extent. When the new writers' agreement comes into effect, what will happen in the market for pay-per-view movies—that is, will supply or demand shift, and how? As a result, how will producer surplus in the market for pay-per-view movies change? Illustrate with a diagram. Do you think the writers' agreement will be popular with cable television companies that show pay-per-view movies?

4. There are six potential consumers of computer games, each willing to buy only one game. Consumer 1 is willing to pay $40 for a computer game, consumer 2 is willing to pay $35, consumer 3 is willing to pay $30, consumer 4 is willing pay $25, consumer 5 is willing to pay $20, and consumer 6 is willing to pay $15.

a. Suppose the market price is $29. What is the total consumer surplus?

b. Now the market price decreases to $19. What is the total consumer surplus now?

c. When the price fell from $29 to $19, how much did each consumer's individual consumer surplus change?

5. In an effort to provide more affordable rental housing for low-income families, the city council of Collegetown decides to impose a rent ceiling well below the current market equilibrium rent.

a. Illustrate the effect of this policy in a diagram. Indicate consumer and producer surplus before and after the introduction of the rent ceiling.

b. Will this policy be popular with renters? With landlords?

c. An economist explains to the city council that this policy is creating a deadweight loss. Illustrate the deadweight loss in your diagram.

6. On Thursday nights, a local restaurant has a pasta special. Ari likes the restaurant's pasta, and his willingness to pay for each serving is shown in the accompanying table.

Quantity of pasta (servings)	Willingness to pay for pasta (per serving)
1	$10
2	8
3	6
4	4
5	2
6	0

a. If the price of a serving of pasta is $4, how many servings will Ari buy? How much consumer surplus does he receive?

b. The following week, Ari is back at the restaurant again, but now the price of a serving of pasta is $6. By how much does his consumer surplus decrease compared to the previous week?

c. One week later, he goes to the restaurant again. He discovers that the restaurant is offering an "all you can eat"

special for $25. How much pasta will Ari eat, and how much consumer surplus does he receive now?

d. Suppose you own the restaurant and Ari is a "typical" customer. What is the highest price you can charge for the "all you can eat" special and still attract customers?

7. The accompanying diagram shows the market for cigarettes. The current equilibrium price per pack is $4, and every day 40 million packs of cigarettes are sold. In order to recover some of the health care costs associated with smoking, the government imposes a tax of $2 per pack. This will raise the equilibrium price to $5 per pack and reduce the equilibrium quantity to 30 million packs.

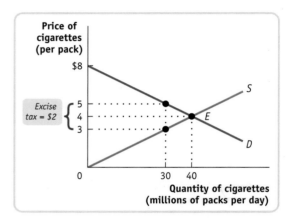

The economist working for the tobacco lobby claims that this tax will reduce consumer surplus for smokers by $40 million per day, since 40 million packs now cost $1 more per pack. The economist working for the lobby for sufferers of second-hand smoke argues that this is an enormous overestimate and that the reduction in consumer surplus will be only $30 million per day, since after the imposition of the tax only 30 million packs of cigarettes will be bought and each of these packs will now cost $1 more. They are both wrong. Why?

8. Consider the original market for pizza in Collegetown, illustrated in the accompanying table. Collegetown officials decide to impose an excise tax on pizza of $4 per pizza.

Price of pizza	Quantity of pizza demanded	Quantity of pizza supplied
$10	0	6
9	1	5
8	2	4
7	3	3
6	4	2
5	5	1
4	6	0
3	7	0
2	8	0
1	9	0

a. What is the quantity of pizza bought and sold after the imposition of the tax? What is the price paid by consumers? What is the price received by producers?

b. Calculate the consumer surplus and the producer surplus after the imposition of the tax. By how much has the imposition of the tax reduced consumer surplus? By how much has it reduced producer surplus?

c. How much tax revenue does Collegetown earn from this tax?

d. Calculate the deadweight loss from this tax.

9. Consider once more the original market for pizza in Collegetown, illustrated in the table in Problem 8. Now Collegetown officials impose a price floor on pizza of $8.

a. What is the quantity of pizza bought and sold after the imposition of the price floor?

b. Calculate the consumer surplus and the producer surplus after the imposition of the price floor.

10. You are the manager of Fun World, a small amusement park. The accompanying diagram shows the demand curve of a typical customer at Fun World.

a. Suppose that the price of each ride is $5. At that price, how much consumer surplus does an individual consumer get? (Recall that the area of a triangle is ½ × the base of the triangle × the height of the triangle.)

b. Suppose that Fun World considers charging an admission fee, even though it maintains the price of each ride at $5. What is the maximum admission fee it could charge? (Assume that all potential customers have enough money to pay the fee.)

c. Suppose that Fun World lowered the price of each ride to zero. How much consumer surplus does an individual consumer get? What is the maximum admission fee Fun World could therefore charge?

11. The accompanying diagram illustrates a taxi driver's individual supply curve (assume that each taxi ride is the same distance).

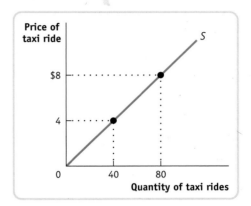

a. Suppose the city sets the price of taxi rides at $4 per ride. What is this taxi driver's producer surplus? (Recall that the area of a triangle is ½ × the base of the triangle × the height of the triangle.)

b. Suppose now that the city keeps the price of a taxi ride set at $4, but it decides to charge taxi drivers a "licensing fee." What is the maximum licensing fee the city could extract from this taxi driver?

c. Suppose that the city allowed the price of taxi rides to increase to $8 per ride. How much producer surplus does an individual taxi driver now get? What is the maximum licensing fee the city could charge this taxi driver?

12. The state needs to raise money, and the governor has a choice of imposing an excise tax of the same amount on one of two previously untaxed goods: the state can tax either sales of restaurant meals or sales of gasoline. Both the demand for and the supply of restaurant meals are more elastic than the demand for and the supply of gasoline. If the governor wants to minimize the deadweight loss caused by the tax, which good should be taxed? For each good, draw a diagram that illustrates the deadweight loss from taxation.

>web... To continue your study and review of concepts in this chapter, please visit the Krugman/Wells website for quizzes, animated graph tutorials, web links to helpful resources, and more.

www.worthpublishers.com/krugmanwells

>> Making Decisions

A TALE OF TWO INVASIONS

O N JUNE 6, 1944, ALLIED SOLDIERS stormed the beaches of Normandy, beginning the liberation of France from German rule. Long before the assault, however, Allied generals had to make a crucial decision: *where* would the soldiers land?

They had to make what we call an "either-or" decision. *Either* the invasion force could cross the English Channel at its narrowest point, Calais—which was what the Germans expected—*or* it could try to surprise the Germans by landing farther west, in Normandy. Since men and landing craft were in limited supply, the Allies could not do both. In fact they chose to rely on surprise. The German defenses in Normandy were too weak to stop the landings, and the Allies went on to liberate France and win the war.

Thirty years earlier, at the beginning of World War I, German generals had to make a different kind of decision. They, too, planned to invade France, in this case via land, and had decided to mount that invasion through Belgium. The decision they had to make was not an "either-or" but a "how much" decision: *how much* of their army should be allocated to the invasion force, and

how much should be used to defend Germany's border with France? The original plan, devised by General Alfred von Schlieffen, allocated most of the German army to the invasion force; on his deathbed, Schlieffen is supposed to have pleaded, "Keep the right wing [the invasion force] strong!" But his successor, General Helmuth von Moltke, weakened the plan: he reallocated some of the divisions that were supposed to race through Belgium to the defense. The weakened invasion force wasn't strong

Decision: Attack here? Or there?

enough: the defending French army stopped it 30 miles from Paris. Most military historians believe that by allocating too few men to the attack, von Moltke cost Germany the war.

So Allied generals made the right decision in 1944; German generals made the wrong decision in 1914. The important

What you will learn in this chapter:

➤ How economists model decision making by individuals and firms

➤ The importance of **implicit** as well as **explicit costs** in decision making

➤ The difference between **accounting profit** and **economic profit,** and why economic profit is the correct basis for decisions

➤ The difference between "either-or" and "how much" decisions

➤ The **principle of marginal analysis**

➤ What **sunk costs** are and why they should be ignored

➤ How to make decisions in cases where time is a factor

point for this chapter is that in both cases the generals had to apply the same logic that applies to economic decisions, like production decisions by businesses and consumption decisions by households.

In this chapter we will survey the principles involved in making economic decisions. These principles will help us understand how any individual—whether a consumer or a producer—makes an economic decision. We begin by taking a deeper look at the sig-nificance of opportunity cost for economic decisions and the role it plays in "either–or" decisions. Next we turn to the problem of making "how much" decisions and the usefulness of *marginal analysis*. We then examine what kind of costs should be ignored in making a decision—costs which economists call *sunk costs*. We end by considering the concept of *present value* and its importance for making decisions when costs and benefits arrive at different times.

Opportunity Cost and Decisions

In Chapter 1 we introduced some core principles underlying economic decisions. We've just seen two of those principles at work in our tale of two invasions. The first is that *resources are scarce*—the invading Allies had a limited number of landing craft, and the invading Germans had a limited number of divisions. Because resources are scarce, the true cost of anything is its *opportunity cost*—that is, the real cost of something is what you must give up to get it. When it comes to making decisions, it is crucial to think in terms of opportunity cost, because the opportunity cost of an action is often considerably more than the simple monetary cost.

Explicit versus Implicit Costs

Suppose that, after graduating from college, you have two options: to go to school for an additional year to get an advanced degree or to take a job immediately. You would like to take the extra year in school but are concerned about the cost.

But what exactly is the cost of that additional year of school? Here is where it is important to remember the concept of opportunity cost: the cost of that year spent getting an advanced degree is what you forgo by not taking a job for that year.

This cost, like any cost, can be broken into two parts: the *explicit cost* of the year's schooling and the *implicit cost*.

An **explicit cost** is a cost that requires an outlay of money. For example, the explicit cost of the additional year of schooling includes tuition. An **implicit cost,** on the other hand, does not involve an outlay of money; instead, it is measured by the value, in dollar terms, of all the benefits that are forgone. For example, the implicit cost of the year spent in school includes the income you would have earned if you had taken that job instead.

A common mistake, both in economic analysis and in real business situations, is to ignore implicit costs and focus exclusively on explicit costs. But often the implicit cost of an activity is quite substantial—indeed, sometimes it is much larger than the explicit cost.

Table 7-1 on page 162 gives a breakdown of hypothetical explicit and implicit costs associated with spending an additional year in school instead of taking a job. The explicit cost consists of tuition, books, supplies, and a home computer for doing assignments—all of which require you to spend money. The implicit cost is the salary you would have earned if you had taken a job instead. As you can see, the forgone salary is $35,000 and the explicit cost is $9,500, making the implicit cost more than three times as much as the explicit cost. So ignoring the implicit cost of an action can lead to a seriously misguided decision.

An **explicit cost** is a cost that involves actually laying out money. An **implicit cost** does not require an outlay of money; it is measured by the value, in dollar terms, of the benefits that are forgone.

TABLE **7-1**

Opportunity Cost of an Additional Year of School

Explicit cost		Implicit cost	
Tuition	$7,000	Forgone salary	$35,000
Books and supplies	1,000		
Home computer	1,500		
Total explicit cost	**9,500**	**Total implicit cost**	**35,000**
Total opportunity cost = Total explicit cost + Total implicit cost = $44,500			

There is another, slightly different way of looking at the implicit cost in this example that can deepen our understanding of opportunity cost. The forgone salary is the cost of using your own resources—your time—in going to school rather than working. The use of your *time* for more schooling, despite the fact that you don't have to spend any money, is nonetheless costly to you. This illustrates an important aspect of opportunity cost: in considering the cost of an activity, you should include the cost of using any of your own resources for that activity. You can calculate the cost of using your own resources by determining what they would have earned in their next best use.

> ### FOR INQUIRING MINDS
>
> ### FAMOUS COLLEGE DROPOUTS
>
> What do Bill Gates, Tiger Woods, and Sarah Michelle Gellar (a.k.a. Buffy the Vampire Slayer) have in common? None of them have a college degree.
>
> Nobody doubts that all three are easily smart enough to have gotten their diplomas. However, they all made the rational decision that the implicit cost of getting a degree would have been too high—by their late teens, each had a very promising career that would have had to be put on hold to get a college degree. Gellar would have had to postpone her acting career; Woods would have had to put off
>
> winning one major tournament after another and becoming the world's best golfer; Gates would have had to delay developing the most successful and most lucrative software ever sold, Microsoft's computer operating system.
>
> In fact, extremely successful people—especially those in careers like acting or athletics, where starting early in life is especially crucial—are often college dropouts. It's a simple matter of economics: the opportunity cost of their time at that stage in their lives is just too high to postpone their careers for a college degree.

Accounting Profit versus Economic Profit

As the example of going to school suggests, taking account of implicit as well as explicit costs can be very important for individuals making decisions. The same is true of businesses.

Consider the case of Kathy's Kopy Shoppe, a small business operating in a local shopping center. Kathy makes copies for customers, who pay for her services. Out of that revenue, she has to pay her expenses: the cost of supplies and the rent for her store space. We suppose that Kathy owns the copy machines themselves. This year Kathy has $100,000 in revenue and $60,000 in expenses. Is her business profitable?

At first it might seem that the answer is obviously yes: she receives $100,000 from her customers and has expenses of only $60,000. Doesn't this mean that she has a profit of $40,000? Not according to her accountant, who reduces the number by $5,000 for the yearly *depreciation* (reduction in value) of the copy machines.

Depreciation occurs because machines wear out over time. The yearly depreciation amount reflects what an accountant estimates to be the reduction in the value of the machines due to wear and tear that year. This leaves $35,000, which is the business's **accounting profit.** Basically, the accounting profit of a company is its revenue minus its explicit cost and depreciation. The accounting profit is the number that Kathy has to report on her income tax forms and that she would be obliged to report to anyone thinking of investing in her business.

> The **accounting profit** of a business is the business's revenue minus the explicit cost and depreciation.

Accounting profit is a very useful number, but suppose that Kathy wants to decide whether to keep her business going or to do something else. To make this decision, she will need to calculate her **economic profit**—the revenue she receives minus her opportunity cost, which may include implicit as well as explicit costs. In general, when economists use the simple term *profit*, they are referring to economic profit. (We will adopt this simplification in later chapters of this book.)

> The **economic profit** of a business is the business's revenue minus the opportunity cost of its resources. It is usually less than the accounting profit.

Why does Kathy's economic profit differ from her accounting profit? Because she may have implicit costs over and above the explicit cost her accountant has calculated. Businesses can face implicit costs for two reasons. First, a business's **capital**—its equipment, buildings, tools, inventory, and financial assets—could have been put to use in some other way. If the business owns its capital, it does not pay any money for its use, but it pays an implicit cost because it does not use the capital in some other way. Second, the owner devotes time and energy to the business that could have been used elsewhere—a particularly important factor in small businesses, whose owners tend to put in many long hours.

> The **capital** of a business is the value of its assets—equipment, buildings, tools, inventory, and financial assets.

If Kathy had rented her copy machines from the manufacturer, their rent would have been an explicit cost. But because Kathy owns her own machines, she does not pay rent on them and her accountant deducts an estimate of their depreciation in the profit statement. However, this does not account for the opportunity cost of the machines— what Kathy forgoes by owning them. Suppose that instead of using the machines for her own business, the best alternative Kathy has is to sell them for $50,000 and put the money into a bank account where it would earn yearly interest of $3,000. This $3,000 is an implicit cost of running the business.

It is generally known as the **implicit cost of capital,** the opportunity cost of the capital used by a business; it reflects the income that could have been realized if the capital had been used in its next best alternative way. It is just as much a true cost as if Kathy had rented the machines instead of owning them.

> The **implicit cost of capital** is the opportunity cost of the capital used by a business—the income the owner could have realized from that capital if it had been used in its next best alternative way.

Finally, Kathy should take into account the opportunity cost of her own time. Suppose that instead of running her own shop, she could earn $34,000 as an office manager. That $34,000 is also an implicit cost of her business.

Table 7-2 summarizes the accounting for Kathy's Kopy Shoppe, taking both explicit and implicit costs into account. It turns out, unfortunately, that although the business makes an accounting profit of $35,000, its economic profit is actually negative.

TABLE 7-2

Profit at Kathy's Kopy Shoppe	
Revenue	$100,000
Explicit cost	– 60,000
Depreciation	– 5,000
Accounting profit	**35,000**
Implicit cost of business	
Income Kathy could have earned on capital in the next best way	– 3,000
Income Kathy could have earned as manager	– 34,000
Economic profit	**–2,000**

"I've done the numbers, and I will marry you."

This means that Kathy would be better off financially if she closed the business and devoted her time and capital to something else.

In real life, discrepancies between accounting profits and economic profits are extremely common. As the following Economics in Action explains, this is a message that has found a receptive audience among real-world businesses.

economics in action

Farming in the Shadow of Suburbia

Beyond the sprawling suburbs, most of New England is covered by dense forest. But this is not the forest primeval: if you hike through the woods, you encounter many stone walls, relics of the region's agricultural past when stone walls enclosed fields and pastures. In 1880, more than half of New England's land was farmed; by 2003, the amount was down to 10 percent.

The remaining farms of New England are mainly located close to large metropolitan areas. There farmers get high prices for their produce from city dwellers who are willing to pay a premium for locally grown, extremely fresh fruit and vegetables.

But now even these farms are under economic pressure caused by a rise in the implicit cost of farming close to a metropolitan area. As metropolitan areas have expanded during the last two decades, farmers increasingly ask themselves whether they could do better by selling their land to property developers.

In 2003, the average value of an acre of farmland in the United States as a whole was $1,270; in Rhode Island, the most densely populated of the New England states, the average was $9,300. The Federal Reserve Bank of Boston has noted that "high land prices put intense pressure on the region's farms to generate incomes that are substantial enough to justify keeping the land in agriculture." The important point is that the pressure is intense even if the farmer owns the land because the land is a form of capital used to run the business. So maintaining the land as a farm instead of selling it to a developer constitutes a large implicit cost of capital. A fact provided by the U.S. Department of Agriculture (USDA) helps us put a dollar figure on the portion of the implicit cost of capital due to development pressure for some Rhode Island farms. In 2003, a USDA program designed to prevent development of Rhode Island farmland by paying owners for the "development rights" to their land paid an average of $4,145 per acre for those rights alone.

About two-thirds of New England's farms remaining in business earn very little money. They are maintained as "rural residences" by people with other sources of income—not so much because they are commercially viable, but more out of a personal commitment and the satisfaction these people derive from farm life. Although many businesses have important implicit costs, they can also have important benefits to their owners that go beyond the revenue earned. ■

< < < < < < < < < < < < < < < < < <

>>**CHECK YOUR UNDERSTANDING 7-1**

1. Karma and Don run a furniture-refinishing business from their home. Which of the following represent an explicit cost of the business and which represent an implicit cost?
   a. Supplies such as paint stripper, varnish, polish, sandpaper, and so on
   b. Basement space that has been converted into a workroom
   c. Wages paid to a part-time helper
   d. A van that they inherited and use only for transporting furniture
   e. The job at a larger furniture restorer that Karma gave up in order to run the business

Solutions appear at back of book.

Making "How Much" Decisions: The Role of Marginal Analysis

As the story of the two wars at the beginning of this chapter demonstrated, there are two types of decisions: "either-or" decisions and "how much" decisions. To help you get a better sense of that distinction, Table 7-3 offers some examples of each kind of decision.

Although many decisions in economics are "either-or," many others are "how much." Not many people will stop driving if the price of gasoline goes up, but many people will drive less. How much less? A rise in wheat prices won't necessarily persuade a lot of people to take up farming for the first time, but it will persuade farmers who were already growing wheat to plant more. How much more?

TABLE 7-3

"How Much" versus "Either-Or" Decisions

"How much" decisions	"Either-or" decisions
How many days before you do your laundry?	Tide or Cheer?
How many miles do you go before an oil change in your car?	Buy a car or not?
How many jalapenos on your nachos?	An order of nachos or a sandwich?
How many workers should you hire in your company?	Run your own business or work for someone else?
How much should a patient take of a drug that generates side effects?	Prescribe drug A or drug B for your patients?
How many troops do you allocate to your invasion force?	Invade at Calais or in Normandy?

To understand "how much" decisions, we use an approach known as *marginal analysis*. Marginal analysis involves comparing the benefit of doing a little bit more of some activity with the cost of doing a little bit more of that activity. The benefit of doing a little bit more of something is what economists call its *marginal benefit*, and the cost of doing a little bit more of something is what they call its *marginal cost*.

Why is this called "marginal" analysis? A margin is an edge; what you do in marginal analysis is push out the edge a bit and see whether that is a good move.

We will begin our study of marginal analysis by focusing on marginal cost, and we'll do that by considering a hypothetical company called Felix's Lawn-Mowing Service, operated by Felix himself with his tractor-mower.

Marginal Cost

Felix is a very hard-working individual; if he works continuously, he can mow 7 lawns in a day. It takes him an hour to mow each lawn. The opportunity cost of an hour of Felix's time is $10 because he could make that much at his next best job.

His one and only mower, however, presents a problem when Felix works this hard. Running his mower for longer and longer periods on a given day takes an increasing toll on the engine and ultimately necessitates more—and more costly—maintenance and repairs.

The second column of Table 7-4 on page 166 shows how the total daily cost of Felix's business depends on the quantity of lawns he mows in a day. For simplicity, we assume that Felix's only costs are the opportunity cost of his time and the cost of upkeep for his mower.

At only 1 lawn per day, Felix's daily cost is $10.50: $10.00 for an hour of his time plus $0.50 for some oil. At 2 lawns per day, his daily cost is $21.75: $20.00 for 2 hours of his time and $1.75 for mower repair and maintenance. At 3 lawns per day, the daily cost has risen to $35.00: $30.00 for 3 hours of his time and $5.00 for mower repair and maintenance.

TABLE 7-4

Felix's Marginal Cost of Mowing Lawns

Quantity of lawns mowed	Felix's total cost	Felix's marginal cost of lawn mowed
0	$0	
		$10.50
1	10.50	
		11.25
2	21.75	
		13.25
3	35.00	
		15.50
4	50.50	
		18.00
5	68.50	
		20.75
6	89.25	
		23.75
7	$113.00	

The third column of Table 7-4 contains the cost incurred by Felix for each *additional* lawn he mows, calculated from information in the second column. The 1st lawn he mows costs him $10.50; this number appears in the third column between the lines representing 0 lawn and 1 lawn because $10.50 is Felix's cost of going from 0 to 1 lawn mowed. The next lawn, going from 1 to 2, costs him an additional $11.25. So $11.25 appears in the third column between the lines representing the 1st and 2nd lawn, and so on.

The increase in Felix's cost when he mows one more lawn is his **marginal cost** of lawn-mowing. In general, the marginal cost of any activity is the additional cost incurred by doing one more unit of that activity.

The marginal costs shown in Table 7-4 have a clear pattern: Felix's marginal cost is greater the more lawns he has already mowed. That is, each time he mows a lawn, the additional cost of doing yet another lawn goes up. Felix's lawn-mowing business has what economists call **increasing marginal cost**: each additional lawn costs more to mow than the previous one. Or, to put it slightly differently, with increasing marginal cost, the marginal cost of an activity rises as the quantity already done rises.

Figure 7-1 is a graphical representation of the third column in Table 7-4. The horizontal axis measures the quantity of lawns mowed, and the vertical axis measures the

> The **marginal cost** of an activity is the additional cost incurred by doing one more unit of that activity.

> There is **increasing marginal cost** from an activity when each additional unit of the activity costs more than the previous unit.

Figure 7-1

The Marginal Cost Curve

The height of each bar is equal to the marginal cost of mowing the corresponding lawn. For example, the 1st lawn mowed has a marginal cost of $10.50, equal to the height of the bar extending from 0 to 1 lawn. The bars ascend in height, reflecting increasing marginal cost: each additional lawn is more costly to mow than the previous one. As a result, the marginal cost curve (drawn by plotting points in the top center of each bar) is upward sloping.

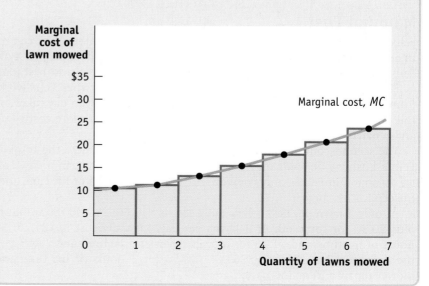

marginal cost of a mowed lawn. The height of each shaded bar indicates the marginal cost incurred by mowing a given lawn. For example, the bar stretching from 4 to 5 lawns is at a height of $18.00, equal to the cost of mowing the 5th lawn. Notice that the bars form a series of ascending steps, a reflection of the increasing marginal cost of lawn-mowing. The **marginal cost curve,** the red curve in Figure 7-1, shows the relationship between marginal cost and the quantity of the activity already done. We draw it by plotting a point in the center at the top of each bar and connecting the points.

The marginal cost curve is upward sloping, due to increasing marginal cost. Not all activities have increasing marginal cost; for example, it is possible for marginal cost to be the same regardless of the number of lawns already mowed. Economists call this case *constant* marginal cost. It is also possible for some activities to have a marginal cost that initially falls as we do more of the activity and then eventually rises. These sorts of activities involve gains from specialization: as more output is produced, more workers are hired, allowing each one to specialize in the task that he or she performs best. The gains from specialization yield a lower marginal cost of production.

Now that we have established the concept of marginal cost, we move to the parallel concept of marginal benefit.

Marginal Benefit

Felix's business is in a town where some of the residents are very busy but others are not so busy. For people who are very busy, the opportunity cost of an hour of their time spent mowing the lawn is very high. So they are willing to pay Felix a fairly high sum to do it for them. People with lots of free time, however, have a lower opportunity cost of an hour of their time spent mowing the lawn. So they are willing to pay Felix only a relatively small sum. And between these two extremes lie other residents who are moderately busy and so are willing to pay a moderate price to have their lawns mowed.

We'll assume that on any given day, Felix has one potential customer who will pay him $35 to mow her lawn, another who will pay $30, a third who will pay $26, a fourth who will pay $23, and so on. Table 7-5 lists what he can receive from each of his seven potential customers per day, in descending order according to price. So if Felix goes from 0 to 1 lawn mowed, he can earn $35; if he goes from 1 to 2 lawns mowed, he can earn an additional $30; and so on. The third column of Table 7-5 shows the **marginal benefit** to Felix of each additional lawn mowed. In general, marginal benefit is the additional benefit derived from undertaking one more unit of an activity. Because it arises from doing one more lawn, each marginal benefit value appears between the lines associated with successive quantities of lawns.

It's clear from Table 7-5 that the more lawns Felix has already mowed, the smaller his marginal benefit from mowing one more. So Felix's lawn-mowing business has what

The **marginal cost curve** shows how the cost of undertaking one more unit of an activity depends on the quantity of that activity that has already been done.

PITFALLS

INCREASING TOTAL COST VERSUS INCREASING MARGINAL COST

The concept of *increasing marginal cost* plays an important role in economic analysis, but students sometimes get confused about what it means. That's because it is easy to wrongly conclude that whenever total cost is increasing, marginal cost must also be increasing. But the following example shows that this conclusion is misguided.

Suppose that we change the numbers of our example: the marginal cost of mowing the 6th lawn is now $20, and the marginal cost of mowing the 7th lawn is now $15. In both instances total cost increases as Felix does an additional lawn: it increases by $20 for the 6th lawn and by $15 for the 7th lawn. But in this example marginal cost is *decreasing*: the marginal cost of the 7th lawn is less than the marginal cost of the 6th lawn. So we have a case of increasing total cost and decreasing marginal cost. What this shows us is that, in fact, totals and marginals can sometimes move in opposite directions.

The **marginal benefit** from an activity is the additional benefit derived from undertaking one more unit of that activity.

TABLE **7-5**

Felix's Marginal Benefit of Mowing Lawns

Quantity of lawns mowed	Felix's total benefit	Felix's marginal benefit of lawn mowed
0	$0	
		$35.00
1	35.00	
		30.00
2	65.00	
		26.00
3	91.00	
		23.00
4	114.00	
		21.00
5	135.00	
		19.00
6	154.00	
		18.00
7	$172.00	

Figure 7-2

The Marginal Benefit Curve

The height of each bar is equal to the marginal benefit of mowing the corresponding lawn. For example, the 1st lawn mowed has a marginal benefit of $35, equal to the height of the bar extending from 0 to 1 lawn. The bars descend in height, reflecting decreasing marginal benefit each additional lawn produces a smaller benefit than the previous one. As a result, the marginal benefit curve (drawn by plotting points in the top center of each bar) is downward sloping. **>web...**

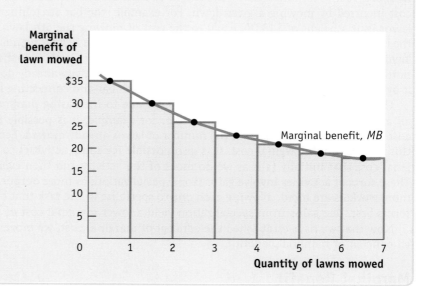

There is **decreasing marginal benefit** from an activity when each additional unit of the activity produces less benefit than the previous unit.

The **marginal benefit curve** shows how the benefit from undertaking one more unit of an activity depends on the quantity of that activity that has already been done.

economists call **decreasing marginal benefit:** each additional lawn mowed produces less benefit than the previous lawn. Or, to put it slightly differently, with decreasing marginal benefit, the marginal benefit of an activity falls as the quantity already done rises.

Just as marginal cost could be represented with a marginal cost curve, marginal benefit can be represented with a **marginal benefit curve,** shown in blue in Figure 7-2. The height of each bar shows the marginal benefit of each additional lawn mowed; the curve through the middle of each bar's top shows how the benefit of each additional unit of the activity depends on the number of units that have already been undertaken.

Felix's marginal benefit curve is downward sloping because he faces decreasing marginal benefit from lawn-mowing. Not all activities have decreasing marginal benefit; in fact, there are many activities for which marginal benefit is constant—that is, it is the same regardless of the number of units already undertaken. In later chapters where we study firms, we will see that the shape of a firm's marginal benefit curve from producing output has important implications for how it behaves within its industry. We'll also see in Chapters 10 and 11 why economists assume that declining marginal benefit is the norm when considering choices made by consumers. Like increasing marginal cost, decreasing marginal benefit is so common that for now we can take it as the norm.

Now we are ready to see how the concepts of marginal benefit and marginal cost can be brought together to answer the question of "how much" of an activity an individual should undertake.

Marginal Analysis

Table 7-6 shows the marginal cost and marginal benefit numbers from Tables 7-4 and 7-5. It also adds an additional column: the net gain to Felix from one more lawn mowed, equal to the difference between the marginal benefit and the marginal cost.

We can use Table 7-6 to determine how many lawns Felix should mow. To see this, imagine for a moment that Felix planned to mow only 3 lawns today. We can immediately see that this is too small a quantity. If Felix mows an additional lawn, increasing the quantity from 3 to 4, he realizes a marginal benefit of $23 and incurs a marginal cost of only $15.50—so his net gain would be $23.00 − $15.50 = $7.50. But even 4 lawns is still too few: if Felix increases the quantity from 4 to 5, his marginal benefit is $21.00 and his marginal cost is only $18.00, for a net gain of $21.00 − $18.00 = $3.00 (as indicated by the highlighting in the table).

TABLE 7-6

Felix's Net Gain from Mowing Lawns

Quantity of lawns mowed	Felix's marginal benefit of lawn mowed	Felix's marginal cost of lawn mowed	Felix's net gain of lawn mowed
0			
	$35.00	$10.50	$24.50
1			
	30.00	11.25	18.75
2			
	26.00	13.25	12.75
3			
	23.00	15.50	7.50
4			
	21.00	18.00	3.00
5			
	19.00	20.75	–1.75
6			
	18.00	23.75	–5.75
7			

But if Felix goes ahead and mows 7 lawns, that is too many. We can see this by looking at the net gain from mowing that 7th lawn: Felix's marginal benefit is $18.00, but his marginal cost is $23.75. So mowing that 7th lawn would produce a net gain of $18.00 − $23.75 = −$5.75; that is, a net *loss* for his business. Even 6 lawns is too many: by increasing the quantity of lawns mowed from 5 to 6, Felix incurs a marginal cost of $20.75 compared with a marginal benefit of only $19.00. He is best off at mowing 5 lawns, the largest quantity of lawns for which marginal benefit is at least as great as marginal cost.

The upshot is that Felix should mow 5 lawns—no more and no less. If he mows fewer than 5 lawns, his marginal benefit from one more is greater than his marginal cost; he would be passing up a net gain by not mowing more lawns. If he mows more than 5 lawns, his marginal benefit from the last lawn mowed is less than his marginal cost, resulting in a loss for that lawn. So 5 lawns is the quantity that generates Felix's maximum possible total net gain; it is what economists call the **optimal quantity** of lawns mowed.

Figure 7-3 on page 170 shows graphically how the optimal quantity can be determined. Felix's marginal benefit and marginal cost curves are both shown. If Felix mows fewer than 5 lawns, the marginal benefit curve is *above* the marginal cost curve, so he can make himself better off by mowing more lawns; if he mows more than 5 lawns, the marginal benefit curve is *below* the marginal cost curve, so he would be better off mowing fewer lawns.

The table in Figure 7-3 confirms our result. The second column repeats information from Table 7-6, showing marginal benefit minus marginal cost—or the net gain—for each lawn. The third column shows total net gain according to the quantity of lawns mowed. The total net gain after doing a given lawn is simply the sum of numbers in the second column up to and including that lawn. For example, the net gain is $24.50 for the first lawn and $18.75 for the second. So the total net gain after doing the first lawn is $24.50, and the total net gain after doing the second lawn is $24.50 + $18.75 = $43.25. Our conclusion that 5 is the optimal quantity is confirmed by the fact that the greatest total net gain, $66.50, occurs when the 5th lawn is mowed.

The example of Felix's lawn-mowing business shows how you go about finding the optimal quantity: increase the quantity as long as the marginal benefit from one more unit is greater than the marginal cost, but stop before the marginal benefit becomes less than the marginal cost.

In many cases, however, it is possible to state this rule more simply. When a "how much" decision involves relatively large quantities, the rule simplifies to this: the optimal quantity is the quantity at which marginal benefit is equal to marginal cost.

> The **optimal quantity** of an activity is the quantity that generates the maximum possible total net gain.

Figure 7-3   The Optimal Quantity

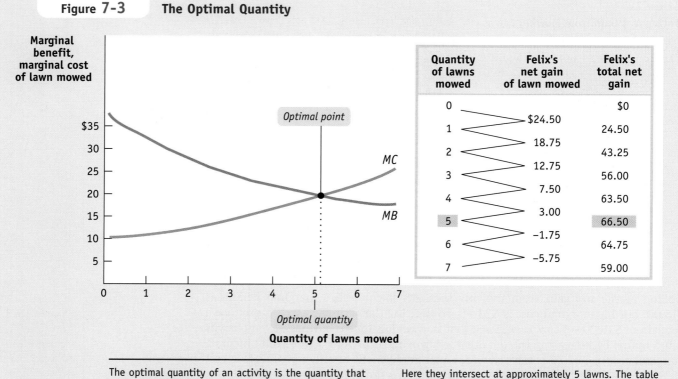

Quantity of lawns mowed	Felix's net gain of lawn mowed	Felix's total net gain
0		$0
	$24.50	
1		24.50
	18.75	
2		43.25
	12.75	
3		56.00
	7.50	
4		63.50
	3.00	
5		66.50
	−1.75	
6		64.75
	−5.75	
7		59.00

The optimal quantity of an activity is the quantity that generates the highest possible total net gain. It is the quantity at which marginal benefit is equal to marginal cost. Equivalently, it is the quantity at which the marginal benefit curve and the marginal cost curve intersect.

Here they intersect at approximately 5 lawns. The table beside the graph confirms that 5 is indeed the optimal quantity: the total net gain is maximized at 5 lawns, generating $66.50 in total net gain for Felix.

The **principle of marginal analysis** says that the optimal quantity of an activity is the quantity at which marginal benefit is equal to marginal cost.

PITFALLS

MUDDLED AT THE MARGIN

The idea of setting marginal benefit *equal* to marginal cost sometimes confuses people. Aren't we trying to maximize the *difference* between benefits and costs? And don't we wipe out our gains by setting benefits and costs equal to each other? But what we are doing is setting *marginal*, not *total*, benefit and cost equal to each other.

Once again, the point is to maximize the total net gain from an activity. If the marginal benefit from the activity is greater than the marginal cost, doing a bit more will increase that gain. If the marginal benefit is less than the marginal cost, doing a bit less will increase the total net gain. So only when the *marginal* benefit and cost are equal is the difference between *total* benefit and cost at a maximum.

To see why this is so, consider the example of a farmer who finds that her optimal quantity of wheat produced is 5,000 bushels. Typically, she will find that in going from 4,999 to 5,000 bushels, her marginal benefit is only very slightly greater than her marginal cost—that is, the difference between marginal benefit and marginal cost is close to zero. Similarly, in going from 5,000 to 5,001 bushels, her marginal cost is only very slightly greater than her marginal benefit—again, the difference between marginal cost and marginal benefit is very close to zero. So a simple rule for her in choosing the optimal quantity of wheat is to produce the quantity at which the difference between marginal benefit and marginal cost is approximately zero—that is, the quantity at which marginal benefit equals marginal cost.

Economists call this rule the **principle of marginal analysis.** It says that the optimal quantity of an activity is the quantity at which marginal benefit equals marginal cost. Graphically, the optimal quantity is the quantity of an activity at which the marginal benefit curve *intersects* the marginal cost curve. In fact, this graphical method works quite well even when the numbers involved aren't that large. For example, in Figure 7-3 the marginal benefit and marginal cost curves cross each other at about 5 lawns mowed—that is, marginal benefit equals marginal cost at about 5 lawns mowed, which we have already seen is Felix's optimal quantity.

A Principle with Many Uses

The principle of marginal analysis can be applied to just about any "how much" decision—including those decisions where the benefits and costs are not necessarily expressed in dollars and cents. Here are a few examples:

- The number of traffic deaths can be reduced by spending more on highways, requiring better protection in cars, and so on. But these measures are expensive. So we can talk about the marginal cost to society of eliminating one more traffic fatality. And we can then ask whether the marginal benefit of that life saved is large enough to warrant doing this. (If you think no price is too high to save a life, see the following Economics in Action.)

- Many useful drugs have side effects that depend on the dosage. So we can talk about the marginal cost, in terms of these side effects, of increasing the dosage of a drug. The drug also has a marginal benefit in helping fight the disease. So the optimal quantity of the drug is the quantity that makes the best of this trade-off.

- Studying for an exam has costs because you could have done something else with the time, such as studying for another exam or sleeping. So we can talk about the marginal cost of devoting another hour to studying for your chemistry final. The optimal quantity of studying is the level at which the marginal benefit in terms of a higher grade is just equal to the marginal cost.

economics in action

The Cost of a Life

What's the marginal benefit to society of saving a human life? You might be tempted to answer that human life is infinitely precious. But in the real world, resources are scarce, so we must decide how much to spend on saving lives since we cannot spend infinite amounts. After all, we could surely reduce highway deaths by dropping the speed limit on interstates to 40 miles per hour, but the cost of such a lower speed limit—in time and money—is more than anyone is willing to pay.

Generally, people are reluctant to talk in a straightforward way about comparing the marginal cost of a life saved with the marginal benefit—it sounds too callous. Sometimes, however, the question becomes unavoidable.

For example, the cost of saving a life became an object of intense discussion in the United Kingdom in 1999, after a horrifying train crash near London's Paddington Station killed 31 people. There were accusations that the British government was spending too little on rail safety. However, the government estimated that improving rail safety would cost an additional $4.5 million per life saved. But if that amount was worth spending—that is, if the estimated marginal benefit of saving a life exceeded $4.5 million—then the implication was that the British government was spending way too little on *traffic safety*. The estimated marginal cost per life saved through highway improvements was only $1.5 million, making it a much better deal than saving lives through greater rail safety. ∎

> >

>>CHECK YOUR UNDERSTANDING 7-2

1. For each of the "how much" decisions listed in Table 7-3, describe the nature of the marginal cost and of the marginal benefit.

2. Suppose that Felix's marginal cost, instead of increasing, is the same for every lawn he mows.
   a. Assume Felix's marginal cost is $18.50. Using Table 7-6, find the optimal quantity of mowed lawns. What is his total net gain?
   b. How high would marginal cost have to be such that Felix's optimal quantity of lawns mowed is 0? Can you specify a marginal cost for which the optimal quantity is 3?

Solutions appear at back of book.

This vet left law school to pursue his dream career. The cost for a year of law school was lost—a sunk cost. But he and his patients are now happy.

A **sunk cost** is a cost that has already been incurred and is nonrecoverable. A sunk cost should be ignored in decisions about future actions.

Sunk Costs

When making decisions, knowing what to ignore is important. Although we have devoted much attention in this chapter to costs that are important to take into account when making a decision, some costs should be ignored when doing so. In this section we will focus on the kinds of costs that people should ignore—what economists call *sunk costs*—and why they should be ignored.

To gain some intuition, consider the following scenario. You own a car that is a few years old, and you have just replaced the brake pads at a cost of $250. But then you find out that the entire brake system is defective and must be replaced—including the newly installed brake pads. This will cost you an additional $1,500. Alternatively, you could sell the car and buy another of comparable quality, but with no brake defects, by spending an additional $1,600. What should you do: fix your old car, or sell it and buy another?

Some might say that you should take the latter option. After all, this line of reasoning goes, if you repair your car, you will end up having spent $1,750: $1,500 for the brake system and $250 for the brake pads you replaced. If you were instead to sell your old car and buy another, you would spend only $1,600.

But this reasoning, although it sounds plausible, is wrong. It is wrong because it ignores the fact that you have *already* spent $250 on brake pads, and that $250 is *nonrecoverable*. That is, having been spent already, the $250 cannot be recouped. Therefore, it should be ignored and should have no effect on your decision whether to repair your car and keep it or not. From an economist's viewpoint, the real cost at this time of repairing and keeping your car is $1,500, not $1,750. Therefore, the correct decision is to repair your car and keep it rather than spend $1,600 on a new car.

In this example, the $250 that has already been spent and cannot be recovered is what economists call a **sunk cost.** Sunk costs should be ignored in making decisions about future actions because they have no influence on their costs and benefits. It's like the old saying, "There's no use crying over spilled milk": once something is gone and can't be recovered, it is irrelevant in making decisions about what to do in the future.

It is often psychologically hard to ignore sunk costs. And if, in fact, the costs haven't yet been incurred, then they should be taken into consideration. That is, if you had known at the beginning that it would cost $1,750 to repair your car, then the right choice *at that time* would have been to buy a new car for $1,600. But once the $250 has already been paid for brake pads, it is no longer something that should be included in your decision making about your next actions. It may be hard to accept that "bygones are bygones," but it is the right thing to do.

economics in action

The Next Generation

Recently, several European countries held "spectrum auctions," auctions in which telephone companies bid for portions of a country's airwave space. The telephone companies planned to use this airwave space to offer new mobile phone services to consumers. Companies believed they could earn large profits by providing these new services, so-called third-generation, or 3G, mobile phone services, which include features such as videocalling and mobile Internet access. Eager to capture what they expected to be large future profits, telephone companies paid billions of dollars for portions of the European airwave space.

But some technology experts were worried. They believed that the companies had exaggerated expectations of future profits and, as a result, had paid too much for the airwave space. These experts feared that once the companies realized that the airwave space was worth much less than what they had paid, the companies would be unwilling to put up the additional money needed for physical infrastructure, such as the towers used to transmit the signals that are necessary to the 3G services.

It turned out that the technology experts were right about the exaggerated expectations: within a few months of the spectrum auctions, telephone companies realized that they had paid far more for the portions of airwave space than they were really worth.

But was the experts' second conjecture correct: would the overpayment for the airwaves really prevent the future investment needed to provide 3G services? The answer at this point is no. Several companies, including Vodaphone, the British company that owns a substantial part of the American company Verizon, have pushed ahead in building the required infrastructure. As of 2004, 3G was available in over 30 countries worldwide.

Technology experts were wrong about the effect of overpayment because they didn't understand the concept of sunk costs. That is, they didn't understand that once made, those payments for airwave space couldn't be recovered; therefore, they wouldn't affect the telephone companies' willingness to spend additional money to complete the project. After the companies came to the painful—and quite embarrassing—realization of their overpayment, it didn't change the fact that it was still profitable to build the infrastructure needed to provide the new services. In the end, they appear to have made the right economic calculation—and in the process admitted to themselves that "there's no use crying over a lost billion or two." ■

> >

>>QUICK REVIEW

➤ *Sunk costs*, costs that have already been incurred and that cannot be recovered, should be ignored in decisions regarding future actions. Because they have already been incurred and are nonrecoverable, they have no influence on future costs and benefits.

>>CHECK YOUR UNDERSTANDING 7-3

1. You have decided to go into the ice-cream business and have bought a used ice-cream truck for $8,000. Now you are reconsidering. What is your sunk cost in the following scenarios?
   a. The truck cannot be resold.
   b. It can be resold, but only at a 50 percent discount.

2. You have gone through two years of medical school but are suddenly wondering whether you wouldn't be happier as a musician. Which of the following statements are potentially valid arguments and which are not?
   a. "I can't give up now, after all the time and money I've put in."
   b. "If I had thought about it from the beginning, I never would have gone to med school, so I should give it up now."
   c. "I wasted two years, but never mind—let's start from here."
   d. "My parents would kill me if I stopped now." (*Hint:* we're discussing *your* decision-making ability, not your parents'.)

Solutions appear at back of book.

The Concept of Present Value

In many cases, individuals must make decisions whose consequences extend some ways into the future. For example, when you decide to attend college, you are committing yourself to years of study, which you expect will pay off for the rest of your life. So the decision to attend college is the decision to embark on a long-term project.

As we have already seen, the basic rule in deciding whether or not to undertake a project is that you should compare the benefits of that project with its costs, implicit as well as explicit. But sometimes there can be a problem in making these comparisons: the benefits and costs of a project may not arrive at the same time.

Sometimes the costs of a project come at an earlier date than the benefits. For example, going to college involves large immediate costs: tuition, income forgone because you are in school, and so on. The benefits, such as a higher salary in your future career, come later, often much later.

In other cases, the benefits of a project come at an earlier date than the costs. If you take out a loan to pay for a vacation cruise, the satisfaction of the vacation will come immediately, but the burden of making payments will come later.

But why is time an issue?

Borrowing, Lending, and Interest

In general, having a dollar today is worth more than having a dollar a year from now. To see why, let's consider two examples.

First, suppose that you get a new job that comes with a $1,000 bonus, which will be paid at the end of the first year. But you would like to spend the extra money now—say, on new clothes for work. Can you do that?

The answer is yes—you can borrow money today and use the bonus to repay the debt a year from now. But if that is your plan, you cannot borrow the full $1,000 today. You must borrow less than that, because a year from now you will have to repay the amount borrowed *plus interest*.

Now consider a different scenario. Suppose that you are paid a bonus of $1,000 today, and you decide that you don't want to spend the money right now. What do you do with it? You put it in the bank; in effect, you are lending the $1,000 to the bank, which in turn lends it out to its customers who wish to borrow. At the end of a year, you will get more than $1,000 back—you will have the $1,000 plus the interest earned.

What all of this means is that $1,000 today is worth more than $1,000 a year from now. The reason is that if you want to have the money today, you must borrow it and pay interest. That is, you must pay a price for using the money today. And, correspondingly, if you forgo using the money today and lend it to someone else, you earn interest on the money. That is, you earn something by letting someone else use your money. When someone borrows money for a year, the **interest rate** is the price, calculated as a percentage of the amount borrowed, charged by the lender.

Because of the interest paid on borrowing, you can't evaluate a project just by adding up all the costs and benefits when those costs and benefits arrive at different times. You must take time into account when evaluating the project because a $1 benefit that comes today is worth more than a $1 benefit that comes a year from now; and a $1 cost that comes today is more burdensome to you than a $1 cost that comes next year. Fortunately, there is a simple way to adjust for these complications.

What we will now see is that the interest rate can be used to convert future benefits and costs into what economists call their *present values*. By using present values in evaluating a project, you can evaluate a project *as if* all its costs and benefits were occurring today rather than at different times. This allows people to "factor out" the complications created by time. We'll start by defining exactly what the concept of present value is.

> When someone borrows money for a year, the **interest rate** is the price, calculated as a percentage of the amount borrowed, charged by the lender.

Defining Present Value

The key to the concept of present value is to understand that you can use the interest rate to compare the value of a dollar realized today with the value of a dollar realized later. Why the interest rate? Because the interest rate correctly measures the cost of delaying a dollar of benefit and, correspondingly, the benefit of delaying a dollar of cost. Let's illustrate this with some examples.

Suppose, first, that you are evaluating whether or not to take a job in which your employer promises to pay you a bonus at the end of the first year. What is the value to you today of $1 of bonus money to be paid to you one year in the future? A slightly different way of asking the same question: what would you be willing to accept today in place of receiving $1 one year in the future?

The way to answer this question is to observe that you need *less* than $1 today in order to be assured of having $1 one year from now. Why? Because any money that you have today can be lent out at interest, turning it into a greater sum at the end of the year.

The symbol r is used to represent the rate of interest, expressed as a fraction—that is, if the interest rate is 10%, then $r = 0.10$. If you lend out X, at the end of a year you will receive your X back, plus the interest on your X, which is $X \times r$. Thus, at the end of the year you will receive $X + $X \times r$, which is $X \times (1 + r)$. What we want to know is how much you would have to lend out today to have $1 a year from now. If the amount you lend out is $X, it must be true that

(7-1) $X \times (1 + r) = 1

Rearranging, we can solve for $X, the amount you need today in order to generate $1 one year from now.

(7-2) $X = $1/(1 + r)$

This means that you would be willing to accept $X today for every $1 to be paid one year from now. The reason is that by lending out $X today, you can be assured of having $1 one year from now. If we plug into the equation the value of the yearly interest rate—say it is 10%, which means that $r = 0.10$—then we can solve for $X: $X is equal to $1/1.10, which is approximately $0.91. So you would be willing to accept $0.91 today in exchange for every $1 to be paid to you one year from now. Economists have a special name for $X—it's called the **present value** of $1.

To see that this technique works for future costs as well as future benefits, consider the following example. Suppose you enter into an agreement that obliges you to pay $1 one year from now—say, to pay off your student loan when you graduate in a year. How much money would you need today to ensure that you have $1 in a year? The answer is $X, the present value of $1, which in our example is $0.91. The reason $0.91 is the right answer is that if you lend it out for one year at an interest rate of 10%, you will receive $1 in return at the end.

> The **present value** of $1 realized one year from now is equal to $1/(1 + r)$: the amount of money you must lend out today in order to have $1 in one year. It is the value to you today of $1 realized one year from now.

What these two examples show us is that the present value concept provides a way to calculate the value today of $1 that is realized in the future—regardless of whether that $1 is realized as a benefit (the bonus) or a cost (the student loan payback). This means that to evaluate a project today that has benefits and/or costs to be realized in the future, we just use the relevant interest rate to convert those future dollars into their present values. In that way we have "factored out" the complication that time creates for decision making.

In the next section we will work out an example of using the present value concept to evaluate a project. But before we do that, it is worthwhile to note that the present value method can be used for projects in which the $1 is realized more than a year later—say, two, three, or even more years.

Suppose you are considering a project that will pay you $1 *two years* from today. What is the value to you today of $1 received two years into the future? We can find the answer to that question by expanding our formula for present value.

Let's call $V the amount of money you need to lend today at an interest rate of r in order to have $1 in two years. So if you lend $V today, you will receive $V \times (1 + r)$ in one year. And if you *re-lend* that sum for yet another year, you will receive $V \times (1 + r) \times (1 + r) = $V \times (1 + r)^2$ at the end of the second year. At the end of two years, $V will be worth $V \times (1 + r)^2$; if $r = 0.10$, then this becomes $V \times (1.10)^2 = $V \times (1.21)$.

Now we are ready to answer the question of what $1 realized two years in the future is worth today. In order for the amount lent today, $V, to be worth $1 two years from now, it must satisfy this formula:

(7-3) $V \times (1 + r)^2 = 1

Rearranging, we can solve for $V:

(7-4) $V = $1/(1 + r)^2$

Given $r = 0.10$, this means that $\$V = \$1/1.21 = \$0.83$. So when the interest rate is 10%, \$1 realized two years from today is worth \$0.83 today because by lending out \$0.83 today you can be assured of having \$1 in two years. And that means that the present value of \$1 realized two years into the future is \$0.83.

From this example we can see how the present value concept can be expanded to a number of years even greater than two. If we ask what value of \$1 realized N number of years into the future is, the answer is given by a generalization of the present value formula: it is equal to $\$1/(1 + r)^N$.

Using Present Value

Suppose you have to choose one of three projects to undertake. Project A has an immediate payoff to you of \$100, while project B requires that you put up \$10 of your own money today in order to receive \$115 a year from now. Project C gives you an immediate payoff of \$119 but requires that you pay \$20 a year from now. We'll assume that the annual interest rate is 10%—that is, $r = 0.10$.

The problem in evaluating these three projects is that they have costs and benefits that are realized at different times. That is, of course, where the concept of present value becomes extremely helpful: by using present value to convert any dollars realized in the future into today's value, you factor out the issue of time. This allows you to calculate the **net present value** of a project—the present value of current and future benefits minus the present value of current and future costs. And the best project is the one with the highest net present value.

Table 7-7 shows how this is done for each of the three projects. The second and third columns show how many dollars are realized and when they are realized; costs are indicated by a minus sign. The fourth column shows the equations used to convert the flows of dollars into their present value, and the fifth column shows the actual amounts of the total net present value for each of the three projects.

For instance, to calculate the net present value of project B, we need to calculate the present value of \$115 received in one year. The present value of \$1 received in one year would be $\$1/(1 + r)$. So the present value of \$115 is 115 times $\$1/(1 + r)$; that is, $\$115/(1 + r)$. The net present value of project B is the present value of today's and future benefits minus the present value of today's and future costs: $-\$10 + \$115/(1 + r)$.

From the fifth column, we can immediately see which is the preferred project—it is project C. That's because it has the highest net present value, \$100.82, which is higher than the net present value of project A (\$100) and much higher than the net present value of project B (\$94.55).

This example shows how important the concept of present value is. If we had failed to use the present value calculations and instead had simply added up the dollars generated by each of the three projects, we could have easily been misled into believing that project B was the best project and project C was the worst one.

The **net present value** of a project is the present value of current and future benefits minus the present value of current and future costs.

TABLE **7-7**

The Net Present Value of Three Projects

Project	Dollars realized today	Dollars realized one year from today	Present value formula	Net present value given $r = 0.10$
A	\$100	—	\$100	\$100.00
B	−\$10	\$115	$-\$10 + \$115/(1 + r)$	\$94.55
C	\$119	−\$20	$\$119 - \$20/(1 + r)$	\$100.82

economics in action

How Big Is That Jackpot, Anyway?

For a clear example of present value at work, consider the case of lottery jackpots.

Recently, the Pennsylvania State Lottery's "Super 6" offered the lucky winner $4 million. Well, sort of. That $4 million was available only if you chose to take your winnings in the form of an "annuity," consisting of $200,000 per year for the next 20 years. If you wanted cash up front, the jackpot was only $2 million.

Why was Pennsylvania so stingy about quick payoffs? It was all a matter of present value.

In fact, the lottery budgeted only $2 million for the jackpot. If the winner had been willing to take the annuity, the lottery would have invested that money, buying U.S. government bonds (in effect lending the money to the federal government). The money would have been invested in such a way that the investments would pay $200,000 each year, just enough to pay the annuity. This worked, of course, because at the interest rates prevailing at the time, the present value of a $4 million annuity spread over 20 years was just about $2 million. Or to put it another way, the opportunity cost to the lottery of that annuity was $2 million.

So why didn't they just call it a $2 million jackpot? Hey, $4 million sounds more impressive! But it was really the same thing. ∎

> > > > > > > > > > > > > > > > > > > >

▶▶ CHECK YOUR UNDERSTANDING 7-4

1. Consider the three alternative projects shown in Table 7-7. This time, however, suppose that the interest rate is only 2%.
   a. Calculate the net present values of the three projects. Which one is now preferred?
   b. Explain why the preferred choice is different with a 2% interest rate than with a 10% rate.

Solutions appear at back of book.

● A LOOK AHEAD ●

This chapter laid out the basic concepts that we need to understand economic decisions. These concepts, as we will soon see, provide the necessary tools for understanding not only the behavior behind the supply and demand curves but also the implications of markets for consumer and producer welfare.

But to get there we need a bit more context—we need to know something more about the kinds of decisions that producers and consumers must make. We start with producers: in the next two chapters we will see how marginal analysis determines how much a profit-maximizing producer chooses to produce.

SUMMARY

1. All economic decisions involve the allocation of scarce resources. Some decisions are "either-or" decisions, in which the question is whether or not to do something. Other decisions are "how much" decisions, in which the question is how many resources to put into some use.

2. The cost of using a resource for a particular activity is the opportunity cost of that resource. Some opportunity costs are **explicit costs;** they involve a direct payment of cash. Other opportunity costs, however, are **implicit** costs; they involve no outlay of money but represent the inflows of cash that are forgone. Both explicit and implicit costs should be taken into account in making decisions. Companies use **capital** and their owners' time. So companies should base decisions on **economic profit,** which takes into account implicit costs such as the opportunity cost of the owners' time and **the implicit cost of capital.** The **accounting profit,** which companies calculate for the purposes of taxes and public reporting, is often considerably larger than the economic

profit because it includes only explicit costs and depreciation, not implicit costs.

3. A "how much" decision is made using marginal analysis, which involves comparing the benefit to the cost of doing an additional unit of an activity. The **marginal cost** of an activity is the additional cost incurred by doing one more unit of the activity, and the **marginal benefit** of an activity is the additional benefit gained by doing one more unit. The **marginal cost curve** is the graphical illustration of marginal cost, and the **marginal benefit curve** is the graphical illustration of marginal benefit.

4. Marginal cost and marginal benefit typically depend on how much of the activity has already been done. In the case of **increasing marginal cost,** each additional unit costs more than the unit before; this is represented by an upward-sloping marginal cost curve. In the case of **decreasing marginal benefit,** each additional unit produces a smaller benefit than the unit before; this is represented by a downward-sloping marginal benefit curve.

5. The **optimal quantity** of an activity is the quantity that generates the maximum possible total net gain. According to the **principle of marginal analysis,** the optimal quantity is the quantity at which marginal benefit is equal to marginal cost. It is the quantity at which the marginal cost curve and the marginal benefit curve intersect.

6. A cost that has already been incurred and that is non-recoverable is a **sunk cost.** Sunk costs should be ignored in decisions about future actions because they have no effect on future benefits and costs.

7. In order to evaluate a project in which costs or benefits are realized in the future, you must first transform them into their **present values** using the **interest rate,** r. The present value of $1 realized one year from now is $1/(1 + r)$, the amount of money you must lend out today to have $1 one year from now. Once this transformation is done, you should choose the project with the highest **net present value.**

KEY TERMS

Explicit cost, p. 161
Implicit cost, p. 161
Accounting profit, p. 163
Economic profit, p. 163
Capital, p. 163
Implicit cost of capital, p. 163

Marginal cost, p. 166
Increasing marginal cost, p. 166
Marginal cost curve, p. 167
Marginal benefit, p. 167
Decreasing marginal benefit, p. 168
Marginal benefit curve, p. 168

Optimal quantity, p. 169
Principle of marginal analysis, p. 170
Sunk cost, p. 172
Interest rate, p. 174
Present value, p. 175
Net present value, p. 176

PROBLEMS

1. Hiro owns and operates a small business that provides economic consulting services. During the year he spends $55,000 on travel to clients and other expenses, and the computer that he owns depreciates by $2,000. If he didn't use the computer, he could sell it and earn yearly interest of $100 on the money created through this sale. Hiro's total revenue for the year is $100,000. Instead of working as a consultant for the year, he could teach economics at a small local college and make a salary of $50,000.

   a. What is Hiro's accounting profit?

   b. What is Hiro's economic profit?

   c. Should Hiro continue working as a consultant, or should he teach economics instead?

2. Jackie owns and operates a web-design business. Her computing equipment depreciates by $5,000 per year. She runs the business out of a room in her home. If she didn't use the room as her business office, she could rent it out for $2,000 per year. Jackie knows that if she didn't run her own business, she could return to her previous job at a large software company that would pay her a salary of $60,000 per year. Jackie has no other expenses.

   a. How much total revenue does Jackie need to make in order to break even in the eyes of her accountant? That is, how much total revenue would give Jackie just zero accounting profit?

   b. How much total revenue does Jackie need to make in order for her to want to remain self-employed? That is, how much total revenue would give Jackie just zero economic profit?

3. You own and operate a bike store. Each year, you receive revenue of $200,000 from your bike sales, and it costs you $100,000 to obtain the bikes. In addition, you pay $20,000 for electricity, taxes, and other expenses per year. Instead of running the bike store, you could become an accountant and receive a yearly salary of $40,000. A large clothing retail chain wants to expand and offers to rent the store from you for $50,000 per year. How do you explain to your friends that despite making a profit, it is too costly for you to continue running your store?

4. Suppose you have just paid your nonrefundable fee of $1,000 for your meal plan for this academic term. This allows you to eat dinner in the cafeteria every evening.

   a. You are offered a part-time job in a restaurant where you can eat for free each evening. Your parents say that you should eat dinner in the cafeteria anyway, since you have already paid for those meals. Are your parents right? Explain why or why not.

   b. Now suppose that you are offered a part-time job in a restaurant, but rather than being able to eat there for free, the restaurant only gives you a large discount on your meals there. Each meal at the restaurant will cost you $2, and if you eat there each evening this semester it will add up to $200. Your roommate says that you should eat in the restaurant since it costs less than the $1,000 that you paid for the meal plan. Is your roommate right? Explain why or why not.

5. You have already bought a $10 ticket for the college soccer game in advance. The ticket cannot be resold. You know that going to the soccer game will give you a benefit equal to $20. After you have bought the ticket, you hear that there will be a professional baseball post-season game at the same time. Tickets to the baseball game cost $20, and you know that going to the baseball game will give you a benefit equal to $35. You tell your friends the following: "If I had known about the baseball game before buying the ticket to the soccer game, I would have gone to the baseball game instead. But now that I already have the ticket to the soccer game, it's better for me to just go to the soccer game." Are you making the correct decision? Justify your answer by calculating the benefits and costs of your decision.

6. Amy, Bill, and Carla all mow lawns for money. Each of them operates a different lawn mower. The accompanying table shows the total cost to Amy, Bill, and Carla of mowing lawns.

Quantity of lawns mowed	Amy's total cost	Bill's total cost	Carla's total cost
0	$0	$0	$0
1	20	10	2
2	35	20	7
3	45	30	17
4	50	40	32
5	52	50	52
6	53	60	82

   a. Calculate Amy's, Bill's, and Carla's marginal costs, and draw each of their marginal cost curves.

   b. Who has increasing marginal cost, who has decreasing marginal cost, and who has constant marginal cost?

7. You are the manager of a gym, and you have to decide how many customers to admit each hour. Assume that each customer stays exactly one hour. Customers are costly to admit because they inflict wear and tear on the exercise equipment. Moreover, each additional customer generates more wear and tear than the customer before. As a result, the gym faces increasing marginal cost. The accompanying table shows the marginal costs associated with each number of customers per hour.

Quantity of customers per hour	Marginal cost of customer
0	
	$14.00
1	
	14.50
2	
	15.00
3	
	15.50
4	
	16.00
5	
	16.50
6	
	17.00
7	

   a. Suppose that each customer pays $15.25 for a one-hour workout. Use the principle of marginal analysis to find the optimal number of customers that you should admit per hour.

   b. You increase the price of a one-hour workout to $16.25. What is the optimal number of customers per hour that you should admit now?

8. Georgia and Lauren are economics students who go to a karate class together. Both have to choose how many classes to go to per week. Each class costs $20. The accompanying table shows Georgia's and Lauren's estimates of the marginal benefit that each of them gets from each class per week.

Quantity of classes	Lauren's marginal benefit of each class	Georgia's marginal benefit of each class
0		
	$23	$28
1		
	19	22
2		
	14	15
3		
	8	7
4		

   a. Use marginal analysis to find Lauren's optimal number of karate classes per week

   b. Will Georgia be willing to go to the same number of classes per week that are optimal for Lauren?

9. The Centers for Disease Control and Prevention (CDC) recommended against vaccinating the whole population against the smallpox virus because the vaccination has undesirable, and sometimes fatal, side effects. Suppose the accompanying

table gives the data that are available about the effects of a smallpox vaccination program.

Percent of population vaccinated	Deaths due to smallpox	Deaths due to vaccination side effects
0	200	0
10	180	4
20	160	10
30	140	18
40	120	33
50	100	50
60	80	74

a. Calculate the marginal benefit (in terms of lives saved) and the marginal cost (in terms of lives lost) of each 10% increment of smallpox vaccination. Calculate the net gain of a 10% increment in population vaccinated.

b. Using marginal analysis, decide what percentage of the population should optimally be vaccinated.

10. Patty delivers pizza using her own car, and she is paid according to how many pizzas she delivers. The accompanying table shows Patty's total benefit and total cost when she works a specific number of hours.

Quantity of hours worked	Total benefit	Total cost
0	$0	$0
1	30	10
2	55	21
3	75	34
4	90	50
5	100	70

a. Use marginal analysis to decide how many hours Patty should work. In other words, what is the optimal number of hours Patty should work?

b. Calculate the total net gain to Patty from working 0 hours, 1 hour, 2 hours, and so on. Now suppose Patty chooses to work for 1 hour. Compare her total net gain from working for 1 hour with her total net gain from working the optimal number of hours. How much would she lose by working for only 1 hour?

11. Assume De Beers is the sole producer of diamonds. When it wants to sell more diamonds, it must lower its price in order to induce consumers to buy more. Furthermore, each additional diamond that is produced costs more than the previous one due to the difficulty of mining for diamonds. De Beers's total benefit schedule is given in the accompanying table, along with its total cost schedule.

Quantity of diamonds	Total benefit	Total cost
0	$0	$0
1	1,000	50
2	1,900	100
3	2,700	200
4	3,400	400
5	4,000	800
6	4,500	1,500
7	4,900	2,500
8	5,200	3,800

a. Draw the marginal cost curve and the marginal benefit curve and, from your diagram, graphically derive the optimal quantity of diamonds to produce.

b. Calculate the total net gain to De Beers from producing each quantity of diamonds. Which quantity gives De Beers the highest total net gain?

12. You have won the state lottery. There are two ways in which you can receive your prize. You can either have $1 million in cash now, or you can have $1.2 million that is paid out as follows: $300,000 now, $300,000 in one year's time, $300,000 in two years' time, and $300,000 in three years' time. The interest rate is 20%. How would you prefer to receive your prize?

13. The drug company Pfizer is considering whether to invest in the development of a new cancer drug. Development will require an initial investment of $10 million now; beginning one year from now, the drug will generate annual profits of $4 million for three years.

a. If the interest rate is 12%, should Pfizer invest in the development of the new drug? Why or why not?

b. If the interest rate is 8%, should Pfizer invest in the development of the new drug? Why or why not?

>web... To continue your study and review of concepts in this chapter, please visit the Krugman/Wells website for quizzes, animated graph tutorials, web links to helpful resources, and more.

www.worthpublishers.com/krugmanwells

>>Behind the Supply Curve: Inputs and Costs

THE FARMER'S MARGIN

OBEAUTIFUL FOR SPACIOUS SKIES, FOR amber waves of grain." So begins the song "America the Beautiful." And those amber waves of grain are for real: though farmers are now only a small minority of America's population, our agricultural industry is immensely productive and feeds much of the world.

If you look at agricultural statistics, however, something may seem a bit surprising: when it comes to yield per acre, U.S. farmers are often nowhere near the top. For example, farmers in western European countries grow about three times as much wheat per acre as their U.S. counterparts. Are the Europeans better at growing wheat than we are?

No: European farmers are very skillful, but no more so than Americans. They produce more wheat per acre because they employ more inputs—more fertilizer and, especially, more labor—per acre. Of course, this means that European farmers have higher costs than their American counterparts. But because of government policies, European farmers receive a much higher price for their wheat than American farmers. This gives them an incentive to use more inputs and to expend more effort at the margin to increase the crop yield per acre.

Notice our use of the phrase "at the margin." Like most decisions that involve a comparison of benefits and costs, decisions about inputs and production involve a comparison of marginal quantities—the marginal cost versus the marginal benefit of producing a bit more from each acre.

In Chapter 7 we used the example of Felix's Lawn-Mowing Service to illustrate the *principle of marginal analysis*, showing

What you will learn in this chapter:

➤ The importance of the firm's **production function,** the relationship between quantity of inputs and quantity of output

➤ Why production is often subject to **diminishing returns to inputs**

➤ What the various forms of a firm's costs are and how they generate the firm's **marginal** and **average cost curves**

➤ Why a firm's costs may differ in the **short run** versus the **long run**

➤ How the firm's technology of production can generate **economies of scale**

American farming practices (at left) or European farming practices (at right)? How intensively an acre of land is worked—a decision at the margin—depends on the price of wheat a farmer faces.

how Felix could use marginal analysis to determine the optimal number of lawns to mow daily—that is, the number that generates the maximum total net gain or profit. In this chapter and in Chapter 9, we will show how marginal analysis can be used to understand the output decisions that lie behind the supply curve. The first step in this analysis is to show how the relationship between a firm's inputs and its output—its *production function*—determines its *cost curves*, the relationship between cost and quantity of output produced. That is what we do in this chapter. In Chapter 9, we will see how to go from the firm's cost curves to the supply curve.

The Production Function

A *firm* is an organization that produces goods or services for sale. To do this, it must transform inputs into output. The quantity of output a firm produces depends on the quantity of inputs; this relationship is known as the firm's **production function**. As we'll see, a firm's production function underlies its *cost curves*. But as a first step, let's look at the characteristics of a hypothetical production function.

Inputs and Output

To understand the concept of a production function, let's consider a farm that we assume, for the sake of simplicity, produces only one output, wheat, and uses only two inputs, land and labor. This particular farm is owned by a couple named George and Martha. They hire workers to do the actual physical labor on the farm. Moreover, we will assume that all potential workers are of the same quality—they are all equally knowledgeable and capable of performing farmwork.

George and Martha's farm sits on 10 acres of land; no more acres are available to them, and they are currently unable to either increase or decrease the size of their farm by selling, buying, or leasing acreage. Land here is what economists call a **fixed input**—an input whose quantity is fixed and cannot be varied. On the other hand, George and Martha are free to decide how many workers to hire. The labor provided by these workers is called a **variable input**—an input whose quantity the firm can vary. (In Chapter 7, when we considered the example of Felix's Lawn-Mowing Service, Felix's fixed input was his lawn mower and his variable input was his own labor.)

In reality, whether or not the quantity of an input is really fixed depends on the time horizon. In the **long run**—that is, given that a long enough period of time has elapsed—firms can adjust the quantity of any input. So there are no fixed inputs in the long run, only in the **short run**. Later in this chapter we'll look more carefully at the distinction between the short run and the long run. But for now, we will restrict our attention to the short run and assume that at least one input is fixed.

George and Martha know that the quantity of wheat they produce depends on the number of workers they hire. Given modern farming techniques, one worker can cultivate the 10-acre farm, albeit not very intensively. When an additional worker is added, the land is divided equally among all the workers: each worker has 5 acres to cultivate when 2 workers are employed, each cultivates 3⅓ acres when 3 are employed, and so on. So as additional workers are employed, the 10 acres of land are cultivated more intensively and more bushels of wheat are produced. The relationship between the quantity of labor and the quantity of output, for a given amount of the fixed input, constitutes the farm's production function. The production function for George and Martha's farm is given in the first two columns of the table in Figure 8-1; the diagram there shows the same information graphically. The curve in Figure 8-1 shows how the quantity of output depends on the quantity of the variable input, for a given quantity of the fixed input; it is called the farm's **total product curve**. The physical quantity of output, bushels of wheat, is measured on the vertical axis, while the quantity of the

A **production function** is the relationship between the quantity of inputs a firm uses and the quantity of output it produces.

A **fixed input** is an input whose quantity is fixed and cannot be varied.

A **variable input** is an input whose quantity the firm can vary.

The **long run** is the time period in which all inputs can be varied.

The **short run** is the time period in which at least one input is fixed.

The **total product curve** shows how the quantity of output depends on the quantity of the variable input, for a given quantity of the fixed input.

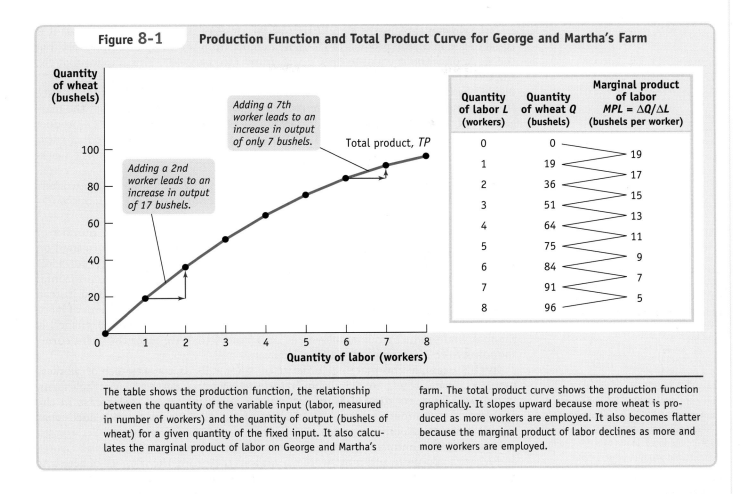

Figure 8-1   Production Function and Total Product Curve for George and Martha's Farm

Quantity of labor L (workers)	Quantity of wheat Q (bushels)	Marginal product of labor MPL = ΔQ/ΔL (bushels per worker)
0	0	
		19
1	19	
		17
2	36	
		15
3	51	
		13
4	64	
		11
5	75	
		9
6	84	
		7
7	91	
		5
8	96	

The table shows the production function, the relationship between the quantity of the variable input (labor, measured in number of workers) and the quantity of output (bushels of wheat) for a given quantity of the fixed input. It also calculates the marginal product of labor on George and Martha's farm. The total product curve shows the production function graphically. It slopes upward because more wheat is produced as more workers are employed. It also becomes flatter because the marginal product of labor declines as more and more workers are employed.

variable input, labor, that is, the number of workers employed, is measured on the horizontal axis. The total product curve here is upward sloping, reflecting the fact that more bushels of wheat are produced as more workers are employed.

Although the total product curve in Figure 8-1 slopes upward along its entire length, the slope isn't constant: as you move up the curve to the right, it flattens out. To understand this changing slope, look at the third column of the table in Figure 8-1, which shows the *change in the quantity of output* that is generated by adding one more worker. That is, it shows the **marginal product** of labor: the additional quantity of output from using one more unit of labor (that is, one more worker).

In this case, we have data at intervals of 1 worker—that is, we have information on the quantity of output when there are 3 workers, 4 workers, and so on. Sometimes data aren't available in increments of 1 unit—for example, you might have information only on the quantity of output when there are 40 workers and when there are 50 workers. In this case, you can use the following equation to figure out the marginal product of labor:

> The **marginal product** of an input is the additional quantity of output that is produced by using one more unit of that input.

$$\textbf{(8-1)} \quad \begin{matrix} \text{Marginal} \\ \text{product} \\ \text{of labor} \end{matrix} = \frac{\text{Change in quantity of output}}{\text{Change in quantity of labor}} = \begin{matrix} \text{Change in quantity of} \\ \text{output generated by one} \\ \text{additional unit of labor} \end{matrix}$$

or

$$MPL = \Delta Q/\Delta L$$

In this equation, Δ, the Greek uppercase delta, represents the change in a variable.

Now we can explain the significance of the slope of the total product curve: it is equal to the marginal product of labor. Remember from the Chapter 2 Appendix that the slope of a line is equal to "rise" over "run" (see page 44). This implies that the slope of the total product curve is the change in the quantity of output (the "rise") divided by the change in the quantity of labor (the "run"). And this, as we can see from Equation 8-1, is simply the marginal product of labor. So the fact that the marginal product of the first worker is 19 also means that the slope of the total product curve in going from 0 to 1 worker is 19. Similarly, the slope of the total product curve in going from 1 to 2 workers is the same as the marginal product of the second worker, 17, and so on.

In this example, the marginal product of labor steadily declines as more workers are hired—that is, each successive worker adds less to output than the previous worker. So as employment increases, the total product curve gets flatter.

Figure 8-2 shows how the marginal product of labor depends on the number of workers employed on the farm. The marginal product of labor, *MPL*, is measured on the vertical axis in units of physical output—bushels of wheat—produced per additional worker, and the number of workers employed is measured on the horizontal axis. You can see from the table in Figure 8-1 that if 5 workers are employed instead of 4, output rises from 64 to 75 bushels; so in this case the marginal product of labor is 11 bushels—the same number found in Figure 8-2. To indicate that 11 bushels is the marginal product when employment rises from 4 to 5, we place the point corresponding to that information halfway between 4 and 5 workers.

In this example the marginal product of labor falls as the number of workers increases. That is, there are *diminishing returns to labor* on George and Martha's farm. In general, there are **diminishing returns to an input** when an increase in the quantity of that input, holding the quantity of all other inputs fixed, reduces that input's marginal product.

To grasp why diminishing returns can occur, think about what happens as George and Martha add more and more workers, without increasing the number of acres. As the number of workers increases, the land is farmed more intensively and the number of bushels increases. But each additional worker is working with a smaller share of the 10 acres—the fixed input—than the previous worker. As a result, the additional

There are **diminishing returns to an input** when an increase in the quantity of that input, holding the levels of all other inputs fixed, leads to a decline in the marginal product of that input.

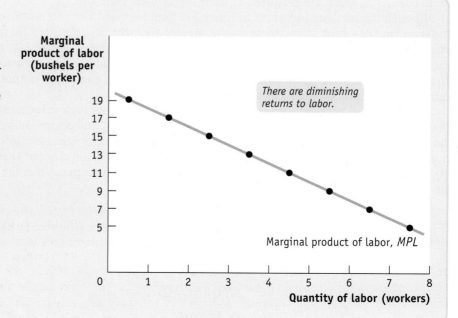

Figure 8-2

Marginal Product of Labor Curve for George and Martha's Farm

The marginal product of labor curve plots each worker's marginal product, the increase in the quantity of output generated by each additional worker. The change in the quantity of output is measured on the vertical axis and the number of workers employed on the horizontal axis. The first worker employed generates an increase in output of 19 bushels, the second worker generates an increase of 17 bushels, and so on. The curve slopes downward due to diminishing returns. >*web*...

There are diminishing returns to labor.

Marginal product of labor, *MPL*

Figure 8-3   Total Product, Marginal Product, and the Fixed Input

This figure shows how the quantity of output—illustrated by the total product curve—and marginal product depend on the level of the fixed input. Panel (a) shows two total product curves for George and Martha's farm, TP_{10} when their farm is 10 acres and TP_{20} when it is 20 acres. With more land, each worker can produce more wheat. So an increase in the fixed input shifts the total product curve up from TP_{10} to TP_{20}. This also implies that the marginal product of each worker is higher when the farm is 20 acres than when it is 10 acres. As a result, an increase in acreage also shifts the marginal product of labor curve up from MPL_{10} to MPL_{20}. Panel (b) shows the marginal product of labor curves. Note that both marginal product of labor curves still slope downward due to diminishing returns.

worker cannot produce as much output as the previous worker. So it's not surprising that the marginal product of the additional worker falls.

The crucial thing to emphasize about diminishing returns is that, like many propositions in economics, it is an "other things equal" proposition: each successive unit of an input will raise production by less than the last *if the quantity of all other inputs is held fixed.*

What would happen if the levels of other inputs were allowed to change? You can see the answer in Figure 8-3. Panel (a) shows two total product curves, TP_{10} and TP_{20}. TP_{10} is the farm's total product curve when its total area is 10 acres (the same curve as in Figure 8-1). TP_{20} is the total product curve when the farm has increased to 20 acres. Except when 0 workers are employed, TP_{20} lies everywhere above TP_{10} because with more acres available, any given number of workers produces more output. Panel (b) shows the corresponding marginal product of labor curves. MPL_{10} is the marginal product of labor curve given 10 acres to cultivate (the same curve as in Figure 8-2) and MPL_{20} is the marginal product of labor curve given 20 acres. Both curves slope downward because, in each case, the amount of land is fixed, albeit at different levels. But MPL_{20} lies everywhere above MPL_{10}, reflecting the fact that the marginal product of the same worker is higher when he or she has more of the fixed input to work with.

Figure 8-3 demonstrates a general result: the position of the total product curve depends on the quantities of other inputs. If you change the quantity of the other inputs, both the total product curve and the marginal product curve of the remaining input will shift. The importance of the "other things equal" assumption in discussing diminishing returns is illustrated in the following For Inquiring Minds.

PITFALLS

WHAT'S A UNIT?

The marginal product of labor (or any other input) is defined as the increase in the quantity of output when you increase the quantity of that input by one unit. But what do we mean by a "unit" of labor? Is it an additional hour of labor, an additional week, or a person-year?

The answer is that it doesn't matter, *as long as you are consistent.* One common source of error in economics is getting units confused—say, comparing the output added by an additional *hour* of labor with the cost of employing a worker for a *week*. Whatever units you use, always be careful that you use the same units throughout your analysis of any problem.

The idea of diminishing returns first became influential with the writings of Thomas Malthus, an English pastor whose 1798 book *An Essay on the Principle of Population* was deeply influential in its own time and continues to provoke heated argument to this day.

Malthus argued that as its population grew (while its land area remained fixed), a country would find it increasingly difficult to grow enough food. Though more intensive cultivation of the land could increase yields, each successive farmer would add less to the total than the last as the marginal product of labor declined. Eventually, food production per capita (the average output of an existing worker) would decline as the population exceeded some level.

He drew a powerful conclusion from this argument—namely, that misery was the normal condition of humankind. Imagine a country in which land was abundant and population low, so that everyone had plenty

to eat. Then families would, he argued, be large (as they were at the time in the United States, where land was abundant), and the population would grow rapidly—until the pressure of population on the land had reduced the condition of most people to a level where starvation and disease held the population in check. (It was arguments like these that led the historian Thomas Carlyle to dub economics the "dismal science").

Happily, Malthus's prediction has turned out to be quite wrong. The world's population has increased from about 1 billion people when Malthus wrote to more than 6 billion today, but in most of the world people eat better now than ever before. In England, in particular, a fivefold increase in population was accompanied by a dramatic rise in the standard of living.

So was Malthus completely wrong? And does the wrongness of his prediction refute the whole idea of diminishing returns? No, on both counts.

First of all, the Malthusian story actually works pretty well as a description of 57 out of the last 59 centuries: peasants in eighteenth-century France probably did not live much better than Egyptian peasants in the age of the pyramids. It just so happens that scientific and technological progress since the eighteenth century has been so rapid that it has far outpaced any problems caused by diminishing returns.

The concept of diminishing returns does not mean that using more labor to grow food, even on a given amount of land, will lead to a decline in the marginal product of labor—*if* there is also a radical improvement in farming technology. It does mean that the marginal product declines when *all* other things—land, farming technology, and a host of other factors—remain the same. And so the happy fact that Malthus's predictions were wrong does not invalidate the concept of diminishing returns.

From the Production Function to Cost Curves

Once George and Martha know their production function, they know the relationship between inputs of labor and land and output of wheat. But if they want to maximize their profits, they need to translate this knowledge into information about the relationship between the quantity of output and cost. Let's see how they can do this.

To translate information about a firm's production function into information about its cost, we need to know how much the firm must pay for its inputs. We will assume that George and Martha face either an explicit or an implicit cost of $400 for the use of the land. As we learned in Chapter 7, it is irrelevant whether George and Martha must rent the land for $400 from someone else, or they own the land themselves and forgo earning $400 by renting it to someone else. Either way, they pay an opportunity cost of $400 by using the land to grow wheat. Moreover, since the land is a fixed input, the $400 George and Martha pay for it is a **fixed cost**, denoted by *FC*—a cost that does not depend on the quantity of output produced. In business, fixed cost is often referred to as "overhead cost."

We also assume that George and Martha must pay each worker $200. Using their production function, George and Martha know that the number of workers they must hire depends on the amount of wheat they intend to produce. So the cost of labor, which is equal to the number of workers multiplied by $200, is a **variable cost**, denoted by *VC*—a cost that depends on the quantity of output produced. Adding the fixed cost and the variable cost of a given quantity of output gives the **total cost**, or *TC*, of that quantity of output. We can express the relationship among fixed cost, variable cost, and total cost as an equation:

A **fixed cost** is a cost that does not depend on the quantity of output produced. It is the cost of the fixed input.

A **variable cost** is a cost that depends on the quantity of output produced. It is the cost of the variable input.

The **total cost** of producing a given quantity of output is the sum of the fixed cost and the variable cost of producing that quantity of output.

(8-2)   Total cost = Fixed cost + Variable cost

or

$$TC = FC + VC$$

The table in Figure 8-4 shows how total cost is calculated for George and Martha's farm. The second column shows the number of workers employed. The third column shows the corresponding level of output, taken from the table in Figure 8-1. The fourth column shows the variable cost, equal to the number of workers multiplied by $200. The fifth column shows the fixed cost, which is $400 regardless of how many workers are employed. The sixth column shows the total cost of output, which is the variable cost plus the fixed cost.

The first column labels each row of the table with a letter, from A to I. These labels will be helpful in understanding our next step: drawing the **total cost curve**, a curve that shows how total cost depends on the quantity of output.

> The **total cost curve** shows how total cost depends on the quantity of output.

George and Martha's total cost curve is shown in the diagram in Figure 8-4, where the horizontal axis measures the quantity of output in bushels of wheat and the vertical

---

Figure 8-4

Total Cost Curve for George and Martha's Farm

The table shows the variable cost, fixed cost, and total cost for various output quantities on George and Martha's 10-acre farm. The total cost curve shows how total cost (measured on the vertical axis) depends on the quantity of output (measured on the horizontal axis). The labeled points on the curve correspond to the rows of the table. The total cost curve slopes upward because the number of workers employed, and hence total cost, increases as the quantity of output increases. The curve gets steeper as output increases due to diminishing returns to labor.

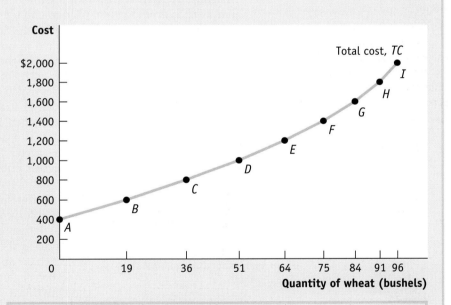

Point on graph	Quantity of labor L (workers)	Quantity of wheat Q (bushels)	Variable cost VC	Fixed cost FC	Total cost TC = FC + VC
A	0	0	$0	$400	$400
B	1	19	200	400	600
C	2	36	400	400	800
D	3	51	600	400	1,000
E	4	64	800	400	1,200
F	5	75	1,000	400	1,400
G	6	84	1,200	400	1,600
H	7	91	1,400	400	1,800
I	8	96	1,600	400	2,000

axis measures total cost in dollars. Each point on the curve corresponds to one row of the table in Figure 8-4. For example, point A shows the situation when 0 workers are employed: output is zero, and total cost is equal to fixed cost, $400. Similarly, point B shows the situation when 1 worker is employed: output is 19 bushels, and total cost is $600, equal to the sum of $400 in fixed cost and $200 in variable cost.

Like the total product curve, the total cost curve is upward sloping: due to the variable cost, the more output produced, the higher the farm's total cost. But unlike the total product curve, which gets flatter as employment rises, the total cost curve gets *steeper*. That is, the slope of the total cost curve is greater as the amount of output produced increases. And as we will soon see, the steepening of the total cost curve is also due to diminishing returns to the variable input. Before we can understand this, we must first look at the relationships among several useful measures of cost.

economics in action

The Mythical Man-Month

The concept of diminishing returns to an input was first formulated by economists during the late eighteenth century. These economists, notably including Thomas Malthus, drew their inspiration from agricultural examples; they noticed, in particular, that as an individual tried to employ more workers in agriculture, he or she was forced to cultivate poorer quality land. Although still valid, such examples can seem somewhat musty and old-fashioned in our modern information economy.

However, the idea of diminishing returns to an input applies with equal force to the most modern of economic activities—such as, say, the design of software. In 1975 Frederick P. Brooks Jr., a project manager at IBM during the days when it dominated the computer business, published a book titled *The Mythical Man-Month* that soon became a classic—so much so that a special anniversary edition was published 20 years later.

The chapter that gave its title to the book is basically about diminishing returns in the writing of software. Brooks observed that multiplying the number of programmers assigned to a project did not produce a proportionate reduction in the time it took to get the program written. A project that could be done by 1 programmer in 12 months could *not* be done by 12 programmers in 1 month—hence the "mythical man-month," the false notion that the number of lines of programming code produced was proportional to the number of code writers employed. In fact, above a certain number, adding another programmer on a project actually *increased* the time to completion.

The argument of *The Mythical Man-Month* is summarized in Figure 8-5. The upper part of the figure shows how the quantity of the project's output, as measured by the number of lines of code produced per month, varies with the number of programmers. Each additional programmer accomplishes less than the previous one, and beyond a certain point an additional programmer is actually counterproductive. The lower part of the figure shows the marginal product of each successive programmer, which falls as more programmers are employed and eventually becomes negative. In other words, programming is subject to diminishing returns so severe that at some point more programmers

Figure 8-5   The Mythical Man-Month

Beyond a certain point, an additional programmer is counterproductive.

Beyond a certain point, adding an additional programmer is counterproductive—output falls and the slope of the total product curve becomes negative. At this point the marginal product of labor curve crosses the horizontal axis—and the marginal product of labor becomes negative.

actually have negative marginal product. The source of the diminishing returns lies in the nature of the production function for a programming project: each programmer must coordinate his or her work with that of all the other programmers on the project, leading to each person spending more and more time communicating with others as the number of programmers increases. In other words, other things equal, there are diminishing returns to labor. It is likely, however, that if fixed inputs devoted to programming projects are increased—say, installing a faster e-mail system—the problem of diminishing returns for additional programmers can be mitigated.

A reviewer of the reissued edition of *The Mythical Man-Month* summarized the reasons for these diminishing returns: "There is an inescapable overhead to yoking up programmers in parallel. The members of the team must 'waste time' attending meetings, drafting project plans, exchanging e-mail, negotiating interfaces, enduring performance reviews, and so on . . . At Microsoft, there will be at least one team member that just designs T-shirts for the rest of the team to wear." (from www.ercb.com, Dr. Dobb's Electronic Review of Computer Books.) ∎

> > > > > > > > > > > > > > > > > > > >

>>CHECK YOUR UNDERSTANDING 8-1

1. Bernie's ice-making company produces ice cubes using a 10-ton machine and electricity. The quantity of output, measured in terms of pounds of ice, is given in this table:

Quantity of electricity (kilowatts)	Quantity of ice (pounds)
0	0
1	1,000
2	1,800
3	2,400
4	2,800

  a. What is the fixed input? What is the variable input?

  b. Construct a table showing the marginal product of the variable input. Does it show diminishing returns?

  c. Suppose a 50 percent increase in the size of the fixed input increases output by 100 percent for any given amount of the variable input. What is the fixed input now? Construct a table showing the quantity of output and marginal product in this case.

Solutions appear at back of book.

Two Key Concepts: Marginal Cost and Average Cost

We've just seen how to derive a firm's total cost curve from its production function. Our next step is to take a deeper look at total cost by deriving two extremely useful measures: *marginal cost* and *average cost*. As we'll see, these two measures of the cost of production have a somewhat surprising relationship to each other. Moreover, they will prove to be vitally important in Chapter 9, where we will use them to analyze the firm's output decision and the market supply curve.

Marginal Cost

We defined marginal cost in Chapter 7: it is the change in total cost generated by producing one more unit of output. We've already seen that marginal product is easiest to calculate if data on output are available in increments of one unit of input. Similarly, marginal cost is easiest to calculate if data on total cost are available in increments of one unit of output. When the data come in less convenient increments, it's still possible to calculate marginal cost over each interval. But for the sake of simplicity, let's work with an example in which the data come in convenient increments.

Ben's Boots produces leather footwear; Table 8-1 shows how its costs per day depend on the number of boots it produces per day. The firm has fixed cost of $108 per day, shown in the second column, which represents the daily cost of its boot-making machine. The third column shows the variable cost, and the fourth column shows the total cost. Panel (a) of Figure 8-6 plots the total cost curve. Like the total cost curve for George and Martha's farm in Figure 8-4, this curve is upward sloping, getting steeper as you move up it to the right.

The significance of the slope of the total cost curve is shown by the fifth column of Table 8-1, which calculates *marginal cost*: the cost of each additional unit. The general formula for marginal cost is

$$\textbf{(8-3)} \quad \text{Marginal cost} = \frac{\text{Change in total cost}}{\text{Change in quantity of output}} = \begin{matrix} \text{Change in total cost} \\ \text{generated by one} \\ \text{additional unit of} \\ \text{output} \end{matrix}$$

or

$$MC = \Delta TC / \Delta Q$$

As in the case of marginal product, marginal cost is equal to "rise" (the increase in total cost) divided by "run" (the increase in the quantity of output). So just as marginal product is equal to the slope of the total product curve, marginal cost is equal to the slope of the total cost curve.

Now we can understand why the total cost curve gets steeper as we move up it to the right: as you can see in Table 8-1, the marginal cost at Ben's Boots rises as output increases. Panel (b) of Figure 8-6 shows the *marginal cost curve* corresponding to the data in Table 8-1. Notice that, as in Figure 8-2, we plot the marginal cost for increasing output from 0 to 1 pair of boots halfway between 0 and 1, the marginal cost for increasing output from 1 to 2 pairs of boots halfway between 1 and 2, and so on.

Why is the marginal cost curve upward sloping? Because there are diminishing returns to inputs in this example. As output increases, the marginal product of the

TABLE **8-1**

Costs at Ben's Boots

Quantity of boots Q (pairs)	Fixed cost FC	Variable cost VC	Total cost $TC = FC + VC$	Marginal cost of pair $MC = \Delta TC / \Delta Q$
0	$108	$0	$108	
				$12
1	108	12	120	
				36
2	108	48	156	
				60
3	108	108	216	
				84
4	108	192	300	
				108
5	108	300	408	
				132
6	108	432	540	
				156
7	108	588	696	
				180
8	108	768	876	
				204
9	108	972	1,080	
				228
10	108	1,200	1,308	

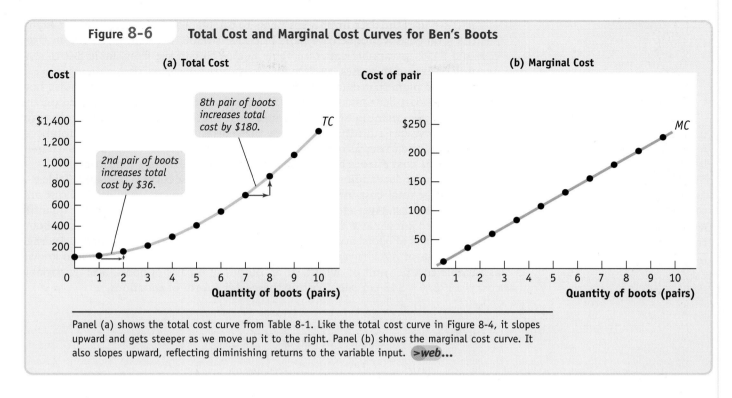

Figure 8-6   **Total Cost and Marginal Cost Curves for Ben's Boots**

Panel (a) shows the total cost curve from Table 8-1. Like the total cost curve in Figure 8-4, it slopes upward and gets steeper as we move up it to the right. Panel (b) shows the marginal cost curve. It also slopes upward, reflecting diminishing returns to the variable input. **>web...**

variable input declines. This implies that more and more of the variable input must be used to produce each additional unit of output as the amount of output already produced rises. And since each unit of the variable input must be paid for, the cost per additional unit of output also rises.

In addition, recall that the flattening of the total product curve is also due to diminishing returns to inputs in production: the marginal product of an input falls as more of that input is used if the quantities of other inputs are fixed. The flattening of the total product curve as output increases and the steepening of the total cost curve as output increases are just flip-sides of the same phenomenon. That is, as output increases, the marginal cost of output also increases because the marginal product of the variable input is falling.

We will return to marginal cost in Chapter 9, when we consider the firm's profit-maximizing output decision. But our next step is to introduce another measure of cost: *average cost.*

Average Cost

In addition to total cost and marginal cost, it's useful to calculate one more measure, **average total cost**, often simply called **average cost**. The average total cost is total cost divided by the quantity of output produced; that is, it is equal to total cost per unit of output. If we let *ATC* denote average total cost, the equation looks like this:

Average total cost, often referred to simply as **average cost**, is total cost divided by quantity of output produced.

$$(8\text{-}4) \quad ATC = \frac{\text{Total cost}}{\text{Quantity of output}} = TC/Q$$

Average total cost is important because it tells the producer how much the *average* or *typical* unit of output costs to produce. Marginal cost, meanwhile, tells the producer how much *one more* unit of output costs to produce. Although they may look very similar, these two measures of cost typically differ. And confusion between them is a major source of error in economics, both in the classroom and in real life, as illustrated by Economics in Action on page 196.

Table 8-2 uses the data from Ben's Boots to calculate average total cost. For example, the total cost of producing 4 pairs of boots is $300, consisting of $108 in fixed cost and $192 in variable cost (see Table 8-1). You can see from Table 8-2 that as quantity of output increases, average total cost first falls, then rises.

Figure 8-7 plots that data to yield the *average total cost curve*, which shows how average total cost depends on output. As before, cost in dollars is measured on the vertical axis and quantity of output is measured on the horizontal axis. The average total cost curve has a distinctive U shape that corresponds to how average total cost first falls and then rises as output increases. Economists believe that such **U-shaped average total cost curves** are the norm for producers in many industries.

To help our understanding of why the average total cost curve is U-shaped, Table 8-2 breaks average total cost into its two underlying components, *average fixed cost* and *average variable cost*. **Average fixed cost**, or *AFC*, is fixed cost divided by the quantity of output, also known as the fixed cost per unit of output. For example, if Ben's Boots produces 4 pairs of boots, average fixed cost is $108/4 = $27 per pair of boots. **Average variable cost**, or *AVC*, is variable cost divided by the quantity of output, also known as variable cost per unit of output. At an output of 4 pairs of boots, average variable cost is $192/4 = $48 per pair. Writing these in the form of equations,

$$(8\text{-}5) \quad AFC = \frac{\text{Fixed cost}}{\text{Quantity of output}} = FC/Q$$

$$AVC = \frac{\text{Variable cost}}{\text{Quantity of output}} = VC/Q$$

Average total cost is the sum of average fixed cost and average variable cost; it has a U shape because these components move in opposite directions as output rises.

Average fixed cost falls as more output is produced because the numerator (the fixed cost) is a fixed number but the denominator (the quantity of output) increases as more is produced. Another way to think about this relationship is that, as more output is produced, the fixed cost is spread over more units of output; the end result is that the fixed cost *per unit of output*—the average fixed cost—falls. You can see this effect in the fourth column of Table 8-2: average fixed cost drops continuously as output increases.

A **U-shaped average total cost curve** falls at low levels of output, then rises at higher levels.

Average fixed cost is the fixed cost per unit of output.

Average variable cost is the variable cost per unit of output.

TABLE 8-2

Average Costs for Ben's Boots

Quantity of boots Q (pairs)	Total cost TC	Average total cost of pair ATC = TC/Q	Average fixed cost of pair AFC = FC/Q	Average variable cost of pair AVC = VC/Q
1	$120	$120.00	$108.00	$12.00
2	156	78.00	54.00	24.00
3	216	72.00	36.00	36.00
4	300	75.00	27.00	48.00
5	408	81.60	21.60	60.00
6	540	90.00	18.00	72.00
7	696	99.43	15.43	84.00
8	876	109.50	13.50	96.00
9	1,080	120.00	12.00	108.00
10	1,308	130.80	10.80	120.00

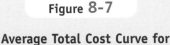

Average Total Cost Curve for Ben's Boots

The average total cost curve at Ben's Boots is U-shaped. At low levels of output, average total cost falls because the "spreading effect" of falling average fixed cost dominates the "diminishing returns effect" of rising average variable cost. At higher levels of output, the opposite is true and average total cost rises. At point *M*, corresponding to an output of three pairs of boots per day, average total cost is at its minimum level, the minimum average total cost. *>web...*

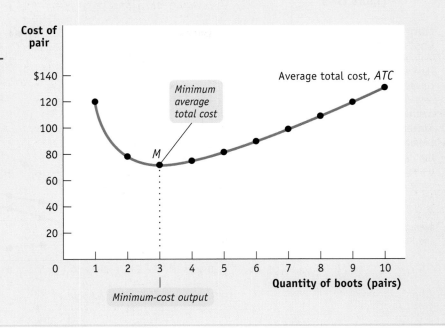

Average variable cost, however, rises as output increases. As we've seen, this reflects diminishing returns to the variable input: each additional unit of output incurs more variable cost to produce than the previous unit. So variable cost rises at a faster rate than the quantity of output increases.

Increasing output, therefore, has two opposing effects on average total cost—the "spreading effect" and the "diminishing returns effect":

- The spreading effect: the larger the output, the more production that can "share" the fixed cost, and therefore the lower the average fixed cost.

- The diminishing returns effect: the more output produced, the more variable input it requires to produce additional units, and therefore the higher the average variable cost.

At low levels of output, the spreading effect is very powerful because even small increases in output cause large reductions in average fixed cost. So at low levels of output, the spreading effect dominates the diminishing returns effect and causes the average total cost curve to slope downward. But when output is large, average fixed cost is already quite small, so increasing output further has only a very small spreading effect. Diminishing returns, on the other hand, usually grow increasingly important as output rises. As a result, when output is large, the diminishing returns effect dominates the spreading effect, causing the average total cost curve to slope upward. At the bottom of the U-shaped average total cost curve, point *M* in Figure 8-7, the two effects exactly balance each other. At this point average total cost is at its minimum level, the minimum average total cost.

Figure 8-8 on page 194 brings together in a single picture four members of the family of cost curves that we have derived from the total cost curve: the marginal cost curve (*MC*), the average total cost curve (*ATC*), the average variable cost curve (*AVC*), and the average fixed cost curve (*AFC*). All are based on the information in Tables 8-1 and 8-2. As before, cost is measured on the vertical axis and the quantity of output is measured on the horizontal axis.

Let's take a moment to note some features of the various cost curves. First of all, marginal cost is upward sloping—the result of diminishing returns that make an additional unit of output more costly to produce than the one before. Average variable cost

Figure 8-8

Marginal Cost and Average Cost Curves for Ben's Boots

Here we have the family of cost curves for Ben's Boots: the marginal cost curve (*MC*), the average total cost curve (*ATC*), the average variable cost curve (*AVC*), and the average fixed cost curve (*AFC*). Note that the average total cost curve is U-shaped and the marginal cost curve crosses the average total cost curve at the bottom of the U, point *M*, corresponding to the minimum average total cost from Table 8-2 and Figure 8-7. **>web...**

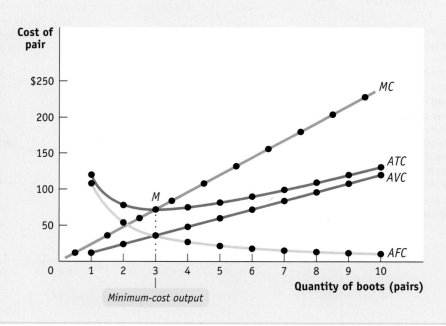

also is upward sloping—again, due to diminishing returns—but is flatter than the marginal cost curve. This is because the higher cost of an additional unit of output is averaged across all units, not just the additional units, in the average variable cost measure. Meanwhile, average fixed cost is downward sloping because of the spreading effect.

Finally, notice that the marginal cost curve intersects the average total cost curve from below, crossing it at its lowest point, point *M* in Figure 8-8. This last feature is our next subject of study.

Minimum Average Total Cost

> The **minimum-cost output** is the quantity of output at which average total cost is lowest—the bottom of the U-shaped average total cost curve.

For a U-shaped average total cost curve, average total cost is at its minimum level at the bottom of the U. Economists call the quantity that corresponds to the minimum average total cost the **minimum-cost output.** In the case of Ben's Boots, the minimum-cost output is three pairs of boots per day.

In Figure 8-8, the bottom of the U is at the level of output at which the marginal cost curve crosses the average total cost curve from below. Is this an accident? No—it reflects general principles that are always true about a firm's marginal cost and average total cost curves:

- At the minimum-cost output, average total cost *is equal to* marginal cost.
- At output less than the minimum-cost output, marginal cost *is less than* average total cost and average total cost is falling.
- And at output greater than the minimum-cost output, marginal cost *is greater than* average total cost and average total cost is rising.

To understand this principle, think about how your grade in one course—say, a 3.0 in physics—affects your overall grade point average. If your GPA before receiving that grade was more than 3.0, the new grade lowers your average.

Similarly, if marginal cost—the cost of producing one more unit—is less than average total cost, producing that extra unit lowers average total cost. This is shown in Figure 8-9 by the movement from A_1 to A_2. In this case, the marginal cost of producing an additional unit of output is low, as indicated by the point MC_L on the marginal cost curve. And when the cost of producing the next unit of output is less

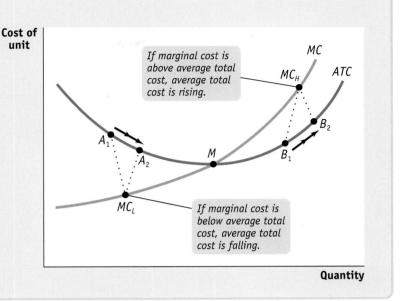

Figure 8-9

The Relationship Between the Average Total Cost and the Marginal Cost Curves

To see why the marginal cost curve (*MC*) must cut through the average total cost curve at the minimum average total cost (point *M*), corresponding to the minimum-cost output, we look at what happens if marginal cost is different from average total cost. If marginal cost is *less* than average total cost, an increase in output must reduce average total cost, as in the movement from A_1 to A_2. If marginal cost is *greater* than average total cost, an increase in output must increase average total cost, as in the movement from B_1 to B_2.

If marginal cost is above average total cost, average total cost is rising.

If marginal cost is below average total cost, average total cost is falling.

than average total cost, increasing production reduces average total cost. So any quantity of output at which marginal cost is less than average total cost must be on the downward-sloping segment of the U.

But if your grade in physics is more than the average of your previous grades, this new grade raises your GPA. Similarly, if marginal cost is greater than average total cost, producing that extra unit raises average total cost. This is illustrated by the move from B_1 to B_2 in Figure 8-9, where the marginal cost, MC_H, is higher than average total cost. So any quantity of output at which marginal cost is greater than average total cost must be on the upward-sloping segment of the U.

Finally, if a new grade is exactly equal to your previous GPA, the additional grade neither raises nor lowers that average—it stays the same. This corresponds to point *M* in Figure 8-9: when marginal cost equals average total cost, we must be at the bottom of the U, because only at that point is average total cost neither falling nor rising.

Does the Marginal Cost Curve Always Slope Upward?

Up to this point, we have emphasized the importance of diminishing returns, which lead to a marginal product curve that is always downward sloping and a marginal cost curve that is always upward sloping. In practice, however, economists believe that marginal cost curves often slope *downward* as a firm increases its production from zero up to some low level, sloping upward only at higher levels of production: they look like the curve *MC* in Figure 8-10 on page 196.

This initial downward slope occurs because a firm that employs only a few workers often cannot reap the benefits of specialization of labor. For example, one individual producing boots would have to perform all the tasks involved: making soles, shaping the upper part, sewing the pieces together, and so on. As more workers are employed, they can divide the tasks, with each worker specializing in one or a few aspects of boot-making. This specialization can lead to *increasing* returns at first, and so to a downward-sloping marginal cost curve. Once there are enough workers to permit specialization, however, diminishing returns set in. So typical marginal cost curves actually have the "swoosh" shape shown by *MC* in Figure 8-10. For the same reason, average variable cost curves typically look like *AVC* in Figure 8-10: they are U-shaped rather than strictly upward sloping.

Figure 8-10

More Realistic Cost Curves

In practice, the marginal cost curve often begins with a section that slopes downward. As output rises from a low level, a firm is capable of engaging in specialization and division of labor, which leads to increasing returns. At higher levels of output, however, diminishing returns lead to upward-sloping marginal cost. When marginal cost has a downward-sloping section, average variable cost is U-shaped. However, the basic results—U-shaped average total cost, and marginal cost that cuts through the minimum average total cost—remain the same. **>web...**

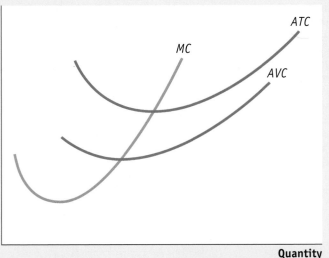

However, as Figure 8-10 also shows, the key features we saw from the example of Ben's Boots remain true: the average total cost curve is U-shaped, and the marginal cost curve passes through the point of minimum average total cost as well as through the point of minimum average variable cost.

economics in action

The Cost of Power

One of the great resources of the western United States is the availability of suitable sites for producing hydroelectric power: electricity generated by the force of water penned up behind a dam. When conditions are right—basically, when a large river runs through a deep but narrow valley—hydroelectric power can be much cheaper than electricity generated using fossil fuels, such as coal, or nuclear power. The western states, although they contain less than one-sixth of America's population, have more than half of the country's hydroelectric generating capacity. This advantage in cheap power has helped them attract industries, such as aluminum smelting, that are heavy users of electricity.

Is it a good idea for the governments of these western states to encourage more industries that make heavy use of electricity to move into their jurisdictions? Until the 1980s, most politicians and business leaders thought so, and many energy-intensive industries did in fact move into the region. But then, to the surprise and anger of consumers, western power companies began demanding higher prices, saying that they were no longer able to cover their costs at the old rates. What went wrong?

The answer is that officials had confused the *average total cost* of producing electricity with its *marginal cost*. Because of this confusion, they underestimated the cost of providing electricity to the new industries moving into their states.

The average total cost of producing power using existing facilities in the West is low, because much of it comes from hydroelectric power. But the marginal cost of providing additional power capacity is high, because it has become increasingly difficult to add new dams—most of the good sites have already been taken, and environmental considerations rule out many of the remaining sites. So when new energy-using businesses move to the West, to satisfy the new demand power

Confusing marginal cost and average total cost proved a very costly mistake for the company that built this dam and its customers.

companies must build expensive new power plants that run on fossil fuels or nuclear energy. So the marginal cost of electricity is much higher than the average total cost.

But electricity is a regulated industry (something we'll discuss in Chapter 14), and the rates electricity companies charge consumers are generally set to reflect average total cost. This gives rise to a seemingly paradoxical effect: when a factory moves into a western state, it pays less for the electricity it consumes than the extra, or marginal, cost incurred by the utility company to provide that electricity—so to cover its higher average total cost, the power company must raise the rates it charges all consumers.

If public officials had understood the difference between average total cost and marginal cost, they might have avoided this trap—either by charging new electricity users higher rates or by discouraging new electricity-using businesses from moving to their states. ■

> > > > > > > > > > > > > > > > > > > >

>> **CHECK YOUR UNDERSTANDING 8-2**

1. Alicia's Apple Pies is a roadside business. Alicia must pay $9.00 in rent each day. In addition, it costs her $1.00 to produce the first pie of the day, and each subsequent pie costs 50% more to produce than the one before. For example, the second pie costs $1.00 \times 1.5 = $1.50 to produce, and so on.

   a. Calculate Alicia's marginal cost, variable cost, average total cost, average variable cost, and average fixed cost as her daily pie output rises from 0 to 6. (*Hint:* The variable cost of two pies is just the marginal cost of the first, plus the marginal cost of the second pie, and so on.)

   b. Indicate the range of pies for which the spreading effect dominates and the range for which the diminishing returns effect dominates.

   c. What is Alicia's minimum-cost output? Explain why making one more pie lowers Alicia's average total cost when output is lower than the minimum-cost output. Similarly, explain why making one more pie raises Alicia's average total cost when output is greater than the minimum-cost output.

Solutions appear at back of book.

Short-Run versus Long-Run Costs

Up to this point, we have treated fixed cost as completely outside the control of a firm because we have focused on the short run. But as we noted earlier, all inputs are variable in the long run: this means that in the long run fixed cost may also be varied. In the long run, in other words, a firm's fixed cost becomes a variable it can choose. For example, given time, Ben's Boots can acquire additional boot-making machinery or dispose of some of its existing machinery. In this section, we will examine how a firm's costs behave in the short run and in the long run. We will also see that the firm will choose its fixed cost in the long run based on the level of output it expects to produce.

Let's begin by supposing that Ben's Boots is considering whether to acquire additional boot-making machines. Acquiring additional machinery will affect its total cost in two ways. First, the firm will have to either rent or buy the additional machinery; either way, that will mean higher fixed cost in the short run. Second, if the workers have more equipment, they will be more productive: fewer workers will be needed to produce any given output, so variable cost for any given output level will be reduced.

The table in Figure 8-11 on page 198 shows how acquiring an additional machine affects costs. In our original example, we assumed that Ben's Boots had a fixed cost of $108. The left half of the table shows variable cost as well as total cost and average total cost assuming a fixed cost of $108. The average total cost curve for this level of fixed cost is given by ATC_1 in Figure 8-11. Let's compare that to a situation in which the firm buys an additional boot-making machine, doubling its fixed cost to $216 but reducing its variable cost at any given level of output. The right half of the table shows the firm's variable cost, total cost, and average total cost with this higher level of fixed cost. The average total cost curve corresponding to $216 in fixed cost is given by ATC_2 in Figure 8-11.

Figure 8-11

Choosing the Level of Fixed Cost for Ben's Boots

There is a trade-off between higher fixed cost and lower variable cost for any given output level, and vice versa. ATC_1 is the average total cost curve corresponding to a fixed cost of $108; it leads to high variable cost. ATC_2 is the average total cost curve corresponding to a higher fixed cost of $216 but lower variable cost. At low output levels, fewer than 4 pairs of boots per day, ATC_1 lies below ATC_2: average total cost is lower with only $108 in fixed cost. But as output goes up, average total cost is lower with the higher amount of fixed cost, $216: at more than 4 pairs of boots per day, ATC_2 lies below ATC_1.

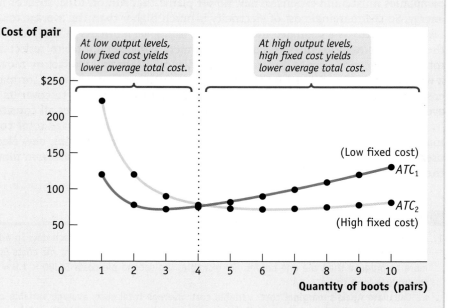

Cost of pair

At low output levels, low fixed cost yields lower average total cost.

At high output levels, high fixed cost yields lower average total cost.

(Low fixed cost) ATC_1

ATC_2 (High fixed cost)

Quantity of boots (pairs)

	Low fixed cost (FC = $108)			High fixed cost (FC = $216)		
Quantity of boots (pairs)	High variable cost	Total cost	Average total cost of pair ATC_1	Low variable cost	Total cost	Average total cost of pair ATC_2
1	$12	$120	$120.00	$6	$222	$222.00
2	48	156	78.00	24	240	120.00
3	108	216	72.00	54	270	90.00
4	192	300	75.00	96	312	78.00
5	300	408	81.60	150	366	73.20
6	432	540	90.00	216	432	72.00
7	588	696	99.40	294	510	72.90
8	768	876	109.50	384	600	75.00
9	972	1,080	120.00	486	702	78.00
10	1,200	1,308	130.80	600	816	81.60

From the figure you can see that when output is small, 4 pairs of boots per day or fewer, average total cost is smaller when Ben's Boots forgoes the additional machinery and maintains the lower fixed cost of $108: ATC_1 lies below ATC_2. For example, at 3 pairs of boots per day, average total cost is $72 without the additional machinery and $90 with the additional machinery. But as output increases beyond 4 pairs per day, the firm's average total cost is lower if it acquires the additional machinery, raising its fixed cost to $216. For example, at 9 pairs of boots per day, average total cost is $120 when fixed cost is $108, but only $78 when fixed cost is $216.

Why does average total cost change like this when fixed cost increases? When output is low, the increase in fixed cost from the additional machinery outweighs the reduction in variable cost from higher worker productivity—that is, there are too few units of output over which to spread the additional fixed cost. So if Ben's Boots plans to produce fewer than 4 pairs of boots per day, it would be better off to choose the lower level of fixed cost, $108, to achieve a lower average total cost of production. When planned output is high, however, it should acquire the additional machinery.

In general, for each output level there is some choice of fixed cost that minimizes the firm's average total cost for that output level. So when the firm has a desired output level that it expects to maintain over time, it should choose the level of fixed cost appropriate to that level—that is, the level of fixed cost that minimizes its average total cost.

Now that we are studying a situation in which fixed cost can change, we need to take time into account when discussing average total cost. All of the average cost curves we have considered until now are defined for a given level of fixed cost—that is, they are defined for the short run, the period of time over which fixed cost doesn't vary. To reinforce that distinction, for the rest of this chapter we will refer to these average total cost curves as "short-run average total cost curves."

For most firms, it is realistic to assume that there are many possible choices of fixed cost, not just two. This implies that for such a firm, many possible short-run average total cost curves will exist, each corresponding to a different choice of fixed cost and so giving rise to what is called a firm's "family" of short-run average total cost curves.

At any given time, a firm will find itself on one of its short-run cost curves, the one corresponding to its current level of fixed cost; a change in output will cause it to move along that curve. If the firm expects that change in output level to be long-standing, then it is likely that the firm's current level of fixed cost is no longer appropriate. Given sufficient time, it will want to adjust its fixed cost to a new level that minimizes average total cost for its new output level. For example, if Ben's Boots had been producing 2 pairs of boots per day with a fixed cost of $108 but found itself increasing its output to 8 pairs per day for the foreseeable future, then in the long run it should increase its fixed cost to a level that minimizes average total cost at the 8-pairs-per-day output level.

Suppose we do a thought experiment and calculate the lowest possible average total cost that can be achieved for each output level if the firm were to choose its fixed cost for each output level. Economists have given this thought experiment a name: the *long-run average total cost curve*. Specifically, the **long-run average total cost curve**, or *LRATC*, is the relationship between output and average total cost when fixed cost has been chosen to minimize average total cost *for each level of output*. If there are many possible choices of fixed cost, the long-run average total cost curve will have the familiar, smooth U shape, as shown by *LRATC* in Figure 8-12.

The **long-run average total cost curve** shows the relationship between output and average total cost when fixed cost has been chosen to minimize average total cost for each level of output.

Figure 8-12

Short-Run and Long-Run Average Total Cost Curves

If Ben's Boots has chosen the level of fixed cost that minimizes short-run average total cost at an output of six pairs of boots per day and actually ends up producing six pairs per day, it will be on *LRATC* at point *C*. But if it produces more or less, in the short run it will be on the short-run average total cost curve *ATC₆* and not on *LRATC*. So if it produces only three pairs per day, its average total cost is shown by point *B*, not point *A*. If it produces nine pairs per day, its average total cost is shown by point *Y*, not point *X*. There are economies of scale when long-run average total cost declines as output increases, and there are diseconomies of scale when long-run average total cost increases as output increases.

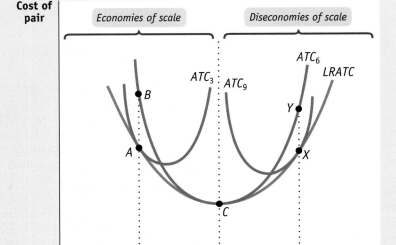

We can now draw the distinction between the short run and the long run more fully. In the long run, when a producer has had time to choose the fixed cost appropriate for its desired level of output, that producer will be on some point on the long-run average total cost curve. But if the output level is altered, the firm will no longer be on its long-run average total cost curve and will instead be moving along its current short-run average total cost curve. It will not be on its long-run average total cost curve again until it readjusts its fixed cost for its new output level.

Figure 8-12 illustrates this point. The curve ATC_3 shows short-run average total cost if a boot producer has chosen the level of fixed cost that minimizes average total cost at an output of 3 pairs of boots per day. This is confirmed by the fact that at 3 pairs per day, ATC_3 touches $LRATC$, the long-run average total cost curve. Similarly, ATC_6 shows short-run average total cost if a boot producer has chosen the level of fixed cost that would minimize average total cost if its output is 6 pairs of boots per day. It touches $LRATC$ at 6 pairs per day. And ATC_9 shows short-run average total cost if a boot producer has chosen the level of fixed cost that would minimize average total cost if its output is 9 pairs of boots per day. It touches $LRATC$ at 9 pairs per day.

Suppose that the firm has initially chosen to be on ATC_6. If the firm actually produces 6 pairs of boots per day, it will be at point C on both its short-run and long-run average total cost curves. Suppose, however, that the firm ends up producing only 3 pairs of boots per day. In the short run, its average total cost is indicated by point B on ATC_6; it is no longer on $LRATC$. If the firm had known that it would be producing only 3 pairs per day, it would have been better off to reduce its fixed cost and achieve lower average total cost. That is, it would have been better off to choose the level of fixed cost corresponding to ATC_3. Then it would have found itself at point A on the long-run average total cost curve, which lies below point B.

Suppose, on the other hand, that the firm ends up producing 9 pairs of boots per day. In the short run its average total cost is indicated by point Y on ATC_6. But it would be better off to incur a higher fixed cost in order to reduce its variable cost and move to ATC_9. This would allow it to reach point X on the long-run average total cost curve, which lies below Y.

The distinction between short-run and long-run average total costs is extremely important in making sense of how real firms operate over time. A company that has to increase output suddenly to meet a surge in demand will typically find that in the short run its average total cost rises sharply because it is hard to get extra production out of the existing facilities. But given time to build new factories or add machinery, short-run average total cost falls.

Economies and Diseconomies of Scale

Finally, what determines the shape of the long-run average total cost curve? The answer is that *scale*, the size of a firm's operations, is often an important determinant of its long-run average total cost of production. Firms that experience scale effects in production find that their long-run average total cost changes substantially depending on the quantity of output they produce. There are **economies of scale** when long-run average total cost declines as output increases. As you can see in Figure 8-12, Ben's Boots experiences economies of scale over output levels ranging from 0 to 6 pairs of boots—the output levels over which the long-run average total cost curve is declining. There are **diseconomies of scale** when long-run average total cost increases as output increases. For Ben's Boots, diseconomies of scale occur at output levels of 6 pairs of boots or more, the output levels over which its long-run average total cost curve is rising.

Although it is not shown in Figure 8-12, there is a third possible relationship between long-run average total cost and scale: firms experience **constant returns to scale** when long-run average total cost is constant as output increases. In this case, the firm's long-run average total cost curve is horizontal over the output levels for which there are constant returns to scale.

There are **economies of scale** when long-run average total cost declines as output increases.

There are **diseconomies of scale** when long-run average total cost increases as output increases.

There are **constant returns to scale** when long-run average total cost is constant as output increases.

What explains these scale effects in production? The answer ultimately lies in the firm's technology of production. Economies of scale often arise from the increased *specialization* that larger output levels allow—a larger scale of operation means that individual workers can limit themselves to more specialized tasks, becoming more skilled and efficient at doing them. Another source of economies of scale is very large initial set-up cost; in some industries—such as auto manufacturing, electricity generating, or petroleum refining—a very large initial cost in the form of plant and equipment is necessary to produce any output. As we'll see in Chapter 14, where we study monopoly, economies of scale have very important implications for how firms and industries interact and behave.

Diseconomies of scale, on the other hand, typically arise in large firms due to problems of coordination and communication: as the firm grows in size, it becomes ever more difficult and therefore costly to communicate and organize its activities. While economies of scale induce firms to get larger, diseconomies of scale tend to limit their size. And when constant returns to scale exist, scale has no effect on a firm's long-run average total cost: it is the same regardless of whether the firm produces 1 unit or 100,000 units.

Summing Up Costs: The Short and Long of It

If a firm is to make the best decisions about how much to produce, it has to understand how its costs relate to the quantity of output it chooses to produce. Table 8-3 provides a quick summary of the concepts and measures of cost you have learned about.

TABLE **8-3**

Concepts and Measures of Cost

	Measurement	Definition	Mathematical term
Short run	Fixed cost	Cost that does not depend on the quantity of output produced	FC
	Average fixed cost	Fixed cost per unit of output	$AFC = FC/Q$
Short run and long run	Variable cost	Cost that depends on the quantity of output produced	VC
	Average variable cost	Variable cost per unit of output	$AVC = VC/Q$
	Total cost	The sum of fixed cost (short-run) and variable cost	$TC = FC$ (short-run) $+ VC$
	Average total cost (average cost)	Total cost per unit of output	$ATC = TC/Q$
	Marginal cost	The change in total cost generated by producing one more unit of output	$MC = \Delta TC/\Delta Q$
Long run	Long-run average total cost	Average cost when fixed cost has been chosen to minimize total cost for each level of output	$LRATC$

economics in action

There's No Business Like Snow Business

Anyone who has lived both in a snowy city, like Chicago, and in a city that only occasionally experiences significant snowfall, like Washington, D.C., is aware of the differences in total cost that arise from making different choices about fixed cost.

In Washington, even a minor snowfall—say, an inch or two overnight—is enough to create chaos during the next morning's commute. The same snowfall in Chicago

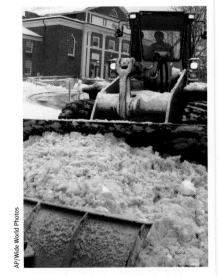

A lesson in economies of scale: cities with higher average annual snowfall maintain larger snowplow fleets.

has hardly any effect at all. The reason is not that Washingtonians are wimps and Chicagoans are made of sterner stuff; it is that Washington, where it rarely snows, has only a fraction as many snowplows and other snow-clearing equipment as cities where heavy snow is a fact of life.

In this sense Washington and Chicago are like two producers who expect to produce different levels of output, where the "output" is snow removal. Washington, which rarely has significant snow, has chosen a low level of fixed cost in the form of snow-clearing equipment. This makes sense under normal circumstances but leaves the city unprepared when major snow does fall. Chicago, which knows that it will face lots of snow, chooses to accept the higher fixed cost that leaves it in a position to respond effectively. ∎

< < < < < < < < < < < < < < < < < <

>> CHECK YOUR UNDERSTANDING 8-3

1. The accompanying table shows three possible combinations of fixed cost and average variable cost.
   a. For each of the three choices, calculate the average total cost of producing 12,000, 22,000, and 30,000 units. For each of these quantities, which choice results in the lowest average total cost?
   b. Suppose that the firm, which has historically produced 12,000 units, experiences a sharp, permanent increase in demand that leads it to produce 22,000 units. Explain how its average total cost will change in the short run and in the long run.

Choice	Fixed cost	Average variable cost
1	$8,000	$1.00
2	12,000	0.75
3	24,000	0.25

   c. Explain what the firm should do instead if it believes the change in demand is temporary.

2. In each of the following cases, explain what kind of scale effects you think the firm will experience and why.
   a. A telemarketing firm in which employees make sales calls using computers and telephones
   b. An interior design firm in which design projects are based on the expertise of the firm's owner
   c. A diamond-mining company

Solutions appear at back of book.

● A LOOK AHEAD ●

We've now seen how to use information about how a firm produces to analyze that firm's costs. Our next step is to go from our analysis of costs to an analysis of the supply curve. To understand the supply curve for a particular good, we will need to look both at how a profit-maximizing firm chooses its quantity of output and at how it decides whether to enter or exit the industry producing that good.

SUMMARY

1. The relationship between inputs and output is a producer's **production function.** In the **short run,** the quantity of a **fixed input** cannot be varied but the quantity of a **variable input** can. In the **long run,** the quantities of all inputs can be varied. For a given amount of fixed input, the **total product curve** shows how the quantity of output changes as the quantity of the variable input changes. We may also calculate the **marginal product** of an input, the increase in output from using one more unit of that input.

2. There are **diminishing returns to an input** when its marginal product declines as more of the input is used, holding the quantity of all other inputs fixed.

3. **Total cost,** represented by the **total cost curve,** is equal to the sum of **fixed cost,** which does not depend on output, and **variable cost,** which does depend on output. Due to diminishing returns, marginal cost, the increase in total cost generated by producing one more unit of output, normally increases as output increases.

4. **Average total cost** (also known as **average cost**), total cost divided by quantity of output, is the cost of the average unit of output while marginal cost is the cost of one more unit produced. Economists believe that **U-shaped average total cost curves** are typical, because average total cost consists of two parts: **average fixed cost,** which falls when output increases (the spreading effect) and **average variable cost,** which rises with output (the diminishing returns effect).

5. When average total cost is U-shaped, the bottom of the U is the level of output at which average total cost is minimized, the point of **minimum-cost output.** This is also the point at which the marginal cost curve crosses the average total cost curve from below. Due to gains from specialization, the marginal cost curve may slope downward initially before sloping upward, giving it a "swoosh" shape.

6. In the long run, a producer can change its fixed input and its level of fixed cost. By accepting higher fixed cost, a firm can lower its variable cost for any given output level, and vice versa. The **long-run average total cost curve** shows the relationship between output and average total cost when fixed cost has been chosen to minimize average total cost at each level of output. A firm moves along its short-run average total cost curve as it increases output, and returns to a point on both its short-run and long-run average total cost curves once it has adjusted fixed cost to its new output level.

7. As output increases, there are **economies of scale** if long-run average total cost declines; **diseconomies of scale** if it increases; and **constant returns to scale** if it remains constant. Scale effects depend on the technology of production.

KEY TERMS

Production function, p. 182
Fixed input, p. 182
Variable input, p. 182
Long run, p. 182
Short run, p. 182
Total product curve, p. 182
Marginal product, p. 183
Diminishing returns to an input, p. 184

Fixed cost, p. 186
Variable cost, p. 186
Total cost, p. 186
Total cost curve, p. 187
Average total cost, p. 191
Average cost, p. 191
U-shaped average total cost curve, p. 192

Average fixed cost, p. 192
Average variable cost, p. 192
Minimum-cost output, p. 194
Long-run average total cost curve, p. 199
Economies of scale, p. 200
Diseconomies of scale, p. 200
Constant returns to scale, p. 200

PROBLEMS

1. Marty's Frozen Yogurt is a small shop that sells cups of frozen yogurt in a university town. Marty owns three frozen-yogurt machines. His other inputs are refrigerators, frozen-yogurt mix, cups, sprinkle toppings, and, of course, workers. He estimates that his daily production function when he varies the number of workers employed (and at the same time, of course, yogurt mix, cups, and so on) is as shown in the accompanying table.

Quantity of labor (workers)	Quantity of frozen yogurt (cups)
0	0
1	110
2	200
3	270
4	300
5	320
6	330

   a. What are the fixed inputs and variable inputs in the production of cups of frozen yogurt?

   b. Draw the total product curve. Put the quantity of labor on the horizontal axis and the quantity of frozen yogurt on the vertical axis.

   c. What is the marginal product of the first worker? The second worker? The third worker? Why does marginal product decline as the number of workers increases?

2. The production function for Marty's Frozen Yogurt is given in Problem 1. Marty pays each of his workers $80 per day. The cost of his other variable inputs is $0.50 per cup of yogurt. His fixed cost is $100 per day.

   a. What is Marty's variable cost and total cost when he produces 110 cups of yogurt? 200 cups? Calculate variable and total cost for every level of output given in Problem 1.

   b. Draw Marty's variable cost curve. On the same diagram, draw his total cost curve.

   c. What is the marginal cost per cup for the first 110 cups of yogurt? For the next 90 cups? Calculate the marginal cost for all remaining levels of output.

3. The production function for Marty's Frozen Yogurt is given in Problem 1. The costs are given in Problem 2.

   a. For each of the given levels of output, calculate the average fixed cost (*AFC*), average variable cost (*AVC*), and average total cost (*ATC*) per cup of frozen yogurt.

b. On one diagram, draw the *AFC*, *AVC*, and *ATC* curves.

c. What principle explains why the *AFC* declines as output increases? What principle explains why the *AVC* increases as output increases? Explain your answers.

d. How many cups of frozen yogurt are produced when average total cost is minimized?

4. The accompanying table shows a car manufacturer's total cost of producing cars.

Quantity of cars	TC
0	$500,000
1	540,000
2	560,000
3	570,000
4	590,000
5	620,000
6	660,000
7	720,000
8	800,000
9	920,000
10	1,100,000

a. What is this manufacturer's fixed cost?

b. For each level of output, calculate the variable cost (*VC*). For each level of output except zero output, calculate the average variable cost (*AVC*), average total cost (*ATC*), and average fixed cost (*AFC*). What is the minimum-cost output?

c. For each level of output, calculate this manufacturer's marginal cost (*MC*).

d. On one diagram, draw the manufacturer's *AVC*, *ATC*, and *MC* curves.

5. Magnificent Blooms is a florist specializing in floral arrangements for weddings, graduations, and other events. Magnificent Blooms has a fixed cost associated with space and equipment of $100 per day. Each worker is paid $50 per day. The daily production function for Magnificent Blooms is shown in the accompanying table.

Quantity of labor (workers)	Quantity of floral arrangements
0	0
1	5
2	9
3	12
4	14
5	15

a. What is the marginal product, *MPL*, of the first, second, third, fourth, and fifth workers? What principle explains why the marginal product per worker declines as the number of workers employed increases?

b. What is the marginal cost (*MC*) of producing each of the first 5 floral arrangements? The sixth through ninth floral arrangements? The remaining levels of output? What principle explains why the marginal cost per floral arrangement increases as the number of arrangements increases?

6. You have the information shown in the accompanying table about a firm's costs. Complete the missing data.

Quantity	TC	MC	ATC	AVC
0	$20			
1	?	$20	?	?
2	?	10	?	?
3	?	16	?	?
4	?	20	?	?
5	?	24	?	?

7. Evaluate each of the following statements: If a statement is true, explain why; if it is false, identify the mistake and try to correct it.

a. A decreasing marginal product tells us that marginal cost must be rising.

b. An increase in fixed cost increases the minimum-cost output.

c. An increase in fixed cost increases marginal cost.

d. When marginal cost is above average total cost, average total cost must be falling.

8. Mark and Jeff operate a small company that produces souvenir footballs. Their fixed cost is $2,000 per month. They can hire workers for $1,000 per worker per month. Their monthly production function for footballs is as given in the accompanying table.

Quantity of labor (workers)	Quantity of footballs
0	0
1	300
2	800
3	1,200
4	1,400
5	1,500

a. For each quantity of labor, calculate average variable cost (*AVC*), average fixed cost (*AFC*), average total cost (*ATC*), and marginal cost (*MC*).

b. On one diagram, draw in the *AVC*, *ATC*, and *MC* curves.

c. At what level of output is Mark and Jeff's average total cost minimized?

9. You produce widgets. Currently you produce 4 widgets at a total cost of $40.

    a. What is your average total cost?

    b. Suppose you could produce one more (the fifth) widget at a marginal cost of $5. If you do produce that fifth widget, what will your average total cost be? Has your average total cost increased or decreased? Why?

    c. Suppose instead that you could produce one more (the fifth) widget at a marginal cost of $20. If you do produce that fifth widget, what will your average total cost be? Has your average total cost increased or decreased? Why?

10. In your economics class, each homework problem set is graded on the basis of a maximum score of 100. You have completed 9 out of 10 of the problem sets for the term, and your current average grade is 88. What range of grades for your 10th problem set will raise your overall average? What range will lower your overall average? Explain.

11. Don owns a small concrete-mixing company. His fixed cost is the cost of the concrete-batching machinery and his mixer trucks. His variable cost is the cost of the sand, gravel, and other inputs for producing concrete; the gas and maintenance for the machinery and trucks; and his workers. He is trying to decide how many mixer trucks to purchase. He has estimated the costs shown in the accompanying table based on estimates of the number of orders his company will receive per week.

Quantity of trucks	FC	VC 20 orders	VC 40 orders	VC 60 orders
2	$6,000	$2,000	$5,000	$12,000
3	7,000	1,800	3,800	10,800
4	8,000	1,200	3,600	8,400

    a. For each level of fixed cost, calculate Don's total cost for producing 20, 40, and 60 orders per week.

    b. If Don is producing 20 orders per week, how many trucks should he purchase and what will his average total cost be? Answer the same questions for 40 and 60 orders per week.

12. Consider Don's concrete-mixing business described in Problem 11. Suppose Don purchased 3 trucks, expecting to produce 40 orders per week.

    a. Suppose that, in the short run, business declines to 20 orders per week. What is Don's average total cost per order in the short run? What will his average total cost per order in the short run be if his business booms to 60 orders per week?

    b. What is Don's long-run average total cost for 20 orders per week? Explain why his short-run average total cost of producing 20 orders per week when the number of trucks is fixed at 3 is greater than his long-run average total cost of producing 20 orders per week.

    c. Sketch Don's long-run average total cost curve. Sketch his short-run average total cost curve if he owns 3 trucks.

13. True or False? Explain your reasoning.

    a. The short-run average total cost can never be less than the long-run average total cost.

    b. The short-run average variable cost can never be less than the long-run average total cost.

    c. In the long run, choosing a higher level of fixed cost shifts the long-run average total cost curve upward.

14. Wolfsburg Wagon (WW) is a small automaker. The accompanying table shows WW's long-run average total cost.

Quantity of cars	LRATC of car
1	$30,000
2	20,000
3	15,000
4	12,000
5	12,000
6	12,000
7	14,000
8	18,000

    a. For which levels of output does WW experience economies of scale?

    b. For which levels of output does WW experience diseconomies of scale?

    c. For which levels of output does WW experience constant returns to scale?

>web... To continue your study and review of concepts in this chapter, please visit the Krugman/Wells website for quizzes, animated graph tutorials, web links to helpful resources, and more.
www.worthpublishers.com/krugmanwells

>> Perfect Competition and the Supply Curve

DOING WHAT COMES NATURALLY

FOOD CONSUMERS IN THE UNITED States are concerned about health issues. Demand for "natural" foods and beverages, such as bottled water and organically grown fruits and vegetables, increased rapidly over the past decade. The small group of farmers who had pioneered organic farming techniques prospered thanks to higher prices.

But everyone knew that the high prices of organic produce were unlikely to persist even if the new, higher demand for naturally grown food continued: the supply of organic food, while not that price-elastic in the short run, was surely much more price-elastic in the long run. Over time, farms already producing organically would increase their capacity, and conventional farmers would enter the organic food business. So the increase in the quantity supplied in response to the increase in price would be much larger in the long run than in the short run.

Where does the supply curve come from? Why is there a difference between the short-run and the long-run supply curve? In this chapter we will use our understanding of costs, developed in Chapter 8, as the basis for an analysis of the supply curve. As we'll see, this will require that we understand the behavior both of individual firms and of an entire industry, composed of these many individual firms.

Our analysis in this chapter assumes that the industry in question is characterized by

perfect competition. We begin by explaining the concept of perfect competition, providing a brief introduction to the conditions that give rise to a perfectly competitive industry. We then show how a producer under perfect competition decides how much to produce. Finally, we use the cost curves of the individual producers to derive the *industry supply curve* under perfect competition. By analyzing the way a competitive industry evolves over time, we will come to understand the distinction between the short-run and long-run effects of changes in demand on a competitive industry—such as, for example, the effect of America's new taste for organic food on the organic farming industry. We will conclude with a deeper discussion of the conditions necessary for perfect competition.

Whether it's organic strawberries or satellites, how a good is produced determines its cost of production.

What you will learn in this chapter:

➤ The meaning of **perfect competition** and the characteristics of a **perfectly competitive industry**

➤ How a **price-taking producer** determines its profit-maximizing quantity of output

➤ How to assess whether or not a producer is profitable and why an unprofitable producer may continue to operate in the short run

➤ Why industries behave differently in the short run and the long run

➤ What determines the **industry supply curve** in both the short run and the long run

Perfect Competition

Suppose that Yves and Zoe are neighboring farmers, both of whom grow organic tomatoes. Both sell their output to the same grocery store chains that carry organic foods; so, in a real sense, Yves and Zoe compete with each other.

Does this mean that Yves should try to stop Zoe from growing tomatoes or that Yves and Zoe should form an agreement to grow less? Almost certainly not: there are hundreds or thousands of organic tomato farmers, and Yves and Zoe are competing with all those other growers as well as with each other. Because so many farmers sell organic tomatoes, if any one of them produced more or less, there would be no measureable effect on market prices.

When people talk about business competition, the image they often have in mind is a situation in which two or three rival firms are intensely struggling for advantage. But economists know that when a business focuses on a few main competitors, it's actually a sign that competition is fairly limited. As the example of organic tomatoes suggests, when there is enough competition it doesn't even make sense to identify your opponents: there are so many competitors that you cannot single out any one of them as a rival.

We can put it another way: Yves and Zoe are **price-taking producers.** A producer is a price-taker when its actions cannot affect the market price of the good it sells. As a result, a price-taking producer considers the market price as given. When there is enough competition—when competition is what economists call "perfect"—then every producer is a price-taker. And there is a similar definition for consumers: a **price-taking consumer** is a consumer who cannot influence the market price of the good by his or her actions. That is, the market price is unaffected by how much or how little of the good the consumer buys.

Defining Perfect Competition

In a **perfectly competitive market**, all market participants, both consumers and producers, are price-takers. That is, neither consumption decisions by individual consumers nor production decisions by individual producers affect the market price of the good.

The supply and demand model, which we introduced in Chapter 3 and have used repeatedly since then, is a model of a perfectly competitive market. It depends fundamentally on the assumption that no individual buyer or seller of a good, such as scalped tickets to a hockey game or organic tomatoes, believes that he or she can affect the price at which he or she can sell or buy the good.

As a general rule, consumers are indeed price-takers. Instances in which consumers are able to affect the prices they pay are rare. It is, however, quite common for producers to have a significant ability to affect the prices they receive, a phenomenon we'll address in Chapter 14. So the model of perfect competition is appropriate for some but not all markets. An industry in which producers are price-takers is called a **perfectly competitive industry.** Clearly, some industries aren't perfectly competitive; in later chapters we'll see how to analyze industries that don't fit the perfectly competitive model.

Under what circumstances will all producers be price-takers? In the next section we will see that there are two necessary conditions for a perfectly competitive industry and that a third condition is often present as well.

Two Necessary Conditions for Perfect Competition

The markets for major grains, like wheat and corn, are perfectly competitive: individual wheat and corn farmers, as well as individual buyers of wheat and corn, take market prices as given. In contrast, the markets for some of the food items made from these grains—in particular, breakfast cereals—are by no means perfectly competitive. There is intense competition among cereal brands, but not *perfect* competition. To understand the difference between the market for wheat and the market for shredded wheat cereal is to understand the two necessary conditions for perfect competition.

First, for an industry to be perfectly competitive, it must contain many producers, none of whom have a large **market share**. A producer's market share is the fraction of the total industry output represented by that producer's output. The distribution of market share constitutes a major difference between the grain industry and the breakfast cereal industry. There are thousands of wheat farmers, none of whom account for more than a small fraction of 1 percent of total wheat sales. The breakfast cereal industry, however, is dominated by four producers: Kellogg's, General Mills, Post, and Quaker Foods. Kellogg's alone accounts for about one-third of all cereal sales. Kellogg's executives know that if they try to sell more corn flakes, they are likely to drive down the market price of corn flakes. That is, they know that their actions influence market prices, simply because they are so large a part of the market that changes in their production will significantly affect the overall quantity supplied. It makes sense to assume that producers are price-takers only when an industry does *not* contain any large players like Kellogg's.

Second, an industry can be perfectly competitive only if consumers regard the products of all producers as equivalent. This clearly isn't true in the breakfast cereal market: consumers don't consider Cap'n Crunch to be a good substitute for Wheaties. As a result, the maker of Wheaties has some ability to increase its price without fear that it will lose all its customers to the maker of Cap'n Crunch. Contrast this with the case of a **standardized product**, sometimes known as a **commodity**. Consumers regard the output of one wheat producer as a perfect substitute for that of another producer. Consequently, one farmer cannot increase the price for his or her wheat without losing all his or her sales to other wheat farmers. So the second necessary condition for a competitive industry is that the industry output is a standardized product.

> A producer's **market share** is the fraction of the total industry output represented by that producer's output.

> A good is a **standardized product**, also known as a **commodity**, when consumers regard the products of different producers as the same good.

FOR INQUIRING MINDS

WHAT'S A STANDARDIZED PRODUCT?

A perfectly competitive industry must produce a standardized product. But is it enough for the products of different firms actually to be the same? No: people must also *think* that they are the same. And producers often go to great lengths to convince consumers that they have a distinctive, or *differentiated*, product, even when they don't.

Consider, for example, champagne—not the superexpensive premium champagnes but the more ordinary stuff. Most people cannot tell the difference between champagne actually produced in the Champagne region of France, where the product originated, and similar products from Spain or California. But the French government has sought and obtained legal protection for the firms of Champagne, ensuring that around the world only bubbly wine from that region

In the end, only kimchi eaters can tell you if there is truly a difference between Korean-produced kimchi and the Japanese-produced variety.

can be called champagne. If it's from someplace else, all the seller can do is say that it was produced by the *méthode Champenoise*. This creates a differentiation in the minds of consumers and lets the champagne producers of Champagne charge higher prices.

In a less Eurocentric example, Korean producers of *kimchi*, the spicy fermented cabbage that is the national side dish, are doing their best to convince consumers that the same product packaged by Japanese firms is just not the real thing. The purpose is, of course, to ensure higher prices for Korean *kimchi*.

So is an industry perfectly competitive if it sells products that are indistinguishable except in name but that consumers, for whatever reason, don't think are standardized? No. When it comes to defining the nature of competition, the consumer is always right.

Free Entry and Exit

All perfectly competitive industries have many producers with small market shares, producing a standardized product. Most perfectly competitive industries are also characterized by one more feature: it is easy for new firms to enter the industry or for firms that are currently in the industry to leave. That is, no obstacles in the form of government regulations or limited access to key resources prevent new producers from entering the market. And no additional costs are associated with shutting down a company and leaving the industry. Economists refer to the arrival of new firms into an industry as *entry*; they refer to the departure of firms from an industry as *exit*. When there are no obstacles to entry into or exit from an industry, we say that the industry has **free entry and exit.**

Free entry and exit is not strictly necessary for perfect competition. In Chapter 4 we described the case of New Jersey clam fishing, where regulations have the effect of limiting the number of fishing boats. Despite this, there are enough boats operating that the fishermen are price-takers. But free entry and exit is a key factor in most competitive industries. It ensures that the number of producers in an industry can adjust to changing market conditions. And, in particular, it ensures that producers in an industry cannot artificially keep other firms out.

There is **free entry and exit** into and from an industry when new producers can easily enter into or leave that industry.

To sum up, then, perfect competition depends on two necessary conditions. First, the industry must contain many producers, each having a small market share. Second, the industry must produce a standardized product. In addition, perfectly competitive industries are normally characterized by free entry and exit.

How does an industry that meets these three criteria behave? As a first step toward answering that question, let's look at how an individual producer in a perfectly competitive industry maximizes profit.

economics in action

The Pain of Competition

Sometimes it is possible to see an industry become perfectly competitive. In fact, it happens on a regular basis in the case of pharmaceuticals: the conditions for perfect competition are often met as soon as the patent on a popular drug expires.

When a company develops a new drug, it is usually able to receive a patent—a legal monopoly that gives it the exclusive right to sell that drug for 20 years from the date of filing. When the patent expires, the field is open for other companies to sell their own versions of the drug—marketed as "generics" and sold under the medical name of the drug rather than the brand name used by the original producer. Generics are standardized products, much like aspirin, and are often sold by many producers.

A good example came in 1984, when Upjohn's patent on ibuprofen—a painkiller that the company still markets under the brand name Motrin—expired. Most people who use ibuprofen, like most people who use aspirin, now purchase a generic version made by one of many producers.

The shift to perfect competition, not coincidentally, is accompanied by a sharp fall in market price. When its patent expired, Upjohn immediately cut the price of Motrin by 35 percent, but as more companies started selling the generic drug, the price of ibuprofen eventually fell by another two-thirds.

Ten years later the patent on the painkiller naproxen—sold under the brand name Naprosyn—expired. The generic version of naproxen was soon selling at only one-tenth of the original price of Naprosyn. ■

> >

> **>> QUICK REVIEW**
>
> ➤ Neither the actions of a *price-taking producer* nor those of a *price-taking consumer* can influence the market price of a good.
>
> ➤ In a *perfectly competitive market* all producers and consumers are price-takers. Consumers are almost always price-takers, but this is often not true of producers. An industry in which producers are price-takers is a *perfectly competitive industry*.
>
> ➤ A perfectly competitive industry contains many producers, each of which produces a *standardized product* (also known as a *commodity*) but none of which has a large *market share*.
>
> ➤ Most perfectly competitive industries are also characterized by *free entry and exit*.

>>CHECK YOUR UNDERSTANDING 9-1

1. In each of the following situations, do you think the industry described will be perfectly competitive or not? Explain your answer.
   a. There are two producers of aluminum in the world, a good sold in many places.
   b. Only a handful of companies produce natural gas from the North Sea. The price of natural gas is determined by global supply and demand, of which North Sea production represents a small share.
   c. Dozens of designers sell high-fashion clothes. Each designer has a distinctive style and a loyal clientele.
   d. There are many baseball teams in the United States, one or two in each major city, and each selling tickets to its events.

Solutions appear at back of book.

Production and Profits

Consider Jennifer and Jason, who run an organic tomato farm. Suppose that the market price of organic tomatoes is $18 per bushel and that Jennifer and Jason are price-takers—they can sell as much as they like at that price. Then we can use the data in Table 9-1 to find their profit-maximizing level of output by direct calculation.

TABLE **9-1**

Profit for Jennifer and Jason's Farm When Market Price Is $18

Quantity of tomatoes Q (bushels)	Total revenue TR	Total cost TC	Profit $TR - TC$
0	$0	$14	$-14
1	18	30	-12
2	36	36	0
3	54	44	10
4	72	56	16
5	90	72	18
6	108	92	16
7	126	116	10

The first column shows the quantity of output in bushels, and the second column shows Jennifer and Jason's total revenue from their output: the market value of their output. Total revenue, TR, is equal to the market price multiplied by the quantity of output:

(9-1) $TR = P \times Q$

In this example, total revenue is equal to $18 per bushel times the quantity of output in bushels.

The third column of Table 9-1 shows Jennifer and Jason's total cost. The fourth column of Table 9-1 shows their profit, equal to total revenue minus total cost:

(9-2) $\text{Profit} = TR - TC$

As indicated by the numbers in the table, profit is maximized at an output of 5 bushels, where profit is equal to $18. But we can gain more insight into the profit-maximizing choice of output by viewing it as a problem of marginal analysis, a task we'll do next.

Using Marginal Analysis to Choose the Profit-Maximizing Quantity of Output

Recall from Chapter 7 the *principle of marginal analysis:* the optimal amount of an activity is the level at which marginal benefit is equal to marginal cost. To apply this principle, consider the effect on a producer's profit of increasing output by 1 unit. The marginal benefit of that unit is the additional revenue generated by selling it; this measure has a name—it is called the **marginal revenue** of that output. The general formula for marginal revenue is:

> **Marginal revenue** is the change in total revenue generated by an additional unit of output.

$$\textbf{(9-3)} \quad \text{Marginal revenue} = \frac{\text{Change in total revenue}}{\text{Change in output}} = \frac{\text{Change in total revenue generated by one additional unit of output}}{}$$

or

$$MR = \Delta TR / \Delta Q$$

So Jennifer and Jason would maximize their profit by producing bushels up to the point at which the marginal revenue is equal to marginal cost. We can summarize this as the producer's **optimal output rule:** profit is maximized by producing the quantity at which the marginal revenue of the last unit produced is equal to its marginal cost. That is, $MR = MC$ at the optimal quantity of output.

> The **optimal output rule** says that profit is maximized by producing the quantity of output at which the marginal revenue of the last unit produced is equal to its marginal cost.

We can learn how to apply the optimal output rule with the help of Table 9-2, which provides various short-run cost measures for Jennifer and Jason's farm. The second column contains the farm's variable cost, and the third column shows its total cost of output based on the assumption that the farm incurs a fixed cost of $14. The fourth column shows their marginal cost. Notice that, in this example, the marginal cost falls as output increases from a low level before rising, so that the marginal cost curve has the "swoosh" shape described in Chapter 8. (Shortly it will become clear that this shape has important implications for short-run production decisions.)

TABLE 9-2

Short-Run Costs for Jennifer and Jason's Farm

Quantity of tomatoes Q (bushels)	Variable cost VC	Total cost TC	Marginal cost of bushel $MC = \Delta TC / \Delta Q$	Marginal revenue of bushel	Net gain of bushel = $MR - MC$
0	$0	$14			
			$16	$18	$2
1	16	30			
			6	18	12
2	22	36			
			8	18	10
3	30	44			
			12	18	6
4	42	56			
			16	18	2
5	58	72			
			20	18	-2
6	78	92			
			24	18	-6
7	102	116			

The fifth column contains the farm's marginal revenue, which has an important feature: Jennifer and Jason's marginal revenue is constant at $18 for every output level. The sixth and final column of Table 9-2 shows the calculation of the net gain per bushel of tomatoes, which is equal to marginal revenue minus marginal cost—or, equivalently, market price minus marginal cost. As you can see, it is positive for the 1st through 5th bushels; producing each of these bushels raises Jennifer and Jason's profit. For the 6th and 7th bushels, however, net gain is negative: producing

WHAT IF MARGINAL REVENUE AND MARGINAL COST AREN'T EXACTLY EQUAL?

The optimal output rule says that to maximize profit, you should produce the quantity at which marginal revenue is equal to marginal cost. But what do you do if there is no output level at which marginal revenue equals marginal cost? In that case, you produce the largest quantity for which marginal revenue exceeds marginal cost. This is the case in Table 9-2 at an output of 5 bushels. The simpler version of the optimal output rule applies when production involves large numbers, such as hundreds or thousands of units. In such cases marginal cost comes in small increments, and there is always a level of output at which marginal cost almost exactly equals marginal revenue.

The **price-taking firm's optimal output rule** says that a price-taking firm's profit is maximized by producing the quantity of output at which the market price is equal to the marginal cost of the last unit produced.

The **marginal revenue curve** shows how marginal revenue varies as output varies.

them would decrease, not increase, profit. (You can verify this by examining Table 9-1.) So 5 bushels are Jennifer and Jason's profit-maximizing output; it is the level of output at which marginal cost is equal to the market price, $18.

This example, in fact, illustrates another general rule derived from marginal analysis—the **price-taking firm's optimal output rule,** which says that a price-taking firm's profit is maximized by producing the quantity of output at which the market price is equal to the marginal cost of the last unit produced. That is, $P = MC$ at the *price-taking firm's* optimal quantity of output. In fact, the price-taking firm's optimal output rule is just an application of the optimal output rule to the particular case of a price-taking firm. Why? Because in the case of a price-taking firm, *marginal revenue is equal to price.* A price-taking firm cannot influence the market price by its actions. It always takes the market price as given because it cannot lower the market price by selling more or raise the market price by selling less. So, for a price-taking firm, the additional revenue generated by producing one more unit is always the market price. We will need to keep this fact in mind in future chapters, where we will learn that marginal revenue is not equal to the market price if the industry is not perfectly competitive and, as a result, firms are not price-takers.

For the remainder of this chapter, we will assume that the firms in question are, like Jennifer and Jason's farm, perfectly competitive. Figure 9-1 shows that Jennifer and Jason's profit-maximizing quantity of output is, indeed, the number of bushels at which the marginal cost of production is equal to price. The figure shows the marginal cost curve, *MC,* drawn from the data in the last column of Table 9-1. As in Chapter 8, we plot the marginal cost of increasing output from 1 to 2 bushels halfway between 1 and 2, and so on. The horizontal line at $18 is Jennifer and Jason's **marginal revenue curve, MR.** Note that whenever a firm is a price-taker, its marginal revenue curve is a horizontal line at the market price: it can sell as much as it likes at the market price. Regardless of whether it sells more or less, the market price is unaffected. In effect, the individual firm faces a horizontal, perfectly elastic demand curve for its output—an individual demand curve for its output that is equivalent to

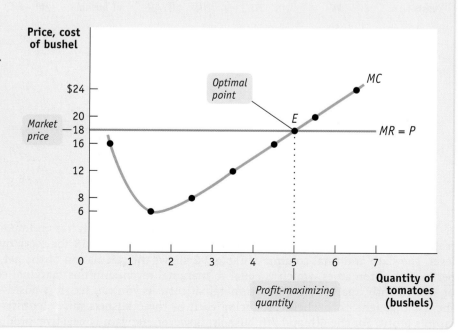

Figure 9-1

The Price-Taking Firm's Profit-Maximizing Quantity of Output

At the profit-maximizing quantity of output, the market price is equal to marginal cost. It is located at the point where the marginal cost curve crosses the marginal revenue curve, which is a horizontal line at the market price. Here, the profit-maximizing point is at an output of 5 bushels of tomatoes, the output quantity at point *E.*

its marginal revenue curve. The marginal cost curve crosses the marginal revenue curve at point *E*. Sure enough, the quantity of output at *E* is 5 bushels.

Does this mean that the firm's production decision can be entirely summed up as "produce up to the point where the marginal cost of production is equal to the price"? No, not quite. Before applying the principle of marginal analysis to determine how much to produce, a potential producer must as a first step answer an "either–or" question: should it produce at all? If the answer to that question is yes, it then proceeds to the second step—a "how much" decision: maximizing profit by choosing the quantity of output at which marginal cost is equal to price.

To understand why the first step in the production decision involves an "either–or" question, we need to ask how we determine whether it is profitable or unprofitable to produce at all.

When Is Production Profitable?

Recall from Chapter 7 that a firm's decision whether or not to stay in a given business depends on its *economic profit*—a measure based on the opportunity cost of resources used in the business. To put it a slightly different way: in the calculation of profit, a firm's total cost incorporates the implicit cost—the benefits forgone in the next best use of the firm's resources—as well as the explicit cost in the form of actual cash outlays.

We will assume that all costs, implicit as well as explicit, are included in the cost numbers given in Table 9-1; as a result, the profit numbers in Table 9-2 are economic profit. So what determines whether Jennifer and Jason's farm earns a profit or generates a loss? The answer is that, given the farm's cost curves, whether or not it is profitable depends on the market price of tomatoes—specifically, *whether the market price is more or less than the farm's minimum average total cost*.

Table 9-3 calculates short-run average variable cost and short-run average total cost for Jennifer and Jason's farm. These are short-run values, because we take fixed cost as given. (We'll turn to the effects of changing fixed cost shortly.) The short-run average total cost curve, *ATC*, is shown in Figure 9-2 on page 214, along with the marginal cost curve, *MC*, from Figure 9-1. As you can see, average total cost is minimized at point *C*, corresponding to an output of 4 bushels—the *minimum-cost output*—and an average total cost of $14 per bushel.

To see how these curves can be used to decide whether production is profitable or unprofitable, recall that profit is equal to total revenue minus total cost, *TR – TC*. This means:

- If *TR* > *TC*, the firm is profitable.
- If *TR* = *TC*, the firm breaks even.
- If *TR* < *TC*, the firm incurs a loss.

TABLE 9-3

Average Costs for Jennifer and Jason's Farm

Quantity of tomatoes Q (bushels)	Variable cost VC	Total cost TC	Average variable cost of bushel AVC = VC/Q	Average total cost of bushel ATC = TC/Q
1	$16.00	$30.00	$16.00	$30.00
2	22.00	36.00	11.00	18.00
3	30.00	44.00	10.00	14.67
4	42.00	56.00	10.50	14.00
5	58.00	72.00	11.60	14.40
6	78.00	92.00	13.00	15.33
7	102.00	116.00	14.57	16.57

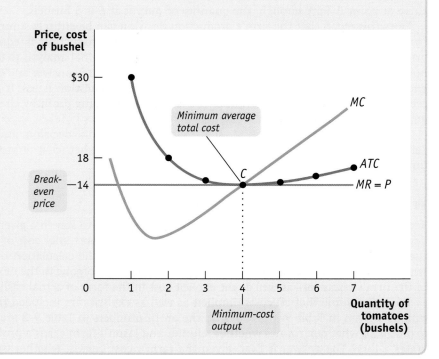

Figure 9-2

Costs and Production in the Short Run

This figure shows the marginal cost curve, *MC*, and the short-run average total cost curve, *ATC*. When the market price is $14, output will be 4 bushels of tomatoes (the minimum-cost output), represented by point *C*. The price of $14, equal to the firm's minimum average total cost, is the firm's *break-even price*. **>web...**

We can also express this idea in terms of revenue and cost per unit of output. If we divide profit by the number of units of output, *Q*, we obtain the following expression for profit per unit of output:

(9-4) $\text{Profit}/Q = TR/Q - TC/Q$

TR/Q is average revenue—that is, the market price. *TC/Q* is average total cost. So a firm is profitable if the market price for its product exceeds the average total cost of the quantity the firm produces; a firm loses money if the market price is less than average total cost of the quantity the firm produces. This means:

- If *P* > *ATC*, the firm is profitable.
- If *P* = *ATC*, the firm breaks even.
- If *P* < *ATC*, the firm incurs a loss.

Figure 9-3 illustrates this result, showing how the market price determines whether a firm is profitable. It also shows how profits are depicted graphically. Each panel shows the marginal cost curve, *MC*, and the short-run average total cost curve, *ATC*. Average total cost is minimized at point *C*. Panel (a) shows the case we have already analyzed, in which the market price of tomatoes is $18 per bushel. Panel (b) shows the case in which the market price of tomatoes is lower, $10 per bushel.

In panel (a), we see that at a price of $18 per bushel the profit-maximizing quantity of output is 5 bushels, indicated by point *E* where the marginal cost curve, *MC*, intersects the marginal revenue curve—which for a price-taking firm is a horizontal line at the market price. At that quantity of output, average total cost is $14.40 per bushel, indicated by point *Z*. Since the price per bushel exceeds average total cost per bushel, Jennifer and Jason's farm is profitable.

Jennifer and Jason's total profits when the market price is $18 are represented by the area of the shaded rectangle in panel (a). To see why, notice that total profit can be expressed in terms of profit per unit:

(9-5) Profit = $TR - TC = (TR/Q - TC/Q) \times Q$

or, equivalently,

Profit = $(P - ATC) \times Q$

since P is equal to TR/Q and ATC is equal to TC/Q. The height of the shaded rectangle in panel (a) corresponds to the vertical distance between points E and Z. It is equal to $P - ATC = \$18.00 - \$14.40 = \$3.60$ per bushel. The shaded rectangle has a width equal to the output: $Q = 5$ bushels. So the area of that rectangle is equal to

---

Figure 9-3

Profitability and the Market Price

In panel (a) the market price is $18. The farm is profitable because price exceeds minimum average total cost, the break-even price, $14. The farm's optimal output choice is indicated by point E, corresponding to an output of 5 bushels. The average total cost of producing 5 bushels is indicated by point Z on the ATC curve, corresponding to an amount of $14.40. The vertical distance between E and Z corresponds to the farm's per-unit profit, $18.00 − $14.40 = $3.60. Total profit is given by the area of the shaded rectangle, 5 × $3.60 = $18.00.

In panel (b) the market price is $10; the farm is unprofitable because the price falls below the minimum average total cost, $14. The farm's optimal output choice when producing is indicated by point A, corresponding to an output of three bushels. The farm's per-unit loss, $14.67 − $10.00 = $4.67, is represented by the vertical distance between A and Y. The farm's total loss is represented by the shaded rectangle, 3 × $4.67 = $14.00 (adjusted for rounding error). **>web...**

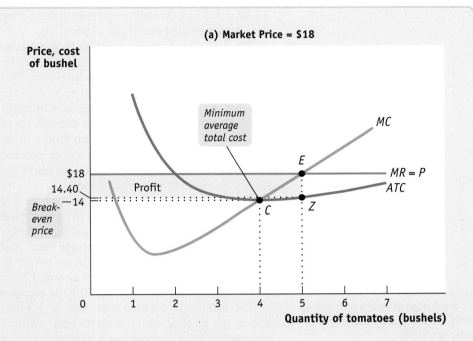

(a) Market Price = $18

(b) Market Price = $10

Jennifer and Jason's profit: 5 bushels × $3.60 profit per bushel = $18—the same number we calculated in Table 9-2.

What about the situation illustrated in panel (b)? Here the market price of tomatoes is $10 per bushel. Setting price equal to marginal cost leads to a profit-maximizing output of 3 bushels, indicated by point A. At this output, Jennifer and Jason have an average total cost of $14.67 per bushel, indicated by point Y. At their profit-maximizing output quantity—3 bushels—average total cost exceeds the market price. This means that Jennifer and Jason's farm generates losses, not profits.

How much do they lose by producing when the market price is $10? On each bushel they lose $ATC - P = \$14.67 - \$10.00 = \$4.67$, an amount corresponding to the vertical distance between points A and Y. And, they would produce 3 bushels, which corresponds to the width of the shaded rectangle. So, the total value of the losses is $\$4.67 \times 3 = \$14.00$ (adjusted for rounding error), an amount that corresponds to the area of the shaded rectangle in panel (b).

But how does a producer know, in general, whether or not its business will be profitable? It turns out that the crucial test lies in a comparison of the market price to the producer's *minimum average total cost.* On Jennifer and Jason's farm, minimum average total cost, which is equal to $14, occurs at an output quantity of 4 bushels. Whenever the market price exceeds minimum average total cost, the producer can find some output level for which the average total cost is less than the market price. That means that the producer can find a level of output at which the firm makes a profit. Jennifer and Jason's farm will be profitable whenever the market price exceeds $14. And they will achieve the highest profit by producing the quantity at which marginal cost equals the market price.

On the other hand, if the market price is less than minimum average total cost, there is no output level at which price exceeds average total cost. As a result, the firm will be unprofitable at any quantity of output. As we saw, at a price of $10—an amount less than minimum average total cost—Jennifer and Jason did indeed lose money. By producing the quantity at which marginal cost equals the market price, Jennifer and Jason did the best they could, but the best that they could do was a loss of $14. Any other quantity would have increased the size of their loss.

The minimum average total cost of a price-taking firm is called its **break-even price,** the price at which it earns zero profits. A firm will earn positive profits when the market price is above the break-even price, and it will suffer losses when the market price is below the break-even price. Jennifer and Jason's break-even price of $14 is the price at point C in Figures 9-2 and 9-3.

So the rule for determining whether a producer of a good is profitable depends on a comparison of the market price of the good to the producer's break-even price—its minimum average total cost:

- Whenever the market price exceeds minimum average total cost, the producer is profitable.

- Whenever the market price equals minimum average total cost, the producer breaks even.

- Whenever the market price is less than minimum average total cost, the producer is unprofitable.

The Short-Run Production Decision

You might be tempted to say that if a firm is unprofitable because the market price is below its minimum average total cost, it shouldn't produce any output. In the short run, however, this conclusion isn't right. In the short run, sometimes the firm should produce even if price falls below minimum average total cost. The reason is that total cost includes *fixed cost*—cost that does not depend on the amount of output produced. In the short run, fixed cost must still be paid, regardless of whether or not a firm produces. For

---

The **break-even price** of a price-taking firm is the market price at which it earns zero profits.

example, if Jennifer and Jason have rented a tractor for the year, they have to pay that rent regardless of whether they produce any tomatoes. Since it cannot be changed in the short run, their fixed cost is irrelevant to their decision about whether to produce or shut down in the short run. Although fixed cost should play no role in the decision about whether to produce at all in the short run, other costs—variable costs—do matter. An example of variable costs is the wages of workers who must be hired to help with planting and harvesting. Variable costs can be saved by *not* producing; so they should play a role in determining whether or not to produce in the short run.

Let's turn to Figure 9-4: it shows both the short-run average total cost curve, *ATC*, and the short-run average *variable* cost curve, *AVC*, drawn from the information in Table 9-3. Recall that the difference between the two curves—the vertical distance between them—represents average fixed cost, the fixed cost per unit of output, *FC/Q*. Because the marginal cost curve has a "swoosh" shape—falling at first before rising— the short-run average variable cost curve is U-shaped: the initial fall in marginal cost causes average variable cost to fall as well, before rising marginal cost eventually pulls it up again. The short-run average variable cost curve reaches its minimum value of $10 at point *A*, at an output of 3 bushels.

We are now prepared to fully analyze the optimal production decision in the short run. We need to consider two cases:

- When the market price is below minimum average *variable* cost
- When the market price is greater than or equal to minimum average *variable* cost

When the market price is below minimum average variable cost, the price the firm receives is not covering its variable cost per unit. A firm in this situation should cease production immediately. Why? Because there is no level of output at which the firm's total revenue covers its variable costs—the costs it can avoid by not operating. In this case the firm maximizes its profits by not producing at all—by, in effect, minimizing its losses. It will still incur a fixed cost in the short run, but it will no longer incur any variable cost. This means that the minimum average variable cost is equal to the **shut-down price,** the price at which the firm ceases production in the short run.

A firm will cease production in the short run if the market price falls below the **shut-down price**, which is equal to minimum average variable cost.

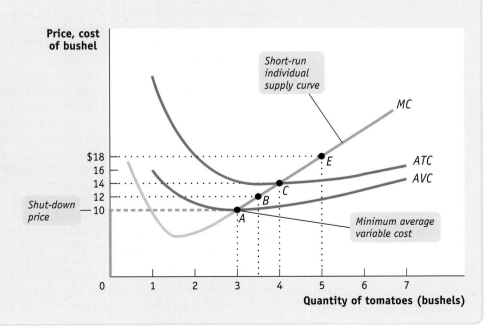

Figure 9-4

The Short-Run Individual Supply Curve

When the market price exceeds Jennifer and Jason's *shut-down price* of $10, the minimum average variable cost indicated by point *A,* they will produce the output quantity at which marginal cost is equal to price. So at any price above minimum average *variable* cost, the short-run individual supply curve is the firm's marginal cost curve; this corresponds to the upward-sloping segment of the individual supply curve. When market price falls below minimum average variable cost, the firm ceases operation in the short run. This corresponds to the vertical segment of the individual supply curve along the vertical axis.

When price is greater than minimum average variable cost, however, the firm should produce in the short run. In this case, the firm maximizes profit—or minimizes its loss—by choosing the output quantity at which its marginal cost is equal to the market price. For example, if the market price of tomatoes is $18 per bushel, Jennifer and Jason should produce at point E in Figure 9-4, corresponding to an output of 5 bushels. Note that point C in Figure 9-4 corresponds to the farm's break-even price of $14 per bushel. Since E lies above C, Jennifer and Jason's farm will be profitable; they will generate a per-bushel profit of $18.00 − $14.40 = $3.60 when the market price is $18.

But what if the market price lies between the shut-down price and the break-even price—that is, between minimum average *variable* cost and minimum average *total* cost? In the case of Jennifer and Jason's farm, this corresponds to prices anywhere between $10 and $14—say, a market price of $12. At $12, Jennifer and Jason's farm is not profitable; since the market price is below minimum average total cost, the farm is losing the difference between price and average total cost per unit produced. Yet, even if it isn't covering its total cost per unit, it is covering its variable cost per unit and some—but not all—of the fixed cost per unit. If a firm in this situation shuts down, it would incur no variable cost but would incur the *full* fixed cost. As a result, shutting down generates an even greater loss than continuing to operate.

This means that whenever price falls between minimum average total cost and minimum average variable cost, the firm is better off producing some output in the short run. The reason is that by producing, it can cover its variable cost per unit and at least some of its fixed cost, even though it is incurring a loss. In this case, the firm maximizes profit—that is, minimizes its loss—by choosing the quantity of output at which its marginal cost is equal to the market price. So if Jennifer and Jason face a market price of $12 per bushel, their profit-maximizing output is given by point B in Figure 9-4, corresponding to an output of 3.5 bushels.

It's worth noting that the decision to produce when the firm is covering its variable costs but not all of its fixed cost is similar to the decision to ignore *sunk costs*, a concept we studied in Chapter 7. You may recall that a sunk cost is a cost that has already been incurred and cannot be recouped; and because it cannot be changed, it should have no effect on any current decision. In the short-run production decision, fixed cost is, in effect, like a sunk cost—it has been spent, and it can't be recovered in the short run. This comparison also illustrates why variable cost does indeed matter in the short run: it can be avoided by not producing.

And what happens if market price is exactly equal to the shut-down price, minimum average variable cost? In this instance, the firm is indifferent between producing 3 units or 0 units. As we'll see shortly, this is an important point when looking at the behavior of an industry as a whole.

The **short-run individual supply curve** shows how an individual producer's profit-maximizing output quantity depends on the market price, taking fixed cost as given.

Putting everything together, we can now draw the **short-run individual supply curve** of Jennifer and Jason's farm; it shows how the profit-maximizing quantity of output in the short run depends on the price, the red line in Figure 9-4. As you can see, the curve is in two segments. The upward-sloping red segment starting at point A shows the short-run profit-maximizing output when market price is above the shut-down price of $10 per bushel. As long as the market price is above the shut-down price, Jennifer and Jason produce the quantity of output at which marginal cost is equal to the market price. That is, at market prices above the shut-down price, the firm's short-run supply curve corresponds to its marginal cost curve. But at any market price below minimum average variable cost—in this case, $10 per bushel—the firm shuts down and output drops to zero in the short run. This corresponds to the vertical segment of the curve that lies on top of the vertical axis.

Do firms really shut down temporarily without going out of business? Yes. In fact, in some businesses temporary shut-downs are routine. The most common examples are industries in which demand is highly seasonal, like outdoor amusement parks in climates with cold winters. Such parks would have to offer very low prices to entice customers during the colder months—prices so low that the owners would not cover their variable costs (principally wages and electricity). The wiser choice economically is to shut down until warm weather brings enough customers who are willing to pay a higher price.

Changing Fixed Cost

Although fixed cost cannot be altered in the short run, in the long run firms can acquire or get rid of machines, buildings, and so on. As we learned in Chapter 8, in the long run the level of fixed cost is a matter of choice. We saw that a firm will choose the level of fixed cost that minimizes the average total cost for its desired output quantity. Now we will focus on an even bigger question facing a firm when choosing its fixed cost: whether to incur *any* fixed cost at all by remaining in its current business.

In the long run, a producer can always eliminate fixed cost by selling off its plant and equipment. If it does so, of course, it can't ever produce—it has exited the industry. In contrast, a potential producer can take on some fixed cost by acquiring machines and other resources, which puts it in a position to produce—it can enter the industry. In most perfectly competitive industries the set of producers, although fixed in the short run, changes in the long run as firms enter or leave the industry.

Consider Jennifer and Jason's farm once again. In order to simplify our analysis, we will sidestep the problem of choosing among several possible levels of fixed cost. Instead, we will assume from now on that Jennifer and Jason have only one possible choice of fixed cost if they operate, the amount of $14 that was the basis for the calculations in Tables 9-1, 9-2, and 9-3. Alternatively, they can choose a fixed cost of zero if they exit the industry. (With this assumption, Jennifer and Jason's short-run average total cost curve and long-run average total cost curve are one and the same.)

Suppose that the market price of organic tomatoes is consistently less than $14 over an extended period of time. In that case, Jennifer and Jason never fully cover their fixed cost: their business runs at a loss. In the long run, then, they can do better by closing their business and leaving the industry. In other words, *in the long run firms will exit an industry if the market price is consistently less than their break-even price*—their minimum average total cost.

On the other hand, suppose, that the price of organic tomatoes is consistently above the break-even price, $14, for an extended period of time. Because their farm is profitable, Jennifer and Jason will remain in the industry and continue producing. But things won't stop there. The organic tomato industry meets the criterion of *free entry*: there are many potential organic tomato producers because the necessary inputs are easy to obtain. And the cost curves of those potential producers are likely to be similar to those of Jennifer and Jason, since the technology used by other producers is likely to be very similar to that used by Jennifer and Jason. If the price is high enough to generate profits for existing producers, it will also attract some of these potential producers into the industry. So *in the long run a price in excess of $14 should lead to entry*: new producers will come into the organic tomato industry.

As we will see in the next section, exit and entry lead to an important distinction between the *short-run industry supply curve* and the *long-run industry supply curve*.

Summing Up: The Perfectly Competitive Firm's Profitability and Production Conditions

In this chapter, we've studied where the supply curve for a perfectly competitive firm comes from. Every perfectly competitive firm makes its production decisions by maximizing profit, and these decisions determine the supply curve. Table 9-4 on page 220 summarizes the competitive firm's profitability and production conditions. It also relates them to entry and exit from the industry.

PITFALLS

ECONOMIC PROFIT, AGAIN
Some readers may wonder why firms would enter an industry when they will do little more than break even. Wouldn't people prefer to go into other businesses that yield a better profit?

The answer is that here, as always, when we calculate cost, we mean *opportunity cost*—that is, cost that includes the return a business owner could get by using his or her resources elsewhere. And so the profit that we calculate is *economic profit*; if the market price is above the break-even level, potential business owners can earn more in this industry than they could elsewhere.

TABLE **9-4**

Summary of the Perfectly Competitive Firm's Profitability and Production Conditions

Profitability Condition (minimum *ATC* = break-even price)	Result
$P >$ minimum *ATC*	Firm profitable. Entry into industry in the long run.
$P =$ minimum *ATC*	Firm breaks even. No entry into or exit from industry in the long run.
$P <$ minimum *ATC*	Firm unprofitable. Exit from industry in the long run.

Production Condition (minimum *AVC* = shut-down price)	Result
$P >$ minimum *AVC*	Firm produces in the short run. If $P <$ minimum *ATC*, firm covers variable cost and some but not all of fixed cost. If $P >$ minimum *ATC*, firm covers all variable cost and fixed cost.
$P =$ minimum *AVC*	Firm indifferent between producing in the short run or not. Just covers variable cost.
$P <$ minimum *AVC*	Firm shuts down in the short run. Does not cover variable cost.

economics in action

California Screaming

Between November 2000 and May 2001, the state of California went through an electricity crisis. Supplies of power were limited, and the wholesale price of electricity—the price at which generators sell power to the local utilities, which then provide it to customers—ran consistently at more than 10 times its normal level.

During the crisis, some economists accused the power generators of deliberately withholding electricity from the market in order to drive up prices. That is, they argued that competition wasn't perfect, that producers weren't taking prices as given. We'll discuss why it might have been in the interests of producers to withhold power in Chapter 14.

The interesting point for now is to ask how you could tell whether or not producers were acting as price-takers. And the answer was that economists used data on electricity generating costs to estimate marginal cost curves for producers. They could then ask whether the producers were actually generating as much power as they should have if they were setting price equal to marginal cost. The conclusion of several influential studies, including a federal investigation by the Justice Department, was that they were not.

Eventually, power companies were caught red-handed: tape recordings revealed they purposely shut down plants in order to drive up prices. Economists applying marginal analysis had gotten it right. ■

< < < < < < < < < < < < < < < < < <

>> CHECK YOUR UNDERSTANDING 9-2

1. Draw a short-run diagram showing a U-shaped average total cost curve, a U-shaped average variable cost curve, and a "swoosh"-shaped marginal cost curve. On it, indicate the range of output and the range of price for which the following actions are optimal.
   a. The firm shuts down immediately.
   b. The firm operates in the short run despite sustaining a loss.
   c. The firm operates while making a profit.

2. The state of Maine has a very active lobster industry, which harvests lobsters during the summer months. During the rest of the year, lobsters can be obtained from other parts of the world but at a much higher price. Maine is also full of "lobster shacks," roadside restaurants serving lobster dishes that are open only during the summer. Explain why it is optimal for lobster shacks to operate only during the summer.

Solutions appear at back of book.

The Industry Supply Curve

Why will an increase in the demand for organic tomatoes lead to a large price increase at first but a much smaller increase in the long run? The answer lies in the behavior of the **industry supply curve**—the relationship between the price and the total output of an industry as a whole. The industry supply curve is what we referred to in earlier chapters as *the* supply curve or the market supply curve. But here we take some extra care to distinguish between the *individual supply curve* of a single firm and the supply curve of the industry as a whole.

As you might guess from the previous section, the industry supply curve must be analyzed in somewhat different ways for the short run and the long run. Let's start with the short run.

The **industry supply curve** shows the relationship between the price of a good and the total output of the industry as a whole.

The Short-Run Industry Supply Curve

Recall that in the short run the number of producers in an industry is fixed—there is no entry or exit. We can best understand how the industry supply curve emerges from individual producer supply curves by imagining that all the producers are alike. So let's assume that there are 100 organic tomato farms, each with the same costs as Jennifer and Jason's farm.

Each of these 100 farms will have an individual short-run supply curve like the one in Figure 9-4. At a price below $10, no farms will produce. At a price of more than $10, each farm will produce the quantity of output at which its marginal cost is equal to the market price. As you can see from Figure 9-4, this will lead them to produce 4 bushels if the price is $14 per bushel, 5 bushels if the price is $18, and so on. So if there are 100 organic tomato farmers and the price of organic tomatoes is $18 per bushel, the industry as a whole will produce 500 bushels, corresponding to 100 farmers × 5 bushels per farmer, and so on. The result is the **short-run industry supply curve**, shown as *S* in Figure 9-5. This curve shows the quantity that producers will supply at each price, *taking the number of producers as given*.

The demand curve *D* in Figure 9-5 crosses the short-run industry supply curve at E_{MKT}, corresponding to a price of $18 and a quantity of 500 bushels. Point E_{MKT} is a **short-run market equilibrium:** the quantity supplied equals the quantity demanded, taking the number of producers as given. But the long run may look quite different, because in the long run farms may enter or exit the industry.

The **short-run industry supply curve** shows how the quantity supplied by an industry depends on the market price given a fixed number of producers.

There is a **short-run market equilibrium** when the quantity supplied equals the quantity demanded, taking the number of producers as given.

Figure 9-5

The Short-Run Market Equilibrium

The short-run industry supply curve, *S*, is the industry supply curve taking the number of producers—here, 100—as given. It is generated by adding together the individual supply curves of the 100 producers. Below the shut-down price of $10, no producer wants to produce in the short run. Above $10, the short-run industry supply curve slopes upward, as each producer increases output as price increases. It intersects the demand curve, *D*, at point E_{MKT}, the point of short-run market equilibrium, corresponding to a market price of $18 and a quantity of 500 bushels. **>web...**

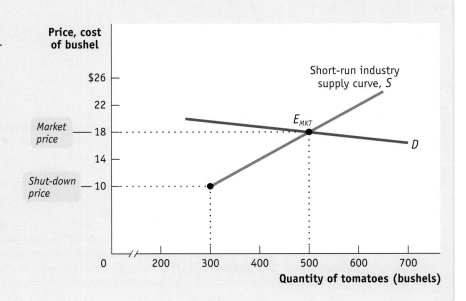

The Long-Run Industry Supply Curve

Suppose that in addition to the 100 farmers currently in the organic tomato business, there are many other potential producers. Suppose also that each of these potential producers would have the same cost curves as existing producers like Jennifer and Jason if it entered the industry

When will additional producers enter the industry? Whenever existing producers are making a profit—that is, whenever the market price is above the break-even price of $14 per bushel, the minimum average total cost of production. For example, at a price of $18 per bushel, new firms will enter the industry.

What will happen as additional producers enter the industry? Clearly, the quantity supplied at any given price will increase. The short-run industry supply curve will shift to the right. This will, in turn, alter the market equilibrium and result in a lower market price. Existing firms will respond to the lower market price by reducing their output, but the total industry output will increase because of the larger number of firms in the industry.

Figure 9-6 illustrates the effects of this chain of events on an existing firm and on the market; panel (a) shows how an individual existing firm responds to entry, and panel (b) shows how the market responds to entry. (Note that these two graphs have been rescaled in comparison to Figure 9-4 to better illustrate how profit changes in response to price.) In panel (b), S_1 is the initial short-run industry supply curve, based on the existence of 100 producers. The initial short-run market equilibrium is at E_{MKT}, with an equilibrium market price of $18 and a quantity of 500 bushels. At this price existing producers are profitable, which is reflected in panel (a): an existing firm makes a total profit represented by the shaded rectangle labeled A when market price is $18.

Figure 9-6   **The Long-Run Market Equilibrium**

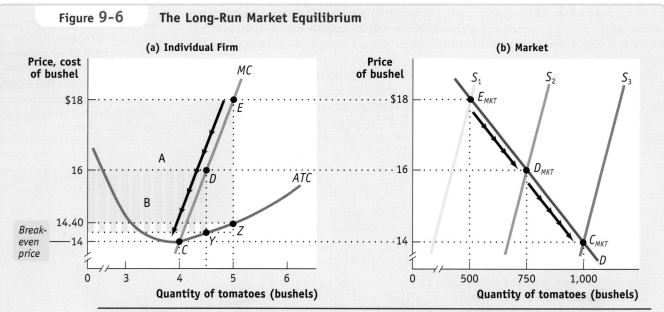

Point E_{MKT} of panel (b) shows the initial short-run market equilibrium, at the intersection of the demand curve, D, and the initial short-run industry supply curve, S_1. Because the market price ($18) is above the break-even price ($14), each of the 100 existing producers makes an economic profit; this is illustrated in panel (a), where the rectangle labeled A shows the profit of an existing firm. These profits induce entry by additional producers, shifting the short-run industry supply curve outward from S_1 to S_2 in panel (b). This results in a new short-run equilibrium at point D_{MKT} with a lower market

price of $16 and higher industry output. The output and profits of existing firms are reduced; but some profit remains, as shown by the rectangle labeled B in panel (a). Entry continues shifting out the short-run industry supply curve, as price falls and industry output increases yet again. Entry finally ceases once an equilibrium, at point C_{MKT} on supply curve S_3, is reached. Here market price is equal to the break-even price; existing producers make zero economic profits and there is no incentive for entry or exit. Therefore C_{MKT} is also a long-run market equilibrium.

These profits will induce new producers to enter the industry, shifting the short-run industry supply curve to the right. For example, the short-run industry supply curve when the number of producers has increased to 167 is S_2. Corresponding to this supply curve is a new short-run market equilibrium labeled D_{MKT}, with a market price of $16 and a quantity of 750 bushels. At $16, each firm produces 4.5 bushels, so that industry output is $167 \times 4.5 = 750$ bushels (rounded). From panel (a) you can see the effect of the entry of 67 new producers on an existing firm: the fall in price causes it to reduce its output, and its profit falls to the area represented by the shaded rectangle labeled B.

Although diminished, the profit of existing firms at D_{MKT} means that entry will continue and the number of firms will continue to rise. If the number of producers rises to 250, the short-run industry supply curve shifts out again to S_3, and the market equilibrium is at C_{MKT}, with a quantity supplied and demanded of 1,000 bushels and a market price of $14 per bushel.

Like E_{MKT} and D_{MKT}, C_{MKT} is a short-run equilibrium. But it is also something more. Because the price of $14 is each firm's break-even price, an existing producer makes zero economic profits—neither a profit nor a loss—when producing its profit-maximizing output of 4 bushels. At this price there is no incentive either for potential producers to enter or for existing producers to exit the industry. So C_{MKT} corresponds to a **long-run market equilibrium**—a situation in which quantity supplied equals the quantity demanded given that sufficient time has elapsed for producers to either enter or exit the industry. In a long-run market equilibrium, all existing and potential producers have fully adjusted to their optimal long-run choices; as a result, no producer has an incentive to either enter or exit the industry.

To explore further the significance of the difference between short-run and long-run equilibrium, consider the effect of an increase in demand on an industry with free entry that is initially in long-run equilibrium. Panel (b) in Figure 9-7 on page 224 shows the market adjustment; panels (a) and (c) show how an existing individual firm behaves during the process.

In panel (b) of Figure 9-7, D_1 is the initial demand curve and S_1 is the initial short-run industry supply curve. Their intersection at point X_{MKT} is both a short-run and a long-run market equilibrium, because the equilibrium price of $14 leads to zero economic profits—and therefore neither entry nor exit. It corresponds to point X in panel (a), where an individual existing firm is operating at the minimum of its average total cost curve.

Now suppose that the demand curve shifts out for some reason to D_2. As shown in panel (b), in the short run, industry output moves along the short-run industry supply curve S_1 to the new short-run market equilibrium at Y_{MKT}, the intersection of S_1 and D_2. The market price rises to $18 per bushel and industry output increases from Q_X to Q_Y. This corresponds to the movement from X to Y in panel (a), as an existing firm increases its output in response to the rise in the market price.

But we know that Y_{MKT} is not a long-run equilibrium, because $18 is higher than minimum average total cost, so existing producers are making economic profits. This will lead additional firms to enter the industry. Over time entry will cause the short-run industry supply curve to shift to the right. In the long run, the short-run industry supply curve will have shifted out to S_2, and the equilibrium will be at Z_{MKT}—with the price falling back to $14 per bushel and industry output increasing yet again, from Q_Y to Q_Z. Like X_{MKT} before the increase in demand, Z_{MKT} is both a short-run and a long-run market equilibrium.

The effect of entry on an existing firm is illustrated in panel (c), in the movement from Y to Z along the firm's individual supply curve. The firm reduces its output in response to the fall in price, ultimately arriving back at its original output quantity, corresponding to the minimum of its average total cost curve. In fact, every firm that is now in the industry—the initial set of firms and the new entrants—will operate at the minimum of its average total cost curves, at point Z. This means that the entire increase in industry output, from Q_X to Q_Z, comes from production by new entrants.

A market is in **long-run market equilibrium** when the quantity supplied equals the quantity demanded, given that sufficient time has elapsed for entry into and exit from the industry to occur.

Figure 9-7   The Effect of an Increase in Demand in the Short Run and the Long Run

Panel (b) shows how an industry adjusts in the short and long run to an increase in demand; panels (a) and (c) show the corresponding adjustments by an existing firm. Initially the market is at point X_{MKT} in panel (b), a short-run and long-run equilibrium at a price of $14 and industry output of Q_X. An existing firm makes zero profit, operating at point X in panel (a) at minimum average total cost. Demand increases as D_1 shifts rightward to D_2, and raises the market price to $18. Existing firms increase their output and industry output moves along the short-run industry supply curve S_1 to a short-run equilibrium at Y_{MKT}. Correspondingly, the existing firm in panel (a) moves from point X to point Y. But at a price of $18 existing firms are profitable. As shown in panel (b), in the long run new entrants arrive and the short-run industry suppply curve shifts rightward, from S_1 to S_2. There is a new equilibrium at point Z_{MKT}, at a lower price of $14 and higher industry output of Q_Z. An existing firm responds by moving from Y to Z in panel (c), returning to its initial output level and zero profit. Production by new entrants accounts for the total increase in industy output, $Q_Z - Q_X$. Like X_{MKT}, Z_{MKT} is also a short-run and long-run equilibrium: with existing firms earning zero economic profits, there is no incentive for any firms to enter or exit the industry. The horizontal line passing through X_{MKT} and Z_{MKT}, LRS, is the *long-run industry supply curve*: at the break-even price of $14, producers will produce any amount that consumers demand in the long run.

The **long-run industry supply curve** shows how the quantity supplied responds to the price once producers have had time to enter or exit the industry.

The line LRS that passes through X_{MKT} and Z_{MKT} in panel (b) is the **long-run industry supply curve.** It shows how the quantity supplied by an industry responds to the price given that producers have had time to enter or exit the industry.

In this particular case, the long-run industry supply curve is horizontal at $14. In other words, in this industry supply is *perfectly elastic* in the long run—given time to enter or exit, producers will supply any quantity consumers demand at a price of $14. Perfectly elastic long-run supply is actually a good assumption for many industries. However, in other industries even the long-run industry supply curve is upward sloping. The usual reason even the long-run industry supply curve is upward sloping is that producers must use some input that is in limited supply and as the industry expands, the price of that input is driven up. For example, beach-resort hotels must compete for a limited quantity of prime beachfront property.

Whether the long-run industry supply curve is horizontal or upward sloping, however, the long-run price elasticity of supply is *higher* than the short-run price elasticity whenever there is free entry and exit. As shown in Figure 9-8, the long-run industry supply curve is always flatter than the short-run industry supply curve. The reason is entry and exit: a high price attracts entry by new producers, resulting in a

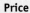

Figure 9-8

Comparing the Short-Run and Long-Run Industry Supply Curves

The long-run industry supply curve may slope upward, but it is always flatter—more elastic—than the short-run industry supply curve. This is because of entry and exit: a higher price attracts new entrants in the long run, resulting in a rise in industry output and a fall in price; a fall in price induces existing producers to exit in the long run, generating a fall in industry output and a rise in price. **>web...**

rise in industry output and a fall in price; a low price induces existing firms to exit, leading to a fall in industry output and an increase in price.

The distinction between the short-run industry supply curve and the long-run industry supply curve is very important in practice. We often see a sequence of events like that shown in Figure 9-7: an increase in demand initially leads to a large price increase, but prices return to their initial level once new firms have entered the industry. Or we see the sequence in reverse: a fall in demand reduces prices in the short run, but they return to their initial level as producers exit the industry.

The Cost of Production and Efficiency in Long-run Equilibrium

Our analysis leads us to three conclusions about the cost of production and efficiency in the long-run equilibrium of a perfectly competitive industry. These results will be important in our discussion in Chapter 14 of how monopoly gives rise to inefficiency.

First, in a perfectly competitive industry in equilibrium, the value of marginal cost is the same for all firms. That's because all firms produce the quantity of output at which marginal cost equals the market price, and as price-takers they all face the same market price.

Second, in a perfectly competitive industry with free entry and exit, each firm will have zero economic profit in long-run equilibrium. Each firm produces the quantity of output that minimizes its average total cost—corresponding to point Z in panel (c) of Figure 9-7. So the total cost of production of the industry's output is minimized in a perfectly competitive industry.

The third and final conclusion is that the long-run market equilibrium of a perfectly competitive industry is efficient: no mutually beneficial transactions go unexploited. To understand this we need to recall a fundamental requirement for efficiency from Chapter 6: all consumers who have a willingness to pay greater than or equal to sellers' costs actually get the good. And we also learned that a market is efficient (except under certain, well-defined conditions)—the market price matches all consumers with a willingness to pay greater than or equal to the market price to all sellers who have a cost of producing the good less than or equal to the market price.

How do we know that the long-run equilibrium of a perfectly competitive industry is efficient? Because each firm produces the output level at which price is equal to marginal cost. And marginal cost is in fact the same as seller's cost—the lowest price the firm is willing to accept for the good. So the long-run equilibrium of a market with a perfectly competitive industry is indeed efficient.

economics in action

A Crushing Reversal

For some reason, starting in the mid-1990s, Americans began drinking a lot more wine. Part of this increase in demand may have reflected a booming economy, but the surge in wine consumption continued even after the economy stumbled in 2001. By 2002, Americans were consuming 35 percent more wine than they did in 1993.

At first, the increase in wine demand led to sharply higher prices; between 1993 and 2000, the price of red wine grapes rose approximately 50 percent, and California grape growers earned high profits. As a result, there was a rapid expansion of the industry, both because existing grape growers expanded their capacity and because new growers entered the market. Between 1994 and 2002, production of red wine grapes almost doubled.

The result was predictable: the price of grapes fell as the supply curve shifted out. As demand growth slowed in 2002, prices plunged by 17 percent. The effect was to end the California wine industry's expansion. In fact, some grape producers began to exit the industry. ∎

As production expanded and prices fell, profits in the California wine industry shriveled.

< < < < < < < < < < < < < < < < < <

>>CHECK YOUR UNDERSTANDING 9-3

1. Which of the following events will induce firms to enter an industry? Which will induce firms to exit? When will entry or exit cease? Explain your answer.
   a. A technological advance lowers the fixed cost of production of every firm in the industry.
   b. The wages paid to workers in the industry go up.
   c. A change in consumer tastes increases demand for the good.
   d. The price of a key input rises due to a shortage of that input.
2. Assume that the egg industry is perfectly competitive and is in long-run equilibrium with a perfectly elastic long-run industry supply curve. Health concerns about cholesterol then lead to a decrease in demand. Construct a figure similar to Figure 9-7, showing the short-run behavior of the industry and how long-run equilibrium is reestablished.

>> QUICK REVIEW

➤ The *industry supply curve* corresponds to the supply curve of earlier chapters. In the short run, the time period over which the number of producers is fixed, the *short-run market equilibrium* is given by the intersection of the *short-run industry supply curve* and the demand curve. In the long run, the time period over which producers can enter or exit the industry, the *long-run market equilibrium* is given by the intersection of the *long-run industry supply curve* and the demand curve. In the long-run market equilibrium, no producer has an incentive to enter or exit the industry.

➤ The long-run industry supply curve is often horizontal, although it may be upward sloping when a necessary input is in limited supply; it is always more elastic than the short-run industry supply curve.

➤ In the long-run market equilibrium of a perfectly competitive industry, each firm produces at the same marginal cost, which is equal to the market price, and the total cost of production of the industry's output is minimized. It is also efficient.

● A LOOK AHEAD ●

In this chapter, we have seen how the rational decisions of producers in a perfectly competitive industry give rise to that industry's supply curve. But this is, of course, only half the story. To complete the picture we must turn next to the decisions made by rational consumers and how these decisions give rise to the demand curve.

SUMMARY

1. In a **perfectly competitive market** all producers are **price-taking producers** and all consumers are **price-taking consumers**—no one's actions can influence the market price. Consumers are normally price-takers, but producers often are not. In a **perfectly competitive industry,** all producers are price-takers.

2. There are two necessary conditions for a perfectly competitive industry: there are many producers, none of whom have a large **market share,** and the industry produces a **standardized product** or **commodity**—goods that consumers regard as equivalent. A third condition is often satisfied as well: **free entry and exit** into and from the industry.

3. A producer chooses output according to the **optimal output rule:** produce the quantity at which **marginal revenue** equals marginal cost. For a price-taking firm, marginal revenue is equal to price and its **marginal revenue curve** is a horizontal line at the market price. It chooses output according to the **price-taking firm's optimal output rule:** produce the quantity at which price equals marginal cost. However, a firm that produces the optimal quantity may not be profitable.

4. A firm is profitable if total revenue exceeds total cost or, equivalently, if the market price exceeds its **break-even price**—minimum average total cost. If market price exceeds the break-even price, the firm is profitable; if it is less, the firm is unprofitable; if it is equal, the firm breaks even. When profitable, the firm's per-unit profit is $P - ATC$; when unprofitable, its per-unit loss is $ATC - P$.

5. Fixed cost is irrelevant to the firm's optimal short-run production decision, which depends on its **shut-down price**—its minimum average variable cost—and the market price. When the market price exceeds the shut-down

price, the firm produces the output quantity where marginal cost equals the market price. When the market price falls below the shut-down price, the firm ceases production in the short run. This generates the firm's **short-run individual supply curve**.

6. Fixed cost matters in the long run. If the market price is below minimum average total cost for an extended period of time, firms will exit the industry. If above, existing firms are profitable and new firms will enter the industry.

7. The **industry supply curve** depends on the time period. The **short-run industry supply curve** is the industry supply curve given that the number of firms is fixed. The **short-run market equilibrium** is given by the intersection of the short-run industry supply curve and the demand curve.

8. The **long-run industry supply curve** is the industry supply curve given sufficient time for entry into and exit from the industry. In the **long-run market equilibrium**—given by the intersection of the long-run industry supply curve and the demand curve—no producer has an incentive to enter or exit. The long-run industry supply curve is often horizontal. It may slope upward if there is limited supply of an input; but it is always flatter than the short-run industry supply curve.

9. In the long-run market equilibrium of a competitive industry, profit maximization leads each firm to produce at the same marginal cost, which is equal to market price. Free entry and exit means that each firm earns zero economic profit—producing the output corresponding to its minimum average total cost. So the total cost of production of an industry's output is minimized. The outcome is efficient because every consumer with a willingness to pay greater or equal to marginal cost gets the good.

KEY TERMS

Price-taking producer, p. 207
Price-taking consumer, p. 207
Perfectly competitive market, p. 207
Perfectly competitive industry, p. 207
Market share, p. 208
Standardized product, p. 208
Commodity, p. 208

Free entry and exit, p. 209
Marginal revenue, p. 211
Optimal output rule, p. 211
Price-taking firm's optimal output rule, p. 212
Marginal revenue curve, p. 212
Break-even price, p. 216

Shut-down price, p. 217
Short-run individual supply curve, p. 218
Industry supply curve, p. 221
Short-run industry supply curve, p. 221
Short-run market equilibrium, p. 221
Long-run market equilibrium, p. 223
Long-run industry supply curve, p. 224

PROBLEMS

1. For each of the following, is the business a price-taking producer? Explain your answers.

   a. A cappuccino café in a university town where there are dozens of very similar cappuccino cafés

   b. The makers of Pepsi-Cola

   c. One of many sellers of zucchini at a local farmers' market

2. For each of the following, is the industry perfectly competitive? Referring to market share, standardization of the product, and/or free entry and exit, explain your answers.

   a. Aspirin

   b. Shania Twain concerts

   c. SUVs

3. Kate's Katering provides catered meals, and the catered meals industry is perfectly competitive. Kate's machinery costs $100 per day and is the only fixed input. Her variable cost is comprised of the wages paid to the cooks and the food ingredients. The variable cost associated with each level of output is given in the accompanying table.

Quantity of meals	VC
0	$0
10	200
20	300
30	480
40	700
50	1,000

a. Calculate the total cost, the average variable cost, the average total cost, and the marginal cost for each quantity of output.

b. What is the break-even price? What is the shut-down price?

c. Suppose that the price at which Kate can sell catered meals is $21 per meal. In the short run, will Kate earn a profit? In the short run, should she produce or shut down?

d. Suppose that the price at which Kate can sell catered meals is $17 per meal. In the short run, will Kate earn a profit? In the short run, should she produce or shut down?

e. Suppose that the price at which Kate can sell catered meals is $13 per meal. In the short run, will Kate earn a profit? In the short run, should she produce or shut down?

4. Bob produces DVD movies for sale, which requires only a building and a machine that copies the original movie onto a DVD. Bob rents a building for $30,000 per month and rents a machine for $20,000 a month. Those are his fixed costs. His variable cost is given in the accompanying table.

Quantity of DVDs	VC
0	$0
1,000	5,000
2,000	8,000
3,000	9,000
4,000	14,000
5,000	20,000
6,000	33,000
7,000	49,000
8,000	72,000
9,000	99,000
10,000	150,000

a. Calculate Bob's average variable cost, average total cost, and marginal cost for each quantity of output.

b. There is free entry into the industry: anyone who enters will face the same costs as Bob. Suppose that currently the price of a DVD is $23. What will Bob's profit be? Is this a long-run equilibrium? If not, what will the price of DVD movies be in the long run?

5. Consider Bob's DVD company described in Problem 4. Assume that DVD production is a perfectly competitive industry. In each case, explain your answers.

a. What is Bob's break-even price? What is his shut-down price?

b. Suppose the price of a DVD is $2. What should Bob do in the short run?

c. Suppose the price of a DVD is $7. What is the profit-maximizing quantity of DVDs that Bob should produce? What will his total profit be? Will he produce or shut down in the short run? Will he stay in the industry or exit in the long run?

d. Suppose instead that the price of DVDs is $20. Now what is the profit-maximizing quantity of DVDs that Bob should produce? What will his total profit be now? Will he produce or shut down in the short run? Will he stay in the industry or exit in the long run?

6. Consider again Bob's DVD company described in Problem 4.

a. Draw Bob's marginal cost curve.

b. Over what range of prices will Bob produce no DVDs in the short run?

c. Draw Bob's individual supply curve.

7. a. A profit-maximizing business incurs an economic loss of $10,000 per year. Its fixed cost is $15,000 per year. Should it produce or shut down in the short run? Should it stay in the industry or exit in the long run?

b. Suppose instead this business has a fixed cost of $6,000 per year. Should it produce or shut down in the short run? Should it stay in the industry or exit in the long run?

8. Four students have each started companies selling late-night snack deliveries to dorms and student apartment complexes. Each student has estimated her or his individual supply schedule as given in the accompanying table.

Delivery charge	Quantity supplied by:			
	Aleesha	Brent	Christine	Dominic
$1	1	5	3	7
2	3	8	6	12
3	5	11	9	17
4	7	15	12	21
5	9	21	15	23

a. Draw the four individual supply curves.

b. Determine the short-run industry supply schedule. Draw the short-run industry supply curve.

9. The first sushi restaurant opens in town. Initially people are very cautious about eating tiny portions of raw fish, as this is a town where large portions of grilled meat have always been popular. Soon, however, an influential health report warns consumers against grilled meat and suggests that they increase their consumption of fish, especially raw fish. The sushi restaurant becomes very popular and its profit increases.

a. What will happen to the short-run profit of the sushi restaurant? What will happen to the number of sushi restaurants in town in the long run? Will the first sushi restaurant be able to sustain its short-run profit over the long run? Explain your answers.

b. Local steakhouses suffer from the popularity of sushi and start incurring losses. What will happen to the number of steakhouses in town in the long run? Explain your answer.

10. A perfectly competitive firm has the following short-run total cost:

Quantity	TC
0	$5
1	10
2	13
3	18
4	25
5	34
6	45

Market demand for the firm's product is given by the following market demand schedule:

Price	Quantity demanded
$12	300
10	500
8	800
6	1,200
4	1,800

a. Calculate this firm's marginal cost and, for all output levels except zero, the firm's average variable cost and average total cost.

b. There are 100 firms in this industry that all have identical costs to those of this firm. Draw the short-run industry supply curve. In the same diagram, draw the market demand curve.

c. What is the market price, and how much profit will each firm make?

11. A new vaccine against a deadly disease has just been discovered. Presently, 55 people die from the disease each year. The new vaccine will save lives, but it is not completely safe. Some recipients of the shots will die from adverse reactions. The projected effects of the inoculation are given in the accompanying table:

Percent of population inoculated	Total deaths due to disease	Total deaths due to inoculation	Marginal benefit of inoculation	Marginal cost of inoculation	"Profit" of inoculation
0	55	0	—	—	—
10	45	0	—	—	—
20	36	1	—	—	—
30	28	3	—	—	—
40	21	6	—	—	—
50	15	10	—	—	—
60	10	15	—	—	—
70	6	20	—	—	—
80	3	25	—	—	—
90	1	30	—	—	—
100	0	35	—	—	—

a. What are the interpretations of "marginal benefit" and "marginal cost" here? Calculate marginal benefit and marginal cost per each 10 percent increase in the rate of inoculation. Write your answers in the table.

b. What proportion of the population should optimally be inoculated?

c. What is the interpretation of "profit" here? Calculate the profit for all levels of inoculation.

12. Evaluate each of the following statements. If a statement is true, explain why; if it is false, identify the mistake and try to correct it.

a. A profit-maximizing firm should select the output level at which the difference between the market price and marginal cost is greatest.

b. An increase in fixed cost lowers the profit-maximizing quantity of output produced in the short run.

>web... To continue your study and review of concepts in this chapter, please visit the Krugman/Wells website for quizzes, animated graph tutorials, web links to helpful resources, and more.

www.worthpublishers.com/krugmanwells

>> The Rational Consumer

A CLAM TOO FAR

To entice customers, restaurants sometimes offer "all-you-can-eat" specials: all-you-can-eat salad bars, all-you-can-eat breakfast buffets, and all-you-can-eat fried-clam dinners.

But how can a restaurant owner who offers such a special be sure she won't be eaten out of business? If she charges $12.99 for an all-you-can-eat clam dinner, what prevents her average customer from wolfing down $30 worth of clams?

The answer is that even though every once in a while you see someone really take advantage of the offer—heaping a plate high with 30 or 40 fried clams—it's a rare occurrence. And even those of us who like fried clams shudder a bit at the sight. Five or even 10 fried clams can be a treat, but 30 clams is ridiculous. Anyone who pays for an all-you-can-eat meal wants to make the most of it, but a sensible person knows when one more clam would be one clam too many.

Notice what we just did in that last sentence. We said that customers in a

When is more of a good thing too much?

restaurant want to "make the most" of their meal; that sounds as if they are trying to maximize something. And we also said that they will stop when consuming one more clam would be a mistake; that sounds as if they are making a marginal decision.

When we analyze the behavior of *producers*, it makes sense to assume that they maximize profits. But what do consumers maximize? Isn't it all a matter of taste?

The answer is yes, it is a matter of taste—and economists can't say much about where tastes come from. But economists *can* say a lot about how a rational individual goes about satisfying his or her tastes. And that is in fact the way that economists think about consumer choice. They work with a model of a *rational consumer*—a consumer who knows what he or she wants and makes the most of the available opportunities.

In this chapter we will show how to analyze the decisions of a rational consumer and how this analysis can be used to derive the market demand curve.

What you will learn in this chapter:

➤ How consumers choose to spend their income on goods and services

➤ Why consumers make choices by maximizing **utility,** a measure of satisfaction from consumption

➤ Why the **principle of diminishing marginal utility** applies to the consumption of most goods and services

➤ How to use marginal analysis to find the **optimal consumption bundle**

➤ How choices by individual consumers give rise to the market demand curve

➤ What **income** and **substitution effects** are

We will begin by showing how the concept of *utility*—a measure of consumer satisfaction—allows us to begin thinking about rational consumer choice. We will then look at how *budget constraints* determine what a consumer can buy and how marginal analysis can be used to determine the consumption choice that maximizes utility. Finally, we will see how to use marginal analysis to derive the demand curve.

Utility: Getting Satisfaction

When analyzing consumer behavior, we're talking about people trying to get what they want—that is, about subjective feelings. Yet there is no simple way to measure subjective feelings. How much satisfaction do I get from my third fried clam? Is it less or more than yours? Does it even make sense to ask the question?

Luckily, it turns out that we don't need to make comparisons between your feelings and mine. All that is required to analyze consumer behavior is to suppose that each individual is trying to maximize some personal measure of the satisfaction gained from consumption of goods and services. That measure is known as the consumer's **utility,** a concept we use to understand behavior but don't expect to measure in practice. Nonetheless, we'll see that the assumption that consumers maximize utility helps us think clearly about consumer choice.

The **utility** of a consumer is a measure of the satisfaction the consumer derives from consumption of goods and services.

Utility and Consumption

An individual's utility depends on everything that individual consumes, from apples to Ziploc bags. The set of all the goods and services an individual consumes is known as the individual's **consumption bundle.** The relationship between an individual's consumption bundle and the total amount of utility it generates is known as the **utility function.** The utility function is a personal matter; two people with different tastes will have different utility functions. Someone who actually likes to consume 40 fried clams at a sitting must have a utility function that looks different from that of someone who would rather stop at 5 clams.

An individual's **consumption bundle** is the collection of all the goods and services consumed by that individual.

An individual's **utility function** gives the total utility generated by his or her consumption bundle.

This terminology is closely parallel to the terminology we used to describe producer decisions in Chapters 8 and 9. A producer uses inputs to produce output according to a production function; a consumer uses consumption to "produce" utility according to a utility function.

Obviously, people do not have a little computer in their heads that calculates the utility generated by their consumption choices. Nonetheless, people must make choices, and they usually base them on at least a rough attempt to decide which choice will give them greater satisfaction. I can have either soup or salad with my dinner. Which will I enjoy more? I can go to Disney World this year or save the money toward buying a new car. Which will make me happier?

The concept of a utility function is just a way of representing the fact that people must make such choices and that they make those choices in a more or less rational way.

How do we measure utility? For the sake of simplicity, it is useful to suppose that we can measure utility in hypothetical units called—what else?—**utils.**

A **util** is a unit of utility.

Figure 10-1, on page 232, illustrates a utility function. It shows the total utility that Cassie, who likes fried clams, gets from an all-you-can-eat clam dinner. We suppose that her consumption bundle consists of a side of cole slaw, which comes with the meal, plus a number of clams to be determined. The table that accompanies the figure shows how Cassie's total utility depends on the number of clams; the curve in panel (a) of the figure shows that same information graphically.

Cassie's utility function is upward sloping over most of the range shown, but it gets flatter as the number of clams consumed increases. And in this example it eventually

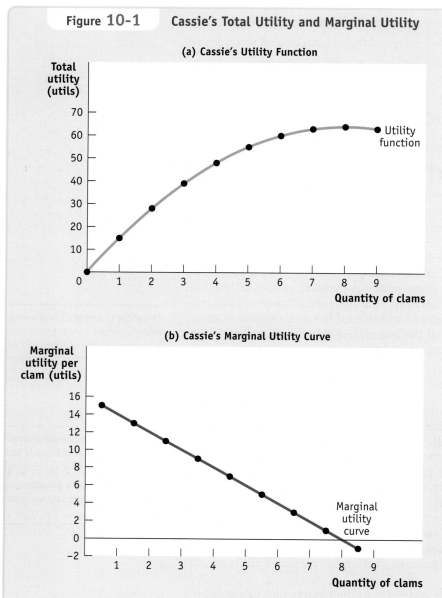

Figure 10-1 Cassie's Total Utility and Marginal Utility

(a) Cassie's Utility Function

Quantity of clams	Total utility (utils)	Marginal utility per clam (utils)
0	0	
		15
1	15	
		13
2	28	
		11
3	39	
		9
4	48	
		7
5	55	
		5
6	60	
		3
7	63	
		1
8	64	
		−1
9	63	

(b) Cassie's Marginal Utility Curve

Panel (a) shows how Cassie's total utility depends on her consumption of fried clams. It increases until it reaches its maximum utility level of 64 utils at 8 clams consumed and decreases after that. Marginal utility is calculated in the table. Panel (b) shows the marginal utility curve, which slopes downward due to diminishing marginal utility. That is, each additional clam gives Cassie less utility than the previous clam.

turns downward. According to the information in the table in Figure 10-1, nine clams is a clam too far: adding that additional clam actually makes Cassie worse off. If she's rational, of course, Cassie will realize that and not consume the ninth clam.

So when Cassie chooses how many clams to consume, she will make this decision by considering the *change* in her total utility from consuming one more clam. This illustrates the general point: to maximize *total* utility, consumers must focus on *marginal* utility.

The Principle of Diminishing Marginal Utility

The **marginal utility** of a good or service is the change in total utility generated by consuming one additional unit of that good or service. The **marginal utility curve** shows how marginal utility depends on the quantity of a good or service consumed.

In addition to showing how Cassie's total utility depends on the number of clams she consumes, the table in Figure 10-1 also shows the **marginal utility** generated by consuming each additional clam—that is, the *change* in total utility from consuming one additional clam. Panel (b) shows the implied **marginal utility curve.** Following our practice in Chapters 7, 8, and 9 with the marginal cost curve, the marginal utility curve is constructed by plotting points at the midpoint of the unit intervals.

FOR INQUIRING MINDS

IS MARGINAL UTILITY REALLY DIMINISHING?

Are all goods really subject to diminishing marginal utility? Of course not; there are a number of goods for which, at least over some range, marginal utility is surely *increasing*.

For example, there are goods that require some experience to enjoy. The first time you do it, downhill skiing involves a lot more fear than enjoyment—or so they say: the authors have never tried it! It only becomes a pleasurable activity if you do it enough to become reasonably competent. And even some less strenuous forms of consumption

take practice; people who are not accustomed to drinking coffee say it has a bitter taste and can't understand its appeal. (The authors, on the other hand, regard coffee as one of the basic food groups.)

Another example would be goods that only deliver if you buy enough; the great Victorian economist Alfred Marshall, who more or less invented the supply and demand model, gave the example of wallpaper: buying only enough to do half a room is worse than useless. If you need two rolls of wallpaper to finish a room, the marginal

utility of the second roll is larger than the marginal utility of the first roll.

So why does it make sense to assume diminishing marginal utility? For one thing, most goods don't suffer from these qualifications: nobody needs to learn to like ice cream. Also, although most people don't ski and some people don't drink coffee, those who do ski or drink coffee do enough of it that the marginal utility of one more ski run or one more cup is less than that of the last. So *in the relevant range,* marginal utility is still diminishing.

The marginal utility curve is downward sloping: each successive clam adds less to total utility than the previous clam. This is reflected in the table: marginal utility falls from a high of 15 utils for the first clam consumed to −1 for the ninth clam consumed. The fact that the ninth clam has negative marginal utility means that consuming it actually reduces total utility. (Restaurants that offer all-you-can-eat meals depend on the proposition that you can have too much of a good thing.) Not all marginal utility curves eventually become negative. But it is a generally accepted proposition that marginal utility curves do slope downward—that consumption of most goods and services is subject to *diminishing marginal utility.*

The basic idea behind the **principle of diminishing marginal utility** is that the additional satisfaction a consumer gets from one more unit of a good or service declines as the amount of that good or service consumed rises. Or, to put it slightly differently, the more of a good or service you consume, the closer you are to being satiated—reaching a point at which an additional unit of the good adds nothing to your satisfaction. For someone who almost never gets to eat a banana, the occasional banana is a marvelous treat (as it was in Eastern Europe before the fall of communism, when bananas were very hard to find). For someone who eats them all the time, a banana is just, well, a banana.

The principle of diminishing marginal utility plays the same role in the analysis of consumer behavior that the principle of diminishing returns to an input plays in the analysis of producer behavior. Like the principle of diminishing returns to an input, the principle of diminishing marginal utility isn't always true. But it is true in the great majority of cases, enough to serve as a foundation for our analysis of consumer behavior.

The **principle of diminishing marginal utility** says that each successive unit of a good or service consumed adds less to total utility than the previous unit.

economics in action

Oysters versus Chicken

Is a particular food a special treat, something you consume on special occasions? Or is it an ordinary, take-it-or-leave-it dish? The answer depends a lot on how much of that food people normally consume, which determines how much utility they get *at the margin* from having a bit more.

Consider chicken. Modern Americans eat a lot of chicken, so much that they regard it as nothing special. Yet this was not always the case. Traditionally chicken was a luxury dish because chickens were expensive to raise. Restaurant menus from two centuries ago show chicken dishes as the most expensive items listed. Even as recently as 1928, Herbert Hoover ran for president on the slogan "A chicken in every pot," a promise of great prosperity.

What changed the status of chicken was the emergence of new, technologically advanced methods for raising and processing the birds. (You don't want to know.) These methods made chicken abundant, cheap, and also—thanks to the principle of diminishing marginal utility—nothing to get excited about.

The reverse evolution took place for oysters. Not everyone likes oysters, or for that matter has ever tried them—they are definitely not ordinary food. But they are regarded as a delicacy by some; at restaurants that serve them, an oyster appetizer often costs more than the main course.

Yet oysters were once very cheap and abundant—and were regarded as poverty food. In *The Pickwick Papers* by Charles Dickens, published in the 1830s, the author remarks that "poverty and oysters always seem to go together."

What changed? Pollution, which destroyed many oyster beds, greatly reduced the supply, but human population growth greatly increased the demand. As a result, thanks to the principle of diminishing marginal utility, oysters went from being a common food, regarded as nothing special, to being a highly prized luxury good. ∎

< < < < < < < < < < < < < < < < < <

>>CHECK YOUR UNDERSTANDING 10-1

1. Explain why a rational consumer who has diminishing marginal utility for a good would not consume an additional unit when it generates negative marginal utility, even when that unit is free.

2. Marta drinks three cups of coffee a day, for which she has diminishing marginal utility. Which of her three cups generates the greatest increase in total utility? Which generates the least?

3. In each of the following cases, does the consumer have diminishing, constant, or increasing marginal utility? Explain your answers.
   a. The more Mabel exercises, the more she enjoys each additional visit to the gym.
   b. Although Mei's classical CD collection is huge, her enjoyment from buying another CD has not changed as her collection has grown.
   c. When Dexter was a struggling student, his enjoyment from a good restaurant meal was greater than now, when he has them more frequently.

Solutions appear at back of book.

Budgets and Optimal Consumption

The principle of diminishing marginal utility explains why most people eventually reach a limit, even at an all-you-can-eat buffet where the cost of another clam is measured only in future indigestion. Under ordinary circumstances, however, it costs some additional resources to consume more of a good, and consumers must take that cost into account when making choices.

What do we mean by cost? As always, the fundamental measure of cost is *opportunity cost*. Because the amount of money a consumer can spend is limited, a decision to consume more of one good is also a decision to consume less of some other good.

Budget Constraints and Budget Lines

Consider Sammy, whose appetite is exclusively for clams and potatoes (there's no accounting for tastes). He has a weekly income of $20 and since, given his appetite, more of either good is better than less, he spends all of it on clams and potatoes. We will assume that clams cost $4 per pound and potatoes cost $2 per pound. What are his possible choices?

Whatever Sammy chooses, we know that the cost of his consumption bundle cannot exceed the amount of money he has to spend. That is,

(10-1)   Expenditure on clams + expenditure on potatoes ≤ total income

Consumers always have limited income, which constrains how much they can consume. So the requirement illustrated by Equation 10-1—that a consumer must choose a consumption bundle that costs no more than his or her total income—is known as the consumer's **budget constraint.** It's a simple way of saying that consumers can't spend more than the total amount of income available to them. In other words, consumption bundles are affordable when they obey the budget constraint. We call the set of all of Sammy's affordable consumption bundles his **consumption possibilities.** As we will see, which consumption bundles are in this set depends on the consumer's income and the prices of goods and services.

Figure 10-2 shows Sammy's consumption possibilities. The quantity of clams in his consumption bundle is measured on the horizontal axis and the quantity of potatoes on the vertical axis. The downward-sloping line connecting points *A* through *F* shows which consumption bundles are affordable and which are not. Every bundle on or inside this line (the shaded area) is affordable; every bundle outside this line is unaffordable. As an example of one of the points, let's look at point *C*, representing 2 pounds of clams and 6 pounds of potatoes, and check whether it satisfies Sammy's budget constraint. The cost of bundle *C* is 6 pounds of potatoes × $2 per pound + 2 pounds of clams × $4 per pound = $12 + $8 = $20. So bundle *C* does indeed satisfy Sammy's budget constraint: it costs no more than his weekly income of $20. In fact,

A **budget constraint** requires that the cost of a consumer's consumption bundle be no more than the consumer's total income.

A consumer's **consumption possibilities** is the set of all consumption bundles that can be consumed given the consumer's income and prevailing prices.

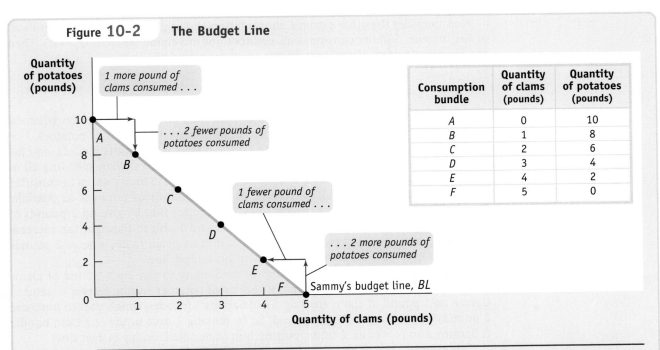

Figure 10-2   The Budget Line

Consumption bundle	Quantity of clams (pounds)	Quantity of potatoes (pounds)
A	0	10
B	1	8
C	2	6
D	3	4
E	4	2
F	5	0

The *budget line* represents all the possible combinations of quantities of potatoes and clams that Sammy can purchase if he spends all of his income. Also, it is the boundary between the set of affordable consumption bundles (the *consumption possibilities*) and unaffordable ones. Given that clams cost $4 per pound and potatoes cost $2 per pound, if Sammy spends all of his income on clams (bundle *F*), he can purchase 5 pounds of clams; if he spends all of his income on potatoes (bundle *A*), he can purchase 10 pounds of potatoes. The slope of the budget line here is −2: 2 pounds of potatoes must be forgone for 1 more pound of clams, reflecting the opportunity cost of clams in terms of potatoes. So the location and slope of the budget line depend on the consumer's income and the prices of the goods.

bundle C costs exactly as much as Sammy's income. By doing the arithmetic, you can check that all the other points lying on the downward-sloping line are also bundles at which Sammy spends all of his income.

The downward-sloping line has a special name, the **budget line.** It shows all the consumption bundles available to Sammy when he spends all of his income. Let's use Figure 10-2 to gain an intuitive understanding of Sammy's budget line. For brevity's sake, we will denote the quantity of clams (in pounds) by Q_C and the quantity of potatoes (in pounds) by Q_P. We will also define P_C to be the price of one pound of clams, P_P to be the price of one pound of potatoes, and N to be Sammy's income. So if we restate Sammy's budget constraint of Equation 10-1 in terms of this new notation, it becomes

(10-2) $(Q_C \times P_C) + (Q_P \times P_P) \leq N$

Whenever Sammy consumes a bundle on his *budget line,* he spends all of his income, so that his expenditure on clams and potatoes is exactly equal to his income. The equation for Sammy's budget line is therefore

(10-3) $(Q_C \times P_C) + (Q_P \times P_P) = N$

Now consider what happens when Sammy spends all $20 of his income on clams (that is, $Q_P = 0$). In that case the greatest amount of clams he can consume is

$Q_C = N/P_C = \$20/\$4$ per pound of clams = 5 pounds of clams

So the horizontal intercept of the budget line—Sammy's clam consumption when he consumes zero potatoes—is at point F, where he consumes 5 pounds of clams.

Now consider the other extreme consumption choice given that Sammy spends all of his income: Sammy consumes all potatoes and no clams (that is, $Q_C = 0$). Then the greatest amount of potatoes he can consume would be

$Q_P = N/P_P = \$20/\$2$ per pound of potatoes = 10 pounds of potatoes

So the vertical intercept of the budget line—Sammy's potato consumption when he consumes zero clams—is at point A, where he consumes 10 pounds of potatoes.

The remaining four bundles indicated on the budget line—points B, C, D, and E—can be understood by considering the trade-offs Sammy faces when spending all of his income. Starting at bundle A, consider what happens if Sammy wants to consume 1 pound of clams while still consuming as many pounds of potatoes as possible. Consuming 1 pound of clams, which costs $4, requires that he give up 2 pounds of potatoes, which cost $2 per pound. In order to move 1 unit to the right (an increase of 1 pound of clams), Sammy must also move 2 units down (a decrease of 2 pounds of potatoes). This places him at bundle B on his budget line.

Similarly, if we start at bundle F and allow Sammy to give up 1 pound of clams (moving 1 unit to the left), how many pounds of potatoes will he receive in return? Giving up 1 pound of clams frees up $4 of Sammy's income, which goes to purchase 2 pounds of potatoes at $2 per pound. So by moving 1 unit to the left from bundle F, Sammy also moves up 2 units, putting him at bundle E on his budget line.

This exercise shows that when Sammy spends all of his income, he trades off more clams for fewer potatoes, or vice versa, by "sliding" along his budget line. In particular, if we assume that Sammy can consume fractions of pounds of clams and potatoes as well as whole pounds, his budget line is indeed the line connecting the points A through F in Figure 10-2.

Do we need to consider the other bundles in Sammy's consumption possibilities, the ones that lie *within* the shaded region in Figure 10-2 bounded by the budget line? The answer is, for all practical situations, no: as long as Sammy doesn't get satiated—that is, his marginal utility from consuming either good is always positive—and he doesn't get any utility from saving income rather than spending it, then he will always choose to consume a bundle that lies on his budget line.

Because changing a consumption bundle involves sliding up or down the budget line, the *slope* of the budget line tells us the opportunity cost of each good in terms of the other. Recall from Chapter 2 that we used the slope of the production possibility frontier to illustrate the opportunity cost to the economy of an additional unit of one good in terms of how much of the other good must be forgone, a cost that arose from the economy's limited productive resources. In this case, the slope of the budget line illustrates the opportunity cost to an individual of consuming one more unit of one good in terms of how much of the other good in his or her consumption bundle must be forgone. The scarce "resource" here is money—the consumer has a limited budget.

The slope of Sammy's budget line—the rise over run—is –2; 2 pounds of potatoes must be forgone to obtain another pound of clams. Economists call the number of pounds of potatoes that must be forgone in order to obtain one more pound of clams the *relative price* of one pound of clams in terms of potatoes. The relative price of the good on the horizontal axis in terms of the good on the vertical axis is equal to minus the slope of the budget line.

One important point about the budget line may be obvious but nonetheless needs emphasizing: the position of a consumer's budget line—how far *out* it is from the origin—depends on that consumer's income. Suppose that Sammy's income were to rise to $32 per week. Then he could afford to buy 8 pounds of clams, or 16 pounds of potatoes, or any consumption bundle in between; as shown in Figure 10-3, his budget line would move *outward*. However, if his income were to shrink to $12 per week, his budget line would shift *inward*: he would be able to consume at most 3 pounds of clams or 6 pounds of potatoes. In all these cases, the slope of the budget line would not change because the relative price of clams in terms of potatoes does not change: for 1 more pound of clams, Sammy still has to give up 2 pounds of potatoes.

Clearly, a larger income would increase Sammy's consumption possibilities; and utility analysis can tell us how he would take advantage of those possibilities to increase his total utility by consuming more of one or both goods. Conversely, a smaller income would reduce Sammy's consumption possibilities. He would be forced to consume less, and his utility would be lower. But for now let's continue to assume that Sammy's income is fixed at $20 per week.

Given that $20 per week budget, what point on his budget line will Sammy choose?

Figure 10-3

Changes in Income Shift the Budget Line

If Sammy's income increases from $20 to $32 per week, he is clearly better off: his consumption possibilities have increased, and his budget line shifts, from BL_1, outward to its new position at BL_2. If Sammy's income decreases from $20 to $12, he is clearly worse off: his consumption possibilities have decreased and his budget line shifts inward toward the origin, from BL_1 to BL_3. **>web...**

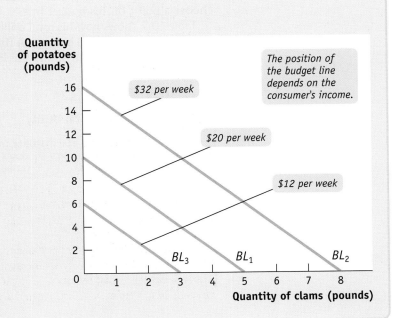

Optimal Consumption Choice

Because Sammy has a budget constraint, which means that he will consume a consumption bundle on the budget line, a choice to consume a given quantity of clams also determines his potato consumption, and vice versa. We want to find the consumption bundle—the point on the budget line—that maximizes Sammy's total utility. This bundle is Sammy's **optimal consumption bundle,** the consumption bundle that maximizes total utility given the budget constraint.

The **optimal consumption bundle** is the consumption bundle that maximizes a consumer's total utility given his or her budget constraint.

TABLE 10-1

Sammy's Utility from Clam and Potato Consumption

Utility from clam consumption		Utility from potato consumption	
Quantity of clams (pounds)	Utility from clams (utils)	Quantity of potatoes (pounds)	Utility from potatoes (utils)
0	0	0	0
1	15	1	11.5
2	25	2	21.4
3	31	3	29.8
4	34	4	36.8
5	36	5	42.5
		6	47.0
		7	50.5
		8	53.2
		9	55.2
		10	56.7

Table 10-1 shows how much utility Sammy gets from different levels of consumption of clams and potatoes, respectively. According to the table, Sammy has a healthy appetite; the more of either good he consumes, the higher his utility.

But because he has a limited budget, he must make a trade-off: the more pounds of clams he consumes, the fewer pounds of potatoes, and vice versa. That is, he must choose a point on his budget line.

Table 10-2 shows how his total utility varies as he slides down his budget line. Each of six possible consumption bundles, A through F from Figure 10-2, is given in the first column. The second column shows the level of clam consumption corresponding to each

TABLE 10-2

Sammy's Budget and Total Utility

Consumption Bundle	Quantity of clams (pounds)	Utility from clams (utils)	Quantity of potatoes (pounds)	Utility from potatoes (utils)	Total utility (utils)
A	0	0	10	56.7	56.7
B	1	15	8	53.2	68.2
C	2	25	6	47.0	72.0
D	3	31	4	36.8	67.8
E	4	34	2	21.4	55.4
F	5	36	0	0	36.0

choice. The third column shows the utility Sammy gets from consuming those clams. The fourth column shows the quantity of potatoes Sammy can afford *given* the level of clam consumption; this quantity goes down as his clam consumption goes up, because he is sliding down the budget line. The fifth column shows the utility he gets from consuming those potatoes. And the final column shows his *total utility*. In this example, Sammy's total utility is the sum of the utility he gets from clams and the utility he gets from potatoes.

Figure 10-4 illustrates the result graphically. Panel (a) shows Sammy's budget line, to remind us that when he decides to consume more clams he is also deciding to consume fewer potatoes. Panel (b) then shows how his total utility depends on that choice. The horizontal axis in panel (b) has two sets of labels: it shows both the quantity of clams, increasing from left to right, and the quantity of potatoes, increasing from right to left. The reason we can use the same axis to represent consumption of both goods is, of course, the budget line: the more pounds of clams Sammy consumes, the fewer pounds of potatoes he can afford, and vice versa.

Figure 10-4

Optimal Consumption Bundle

Panel (a) shows Sammy's budget line and his six possible consumption bundles. Panel (b) shows how his total utility is affected by his consumption bundle, which must lie on his budget line. The quantity of clams is measured from left to right on the horizontal axis, and the quantity of potatoes is measured from right to left. His total utility is maximized at bundle *C*, where he consumes 2 pounds of clams and 6 pounds of potatoes. This is Sammy's *optimal consumption bundle.* **>web...**

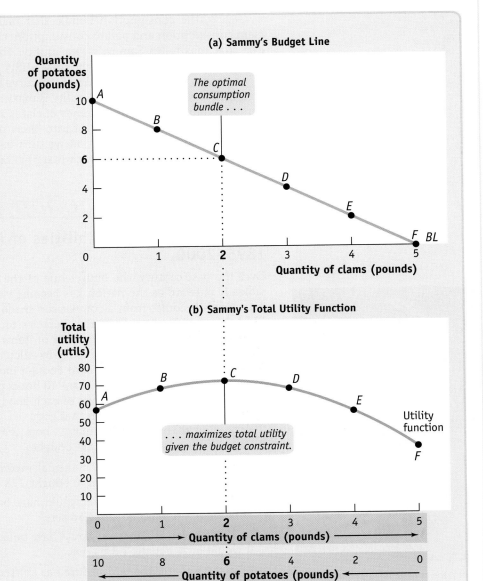

FOOD FOR THOUGHT ON BUDGET CONSTRAINTS

Budget constraints aren't just about money. In fact, there are many other budget constraints affecting our lives. You face a budget constraint if you have a limited amount of closet space for your clothes. All of us face a budget constraint on time: there are only so many hours in the day.

And people trying to lose weight on the Weight Watchers plan face a budget constraint on the foods they eat.

The Weight Watchers plan assigns each food a certain number of "points." A scoop of ice cream gets 4 points, a slice of pizza 7 points, a cup of grapes 1 point. You are allowed a maximum number of points each day but are free to choose which foods you eat. In other words, a dieter on the Weight Watchers plan is just like a consumer choosing a consumption bundle: points are the equivalent of prices, and the overall point limit is the equivalent of income.

Clearly, the consumption bundle that makes the best of the trade-off between clam consumption and potato consumption, the optimal consumption bundle, is the one that maximizes Sammy's total utility. That is, Sammy's optimal consumption bundle puts him at the top of the total utility curve.

As always, we can find the top of the curve by direct observation. We can see from Figure 10-4 that Sammy's total utility is maximized at point C—that his optimal consumption bundle contains 2 pounds of clams and 6 pounds of potatoes. But we know that we usually gain more insight into "how much" problems when we use marginal analysis. So in the next section we turn to representing and solving the optimal consumption choice problem with marginal analysis.

economics in action

The Consumption Possibilities of American Workers, 1895–2000

Over the past century, the budget line of the average American worker has shifted radically outward as the nation has become vastly richer. A good illustration of this outward shift comes from a comparison made by the economist J. Bradford DeLong (find the article at http://econ161.berkeley.edu/TCEH/Slouch_wealth2.html).

He compared the cost of a number of items in the 1895 Montgomery Ward catalog to the cost of similar items today by calculating the number of hours an average worker would need to work to earn enough money to buy them. If we assume that a worker puts in 2,000 hours per year—40 hours per week, with two weeks of vacation—we can calculate how many units of each good a worker could purchase by spending an entire year's income only on that good.

According to DeLong's estimates, here are the amounts of various goods that workers then and now could have bought:

- In 1895, an average worker's annual income would have bought 7.7 one-speed bicycles; in 2000, it would have bought 278 bicycles.

- In 1895, the worker's income would have bought 45 full sets of dinner plates; in 2000, it would have bought 556 sets.

- In 1895, a worker's income would have bought 0.83 of a Steinway piano; in 2000, it would have bought 1.8 pianos.

By any standard, the budget line has shifted out enormously. DeLong estimates that the shift for the average good is approximately sevenfold. That is, today's workers can on average purchase seven times as much of a randomly chosen good

Today, the average American worker's annual income buys a lot more bicycle than it did in 1895.

as their predecessors could have in 1895. Of course, in a way this understates the rise in purchasing power: there are many goods, like computers, that were not available in 1895 at any price. ∎

> > > > > > > > > > > > > > > > > >

1. In the following two examples, draw the budget line. Make sure that you calculate the following: (i) the vertical intercept of the budget line; (ii) the horizontal intercept of the budget line; (iii) the slope of the budget line; (iv) the opportunity cost of the good on the horizontal axis in terms of the good on the vertical axis.
   a. A consumption bundle consisting of movie tickets and buckets of popcorn. Each ticket costs $5.00, each bucket of popcorn costs $2.50, and the consumer's income is $10.00. Movie tickets are on the vertical axis and buckets of popcorn are on the horizontal axis.
   b. A consumption bundle consisting of underwear and socks. Each pair of underwear costs $4.00, each pair of socks costs $1.50, and the consumer's income is $12.00. Pairs of socks are on the vertical axis and pairs of underwear are on the horizontal axis.

Solutions appear at back of book.

Spending the Marginal Dollar

Marginal analysis is often the best way to think about "how much" decisions. In this case, Sammy is making a decision about the quantity of clams to consume, taking into account the fact that the more clams he consumes, the fewer potatoes he can afford. As we've seen, we can find his optimal consumption choice by finding the total utility he receives from each consumption bundle on his budget line and then choosing the bundle at which total utility is maximized. But is there a way to use marginal analysis instead?

The answer is yes: we can think about the problem of choosing an optimal consumption bundle in terms of the decision a consumer must make about how much to spend on each good. The marginal decision then becomes one of how to *spend the marginal dollar*—how to allocate an additional dollar between clams and potatoes. As we'll see in a moment, looking at Sammy's decision in terms of how he allocates his income gives us an important insight into the relationship between prices and consumer decisions.

Our first step is to ask how much additional utility Sammy gets from spending an additional dollar on either good—the **marginal utility per dollar** spent on either clams or potatoes.

Marginal Utility per Dollar

We've already introduced the concept of marginal utility, the additional utility a consumer gets from consuming one more unit of a good or service; now let's see how this concept can be used to derive the related measure of marginal utility per dollar.

Table 10-3, on page 242, shows how to calculate the marginal utility per dollar spent on clams and potatoes, respectively.

In panel (a) of the table, the first column shows different possible levels of clam consumption. The second column shows the utility Sammy derives from each level of clam consumption; the third column then shows the marginal utility, the increase in utility Sammy gets from consuming an additional pound of clams. Panel (b) does the same thing for potatoes. The next step is to derive marginal utility *per dollar* for each good. To do this, we must divide the marginal utility of the good by its price in dollars.

To see why we must divide by the price, compare the third and fourth columns of panel (a). Consider what happens if Sammy increases his clam consumption from 2 pounds to 3 pounds. As we can see, this increase in clam consumption raises his total utility by 6 utils. But he must spend $4 for that additional pound, so the increase in his utility per additional dollar spent on clams is 6 utils/$4 = 1.5 utils per dollar.

The **marginal utility per dollar** spent on a good or service is the additional utility from spending one more dollar on that good or service.

TABLE 10-3

Marginal Utility per Dollar

(a) Clams (price of clams = $4 per pound)				(b) Potatoes (price of potatoes = $2 per pound)			
Quantity of clams (pounds)	Utility from clams (utils)	Marginal utility per pound of clams (utils)	Marginal utility per dollar (utils)	Quantity of potatoes (pounds)	Utility from potatoes (utils)	Marginal utility per pound of potatoes (utils)	Marginal utility per dollar (utils)
0	0			0	0		
		15	3.75			11.5	5.75
1	15			1	11.5		
		10	2.50			9.9	4.95
2	25			2	21.4		
		6	1.50			8.4	4.20
3	31			3	29.8		
		3	0.75			7.0	3.50
4	34			4	36.8		
		2	0.50			5.7	2.85
5	36			5	42.5		
						4.5	2.25
				6	47.0		
						3.5	1.75
				7	50.5		
						2.7	1.35
				8	53.2		
						2.0	1.00
				9	55.2		
						1.5	0.75
				10	56.7		

Similarly, if he increases his clam consumption from 3 pounds to 4 pounds, his marginal utility is 3 utils per clam but his marginal utility per dollar is 3 utils/$4 = 0.75 utils per dollar. Notice that because of diminishing marginal utility per pound of clams, Sammy's marginal utility per pound of clams falls as the quantity of clams he consumes rises. As a result, his marginal utility per dollar spent on clams also falls as the quantity of clams he consumes rises.

So the last column of panel (a) shows how Sammy's marginal utility per dollar spent on clams depends on the quantity of clams he consumes. Similarly, the last column of panel (b) shows how his marginal utility per dollar spent on potatoes depends on the quantity of potatoes he consumes. Again, marginal utility per dollar spent on each good declines as the quantity of that good consumed rises, because of diminishing marginal utility.

We will use the symbols MU_C and MU_P to represent the marginal utility per pound of clams and potatoes, respectively. Then the marginal utility per dollar spent on clams is MU_C/P_C and the marginal utility per dollar spent on potatoes is MU_P/P_P. In general, the additional utility generated from an additional dollar spent on a good is equal to:

(10-4)   Marginal utility per dollar spent on a good
= Marginal utility of one unit of the good / Price of one unit of the good
= MU_{good}/P_{good}

Now let's see how this concept helps us derive a consumer's optimal consumption using marginal analysis.

Optimal Consumption

The curve in panel (a) of Figure 10-5 shows Sammy's marginal utility per dollar spent on clams, MU_C/P_C, as derived in Table 10-3. The curve in panel (b) shows his marginal utility per dollar spent on potatoes, MU_P/P_P. We already know from Figure

Figure 10-5 Marginal Utility per Dollar

Panel (a) shows Sammy's marginal utility per dollar spent on clams; panel (b) shows his marginal utility per dollar spent on potatoes. Points C_C in panel (a) and C_P in panel (b) correspond to bundle C in Figure 10-4, Sammy's optimal consumption bundle of 2 pounds of clams and 6 pounds of potatoes. At these points his marginal utility per dollar spent on each good is 2. This illustrates the *optimal consumption rule*: at the optimal consumption bundle, the marginal utility per dollar spent on each good and service is the same. At any other consumption bundle along Sammy's budget line, such as bundle B in Figure 10-4, which is represented here by points B_C and B_P, consumption is not optimal: he can increase his utility at no additional cost by reallocating his spending.

10-4 that Sammy's optimal consumption bundle, C, consists of 2 pounds of clams and 6 pounds of potatoes. From Figure 10-5 we can read off the marginal utility per dollar spent on clams and potatoes, respectively, at that optimal consumption bundle, which corresponds to points C_C and C_P. And we see something interesting: when Sammy consumes 2 pounds of clams and 6 pounds of potatoes, his marginal utility per dollar spent is the same, 2, for both goods. That is, at the optimal consumption bundle $MU_C/P_C = MU_P/P_P = 2$.

This isn't an accident. Consider another one of Sammy's possible consumption bundles, say B in Figure 10-4, at which he consumes 1 pound of clams and 8 pounds of potatoes. The marginal utility per dollar spent on each good is shown by points B_C and B_P in Figure 10-5. At that consumption bundle, Sammy's marginal utility per dollar spent on clams would be approximately 3, but his marginal utility per dollar spent on potatoes would be only approximately 1. This shows that he has made a mistake: he is consuming too many potatoes and not enough clams.

How do we know this? If Sammy's marginal utility per dollar spent on clams is higher than his marginal utility per dollar spent on potatoes, he has a simple way to make himself better off while staying within his budget: spend $1 less on potatoes and $1 more on clams. By spending an additional dollar on clams, he adds about 3 utils to his total utility; meanwhile, by spending $1 less on potatoes, he subtracts only about 1 util from his total utility. Because his marginal utility per dollar spent is higher for clams than for potatoes, reallocating his spending toward clams and away from potatoes would increase his total utility. On the other hand, if his marginal utility per dollar spent on potatoes is higher, he can increase his utility by spending less on clams and more on potatoes. So if Sammy has in fact chosen his optimal consumption bundle, his marginal utility per dollar spent on clams and potatoes must be equal.

BUT ARE CONSUMERS REALLY RATIONAL?

Many companies offer retirement plans that allow their employees to put aside part of their salaries tax-free. These plans, called 401(k)s, can save a worker thousands of dollars in taxes each year. But the plans sometimes have disadvantages: some companies invest their employees' savings mainly in their own stock, which can be disastrous if the company gets in trouble, leaving the employee with no savings *and* no job. (That's what happened to the employees of Enron.)

Clearly, then, people should carefully decide how much of their money to put in an employer-administered retirement plan. They should compare the marginal utility of a dollar spent on current consumption with the marginal utility of a dollar saved for retirement. They should weigh the tax advantages of saving through the employer plan against the risks of letting the employer decide where their savings are invested.

But recent economic research suggests that most people aren't careful at all. For example, some companies have an "opt-in" system for 401(k)s—that is, in some companies employees must ask to be enrolled. Other companies have an "opt-out" system—employees are automatically enrolled unless they request otherwise. This shouldn't make a difference—if the plan is managed well, people should opt in; if it's managed poorly (that is, investing mainly in company's own stock), they should opt out. Yet when companies switch to automatic enrollment, the number of employees in their 401(k) plans

rises dramatically. As the National Bureau of Economic Research put it, workers seem to follow the path of least resistance, instead of comparing their options and maximizing their utility.

Studies of saving behavior are one example of a growing field known as "behavioral economics." Behavioral economists question the whole concept of the rational consumer. Their research focuses on situations in which people don't seem to be rational—that is, when they behave in ways that can't easily be explained by utility maximization.

One key insight in behavioral economics comes from the work of Herbert Simon, who won the Nobel prize in economics in 1978. Simon argued that sometimes individuals find that it isn't actually rational to go to great lengths to maximize utility, since searching for the perfect answer is itself a costly activity. Instead, he argued, they engage in *bounded rationality*: individuals save time and effort by making decisions that are "good enough," rather than perfect. In the case of savings plans, this might involve following the path of least resistance: not bothering to participate in a well-managed

opt-in plan, and not bothering to opt out of a poorly managed automatic plan.

Today's behavioral economists use insights from psychology to understand behavior seemingly at odds with rationality. The 2002 Nobel prize went to Daniel Kahneman, a psychologist who, with his late co-author Amos Tversky, laid out a theory of how people make choices in the face of uncertainty. This work and other insights into nonrational behavior are having an important influence on analysis of financial markets, labor markets, and other economic concerns.

But it's hard to find a behavioral economist who thinks that the insights of this field should replace the analysis of utility maximization. The theory of the rational consumer remains the main way in which economists analyze consumer behavior.

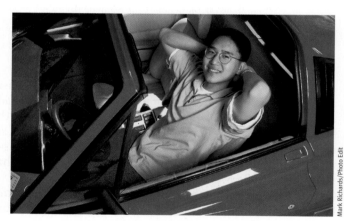

Great new car, but are you saving enough for retirement?

The **optimal consumption rule** says that when a consumer maximizes utility, the marginal utility per dollar spent must be the same for all goods and services in the consumption bundle.

This is a general principle, known as the **optimal consumption rule**: when a consumer maximizes utility in the face of a budget constraint, the marginal utility per dollar spent on each good or service in the consumption bundle is the same. That is, for any two goods C and P the optimal consumption rule says that at the optimal consumption bundle

(10-5) $MU_C/P_C = MU_P/P_P$

It's easiest to understand this rule using examples in which the consumption bundle contains only two goods, but it applies no matter how many goods or services a consumer buys: in the optimal consumption bundle, the marginal utilities per dollar spent for each and every good or service in that bundle are equal.

economics in action

Self-Service Gasoline

At the end of the 1970s the price of gasoline in the United States shot up because of a combination of world oil shortages and deregulation. At the same time, many gas stations began offering drivers a discount if they pumped their own gas.

Many people argued that the rise of self-service gas was a response to higher gas prices and that if gas prices ever went down again, people would once again be willing to pay the price of full service.

But economists in general were skeptical of this conclusion. Consumers, they argued, were making a calculation: the extra utility gained from spending on other goods was worth the extra effort. And gas stations offered a price break on self-service gas because it saved them labor; so the price break would remain even if gas prices went down. So economists argued that people would continue to use self-service pumps even if gas prices fell back to traditional levels.

In the event, gas prices did fall; by the late 1990s they were actually lower, adjusted for inflation, than they had been for generations. But most drivers continued to use self-service gas. ■

> >

>> CHECK YOUR UNDERSTANDING 10-3

1. In Figure 10-5 you can see that marginal utility per dollar spent on clams and marginal utility per dollar spent on potatoes are approximately equal at a consumption bundle consisting of 3 pounds of clams and 8 pounds of potatoes. Explain why this is not Sammy's optimal consumption bundle. Illustrate your answer using the budget line in Figure 10-4.

2. Explain what is faulty about the following statement, using data from Table 10-3: "In order to maximize utility, Sammy should consume the bundle that gives him the maximum marginal utility per dollar for each good."

Solutions appear at back of book.

From Utility to the Demand Curve

We have now analyzed the optimal consumption choice of a consumer whose income we take as given and who faces one particular set of prices—in our Sammy example, $20 of income per week, $4 per pound of clams, and $2 per pound of potatoes.

But the main reason we want to understand consumer behavior is to go behind the market demand curve—to understand how the market demand curve is explained by the utility-maximizing behavior of individual consumers.

Individual Demand and Market Demand

Let's begin by reviewing the relationship between prices and quantity demanded, both at the individual level and at the level of the market as a whole.

The **individual demand curve** for a good shows the relationship between the quantity of a good demanded by an individual consumer and the market price of that good. For example, suppose that Bert is a consumer of fried clams and that panel (a) of Figure 10-6 page 246 shows how many pounds of clams he will buy at any given market price per pound. Then D_{Bert} is Bert's individual demand curve.

The *market demand curve* shows how the quantity of a good demanded by all consumers depends on the market price of that good. The market demand curve is the *horizontal sum* of the individual demand curves of all consumers. To see what we mean by the term *horizontal sum*, assume for a moment that there are only two consumers of fried clams, Bert and Ernie. Ernie's individual demand curve is shown in panel (b). Panel (c) shows the market demand curve. At any given price, the quantity demanded

The **individual demand curve** for a good shows the relationship between quantity demanded and price for an individual consumer.

Figure 10-6   Individual and Market Demand

Bert and Ernie are the only two consumers of clams in the market. Panel (a) shows Bert's individual demand curve for clams and panel (b) shows Ernie's. The market demand curve, shown in panel (c), is the horizontal sum of the individual demand curves. That is, the quantity demanded by the market at any given price is the sum of the quantities demanded by Bert and by Ernie at that price. **>web...**

by the market is the sum of the quantities demanded by Bert and Ernie. For example, at a price of $6 per pound, Bert demands 2 pounds of clams and Ernie demands 1 pound; so the quantity demanded by the market is 3 pounds. At a price of $4 per pound, Bert demands 4 pounds and Ernie demands 2 pounds; so the quantity demanded by the market is 6 pounds—and so on.

But what lies behind the individual demand curves? The *law of demand* tells us that if the price of a good increases, the quantity demanded of that good decreases. But let's now use our analysis of consumer choice to get a deeper understanding of the law of demand.

Marginal Utility, the Substitution Effect, and the Law of Demand

Suppose that the price of fried clams, P_C, rises. This doesn't change the marginal utility a consumer gets from an additional pound of clams, MU_C, at any given level of clam consumption. However, it reduces the marginal utility *per dollar spent* on fried clams, MU_C/P_C. And the decrease in marginal utility per dollar spent on clams gives the consumer an incentive to consume fewer clams.

To see why, recall the optimal consumption rule: a utility-maximizing consumer chooses a consumption bundle for which the marginal utility per dollar spent on all goods is the same. If the marginal utility per dollar spent on clams falls because the price of clams rises, the consumer can increase his or her utility by purchasing fewer clams and more of other goods.

The opposite happens if the price of clams falls. In that case the marginal utility per dollar spent on clams, MU_C/P_C, increases at any given level of clam consumption. A consumer can increase his or her utility by purchasing more clams and less of other goods.

So when the price of a good increases, an individual will normally consume less of that good and more of other goods. Correspondingly, when the price of a good decreases, an individual will normally consume more of that good and less of other goods. This means that the individual demand curve, which relates an individual's consumption of a good to the price of that good, is normally downward sloping—that is, it obeys the law of demand.

An alternative way to think about why individual demand curves slope downward is to focus on opportunity costs. When the price of clams—or any other good—decreases, an individual doesn't have to give up as many units of other goods in order to buy one more unit of clams. So consuming clams becomes more attractive. Conversely, when the price of a good increases, consuming that good becomes a less attractive use of resources, and the consumer buys less.

This effect of a price change on the quantity consumed by a consumer is always present. It is known as the **substitution effect**—the change in the quantity consumed as the consumer substitutes the good that has become relatively cheaper for the good that has become relatively more expensive. When a good absorbs only a small share of the consumer's spending, the substitution effect is essentially the whole story about why the individual demand curve of that consumer slopes downward. And, by implication, when a good absorbs only a small share of the typical consumer's spending, the substitution effect is essentially the sole explanation of why the market demand curve slopes downward. However, some goods, such as housing, absorb a large share of a typical consumer's spending. For such goods, the story behind the individual demand curve and the market demand curve becomes slightly more complicated.

> The **substitution effect** of a change in the price of a good is the change in the quantity consumed of that good as the consumer substitutes the good that has become relatively cheaper for the good that has become relatively more expensive.

The Income Effect

For the vast majority of goods, the substitution effect is pretty much the whole story behind the slopes of the individual and market demand curves. There are, however, some goods, like food or housing, that account for a substantial share of many consumers' spending. In such cases another effect, called the income effect, also comes into play.

Consider the case of a family that spends half its income on rental housing. Now suppose that the price of housing increases. This will have a substitution effect on the family's demand: other things equal, the family will have an incentive to consume less housing—say, by moving to a smaller apartment—and more of other goods. But the family will also, in a real sense, be made poorer by that higher housing price—its income will buy less housing than before. And this reduction in its purchasing power will have an additional effect, beyond the substitution effect, on the family's consumption bundle, including its consumption of housing.

The change in the quantity consumed of a good that results from a change in the overall purchasing power of the consumer due to the change in the price of a good is known as the **income effect** of the price change. Here we find that a change in the price of a good in effect changes a consumer's income, because such a price change alters the consumer's purchasing power. This is part of the effect of prices on consumption choices.

> The **income effect** of a change in the price of a good is the change in the quantity consumed of that good that results from a change in the consumer's purchasing power due to the change in the price of the good.

It's possible to give more precise definitions of the substitution effect and the income effect of a price change, and we do this in Chapter 11. For most purposes, however, there are only two things you need to know about the distinction between these two effects.

First, for the great majority of goods and services, the income effect is not important and has no significant effect on individual consumption. So most market demand curves slope downward solely because of the substitution effect—end of story.

Second, when it matters at all, the income effect usually reinforces the substitution effect. That is, when the price of a good that absorbs a substantial share of income rises, consumers of that good become a bit poorer because their purchasing power falls. And the vast majority of goods are *normal* goods, goods for which demand decreases when income falls. So this effective reduction in income leads to a reduction in the quantity demanded and reinforces the substitution effect.

However, in the case of an *inferior* good, a good for which demand increases when income falls, the income and substitution effects work in opposite directions. Although the substitution effect tends to produce a decrease in the quantity of any good demanded as its price increases, in the case of an inferior good the income effect of a price increase tends to produce an *increase* in the quantity demanded.

GIFFEN GOODS

Back when Ireland was a desperately poor country—not the prosperous "Celtic Tiger" it has lately become—it was claimed that the Irish would eat *more* potatoes when the price of potatoes went up. That is, some observers claimed that Ireland's demand curve for potatoes sloped upward, not downward.

Can this happen? In theory, yes. If Irish demand for potatoes actually sloped upward, it would have been a real-life case of a "Giffen good," named after a nineteenth-century statistician who thought (probably wrongly) that he saw an upward-sloping demand curve in some data he was studying.

Here's the story. Suppose that there is some good that absorbs a large share of consumers' budgets and that this good is also *inferior*—people demand less of it when their income rises. The classic supposed example was, as you might guess, potatoes in Ireland, back when potatoes were an inferior good—they were what poor people ate—and when the Irish were very poor.

Now suppose that the price of potatoes increases. This would, *other things equal*, cause people to substitute other goods for potatoes. But other things are not equal: given the higher price of potatoes, people are poorer. And this *increases* the demand for potatoes, because potatoes are an inferior good.

If this income effect outweighs the substitution effect, a rise in the price of potatoes would increase the quantity demanded; the law of demand would not hold.

In a way the point of this story—which has never been validated in any real situation, nineteenth-century Ireland included—is how unlikely such an event is. The law of demand really is a law, with few exceptions.

As a result, there are hypothetical cases involving inferior goods in which the distinction between income and substitution effects are important (see For Inquiring Minds). As a practical matter, however, it's not a subject we need to worry about when discussing the demand for most goods. Typically, income effects are important only for a very limited number of goods and when discussing *factor markets*, as we'll see in Chapter 12.

economics in action

Mortgage Rates and Consumer Demand

Most people buy houses with mortgages—loans backed by the value of the house. The interest rates on such mortgages change over time; for example, they fell quite a lot over the period from 2000 to 2003. When that happens, the cost of housing falls for millions of people—even people who have mortgages at high interest rates are often able to "refinance" them at lower rates.

It's not surprising that the demand for housing goes up when mortgage rates go down. Economists have noticed, however, that the demand for many other goods also rises when mortgage rates fall. Some of these goods are items connected with new or bigger houses, such as furniture. But people also buy new cars, eat more meals in restaurants, and take more vacations. Why?

The answer illustrates the distinction between substitution and income effects. When housing becomes cheaper, there is a *substitution effect*: people have an incentive to substitute housing for other goods in their consumption bundle. But housing also happens to be a good that absorbs a large part of consumer spending, with many families spending a quarter or more of their income on mortgage payments. So when the price of housing falls, people are in effect richer—there is a noticeable *income effect*.

The increase in the quantity of housing demanded when mortgage rates fall is the result of both effects: housing becomes a better buy compared with other consumer goods, and people also buy more and bigger houses because they feel richer. And because they feel richer, they also buy more of all other normal goods, such as cars, restaurant meals, and vacations. ∎

> ## QUICK REVIEW
>
> ➤ The market demand curve for a good is the horizontal sum of each consumer's *individual demand curve*.
>
> ➤ Most goods absorb only a small fraction of a consumer's spending. For such goods, the *substitution effect* of a price change is the only important effect of the price change on demand. It causes individual demand curves and the market demand curve to slope downward.
>
> ➤ When a good absorbs a large fraction of a consumer's spending, the *income effect* of a price change is present in addition to the substitution effect.
>
> ➤ For normal goods, demand rises when a consumer is richer and falls when a consumer is poorer, so that the income effect reinforces the substitution effect. For inferior goods, demand rises when a consumer is poorer and falls when a consumer is richer, so that the income and substitution effects move in the opposite direction.

< < < < < < < < < < < < < < < < < < < <

>>CHECK YOUR UNDERSTANDING 10-4

In each of the following cases, state whether the income effect, the substitution effect, or both are significant. In which cases do they move in the same direction? In opposite directions? Why?

1. Orange juice represents a small share of Clare's spending. She buys more lemonade and less orange juice when the price of orange juice goes up. She does not change her spending on other goods.

2. Apartment rents have risen dramatically this year. Since rent absorbs a major part of her income, Delia moves to a smaller apartment. Assume that rental housing is a normal good.

3. The cost of a semester-long meal ticket at the student cafeteria rises, representing a significant increase in living costs. As a result, many students have less money to spend on weekend meals at restaurants so eat in the cafeteria instead. Assume that cafeteria meals are an inferior good.

Solutions appear at back of book.

• A LOOK AHEAD •

At this point we have the basic tools to understand consumer behavior; taken together with our analysis of producer behavior (which is in Chapters 8 and 9), we have the background behind both the supply and the demand curves.

There is more to say about consumer choice; those who want to pursue the subject further should proceed to Chapter 11. Those eager to move on can, however, skip to Chapter 12 and the next subject: how the same tools that we have used to analyze the markets for *goods and services* can also be used to analyze the markets for *factors of production.*

SUMMARY

1. Consumers maximize a measure of satisfaction called **utility.** Each consumer has a **utility function** that determines the level of total utility from his or her **consumption bundle,** the goods and services that are consumed. We measure utility in hypothetical units called **utils.**

2. A good's or service's **marginal utility** is the additional utility generated by consuming one more unit of the good or service. We usually assume that the **principle of diminishing marginal utility** holds: consumption of another unit of a good or service yields less additional utility than the previous unit. As a result, the **marginal utility curve** is downward sloping.

3. A **budget constraint** limits a consumer's spending to no more than his or her income. It defines the consumer's **consumption possibilities,** the set of all affordable consumption bundles. A consumer who spends all of his or her income will choose a consumption bundle on the **budget line,** the slope of which is equal to the opportunity cost of the good on the horizontal axis in terms of the good on the vertical axis. An individual chooses the consumption bundle that maximizes total utility, the **optimal consumption bundle.**

4. We use marginal analysis to find the optimal consumption bundle by analyzing how to allocate the marginal dollar. The **optimal consumption rule** says that at the optimal consumption bundle the **marginal utility per dollar** spent on each good and service—the marginal utility of a good divided by its price—is the same.

5. An **individual demand curve** for a good shows how an individual consumer's quantity demanded depends on price. Individual demand curves are summed horizontally to yield the market demand curve. Changes in the price of a good affect the quantity consumed in two possible ways: the **substitution effect** and the **income effect.** Most goods absorb only a small share of a consumer's spending; for these goods, only the substitution effect—buying less of the good that has become relatively more expensive and more of the good that has become relatively cheaper—is significant. It causes the individual and the market demand curves to slope downward. When a good absorbs a large fraction of spending, the income effect is also significant: an increase in a good's price makes a consumer poorer, but a decrease in price makes a consumer richer. This change in purchasing power makes consumers demand more or less of a good, depending on whether the good is normal or inferior. For normal goods, the substitution and income effects reinforce each other. For inferior goods, however, they work in opposite directions.

KEY TERMS

Utility, p. 231
Consumption bundle, p. 231
Utility function, p. 231
Util, p. 231
Marginal utility, p. 232
Marginal utility curve, p. 232

Principle of diminishing marginal utility, p. 233
Budget constraint, p. 235
Consumption possibilities, p. 235
Budget line, p. 236
Optimal consumption bundle, p. 238

Marginal utility per dollar, p. 241
Optimal consumption rule, p. 244
Individual demand curve, p. 245
Substitution effect, p. 247
Income effect, p. 247

PROBLEMS

1. For each of the following situations, decide whether Al has increasing, constant, or diminishing marginal utility.

   a. The more economics classes Al takes, the more he enjoys the subject. And the more classes he takes, the easier each one gets, making him enjoy each additional class even more than the one before.

   b. Al likes loud music. In fact, according to him, "the louder, the better." Each time he turns the volume up a notch, he adds 5 utils to his total utility.

   c. Al enjoys watching old episodes of the sitcom *Friends*. He claims that old episodes are always funny, but he does admit that the more he sees an episode, the less funny it gets.

   d. Al loves toasted marshmallows. The more he eats, however, the fuller he gets and the less he enjoys each additional marshmallow. And there is a point at which he becomes satiated: beyond that point, more marshmallows actually make him feel worse rather than better.

2. Use the concept of marginal utility to explain the following: Newspaper vending machines are designed so that once you have paid for one paper, you could take more than one paper at a time. But soda vending machines, once you have paid for one soda, dispense only one soda at a time.

3. Brenda likes to have bagels and coffee for breakfast. The accompanying table shows Brenda's total utility from various consumption bundles of bagels and coffee.

Consumption bundle		Total utility (utils)
Quantity of bagels	Quantity of coffee (cups)	
0	0	0
0	2	28
0	4	40
1	2	48
1	3	54
2	0	28
2	2	56
3	1	54
3	2	62
4	0	40
4	2	66

Suppose Brenda knows she will consume 2 cups of coffee for sure. However, she can choose to consume different quantities of bagels: she can choose either 0, 1, 2, 3, or 4 bagels.

   a. Calculate Brenda's marginal utility from bagels as she goes from consuming 0 bagel to 1 bagel, from 1 bagel to 2 bagels, from 2 bagels to 3 bagels, and from 3 bagels to 4 bagels.

   b. Draw Brenda's marginal utility curve of bagels. Does Brenda have increasing, diminishing, or constant marginal utility of bagels?

4. Brenda from Problem 3 now has to make a decision about how many bagels and how much coffee to have for breakfast. She has $8 of income to spend on bagels and coffee. Use the information on her utility given in the table in Problem 3.

   a. Bagels cost $2 each, and coffee costs $2 per cup. Which bundles are on Brenda's budget line? For each of these bundles, what is the level of utility (in utils) that Brenda experiences? Which bundle is therefore her optimal bundle?

   b. The price of bagels increases to $4, but the price of coffee remains at $2 per cup. Which bundles are now on Brenda's budget line? For each of these bundles, what is the level of utility (in utils) that Brenda experiences? Which bundle is therefore her optimal bundle?

   c. Compare your answers from parts a and b. As the price of bagels increased from $2 to $4, what happened to the quantity of bagels that Brenda chose to consume? What does this imply about the slope of Brenda's demand curve for bagels? In words, describe the substitution effect and the income effect of this increase in the price of bagels. (Bagels are a normal good.)

5. Bruno can spend his income on two different goods: Britney Spears CDs and notebooks for his class notes. He is thinking about the following three bundles: bundle A contains 5 CDs and 5 notebooks; bundle B contains 10 CDs and 2 notebooks; and bundle C contains 3 CDs and 6 notebooks. For each of the following situations, draw the budget line and decide which of these bundles are possible consumption bundles. That is, determine which of these bundles he can consume given his income and prices. Place CDs on the horizontal axis and notebooks on the vertical axis.

   a. CDs cost $10 each, and notebooks cost $2 each. Bruno has income of $60.

   b. CDs cost $10 each, and notebooks cost $5 each. Bruno has income of $110.

c. [...]
s[...]
c[...]
n[...]

6. Bru[...]
his[...]
nyir[...]
Brit[...]

Quantity of notebooks	(utils)	Quantity of CDs	CDs (utils)
0	0	0	0
2	70	1	80
4	130	2	150
6	180	3	210
8	220	4	260
10	250	5	300

The price of a notebook is $5, the price of a CD is $10, and Bernie has $50 of income to spend.

a. Which consumption bundles of notebooks and CDs can Bernie consume if he spends all his income? Draw Bernie's budget line with CDs on the horizontal axis and notebooks on the vertical axis.

b. Calculate the marginal utility of each notebook and the marginal utility of each CD. Then calculate the marginal utility per dollar spent on notebooks and the marginal utility per dollar spent on CDs.

c. Draw a diagram like Figure 10-5 in which the marginal utility per dollar spent on notebooks is shown in one panel and the marginal utility per dollar spent on CDs in the other panel. Using this diagram and the optimal spending rule, predict which bundle—from all the bundles on his budget line—Bernie will choose.

7. For each of the following situations, decide whether the bundle Lakshani is thinking about consuming is optimal or not. If it is not optimal, how could Lakshani improve her overall level of utility? That is, determine which good she should spend more on and which good should spend less on.

a. Lakshani has $200 to spend on sneakers and sweaters. Sneakers cost $50 per pair, and sweaters cost $20 each. She is thinking about buying 2 pairs of sneakers and 5 sweaters. She tells her friend that the additional utility she would get from the second pair of sneakers is the same as the additional utility she would get from the fifth sweater.

b. Lakshani has $5 to spend on pens and pencils. Each pen costs $0.50 and each pencil costs $0.10. She is thinking about buying 6 pens and 20 pencils. The last pen added five times as much to her total utility as the last pencil.

c. Lakshani has $50 per season to spend on tickets to football games and tickets to soccer games. Each football ticket costs $10 and each soccer ticket costs $5. She is thinking about buying 3 football tickets and 2 soccer tick-

ets. Her marginal utility from the third football ticket is twice as much as her marginal utility from the second soccer ticket.

8. Cal "Cool" Cooper has $200 to spend on cell phones and sunglasses.

a. Each cell phone costs $100 and each pair of sunglasses costs $50. Which bundles lie on Cal's budget line? Draw a diagram like Figure 10-5 in which the marginal utility per dollar spent on cell phones is shown in one panel and the marginal utility per dollar spent on sunglasses is shown in the other panel. Using this diagram and the optimal spending rule, decide how Cal should allocate his money. That is, from all the bundles on his budget line, which bundle will Cal choose? The accompanying table gives his utility of cell phones and sunglasses.

Quantity of cell phones	Utility from cell phones (utils)	Quantity of sunglasses	Utility from sunglasses (utils)
0	0	0	0
1	400	2	600
2	700	4	700

b. The price of cell phones falls to $50 each, but the price of sunglasses remains at $50 per pair. Which bundles lie on Cal's budget line? Draw a diagram like Figure 10-5 in which the marginal utility per dollar spent on cell phones is shown in one panel and the marginal utility per dollar spent on sunglasses is shown in the other panel. Using this diagram and the optimal spending rule, decide how Cal should allocate his money. That is, from all the bundles on his budget line, which bundle will Cal choose? The accompanying table gives his utility of cell phones and sunglasses.

Quantity of cell phones	Utility from cell phones (utils)	Quantity of sunglasses	Utility from sunglasses (utils)
0	0	0	0
1	400	1	325
2	700	2	600
3	900	3	825
4	1,000	4	700

c. How does Cal's consumption of cell phones change as the price of cell phones falls? In words, describe the income effect and the substitution effect of this fall in the price of cell phones. (Cell phones are a normal good.)

9. Damien Matthews is a busy actor. He allocates his free time to watching movies and working out at the gym. The accompanying table shows his utility from the number of times per week he watches a movie or goes to the gym.

Quantity of gym visits per week	Utility from gym visits (utils)	Quantity of movies per week	Utility from movies (utils)
1	100	1	60
2	180	2	110
3	240	3	150
4	280	4	180
5	310	5	190
6	330	6	195
9	340	7	197

Damien has 14 hours per week to spend on watching movies and going to the gym. Each movie takes 2 hours and each gym visit takes 2 hours. (*Hint:* Damien's free time is analogous to income he can spend. The hours needed for each activity are analogous to the price of that activity.)

a. Which bundles of gym visits and movies can Damien consume per week if he spends all his time either going to the gym or watching movies? Draw Damien's budget line in a diagram with gym visits on the horizontal axis and movies on the vertical axis.

b. Calculate the marginal utility of each gym visit and the marginal utility of each movie. Then calculate the marginal utility per hour spent at the gym and the marginal utility per hour spent watching movies.

c. Draw a diagram like Figure 10-5 in which the marginal utility per hour spent at the gym is shown in one panel and the marginal utility per hour spent watching movies is shown in the other panel. Using this diagram and the optimal spending rule, decide how Damien should allocate his time.

10. Anna Jenniferson is an actress, and on the set of a new movie she meets Damien from Problem 9. She tells him that she likes watching movies much more than going to the gym. In fact, she says that if she had to give up seeing 1 movie, she would need to go to the gym twice to make up for the loss in utility from not seeing the movie. A movie takes 2 hours, and a gym visit also lasts 2 hours. Damien tells Anna that she is not watching enough movies. Is he right?

11. Sven is a poor student who covers most of his dietary needs by eating cheap breakfast cereal, since it contains most of the important vitamins. As the price of cereal increases, he decides to buy even less of other foods and even more breakfast cereal to maintain his intake of important nutrients. This makes breakfast cereal a Giffen good for Sven. Describe in words the substitution effect and the income effect from this increase in the price of cereal. In which direction does each effect move, and why? What does this imply for the slope of Sven's demand curve for cereal?

12. In each of the following situations, describe the substitution effect and (if it is significant) the income effect. In which direction does each of these effects move? Why?

a. Ed spends a large portion of his income on his children's education. Because tuition fees rise, one of his children has to withdraw from college.

b. Homer spends much of his monthly income on home mortgage payments. The interest on his adjustable-rate mortgage falls, lowering his mortgage payments, and Homer decides to move to a larger house.

c. Pam thinks that Spam is an inferior good. Yet as the price of Spam rises, she decides to buy less of it.

>web... To continue your study and review of concepts in this chapter, please visit the Krugman/Wells website for quizzes, animated graph tutorials, web links to helpful resources, and more.

www.worthpublishers.com/krugmanwells

>>Consumer Preferences and Consumer Choice

A TALE OF TWO CITIES

DO YOU WANT TO EARN A HIGH SALARY? Maybe you should consider moving to San Jose, California, the metropolitan area that contains much of Silicon Valley, America's leading cluster of high-tech industries. The average family in San Jose has an income far higher than that of the average American family. According to bestplaces.net, a website that compares living conditions in different cities, average household income in San Jose is more than twice as high as that in Cincinnati.

But before you rush to San Jose, there's something else you should know: housing is very expensive there—about four times as expensive per square foot of living space as in Cincinnati. Understandably, the average apartment or house in San Jose is small by American standards.

So is life better or worse in San Jose than in Cincinnati? It depends a lot on what you want. For young people without children, the high wage they can earn in San Jose probably outweighs the high price of housing. They are willing to accept more cramped living quarters in return for the ability to consume greater quantities of other goods such as restaurant meals or clothing. People with large families, however, might prefer midwestern locations like Cincinnati, where the average wage is lower than in San Jose but a dollar buys many more square feet of living space. That is, they would choose to eat fewer restaurant meals but live in more spacious housing.

For individuals whose preferences lie somewhere between those of childless yuppies and those of proud parents, the choice between San Jose and Cincinnati may not be easy. In fact, some people would be *indifferent* between living in the two locations. That's not to say that they would live the same way in San Jose and in Cincinnati; in San Jose they would live in small apartments and eat out a lot, but in Cincinnati they would be homebodies.

What you will learn in this chapter:

➤ Why economists use **indifference curves** to illustrate a person's preferences

➤ The importance of the **marginal rate of substitution,** the rate at which a consumer is just willing to substitute one good for another

➤ An alternative way of finding a consumer's optimal consumption bundle using indifference curves and the budget line

➤ How the shape of indifference curves helps determine whether goods are substitutes or complements

➤ An in-depth understanding of income and substitution effects

Ariel Skelley/Masterfile

Carol Halebein for the *New York Times*

Spacious house in the suburbs or cozy apartment in the city—how would you choose?

And they would find both lifestyles equally good.

Our comparison of San Jose and Cincinnati has several morals. One is that different people have different preferences. But we also see that even given an individual's preferences, there may be different consumption bundles that yield the same total utility. This insight leads to the concept of *indifference curves,* a useful way to represent individual preferences.

The example also shows that an individual's total utility depends not only on income but also on prices—and that both income and prices affect consumer choices. We will apply this more complete analysis of consumer choice to the important distinction between *complements* and *substitutes.* Finally, we will use this insight to examine further the *income* and *substitution effects* we covered briefly in Chapter 10.

But, let's begin with indifference curves.

Mapping the Utility Function

In Chapter 10 we introduced the concept of a utility function, which determines a consumer's total utility given his or her consumption bundle. In Figure 10-1 we saw how Cassie's total utility changed as we changed the quantity of fried clams consumed, holding fixed the quantities of other items in her bundle. That is, in Figure 10-1 we showed how total utility changed as consumption of only *one* good changed. But we also learned in Chapter 10, from our example of Sammy, that finding the optimal consumption bundle involves the problem of how to allocate the last dollar spent between *two* goods, clams and potatoes. In this chapter we will extend the analysis by learning how to express total utility as a function of consumption of two goods. In this way we will deepen our understanding of the trade-off involved when choosing the optimal consumption bundle and of how the optimal consumption bundle itself changes in response to changes in the prices of goods. In order to do that, we now turn to a different way of representing a consumer's utility function, based on the concept of *indifference curves.*

Indifference Curves

Ingrid is a consumer who buys only two goods: housing, measured in the number of rooms, and restaurant meals. How can we represent her utility function in a way that takes account of her consumption of both goods?

One way is to draw a three-dimensional picture. Figure 11-1 shows a three-dimensional "utility hill." The distance along the horizontal axis measures the quantity of housing Ingrid consumes in terms of numbers of rooms; the distance along the vertical axis measures the number of restaurant meals she consumes. The altitude or height of the hill at each point is indicated by a contour line, along which the height of the hill is constant. For example, point *A*, which corresponds to a consumption bundle of 3 rooms and 30 restaurant meals, lies on the contour line labeled 450. So the total utility Ingrid receives from consuming 3 rooms and 30 restaurant meals is 450 utils.

A three-dimensional picture like Figure 11-1 helps us think about the relationship between consumption bundles and total utility. But anyone who has ever used a topographical map to plan a hiking trip knows that it is possible to represent a three-dimensional surface in only two dimensions. A topographical map doesn't offer a three-dimensional view of the terrain; instead, it conveys information about altitude solely through the use of contour lines.

The same principle can be applied to representing the utility function. In Figure 11-2 Ingrid's consumption of rooms is measured on the horizontal axis and her consumption of restaurant meals on the vertical axis. The curve here corresponds to the contour line in Figure 11-1, drawn at a total utility of 450 utils. This curve shows all

Figure 11-1

Ingrid's Utility Function

The three-dimensional hill shows how Ingrid's total utility depends on her consumption of housing and restaurant meals. Point A corresponds to consumption of 3 rooms and 30 restaurant meals. That consumption bundle yields Ingrid 450 utils, corresponding to the height of the hill at point A. The lines running around the hill are contour lines, along which the height is constant. So every point on a given contour line generates the same level of utility.

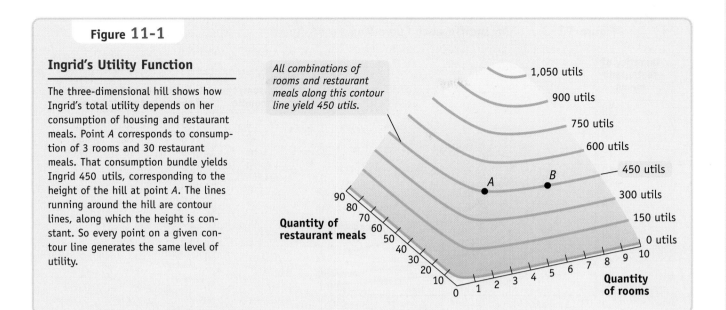

All combinations of rooms and restaurant meals along this contour line yield 450 utils.

1,050 utils
900 utils
750 utils
600 utils
450 utils
300 utils
150 utils
0 utils

Quantity of restaurant meals

Quantity of rooms

the consumption bundles that yield a total utility of 450 utils. One point on that contour line is A, a consumption bundle consisting of 3 rooms and 30 restaurant meals. Another point on that contour line is B, a consumption bundle consisting of 6 rooms but only 15 restaurant meals. Because B also lies on the contour line, it yields Ingrid the same total utility—450 utils—as A. We say that Ingrid is *indifferent* between A and B: because A and B yield the same total utility level, Ingrid is equally well off with either bundle.

A contour line that maps consumption bundles yielding the same amount of total utility is known as an **indifference curve.** An individual is always indifferent between any two bundles that lie on the same indifference curve. Given a consumer's tastes, there is an indifference curve corresponding to each possible level of total utility. The indifference curve in Figure 11-2 shows consumption bundles that yield Ingrid 450 utils; different indifference curves would show consumption bundles that yield Ingrid 400 utils, 500 utils, and so on.

An **indifference curve** is a line that shows all the consumption bundles that yield the same amount of total utility for an individual.

Figure 11-2

An Indifference Curve

An indifference curve is a contour line along which total utility is constant. In this case we show all the consumption bundles that yield Ingrid 450 utils. Consumption bundle A, consisting of 3 rooms and 30 restaurant meals, yields the same total utility as bundle B, consisting of 6 rooms and 15 restaurant meals. That is, Ingrid is indifferent between bundle A and bundle B.

>*web*...

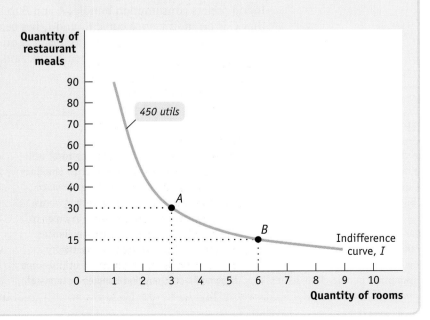

Quantity of restaurant meals

450 utils

A

B

Indifference curve, *I*

Quantity of rooms

Figure 11-3   **An Indifference Curve Map**

Consumption bundle	Quantity of rooms	Quantity of meals	Total utility (utils)
A	3	30	450
B	6	15	450
C	5	10	391
D	4	45	519

The utility function can be represented in as much detail as we want by showing a number of indifference curves, each corresponding to a different level of total utility. In this figure bundle C lies on an indifference curve corresponding to a total utility of 391 utils. As in Figure 11-2, bundles A and B lie on an indifference curve corresponding to a total utility of 450 utils. Bundle D lies on an indifference curve corresponding to a total utility of 519 utils. Ingrid prefers any bundle on I_2 to any bundle on I_1, and she prefers any bundle on I_3 to any bundle on I_2. **>web...**

The entire utility function of an individual can be represented by an **indifference curve map**, a collection of indifference curves in which each curve corresponds to a different total utility level.

A collection of indifference curves that represents a consumer's entire utility function, with each indifference curve corresponding to a different level of total utility, is known as an **indifference curve map.** Figure 11-3 shows three indifference curves, I_1, I_2, and I_3, from Ingrid's indifference curve map, as well as several consumption bundles, A, B, C, and D. The accompanying table lists each bundle, its composition of rooms and restaurant meals, and the total utility it yields. Because bundles A and B generate the same number of utils, 450, they lie on the same indifference curve, I_2. Although Ingrid is indifferent between A and B, she is certainly not indifferent between A and C: as you can see from the table, C generates only 391 utils, a lower total utility than A or B. So Ingrid prefers consumption bundles A and B to bundle C. This is represented by the fact that C is on indifference curve I_1, and I_1 lies below I_2. Bundle D, though, generates 519 utils, a higher total utility than A and B. It is on I_3, an indifference curve that lies above I_2. Clearly, Ingrid prefers D to either A or B. And, even more strongly, she prefers D to C.

In the table that accompanies Figure 11-3 we give the number of utils achieved at each of the indifference curves shown in the figure. But is this information actually needed?

The answer is no. As you will see shortly, the indifference curve map tells us all we need to know in order to find a consumer's optimal consumption bundle. That is, it's important that Ingrid has higher total utility along indifference curve I_2 than she does along I_1, but it doesn't matter *how much* higher her total utility is. In other words, we don't have to measure utils in order to understand how consumers make choices.

Economists say that consumer theory requires an "ordinal" measure of utility—one that ranks consumption bundles in terms of desirability—so that we can say that bundle X is better than bundle Y. The theory does not, however, require "cardinal" utility, which actually assigns a specific number to the total utility yielded by each bundle.

So why introduce the concept of utils at all? The answer is that it is much easier to understand the basis of rational choice by using the concept of measurable utility.

Properties of Indifference Curves

No two individuals have the same indifference curve map because no two individuals have the same preferences. But economists believe that every indifference curve map has two general properties, illustrated in panel (a) of Figure 11-4:

- *Indifference curves never cross.* Suppose that we tried to draw an indifference curve map like the one depicted in the left diagram in panel (a), in which two indifference curves cross at *A*. What is the total utility at *A*? Is it 100 utils or 200 utils? Indifference curves cannot cross because each consumption bundle must correspond to a unique total utility level—not, as shown at *A*, two different total utility levels.

Figure 11-4   Properties of Indifference Curves

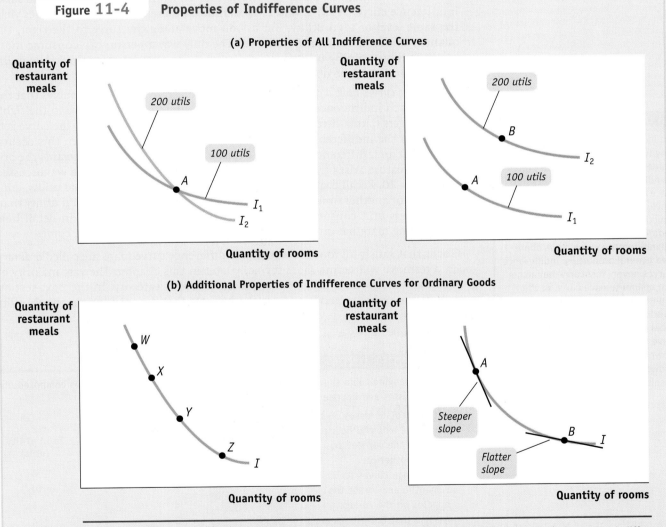

Panel (a) represents two general properties that all indifference curve maps share. The left diagram shows why indifference curves cannot cross: if they did, a consumption bundle such as *A* would yield both 100 and 200 utils, a contradiction. The right diagram of panel (a) shows that indifference curves that are farther out yield higher total utility: bundle *B*, which contains more of both goods than bundle *A*, yields higher total utility. Panel (b) depicts two additional properties of indifference curves for ordinary goods. The left diagram of panel (b) shows that indifference curves slope downward: as you move down the curve from bundle *W* to bundle *Z*, consumption of rooms increases. To keep total utility constant, this must be offset by a reduction in quantity of restaurant meals. The right diagram of panel (b) shows a convex-shaped indifference curve. The slope of the indifference curve gets flatter as you move down the curve to the right, a feature arising from diminishing marginal utility.

■ *The farther out an indifference curve lies—the farther it is from the origin—the higher the level of total utility it indicates.* The reason, illustrated in the right diagram in panel (a), is that we assume that more is better—over the set of consumption bundles we are considering, the consumer is not satiated. Bundle *B*, on the outer indifference curve, contains more of both goods than bundle *A* on the inner indifference curve. So *B* generates a higher total utility level (200 utils) and therefore lies on a higher indifference curve than *A*.

Furthermore, economists believe that, for most goods, consumers' indifference curve maps also have two additional properties. They are illustrated in panel (b) of Figure 11-4:

■ *Indifference curves are downward sloping.* Here, too, the reason is that more is better. The left diagram in panel (b) shows four consumption bundles on the same indifference curve: *W, X, Y,* and *Z*. By definition these consumption bundles yield the same level of total utility. But as you move along the curve to the right, the quantity of rooms consumed increases. The only way a person can consume more rooms without gaining utility is by giving up some restaurant meals. So the indifference curve must be downward sloping.

■ *Indifference curves have a convex shape.* The right diagram in panel (b) shows that the slope of each indifference curve changes as you move down the curve to the right: the curve gets flatter. If you move up an indifference curve to the left, the curve gets steeper. So the indifference curve is steeper at *A* than it is at *B*. When this occurs, we say that an indifference curve has a *convex* shape—it is bowed-in towards the origin. This feature arises from diminishing marginal utility, a principle we discussed in Chapter 10. Recall that when a consumer has diminishing marginal utility, consumption of another unit of a good generates a smaller increase in total utility than the previous unit consumed. In the next section, we will examine in detail how diminishing marginal utility gives rise to convex-shaped indifference curves.

Goods that satisfy all four properties of indifference curve maps are called *ordinary goods*, a term we will define more formally later in this chapter. The vast majority of goods in any consumer's utility function fall into this category. In the next section we will define ordinary goods and see the key role that diminishing marginal utility plays for them. ■

< < < < < < < < < < < < < < < < <

>> CHECK YOUR UNDERSTANDING 11-1

1. The accompanying table shows Samantha's preferences for consumption bundles composed of chocolate kisses and licorice drops.

    a. With chocolate kisses on the horizontal axis and licorice drops on the vertical axis, draw hypothetical indifference curves for Samantha and locate the bundles on the curves. Assume that both items are ordinary goods.

Consumption bundle	Quantity of chocolate kisses	Quantity of licorice drops	Total utility (utils)
A	1	3	6
B	2	3	10
C	3	1	6
D	2	1	4

    b. Suppose you don't know the number of utils provided by each bundle. Assuming that more is better, predict Samantha's ranking of each of the four bundles to the extent possible.

2. On the left diagram in panel (a) of Figure 11-4, draw a point *B* anywhere on the 200 utils indifference curve and a point *C* anywhere on the 100 utils indifference curve (but *not* at the same location as point *A*). By comparing the utils generated by bundles *A* and *B* and those generated by bundles *A* and *C*, explain why indifference curves cannot cross.

Indifference Curves and Consumer Choice

At the beginning of the last section we used indifference curves to represent the preferences of Ingrid, whose consumption bundles consist of rooms and restaurant meals. Our next step is to show how to use Ingrid's indifference curve map to find her utility-maximizing consumption bundle given her budget constraint.

It's important to understand how our analysis here relates to what we did in Chapter 10. We are not offering a new theory of consumer behavior in this chapter—just as in Chapter 10, consumers are assumed to maximize total utility. In particular, we know that consumers will follow the *optimal consumption rule* from Chapter 10: the optimal consumption bundle lies on the budget line, and the marginal utility per dollar is the same for every good in the bundle.

But as we'll see shortly, we can derive this optimal consumer behavior in a somewhat different way—a way that yields deeper insights into consumer choice.

The Marginal Rate of Substitution

The first component of our approach is a new concept, the *marginal rate of substitution*. The essence of this concept is illustrated in Figure 11-5.

Recall from the last section that for most goods, consumers' indifference curves are downward sloping and convex. Figure 11-5 shows such an indifference curve. The points labeled *V, W, X, Y,* and *Z* all lie on this indifference curve—that is, they represent consumption bundles that yield Ingrid the same level of total utility. The table accompanying the figure shows the components of each of the bundles. As we move along the indifference curve from *V* to *Z*, Ingrid's consumption of housing steadily increases from 2 rooms to 6 rooms, but her total utility is kept constant. As we move

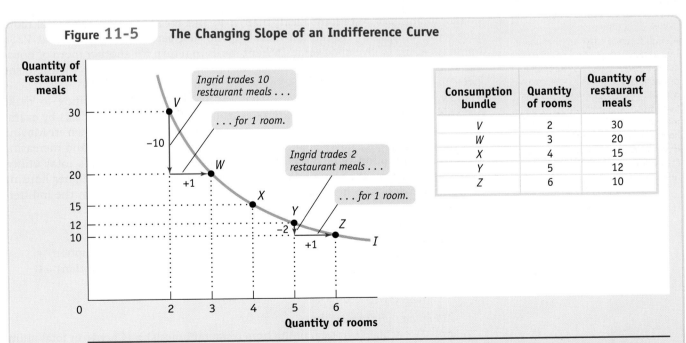

Figure 11-5 The Changing Slope of an Indifference Curve

Consumption bundle	Quantity of rooms	Quantity of restaurant meals
V	2	30
W	3	20
X	4	15
Y	5	12
Z	6	10

Ingrid trades 10 restaurant meals . . . . . . for 1 room.

Ingrid trades 2 restaurant meals . . . . . . for 1 room.

This indifference curve is downward sloping and convex, implying that restaurant meals and rooms are ordinary goods for Ingrid. As Ingrid moves down her indifference curve from *V* to *Z*, she trades off reduced consumption of restaurant meals for increased consumption of housing. However, the terms of that trade-off change. As she moves from *V* to *W*, she is willing to give up 10 restaurant meals in return for 1 more room. As her consumption of rooms rises and her consumption of restaurant meals falls, she is willing to give up fewer restaurant meals in return for each additional room. The flattening of the slope as you move from left to right arises from diminishing marginal utility. **>web...**

down the indifference curve, then, Ingrid is trading more of one good for less of the other, with the *terms* of that trade-off—the ratio of additional rooms consumed to restaurant meals sacrificed—chosen to keep her total utility constant.

Notice that the quantity of restaurant meals that Ingrid is willing to give up in return for an additional room changes along the indifference curve. As we move from *V* to *W*, housing consumption rises from 2 to 3 rooms and restaurant meal consumption falls from 30 to 20—a trade-off of 10 restaurant meals for 1 additional room. But as we move from *Y* to *Z*, housing consumption rises from 5 to 6 rooms and restaurant meal consumption falls from 12 to 10, a trade-off of only 2 restaurant meals for an additional room.

To put it in terms of slopes, the slope of the indifference curve between *V* and *W* is −10: the change in restaurant meal consumption, −10, divided by the change in housing consumption, 1. Similarly, the slope of the indifference curve between *Y* and *Z* is −2. So the indifference curve gets flatter as we move down it to the right—that is, it has a convex shape, one of the four properties of an indifference curve for ordinary goods.

Why does the trade-off change in this way? Let's think about it intuitively, then work through it more carefully. When Ingrid moves down her indifference curve, whether from *V* to *W* or from *Y* to *Z*, she gains utility from her additional consumption of housing but loses an equal amount of utility from her reduced consumption of restaurant meals. But at each step, the initial position from which Ingrid begins is different. At *V*, Ingrid consumes only a small quantity of rooms, so because of diminishing marginal utility her marginal utility per room at that point is high. At *V*, then, an additional room adds a lot to Ingrid's total utility. But at *V* she already consumes a large quantity of restaurant meals, so her marginal utility of restaurant meals is low at that point. This means that it takes a large reduction in her quantity of restaurant meals consumed to offset the increased utility she gets from the extra room of housing.

At *Y*, in contrast, Ingrid consumes a much larger quantity of rooms and a much smaller quantity of restaurant meals than at *V*. This means that an additional room adds fewer utils, and a restaurant meal forgone subtracts more utils, than at *V*. So Ingrid is willing to give up fewer restaurant meals in return for another room of housing at *Y* (where she gives up two meals for one room) than she is at *V* (where she gives up 10 meals for one room).

Now let's express the same idea—that the trade-off Ingrid is willing to make depends on where she is starting from—by using a little math. We do this by examining how the slope of the indifference curve changes as we move down it. Moving down the indifference curve—reducing restaurant meal consumption and increasing housing consumption—will produce two opposing effects on Ingrid's total utility: lower restaurant meal consumption will reduce her total utility, but higher housing consumption will raise her total utility. And since we are moving down the indifference curve, these two effects must exactly cancel out:

> *Along the indifference curve:*
> **(11-1)** (Change in total utility because of lower restaurant consumption) +
>   (Change in total utility because of higher housing consumption) = 0

or, rearranging terms,

> *Along the indifference curve:*
> **(11-2)** −(Change in total utility from restaurant meals) = (Change in total utility from housing)

Let's now focus on what happens as we move only a short distance down the indifference curve, trading off a small increase in housing consumption for a small decrease in restaurant meal consumption. Following our notation from Chapter 10, let's use MU_R and MU_M to represent the marginal utility of rooms and restaurant meals, respectively, and ΔQ_R and ΔQ_M to represent the changes in room and meal consumption, respectively. In general, the change in total utility caused by a small change in consumption of a good is equal to the change in consumption multiplied by the *marginal utility* of that good. This means that we can calculate the change in Ingrid's total utility generated by a change in her consumption bundle using the following equations:

(11-3) Change in total utility arising from a change in consumption of restaurant meals = $MU_M \times \Delta Q_M$

and

(11-4) Change in total utility arising from a change in consumption of rooms = $MU_R \times \Delta Q_R$

So we can write Equation 11-2 in symbols as

(11-5) *Along the indifference curve:* $-MU_M \times \Delta Q_M = MU_R \times \Delta Q_R$

Note that the left-hand side of Equation 11-5 has a minus sign; it represents minus the loss in total utility from decreased restaurant meal consumption. This must equal the gain in total utility from increased room consumption, represented by the right-hand side of the equation.

What we want, of course, is to know how this translates into the slope of the indifference curve. To find the slope, we divide both sides of Equation 11-5 by ΔQ_R, and again by MU_M, in order to get the ΔQ_M, ΔQ_R terms on one side and the MU_R, MU_M terms on the other. This results in:

(11-6) *Along the indifference curve:* $\dfrac{-\Delta Q_M}{\Delta Q_R} = \dfrac{MU_R}{MU_M}$

The left-hand side of Equation 11-6 is *minus* the slope of the indifference curve; it is the rate at which Ingrid is willing to trade a higher quantity of rooms (the good on the horizontal axis) in place of restaurant meals (the good on the vertical axis). The right-hand side of Equation 11-6 is the ratio of the marginal utility of rooms to the marginal utility of restaurant meals—that is, the ratio of what she gains from one more room to what she gains from one more meal.

Putting all this together, we see that Equation 11-6 shows that, along the indifference curve, the quantity of restaurant meals Ingrid is willing to give up in return for a room, $\Delta Q_M / \Delta Q_R$, is exactly equal to the ratio of the marginal utility of a room to that of a meal, MU_R / MU_M. Only when this condition is met will her total utility level remain constant as she consumes more rooms and fewer restaurant meals.

Economists have a special name for the ratio of the marginal utilities found in the right-hand side of Equation 11-6: it is called the **marginal rate of substitution,** or **MRS,** of rooms (the good on the horizontal axis) in place of restaurant meals (the good on the vertical axis). That's because as we slide down Ingrid's indifference curve, we are substituting more rooms for fewer restaurant meals in her consumption bundle. As we'll see shortly, the marginal rate of substitution plays an important role in finding the optimal consumption bundle.

> The **marginal rate of substitution**, or **MRS**, of good *R* in place of good *M* is equal to MU_R / MU_M, the ratio of the marginal utility of *R* to the marginal utility of *M*.

Recall that indifference curves get flatter as you move down them to the right. The reason, as we've just discussed, is diminishing marginal utility: as Ingrid consumes more housing and fewer restaurant meals, her marginal utility from housing falls and her marginal utility from restaurant meals rises. So her marginal rate of substitution, which is equal to minus the slope of her indifference curve, falls as she moves down the indifference curve.

The flattening of indifference curves as you slide down them to the right—which reflects the same logic as the principle of diminishing marginal utility—is known as the principle of **diminishing marginal rate of substitution.** It says that an individual who consumes only a little bit of good *A* and a lot of good *B* will be willing to trade off a lot of *B* in return for one more unit of *A*; an individual who already consumes a lot of *A* and not much *B* will be less willing to make that trade-off.

> The principle of **diminishing marginal rate of substitution** states that the more of good *R* a person consumes in proportion to good *M*, the less *M* he or she is willing to substitute for another unit of *R*.

We can illustrate this point by referring back to Figure 11-5. At point *V*, a bundle with a high proportion of restaurant meals to rooms, Ingrid is willing to forgo 10 restaurant meals in return for 1 room. But at point *Y*, a bundle with a low proportion of restaurant meals to rooms, she is willing to forgo only 2 restaurant meals in return for 1 room.

From this example we can see that, in Ingrid's utility function, rooms and restaurant meals possess the two additional properties that characterize ordinary goods. Ingrid requires additional rooms to compensate her for the loss of a meal, and vice versa; so her indifference curves for these two goods are downward sloping. And her indifference curves are convex: the slope of her indifference curve—*minus* the marginal rate of substitution—becomes flatter as we move down it. In fact, an indifference curve is convex only when it has diminishing marginal rate of substitution—these two conditions are equivalent.

With this information we can define **ordinary goods,** which account for the great majority of goods in any consumer's utility function. A pair of goods are ordinary goods in a consumer's utility function if they possess two properties: the consumer requires more of one good to compensate for less of the other, and the consumer experiences a diminishing marginal rate of substitution when substituting one good for the other.

Next we will see how to determine Ingrid's optimal consumption bundle using indifference curves.

Two goods, *R* and *M*, are **ordinary goods** in a consumer's utility function when (1) the consumer requires additional units of *R* to compensate for less *M*, and vice versa; and (2) the consumer experiences a diminishing marginal rate of substitution in substituting one good for another.

The Tangency Condition

Now let's put some of Ingrid's indifference curves on the same diagram as her budget line, to get an alternative way of representing her optimal consumption choice. Figure 11-6 shows Ingrid's budget line, *BL*, when her income is $2,400 per month, housing costs $150 per room each month, and restaurant meals cost $30 each. What is her optimal consumption bundle?

To answer this question, we show several of Ingrid's indifference curves: I_1, I_2, and I_3. Ingrid would like to achieve the total utility level represented by I_3, the highest of the three curves, but she cannot afford to because she is constrained by her income: no consumption bundle on her budget line yields that much total utility. But she shouldn't

Figure 11-6

The Optimal Consumption Bundle

The budget line, *BL*, shows Ingrid's possible consumption bundles given an income of $2,400 per month, when rooms cost $150 per month and restaurant meals cost $30 each. I_1, I_2, and I_3 are indifference curves. Consumption bundles such as *B* and *C* are not optimal because Ingrid can get onto a higher indifference curve. The optimal consumption bundle is at *A*, where the budget line is just tangent to the highest possible indifference curve. *>web...*

settle for the level of total utility generated by B, which lies on I_1: there are other bundles on her budget line, such as A, that clearly yield higher total utility than B.

In fact, A—a consumption bundle consisting of 8 rooms and 40 restaurant meals per month—is Ingrid's optimal consumption choice. The reason is that A lies on the highest indifference curve Ingrid can reach given her income.

At the optimal consumption bundle A, Ingrid's budget line just touches the relevant indifference curve—the budget line is *tangent* to the indifference curve. This **tangency condition** between the indifference curve and the budget line applies to the optimal consumption bundle when the indifference curves have the typical convex shape: *At the optimal consumption bundle, the budget line just touches the indifference curve.*

To see why, let's look more closely at how we know that a consumption bundle that *doesn't* satisfy the tangency condition can't be optimal. Re-examining Figure 11-6, we can see that the consumption bundles B and C are both affordable because they lie on the budget line. However, neither is optimal. Both of them lie on the indifference curve I_1, which cuts through the budget line at both points. But because I_1 cuts through the budget line, Ingrid can do better: she can move down the budget line from B or up the budget line from C, as indicated by the arrows. In each case this allows her to get onto a higher indifference curve, I_2, which increases her total utility.

Ingrid cannot, however, do any better than I_2: any other indifference curve either cuts through her budget line or doesn't touch it at all. And the bundle that allows her to achieve I_2 is, of course, her optimal consumption bundle, A.

Prices and the Marginal Rate of Substitution

Let's note one final point about the optimal consumption bundle shown in Figure 11-6. At point A, the slope of the indifference curve is just equal to the slope of the budget line.

From rearranging Equation 11-6 we know that the slope of the indifference curve at any point is equal to minus the marginal rate of substitution:

(11-7) Slope of indifference curve $= -MU_R/MU_M$

But what is the slope of the budget line? As in Chapter 10, let's use the symbol N to represent Ingrid's income. As we saw in Chapter 10, the horizontal intercept of her budget line—the number of rooms she can afford if she spends all her income on rooms—is N/P_R. The vertical intercept of her budget line—the number of restaurant meals she can afford if she spends all her income on restaurant meals—is N/P_M. So the slope of her budget line when R is measured on the horizontal axis and M is measured on the vertical axis is:

(11-8) Slope of budget line $= -\dfrac{N/P_M}{N/P_R} = -P_R/P_M$

The quantity P_R/P_M is known as the **relative price** of rooms in terms of restaurant meals (to distinguish it from an ordinary price in terms of dollars). Because giving up one room allows you to buy P_R/P_M quantity of restaurant meals, or 5 meals, we can interpret the relative price P_R/P_M as the rate at which a room trades for restaurant meals in the market.

Putting Equations 11-7 and 11-8 together, we arrive at the **relative price rule,** which says:

(11-9) *At the optimal consumption bundle:* $\dfrac{MU_R}{MU_M} = \dfrac{P_R}{P_M}$

That is, at the optimal consumption bundle, the marginal rate of substitution between any two goods is equal to the ratio of their prices. Or to put it in a more intuitive way, at Ingrid's optimal consumption bundle, the rate at which she would trade a room in exchange for having more restaurant meals along her indifference curve, MU_R/MU_M, is *equal* to the rate at which rooms are traded for restaurant meals in the market, P_R/P_M.

The **tangency condition** between the indifference curve and the budget line holds when the indifference curve and the budget line just touch. This condition determines the optimal consumption bundle when the indifference curves have the typical convex shape.

The **relative price** of good R in terms of good M is equal to P_R/P_M.

The **relative price rule** says that at the optimal consumption bundle, the marginal rate of substitution between two goods is equal to their relative price.

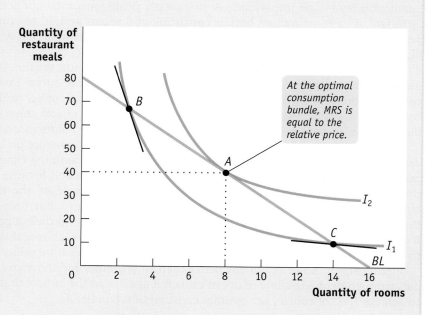

Figure 11-7

Understanding the Relative Price Rule

The *relative price* of rooms in terms of restaurant meals is equal to minus the slope of the budget line. The *marginal rate of substitution* of rooms in place of restaurant meals is equal to minus the slope of the indifference curve. The *relative price rule* says that at the optimal consumption bundle, the marginal rate of substitution must equal the relative price. This point can be demonstrated by considering what happens when the marginal rate of substitution is not equal to the relative price. At consumption bundle *B*, the marginal rate of substitution is larger than the relative price; Ingrid can increase her total utility by moving down her budget line, *BL*. At *C*, the marginal rate of substitution is smaller than the relative price, and Ingrid can increase her total utility by moving up the budget line. Only at *A*, where the relative price rule holds, is her total utility maximized, given her budget constraint.

At the optimal consumption bundle, MRS is equal to the relative price.

What would happen if this equality did not hold? We can see by examining Figure 11-7. There, at point *B*, the slope of the indifference curve, $-MU_R/MU_M$, is greater in absolute value than the slope of the budget line, $-P_R/P_M$. This means that, at *B*, Ingrid values an additional room in place of meals *more* than it costs her to buy an additional room and forgo some meals. As a result, Ingrid would be better off moving down her budget line toward *A*, consuming more rooms and fewer restaurant meals—and that *B* could not have been her optimal bundle! Likewise, at *C*, the slope of Ingrid's indifference curve is less than the slope of the budget line. The implication is that, at *C*, Ingrid values additional meals in place of a room *more* than it costs her to buy additional meals and forgo a room. Again, Ingrid would be made better off by moving along her budget line—consuming more restaurant meals and fewer rooms—until she reaches *A*, her optimal consumption bundle.

But suppose that we do the following transformation to Equation 11-9: divide both sides by P_R and multiply both by MU_M. Then the relative price rule becomes:

(11-10) *At the optimal consumption bundle:* $\dfrac{MU_R}{P_R} = \dfrac{MU_M}{P_M}$

which is the *optimal consumption rule*, from Chapter 10, Equation 10-5. So using either the optimal consumption rule (from Chapter 10) or the relative price rule (from this chapter), we find the same optimal consumption bundle.

Preferences and Choices

Now that we have seen how to represent optimal consumption choice in an indifference curve diagram, we can turn briefly to the relationship between consumer preferences and consumer choices.

When we say that two consumers have different preferences, we mean that they have different utility functions. This in turn means that they will have indifference curve maps with different shapes. And those different maps will translate into different consumption choices, even among consumers with the same income who face the same prices.

To see this, suppose that Ingrid's friend Lars also consumes only housing and restaurant meals. However, Lars has a stronger preference for restaurant meals and a

Figure 11-8

Differences in Preferences

Ingrid and Lars have different preferences, reflected in the different shapes of their indifference curve maps. So they will choose different consumption bundles even when they have the same possible choices. Both of them have an income of $2,400 per month and face prices of $30 per meal and $150 per room. Panel (a) shows Ingrid's consumption choice: 8 rooms and 40 restaurant meals. Panel (b) shows Lars's choice: even though he has the same budget line, he consumes fewer rooms and more restaurant meals.

(a) Ingrid's Preferences and Her Optimal Consumption Bundle

(b) Lars's Preferences and His Optimal Consumption Bundle

weaker preference for housing. This difference in preferences is shown in Figure 11-8, which shows *two* sets of indifference curves: panel (a) shows Ingrid's preferences and panel (b) shows Lars's preferences. Note the difference in their shapes.

Suppose, as before, that rooms cost $150 per month and restaurant meals cost $30. Let's also assume that both Ingrid and Lars have incomes of $2,400 per month, giving them identical budget lines. Nonetheless, because they have different preferences, they will make different consumption choices, as shown in Figure 11-8. Ingrid will choose 8 rooms and 40 restaurant meals; Lars will choose 4 rooms and 60 restaurant meals.

economics in action

Rats and Rational Choice

Let's admit it: the theory of consumer choice does not bear much resemblance to the way most of us think about our consumption decisions. The purpose of the theory is, however, to help economists think systematically about how a rational consumer would behave. The practical question is whether consumers actually behave rationally.

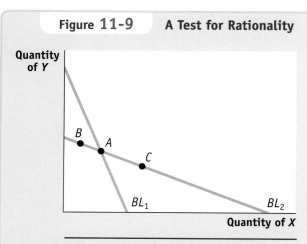

Figure 11-9 **A Test for Rationality**

Suppose that a consumer has the budget line BL_1 and chooses the consumption bundle A. If that consumer is now given a new budget line such as BL_2, it would be irrational to choose a bundle such as B; the consumer could have afforded that bundle before but chose A instead. A rational consumer would always at least stay at A or choose a new consumption bundle that was not affordable before, such as C. It's difficult to test people in this way—but it works for rats!

One simple test for rationality would look like the one shown in Figure 11-9. First, give a consumer the budget line labeled BL_1, and observe what consumption bundle the consumer chooses; the result is indicated in the figure as A. Then change the budget constraint, so that the new budget line is BL_2. Here the consumer is still able to afford the original consumption bundle A but also has some new choices available.

Would a rational consumer then choose a bundle like B? No. The reason is that B lies *inside* the original budget line—that is, when the budget line was BL_1, the consumer could have afforded it but chose A instead. It would be irrational to choose it now, when A is still available. So the new choice for a rational consumer must be either A or some bundle that has just become available, such as C.

It's hard to perform experiments like this on people—at any rate, it's not ethical (though more indirect experiments do suggest that people behave more or less rationally in their consumption choices). However, there is clear evidence that animals, such as rats, are able to make rational choices!

Economists have conducted experiments in which rats are presented with a "budget constraint"—a limited number of times per hour they can push either of two levers. One of the levers yields small cups of water; the other yields pellets of food. After the rat's choices have been observed, the budget constraint is changed by varying the number of lever pushes required to get each good. Sure enough, the rats satisfy the rule for rational choice.

If rats are rational, can people be far behind? ∎

< < < < < < < < < < < < < < < < < < < <

>> QUICK REVIEW

➤ The *marginal rate of substitution* (*MRS*) of R in place of M, MU_R/MU_M, is equal to minus the slope of the indifference curve.

➤ With *diminishing marginal rate of substitution*, a consumer requires more and more R to compensate for each forgone unit of M as the amount of R consumed grows relative to the amount of M consumed.

➤ Most goods are *ordinary goods*—goods with diminishing marginal rate of substitution.

➤ P_R/P_M, the *relative price* of good R in terms of good M, is equal to minus the slope of the budget line when R is measured on the horizontal axis and M is measured on the vertical axis. A utility-maximizing consumer chooses the bundle that satisfies the *tangency condition*: the indifference curve and the budget line just touch. So at the optimal consumption bundle, $MU_R/MU_M = P_R/P_M$, a condition called the *relative price rule*.

➤ Any two consumers will have different indifference curve maps because they have different preferences. Faced with the same budget and prices, they will make different consumption choices.

>> CHECK YOUR UNDERSTANDING 11-2

1. Lucinda and Kyle each consume 3 comic books and 6 video games. Lucinda's marginal rate of substitution of books in place of games is 2 and Kyle's is 5.

   a. For each person, find another consumption bundle that yields the same total utility as the current bundle. Who is less willing to trade games for books? In a diagram with books on the horizontal axis and games on the vertical axis, how would this be reflected in differences in the shapes of their indifference curves?

   b. Find the relative price of books in terms of games at which Lucinda's current bundle is optimal. Is Kyle's bundle optimal given this relative price? If not, how should Kyle rearrange his consumption?

Solutions appear at back of book.

Using Indifference Curves: Substitutes and Complements

Now that we've seen how to analyze consumer choice using indifference curves, we can get some payoffs from our new technique. First up is a new insight into the distinction between *substitutes* and *complements*.

Way back in Chapter 3 we pointed out that the price of one good often affects the demand for another but that the direction of this effect can go either way: a rise in the price of tea increases the demand for coffee, but a rise in the price of cream reduces the demand for coffee. Tea and coffee are substitutes; cream and coffee are complements.

But what determines whether two goods are substitutes or complements? It depends on the shape of a consumer's indifference curves. This relationship can be illustrated with two extreme cases: the cases of *perfect substitutes* and *perfect complements*.

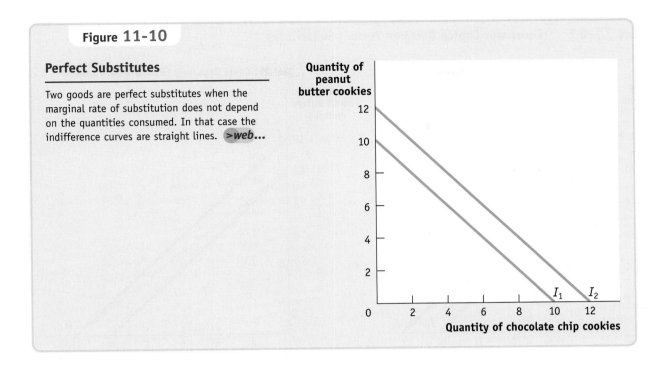

Figure 11-10

Perfect Substitutes

Two goods are perfect substitutes when the marginal rate of substitution does not depend on the quantities consumed. In that case the indifference curves are straight lines. **>web...**

Perfect Substitutes

Consider Cokie, who likes cookies. She isn't particular: it doesn't matter to her whether she has 3 peanut butter cookies and 7 chocolate chip cookies, or vice versa. What would her indifference curves between peanut butter and chocolate chip cookies look like?

The answer is that they would be straight lines like I_1 and I_2 in Figure 11-10. For example, I_1 shows that any combination of peanut butter cookies and chocolate chip cookies that adds up to 10 cookies yields Cokie the same utility.

A consumer whose indifference curves are straight lines is always willing to substitute the same amount of one good for one unit of the other, regardless of how much of either good he or she consumes. Cokie, for example, is always willing to accept one fewer peanut butter cookie in exchange for one more chocolate chip cookie, making her marginal rate of substitution *constant*.

When indifference curves are straight lines, we say that goods are **perfect substitutes.** When two goods are perfect substitutes, there is only one relative price at which consumers will be willing to purchase both goods; a slightly higher or lower relative price will cause consumers to buy only one of the two goods.

Figure 11-11 illustrates this point. The indifference curves are the same as those in Figure 11-10, but now we include Cokie's budget line, *BL*. In each panel we assume that Cokie has $12 to spend. In panel (a) we assume that chocolate chip cookies cost $1.20 and peanut butter cookies cost $1.00. Cokie's optimal consumption bundle is then at point *A*: she buys 12 peanut butter cookies and no chocolate chip cookies. In panel (b) the situation is reversed: chocolate chip cookies cost $1.00 and peanut butter cookies cost $1.20. In this case her optimal consumption is at point *B*, where she consumes only chocolate chip cookies.

Why does such a small change in the price cause Cokie to switch all her consumption from one good to the other? Because her marginal rate of substitution doesn't depend on the composition of her consumption bundle. If the relative price of chocolate chip cookies is more than the marginal rate of substitution, she buys only peanut butter cookies; if it is less, she buys only chocolate chip. And if the relative price of chocolate chip cookies is equal to the marginal rate of substitution, Cokie can maximize her utility by buying any bundle on her budget line. That is, she will be

Two goods are **perfect substitutes** if the marginal rate of substitution of one good in place of the other good is constant, regardless of how much of each an individual consumes.

Figure 11-11 Consumer Choice Between Perfect Substitutes

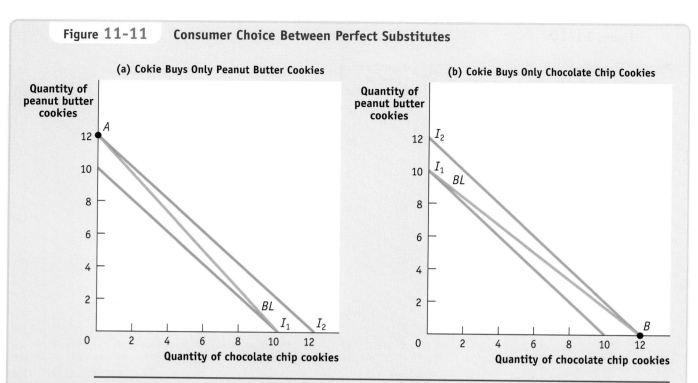

(a) Cokie Buys Only Peanut Butter Cookies

(b) Cokie Buys Only Chocolate Chip Cookies

When two goods are perfect substitutes, small price changes can lead to large changes in the consumption bundle. In panel (a), the relative price of chocolate chip cookies is slightly higher than the marginal rate of substitution of chocolate chip in place of peanut butter cookies; this is enough to induce Cokie to choose consumption bundle A, which consists entirely of peanut butter cookies. In panel (b), the relative price of chocolate chip cookies is slightly lower than the marginal rate of substitution; this induces Cokie to choose bundle B, consisting entirely of chocolate chip cookies.

equally happy with any combination of chocolate chip cookies and peanut butter cookies that she can afford. As a result, we cannot predict which particular bundle she will choose among all the bundles that lie on her budget line.

Perfect Complements

Two goods are **perfect complements** when a consumer wants to consume the goods in the same ratio regardless of their relative price.

The case of perfect substitutes represents one extreme form of consumer preferences; the case of perfect complements represents the other. Goods are **perfect complements** when a consumer wants to consume two goods in the same ratio, regardless of their relative price.

Suppose that Aaron likes cookies and milk—but only together. An extra cookie without an extra glass of milk yields no utility; neither does an extra glass of milk without another cookie. In this case, his indifference curves will form right angles, as shown in Figure 11-12.

To see why, consider the three bundles labeled A, B, and C. At B, on I_4, Aaron consumes 4 cookies and 4 glasses of milk. At A, directly above B, he consumes 4 cookies and 5 glasses of milk; but the extra glass of milk adds nothing to his utility. So A is on the same indifference curve as B, I_4. Similarly, at C he consumes 5 cookies and 4 glasses of milk, but this yields the same total utility as 4 cookies and 4 glasses of milk. So C is also on the same indifference curve, I_4.

Also shown in Figure 11-12 is a budget line that would allow Aaron to choose bundle B. The important point is that the slope of the budget line has no effect on his

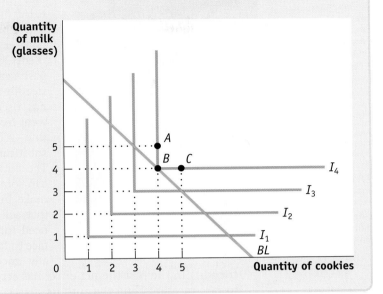

Figure 11-12

Perfect Complements

When two goods are perfect complements, a consumer wants to consume the goods in the same ratio regardless of their relative price. Indifference curves take the form of right angles. In this case, Aaron will choose to consume 4 glasses of milk and 4 cookies (bundle *B*) regardless of the slope of the budget line passing through *B*. The reason is that neither an additional glass of milk without an additional cookie (bundle *A*) nor an additional cookie without an additional glass of milk (bundle *C*) adds to his total utility.

>*web*...

relative consumption of cookies and milk. This means that he will always consume the two goods in the same proportions regardless of prices—which makes the goods perfect complements.

You may be wondering what happened to the marginal rate of substitution in Figure 11-12. That is, exactly what is Aaron's marginal rate of substitution between cookies and milk, given that he is unwilling to make any substitutions between them? The answer is that in the case of perfect complements, the marginal rate of substitution is *undefined* because an individual's preferences don't allow *any* substitution between goods.

Less Extreme Cases

There are real-world examples of pairs of goods that are very close to being perfect substitutes. For example, the list of ingredients on a package of Bisquick pancake mix says that it contains "soybean and/or cottonseed oil": the producer uses whichever is cheaper, since consumers can't tell the difference. There are other pairs of goods that are very close to being perfect complements—for example, cars and tires.

In most cases, however, the possibilities for substitution lie somewhere between these extremes. In some cases, as illustrated by the following Economics in Action, it isn't easy to be sure whether goods are substitutes or complements.

economics in action

Who Needs Fleshmeets?

In the information technology community, "fleshmeet" is slang for a face-to-face (sorry, F2F) meeting, as opposed to an electronic interaction. Clearly the term is meant to be a bit derogatory; actually getting together with someone in the same room is so, well, twentieth-century—a crude, old-fashioned way of doing business.

Video conferencing might cut your commute time, but there's really no substitute for being there.

But are electronic communication and face-to-face meetings really substitutes? In a 1996 paper titled "Information Technology and the Future of Cities," the economists Jess Gaspar and Edward Glaeser argued that they might well be complements. Gaspar and Glaeser pointed out that over the past century the cost of telecommunications has steadily fallen and the quality of the communication has risen: long-distance phone calls, for example, went from being impossible to being cheap and routine—yet activities you might have thought were substitutes, like business travel, continued to boom. The authors suggested that although a phone call can sometimes replace a business trip, the ability to make inexpensive phone calls also generates more interaction among businesses and therefore more need for communication—both on the phone and face to face. (Think of the way that cell phones actually encourage people to get together with their friends.) In the past the net effect has actually been to increase the demand for face-to-face meetings, and the authors suggested that newer technologies will continue to be complements rather than substitutes for direct personal interaction.

Some futurists believe that we are heading for a world in which people live wherever they please and interact via the Internet; in such a world not only business travel but also big cities, which exist mainly to facilitate face-to-face interaction, would lose much of their purpose. Gaspar and Glaeser argued, however, that this remains unlikely for the foreseeable future. ■

< < < < < < < < < < < < < < < < < < <

➤ When two goods are *perfect substitutes*, the marginal rate of substitution is constant and the indifference curves are straight lines.

➤ When two goods are *perfect complements*, the indifference curves form right angles and the marginal rate of substitution is undefined.

➤ The relationship between most goods for most people falls somewhere between these two extremes.

>>CHECK YOUR UNDERSTANDING 11-3

In each of the following cases, determine whether the two goods are perfect substitutes, perfect complements, or ordinary goods. Explain your answer, paying particular attention to the marginal rate of substitution of one good in place of the other good.

1. Sanjay cares only about the number of jelly beans he receives and not about whether they are banana-flavored or pineapple-flavored.

2. Hillary's marginal utility of cherry pie goes up as she has more scoops of vanilla ice cream to go with each slice. But she is willing to consume some cherry pie without any vanilla ice cream.

3. Despite repeated reductions in price, customers won't buy software programs made by Omnisoft Corporation unless the company also sells the computer operating system that enables a computer to read these software programs.

4. Darnell works part time at the campus bookstore. The manager has asked him to work additional hours this week. Darnell is willing to do additional work, but he finds that the more hours he has already worked, the less willing he is to work yet another hour. (*Hint:* Think of the goods in question as being income and leisure time.)

Solutions appear at back of book.

Prices, Income, and Demand

Let's now return to Ingrid's consumption choices. In the situation we've considered, her income was $2,400 per month, housing cost $150 per room, and restaurant meals cost $30 each. Her optimal consumption bundle, as seen in Figure 11-7 on page 264, contained 8 rooms and 40 restaurant meals.

Let's now ask how her consumption choice would change if either the rent per room or her income changed. As we'll see, we can put these pieces together to deepen our understanding of consumer demand.

Figure 11-13

Effects of a Price Increase on the Budget Line

An increase in the price of rooms, holding the price of restaurant meals constant, increases the relative price of rooms in terms of restaurant meals. As a result, Ingrid's original budget line, BL_1, rotates inward to BL_2. Her maximum possible purchase of restaurant meals is unchanged, but her maximum possible purchase of rooms is reduced. **>web...**

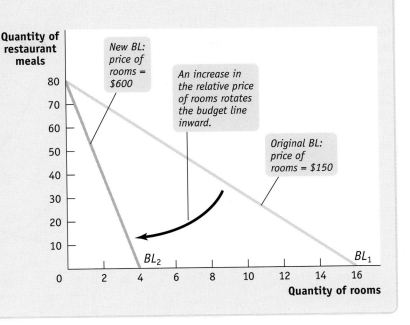

The Effects of a Price Increase

Suppose that for some reason there is a sharp increase in housing prices. Ingrid must now pay $600 per room instead of $150. Meanwhile, the price of restaurant meals and her income remain unchanged. How does this change affect her consumption choices?

When the price of rooms rises, the relative price of rooms in terms of restaurant meals rises; as a result, Ingrid's budget line changes (for the worse—but we'll get to that). She responds to that change by choosing a new consumption bundle.

Figure 11-13 shows Ingrid's original (BL_1) and new (BL_2) budget lines—again, under the assumption that her income remains constant at $2,400 per week. With housing costing $150 per room and a restaurant meal costing $30, her budget line, BL_1, intersected the horizontal axis at 16 rooms and the vertical axis at 80 restaurant meals. After the price of a room rises to $600 per room, the budget line, BL_2, still hits the vertical axis at 80 restaurant meals, but it hits the horizontal axis at only 4 rooms. Her budget line has rotated inward, reflecting the new, higher relative price of a room in terms of restaurant meals.

Figure 11-14, on page 272, shows how Ingrid responds to her new circumstances. Her original optimal consumption bundle consists of 8 rooms and 40 meals. After her budget line rotates in response to the change in relative price, she finds her new optimal consumption bundle by choosing the point on BL_2 that brings her to as high an indifference curve as possible. At the new optimal consumption bundle, she consumes fewer rooms and more restaurant meals than before: 1 room and 60 restaurant meals.

PITFALLS

"OTHER THINGS EQUAL," REVISITED

One of the biggest sources of confusion and error in economics—both in the classroom and in the real world—is failure to keep in mind the principle that all economic relationships are defined "other things equal." You may recall from Chapter 3 that a demand curve shows the effect of a good's price on its quantity demanded, *other things equal*—that is, all other things that influence demand being unchanged. Among those "other things" are the prices of other goods and the incomes of consumers.

To see how important it is to be clear about what is being held constant, let's compare two experiments. First, what happens to Ingrid's budget line if we increase the price of rooms, holding the price of restaurant meals and Ingrid's income constant? Second, what happens to her budget line if we increase the price of housing and *at the same time also increase the price of restaurant meals and Ingrid's income*?

We've just seen the effects of raising the price of rooms from $150 per month to $600. But now imagine that the price of restaurant meals also quadruples from $30 to $120 and that Ingrid's income quadruples from $2,400 to $9,600 per month. How does her budget line change?

The answer (check it yourself) is that quadrupling all three numbers—the price of rooms, the price of restaurant meals, and Ingrid's income—has *no* effect on her budget line. Because the relative price is unchanged, it won't affect her consumption choice. So the law of demand, which says that increasing the price of a good reduces the quantity demanded, is only an "other things equal" proposition; a higher price results in a lower quantity demanded, holding other prices and income constant.

Figure 11-14

Responding to a Price Increase

Ingrid responds to the higher relative price of rooms by choosing a new consumption bundle with fewer rooms and more restaurant meals. Her new bundle, *C*, contains 1 room instead of 8 and 60 restaurant meals instead of 40.

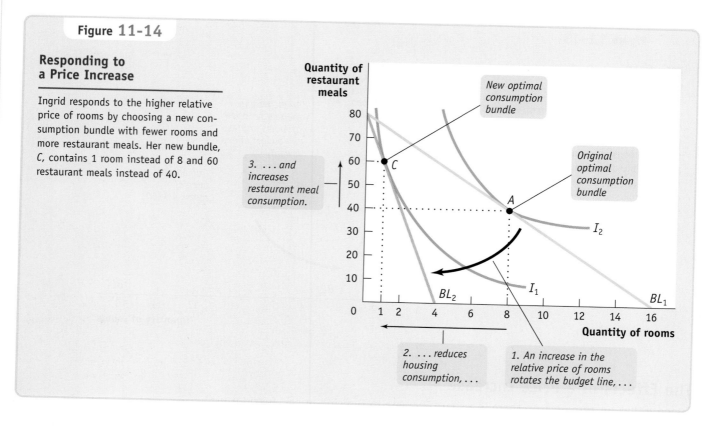

New optimal consumption bundle

Original optimal consumption bundle

3. . . . and increases restaurant meal consumption.

2. . . . reduces housing consumption, . . .

1. An increase in the relative price of rooms rotates the budget line, . . .

Why does Ingrid's consumption of rooms fall? Part—but only part—of the reason is that the rise in the price of rooms reduces her purchasing power, making her poorer. That is, the higher relative price of rooms rotates her budget line inward towards the origin, reducing her consumption possibilities and putting her on a lower indifference curve. In a sense, when she faces a higher price of housing, it's as if her income declined.

To understand this effect, and to see why it isn't the whole story, let's consider a different change in Ingrid's circumstances: a change in her income.

Income and Consumption

In Chapter 10 we learned about the individual demand curve, which shows how a consumer's consumption choice will change as the price of one good changes, holding income and the prices of other goods constant. That is, movement along the individual demand curve shows the substitution effect—how quantity consumed changes in response to changes in the *relative price* of the two goods. But we can also ask how the consumption choice will change if *income* changes, holding relative price constant.

In the previous section we considered an example in which a rise in the price of housing put Ingrid on a lower indifference curve. As we noted, it was as if her income had fallen. In this section we will consider how Ingrid responds to a direct change in income—that is, a change in her income level holding relative price constant. Figure 11-15 compares Ingrid's budget line and

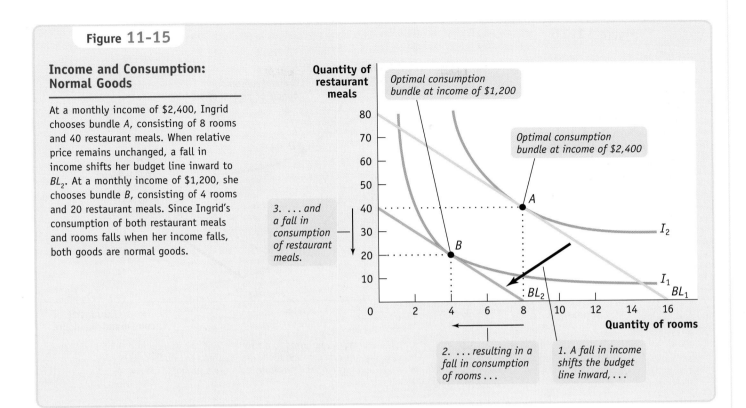

Figure 11-15

Income and Consumption: Normal Goods

At a monthly income of $2,400, Ingrid chooses bundle *A*, consisting of 8 rooms and 40 restaurant meals. When relative price remains unchanged, a fall in income shifts her budget line inward to BL_2. At a monthly income of $1,200, she chooses bundle *B*, consisting of 4 rooms and 20 restaurant meals. Since Ingrid's consumption of both restaurant meals and rooms falls when her income falls, both goods are normal goods.

optimal consumption choice with an income of $2,400 per month ($BL_1$) with her budget line and optimal consumption choice with an income of $1,200 per month ($BL_2$), while keeping prices at $150 per room and $30 per restaurant meal. *A* is Ingrid's optimal consumption bundle at an income of $2,400 and *B* is her optimal consumption bundle at an income of $1,200. In each case, her optimal consumption bundle is given by the point at which the budget line is tangent to the indifference curve. As you can see, at the lower income her budget line shifts *inward* compared to her budget line at the higher income but maintains the same slope because relative price has not changed. This means that she must reduce her consumption of either housing or restaurant meals, or both. As a result she is at a lower level of total utility, represented by a lower indifference curve.

As it turns out, Ingrid chooses to consume less of both goods when her income falls: as her income goes from $2,400 to $1,200, her consumption of housing falls from 8 to 4 rooms and her consumption of restaurant meals falls from 40 to 20. This is because in her utility function both goods are *normal goods*, as defined in Chapter 5: goods for which demand increases when income rises and for which demand decreases when income falls.

Although most goods are normal goods, we also pointed out in Chapter 5 that some goods are *inferior goods*, goods for which demand moves in the opposite direction to the change in income: demand decreases when income rises, and demand increases when income falls. An example might be second-hand furniture. Whether a good is an inferior good depends on the consumer's indifference curve map. Figure 11-16 on page 274 illustrates such a case, where second-hand furniture is measured on the horizontal axis and restaurant meals are measured on the vertical axis. Note that when Ingrid's income falls from $2,400 ($BL_1$) to $1,200 ($BL_2$), and her optimal consumption bundle goes from *D* to *E*, her consumption of second-hand furniture increases—implying that second-hand furniture is an inferior good. Simultaneously, her consumption of restaurant meals decreases—implying that restaurant meals are a normal good.

Figure 11-16

Income and Consumption: An Inferior Good

When Ingrid's income falls from $2,400 to $1,200, her optimal consumption bundle changes from D to E. Her consumption of second-hand furniture increases, implying that second-hand furniture is an inferior good. In contrast, her consumption of restaurant meals falls, implying that restaurant meals are a normal good.

>web...

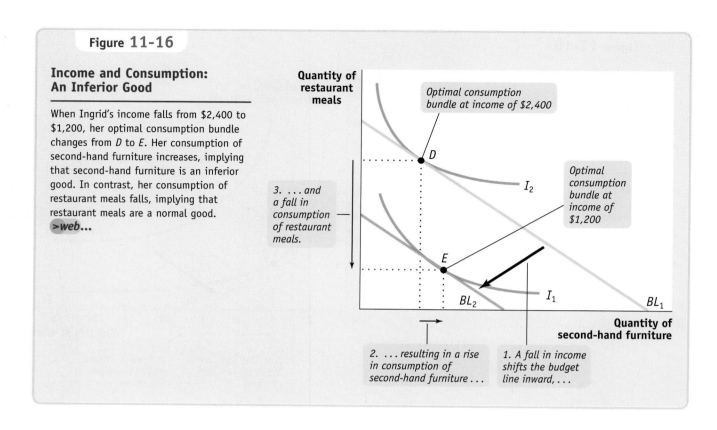

Quantity of restaurant meals

Optimal consumption bundle at income of $2,400

D

I_2

Optimal consumption bundle at income of $1,200

3. ...and a fall in consumption of restaurant meals.

E

BL_2 I_1 BL_1

Quantity of second-hand furniture

2. ...resulting in a rise in consumption of second-hand furniture...

1. A fall in income shifts the budget line inward, ...

Income and Substitution Effects

Now that we have examined the effects of a change in income, we can return to the issue of a change in price—and show in a more specific way that the effect of a higher price on demand has an income component.

Figure 11-17 shows, once again, Ingrid's original (BL_1) and new (BL_2) budget lines and consumption choices with a monthly income of $2,400. At a housing price of $150 per room, Ingrid chooses the consumption bundle at A; at a housing price of $600 per room, she chooses the consumption bundle at C.

Let's notice again what happens to Ingrid's budget line. It continues to hit the vertical axis at 80 restaurant meals; that is, if Ingrid were to spend all her income on restaurant meals, the increase in the price of housing would not affect her. But the new budget line hits the horizontal axis at only 4 rooms. So the budget line has rotated, *shifting inward* and *becoming steeper,* as a consequence of the rise in the relative price of rooms.

We already know what happens: Ingrid's consumption of housing falls from 8 rooms to 1 room. But the figure suggests that there are *two* reasons for the fall in Ingrid's housing consumption. One reason she consumes fewer rooms is that, because of the higher relative price of rooms, the opportunity cost of a room measured in restaurant meals—the quantity of restaurant meals she must give up to consume an additional room—has increased. This change in opportunity cost, which is reflected in the steeper slope of the budget line, gives her an incentive to substitute restaurant meals for rooms in her consumption.

But the other reason Ingrid consumes fewer rooms after their price increases is that the rise in the price of rooms makes her *poorer.* True, her money income hasn't changed. But she must pay more for rooms, and as a result her budget line has rotated inward. So she cannot reach the same level of total utility as before. That is why she ends up on a lower indifference curve.

In the real world these effects—an increase in the price of a good raises its opportunity cost, and also makes consumers poorer—usually go together. But in our

Figure 11-17

Income and Substitution Effects

The movement from Ingrid's original optimal consumption bundle when the price of rooms is $150, A, to her new optimal consumption bundle when the price of rooms is $600, C, can be decomposed into two parts. The movement from A to B—the movement along the original indifference curve, I_2, as relative price changes—is the pure substitution effect. It captures how her consumption would change if she were given a hypothetical increase in income that just compensates her for the increase in the price of rooms. The movement from B to C, the change in consumption when we remove that hypothetical income compensation, is the income effect of the price increase—how her consumption changes as a result of the fall in her purchasing power.

imagination we can separate them. In Chapter 10 we introduced the distinction between the *substitution effect* of a price change (the change in consumption that arises from the substitution of the good that is now relatively cheaper for the good that is now relatively more expensive) and the *income effect* (the change in consumption caused by the change in purchasing power arising from a price change). Now we can show these two effects more clearly.

To isolate the substitution effect, let's temporarily change the story about why Ingrid faces an increase in rent: it's not that housing has become more expensive, it's the fact that she has moved from Cincinnati to San Jose, where the rents are higher. But let's consider a hypothetical scenario—let's suppose momentarily that she earns more in San Jose and that the higher income is just enough to *compensate* her for the higher price of housing, so that her total utility is exactly the same as before.

Figure 11-17 shows her situation before and after the move. The bundle labeled A represents Ingrid's original consumption choice: 8 rooms, 40 restaurant meals. When she moves to San Jose, she faces a higher price of housing, so her budget line becomes steeper. But we have just assumed that her move increases her income by just enough to compensate for the higher price of housing—that is, just enough to let her reach the original indifference curve. So her new *hypothetical* optimal consumption bundle is at B, where the steeper dashed hypothetical budget line (BL_S) is just tangent to the original indifference curve (I_2). By assuming that we have compensated Ingrid for the loss in purchasing power due to the increase in the price of housing, we isolate the *pure substitution* effect of the change in relative price on her consumption.

At B, Ingrid's consumption bundle contains 2 rooms and 120 restaurant meals. This costs $4,800 (2 rooms at $600 each, and 120 meals at $30). So if Ingrid faces an increase in the price of housing from $150 to $600 per room, but also experiences a rise in her income from $2,400 to $4,800 per month, she ends up with the same level of total utility.

The movement from A to B is the pure substitution effect of the price change. It is the effect on Ingrid's consumption choice when we change the relative price of housing while keeping her total utility constant.

Now that we have isolated the substitution effect, we can bring back the income effect of the price change. That's easy: we just go back to the original story, in which Ingrid faces an increase in the price of housing *without* any rise in income. We already know that this leads her to *C* in Figure 11-17. But we can think of the move from *A* to *C* as taking place in two steps. First, Ingrid moves from *A* to *B,* the substitution effect of the change in relative price. Then we take away the extra income needed to keep her on the original indifference curve, causing her to move to *C.* The movement from *B* to *C* is the additional change in Ingrid's demand that results because the increase in housing prices actually does reduce her utility. So this is the income effect of the price change.

We can use Figure 11-17 to confirm that restaurant meals and rooms are both normal goods in Ingrid's preferences. For normal goods, the income effect and the substitution effect work in the same direction: a price increase induces a fall in quantity consumed by the substitution effect (the move from *A* to *B*) and a fall in quantity consumed by the income effect (the move from *B* to *C*). That's why demand curves for normal goods always slope downward.

What would have happened as a result of the increase in the price of housing if, instead of being a normal good, rooms had been an inferior good for Ingrid? First, the movement from *A* to *B* depicted in Figure 11-17, the substitution effect, would remain unchanged. But an income change causes quantity consumed to move in the opposite direction for an inferior good. So the movement from *B* to *C* shown in Figure 11-17, the income effect for a normal good, would no longer hold. Instead, the income effect for an inferior good would cause Ingrid's quantity of rooms consumed to *increase* from *B*—say, to a bundle consisting of 3 rooms and 20 restaurant meals.

In the end, the demand curves for inferior goods normally slope downward: if Ingrid consumes 3 rooms after the increase in the price of housing, it is still 5 fewer rooms than she consumed before. So although the income effect moves in the opposite direction of the substitution effect in the case of an inferior good, in this example the substitution effect is stronger than the income effect.

But what if there existed a type of inferior good in which the income effect is so strong that it dominates the substitution effect? Would a demand curve for that good then slope upward—that is, would quantity demanded increase when price increases? The answer is yes: you have encountered such a good already—it is called a *Giffen good,* and it was described in For Inquiring Minds on page 248 of Chapter 10. As we noted there, Giffen goods are rare creatures, but they cannot be ruled out.

Is the distinction between income and substitution effects important in practice? For analyzing the demand for goods, the answer is that it usually isn't that important. However, in Chapter 12 we'll discuss how individuals make decisions about how much of their labor to supply to employers. In that case income and substitution effects work in opposite directions, and the distinction between them becomes crucial.

economics in action

How Much Housing?

To illustrate the substitution effect, we offered a hypothetical example in which Ingrid moves from Cincinnati to San Jose, gaining a higher income but facing a higher price of housing. We made up the numbers for that example, but the real comparison between the two cities is not that different.

As we mentioned at the beginning of this chapter, the website bestplaces.net reports that household incomes are more than twice as high in San Jose as they are in Cincinnati but that housing is also far more expensive. The website also offers an estimate of the cost of living—that is, an estimate of how much income a family would need to achieve a "typical" level of utility. According to this estimate, the cost of living in San Jose is also about twice that in Cincinnati. So, on average, families live about as well in the two metropolitan areas.

But they don't live the same way because relative prices are different. Houses are somewhat smaller in San Jose, with fewer rooms and fewer square feet. Most noticeably, the great majority of new homes in the Cincinnati area are single-family houses on big lots; in San Jose, people are much more likely to live in townhouses or apartments. ∎

> > > > > > > > > > > > > > > > > > >

1. Sammy has $60 in weekly income, the current price of clams is $5 per pound, and the current price of potatoes is $1 per pound. Both are normal goods for Sammy. For each of the following situations, construct a diagram that, like Figure 11-17, shows the substitution effect alone and also shows the substitution and income effects together. Put the quantity of clams (in pounds) on the horizontal axis and the quantity of potatoes (in pounds) on the vertical axis.
   a. The price of a pound of clams falls from $5 to $2.50 and the price of a pound of potatoes remains at $1.
   b. The price of a pound of clams rises from $5 to $10 and the price of a pound of potatoes remains at $1.

Solutions appear at back of book.

• A LOOK AHEAD •

With the end of this chapter, our analysis of consumer behavior is complete. Chapters 8 and 9 present a complete analysis of producer behavior under perfect competition. Next we turn to the study of factor markets, which allocate factors of production such as physical capital and labor to various producers. In Chapter 12, we will see that producer and consumer behaviors are much like flip-sides of the same coin. For example, a producer decides whether or not to hire another worker based on a comparison of the worker's cost, the wage rate, to the value of what that worker can produce. Meanwhile, an individual decides whether or not to work based on a comparison of the wage rate to the value that he or she places on leisure. The study of factor markets initiates a higher level of analysis, a first step on the path toward understanding how the market coordinates economic activity in order to, in most cases, bring about the best outcome possible.

SUMMARY

1. Preferences can be represented by an **indifference curve map,** a series of **indifference curves.** Each curve shows all the consumption bundles that yield a given level of total utility. Indifference curves have two general properties: they never cross; and greater distance from the origin indicates higher total utility levels. The indifference curves of ordinary goods have two additional properties: they are downward sloping and are *convex* in shape.

2. The **marginal rate of substitution,** or **MRS,** of R in place of M—the rate at which a consumer is willing to substitute more R for less M—is equal to MU_R/MU_M and is also equal to minus the slope of the indifference curve. Convex indifference curves get flatter as you move to the right along the horizontal axis and steeper as you move upward along the vertical axis because of *diminishing marginal utility*: a consumer requires more and more units of

   R to substitute for a forgone unit of M as the amount of R consumed relative to the amount of M consumed rises.

3. Most goods are **ordinary goods,** goods for which a consumer requires additional units of some other good as compensation for giving up some of the good, and for which there is **diminishing marginal rate of substitution.**

4. A consumer maximizes utility by getting on the highest indifference curve his or her budget constraint allows. Using the **tangency condition,** the consumer chooses the bundle at which the indifference curve just touches the budget line. At this point, the **relative price** of R in terms of M, P_R/P_M (which is equal to minus the slope of the budget line when R is on the horizontal axis and M is on the vertical axis), is equal to the marginal rate of substitution of R in place of M, MU_R/MU_M (which is equal to minus the slope of the indifference curve). This gives us

the **relative price rule:** at the optimal consumption bundle, the relative price is equal to the marginal rate of substitution. Rearranging this equation also gives us the optimal consumption rule of Chapter 10. Two consumers faced with the same prices and income, but with different preferences and therefore different indifference curve maps, will make different consumption choices.

5. When the marginal rate of substitution is constant, two goods are **perfect substitutes** and indifference curves are straight lines: there is only one relative price at which the consumer is willing to purchase both goods. When a consumer wants to consume the two goods in the same ratio, regardless of the relative price, the goods are **perfect complements.** In this case the indifference curves form right angles and the marginal rate of substitution is undefined. The relationship between most goods for most people lies between these two extremes.

6. The effect of a change in relative price on consumer choice can be decomposed into the substitution effect and the income effect. The substitution effect is shown by the movement along the original indifference curve in response to the change in relative price, as the consumer substitutes more of the cheaper good in place of the more expensive good. The income effect is shown by a change to a new indifference curve, reflecting the fact that a change in a good's price alters the purchasing power of a given level of income.

7. The income and substitution effects work in the same direction for normal goods, ensuring that demand curves slope downward.

KEY TERMS

Indifference curve, p. 255
Indifference curve map, p. 256
Marginal rate of substitution (*MRS*), p. 261
Diminishing marginal rate of substitution, p. 261

Ordinary goods, p. 262
Tangency condition, p. 263
Relative price, p. 263

Relative price rule, p. 263
Perfect substitutes, p. 267
Perfect complements, p. 268

PROBLEMS

1. For each of the following situations, draw a diagram containing three of Isabella's indifference curves.

   a. For Isabella, cars and tires are perfect complements, but in a ratio of 1:4; that is, for each car, Isabella wants exactly four tires. Be sure to label and number the axes of your diagram. Place tires on the horizontal axis and cars on the vertical axis.

   b. Isabella gets utility only from her caffeine intake. She can consume Valley Dew or cola, and Valley Dew contains twice as much caffeine as cola. Be sure to label and number the axes of your diagram. Place cola on the horizontal axis and Valley Dew on the vertical axis.

   c. Isabella gets utility from consuming two goods: leisure time and income. Both have diminishing marginal utility. Be sure to label the axes of your diagram. Place leisure on the horizontal axis and income on the vertical axis.

   d. Isabella can consume two goods: skis and bindings. For each ski she wants exactly one binding. Be sure to label and number the axes of your diagram. Place bindings on the horizontal axis and skis on the vertical axis.

   e. Isabella gets utility from consuming soda. But she gets no utility from consuming water: any more, or any less, water leaves her utility level unchanged. Be sure to label the axes of your diagram. Place water on the horizontal axis and soda on the vertical axis.

2. Use the four properties of indifference curves for ordinary goods illustrated in Figure 11-4 to answer the following questions.

   a. Can you rank the following two bundles? If so, which property of indifference curves helps you rank them?

   Bundle *A*: 2 movie tickets and 3 cafeteria meals
   Bundle *B*: 4 movie tickets and 8 cafeteria meals

   b. Can you rank the following two bundles? If so, which property of indifference curves helps you rank them?

   Bundle *A*: 2 movie tickets and 3 cafeteria meals
   Bundle *B*: 4 movie tickets and 3 cafeteria meals

   c. Can you rank the following two bundles? If so, which property of indifference curves helps you rank them?

   Bundle *A*: 12 videos and 4 bags of chips
   Bundle *B*: 5 videos and 10 bags of chips

   d. Suppose you are indifferent between the following two bundles:

   Bundle *A*: 10 breakfasts and 4 dinners
   Bundle *B*: 4 breakfasts and 10 dinners

   Now compare bundle *A* and the following bundle:

   Bundle *C*: 7 breakfasts and 7 dinners

   Can you rank bundle *A* and bundle *C*? If so, which property of indifference curves helps you rank them? (*Hint:* It may help if you draw this, placing dinners on the horizontal axis and breakfasts on the vertical axis. And remember that breakfasts and dinners are ordinary goods.)

3. The four properties of indifference curves for ordinary goods illustrated in Figure 11-4 rule out certain indifference curves. Determine whether those general properties allow each of the following indifference curves. If not, state which of the general principles rules out the curves.

a.

b.

c.

d.

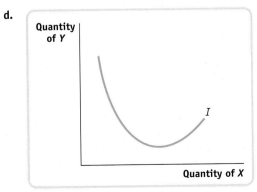

4. Kory has an income of $50, which she can spend on two goods: CDs and cups of hot chocolate. Both are normal goods for her; each CD costs $10, and each cup of hot chocolate costs $2. For each of the following situations, decide whether this is Kory's optimal consumption bundle. If not, what should Kory do to achieve her optimal consumption bundle?

   a. Kory is thinking about buying 4 CDs and 5 cups of hot chocolate. At that bundle, her marginal rate of substitution of CDs in place of hot chocolate is 1; that is, she would be just willing to exchange 1 fewer cup of hot chocolate for 1 more CD.

   b. Kory is thinking about buying 2 CDs and 15 cups of hot chocolate. Kory's marginal utility of the second CD is 25, and her marginal utility of the fifteenth cup of hot chocolate is 5.

   c. Kory is thinking about buying 1 CD and 10 cups of hot chocolate. At that bundle, her marginal rate of substitution of CDs in place of hot chocolate is 5; that is, she would be just willing to exchange 5 cups of hot chocolate for 1 CD.

5. Raul has 4 Cal Ripken and 2 Nolan Ryan baseball cards. The prices of these baseball cards are $24 for Cal and $12 for Nolan. Raul, however, would be willing to exchange 1 Cal card for 1 Nolan card.

   a. What is Raul's marginal rate of substitution of Cal Ripken in place of Nolan Ryan baseball cards?

   b. Can Raul buy and sell baseball cards to make himself better off? How?

   c. Suppose Raul has traded baseball cards and now no longer wants to make any more trades. What is his marginal rate of substitution of Cal Ripken in place of Nolan Ryan cards now?

6. Ralph and Lauren are talking about how much they like going to the gym and how much they like eating out at their favorite restaurant. A session at the gym costs the same as a meal at the restaurant. Ralph says that, for his current consumption of gym sessions and restaurant meals, he values one more meal twice as much as he values one more session at the gym. Lauren is studying economics, and she tells him that he cannot be choosing his optimal consumption bundle.

   a. Is Lauren right? Why or why not? Draw a diagram of Ralph's budget line and the indifference curve that he is on by making his current consumption choice. Place restaurant meals on the horizontal axis and gym sessions on the vertical axis.

   b. How should Ralph adjust his consumption so that it is optimal? Illustrate an optimal choice in your diagram.

7. Sabine can't tell the difference of Coke in place of Pepsi—the two taste exactly the same to her.

   a. What is Sabine's marginal rate of substitution of Coke in place of Pepsi?

   b. Draw a few of Sabine's indifference curves for Coke and Pepsi. Place Coke on the horizontal axis and Pepsi on the vertical axis.

   c. Sabine has $6 to spend on cola this week. Coke costs $1.50 per six-pack and Pepsi costs $1.00 per six-pack.

Draw Sabine's budget line for Coke and Pepsi on the same diagram.

d. What is Sabine's optimal consumption bundle? Show this on your diagram.

e. If the price of Coke and Pepsi is the same, what combination of Coke and Pepsi will Sabine buy?

8. For Norma, both nachos and salsa are normal goods. Although she likes consuming them together, they are not perfect complements (her indifference curves are convex-shaped, not right angle–shaped). The price of nachos rises, while the price of salsa remains unchanged.

   a. Can you determine definitively whether she consumes more or fewer nachos? Explain with a diagram, placing nachos on the horizontal axis and salsa on the vertical axis.

   b. Can you determine definitively whether she consumes more or less salsa? Explain with a diagram, placing nachos on the horizontal axis and salsa on the vertical axis.

9. Tyrone is a utility maximizer. His income is $100, which he can spend on cafeteria meals and on notepads. Each meal costs $5, and each notepad costs $2. At these prices Tyrone chooses to buy 16 cafeteria meals and 10 notepads.

   a. Draw a diagram that shows Tyrone's choice using an indifference curve and his budget line, placing notepads on the vertical axis and cafeteria meals on the horizontal axis. Label the indifference curve I_1 and the budget line BL_1.

   b. The price of notepads falls to $1; the price of cafeteria meals remains the same. On the same diagram, draw Tyrone's budget line with the new prices and label it BL_H.

   c. Lastly, Tyrone's income falls to $90. On the same diagram, draw his budget line with this income and the new prices and label it BL_2. Is he worse off, better off, or equally as well off with these new prices and lower income than compared to the original prices and higher income? (Hint: Determine whether Tyrone can afford to buy his original consumption bundle of 16 meals and 10 notepads with the lower income and new prices.) Illustrate your answer using an indifference curve and label it I_2.

   d. Give an intuitive explanation of your answer to (c).

10. Gus spends his income on gas for his car and food. The government raises the tax on gas, thereby raising the price of gas. But the government also lowers the income tax, thereby increasing Gus's income. And this rise in income is just enough to place Gus on the same indifference curve as the one he was on before the price of gas rose. Will Gus buy more, less, or the same amount of gas as before these changes?

11. Pam spends her money on bread and Spam, and her indifference curves obey the four properties of indifference curves for ordinary goods. Suppose that, for Pam, Spam is an inferior, but not a Giffen, good; bread is a normal good. Bread costs $2 per loaf, and Spam costs $2 per can. Pam has $20 to spend.

   a. Draw a diagram of Pam's budget line, placing Spam on the horizontal axis and bread on the vertical axis. Suppose

her optimal consumption bundle is 4 cans of Spam and 6 loaves of bread. Illustrate that bundle also, and draw the indifference curve on which it lies.

   b. The price of Spam falls to $1; the price of bread remains the same. Pam now buys 7 loaves of bread and 6 cans of Spam. Illustrate her new budget line and new optimal consumption bundle in your diagram. Also draw the indifference curve on which this bundle lies.

   c. In your diagram, show the income and substitution effects from this fall in the price of Spam. Remember that Spam is an inferior good for Pam.

12. Katya commutes to work. She can either use public transport or her own car. Her indifference curves obey the four properties of indifference curves for ordinary goods.

   a. Draw Katya's budget line with car travel on the vertical axis and public transport on the horizontal axis. Suppose that Katya consumes some of both goods. Draw an indifference curve that helps you illustrate that optimal consumption bundle.

   b. Now the price of public transport falls. Draw Katya's new budget line.

   c. For Katya, public transport is an inferior, but not a Giffen, good. Draw an indifference curve that illustrates her optimal consumption bundle after the price of public transport has fallen. Is Katya consuming more or less public transport?

   d. Show the income and substitution effects from this fall in the price of public transport.

13. For Crandall, cheese cubes and crackers are perfect complements: he wants to consume exactly 1 cheese cube with each cracker. He has $2.40 to spend on cheese and crackers. One cheese cube costs 20 cents, and 1 cracker costs 10 cents. Draw a diagram, with crackers on the horizontal axis and cheese cubes on the vertical axis, to answer the following questions.

   a. Which bundle will Crandall consume?

   b. The price of crackers rises to 20 cents. How many cheese cubes and how many crackers will Crandall consume?

   c. In your diagram, show the income and substitution effects from this price rise.

14. Carmen consumes nothing but cafeteria meals and CDs. Her indifference curves exhibit the four general properties of indifference curves. Cafeteria meals cost $5 each, and CDs cost $10. Carmen has $50 to spend.

   a. Draw Carmen's budget line and an indifference curve that illustrates her optimal consumption bundle. Place cafeteria meals on the horizontal axis and CDs on the vertical axis. You do not have enough information to know the specific tangency point, so choose one arbitrarily.

   b. Now Carmen's income rises to $100. Draw her new budget line on the same diagram, as well as an indifference curve that illustrates her optimal consumption bundle. Assume that cafeteria meals are an inferior good.

   c. Can you draw an indifference curve showing that cafeteria meals and CDs are both inferior goods?

>> Factor Markets and the Distribution of Income

THE VALUE OF A DEGREE

DOES HIGHER EDUCATION PAY? YES, IT does: in the modern economy, employers are willing to pay a premium for workers with more education. And the size of that premium has increased a lot over the last few decades. Back in 1973 workers with advanced degrees, such as law degrees or MBAs, earned only 76 percent more than those who had only graduated from high school. By 2003 the premium for an advanced degree had risen to 120 percent.

Who decided that the wages of workers with advanced degrees would rise so much compared with those of high school grads? The answer, of course, is that nobody decided it. Wage rates are prices, the prices of different kinds of labor; and they are decided, like other prices, by supply and demand.

Still, there is a difference between the wage rate of high school grads and the price of used textbooks: the wage rate isn't the price of a *good,* it's the price of a *factor of production.* And although markets for factors of production are in many ways similar to those

for goods, there are also some important differences.

In this chapter, we examine *factor markets,* the markets in which factors of production such as labor are traded. Factor markets, like goods markets, play a crucial role in the economy: they allocate productive resources to producers and help ensure that those resources are used efficiently.

This chapter begins by describing the major factors of production. Then we consider the demand for factors of production, which leads us to a crucial insight: the *marginal productivity theory of income distribution.*

If you've ever had doubts about attending college, consider this: factory workers with only high school degrees will make much less than college grads. The present discounted value of the difference in lifetime earnings is as much as $300,000.

We then consider some challenges to the marginal productivity theory. The final section of the chapter looks at the supply of the most important factor, labor.

What you will learn in this chapter:

► How factors of production—resources like land, labor, and both **physical capital** and **human capital**—are traded in factor markets, determining the **factor distribution of income**

► How the demand for factors leads to the **marginal productivity theory of income distribution**

► An understanding of the sources of wage disparities and the role of discrimination

► The way in which a worker's decision about **time allocation** gives rise to labor supply

The Economy's Factors of Production

You may recall that we defined a *factor of production* in Chapter 2 in the context of the circular-flow model; it is any resource that is used by firms to produce *goods* and *services,* items that are consumed by households. Factors of production are bought and sold in *factor markets,* and the prices in factor markets are known as *factor prices.*

What are these factors of production, and why do factor prices matter?

The Factors of Production

Physical capital—often referred to simply as "capital"—consists of manufactured resources such as buildings and machines.

Human capital is the improvement in labor created by education and knowledge that is embodied in the workforce.

As we learned in Chapter 2, economists divide factors of production into four principal classes: land, labor, physical capital, and human capital. *Land* is a resource provided by nature; *labor* is the work done by human beings.

In Chapter 7 we defined *capital*; it is the assets that are used by a firm in producing its output. There are two broad types of capital. **Physical capital**—often referred to simply as "capital"—consists of manufactured resources such as buildings and machines.

In the modern economy, **human capital,** the improvement in labor created by education and knowledge, and embodied in the workforce, is at least equally significant. The importance of human capital has been greatly increased by the progress of technology, which has made a high level of technical sophistication essential to many jobs—one cause of the increased premium paid for workers with advanced degrees.

Why Factor Prices Matter: The Allocation of Resources

Factor markets and factor prices play a key role in one of the most important processes that must take place in any economy: the allocation of resources among producers.

Consider the example of Florida in 1992, in the aftermath of Hurricane Andrew, which was the costliest hurricane to hit the U.S. mainland to date. The state had an urgent need for workers in the building trades—carpenters, plumbers, and so on—to repair or replace damaged homes and businesses. What ensured that those needed workers actually came? The high demand for construction workers in Florida drove up their wages, which led large numbers of workers with the right skills to move temporarily to the state to do the work. In other words, the market for a factor of production—construction workers—allocated that factor of production to where it was needed.

In this sense factor markets are similar to goods markets, which allocate goods among consumers. But there are two features that make factor markets somewhat special. Unlike in a goods market, demand in a factor market is what we call *derived demand.* That is, demand for the factor is derived from the firm's output choice. The second feature is that factor markets are where most of us get the largest shares of our income (government transfers being the next largest source of income in the economy).

Factor Incomes and the Distribution of Income

Most American families get most of their income in the form of wages and salaries—that is, they get their income by selling labor. Some people, however, get most of their income from physical capital: when you own stock in a company, what you really own is a share of that company's physical capital. And some people get much of their income from the rents on land they own.

Obviously, then, the prices of factors of production have a major impact on how the economic "pie" is sliced among different groups. For example, a higher wage rate, other things equal, means that more of the income in the economy goes to people who derive their income from labor, as opposed to capital. Economists refer to how the economic pie is sliced as the "distribution of income."

Specifically, factor prices determine the **factor distribution of income**—how the total income of the economy is divided among labor, land, and capital.

PITFALLS

WHAT IS A FACTOR, ANYWAY?

Imagine a business that produces shirts. The business will make use of workers and machines—that is, of labor and capital. But it will also use other inputs, such as electricity and cloth. Are all of these inputs factors of production? No: labor and capital are factors of production, but cloth and electricity are not.

The key distinction is that a factor of production earns income from the selling of its services over and over again but an input cannot. For example, a worker earns income over time from repeatedly selling his or her efforts; the owner of a machine earns income over time from repeatedly selling the use of that machine. So a factor of production, such as labor and capital, represents an enduring source of income. An input like electricity or cloth, however, is used up in the production process. Once exhausted, it cannot be a source of future income for its owner.

The **factor distribution of income** is the division of total income among labor, land, and capital.

THE FACTOR DISTRIBUTION OF INCOME AND SOCIAL CHANGE IN THE INDUSTRIAL REVOLUTION

Have you read any novels by Jane Austen? How about Charles Dickens? If you've read both, you probably noticed that they seem to be describing quite different societies. Austen's novels, set around 1800, describe a world in which the leaders of society are land-owning aristocrats. Dickens, writing about 50 years later, describes a world in which businessmen, especially factory owners, seem to be in control.

This literary shift reflects a dramatic transformation in the factor distribution of income. The Industrial Revolution, which took place between the late

By altering how people lived and worked, the Industrial Revolution led to huge economic and social changes.

eighteenth century and the middle of the nineteenth century, changed England from a mainly agricultural country, in which land earned a fairly substantial share of income, to an urbanized and industrial one, in which land rents were dwarfed by capital income. Recent estimates by the economist Nancy Stokey show that between 1780 and 1850 the share of land represented in national income fell from 20 to 9 percent, while the share represented by capital rose from 35 to 44 percent. That shift changed everything—even literature.

As the following Economics in Action explains, the factor distribution of income in the United States has been quite stable over the past few decades. In other times and places, however, large changes have taken place in the factor distribution. One notable example: during the Industrial Revolution, the share of total income earned by land owners fell sharply, while that earned by capital owners rose. As explained in For Inquiring Minds, this shift had a profound effect on society.

economics in action

The Factor Distribution of Income in the United States

When we talk about the factor distribution of income, what are we talking about in practice?

In the United States, as in all advanced economies, payments to labor account for most of the economy's total income. Figure 12-1 shows the factor distribution of income in the United States in 2003: in that year, 71 percent of total income in the economy took the form of "compensation of employees"—a number that includes both

Figure 12-1

Factor Distribution of Income in the United States in 2003

In 2003, compensation of employees accounted for most income earned in the United States—71 percent of the total. Most of the remainder—consisting of earnings paid in the form of interest, corporate profits, and rent—went to owners of physical capital. Finally, proprietors' income—9 percent of the total—went to individual owners of businesses as compensation for their labor and capital expended in their businesses.

Source: Bureau of Economic Analysis.

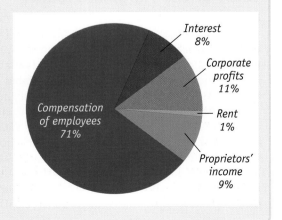

wages and benefits such as health insurance. This number has been quite stable over the long run; roughly 30 years earlier, in 1971, compensation of employees was very similar, at 73 percent of total income.

However, measured wages and benefits don't capture the full income of "labor" because a significant fraction of total income in the United States (usually between 8 and 9 percent) is "proprietors' income"—the earnings of people who own their own businesses. Part of that income should be considered wages these business owners pay themselves. So the true share of labor in the economy is probably a few percentage points higher than the "compensation of employees" share.

But much of what we call compensation of employees is really a return on human capital. A surgeon isn't just supplying the services of a pair of ordinary hands (at least the patient hopes not!): that individual is also supplying the result of many years and hundreds of thousands of dollars invested in training and experience. We can't directly measure what fraction of wages is really a payment for education and training, but many economists believe that human capital has become *the* most important factor of production in modern economies. ∎

< < < < < < < < < < < < < < < < < <

>> CHECK YOUR UNDERSTANDING 12-1

1. Suppose that the government places price controls on the market for college professors, imposing a wage that is lower than the market wage. Describe the effect of this policy on the production of college degrees. What sectors of the economy do you think will be adversely affected by this policy? What sectors of the economy might benefit?

Solutions appear at back of book.

Marginal Productivity and Factor Demand

All economic decisions are about comparing costs and benefits—and usually about comparing marginal costs and marginal benefits. This goes both for a consumer, deciding whether to buy another pound of fried clams, and for a producer, deciding whether to hire an additional worker.

Although there are some important exceptions, most factor markets in the modern American economy are perfectly competitive, meaning that buyers and sellers of a given factor are price-takers. And in a competitive labor market, it's clear how to define an employer's marginal cost of a worker: it is simply the worker's wage rate. But what is the marginal benefit of that worker? To answer that question, we return to a concept first introduced in Chapter 8: the *production function,* which relates inputs to output. And as in Chapter 9, we will assume throughout this chapter that all producers are price-takers—they operate in a perfectly competitive industry.

Value of the Marginal Product

Figure 12-2 reproduces Figures 8-1 and 8-2, which showed the production function for wheat on George and Martha's farm. Panel (a) uses the total product curve to show how total wheat production depends on the number of workers employed on the farm; panel (b) shows how the *marginal product* of labor, the increase in output from employing one more worker, depends on the number of workers employed. Table 12-1, which reproduces the table in Figure 8-1, shows the numbers behind the figure.

Assume that George and Martha want to maximize their profit, that workers must be paid $200 each, and that wheat sells for $20 per bushel. What is their optimal number of workers? That is, how many workers should they employ to maximize profit?

In Chapters 8 and 9 we showed how to answer this question in several steps. In Chapter 8 we used information from the producer's production function to derive the firm's total cost and its marginal cost. And in Chapter 9 we derived the *price-taking firm's optimal output rule:* a price-taking firm's profit is maximized by producing the

Figure 12-2   The Production Function for George and Martha's Farm

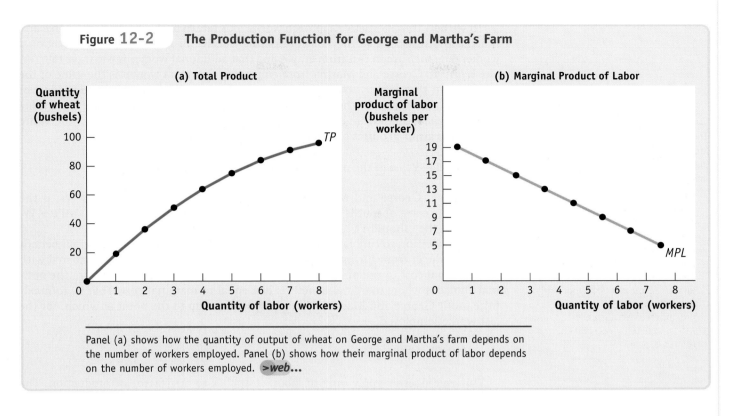

Panel (a) shows how the quantity of output of wheat on George and Martha's farm depends on the number of workers employed. Panel (b) shows how their marginal product of labor depends on the number of workers employed. **>web...**

quantity of output at which the marginal cost of the last unit produced is equal to the market price. Having determined the optimal quantity of output, we can go back to the production function and find the optimal number of workers—it is simply the number of workers needed to produce the optimal quantity of output.

There is, however, another way to find the number of workers that maximizes a producer's profit. We can go directly to the question of what level of employment maximizes profit. This alternative approach is equivalent to the approach we outlined in the preceding paragraph—it's just a different way of looking at the same thing, which gives us more insight into the demand for factors as opposed to the supply of goods.

TABLE 12-1

Employment and Output for George and Martha's Farm

Quantity of labor L (workers)	Quantity of wheat Q (bushels)	Marginal product of labor $MPL = \dfrac{\Delta Q}{\Delta L}$ (bushels per worker)
0	0	
		19
1	19	
		17
2	36	
		15
3	51	
		13
4	64	
		11
5	75	
		9
6	84	
		7
7	91	
		5
8	96	

To see how this alternative approach works, let's return to the example of George and Martha and suppose that they are considering whether or not to employ an additional worker. The increase in *cost* from employing that additional worker is the wage rate, *W*. The *benefit* to George and Martha from employing that extra worker is the value of the extra output that worker can produce. What is this value? It is the marginal product of labor, *MPL*, multiplied by the price per unit of output, *P*. This quantity—the extra value of output that comes from employing one more unit of labor—is known as the **value of the marginal product** of labor, or *VMPL*:

> The **value of the marginal product** of a factor is the value of the additional output generated by employing one more unit of that factor.

(12-1)   Value of the marginal product of labor = $VMPL = P \times MPL$

So should George and Martha hire that extra worker? The answer is yes, if the value of the extra output is more than the cost of the worker—that is, if $VMPL > W$. Otherwise they shouldn't hire that worker.

So the decision to hire labor is a marginal decision, in which the marginal benefit to the producer from hiring an additional worker (*VMPL*) should be compared with the marginal cost to the producer (*W*). And as with any marginal decision, the optimal choice is where marginal benefit is just equal to marginal cost. That is, to maximize profit George and Martha will employ workers up to the point at which, for the last worker employed,

(12-2) $VMPL = W$

This rule doesn't apply only to labor; it applies to any factor of production. The value of the marginal product of any factor is its marginal product times the price of the good it produces. The general rule is that *a profit-maximizing price-taking producer employs each factor of production up to the point at which the value of the marginal product of the last unit of the factor employed is equal to that factor's price.*

It's important to realize that this rule doesn't conflict with our analysis in Chapters 8 and 9. There we saw that a profit-maximizing producer of a good chooses the level of output at which the price of that good is equal to the marginal cost of production. It's just a different way of looking at the same rule. If the level of output is chosen so that price equals marginal cost, then it is also true that at that output level the value of the marginal product of labor will equal the wage rate.

Now let's look more closely at why choosing the level of employment at which the value of the marginal product of the last worker employed is equal to the wage rate works—and at how it helps us understand factor demand.

Value of the Marginal Product and Factor Demand

> The **value of the marginal product curve** of a factor shows how the value of the marginal product of that factor depends on the quantity of the factor employed.

Table 12-2 calculates the value of the marginal product of labor on George and Martha's farm, on the assumption that the price of wheat is $20 per bushel. In Figure 12-3 the horizontal axis shows the number of workers employed; the vertical axis measures the value of the marginal product of the last worker employed *and* the wage rate. The curve shown is the **value of the marginal product curve** of labor. This curve, like the marginal product of labor curve, is downward sloping due to diminishing returns to labor in production. That is, the value of the marginal product of each worker is less than that of the preceding worker, because the marginal product of each worker is less than that of the preceding worker.

We have just seen that to maximize profit, George and Martha must hire workers up to the point at which the wage rate is equal to the value of the marginal product of the last worker employed. Let's use the example to see that this principle really works.

Assume that George and Martha currently employ 3 workers and that workers must be paid the market wage rate of $200. Should they employ an additional worker?

TABLE 12-2

Value of the Marginal Product of Labor for George and Martha's Farm

Quantity of labor L (workers)	Marginal product of labor MPL (bushels per worker)	Value of the marginal product of labor VMPL = P × MPL
0		
	19	$380
1		
	17	340
2		
	15	300
3		
	13	260
4		
	11	220
5		
	9	180
6		
	7	140
7		
	5	100
8		

Looking at Table 12-2, we see that if George and Martha currently employ 3 workers, the value of the marginal product of an additional worker is $260. So if they employ an additional worker, they will increase the value of their production by $260 but increase their cost by only $200, yielding an increase of $60 in the farm's profit. In fact, a producer can always increase profit by employing one more unit of a factor of production as long as the value of the marginal product produced by that unit exceeds the factor price.

Figure 12-3

The Value of the Marginal Product Curve

This curve shows how the value of the marginal product of labor depends on the number of workers employed. It is downward sloping due to diminishing returns to labor in production. To maximize profit, George and Martha choose the level of employment at which the value of the marginal product of labor is equal to the market wage rate. For example, at a wage rate of $200 the profit-maximizing level of employment is 5 workers, shown by point A. The value of the marginal product curve for a factor is the producer's individual demand curve for that factor. >web...

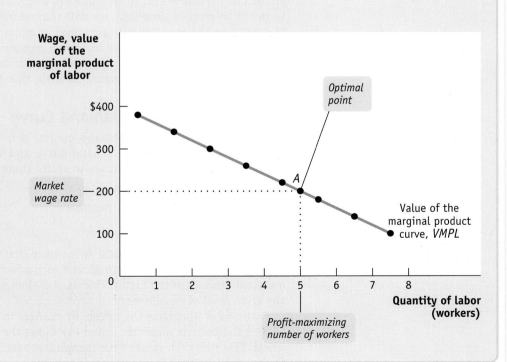

Alternatively, suppose that George and Martha employ 8 workers. By reducing the number of workers to 7, they can save $200 in wages. Meanwhile, the value of the marginal product of that last worker was only $100. So, by reducing employment by one worker they can increase profit by $100. A producer can always increase profit by employing one less unit of a factor of production as long as the value of the marginal product produced by that unit is less than the factor price.

Using this method, we can see from Table 12-2 that the profit-maximizing employment level is 5 workers given a wage rate of $200. The value of the marginal product of the 5th worker is $220, so adding that worker results in $20 of additional profit. But George and Martha should not hire more than 5 workers: the value of the marginal product of the 6th worker is only $180, $20 less than the cost of that worker. So, to maximize profit, George and Martha should employ workers up to but not beyond the point at which the value of the marginal product of the last worker employed is equal to the wage rate.

Now look again at the value of the marginal product curve in Figure 12-3. To determine the profit-maximizing level of employment, we set the price of labor—$200 per worker—equal to the value of the marginal product of labor. This means that the profit-maximizing level of employment is at point *A*, corresponding to an employment level of 5 workers. If the price of labor were higher or lower, we would simply move up or down the curve.

In this example, George and Martha have a small farm in which the potential employment level varies from 0 to 8 workers, and they hire workers up to the point where the value of the marginal product of the last worker is no less than the wage rate. Suppose, however, that the firm in question is large and has the potential of hiring many workers. When there are many employees, the value of the marginal product of labor falls only slightly when an additional worker is employed. As a result, there will be some worker whose value of the marginal product almost exactly equals the wage rate. (In keeping with the George and Martha example, this means that some worker has a value of the marginal product of approximately $200.) In this case, the firm maximizes profit by choosing a level of employment at which the value of the marginal product of the last worker hired *equals* (to a very good approximation) the wage rate.

In the interest of simplicity, we will assume from now on that firms use this rule to determine the profit-maximizing level of employment. *This means that the value of the marginal product curve is the individual producer's labor demand curve.* And in general, a producer's value of the marginal product curve for any factor of production is that producer's individual demand curve for that factor of production.

Shifts of the Factor Demand Curve

As in the case of ordinary demand curves, it is important to distinguish between movements along the factor demand curve and *shifts* of the factor demand curve. What causes factor demand curves to shift? There are three main causes:

- Changes in prices of goods
- Changes in supply of other factors
- Changes in technology

Changes in Prices of Goods Remember that factor demand is derived demand: if the price of the good that is produced with a factor changes, so will the value of the marginal product of the factor. That is, if P changes, $VMPL = P \times MPL$ will change at any given level of employment.

Figure 12-4 illustrates the effects of changes in the price of wheat, assuming that $200 is the current wage rate. Panel (a) shows the effect of an *increase* in the price of wheat. This shifts the value of the marginal product curve upward, because *VMPL* rises at any given level of employment. If the wage rate remains unchanged at $200, the optimal point moves from *A* to *B*: the profit-maximizing level of employment rises.

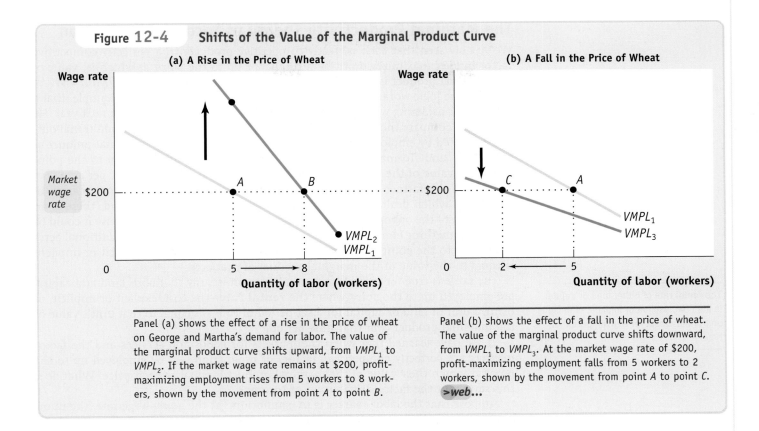

Figure 12-4   Shifts of the Value of the Marginal Product Curve

(a) A Rise in the Price of Wheat

(b) A Fall in the Price of Wheat

Panel (a) shows the effect of a rise in the price of wheat on George and Martha's demand for labor. The value of the marginal product curve shifts upward, from $VMPL_1$ to $VMPL_2$. If the market wage rate remains at $200, profit-maximizing employment rises from 5 workers to 8 workers, shown by the movement from point A to point B.

Panel (b) shows the effect of a fall in the price of wheat. The value of the marginal product curve shifts downward, from $VMPL_1$ to $VMPL_3$. At the market wage rate of $200, profit-maximizing employment falls from 5 workers to 2 workers, shown by the movement from point A to point C. >web...

Panel (b) shows the effect of a *decrease* in the price of wheat. This shifts the value of the marginal product curve downward. If the wage rate remains unchanged at $200, the optimal point moves from A to C: the profit-maximizing level of employment falls.

Changes in Supply of Other Factors Suppose that George and Martha acquire more land to cultivate—say, by clearing a woodland on their property. Each worker could then produce more wheat because each one would have more land to work with. So the marginal product of labor on the farm would rise at any given level of employment. This would have the same effect as an increase in the price of wheat, which we have already seen in panel (a) of Figure 12-4: the value of the marginal product curve would shift upward, and at any given wage rate the profit-maximizing level of employment would increase. Similarly, if George and Martha cultivate less land, the marginal product of labor at any given employment level would fall—each worker would produce less wheat because of having less land to work with. As a result, the value of the marginal product curve would shift downward—as in panel (b) of Figure 12-4—and the profit-maximizing level of employment would decrease.

Changes in Technology In general, the effect of technological progress on the demand for any given factor can go either way: improved technology can either increase or decrease the demand for a given factor of production.

How can technological progress decrease factor demand? Consider horses, which were once an important factor of production. The development of substitutes for horse power, such as automobiles and tractors, greatly reduced the demand for horses.

The usual effect of technological progress, however, is to increase factor demand. In particular, although there have been persistent fears that machinery would reduce the demand for labor, over the long run the U.S. economy has seen both large wage increases and large increases in employment, suggesting that technological progress has greatly increased labor demand.

The Marginal Productivity Theory of Income Distribution

We've now seen that each perfectly competitive producer in a perfectly competitive factor market maximizes profit by hiring labor up to the point at which its value of the marginal product is equal to its price—that is, to the point where $VMPL = W$.

The same logic works for other factors of production. Suppose, for example, that a farmer is considering whether to rent an additional acre of land for the next year. He or she will compare the cost of renting that acre with the value of the additional output generated by employing an additional acre—the value of the marginal product of an acre of land. To maximize profit, the farmer must employ land up to the point where the value of the marginal product of an acre is equal to the rent per acre.

What if the farmer already owns the land? We already saw the answer back in Chapter 7, which dealt with economic decisions: even if you own land, there is an implicit cost—the opportunity cost—of using it for a given activity, because it could be used for something else. So a profit-maximizing producer will employ additional acres of land up to the point where the cost of the last acre employed, explicit or implicit, is equal to the value of the marginal product of that acre.

The same is true for capital. In general, economists say that both land and capital are employed up to the point where the **rental rate**—the cost, explicit or implicit, of using a unit of land or capital for a set period of time—is equal to that unit's value of the marginal product over that time period.

So we have learned that when the markets for goods and services and the factor markets are perfectly competitive, factors of production will be employed up to the point at which their value of the marginal product is equal to their price. What does this say about the factor distribution of income?

Suppose that the labor market is in equilibrium: at the going wage rate, the number of workers that producers want to employ is equal to the number of workers willing to work. Then all employers will pay the *same* wage rate, and *each* employer, whatever he or she is producing, will employ labor up to the point where the value of the marginal product of one more worker is equal to that wage rate.

This situation is illustrated in Figure 12-5, which shows the value of the marginal product curves of two producers—Farmer Jones, who produces wheat, and Farmer

---

The **rental rate** of either land or capital is the cost, explicit or implicit, of using a unit of that asset for a given period of time.

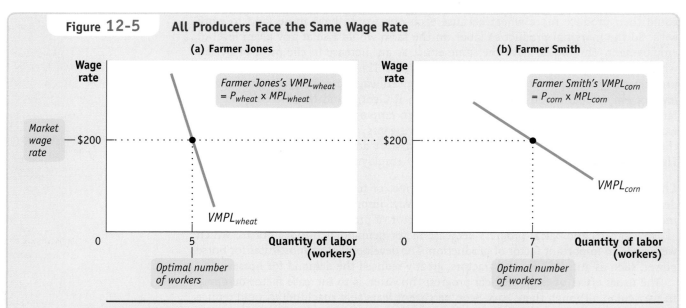

Figure 12-5   All Producers Face the Same Wage Rate

(a) Farmer Jones

Farmer Jones's $VMPL_{wheat}$ = $P_{wheat} \times MPL_{wheat}$

$VMPL_{wheat}$

Optimal number of workers

(b) Farmer Smith

Farmer Smith's $VMPL_{corn}$ = $P_{corn} \times MPL_{corn}$

$VMPL_{corn}$

Optimal number of workers

Although Farmer Jones grows wheat and Farmer Smith grows corn, they both compete in the same market for labor and must therefore pay the same wage rate, $200.

Each producer hires labor up to the point at which $VMPL$ = $200: 5 workers for Jones, 7 workers for Smith.

Smith, who produces corn. Despite the fact that they produce different products, they compete for the same workers, and so must pay the same wage rate, $200. So when both farmers maximize profit, both hire labor up to the point where its value of the marginal product is equal to the wage rate. In the figure, this corresponds to employment of 5 workers by Jones and 7 by Smith.

Figure 12-6 illustrates the general situation in the labor market as a whole. The *market labor demand curve*, like the market demand curve for a good (shown in Figure 10-6), is the horizontal sum of all the individual labor demand curves—which is the same as each producer's value of the marginal product curve. For now, let's simply assume an upward-sloping supply curve for labor; we'll discuss labor supply later in this chapter. Then the equilibrium wage rate is the wage rate at which the quantity of labor supplied is equal to the quantity of labor demanded. In Figure 12-6, this equilibrium wage rate is W^* and the corresponding equilibrium employment level is L^*.

And as we showed in the examples of the farms of George and Martha and of Farmer Jones and Farmer Smith (where the equilibrium wage rate corresponds to $200), each firm will hire labor up to the point at which the value of the marginal product of labor is equal to the equilibrium wage rate. This means that, in equilibrium, the marginal product of labor will be the same for all employers. So the equilibrium (or market) wage rate is equal to the **equilibrium value of the marginal product** of labor—the additional value produced by the last unit of labor employed in the labor market as a whole. It doesn't matter where that additional unit is employed, since VMPL is the same for all producers.

What we have just learned, then, is that the market wage rate is equal to the equilibrium value of the marginal product of labor. And the same is true of each factor of production: in a perfectly competitive market economy, the market price of each factor is equal to its equilibrium value of the marginal product.

The theory that each factor is paid the value of the output generated by the last unit employed in the factor market as a whole is known as the **marginal productivity theory of income distribution**.

> The **equilibrium value of the marginal product** of a factor is the additional value produced by the last unit of that factor employed in the factor market as a whole.

> According to the **marginal productivity theory of income distribution**, every factor of production is paid its equilibrium value of the marginal product.

Figure 12-6

Equilibrium in the Labor Market

The market labor demand curve is the horizontal sum of the individual labor demand curves of all producers. Here the equilibrium wage rate is W^*, the equilibrium employment level is L^*, and every producer hires labor up to the point at which $VMPL = W^*$. So labor is paid its equilibrium value of the marginal product, the value of the marginal product of the last worker hired in the labor market as a whole. **>web...**

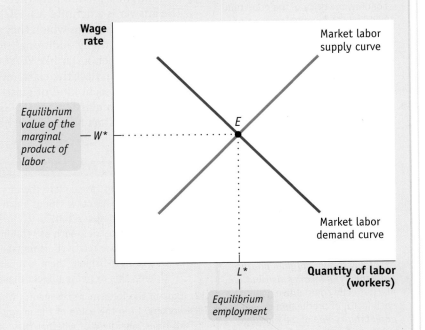

PITFALLS

GETTING MARGINAL PRODUCTIVITY RIGHT

It's important to be careful about what the marginal productivity theory of income distribution says: it says that *all* units of a factor get paid the factor's equilibrium value of the marginal product—the additional value produced by the *last* unit of the factor employed.

The most common source of error is to forget that the relevant value of the marginal product is the equilibrium value, not the value of the marginal products you calculate on the way to equilibrium. In looking at Table 12-2, you might be tempted to think that because the first worker has a value of the marginal product of $380 that worker is paid $380 in equilibrium. Not so: if the equilibrium value of the marginal product in the labor market is equal to $200, then *all* workers receive $200.

> In a perfectly competitive market economy, the price of the good multiplied by the marginal product of labor is equal to the *value of the marginal product of labor:* $VMPL = P \times MPL$. A profit-maximizing producer hires labor up to the point at which the value of the marginal product of labor is equal to the wage rate: $VMPL = W$. The *value of the marginal product of labor curve* slopes downward due to diminishing returns to labor in production.

> The market demand curve for labor is the horizontal sum of all the individual demand curves of producers in that market. It shifts for three main reasons: changes in output price, changes in the supply of other factors, and technological progress.

> According to the *marginal productivity theory of income distribution,* in a perfectly competitive economy each factor of production is paid its *equilibrium value of the marginal product.*

To understand why the marginal productivity theory of income distribution is an important theory, take a look back at Figure 12-1, which showed the factor distribution of income in the United States, and ask yourself this question: who or what decided that labor would get 71 percent of total U.S. income? Why not 90 percent or 50 percent?

The answer, according to the marginal productivity theory of income distribution, is that the division of income among the economy's factors of production isn't arbitrary: it is determined by each factor's marginal productivity at the economy's equilibrium. The wage rate earned by *all* workers in the economy is equal to the increase in the value of output generated by the last worker employed in the economy-wide labor market.

Here we have assumed that all workers are of the same ability. But in reality workers may differ considerably in ability. Rather than thinking of one labor market for all workers in the economy, we can instead think of different markets for different types of workers, where workers are of equivalent ability within each market. For example, the market for computer programmers is different from the market for pastry chefs. And in the market for computer programmers, all participants are assumed to have equal ability; likewise for the market for pastry chefs. In this scenario, the marginal productivity theory of income distribution still holds. That is, when the labor market for computer programmers is in equilibrium, the wage rate earned by all computer programmers is equal to the market's equilibrium value of the marginal product—the value of the marginal product of the last computer programmer hired in that market.

economics in action

Star Power

If you want to be rich, don't become a classical musician or an opera singer. Most musical artists earn quite little considering the many years of training required.

There are, however, a handful of performers who command very large fees, in the vicinity of $30,000 for a single performance. Can the fees paid to stars be explained by the marginal productivity theory of income distribution?

The answer is a definite yes. High fees for stars reflect a careful calculation by managers of the theaters in which they perform. These managers know—with considerable precision—how many additional tickets they will sell, and how much they can raise ticket prices, when a star like Yo-Yo Ma is performing. The high fees paid to these classical superstars reflect the extra revenues they will generate from ticket sales.

All this may seem kind of crass—aren't we talking about art and beauty here? Yes, but music—even classical music—is also a business, and the principles of economics apply to opera stars as much as they do to fast-food workers. ■

< < < < < < < < < < < < < < < < < <

1. In the following cases, state the direction of the shift of the demand curve for labor and what will happen, other things equal, to the market equilibrium wage rate and quantity of labor employed as a result.
   a. Service industries, such as retailing and banking, experience an increase in demand. These industries use relatively more labor than nonservice industries.
   b. Due to over-fishing, there is a fall in the amount of fish caught per day by commercial fishers; this decrease affects their demand for workers.

2. Explain the following statement: "When firms in different industries all compete for the same workers, then the value of the marginal product of the last worker hired will be equal across all firms regardless of whether they are in different industries."

Solutions appear at back of book.

Is the Marginal Productivity Theory of Income Distribution Really True?

Although the marginal productivity theory of income distribution is a well-established part of economic theory, closely linked to the analysis of markets in general, it is a source of some controversy. There are two main objections to it.

First, in the real world we see large disparities in income between factors of production that, in the eyes of some observers, should receive the same payment. Perhaps the most conspicuous examples in the United States are the large differences in the average wages between women and men and among various racial and ethnic groups. Do these wage differences really reflect differences in marginal productivity, or is something else going on?

Second, many people wrongly believe that the marginal productivity theory of income distribution gives a *moral* justification for the distribution of income, implying that the existing distribution is fair and appropriate. (We'll explain in Chapter 13 why this is a misconception.) This misconception sometimes leads people who believe that the current distribution of income is unfair to reject marginal productivity theory.

To address these controversies, we'll start by looking at income disparities across gender and ethnic groups. Then we'll ask what factors might account for these disparities and whether these explanations are consistent with the marginal productivity theory of income distribution.

Wage Disparities in Practice

Wage rates in the United States cover a very wide range. In 2003, hundreds of thousands of workers received the legal federal minimum of $5.15 per hour. At the other extreme, the chief executives of several companies were paid more than $100 million, which is $20,000 per hour even if they worked 100-hour weeks. Even leaving out these extremes, there is a huge range of wage rates. Are people really that different in their marginal productivities?

A particular source of concern is the existence of systematic wage differences across gender and ethnicity. Figure 12-7 compares annual median earnings in 2002 of workers classified by gender and ethnicity. As a group, white males had the highest

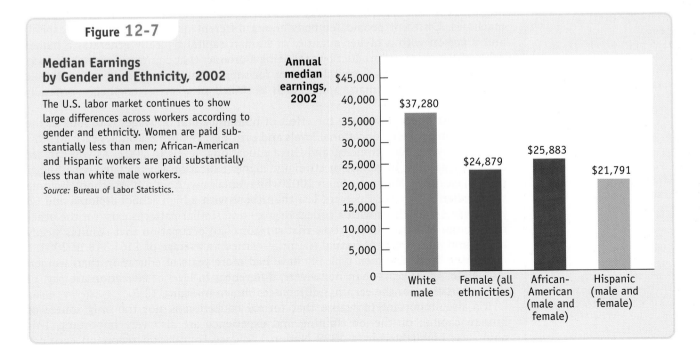

Figure 12-7

Median Earnings by Gender and Ethnicity, 2002

The U.S. labor market continues to show large differences across workers according to gender and ethnicity. Women are paid substantially less than men; African-American and Hispanic workers are paid substantially less than white male workers.

Source: Bureau of Labor Statistics.

earnings. Other data show that women (averaging across all ethnicities) earned only about 67 percent as much; African-American workers (male and female combined) only 69 percent as much; Hispanic workers only 58 percent as much.

We are a nation founded on the belief that all men are created equal—and if the Constitution were rewritten today, we would say that *all people* are created equal. So why do they receive such unequal pay? Let's start with the marginal productivity explanations, then look at other influences.

Marginal Productivity and Wage Inequality

A large part of the observed inequality in wages can be explained by considerations that are consistent with the marginal productivity theory of income distribution. In particular, there are three well-understood sources of wage differences across occupations and individuals.

Compensating differentials are wage differences across jobs that reflect the fact that some jobs are less pleasant than others.

First is the existence of **compensating differentials:** across different types of jobs, wages are often higher or lower depending on how attractive or unattractive the job is. Workers with unpleasant or dangerous jobs demand a higher wage in comparison to workers with jobs that require the same skill and effort but lack the unpleasant or dangerous qualities. For example, truckers who haul hazardous loads are paid more than truckers who haul normal loads. But for any *given* job, the marginal productivity theory of income distribution generally holds true. For example, hazardous-load truckers are paid a wage equal to the equilibrium value of the marginal product of the last person employed in the market for hazardous-load truckers.

A second reason for wage inequality that is clearly consistent with marginal productivity theory is differences in talent. People differ in their abilities: a high-ability person, by producing a better product that commands a higher price compared to a lower-ability person, generates a higher value of the marginal product. And these differences in the value of the marginal product translate into differences in earning potential. We all know that this is true in sports: practice is important, but 99.99 percent (at least) of the population just doesn't have what it takes to hit golf balls like Tiger Woods or skate like Michelle Kwan. The same is true, though less obvious, in other fields of endeavor.

A third, very important reason for wage differences is differences in the quantity of *human capital*. Recall that human capital—education and training—is at least as important in the modern economy as physical capital in the form of buildings and machines. Different people "embody" quite different quantities of human capital, and a person with a higher quantity of human capital typically generates a higher value of the marginal product by producing a product that commands a higher price. So differences in human capital account for substantial differences in wages. People with high levels of human capital, such as skilled surgeons or engineers, generally receive high wages.

The most direct way to see the effect of human capital on wages is to look at the relationship between educational levels and earnings. Figure 12-8 shows earnings differentials by gender, ethnicity, and three educational levels in 2002. As you can see from it, regardless of gender or ethnicity, higher education is associated with higher median earnings. For example, in 2002 white females without a high school diploma had median earnings 31 percent less than those with a high school diploma and 58 percent less than those with a college degree—and similar patterns exist for the other five groups. Additional data show that surgeons—an occupation that requires steady hands and many years of formal training—earned an average of $161,348 in 2001.

Because even now men typically have had more years of education than women and whites more years than nonwhites, differences in level of education are part of the explanation for the earnings differences shown in Figure 12-7.

It's also important to realize that formal education is not the only source of human capital; on-the-job training and experience are also very important. This point was highlighted by a 1999 National Science Foundation report on earnings

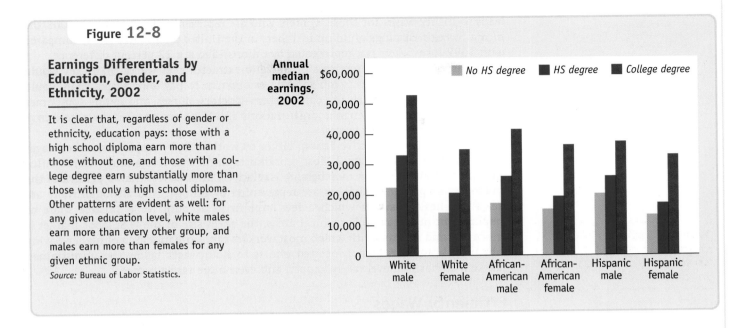

Figure 12-8

Earnings Differentials by Education, Gender, and Ethnicity, 2002

It is clear that, regardless of gender or ethnicity, education pays: those with a high school diploma earn more than those without one, and those with a college degree earn substantially more than those with only a high school diploma. Other patterns are evident as well: for any given education level, white males earn more than every other group, and males earn more than females for any given ethnic group.

Source: Bureau of Labor Statistics.

differences between male and female engineers. The study was motivated by concerns over the male–female earnings gap: on average, men with engineering degrees earn about 25 percent more than women with equivalent degrees. The study found that women in engineering are, on average, younger than men and have considerably less experience than their male counterparts. This difference in age and experience, according to the study, explained most of the earnings differential. Differences in job tenure and experience can partly explain one notable aspect of Figure 12-8: that, across all ethnicities, women's median earnings are less than men's median earnings for any given education level.

But it's also important to emphasize that earnings differences that arise from differences in human capital are not necessarily "fair." A society in which nonwhite children typically receive a poor education because they live in underfunded school districts, then go on to earn low wages because they are poorly educated, may have labor markets that are well described by marginal productivity theory (and would be consistent with the earnings differentials across ethnic groups shown in Figure 12-7). Yet many people would still consider the resulting distribution of income unfair.

Still, many observers think that actual wage differentials cannot be entirely explained by compensating differentials, differences in talent, and human capital. They believe that market power, *efficiency wages,* and discrimination also play an important role. We will examine these forces next.

Market Power

The marginal productivity theory of income distribution is based on the assumption that factor markets are perfectly competitive. In such markets we can expect workers to be paid the equilibrium value of their marginal product, regardless of who they are. But how valid is this assumption?

We haven't yet studied markets that are *not* perfectly competitive (we'll get there in Chapter 14), but let's touch briefly on the ways in which labor markets may deviate from the competitive assumption.

One undoubted source of differences in wages between otherwise similar workers is the role of **unions**—organizations that try to raise wages and improve working conditions for their members. Labor unions, when they are successful, replace one-on-one wage deals between workers and employers with "collective bargaining," in which the employer must negotiate wages with union representatives. Without question, this

Unions are organizations of workers that try to raise wages and improve working conditions for their members.

leads to higher wages for those workers who are represented by unions. In 2003 the median weekly earnings of union members in the United States were $760, compared with $599 for workers not represented by unions—about a 22 percent difference.

Just as workers can sometimes organize to extract higher wages than they would otherwise receive, employers can sometimes organize to pay *lower* wages than would result from competition. Health care workers—doctors, nurses, and so on—sometimes argue that health maintenance organizations (HMOs) are engaged in a collective effort to hold down their wages.

How much does collective action, either by workers or by employers, affect wages in the modern United States? Most economists think that it is a fairly minor influence. To begin with, union membership is relatively limited: less than 9 percent of the employees of private businesses are represented by unions. And although there are fields like health care in which a few large firms account for a sizeable share of employment in certain geographical areas, the sheer size of the U.S. labor market is enormous and the ease with which most workers can move in search of higher-paying jobs probably means that concerted efforts to hold wages below the unrestrained market equilibrium level rarely happen and even more rarely succeed.

Efficiency Wages

A second source of wage inequality is the phenomenon of *efficiency wages*—a type of incentive scheme to motivate workers to work hard and reduce worker turnover used by employers. Suppose that a worker performs a job that is extremely important but in which the employer can observe only at infrequent intervals how well the job is being performed—say, serving as a caregiver for the employer's child. Then it often makes sense for the employer to pay more than the worker could earn in an alternative job—that is, more than the equilibrium wage. Why? Because earning a premium makes losing this job and having to take the alternative job quite costly for the worker. So a worker who happens to be observed performing poorly and is therefore fired is now worse off for having to accept a lower-paying job. The threat of losing a job that pays a premium motivates the worker to perform well and avoid being fired. Likewise, paying a premium also reduces worker turnover—the frequency with which an employee leaves a job voluntarily. Despite the fact that it may take no more effort and skill to be a child's caregiver than to be an office worker, efficiency wages show why it often makes economic sense for a parent to pay a caregiver more than the equilibrium wage of an office worker.

The **efficiency-wage model** explains why we may observe wages offered above their equilibrium level. Like the price floors that we studied in Chapter 4—and, in particular, much like the minimum wage—this phenomenon leads to a surplus of labor supplied in the markets for labor that are characterized by the efficiency wage model. This surplus of labor translates into unemployment—some workers are actively searching for a high-paying efficiency-wage job but are unable to get one, and other more fortunate but no more deserving workers are able to acquire one. As a result, two workers with exactly the same profile—the same skills and same job history—may earn unequal wages: the worker who is lucky enough to get an efficiency-wage job earns more than the worker who gets a standard job (or who remains unemployed while searching for a higher-paying job). Efficiency wages are a type of market failure that arises from the fact that some employees don't always perform as well as they should and are able to hide that fact. As a result, employers use nonequilibrium wages in order to motivate their employees, leading to an inefficient outcome.

Discrimination

It is a real and ugly fact that throughout history there has been discrimination against workers who are considered to be the wrong race, ethnicity, or gender. How does this fit into our economic models?

The main insight economic analysis offers is that discrimination is *not* a natural consequence of market competition. On the contrary, market forces tend to work

According to the **efficiency-wage model,** some employers pay an above-equilibrium wage as an incentive for better performance.

against discrimination. To see why, consider the incentives that would exist if social convention dictated that women be paid, say, 30 percent less than men with equivalent qualifications and experience. A company whose management was itself unbiased would then be able to reduce its costs by hiring women rather than men—and such companies would have an advantage over other companies that hired men despite their higher cost. The result would be to create an excess demand for female workers, which would tend to drive up their wages.

But if market competition works against discrimination, how is it that so much discrimination has taken place? The answer is twofold. First, when labor markets don't work well, employers may have the ability to discriminate without hurting their profits. For example, market interferences (such as unions or minimum-wage laws) or market failures (such as efficiency wages) can lead to wages that are above their equilibrium levels. In these cases, there are more job applicants than there are jobs—leaving employers free to discriminate among applicants. In research published in 2003, two economists, Marianne Bertrand and Sendhil Mullainathan, documented discrimination in hiring by sending fictitious résumés to prospective employers on a random basis. Applicants with "white-sounding" names such as Emily Walsh were 50 percent more likely to be contacted than applicants with "African-American-sounding" names such as Lakisha Washington. Also, applicants with white-sounding names and good credentials were much more likely to be contacted than those without such credentials. By contrast, potential employers seemed to ignore the credentials of applicants with African-American-sounding names.

Second, discrimination has sometimes been institutionalized in government policy. This institutionalization of discrimination has made it easier to maintain it against market pressure, and historically it is the form that discrimination has typically taken. For example, at one time in the United States, African-Americans were barred from attending "whites-only" public schools and universities in many parts of the country and forced to attend inferior schools. So although market competition tends to work against *current* discrimination, it is not a remedy for past discrimination, which typically has had an impact on the education and experience of its victims and thereby reduces their income. Economics in Action below illustrates the way in which government policy enforced discrimination in the world's most famous racist regime, that of South Africa.

So Does Marginal Productivity Theory Work?

The main conclusion you should draw from this discussion is that marginal productivity theory is not a perfect description of how factor incomes are determined but that it works pretty well. The deviations are important. But, by and large, in a modern economy with well-functioning labor markets, factors of production are paid the equilibrium value of the marginal product—the value of the marginal product of the last unit employed in the market as a whole.

It's important to emphasize, once again, that this does not mean that the factor distribution of income is morally justified. We'll turn to issues of fairness and equity in Chapter 13.

economics in action

The Economics of Apartheid

The Republic of South Africa is the richest nation in Africa, but it also has a harsh political history. Until the peaceful transition to majority rule in 1994, the country was controlled by its white minority, Afrikaners, the descendants of European (mainly Dutch) immigrants. This minority imposed an economic system known as apartheid, which overwhelmingly favored white interests over those of native Africans and other groups considered "nonwhite," such as Asians.

South Africa is a democracy now, but the human legacy of apartheid persists.

The origins of apartheid go back to the early years of the twentieth century, when large numbers of white farmers began moving into South Africa's growing cities. There they discovered, to their horror, that they did not automatically earn higher wages than other races. But they had the right to vote—and nonwhites did not. And so the South African government instituted "job-reservation" laws designed to ensure that only whites got jobs that paid well. The government also set about creating jobs for whites in government-owned industries. As Allister Sparks notes in *The Mind of South Africa* (1990), in its efforts to provide high-paying jobs for whites, the country "eventually acquired the largest amount of nationalized industry of any country outside the Communist bloc."

In other words, racial discrimination was possible because it was backed by the power of the government, which prevented markets from following their natural course.

A postscript: in 1994, in one of the political miracles of modern times, the white regime ceded power and South Africa became a full-fledged democracy. Apartheid was abolished. Unfortunately, large racial differences in earnings remain. The main reason is that apartheid created huge disparities in human capital, which will persist for many years to come. ■

< < < < < < < < < < < < < < < < < <

>>CHECK YOUR UNDERSTANDING 12-3

1. Assess each of the following statements. Do you think they are true, false, or ambiguous? Explain.
   a. The marginal productivity theory of income distribution is inconsistent with the presence of income disparities associated with gender, race, or ethnicity.
   b. Companies that engage in workplace discrimination but whose competitors do not are likely to have lower profits as a result of their actions.
   c. Workers who are paid less because they have less experience are not the victims of discrimination.

The Supply of Labor

Up to this point we have focused on the demand for factors, which determines the quantities demanded of labor, capital or land by producers as a function of their factor prices. What about the supply of factors?

In this section we focus exclusively on the supply of labor. We do this for two reasons. First, in the modern U.S. economy, labor is the most important factor of production, accounting for most of factor income. Second, as we'll see, labor supply is the area in which factor markets look most different from markets for goods and services.

Work Versus Leisure

In the labor market, the roles of firms and households are the reverse of what they are in markets for goods and services. On the one hand, a good such as wheat is supplied by firms and demanded by households; on the other hand, labor is demanded by firms and supplied by households. How do people decide how much labor to supply?

As a practical matter, most people have limited control over their work hours: either you take a job that involves working a set number of hours per week, or you don't get the job at all. To understand the logic of labor supply, however, it helps to put realism to one side for a bit and imagine an individual who can choose to work as many or as few hours as he or she likes.

Why wouldn't such an individual work as many hours as possible? Because workers are human beings, too, and have other uses for their time. An hour spent on the job is an hour not spent on other, presumably more pleasant, activities. So the decision about how much labor to supply involves making a decision about **time allocation**—how many hours to spend on different activities.

Decisions about labor supply result from decisions about **time allocation:** how many hours to spend on different activities.

By working, people earn income that they can use to buy goods. The more hours an individual works, the more goods he or she can afford to buy. But this increased purchasing power comes at the expense of a reduction in **leisure,** the time spent not working. (Leisure doesn't necessarily mean time goofing off. It could mean time spent with one's family, pursuing hobbies, exercising, and so on). And though purchased goods yield utility, so does leisure. Indeed, we can think of leisure itself as a normal good, which most people would like to consume more of as their incomes increase.

How does a rational individual decide how much leisure to consume? By making a marginal comparison, of course. In analyzing consumer choice, we asked how a utility-maximizing consumer uses a marginal *dollar*. In analyzing labor supply, we ask how an individual uses a marginal *hour*.

Leisure is time available for purposes other than earning money to buy marketed goods.

Consider Clive, an individual who likes both leisure and the goods money can buy. And suppose that his wage rate is $10 per hour. In deciding how many hours he wants to work, he must compare the marginal utility of an additional hour of leisure with the additional utility he gets from $10 worth of goods. If $10 worth of goods adds more to his total utility than an additional hour of leisure, he can increase his total utility by giving up an hour of leisure in order to work an additional hour. If an extra hour of leisure adds more to his total utility than $10 in income, he can increase his total utility by working one fewer hour in order to gain an hour of leisure.

At Clive's optimal labor supply choice, then, his marginal utility of one hour of leisure is equal to the marginal utility he gets from the goods that his hourly wage can purchase. This is very similar to the *optimal consumption rule* we encountered in Chapter 10, except that it is a rule about time rather than money.

Our next step is to ask how Clive's decision about time allocation is affected when his wage rate changes.

Wages and Labor Supply

Suppose that Clive's wage rate doubles, from $10 to $20 per hour. How will he change his time allocation?

You could argue that Clive will work longer hours, because his incentive to work has increased: by giving up an hour of leisure, he can now gain twice as much money as before. But you could equally well argue that he will work less, because he doesn't need to work as many hours to generate the income to pay for the goods he wants.

As these opposing arguments suggest, the quantity of labor Clive supplies can either rise or fall when his wage rate rises. To understand why, let's recall the distinction between *substitution effects* and *income effects* that we learned in Chapters 10 and 11. We saw there that a price change affects consumer choice in two ways: by changing the opportunity cost of a good in terms of other goods (the substitution effect) and by making the consumer richer or poorer (the income effect).

Now think about how a rise in Clive's wage rate affects his demand for leisure. On the one hand, the opportunity cost of leisure—the amount of money he gives up by taking an hour off instead of working—rises. That substitution effect gives him an incentive, other things equal, to consume less leisure and work longer hours. But on the other hand, a higher wage rate makes Clive richer—and this income effect leads him, other things equal, to want to consume *more* leisure and supply less labor, because leisure is a normal good.

So in the case of labor supply, the substitution effect and the income effect work in opposite directions. If the substitution effect is so powerful that it dominates the income effect, an increase in Clive's wage rate leads him to supply more hours of labor. If the income effect is so powerful that it dominates the substitution effect, an increase in the wage rate leads him to supply *fewer* hours of labor.

We see, then, that the **individual labor supply curve**—the relationship between the wage rate and the number of hours of labor supplied by an individual worker—is not necessarily upward sloping. If the income effect dominates, a higher wage rate will reduce the quantity of labor supplied.

The **individual labor supply curve** shows how the quantity of labor supplied by an individual depends on that individual's wage rate.

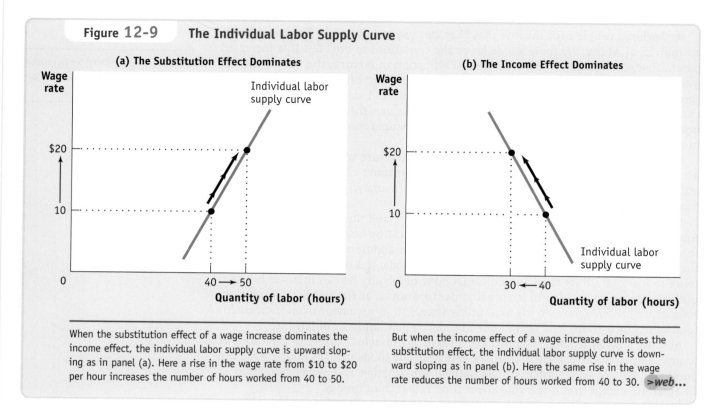

Figure 12-9   The Individual Labor Supply Curve

When the substitution effect of a wage increase dominates the income effect, the individual labor supply curve is upward sloping as in panel (a). Here a rise in the wage rate from $10 to $20 per hour increases the number of hours worked from 40 to 50.

But when the income effect of a wage increase dominates the substitution effect, the individual labor supply curve is downward sloping as in panel (b). Here the same rise in the wage rate reduces the number of hours worked from 40 to 30. **>web...**

Figure 12-9 illustrates the two possibilities for labor supply. If the substitution effect dominates the income effect, the individual labor supply curve slopes upward; panel (a) shows an increase in the wage rate from $10 to $20 per hour leading to a rise in the number of hours worked from 40 to 50. However, if the income effect dominates, the quantity of labor supplied goes down when the wage rate increases. Panel (b) shows the same rise in the wage rate leading to a *fall* in the number of hours worked from 40 to 30. (Economists refer to an individual labor supply curve that contains both upward-sloping and downward-sloping segments as a "backward-bending labor supply curve"— a concept that we analyze in detail in this chapter's appendix.)

Is a negative response of the quantity of labor supplied to the wage rate a real possibility? Yes: many labor economists believe that income effects on the supply of labor may be somewhat stronger than substitution effects. The most compelling piece of evidence for this belief comes from Americans' increasing consumption of leisure over the past century. At the end of the nineteenth century, wages adjusted for inflation

FOR INQUIRING MINDS

WHY YOU CAN'T FIND A CAB WHEN IT'S RAINING

Everyone says that you can't find a taxi in New York when you really need one—say, when it's raining. That could be because everyone else is trying to get a taxi at the same time. But according to a study published in the *Quarterly Journal of Economics*, it's more than that: cab drivers actually go home early when it's raining.

The reason is that the hourly wage rate of a taxi driver depends on the weather:

when it's raining, drivers get more fares and therefore earn more per hour. And it seems that the income effect of this higher wage rate outweighs the substitution effect.

This behavior leads the authors of the study to question drivers' rationality. They point out that if taxi drivers thought in terms of the long run, they would realize that rainy days and nice days tend to average out and that their high earnings on a

rainy day don't really affect their long-run income very much. Indeed, experienced drivers (who have probably figured this out) are less likely than inexperienced drivers to go home early on a rainy day. But leaving such issues to one side, the study does seem to show clear evidence of a labor supply curve that slopes downward instead of upward, thanks to income effects. (See source note on page xxii.)

were only about one-eighth what they are today; the typical work week was 70 hours, and very few workers retired at 65. Today the typical work week is less than 40 hours, and most people retire at 65 or earlier. So it seems that Americans have chosen to take advantage of higher wages in part by consuming more leisure.

Shifts of the Labor Supply Curve

Now that we have examined how income and substitution effects shape the individual labor supply curve, we can turn to the market labor supply curve. In any labor market, the market supply curve is the horizontal sum of the individual labor supply curves of all workers in that market. A change in any factor *other than the wage* that alters workers' willingness to supply labor causes a shift of the labor supply curve. A variety of factors can lead to such shifts, including changes in preferences and social norms, changes in population, changes in opportunities, and changes in wealth.

Changes in Preferences and Social Norms Changes in preferences and social norms can lead workers to increase or decrease their willingness to work at any given wage. A striking example of this phenomenon is the large increase in the number of employed women—particularly married employed women—that has occurred in the United States since the 1960s. Until that time, women who could afford to largely avoided working outside the home. Changes in preferences and norms in post–World War II America (helped along by the invention of labor-saving home appliances such as washing machines, increasing urbanization of the population, and higher female education levels) have induced large numbers of American women to join the workforce—a phenomenon often repeated in other countries that experience similar social and technological forces.

Changes in Population Changes in the population size generally lead to shifts of the labor supply curve. A larger population tends to shift the labor supply rightward as more workers are available at any given wage; a smaller population tends to shift the labor supply curve leftward. Currently the size of the U.S. labor force grows by approximately 1 percent per year, a result of immigration from other countries and, in comparison to other developed countries, a relatively high U.S. birth rate. As a result, many labor markets in the United States are experiencing rightward shifts of their labor supply curves.

Changes in Opportunities At one time, teaching was the only occupation considered suitable for well-educated women. However, as opportunities in other professions opened up to women starting in the 1960s, many women left teaching and potential female teachers chose other careers. This generated a leftward shift of the supply curve for teachers, reflecting a fall in the willingness to work at any given wage and forcing school districts to pay more to maintain an adequate teaching staff. These events illustrate a general result: when superior alternatives arise for workers in another labor market, the supply curve in the original labor market shifts leftward as workers move to the new opportunities. Similarly, when opportunities diminish in one labor market—say, layoffs in the manufacturing industry occur because of increased foreign competition—the supply in alternative labor markets increases as workers move to these other markets.

Changes in Wealth A person whose wealth increases will buy more normal goods, including leisure. So when a class of workers experiences a general rise in their wealth levels—say, due to a stock market boom—the income effect from the wealth increase will shift the labor supply curve associated with those workers leftward as workers consume more leisure and work less. Note that *the income effect caused by a change in wealth shifts the labor supply curve,* but *the income effect from a wage increase*—as we discussed in the case of the individual labor supply curve—*is a movement along the labor supply curve.* The following Economics in Action illustrates how such a change in the wealth levels of many families during the late 1990s led to a shift of the market labor supply curve associated with their employable children.

economics in action

The Decline of the Summer Job

In the summer of 2000, according to the *New York Times,* the New Jersey resort town of Ocean City found itself facing a serious shortage of lifeguards. Traditionally lifeguard positions, together with many other seasonal jobs, have been filled mainly by high school and college students. But in recent years a growing number of young Americans have chosen not to take summer jobs. In 1979, 71 percent of Americans between the ages of 16 and 19 were in the summer workforce. Twenty years later that number had fallen to 63 percent; and by 2003, it was 54 percent. Data show that it was young men in particular who became much less willing to take summer jobs during the 1990s.

One explanation for the decline in summer labor supply is that more students feel that they should devote their summers to additional study. But an important factor in the decline, according to the article, was that an economic and stock market boom in the late 1990s had made many more American families affluent—affluent enough that their children no longer felt pressure to make a financial contribution by working all summer.

In short, the income effect led to a reduced labor supply. ■

< < < < < < < < < < < < < < < < < < < <

>> CHECK YOUR UNDERSTANDING 12-4

1. Formerly, Clive was free to work as many or as few hours per week as he wanted. But a new law limits the maximum number of hours he can work per week to 35. Explain under what circumstances, if at all, he is made:
   a. Worse off
   b. Equally as well off
   c. Better off

2. Explain in terms of the income and substitution effects how a fall in Clive's wage can induce him to work more hours than before.

Solutions appear at back of book.

• A LOOK AHEAD •

We have now put together all the pieces for understanding how a perfectly competitive market economy works. We've seen how supply and demand determine market prices, how profit maximization gives rise to the supply curve for each good, and how utility maximization gives rise to the demand curve. We've also just seen how factor markets determine the prices of factors of production and therefore the factor incomes of individuals.

But the ultimate purpose of an economy is to provide people with what they want. How well does a market economy do that job? In the next chapter we finally examine the *efficiency* of a market economy and the related but different question of *equity.*

SUMMARY

1. Just as there are markets for goods and services, there are markets for factors of production, including labor, land, and both **physical capital** and **human capital.** These markets determine the **factor distribution of income.**

2. Profit-maximizing price-taking producers will employ a factor up to the point at which its price is equal to its **value of the marginal product**—the marginal product of the factor multiplied by the price of the good. The **value of the marginal product curve** is therefore the individual price-taking producer's demand curve for a factor.

3. The market demand curve for labor is the sum of the individual demand curves of producers in that market. It shifts for three main reasons: changes in output price, changes in the supply of other factors, and technological changes.

4. When a competitive labor market is in equilibrium, the market wage is equal to the **equilibrium value of the marginal product** of labor, the additional value produced by the last worker hired in the labor market as a whole. The same principle applies to other factors of production: the **rental rate** of land or capital is equal to the equilibrium value of the marginal products. This insight leads to the **marginal productivity theory of income distribution,** according to which each factor is paid the value of the marginal product of the last unit of that factor employed in the factor market as a whole.

5. Large disparities in wages raise questions about the validity of the marginal productivity theory of income distribution. Many disparities can be explained by **compensating differentials** and by differences in talent, job experience, and human capital across workers. Market interference in the forms of **unions** and collective action by employers also creates wage disparities. The **efficiency-wage model,** which arises from a type of market failure, shows how wage disparities can arise from employers' attempts to increase worker performance. Free markets tend to diminish dis-

crimination, but discrimination remains a real source of wage disparity. Discrimination is typically maintained either through problems in labor markets or (historically) through institutionalization in government policies.

6. Labor supply is the result of decisions about **time allocation,** where each worker faces a trade-off between **leisure** and work. An increase in the hourly wage rate tends to increase work hours by the substitution effect but to reduce work hours by the income effect. If the net result is that a worker increases the quantity of labor supplied in response to a higher wage, the **individual labor supply curve** slopes upward. If the net result is that a worker reduces their work hours, the individual labor supply curve—unlike supply curves for goods and services—slopes downward.

7. The market labor supply curve is the sum of the individual labor supply curves of all workers in that market. It shifts for four main reasons: changes in preferences and social norms, changes in population, changes in opportunities, and changes in wealth.

KEY TERMS

Physical capital, p. 282
Human capital, p. 282
Factor distribution of income, p. 282
Value of the marginal product, p. 286
Value of the marginal product curve, p. 286
Rental rate, p. 290

Equilibrium value of the marginal product, p. 291
Marginal productivity theory of income distribution, p. 291
Compensating differentials, p. 294
Unions, p. 295

Efficiency-wage model, p. 296
Time allocation, p. 298
Leisure, p. 299
Individual labor supply curve, p. 299

PROBLEMS

1. In 2001, national income in the United States was $8,122.0 billion. In the same year, 135 million workers were employed, at an average wage of $43,518 per worker per year.

   a. How much compensation of employees was paid in the United States in 2001?

   b. Analyze the factor distribution of income. What percentage of national income was received in terms of compensation of employees in 2001?

   c. Suppose that a huge wave of corporate downsizing leads many terminated employees to open their own businesses. What is the effect on the factor distribution of income?

   d. Suppose the supply of labor rises due to an increase in the retirement age. What happens to the percentage of national income received in terms of compensation of employees?

2. Marty's Frozen Yogurt has the production function per day shown in the accompanying table. The equilibrium wage rate for a worker is $80 per day. Each cup of frozen yogurt sells for $2.

Quantity of labor (workers)	Quantity of frozen yogurt (cups)
0	0
1	110
2	200
3	270
4	300
5	320
6	330

   a. Calculate the marginal product of labor for each worker and the value of the marginal product per worker.

   b. How many workers should Marty employ?

3. Patty's Pizza Parlor has the production function per hour shown in the accompanying table. The hourly wage rate for each worker is $10. Each pizza sells for $2.

Quantity of labor (workers)	Quantity of pizza
0	0
1	9
2	15
3	19
4	22
5	24

a. Calculate the marginal product of labor for each worker and the value of the marginal product per worker.

b. Draw the value of the marginal product curve. Use your diagram to determine how many workers Patty should employ.

c. Now the price of pizza increases to $4. Calculate the value of the marginal product per worker, and draw the new value of the marginal product curve into your diagram. Use your diagram to determine how many workers Patty should employ now.

4. The production function for Patty's Pizza Parlor is given in the table in Problem 3. The price of pizza is $2, but the hourly wage rate rises from $10 to $15. Use a diagram to determine how Patty's demand for workers responds as a result of this wage rate increase.

5. Patty's Pizza Parlor initially had the production function given in the table in Problem 3. A worker's hourly wage rate was $10, and pizza sold for $2. Now Patty buys a new high-tech pizza oven that allows her workers to become twice as productive as before. That is, the first worker now produces 18 pizzas per hour instead of 9, and so on.

a. Calculate the new marginal product of labor and the new value of the marginal product of labor.

b. Use a diagram to determine how Patty's hiring decision responds to this increase in the productivity of her workforce.

6. Jameel runs a driver education school. The more driving instructors he hires, the more driving lessons he can sell. But because he owns a limited number of training automobiles, each additional driving instructor adds less to Jameel's output of driving lessons. The accompanying table shows Jameel's production function per day. Each driving lesson can be sold at $35 per hour.

Quantity of labor (driving instructors)	Quantity of driving lessons (hours)
0	0
1	8
2	15
3	21
4	26
5	30
6	33

Determine Jameel's labor demand schedule (his demand schedule for driving instructors) for each of the following daily wage rates for driving instructors: $160, $180, $200, $220, $240, and $260.

7. Dale and Dana work at a self-service gas station and convenience store. Dale opens up everyday and Dana arrives later to help stock the store. They are both paid the current market wage of $9.50 per hour. But Dale feels he should be paid much more because the revenue generated from the gas pumps he turns on every morning is much higher than the revenue generated by the items that Dana stocks. Assess this argument.

8. In the Shire, farmers can rent land for $100 per acre per year. All the acres are identical. Merry Brandybuck rents 30 acres on which he grows carrots. Pippin Took rents 20 acres on which he grows corn. They sell their produce in a perfectly competitive market. Merry boasts that his value of the marginal product of land is twice as large as Pippin's. Pippin replies that, if this is true and if Merry wants to maximize his profit, Merry is renting too much land. Is Pippin right? Explain your answer.

9. For each of the following situations in which similar workers are paid different wages, give the most likely explanation for these wage differences.

a. Test pilots for new jet aircraft earn higher wages than airline pilots.

b. College graduates usually have higher earnings in their first year on the job than workers without college degrees have in their first year on the job.

c. Full professors command higher salaries than assistant professors for teaching the same class.

d. Unionized workers are generally better paid than non-unionized workers.

10. Research consistently finds that despite nondiscrimination policies, African-American workers on average receive lower wages than white workers do. What are the possible reasons for this? Are these reasons consistent with marginal productivity theory?

11. Greta is an enthusiastic amateur gardener and spends a lot of her free time working in her yard. She also has a demanding and well-paid job as a freelance advertising consultant. The advertising business is going through a difficult time and the hourly consulting fee Greta can charge falls. Greta decides to spend more time gardening and less time consulting. Explain her decision in terms of income and substitution effects.

12. Wendy works at a fast-food restaurant. When her wage rate was $5 per hour, she worked 30 hours per week. When her wage rate rose to $6 per hour, she decided to work 40 hours. But when her wage rate rose further to $7, she decided to work only 35 hours.

a. Draw Wendy's individual labor supply curve.

b. Is Wendy's behavior irrational, or can you find a rational explanation? Explain your answer.

13. You are the governor's economic policy adviser. The governor wants to put in place policies that encourage employed people to work more hours at their jobs and that encourage unemployed people to find and take jobs. Assess each of the following policies in terms of reaching that goal. Explain your

reasoning in terms of income and substitution effects, and indicate when the impact of the policy may be ambiguous.

a. The state income tax rate is lowered, which has the effect of increasing workers' after-tax wage rate.

b. The state income tax rate is increased, which has the effect of decreasing workers' after-tax wage rate.

c. The state property tax rate is increased, which reduces workers' after-tax income.

>web... To continue your study and review of concepts in this chapter, please visit the Krugman/Wells website for quizzes, animated graph tutorials, web links to helpful resources, and more.

www.worthpublishers.com/krugmanwells

Chapter 12 Appendix: Indifference
>>Curve Analysis of Labor Supply

In the body of this chapter, we explained why the labor supply curve can slope downward instead of upward: the substitution effect of a higher wage rate, which provides an incentive to work longer hours, can be outweighed by the income effect of a higher wage rate, which may lead individuals to consume more leisure. In this appendix we show how this analysis can be carried out using the *indifference curves* introduced in Chapter 11.

The Time Allocation Budget Line

Let's return to the example of Clive, who likes leisure but also likes having money to spend. We now assume that Clive has a total of 80 hours per week that he could spend either working or enjoying as leisure time. (The remaining hours in his week, we assume, are taken up with necessary activities, mainly sleeping). Let's also assume, initially, that his hourly wage rate is $10.

His consumption possibilities are defined by the **time allocation budget line** in Figure 12A-1, a budget line that shows Clive's trade-offs between consumption of leisure and income. Hours of leisure per week are measured on the horizontal axis, and the money he earns from working is measured on the vertical axis.

The horizontal intercept, point X, is at 80 hours: if Clive didn't work at all, he would have 80 hours of leisure per week but would not earn any money. The vertical intercept, point Y, is at $800: if Clive worked all the time, he would earn $800 per week.

Why can we use a budget line to describe Clive's time allocation choice? The budget lines found in Chapters 10 and 11 represented the trade-offs facing consumers deciding how to allocate their income among different goods. Here, instead of asking how

> A **time allocation budget line** shows an individual's trade-offs between consumption of leisure and the income that allows consumption of marketed goods.

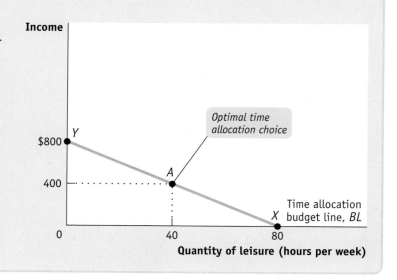

Figure 12A-1

The Time Allocation Budget Line

Clive's time allocation budget line shows his tradeoff between work, which pays a wage rate of $10 per hour, and leisure. At point X he allocates all his time, 80 hours, to leisure but has no income. At point Y he allocates all his time to work, earning $800, but consumes no leisure. His hourly wage rate of $10, the opportunity cost of an hour of leisure, is equal to minus the slope of the time allocation budget line. We have assumed that point A, at 40 hours of leisure and $400 in income, is Clive's optimal time allocation. It obeys the optimal time allocation rule: the additional utility Clive gets from one more hour of leisure must equal the additional utility he gets from the goods he can purchase with one hour's wages.

Clive allocates his income, we ask how he allocates his *time*. But the principles under-lying the allocation of income and the allocation of time are the same: each involves allocating a fixed amount of a resource (80 hours of time in this case) with a constant trade-off (Clive must forgo $10 for each additional hour of leisure). So using a budget line is just as appropriate for time allocation as it is for income allocation.

As in the case of ordinary budget lines, opportunity cost plays a key role. The opportunity cost of an hour of leisure is what Clive must forgo by working one less hour—$10 in income. This opportunity cost is, of course, Clive's hourly wage rate and is equal to minus the slope of his time allocation budget line. You can verify this by noting that the slope is equal to minus the vertical intercept, point Y, divided by the horizontal intercept, point X—that is, −$800/(80 hours) = −$10 per hour.

To maximize his utility, Clive must choose the optimal point on the time alloca-tion budget line in Figure 12A-1. In Chapter 10 we saw that a consumer who allo-cates spending to maximize utility finds the point on the budget line that satisfies the *optimal consumption rule:* the marginal utility per dollar spent on two goods must be equal. Although Clive's choice involves allocating time rather than money, the same principles apply.

Since Clive "spends" time rather than money, the counterpart of the optimal con-sumption rule is the **optimal time allocation rule:** the marginal utility Clive gets from the extra money earned from an additional hour spent working must equal the marginal utility of an additional hour of leisure.

> The **optimal time allocation rule** says that an individual should allocate time so that the marginal utility per hour spent working is equal to the marginal utility of an additional hour of leisure.

The Effect of a Higher Wage Rate

Depending on his tastes, Clive's utility-maximizing choice of hours of leisure and income could lie anywhere on the time allocation budget line in Figure 12A-1. Let's assume that his optimal choice is point A, at which he consumes 40 hours of leisure and earns $400. Now we are ready to link the analysis of time allocation to labor supply.

When Clive chooses a point like A on his time allocation budget line, he is also choosing the quantity of labor he supplies to the labor market. By choosing to con-sume 40 of his 80 available hours as leisure, he has also chosen to supply the other 40 hours as labor.

Now suppose that Clive's wage rate doubles, from $10 to $20 per hour. The effect of this increase in his wage rate is shown in Figure 12A-2 on page 308. His time allo-cation budget line rotates outward: the vertical intercept, which represents the amount he could earn if he devoted all 80 hours to work, shifts upward from point Y to point Z. As a result of the doubling of his wage, Clive would earn $1,600 instead of $800 if he devoted all 80 hours to working.

But how will Clive's time allocation actually change? As we saw in the chapter, this depends on the *income effect* and *substitution effect* that we learned about in Chapters 10 and 11.

The substitution effect of an increase in the wage rate works as follows. When the wage rate increases, the opportunity cost of an hour of leisure increases; this induces Clive to consume less leisure and work more hours—that is, to substitute hours of work for hours of leisure as the wage rate rises. If the substitution effect were the whole story, the individual labor supply curve would look like any ordinary supply curve and would always be upward sloping—a higher wage rate leads to greater labor supply.

What we learned in our analysis of demand was that for most consumer goods, the income effect isn't very important because most goods account for only a very small share of a consumer's spending. In addition, in the few cases of goods where the income effect is significant—for example, major purchases like housing—it usual-ly reinforces the substitution effect: most goods are normal goods, so when a price increase makes a consumer poorer, he or she buys less of that good.

Figure 12A-2

An Increase in the Wage Rate

The two panels show Clive's initial optimal choice, point *A*, on BL₁ the time allocation budget line corresponding to a wage rate of $10. After his wage rate rises to $20, his budget line rotates out to the new budget line, BL₂: if he spends all his time working, the amount of money he earns rises from $800 to $1,600, reflected in the movement from *Y* to *Z*. This generates two opposing effects: the substitution effect pushes him to consume less leisure and to work more hours; the income effect pushes him to consume more leisure and to work fewer hours. Panel (a) shows the change in time allocation when the substitution effect is stronger: Clive's new optimal choice is point *B*, representing a decrease in hours of leisure to 30 hours and an increase in hours of labor to 50 hours. In this case the individual labor supply curve slopes upward. Panel (b) shows the change in time allocation when the income effect is stronger: point *C* is the new optimal choice, representing an increase in hours of leisure to 50 hours and a decrease in hours of labor to 30 hours. Now the individual labor supply curve slopes downward.

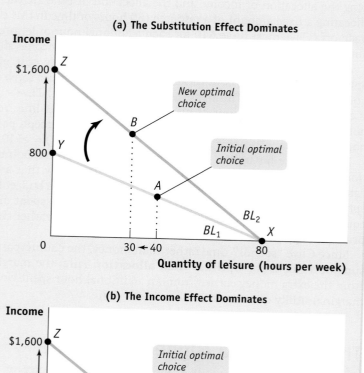

(a) The Substitution Effect Dominates

(b) The Income Effect Dominates

In the labor/leisure choice, however, the income effect takes on a new significance, for two reasons. First, most people get the great majority of their income from wages. This means that the income effect of a change in the wage rate is *not* small: an increase in the wage rate will generate a significant increase in income. Second, leisure is a normal good: when income rises, other things equal, people tend to consume more leisure and work fewer hours.

So the income effect of a higher wage rate tends to *reduce* the quantity of labor supplied, working in opposition to the substitution effect, which tends to *increase* the quantity of labor supplied. So the net effect of a higher wage rate on the quantity of labor Clive supplies could go either way—depending on his preferences, he might choose to supply more labor, or he might choose to supply less labor. The two panels of Figure 12-A2 illustrate these two outcomes. In each panel, point *A* represents Clive's initial consumption choice. Panel (a) shows the case in which Clive works more hours in response to a higher wage rate. An increase in the wage rate induces him to move from point *A* to point *B*, where he consumes less leisure than

Figure 12A-3

A Backward-Bending Individual Labor Supply Curve

At lower wage rates, the substitution effect dominates the income effect for this individual. This is
illustrated by the movement along the individual
labor supply curve from point A to point B: a rise in
the wage rate from W_1 to W_2 leads the quantity of
labor supplied to increase from L_1 to L_2. But at higher
wage rates, the income effect dominates the substitution effect, shown by the movement from point B
to point C: here, a rise in the wage rate from W_2 to
W_3 leads the quantity of labor supplied to decrease
from L_2 to L_3.

at A and therefore works more hours. Here the substitution effect prevails over the
income effect. Panel (b) shows the case in which Clive works fewer hours in
response to a higher wage rate. Here, he moves from A to C, where he consumes
more leisure and works *fewer* hours than at A. Here the income effect prevails over
the substitution effect.

When the income effect of a higher wage rate is stronger than the substitution
effect, the individual labor supply curve, which shows how much labor an individual
will supply at any given wage rate, slopes the "wrong" way—downward: a higher wage
rate leads to a smaller quantity of labor supplied.

Economists believe that the substitution effect usually dominates the income
effect in the labor supply decision when an individual's wage rate is low. An individual labor supply curve is typically upward sloping for lower wage rates as people
work more in response to rising wage rates. But they also believe that many individuals have stronger preferences for leisure and will choose to cut back the number of
hours worked as their wage rate continues to rise. For these individuals, the income
effect eventually dominates the substitution effect as the wage rate rises, leading
their individual labor supply curves to change slope and to "bend backward" at high
wage rates. An individual labor supply curve with this feature, called a **backward-
bending individual labor supply curve,** is shown in Figure 12A-3. Although an
individual labor supply curve may bend backward, *market* labor supply curves are
almost always upward sloping over their entire range as higher wage rates draw more
new workers into the labor market.

A **backward-bending individual labor
supply curve** is an individual labor supply curve that is upward sloping at low
to moderate wage rates and is
downward sloping at higher wage rates.

Indifference Curve Analysis

In Chapter 11, we showed that consumer choice can be represented using the concept of *indifference curves,* which provide a "map" of consumer preferences. If you
have covered Chapter 11, you may find it interesting to learn that indifference curves
are also useful for addressing the issue of labor supply. In fact, this is one place where
they are particularly helpful.

Figure 12A-4

Labor Supply Choice: The Indifference Curve Approach

Point A, on BL_1, is Clive's initial optimal choice. After a wage rate increase his income and utility level increase: his new time budget allocation line is BL_2 and his new optimal choice is point C. This change can be decomposed into the substitution effect—the fall in the hours of leisure from point A to point S, and the income effect—the increase in the number of hours of leisure from point S to point C. As shown here, the income effect dominates the substitution effect: the net result of an increase in the wage rate is an increase in the hours of leisure consumed and a decrease in the hours of labor supplied.

Using indifference curves, Figure 12A-4 shows how an increase in the wage rate can lead to a fall in the quantity of labor supplied. Point A is Clive's initial optimal choice, given an hourly wage rate of $10. It is the same as point A in Figure 12A-2; this time, however, we include an indifference curve to show that it is a point at which the budget line is tangent to the highest possible indifference curve.

Now consider the effect of a rise in the wage rate to $20. Imagine, for a moment, that at the same time Clive was offered a higher wage, he was told that he had to start repaying his student loan and that the good-news/bad-news combination left his utility unchanged. Then he would find himself at point S: on the same indifference curve as at A, but tangent to a steeper budget line, the dashed line BL_S in Figure 12A-4, which is parallel to BL_2. The move from A to S is the substitution effect of his wage increase: it leads him to consume less leisure and therefore supply more labor.

But now cancel the repayment on the student loan, and Clive is able to move to a higher indifference curve. His new optimum is at C, which corresponds to C in panel (b) of Figure 12A-2. The move from S to C is the income effect of his wage increase. And we see that this income effect can outweigh the substitution effect: at C he consumes more leisure, and therefore supplies less labor, than he did at A.

PROBLEMS

1. Leandro has 16 hours per day that he can allocate to work or leisure. His job pays a wage rate of $20. Leandro decides to consume 8 hours of leisure. His indifference curves have the usual shape: they are downward sloping, they do not cross, and they have the characteristic convex shape.

a. Draw Leandro's time allocation budget line for a typical day. Then illustrate the indifference curve at his optimal choice.

Now Leandro's wage rate falls to $10.

b. Draw Leandro's new budget line.

c. Suppose that Leandro now works only 4 hours as a result of his reduced wage rate. Illustrate the indifference curve at his new optimal choice.

d. Leandro's decision to work less as the wage rate falls is the result of a substitution effect and an income effect. In your diagram, show the income effect and the substitution effect from this reduced wage rate. Which effect is stronger?

2. Florence is a highly paid fashion consultant who earns $100 per hour. She has 16 hours per day that she can allocate to work or leisure, and she decides to work for 12 hours.

a. Draw Florence's time allocation budget line for a typical day, and illustrate the indifference curve at her optimal choice.

One of Florence's clients is featured on the front page of *Vague*, an influential fashion magazine. As a result, Florence's consulting fee now rises to $500 per hour. Florence decides to work only 10 hours per day.

b. Draw Florence's new time allocation budget line, and illustrate the indifference curve at her optimal choice.

c. In your diagram, show the income effect and the substitution effect from this increase in the wage rate. Which effect is stronger?

3. Tamara has 80 hours per week that she can allocate to work or leisure. Her job pays a wage rate of $20 per hour, but Tamara is being taxed on her income in the following way. On the first $400 that Tamara makes, she pays no tax. That is, for the first 20 hours she works, her net wage—what she takes home after taxes—is $20 per hour. On all income above $400, Tamara pays a 75% tax. That is, for all hours above the first 20 hours, her net wage rate is only $5 per hour. Tamara decides to work 30 hours. Her indifference curves have the usual shape.

a. Draw Tamara's time allocation budget line for a typical week. Also illustrate the indifference curve at her optimal choice.

The government changes the tax scheme. Now only the first $100 of income are tax-exempt. That is, for the first 5 hours she works, Tamara's net wage rate is $20 per hour. But the government reduces the tax rate on all other income to 50%. That is, for all hours above the first 5 hours, Tamara's net wage rate is now $10. After these changes, Tamara finds herself exactly equally as well off as before. That is, her new optimal choice is on the same indifference curve as her initial optimal choice.

b. Draw Tamara's new time allocation budget line on the same diagram. Also illustrate her optimal choice. Bear in mind that she is equally as well off (on the same indifference curve) as before the tax changes occurred.

c. Will Tamara work more or less than before the changes to the tax scheme? Why?

>web... To continue your study and review of concepts in this chapter, please visit the Krugman/Wells website for quizzes, animated graph tutorials, web links to helpful resources, and more.

www.worthpublishers.com/krugmanwells

>> Efficiency and Equity

AFTER THE FALL

WHEN THE BERLIN WALL CAME down in 1989, Western observers got their first good look at the centrally planned economy of East Germany. What they found was a stunningly inefficient system. Although investment had been lavished on politically favored industries such as energy production, producers of consumer goods and services were starved for capital. And the consumer goods that were produced were often not what consumers wanted to buy.

The revelation of East German inefficiency showed how badly such a planned economy worked compared with a market economy, like that of West Germany.

But even after the wall had come down, the government of the newly unified Federal Republic of Germany was not willing to let the free market run its course. Instead, both industry and individuals in East Germany received huge amounts of financial aid. The goal was to prevent the emergence of a politically unacceptable level of inequality between the former East Germans, many of whom lost their jobs in the aftermath of reunification, and West Germans.

Over time, many economists have come to believe that this aid actually delayed the reconstruction of the East German economy. They argue that the aid reduced incentives for workers to relocate to areas where more jobs were available or to learn new skills. But German officials insist that the price was well worth paying: sometimes a sense of fairness, they argue, is more important than efficiency.

Germany's experience reminds us that although we want our economy to be efficient, we also want it to be fair. In this chapter we will address both concerns. We begin by discussing the *efficiency* of a competitive market economy—the effectiveness of a competitive market economy at producing the goods and services that people want to consume. We then turn to the less well-defined

What you will learn in this chapter:

➤ How the overall concept of efficiency can be broken down into three components—**efficiency in consumption, efficiency in production,** and **efficiency in output levels**

➤ How a perfectly competitive market for a single good achieves efficiency in all three components

➤ Why an economy consisting of many perfectly competitive markets is typically, but not always, efficient

➤ The limits of the concept of efficiency—in particular, why efficiency is about how to achieve goals but not about which goals are chosen

Goods produced in centrally planned economies (consider the East German–produced Trabant at left) are notorious for their poor quality compared to stylish, high-quality goods produced in market economies (consider the West German–produced Mercedes at right).

but equally important issue of *equity*—is the distribution of consumption among individuals "fair"? As we'll see, there is no generally accepted definition of *fairness*; nonetheless, societies often choose to sacrifice some efficiency in the pursuit of equity.

Supply, Demand, and the Virtues of the Market

Back in Chapter 6 we introduced the concepts of *consumer surplus* and *producer surplus*. Recall that consumer surplus is the difference between what buyers are willing to pay for a good and what they actually pay; it measures the gains to consumers from participating in the market. Similarly, producer surplus is the difference between the price that sellers of a good receive and their cost; it measures the gains to producers from participating in the market. The sum of consumer and producer surplus, *total surplus,* measures the gains from trade: the total benefits to buyers and sellers from participating in the market.

What we learned in that chapter was a remarkable fact: in equilibrium, a perfectly competitive market—a market in which both buyers and sellers are price-takers—is usually efficient. That is, in most cases such a market *maximizes total surplus*. Except in cases of market failure, there is no way to increase the gains from trade once a market has done its work.

But why is this true, and what are the conditions that make it possible?

To answer these questions, let's briefly look at this story again. It will set the stage for our discussion of efficiency in the economy as a whole.

Why a Market Maximizes Total Surplus

In Chapter 6 we showed that a market maximizes total surplus by considering the alternatives. That is, any attempt to rearrange consumption or production from the market equilibrium reduces total surplus.

How did we demonstrate this result? Figure 13-1 shows, once again, the example of a market in used textbooks. In this example the equilibrium is at *E*, where the price

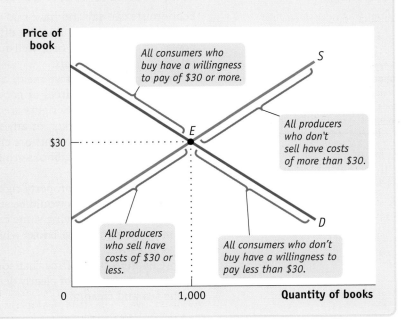

Figure 13-1

Why a Market Maximizes Total Surplus

How do we know that total surplus is maximized at the equilibrium price of $30 per book and the equilibrium quantity of 1,000 books? First, books go to the "right" consumers: every consumer who buys a book has a willingness to pay of $30 or more, and every potential consumer who does *not* buy a book has a willingness to pay less than $30. Second, books are supplied by the "right" producers: every seller who supplies a book has a cost of $30 or less, and every potential seller who does *not* supply a book has a cost of more than $30. Finally, the "right" quantity of 1,000 books are bought and sold: any additional books would cost more than $30 to produce but would be worth less than $30 to the consumers who receive them. If any fewer books were bought and sold, some consumers would be willing to pay more than it costs producers to supply these books.

is $30, and the quantity bought and sold is 1,000 books. We then laid out the three ways in which you might try to improve on this equilibrium and showed that none of them will succeed:

- *Reallocating consumption.* You might try to increase total surplus by giving books to different consumers. But in equilibrium every consumer who gets a book is to the left of *E* on the demand curve, and every consumer who does not get a book is to the right of *E*. That is, every consumer who gets a book has a higher willingness to pay than every consumer who does not get a book. So any reallocation of consumption away from the market equilibrium would reduce the total surplus.

- *Reallocating production.* You might try to increase total surplus by getting different people to sell books. (For simplicity, let's think of sellers as "producing" the books.) But every potential seller who sells a book is to the left of *E* on the supply curve, and every potential seller who does not sell a book is to the right of *E*. That is, every potential seller who sells a book has a lower cost than every potential seller who does not. So any reallocation of production away from the market equilibrium would reduce the total surplus.

- *Changing the level of production.* You might try to increase total surplus by either increasing or decreasing the number of books sold. But at point *E*, the willingness to pay of the last buyer is just equal to the cost of the last seller. So any change in production means either producing a book that is not worth as much to the buyer as it costs to provide or *not* producing a book that is worth more to a consumer than it costs.

So we saw in Chapter 6 that when an individual competitive market is in equilibrium, the consumers who are willing to pay the most for a good are the ones who get it; the producers with the lowest cost are the ones who produce it; and the quantity produced and consumed is right, in the sense that producing either more or less would reduce total surplus.

As we'll see in the next section, a similar case for efficiency applies to the economy as a whole. But before we lay out that case, let's look at the reasons why a market manages to get so much right.

Why Markets Work So Well: Property Rights

Economists can say and have said volumes about why markets are an effective way to organize an economy. But the effectiveness of markets comes down largely to the power of two features of a well-functioning market: *property rights* and the role of prices as *economic signals*.

By **property rights** we mean a system in which valuable items in the economy—whether they are resources or goods—have specific owners who can dispose of them as they choose. Property rights are what make the mutually beneficial transactions in the used-textbook market, or any market, possible.

To see why property rights are crucial, imagine that students do not have full property rights in their textbooks—that they are not allowed to resell books when the semester is over.

This restriction on property rights would prevent many mutually beneficial transactions. Some students would be stuck with textbooks they do not plan to reread and would be happier receiving some cash instead. Other students would be forced to pay full price for shiny new books when they would be happier getting slightly battered copies at a lower price.

In Chapter 20, we'll see that some of the major ways in which markets go wrong have to do with a lack of clearly defined property rights in valuable goods such as fish in the sea and clean air.

Property rights are the rights of owners of valuable items, whether resources or goods, to dispose of those items as they choose.

Why Markets Work So Well: Prices as Economic Signals

Because well-defined property rights give individuals the right to engage in mutually beneficial trades, the second necessary feature of well-functioning markets—economic signals—tell individuals *which* trades are mutually beneficial. An **economic signal** is any piece of information that helps people make better economic decisions. There are thousands of signals that businesses watch in the real world. For example, business forecasters say that sales of cardboard boxes are a good early indicator of changes in industrial production: if businesses are buying lots of cardboard boxes, you can be sure that they will soon increase their production.

But prices are far and away the most important signals in a market economy, because they convey essential information about other people's costs and their willingness to pay. If the equilibrium price of used books is $30, this in effect tells everyone both that there are consumers willing to pay $30 and up and that there are producers with a cost of $30 or less.

The signal given by the market price is what ensures that total surplus is maximized, by telling people whether to buy or sell books. If the price of a book is $30, any consumer who would not be willing to pay $30 knows that there are other consumers who are willing to pay more; any producer whose cost is more than $30 knows that there are other producers with lower costs. And consumers who *are* willing to pay $30 or more, like producers with costs of $30 or less, are in effect told that it is a good idea for them to consume and produce.

> An **economic signal** is any piece of information that helps people make better economic decisions.

Why Markets Sometimes Don't Work Well: Market Failure

We'll want to keep these two crucial features of competitive markets—property rights and prices as economic signals—in mind in later chapters when we analyze in detail how markets sometimes fail. It's worth revisiting the caution found in Chapter 6 about cases of market failure—the situation in which a market fails to maximize total surplus. First, markets can fail when one party, in an attempt to capture more resources, prevents mutually beneficial trades from occurring. Second, markets can fail when actions have side effects on others that aren't properly taken into account by the market—side effects like pollution. Finally, markets can fail because some goods, by their very nature, are unsuited for efficient management by markets. We will see in the next section how all three of these cases can be interpreted as instances in which prices give incorrect signals—that is, they fail to help people make better economic decisions. And as we will discover shortly, the failure of a particular market in an economy has implications for how well the entire economy operates.

economics in action

Smoothing Out the Bumps

The area around the departure gate is crowded, so it's obvious the plane will be full. In fact, it turns out that it's more than full. The gate agent announces that the flight is overbooked and asks for volunteers to give up their seats in return for rebooking on a later flight plus additional incentives, such as $200 toward a future ticket. If not enough volunteers come forward immediately, the incentives are increased.

This scene is familiar to any frequent flier. But it didn't always work that way. In fact, it took a couple of economists to teach the airlines how to deal efficiently with overbooking.

On busy flights, airlines have always sold tickets for more seats than actually exist. There's a good reason for this: some people with reservations always fail to show up, and an empty seat is a seat wasted. But sometimes fewer people than expected are no-shows, and a flight ends up overbooked. What happens then?

Until 1978, airlines simply "bumped" some of their passengers—informed them that their reservations had been canceled. There were no uniform rules about who got bumped; some airlines, for example, bumped older passengers because they were less likely to complain. Needless to say, those who got bumped were not happy.

In 1968, however, the economist Julian Simon proposed a market approach, in which airlines would treat a flight reservation as if a seat were a property right given to the passenger, so that the airlines would have to buy that right back if the plane was overbooked. Airlines didn't think this idea was practical. But in 1978 another economist, Alfred Kahn, was appointed to head the Civil Aeronautics Board, which regulated airlines at that time. He required airlines to use an auction system to deal with overbooking, resulting in the familiar process of asking for volunteers.

What's the advantage of this voluntary, market solution? Under the old system, someone who urgently needed to get on the scheduled flight was as likely to get bumped as someone who could easily take a later connection. Since 1978, those who absolutely have to make the flight don't volunteer; those who aren't that anxious to board get something that's worth more to them. The airline pays a cost to get passengers to give up their reserved seats but more than makes up for it in higher overall customer satisfaction. In short, everyone gains. By using property rights to create a market, Simon and Kahn moved that piece of the economy toward efficiency. ∎

< < < < < < < < < < < < < < < < < < < <

1. Imagine that eMarkets! is a company that implements a competitive market in MP3 players. Based on information it gathers, it tells producers what the equilibrium price will be so that they can decide how much to produce. And once production has occurred, it allocates output to consumers based on the price and their willingness to pay.
   a. What information would they need to know from consumers and producers in order to find the equilibrium price and quantity of MP3 players?
   b. Suppose that eMarkets! has determined that, once production occurs and trading happens, the equilibrium price will be $199 and the equilibrium quantity will be 10,000 units. But also suppose that due to a computer glitch, it informs some producers that the price will be $299, while it informs some producers that the price will be $99. How will producer surplus be affected? Can you determine the effect on the quantity produced—will it be equal to, less than, or more than the equilibrium quantity?
   c. Also suppose that due to the computer glitch, some consumers with a willingness to pay of $299 are told that the price is $399. An equal number of consumers who have a willingness to pay of $119 are allowed to buy the good at a price of $99. How will consumer surplus be affected?

   Solutions appear at back of book.

Efficiency in the Economy as a Whole

We've seen how the equilibrium outcome of an individual competitive market usually maximizes the total surplus of participants in that market. Is there an equivalent result for the economy as a whole? That is, is there a corresponding concept of equilibrium for the whole economy? And if so, does this equilibrium outcome maximize the welfare of the economy's participants?

The economy as a whole consists not of one but of many, many markets, all interrelated in two ways:

■ On the consumption side, the demand for each good is affected by the prices of other goods.

■ On the production side, producers of different goods compete for the same factors of production.

To think about the economy as a whole, then, we have to think of many markets, for both goods and factors. A **competitive market economy** is an economy in which all of these markets are perfectly competitive, with equilibrium prices determined by

A **competitive market economy** is an economy in which all markets, for goods and for factors, are perfectly competitive.

supply and demand. In each market both the supply and demand curves are likely to be affected by events in other markets.

When all markets have reached equilibrium—when the quantity of each good and factor demanded is equal to the quantity of each good and factor supplied at the going market prices—we say that the economy is in **general equilibrium.** To put it another way, general equilibrium is the economy-wide counterpart of ordinary equilibrium in a single market.

Our next task is to show that, as with an individual competitive market in equilibrium, a competitive market economy in general equilibrium is usually *efficient*—that is, it is efficient except in certain well-defined cases. What do we mean by saying that the economy as a whole is efficient? Actually, we defined efficiency way back in Chapter 1. We will start by revisiting that definition to see why it is the right approach to analyzing the economy as a whole. Next, we will describe the three criteria that an economy as a whole must satisfy in order to be efficient. Finally, we will learn how failures of individual markets can lead to inefficiency in the economy as a whole—failures we can view as cases in which prices fail to perform as economic signals.

> An economy is in **general equilibrium** when the quantity supplied is equal to the quantity demanded in all markets.

Efficiency, Revisited

When economists discuss efficiency in an individual market, they usually use the concepts of consumer and producer surplus, which measure costs and benefits in monetary terms. This makes sense when you are talking about the market for just one good, because you can take the prices of other goods—and therefore the value of a dollar—as given. When we are analyzing the economy as a whole, however, measuring costs and benefits in dollar terms no longer makes sense, because all prices are "to be determined."

FOR INQUIRING MINDS

DEFINING ECONOMIC EFFICIENCY

The economist's definition of *efficiency*—that an economy is efficient if nobody can be made better off without making others worse off—may seem to be oddly indirect. Why can't we define efficiency in terms of a positive achievement rather than the absence of something?

Many other definitions of efficiency have been proposed, but none of them have survived careful scrutiny—all of them turn out either to be incomplete or to involve unacceptable implications. A good example is the fate of the principle known as utilitarianism, proposed by the nineteenth-century English philosopher Jeremy Bentham.

Bentham offered a simple principle: "the greatest good for the greatest number." In effect, he argued that society should try to maximize the total utility of its members. This sounded persuasive but eventually ran into two problems. First, how do we add up the utility of different people? We may loosely say that Ms. Martineau is happier than Mr. Ricardo, but is she twice as happy or three

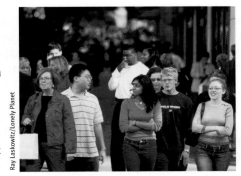

Whose util counts more? Efficiency has been difficult to define because we can't compare utility across people.

times as happy? You may argue that it makes no sense even to ask that question—but in that case Bentham's principle becomes meaningless because we have no way to add up the total utility of all members of society.

Second, even if we imagine that it is somehow possible to add up the utility of different people, critics of Bentham point out that his doctrine has the disturbing

implication that we should cater to the tastes of "utility monsters"—people who derive especially high pleasure from excessive consumption. Bentham's criterion implies that if Martineau really likes owning luxury automobiles and going to fancy restaurants but Ricardo is a modest sort who can make do with a bicycle and macaroni-and-cheese dinners, we should take money from Ricardo and give it to Martineau—even if Ricardo is a hard worker and Martineau notably lazy. This doesn't seem right.

Because of these difficulties, Bentham's principle has pretty much vanished from economic thought. The same is true of other ideas, such as the Marxist slogan "from each according to his ability, to each according to his needs." The only definition of efficiency that has managed to survive practical and logical criticism is the negative one: an economy is inefficient if there is a way to make at least one person better off without making others worse off, and it is efficient if it is not inefficient.

Instead, economists focus on the basic definition of efficiency. Recall from Chapter 1: an economy is efficient if it does not pass up any opportunities to make some people better off without making other people worse off.

To achieve efficiency, an economy must meet three criteria, which closely parallel the three features ensuring that total surplus is maximized in an individual market. The economy must be *efficient in consumption*, *efficient in production*, and *efficient in output levels*. Let's look at these criteria and see how a competitive market economy satisfies them.

Efficiency in Consumption

An economy is efficient in consumption
if there is no way to redistribute goods
among consumers that makes some
consumers better off without making
others worse off.

An economy is **efficient in consumption** if there is no way to redistribute goods among consumers that makes some consumers better off without making others worse off.

To see what efficiency in consumption involves, it helps to imagine scenarios for inefficiency. Imagine, for example, an economy that produces both cornflakes and shredded wheat but that provides those who prefer shredded wheat with cornflakes, and vice versa. Then it would be possible to make at least one person better off without making anyone else worse off by redistributing the goods, giving people the breakfast cereal they prefer.

The first piece of good news is that as long as prices perform properly as economic signals, this kind of inefficiency won't occur in a competitive market economy. We've seen this already in the case of market equilibrium in one individual market: the consumers who actually receive a good at the market equilibrium are those with the greatest willingness to pay—thanks to the role prices play in helping people make the right economic decisions. Consumers who prefer an additional box of cornflakes will be willing to pay more for that box than consumers who would rather have an additional box of shredded wheat. So if the markets for cornflakes and shredded wheat are both in equilibrium, there won't be any way to make at least one consumer better off without making others worse off by redistributing the available quantities of breakfast cereals.

In other words, prices in goods markets ensure that you can't increase total surplus in a single market by taking a good away from one person and giving it to another. Similarly, prices also ensure that when all markets in an economy are in perfectly competitive general equilibrium, there is no way to redistribute goods that makes some consumers better off without making others worse off.

It's important, however, to realize the limitations of that statement: even though an economy is efficient, you can always make *some* consumers better off if you are willing to make others worse off. We'll come back to that point shortly.

Efficiency in Production

An economy is **efficient in production** if
there is no way to produce more of
some goods without producing less of
other goods.

Economists say that an economy is **efficient in production** if it is not possible to produce more of some goods without producing less of others.

We can use the *production possibility frontier* model from Chapter 2 to understand this. This model uses a diagram like Figure 13-2 to illustrate the economy's trade-offs: the more wheat it produces, the less corn it can produce, and vice versa. If the economy produces the quantities at either point *A* or point *B* on the production possibility frontier, it is efficient in production: it is possible to produce more corn than the economy produces at *A*, but only by producing less wheat; it is possible to produce more wheat than the economy produces at *B*, but only by producing less corn. The economy is not efficient in production, however, if it produces at point *C:* it is possible to produce more wheat *and* more corn than the economy does at that point.

An economy has an **efficient allocation
of resources** if there is no way to reallocate factors of production among producers to produce more of some goods
without producing less of others.

An economy will be efficient in production if it has an **efficient allocation of resources**—if there is no way to reallocate factors of production among producers to produce more of some goods without producing less of others. This is an important result: *An economy that is efficient in allocation of resources is efficient in production, and vice versa.*

Here is another way to think about Figure 13-2: at point *A* the economy can produce more corn only by taking resources away from wheat production. Similarly, at

Figure 13-2

The Production Possibility Frontier and Efficiency in Production

An economy is efficient in production if it cannot produce more of one good without producing less of other goods. Equivalently, an economy is efficient in production if it is on its production possibility frontier. Here A and B are efficient production points—at each point the economy can produce more of one good only by producing less of the other. C is not an efficient production point because more corn *and* more wheat can be produced.

point B the economy can produce more wheat only by taking resources away from corn production.

Just as in the case of efficiency in consumption, it helps to imagine scenarios for inefficiency. In the United States, land in Iowa is ideally suited for growing corn, land in Minnesota is much better suited for growing wheat, and most land in Maine isn't suitable for growing either. It would clearly be inefficient if good land in the Midwest were left idle but farmers struggled with the stony soil of Maine; it would also be inefficient if Iowa farms grew wheat and Minnesota farms grew corn.

The second piece of good news is that, just as in the case of consumption, the role of prices as economic signals ensures that a competitive market economy in general equilibrium achieves efficiency in production. The logic is similar, but this time it applies to prices in factor markets rather than prices in goods markets. Corn farmers are willing to pay more for Iowa land than wheat farmers; wheat farmers are willing to pay more for Minnesota land than are corn farmers. And much of New England is no longer farmed but has returned to forest, because labor and capital can be more productively employed on richer lands elsewhere. In short, when factor markets are competitive, resources are allocated to the producers that can make the best use of them, and the economy is indeed efficient in production.

Notice, however, that this does not say *what* the economy produces. Both A and B in Figure 13-2 represent efficient production. We still need to ask whether the economy produces at the "right" place on the production possibility frontier—or, rather, *a* right place, because there may be many efficient outcomes. But let's hold off on that for a moment and finish our description of efficiency in the competitive market economy as a whole.

Efficiency in Output Levels

Suppose that a competitive market economy is efficient in production—it cannot produce more of some goods without producing less of others. Suppose also that it is efficient in consumption—there is no way to redistribute the goods produced that will make some consumers better off without making others worse off. There is still the question of whether the competitive market economy is producing the *right mix* of goods to start with. For example, suppose that point A in Figure 13-3 on page 320 corresponds to

An economy is **efficient in output levels** if there isn't a different mix of output that would make some people better off without making others worse off.

producing enough wheat to let everyone have shredded wheat five times a week and cornflakes two times a week. This will still be inefficient if everyone prefers to have shredded wheat only three times a week but cornflakes four times a week—*and* if point *B* would allow them to do so. In that case, moving from *A* to *B*—that is, shifting resources into corn production—would make everyone better off. Our third criterion for efficiency, then, is that the economy be **efficient in output levels:** there must not be a different mix of output that would make some people better off without making others worse off.

The third and final piece of good news about the equilibrium of a competitive market economy is that it will be efficient in output levels when prices perform properly as economic signals.

How do we know this? We already saw that in an individual competitive market producers produce the quantity of output that maximizes total surplus. The reason is that consumers and producers face the same price—the market price is an economic signal telling producers what one more unit of output is worth to consumers. This signal induces producers to produce that extra unit of output if the cost of the resources they would need to produce it is less than the market price.

In the economy as a whole, producers learn how much consumers are willing to pay for a bit more of one good versus a bit more of another when market prices operate as economic signals. This process ensures that a competitive market economy in general equilibrium produces the right mix of goods.

To see how this happens, imagine an economy in which the only resource that can be shifted between industries is labor, and all producers are hiring from the same labor market. (We'll also assume there are no complications like compensating differentials that make wages differ.) Imagine that right now consumers would prefer more corn and less wheat than the economy is currently producing. The economy can provide what consumers want by transferring labor from wheat production to corn production—by forgoing some wheat output in order to produce more corn. But will this adjustment take place?

Yes, it will, because consumers are willing to pay more for the additional corn that one more worker employed in corn production can produce than they are willing to pay for the wheat forgone by employing one fewer worker in wheat production. We can express this algebraically. The extra corn that a unit of labor can produce is MPL_{corn}, the marginal product of labor in corn. The wheat that unit of labor would have produced is MPL_{wheat}, the marginal product of labor in wheat. When we say that

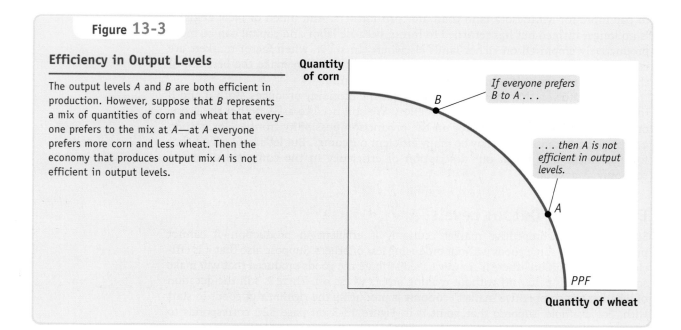

Figure 13-3

Efficiency in Output Levels

The output levels *A* and *B* are both efficient in production. However, suppose that *B* represents a mix of quantities of corn and wheat that everyone prefers to the mix at *A*—at *A* everyone prefers more corn and less wheat. Then the economy that produces output mix *A* is not efficient in output levels.

Quantity of corn

If everyone prefers B to A . . .

B

. . . then A is not efficient in output levels.

A

PPF

Quantity of wheat

consumers are willing to pay more for the extra corn than for the wheat, we are saying that at the current employment and output levels in the corn and wheat sectors

(13-1) $P_{corn} \times MPL_{corn} > P_{wheat} \times MPL_{wheat}$

where P_{corn} and P_{wheat} are the prices of corn and wheat respectively.

We've already seen the expressions in Equation 13-1 in Chapter 12. $P_{corn} \times MPL_{corn}$ is the *value of the marginal product* of labor in corn production, and $P_{wheat} \times MPL_{wheat}$ is the value of the marginal product of labor in wheat production. So we can restate Equation 13-1 as

(13-2) $VMPL_{corn} > VMPL_{wheat}$

This expression says that the value produced by an additional unit of labor employed in corn production is greater than that of an additional unit of labor employed in wheat production when consumers prefer more corn and less wheat than is being produced.

Can this be an equilibrium? No; we learned in Chapter 12 that producers maximize profits by hiring labor up until the point that $VMPL = W$, where W is the wage rate. That is, a producer hires labor until the value of the output produced by the last worker employed is equal to the current market wage rate. In this example, corn producers and wheat producers hire workers from the same labor market. So the direct implication of $VMPL_{corn} > VMPL_{wheat}$ is that, at current employment levels, corn producers are willing to pay a higher wage rate than wheat producers. Corn producers will hire workers away from wheat producers.

When will this process stop? When the wage rate that corn producers are willing to pay is equal to the wage rate that wheat producers are willing to pay; that is, when $VMPL_{corn} = VMPL_{wheat}$. The evolution of this process is illustrated in Figure 13-4.

Figure 13-4   How an Economy Achieves Efficiency in Output Levels

If at current employment levels $VMPL_{corn} > VMPL_{wheat}$, then corn producers will increase their profits by hiring workers away from wheat producers, who will, in turn, increase their profits by laying off workers. This process is illustrated for a corn producer in panel (a). As a corn producer hires workers, she increases her corn production and moves down her $VMPL$ curve until she reaches her optimal employment level, the number of workers at which $VMPL_{corn} = W$, the market wage rate. Panel (b) shows the corresponding changes for a wheat producer:

he decreases his wheat production and moves up his $VMPL$ curve as he lays off workers. He also reaches his optimal employment level at $VMPL_{wheat} = W$. Workers cease moving between sectors once $VMPL_{corn} = VMPL_{wheat}$. It is an equilibrium because at that point the value of the additional output produced by a worker in the corn sector no longer exceeds the value of the additional output produced by a worker in the wheat sector and corn producers are no longer willing to pay a higher wage than wheat producers.

In panel (a), a corn producer starts at a $VMPL_{corn}$ greater than the current market wage rate. She increases her profits by hiring more workers and moves down her $VMPL$ curve until she reaches her optimal employment level, at which $VMPL_{corn} = W$.

Where are these new workers in the corn sector coming from? They are coming from the wheat sector. This is illustrated in panel (b), where a wheat producer is losing workers and in the process is moving up his $VMPL$ curve. He increases his profits by laying off workers, letting them go until he reaches his optimal employment level, at which $VMPL_{wheat} = W$.

So as labor in the economy is reallocated from wheat production to corn production, the output of corn rises and the output of wheat falls. Eventually, workers cease moving from the wheat sector to the corn sector when $VMPL_{corn} = VMPL_{wheat}$. At this point the value of the additional output produced by a worker in the corn sector no longer exceeds the value of the additional output produced by a worker in the wheat sector. That is, we have finally reached an equilibrium.

This example helps us understand that, in a market economy, markets for goods and services are linked via the factor markets. Or to put it a slightly different way, any change in the amount of one good or service produced will ultimately affect the amounts of other goods and services as factors of production shift from one sector to another. Figure 13-5 helps us make sense of the interconnectedness of markets for goods and services and factor markets in a market economy. To appreciate its signifi-

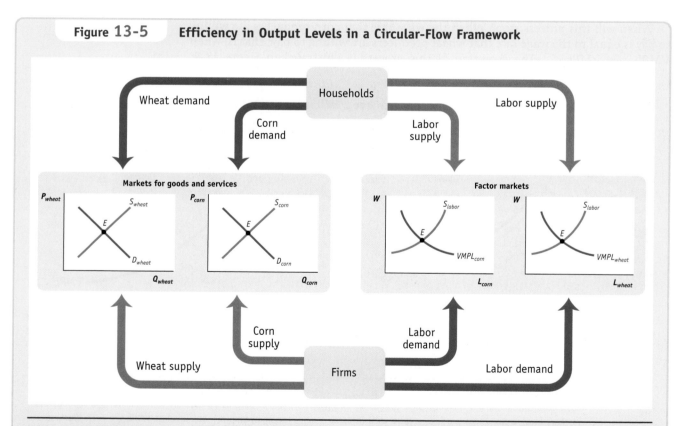

Figure 13-5   Efficiency in Output Levels in a Circular-Flow Framework

Using a hypothetical economy in which corn and wheat are the only goods and labor is the only factor of production, we can see how the markets for goods and services are linked via the factor markets. The factor markets bring the supply of labor from households and the demand for labor by firms into equilibrium, and the markets for goods and services bring the supply of goods and services from firms and the demand for goods and services by households into equilibrium. But supply and demand in all these markets are interrelated: households' earnings in the labor market determine their demand for goods and services, and vice versa; firms' profits from hiring labor in the labor market and producing output determine their supply of goods and services, and vice versa. Any change in one market will ultimately generate corresponding changes in all the other markets. When every market for goods and services and every factor market in the economy is in equilibrium, the economy as a whole is in general equilibrium.

cance, it may help recalling the circular-flow diagram of Chapter 2. There we saw how firms and households are linked via the factor markets and the markets for goods and services through flows of money. That is, in the factor markets, firms pay households for factors of production; in the markets for goods and services, households pay firms for goods and services.

Figure 13-5 presents an alternative and richer version of the same phenomenon, this time expressed in terms of the forces of supply and demand for resources that underlie the money flows of the circular-flow diagram. Here, we imagine that the only goods in the economy are corn and wheat and that labor is the only factor of production. The right portion of the figure represents how the supply of labor from households and the demand for labor from firms meet and are brought into equilibrium in the factor markets. But supply and demand in the labor market are themselves affected by supply and demand in the markets for goods and services: firms' demand for labor is derived from the demand for their goods and services, and households' supply of labor is determined by the earnings required for purchases in the markets for goods and services.

Similarly, the left portion of Figure 13-5 represents how the supply of goods and services from firms and the demand for goods and services from households meet and are brought into equilibrium in the markets for goods and services. Again, there is an interrelationship between the market for goods and services and factor markets: households' demand for goods and services is determined by the wages they earn in the labor market, and firms' supply of goods and services is determined by the returns they generate from hiring labor in the labor market.

Moreover, any change in the demand for a good will initiate a cascade of events that will ripple through the entire economy as resources shift among various sectors in response. So, for example, an increase in demand for corn relative to wheat causes a rightward shift of the demand for corn and a leftward shift in the demand for wheat. This results in an increase in the equilibrium quantity of corn supplied and a decrease in the equilibrium quantity of wheat supplied, which in turn causes an increase in the equilibrium employment level in the corn sector and a decrease in the equilibrium employment in the wheat sector. So the incentives in a competitive market economy in which prices perform properly as economic signals will lead the economy to produce the mix of goods that consumers prefer—that is, the economy will indeed be efficient in output levels. When each market for goods and services and each factor market is in equilibrium, the economy as a whole is in general equilibrium.

How does a competitive market economy achieve this amazing result? It comes down to the point we have emphasized throughout this discussion: the role of prices as *economic signals*. The fact that everyone faces the same prices ensures that goods and services are efficiently allocated among consumers, that factors of production are efficiently allocated among producers, and that the mix of goods and services produced reflects what people want.

Inefficiency in the Economy: When Prices Go Astray

The efficiency of a competitive market economy, however, is not something we should take for granted. Just as individual markets can fail, the general equilibrium of a competitive market economy may be inefficient. When this happens, some mutually beneficial trades will go unexploited. That is, there is some reallocation of consumption or production, or some change in output levels, that would make someone better off without making others worse off.

Why is a competitive market economy sometimes inefficient? For the same three reasons that individual markets sometimes fail. And when markets fail, prices fail to serve as economic signals.

First, recall that a market fails when attempts by one party to capture more resources prevents mutually beneficial transactions from occurring. We can illustrate this phenomenon by returning to our Chapter 4 example of quotas and New York taxi licenses. Recall that the current quota on taxi licenses in New York City results in a shortage of taxi rides compared to the unrestricted competitive market equilibrium. As a result, existing owners of taxi licenses gain (earning higher returns than they would have otherwise), but mutually beneficial transactions in taxi rides go unexploited. If the quota didn't exist, the fact that the market price of a ride exceeds the unrestricted competitive market price would draw new taxi drivers into the market. So supply would increase until the willingness to pay of the last rider in the market is equal to the cost of the last driver in the market, and the market would achieve efficiency. Or, to put it slightly differently, the quota prevents the market price from operating as an economic signal that would draw new taxi drivers into the market to eliminate the shortage. As a result, the larger economy (of which the New York City taxi ride market is a part) is inefficient. It's not efficient in consumption because some riders with a higher willingness to pay can't get a taxi but some with a lower willingness to pay are able to. It is not efficient in production because some drivers with higher costs have licenses but some with lower costs do not, implying that output could be increased without using more resources by reallocating production to those drivers with the lowest cost. And it is not efficient in output levels because there are too few taxi rides provided relative to other goods. We will study a similar kind of inefficiency in detail in Chapter 14, where we investigate monopoly, an industry that has only a single seller.

The second source of market failure is the side effects of actions that aren't properly accounted for in the existing markets. For example, consider the pollution caused by a large poultry farm whose wastes foul nearby streams and reduce the welfare of nearby residents. The cost savings that the farm gains by dumping its waste rather than having it properly disposed of are smaller in value than the discomfort experienced by its neighbors—that is, what the neighbors would be willing to pay to get rid of the pollution. But a mutually beneficial trade between the farm and the neighbors is going unexploited. Efficiency could be achieved if there were a "market for pollution"—if either the farm could purchase from the residents the right to dump so many barrels of waste or the residents could purchase from the farm the right to water of a certain purity. Either way, efficiency would be achieved: consumers would buy and the seller would sell until the willingness to pay for the last unit bought and sold equals the seller's cost of producing it. The problem here arises because the relevant market doesn't exist—there is no market for either pollution rights or water-purity rights. As a result, there is no relevant market price that can function as an economic signal to direct individuals to buy and sell. This economy is inefficient: the total welfare of individuals in the economy would be higher if less pollution and, correspondingly, less poultry were produced. We will analyze these side effects, called *externalities*, in detail in Chapter 19. There we will see how governments can intervene in ways that assure that market prices do indeed provide the proper economic signals.

The third and final reason that markets fail is that some goods, by their nature, are unsuited for efficient management by markets. Consider a song that can be downloaded from the Internet. Once the song is recorded, the marginal cost to the record company of allowing someone to download it is virtually zero. So efficiency implies that people should be allowed to download the song until the last downloader's willingness to pay is equal to zero. That is, efficiency is achieved only if there is free and unrestricted downloading of music. But an inconvenient fact arises at this point: if the record company can't charge for downloads, then it won't have revenues to pay its artists. And if it can't pay its artists, then artists won't record in the first place. And that, too, is inefficient. The problem here lies in the nature of the good itself, called an *information good*, which is the subject of Chapter 22. For information goods, efficiency in consumption means that the price to consumers must be zero, but efficiency in output levels means that the price received by producers must be greater than zero. For these goods, inefficiency is simply unavoidable. A similar inefficiency arises for what are called *public goods* and *common resources*—goods for which, by their nature, the producer cannot charge consumers. We will study public goods and common resources in Chapter 20.

In most cases, however, market failures can be corrected. Indeed, although it is important to understand how they occur, this analysis isn't a reason to reject markets. Instead, the analysis of market failures tells policy makers how to correct them and take advantage of the remarkable ability of a competitive market economy to allocate resources efficiently.

economics in action

A Great Leap—Backward

We began this chapter with the observation that the planned economy of East Germany did not, as its founders had hoped, surpass the market economies of the West. But possibly the most compelling example of inefficiency in a planned economy comes from China.

In the late 1950s, China's leader Mao Zedong put into effect an ambitious plan, the so-called Great Leap Forward, to speed up the nation's industrialization. Key to this plan was a shift from urban to rural manufacturing: farming villages were supposed to start producing such heavy industrial goods as steel.

Unfortunately, this plan backfired. Diverting farmers from their usual work led to a sharp fall in food production. Meanwhile, because raw materials like coal and iron ore were sent to ill-equipped and inexperienced rural producers rather than to urban factories, industrial output declined as well. The plan, in short, led to a fall in the production of everything.

Because China was a very poor nation to start with, the results were catastrophic. The famine that followed is estimated to have reduced China's population by as much as 30 million. ■

>> CHECK YOUR UNDERSTANDING 13-2

1. In the small country of Bountiful, labor is the only factor of production, all workers are paid the same wage, all food is produced domestically, and all markets are perfectly competitive. Imagine that, due to health concerns, each Bountifullian experiences a greater demand for breakfast cereals and a lower demand for sausage.
   a. Explain how the change in preferences will lead to a reallocation of labor between the sausage and breakfast cereal industries. Use the concepts of $VMPL_S$, $VMPL_C$, and wage rate in your answer (the subscript S refers to sausage and C to cereal).
   b. How will you know that the Bountiful economy has fully adjusted to the change in preferences? Use the three conditions of efficiency in your answer.

Solutions appear at back of book.

Efficiency and Equity

We have now shown why a perfectly competitive market economy is typically efficient: there is no way to make some people better off without making others worse off.

This conclusion refutes the claims of would-be economic planners, who insist that markets are disorganized free-for-alls and that centralized decision making would be more efficient. But we need to be careful: it is easy to get carried away with the idea that markets get it right and to then draw inappropriate conclusions about economic policy.

It's important to remember that efficiency is about *how to achieve goals*; it does not say anything about what your goals should be. Saying that the market outcome is efficient doesn't mean that that outcome is necessarily desirable. In fact, in some circumstances a well-thought-out economic policy may deliberately choose an outcome that is *not* efficient.

When can an outcome be efficient without being desirable? When it's not fair.

FOR INQUIRING MINDS

THEORIES OF JUSTICE

In 1971 the philosopher John Rawls published *A Theory of Justice*, which represents the most famous attempt to date to develop a theory of economic fairness. He asked readers to imagine deciding economic and social policies behind a "veil of ignorance" about their identity. That is, suppose that you knew you would be a human being but you did not know whether you would be rich or poor, healthy or sick, and so on. What kind of policies would you want?

Rawls answered that you would probably choose policies that placed a high weight on the utility of the worst-off members of society: after all, you might end up being one of them. And because of diminishing marginal utility, having a few dollars more would do you a lot of good if you find yourself poor, but having a few dollars less wouldn't do you much harm if you find yourself well-off.

Although no nation has ever made this theory the basis for its economic policy, Rawls-type arguments do play an important role in the debate over economic and social policy. For example, when Congress debated a plan to cut tax rates on large estates—those valued at over $1.3 million—from their 2000 rate of 55 percent, Bill Gates, Sr., father of the Microsoft billionaire, offered a defense of the existing tax based on a Rawlsian view of fairness. He made his case by asking people to imagine traveling back to the moment of their birth. At that point, you get to decide, for a price, where you are going to be born—the hugely rich United States or impoverished Ethiopia. The price for choosing Ethiopia is zero; the price for choosing the United States is 55 percent of the value of your estate should it exceed $1.3 million when you die. Or to put it another way, imagine that the price of being born in the United States instead of Ethiopia is your commitment to pay the current level of the U.S. estate tax. What would you choose?

What's Fair?

Imagine an economy in which a dictator controls everything, keeping almost everything the economy produces for himself and allowing his subjects only the bare minimum they need to survive. Could such an economy be efficient?

Yes, it could. If there is no way to make one of the suffering citizens better off without making the dictator worse off, then the economy is efficient. But that doesn't mean we have to approve of it. The situation is clearly unjust; the contrast between the dictator's wealth and his subjects' poverty isn't fair.

This extreme example shows that we want something more than efficiency from an economy. We also want *equity*: we want the distribution of utility among individuals to be reasonably fair.

But what exactly is "fair"? That turns out to be a very hard question to answer. To see why it's such a tricky question, let's consider how plausible ideas about fairness become problematic when you start to think about them carefully.

"FAIR IS FAIR... IF IT'S TURN-OFF-YOUR-TV WEEK FOR ME, THEN IT'S UNPLUG-YOUR-EMAIL WEEK FOR YOU."

First, you sometimes hear that people should be given an equal chance at the starting line—that is, at birth, or maybe at the age of 18, everyone should have the same opportunities to be successful in life. That sounds fair—but what about the natural desire of parents to do well by their children? Shouldn't parents who own their own businesses have the right to appoint their children to executive positions in those businesses? Shouldn't parents who can afford to do so have the right to send their children to expensive private schools? It seems unfair that children of successful parents should have an advantage over children whose parents don't have the same resources. Yet it would also seem unfair to prevent successful parents from helping their children. How do you resolve this contradiction?

Another familiar concept is that people should be rewarded for the work they do. And that, too seems reasonable: if you are a skilled worker, with twice my marginal product, it seems only fair that you should receive twice my wage. But what about someone who suffers an injury and cannot work? To say that that person should go without any income seems unfair.

The attempt to define fairness has led to some fascinating debates among philosophers; we describe the views of one influential thinker, John Rawls, in For Inquiring Minds on page 326. However, those debates have not led to any generally accepted definition.

Do we need a definition of *fairness*? Not necessarily—virtually everyone agrees that some outcomes, like our hypothetical dictator-dominated economy, are unfair, and in other cases we can agree to differ. But sometimes the lack of agreement on fairness means that economic analysis alone cannot be used to decide between alternative policies. To see why, let's introduce a new concept, the *utility possibility frontier*.

The Utility Possibility Frontier

Let's think of an economy that contains only two kinds of people, Easterners and Westerners. In Figure 13-6, the horizontal axis measures the total utility of the typical Westerner and the vertical axis measures the total utility of the typical Easterner.

An efficient outcome in this economy would be one in which there was no way to make either Easterners or Westerners better off without making members of the other group worse off. But there may be many such possible outcomes. In the figure we show what the possibilities might look like by drawing a **utility possibility frontier,** which shows how well-off each group *could* be given the economy's resources and the total utility of the other. Any point on the utility possibility frontier is efficient—that is, once you are on the frontier, the only way to make some people better off is to make others worse off. Any point inside the frontier is inefficient.

So suppose that you were asked to choose between two sets of economic policies—one that would bring the economy to point *A* and one that would bring it to point *B*. For example, suppose there is a question of who should receive ownership of some disputed land. As long as the property rights are clearly defined, the economy will be efficient, but Westerners would prefer that they get the rights, and Easterners would prefer the reverse. So which outcome is better?

A **utility possibility frontier** shows how well-off one individual or group could be for each given total utility level of another individual or group.

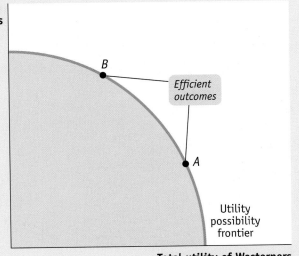

Figure 13-6

The Utility Possibility Frontier

The utility possibility frontier reminds us that there may be many efficient outcomes for an economy. The utility possibility frontier shows the maximum level of total utility of a typical Easterner, given the level of total utility of a typical Westerner. Any point on the curve is efficient because at such a point there is no way to make a typical Easterner better off without making a typical Westerner worse off, and vice versa. But this means that we cannot decide on economic grounds alone whether point *A* or *B* is better.

Total utility of Easterners

B

Efficient outcomes

A

Utility possibility frontier

Total utility of Westerners

The answer is that it's a matter of taste. Westerners would, of course, prefer *A*; Easterners would prefer *B*. For government officials trying to decide how to assign the property rights, the answer would depend on what relative weight they give to the welfare of the two groups. The question of whether *A* or *B* is better is, in other words, a question of values that economics cannot answer.

Notice, by the way, that *A* and *B* don't differ just in how goods and services are distributed to individuals; they might well involve producing a different mix of goods and services. If Westerners like cornflakes but Easterners prefer shredded wheat, the economy probably produces more corn and less wheat at *B* than at *A*. Is it more efficient to produce corn or wheat? There is no answer to this question, because both can be efficient, depending on our goals.

The point that efficiency is a means to achieve goals, not a goal in itself, can be further illustrated by considering what is wrong with *inefficient* policies. Figure 13-7 shows the same utility possibility frontier as Figure 13-6 but now also shows point *C*—an inefficient outcome, one that lies inside the frontier. You might think of *C* as the result of a policy that favors Easterners in an inefficient way. In fact, many economists believe that the actual policies the newly reunited Germany followed to help the former East Germans were poorly designed, providing them with few incentives to take new jobs or acquire new skills. That is, many economists believe that Germany as a whole ended up at a point like *C*.

Is there any reason why you might want to choose an inefficient point such as *C*? Not if better choices are genuinely available: there are points on the utility possibility frontier that are better than *C* whatever relative weight you give to the welfare of the two groups. For example, *B* is better than *C* by any standard.

But what if the real choices are limited to *A* or *C*? Should you as a voter prefer the efficient policies proposed by the Western party?

Not necessarily. *A* is efficient, and *C* is not; but it is still true that Easterners are better off at *C* than they are at *A*. So if the utility of Easterners matters enough to you, you might well prefer *C* to *A* even though you would prefer *B* to either. As economists say, it is often—but by no means always—worth trading less efficiency for more equity.

So it's important to remember what efficiency is *not*. Efficiency is not a goal in itself, to be pursued at the expense of other goals. It is only a way to achieve our goals more effectively—whatever those goals may be.

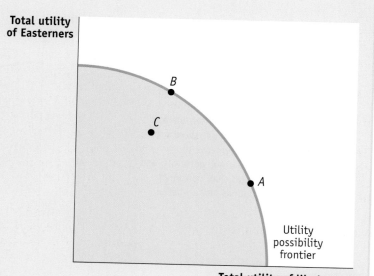

Figure 13-7

Efficiency Versus Equity

Suppose that for some reason the policy choices that are available are restricted: you can choose only between the efficient outcome *A* and the inefficient outcome *C*. Does this mean that *A* is preferable? Not necessarily. If you place a high enough weight on the utility of Easterners, you may be willing to trade *efficiency* for *equity*: even though the economy is not efficient at *C*, the utility of Easterners is higher at *C* than at *A*.

economics in action

Death and Taxes

Earlier, we used the example of parents giving their children a head start by paying for expensive private schooling to show how simple questions of fairness can give conflicting answers. In fact, inheritance is one of those areas in which differing notions of fairness translate directly into different policy conclusions.

One notion of fairness focuses on individual positions at the starting line: it says that it is unfair that some children should inherit large sums but others get nothing. The natural conclusion from this notion is that inheritances should be heavily taxed. This has, in fact, been the policy of many countries, including to some extent the United States.

The alternative notion of fairness focuses on the right of people to choose what to do with their money: it says that it is unfair to deny parents the right to pass on their savings to their children.

These competing notions are reflected in different names for the "estate tax," the tax levied on the assets individuals leave behind them at death. Politicians who focus on the starting line call it the "inheritance tax," emphasizing the position of the heirs. Politicians who focus on individual choice call it the "death tax," emphasizing the position of the parents.

Who's right? Economic analysis can't say. However, legislation passed in 2001 will eliminate the estate tax by 2010. ∎

> > > > > > > > > > > > > > > > > > > >

>>CHECK YOUR UNDERSTANDING 13-3

1. Explain why it is easier to determine whether an economy is efficient than to determine whether it is fair.

2. Explain why the following statements are problematic to use in determining whether or not a society is fair.
   a. In a fair society, each person contributes to society according to his or her means, and each person receives benefits according to his or her needs.
   b. In a fair society, a person is rewarded in proportion to how hard he or she works.

Solutions appear at back of book.

• A LOOK AHEAD •

We have now answered the first of the big questions we raised in the Introduction: *Why does a competitive market economy generally work so well?* Part of the answer involved defining what it means to work "well": an economy works badly if it misses opportunities to make at least one person better off without making others worse off, and it works well if it does not miss those opportunities.

What we've now seen is that in a well-functioning competitive market economy in equilibrium, consumers can buy as much or as little as they choose at the same price, and producers can sell as much or as little as they choose, also at the same price. And this means that all the opportunities to make at least one person better off without making others worse off—whether by redistributing goods among consumers, rearranging output among producers, or changing what the economy produces—will *already have been taken*.

One question down, another to go. Why do things sometimes go wrong? Why do market economies sometimes work badly? The short answer, as we saw in Chapter 6, is "market failure." The long answer will require a few more chapters!

SUMMARY

1. Except in cases of market failure, an individual competitive market in equilibrium maximizes total surplus, the sum of consumer and producer surplus. Rearranging consumption, rearranging production, or changing the level of output will all reduce total surplus.

2. **Property rights** and prices as **economic signals** are two features of competitive markets that are crucial to their ability to work well. The three causes of market failure—mutually beneficial transactions that are unexploited due to attempts to capture surplus, side effects that are not accounted for in the market, and goods whose nature prevents their efficient management by markets—can all be linked to the failure of prices to perform properly as economic signals.

3. When we turn to the performance of the economy as a whole, we use the economic definition of efficiency: the **general equilibrium** of a **competitive market economy** is efficient if there is no way to make some people better off without making others worse off.

4. Economic efficiency requires **efficiency in consumption**—there is no way to redistribute goods and services that makes some consumers better off without making others worse off. It requires **efficiency in production**, which arises from an **efficient allocation of**

resources—there is no way to reallocate resources that allows the economy to produce more of some goods and services without producing less of others. And it requires **efficiency in output levels**—there is no other choice of output mix that makes some people better off without making others worse off. In the same way in which a competitive market maximizes total surplus, the general equilibrium of a competitive market economy as a whole is efficient—in consumption, in production, and in output levels—when prices perform properly as market signals. In cases of market failure, however, prices fail to lead people to exploit all mutually beneficial transactions; as a result, when markets fail, the economy as a whole is inefficient.

5. It is not enough for an economy to be efficient. We also want it to deliver an outcome that is "fair" in terms of the distribution of utility among individuals. Economic fairness is known as equity.

6. Unfortunately, there is no generally accepted definition of *fairness*. The ambiguity this sometimes creates for evaluating economic policy can be illustrated with the **utility possibility frontier,** which shows the trade-offs between the utility achieved by one individual or group and that achieved by other individuals or groups.

KEY TERMS

Property rights, p. 314
Economic signal, p. 315
Competitive market economy, p. 316

General equilibrium, p. 317
Efficient in consumption, p. 318
Efficient in production, p. 318

Efficient allocation of resources, p. 318
Efficient in output levels, p. 320
Utility possibility frontier, p. 327

PROBLEMS

1. The Medici family in Florence produces all the wool in Italy. The five Medici children each have a factory in which they can produce one pound of wool per day. Their costs of producing each pound of wool are given on the left side of the accompanying table. Wool is demanded by the Visconti family in Milan. Each of the five Visconti children can demand one pound of wool per day. Their willingness to pay is given on the right side of the table.

Medici family		Visconti family	
Name	Cost (per pound)	Name	Willingness to pay (per pound)
Lucrezia	$8	Ennio	$14
Bianca	10	Lucchino	13
Luisa	12	Matteo	12
Contessina	14	Giovanni	11
Maddalena	16	Filippo	10

a. The market in wool is perfectly competitive. What will the equilibrium price be?

b. Does the equilibrium price lead to efficiency in this market?

c. The Visconti family argues that the price of wool should be fixed at a maximum of $10 so that all their operations can buy wool. Is this efficient? Why or why not?

2. Lakshmi and Sam have a cake that they want to divide in an efficient way, and the cake is the only good in their little economy. Both Lakshmi and Sam like cake and would always prefer to have more of it. Using the standard of efficiency in consumption, determine whether the following ways of dividing the cake are efficient.

a. Lakshmi and Sam each get half of the cake.

b. Lakshmi and Sam each get one-third of the cake and one-third is thrown away.

c. Lakshmi gets the whole cake and Sam gets nothing.

3. A city block with 25 residents has a garden in the center. Some of the residents are very busy, but others have lots of leisure time. And their preferences also differ: some enjoy yard work, others don't. The garden requires a total of 1,000 hours of work per year—planting, mowing grass, and so on. One resident suggests that each resident should contribute 40 hours per year to maintain the garden. Another resident, an economist, objects that this will be inefficient.

a. Explain why the economist thinks that the proposal will be inefficient.

b. Describe how a market in which residents can trade hours of yard work leads to an efficient allocation of yard work among residents.

4. In the town of Rockport, only two goods are produced: left shoes and right shoes. And this economy produces on the production possibility frontier. That is, there is no way of producing more left shoes without producing fewer right shoes, and vice versa. What else would you need to know, if anything, to determine whether the economy of Rockport as a whole is efficient? That is, does it satisfy efficiency in production, efficiency in consumption, and efficiency in output levels? Explain your answer.

5. The economy of Dunk, IN, produces only two goods, bagels and doughnuts, using labor as the only factor of production. There are 8 workers in Dunk and all are paid the same wage. The accompanying table shows the amount of output that can be produced with a certain number of workers.

Quantity of labor in doughnut production (workers)	Quantity of doughnuts	Quantity of labor in bagel production (workers)	Quantity of bagels
0	0	0	0
1	34	1	50
2	40	2	86
3	46	3	92
4	49	4	98
5	52	5	104
6	53	6	106

a. Suppose that the price of a doughnut is $0.50 and the price of a bagel is also $0.50. There are 2 workers producing doughnuts and 3 workers producing bagels. The other 3 workers are unemployed. Given what you know about the relationship between the value of the marginal products and efficiency, determine whether this economy is efficient in the production of doughnuts versus the production of bagels—that is, is the economy efficient in output levels? Also determine whether the economy is efficient in production—that is, is it producing on the production possibility frontier?

b. Suppose that the price of doughnuts is $0.20, and the price of bagels is $0.10. There are 4 workers producing doughnuts and 4 workers producing bagels, and nobody is unemployed. Is this economy efficient in production? Is it efficient in output levels?

c. Initially, the price of doughnuts is $0.20, the price of bagels is $0.10, and there are 4 workers producing doughnuts and 4 workers producing bagels, just as in part b. Now consumers' tastes change: due to health concerns, consumers are now willing to pay $0.75 per bagel but only $0.10 per doughnut. These new prices act as signals of consumers' preferences. In response to this change, will the allocation of workers to bagel or doughnut production change?

6. Land in the Shire can be used for growing carrots or potatoes, and the only variable input into production is labor (land is fixed). All workers are paid the same wage. There are two farmers: Sam grows carrots, and the marginal product of labor on his farm is 30 pounds of carrots per month. Merry grows potatoes, and the marginal product of labor on his farm is 44 pounds of potatoes per month. Each experiences diminishing returns to labor. The price of carrots is $3 per pound, and the price of potatoes is $2 per pound.

a. Calculate the value of the marginal product of labor in carrots and in potatoes to assess whether the economy of the Shire is efficient in output levels. Is the economy in general equilibrium?

b. Do the prices of carrots and potatoes signal that farmers should produce more or less of their crops? In which direction will employment levels adjust in response to the market prices for the two crops? Describe how the economy reaches general equilibrium.

7. The economy of Leisureville, CO, produces only two goods: skis and bikes. Labor is the only variable input into production, there are diminishing returns to labor, and all workers are paid the same wage. All markets are competitive, and initially the economy is in general equilibrium. Now, due to a change in tastes, consumers' preferences change away from skis and toward bikes.

a. What will happen to consumers' willingness to pay for bikes and for skis? What will therefore happen to the market prices for bikes and skis?

b. As the prices adjust, what will happen to the value of the marginal product of labor in bikes and in skis? What will happen to bike producers' and ski producers' willingness to pay for workers?

c. As adjustments are made in employment, what happens to the output of bikes and of skis? How does the marginal product of labor in bikes and in skis respond? What therefore happens to the value of the marginal product of labor in bikes and in skis?

d. At what point does this process stop?

8. Gulliver travels to a country in which there are two types of creatures, the Houyhnhnms and the Yahoos, and there are equally as many Houyhnhnms as there are Yahoos. The accompanying table lists the possible combinations of utility levels. That is, the points in the table lie on this economy's utility possibility frontier.

Point	Total utility of Houyhnhnms (utils)	Total utility of Yahoos (utils)
A	200	0
B	180	30
C	140	60
D	80	90
E	0	120

a. Draw the utility possibility frontier. When Gulliver arrives, he notices that the Houyhnhnms have a utility of 120 and the Yahoos have a utility of 50. Is this an efficient outcome?

b. Gulliver remembers that Jeremy Bentham argued that the best outcome is the one that maximizes the sum of everyone's utility. Which of the points A through E on the utility frontier would Bentham have chosen as the best outcome?

c. Gulliver then recalls that John Rawls argued that the best outcome is the one that gives the most utility to whoever happens to be the worst-off member in society. Which of the points A through E would Rawls have chosen?

9. Consider the utility possibility frontier in the accompanying diagram.

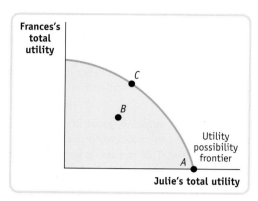

a. Is point A efficient? Would you describe point A as fair? Why or why not?

b. Is point B efficient?

c. Is point C better than point B? Why or why not?

d. Is point A better than point B? Why or why not?

>web... To continue your study and review of concepts in this chapter, please visit the Krugman/Wells website for quizzes, animated graph tutorials, web links to helpful resources, and more.

www.worthpublishers.com/krugmanwells

>> Monopoly

EVERYBODY MUST GET STONES

A FEW YEARS AGO DE BEERS, THE world's main supplier of diamonds, ran an ad urging men to buy their wives diamond jewelry. "She married you for richer, for poorer," read the ad. "Let her know how it's going."

Crass? Yes. Effective? No question. For generations diamonds have been a symbol of luxury, valued not only for their appearance but also for their rarity.

But geologists will tell you that diamonds aren't all that rare. In fact, according to the *Dow Jones-Irwin Guide to Fine Gems and Jewelry*, diamonds are "more common than any other gem-quality colored stone. They only seem rarer . . ."

Why do diamonds seem rarer than other gems? Part of the answer is a brilliant marketing campaign (We'll talk more about marketing and product

Got stones?

differentiation in Chapter 16.) But mainly diamonds seem rare because De Beers *makes* them rare: the company controls most of the world's diamond mines and limits the quantity of diamonds supplied to the market.

Up to now we have concentrated exclusively on perfectly competitive markets—markets in which the producers are perfect competitors. But De Beers isn't like the producers we've studied so far: it is a *monopolist*, the sole (or almost sole) producer of a good. Monopolists behave differently from producers in perfectly competitive industries: whereas perfect competitors take the price at which they can sell their output as given, monopolists know that their actions affect market prices and take that effect into account when deciding how much to produce. Before we begin our analysis, let's step back and look at monopoly and perfect competition as parts of a broader system for classifying markets.

Perfect competition and monopoly are particular types of *market structure*. They are particular categories in a system economists use to classify markets and industries according to two main dimensions. This chapter begins with a brief overview of types of market structure. It will help us here and in subsequent chapters to understand on a deeper level why markets differ and why producers in those markets behave quite differently.

What you will learn in this chapter:

► The significance of **monopoly,** where a single **monopolist** is the only producer of a good

► How a monopolist determines its profit-maximizing output and price

► The difference between monopoly and perfect competition, and the effects of that difference on society's welfare

► How policy makers address the problems posed by monopoly

► What **price discrimination** is, and why it is so prevalent when producers have **market power.**

Types of Market Structure

In the real world, there is a mind-boggling array of different markets. We observe widely different behavior patterns by producers across markets: in some markets producers are extremely competitive; in others, they seem somehow to coordinate their actions to avoid competing with one another; and, as we have just described, some markets are monopolies in which there is no competition at all. In order to develop principles and make predict-------- ve in them, economists have deve   *erfect competition, monopoly, oligopo*

This system of market stru

- The number of producers ir
- Whether the goods offered

Differentiated goods are good: sti- tutable by consumers (think C

Figure 14-1 provides a simple   ructure clas- sified according to the two dim   producer sells a single, undifferentiated product. In *olig*   s—more than one but not a large number—sell products that may   ntical or differentiated. In *monopolistic competition*, many producers eac. sell a differentiated product (think of producers of economics textbooks). And finally, as we know, in *perfect competition* many producers each sell an identical product.

You might wonder what determines the number of firms in a market: whether there is one (monopoly), few (oligopoly), or many (perfect competition and monopolistic competition). We won't answer that question here, because it will be covered in detail later in this chapter and in Chapters 15 and 16, which analyze oligopoly and monopolistic competition. We will just briefly note that in the long run it depends on whether there are conditions that make it difficult for new firms to enter the market, such as government regulations that discourage entry, economies of scale in production, technological superiority, or control of necessary resources or inputs. When these conditions are present, industries tend to be monopolies or oligopolies; when they are not present, industries tend to be perfectly competitive or monopolistically competitive.

You might also wonder why some markets have differentiated products but others have identical ones. The answer is that it depends on the nature of the good and consumers' preferences. Some goods—soft drinks, economics textbooks, breakfast cereals—

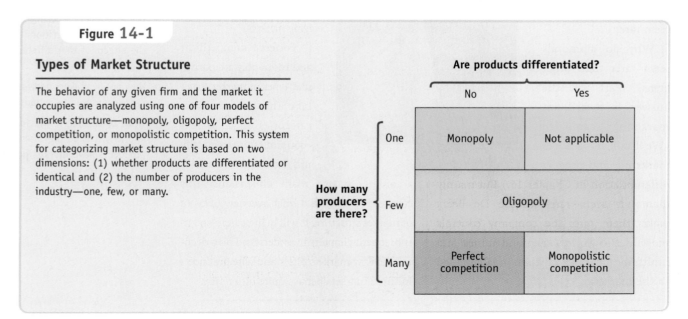

Figure 14-1

Types of Market Structure

The behavior of any given firm and the market it occupies are analyzed using one of four models of market structure—monopoly, oligopoly, perfect competition, or monopolistic competition. This system for categorizing market structure is based on two dimensions: (1) whether products are differentiated or identical and (2) the number of producers in the industry—one, few, or many.

		Are products differentiated?	
		No	Yes
How many producers are there?	One	Monopoly	Not applicable
	Few	Oligopoly	
	Many	Perfect competition	Monopolistic competition

can readily be made into different varieties in the eyes and tastes of consumers. Other goods—hammers, for example—are much less easy to differentiate.

Although this chapter is devoted to monopoly, important aspects of monopoly carry over to other market structures—to oligopoly and monopolistic competition. In the next section, we will define monopoly and review the conditions that make it possible. These same conditions, in less extreme form, also give rise to oligopoly. We then show how a monopolist can increase profit by limiting the quantity supplied to a market—behavior that also occurs in oligopoly and monopolistic competition. As we'll see, this kind of behavior is good for the producer but bad for consumers; it also causes inefficiency. An important topic of study will be the ways in which public policy tries to limit the damage. Finally, we turn to one of the surprising effects of monopoly—one that is very often present in oligopoly and monopolistic competition as well: the fact that different consumers often pay different prices for the same good.

The Meaning of Monopoly

The De Beers monopoly of South Africa was created in the 1880s by Cecil Rhodes, a British businessman. By 1880 mines in South Africa already dominated the world's supply of diamonds. There were, however, many mining companies, all competing with each other. During the 1880s Rhodes bought the great majority of those mines and consolidated them into a single company, De Beers. By 1889 De Beers controlled almost all of the world's diamond production.

De Beers, in other words, became a **monopolist.** A producer is a monopolist if it is the sole supplier of a good that has no close substitutes. When a firm is a monopolist, the industry is a **monopoly.**

> A **monopolist** is a firm that is the only producer of a good that has no close substitutes. An industry controlled by a monopolist is known as a **monopoly.**

Monopoly: Our First Departure from Perfect Competition

As we saw in the Chapter 9 section "Defining Perfect Competition," the supply and demand model of a market is not universally valid. Instead, it's a model of perfect competition, which is only one of several different types of market structure.

Back in Chapter 9 we learned that a market will be perfectly competitive only if there are many producers, all of whom produce the same good. Monopoly is the most extreme departure from perfect competition.

In practice, true monopolies are hard to find in the modern American economy, partly because of legal obstacles. A contemporary entrepreneur who tried to consolidate all the firms in an industry the way that Rhodes did would soon find himself in court, accused of breaking *antitrust* laws, which are intended to prevent monopolies from emerging. Oligopoly, a market structure in which there is a small number of large producers, is much more common. In fact, most of the goods you buy, from autos to airline tickets, are supplied by oligopolies, which we will examine in detail in Chapter 15.

Monopolies do, however, play an important role in some sectors of the economy, such as pharmaceuticals. Furthermore, our analysis of monopoly will provide a foundation for our later analysis of other departures from perfect competition, such as oligopoly and monopolistic competition.

What Monopolists Do

Why did Rhodes want to consolidate South African diamond producers into a single company? What difference did it make to the world diamond market?

Figure 14-2 (on page 336) offers a preliminary view of the effects of monopoly. It shows an industry in which the supply curve under perfect competition intersects the demand curve at C, leading to the price P_C and the output Q_C.

Figure 14-2

What a Monopolist Does

Under perfect competition, the price and quantity are determined by supply and demand. Here, the equilibrium is at C, where the price is P_C and the quantity is Q_C. A monopolist reduces the quantity supplied to Q_M, and moves up the demand curve from C to M, raising the price to P_M. **>web...**

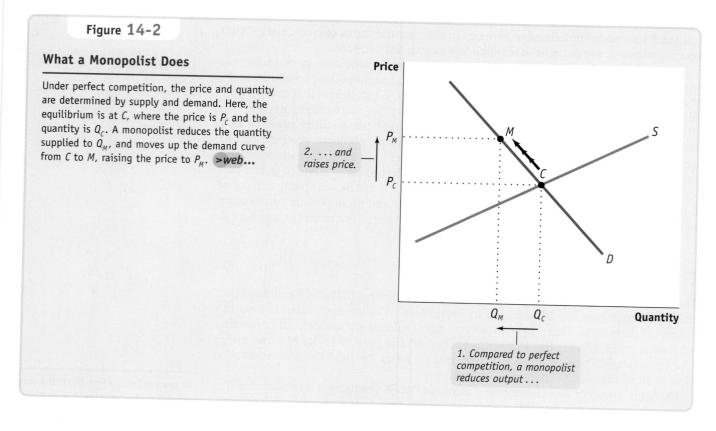

2. . . . and raises price.

1. Compared to perfect competition, a monopolist reduces output . . .

Market power is the ability of a firm to raise prices.

Suppose that this industry is consolidated into a monopoly. The monopolist *moves up the demand curve* by reducing quantity supplied to a point like M, at which the quantity produced, Q_M, is lower and the price P_M, is higher than under perfect competition.

The ability of a monopolist to raise its price above the competitive level by reducing output is known as **market power.** And market power is what monopoly is all about. A wheat farmer who is one of 100,000 wheat farmers has no market power: he or she must sell wheat at the going market price. Your local cable TV company, though, does have market power: it can raise prices and still keep many (though not all) of its customers, because they have nowhere else to go. In short, it's a monopolist.

The reason a monopolist reduces output and raises price compared to the perfectly competitive industry levels is to increase profit. Cecil Rhodes consolidated the diamond producers into De Beers because he realized that the whole would be worth more than the sum of its parts—the monopoly would generate more profit than the sum of the profits of the individual competitive firms. In fact, we saw in Chapter 9 that under perfect competition economic profits normally vanish in the long run. Under monopoly the profits don't go away—a monopolist is able to continue earning profits in the long run.

In fact, monopolists are not the only types of firms that possess market power. In the next chapter we will study *oligopolists*, firms that can have market power as well. Under certain conditions, oligopolists can earn positive economic profits in the long run by restricting output like monopolists do.

But why don't profits get competed away? What allows monopolists to be monopolists?

Why Do Monopolies Exist?

A monopolist making profits will not go unnoticed by others. But won't other firms crash the party, grab a piece of the action, and drive down prices and profits in the long run? For a profitable monopoly to persist, something must keep others from going into the same business; that "something" is known as a **barrier to entry.** There are four principal types of barriers to entry: control of scarce resources or inputs, economies of scale, technological superiority, and government-created barriers.

Control of a Scarce Resource or Input A monopolist that controls a resource or input crucial to an industry can prevent other firms from entering its market. Cecil Rhodes created the De Beers monopoly by establishing control over the mines that produced the great bulk of the world's diamonds.

Economies of Scale Many Americans have natural gas piped into their homes, for cooking and heating. Invariably, the local gas company is a monopolist. But why don't rival companies compete to provide gas?

In the early nineteenth century, when the gas industry was just starting up, companies did compete for local customers. But this competition didn't last long; soon local gas supply became a monopoly in almost every town because of the large fixed costs involved in providing a town with gas lines. Since the cost of laying gas lines didn't depend on how much gas a company sold, firms with a larger volume of sales had a cost advantage: because they were able to spread the fixed costs over a larger volume, they had lower average total costs than smaller firms.

Local gas supply is an industry in which average total cost always falls as output increases. As we learned in Chapter 8, this phenomenon is called *economies of scale.* There we learned that when average total cost falls as output increases, firms tend to grow larger. In an industry characterized by economies of scale, larger companies are more profitable and drive out smaller ones. For the same reason, established companies have a cost advantage over any potential entrant—a potent barrier to entry. So economies of scale can both give rise to and sustain monopoly.

A monopoly created and sustained by economies of scale is called a **natural monopoly.** The defining characteristic of a natural monopoly is that it possesses economies of scale over the range of output that is relevant for the industry. This is illustrated in Figure 14-3, showing the firm's average total cost curve and the market demand curve. Here we can see that the natural monopolist's *ATC* curve declines over the output levels at which price is greater than or equal to average total cost. So the

A **natural monopoly** exists when economies of scale provide a large cost advantage to having all of an industry's output produced by a single firm.

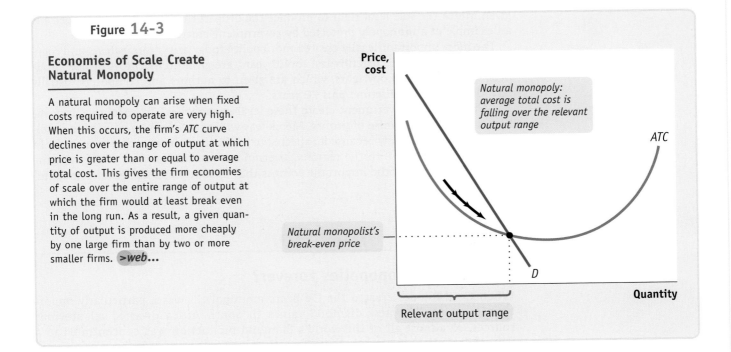

Figure 14-3

Economies of Scale Create Natural Monopoly

A natural monopoly can arise when fixed costs required to operate are very high. When this occurs, the firm's *ATC* curve declines over the range of output at which price is greater than or equal to average total cost. This gives the firm economies of scale over the entire range of output at which the firm would at least break even in the long run. As a result, a given quantity of output is produced more cheaply by one large firm than by two or more smaller firms. **>web...**

Natural monopoly: average total cost is falling over the relevant output range

ATC

Natural monopolist's break-even price

D

Price, cost

Quantity

Relevant output range

natural monopolist has economies of scale over the entire range of output for which any firm would want to remain in the industry—the range of output at which the firm would at least break even in the long run. The source of this condition is large fixed costs: when large fixed costs are required to operate, a given quantity of output is produced at lower average total cost by one large firm than by two or more smaller firms.

The most visible natural monopolies in the modern economy are local utilities—water, gas, electricity, local phone service, and cable television. As we'll see later in this chapter, natural monopolies pose a special challenge to public policy.

Technological Superiority A firm that maintains a consistent technological advantage over potential competitors can establish itself as a monopolist. For example, from the 1970s through the 1990s the chip manufacturer Intel was able to maintain a consistent advantage over potential competitors in both the design and the production of microprocessors, the chips that run computers. But technological superiority is typically a short-run, not a long-run, barrier to entry: over time competitors will invest in upgrading their technology to match that of the technology leader. In fact, in the last few years Intel found its technological superiority eroded by a competitor, Advanced Micro Devices (also known as AMD), which now produces chips approximately as fast and as powerful as Intel chips.

We should note, however, that in certain high-tech industries, technological superiority is not a guarantee of success against competitors. Some high-tech industries are characterized by *network externalities*, a condition that arises when the value to the consumer of a good rises as the number of people who also use the good rises. In these industries, the firm possessing the largest network—the largest number of consumers currently using its product—has an advantage over its competitors in attracting new customers, an advantage that may allow it to become a monopolist. Microsoft is often cited as an example of a company with a technologically inferior product—its computer operating system—that grew into a monopolist through the phenomenon of network externalities. (You can read more about network externalities in Chapter 22.)

Government-Created Barriers In 1998 the pharmaceutical company Merck introduced Propecia, a drug effective against baldness. Despite the fact that Propecia was very profitable and other drug companies had the know-how to produce it, no other firms challenged Merck's monopoly. That's because the U.S. government had given Merck the sole legal right to produce the drug in the United States. Propecia is an example of a monopoly protected by government-created barriers.

The most important legally created monopolies today arise from *patents* and *copyrights*. Patents, which currently last for 20 years, are given to inventors of new products, such as drugs; copyrights, which are given to authors and composers, usually last for the creator's lifetime plus 70 years.

Why does the government create these legal monopolies? To encourage innovation through the promise of profits. Merck was willing to invest large sums in developing Propecia precisely because it expected to profit from the resulting monopoly. In Chapter 22, we'll go into the reasons governments use this method of encouraging innovation. For now, the important point is that in some cases the government creates monopolies.

economics in action

Are Diamond Monopolies Forever?

When Cecil Rhodes created the De Beers monopoly, it was a particularly opportune moment. The new diamond mines in South Africa dwarfed all previous sources, so almost all of the world's diamond production was concentrated in a few square miles.

Since that time, however, diamond deposits similar to those in South Africa have been found in a number of places—other African countries, Russia, and Australia, which is now the largest producer. So how does De Beers remain a monopolist?

Until quite recently De Beers was able to extend its control of resources even as new mines were opened. De Beers either bought out new producers or entered into agreements with local governments which controlled some of the new mines, effectively making them part of the De Beers monopoly. The most remarkable of these was an agreement with the former Soviet Union, which ensured that Russian diamonds would be marketed through De Beers, preserving its ability to control world supplies.

In recent years, however, the spread of diamond production—together with competition from synthetic diamonds, which are becoming better substitutes for natural stones—has led to some erosion of De Beers's control, and prices have even dropped somewhat. De Beers is arguably the most successful monopolist in history—but even diamond monopolies may not be forever. ■

> > > > > > > > > > > > > > > > > > >

>> QUICK REVIEW

> A *monopolist* has *market power* and as a result will charge higher prices and produce less output than a competitive industry. This generates profit for the monopolist in the short run and long run.

> Profits will not persist in the long run unless there is a *barrier to entry*. This can take the form of control of natural resources or inputs, economies of scale, technological superiority, or legal restrictions imposed by governments, including patents and copyrights.

> A *natural monopoly* arises when average total cost is declining over the output range relevant for the industry. This creates a barrier to entry because an established monopolist has lower average total cost than any smaller firm.

>> CHECK YOUR UNDERSTANDING 14-1

1. Currently, Texas Tea Oil Co. is the only local supplier of home heating oil in Frigid, Alaska. This winter residents were shocked that the cost of a gallon of heating oil had doubled and believed that they were the victims of market power. Explain which of the following pieces of evidence support or undermine that conclusion.
   a. There is a national shortage of heating oil, and Texas Tea could procure only a limited amount.
   b. Last year, Texas Tea and several other competing local oil-supply firms merged into a single firm.
   c. The cost to Texas Tea of purchasing heating oil from refineries has gone up significantly.
   d. Recently, some nonlocal firms have begun to offer heating oil to Texas Tea's regular customers at a price much lower than Texas Tea's.
   e. Texas Tea has acquired an exclusive government license to draw oil from the only heating oil pipeline in the state.

Solutions appear at back of book.

How a Monopolist Maximizes Profit

As we've suggested, once Cecil Rhodes consolidated the competing diamond producers of South Africa into a single company, the industry's behavior changed: the quantity supplied fell and the market price rose. In this section we will learn how a monopolist increases its profits by reducing output. And we will see the crucial role that market demand plays in leading a monopolist to behave differently from a perfectly competitive industry.

The Monopolist's Demand Curve and Marginal Revenue

In Chapter 9 we derived the firm's optimal output rule: a profit-maximizing firm produces the quantity of output at which the marginal cost of producing the last unit of output equals marginal revenue—the change in total revenue generated by that last unit of output. That is, $MR = MC$ at the profit-maximizing quantity of output. Although the optimal output rule holds for *all* firms, we will see shortly that its application leads to different profit-maximizing output levels for a monopolist compared to a perfectly competitive firm—that is, a price-taking firm. The source of that difference lies in the comparison of the demand curve faced by a monopolist to the demand curve faced by an individual, perfectly competitive firm.

In addition to the optimal output rule, we also learned in Chapter 9 that even though the *market* demand curve is always downward sloping, each of the firms that make up a perfectly competitive industry faces a horizontal, *perfectly elastic* demand curve, like D_C in panel (a) of Figure 14-4 (on page 340). Any attempt by an individual firm in a perfectly competitive industry to charge more than the going market price will cause it to lose all its sales. It can, however, sell as much as it likes at the market price. As we saw in Chapter 9,

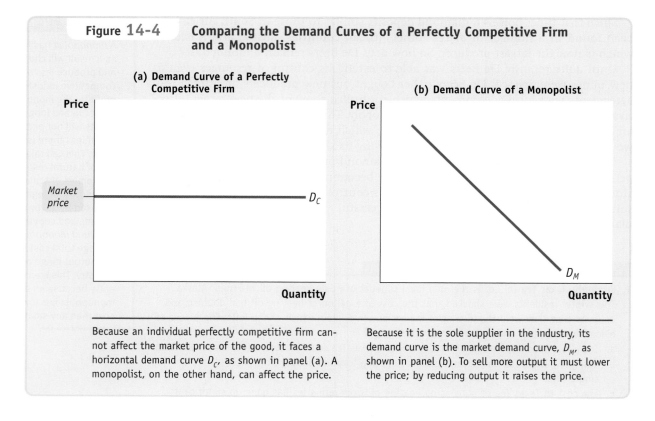

Figure 14-4   Comparing the Demand Curves of a Perfectly Competitive Firm and a Monopolist

(a) Demand Curve of a Perfectly Competitive Firm

(b) Demand Curve of a Monopolist

Because an individual perfectly competitive firm cannot affect the market price of the good, it faces a horizontal demand curve D_C, as shown in panel (a). A monopolist, on the other hand, can affect the price.

Because it is the sole supplier in the industry, its demand curve is the market demand curve, D_M, as shown in panel (b). To sell more output it must lower the price; by reducing output it raises the price.

the marginal revenue of a perfectly competitive producer is simply the market price. As a result, the price-taking firm's optimal output rule is to produce the output level at which the marginal cost of the last unit produced is equal to the market price.

A monopolist, in contrast, is the sole supplier of its good. So its demand curve is simply the market demand curve, which is downward sloping, like D_M in panel (b). This downward slope creates a "wedge" between the price of the good and the marginal revenue of the good—the change in revenue generated by producing one more unit.

Table 14-1 shows this wedge between price and marginal revenue for a monopolist, by calculating the monopolist's total revenue and marginal revenue schedules from its demand schedule.

The first two columns of Table 14-1 show a hypothetical demand schedule for De Beers diamonds. For the sake of simplicity, we assume that all diamonds are exactly alike. And to make the arithmetic easy, we suppose that the number of diamonds sold is far smaller than is actually the case. For instance, at a price of $500 per diamond, we assume that only 10 diamonds are sold. The demand curve implied by this schedule is shown in panel (a) of Figure 14-5 on page 342.

The third column of Table 14-1 shows De Beers's total revenue from selling each quantity of diamonds—the price per diamond multiplied by the number of diamonds sold. The last column calculates marginal revenue, the change in total revenue from producing and selling another diamond.

Clearly, after the 1st diamond, the marginal revenue a monopolist receives from selling one more unit is less than the price at which that unit is sold. For example, if De Beers sells 10 diamonds, the price at which the 10th diamond is sold is $500. But the marginal revenue—the change in total revenue in going from 9 to 10 diamonds—is only $50.

Why is the marginal revenue from that 10th diamond less than the price? An increase in production by a monopolist has two opposing effects on revenue:

■ *A quantity effect.* One more unit is sold, increasing total revenue by the price at which the unit is sold (in this case, $500).

- *A price effect*. In order to sell that last unit, the monopolist must cut the market price on *all* units sold. This decreases total revenue (in this case, by 9 × −$50 = −$450).

The quantity effect and the price effect are illustrated by the two shaded areas in panel (a) of Figure 14-5 on page 342. Increasing diamond sales from 9 to 10 means moving down the demand curve from *A* to *B*, reducing the price per diamond from $550 to $500. The green-shaded area represents the quantity effect: De Beers sells the 10th diamond at a price of $500. This is offset, however, by the price effect, represented by the orange-shaded area. In order to sell that 10th diamond, De Beers must reduce the price on all its diamonds from $550 to $500. So it loses 9 × $50 = $450 in revenue, the orange-shaded area. So, as point *C* indicates, the total effect on revenue of selling one more diamond—the marginal revenue—derived from an increase in diamond sales from 9 to 10 is only $50.

Point *C* lies on the monopolist's marginal revenue curve, labeled *MR* in panel (a) of Figure 14-5 and taken from the last column of Table 14-1. The crucial point about the monopolist's marginal revenue curve is that it is always *below* the demand curve.

TABLE **14-1**

Demand, Total Revenue, and Marginal Revenue for the De Beers Monopoly

Price of diamond P	Quantity of diamonds Q	Total revenue $TR = P \times Q$	Marginal revenue $MR = \Delta TR/\Delta Q$
$1,000	0	$0	
			$950
950	1	950	
			850
900	2	1,800	
			750
850	3	2,550	
			650
800	4	3,200	
			550
750	5	3,750	
			450
700	6	4,200	
			350
650	7	4,550	
			250
600	8	4,800	
			150
550	9	4,950	
			50
500	10	5,000	
			−50
450	11	4,950	
			−150
400	12	4,800	
			−250
350	13	4,550	
			−350
300	14	4,200	
			−450
250	15	3,750	
			−550
200	16	3,200	
			−650
150	17	2,550	
			−750
100	18	1,800	
			−850
50	19	950	
			−950
0	20	0	

Figure 14-5

A Monopolist's Demand, Total Revenue, and Marginal Revenue Curves

Panel (a) shows the monopolist's demand and marginal revenue curves for diamonds from Table 14-1. The marginal revenue curve lies below the demand curve. To see why, consider point A on the demand curve, where 9 diamonds are sold at $550 each, generating total revenue of $4,950. To sell a 10th diamond, the price on all 10 diamonds must be cut to $500, as shown by point B. As a result, total revenue increases by the green area (the quantity effect: $500) but decreases by the orange area (the price effect: –$450). So the marginal revenue from the 10th diamond is $50 (the difference between the green and orange areas) which is much lower than its price, $500.

Panel (b) shows the monopolist's total revenue curve for diamonds. As output goes from 0 to 10 diamonds, total revenue increases. It reaches its maximum at 10 diamonds—the level at which marginal revenue is equal to 0—and declines thereafter. The quantity effect dominates the price effect when total revenue is rising; the price effect dominates the quantity effect when total revenue is falling. **>web...**

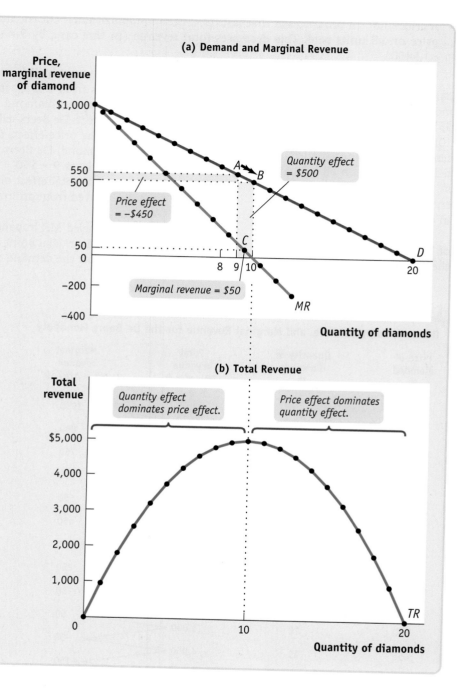

That's because of the price effect, which means that a monopolist's marginal revenue from selling an additional unit is always less than the price the monopolist receives for that unit. It is the price effect that creates the wedge between the monopolist's marginal revenue curve and the demand curve: in order to sell an additional diamond, De Beers must cut the market price on all units sold.

In fact, this wedge exists for any firm that possesses market power, such as oligopolists. Having market power means that the firm faces a downward-sloping demand curve. As a result, there will always be a price effect from an increase in its output. So for a firm with market power, the marginal revenue curve always lies below its demand curve.

Take a moment to compare the monopolist's marginal revenue curve with the marginal revenue curve for a perfectly competitive firm, one without market power. For such a firm there is no price effect from an increase in output: its marginal revenue curve is simply its horizontal demand curve. So for a perfectly competitive firm, market price and marginal revenue are always equal.

To emphasize how the quantity and price effects offset each other for a firm with market power, De Beers's total revenue curve is shown in panel (b) of Figure 14-5. Notice that it is hill-shaped: as output rises from 0 to 10 diamonds, total revenue increases. This reflects the fact that *at low levels of output, the quantity effect is stronger than the price effect:* as the monopolist sells more, it has to lower the price on only very few units, so the price effect is small. As output rises beyond 10 diamonds, total revenue actually falls. This reflects the fact that *at high levels of output, the price effect is stronger than the quantity effect:* as the monopolist sells more, it now has to lower the price on many units of output, making the price effect very large. Correspondingly, the marginal revenue curve lies below zero at output levels above 10 diamonds. For example, an increase in diamond production from 11 to 12 yields only $400 for the 12th diamond, simultaneously reducing the revenue from diamonds 1 through 11 by $550. As a result, the marginal revenue of the 12th diamond is −$150.

The Monopolist's Profit-Maximizing Output and Price

To complete the story of how a monopolist maximizes profit, we now bring in the monopolist's marginal cost. Let's assume that there is no fixed cost of production, and we'll also assume that the marginal cost of producing an additional diamond is constant at $200, no matter how many diamonds De Beers produces. Then marginal cost will always equal average total cost and the marginal cost curve (and the average total cost curve) is a horizontal line at $200, as shown in Figure 14-6.

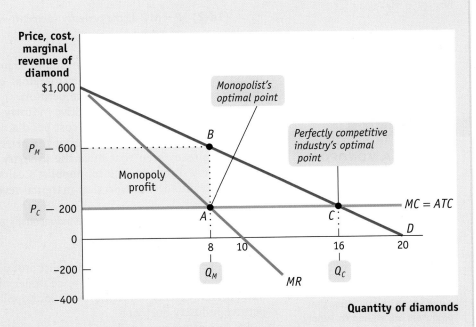

Figure 14-6

The Monopolist's Profit-Maximizing Output and Price

This figure shows the demand, marginal revenue, and marginal cost curves. Marginal cost per diamond is $200, so the marginal cost curve is horizontal at $200. According to the optimal output rule, the profit-maximizing level of output for the monopolist is at $MR = MC$, shown by point *A*, where the marginal cost and marginal revenue curves cross at an output of 8 diamonds. The price De Beers can charge per diamond is found by going to the point on the demand curve directly above point *A*, which is point *B* here—a price of $600 per diamond. It makes a profit of $400 × 8 = $3,200. A perfectly competitive industry produces the output level at which $P = MC$, given by point *C*, where the demand curve and marginal cost curves cross. So a competitive industry produces 16 diamonds, sells at a price of $200, and makes zero profit.

To maximize profit, the monopolist compares marginal cost with marginal revenue. If marginal revenue exceeds marginal cost, De Beers increases profit by producing more; if marginal revenue is less than marginal cost, De Beers increases profit by producing less. So the monopolist maximizes its profit by using the optimal output rule:

(14-1) $MR = MC$ at the monopolist's profit-maximizing quantity of output

The monopolist's optimal point is shown in Figure 14-6. At *A*, the marginal cost curve, *MC*, crosses the marginal revenue curve, *MR*. The corresponding output level, 8 diamonds, is the monopolist's profit-maximizing quantity of output, Q_M. The price at which consumers demand 8 diamonds is $600, so the monopolist's price, P_M, is $600—corresponding to point *B*. The cost of producing each diamond is $200, so the monopolist earns a profit of $600 − $200 = $400 per diamond, and total profit is 8 × $400 = $3,200, as indicated by the shaded area.

Monopoly versus Perfect Competition

When Cecil Rhodes consolidated many independent diamond producers into De Beers, he converted a perfectly competitive industry into a monopoly. We can now use our analysis to see the effects of such a consolidation.

Let's look again at Figure 14-6 and ask how this same market would work if, instead of being a monopoly, the industry were perfectly competitive. We will continue to assume that there is no fixed cost, and that marginal cost is constant, so average total cost and marginal cost are equal.

If the diamond industry consists of many perfectly competitive firms, each of those producers takes the market price as given. That is, each producer acts as if its marginal revenue is equal to the market price. So each firm within the industry uses the price-taking firm's optimal output rule:

(14-2) $P = MC$ at the perfectly competitive firm's profit-maximizing quantity of output

In Figure 14-6, this would correspond to producing at *C*, where the price per diamond, P_C, is $200, equal to the marginal cost of production. Profit-maximizing industry output under perfect competition, Q_C, is therefore 16 diamonds.

But does the perfectly competitive industry earn any profits at *C*? No: the price of $200 is equal to the production cost per diamond. So there are no economic profits for this industry when it produces at the perfectly competitive output level.

We've already seen that once the industry is consolidated into a monopoly, the result is very different. The monopolist's calculation of marginal revenue takes the price effect into account, so that marginal revenue is less than the price. That is,

(14-3) $P > MR = MC$ at the monopolist's profit-maximizing quantity of output

As we've already seen, the monopolist produces less than the competitive industry—8 diamonds rather than 16. The price under monopoly is $600, compared with only $200 under perfect competition. The monopolist earns a positive profit, but the competitive industry does not.

So, just as we suggested earlier, we see that compared with a competitive industry, a monopolist does the following:

- Produces a smaller quantity: $Q_M < Q_C$
- Charges a higher price: $P_M > P_C$
- Earns a profit

A monopolist faces marginal revenue that is less than the market price. But how much lower? The answer depends on the *price elasticity of demand*.

Remember from Chapter 5 that the price elasticity of demand determines how *total revenue* from sales changes when the price falls. If the price elasticity is greater than 1, a fall in the price increases total revenue, because the rise in the quantity demanded outweighs the lower price of each unit sold. If the elasticity is less than 1, a lower price reduces total revenue.

When a monopolist increases output by one unit, it must reduce the market price in order to sell that unit. If the price elasticity of demand is less than 1, this will actually reduce revenue—that is, marginal revenue will be negative. The monopolist can only increase revenue by producing more if the price elasticity of demand is greater than 1; the higher the elasticity, the closer the additional revenue is to the initial market price.

What this tells us is that the difference between monopoly behavior and perfect competition depends on the price elasticity of demand. A monopolist that faces highly elastic demand will behave almost like a firm in a perfectly competitive industry.

For example, Amtrak has a monopoly of intercity passenger service in the Northeast Corridor, but it has very little ability to raise prices: potential train travelers will switch to cars and planes. In contrast, a monopolist that faces less elastic demand—like most cable TV companies—will behave very differently from a perfect competitor: it will charge much higher prices and restrict output more.

Monopoly: The General Picture

Figure 14-6 involved specific numbers and assumed that the marginal cost curve was a horizontal line. Figure 14-7 shows a more general picture of monopoly in action: D is the market demand curve; MR, the marginal revenue curve; MC, the marginal cost curve; and ATC, the average total cost curve. Here we return to the usual assumption that the marginal cost curve is upward sloping and the average total cost curve is U-shaped.

Figure 14-7

The Monopolist's Profit

In this case, the marginal cost curve is upward sloping and the average total cost curve is U-shaped. The monopolist maximizes profit by producing the level of output at which $MR = MC$, given by point A, generating quantity Q_M. It finds its monopoly price, P_M, from the point on the demand curve directly above point A, point B here. The average total cost of Q_M is shown by point C. Profit is given by the area of the shaded rectangle. **>web...**

Applying the optimal output rule, we see that the profit-maximizing level of output is the output at which marginal revenue equals marginal cost, indicated by point A. The profit-maximizing quantity of output is Q_M, and the price charged by the monopolist is P_M. At the profit-maximizing level of output, the monopolist's average total cost is ATC_M, shown by point C.

Recalling how we calculated profit in Equation 9-5 on page 215, profit is equal to the difference between total revenue and total cost. So we have

$$
\begin{aligned}
\textbf{(14-4)} \quad \text{Profit} &= TR - TC \\
&= (P_M \times Q_M) - (ATC_M \times Q_M) \\
&= (P_M - ATC_M) \times Q_M
\end{aligned}
$$

Profit is equal to the area of the shaded rectangle in Figure 14-7, with a height of $P_M - ATC_M$ and a width of Q_M.

In Chapter 9 we learned that a perfectly competitive industry can have profits *in the short run but not in the long run*. In the short run price can exceed average total cost, allowing a perfectly competitive firm to make a profit. But we also know that this cannot persist. In the long run, any profit in a perfectly competitive industry will be competed away as new firms enter the market. In contrast, a monopolist will make profits in both the short run and the long run.

economics in action

California Power Play?

The winter of 2000–2001 was a grim time for California, as power shortages gripped the state. One factor involved was the soaring price of natural gas, especially in the southern part of the state.

The strange thing was that natural gas prices in California were much higher than in Texas, the source of most of the state's natural gas. That is, the marginal cost of supplying natural gas to California—the cost of buying it in Texas, plus the small expense of shipping it across state lines—was much less than the price of California gas. So why wasn't more gas supplied?

The answer appears to have been that natural gas is transported via interstate pipelines and that the El Paso Corporation, which held a near-monopoly of pipelines supplying southern California, deliberately restricted the quantity of gas available in order to drive up market prices.

Because pipelines tend to be monopolies, they are subject to *price regulation*, discussed later in this chapter. As a result, the price a pipeline company can charge for shipping natural gas is limited. However, El Paso, in addition to running the pipelines, also has an unregulated subsidiary that sells natural gas in California. A judge at the Federal Energy Regulatory Commission concluded that the company used its control of the pipeline to drive up the prices received by its marketing subsidiary. It did this by reducing output—by running pipelines at low pressure and by scheduling non-essential maintenance during periods of peak demand. This conclusion was partly based on internal memos at El Paso, which seemed to say that the company was "idling large blocks of transport" to widen price spreads between natural gas delivered to Texas and to California.

El Paso denied the charges and has never admitted exercising market power. In 2003, however, the company agreed to a settlement in which it paid the state of

The STRUGGLING U.S. Postal Service takes a LESSON from the POWER COMPANIES...

WHOOPS! STAMP SHORTAGE! NOW THEY'RE TWO BUCKS EACH

California $1.7 billion. Many analysts—including the staff at the Federal Energy Regulatory Commission—believe that El Paso's exercise of market power in the natural gas market was part of a broad pattern of market manipulation that played a key role in California's energy crisis during 2000–2001. ■

> > > > > > > > > > > > > > > > > > > >

>>CHECK YOUR UNDERSTANDING 14-2

1. Use the accompanying total revenue schedule of Emerald, Inc., a monopoly producer of 10-carat emeralds, to calculate the answers to parts a–d. Then answer part e.
   a. The demand schedule
   b. The marginal revenue schedule
   c. The quantity effect component of marginal revenue per output level
   d. The price effect component of marginal revenue per output level
   e. What additional information is needed to determine Emerald, Inc.'s profit-maximizing output?

Quantity of emeralds demanded	Total revenue
1	$100
2	186
3	252
4	280
5	250

2. Use Figure 14-6 to show what happens to the following when the marginal cost of diamond production rises from $200 to $400.
   a. Marginal cost curve
   b. Profit-maximizing quantity
   c. Profit of the monopolist
   d. Perfectly competitive industry profits

Solutions appear at back of book.

Monopoly and Public Policy

It's good to be a monopolist, but it's not so good to be a monopolist's customer. A monopolist, by reducing output and raising prices, benefits at the expense of consumers. But buyers and sellers always have conflicting interests. Is the conflict of interest under monopoly any different than it is under perfect competition?

The answer is yes, because monopoly is a source of inefficiency: the losses to consumers from monopoly behavior are larger than the gains to the monopolist. Because monopoly leads to net losses for the economy, governments often try either to prevent the emergence of monopolies or to limit their effects. In this section we will see why monopoly leads to inefficiency and examine the policies governments adopt in an attempt to prevent this inefficiency.

Welfare Effects of Monopoly

By restricting output below the level at which marginal cost is equal to the market price, a monopolist increases its profit but hurts consumers. To assess whether this is a net benefit or loss to society, we must compare the monopolist's gain in profit to the consumer loss. And what we learn is that the consumer loss is larger than the monopolist's gain. Monopoly causes a net loss for the economy.

To see why, let's return to the case where the marginal cost curve is horizontal, as shown in the two panels of Figure 14-8 on page 348. Here the marginal cost curve is MC, the demand curve is D, and, in panel (b), the marginal revenue curve is MR.

Panel (a) shows what happens if this industry is perfectly competitive. Equilibrium output is Q_C; the price of the good, P_C, is equal to marginal cost, and marginal cost is also equal to average total cost because there is no fixed cost and marginal cost is constant. Each firm is earning exactly its cost per unit of output, so there is no producer surplus in this equilibrium. The consumer surplus generated by the market is equal to the area of the blue-shaded triangle CS_C shown in panel (a). Since there is no producer surplus when the industry is perfectly competitive, CS_C also represents the total surplus.

Figure 14-8   Monopoly Causes Inefficiency

(a) Total Surplus with Perfect Competition

Price, cost

Consumer surplus with perfect competition

CS_C

P_C MC

Q_C Quantity   D

(b) Total Surplus with Monopoly

Price, cost, marginal revenue

Consumer surplus with monopoly

P_M CS_M

PS_M Profit

Deadweight loss

DL MC

Q_M MR   D

Quantity

Panel (a) depicts a perfectly competitive industry: output is Q_C and market price, P_C, is equal is to MC. Since price is exactly equal to each producer's cost of production per unit, there is no producer surplus. Total surplus is therefore equal to consumer surplus, the entire shaded area. Panel (b) depicts the industry under monopoly: the monopolist decreases output to Q_M and charges P_M.

Consumer surplus (blue area) has shrunk because a portion of it is has been captured as profit (green area). Total surplus falls: the deadweight loss (orange area) represents the value of mutually beneficial transactions that do not occur because of monopoly behavior. **>web...**

Panel (b) shows the results for the same market, but this time assuming that the industry is a monopoly. The monopolist produces the level of output, Q_M, at which marginal cost is equal to marginal revenue, and it charges the price P_M. The industry now earns profit—which is also the producer surplus—equal to the area of the green rectangle, PS_M. Note that this profit is surplus that has been captured from consumers as consumer surplus shrinks to the area of the blue triangle, CS_M.

By comparing panels (a) and (b), we see that in addition to the redistribution of surplus from consumers to the monopolist, another important change has occurred: the sum of profit and consumer surplus—total surplus—is *smaller* under monopoly than under perfect competition. That is, the sum of CS_M and PS_M is less than the area CS_C in panel (a). In Chapter 6, we analyzed the concept of *deadweight loss*, the net loss caused by government policies such as taxes. Here we show that monopoly creates a deadweight loss to society equal to the area of the orange triangle, *DL*. So monopoly produces a net loss for the economy.

This net loss exists because some mutually beneficial transactions do not occur. There are people for whom an additional unit of the good is worth more than the marginal cost of producing it, but who don't consume it because they are not willing to pay P_M.

Those who recall our discussion of the deadweight loss from taxes in Chapter 6 will notice that the deadweight loss from monopoly looks quite similar. Indeed, by driving a wedge between price and marginal cost, monopoly acts much like a tax on consumers and produces the same kind of inefficiency.

So monopoly hurts the welfare of society as a whole and is a source of market failure. Is there anything government policy can do about it?

Preventing Monopoly

Policy toward monopoly depends crucially on whether or not the industry in question is a natural monopoly, one in which economies of scale ensure that bigger producers have lower average total cost. If the industry is *not* a natural monopoly, the best policy is to prevent monopoly from arising or break it up if it already exists. Let's focus on that case first, then turn to the more difficult problem of dealing with natural monopoly.

The De Beers monopoly on diamonds didn't have to happen. Diamond production is not a natural monopoly: the industry's costs would be no higher if it consisted of a number of independent, competing producers (as is the case, for example, in gold production).

So if the South African government had been worried about how a monopoly would have affected consumers, it could have blocked Cecil Rhodes in his drive to dominate the industry or broken up his monopoly after the fact. Today, governments often try to prevent monopolies from forming and break up existing ones.

De Beers is a rather unique case: for complicated historical reasons, it was allowed to remain a monopoly. But over the last century, most similar monopolies have been broken up. The most celebrated example in the United States is Standard Oil, founded by John D. Rockefeller in 1870. By 1878 Standard Oil controlled almost all U.S. oil refining; but in 1911 a court order broke the company into a number of smaller units, including the companies that later became Exxon and Mobil (and more recently merged to become ExxonMobil).

The government policies used to prevent or eliminate monopolies are known as *antitrust policy*, which we will discuss in the next chapter.

Dealing with Natural Monopoly

Breaking up a monopoly that isn't natural is clearly a good idea: the gains to consumers outweigh the loss to the producer. But it's not so clear whether a natural monopoly, one in which large producers have lower average total costs than small producers, should be broken up, because this would raise average total cost. For example, a town government that tried to prevent a single company from dominating local gas supply—which, as we've discussed, is almost surely a natural monopoly—would raise the cost of providing gas to its residents.

Yet even in the case of a natural monopoly, a profit-maximizing monopolist acts in a way that causes inefficiency—it charges consumers a price that is higher than marginal cost, and therefore prevents some potentially beneficial transactions. Also, it can seem unfair that a firm that has managed to establish a monopoly position earns large profits at the expense of consumers.

What can public policy do about this? There are two common answers.

Public Ownership In many countries, the preferred answer to the problem of natural monopoly has been **public ownership.** Instead of allowing a private monopolist to control an industry, the government establishes a public agency to provide the good and protect consumers' interests. For example, before 1984 in Britain, telephone service was provided by the state-owned British Telecom, and before 1987 airline travel was provided by the state-owned British Airways. (These companies still exist, but they have been privatized, competing with other firms in their respective industries.)

There are some examples of public ownership in the United States. Passenger rail service is provided by the public company Amtrak; regular mail delivery is provided by the U.S. Postal Service; some cities, including Los Angeles, have publicly owned electric power companies.

The advantage of public ownership, in principle, is that a publicly owned natural monopoly can set prices based on the criterion of efficiency rather than profit maximization. In a perfectly competitive industry, profit-maximizing behavior *is* efficient, because producers set prices equal to marginal cost; that is why there is no economic argument for public ownership of, say, wheat farms.

Experience suggests, however, that public ownership as a solution to the problem of natural monopoly often works badly in practice. One reason is that publicly owned firms are often less eager than private companies to keep costs down or offer high-quality products. Another is that publicly owned companies all too often end up serving political

In **public ownership** of a monopoly, the good is supplied by the government or by a firm owned by the government.

interests—providing contracts or jobs to people with the right connections. For example, Amtrak has notoriously provided train service at a loss to destinations that attract few passengers—but that are located in the districts of influential members of Congress.

Regulation In the United States, the more common answer has been to leave the industry in private hands but subject it to regulation. In particular, most local utilities like electricity, telephone service, natural gas, and so on are covered by **price regulation** that limits the prices they can charge.

We saw in Chapter 4 that imposing a *price ceiling* on a competitive industry is a recipe for shortages, black markets, and other nasty side effects. Doesn't imposing a limit on the price that, say, a local gas company can charge have the same effects?

Not necessarily: a price ceiling on a monopolist need not create a shortage—in the absence of a price ceiling, a monopolist would charge a price that is higher than its marginal cost of production. So even if forced to charge a lower price—as long as that price is above *MC* and the monopolist at least breaks even on total output—the monopolist still has an incentive to produce the quantity demanded at that price.

Figure 14-9 shows an example of price regulation of a natural monopoly—a highly simplified version of a local gas company. The company faces a demand curve *D*, with an associated marginal revenue curve *MR*. For simplicity, we assume that the firm's total costs consist of two parts: a fixed cost and variable costs that are incurred at a constant proportion to output. So marginal cost is constant in this case, and the marginal cost curve (which here is also the average variable cost curve) is a horizontal line at *MC*. The average total cost curve is the downward-sloping curve *ATC*; it is downward sloping because the higher the output, the lower the average fixed cost (the fixed cost per unit of output). Because average total cost is downward sloping over the range of output relevant for market demand, this is a natural monopoly.

> **Price regulation** limits the price that a monopolist is allowed to charge.

Figure 14-9   **Regulated and Unregulated Natural Monopoly**

(a) Total Surplus with an Unregulated Natural Monopolist

(b) Total Surplus with a Regulated Natural Monopolist

This figure shows the case of a natural monopolist. In panel (a), if the monopolist is allowed to charge P_M, it makes a profit, shown by the green area; consumer surplus is shown by the blue area. If it is regulated and must charge the lower price P_R, output increases from Q_M to Q_R, and consumer surplus increases.

Panel (b) shows what happens when the monopolist must charge a price equal to average total cost, the price P_R^*. Output expands to Q_R^*, and consumer surplus is now the entire blue area. The monopolist makes zero profit. This is the greatest consumer surplus possible when the monopolist is allowed to at least break even, making P_R^* the best regulated price.

Panel (a) illustrates a case of natural monopoly without regulation. The unregulated natural monopolist chooses the monopoly output Q_M and charges the price P_M. Since the monopolist receives a price greater than its average total cost, it earns a profit. This profit is exactly equal to the producer surplus in this market, represented by the green-shaded rectangle. Consumer surplus is given by the blue-shaded triangle.

Now suppose that regulators impose a price ceiling on local gas deliveries—one that falls below the monopoly price P_M but above ATC, say, at P_R in panel (a). At that price the quantity demanded is Q_R.

Does the company have an incentive to produce that quantity? Yes. If the price at which the monopolist can sell its product is fixed by regulators, the firm's output no longer affects the market price—so it ignores the MR curve and is willing to expand output to meet the quantity demanded as long as the price it receives for the next unit is greater than marginal cost and the monopolist at least breaks even on total output. So with price regulation, the monopolist produces more, at a lower price.

Of course, the monopolist will not be willing to produce at all if the imposed price means producing at a loss. That is, the price ceiling has to be set high enough to allow the firm to cover its average total cost. Panel (b) shows a situation in which regulators have pushed the price down as far as possible, at the level where the average total cost curve crosses the demand curve. At any lower price the firm loses money. The price here, P_R^*, is the best regulated price: the monopolist is just willing to operate and produces Q_R^*, the quantity demanded at that price. Consumers and society gain as a result.

The welfare effects of this regulation can be seen by comparing the shaded areas in the two panels of Figure 14-9. Consumer surplus is increased by the regulation, with the gains coming from two sources. First, profits are eliminated and added instead to consumer surplus. Second, the larger output and lower price leads to an overall welfare gain—an increase in total surplus.

This all looks terrific: consumers are better off, profits are eliminated, and overall welfare increases. Unfortunately, things are rarely that easy in practice. The main problem is that regulators don't have the information required to set the price exactly at the level at which the demand curve crosses the average total cost curve. Sometimes they set it too low, creating shortages; at other times they set it too high. Also, regulated monopolies, like publicly owned firms, tend to exaggerate their costs to regulators and to provide inferior quality to consumers.

Must Monopoly Be Controlled? Sometimes the cure is worse than the disease. Some economists have argued that the best solution, even in the case of natural monopoly, may be to live with it. The case for doing nothing is that attempts to control monopoly will, one way or another, do more harm than good—for example, by the politicization of pricing, which leads to shortages or by the creation of opportunities for political corruption.

The following Economics in Action describes the case of cable television, a natural monopoly that has been alternately regulated and deregulated as politicians change their minds about the appropriate policy.

economics in action

Cable Dilemmas

Most price regulation in the United States goes back a long way: electricity, local phone service, water, and gas have been regulated in most places for generations. But cable television is a relatively new industry. Until the late 1970s only rural areas too remote to support local broadcast stations were served by cable. After 1972 new technology and looser rules made it profitable to offer cable service to major metropolitan areas; new networks like HBO and CNN emerged to take advantage of the possibilities.

But local cable TV is clearly a natural monopoly: there are large fixed costs to running cable through a town that don't depend on how many people actually subscribe, so that having more than one cable company would involve a lot of wasteful duplication. But if the local cable company is a monopoly, should its prices be regulated?

At first most local governments thought so, and cable TV was subject to price regulation. In 1984, however, Congress passed a law prohibiting most local governments from regulating cable prices. (The law was the result both of widespread skepticism about whether price regulation was actually a good idea and of intensive lobbying by the cable companies.)

After the law went into effect, however, cable television rates increased sharply. The resulting consumer backlash led to a new law, in 1992, which once again allowed local governments to set limits on cable prices.

Was the new regulation a success? As measured by the prices of "basic" cable service, it was: after rising rapidly during the period of deregulation, the cost of basic service leveled off.

However, price regulation in cable applies only to "basic" service. Cable operators can try to evade the restrictions by charging more for premium channels like HBO or by offering fewer channels in the "basic" package. So some skeptics have questioned whether the regulation has actually been effective.

The story of cable television shows that making policy for natural monopolies is harder than the simplified model suggests. It also shows that sometimes governments have a hard time making up their minds! ■

< < < < < < < < < < < < < < < < < < < <

>> CHECK YOUR UNDERSTANDING 14-3

1. What policy should the government adopt in the following cases? Explain.
   a. Internet service in Anytown, OH, is provided by cable. Customers feel they are being overcharged, but the cable company claims it must charge prices that let it recover the costs of laying cable.
   b. The only two airlines that currently fly to Alaska need government approval to merge. Other airlines wish to fly to Alaska but need government-allocated landing slots to do so.

2. True or false? Explain your answer.
   a. Society's welfare is lower under monopoly because some consumer surplus is transformed into profit for the monopolist.
   b. A monopolist causes inefficiency because there are consumers who are willing to pay a price greater than or equal to marginal cost but less than the monopoly price.

3. Suppose a monopolist mistakenly believes that its marginal revenue is always equal to the market price. Assuming constant marginal cost and no fixed cost, draw a diagram comparing the level of profit, consumer surplus, total surplus, and deadweight loss for this misguided monopolist compared to a smart monopolist.

Solutions appear at back of book.

Price Discrimination

Up to this point we have considered only the case of a **single-price monopolist,** one who charges all consumers the same price. As the term suggests, not all monopolists do this. In fact, many if not most monopolists find that they can increase their profits by charging different customers different prices for the same good: they engage in **price discrimination.**

The most striking example of price discrimination most of us encounter regularly involves airline tickets. Although there are a number of airlines, most routes in the United States are serviced by only one or two carriers, which, as a result, have market power and can set prices. So any regular airline passenger quickly becomes aware that the question "How much will it cost me to fly there?" rarely has a simple answer. If you are willing to buy a nonrefundable ticket a month in advance and stay over a Saturday night, the round trip may cost only $150—or less if you are a senior citizen or a student. But if you have to go on a business trip tomorrow, which happens to be Tuesday, and come back on Wednesday, the round trip might cost $550. Yet the business traveler and the visiting grandparent receive the same product—the same cramped seat, the same awful food.

You might object that airlines are not usually monopolists—that the airline industry is an oligopoly. In fact, price discrimination takes place under oligopoly and monopolistic competition as well as monopoly. But it doesn't happen under perfect competition. And once we've seen why monopolists sometimes price discriminate, we'll be in a good position to understand why it happens in other cases, too.

The Logic of Price Discrimination

To get a preliminary view of why price discrimination might be more profitable than charging all consumers the same price, imagine that Air Sunshine offers the only nonstop flights between Bismarck, North Dakota, and Ft. Lauderdale, Florida. Assume that there are no capacity problems—the airline can fly as many planes as the number of passengers warrants. Also assume that there is no fixed cost. The marginal cost to the airline of providing a seat is $125, however many passengers it carries.

Further assume that the airline knows there are two kinds of potential passengers. First, there are business travelers, 2,000 of whom want to travel between the destinations each week. Second, there are students, 2,000 of whom also want to travel each week.

Will potential passengers take the flight? It depends on the price. The business travelers, it turns out, really want to fly; they will take the plane as long as the price is no more than $550. The students, however, have less money and more time; if the price goes above $150, they will take the bus.

So what should the airline do? If it has to charge everyone the same price, its options are limited. It could charge $550; that way it would get as much as possible out of the business travelers but lose the student market. Or it could charge only $150; that way it would get both types of travelers but would not make as much money on the business travelers as it might have.

We can quickly calculate the profits from each of these alternatives. If the airline charged $550, it would sell 2,000 tickets to the business travelers, getting total revenues of 550 × 2,000 = $1.1 million and incurring costs of 125 × 2,000 = $250,000; so its profit would be $850,000. If the airline charged only $150, it would sell 4,000 tickets, receiving revenue of 4,000 × 150 = $600,000 and incurring costs of 4,000 × 125 = $500,000; so its profit would be $100,000. If the airline must charge everyone the same price, charging the higher price is clearly more profitable.

What the airline would really like to do, however, is charge the business travelers the full $550 but offer $150 tickets to the students. That's a lot less than the price paid by business travelers, but it's still above marginal cost; so if the airline could sell those extra 2,000 tickets to students, it would make an additional $50,000 in profit.

In this example we assume that cutting the price below $550 will not lead to *any* additional business travel and that at a price above $150 *no* students will fly. The implied demand curve is shown in Figure 14-10 on page 354.

It would be more realistic to suppose that there is some "give" in the demand of each group. But this, it turns out, does not do away with the argument for price discrimination. The important point is that the two groups of consumers differ in their *sensitivity to price*—that a high price has a larger effect in discouraging purchases by students than by business travelers. As long as different groups of customers respond differently to the price, a monopolist will find that it can capture more consumer surplus and increase its profit by charging them different prices.

Figure 14-10

Two Types of Airline Customers

Air Sunshine has two types of customers, business travelers willing to pay $550 per ticket and students willing to pay $150 per ticket. There are 2,000 of each kind of customer. Air Sunshine has constant marginal cost of $125 per seat. If Air Sunshine could charge these two types of customers different prices, it would maximize its profit by charging business travelers $550 and students $150 per ticket. It would capture all of the consumer surplus as profit.
>web...

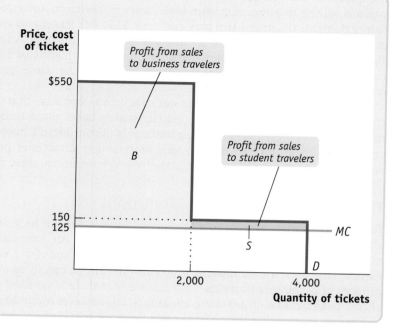

Price Discrimination and Elasticity

A more realistic description of the demand that airlines face would not specify particular prices at which different types of travelers would choose to fly. Instead, it would distinguish between the groups on the basis of their sensitivity to the price—their price elasticity of demand.

Suppose that a company sells its product to two easily identifiable groups of people—business travelers and students. It just so happens that business travelers are very insensitive to the price: there is a certain amount of the product they just have to have whatever the price, but they cannot be persuaded to buy much more than that no matter how cheap it is. Students, though, are more flexible: offer a good enough price and they will buy quite a lot, but raise the price too high and they will switch to something else. What should the company do?

The answer is the one already suggested by our simplified example: the company should charge business travelers, with their low price elasticity of demand, a higher price than it charges students, with their high price elasticity of demand.

The actual situation of the airlines is very much like this hypothetical example. Business travelers typically place a high priority on being at the right place at the right time and are not too sensitive to the price. But nonbusiness travelers faced with a high price might take the bus, drive to another airport to get a lower fare, or skip the trip altogether.

So why doesn't an airline simply announce different prices for business and nonbusiness customers? First, this would probably be illegal (U.S. law places severe limits on the ability of companies to practice open price discrimination). Second, even if it were legal, it would be a hard policy to enforce: business travelers might be willing to wear casual clothing and claim they were visiting family in Ft. Lauderdale in order to save $400.

So what the airlines do—quite successfully—is impose rules that indirectly have the effect of charging business and non-business travelers different fares. Business travelers usually

On many airline routes, the fare you pay depends on the type of traveller you are.

Mark Peterson

travel during the week and want to be home on the weekend; so the round-trip fare is much higher if you don't stay over a Saturday night. The requirement of a weekend stay for a cheap ticket effectively separates business from nonbusiness travelers. Similarly, business travelers often visit several cities in succession rather than make a simple round trip; so round-trip fares are much lower than twice the one-way fare. Many business trips are scheduled on short notice; so fares are much lower if you book far in advance. Fares are also lower if you travel standby, taking your chances on whether you actually get a seat—business travelers have to make it to that meeting; people visiting their relatives don't. And by requiring customers to show their ID upon check-in, airlines make sure there are no resales of tickets between the two groups that would undermine their ability to price-discriminate—students can't buy cheap tickets and resell them to business travelers. Look at the rules that govern ticket-pricing, and you will see an ingenious implementation of profit-maximizing price discrimination.

Perfect Price Discrimination

Let's return to the example of business travelers and students traveling between Bismarck and Ft. Lauderdale, illustrated in Figure 14-10, and ask what would happen if the airline could distinguish between the two groups of customers in order to charge each a different price.

Clearly, the airline would charge each group its willingness to pay—that is, as we learned in Chapter 6, the maximum that each group is willing to pay. For business travelers, the willingness to pay is $550, and it is $150 for students. As we have assumed, the marginal cost is $125 and does not depend on output, so that the marginal cost curve is a horizontal line. We can easily read off the airline's profit: it is the sum of the areas of the rectangle *B* and the rectangle *S*.

In this case, the consumers do not get any consumer surplus! The entire surplus is captured by the monopolist in the form of profit. When a monopolist is able to capture the entire surplus in this way, we say that it achieves **perfect price discrimination.**

In general, the greater the number of different prices a monopolist is able to charge, the closer it can get to perfect price discrimination. Figure 14-11 on page 356 shows a monopolist facing a downward-sloping demand curve; we suppose that this monopolist is able to charge different prices to different groups of consumers, with the consumers who are willing to pay the most being charged the most. In panel (a) the monopolist charges two different prices; in panel (b) the monopolist charges three different prices. Two things are apparent:

- The greater the number of prices the monopolist charges, the lower the lowest price—that is, some consumers will pay prices that approach marginal cost.

- The greater the number of prices the monopolist charges, the more money it extracts from consumers.

With a very large number of different prices, the picture would look like panel (c), a case of perfect price discrimination. Here, consumers least willing to buy the good pay marginal cost, and the entire consumer surplus is extracted as profit.

Both our airline example and the example in Figure 14-11 can be used to make another point: a monopolist that can engage in perfect price discrimination doesn't cause any inefficiency! The reason is that the source of inefficiency is eliminated: there are no potential consumers who would be willing to purchase the good at a price equal to or above marginal cost but do not get the chance to do so. Instead, the monopolist manages to "scoop up" these consumers by offering them lower prices than it charges others.

Perfect price discrimination is probably never possible in practice. At a fundamental level, the inability to achieve perfect price discrimination is a problem of prices as economic signals, a phenomenon we noted in Chapter 13. When prices work as economic signals, they convey the information needed to ensure that all mutually beneficial transactions will indeed occur: the market price signals the seller's cost, and a

Perfect price discrimination takes place when a monopolist charges each consumer his or her willingness to pay—the maximum that consumer is willing to pay.

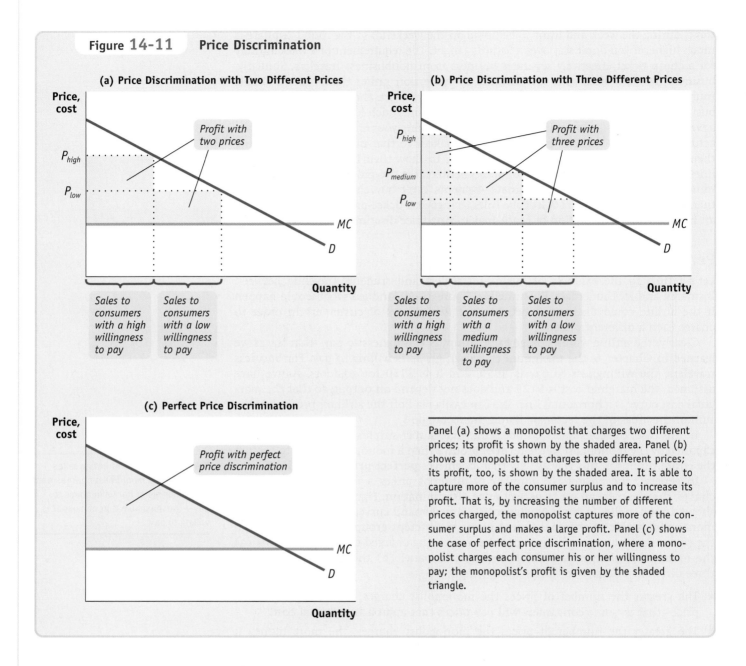

Figure 14-11   Price Discrimination

(a) Price Discrimination with Two Different Prices

Profit with two prices

(b) Price Discrimination with Three Different Prices

Profit with three prices

It is able to capture more of the consumer surplus and to increase its profit. That is, by increasing the number of different prices charged, the monopolist captures more of the consumer surplus and makes a large profit. Panel (c) shows the case of perfect price discrimination, where a monopolist charges each consumer his or her willingness to pay; the monopolist's profit is given by the shaded triangle.

(c) Perfect Price Discrimination

Profit with perfect price discrimination

Panel (a) shows a monopolist that charges two different prices; its profit is shown by the shaded area. Panel (b) shows a monopolist that charges three different prices; its profit, too, is shown by the shaded area.

consumer signals willingness to pay by purchasing the good whenever that willingness to pay is at least as high as the market price. The problem in reality, however, is that prices are often not perfect signals: a consumer's true willingness to pay can be disguised, as by a business traveler who claims to be a student when buying a ticket in order to obtain a lower fare. When such disguises work, a monopolist cannot achieve perfect price discrimination. However, monopolists do try to move in the direction of perfect price discrimination through a variety of pricing strategies. Common techniques for price discrimination include the following:

- *Advance purchase restrictions.* Prices are lower for those who purchase well in advance (or in some cases for those who purchase at the last minute). This separates those who are likely to shop for better prices from those who won't.

- *Volume discounts.* Often the price is lower if you buy a large quantity. For a consumer who plans to consume a lot of a good, the cost of the last unit—the marginal cost to the consumer—is considerably less than the average price. This separates those who plan to buy a lot and are therefore likely to be more sensitive to price from those who don't.

- *Two-part tariffs.* In a discount club like Sam's Club (which is not a monopolist but a monopolistic competitor), you pay an annual fee in addition to the cost of the items you purchase. So the cost of the first item you buy is in effect much higher than that of subsequent items, thereby making the two-part tariff behave like a volume discount.

Our discussion also helps explain why government policies on monopoly typically focus on preventing deadweight losses, not preventing price discrimination—unless it causes serious issues of equity. Compared to a single-price monopolist, price discrimination—even when it is not perfect—can increase the efficiency of the market. If sales to consumers formerly priced out of the market but now able to purchase the good at a lower price generate enough surplus to offset the loss in surplus to those now facing a higher price and no longer buying the good, then total surplus increases when price discrimination is introduced. An example of this might be a drug that is disproportionately prescribed to senior citizens, who are often on fixed incomes and so are very sensitive to price. A policy that allows a drug company to charge senior citizens a low price and everyone else a high price may indeed increase total surplus compared to a situation in which everyone is charged the same price. But price discrimination that creates serious concerns about equity is likely to be prohibited—for example, an ambulance service that charges patients based on the severity of their emergency.

economics in action

Sales, Factory Outlets, and Ghost Cities

Have you ever wondered why department stores occasionally hold sales, offering their merchandise for considerably less than the usual prices? Or why, driving along America's highways, you sometimes encounter clusters of "factory outlet" stores, often a couple of hours' drive from the nearest city? These familiar features of the economic landscape are actually rather peculiar if you think about them: why should sheets and towels be suddenly cheaper for a week each winter, or raincoats be offered for less in Freeport, Maine, than in Boston? In each case the answer is that the sellers—who are often oligopolists or monopolistic competitors—are engaged in a subtle form of price discrimination.

Why hold regular sales of sheets and towels? Stores are aware that some consumers buy these goods only when they discover that they need them; they are not likely to put a lot of effort into searching for the best price and so have a relatively low price elasticity of demand. So the store wants to charge high prices for customers who come in on an ordinary day. But shoppers who plan ahead, looking for the lowest price, will wait until there is a sale. So by scheduling such sales only now and then, the store is in effect able to discriminate between high-elasticity and low-elasticity customers.

An outlet store serves the same purpose: by offering merchandise for low prices, but only a considerable distance away from downtown, a seller is able to establish a separate market for those customers who are willing to make a significant effort to search out lower prices—and who therefore have a relatively high price elasticity of demand.

Finally, let's return to airline tickets to mention one of the truly odd features of their prices. Often a flight from one major destination to another—say, from Chicago to Los Angeles—is cheaper than a much shorter flight to a smaller city—say, from Chicago to Salt Lake City. Again, the reason is a difference in the price elasticity of demand: customers have a choice of many airlines between Chicago and Los Angeles, so the demand for any one flight is quite elastic; customers have very little choice in flights to a small city, so the demand is much less elastic.

But often there is a flight between two major destinations that makes a stop along the way—say, a flight from Chicago to Los Angeles with a stop in Salt Lake. In these cases, it is sometimes cheaper to fly to the more distant city than to the city that is a stop along the way. For example, it may be cheaper to purchase a ticket to Los Angeles and get off in Salt Lake City than to purchase a ticket to Salt Lake City! It sounds ridiculous but makes perfect sense given the logic of monopoly pricing.

So why don't passengers simply buy a ticket from Chicago to Los Angeles, but get off at Salt Lake? Well, some do—but the airlines, understandably, make it difficult for customers to find out about such "ghost cities." In addition, the airline will not allow you to check baggage only part of the way if you have a ticket for the final destination. (And airlines refuse to honor tickets for return flights when a passenger has not completed all the legs of the outbound flight.) All these restrictions are meant to enforce the separation of markets necessary to allow price discrimination. ∎

< < < < < < < < < < < < < < < < < < <

>>CHECK YOUR UNDERSTANDING 14-4

1. True or false? Explain your answer.
   a. A single-price monopolist sells to some customers that a price-discriminating monopolist refuses to.
   b. A price-discriminating monopolist creates more inefficiency than a single-price monopolist because it captures more of the consumer surplus.
   c. Under price discrimination, a customer with highly elastic demand will pay a lower price than a customer with inelastic demand.

2. Which of the following are cases of price discrimination and which are not? In the cases of price discrimination, identify the consumers with high and those with low price elasticity of demand.
   a. Damaged merchandise is marked down.
   b. Restaurants have senior citizen discounts.
   c. Food manufacturers place discount coupons for their merchandise in newspapers.
   d. Airline tickets cost more during the summer peak flying season.

Solutions appear at back of book.

• A LOOK AHEAD •

We've now taken one large step away from the world of perfect competition. As we have seen, a monopolistic industry behaves quite differently from a perfectly competitive one.

But pure monopoly is actually quite rare in the modern economy. More typical are industries in which there is some competition, but not perfect competition—that is, where there is *imperfect competition*. In the next two chapters we examine two types of imperfect competition: oligopoly and monopolistic competition.

You might expect an oligopoly to act something like a cross between a monopoly and a perfectly competitive industry, but it turns out that oligopoly raises issues that arise neither in perfect competition nor in monopoly, issues of *strategic interaction* and *collusion* between firms. Likewise, monopolistic competition creates yet another set of issues, such as tastes, product differentiation, and advertising.

SUMMARY

1. There are four main types of market structure based on number of firms in the industry and product differentiation: perfect competition, monopoly, oligopoly, and monopolistic competition.

2. A **monopolist** is a producer who is the sole supplier of a good without close substitutes. An industry controlled by a monopolist is a **monopoly.**

3. The key difference between a monopoly and a perfectly competitive industry is that a perfectly competitive firm faces a horizontal demand curve but a monopolist faces a downward-sloping demand curve. This gives the monopolist **market power,** the ability to raise the market price by reducing output compared to a perfectly competitive industry.

4. To persist, a monopoly must be protected by a **barrier to entry.** This can take the form of control of natural resources or inputs, economies of scale that give rise to **natural monopoly,** technological advantage, or government rules that prevent entry by other firms.

5. The marginal revenue of a monopolist is composed of a quantity effect (the price received from the additional unit) and a price effect (the reduction in the price at which all units are sold). Because of the price effect, a monopolist's marginal revenue is always less than the market price, and the marginal revenue curve lies below the demand curve.

6. At the monopolist's profit-maximizing output level, marginal cost equals marginal revenue, which is less than market price. At the perfectly competitive firm's profit-maximizing output level, marginal cost equals the market price. So in comparison to perfectly competitive industries, monopolies produce less, charge higher prices, and earn higher profits in both the short run and the long run.

7. A monopoly creates deadweight losses by charging a price above marginal cost: the loss in consumer surplus exceeds the monopolist's profit. Thus monopolies are a source of market failure and should be prevented or broken up, except in the case of natural monopolies.

8. Natural monopolies can still cause deadweight losses. To limit these losses, governments sometimes impose **public ownership** and at other times impose **price regulation.** A price ceiling on a monopolist, as opposed to a perfectly competitive industry, need not cause shortages and can increase total surplus.

9. Not all monopolists are **single-price monopolists.** Monopolists, as well as oligopolists and monopolistic competitors, often engage in **price discrimination** to make higher profits, using various techniques to differentiate consumers based on their sensitivity to price and charging those with less elastic demand higher prices. A monopolist that achieves **perfect price discrimination** charges each consumer a price equal to his or her willingness to pay and captures the total surplus in the market. Although perfect price discrimination creates no inefficiency, it is practically impossible to implement.

KEY TERMS

Monopolist, p. 335
Monopoly, p. 335
Market power, p. 336
Barrier to entry, p. 337

Natural monopoly, p. 337
Public ownership, p. 349
Price regulation, p. 350
Single-price monopolist, p. 352

Price discrimination, p. 352
Perfect price discrimination, p. 355

PROBLEMS

1. Each of the following firms possesses market power. Explain its source.

   a. Merck, the producer of the patented cholesterol-lowering drug Zetia

   b. Verizon, a provider of local telephone service

   c. Chiquita, a supplier of bananas and owner of most banana plantations

2. Skyscraper City has a subway system, for which a one-way fare is $1.50. There is pressure on the mayor to reduce the fare by one-third, to $1.00. The mayor is dismayed, thinking that this will mean Skyscraper City is losing one-third of its revenue from sales of subway tickets. The mayor's economic adviser reminds her that she is focusing only on the price effect and ignoring the quantity effect. Explain why the mayor's estimate of a one-third loss of revenue is likely to be an overestimate. Illustrate with a diagram.

3. Consider an industry with the demand curve and marginal cost (MC) curve shown in the accompanying diagram. There is no fixed cost. If the industry is a single-price monopoly, the monopolist's marginal revenue curve would be MR. Answer the following questions by naming the appropriate points or areas.

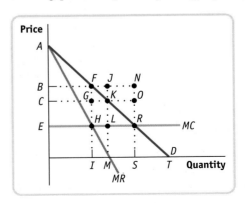

   a. If the industry is perfectly competitive, what will be the total quantity produced? At what price?

b. Which area reflects consumer surplus under perfect competition?

c. If the industry is a single-price monopoly, what quantity will the monopolist produce? Which price will it charge?

d. Which area reflects the single-price monopolist's profit?

e. Which area reflects consumer surplus under single-price monopoly?

f. Which area reflects the deadweight loss to society from single-price monopoly?

g. If the monopolist can price-discriminate perfectly, what quantity will the perfectly price-discriminating monopolist produce?

4. Bob, Bill, Ben, and Brad Baxter have just made a documentary movie about their basketball team. They are thinking about making the movie available for download on the Internet, and they can act as a single-price monopolist if they choose to. Each time the movie is downloaded, their Internet service provider charges them a fee of $4. The Baxter brothers are arguing about which price to charge customers per download. The accompanying table shows the demand schedule for their film.

Price of download	Quantity of downloads demanded
$10	0
8	1
6	3
4	6
2	10
0	15

a. Calculate the total revenue and the marginal revenue per download.

b. Bob is proud of the film and wants as many people as possible to download it. Which price would he choose? How many downloads would be sold?

c. Bill wants as much total revenue as possible. Which price would he choose? How many downloads would be sold?

d. Ben wants to maximize profit. Which price would he choose? How many downloads would be sold?

e. Brad wants to charge the efficient price. Which price would he choose? How many downloads would be sold?

5. Jimmy has a room that overlooks, from some distance, a major league baseball stadium. He decides to rent a telescope for $50.00 a week and charge his friends and classmates to use it to peep at the game for 30 seconds. He can act as a single-price monopolist for renting out "peeps." For each person who takes a 30-second peep, it costs Jimmy $0.20 to clean the eyepiece. The accompanying table shows the information Jimmy has gathered about the demand for the service.

Price of peep	Quantity of peeps demanded
$1.20	0
1.00	100
0.90	150
0.80	200
0.70	250
0.60	300
0.50	350
0.40	400
0.30	450
0.20	500
0.10	550

a. For each price in the table, calculate the total revenue from selling peeps and the marginal revenue per peep.

b. At what quantity will Jimmy's profit be maximized? What price will he charge? What will his total profit be?

c. Jimmy's landlady complains about all the visitors coming into the building and tells Jimmy to stop selling peeps. Jimmy discovers, however, that if he gives the landlady $0.20 for every peep he sells, she will stop complaining. What effect does the $0.20-per-peep bribe have on Jimmy's marginal cost per peep? What is the new profit-maximizing quantity of peeps? What effect does the $0.20-per-peep bribe have on Jimmy's total profit?

6. Suppose that De Beers is a single-price monopolist in the market for diamonds. De Beers has five potential customers: Raquel, Jackie, Joan, Mia, and Sophia. Each of these customers will buy at most one diamond—and only if the price is just equal to, or lower than, her willingness to pay. Raquel's willingness to pay is $400; Jackie's, $300; Joan's, $200; Mia's, $100; and Sophia's, $0. De Beers's marginal cost per diamond is $100. This leads to the demand schedule for diamonds shown in the accompanying table.

Price of diamond	Quantity of diamonds demanded
$500	0
400	1
300	2
200	3
100	4
0	5

a. Calculate De Beers's total revenue and its marginal revenue. From your calculation, draw the demand curve and the marginal revenue curve.

b. Explain why De Beers faces a downward-sloping demand curve.

c. Explain why the marginal revenue from an additional diamond sale is less than the price of the diamond.

d. Suppose De Beers currently charges $200 for its diamonds. If it lowered the price to $100, how large is the price effect? How large is the quantity effect?

e. Draw the marginal cost curve into your diagram and determine which quantity maximizes De Beers's profit and which price De Beers will charge.

7. Use the demand schedule for diamonds given in Problem 6. The marginal cost of producing diamonds is constant at $100.

a. If De Beers charges the monopoly price, how large is the individual consumer surplus that each buyer experiences? Calculate total consumer surplus by summing the individual consumer surpluses. How large is producer surplus?

Suppose that upstart Russian and Asian producers enter the market and the market becomes perfectly competitive.

b. What is the perfectly competitive price? What quantity will be sold in this perfectly competitive market?

c. At the competitive price and quantity, how large is the consumer surplus that each buyer experiences? How large is total consumer surplus? How large is producer surplus?

d. Compare your answer to part c to your answer to part a. How large is the deadweight loss associated with monopoly in this case?

8. Use the demand schedule for diamonds given in Problem 6. De Beers is a monopolist, but it can now price-discriminate perfectly among all five of its potential customers. De Beers's marginal cost is constant at $100.

a. If De Beers can price-discriminate perfectly, to which customers will it sell diamonds and at what prices?

b. How large is each individual consumer surplus? How large is total consumer surplus? Calculate producer surplus by summing the producer surplus generated by each sale.

9. Download Records decides to release an album by the group Mary and the Little Lamb. It produces the album with no fixed cost, but the total cost of downloading an album to a CD and paying Mary her royalty is $6 per album. Download Records can act as a single-price monopolist. Its marketing division finds that the demand schedule for the album is as shown in the accompanying table.

Price of album	Quantity of albums demanded
$22	0
20	1,000
18	2,000
16	3,000
14	4,000
12	5,000
10	6,000
8	7,000

a. Calculate the total revenue and the marginal revenue per album.

b. The marginal cost of producing each album is constant at $6. To maximize profit, what level of output should Download Records choose, and which price should it therefore charge?

c. Mary renegotiates her contract and now needs to be paid a royalty of $14 per album. So the marginal cost rises to be constant at $14. To maximize profit, what level of output should Download Records now choose, and which price should it charge for each album?

10. The accompanying diagram illustrates your local electricity company's natural monopoly. The diagram shows the demand curve for kilowatt-hours (kWh) of electricity, the company's marginal revenue (*MR*) curve, the marginal cost (*MC*) curve, and its average total cost (*ATC*) curve. The government wants to regulate the monopolist by imposing a price ceiling.

a. If the government does not regulate this monopolist, which price will it charge? Illustrate the inefficiency this creates by shading the deadweight loss from monopoly.

b. If the government imposes a price ceiling equal to the marginal cost, $0.30, will the monopolist make profits or lose money? Shade the area of profit (or losses) for the monopolist. If the government does impose this price ceiling, do you think the firm will continue to produce in the long run?

c. If the government imposes a price ceiling of $0.50, will the monopolist make a profit or lose money?

11. The movie theater in Collegetown serves two kinds of customers: students and professors. There are 900 students and 100 professors in Collegetown. Each student's willingness to pay for a movie ticket is $5. Each professor's willingness to pay for a movie ticket is $10. Each will buy at most one ticket. The movie theater's marginal cost per ticket is constant at $3, and there is no fixed cost.

a. Suppose the movie theater cannot price-discriminate and needs to charge both students and professors the same price per ticket. If the movie theater charges $5, who will buy tickets and what will the movie theater's profit be? How large is consumer surplus?

b. If the movie theater charges $10, who will buy movie tickets and what will the movie theater's profit be? How large is consumer surplus?

c. Now suppose that, if it chooses to, the movie theater can price-discriminate between students and professors by requiring students to show their student ID. If the movie theater charges students $5 and professors $10, how much profit will the movie theater make? How large is consumer surplus?

>web... To continue your study and review of concepts in this chapter, please visit the Krugman/Wells website for quizzes, animated graph tutorials, web links to helpful resources, and more.

www.worthpublishers.com/krugmanwells

>>Oligopoly

CAUGHT IN THE ACT

THE AGRICULTURAL PRODUCTS COMPANY Archer Daniels Midland (also known as ADM) likes to describe itself as "supermarket to the world." Its name is familiar to many Americans not only because of its important role in the economy but also because of its advertising and sponsorship of public television programs. But on October 25, 1993, ADM itself was on camera.

On that day executives from ADM and its Japanese competitor Ajinomoto met at the Marriott Hotel in Irvine, California, to discuss the market for lysine, an additive used in animal feed. (How is lysine produced? It's excreted by genetically engineered bacteria.) In this and subsequent meetings, the two companies joined with several other competitors to set targets for the market price of lysine. Each company agreed to limit its production in order to achieve those targets. Agreeing on specific limits would be their biggest challenge—or so they thought.

What the participants in the meeting didn't know was that they had a bigger problem: the FBI had bugged the room and was filming them with a camera hidden in a lamp.

What the companies were doing was illegal. To understand why it was illegal and why the companies were doing it anyway, we need to examine the issues posed by industries that are neither perfectly competitive nor pure monopolies. In this chapter we focus on *oligopoly*, an industry in which there are only a few producers. As we'll see, oligopoly is a very important reality—much more important, in fact, than monopoly and arguably more typical of modern economies than perfect competition.

Although much that we have learned about both perfect competition and monopoly is relevant to oligopoly, oligopoly

AP/Wide World Photos

The law catches up with a colluding oligopolist.

also raises some entirely new issues. Among other things, firms in an oligopoly are often tempted to engage in the kind of behavior that got ADM, Ajinomoto, and other lysine producers into trouble with the

What you will learn in this chapter:

➤ The meaning of **oligopoly,** and why it occurs

➤ Why **oligopolists** have an incentive to act in ways that reduce their combined profit, and why they can benefit from **collusion**

➤ How our understanding of oligopoly can be enhanced by using **game theory,** especially the concept of the **prisoners' dilemma**

➤ How repeated interactions among oligopolists can help them achieve **tacit collusion**

➤ How oligopoly works in practice, under the legal constraints of **antitrust policy** law. For example, in 2002 five of the largest music companies and three of the largest music retailers in the United States settled government charges that they worked together to keep the prices of CDs artificially high during the 1990s.

We will begin by examining what oligopoly is and why it is so important. Then we'll turn to the behavior of oligopolistic industries. Finally, we'll look at *antitrust policy,* which is primarily concerned with trying to keep oligopolies "well behaved."

The Prevalence of Oligopoly

At the time of that elaborately bugged meeting, no one company controlled the world lysine industry, but there were only a few major producers. An industry with only a few sellers is known as an **oligopoly;** a firm in such an industry is known as an **oligopolist.**

Oligopolists obviously compete with each other for sales. But ADM and Ajinomoto weren't like firms in a perfectly competitive industry, which take the price at which they can sell their product as given. Each of these firms knew that its decision about how much to produce would affect the market price. That is, like monopolists, each of the firms had some *market power.* So the competition in this industry wasn't "perfect."

Economists refer to a situation in which firms compete but also possess market power—which enables them to affect market prices—as **imperfect competition.** As we saw in Chapter 14, there are actually two important forms of imperfect competition: oligopoly and *monopolistic competition.* Of these, oligopoly is probably the more important in practice.

Although lysine is a multibillion-dollar business, it is not exactly a product familiar to most consumers. However, many familiar goods and services are supplied by only a few competing sellers, which means the industries in question are oligopolies. For example, most air routes are served by only two or three airlines: in recent years, regularly scheduled shuttle service between New York and either Boston or Washington, D.C. has been provided only by Delta and US Airways. Similarly, most long-distance telephone service is supplied by one of three carriers: AT&T, MCI, or Sprint. Most cola beverages are sold by Coca-Cola and Pepsi. This list could go on for many pages.

It's important to realize that an oligopoly isn't necessarily made up of large firms. What matters isn't size per se; the question is how many competitors there are. When a small town has only two grocery stores, grocery service there is just as much an oligopoly as air shuttle service between New York and Washington.

Why are oligopolies so prevalent? Essentially, oligopoly is the result of the same factors that sometimes produce monopoly, but in somewhat weaker form. Probably the most important source of oligopoly is the existence of *economies of scale,* which give bigger producers a cost advantage over smaller ones. When these economies of scale are very strong, they lead to monopoly, but when they are not that strong they lead to competition among a small number of firms. For example, larger grocery stores typically have lower costs than smaller stores. But the advantages of large scale taper off once grocery stores are reasonably large, which is why two or three stores often survive in small towns.

If oligopoly is so common, why has most of this book focused on competition in industries where the number of sellers is very

> An **oligopoly** is an industry with only a small number of producers. A producer in such an industry is known as an **oligopolist.**

> When no one firm has a monopoly, but producers nonetheless realize that they can affect market prices, an industry is characterized by **imperfect competition.**

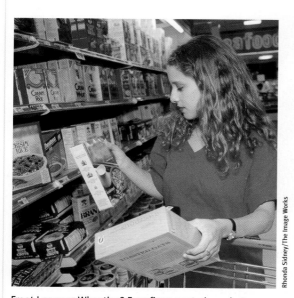

Froot Loops or Wheaties? Four firms control nearly 83 percent of the breakfast cereal market.

Rhonda Sidney/The Image Works

large? And why did we study monopoly, which is relatively uncommon, first? The answer has two parts. First, much of what we learn from the study of perfectly competitive markets—about costs, entry and exit, and efficiency—remains valid despite the fact that many industries are not perfectly competitive. Second, the analysis of oligopoly turns out to present some puzzles for which there is no easy solution. It is almost always a good idea—in exams and in life—first to deal with the questions you can answer, then to puzzle over the harder ones. We have simply followed the same strategy, developing the relatively clear-cut theories of perfect competition and monopoly first, and only then turning to the puzzles presented by oligopoly.

economics in action

Some Oligopolistic Industries

In practice, it is not always easy to determine an industry's market structure just by looking at the number of sellers. Many oligopolistic industries contain a number of small "niche" producers, which don't really compete with the major players. For example, the U.S. airline industry includes a number of regional airlines like Shuttle America, which flies propeller planes between places like Trenton, New Jersey, and Bedford, Massachusetts; if you count these carriers, the U.S. airline industry contains dozens of sellers, which doesn't sound like competition among a small group. But there are only a handful of national competitors like American and United, and on many routes, as we've seen, there are only two or three competitors.

To get a better picture of market structure, economists often use the "four-firm concentration ratio," which asks what share of industry sales is accounted for by the top four firms. (Why four? The federal government normally doesn't release data on share of industry sales by individual firms within the top four, lest it be accused of giving away corporate secrets.)

TABLE 15-1

Four-Firm Concentration Ratios

Industry	Concentration ratio	Largest firms
1. Cigarettes	98.9	Philip Morris, R. J. Reynolds, Lorillard, Brown and Williamson
2. Batteries	90.1	Duracell, Energizer, Rayovac
3. Breweries	89.7	Anheuser-Busch, Miller, Coors, Stroh's
4. Light bulbs	88.9	Westinghouse, General Electric
5. Breakfast cereals	82.9	Kellogg's, General Mills, Post, Quaker Oats
6. Automobiles	79.5	General Motors, Ford, DaimlerChrysler

Source: U.S. Census Bureau.

Table 15-1 shows some industries with very high four-firm concentration ratios, along with the names of the largest firms in each industry. These names are familiar—not only because these are big companies but also because they advertise a lot. And that is not an accident. As we will see shortly, oligopolistic firms often choose *not* to compete much on price, trying to win customers in other ways—such as through ad campaigns. ∎

> > > > > > > > > > > > > > > > > >

>> QUICK REVIEW

➤ In addition to perfect competition and monopoly, *oligopoly* and monopolistic competition are also important types of market structure. They are forms of *imperfect competition*.

➤ Oligopoly is a common market structure. It arises from the same forces that lead to monopoly, except in weaker form.

1. Explain why each of the following industries is an oligopoly, not a perfectly competitive industry.
   a. The world oil industry, where a few countries near the Persian Gulf control much of the world's oil reserves
   b. The microprocessor industry, where two firms, Intel and its bitter rival AMD, dominate the technology
   c. The wide-bodied passenger jet industry, composed of the American firm Boeing and the European firm Airbus, where production is characterized by extremely large fixed cost

Solutions appear at back of book.

Understanding Oligopoly

How much will a firm produce? Up to this point we have always answered: the quantity that maximizes its profit. The assumption that firms maximize profit is enough to determine their output when they are perfect competitors or when the industry is a monopoly.

When it comes to oligopoly, however, we run into some difficulties. Indeed, economists often describe the behavior of oligopolistic firms as a "puzzle."

A Duopoly Example

Let's begin looking at the puzzle of oligopoly with the simplest version, an industry in which there are only two producing firms—a **duopoly**—and each is known as a **duopolist.**

Going back to our opening story, imagine that ADM and Ajinomoto are the only two producers of lysine. To make things even simpler, suppose that once a company has incurred the fixed cost needed to produce lysine, the marginal cost of producing another pound is zero. So the companies are concerned only with the revenue they receive from sales.

Table 15-2 shows a hypothetical demand schedule for lysine and the total revenue of the industry at each price-quantity combination.

If this were a perfectly competitive industry, each firm would have an incentive to produce more as long as the market price was above marginal cost. Since the

An oligopoly consisting of only two firms is a **duopoly**. Each firm is known as a **duopolist**.

TABLE **15-2**

Demand Schedule for Lysine

Price of lysine (per pound)	Quantity of lysine demanded (millions of pounds)	Total revenue (millions)
$12	0	$0
11	10	110
10	20	200
9	30	270
8	40	320
7	50	350
6	60	360
5	70	350
4	80	320
3	90	270
2	100	200
1	110	110
0	120	0

marginal cost is assumed to be zero, this would mean that at equilibrium lysine would be provided free. Firms would produce until price equals zero, yielding a total output of 120 million pounds and zero revenue for all firms.

However, surely the firms would not be that stupid. With only two firms in the industry, each would realize that by producing more it would drive down the market price. So each firm would, like a monopolist, realize that profits would be higher if it limited its production.

So how much will the two firms produce?

One possibility is that the two companies will engage in **collusion**—they will cooperate to raise each other's profits. The strongest form of collusion is a **cartel,** an arrangement that determines how much each firm is allowed to produce. The world's most famous cartel is the Organization of Petroleum Exporting Countries, described in Economics in Action on page 377. As its name indicates, it's actually an agreement among governments rather than firms. There's a reason this most famous of cartels is an agreement among governments: cartels among firms are illegal in the United States and many other jurisdictions. But let's ignore the law for a moment (which is, of course, what ADM and Ajinomoto did in real life—to their own detriment).

So suppose that ADM and Ajinomoto were to form a cartel and that this cartel decided to act as if it were a monopolist, maximizing total industry profits. It's obvious from Table 15-2 that in order to maximize the combined profits of the firms, this cartel should set total industry output at 60 million pounds of lysine, which would sell at a price of $6 per pound, leading to revenue of $360 million, the maximum possible. Then the only question would be how much of that 60 million pounds each firm gets to produce. A "fair" solution might be for each firm to produce 30 million pounds.

But even if the two firms agreed on such a deal, they might have a problem: each of the firms would have an incentive to break its word and produce more than the agreed-upon quantity.

> Sellers engage in **collusion** when they cooperate to raise each others' profits. A **cartel** is an agreement by several producers that increases their combined profits by telling each one how much to produce.

Collusion and Competition

Suppose that the presidents of ADM and Ajinomoto were to agree that each would produce 30 million pounds of lysine over the next year. Both would understand that this plan maximizes their combined profits. And both would have an incentive to cheat.

To see why, consider what would happen if Ajinomoto honored its agreement, producing only 30 million pounds, but ADM ignored its promise and produced 40 million pounds. This increase in total output would drive the price down from $6 to $5 per pound, the price at which 70 million pounds are demanded. The industry's total revenue would fall from $360 million ($6 × 60 million pounds) to $350 million ($5 × 70 million pounds). However, ADM's revenue would *rise*, from $180 million to $200 million. Since we are assuming a marginal cost of zero, this would mean a $20 million increase in ADM's profits.

But Ajinomoto's president might make exactly the same calculation. And if *both* firms were to produce 40 million pounds of lysine, the price would drop to $4 per pound. So each firm's profits would fall, from $180 million to $160 million.

Why do individual firms have an incentive to produce more than the quantity that maximizes their joint profits? Because neither firm has as strong an incentive to limit its output as a true monopolist would.

Let's go back for a minute to the theory of monopoly. We know that a profit-maximizing monopolist sets marginal cost (which in this case is zero) equal to marginal revenue. But what is marginal revenue? Producing an additional unit of a good has two effects:

1. A positive *quantity* effect: one more unit is sold, increasing total revenue by the price at which that unit is sold.

2. A negative *price* effect: in order to sell one more unit, the monopolist must cut the market price on *all* units sold.

The negative price effect is the reason marginal revenue for a monopolist is less than the market price. But when considering the effect of increasing production, a firm is concerned only with the price effect on its own units of output, not those of its fellow oligopolists. Both ADM and Ajinomoto suffer a negative price effect if ADM decides to produce extra lysine and so drives down the price. But ADM cares only about the negative price effect on the units it produces, not about the loss to Ajinomoto.

This tells us that an individual firm in an oligopolistic industry faces a smaller price effect from an additional unit of output than a monopolist; therefore, the marginal revenue that such a firm calculates is higher. So it will seem to be profitable for any one company in an oligopoly to increase production, even if that increase reduces the profits of the industry as a whole. But if everyone thinks that way, the result is that everyone earns a lower profit!

Until now, we have been able to analyze producer behavior by asking what a producer should do to maximize profits. But even if ADM and Ajinomoto are both trying to maximize profits, what does this predict about their behavior? Will they engage in collusion, reaching and holding to an agreement that maximizes their combined profits? Or will they engage in **noncooperative behavior,** with each firm acting in its own self-interest, even though this has the effect of driving down everyone's profits? Both strategies sound like profit maximization. Which will actually describe their behavior?

Now you see why oligopoly presents a puzzle: there are only a small number of players, making collusion a real possibility. If there were dozens or hundreds of firms, it would be safe to assume they would behave noncooperatively. When there are only a handful of firms in an industry, however, it's hard to determine whether collusion will actually materialize.

Since collusion is ultimately more profitable than noncooperative behavior, firms have an incentive to collude if they can. One way to do so is to formalize it—sign an agreement (maybe even make a legal contract) or establish some financial incentives for the companies to set their prices high. But in the United States and many other nations, you can't do that—at least not legally. Companies cannot make a legal contract to keep prices high: not only is the contract unenforceable, but writing it is a one-way ticket to jail. Neither can they sign a gentlemen's agreement, which lacks the force of law but perhaps exerts moral force—that's illegal, too. In fact, executives from rival companies rarely meet without lawyers present, who make sure that the conversation does not stray into inappropriate territory. Even hinting at how nice it would be if prices were higher can bring you an unwelcome interview with the Justice Department or the Federal Trade Commission, both of which enforce the laws against oligopolistic collusion. For example, at the time of writing, the Justice Department had begun to consider whether to open a formal inquiry into a series of meetings held between Monsanto and Pioneer Hi-Bred International, two companies that account for 60 percent of the U.S. market in maize and soybean seed. The two companies, parties to a licensing agreement involving genetically modified seed, claimed that no illegal discussions of price fixing occurred in those meetings. But the fact that the two firms discussed prices as part of the licensing agreement is enough to ensure, according to some experts, that a formal investigation will eventually be launched.

Sometimes, as we've seen, oligopolistic firms just ignore the rules. But more often they find ways to achieve collusion without a formal agreement. As we'll see in the next section, one important factor in determining how hard it is to achieve collusion without a formal agreement is how easy it is for a firm to increase its output quickly in order to capture sales from its rival.

Competing in Prices versus Competing in Quantities

In our duopoly example, we've assumed that firms choose a quantity of output and sell that output at whatever the market price turns out to be. That's actually a pretty good description of the way the lysine market works. But in other industries, such

> When firms ignore the effects of their actions on each other's profits, they engage in **noncooperative behavior.**

as automobiles, firms don't choose a level of output; they choose a *price* and sell as much as they can at that price. Does this make any difference?

Yes, it does, at least when we analyze noncooperative behavior. In choosing what to do, an oligopolist must always be concerned about whether a noncooperative rival firm will respond by *undercutting* her. The oligopolist must be concerned that a rival firm will take some action that allows it to steal some of her sales and capture a larger share of the market. And, it turns out, the answer to whether a rival is willing to engage in undercutting behavior depends on how difficult it is for him to increase output to satisfy the additional customers he gains by his undercutting.

Let's consider a hypothetical example using Airbus and Boeing, duopolists in the large passenger aircraft industry, to gain some intuition. For these firms, deciding their production capacity—how much output they can produce over, say, the next two or three years—is their most important decision. Why? Passenger aircraft are very large and are built in batches, a few planes at a time, in huge hangars. The determining factor in how many planes can be built at any given time is the size of the company's existing production facilities, which can take years to build.

So this means that when Airbus, for example, sets its maximum production capacity at 50 planes per year, Boeing can feel comfortably assured that Airbus won't easily be able to increase this number anytime soon. This, in turn, has important implications for Boeing's actions. If Boeing also sets its production capacity at 50 planes per year, it can safely assume that Airbus's production capacity is *given* and that, as a result, the market will be split 50–50 between the two manufacturers. Airbus won't be able to quickly increase its output and steal some of Boeing's customers by offering them a lower price. The end result is that the total output of the industry is less than the output under perfect competition, and each firm earns a profit. Economists refer to this kind of behavior as *quantity competition* or *Cournot behavior,* after the nineteenth-century French economist who devised the model. The basic insight of the Cournot model is that when firms are restricted in how much they can produce, it is easier for them to avoid excessive competition and to "divvy up" the market, thereby pricing above marginal cost and earning profits. It is easier for them to achieve an outcome that looks like collusion without a formal agreement.

But how does the behavior of oligopolists change when they are not constrained by limited production capacity? Let's assume that American Airlines and British Airways are duopolists and that they have exclusive rights to fly the Chicago–London route. When the economy is strong and lots of people want to fly between Chicago and London, American Airlines and British Airways are likely to find the number of passengers they can carry constrained by their production capacity—for example, the number of landing slots available. So in this environment they are likely to behave according to the Cournot model and price above marginal cost—say, charging $800 per round trip. But when the business climate is poor, the two airlines are likely to find that they have lots of empty seats at a fare of $800 and that capacity constraints are no longer an issue. What will they do?

Recent history tells us they will engage in a price war by slashing ticket prices. They are no longer able to maintain Cournot behavior because at the ticket price of $800, each has excess capacity. If American Airlines were to try to maintain a price of $800, it would soon find itself undercut by British Airways, which would charge $750 and steal all its customers. In turn, American Airlines would undercut British Airways by charging $700—and so on. As long as each firm finds that it can make additional sales by cutting price, each will continue cutting until price is equal to marginal cost. (Going any lower would cause them to incur an avoidable loss.) This type of behavior is known as *price competition* or *Bertrand* behavior, after another nineteenth-century French economist. The logic behind the Bertrand model is that when firms produce perfect substitutes and have sufficient capacity to satisfy demand when price is equal to marginal cost, then each firm will be compelled to engage in competition by undercutting its rival's price until the price reaches marginal cost—that is, perfect competition.

Oligopolists would, understandably, prefer to avoid Bertrand behavior because it earns them zero profits. Lacking an environment that imposes constraints on their output capacity, firms try other means to avoid direct price competition—such as producing products that are not perfect substitutes but are instead differentiated. We'll examine this strategy in more detail later in this chapter, just noting here that producing differentiated products allows oligopolists to cultivate a loyal set of customers and to charge prices higher than marginal cost.

Even in the absence of limitations on production capacity, firms are often able to maintain collusive behavior (although it may be somewhat harder to do). In the next section, we'll see why such informal collusion often works but sometimes fails.

economics in action

The Great Vitamin Conspiracy

It was a bitter pill to swallow. In late 1999 some of the world's largest drug companies (mainly European and Japanese) agreed to pay billions of dollars in damages to customers after being convicted of a huge conspiracy to rig the world vitamin market.

The conspiracy began in 1989 when the Swiss company Roche and the German company BASF began secret talks about raising prices for vitamins. Soon a French company, Rhone-Poulenc, joined in, followed by several Japanese companies and other companies around the world. The members of the group, which referred to itself as "Vitamins Inc.," met regularly—sometimes at hotels, sometimes at the private homes of executives—to set prices and divide up markets for "bulk" vitamins (like vitamin A, vitamin C, and so on). These bulk vitamins are sold mainly to other companies, such as animal feed makers, food producers, and so on, which include them in their products. Indeed, it was the animal feed companies that grew suspicious about the prices they were being charged, which led to a series of investigations. The case eventually broke open when Rhone-Poulenc made a deal with U.S. officials to provide evidence about the conspiracy. The French company was concerned that rumors about price-fixing would lead U.S. officials to block its planned merger with another company.

This was a huge conspiracy—it makes the lysine case look like, well, chicken feed. How could it have happened?

The main answer probably lies in different national traditions about how to treat oligopolists. The United States has a long tradition of taking tough legal action against price-fixing, as we have just described. European governments, however, have historically been much less stringent. Indeed, in the past some European governments have actually encouraged major companies to form cartels. Modern European law on competition is not that different from that in the United States, but the European cultural tradition of viewing conspiracies to raise prices as normal business practice has not entirely died out. ∎

‹ ‹ ‹ ‹ ‹ ‹ ‹ ‹ ‹ ‹ ‹ ‹ ‹ ‹ ‹ ‹ ‹ ‹ ‹ ‹

>> CHECK YOUR UNDERSTANDING 15-2

1. Which of the following factors increase the likelihood that an oligopolist will collude with other firms in the industry? The likelihood that an oligopolist will act noncooperatively and raise output? Explain your answers.
   a. The firm's initial market share is small.
   b. The firm has a cost advantage over its rivals.
   c. The firm's customers face additional costs when they switch from the use of one firm's product to another firm's product.
   d. The firm and its rivals are currently operating at maximum production capacity, which cannot be altered in the short run.

Solutions appear at back of book.

Games Oligopolists Play

In our duopoly example and in real life, each oligopolistic firm realizes both that its profit depends on what its competitor does and that its competitor's profit depends on what it does. That is, the two firms are in a situation of **interdependence.**

In effect, the two firms are playing a "game" in which the profit of each player depends not only on its own actions but on those of the other player. The area of study of such games, known as **game theory,** has many applications, not just to economics but also to military strategy, politics, and other social sciences.

Let's see how game theory helps us understand oligopoly.

The Prisoners' Dilemma

Game theory deals with any situation in which the reward to any one player—the **payoff**—depends not only on his or her own actions but also on those of other players in the game. In the case of oligopolistic firms, the payoff is simply the firm's profit.

When there are only two players, as in a duopoly, the interdependence between the players can be represented with a **payoff matrix** like that shown in Figure 15-1. Each row corresponds to an action by one player (in this case, ADM); each column corresponds to an action by the other (in this case, Ajinomoto). For simplicity, let's assume that ADM can pick only one of two alternatives: produce 30 million pounds of lysine or produce 40 million pounds. Ajinomoto has the same pair of choices.

The matrix contains four boxes, each divided by a diagonal line. Each box shows the payoff to the two firms that results from a pair of choices; the number below the diagonal shows ADM's profits, the number above the diagonal shows Ajinomoto's profits.

These payoffs show what we concluded from our earlier analysis: the combined profit of the two firms is maximized if they each produce 30 million pounds. Either firm can, however, increase its own profits by producing 40 million pounds while the

When the decisions of two or more firms significantly affect each others' profits, they are in a situation of **interdependence.**

The study of behavior in situations of interdependence is known as **game theory.**

The reward received by a player in a game, such as the profit earned by an oligopolist, is that player's **payoff.**

A **payoff matrix** shows how the payoff to each of the participants in a two-player game depends on the actions of both. Such a matrix helps us analyze interdependence.

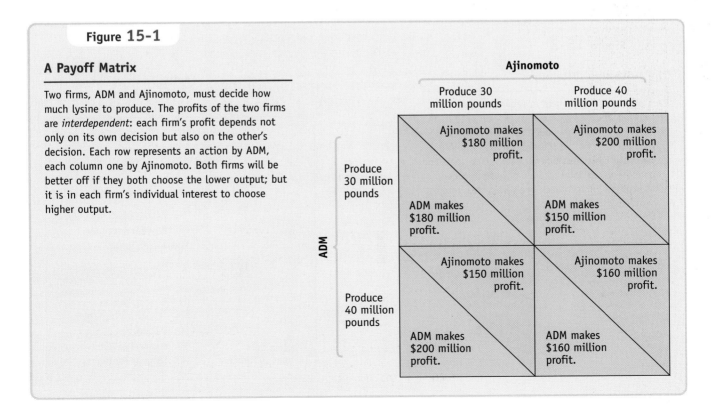

Figure 15-1

A Payoff Matrix

Two firms, ADM and Ajinomoto, must decide how much lysine to produce. The profits of the two firms are *interdependent*: each firm's profit depends not only on its own decision but also on the other's decision. Each row represents an action by ADM, each column one by Ajinomoto. Both firms will be better off if they both choose the lower output; but it is in each firm's individual interest to choose higher output.

other produces only 30 million pounds. But if both produce the larger quantity, both will have lower profits than if they had both held their output down.

The particular situation shown here is a version of a famous—and seemingly paradoxical—case of interdependence that appears in many contexts. Known as the **prisoners' dilemma,** it is a type of game in which the payoff matrix implies the following:

- Each player has an incentive, regardless of what the other player does, to cheat—to take an action that benefits it at the other's expense.

- When both players cheat, both are worse off than they would have been if neither had cheated.

The original illustration of the prisoners' dilemma occurred in a fictional story about two accomplices in crime—let's call them Thelma and Louise—who have been caught by the police. The police have enough evidence to put them behind bars for 5 years. They also know that the pair have committed a more serious crime, one that carries a 20-year sentence; unfortunately, they don't have enough evidence to convict the women on that charge. To do so, they would need each of the prisoners to implicate the other in the second crime.

So the police put the miscreants in separate cells and say the following to each: "Here's the deal: If neither of you confesses, you know that we'll send you to jail for 5 years. If you confess and implicate your partner, and she doesn't do the same, we'll reduce your sentence from 5 years to 2. But if your partner confesses and you don't, you'll get the maximum 20 years. And if both of you confess, we'll give you both 15 years."

Figure 15-2 shows the payoffs that face the prisoners, depending on the decision of each to remain silent or to confess. (Usually the payoff matrix reflects the players' payoffs, and higher payoffs are better than lower payoffs. This case is an exception: a higher number of years in prison is bad, not good!) Let's assume that the prisoners have no way to communicate and that they have not sworn an oath not to harm each other or anything of that sort. So each acts in her own self-interest. What will they do?

> **Prisoners' dilemma** is a game based on two premises: (1) Each player has an incentive to choose an action that benefits itself at the other player's expense. (2) When both players act in this way, both are worse off than if they had chosen different actions.

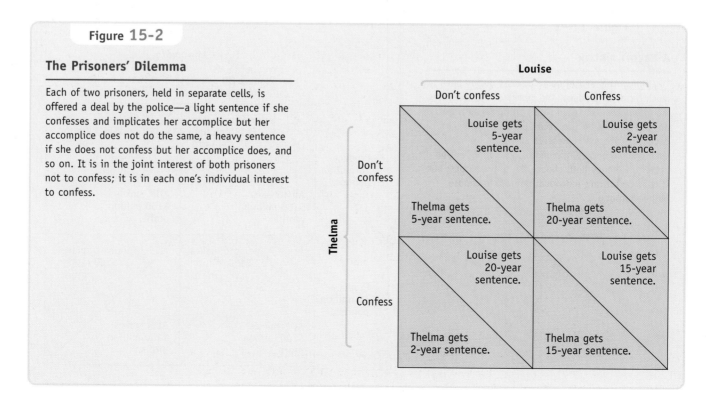

Figure 15-2

The Prisoners' Dilemma

Each of two prisoners, held in separate cells, is offered a deal by the police—a light sentence if she confesses and implicates her accomplice but her accomplice does not do the same, a heavy sentence if she does not confess but her accomplice does, and so on. It is in the joint interest of both prisoners not to confess; it is in each one's individual interest to confess.

The answer is clear: both will confess. Look at it first from Thelma's point of view: she is better off confessing, regardless of what Louise does. If Louise doesn't confess, Thelma's confession reduces her own sentence from 5 years to 2. If Louise *does* confess, Thelma's confession reduces her sentence from 20 to 15 years. Either way, it's clearly in Thelma's interest to confess. And because she faces the same incentives, it's clearly in Louise's interest to confess, too. To confess in this situation is a type of action that economists call a *dominant strategy*. An action is a **dominant strategy** when it is the player's best action regardless of what action the other player takes. It's important to note that not all games have a dominant strategy—it depends on the structure of payoffs in the game. But in the case of Thelma and Louise, it is clearly in the interest of the police to structure the payoffs so that confessing is a dominant strategy for each person. So as long as the two prisoners have no way to make an enforceable agreement that neither will confess (something they can't do if they can't communicate, and the police certainly won't allow them to do because the police want to compel each one to confess), Thelma and Louise will each act in a way that hurts the other.

So if each prisoner acts rationally in her own interest, both will confess. Yet if neither of them had confessed, both would have received a much lighter sentence! In a prisoners' dilemma, each player has a clear incentive to act in a way that hurts the other player—but when both make that choice, it leaves both of them worse off.

When Thelma and Louise both confess, they reach an *equilibrium* of the game. We have used the concept of equilibrium many times in this book; it is an outcome in which no individual or firm has any incentive to change his or her action. In game theory, this kind of equilibrium, in which each player takes the action that is best for her given the actions taken by other players, and vice versa, is known as a **Nash equilibrium,** after the mathematician and Nobel Laureate John Nash. (Nash's life was chronicled in the best-selling biography *A Beautiful Mind,* which was made into a movie.) Because the players in a Nash equilibrium do not take into account the effect of their actions on others, this is also known as a **noncooperative equilibrium.**

Now look back at Figure 15-1; ADM and Ajinomoto are in the same situation as Thelma and Louise. Each firm is better off producing the higher output, regardless of what the other firm does. Yet if both produce 40 million pounds, both are worse off than if they had followed their agreement and produced only 30 million pounds. In both cases, then, the pursuit of individual self-interest—the effort to maximize profits or to minimize jail time—has the perverse effect of hurting both players.

Prisoners' dilemmas appear in many situations. The For Inquiring Minds on page 374 describes an example from the days of the Cold War. Clearly, the players in any prisoners' dilemma would be better off if they had some way of enforcing cooperative behavior—if Thelma and Louise had both sworn to a code of silence, or if ADM and Ajinomoto had signed an enforceable agreement not to produce more than 30 million pounds of lysine.

But in the United States an agreement setting the output levels of two oligopolists isn't just unenforceable, it's illegal. So it seems that the undesirable noncooperative equilibrium is the only possible outcome. Or is it?

Overcoming the Prisoners' Dilemma: Repeated Interaction and Tacit Collusion

Thelma and Louise in their cells are playing what is known as a *one-shot* game—that is, they play the game with each other only once. They get to choose once and for all whether to confess or hang tough, and that's it. However, most of the games that

PITFALLS

PLAYING FAIR IN THE PRISONERS' DILEMMA

One common reaction to the prisoners' dilemma is to assert that it isn't really rational for either prisoner to confess. Thelma wouldn't confess because she'd be afraid Louise would beat her up, or Thelma would feel guilty because Louise wouldn't do that to her.

But this kind of answer is, well, cheating—it amounts to changing the payoffs in the payoff matrix. To understand the dilemma, you have to play fair and imagine prisoners who care *only* about the length of their sentences.

Luckily, when it comes to oligopoly, it's a lot easier to believe that the firms care only about their profits. There is no indication that anyone at ADM felt either fear of or affection for Ajinomoto, or vice versa; it was strictly about business.

An action is a **dominant strategy** when it is a player's best action regardless of the action taken by the other player.

A **Nash equilibrium,** also known as a **noncooperative equilibrium,** is the result when each player in a game chooses the action that maximizes his or her payoff given the actions of other players, ignoring the effects of his or her action on the payoffs received by those other players.

PRISONERS OF THE ARMS RACE

Between World War II and the late 1980s, the United States and the Soviet Union were locked in a seemingly endless struggle that never broke out into open war. During this Cold War, both countries spent huge sums on arms, sums that were a significant drain on the U.S. economy and eventually proved a crippling burden for the Soviet Union, whose underlying economic base was much weaker. Yet neither country was ever able to achieve a decisive military advantage.

As many people pointed out, both nations would have been better off if they had both spent less on arms. Yet the arms race continued for 40 years.

Why? As political scientists were quick to notice, one way to explain the arms race was to suppose that the two countries were locked in a classic prisoners' dilemma. Each government would have

Caught in the prisoners' dilemma: heavy military spending hastened the collapse of the Soviet Union.

liked to achieve decisive military superiority, and each feared military inferiority. But both would have preferred a stalemate with low military spending to one with high spending. However, each government rationally chose to engage in high spending. If its rival did not spend heavily, this would lead to military superiority; *not* spending heavily would lead to inferiority if the other government continued its arms buildup. So the countries were trapped.

The answer to this trap could have been an agreement not to spend as much; indeed, the two sides tried repeatedly to negotiate limits on some kinds of weapons. But these agreements weren't very effective. In the end the issue was resolved as heavy military spending hastened the collapse of the Soviet Union in 1991.

---

oligopolists play aren't one-shot; instead, they expect to play the game repeatedly with the same competitors. An oligopolist usually expects to be in business for many years, and it knows that its decision today about whether to cheat is likely to affect the way other firms treat it in the future. So a smart oligopolist doesn't just decide what to do based on the effect on profit in the short run. Instead, he or she engages in **strategic behavior,** taking account of the effects of the action he or she chooses today on the future actions of other players in the game. And under some conditions oligopolists that behave strategically can manage to behave as if they had a formal agreement to collude.

> A firm engages in **strategic behavior** when it attempts to influence the future behavior of other firms.

Suppose that ADM and Ajinomoto expect to be in the lysine business for many years and therefore expect to play the game of cheat versus collude shown in Figure 15-1 many times. Would they really betray each other time and again?

Probably not. Suppose that ADM considers two strategies. In one strategy it always cheats, producing 40 million pounds of lysine each year, regardless of what Ajinomoto does. In the other strategy, it starts off with good behavior, producing only 30 million pounds in the first year, and watches to see what its rival does. If Ajinomoto also keeps its production down, ADM will stay cooperative, producing 30 million pounds again for the next year. But if Ajinomoto produces 40 million pounds, ADM will take the gloves off and also produce 40 million pounds next year. This latter strategy—start off behaving cooperatively, but thereafter do whatever the other player did in the previous period—is generally known as **tit for tat**.

> A strategy of **tit for tat** involves playing cooperatively at first, then doing whatever the other player did in the previous period.

"Tit for tat" is a form of strategic behavior, which we have just defined as behavior intended to influence the future actions of other players. "Tit for tat" offers a reward to the other player for cooperative behavior—if you behave cooperatively, so will I. It also provides a punishment for cheating—if you cheat, don't expect me to be nice in the future.

The payoff to ADM of each of these strategies would depend on which strategy Ajinomoto chooses. Consider the four possibilities, shown in Figure 15-3:

Figure 15-3

How Repeated Interaction Can Support Collusion

A strategy of "tit for tat" involves playing cooperatively at first, then following the other player's move. This rewards good behavior and punishes bad behavior. If the other player cheats, playing "tit for tat" will lead to only a short-term loss in comparison to playing "always cheat." But if the other player plays "tit for tat," also playing "tit for tat" leads to a long-term gain. So a firm that expects other firms to play "tit for tat" may well choose to do the same, leading to successful tacit collusion.

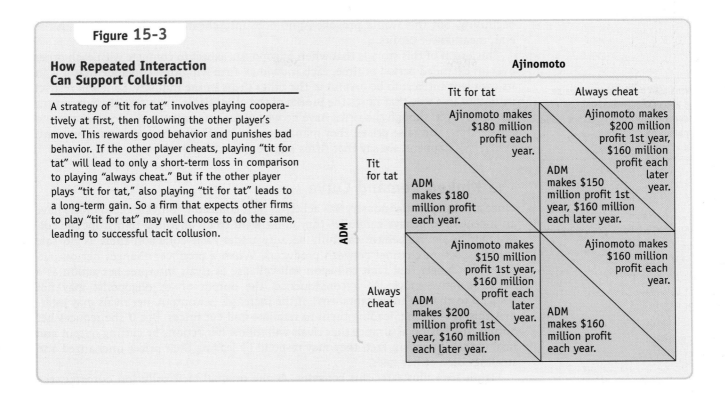

1. If ADM plays "tit for tat" and so does Ajinomoto, both firms will make a profit of $180 million each year.

2. If ADM plays "always cheat" but Ajinomoto plays "tit for tat," ADM makes a profit of $200 million the first year but only $160 million per year thereafter.

3. If ADM plays "tit for tat" but Ajinomoto plays "always cheat," ADM makes a profit of only $150 million in the first year but $160 million per year thereafter.

4. If ADM plays "always cheat" and Ajinomoto does the same, both firms will make a profit of $160 million each year.

Which strategy is better? In the first year, ADM does better playing "always cheat," whatever its rival's strategy: it assures itself that it will get either $200 million or $160 million (which of the two payoffs it actually receives depends upon whether Ajinomoto plays "always cheat" or "tit for tat"). This is better than what it would get in the first year if it played "tit for tat": either $180 million or $150 million. But by the second year, a strategy of "always cheat" gains ADM only $160 million per year for the second and all subsequent years, regardless of Ajinomoto's actions. This amount is inferior to the amount ADM would gain by playing "tit for tat": for the second and all subsequent years, it would never get any less than $160 million and would get as much as $180 million if Ajinomoto played "tit for tat" as well. So which strategy is more profitable depends on two things: how many years ADM expects to play the game and what strategy its rival follows.

If ADM expects the lysine business to end in the near future, it is in effect playing a one-shot game. So it might as well grab what it can. Even if ADM expects to remain in the lysine business for many years (therefore to find itself repeatedly playing this game with Ajinomoto) and expects, for some reason, Ajinomoto always to cheat, it should also always cheat. That is, ADM should follow the old rule "Do unto others before they do unto you."

But if ADM expects to be in the business for a long time and thinks Ajinomoto is likely to play "tit for tat," it will make more profits over the long run by playing "tit for tat," too. It could have made some extra short-term profits by cheating at the beginning, but this would provoke Ajinomoto into cheating too, and would, in the end, mean lower profits.

The lesson of this story is that when oligopolists expect to compete with each other over an extended period of time, each individual firm will often conclude that it is in its own best interest to be helpful to the other firms in the industry. So it will restrict its output in a way that raises the profits of the other firms, expecting them to return the favor. Even though the firms have no way of making an enforceable agreement to limit output and raise prices, they manage to act "as if" they had such an agreement. When this happens, we say that firms engage in **tacit collusion.**

When firms limit production and raise prices in a way that raises each others' profits, even though they have not made any formal agreement, they are engaged in **tacit collusion.**

The Kinked Demand Curve

Once an oligopolistic industry has achieved tacit collusion, individual producers have an incentive to behave carefully—they don't want to do anything to disrupt the collusion. They must behave carefully because under tacit collusion there is no safe communication channel between producers. When a producer changes her output, there is a danger that tacit collusion will collapse as rivals interpret her action as a noncooperative move. As a consequence, the output of an oligopolist may not respond to changes in marginal cost. If she increases her output, her rivals may interpret this as cheating, leading them to retaliate and cut prices. But if she reduces her output, she has no assurance that rivals will follow her actions by cutting output and raising their prices. In fact, they may respond by leaving their prices unchanged and stealing some of her sales.

Figure 15-4 illustrates this behavior. At the original tacit collusion outcome, the oligopolist produces the quantity Q^* and receives the price P^*, located on her demand curve, D. This demand curve shows how the price she receives for her good varies as she changes her output. As you can see, this demand curve has a special shape—it is *kinked* at the price and quantity combination associated with the tacit collusion outcome, P^* and Q^*.

Figure 15-4

The Kinked Demand Curve

This oligopolist believes that her demand curve is kinked at the tacit collusion price and quantity levels, P^* and Q^*. That is, she believes that if she increases her output and lowers her price her rivals will retaliate, increasing their output and lowering their prices as well, leading to only a small gain in sales. So her demand curve is very steep to the right of Q^*. But the oligopolist believes that if she lowers her output and raises her price her rivals will refuse to reciprocate and will steal a substantial number of her customers, leading to a large fall in sales. So her demand curve is very flat to the left of Q^*. The kink in the demand curve leads to the break XY in the marginal revenue curve. As shown by the marginal cost curves, MC_1 and MC_2, any marginal cost curve that lies within the break leads the oligopolist to produce the same output level, Q^*. So starting at the tacit collusion outcome, changes in marginal cost within a certain range will leave the firm's output unchanged. But large changes in marginal cost—changes that cause the marginal cost curve to cut the marginal revenue curve in the segment WX or the segment YZ—will lead to changes in output. **>web...**

On one side, the demand curve slopes steeply downward at output levels greater than Q^*. The reason is that the oligopolist believes that if she produces more than Q^*, she will gain very few sales because her rivals will retaliate by also producing more and cutting their prices.

On the other side, the demand curve is very flat. If the oligopolist reduces her output below Q^*, she does not expect rivals to reduce their output as well. Consequently, she will lose a relatively large number of sales if she lowers her output and raises her price as her rivals capture a substantial share of her customers. You might ask why the industry can't reestablish tacit collusion at a higher price and lower output after our oligopolist cuts her output and raises her price. It is possible, but by no means assured, that the industry can reestablish tacit collusion. So it is reasonable for an oligopolist to fear that tacit collusion will not be reestablished and to behave as if her demand curve is kinked as in Figure 15-4.

Now that we have explained the source of the oligopolist's **kinked demand curve,** let's examine how this affects her response to a change in marginal cost. The kink in the demand curve D generates a break in the oligopolist's marginal revenue curve, MR, shown by the gap between the points X and Y. Two marginal cost curves pass through that break in the marginal revenue curve: MC_1 corresponds to a situation of higher marginal cost, and MC_2 corresponds to a situation of lower marginal cost.

Recall that according to the optimal output rule, a firm will maximize profits by producing the output level at which marginal revenue is equal to marginal cost. But given the break between X and Y in the oligopolist's marginal revenue curve, any marginal cost curves that lie within that break—like MC_1 and MC_2—will generate the same output level, Q^*. To put it in a slightly different way, starting from the tacit collusive output level Q^*, the oligopolist's output level is unresponsive to changes in marginal cost within a certain range. If marginal cost falls substantially, the oligopolist is more likely to risk a breakdown in collusion and increase her output; in this case, the marginal cost curve cuts the marginal revenue curve in the segment YZ. And if marginal cost rises substantially, shifting the marginal cost curve up so that it cuts the marginal revenue curve in the segment WX, then the oligopolist is likely to reduce output and raise her price despite the risk of losing significant sales to rivals. But if marginal cost changes within a limited range—the range defined by XY—the producer will leave her output level unchanged rather than risk a breakdown in tacit collusion.

The behavior described by the kinked demand curve appears justified when a producer believes that she alone is facing a change in marginal cost—that is, when the change is unique to her. But when the change in marginal cost is clearly shared throughout the industry, this behavior is much less plausible. In that case, each producer knows that a change in a rival's output level and price is just a response to a change in the general level of marginal cost, not a hostile act of noncooperation. Consequently, all the producers in the industry are likely to respond to a change in marginal cost by adjusting their output and prices and thereby maintain collusion.

An oligopolist who believes she will lose a substantial number of sales if she reduces output and increases her price but will gain only a few additional sales if she increases output and lowers her price, away from the tacit collusion outcome, faces a **kinked demand curve.**

economics in action

The Rise and Fall and Rise of OPEC

Call it the cartel that does not need to meet in secret. The Organization of Petroleum Exporting Countries, usually referred to as OPEC, includes 11 national governments (Algeria, Indonesia, Iran, Iraq, Kuwait, Libya, Nigeria, Qatar, Saudi Arabia, United Arab Emirates, and Venezuela). Two other oil-exporting countries, Norway and Mexico, are not formally part of the cartel but act as if they were. (Russia, also an important oil exporter, has not yet become part of the club.) Unlike corporations, which are often legally prohibited by governments from reaching agreements about production and prices, national governments can talk about whatever they feel like. OPEC members routinely meet to try to set targets for production.

Figure 15-5 The Ups and Downs of the Oil Cartel

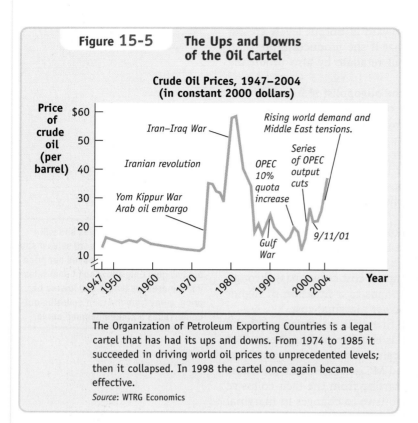

**Crude Oil Prices, 1947–2004
(in constant 2000 dollars)**

- Iran–Iraq War
- Rising world demand and Middle East tensions.
- Iranian revolution
- Series of OPEC output cuts
- OPEC 10% quota increase
- Yom Kippur War Arab oil embargo
- 9/11/01
- Gulf War

The Organization of Petroleum Exporting Countries is a legal cartel that has had its ups and downs. From 1974 to 1985 it succeeded in driving world oil prices to unprecedented levels; then it collapsed. In 1998 the cartel once again became effective.

Source: WTRG Economics

These nations are not particularly friendly with one another. Indeed, OPEC members Iraq and Iran fought a spectacularly bloody war with each other in the 1980s. And, in 1990, Iraq invaded another member, Kuwait. (A mainly American force based in yet another OPEC member, Saudi Arabia, drove the Iraqis out of Kuwait.)

Yet the members of OPEC, like one another or not, are effectively players in a game with repeated interactions. In any given year it is in their combined interest to keep output low and prices high. But it is also in the interest of any one producer to cheat and produce more than the agreed-upon quota—unless that producer believes that this action will bring future retaliation.

So how successful is the cartel? Well, it's had its ups and downs.

Figure 15-5 shows the price of oil in constant dollars (that is, the value of a barrel of oil in terms of other goods) since 1947. OPEC first demonstrated its muscle in 1974: in the aftermath of a war in the Middle East, several OPEC producers limited their output—and they liked the results so much that they decided to continue the practice. Following a second wave of turmoil in the aftermath of Iran's 1979 revolution, prices shot still higher.

By the mid-1980s, however, there was a growing glut of oil on world markets, and cheating by cash-short OPEC members became widespread. The result, in 1985, was that producers who had tried to play by the rules—especially Saudi Arabia, the largest producer—got fed up, and collusion collapsed.

The cartel began to act effectively again at the end of the 1990s, thanks largely to the efforts of Mexico's oil minister to orchestrate output reductions. To assure greater adherence to production targets, OPEC meets very frequently—seven times in 2003 alone—seeking to keep the price of a barrel of oil in the range of $22 to $28. And this discipline appears to be paying off; a decrease of 900,000 barrels per day in late 2003 coupled with rising demand from China and production difficulties in Iraq resulted in oil prices above $40 a barrel in 2004. ■

< < < < < < < < < < < < < < < < < <

>>QUICK REVIEW

- ➤ Economists use *game theory* to study firms' behavior when there is *interdependence* between their *payoffs*. The game can be represented with a *payoff matrix*. Depending on the payoffs, a player may or may not have a *dominant strategy*.
- ➤ When each firm has an incentive to cheat, but both are worse off if both cheat, the situation is known as a *prisoners' dilemma*.
- ➤ Players who don't take their interdependence into account arrive at a *Nash*, or *noncooperative, equilibrium*. But if a game is played repeatedly, players may engage in *strategic behavior*, sacrificing short-run profit to influence future behavior.
- ➤ In repeated prisoners' dilemma games, *tit for tat* is often a good strategy, leading to successful *tacit collusion*.
- ➤ The *kinked demand curve* illustrates how tacit collusion can make an oligopolist unresponsive to changes in marginal cost within a certain range when those changes are unique to her.

>>CHECK YOUR UNDERSTANDING 15-3

1. Find the Nash (noncooperative) equilibrium actions for the accompanying payoff matrix. Which actions maximize the total payoff of Nikita and Margaret? Why is it unlikely that they will choose those actions without some communication?

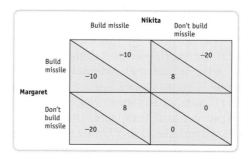

2. Which factors make it more likely that oligopolists will play noncooperatively? Which make it more likely that they will engage in tacit collusion? Explain.
   a. Each oligopolist expects several new firms to enter the market in the future.
   b. It is very difficult for a firm to detect whether another firm has raised output.
   c. The firms have coexisted while maintaining high prices for a long time.

Oligopoly in Practice

In Economics in Action on page 370 we described the cartel known as "Vitamins Inc.," which effectively promoted collusion for many years. The conspiratorial dealings of the vitamin makers were not, fortunately, the norm. But how do oligopolies usually work in practice? The answer depends both on the legal framework that limits what firms can do and on the underlying ability of firms in a given industry to cooperate without formal agreements.

The Legal Framework

To understand oligopoly pricing in practice, we must be familiar with the legal constraints under which oligopolistic firms operate. In the United States, oligopoly first became an issue during the second half of the nineteenth century, when the growth of railroads—themselves an oligopolistic industry—created a national market for many goods. Large firms producing oil, steel, and many other products soon emerged. The industrialists quickly realized that profits would be higher if they could limit price competition. So many industries formed cartels—that is, they signed formal agreements to limit production and raise prices. Until 1890, when the first federal legislation against such cartels was passed, this was perfectly legal.

However, although these cartels were legal, they weren't legally *enforceable*—members of a cartel couldn't ask the courts to force a firm that was violating its agreement to reduce its production. And firms often did violate their agreements, for the reason already suggested by our duopoly example: there is always a temptation for each firm in a cartel to produce more than it is supposed to.

In 1881 clever lawyers at John D. Rockefeller's Standard Oil Company came up with a solution—the so-called *trust*. In a trust, shareholders of all the major companies in an industry placed their shares in the hands of a board of trustees who controlled the companies. This, in effect, merged the companies into a single firm that could then engage in monopoly pricing. In this way, the Standard Oil Trust established what was essentially a monopoly of the oil industry, and it was soon followed by trusts in sugar, whiskey, lead, cottonseed oil, and linseed oil.

Eventually there was a public backlash, driven partly by concern about the economic effects of the trust movement, partly by fear that the owners of the trusts were simply becoming too powerful. The result was the Sherman Antitrust Act of 1890, which was intended both to prevent the creation of more monopolies and to break up existing ones. At first this law went largely unenforced. But over the decades that followed, the federal government became increasingly committed to making it difficult for oligopolistic industries either to become monopolies or to behave like them. Such efforts are known to this day as **antitrust policy.**

One of the most striking early actions of antitrust policy was the breakup of Standard Oil in 1911. (Its components formed the nuclei of many of today's large oil companies—Standard Oil of New Jersey became Exxon, Standard Oil of New York became Mobil, and so on.) In the 1980s a long-running case led to the breakup of Bell Telephone, which once had a monopoly of both local and long-distance phone service in the United States.

The details of antitrust policy can be exceedingly complex, especially because corporations can and do fight costly legal battles against decisions they dislike. The core of what antitrust means in practice can, however, be understood by turning, once again, to our lysine example. In that example, there are two obvious ways for the companies to avoid getting trapped in the prisoners' dilemma. One is the solution they actually tried: for the companies to meet with each other to agree to produce less and get higher prices. The other is to eliminate conflict by combining the two companies into one—let one company buy the other, or let them exchange their shares and merge.

Antitrust policy refers to the efforts of the government to prevent oligopolistic industries from becoming or behaving like monopolies.

Antitrust law makes both of these solutions illegal. If the executives meet to collude on prices, they can be sent to jail and their companies fined. If the companies try to merge, the Justice Department or the Federal Trade Commission will tell them that they cannot.

So what's an oligopolist to do?

Tacit Collusion and Price Wars

If a real industry were as simple as our lysine example, it probably wouldn't be necessary for the company presidents to meet or do anything that could land them in jail. Both firms would realize that it was in their mutual interest to restrict output to 30 million pounds each and that any short-term gains to either firm from producing more would be much less than the later losses as the other firm retaliated. So even without any explicit agreement, the firms would probably achieve the tacit collusion needed to maximize their combined profits.

Real industries are nowhere near that simple; nonetheless, in most oligopolistic industries, most of the time, the sellers do appear to succeed in keeping prices above their noncooperative level. Tacit collusion, in other words, is the normal state of oligopoly.

Although tacit collusion is common, it rarely allows an industry to push prices all the way up to their monopoly level; collusion is usually far from perfect. A variety of factors make it hard for an industry to coordinate on high prices.

Large Numbers   Suppose that there were three instead of two firms in the lysine industry and that each was currently producing only 20 million pounds. You can confirm for yourself that in that case any one firm that decided to produce an extra 10 million pounds would gain more in short-term profits—and lose less once another firm responded in kind—than in our original example. The general point is that the more firms there are in an oligopoly, the less is the incentive of any one firm to behave cooperatively, taking into account the impact of its actions on the profits of the other firms. Large numbers of firms in an industry typically are an indication that there are low barriers to entry.

Complex Products and Pricing Schemes   In our lysine example the two firms produce only one product. In reality, however, oligopolists often sell thousands or even tens of thousands of different products. Under these circumstances, keeping track of what other firms are producing and what prices they are charging is difficult. This makes it hard to determine whether a firm is cheating on the tacit agreement.

Differences in Interests   In the lysine example, a tacit agreement for the firms to split the market equally is a natural outcome, probably acceptable to both firms. In real industries, however, firms often differ both in their perceptions about what is fair and in their real interests.

For example, suppose that Ajinomoto was a long-established lysine producer and ADM a more recent entrant to the industry. Ajinomoto might feel that it deserved to continue producing more than ADM, but ADM might feel that it was entitled to 50 percent of the business. (A disagreement along these lines was one of the contentious issues in those meetings the FBI was filming.)

Alternatively, suppose that ADM's marginal costs were lower than Ajinomoto's. Even if they could agree on market shares, they would then disagree about the profit-maximizing level of output.

Bargaining Power of Buyers   Often oligopolists sell not to individual consumers but to large buyers—other industrial enterprises, nationwide chains of stores, and so on. These large buyers are in a position to bargain for lower prices from the oligopolists: they can ask for a discount from an oligopolist, and warn that they will go to a competitor if they don't get it. An important reason why large retailers like Wal-Mart are able to offer lower prices to customers than small retailers is precisely their ability to use their size to extract lower prices from their suppliers.

These difficulties in enforcing tacit collusion have sometimes led companies to defy the law and create illegal cartels. We've already examined the cases of the lysine industry and the bulk vitamin industry. An older, classic example was the U.S. electrical equipment conspiracy of the 1950s, which led to the indictment of and jail sentences for some executives. The industry was one in which tacit collusion was especially difficult because of all the reasons just mentioned. There were many firms—40 companies were indicted. They produced a very complex array of products, often more or less custom-built for particular clients. They differed greatly in size, from giants like General Electric to family firms with only a few dozen employees. And the customers in many cases were large buyers like electrical utilities, which would normally try to force suppliers to compete for their business. Tacit collusion just didn't seem practical—so executives met secretly and illegally to decide who would bid what price for which contract.

The following For Inquiring Minds describes yet another price-fixing conspiracy: the one between the very posh auction houses Sotheby's and Christie's.

FOR INQUIRING MINDS
THE ART OF CONSPIRACY

If you want to sell a valuable work of art, there are really only two places to go: Christie's, the London-based auction house, or Sotheby's, its New York counterpart and competitor. Both are classy operations—literally: many of the employees of Christie's come from Britain's aristocracy, and many of Sotheby's come from blue-blooded American families that might as well have titles. They're not the sort of people you would expect to be seeking plea bargains from prosecutors.

But on October 6, 2000, Diana D. Brooks, the very upper-class former president of Sotheby's, pleaded guilty to a conspiracy. With her counterpart at Christie's, she had engaged in the illegal practice of price-fixing—agreeing on the fees they would charge people who sold artwork through either house. As part of her guilty plea, and in an effort to avoid going to jail, she agreed to help in the investigation of her boss, the former chairman of Sotheby's.

Why would such upper-crust types engage in illegal practices? For the same reasons that respectable electrical equipment industry executives did. By definition, no two works of art are alike; it wasn't easy for the two houses to collude tacitly, because it was too hard to determine what commissions they were charging on any given transaction. To increase profits, then, the companies felt that they needed to reach a detailed agreement. They did, and they got caught.

Because tacit collusion is often hard to achieve, most oligopolies charge prices that are well below what the same industry would charge if it were controlled by a single firm—or what they would charge if they were able to collude explicitly. In addition, sometimes collusion breaks down and there is a **price war**. A price war sometimes involves simply a collapse of prices to their noncooperative level. Sometimes they even go *below* that level, as sellers try to put each other out of business or at least punish what they regard as cheating.

A **price war** occurs when tacit collusion breaks down and prices collapse.

Product Differentiation and Price Leadership

Lysine is lysine: there was no question in anyone's mind that ADM and Ajinomoto were producing the same good and that consumers would make their decision about which company's lysine to buy based on the price.

In many oligopolies, however, firms produce products that consumers regard as similar but not identical. A $10 difference in the price won't make many customers switch from a Ford to a Chrysler, or vice versa. Sometimes the differences between products are real, like differences between Froot Loops and Wheaties; sometimes, like differences between brands of vodka (which is *supposed* to be tasteless), they exist mainly in the minds of consumers. Either way, the effect is to reduce the intensity of the competition among the firms: consumers will not all rush to buy whichever product is cheapest.

Firms engage in **product differentiation** when they try to convince buyers that their product is different from the products of other firms in the industry.

As you might imagine, oligopolists welcome the extra market power that comes when consumers think that their product is different from that of competitors. So in many oligopolistic industries, firms make considerable efforts to create the perception that their product is different—that is, they engage in **product differentiation.**

A firm that tries to differentiate its product may do so by altering what it actually produces, adding "extras," or choosing a different design. It may also use advertising and marketing campaigns to create a differentiation in the minds of consumers, even though its product is more or less identical to the products of rivals.

A classic case of how products may be perceived as different even when they are really pretty much the same is over-the-counter medication. For many years there were only three widely sold pain relievers—aspirin, ibuprofen, and acetaminophen. Yet these generic pain relievers were marketed under a number of brand names, each brand using a marketing campaign implying some special superiority (one classic slogan was "contains the pain reliever doctors recommend most"—that is, aspirin).

Whatever the nature of product differentiation, oligopolists producing differentiated products often reach a tacit understanding not to compete on price. For example, during the years when the great majority of cars sold in the United States were produced by the Big Three auto companies, there was a sort of unwritten rule that none of the three companies would try to gain market share by making its cars noticeably cheaper than those of the other two.

But then who would decide on the overall price of cars? The answer was normally that General Motors, the biggest of the three, would announce its prices for the year first; then the other companies would match it. This pattern of behavior, in which some company tacitly sets prices for the industry as a whole, is known as **price leadership.**

In **price leadership**, one firm sets its price first, and other firms then follow.

Firms that have a tacit understanding not to compete on price often engage in intense **nonprice competition,** using advertising and other means to try to increase their sales.

Interestingly, firms that have a tacit agreement not to compete on price often engage in vigorous **nonprice competition**—adding new features to their products, spending large sums on ads that proclaim the inferiority of their rivals' offerings, and so on.

Perhaps the best way to understand the mix of cooperation and competition in such industries is with a political analogy. During the long Cold War between the United States and the Soviet Union, the two countries engaged in intense rivalry for global influence. They not only provided financial and military aid to their allies; they sometimes supported forces trying to overthrow governments allied with their rival (as the Soviet Union did in Vietnam in the 1960s and early 1970s, and as the United States did in Afghanistan from 1979 until the collapse of the Soviet Union in 1991). They even sent their own soldiers to support allied governments against rebels (as the United States did in Vietnam and the Soviet Union did in Afghanistan). But they did *not* get into direct military confrontations with each other; open warfare between the two superpowers was regarded by both as too dangerous—and tacitly avoided.

Price wars aren't as serious as shooting wars, but the principle is the same.

economics in action

Air Wars

The first time Robert Crandall, then CEO of American Airlines, tried to collude on prices, he was blunt: in 1983 he called the head of rival Braniff (now defunct) and proposed in so many words (many of them unprintable) that the two airlines both raise fares 20 percent. Alas for Crandall, the conversation was being taped.

Eight years later, Crandall tried a more legal approach: declaring himself a "statesman," he raised American's fares in the hopes that rivals would follow suit. But they didn't, and the airline lost many passengers.

On both occasions the airline industry was in the midst of a price war. Indeed, price wars—in which fares fall 50 percent or more for a time, then soar again—are something of an industry specialty.

Why are airlines so prone to price wars? There are at least three reasons, all bearing on the problems of tacit collusion we have just discussed. First, although each airline tries to differentiate its product, creating a perception among consumers that it offers better service, most fliers choose airlines on the basis of schedule and price—period. So competition is intense. Second, airline pricing is complex: as discussed in Chapter 14, airlines engage in complex price-discrimination schemes that make it hard to figure out when tacit collusion is being broken. Third, airlines often differ in their interests: many of the most severe price wars have been set off by attempts of a new competitor to break into established markets. And this indicates yet another source of airline price wars: low barriers to entry. ∎

> > > > > > > > > > > > > > > > > > >

1. Which of the following factors are likely to support the conclusion that there is tacit collusion in this industry? Which are not? Explain.
   a. For many years the price in the industry has changed infrequently, and all the firms in the industry charge the same price. The largest firm publishes a catalog containing a "suggested" retail price. Changes in price coincide with changes in the catalog.
   b. There has been considerable variation in the market shares of the firms in the industry over time.
   c. Firms in the industry build into their products unnecessary features that make it hard for consumers to switch from one company's products to another's.
   d. Firms meet yearly to discuss their annual sales forecasts.
   e. Firms tend to adjust their prices upward at the same times.

How Important Is Oligopoly?

We have seen that, across industries, oligopoly is far more common than either perfect competition or monopoly. When we try to analyze oligopoly, the economist's usual way of thinking—asking how self-interested individuals would behave, then analyzing their interaction—does not work as well as we might hope, because we do not know whether rival firms will engage in noncooperative behavior or manage to engage in some kind of collusion. Given the prevalence of oligopoly, then, is the analysis we developed in earlier chapters, which was based on perfect competition, still useful?

The conclusion of the great majority of economists is yes. For one thing, important parts of the economy are fairly well described by perfect competition. And even though many industries are oligopolistic, in many cases the limits to collusion keep prices relatively close to marginal costs—in other words, the industry behaves "almost" as if it were perfectly competitive.

It is also true that predictions from supply and demand analysis are often valid for oligopolies. For example, in Chapter 4 we saw that price controls will produce shortages. Strictly speaking, this conclusion is certain only for perfectly competitive industries. But in the 1970s, when the U.S. government imposed price controls on the definitely oligopolistic oil industry, the result was indeed to produce shortages and lines at the gas pumps.

So how important is it to take account of oligopoly? Most economists adopt a pragmatic approach. As we have seen in this chapter, the analysis of oligopoly is far more difficult and messy than that of perfect competition; so in situations where they do not expect the complications associated with oligopoly to be crucial, economists prefer to adopt the working assumption of perfectly competitive markets. They always keep in mind the possibility that oligopoly might be important; they recognize that there are important issues, from antitrust policies to price wars, where trying to understand oligopolistic behavior is crucial.

We will follow the same approach in the chapters that follow.

• A LOOK AHEAD •

We're not yet done with our investigation of market structures other than perfect competition. There are quite a few industries that don't seem to fit either the definition of oligopoly or the definition of perfect competition. Consider, for example, the restaurant business. There are many restaurants, so it's not an oligopoly. But restaurants aren't price-takers, like wheat farmers, so it's not perfectly competitive. What is it?

The answer lies in the next chapter, which turns to the concept of *monopolistic competition.*

SUMMARY

1. Many industries are **oligopolies:** there are only a few sellers. In particular, a **duopoly** has only two sellers. Oligopolies exist for more or less the same reasons that monopolies exist, but in weaker form. They are characterized by **imperfect competition:** firms compete but possess market power.

2. Predicting the behavior of **oligopolists** poses something of a puzzle. The firms in an oligopoly could maximize their combined profits by acting as a **cartel,** setting output levels for each firm as if they were a single monopolist; to the extent that firms manage to do this, they engage in **collusion.** But each individual firm has an incentive to produce more than it would in such an arrangement—to engage in **noncooperative behavior.** Informal collusion is likely to be easier to achieve in industries in which firms face capacity constraints.

3. The situation of **interdependence,** in which each firm's profit depends noticeably on what other firms do, is the subject of **game theory.** In the case of a game with two players, the **payoff** of each player depends both on its own actions and on the actions of the other; this interdependence can be represented as a **payoff matrix.** Depending upon the structure of payoffs in the payoff matrix, a player may have a **dominant strategy**—an action that is always the best regardless of the other player's actions.

4. **Duopolists** face a particular type of game known as a **prisoners' dilemma;** if each acts independently in its own interest, the resulting **Nash equilibrium** or **noncooperative equilibrium** will be bad for both. However, firms that expect to play a game repeatedly tend to engage in **strategic behavior,** trying to influence each other's future actions. A particular strategy that seems to work well in such situations is **tit for tat,** which often leads to **tacit collusion.**

5. The **kinked demand curve** illustrates how an oligopolist who faces unique changes in her marginal cost within a certain range may choose not to adjust her output and price in order to avoid a breakdown in tacit collusion.

6. In order to limit the ability of oligopolists to collude and act like monopolists, most governments pursue an **antitrust policy** designed to make collusion more difficult. In practice, however, tacit collusion is widespread.

7. A variety of factors make tacit collusion difficult: large numbers of firms, complex products and pricing, differences in interests, and bargaining power of buyers. When tacit collusion breaks down, there is a **price war.** Oligopolists try to avoid price wars in various ways, such as through **product differentiation** and through **price leadership,** in which one firm sets prices for the industry. Another is through **nonprice competition,** like advertising.

KEY TERMS

Oligopoly, p. 364
Oligopolist, p. 364
Imperfect competition, p. 364
Duopoly, p. 366
Duopolist, p. 366
Collusion, p. 367
Cartel, p. 367
Noncooperative behavior, p. 368
Interdependence, p. 371

Game theory, p. 371
Payoff, p. 371
Payoff matrix, p. 371
Prisoners' dilemma, p. 372
Dominant strategy, p. 373
Nash equilibrium, p. 373
Noncooperative equilibrium, p. 373
Strategic behavior, p. 374

Tit for tat, p. 374
Tacit collusion, p. 376
Kinked demand curve, p. 377
Antitrust policy, p. 379
Price war, p. 381
Product differentiation, p. 382
Price leadership, p. 382
Nonprice competition, p. 382

PROBLEMS

1. The accompanying table shows the demand schedule for vitamin D. Suppose that the marginal cost of producing vitamin D is zero.

Price of vitamin D (per ton)	Quantity of vitamin D demanded (tons)
$8	0
7	10
6	20
5	30
4	40
3	50
2	60
1	70

a. Assume that BASF is the only producer of vitamin D and acts as a monopolist. It currently produces 40 tons of vitamin D at $4 per ton. If BASF were to produce 10 tons more, what would be the price effect for BASF? What would be the quantity effect? Would BASF therefore have an incentive to produce those 10 additional tons?

b. Now assume that Roche enters the market by also producing vitamin D and the market is now a duopoly. BASF and Roche agree to produce 40 tons of vitamin D in total, 20 tons each. BASF cannot be punished for deviating from the agreement with Roche. If BASF, on its own, were to deviate from that agreement and produce 10 tons more, what would be the price effect for BASF? What would be the quantity effect for BASF? Would BASF have an incentive to produce those 10 additional tons?

2. The market for olive oil in New York City is controlled by two families, the Sopranos and the Contraltos. Both families will ruthlessly eliminate any other family that attempts to enter the New York City olive oil market. The marginal cost of producing olive oil is constant and equal to $40 per gallon. There is no fixed cost. The accompanying table gives the market demand schedule for olive oil.

Price of olive oil (per gallon)	Quantity of olive oil demanded (gallons)
$100	1,000
90	1,500
80	2,000
70	2,500
60	3,000
50	3,500
40	4,000
30	4,500
20	5,000
10	5,500

a. Suppose the Sopranos and the Contraltos form a cartel. For each of the quantities given in the table, calculate the total revenue for their cartel and the marginal revenue for each additional gallon. How many gallons of olive oil would the cartel sell in total and at what price? The two families share the market equally (each produces half of the total output of the cartel). How much profit does each family make?

b. Uncle Junior, the head of the Soprano family, breaks the agreement and sells 500 more gallons of olive oil than under the cartel agreement. Assuming the Contraltos maintain the agreement, how does this affect the price for olive oil and the profits earned by each family?

c. Anthony Contralto, the head of the Contralto family, decides to punish Uncle Junior by increasing his sales by 500 gallons as well. How much profit does each family earn now?

3. In France, the market for bottled water is controlled by two large firms, Perrier and Evian. Each firm has a fixed cost of €1 and a constant marginal cost of €2 per liter of bottled water (€ = 1 euro). The accompanying table gives the market demand schedule for bottled water in France.

Price of bottled water (per liter)	Quantity of bottled water demanded (liters)
€10	0
9	1
8	2
7	3
6	4
5	5
4	6
3	7
2	8
1	9

a. Suppose the two firms form a cartel and act as a monopolist. Calculate marginal revenue for the cartel. What will the monopoly price and output be? Assuming the firms divided the output evenly, how much will each produce and what will each firm's profits be?

b. Now suppose Perrier decides to increase production by 1 liter. Evian doesn't change its production. What will the new market price and output be? What is Perrier's profit? What is Evian's profit?

c. What if Perrier increases production by 3 liters? Evian doesn't change its production. What would its output and profits be relative to those in part b?

d. What do your results tell you about the likelihood of cheating on such agreements?

4. To preserve the North Atlantic fish stocks, it is decided that only two fishing fleets, one from the United States and the other from the European Union (EU) can fish in those waters. The accompanying table shows the market demand schedule per week for fish from these waters. The only costs are fixed costs, so fishing fleets maximize profit by maximizing revenue.

Price of fish (per pound)	Quantity of fish demanded (pounds)
$17	1,800
16	2,000
15	2,100
14	2,200
12	2,300

a. If both fishing fleets collude, what is the revenue-maximizing output for the North Atlantic fishery? What price will a pound of fish sell for?

b. If both fishing fleets collude and share the output equally, what is the revenue to the EU fleet? To the U.S. fleet?

c. Suppose the EU fleet cheats by expanding its own catch by 100 pounds per week. The U.S. fleet doesn't change its catch. What is the revenue to the U.S. fleet? To the EU fleet?

d. In retaliation for the cheating by the EU fleet, the U.S. fleet also expands its catch by 100 pounds per week. What is the revenue to the U.S. fleet? to the EU fleet?

5. Suppose that the fisheries agreement in Problem 4 breaks down, so that the fleets behave noncooperatively. Assume that the U.S. and the EU each can send out either one or two fleets. Also assume that the more fleets in the area, the more fish they catch in total but the lower the catch of each fleet. The accompanying matrix shows the profit (in dollars) per week earned by the two sides.

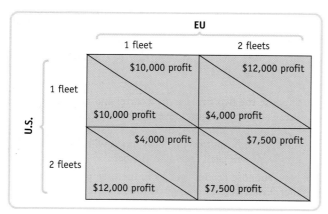

a. What is the noncooperative Nash equilibrium? Will each side choose to send out one or two fleets?

b. Suppose that the fish stocks are being depleted. Each region considers the future and comes to a "tit-for-tat" agreement whereby each side will send only one fleet out as long as the other does the same. If either of them breaks the agreement and sends out a second fleet, the other will also send out two and will continue to do so until its competitor sends out only one fleet. If both play this "tit-for-tat" strategy, how much profit will each make every week?

6. Untied and Air 'R' Us are the only two airlines operating flights between Collegeville and Bigtown. That is, they operate in a duopoly. Each airline can charge either a high price or a low price for a ticket. The accompanying matrix shows their payoffs, in profits per seat (in dollars), for any choice that the two airlines can make.

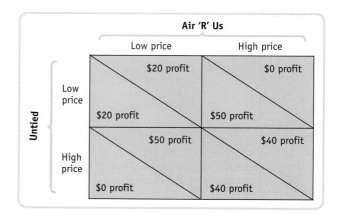

a. Suppose the two airlines play a one-shot game—that is, they interact only once and never again. What will be the Nash (noncooperative) equilibrium in this one-shot game?

b. Now suppose the two airlines play this game twice. And suppose each airline can play one of two strategies: it can play either "always charge the low price" or "tit for tat"—that is, it starts off charging the high price in the first period, and then in the second period it does whatever the other airline did in the previous period. Write down the payoffs to Untied from the following four possibilities:

   i. Untied plays "always charge the low price" when Air 'R' Us also plays "always charge the low price."

   ii. Untied plays "always charge the low price" when Air 'R' Us plays "tit for tat."

   iii. Untied plays "tit for tat" when Air 'R' Us plays "always charge the low price."

   iv. Untied plays "tit for tat" when Air 'R' Us also plays "tit for tat."

7. Suppose that Coke and Pepsi are the only two producers of cola drinks, so they are duopolists. Both companies have zero marginal cost and a fixed cost of $100,000.

a. Assume first that consumers regard Coke and Pepsi as perfect substitutes. Currently both are sold for $0.20 per can, and at that price each company sells 4 million cans per day.

   i. How large is Pepsi's profit?

   ii. If Pepsi were to raise its price to $0.30 cents per can, what would happen to its profit?

b. Now suppose that each company advertises to differentiate its product from the other company's. As a result of advertising, Pepsi realizes that if it raises or lowers its price, it will sell less or more of its product, as shown by the demand schedule in the accompanying table.

Price of Pepsi (per can)	Quantity of Pepsi demanded (millions of cans)
$0.10	5
0.20	4
0.30	3
0.40	2
0.50	1

If Pepsi now were to raise its price to $0.30 per can, what would happen to its profit?

c. Comparing your answer to part a(i) and to part b, what is the maximum amount Pepsi would be willing to spend on advertising?

8. Philip Morris and R.J. Reynolds spend huge sums of money each year to advertise their tobacco products in an attempt to steal customers from each other. Suppose each year Philip Morris and R.J. Reynolds have to decide whether or not they want to spend money on advertising. If neither firm advertises, each will earn a profit of $2 million. If they both advertise, each will earn a profit of $1.5 million. If one firm advertises and the other does not, the firm that advertises will earn a profit of $2.8 million and the other firm will earn $1 million.

a. Use a payoff matrix to depict this problem.

b. Suppose Philip Morris and R.J. Reynolds can write an enforceable contract about what they will do. What is the cooperative solution to this game?

c. What is the Nash equilibrium without an enforceable contract? Explain why this is the likely outcome.

9. Over the last 30 years the Organization of Petroleum Exporting Countries (OPEC) has had varied success in forming and maintaining its cartel agreements. Explain how the following factors may contribute to the difficulty of forming and/or maintaining its price and output agreements.

a. New oil fields are discovered and increased drilling is undertaken in the Gulf of Mexico and the North Sea by nonmembers of OPEC.

b. Crude oil is a product that is differentiated by sulfur content: it costs less to refine low-sulfur crude oil into gasoline. Different OPEC countries possess oil reserves of different sulfur content.

c. Cars powered by hydrogen are developed.

10. Suppose you are an economist working for the Antitrust Division of the Department of Justice. In each of the following cases you are given the task of determining whether the behavior warrants an antitrust investigation for possible illegal acts, or is just an example of undesirable, but not illegal, tacit collusion. Explain your reasoning.

a. Two companies dominate the industry for industrial lasers. Several people sit on the boards of directors of both companies.

b. Three banks dominate the market for banking in a given state. Their profits have been going up recently as they add new fees for customer transactions. Advertising among the banks is fierce, and new branches are springing up in many locations.

c. The two oil companies that produce most of the petroleum for the western half of the United States have decided to forgo building their own pipelines and to share a common pipeline, the only means of transporting petroleum products to that market.

d. The two major companies that dominate the market for herbal supplements have each created a subsidiary that sells the same product as the parent company in large quantities but with a generic name.

e. The two largest credit card companies, Passport and OmniCard, have required all banks and retailers who accept their cards to agree to limit their use of rival credit cards.

11. The industry for small, single-engine airplanes is oligopolistic, and it has achieved tacit collusion. Each firm currently sells 10 airplanes at a price of $200,000 each. Each firm believes that it will sell 1 fewer airplane if it raises the price by $5,000. And each firm also believes that it can sell 1 more airplane if it lowers the price by $10,000. That is, each firm has a kinked demand curve.

a. How much additional revenue will a firm generate if it produces 1 more (the 11th) airplane?

b. How much revenue will a firm lose if it produces 1 fewer airplane?

c. If the marginal cost of producing an airplane is $120,000, how many airplanes will each firm produce, and at what price?

d. If the marginal cost of producing an airplane is $140,000, how many airplanes will each firm produce, and at what price?

>web... To continue your study and review of concepts in this chapter, please visit the Krugman/Wells website for quizzes, animated graph tutorials, web links to helpful resources, and more.

www.worthpublishers.com/krugmanwells

chapter

>> Monopolistic Competition and Product Differentiation

FAST-FOOD DIFFERENTIATION

A RECENT BEST-SELLING BOOK TITLED *Fast Food Nation* offered a fascinating if rather negative report on the burgers, pizza, tacos, and fried chicken that make up so much of the modern American diet. According to the book, all fast-food chains produce and deliver their food in pretty much the same way. In particular, a lot of the taste of your fast food—whatever kind of fast food it is—comes from food additives manufactured in New Jersey.

But each fast-food provider goes to great lengths to convince you that it has something special to offer. Everyone recognizes Ronald McDonald the clown, a symbol of McDonald's carefully cultivated image as the place kids love. Rival Wendy's took a bite out of McDonald's market share with a little old lady yelling "Where's the beef?", a campaign that emphasized Wendy's somewhat bigger burgers.

So how would you describe the fast-food industry? On the one hand, it clearly isn't a monopoly. When you go to a fast-food court, you have a choice among vendors, and there is real competition between the different burger outlets and between the burgers and the fried chicken. On the other hand, in a way each vendor *does* possess some aspects of a monopoly: at one point McDonald's had the slogan "Nobody does it like McDonald's." That was literally true—though McDonald's competitors would say that they did it *better*. In any case, the point is that each fast-food provider offers a product that is *differentiated* from its rivals' products.

Competing for your tastebuds.

In the fast-food industry, many firms compete to satisfy more or less the same demand—the desire of consumers for something tasty but quick. But each firm offers to satisfy that demand with a distinctive, differentiated product—products that consumers typically view as close but not perfect substitutes. When there are many firms offering competing, differentiated products, as there are in the fast-food industry, economists say that the industry is characterized by *monopolistic competition*.

What you will learn in this chapter:

➤ The meaning of **monopolistic competition**

➤ Why oligopolists and monopolistically competitive firms differentiate their products

➤ How prices and profits are determined in monopolistic competition in the short run and the long run

➤ Why monopolistic competition poses a trade-off between lower prices and greater product diversity

➤ The economic significance of advertising and brand names

Jeff Greenberg/PhotoEdit

This is the fourth and final market structure that we will discuss, after perfect competition, monopoly, and oligopoly.

We'll start by defining monopolistic competition more carefully and explain its characteristic features. Then we'll explore how firms differentiate their products; this will allow us to analyze how monopolistic competition works. The chapter concludes with a discussion of some ongoing controversies about product differentiation—in particular, the question of why advertising is effective.

The Meaning of Monopolistic Competition

Joe manages the Wonderful Wok stand in the food court of a big shopping mall. He offers the only Chinese food there, but there are more than a dozen alternatives, from Bodacious Burgers to Pizza Paradise. When deciding what to charge for a meal, Joe knows that he must take those alternatives into account: even people who normally prefer stir-fry won't order a $15 lunch from Joe when they can get a burger, fries, and drink for $4.

But Joe also knows that he won't lose all his business even if his lunches cost a bit more than the alternatives. Chinese food isn't the same thing as burgers or pizza. Some people will really be in the mood for Chinese that day, and they will buy from Joe even if they could have dined more cheaply on burgers. Of course, the reverse is also true: even if Chinese is a bit cheaper, some people will choose burgers instead. In other words, Joe does have some market power: he has *some* ability to set his own price.

So how would you describe Joe's situation? He definitely isn't a price-taker, so he isn't in a situation of perfect competition. But you wouldn't exactly call him a monopolist, either. Although he's the only seller of Chinese food in that food court, he does face competition from other food vendors.

Yet it would also be wrong to call him an oligopolist. Oligopoly, remember, involves competition among a small number of firms in an industry protected by some—albeit limited—barriers to entry and whose profits are highly interdependent. This interdependence provides an incentive for oligopolists to try to find a way to collude, if only tacitly. But in Joe's case there are *lots* of vendors in the shopping mall, too many to make tacit collusion feasible.

Economists describe Joe's situation as one of **monopolistic competition.** Monopolistic competition is particularly common in service industries like restaurants and gas stations, but it also exists in some manufacturing industries. It involves three conditions: large numbers of competing producers, differentiated products, and free entry into and exit from the industry in the long run. In a monopolistically competitive industry, each producer has some ability to set the price of her differentiated good. But exactly how high she can set it is limited by the competition she faces from other existing and potential producers that produce close, but not identical, products.

> **Monopolistic competition** is a market structure in which there are many competing producers in an industry, each producer sells a differentiated product, and there is free entry into and exit from the industry in the long run.

Large Numbers

In a monopolistically competitive industry there are many producers. Such an industry does not look either like a monopoly, where the firm faces no competition, or an oligopoly, where each firm has only a few rivals. Instead, each seller has many competitors. There are many vendors in a big food court, many gas stations along a major highway, and many hotels in a popular beach resort.

Differentiated Products

In a monopolistically competitive industry, each producer has a product that consumers view as somewhat distinct from the products of competing firms but at the same time are considered close substitutes. If Joe's food court contained 15 vendors selling exactly the same kind and quality of food, there would be perfect competition: any seller who tried to charge a higher price would have no customers. But suppose that Wonderful Wok is the only Chinese food vendor, Bodacious Burgers is the only hamburger stand, and so on. The result of this differentiation is that each seller has some ability to set his own price: each producer has some—albeit limited—market power.

Free Entry and Exit in the Long Run

In monopolistically competitive industries, new producers, with their own distinct products, can enter the industry freely in the long run. For example, other food vendors would open outlets in the shopping mall if they thought it would be profitable to do so. In addition, firms will exit the industry if they find they are not covering their costs in the long run.

Monopolistic competition, then, differs from the three market structures we have examined so far. It's not the same as perfect competition: firms have some power to set prices. It's not pure monopoly: firms face some competition. And it's not the same as oligopoly: because there are many firms and free entry, the potential for collusion so important in oligopoly no longer exists.

We'll see in a moment how prices, output, and the number of products available are determined in monopolistically competitive industries. But first, let's look a little more closely at what it means to have differentiated products.

Product Differentiation

We pointed out in Chapter 15 that product differentiation often plays an important role in oligopolistic industries. In such industries, product differentiation reduces the intensity of competition between firms when tacit collusion cannot be achieved. Product differentiation plays an even more crucial role in monopolistically competitive industries. Because tacit collusion is virtually impossible when there are many producers, product differentiation is the only way monopolistically competitive firms can acquire some market power.

How do firms in the same industry—such as fast-food vendors, gas stations, or chocolate companies—differentiate their products? Sometimes the difference is mainly in the minds of consumers rather than in the products themselves. We'll discuss the role of advertising and the importance of brand names in achieving this kind of product differentiation later in the chapter. But, in general, firms differentiate their products by—surprise!—actually making them different.

The key to product differentiation is that consumers have different preferences and that each producer can carve out a market niche by producing something that caters to the particular preferences of some group of consumers better than the products of other firms. There are three important forms of product differentiation: differentiation by style or type, differentiation by location, and differentiation by quality.

Differentiation by Style or Type

The sellers in Joe's food court offer different types of fast food: hamburgers, pizza, Chinese food, Mexican food, and so on. Each consumer arrives at the food court with some preference for one or another of these offerings. This preference may depend on the consumer's mood, her diet, or what she has already eaten that day. These preferences will not make consumers indifferent to price: If Wonderful Wok were to charge $15 for an egg roll, everybody would go to Bodacious Burgers or Pizza Paradise instead. But, some people will choose a more expensive meal if that type of food is closer to their preference. So the products of the different vendors are substitutes, but they aren't *perfect* substitutes—they are *imperfect substitutes*.

FOR INQUIRING MINDS

BUCKS FOR STARBUCKS

The coffee shop industry has always been monopolistically competitive, with each local shop selling a somewhat differentiated product. Until the middle of the 1980s, however, products were mainly differentiated by location: customers chose a coffee shop because it was near their workplace or on the way to work. There was also a bit of differentiation by quality—some places made better coffee than others—but that was it. After all, coffee was coffee.

That is, coffee was coffee until it started becoming cappuccino, latte, frappuccino, and other more or less Italian-style beverages. Call it the Starbucks revolution: the Seattle-based chain led the transformation of America's caffeine intake, growing from 15 stores in Seattle in 1987 to more than 7,500 around the world by 2004.

Is this a true expansion of the choices available to consumers? Are the coffee varieties now available really different? Yes, they are. The authors are old enough to remember what typical coffee shop coffee tasted like in the dark ages: things really have improved. Is the

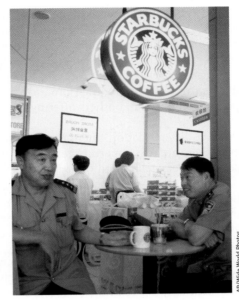

Mocha lattes served here—the Starbucks revolution comes to Beijing.

improvement worth the price of a Starbucks latte? Well, people are willing to pay those prices, and the customer is always right.

Vendors in a food court aren't the only sellers who differentiate their offerings by type. Clothing stores concentrate on women's or men's clothes, on business attire or sportswear, on trendy or classic styles, and so on. Auto manufacturers offer sedans, minivans, sport-utility vehicles, and sports cars, each type aimed at drivers with different needs and tastes.

Books offer yet another example of differentiation by type and style. Mysteries are differentiated from romances; among mysteries, we can differentiate among hard-boiled detective stories, whodunits, and police procedurals. And no two writers of hard-boiled detective stories are exactly alike: Raymond Chandler and Sue Grafton each have their devoted fans.

In fact, product differentiation is characteristic of most consumer goods. As long as people differ in their tastes, producers find it possible and profitable to produce a range of varieties.

Differentiation by Location

Gas stations along a road offer differentiated products. True, the gas may be exactly the same. But the location of the stations is different, and location matters to consumers: it's more convenient to stop for gas near your home, near your workplace, or near wherever you are when the gas gauge gets low.

In fact, many monopolistically competitive industries supply goods differentiated by location. This is especially true in service industries, from dry cleaners to hairdressers, where customers often choose the seller who is closest rather than cheapest.

Differentiation by Quality

Do you have a craving for chocolate? How much are you willing to spend on it? You see, there's chocolate and then there's chocolate: although ordinary chocolate may not be very expensive, gourmet chocolate can cost dollars for every bite.

With chocolate, as with many goods, there is a range of possible qualities. You can get a usable bicycle for less than $100; you can get a much fancier bicycle for 10 times as much. It all depends on how much the additional quality matters to you and how much you will miss the other things you could have purchased with that money.

Because consumers vary in what they are willing to pay for higher quality, producers can differentiate their products by quality—some offering lower-quality, inexpensive products and others offering higher-quality products at a higher price.

Product differentiation, then, can take several forms. Whatever form it takes, however, there are two important features of industries with differentiated products: *competition among sellers* and *value in diversity*.

Competition among sellers means that even though sellers of differentiated products are not offering identical goods, they are to some extent competing for a limited market. If more businesses enter the market, each will find that it sells less quantity at any given price. For example, if a new gas station opens along a road, each of the existing gas stations will sell a bit less.

Value in diversity refers to the gain to consumers from the proliferation of differentiated products. A food court with eight vendors makes consumers happier than one with only six vendors, even if the prices are the same, because some customers will get a meal that is closer to what they had in mind. A road on which there is a gas station every two miles is more convenient for motorists than a road where gas stations are five miles apart. When a product is available in many different qualities, fewer people are forced to pay for more quality than they need or to settle for lower quality than they want. There are, in other words, benefits to consumers from a greater diversity of available products.

As we'll see next, competition among the sellers of differentiated products is the key to understanding how monopolistic competition works.

economics in action

Any Color, So Long as It's Black

The early history of the auto industry offers a classic illustration of the power of product differentiation.

The modern automobile industry was created by Henry Ford, who first introduced assembly-line production. This technique made it possible for him to offer the famous Model T at a far lower price than anyone else was charging for a car; by 1920, Ford dominated the automobile business.

Ford's strategy was to offer just one style of car, which maximized his economies of scale but made no concessions to differences in taste. He supposedly declared that customers could get the Model T in "any color, so long as it's black."

This strategy was challenged by Alfred P. Sloan, who had merged a number of smaller automobile companies into General Motors. Sloan's strategy was to offer a range of car types, differentiated by quality and price. Chevrolets were basic cars that directly challenged the Model T, Buicks were bigger and more expensive, and so on up to Cadillacs. And you could get each model in several different colors.

By the 1930s the verdict was clear: customers preferred a range of styles, and General Motors, not Ford, became the dominant auto manufacturer for the rest of the twentieth century. ■

< < < < < < < < < < < < < < < <

1. Each of the following goods and services are differentiated products. Which are differentiated as a result of monopolistic competition and which are not? Explain.
    a. Ladders
    b. Soft drinks
    c. Department stores
    d. Steel

2. You must determine which of two types of market structure best describes an industry, but you are allowed to ask only one question about the industry. What question should you ask to determine if an industry is:
    a. Perfectly competitive or monopolistically competitive?
    b. Monopoly or monopolistically competitive?

Solutions appear at back of book.

Understanding Monopolistic Competition

Suppose an industry is monopolistically competitive: it consists of many producers, all competing for the same consumers but offering differentiated products. How does such an industry behave?

As the term *monopolistic competition* suggests, this market structure combines some features typical of monopoly with others typical of perfect competition. Because each firm is offering a distinct product, it is in a way like a monopolist: it faces a downward-sloping demand curve and has some market power—the ability within limits to determine the price of its product. However, unlike a pure monopolist, a monopolistically competitive firm does face competition: the amount of its product it can sell depends on the prices and products offered by other firms in the industry.

The same, of course, is true of an oligopoly. In a monopolistically competitive industry, however, there are *many* producers, as opposed to the small number that defines an oligopoly. This means that the "puzzle" of oligopoly—will firms collude or will they behave noncooperatively?—does not arise in the case of monopolistically competitive industries. True, if all the gas stations or all the restaurants in a town could agree—explicitly or tacitly—to raise prices, it would be in their mutual interest to do so. But such collusion is virtually impossible when the number of firms is large and, by implication, there are no barriers to entry. So in situations of monopolistic competition, we can safely assume that firms behave noncooperatively and ignore the potential for collusion.

Monopolistic Competition in the Short Run

We introduced the distinction between short-run and long-run equilibrium back in Chapter 9. The short-run equilibrium of an industry takes the number of firms as given. The long-run equilibrium, by contrast, is reached only after enough time has elapsed for firms to enter or exit the industry. To analyze monopolistic competition, we focus first on the short run and then on how an industry moves from the short run to the long run.

Panels (a) and (b) of Figure 16-1 on page 394 show two possible situations that a typical firm in a monopolistically competitive industry might face in the short run. In each case the firm looks like any monopolist: it faces a downward-sloping demand curve, which implies a downward-sloping marginal revenue curve.

We assume that every firm has an upward-sloping marginal cost curve but that it also faces some fixed costs, so that its average total cost curve is U-shaped. This assumption doesn't matter in the short run, but, as we'll see shortly, it is crucial to understanding the long-run equilibrium.

In each case the firm, in order to maximize profit, sets marginal revenue equal to marginal cost. So how do these two figures differ? In panel (a) the firm is profitable; in panel (b) it is unprofitable.

Figure 16-1   **The Monopolistically Competitive Firm in the Short Run**

The firm in panel (a) can be profitable for some output quantity: the quantity at which its average total cost curve, *ATC*, lies below its demand curve, D_P. The profit-maximizing output quantity is Q_P, the output at which marginal revenue, MR_P, is equal to marginal cost, *MC*. The firm charges price P_P and earns a profit, represented by the area of the shaded rectangle. The firm in panel (b), however, can never be profitable because its average total cost curve lies above its demand curve, D_U, for every output quantity. The best that it can do if it produces at all is to produce quantity Q_U and charge price P_U. This generates a loss, indicated by the area of the shaded rectangle. Any other output quantity results in a greater loss. **>web...**

In panel (a) the firm faces the demand curve D_P and the marginal revenue curve MR_P. It produces the profit-maximizing output Q_P, the quantity at which marginal revenue is equal to marginal cost, and sells it at the price P_P. This price is above the average total cost at this output, ATC_P. The firm's profit is indicated by the area of the shaded rectangle.

In panel (b) the firm faces the demand curve D_U and the marginal revenue curve MR_U. It chooses the quantity Q_U at which marginal revenue is equal to marginal cost. However, in this case the price P_U is *below* the average total cost ATC_U; so at this quantity the firm loses money. Its loss is equal to the area of the shaded rectangle. Since Q_U is the profit-maximizing quantity—which means, in this case, the loss-minimizing quantity—there is no way for a firm in this situation to make a profit. We can confirm this by noting that at *any* quantity of output, the average total cost curve in panel (b) lies above the demand curve D_U. Because $ATC > P$ at all quantities of output, this firm always suffers a loss.

As this comparison suggests, the key to whether a firm with market power is profitable or unprofitable in the short run lies in the relationship between its demand curve and its average total cost curve. In panel (a) the demand curve D_P crosses the average total cost curve, meaning that some of the demand curve lies above the average total cost curve. So there are some price–quantity combinations available at which price is higher than average total cost, indicating that the firm can choose a quantity at which it makes positive profit.

In panel (b), by contrast, the demand curve D_U does not cross the average total cost curve—it always lies below it. So the price corresponding to each quantity demanded is always less than the average total cost of producing that quantity. There is no quantity at which the firm can avoid losing money.

These figures, showing firms facing downward-sloping demand curves and their associated marginal revenue curves, look just like ordinary monopoly analysis. The "competition" aspect of monopolistic competition comes into play, however, when we move from the short run to the long run.

Monopolistic Competition in the Long Run

Obviously, an industry in which existing firms are losing money, like the one in panel (b) of Figure 16-1, is not in long-run equilibrium. When existing firms are losing money, some firms will *exit* the industry. The industry will not be in long-run equilibrium until the persistent losses have been eliminated by the exit of some firms.

It may be less obvious that an industry in which existing firms are earning profits, like the one in panel (a) of Figure 16-1, is also not in long-run equilibrium. Given there is *free entry* into the industry, persistent profits by the firms already existing will lead to the entry of additional producers. The industry will not be in long-run equilibrium until the persistent profits have been eliminated by the entry of new producers.

How will entry or exit by other firms affect the profits of a typical existing firm? Because the differentiated products offered by firms in a monopolistically competitive industry compete for the same set of customers, entry or exit by other firms will affect the demand curve facing every existing producer. If new gas stations open along a highway, each of the existing gas stations will sell less gas at any given price. So, as illustrated in panel (a) of Figure 16-2, entry of additional producers into a monopolistically competitive industry will lead to a *leftward* shift of the demand curve and the marginal revenue curve facing a typical existing producer.

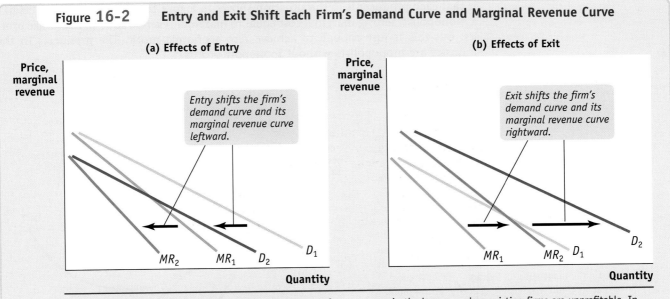

Figure 16-2   Entry and Exit Shift Each Firm's Demand Curve and Marginal Revenue Curve

(a) Effects of Entry

Price, marginal revenue

Entry shifts the firm's demand curve and its marginal revenue curve leftward.

MR_2 MR_1 D_2 D_1

Quantity

(b) Effects of Exit

Price, marginal revenue

Exit shifts the firm's demand curve and its marginal revenue curve rightward.

MR_1 MR_2 D_1 D_2

Quantity

Entry will occur in the long run when existing firms are profitable. In panel (a), entry causes each existing firm's demand curve and marginal revenue curve to shift to the left. The firm receives a lower price for every unit it sells, and its profit falls. Entry will cease when firms make zero profit. Exit will occur in the long run when existing firms are unprofitable. In panel (b), exit out of the industry shifts each remaining firm's demand curve and marginal revenue curve to the right. The firm receives a higher price for every unit it sells, and profit rises. Exit will cease when the remaining firms make zero profit.

In the long run, a monopolistically competitive industry ends up in **zero-profit equilibrium**: each firm makes zero profit at its profit-maximizing quantity.

Conversely, suppose that some of the gas stations along the highway close. Then each of the remaining stations will sell more gasoline at any given price. So as illustrated in panel (b), exit of firms from an industry leads to a *rightward* shift of the demand curve and marginal revenue curve facing a typical remaining producer.

The industry will be in long-run equilibrium when there is neither entry nor exit. This will occur only when every firm earns zero profit. So in the long run, a monopolistically competitive industry will end up in **zero-profit equilibrium,** in which firms just manage to cover their costs at their profit-maximizing output quantities.

We have seen that a firm facing a downward-sloping demand curve will earn positive profits if any part of that demand curve lies above its average total cost curve; it will incur a loss if its demand curve lies everywhere below its average total cost curve. So in zero-profit equilibrium, the firm must be in a borderline position between these two cases; its demand curve must just touch its average total cost curve. That is, it must be just *tangent* to it at the firm's profit-maximizing output quantity—the output quantity at which marginal revenue equals marginal cost.

If this is not the case, the firm operating at its profit-maximizing quantity will find itself making either a profit or loss, as illustrated in the panels of Figure 16-1. But we also know that free entry and exit means that this cannot be a long-run equilibrium. Why? In the case of a profit, new firms will enter the industry, shifting the demand curve of every existing firm leftward until all profits are extinguished. In the case of a loss, some existing firms exit and so shift the demand curve of every remaining firm to the right until all losses are extinguished. All entry and exit ceases only when every existing firm makes zero profit at its profit-maximizing quantity of output.

Figure 16-3 shows a typical monopolistically competitive firm in such a zero-profit equilibrium. The firm produces Q_{MC}, the output at which $MR = MC$, and charges price P_{MC}. At this price and quantity, represented by point Z, the demand curve is just tangent to its average total cost curve. The firm earns zero profit because price, P_{MC}, is equal to average total cost, ATC_{MC}.

The normal long-run condition of a monopolistically competitive industry, then, is that each producer is in the situation shown in Figure 16-3. Each producer acts like a monopolist, setting marginal cost equal to marginal revenue so as to maximize profits. But this is just enough to achieve zero economic profit. The producers in the industry are monopolists without monopoly profits.

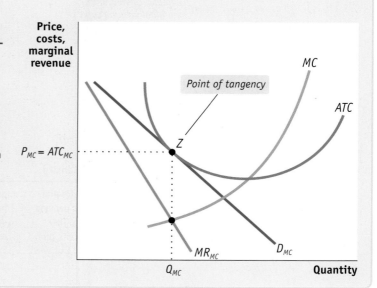

Figure 16-3

The Long-Run Zero-Profit Equilibrium

If existing firms are profitable, entry will occur and shift each existing firm's demand curve leftward. If existing firms are unprofitable, each existing firm's demand curve shifts rightward as some firms exit the industry. Entry and exit will cease when every existing firm makes zero profit at its profit-maximizing quantity. So, in long-run zero-profit equilibrium, the demand curve of each firm is tangent to its average total cost curve at its profit-maximizing quantity: at the profit-maximizing quantity, Q_{MC}, price, P_{MC}, equals average total cost, ATC_{MC}. A monopolistically competitive firm is like a monopolist without monopoly profits. **>web...**

On the face of it, the movie business seems to meet the criteria for monopolistic competition. Movies compete for the same consumers; each movie is different from the others; new companies can and do enter the business. But where's the zero-profit equilibrium? After all, some movies are enormously profitable.

The key is to realize that for every successful blockbuster, there are several flops—and that the movie studios don't know in advance which will be which. (One observer of Hollywood summed up his conclusions as follows: "Nobody knows anything.") And by the time it becomes clear that a movie will be a flop, it's too late to cancel it.

The difference between movie-making and the type of monopolistic competition we model in this chapter is that the fixed costs of making a movie are also *sunk costs*—once they've been incurred, they can't be recovered.

Yet there is still, in a way, a zero-profit equilibrium. If movies on average were highly profitable, more studios would enter the industry and more movies would be made. If movies on average lost money, fewer movies would be made. In fact, as you might expect, the movie industry on average earns just about enough to cover the cost of production—that is, it earns roughly zero economic profit.

This kind of situation—in which firms earn zero profit on average but have a mixture of highly profitable hits and money-losing flops—can be found in other industries, characterized by high, up-front sunk costs. A notable example is the pharmaceutical industry, where many research projects lead nowhere, but a few lead to highly profitable drugs.

economics in action

Bagels from Boom to Bust

Bagels have always been big in New York City, but in the mid-1990s they suddenly became popular across the entire country. Nobody was quite sure why. One factor may have been health consciousness (bagels are low in fat and cholesterol—until you smother them in cream cheese). Another may have been the popularity of New York–based TV shows, like *Seinfeld*. In any case, bagel consumption surged. Those who already owned bagel shops suddenly found their businesses highly profitable.

The fresh-bagel sector fits the definition of monopolistic competition quite well: there are many shops, all competing with one another, but the shops are differentiated by location as well as by style (some shops offer traditional bagels; others offer new items like bagels with blueberries or jalapenos). Each has some market power—it will not lose all its business if it charges slightly higher prices than other shops. And the industry is also characterized by free entry. Sure enough, once bagel shops became highly profitable, many new competitors entered the business. This, in turn, reduced the profitability of every bagel shop. By the end of the 1990s bagels were no longer a highly profitable business. Indeed, quite a few companies dropped out of the business or went bankrupt.

Meanwhile, a similar story seems to be emerging among specialty coffee shops: Starbucks is the most visible company but by no means the only one. When Americans developed a taste for espresso-based drinks like lattes, the business became highly profitable, and many firms entered the industry. In 1991 there were only 500 high-end coffee shops in the United States, but today there are more than 10,000. Demand for specialty coffee is still going up, but thanks to the rapid growth in the number of coffee shops, experts no longer think that the business offers easy opportunities for high profits. ∎

> >

>> QUICK REVIEW

➤ Like a monopolist, each firm in a monopolistically competitive industry faces a downward-sloping demand curve and marginal revenue curve. In the short run, it may earn a profit or incur a loss at its profit-maximizing quantity.

➤ If the typical firm earns positive profit, new firms will enter the industry in the long run, shifting each existing firm's demand curve to the left. If the typical firm incurs a loss, some existing firms will exit the industry in the long run, shifting the demand curve of each remaining firm to the right.

➤ In the long-run equilibrium of a monopolistically competitive industry, the *zero-profit equilibrium*, firms just break even. The typical firm's demand curve is tangent to its average total cost curve at its profit-maximizing quantity.

1. Currently a monopolistically competitive industry, composed of firms with U-shaped average total cost curves, is in long-run equilibrium. Describe how the industry adjusts, in both the short and long run, in each of the following situations.
   a. A technological change that increases fixed cost for every firm in the industry
   b. A technological change that decreases marginal cost for every firm in the industry
2. Why, in the long run, is it impossible for firms in a monopolistically competitive industry to create a monopoly by joining together to form a single firm?

Solutions appear at back of book.

Monopolistic Competition versus Perfect Competition

In a way, long-run equilibrium in a monopolistically competitive industry looks a lot like long-run equilibrium in a perfectly competitive industry. In both cases, there are many firms; in both cases, profits have been competed away; in both cases, the price received by every firm is equal to the average total cost of production.

However, the two versions of long-run equilibrium are different—in ways that are economically significant.

Price, Marginal Cost, and Average Total Cost

Figure 16-4 compares the long-run equilibrium of a typical firm in a perfectly competitive industry with that of a typical firm in a monopolistically competitive industry. Panel (a) shows a perfectly competitive firm facing a market price equal to its minimum average total cost; panel (b) reproduces Figure 16-3. Comparing the panels, we see two important differences.

First, in the case of the perfectly competitive firm shown in panel (a), the price, P_C, received by the firm at the profit-maximizing quantity, Q_C, is equal to the firm's marginal cost of production, MC_C, at that quantity of output. By contrast, at the profit-maximizing quantity chosen by the monopolistically competitive firm in panel (b), Q_{MC}, the price, P_{MC}, is *higher* than the marginal cost of production, MC_{MC}.

This difference translates into a difference in the attitude of firms toward consumers. A wheat farmer, who can sell as much wheat as he likes at the going market price, would not get particularly excited if you offered to buy some wheat at the market price. Since he has no desire to produce more at that price and can sell the wheat to someone else, you are not doing him a favor.

But if you decide to fill up your tank at Jamil's gas station rather than at Katy's, you are doing Jamil a favor. He is not willing to cut his price to get more customers—he's already made the best of that trade-off. But if he gets a few more customers than he expected at the *posted* price, that's good news: an additional sale at the posted price increases his revenue more than it increases his costs because the posted price exceeds marginal cost.

The fact that monopolistic competitors, unlike perfect competitors, want to sell more at the going price is crucial to understanding why they engage in activities like advertising that help increase sales.

The other difference between monopolistic competition and perfect competition that is visible in Figure 16-4 involves the position of each firm on its average total cost curve. In panel (a), the perfectly competitive firm produces at point Q_C, at the bottom of the U-shaped average total cost curve. That is, each firm produces the quantity at which average total cost is minimized—the *minimum-cost output*. As a consequence, the total cost of industry output is also minimized.

Under monopolistic competition, in panel (b), the firm produces at Q_{MC}, on the *downward-sloping* part of the U-shaped *ATC* curve: it produces less than the quantity

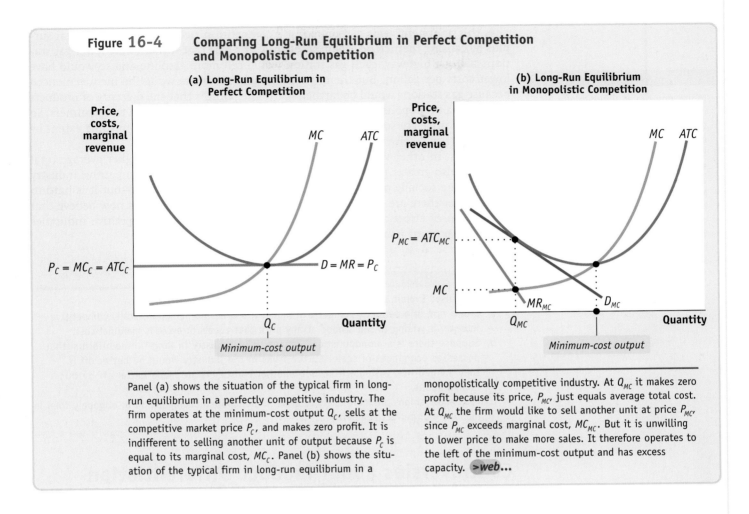

Figure 16-4   **Comparing Long-Run Equilibrium in Perfect Competition and Monopolistic Competition**

(a) Long-Run Equilibrium in Perfect Competition

(b) Long-Run Equilibrium in Monopolistic Competition

Panel (a) shows the situation of the typical firm in long-run equilibrium in a perfectly competitive industry. The firm operates at the minimum-cost output Q_C, sells at the competitive market price P_C, and makes zero profit. It is indifferent to selling another unit of output because P_C is equal to its marginal cost, MC_C. Panel (b) shows the situation of the typical firm in long-run equilibrium in a monopolistically competitive industry. At Q_{MC} it makes zero profit because its price, P_{MC}, just equals average total cost. At Q_{MC} the firm would like to sell another unit at price P_{MC}, since P_{MC} exceeds marginal cost, MC_{MC}. But it is unwilling to lower price to make more sales. It therefore operates to the left of the minimum-cost output and has excess capacity. **>web...**

that would minimize average total cost. This failure to produce enough to minimize average total cost is sometimes described as the **excess capacity** issue. The typical vendor in a food court or gas station along a road is not big enough to take maximum advantage of available cost savings. So, the total cost of industry output is not minimized in the case of a monopolistically competitive market.

Some people have argued that, because every monopolistic competitor has excess capacity, monopolistically competitive industries are inefficient. But the issue of efficiency under monopolistic competition turns out to be a subtle one that does not have a clear answer.

> Firms in a monopolistically competitive industry have **excess capacity**: they produce less than the output at which average total cost is minimized.

Is Monopolistic Competition Inefficient?

A monopolistic competitor, like a monopolist, charges a price that is above marginal cost. As a result, some people are willing to pay at least as much for an egg roll at Wonderful Wok as it costs to produce it, but who are deterred from doing so. In monopolistic competition, some mutually beneficial transactions go unexploited.

Furthermore, it is often argued that monopolistic competition is subject to a further kind of inefficiency: that the excess capacity of every monopolistic competitor implies *wasteful duplication*: monopolistically competitive industries offer too many varieties. According to this argument, it would be better if there were only two or three vendors in the food court, not six or seven. If there were fewer vendors, they would each have lower average total costs and so could offer food more cheaply.

Is this argument against monopolistic competition right—that it lowers total surplus by causing inefficiency? Not necessarily. It's true that if there were fewer gas stations along a highway, each gas station would sell more gasoline and so would have lower costs per gallon. But there is a drawback: motorists would be inconvenienced because gas stations would be farther apart. The point is that the diversity of products offered in a monopolistically competitive industry is itself beneficial to consumers. So the higher price consumers pay because of excess capacity is offset to some extent by the value they receive from greater diversity.

There is, in other words, a trade-off: more producers means higher average total costs but also greater product diversity. Does a monopolistically competitive industry arrive at the socially optimal point on this trade-off? Probably not—but it is hard to say whether there are too many firms or too few! Most economists now believe that duplication of effort and excess capacity in monopolistically competitive industries are not important issues in practice. ∎

< < < < < < < < < < < < < < < < < < <

>> CHECK YOUR UNDERSTANDING 16-3

1. True or false? Explain your answer.
   a. Like a firm in a perfectly competitive industry, a firm in a monopolistically competitive industry is willing to sell a good at any price that equals or exceeds marginal cost.
   b. Suppose there is a monopolistically competitive industry in long-run equilibrium that possesses economies of scale. All the firms in the industry would be better off if they merged into a single firm, but whether consumers are made better off by this is ambiguous.
   c. Fads and fashions are more likely to arise in monopolistic competition or oligopoly than in monopoly or perfect competition.

Solutions appear at back of book.

Controversies about Product Differentiation

Up to this point, we have assumed that products are differentiated in a way that corresponds to some real desire of consumers. There is real convenience in having a gas station in your neighborhood; Chinese food and Mexican food are really different from each other.

In the real world, however, some instances of product differentiation can seem puzzling if you think about them. What is the real difference between the long-distance phone service of AT&T and MCI? Between Energizer and Duracell batteries? Or a Marriot and a Ramada hotel room? Most people would be hard-pressed to answer any of these questions. Yet the producers of these goods make considerable efforts to convince consumers that their products are different from and better than those of their competitors.

No discussion of product differentiation is complete without spending at least a bit of time on the two related issues—and puzzles—of *advertising* and *brand names*.

The Role of Advertising

Wheat farmers don't advertise their wares on TV; car dealers do. That's not because farmers are shy and car dealers are outgoing; it's because advertising is worthwhile only in industries in which firms have at least some market power. The purpose of advertisements is to get people to buy more of a seller's product at the going price. A perfectly competitive firm, which can sell as much as it likes at the going market price, would have no incentive to spend money convincing consumers to buy more. Only a firm that has some market power, and which therefore charges a price that is above marginal cost, can gain from advertising. (Industries that are more or less perfectly competitive, like the milk industry, do advertise—but these ads are sponsored by an association on behalf of the industry as a whole, not on behalf of the milk that comes from the cows on a particular farm.)

Given that advertising "works," it's not hard to see why firms with market power would spend money on it. But the big question about advertising is *why* it works. A related question is whether advertising is, from society's point of view, a waste of resources.

Not all advertising poses a puzzle. Much of it is straightforward: it's a way for sellers to inform potential buyers about what they have to offer (or, occasionally, for buyers to inform potential sellers about what they want). Nor is there much controversy about the economic usefulness of ads that provide information: the real estate ad that declares "sunny, charming, 2 br, 1 ba, a/c" tells you things you need to know (even if a few euphemisms are involved—"charming," of course, means "small").

But what information is being conveyed when a TV actress proclaims the virtues of one or another long-distance telephone service or a sports hero declares that some company's batteries are better than those inside that pink mechanical rabbit? Surely nobody believes that the sports star is an expert on batteries—or that he chose the company that he personally believes makes the best batteries, as opposed to the company that offered to pay him the most. Yet companies believe, with good reason, that money spent on such promotions increases their sales—and that they would be in big trouble if they stopped advertising but their competitors continued to do so.

Why are consumers influenced by ads that do not really provide any information about the product? One answer is that consumers are not as rational as economists typically assume. Perhaps consumers' judgments, or even their tastes, can be influenced by things that economists think ought to be irrelevant, such as which company has hired the most charismatic celebrity to endorse its product. And there is surely some truth to this. Consumer rationality is a useful working assumption; it is not an absolute truth.

However, another answer is that consumer response to advertising is not entirely irrational, because ads can serve as indirect "signals" in a world where consumers don't have good information about products. Suppose, to take a common example, that you need to avail yourself of some local service that you don't use regularly—body work on your car, say, or furniture moving. You turn to the Yellow Pages, where you see a number of small listings and several large display ads. You know that those display ads are large because the firms paid extra for them; still, it may be quite rational to call one of the firms with a big display ad. After all, the big ad probably means that it's a relatively large, successful company—otherwise, the company wouldn't have found it worth spending the money for the larger ad.

The same principle may partly explain why ads feature celebrities. You don't really believe that the supermodel prefers that watch; but the fact that the watch manufacturer is willing and able to pay her fee tells you that it is a major company that is likely to stand behind its product. According to this reasoning, an expensive advertisement serves to establish the quality of a firm's products in the eyes of consumers.

The possibility that it is rational for consumers to respond to advertising also has some bearing on the question of whether advertising is a waste of resources. If ads only work by manipulating the weak-minded, the $128 billion U.S. businesses spent on advertising in 2003 would have been an economic waste—except to the extent that ads sometimes provide entertainment. To the extent that advertising conveys important information, however, it is an economically productive activity after all.

Brand Names

You've been driving all day, and you decide that it's time to find a place to sleep. On your right, you see a sign for the Bates Motel; on your left, you see a sign for a Motel 6, or a Best Western, or some other national chain. Which one do you choose?

Unless they were familiar with the area, most people would head for the chain. In fact, most motels in the United States are members of major chains; the same is true of most fast-food restaurants and many, if not most, stores in shopping malls.

Motel chains and fast-food restaurants are only one aspect of a broader phenomenon: the role of **brand names,** names owned by particular companies that differentiate their products in the minds of consumers. In many cases, a company's brand name is the most important asset it has: clearly, McDonald's is worth far more than the sum of the deep-fat fryers and hamburger grills the company owns.

In fact, companies often go to considerable lengths to defend their brand names, suing anyone else who uses them without permission. You may talk about blowing your nose on a kleenex or xeroxing a term paper, but unless the product in question comes from Kleenex or Xerox, the seller must describe it as a facial tissue or a photocopier.

As with advertising, with which they are closely linked, the social usefulness of brand names is a source of dispute. Does the preference of consumers for known brands reflect consumer irrationality? Or do brand names convey real information? That is, do brand names create unnecessary market power, or do they serve a real purpose?

As in the case of advertising, the answer is probably some of both. On the one hand, brand names often do create unjustified market power. Consumers often pay more for brand-name goods in the supermarket even though consumer experts assure us that the cheaper store brands are equally good. Similarly, many common medicines, like aspirin, are cheaper—with no loss of quality—in their generic form.

On the other hand, for many products the brand name does convey information. A traveler arriving in a strange town can be sure of what awaits in a Holiday Inn or a McDonald's; a tired and hungry traveler may find this preferable to trying an independent hotel or restaurant that might be better—but might be worse.

In addition, brand names offer some assurance that the seller is engaged in repeated interaction with its customers and so has a reputation to protect. If a traveler eats a bad meal at a restaurant in a tourist trap and vows never to eat there again, the restaurant owner may not care, since the chance is small that the traveler will be in the same area again in the future. But if that traveler eats a bad meal at McDonald's and vows never to eat at a McDonald's again, that matters to the company. This gives McDonald's an incentive to provide consistent quality and so gives travelers some assurance that quality controls are in place.

> A **brand name** is a name owned by a particular firm that distinguishes its products from those of other firms.

economics in action

Absolut Irrationality

Advertising often serves a useful function. Among other things, it can make consumers aware of a wider range of alternatives, which leads to increased competition and lower prices. Indeed, in some cases the courts have viewed industry agreements *not* to advertise as violations of antitrust law. For example, in 1995 the California Dental Association was convicted of conspiracy to prevent competition by discouraging its members from advertising. It had, according to the judge, "withheld from the public information about prices, quality, superiority of service, guarantees, and the use of procedures to allay patient anxiety."

Conversely, advertising sometimes creates product differentiation and market power where there is no real difference in the product. Consider, in particular, the spectacularly successful advertising campaign of Absolut vodka.

In *Twenty Ads That Shook the World*, James B. Twitchell puts it this way: "The pull of Absolut's magnetic advertising is curious because the product itself is so bland. Vodka is aquavit, and aquavit is the most unsophisticated of alcohols. . . . No taste, no smell. . . . In fact, the Swedes, who make the stuff, rarely drink Absolut. They prefer cheaper brands such as Explorer, Renat Brannwinn, or Skane. That's because Absolut can't advertise in Sweden, where alcohol advertising is against the law."

But here's a metaphysical question: if Absolut doesn't really taste any different from other brands, but advertising convinces consumers that they are getting a distinctive product, who are we to say that they aren't? Isn't distinctiveness in the mind of the beholder? ∎

> > > > > > > > > > > > > > > > > > > >

>> **QUICK REVIEW**

- In industries with product differentiation, firms advertise in order to increase the demand for their products.
- Advertising is not a waste of resources when it gives consumers useful information about products.
- Advertising that simply touts a product is harder to explain. Either consumers are irrational, or expensive advertising communicates that the firm's products are of high quality.
- Some firms create *brand names*. As with advertising, the economic value of brand names can be ambiguous. They convey real information when they assure consumers of the quality of a product.

>> CHECK YOUR UNDERSTANDING 16-4

1. In which of the following cases is advertisement likely to be economically useful? Economically wasteful? Explain.
   a. Advertisements on the benefits of aspirin
   b. Advertisements for Bayer aspirin
   c. Advertisements on the benefits of drinking orange juice
   d. Advertisements for Tropicana orange juice
   e. Advertisements that state how long a plumber or an electrician has been in business
2. Some industry analysts have stated that a successful brand name is like a barrier to entry. Explain.

Solutions appear at back of book.

• A LOOK AHEAD •

Over the last three chapters we have taken the basic analysis of a perfectly competitive market and extended it in one important direction: to include other kinds of *market structures*. Next we turn to a different kind of extension: to different kinds of *markets*. We begin by asking how economic analysis changes when a national economy can exchange goods and services with other national economies. Next stop: international trade.

SUMMARY

1. **Monopolistic competition** is a market structure in which there are many competing producers, each producing a differentiated product, and there is free entry and exit in the long run. Product differentiation takes three main forms: by style or type, by location, or by quality. Products of competing sellers are considered imperfect substitutes, and each firm has its own downward-sloping demand curve and marginal revenue curve.

2. Short-run profits will attract entry of new firms. This reduces the quantity each existing producer sells at any given price and shifts its demand curve to the left. Short-run losses will induce exit by some firms. This shifts the demand curve of each remaining firm to the right.

3. In the long run, a monopolistically competitive industry is in **zero-profit equilibrium:** at its profit-maximizing quantity, the demand curve for each existing firm is tangent to its average total cost curve. There are zero profits in the industry and no entry or exit.

4. In long-run equilibrium, firms in a monopolistically competitive industry sell at a price greater than marginal cost. They also have **excess capacity** because they produce less than the minimum-cost output; as a result, they have higher costs than firms in a competitive industry. Whether or not monopolistic competition is inefficient is ambiguous because consumers value the diversity of products that it creates.

5. A monopolistically competitive firm will always prefer to make an additional sale at the going price, so it will engage in advertising to increase demand for its product and enhance its market power. Advertising and **brand names** that provide useful information to consumers are economically valuable. But they are economically wasteful when their only purpose is to create market power. In reality, advertising and brand names are likely to be some of both: economically valuable and economically wasteful.

KEY TERMS

Monopolistic competition, p. 389
Zero-profit equilibrium, p. 396

Excess capacity, p. 399

Brand name, p. 402

PROBLEMS

1. Use the three conditions for monopolistic competition discussed in the chapter to decide which of the following firms are likely to be operating as monopolistic competitors. If they are not monopolistically competitive firms, are they monopolists, oligopolists, or perfectly competitive firms?

   a. A local band that plays for weddings, parties, and so on

   b. Minute Maid, a producer of individual-serving juice boxes

   c. Your local dry cleaner

   d. A farmer who produces soybeans

2. You are thinking of setting up a coffee shop. The market structure for coffee shops is monopolistic competition. There are three Starbucks shops, and two other coffee shops very much like Starbucks, in your town already. In order for you to have some degree of market power, you may want to differentiate your coffee shop. Thinking about the three different ways in which products can be differentiated, explain how you would decide whether you should copy Starbucks or whether you should sell coffee in a completely different way.

3. The restaurant business in town is a monopolistically competitive industry in long-run equilibrium. One restaurant owner asks for your advice. She tells you that, each night, not all tables in her restaurant are full. She also tells you that if she lowered the prices on her menu, she would attract more customers and that doing so would lower her average total cost. Should she lower her prices? Draw a diagram showing the demand curve, marginal revenue curve, marginal cost curve, and average total cost curve for this restaurant to explain your advice. Show in your diagram what would happen to the restaurant owner's profit if she were to lower the price so that she sells the minimum-cost output.

4. The structure of the local gas station industry is monopolistic competition. Suppose that currently each gas station incurs a loss. Draw a diagram for a typical gas station to show this short-run situation. Then, in a separate diagram, show what will happen to the typical gas station in the long run. Explain your reasoning.

5. The local hairdresser industry has the structure of monopolistic competition. Your hairdresser boasts that he is making a profit and that if he continues to do so, he will be able to retire in five years. Use a diagram to illustrate your hairdresser's current situation. Do you expect this to last? In a separate diagram, draw what you expect to happen in the long run. Explain your reasoning.

6. Magnificent Blooms is a florist in a monopolistically competitive industry. It is a successful operation, producing the quantity that minimizes its average total cost and making a profit. The owner also boasts that at its current level of output, its marginal cost is above marginal revenue. Illustrate the current situation of Magnificent Blooms in a diagram. Answer the following questions by illustrating with a diagram.

   a. In the short run, could Magnificent Blooms increase its profit?

   b. In the long run, could Magnificent Blooms increase its profit?

7. "In the long run, there is no difference between monopolistic competition and perfect competition." True, false, or ambiguous? Discuss this statement with respect to the following:

   a. The price charged to consumers

   b. The average total cost of production

   c. The efficiency of the market outcome

   d. The typical firm's profit in the long run

8. "In both the short run and in the long run, the typical firm in monopolistic competition and a monopolist each make a profit." Do you agree with this statement? Explain your reasoning.

9. The market for clothes has the structure of monopolistic competition. What impact will fewer firms in this industry have on you as a consumer? Address the following issues:

   a. Variety of clothes

   b. Differences in quality of service

   c. Price

10. For each of the following situations, decide whether advertising is directly informative about the product or simply an indirect signal of its quality. Explain your reasoning.

    a. Golf champion Tiger Woods drives a Buick in a TV commercial and claims that he prefers it to any other car.

    b. A newspaper ad states "For sale: 1989 Honda Civic, 160,000 miles, new transmission."

    c. McDonald's spends millions of dollars on an advertising campaign that proclaims: "I'm lovin' it."

    d. Subway advertises one of its sandwiches claiming that it contains 6 grams of fat and fewer than 300 calories.

11. In each of the following cases, explain how the advertisement functions as a signal to a potential buyer. Explain what information the buyer lacks that is being supplied by the advertisement and how the information supplied by the advertisement is likely to affect the buyer's willingness to buy the good.

    a. "Looking for work. Excellent references from previous employers available."

    b. "Electronic equipment for sale. All merchandise carries a one-year, no-questions-asked warranty."

    c. "Car for sale by original owner. All repair and maintenance records available."

12. McDonald's spends millions of dollars each year on legal protection of its brand name, thereby preventing any unauthorized use of it. Explain what information this conveys to you as a consumer about the quality of McDonald's products.

> **web...** To continue your study and review of concepts in this chapter, please visit the Krugman/Wells website for quizzes, animated graph tutorials, web links to helpful resources, and more.
>
> ### www.worthpublishers.com/krugmanwells

17

>> International Trade

A ROSE BY ANY OTHER NATION

GIVING YOUR BELOVED ROSES ON Valentine's Day is a well-established tradition in the United States. But in the past it was a very expensive gesture: in the northern hemisphere, Valentine's Day falls not in summer, when roses are in bloom, but in the depths of winter. Until recently, that meant that the roses in the florist's shop were grown at great cost in heated greenhouses. Nowadays, however, most of the Valentine's Day roses sold in this country are flown in from South America, mainly from Colombia, where growing a rose in February is no trouble at all.

Is it a good thing that we now buy our winter roses from abroad? The vast majority of economists say yes: international trade, in which countries specialize in producing different goods and trade those goods with each other, is a source of mutual benefit to the countries involved. In Chapter 2 we laid out the basic principle that there are *gains from trade*; it's a principle that applies to countries as well as individuals.

But politicians and the public are often not convinced. In fact, during the 1996 presidential campaign one contender used the occasion of Valentine's Day to visit a flower-growing greenhouse in New Hamp-

shire, where he denounced imports of South American roses as a threat to U.S. jobs.

Up to now this book has analyzed the economy as if it were self-sufficient, as if the economy produced all the goods and services it consumes, and vice versa. This is, of course, true of the world economy as a whole. But it is not true of any individual country. It's true that 40 years ago the United States exported only a small fraction of what it produced and imported only a

What do these sweethearts and this rose farmer have in common? They are enjoying the mutual benefits of international trade.

What you will learn in this chapter:

➤ How comparative advantage leads to mutually beneficial international trade

➤ The sources of international comparative advantage

➤ Who gains and who loses from international trade, and why the gains exceed the losses

➤ How **tariffs** and **import quotas** cause inefficiency and reduce total surplus

➤ Why governments often engage in **trade protection** to shelter domestic industries from imports and how **international trade agreements** counteract this small fraction of what it consumed. Since then, however, both U.S. imports and U.S. exports have grown much faster than the U.S. economy as a whole. And other countries engage in far more foreign trade, relative to the size of their economies, than does the United States. To have a full picture of how national economies work, we must understand international trade.

This chapter examines the economics of international trade. We start from the model of comparative advantage, which, as we saw in Chapter 2, explains why there are gains from international trade. It's also important, however, to understand how some individuals can be hurt by international trade and the effects of trade policies that countries use to limit imports or promote exports.

Comparative Advantage and International Trade

The United States buys roses—and many other goods and services—from other countries. At the same time, it sells many goods and services to other countries. Goods and services purchased from abroad are **imports;** goods and services sold abroad are **exports.**

As illustrated by the opening story, imports and exports have taken on an increasingly important role in the U.S. economy. Over the last 40 years, both imports into the United States and exports from the United States have grown faster than the U.S. economy; panel (a) of Figure 17-1 shows how the value of imports and exports have grown as a percentage of gross domestic product. As panel (b) demonstrates, foreign trade is even more important for many other countries than for the United States.

To understand why international trade occurs and why economists believe it is beneficial to the economy, we will first review the concept of comparative advantage.

> Goods and services purchased from other countries are **imports;** goods and services sold to other countries are **exports.**

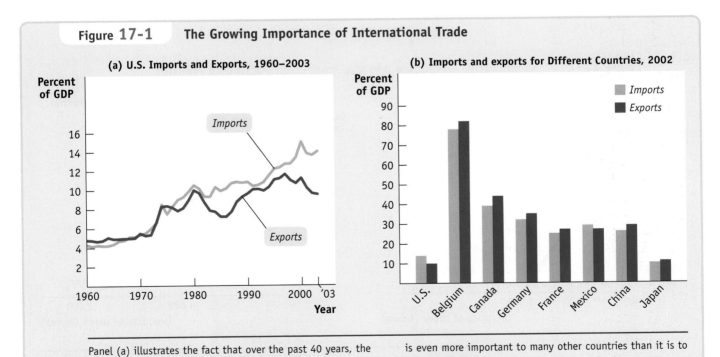

Figure 17-1 **The Growing Importance of International Trade**

(a) U.S. Imports and Exports, 1960–2003

(b) Imports and exports for Different Countries, 2002

Panel (a) illustrates the fact that over the past 40 years, the United States has exported a steadily growing share of its output (that is, its gross domestic product) to other countries and imported a growing share of what it consumes from abroad. Panel (b) demonstrates that international trade is even more important to many other countries than it is to the United States.

Source: U.S. Department of Commerce, National Income and Product Accounts [for panel (a)] and United Nations Human Development Report 2004 [for panel (b)].

Production Possibilities and Comparative Advantage, Revisited

To grow Valentine's Day roses, any country must use resources—labor, energy, capital, and so on—that could have been used to produce other things. The potential production of other goods a country must forgo to produce a rose is the opportunity cost of that rose.

It's a lot easier to grow Valentine's Day roses in Colombia, where the weather in January and February is nearly ideal, than it is in the United States. Conversely, other goods are not produced as easily in Colombia as in the United States. For example, Colombia doesn't have the base of skilled workers and technological know-how that makes the United States so good at producing high-technology goods. So the opportunity cost of a Valentine's Day rose, in terms of other goods such as computers, is much less in Colombia than it is in the United States.

And so we say that Colombia has a comparative advantage in producing roses. Let's repeat the definition of comparative advantage from Chapter 2: *a country has a comparative advantage in producing a good if the opportunity cost of producing the good is lower for that country than for other countries.*

Figure 17-2 provides a hypothetical numerical example of comparative advantage in international trade. We assume that only two goods are produced and consumed, roses and computers, and there are only two countries in the world, the United States and Colombia. We also assume that roses are shipped in standard refrigerated boxes, each containing 100 roses. The figure shows hypothetical production possibility frontiers for the United States and Colombia. As in Chapter 2, we simplify the model by assuming that the production possibility frontiers are straight lines, rather than the more realistic bowed-out shape shown in Figure 2-1. The straight-line shape implies that the opportunity cost of a box of roses in terms of computers in each country is constant—it does not depend on how many units of each good the country produces. The analysis of international trade under the assumption that opportunity costs are constant and therefore production possibility frontiers are

---

Figure 17-2   **Comparative Advantage and the Production Possibility Frontier**

The U.S. opportunity cost of a box of roses in terms of a computer is 2: 2 computers must be forgone for every additional box of roses produced. The Colombian opportunity cost of a box of roses in terms of a computer is 0.5: only 0.5 computer must be forgone for every additional box of roses produced. Therefore, Colombia has a comparative advantage in roses and the United States has a comparative advantage in computers. In autarky, C_{US} is the U.S. production and consumption bundle and C_{CO} is the Colombian production and consumption bundle.

TABLE 17-1

Production Possibilities

(a) United States	Production	
	One possibility	Another possibility
Quantity of roses (boxes)	1,000	0
Quantity of computers	0	2,000

(b) Colombia	Production	
	One possibility	Another possibility
Quantity of roses (boxes)	2,000	0
Quantity of computers	0	1,000

straight lines is known as the **Ricardian model of international trade,** named after the English economist David Ricardo, who introduced this analysis in the early nineteenth century.

Table 17-1 presents the same information that is shown in Figure 17-2. We assume that the United States can produce 1,000 boxes of roses if it produces no computers or 2,000 computers if it produces no roses. The slope of the production possibility frontier in panel (a) is –2,000/1,000, or –2: to produce an additional box of roses, the United States must forgo the production of 2 computers.

Similarly, we assume that Colombia can produce 2,000 boxes of roses if it produces no computers or 1,000 computers if it produces no roses. The slope of the production possibility frontier in panel (b) is –1,000/2,000, or –0.5: to produce an additional box of roses, Colombia must forgo the production of 0.5 computer.

Economists use the term **autarky** to describe a situation in which a country cannot trade with other countries. We assume that in autarky the United States would choose to produce and consume 500 boxes of roses and 1,000 computers. This autarky production and consumption bundle is shown by point C_{US} in panel (a) of Figure 17-2. We also assume that in autarky Colombia would choose to produce and consume 1,000 boxes of roses and 500 computers, shown by point C_{CO} in panel (b). The outcome in autarky is summarized in Table 17-2, where world production and consumption is the sum of U.S. and Colombian production and consumption.

If the countries trade with each other, they can do better than they can in autarky. In this example, Colombia has a comparative advantage in the production of roses. That

The **Ricardian model of international trade** analyzes international trade under the assumption that opportunity costs are constant.

Autarky is a situation in which a country cannot trade with other countries.

TABLE 17-2

Production and Consumption Under Autarky

(a) United States	Production	Consumption
Quantity of roses (boxes)	500	500
Quantity of computers	1,000	1,000

(b) Colombia	Production	Consumption
Quantity of roses (boxes)	1,000	1,000
Quantity of computers	500	500

(c) World (United States and Colombia)	Production	Consumption
Quantity of roses (boxes)	1,500	1,500
Quantity of computers	1,500	1,500

is, the opportunity cost of roses is lower in Colombia than in the United States: 0.5 computer per box of roses in Columbia versus 2 computers per box of roses in the United States. Conversely, the United States has a comparative advantage in the production of computers: to produce an additional computer, the United States must forgo the production of 0.5 box of roses, but producing an additional computer in Colombia requires forgoing the production of 2 boxes of roses. International trade allows each country to specialize in producing the good in which it has a comparative advantage: computers in the United States, roses in Colombia. And that leads to gains for both when they trade.

The Gains from International Trade

Figure 17-3 illustrates how both countries gain from specialization and trade. Again, panel (a) represents the United States and panel (b) represents Colombia. As a result of international trade, the United States produces at point Q_{US}: 2,000 computers but no roses. Colombia produces at Q_{CO}: 2,000 boxes of roses but no computers. The new production choices are given in the second column of Table 17-3.

By comparing Table 17-3 with Table 17-2, you can see that specialization increases total world production of *both* goods. In the absence of specialization, total world production consists of 1,500 computers and 1,500 boxes of roses. After specialization, total world production rises to 2,000 computers and 2,000 boxes of roses. These goods can now be traded, with the United States consuming roses produced in Colombia and Colombia consuming computers produced in the United States. The result is that each country can consume more of *both* goods than it did in autarky.

In addition to showing production under trade, Figure 17-3 shows one of many possible pairs of consumption bundles for the United States and Colombia, which is also given in Table 17-3. In this example, the United States moves from its autarky consumption of 1,000 computers and 500 boxes of roses, shown by C_{US}, to consumption after trade of 1,250 computers and 750 boxes of roses, represented by C'_{US}. Colombia moves from its autarky consumption of 500 computers and 1,000 boxes of

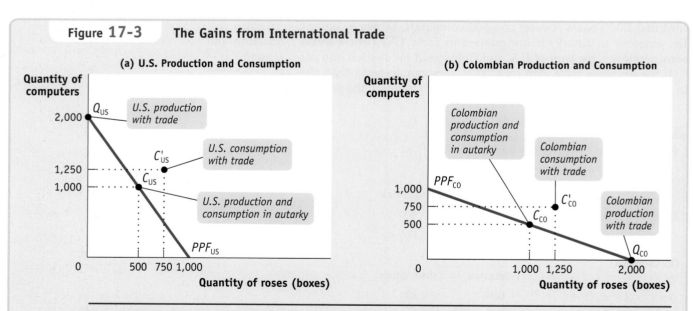

Figure 17-3   **The Gains from International Trade**

(a) U.S. Production and Consumption

(b) Colombian Production and Consumption

Trade increases world production of both goods, allowing both countries to consume more. Here, each country specializes its production as a result of trade: the United States produces at Q_{US} and Colombia produces at Q_{CO}. Total world production of computers has risen from 1,500 to 2,000

and of roses from 1,500 boxes to 2,000 boxes. The United States can now consume bundle C'_{US}, and Colombia can now consume bundle C'_{CO}—consumption bundles that were unattainable without trade.

TABLE 17-3

Production and Consumption After International Trade

(a) United States

	Production	Consumption
Quantity of roses (boxes)	0	750
Quantity of computers	2,000	1,250

(b) Colombia

	Production	Consumption
Quantity of roses (boxes)	2,000	1,250
Quantity of computers	0	750

(c) World (United States and Columbia)

	Production	Consumption
Quantity of roses (boxes)	2,000	2,000
Quantity of computers	2,000	2,000

roses, shown by C_{CO}, to consumption after trade of 750 computers and 1,250 boxes of roses, shown by C'_{CO}.

What makes this possible is the fact that with international trade countries are no longer required to consume the same bundle of goods that they produce. Each country produces at one point (Q_{US} for the United States, Q_{CO} for Colombia) but consumes at a different point (C'_{US} for the United States, C'_{CO} for Colombia). The difference reflects imports and exports: the 750 boxes of roses the United States consumes are imported from Colombia; the 750 computers Colombia consumes are imported from the United States.

In this example we have simply assumed the post-trade consumption bundles of the two countries. In fact, just as in the case of individual consumption choices, the consumption choices of countries reflect both the preferences of its residents and the *relative prices* in international markets—the prices of one good in terms of another. Although we have not explicitly given the price of computers in terms of roses, that price is implicit in our example: Colombia exports 750 boxes of roses and receives 750 computers in return, so that each box of roses is traded for 1 computer. This tells us that the price of a computer on world markets must be equal to the price of a box of roses in our example.

What determines the actual relative prices in international trade? The answer is supply and demand—and we'll turn to supply and demand in international trade in the next section. However, first let's look behind the production possibility frontiers and ask what determines a country's comparative advantage.

Sources of Comparative Advantage

International trade is driven by comparative advantage, but where does comparative advantage come from? Economists who study international trade have found three main sources of comparative advantage: international differences in *climate*, international differences in *factor endowments*, and international differences in *technology*.

Differences in Climate A key reason the opportunity cost of producing a Valentine's Day rose in Colombia is less than in the United States is that nurseries in Colombia can grow roses outdoors all year

PITFALLS

THE PAUPER LABOR FALLACY
One common argument about international trade goes as follows: it's true that Bangladesh (to pick an example) can produce some goods, such as clothing, more cheaply than we can—but that cost advantage is based only on lower wages. In fact, it takes *fewer* hours of labor to produce a shirt in the United States than in Bangladesh. So importing goods produced by "pauper labor" (workers who are paid very low wages), goes the argument, reduces the American standard of living.

Why is this a misconception? Because it confuses *comparative advantage* with *absolute advantage*. Yes, it takes less labor to produce a shirt in the United States than it does in Bangladesh. But what determines comparative advantage is not the amount of resources used to produce a good but the opportunity cost of that good—the quantity of other goods forgone in order to produce a shirt.

Low wages in countries such as Bangladesh reflect low productivity of labor across the board. Because labor productivity in other Bangladeshi industries is very low, using a lot of labor to produce a shirt does not require forgoing the production of large quantities of other goods. But in the United States, the opposite is true: very high productivity in other industries (such as high-technology goods) means that producing a shirt in the United States requires sacrificing lots of other goods. So the opportunity cost of producing a shirt is less in Bangladesh than in the United States. Despite its lower labor productivity, Bangladesh has a comparative advantage in clothing production, although the United States has an absolute advantage. As a result, importing clothing from Bangladesh actually raises the standard of living in the United States.

round but nurseries in the United States can't. In general, differences in climate are a significant source of international trade. Tropical countries export tropical products like coffee, sugar, and bananas. Countries in the temperate zones export crops like wheat and corn. Some trade is even driven by the difference in seasons between the northern and southern hemispheres: winter deliveries of Chilean grapes and New Zealand apples have become commonplace in U.S. and European supermarkets.

Differences in Factor Endowments Canada is a major exporter of forest products—lumber and products derived from lumber, like pulp and paper—to the United States. These exports don't reflect the special skill of Canadian lumberjacks. Instead, Canada has a comparative advantage in forest products because its forested area is much greater compared to the size of its labor force than the ratio of forestland to the labor force in the United States.

Forestland, like labor and capital, is a factor of production. Due to history and geography, the mix of available factors of production differs among countries, providing an important source of comparative advantage. The relationship between comparative advantage and factor availability is found in an influential model of international trade, the *Heckscher–Ohlin model* (developed by two Swedish economists in the first half of the twentieth century).

A key concept in the model is *factor intensity*. Producers use different ratios of factors of production in the production of different goods. For example, at any given wage rate and rental rate of capital, oil refineries will use much more capital per worker than clothing factories. Economists use the term **factor intensity** to describe this difference among goods: oil refining is capital-intensive, because it tends to use a high ratio of capital to labor, but clothing manufacture is labor-intensive, because it tends to use a high ratio of labor to capital.

According to the **Heckscher–Ohlin model,** a country will have a comparative advantage in a good whose production is intensive in the factors that are abundantly available in that country. So a country that has an abundance of capital will have a comparative advantage in capital-intensive industries such as oil refining, but a country that has an abundance of labor will have a comparative advantage in labor-intensive industries such as clothing production. The basic intuition behind this result is simple and based on opportunity cost. The opportunity cost of a given factor—the value that the factor would generate in alternative uses—is low for a country when it possesses an abundance of that factor. (For example, in rainy parts of the United States, the opportunity cost of water for residences is low because there is a plentiful supply for other uses, such as agriculture.) So the opportunity cost of producing goods that are intensive in the use of an abundantly available factor is also low.

> The **factor intensity** of production of a good is a measure of which factor is used in relatively greater quantities than other factors in production.
>
> According to the **Heckscher–Ohlin model**, a country has a comparative advantage in a good whose production is intensive in the factors that are abundantly available in that country.

FOR INQUIRING MINDS

DOES TRADE HURT POOR COUNTRIES?

It's a good bet that the clothes you are wearing right now were produced in a labor-abundant country such as Bangladesh or Sri Lanka. If so, the workers who produced those clothes were paid very low wages by Western standards: in 2002 (the most recent data available) workers in Sri Lankan factories were paid an average of $0.33 an hour. Doesn't this mean that Sri Lankan workers are getting a bad deal?

The answer of most economists is that it doesn't. The wages paid to export workers in poor countries should be compared not to what workers get in rich countries but to what they would get if those export jobs weren't available. The reason Sri Lankans are willing to work for so little is that in an underdeveloped economy, with lots of labor but very little of other factors of production like capital, the opportunities available to workers are very limited. It's almost certain that international trade makes Sri Lanka and other low-wage countries *less* poor than they would be otherwise and raises workers' wages relative to what they would be without international trade.

Nonetheless, many people in advanced countries—students in particular—are disturbed by the thought that their consumer goods are produced by such poorly paid workers and want to see those workers receive higher pay and better working conditions. The dilemma is whether it is possible to insist on higher wages and better working conditions without eliminating the job altogether, thereby choking off the benefits of international trade.

The most dramatic example of the validity of the Heckscher–Ohlin model is world trade in clothing. Clothing production is a labor-intensive activity: it doesn't take much physical capital, nor does it require a lot of human capital in the form of highly educated workers. So you would expect labor-abundant countries such as China and Bangladesh to have a comparative advantage in clothing production. And they do.

That much international trade is the result of differences in factor endowments helps explain another fact: international specialization of production is often *incomplete*. That is, a country often maintains some domestic production of a good that it imports. A good example of this is the United States and oil. Saudi Arabia exports oil to the United States because Saudi Arabia has an abundant supply of oil relative to its other factors of production; the United States exports medical devices to Saudi Arabia because it has an abundant supply of medical technical expertise relative to its other factors of production. But the United States also produces some oil domestically because the size of its domestic oil reserves make it economical to do so. In our demand and supply analysis in the next section, we'll consider incomplete specialization by a country to be the norm. We should emphasize, however, that the fact that countries often incompletely specialize does not in any way change the conclusion that there are gains from trade.

Differences in Technology In the 1970s and 1980s, Japan became by far the world's largest exporter of automobiles, selling large numbers to the United States and the rest of the world. Japan's comparative advantage in automobiles wasn't the result of climate. Nor can it easily be attributed to differences in factor endowments: aside from a scarcity of land, Japan's mix of available factors is quite similar to that in other advanced countries. Instead, Japan's comparative advantage in automobiles was based on the superior production techniques developed by that country's manufacturers, which allowed them to produce more cars with a given amount of labor and capital than their American or European counterparts.

Japan's comparative advantage in automobiles was a case of comparative advantage caused by differences in technology—the techniques used in production.

The causes of differences in technology are somewhat mysterious. Sometimes they seem to be based on knowledge accumulated through experience—for example, Switzerland's comparative advantage in watches reflects a long tradition of watchmaking. Sometimes they are the result of a set of innovations that for some reason occur in one country but not in others. Technological advantage is also often transitory. American auto manufacturers have now closed much of the gap in productivity with their Japanese competitors; Europe's aircraft industry has closed a similar gap with the U.S. aircraft industry. At any given point in time, however, differences in technology are a major source of comparative advantage.

FOR INQUIRING MINDS

INCREASING RETURNS AND INTERNATIONAL TRADE

Most analysis of international trade focuses on how differences between countries—differences in climate, factor endowments, and technology—create national comparative advantage. However, economists have also pointed out another reason for international trade: the role of *increasing returns*.

Production of a good is characterized by increasing returns if the productivity of labor and other resources rises with the quantity of output. For example, in an industry characterized by increasing returns, increasing output by 10 percent might require only 8 percent more labor and 9 percent more raw materials. Increasing returns (sometimes also called economies of scale) can give rise to monopoly, because they give large firms an advantage over small firms.

But increasing returns can also give rise to international trade. The logic runs as follows: if production of a good is characterized by increasing returns, it makes sense to concentrate production in only a few locations, so as to achieve a high level of production in each location. But that also means that the good is produced in only a few countries, which export that good to other countries. A commonly cited example is the North American auto industry: although both the United States and Canada produce automobiles and their components, each particular model or component tends to be produced in only one of the two countries and exported to the other. Increasing returns probably play a large role in the trade in manufactured goods between advanced countries, which is about 25 percent of the total value of world trade.

In the United States, an abundance of engineering know-how has led to a comparative advantage in aircraft.

economics in action

The Comparative Advantage of the United States

The United States is a country of superlatives: a nation richly endowed with many resources, human and natural, it has an *absolute* advantage in almost everything—that is, it is better at producing almost everything than anyone else. But what is its *comparative* advantage?

In 1953 the economist Wassily Leontief made a surprising discovery. Until his work, many economists had assumed that because U.S. workers were clearly better-equipped with machinery than their counterparts in other countries, the production of U.S. exports was more capital-intensive than the production of U.S. imports. That is, they expected that U.S. exports were more capital-intensive than U.S. imports. But Leontief's work showed that this wasn't true: in fact, goods that the United States exported were slightly less capital-intensive than goods the country imported. The "Leontief paradox" led to a sustained effort to make sense of U.S. trade patterns.

The main resolution of this paradox, it turns out, depends on the definition of capital. U.S. exports aren't intensive in *physical* capital—machines and buildings. Instead, they are intensive in *human* capital. U.S. exporting industries use a substantially higher ratio of highly educated workers to other workers than is found in U.S. industries that compete against imports. For example, one of America's biggest export sectors is aircraft; the aircraft industry employs large numbers of engineers and other people with graduate degrees relative to the number of manual laborers. Conversely, we import a lot of clothing, which is often produced by workers with little formal education. ■

< < < < < < < < < < < < < < < < <

>>CHECK YOUR UNDERSTANDING 17-1

1. In the United States, the opportunity cost of 1 ton of corn is 50 bicycles. In China, the opportunity cost of 1 bicycle is 0.01 ton of corn.
   a. Determine the pattern of comparative advantage.
   b. In autarky, the United States can produce 200,000 bicycles if no corn is produced, and China can produce 3,000 tons of corn if no bicycles are produced. Draw each country's production possibility frontier assuming constant opportunity cost, with tons of corn on the vertical axis and bicycles on the horizontal axis.
   c. With trade, each country specializes its production. The United States consumes 1,000 tons of corn and 200,000 bicycles; China consumes 3,000 tons of corn and 100,000 bicycles. Indicate the production and consumption points on your diagrams, and use them to explain the gains from trade.

2. Explain the following patterns of trade using the Heckscher–Ohlin model:
   a. France exports wine to the United States, and the United States exports movies to France.
   b. Brazil exports shoes to the United States, and the United States exports shoe-making machinery to Brazil.

Solutions appear at back of book.

Supply, Demand, and International Trade

Simple models of comparative advantage are helpful for understanding the fundamental causes of international trade. However, to analyze the effects of international trade at a more detailed level and to understand trade policy, it helps to return to the supply and demand model. We'll start by looking at the effects of imports on domestic producers and consumers, then turn to the effect of exports.

The Effects of Imports

Figure 17-4 shows the U.S. market for roses, ignoring international trade for a moment. It introduces a few new concepts: the *domestic demand curve,* the *domestic supply curve,* and the domestic or autarky price.

The **domestic demand curve** shows how the quantity of a good demanded by residents of a country depends on the price of that good. Why "domestic"? Because people living in other countries may demand the good, too. Once we introduce international trade, we need to distinguish between purchases of a good by domestic consumers and purchases by foreign consumers. So the domestic demand curve reflects only the demand of residents of our own country. Similarly, the **domestic supply curve** shows how the quantity of a good supplied by producers inside a country depends on the price of that good. Once we introduce international trade, we need to distinguish between the supply of domestic producers and foreign supply—supply brought in from abroad.

In autarky, with no international trade in roses, the equilibrium in this market would be determined by the intersection of the domestic demand and domestic supply curves, point A. The equilibrium price of roses would be P_A, and the equilibrium quantity of roses produced and consumed would be Q_A. As always, both consumers and producers would gain from the existence of the domestic market. Consumer surplus would be equal to the area of the upper shaded triangle in Figure 17-4. Producer surplus would be equal to the area of the lower shaded triangle. And total surplus would be equal to the sum of these two shaded triangles.

Now let's imagine opening up this market to imports. To do this, we must make some assumption about the supply of imports. The simplest assumption, which we will adopt here, is that unlimited quantities of roses can be purchased from abroad at a fixed price, known as the **world price** of roses. Figure 17-5 on page 416 shows a situation in which the world price of roses, P_W, is lower than the price of roses that would prevail in the domestic market in autarky, P_A.

Given the world price of roses is below the domestic price of roses, it is profitable for importers to buy roses abroad and resell them domestically. The imported roses increase the supply of roses to the domestic market, driving down the domestic market price. Roses will continue to be imported until the domestic price falls to a level equal to the world price.

The result is shown in Figure 17-5. Because of imports, the domestic price of roses falls from P_A to P_W. The quantity of roses demanded by domestic consumers rises from Q_A to C_T, and the quantity supplied by domestic producers falls from Q_A to Q_T.

> The **domestic demand curve** shows how the quantity of a good demanded by domestic consumers depends on the price of that good.
>
> The **domestic supply curve** shows how the quantity of a good supplied by domestic producers depends on the price of that good.

> The **world price** of a good is the price at which that good can be bought or sold abroad.

Figure 17-4

Consumer and Producer Surplus in Autarky

In the absence of trade, domestic price is P_A, the price at which the domestic supply curve and the domestic demand curve intersect. The quantity produced and consumed domestically is Q_A. Consumer surplus is represented by the blue-shaded area, and producer surplus is represented by the red-shaded area.

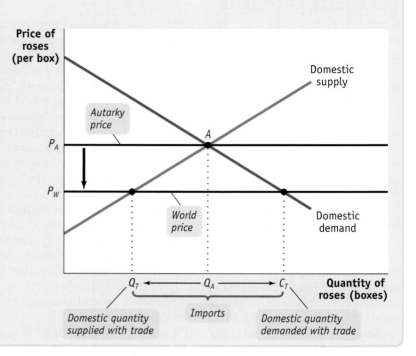

Figure 17-5

The Domestic Market with Imports

Here the world price of roses, P_W, is below the autarky price, P_A. When the economy is opened to international trade, imports enter the domestic market, and the domestic price, P_A, falls to the world price, P_W. As the price falls, the domestic quantity demanded rises from Q_A to C_T and domestic production falls from Q_A to Q_T. The difference between domestic quantity demanded and domestic quantity supplied at P_W, the quantity $C_T - Q_T$, is filled by imports.

The difference between the domestic quantity demanded and the domestic quantity supplied, $C_T - Q_T$, is filled by imports.

Now let's turn to the effects of imports on consumer surplus and producer surplus. Because imports of roses lead to a fall in their domestic price, consumer surplus rises and producer surplus falls. Figure 17-6 shows how this works. We label four areas: W,

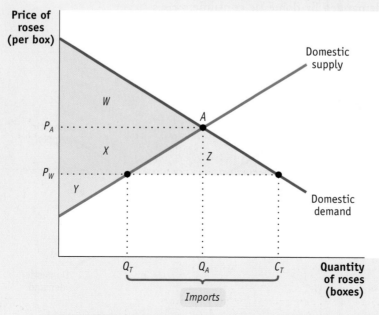

Figure 17-6 **The Effects of Imports on Surplus**

	Changes in surplus	
	Gain	**Loss**
Consumer surplus	$X + Z$	
Producer surplus		$-X$
Change in total surplus	**$+Z$**	

When the domestic price falls to P_W as a result of international trade, consumers gain additional surplus (areas $X + Z$) and producers lose surplus (area X). Because the gains to consumers outweigh the losses to producers, there is an increase in the total surplus in the economy as a whole (area Z).

X, Y, and Z. The autarky consumer surplus we identified in Figure 17-4 corresponds to W, and the autarky producer surplus corresponds to the sum of X and Y. The fall in the domestic price to the world price leads to an increase in consumer surplus; it increases by the areas X and Z, so that it now equals the sum of W, X, and Z. At the same time, producers lose the area X in surplus, so that producer surplus now equals only Y.

The table in Figure 17-6 summarizes the changes in consumer and producer surplus when the rose market is opened to imports. Consumers gain surplus equal to the area $X + Z$. Producers lose surplus equal to the area X. So the sum of producer and consumer surplus—the total surplus generated in the rose market—increases by the area Z. As a result of trade, consumers gain and producers lose, but the gain to consumers exceeds the loss to producers.

This is an important result. We have just shown that opening up a market to imports leads to a net gain in total surplus, which is what we should have expected given the proposition that there are gains from international trade. However, we have also learned that although the country as a whole gains, some groups—in this case, domestic producers of roses—lose as a result of international trade. As we'll see shortly, the fact that international trade typically creates losers as well as winners is crucial for understanding the politics of trade policy.

We turn next to the case in which a country exports a good.

The Effects of Exports

Figure 17-7 shows the effects on a country when it exports a good, in this case computers. For this example, we assume that unlimited quantities of computers can be sold abroad at a given world price, P_W, which is higher than the price that would prevail in the domestic market in autarky, P_A.

The higher world price makes it profitable for exporters to buy computers domestically and sell them overseas. The purchases of domestic computers drives the domestic price up until the domestic price is equal to the world price. As a result, the quantity demanded by domestic consumers falls from Q_A to C_T, and the quantity supplied by domestic producers rises from Q_A to Q_T. This difference between domestic production and domestic consumption, $Q_T - C_T$, is exported.

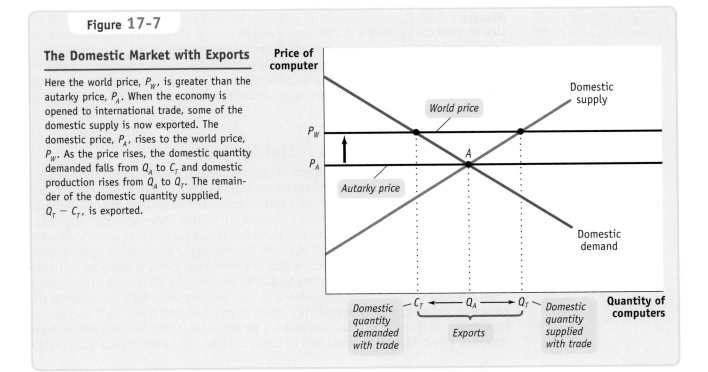

Figure 17-7

The Domestic Market with Exports

Here the world price, P_W, is greater than the autarky price, P_A. When the economy is opened to international trade, some of the domestic supply is now exported. The domestic price, P_A, rises to the world price, P_W. As the price rises, the domestic quantity demanded falls from Q_A to C_T and domestic production rises from Q_A to Q_T. The remainder of the domestic quantity supplied, $Q_T - C_T$, is exported.

Figure 17-8   The Effect of Exports on Surplus

	Changes in surplus	
	Gain	**Loss**
Consumer surplus		$-X$
Producer surplus	$X + Z$	
Change in total surplus	**+Z**	

When the domestic price rises to P_W as a result of trade, producers gain additional surplus (areas $X + Z$) but consumers lose surplus (area X). Because the gains to producers outweigh the losses to consumers, there is an increase in the total surplus in the economy as a whole (area Z).

Like imports, exports lead to an overall gain in total surplus for the exporting country, but also create losers as well as winners. Figure 17-8 shows the effects of computer exports on producer and consumer surplus. In the absence of trade, the price of computers would be P_A. Consumer surplus in the absence of trade is the sum of the areas W and X, and producer surplus would be the area Y. As a result of trade, price rises from P_A to P_W, consumer surplus falls to W, and producer surplus rises to $Y + X + Z$. So producers gain $X + Z$, consumers lose X, and, as shown in the table accompanying the figure, the economy as a whole gains total surplus in the amount of Z.

We have learned, then, that imports of a particular good hurt domestic producers of that good but help domestic consumers, whereas exports of a particular good hurt domestic consumers but help domestic producers of that good. In each case, the gains are larger than the losses.

International Trade and Factor Markets

So far we have focused on the effects of international trade on producers and consumers in a particular industry. For many purposes this is a very helpful approach. But to understand the long-run effects of international trade on income distribution, this approach can be inadequate, because factors of production move between industries.

To see the problem, consider the position of Maria, a trained accountant who currently works for a U.S. company that grows flowers. If the economy is opened up to imports of roses from South America, the domestic rose-growing industry will contract, and it will hire fewer accountants. But accounting is a profession with employment opportunities in many industries, and Maria might well find a better job in the computer industry, which expands as a result of international trade. So it may not be appropriate to think of her as a producer of flowers who is hurt by competition from imported roses. Rather, what matters to her is the effect of international trade on the salaries of accountants, wherever they are employed. In other words, sometimes it is important to analyze the effect of trade on *factor prices*.

Earlier in this chapter we described the Heckscher–Ohlin model of trade, which states that comparative advantage is determined by a country's factor endowment. This model also suggests how international trade affects factor prices in a country: compared to autarky, international trade tends to raise the prices of factors that are abundantly available and reduce the prices of factors that are scarce.

We won't work this out in detail, but the idea is intuitively simple. Think of a country's industries as consisting of two kinds: **exporting industries,** which produce goods and services that are sold abroad, and **import-competing industries,** which produce goods and services that are also imported. Compared with autarky, international trade leads to higher production in exporting industries and lower production in import-competing industries. This indirectly increases the demand for the factors used by exporting industries and decreases the demand for factors used by import-competing industries. In addition, the Heckscher–Ohlin model says that a country tends to export goods that are intensive in its abundant factors and to import goods that are intensive in its scarce factors. *So international trade tends to increase the demand for factors that are abundant in our country compared with other countries, and to decrease the demand for factors that are scarce in our country compared with other countries. As a result, the prices of abundant factors tend to rise, and the prices of scarce factors tend to fall.*

> **Exporting industries** produce goods and services that are sold abroad.
>
> **Import-competing industries** produce goods and services that are also imported.

The Economics in Action on page 414 pointed out that U.S. exports tend to be human-capital-intensive and U.S. imports tend to be unskilled-labor-intensive. This suggests that the effect of international trade on U.S. factor markets is to raise the wage rate of highly educated workers and to reduce the wage rate of unskilled workers.

This effect has been a source of some concern in recent years. Wage inequality—the gap between the wages of highly paid and low-paid workers—has increased substantially over the last 25 years. Some economists believe that growing international trade is an important factor in that trend. If international trade has the effects predicted by the Heckscher–Ohlin model, it raises the wages of highly educated workers, who already have relatively high wages, and lowers the wages of less educated workers, who already have relatively low wages.

How important are these effects? In some historical episodes, the impacts of international trade on factor prices have been very large. As we explain in the Economics in Action that follows, the opening of transatlantic trade in the late nineteenth century had a large negative impact on land rents in Europe, hurting landowners but helping workers and owners of capital. The effects of trade on wages in the United States have generated considerable controversy in recent years. Most economists who have studied the issue agree that growing imports of labor-intensive products from newly industrializing economies, and the export of high-technology goods in return, have helped cause a widening wage differential between highly educated and less educated workers in this country. However, other forces, especially technological change, are probably more important in explaining growing wage inequality.

economics in action

Trade, Wages, and Land Prices in the Nineteenth Century

Beginning around 1870, there was an explosive growth of world trade in agricultural products, based largely on the steam engine. Steam-powered ships could cross the ocean much more quickly and reliably than sailing ships. Until about 1860, steamships had higher costs than sailing ships, but after that rates dropped sharply. At the same time, steam-powered rail transport made it possible to bring grain and other bulk goods cheaply from the interior to ports. The result was that land-abundant countries—the United States, Canada, Argentina, Australia—began shipping large quantities of agricultural goods to the densely populated, land-scarce countries of Europe.

An economy has **free trade** when the government does not attempt either to reduce or to increase the levels of exports and imports that occur naturally as a result of supply and demand.

Policies that limit imports are known as **trade protection** or simply as **protection.**

A **tariff** is a tax levied on imports.

This opening up of international trade led to higher prices of agricultural products, such as wheat, in exporting countries and a decline in their prices in importing countries. Notably, the difference between wheat prices in the midwestern United States and England plunged.

The change in agricultural prices created both winners and losers on both sides of the Atlantic as factor prices adjusted. In England, land prices fell by half compared with average wages; landowners found their purchasing power sharply reduced, but workers benefited from cheaper food. In the United States, the reverse happened: land prices doubled compared with wages. Landowners did very well, but workers found the purchasing power of their wages dented by rising food prices. ∎

< < < < < < < < < < < < < < < < < <

>> CHECK YOUR UNDERSTANDING 17-2

1. Due to a strike by truckers, trade in food between the United States and Mexico is halted. In autarky, the price of Mexican grapes is lower than that of U.S grapes. Using a diagram of the U.S. domestic demand curve and the U.S domestic supply curve for American grapes, explain the effect of these events on the following:
   a. U.S grape consumers' surplus
   b. U.S grape producers' surplus
   c. U.S total surplus

2. What effect do you think these events have on Mexican grape producers? Mexican grape pickers? Mexican grape consumers? U.S. grape pickers?

Solutions appear at back of book.

The Effects of Trade Protection

Ever since David Ricardo laid out the principle of comparative advantage in the early nineteenth century, most economists have advocated **free trade.** That is, they have argued that government policy should not attempt either to reduce or to increase the levels of exports and imports that occur naturally as a result of supply and demand. Despite the free-trade arguments of economists, however, many governments use taxes and other restrictions to limit imports. Much less frequently, governments offer subsidies to encourage exports. Policies that limit imports, usually with the goal of protecting domestic producers in import-competing industries from foreign competition, are known as **trade protection** or simply as **protection.**

Let's look at the two most common protectionist policies, tariffs and import quotas, then turn to the reasons governments follow these policies.

The Effects of a Tariff

A **tariff** is a form of excise tax, one that is levied only on sales of imported goods. For example, the U.S. government could declare that anyone bringing in roses from Colombia must pay a tariff of $2 per rose, or $200 per box of 100 roses. In the distant past, tariffs were an important source of government revenue because they were relatively easy to collect. But in the modern world, tariffs are usually intended to discourage imports and protect import-competing domestic producers rather than as a source of government revenue.

The effect of a tariff is to raise both the price received by domestic producers and the price paid by domestic consumers. Suppose, for example, that our country imports roses, and a box of 100 roses is available on the world market at $400. As we saw earlier, under free trade the domestic price would also be $400. But if a tariff of $200 per box is imposed, the domestic price will rise to $600, and it won't be profitable to import roses unless the price in the domestic market is high enough to compensate importers for the cost of paying the tariff.

Figure 17-9 illustrates the effects of a tariff on rose imports. As before, we assume that P_W is the world price of roses. Before the tariff is imposed, imports have driven the domestic price down to P_W, so that pre-tariff domestic production is Q_1, pre-tariff domestic consumption is C_1, and pre-tariff imports are $C_1 - Q_1$.

Now suppose that the government imposes a tariff on each box of roses imported. As a consequence, it is no longer profitable to import roses unless the domestic price

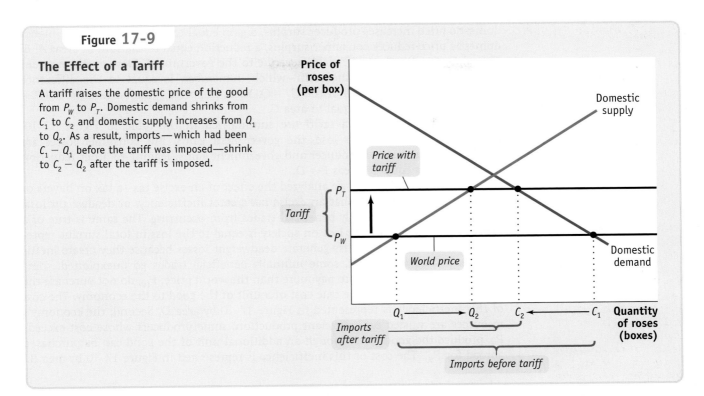

Figure 17-9

The Effect of a Tariff

A tariff raises the domestic price of the good from P_W to P_T. Domestic demand shrinks from C_1 to C_2 and domestic supply increases from Q_1 to Q_2. As a result, imports—which had been $C_1 - Q_1$ before the tariff was imposed—shrink to $C_2 - Q_2$ after the tariff is imposed.

received by the importer is greater than or equal to the world price *plus* the tariff. So the domestic price rises to P_T, which is equal to the world price, P_W, plus the tariff. Domestic production rises to Q_2, domestic consumption falls to C_2, and imports fall to $C_2 - Q_2$.

A tariff, then, raises domestic prices, and leads to increased domestic production and reduced domestic consumption compared to the situation under free trade. Figure 17-10 shows the effects on surplus. There are three effects. First, the higher

Figure 17-10   A Tariff Reduces Total Surplus

	Changes in surplus	
	Gain	**Loss**
Consumer surplus		$-(A + B + C + D)$
Producer surplus	A	
Government revenue	C	
Change in total surplus		$-(B + D)$

When the domestic price rises as a result of a tariff, producers gain additional surplus (area A), the government gains revenue (area C), and consumers lose surplus (areas $A + B + C + D$). Because the losses to consumers outweigh the gains to producers and the government, the economy as a whole loses surplus (areas B + D).

domestic price increases producer surplus, a gain equal to area *A*. Second, the higher domestic price reduces consumer surplus, a reduction equal to the sum of areas *A*, *B*, *C*, and *D*. Finally, the tariff yields revenue to the government. How much revenue? The government collects the tariff—which, remember, is equal to the difference between P_T and P_W on each of the $C_2 - Q_2$ roses imported. So total revenue is $(P_T - P_W) \times (C_2 - Q_2)$. This is equal to area *C*.

The welfare effects of a tariff are summarized in the table in Figure 17-10. Producers gain, consumers lose, the government gains. But consumer losses are greater than the sum of producer and government gains, leading to a net reduction in total surplus equal to areas *B* + *D*.

Recall that in Chapter 4 we analyzed the effect of an excise tax—a tax on buyers or sellers of a good. We saw that an excise tax creates inefficiency, or deadweight loss, because it prevents mutually beneficial trades from occurring. The same is true of a tariff, where its deadweight loss on society is equal to the loss in total surplus represented by areas *B* + *D*. Tariffs generate deadweight losses because they create inefficiencies in two ways. First, some mutually beneficial trades go unexploited: some consumers who are willing to pay more than the world price, P_W, do not purchase the good, even though P_W is the true cost of a unit of the good to the economy. The cost of this inefficiency is represented in Figure 17-10 by area *D*. Second, the economy's resources are wasted on inefficient production: some producers whose cost exceeds P_W produce the good, even though an additional unit of the good can be purchased abroad for P_W. The cost of this inefficiency is represented in Figure 17-10 by area *B*.

The Effects of an Import Quota

An **import quota** is a legal limit on the quantity of a good that can be imported.

An **import quota,** another form of trade protection, is a legal limit on the quantity of a good that can be imported. For example, a U.S. import quota on Colombian roses might limit the number imported each year to 50 million. Import quotas are usually administered through licenses: a number of licenses are issued, each giving the license-holder the right to import a limited quantity of the good each year.

We discussed quotas in Chapter 4, where we saw that a quota on sales has the same effect as an excise tax, with one difference: the money that would otherwise have accrued to the government as tax revenue under an excise tax becomes quota rents to license-holders under a quota. Similarly, an import quota has the same effect as a tariff, with one difference: the money that would otherwise have been government revenue becomes quota rents to license-holders. Look again at Figure 17-10. An import quota that limits imports to $C_2 - Q_2$ will raise the domestic price of roses by the same amount as the tariff we considered previously. That is, it will raise the domestic price from P_W to P_T. However, area *C* will now represent quota rents rather than government revenue.

Who receives import licenses and so collects the quota rents? In the case of U.S. import protection, the answer may surprise you: the most important import licenses—mainly for clothing, to a lesser extent for sugar—are granted to foreign governments.

Because the quota rents for most U.S. import quotas go to foreigners, the cost to the nation of such quotas is larger than that of a comparable tariff (a tariff that leads to the same level of imports). In Figure 17-10 the net loss to the United States from such an import quota would be equal to *B* + *C* + *D*, the difference between consumer losses and producer gains.

economics in action

Trade Protection in the United States

The United States today generally follows a policy of free trade, at least in comparison with other countries and also in comparison with its own past. Most manufactured goods are subject either to no tariff or to a low tariff. However, there are two areas in which the United States does significantly limit imports.

One is agriculture. The typical U.S. policy here is something called a "tariff quota." A certain amount of the imports are subject to a low tariff rate; this acts like an import quota because an importer is allowed to pay the low rate only if she has a license. Any additional imports are subject to a much higher tariff rate. We have tariff quotas on beef, dairy products, sugar, peanuts, and other things. For Inquiring Minds on page 424 discusses the sugar quota in the context of worldwide sugar policy.

The other area in which the United States significantly limits imports is clothing and textiles, where the government applies an elaborate system of import quotas.

The peculiar thing about U.S. trade protection is that in most cases quota licenses are assigned to foreigners, often foreign governments. For example, rights to sell clothing in the United States are allotted to various exporting countries, which can then hand those rights out as they see fit. This means that the quota rents go overseas, greatly increasing the cost to the United States of the import limitations. In fact, according to some estimates, about 70 percent of the total cost of U.S. import restrictions comes not from deadweight loss but from the transfer of quota rents to foreigners. ■

> >

>>CHECK YOUR UNDERSTANDING 17-3

1. Suppose that the world price of butter is $0.50 per pound and the domestic price in autarky is $1.00 per pound. Use a diagram similar to Figure 17-9 to show the following:
   a. If there is free trade, domestic butter producers want the government to impose a tariff of no less than $0.50 per pound.
   b. What happens if a tariff greater than $0.50 per pound is imposed.

2. Suppose the government imposes an import quota rather than a tariff on butter. What quota limit would generate the same quantity of imports as a tariff of $0.50 per pound?

Solutions appear at back of book.

The Political Economy of Trade Protection

We have seen that international trade produces mutual benefits to the countries that engage in it. We have also seen that tariffs and import quotas, although they produce winners as well as losers, reduce total surplus. Yet many countries continue to impose tariffs and import quotas, and to enact other protectionist measures.

To understand why trade protection takes place, we will first look at some common justifications for protection. Then we will look at the politics of trade protection. Finally, we will look at an important feature of trade protection in today's world: tariffs and import quotas are the subject of international negotiation and are policed by international organizations.

Arguments for Trade Protection

Advocates of tariffs and import quotas offer a variety of arguments. Three common arguments are *national security*, *job creation*, and the *infant industry argument*.

The national security argument is based on the proposition that overseas sources of goods are vulnerable to disruption in times of international conflict; therefore a country should protect domestic suppliers of crucial goods with the aim to be self-sufficient in those goods. In the 1960s, the United States—which had begun to import oil as domestic oil reserves ran low—had an import quota on oil, justified on national

>> QUICK REVIEW

➤ Most economists advocate *free trade*, although many governments engage in *trade protection* of import-competing industries. The two most common protectionist policies are tariffs and import quotas. In rare instances, governments subsidize export industries.

➤ A *tariff* is a tax on imports. It raises the domestic price above the world price, leading to a fall in trade and total consumption and a rise in domestic production. Domestic producers and the government gain, but consumer losses more than offset this gain, leading to deadweight loss in total surplus.

➤ An *import quota* is a legal quantity limit on imports. Its effect is like that of a tariff, except that revenues—the quota rents—accrue to the license-holder, not to the government.

FOR INQUIRING MINDS

BITTERSWEET

If there's one good in which we can be absolutely sure that neither the European Union nor the United States has a comparative advantage, it's sugar. The cheapest way to produce sugar is by growing sugar cane, a crop that requires a tropical climate. A few places in the United States can grow cane sugar (basically along the Gulf of Mexico and in Hawaii), but they are no match for the sugar-growing capacity of genuinely tropical countries. And it's almost impossible to grow sugar cane in Western Europe.

Yet Europe is a net *exporter* of sugar, and the United States imports only a fraction of its consumption. How is this possible, and why does it happen?

It's possible because there is another less efficient way to produce sugar: sugar beets can survive even in cold climates. On both sides of the Atlantic, sugar producers receive huge amounts of government support. In the United States, an import quota keeps prices on average at twice world levels. In Europe, import restrictions are supplemented by huge government subsidies to farmers.

What's the rationale for this trade protection? Governments hardly even bother to make excuses: on both sides of the Atlantic, there's a powerful farm lobby. In fact, agriculture in industrial countries is heavily subsidized, at the expense of both consumers and taxpayers.

The really sad thing is that some of the protected goods—sugar in particular—would be major exports of poor countries (and major sources of income for their poor farmers) if it weren't for the import quotas and subsidies in advanced countries.

security grounds. Some people have argued that we should again have policies to discourage imports of oil, especially from the Middle East.

The job creation argument points to the additional jobs created in import-competing industries as a result of trade protection. Economists argue that these jobs are offset by the jobs lost elsewhere, such as industries that use imported inputs and now face higher input costs. But noneconomists don't always find this argument persuasive.

Finally, the infant industry argument, often raised in newly industrializing countries, holds that new industries require a temporary period of trade protection to get established. For example, in the 1950s many countries in Latin America imposed tariffs and import quotas on manufactured goods, in an effort to switch from their traditional role as exporters of raw materials to a new status as industrial countries.

The Politics of Trade Protection

In reality, much trade protection has little to do with the arguments just described. Instead, it reflects the political influence of import-competing producers.

We've seen that a tariff or import quota leads to gains for import-competing producers and losses for consumers. Producers, however, usually have much more influence over trade policy decisions. The producers who compete with imports of a particular good are usually a smaller, more cohesive group than the consumers of that good.

An example is trade protection for sugar, discussed in For Inquiring Minds above. The United States has an import quota on sugar, which on average leads to a domestic price about twice the world price. This quota is difficult to rationalize in terms of any economic argument. However, consumers rarely complain about the quota because they are unaware that it exists: Because no individual consumer buys large amounts of sugar, the cost of the quota is only a few dollars per family each year, not enough to attract notice. But there are only a few thousand sugar growers in the United States. They are very aware of the benefits they receive from the quota and make sure that their representatives in Congress are aware of their interest in the matter.

Given these political realities, it may seem surprising that trade is as free as it is. As explained in Economics in Action on page 425, the United States has low tariffs, and its import quotas are mainly confined to clothing and a few agricultural products. It would be nice to say that the main reason trade protection is so limited is that economists have convinced governments of the virtues of free trade. A more important reason, however, is the role of *international trade agreements*.

International Trade Agreements and the World Trade Organization

When a country engages in trade protection, it hurts two groups. We've already emphasized the adverse effect on domestic consumers, but protection also hurts foreign export industries. This means that countries care about each others' trade policies: the Canadian lumber industry has a strong interest in keeping U.S. tariffs on forest products low.

Because countries care about each others' trade policies, they engage in **international trade agreements:** treaties in which a country promises to engage in less trade protection against the exports of another country in return for a promise by the other country to do the same for its exports. Most world trade is now governed by such agreements.

Some international trade agreements involve just two countries or a small group of countries. In 1993, the U.S. Congress approved the North American Free Trade Agreement (NAFTA) between the United States, Canada, and Mexico. Once fully implemented, this agreement will remove all barriers to trade among the three nations. Free trade has already been implemented among the 25 nations of the European Union.

There are also global trade agreements, covering most of the world. Such global agreements are overseen by the **World Trade Organization,** or WTO, which plays two roles. First, it provides the framework for the massively complex negotiations involved in a major international trade agreement (the full text of the last major agreement, approved in 1994, was 24,000 pages long). Second, the WTO resolves disputes between members. These disputes typically arise when one country claims that another country's policies violate its previous agreements.

Here are two examples that illustrate the WTO's role. First, in 1999 the WTO ruled that the European Union's import restrictions on bananas, which discriminate in favor of producers in former European colonies and against Central American producers, are in violation of international trade rules. The banana dispute had threatened to become a major source of conflict between the European Union and the United States because the United States has taken the side of the Central American countries. Europe is currently in the process of revising its system. In 2002 the United States was on the losing side of a WTO decision: the European Union complained that a provision in U.S. tax law, intended to help exporting companies, is in effect an export subsidy—which is not allowed according to international agreements. The WTO ruled in Europe's favor and the United States is now obliged to revise its tax law.

The WTO is sometimes, with great exaggeration, described as a world government. In fact, it has no army, no police, and no direct enforcement power. The grain of truth in that description is that when a country joins the WTO, it agrees to accept the organization's judgments—and these judgments apply not only to tariffs and import quotas but also to domestic policies that, according to the organization, are in effect trade protection under another name. So in joining the WTO a country does give up a bit of its sovereignty.

> **International trade agreements** are treaties in which a country promises to engage in less trade protection against the exports of other countries in return for a promise by other countries to do the same for its own exports.

> The **World Trade Organization** oversees international trade agreements and rules on disputes between countries over those agreements.

economics in action

Declining Tariffs

The United States began basing its trade policy on international agreements in the 1930s, and global trade negotiations began soon after World War II. The success of these agreements in reducing trade protection is illustrated by Figure 17-11 on page 426 which shows the average U.S. tariff rate on imports subject to tariffs since the 1920s.

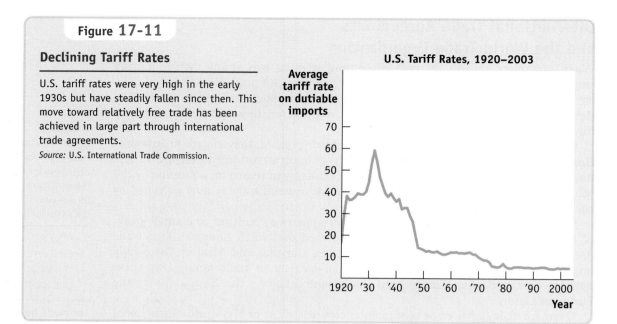

Figure 17-11

Declining Tariff Rates

U.S. tariff rates were very high in the early 1930s but have steadily fallen since then. This move toward relatively free trade has been achieved in large part through international trade agreements.

Source: U.S. International Trade Commission.

U.S. Tariff Rates, 1920–2003

>>QUICK REVIEW

➤ The three major justifications for trade protection are national security, job creation, and protection of infant industries.

➤ Despite the deadweight losses, import protections are often imposed because groups representing import-competing industries are smaller and more cohesive, and therefore more influential, than groups of consumers.

➤ To further trade liberalization, countries engage in *international trade agreements*. Some agreements are for only a small number of countries, such as the North American Free Trade Agreement. The *World Trade Organization* (WTO) is a multinational organization that seeks to negotiate global trade agreements as well as adjudicate trade disputes between members.

Tariffs reached a peak in the early 1930s after the passage of a very protectionist bill, known as the Smoot-Hawley tariff, in 1930. (Some people blame Smoot-Hawley for causing the Great Depression of the 1930s, though few economists think it was *that* bad.) From then on, tariff rates have steadily ratcheted down, with U.S. moves matched in other advanced countries, and later in many poorer countries as well.

At this point world trade in manufactured goods is subject to low tariffs and relatively few import quotas, with clothing the main exception. Agricultural products are subject to many more restrictions, reflecting the political power of farmers in advanced countries. ∎

< < < < < < < < < < < < < < < < < <

>>CHECK YOUR UNDERSTANDING 17-4

1. In 2002 the U.S. imposed tariffs on steel imports, which are an input in a large number and variety of U.S. industries. Explain why political lobbying to eliminate these tariffs is more likely to be effective than political lobbying to eliminate tariffs on consumer goods such as sugar or clothing.

2. Over the years, the WTO has increasingly found itself adjudicating trade disputes that involve not just tariffs or quota restrictions but also restrictions based on quality, health, and environmental considerations. Why do you think this has occurred? What method would you, as a WTO official, use to decide whether a quality, health, or environmental restriction is in violation of a free-trade agreement?

Solutions appear at back of book.

• A LOOK AHEAD •

As we move ahead to new topics, it is important that we carry with us the insights learned here about the logic of comparative advantage and the gains from international trade. They will provide us with a deeper understanding of what drives the world economy and of the reasons countries differ economically. In addition, the study of international trade teaches us how economic policies can create both winners and losers despite the fact that society as a whole gains, an important consideration in any study of how policies are actually made.

SUMMARY

1. International trade is of growing importance to the United States and of even greater importance to most other countries. International trade, like trade among individuals, arises from comparative advantage: the opportunity cost of producing an additional unit of a good is lower in some countries than in others. Goods and services purchased abroad are **imports;** those sold abroad are **exports.**

2. The **Ricardian model of international trade** assumes that opportunity costs are constant. It shows that there are gains from trade: two countries are better off with trade than in **autarky.**

3. In practice, comparative advantage reflects differences between countries in climate, factor endowments, and technology. The **Heckscher–Ohlin model** shows how differences in factor endowments determine comparative advantage: goods differ in **factor intensity,** and countries tend to export goods that are intensive in the factors they have in abundance.

4. The **domestic demand curve** and the **domestic supply curve** determine the price of a good in autarky. When international trade occurs, the domestic price is driven to equality with the **world price,** the price at which the good may be bought or sold abroad.

5. If the world price is below the autarky price, a good is imported. This leads to an increase in consumer surplus, a fall in producer surplus, and a gain in total surplus. If the world price is above the autarky price, a good is exported. This leads to an increase in producer surplus, a fall in consumer surplus, and a gain in total surplus.

6. International trade leads to expansion in **exporting industries** and contraction in **import-competing industries.** This raises the domestic demand for abundant factors of production, reduces the demand for scarce factors, and so affects factor prices.

7. Most economists advocate **free trade,** but in practice many governments engage in **trade protection.** The two most common forms of **protection** are tariffs and quotas; in rare occasions, export industries are subsidized.

8. A **tariff** is a tax levied on imports. It raises the domestic price above the world price, hurting consumers, benefiting domestic producers, and generating government revenue. As a result, total surplus falls. An **import quota** is a legal limit on the quantity of a good that can be imported. It has the same effects as a tariff, except that the revenue goes not to the government but to those who receive import licenses.

9. Although several popular arguments have been made in favor of trade protection, in practice the main reason for protection is probably political: import-competing industries are well organized and well informed about how they gain from trade protection, while consumers are unaware of the costs they pay. Still, U.S. trade is fairly free, mainly because of the role of **international trade agreements,** in which countries agree to reduce trade protection against each others' exports. Trade negotiations are overseen, and the resulting agreements are enforced, by the **World Trade Organization.**

KEY TERMS

Imports, p. 407
Exports, p. 407
Ricardian model of international trade, p. 409
Autarky, p. 409
Factor intensity, p. 412
Heckscher–Ohlin model, p. 412

Domestic demand curve, p. 415
Domestic supply curve, p. 415
World price, p. 415
Exporting industries, p. 419
Import-competing industries, p. 419
Free trade, p. 420
Trade protection, p. 420

Protection, p. 420
Tariff, p. 420
Import quota, p. 422
International trade agreements, p. 425
World Trade Organization, p. 425

PROBLEMS

1. Assume Saudi Arabia and the United States face the production possibilities for oil and cars shown in the accompanying table.

Saudi Arabia		United States	
Quantity of oil (millions of barrels)	Quantity of cars (millions)	Quantity of oil (millions of barrels)	Quantity of cars (millions)
0	4	0	10.0
200	3	100	7.5
400	2	200	5
600	1	300	2.5
800	0	400	0

a. What is the opportunity cost of producing a car in Saudi Arabia? In the United States? What is the opportunity cost of producing a barrel of oil in Saudi Arabia? In the United States?

b. Which country has the comparative advantage in producing oil? In producing cars?

c. Suppose that in autarky, Saudi Arabia produces 200 million barrels of oil and 3 million cars; and that the United States produces 300 million barrels of oil and 2.5 million cars. Without trade, can Saudi Arabia produce more oil *and* more cars? Without trade, can the United States produce more oil *and* more cars?

2. The production possibilities for the United States and Saudi Arabia are given in Problem 1. Suppose now that each country specializes in the good in which it has the comparative advantage, and the two countries trade. Also assume that for each country the value of imports must equal the value of exports.

a. What is the total quantity of oil produced? What is the total quantity of cars produced?

b. Is it possible for Saudi Arabia to consume 400 million barrels of oil and 5 million cars, and for the United States to consume 400 million barrels of oil and 5 million cars?

c. Suppose that, in fact, Saudi Arabia consumes 300 million barrels of oil and 4 million cars and the United States consumes 500 million barrels of oil and 6 million cars. How many barrels of oil does the United States import? How many cars does the United States export? Suppose a car costs $10,000 on the world market. How much, then, does a barrel of oil cost on the world market?

3. Both Canada and the United States produce lumber and music CDs with constant opportunity costs. The United States can produce either 10 tons of lumber and no CDs, or 1,000 CDs and no lumber, or any combination in between. Canada can produce either 8 tons of lumber and no CDs, or 400 CDs and no lumber, or any combination in between.

a. Draw the U.S. and Canadian production possibility frontiers in two separate diagrams, with CDs on the horizontal axis and lumber on the vertical axis.

b. In autarky, if the United States wants to consume 500 CDs, how much lumber can it consume at most? Label this point A in your diagram. Similarly, if Canada wants to consume 1 ton of lumber, how many CDs can it consume in autarky? Label this point C in your diagram.

c. Which country has the absolute advantage in lumber production?

d. Which country has the comparative advantage in lumber production?

Suppose each country specializes in the good in which it has the comparative advantage, and there is trade.

e. How many CDs does the United States produce? How much lumber does Canada produce?

f. Is it possible for the United States to consume 500 CDs and 7 tons of lumber? Label this point B in your diagram. Is it possible for Canada at the same time to consume 500 CDs and 1 ton of lumber? Label this point D in your diagram.

4. For each of the following trade relationships, explain the likely source of the comparative advantage of each of the exporting countries.

a. The United States exports software to Venezuela, and Venezuela exports oil to the United States.

b. The United States exports airplanes to China, and China exports clothing to the United States.

c. The United States exports wheat to Colombia, and Colombia exports coffee to the United States.

5. Shoes are labor-intensive and satellites are capital-intensive to produce. The United States has abundant capital. China has abundant labor. According to the Heckscher–Ohlin model, which good will China export? Which good will the United States export? In the United States, what will happen to the price of labor (the wage) and to the price of capital?

6. Before the North American Free Trade Agreement (NAFTA) gradually eliminated import tariffs on goods, the autarky price of tomatoes in Mexico was below the world price and in the United States was above the world price. Similarly, the autarky price of poultry in Mexico was above the world price and in the United States was below the world price. Draw diagrams with domestic supply and demand curves for each country and each of the two goods. As a result of NAFTA, the United States now imports tomatoes from Mexico and the United States now exports poultry to Mexico. How would you expect the following groups to be affected?

a. Mexican and U.S. consumers of tomatoes. Illustrate the effect on consumer surplus in your diagram.

b. Mexican and U.S. producers of tomatoes. Illustrate the effect on producer surplus in your diagram.

c. Mexican and U.S. tomato workers.

d. Mexican and U.S. consumers of poultry. Illustrate the effect on consumer surplus in your diagram.

e. Mexican and U.S. producers of poultry. Illustrate the effect on producer surplus in your diagram.

f. Mexican and U.S. poultry workers.

7. The accompanying table indicates the U.S. domestic demand schedule and domestic supply schedule for commercial jet airplanes. Suppose that the world price of a commercial jet airplane is $100 million.

Price of jet (millions)	Quantity of jets demanded	Quantity of jets supplied
$120	100	1,000
110	150	900
100	200	800
90	250	700
80	300	600
70	350	500
60	400	400
50	450	300
40	500	200

a. In autarky, how many commercial jet airplanes does the United States produce, and at what price are they bought and sold?

b. With trade, what will the price for commercial jet airplanes be? Will the United States import or export airplanes? How many?

8. The accompanying table shows the U.S. domestic demand schedule and domestic supply schedule for oranges. Suppose that the world price of oranges is $0.30 per orange.

Price of orange	Quantity of oranges demanded (thousands)	Quantity of oranges supplied (thousands)
$1.00	2	11
0.90	4	10
0.80	6	9
0.70	8	8
0.60	10	7
0.50	12	6
0.40	14	5
0.30	16	4
0.20	18	3

a. Draw the U.S. domestic supply curve and domestic demand curve.

b. With free trade, how many oranges will the United States import or export?

Suppose that the U.S. government imposes a tariff on oranges of $0.20 per orange.

c. How many oranges will the United States import or export after introduction of the tariff?

d. In your diagram, shade the gain or loss to the economy as a whole from the introduction of this tariff.

9. The U.S. domestic demand schedule and domestic supply schedule for oranges was given in Problem 8. Suppose that the world price of oranges is $0.30. The United States introduces an import quota of 3,000 oranges. Draw the domestic demand and supply curves and answer the following questions.

a. What will the domestic price of oranges be after introduction of the quota?

b. What is the value of the quota rents that importers of oranges receive?

10. The accompanying diagram illustrates the U.S. domestic demand curve and domestic supply curve for beef.

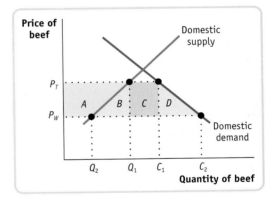

The world price of beef is P_W. The United States currently imposes an import tariff on beef, so the price of beef is P_T. Congress decides to eliminate the tariff. In terms of the areas marked in the diagram, answer the following questions.

a. What is the gain/loss in consumer surplus?

b. What is the gain/loss in producer surplus?

c. What is the gain/loss to the government?

d. What is the gain/loss to the economy as a whole?

11. As the United States has opened up to trade, it has lost many of its low-skill manufacturing jobs, but it has gained jobs in high-skill industries, such as the software industry. Explain whether the United States as a whole has been made better off by trade.

12. The United States is highly protective of its agricultural industry, imposing import tariffs, and sometimes quotas, on imports of agricultural goods. The chapter has presented three arguments for trade protection. For each argument, discuss whether it is a valid justification for trade protection of U.S. agricultural products.

13. In World Trade Organization (WTO) negotiations, if a country agrees to reduce trade barriers (tariffs or quotas), it usually refers to this as a *concession* to other countries. Do you think that this terminology is appropriate?

14. Producers in import-competing industries often make the following argument: "Other countries have an advantage in production of certain goods purely because workers abroad are paid lower wages. In fact, American workers are much more productive than foreign workers. So import-competing industries need to be protected." Is this a valid argument? Explain your answer.

>web... To continue your study and review of concepts in this chapter, please visit the Krugman/Wells website for quizzes, animated graph tutorials, web links to helpful resources, and more.

www.worthpublishers.com/krugmanwells

Uncertainty, Risk, and Private Information

18

AFTER THE FLOOD

IN MARCH 1998 THE FLINT RIVER OVERflowed its banks and flooded the town of Albany, Georgia. It was a catastrophe. The town's residents were especially distraught because many of them had no flood insurance—they had dropped their coverage after a similar flood in 1994 led insurance companies to raise their *premiums*.

The case of Albany's floods reminds us that uncertainty is an important feature of real-world economies. Up to this point, we have assumed that people make decisions with knowledge of exactly how those decisions will affect their welfare. In reality, people often make economic decisions—such as whether to build a house near a river—without full knowledge of their future consequences. As the residents of Albany learned, making decisions when the future is uncertain carries with it the *risk* of loss.

Yet it is often possible for individuals to use markets to reduce the risk they face. The Flint River flood made headlines because it's unusual for so many victims of a disaster to be without insurance. In fact, through insurance and other devices, the modern economy offers many ways for individuals to reduce their exposure to risk.

Does this mean that a market economy can solve all the problems created by uncertainty? Alas, no. Markets do very well at coping with situations in which nobody knows what will happen. But they run into trouble when some people know things that others do not—a situation known as *private information*. We'll see that private information can cause inefficiency by preventing mutually beneficial transactions.

By failing to maintain their flood insurance, these Albany, Georgia, homeowners incurred huge losses in 1998.

What you will learn in this chapter:

➤ That **risk** is an important feature of the economy, and that most people are **risk-averse**—they would like to avoid risk

➤ Why diminishing marginal utility makes people risk-averse and determines the **premium** they are willing to pay to reduce risk

➤ How risk can be traded, with risk-averse people paying others to assume part of their risk

➤ How exposure to risk can be reduced through **diversification** and **pooling**

➤ The special problems posed by **private information**—situations in which some people know things that other people do not

In this chapter we'll examine the economics of risk and private information. We'll start by looking at why people dislike risk. Then we'll explore how a market economy allows people to reduce risk, at a price. Finally, we'll turn to the special problems created when some people have information that others don't.

The Economics of Risk Aversion

In general, people don't like risk and are willing to pay a price to avoid it. Just ask the U.S. insurance industry, which collects more than $1 trillion in premiums every year. But what exactly is risk? And why don't people like it? To answer these questions, we need to look briefly at the concept of *expected value* and the meaning of uncertainty. Then we can turn to why people dislike *risk*.

Expectations and Uncertainty

The Lee family doesn't know how big its medical bills will be next year. If all goes well, it won't have any medical expenses at all. Let's assume that there's a 50 percent chance of that happening. But if family members require hospitalization or expensive drugs, they will face medical expenses of $10,000. Let's assume that there's also a 50 percent chance that these high medical expenses will materialize.

In this example—which is designed to illustrate a point, rather than to be realistic—the Lees' medical expenses for the coming year are a **random variable,** a variable that has an uncertain future value. No one can predict which of its possible values, or outcomes, a random variable will take. But that doesn't mean we can say nothing about the Lees' future medical expenses. On the contrary, an actuary (a person trained in evaluating uncertain future events) could calculate the **expected value** of expenses next year—the weighted average of all possible values, where the weights on each possible value correspond to the probability of that value occurring. In this example, the expected value of the Lees' medical expenses is $(0.5 \times \$0) + (0.5 \times \$10,000) = \$5,000$.

To derive the general formula for the expected value of a random variable, we imagine that there are a number of different **states of the world,** possible future events. Each state is associated with a different realized value—the value that actually occurs—of the random variable. You don't know which state of the world will actually occur, but you can assign probabilities, one for each state of the world. Let's assume that P_1 is the probability of state 1, P_2 the probability of state 2, and so on. And you know the realized value of the random value in each state of the world: S_1 in state 1, S_2 in state 2, and so on. Let's also assume that there are N possible states. Then the expected value of the random variable is:

(18-1) *Expected value of a random variable*
$$EV = (P_1 \times S_1) + (P_2 \times S_2) + \dots + (P_N \times S_N)$$

In the case of the Lee family, there are only two possible states of the world, each with a probability of 0.5.

Notice, however, that the Lee family doesn't actually expect to pay $5,000 in medical bills next year, regardless of what occurs. That's because in this example there is no state of the world in which the family pays exactly $5,000. Either the family pays nothing, or it pays $10,000. So the Lees face considerable uncertainty about their future medical expenses.

But what if the Lee family can buy health insurance that will cover its medical expenses, whatever they turn out to be? Suppose, in particular, that the family can pay $5,000 up front in return for full coverage of whatever medical expenses actually arise during the coming year. Then the Lees' future medical expenses are no longer uncer-

---

A **random variable** is a variable with an uncertain future value.

The **expected value** of a random variable is the weighted average of all possible values, where the weights on each possible value correspond to the probability of that value occurring.

A **state of the world** is a possible future event.

tain *for them*: in return for $5,000—an amount equal to the expected value of the medical expenses—the insurance company assumes all responsibility for paying those medical expenses. Would this be a good deal from the Lees' point of view?

Yes, it would—or at least most families would think so. Most people prefer, other things equal, to reduce **risk**—uncertainty about future outcomes. (We'll focus here on **financial risk,** in which the uncertainty is about monetary outcomes, as opposed to uncertainty about outcomes that can't be assigned a monetary value.) In fact, most people are willing to pay a substantial price to reduce their risk; that's why we have an insurance industry. But before we study the market for insurance, we need to understand why people feel that risk is a bad thing, an attitude that economists call *risk aversion*. The answer, as we'll now see, is a concept we first encountered in our analysis of consumer demand, back in Chapter 10: *diminishing marginal utility*.

> **Risk** is uncertainty about future outcomes. When the uncertainty is about monetary outcomes, it becomes **financial risk**.

The Logic of Risk Aversion

To understand how diminishing marginal utility gives rise to risk aversion, we need to look not only at the Lees' medical costs but also at how those costs affect the income the family has left after medical expenses. Let's assume that the family knows that it will have an income of $30,000 next year. If the family has no medical expenses, it will be left with all of that income. If its medical expenses are $10,000, its income after medical expenses will be only $20,000. Since we have assumed that there is an equal chance of these two outcomes, the expected value of the Lees' income after medical expenses is $(0.5 \times \$30,000) + (0.5 \times \$20,000) = \$25,000$. At times we will simply refer to this as expected income.

But as we'll now see, if the family's utility function has the shape typical of most families', its **expected utility**—the expected value of its total utility given uncertainty about future outcomes—is less than it would be if the family didn't face any risk and knew with certainty that its income after medical expenses would be $25,000.

> **Expected utility** is the expected value of an individual's total utility given uncertainty about future outcomes.

To see why, we need to look at how total utility depends on income. Panel (a) of Figure 18-1 on page 434 shows a hypothetical utility function for the Lee family, where total utility depends on income—the amount of money the Lees have available for consumption of goods and services (after they have paid any medical bills). The table within the figure shows how the family's total utility varies over the income range of $20,000 to $30,000. As usual, the utility function is upward sloping, because more income leads to higher total utility. Notice as well that the curve gets flatter as we move up and to the right, which reflects diminishing marginal utility.

In Chapter 10 we applied the principle of diminishing marginal utility to individual goods and services: each successive unit of a good or service that a consumer purchases adds less to his or her total utility. The same principle applies to income used for consumption: each successive dollar of income adds less to total utility than the previous dollar. Panel (b) shows how marginal utility varies with income, confirming that marginal utility of income falls as income rises. As we'll see in a moment, diminishing marginal utility is the key to understanding the desire of individuals to reduce risk.

To analyze how a person's utility is affected by risk, economists start from the assumption that individuals facing uncertainty maximize their *expected* utility. We can use the data in Figure 18-1 to calculate the Lee family's expected utility. We'll first do the calculation assuming that the Lees have no insurance, and then we'll recalculate it assuming that they have purchased insurance.

Without insurance, if the Lees are lucky and don't incur any medical expenses, they will have an income of $30,000, generating total utility of 1,080 utils. But if they have no insurance and are unlucky, incurring $10,000 in medical expenses, they will have just $20,000 of their income to spend on consumption and total utility of only 920 utils. So *without insurance,* the family's expected utility is $(0.5 \times 1,080) + (0.5 \times 920) = 1,000$ utils.

Now let's suppose that an insurance company offers to pay whatever medical expenses the family incurs during the next year in return for a **premium**—a payment

> A **premium** is a payment to an insurance company in return for the insurance company's promise to pay a claim in certain states of the world.

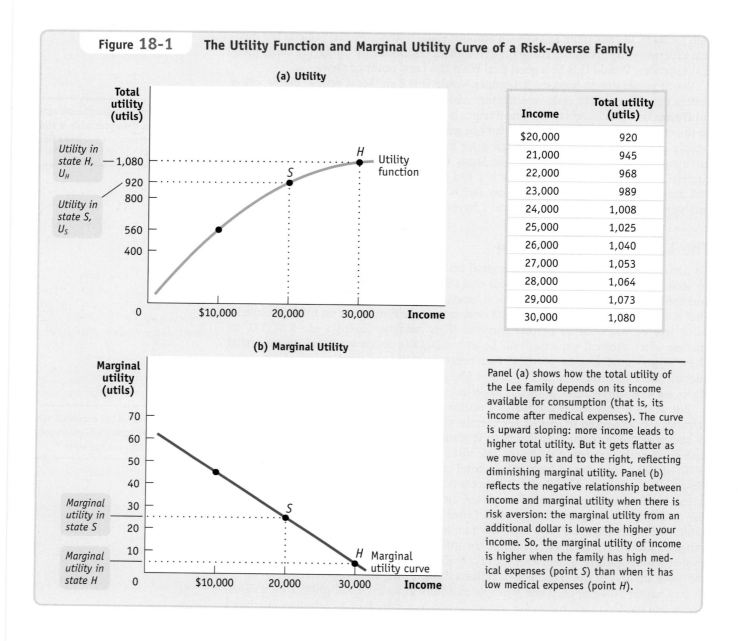

Figure 18-1 **The Utility Function and Marginal Utility Curve of a Risk-Averse Family**

(a) Utility

Income	Total utility (utils)
$20,000	920
21,000	945
22,000	968
23,000	989
24,000	1,008
25,000	1,025
26,000	1,040
27,000	1,053
28,000	1,064
29,000	1,073
30,000	1,080

(b) Marginal Utility

Panel (a) shows how the total utility of the Lee family depends on its income available for consumption (that is, its income after medical expenses). The curve is upward sloping: more income leads to higher total utility. But it gets flatter as we move up it and to the right, reflecting diminishing marginal utility. Panel (b) reflects the negative relationship between income and marginal utility when there is risk aversion: the marginal utility from an additional dollar is lower the higher your income. So, the marginal utility of income is higher when the family has high medical expenses (point S) than when it has low medical expenses (point H).

A fair insurance policy is an insurance policy for which the premium is equal to the expected value of the claim.

---

to the insurance company—of $5,000. Note that the amount of the premium in this case is equal to the expected value of the Lees' medical expenses—the expected value of their future claim against the policy. An insurance policy with this feature, for which the premium is equal to the expected value of the claim, has a special name— a **fair insurance policy.**

If the family purchases this fair insurance policy, the expected value of its income available for consumption is the *same* as it would be without insurance: $25,000— that is, $30,000 minus the $5,000 premium. But the family's risk has been eliminated: the family has an income available for consumption of $25,000 *for sure*, which means that it receives the utility level associated with an income of $25,000. Reading from the table in Figure 18-1, we see that this utility level is 1,025 utils. Or to put it a slightly different way, their expected utility with insurance is $1 \times 1,025 = 1,025$ utils, because with insurance they will receive a utility of 1,025 utils with a probability of 1. And this is higher than the level of expected utility without insurance—only 1,000 utils. So by eliminating risk through the purchase of a fair insurance policy, the family increases its expected utility even though its expected income hasn't changed.

TABLE 18-1

The Effect of Fair Insurance on the Lee Family's Expected Income and Expected Utility

	Income in different states of the world		Expected income	Expected utility
	$0 in medical expenses (0.5 probability)	$10,000 in medical expenses (0.5 probability)		
Without insurance	$30,000	$20,000	(0.5 × $30,000) + (0.5 × $20,000) = $25,000	(0.5 × 1,080 utils) + (0.5 × 920 utils) = 1,000 utils
With fair insurance	$25,000	$25,000	(0.5 × $25,000) + (0.5 × $25,000) = $25,000	(0.5 × 1,025 utils) + (0.5 × 1,025 utils) = 1,025 utils

The calculations for this example are summarized in Table 18-1. This example shows that the Lees, like most people in real life, are **risk-averse:** they will choose to reduce the risk they face when the cost of that reduction leaves the expected value of their income or wealth unchanged. So the Lees, like most people, will be willing to buy fair insurance.

You might think that this result depends on the specific numbers we have chosen. In fact, however, the proposition that purchase of a fair insurance policy increases expected utility depends on only one assumption: diminishing marginal utility. The reason is that *with diminishing marginal utility, a dollar gained when income is low adds more to utility than a dollar lost when income is high.* That is, having an additional dollar matters more when you are facing hard times than when you are facing good times. And as we will shortly see, a fair insurance policy is desirable because it transfers a dollar from high-income states (where it is valued less) to low-income states (where it is valued more).

But first, let's see how diminishing marginal utility leads to risk aversion by examining expected utility more closely. In the case of the Lee family, there are two states of the world; let's call them H and S, for healthy and sick. In state H the family has no medical expenses; in state S it has $10,000 in medical expenses. Let's use the symbols U_H and U_S to represent the Lee family's utility in each state. Then the family's expected utility is

(18-2)   Expected utility = (Probability of healthy state × Total utility in healthy state)
   + (Probability of sick state × Total utility in sick state)
   = $(0.5 \times U_H) + (0.5 \times U_S)$

The fair insurance policy *reduces* the family's income available for consumption in state H by $5,000, but it *increases* it in state S by the same amount. As we've just seen, we can use the utility function to directly calculate the effects of these changes on expected utility. But as we have also seen in many other contexts, we gain more insight into individual choice by focusing on *marginal* utility.

To use marginal utility to analyze the effects of fair insurance, let's imagine introducing the insurance a bit at a time, say in 5,000 small steps. At each of these steps, we reduce income in state H by $1 and simultaneously increase income in state S by $1. At each of these steps, utility in state H falls by the marginal utility of income in that state but utility in state S rises by the marginal utility of income in that state.

Now look again at panel (b) of Figure 18-1, which shows how marginal utility varies with income. Point S shows marginal utility when the Lee family's income is $20,000; point H shows marginal utility when income is $30,000. Clearly, marginal utility is higher when income after medical expenses is low. Because of diminishing marginal utility, an additional dollar of income adds more to utility when the family has low income (point S) than when it has high income (point H).

Risk-averse individuals will choose to reduce the risk they face when that reduction leaves the expected value of their income or wealth unchanged.

This tells us that the gain in expected utility from increasing income in state S is larger than the loss in expected utility from reducing income in state H. So at each step of the process of reducing risk, by transferring $1 of income from state H to state S, expected utility increases. This is the same as saying that the family is risk-averse; that is, risk aversion is a result of diminishing marginal utility.

Almost everyone is risk-averse, because almost everyone has diminishing marginal utility. But the degree of risk aversion varies among individuals—some people are more risk-averse than others. To illustrate this point, Figure 18-2 compares two individuals, Danny and Mel. We suppose that each of them earns the same income now but is confronted with the possibility of earning either $1,000 more or $1,000 less. Panel (a) shows how each individual's total utility would be affected by the change in income. Danny would gain very few utils from a rise in income, which moves him from N to H_D, but lose a large number of utils from a fall in income, which moves him from N to L_D. That is, he is highly risk-averse. This is reflected in the lower part of the figure by his steeply declining marginal utility curve. Mel, though, would gain almost as

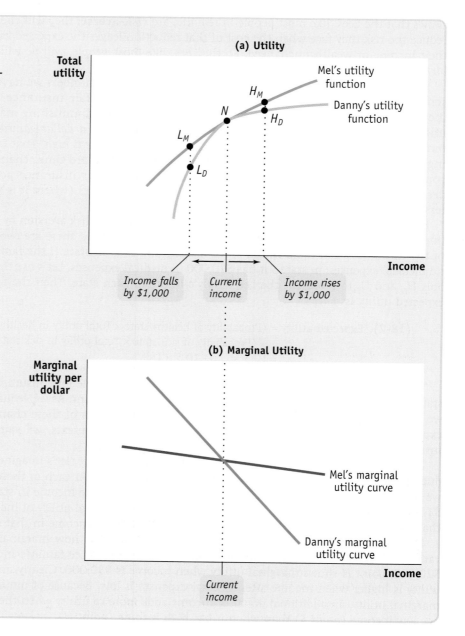

Figure 18-2

Differences in Risk Aversion

Danny and Mel have different utility functions. Danny is highly risk-averse: a gain of $1,000 in income, which moves him from N to H_D, adds only a few utils to his total utility, but a $1,000 fall in income, which moves him from N to L_D, reduces his total utility by a large number of utils. By contrast, Mel gains almost as many utils from a $1,000 rise in income (the movement from N to H_M) as he loses from a $1,000 fall in income (the movement from N to L_M). This difference—reflected in the differing slopes of the two men's marginal utility curves—means that Danny would be willing to pay much more than Mel for insurance.

THE PARADOX OF GAMBLING

If most people are risk-averse and risk-averse individuals won't take a fair gamble, how come Las Vegas, Atlantic City, and other places where gambling is legal do so much business?

After all, a casino doesn't even offer gamblers a fair gamble: all the games in any gambling facility are designed so that, on average, the casino makes money. So why would anyone play their games?

You might argue that the gambling industry caters to the minority of people who are actually the opposite of risk-averse: risk-loving. But a glance at the

James Marshall/Corbis

Gambling: Enjoyment or addiction?

customers of Las Vegas hotels quickly refutes that hypothesis: most of them aren't daredevils who also sky-dive and

hang-glide. Instead, most of them are ordinary people who have health and life insurance and who wear seat belts. In other words, they are risk-averse like the rest of us.

So why do people gamble? Presumably because they enjoy the experience.

Also, gambling may be one of those areas where the assumption of rational behavior goes awry. Psychologists have concluded that gambling can be addictive in ways that are not that different from the addictive effects of drugs. Taking dangerous drugs is irrational; so is excessive gambling. Alas, both happen all the same.

---

many utils from higher income, which moves him from N to H_M, as he would lose from lower income, which moves him from N to L_M. He is barely risk-averse at all. This is reflected in his marginal utility curve, which is almost horizontal. So other things equal, Danny will gain a lot more utility from insurance than Mel will.

Individuals differ in risk aversion for two main reasons: differences in preferences and differences in initial income or wealth.

- *Differences in preferences.* Other things equal, people simply differ in how much their marginal utility is affected by their level of income. Someone whose marginal utility does not depend very much on income won't be highly risk-averse.

- *Differences in initial income or wealth.* The possible loss of $1,000 makes a big difference to a family living below the poverty line; it makes very little difference to someone who earns $1 million a year. In general, people with high incomes or high wealth will be less risk-averse.

Differences in risk aversion have an important consequence: they affect how much an individual is willing to pay to avoid risk.

Paying to Avoid Risk

The risk-averse Lee family is clearly better off taking out a fair insurance policy—a policy that leaves their expected income unchanged but eliminates their risk. Unfortunately, real insurance policies are rarely fair: because insurance companies have to cover other costs, such as salaries for salespeople and actuaries, they charge more than they expect to pay in claims. Will the Lee family still want to purchase an "unfair" insurance policy—one for which the premium is larger than the expected claim?

It depends on the size of the premium. Look again at Table 18-1. We know that without insurance expected utility is 1,000 utils and

PITFALLS

BEFORE THE FACT VERSUS AFTER THE FACT

Why is an insurance policy different from a doughnut?

No, it's not a riddle. Although the supply and demand for insurance behave like the supply and demand for any good or service, the payoff is very different. When you buy a doughnut, you know what you're going to get; when you buy insurance, by definition you *don't* know what you're going to get. If you bought car insurance and then didn't have an accident, you got nothing from the policy, except peace of mind, and might wish that you hadn't bothered. But if you did have an accident, you probably wished that you had bought insurance that covered the cost.

This means we have to be careful in assessing the rationality of insurance purchases (or, for that matter, any decision made in the face of uncertainty). *After the fact*—after the uncertainty has been resolved—such decisions are almost always subject to second-guessing. But that doesn't mean that the decision was wrong *before the fact*, given the information available at the time.

One highly successful Wall Street investor told us that he never looks back—that as long as he believes he made the right decision given what he knew when he made it, he never reproaches himself if things turn out badly. That's the right attitude, and it almost surely contributes to his success.

that insurance costing $5,000 raises expected utility to 1,025 utils. If the premium were $6,000, the Lees would be left with an income of $24,000, which, as you can see from Figure 18-1, would give them a total utility of 1,008 utils—which is still higher than their expected utility if they had no insurance at all. So the Lees would be willing to buy insurance with a $6,000 premium. But they wouldn't be willing to pay $7,000, which would reduce their income to $23,000 and their total utility to 989 utils.

This example shows that risk-averse individuals are willing to make deals that reduce their expected income but also reduce their risk: they are willing to pay a premium that exceeds their expected claim. The more risk-averse they are, the higher the premium they are willing to pay. That willingness to pay is what makes the insurance industry possible.

economics in action

Warranties

Many expensive consumer goods—stereos, major appliances, cars—come with some form of *warranty*. Typically, the manufacturer guarantees to repair or replace the item if something goes wrong with it during some specified period after purchase—usually six months or one year.

Why do manufacturers offer warranties? Part of the answer is that warranties *signal* to consumers that the goods are of high quality (see the discussion of private information later in this chapter). But mainly warranties are a form of consumer insurance. For many people, the cost of repairing or replacing an expensive item like a refrigerator—or, worse yet, a car—would be a serious burden. If they were obliged to come up with the cash, their consumption of other goods would be restricted; as a result, their marginal utility of income would be higher than if they didn't have to pay for repairs.

So a warranty that covers the cost of repair or replacement increases the consumer's expected utility, even if the cost of the warranty is greater than the expected future claim paid by the manufacturer. ■

< < < < < < < < < < < < < < < < < <

>> CHECK YOUR UNDERSTANDING 18-1

1. In which of the following circumstances would you be more likely to buy car insurance?
   a. You must work to pay your living expenses, and you need a car to get to work.
   b. Your parents are wealthy and can easily buy you another car if you need it.

2. Karma's income next year is uncertain: there is a 60% probability she will make $22,000 and a 40% probability she will make $35,000. The accompanying table shows some income and utility levels for Karma:

Income	Total utility (utils)
$22,000	850
25,000	1,014
26,000	1,056
35,000	1,260

   a. What is Karma's expected income? her expected utility?
   b. What certain income level leaves her as well off as her uncertain income? What does this imply about Karma's attitudes toward risk? Explain.
   c. Would Karma be willing to pay some amount of money greater than zero for an insurance policy that guarantees her an income of $26,000? Explain.

Solutions appear at back of book.

Buying, Selling, and Reducing Risk

Lloyd's of London is the oldest existing commercial insurance company, and it is an institution with an illustrious past. Originally formed in the eighteenth century as a commercial venture to help merchants cope with the risks of commerce, it grew in the heyday of the British Empire into a mainstay of imperial trade.

The basic idea of Lloyd's was simple. In the eighteenth century, shipping goods via sailing vessels was risky: the chance that a ship would sink in a storm or be captured by pirates was fairly high. The merchant who owned the ship and its cargo could easily be ruined financially by such an event. Lloyd's matched shipowners seeking insurance with wealthy investors who promised to compensate a merchant if his ship was lost. In return, the merchant paid the investor a fee in advance; if his ship *didn't* sink, the investor still kept the fee. In effect, the merchant paid a price to relieve himself of risk. By matching people who wanted to purchase insurance with people who wanted to provide it, Lloyd's performed the functions of a market. The fact that British merchants could use Lloyd's to reduce their risk made many more people in Britain willing to undertake merchant trade.

Insurance companies have changed quite a lot from the early days of Lloyd's. They no longer consist of wealthy individuals deciding on insurance deals over port and boiled mutton. But asking why Lloyd's worked to the mutual benefit of merchants and investors is a good way to understand how the market economy as a whole "trades" and thereby transforms risk.

The insurance industry rests on two principles. The first is that trade in risk, like trade in any good or service, can produce mutual gains. In this case, the gains come when people who are less willing to bear risk transfer it to people who are more willing to bear it. The second is that some risk can be made to disappear through *diversification*. Let's consider each principle in turn.

Trading Risk

It may seem a bit strange to talk about "trading" risk. After all, risk is a bad thing—and aren't we supposed to be trading goods and services?

But people often trade away things they don't like to other people who dislike them less. Suppose you have just bought a house for $100,000, the average price for a house in your community. But you have now learned, to your horror, that the building next door is being turned into an all-night disco. You want to sell the house immediately and are willing to accept $95,000 for it. But who will now be willing to buy it? The answer: a person who doesn't really mind late-night noise. Such a person might be willing to pay up to $100,000. So there is an opportunity here for a mutually beneficial deal—you are willing to sell for as little as $95,000, and the other person is willing to pay as much as $100,000, so any price in between will benefit both of you.

The key point is that the two parties have different sensitivities to noise, which enables those who most dislike noise, in effect, to pay other people to make their lives quieter. Trading risk works exactly the same way: people who want to reduce the risk they face can pay other people who are less sensitive to risk to take some of their risk away.

As we saw in the previous section, individual preferences account for some of the variations in people's attitudes toward risk, but differences in income and wealth are probably the principal reason behind different risk sensitivities. Lloyd's made money by matching wealthy investors who were more risk-tolerant with less wealthy and therefore more risk-averse shipowners.

Suppose, staying with our Lloyd's of London story, that a merchant whose ship went down would lose £1,000, and that there was a 10% chance of such a disaster. The expected loss in this case, then, would be $0.10 \times £1,000 = £100$. But the merchant, whose whole livelihood was at stake, might have been willing to pay £150 to be compensated in the amount of £1,000 if the ship sank. Meanwhile, a wealthy investor for whom the loss of £1,000 was no big deal would have been willing to take this risk for a return only slightly better than the expected loss—say, £110. Clearly, there is room for a mutually beneficial deal here: the merchant pays something less than £150 and more than £110—say, £130—in return for compensation if the ship goes down. In effect, he has paid a less risk-averse individual to bear the burden of his risk. Everyone has been made better off by this transaction.

The funds that an insurer places at risk when providing insurance is called his or her **capital at risk**.

The funds that an insurer places at risk when providing insurance are called his or her **capital at risk.** In our example, the wealthy Lloyd's investor places capital of £1,000 at risk in return for a premium of £130. In general, the amount of capital that potential insurers are willing to place at risk depends, other things equal, on the premium offered. If every ship is worth £1,000 and has a 10% chance of going down, nobody would offer insurance for less than a £100 premium, equal to the expected claim. In fact, only an investor who isn't risk-averse at all would be willing to offer a policy at that price, because accepting a £100 premium would leave the insurer's expected income unchanged while increasing his or her risk. Suppose there is one investor who isn't risk-averse; but the next most willing investor is slightly risk-averse and insists on a £105 premium. The next investor, being somewhat more risk-averse, demands a premium of £110, and so on. By varying the premium and asking how many insurers would be willing to provide insurance at that premium, we can trace out a supply curve for insurance, as shown in Figure 18-3. As the premium increases as we move up the supply curve, more risk-averse investors are induced to provide coverage.

Meanwhile, potential buyers will consider their willingness to pay a given premium, defining the demand curve for insurance. In Figure 18-4, the highest premium that any shipowner is willing to pay is £200. Who's willing to pay this? The most risk-averse shipowner, of course. A slightly less risk-averse shipowner might be willing to pay £190, an even slightly less risk-averse ship owner is willing to pay £180, and so on.

Now imagine a market in which there are thousands of shipowners and potential insurers, so that the supply and demand curves for insurance are smooth lines. In this market, as in markets for ordinary goods and services, there will be an equilibrium price and quantity. Figure 18-5 illustrates such a market equilibrium at a premium of £130, with a total quantity of 5,000 policies bought and sold, representing a total capital at risk of £5,000,000.

An **efficient allocation of risk** is an allocation of risk in which those who are most willing to bear risk are those who end up bearing it.

Notice that in this market risk is transferred from the people who most want to get rid of it (the most risk-averse shipowners) to the people least bothered by risk (the least risk-averse investors). So just as markets for goods and services typically produce an efficient allocation of resources, markets for risk also typically lead to an **efficient allocation of risk**—an allocation of risk in which those who are most willing to bear

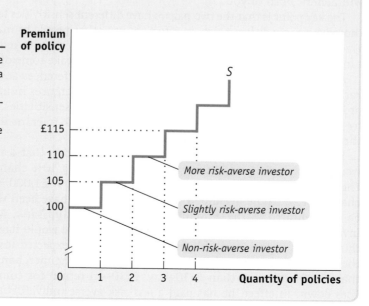

Figure 18-3

The Supply of Insurance

This is the supply of insurance policies to provide £1,000 in coverage to a merchant ship that has a 10% chance of being lost. Each investor has £1,000 of capital at risk. The lowest possible premium at which a policy is offered is £100, equal to the expected claim, and only a non-risk-averse investor is willing to supply this policy. As the premium increases, investors who are more risk-averse are induced to supply policies to the market, increasing the quantity of policies supplied.

Figure 18-4

The Demand for Insurance

This is the demand for insurance policies for £1,000 in coverage of a merchant ship that has a 10% chance of being lost. In this example, the highest premium at which anyone demands a policy is £200, which only the most risk-averse shipowner will desire. As the premium falls, shipowners who are less risk-averse are induced to demand policies, increasing the quantity of policies demanded.

risk are those who end up bearing it. But as in the case of the markets for goods and services, there is an important qualification to this result: there are well-defined cases in which the market for risk fails to achieve efficiency. These arise from the presence of private information, an important topic that we will cover in the next section.

The trading of risk between individuals who differ in their degree of risk aversion plays an extremely important role in the economy, but it is not the only way that markets can help people cope with risk. Under some circumstances, markets can perform a sort of magic trick: they can make some (though rarely all) of the risk that individuals face simply disappear.

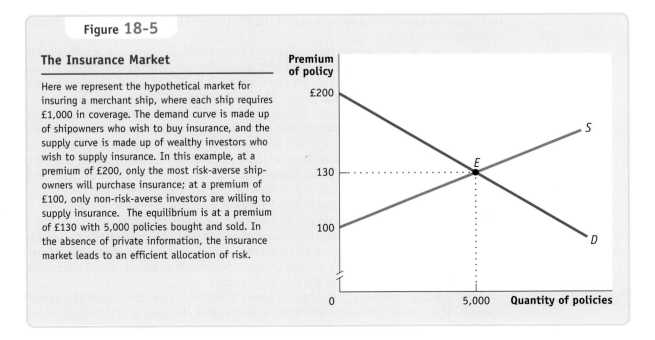

Figure 18-5

The Insurance Market

Here we represent the hypothetical market for insuring a merchant ship, where each ship requires £1,000 in coverage. The demand curve is made up of shipowners who wish to buy insurance, and the supply curve is made up of wealthy investors who wish to supply insurance. In this example, at a premium of £200, only the most risk-averse ship-owners will purchase insurance; at a premium of £100, only non-risk-averse investors are willing to supply insurance. The equilibrium is at a premium of £130 with 5,000 policies bought and sold. In the absence of private information, the insurance market leads to an efficient allocation of risk.

Making Risk Disappear: The Power of Diversification

In the early days of Lloyd's, British merchant ships traversed the world, trading spices and silk from Asia, tobacco and rum from the New World, and textiles and wool from Britain, among many other goods. Each of the many routes that British ships took had its own unique risks—pirates in the Caribbean, gales in the North Atlantic, typhoons in the Indian Ocean.

In the face of all these risks, how were merchants able to survive? One important way was by reducing their risks by not putting all their eggs in one basket: by sending different ships to different destinations, they could reduce the probability that all their ships would be lost. A strategy of investing in such a way as to reduce the probability of severe losses is known as *diversification*. As we'll now see, diversification can often make some of the economy's risk disappear.

Let's stay with our shipping example. It was all too likely that a pirate might seize a merchant ship in the Caribbean or that a typhoon might sink another ship in the Indian Ocean. But the key point here is that the various threats to shipping didn't have much to do with each other. So it was considerably less likely that a merchant who had one ship in the Caribbean and another ship in the Indian Ocean in a given year would lose them both, one to a pirate and the other to a typhoon. After all, there was no connection: the actions of cut-throats in the Carribean had no influence on weather in the Indian Ocean, or vice versa.

Statisticians refer to such events—events that have no connection, so that one is no more likely to happen if the other does than if it does not—as **independent events.** Many unpredictable events are independent of each other. If you toss a coin twice, the probability that it will come up heads on the second toss is the same whether it came up heads or tails on the first toss. If your house burns down today, it does not affect the probability that my house will burn down the same day (unless we live next door to each other or share the services of the same incompetent electrician.)

There is a simple rule for calculating the probability that two independent events will both happen: multiply the probability that one event would happen on its own by the probability that the other event would happen on its own. If you toss a coin once, the probability that it will come up heads is 0.5; if you toss the coin twice, the probability that it will come up heads *both* times is $0.5 \times 0.5 = 0.25$.

But what did it matter to shipowners or Lloyd's investors that ship losses in the Caribbean and ship losses in the Indian Ocean were independent events? The answer is that by spreading their investments across different parts of the world, shipowners or Lloyd's investors could make some of the riskiness of the shipping business simply disappear.

Let's suppose that Joseph Moneypenny, Esq., is wealthy enough to outfit two ships—and let's ignore for a moment the possibility of insuring his ships. Should Mr. Moneypenny equip two ships for the Caribbean trade and send them off together? Or should he send one ship to Barbados and one to Calcutta?

Assume that both voyages will be equally profitable if successful, yielding £1,000 if the voyage is completed. Also assume that there is a 10% chance both that a ship sent to Barbados will run into a pirate or that a ship sent to Calcutta will be sunk by a typhoon. And if two ships travel to the same destination, we will assume that they share the same fate. So if Mr. Moneypenny were to send both his ships to either destination, he would face a probability of 10% of losing all his investment.

But if Mr. Moneypenny were instead to send one ship to Barbados and one to Calcutta, the probability that he would lose both of them would be only $0.1 \times 0.1 = 0.01$, or just 1%. As we will see shortly, his expected payoff would be the same—but the chance of losing it all would be much less. So by engaging in **diversification**—investing in several different things, where the possible losses are independent events—he could make some of his risk disappear.

Table 18-2 summarizes Mr. Moneypenny's options and their possible consequences. If he sends both ships to the same destination, he runs a 10% chance of los-

TABLE 18-2

How Diversification Reduces Risk

(a) If both ships sent to the same destination

State	Probability	Payoff	Expected payoff
Both ships arrive	0.9 = 90%	£2,000	$(0.9 \times £2{,}000) + (0.1 \times £0) = £1{,}800$
Both ships lost	0.1 = 10%	0	

(b) If one ship sent east, one west

State	Probability	Payoff	Expected payoff
Both ships arrive	0.9 × 0.9 = 81%	£2,000	$(0.81 \times £2{,}000) + (0.01 \times £0) +$
Both ships lost	0.1 × 0.1 = 1%	0	$(0.18 \times £1{,}000) = £1{,}800$
One ship arrives	(0.1 × 0.9) + (0.1 × 0.9) = 18%	1,000	

ing them both. If he sends them to different destinations, there are three possible outcomes. Both ships could arrive safely: because there is a 0.9 probability of either one making it, the probability that both will make it is 0.9 × 0.9 = 81%. Both could be lost—but the probability of that happening is only 0.1 × 0.1 = 1%. Finally, there are two ways that only one ship can arrive. The probability that the first ship arrives and the second ship is lost is 0.9 × 0.1 = 9%. The probability that the first ship is lost but the second ship arrives is 0.1 × 0.9 = 9%. So the probability that only one ship makes it is 9% + 9% = 18%.

You might think that diversification is a strategy available only to those with a lot of money to begin with. How could Mr. Moneypenny have diversified if he were able to finance only one ship? But there are ways for even small investors to diversify. Even if Mr. Moneypenny were only wealthy enough to equip one ship, he could enter a partnership with another merchant. They could jointly outfit two ships, agreeing to share the profits equally, and then send those ships to different destinations. That way each would face less risk than if he equipped one ship on his own.

In the modern economy, diversification is made much easier for investors by the fact that they can easily buy shares in many companies by using the *stock market*. The owner of a **share** in a company is the owner of part of that company—typically a very small part, one-millionth or less. An individual who put all of his or her wealth in shares of a single company would lose all of that wealth if the company went bankrupt. But most investors hold shares in many companies, which makes the chance of losing all their investment very small.

In fact, Lloyd's of London wasn't just a way to trade risks; it was also a way for investors to diversify. To see how this worked, let's introduce Lady Penelope Smedley-Smythe, a wealthy aristocrat, who decides to increase her income by placing £1,000 of her capital at risk via Lloyd's. She could use that capital to insure just one ship. But more typically she would enter a "syndicate," a group of investors, who would jointly insure a number of ships going to different destinations, agreeing to share the cost if any one of those ships went down. Because it would be much less likely for all the ships insured by the syndicate to sink than for any one of them to go down, Lady Smedley-Smythe would be at much less risk of losing her entire capital.

In some cases, an individual can make risk almost entirely disappear by taking a small share in many

A **share** in a company is a partial ownership of that company.

"*Your mother called to remind you to diversify.*"

Pooling is a strong form of diversification in which an individual takes a small share in many independent events. This produces a payoff with very little risk.

independent events. This strategy is known as **pooling.** Consider the case of a health insurance company, which has millions of policyholders, with thousands of them requiring expensive treatment each year. The insurance company can't know whether any given individual will, say, require a heart bypass operation. But heart problems for two different individuals are pretty much independent events. And when there are many possible independent events, it is possible, using statistical analysis, to predict with great accuracy *how many* events of a given type will happen. For example, if you toss a coin 1,000 times, it will come up heads about 500 times—and it is very unlikely to be more than a percent or two off that figure. So a company offering fire insurance can predict very accurately how many of its clients' homes will burn down in a given year; a company offering health insurance can predict very accurately how many of its clients will need heart surgery in a given year; a life insurance company can predict how many of its clients will . . . Well, you get the idea.

When an insurance company is able to take advantage of the predictability that comes from looking at large numbers of independent events, it is said to engage in *pooling of risks.* And this pooling often means that even though insurance companies protect people from risk, the owners of the insurance companies may not themselves face much risk.

Lloyd's of London wasn't just a way for wealthy individuals to get paid for taking on some of the risks of less wealthy merchants. It was also a vehicle for pooling some of those risks. The effect of that pooling was to shift the supply curve in Figure 18-5 rightward: to make people willing to accept more risk, at a lower price, than would otherwise have been possible.

FOR INQUIRING MINDS

401(k) FOLLIES

It's important to save for your retirement. In the United States, many people save using what is known as a 401(k) plan—a plan that puts aside part of their salary in a special account, which can only be drawn down after retirement. The name comes from a special provision of the tax law, which exempts money set aside in these plans from income tax until the money is withdrawn.

The money in a 401(k) plan can be invested in stocks and other financial assets. Of course, this exposes the worker to the risk of losing some of his or her savings if the value of the stock falls.

The sensible thing is therefore to diversify 401(k) investments. But in 2001 and 2002, when the prices of some stocks plunged, it became clear that in some cases workers had been persuaded to invest most or all of their retirement savings in the stock of the companies that employed them. Most spectacularly, many employees at Enron, a seemingly solid company that suddenly collapsed in 2001, had their entire retirement savings in Enron stock—and were left with nothing. Other stock prices also fell at the time, but a broadly diversified 401(k) would have lost no more than 20 percent of its value in those years.

The Limits of Diversification

Diversification can reduce risk. In some cases it can eliminate it. But these cases are not typical, because there are important limits to diversification. We can see the most important reason for these limits by returning to Lloyd's one more time.

During the period when Lloyd's was creating its legend, there was one important hazard facing British shipping other than pirates or storms: war. Between 1690 and 1815, Britain fought a series of wars, mainly with France (which, among other things, went to war with Britain in support of the American Revolution). Each time, France would sponsor "privateers"—basically pirates with official backing—to raid British shipping and thus indirectly damage Britain's war effort.

Whenever war broke out between Britain and France, losses of British merchant ships would suddenly increase. Unfortunately, merchants could not protect themselves against this eventuality by sending ships to different ports: the privateers would prey on British ships anywhere in the world. So the loss of a ship to French privateers in the Caribbean and the loss of another ship to French privateers in the Indian Ocean would *not* be independent events. It would be quite likely that they would happen in the same year.

When an event is more likely to occur if some other event occurs, these two events are said to be **positively correlated.** And like the risk of having a ship seized by French privateers, many financial risks are, alas, positively correlated.

Here are some of the positively correlated financial risks that investors in the modern world face:

- *Severe weather.* Within any given region of the United States, losses due to weather are definitely not independent events. When a hurricane hits Florida, a lot of Florida homes will suffer hurricane damage. To some extent, insurance companies can diversify away this risk by insuring homes in many states. But events like El Niño (a recurrent temperature anomaly in the Pacific Ocean that disrupts weather around the world) can cause simultaneous flooding across the United States.

- *Political events.* Modern governments do not, thankfully, license privateers—although submarines served much the same function during World War II. Even today, however, some kinds of political events—say, a war or revolution in a key raw-material-producing area—can damage business around the globe.

- *Business cycles.* The causes of *business cycles*, fluctuations in the output of the economy as a whole, are a subject for macroeconomics. What we can say here is that if one company suffers a decline in business because of a nationwide economic slump, many other companies will also suffer such declines. So these events will be positively correlated.

When events are positively correlated, the risks they pose cannot be diversified away. An investor can protect herself from the risk that any one company will do badly by investing in many companies; she cannot use the same technique to protect against an economic slump in which *all* companies do badly. An insurance company can protect itself against the risk of losses from local flooding by insuring houses in many different places; but a global weather pattern that produces floods in many places will defeat this strategy.

So institutions like insurance companies and stock markets cannot make risk go away completely. There is always an irreducible core of risk that cannot be diversified. Markets for risk, however, do accomplish two things: First, they enable the economy to eliminate the risk that can be diversified. Second, they allocate the risk that remains to the people most willing to bear it.

Two events are **positively correlated** if each event is more likely to occur if the other event also occurs.

economics in action

When Lloyd's Almost Llost It

At the end of the 1980s, the venerable institution of Lloyd's found itself in severe trouble. Investors who had placed their capital at risk, believing that the risks were small and the return on their investments more or less assured, found themselves required to make large payments to satisfy enormous claims. A number of investors, including members of some very old aristocratic families, found themselves pushed into bankruptcy.

What happened? Part of the answer is that ambitious managers at Lloyd's had persuaded investors to take on risks that were much larger than the investors realized. (Or to put it a different way, the premiums the investors accepted were too small for the true level of risk contained in the policies.)

➤ Insurance markets exist because there are gains from trade in risk. Except in the case of private information, they lead to an *efficient allocation of risk*: those who are most willing to bear risk place their *capital at risk* to cover the financial losses of those least willing to bear risk.

➤ When *independent events* are involved, a strategy of *diversification* can substantially reduce risk. Diversification is made easier by the existence of institutions like the stock market, in which people trade *shares* of companies. A form of diversification, relevant especially to insurance companies, is *pooling*.

➤ When events are *positively correlated*, there is a core of risk that will not go away no matter how much individuals diversify.

But the biggest single problem was that many of the events against which Lloyd's had become a major insurer were *not* independent. In the 1970s and 1980s, Lloyd's had become a major provider of corporate liability insurance in the United States: it protected American corporations against the possibility that they might be sued for selling defective or harmful products. Everyone expected such suits to be more or less independent events. Why should one company's legal problems have much to do with another's?

The answer turned out to lie in one word: asbestos. For decades, this fireproofing material had been used in many products, which meant that many companies were responsible for its use. Then it turned out that asbestos can cause severe damage to the lungs, especially in children. The result was a torrent of lawsuits by people who believed they were injured by asbestos and billions of dollars in damage awards—many of them ultimately paid by Lloyd's investors. ■

< < < < < < < < < < < < < < < < < <

1. Explain how each of the following events would change the equilibrium premium and quantity of insurance in the market, indicating any shifts in the supply and demand curves.
   a. An increase in the number of ships traveling the same trade routes and so facing the same kinds of risks
   b. An increase in the number of trading routes, with the same number of ships traveling a greater variety of routes and so facing different kinds of risk
   c. An increase in the degree of risk aversion among the ship-owners in the market
   d. An increase in the degree of risk aversion among the investors in the market
   e. An increase in the risk affecting the economy as a whole
   f. A fall in the wealth levels of investors in the market

Solutions appear at back of book.

Private Information: What You Don't Know Can Hurt You

Markets do very well at dealing with risk due to uncertainty: situations in which nobody knows what is going to happen, whose house will be flooded, or who will get sick. However, markets have much more trouble with situations in which *some people know things that other people don't know*—situations of **private information.** As we will see, private information can distort economic decisions and sometimes prevent mutually beneficial economic transactions from taking place. (Sometimes economists use the term *asymmetric information* rather than private information, but they are equivalent.)

Private information is information that some people have that others do not.

Why is some information private? The most important reason is that people generally know more about themselves than other people do. You know whether or not you are a careful driver; but unless you have already been in several accidents, your insurance company does not. You also probably know more about objects you deal with regularly than anyone else. So if you are selling me your used car, you are more likely to be aware of any problems with it than I am.

But why should such differences in who knows what be a problem? It turns out that there are two distinct sources of trouble: *adverse selection,* which arises from having private information about the way things are, and *moral hazard,* which arises from having private information about what people do.

Adverse Selection: The Economics of Lemons

Suppose that someone offers to sell you an almost brand-new car—purchased just three months ago, with only 2,000 miles on the odometer and no dents or scratches. Will you be willing to pay almost the same for it as for a car direct from the dealer?

Probably not, for one main reason: you cannot help but wonder why this car is being sold. Is it because the owner has discovered that something is wrong with it—that it is a "lemon"? Having driven the car for a while, the owner knows more about it than you do—and people are more likely to sell cars that give them trouble.

You might think that the fact that sellers of used cars know more about them than the buyers do represents an advantage to the sellers. But potential buyers know that potential sellers are likely to offer them lemons—they just don't know exactly which car is a lemon. Because potential buyers of a used car know that potential sellers are more likely to sell lemons than good cars, buyers will offer a lower price than they would if they had a guarantee of the car's quality. Worse yet, this poor opinion of used cars tends to be self-reinforcing, precisely because it depresses the prices that buyers offer. Used cars sell at a discount because buyers expect a disproportionate share of those cars to be lemons. Even a used car that is not a lemon would sell only at a large discount, because buyers don't know whether it's a lemon or not. But potential sellers who have good cars are unwilling to sell them at a deep discount, except under exceptional circumstances. So good used cars are rarely offered for sale; and used cars that are offered for sale have a strong tendency to be lemons. (This is why people who have a compelling reason to sell a car, such as moving overseas, make a point of revealing that information to potential buyers—as if to say "This car is not a lemon!")

The end result, then, is not only that used cars sell for low prices and that there are a large number of used cars with hidden problems. Equally important, many potentially beneficial transactions—sales of good cars by people who would like to get rid of them to people who would like to buy them—end up being frustrated by the inability of potential sellers to convince potential buyers that their cars are actually worth the higher price demanded. So some mutually beneficial trades between those who want to sell used cars and those who want to buy them go unexploited.

Although economists sometimes refer to situations like this as the "lemons problem" (the issue was introduced in a famous 1970 paper by economist and Nobel Laureate George Akerlof entitled "The Market for Lemons"), the more formal name of the problem is **adverse selection.** The reason for the name is obvious: because the potential sellers know more about the quality of what they are selling than the potential buyers, they have an incentive to select the worst things to sell.

Adverse selection does not apply only to used cars. It is a problem for many parts of the economy—most notably for insurance companies. Suppose that an insurance company were to offer a standard policy for repairing cars after accidents, with the same premium for all drivers. This premium would reflect the *average* risk of accidents across all drivers. But that would make the policy look very expensive to drivers who know they are particularly careful or skillful and so less likely than the average driver to have an accident. So safe drivers would be less likely than less-safe drivers to buy this policy, leaving the insurance company with exactly the customers it doesn't want: people who have a higher-than-average risk of having accidents. Mutually beneficial transactions between safe drivers and insurance companies go unexploited because when drivers possess private information about their risk characteristics, the insurance company cannot set premiums according to the true riskiness of the driver. Safe drivers would get "priced out" of the market.

In practice, people or firms faced with the problem of adverse selection follow one of several well-established strategies for dealing with it. One strategy is **screening:** using observable information to make inferences about private information. Auto insurance provides a very good example. An insurance company may not know whether you are a careful driver, but it has statistical data on the accident rates of people who resemble your profile—and it uses those data in setting premiums. A 19-year-old male who drives a sports car and has already had a fender-bender is likely to pay a very high premium. A 40-year-old female who drives a minivan and has

Adverse selection occurs when an individual knows more about the way things are than other people do. Private information leads buyers to expect hidden problems in items offered for sale, leading to low prices and the best items being kept off the market.

Adverse selection can be reduced through **screening:** using observable information about people to make inferences about their private information.

Adverse selection can be diminished by people **signaling** their private information through actions that credibly reveal what they know.

A long-term **reputation** allows an individual to reassure others that he or she isn't concealing adverse private information.

never had an accident is likely to pay much less. In some cases, this may be quite unfair: some adolescent males are very careful drivers, and some mature women drive their minivans as if they were F-16s. But nobody can deny that the insurance companies are right on average.

Another strategy is for people who are good prospects to do something **signaling** their private information—taking some action that wouldn't be worth taking unless they were indeed good prospects. Reputable used-car dealers often offer warranties—promises to repair any problems with the cars they sell that arise within a given amount of time. This isn't just a way of insuring their customers against possible expenses; it's a way of credibly showing that they are not selling lemons. As a result, more sales occur and dealers can command higher prices for their used cars.

Finally, in the face of adverse selection, it can be very valuable to establish a good **reputation:** a used-car dealer will often advertise how long it has been in business to show that it has continued to satisfy its customers. New customers, therefore, will be willing to purchase cars and to pay more for that dealer's cars.

Moral Hazard

In the late 1970s, New York and other major cities experienced an epidemic of "suspicious" fires—fires that appeared to be deliberately set. Some of the fires were probably started by teenagers on a lark, others by gang members struggling over turf. But investigators eventually became aware of patterns in a number of the fires. Particular landlords, who owned several buildings, seemed to have an unusually large number of their buildings burn down. Although it was difficult to prove, police had few doubts that most of these "fire-prone" landlords were hiring professional arsonists to torch their own properties.

Why burn your own building? These buildings were typically in declining neighborhoods, where rising crime and middle-class flight had led to a decline in property values. But the insurance policies on the buildings were written to compensate owners based on historical property values, and so would actually pay the owner of a destroyed building more than the building was worth in the current market. For an unscrupulous landlord who knew the right people, this presented a profitable opportunity.

The arson epidemic became less severe during the 1980s, partly because insurance companies began making it difficult to overinsure properties, and partly because a boom in real estate values made many previously arson-threatened buildings worth more unburned.

The episode makes it clear that it is a bad idea for insurance companies to let customers insure buildings for more than their value—it gives the customers some destructive incentives. You might think, however, that the incentive problem goes away as long as the insurance is no more than 100 percent of the value of what is being insured.

But, unfortunately, anything close to 100 percent insurance still distorts incentives—it induces policyholders to behave differently than they would in the absence of insurance. The reason is that preventing fires requires effort and cost on the part of a building's owner. Fire alarms and sprinkler systems have to be kept in good repair, fire safety rules have to be strictly enforced, and so on. All of this takes time and money—time and money that the owner may not find worth spending if the insurance policy will provide close to full compensation for any losses.

Of course, the insurance company could specify in the policy that it won't pay if basic safety precautions have not been taken. But it isn't always easy to tell how careful a building's owner has been—the owner knows, but the insurance company does not.

Moral hazard occurs when an individual knows more about his or her own actions than other people do. This leads to a distortion of incentives to take care or to exert effort when someone else bears the costs of the lack of care or effort.

The point is that the building's owner has private information about his or her own actions, about whether he or she has really taken all appropriate precautions. As a result, the insurance company is likely to face greater claims than if it were able to determine exactly how much effort a building owner exerts to prevent a loss. The problem of distorted incentives arises when an individual has private information about his own actions but someone else bears the costs of a lack of care or effort. This is known as **moral hazard.**

To deal with moral hazard, it is necessary to give individuals with private information some personal stake in what happens, a stake that gives them a reason to exert effort even if others cannot verify that they have done so. Moral hazard is the reason salespeople in many stores receive a commission on sales: it's hard for managers to be sure how hard the salespeople are really working, and if they were paid only straight salary, they would not have an incentive to exert effort to make those sales. As described in the Economics in Action below, similar logic explains why many stores and restaurants, even if they are part of national chains, are actually franchises, licensed outlets owned by the people who run them.

Insurance companies deal with moral hazard by requiring a **deductible:** they compensate for losses only above a certain amount, so that coverage is always less than 100 percent. The insurance on your car, for example, may pay for repairs only after the first $500 in loss. This means that a careless driver who gets into a fender-bender will end up paying $500 for repairs even if he is insured, which provides at least some incentive to be careful and reduce moral hazard.

A **deductible** in an insurance policy is a sum that the insured individual must pay before being compensated for a claim.

In addition to reducing moral hazard, deductibles provide a partial solution to the problem of adverse selection. Your insurance premium often drops substantially if you are willing to accept a large deductible. This is an attractive option to people who know they are low-risk customers; it is less attractive to people who know they are high-risk—and so are likely to have an accident and end up paying the deductible. By offering a menu of policies with different premiums and deductibles, insurance companies can screen their customers, inducing them to sort themselves out on the basis of their private information.

As the example of deductibles suggests, moral hazard limits the ability of the economy to allocate risks efficiently. You generally can't get full (100 percent) insurance on your home or car, even though you would like to buy it, and you bear the risk of large deductibles even though you would prefer not to. The following Economics in Action illustrates how in some cases moral hazard limits the ability of investors to diversify their investments.

economics in action

Franchise Owners Try Harder

When Americans go out for a quick meal, they often end up at one of the fast-food chains—McDonald's, Burger King, and so on. Because these are large corporations, most customers probably imagine that the people who serve them are themselves employees of large corporations. But usually they aren't. Most fast-food restaurants—for example, 85 percent of McDonald's outlets—are franchises. That is, some individual has paid the parent company for the right to operate a restaurant selling its product; he or she may look like an arm of a giant company but is in fact a small-business owner.

Becoming a franchisee is not a guarantee of success. You must put up a large amount of money, both to buy the license and to set up the restaurant itself (to open a Taco Bell, for example, cost $1 million in 1997). And although McDonald's takes care that its franchises are not too close to each other, they often face stiff competition from rival chains and even from a few truly independent restaurants. Becoming a franchise owner, in other words, involves taking on quite a lot of risk.

But why should people be willing to take these risks? Didn't we just learn that it is better to diversify, to spread your wealth among many investments? The logic of diversification would seem to say that it's better for someone with $1 million to invest in a wide range of stocks rather than put it all into one Taco Bell. This implies that Taco Bell would find it hard to attract franchisees: nobody would be willing to be a franchisee unless they expected to earn considerably more than they would as a simple hired manager having invested their wealth in a diversified portfolio of stocks. So wouldn't it be more profitable for McDonald's or Taco Bell simply to hire managers to run their restaurants?

It turns out that it isn't, because the success of a restaurant depends a lot on how hard the manager works, on the effort he or she puts into choosing the right employees, on keeping the place clean and attractive to customers, and so on. Could McDonald's get the right level of effort from a salaried manager? Probably not. The problem is moral hazard: the manager knows whether he or she is really putting 100 percent into the job; but company headquarters, which bears the costs of a poorly run restaurant, does not. So a salaried manager, who gets a salary even without doing everything possible to make the restaurant a success, does not have the incentive to do that extra bit—an incentive the owner does have because he or she has a substantial personal stake in the success of the restaurant.

In other words, there is a moral hazard problem when a salaried manager runs a McDonald's, where the private information is how hard the manager works. Franchising resolves this problem. A franchisee, whose wealth is tied up in the business and who stands to profit personally from its success, has every incentive to work extremely hard.

The result is that fast-food chains rely mainly on franchisees to operate their restaurants, even though the contracts with these owner-managers allow the franchisees on average to make much more than it would have cost the companies to employ store managers. The higher earnings of franchisees compensate them for the risk they accept, and the companies are compensated by higher sales that lead to higher license fees. In addition, franchisees are forbidden by the licensing agreement with the company from reducing their risk by taking actions such as selling shares of the franchise to outside investors and using the proceeds to diversify. It's an illustration of the fact that moral hazard prevents the elimination of risk through diversification. ∎

< < < < < < < < < < < < < < < < < < <

>>CHECK YOUR UNDERSTANDING 18-3

1. Your car insurance premiums are lower if you have had no moving violations for several years. Explain how this feature tends to decrease the potential inefficiency caused by adverse selection.

2. A common feature of home construction contracts is that when it costs more to construct a building than was originally estimated, the contractor must absorb the additional cost. Explain how this feature reduces the problem of moral hazard but also forces the contractor to bear more risk than she would like.

3. True or false? Explain your answer, stating what concept analyzed in this chapter accounts for the feature.

   People with higher deductibles on their auto insurance:
   a. Generally drive more carefully
   b. Pay lower premiums
   c. Generally are wealthier

• A LOOK AHEAD •

We began this chapter with a discussion of yet another thing markets can do right: they allow individuals to trade risk, to their mutual benefit. But our discussion of private information shows that markets have difficulty handling some problems.

In the next two chapters, we will begin discussing in earnest the problem of *market failure*—situations in which markets, left to themselves, can lead to inefficient outcomes. As we'll see, one of the key roles of government is to correct market failure.

SUMMARY

1. The **expected value** of a **random variable** is the weighted average of all possible values, where the weight corresponds to the probability of a given value occurring.

2. **Risk** is uncertainty about future events or **states of the world**. It is **financial risk** when the uncertainty is about monetary outcomes.

3. Under uncertainty, people maximize **expected utility**. A **risk-averse** person will choose to reduce risk when that reduction leaves the expected value of his or her income or wealth unchanged. A **fair insurance policy** has that feature: the **premium** is equal to the expected value of the claim.

4. Risk aversion arises from diminishing marginal utility: an additional dollar of income generates higher marginal utility in low-income states than in high-income states. A fair insurance policy increases a risk-averse person's utility because it transfers a dollar from a high-income state (a state when no loss occurs) to a low-income state (a state when a loss occurs).

5. Differences in preferences and income or wealth lead to differences in risk aversion. Depending on the size of the premium, a risk-averse person is willing to purchase unfair insurance, a policy for which the premium exceeds the expected value of the claim. The greater your risk aversion, the higher the premium you are willing to pay.

6. There are gains from trade in risk, leading to an **efficient allocation of risk:** those who are most willing to bear risk put their **capital at risk** to cover the losses of those least willing to bear risk.

7. Risk can also be reduced through **diversification,** investing in several different things that correspond to **independent events.** The stock market, where **shares** in companies are traded, offers one way to diversify. Insurance companies can engage in **pooling,** insuring many independent events so as to eliminate almost all risk. But when the underlying events are **positively correlated,** all risk cannot be diversified away.

8. **Private information** can cause inefficiency in the allocation of risk. One problem is **adverse selection,** private information about the way things are. It creates the "lemons problem" in used car markets where sellers of high-quality cars drop out of the market. Adverse selection can be limited in several ways—through **screening** of individuals, through **signaling** that people use to reveal their private information, and through the building of a **reputation.**

9. A related problem is **moral hazard:** individuals have private information about their actions, which distorts their incentives to exert effort or care when someone else bears the costs of that lack of effort or care. It limits the ability of markets to allocate risk efficiently. Insurance companies try to limit moral hazard by imposing **deductibles,** placing more risk on the insured.

KEY TERMS

Random variable, p. 432
Expected value, p. 432
State of the world, p. 432
Risk, p. 433
Financial risk, p. 433
Expected utility, p. 433
Premium, p. 433
Fair insurance policy, p. 434

Risk-averse, p. 435
Capital at risk, p. 440
Efficient allocation of risk, p. 440
Independent events, p. 442
Diversification, p. 442
Share, p. 443
Pooling, p. 444
Positively correlated, p. 445

Private information, p. 446
Adverse selection, p. 447
Screening, p. 447
Signaling, p. 448
Reputation, p. 448
Moral hazard, p. 448
Deductible, p. 449

PROBLEMS

1. For each of the following situations, calculate the expected value.

   a. Tanisha owns one share of IBM stock, which is currently trading at $80. There is a 50% chance that the share price will rise to $100 and a 50% chance that the share price will fall to $70. What is the expected value of the future share price?

   b. Sharon buys a ticket in a small lottery. There is a probability of 0.7 that she will win nothing, of 0.2 that she will win $10, and of 0.1 that she will win $50. What is the expected value of Sharon's winnings?

   c. Aaron is a farmer whose rice crop depends on the weather. If the weather is favorable, he will make a profit of $100. If the weather is unfavorable, he will make a profit of −$20 (that is, he will lose money). The weather forecast reports that the probability of weather being favorable is 0.9 and the probability of weather being unfavorable is 0.1. What is the expected value of Aaron's profit?

2. Vicky N. Vestor is considering investing some of her money in a start-up company. She currently has income of $4,000, and she is considering investing $2,000 of that in the company. There is a 0.5 probability that the company will succeed and

will pay out $8,000 to Vicky (her original investment of $2,000 plus $6,000 of the company's profits). And there is a 0.5 probability that the company will fail and Vicky will get nothing (and lose her investment). The accompanying table illustrates Vicky's utility function.

Income	Total utility (utils)
$0	0
1,000	50
2,000	85
3,000	115
4,000	140
5,000	163
6,000	183
7,000	200
8,000	215
9,000	229
10,000	241

a. Calculate Vicky's marginal utility of income for each income level. Is Vicky risk-averse?

b. Calculate the expected value of Vicky's income from this investment.

c. Calculate Vicky's expected utility from making the investment.

d. What is Vicky's utility from not making the investment? Will Vicky therefore invest in the company?

3. Vicky N. Vestor's utility function was given in Problem 2. As in Problem 2, Vicky currently has income of $4,000. She is considering investing in a start-up company, but the investment now costs $4,000 to make. If the company fails, Vicky will get nothing from the company. But if the company succeeds, she will get $10,000 from the company (her original investment of $4,000 plus $6,000 of the company's profits). Each event has a 0.5 probability of occurring. Will Vicky invest in the company?

4. You have $1,000 that you can invest. If you buy Ford stock, you face the following returns and probabilities from holding the stock for one year: with a probability of 0.2 you will get $1,500; with a probability of 0.4 you will get $1,100; and with a probability of 0.4 you will get $900. If you put the money into the bank, in one year's time you will get $1,100 for certain.

a. What is the expected value of your earnings from investing in Ford stock?

b. Suppose you are risk-averse. Can we say for sure whether you will invest in Ford stock or put your money into the bank?

5. You have $1,000 that you can invest. If you buy General Motors stock, then, in one year's time: with a probability of 0.4 you will get $1,600; with a probability of 0.4 you will get $1,100; and with a probability of 0.2 you will get $800. If you put the money into the bank, in one year's time you will get $1,100 for certain.

a. What is the expected value of your earnings from investing in General Motors stock?

b. Suppose you prefer putting your money into the bank to investing it in General Motors stock. What does that tell us about your attitude to risk?

6. Wilbur is an airline pilot who currently has income of $60,000. If he gets sick and loses his flight medical certificate, he loses his job and has only $10,000 income. His probability of staying healthy is 0.6, and his probability of getting sick is 0.4. Wilbur's utility function is given in the accompanying table.

Income	Total utility (utils)
$0	0
10,000	60
20,000	110
30,000	150
40,000	180
50,000	200
60,000	210

a. What is the expected value of Wilbur's income?

b. What is Wilbur's expected utility?

Wilbur thinks about buying "loss-of-license" insurance that will compensate him if he loses his flight medical certificate.

c. One insurance company offers Wilbur full compensation for his income loss (that is, the insurance company pays Wilbur $50,000 if he loses his flight medical certificate), and it charges a premium of $40,000. That is, regardless of whether he loses his flight medical certificate, Wilbur's income after insurance will be $20,000. What is Wilbur's utility? Will he buy the insurance?

d. What is the highest premium Wilbur would just be willing to pay for full insurance (insurance that completely compensates him for the income loss)?

7. Hugh's income is currently $5,000. His utility function is shown in the accompanying table.

Income	Total utility (utils)
$0	0
1,000	100
2,000	140
3,000	166
4,000	185
5,000	200
6,000	212
7,000	222
8,000	230
9,000	236
10,000	240

a. Calculate Hugh's marginal utility of income. What is his attitude toward risk?

b. Hugh is thinking about gambling in a casino. With a probability of 0.5 he loses $4,000, and with a probability of 0.5 he wins $4,000. What is the expected value of Hugh's income? What is Hugh's expected utility? Will he decide to gamble? (Suppose that he gets no extra utility from going to the casino.)

c. Suppose that the "spread" (how much he can win versus how much he can lose) of the gamble narrows, so that with a probability of 0.5 Hugh loses $2,000, and with a probability of 0.5 he wins $2,000. What is the expected value of Hugh's income? What is his expected utility? Is this gamble better for him than the gamble in part b? Will he decide to gamble?

8. Eva is risk-averse. Currently she has $50,000 to invest. She faces the following choice: she can invest in the stock of a dot-com company, or she can invest in IBM stock. If she invests in the dot-com company, then with probability 0.5 she will lose $30,000, but with probability 0.5 she will gain $50,000. If she invests in IBM stock, then with probability 0.5 she will lose only $10,000, but with probability 0.5 she will gain only $30,000. Can you tell which investment she will prefer to make?

9. Suppose you have $1,000 that you can invest in Ted and Larry's Ice Cream Parlor and Ethel's House of Cocoa. The price of a share of stock in either company is $100. The fortunes of each company are closely linked to the weather. When it is warm, the value of Ted and Larry's stock rises to $150 but the value of Ethel's stock falls to $60. When it is cold, the value of Ethel's stock rises to $150 but the value of Ted and Larry's stock falls to $60. There is an equal chance of the weather being warm or cold.

a. If you invest all your money in Ted and Larry's, what is your expected stock value? What if you invest all your money in Ethel's?

b. Suppose you diversify and invest half of your $1,000 in each company. How much will your total stock be worth if the weather is warm? What if it is cold?

c. Suppose you are risk-averse. Would you prefer to put all your money in Ted and Larry's, as in part a? Or would you prefer to diversify, as in part b? Explain your reasoning.

10. You are considering buying a second-hand Volkswagen. From reading car magazines, you know that half of all Volkswagens have problems of some kind (they are "lemons") and the other half run just fine (they are "plums"). If you knew that you were getting a plum, you would be willing to pay $10,000 for it: this is how much a plum is worth to you. You would also be willing to buy a lemon, but only if its price was no more than $4,000: this is how much a lemon is worth to you. And someone who owns a plum would be willing to sell it at any price above $8,000. Someone who owns a lemon would be willing to sell it for any price above $2,000.

a. For now, suppose that you can immediately tell whether the car that you are being offered is a lemon or a plum. Suppose someone offers you a plum. Will there be trade?

Now suppose that the seller has private information about the car she is selling: the seller knows whether she has a lemon or a plum. But when the seller offers you a Volkswagen, you do not know whether it is a lemon or a plum. So this is a situation of adverse selection.

b. Since you do not know whether you are being offered a plum or a lemon, you base your decision on the expected value to you of a Volkswagen, assuming you are just as likely to buy a lemon as a plum. Calculate this expected value.

c. Suppose, from driving the car, the seller knows she has a plum. However, you don't know whether this particular car is a lemon or a plum, so the most you are willing to pay is your expected value. Will there be trade?

11. You own a company that produces chairs, and you are thinking about hiring one more employee. Each chair produced gives you revenue of $10. There are two potential employees, Fred Ast and Sylvia Low. Fred is a fast worker who produces ten chairs per day, creating revenue for you of $100. Fred knows that he is fast and so will work for you only if you pay him more than $80 per day. Sylvia is a slow worker who produces only five chairs per day, creating revenue for you of $50. Sylvia knows that she is slow and so will work for you if you pay her more than $40 per day. Although Sylvia knows she is slow and Fred knows he is fast, you do not know who is fast and who is slow. So this is a situation of adverse selection.

a. Since you do not know which type of worker you get, you think about what the expected value of your revenue will be if you hire one of the two. What is that expected value?

b. Suppose you offered to pay a daily wage equal to the expected revenue you calculated in part a. Who would you be able to hire: Fred, or Sylvia, or either?

12. For each of the following situations, do the following: First describe whether it is a situation of moral hazard or of adverse selection. Then explain what inefficiency can arise from this situation and explain how the proposed solution reduces the inefficiency.

a. When you buy a second-hand car, you do not know whether it is a lemon (low quality) or a plum (high quality), but the seller knows. A solution is for sellers to offer a warranty with the car that pays for repair costs.

b. Some people are prone to see doctors unnecessarily for minor complaints like headaches and health maintenance organizations do not know how urgently you need a doctor. A solution is for insurees to have to make a co-payment of a certain dollar amount (for example, $10) each time they visit a health care provider. All insurees are risk-averse.

c. When airlines sell tickets, they do not know whether a buyer is a business traveler (who is willing to pay a lot for a seat), or a leisure traveler (who has a low willingness to pay). A solution for a profit-maximizing airline is to offer an expensive ticket that is very flexible (it allows date and route changes) and a cheap ticket that is very inflexible (it has to be booked in advance and cannot be changed).

d. A company does not know whether workers on an assembly line work hard or whether they shirk. A solution is to pay the workers "piece rates," that is, pay them according to how much they have produced each day. All workers are risk-averse while the company is not risk-averse.

e. When making a decision about hiring you, prospective employers do not know whether you are a productive or unproductive worker. A solution is for productive workers to provide potential employers with references from previous employers.

>*web*... To continue your study and review of concepts in this chapter, please visit the Krugman/Wells website for quizzes, animated graph tutorials, web links to helpful resources, and more.

www.worthpublishers.com/krugmanwells

>> **Externalities**

WHO'LL STOP THE RAIN?

MILLIONS OF PEOPLE IN THE NORTH-eastern United States can think of no better way to relax than fishing in one of the region's thousands of lakes. But in the 1960s avid fishermen noticed something alarming: lakes that had formerly teemed with fish were now almost empty. What had happened?

The answer turned out to be acid rain, caused mainly by coal-burning power plants. When coal is burned, it releases sulfur dioxide and nitric oxide into the atmosphere; these gases react with water, producing sulfuric acid and nitric acid. The result in the Northeast, downwind from the nation's industrial heartland, was rain sometimes as acidic as lemon juice. Acid rain didn't just kill fish; it also damaged trees and crops and in time even began to dissolve limestone buildings.

You'll be glad to hear that the acid rain problem today is much less serious than it was in the 1960s. Power plants have reduced their emissions by switching to low-sulfur coal and installing scrubbers in their smokestacks. But they didn't do this out of the goodness of their hearts; they did it in response to government policy. Without such intervention, power companies would have had no incentive to take the environmental effects of their actions into account.

When individuals impose costs on or provide benefits for others, but don't have an economic incentive to take those costs or benefits into account, economists say that the situation includes *externalities*. You may recall that we briefly noted this phenomenon in Chapters 1, 6, and 13. There we stated that one of the principal sources of market failure are actions that create *side effects* that are not

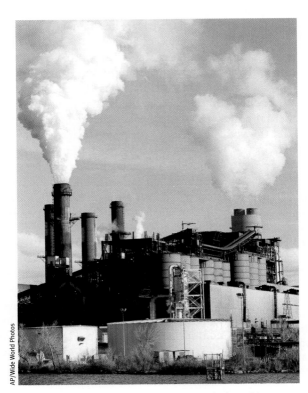

For many polluters, acid rain is someone else's problem.

What you will learn in this chapter:

➤ What **externalities** are and why they can lead to inefficiency in a market economy and support for government intervention

➤ The difference between **negative** and **positive externalities**

➤ The importance of the **Coase theorem,** which explains how private individuals can sometimes solve externalities

➤ Why some government policies to deal with externalities, such as **emissions taxes, tradable permits,** or **Pigouvian subsidies,** are efficient, although others, like **environmental standards,** are inefficient

➤ How positive externalities give rise to arguments for **industrial policy** properly taken into account—that is, externalities. In this chapter, we'll examine the economics of externalities, seeing how they can get in the way of economic efficiency and lead to market failure, why they provide a reason for government intervention in markets, and how economic analysis can be used to guide government policy.

Because externalities arise from the side effects of actions, we need to study them from two slightly different vantage points. First, we consider the situation in which the side effect—that is, pollution—can be directly observed and quantified. Whenever an activity can be directly observed and quantified, it can be regulated: by imposing direct controls on it, by taxing it, or by subsidizing it. As we will see, government intervention in this case should be aimed

directly at moving the market to the right quantity of the side effect.

But in many situations, only the original activity, not its side effect, can be observed. For example, we can't observe the congestion caused by a single car, so the government is unable to implement policies that control the side effect directly. What it can do is employ policies that affect the *original* activity—driving. So in the second part of our analysis we will consider how governments can indirectly achieve the right quantity of the side effect through influencing the activity that generates it. In a fundamental way, however, the two approaches are equivalent: each one involves, at the margin, setting the benefit of doing a little bit more of something equal to the cost of doing that little bit more.

The Economics of Pollution

Pollution is a bad thing. Yet most pollution is a side effect of activities that provide us with good things: our air is polluted by power plants generating the electricity that lights our cities, and our rivers are damaged by fertilizer runoff from farms that grow our food. Why don't we accept a certain amount of pollution as the cost of a good life?

Actually, we do. Even highly committed environmentalists don't think that we can or should completely eliminate pollution—even an environmentally conscious society would accept *some* pollution as the cost of producing useful goods and services. What environmentalists argue is that unless there is a strong and effective environmental policy, our society will generate *too much* pollution—too much of a bad thing. And the great majority of economists agree.

To see why, we need a framework that lets us think about how much pollution a society *should* have. We'll then be able to see why a market economy, left to itself, will produce more pollution than it should. We'll start by adopting the simplest framework to study the problem—assuming that the amount of pollution emitted by a polluter is directly observable and controllable.

Costs and Benefits of Pollution

How much pollution should society allow? We learned in Chapter 7 that "how much" decisions always involve comparing the marginal benefit from an additional unit of something with the marginal cost of that additional unit. The same is true of pollution.

The **marginal social cost of pollution** is the additional cost imposed on society as a whole by an additional unit of pollution. For example, acid rain damages fisheries, crops, and forests, and each additional ton of sulfur dioxide released into the atmosphere increases the damage.

The **marginal social cost of pollution** is the additional cost imposed on society as a whole by an additional unit of pollution.

PITFALLS

SO HOW DO YOU MEASURE THE MARGINAL SOCIAL COST OF POLLUTION?
It might be confusing to think of marginal *social* cost—after all, we have up to this point always defined marginal cost as being incurred by an individual or a firm, not society as a whole. But it is easily understandable once we link it to the familiar concept of willingness to pay: the marginal social cost of a unit of pollution is equal to the *highest willingness to pay among all members of society* to avoid that unit of pollution. But calculating the true cost to society of pollution—marginal or average—is a difficult matter, requiring a great deal of scientific knowledge, as the Economics in Action on page 461 illustrates. As a result, society often underestimates the true marginal social cost of pollution.

The **marginal social benefit of pollution**—the additional gain to society from an additional unit of pollution—may seem like a confusing concept. What's good about pollution? However, avoiding pollution requires using scarce resources that could have been used to produce other goods and services. For example, to reduce the quantity of sulfur dioxide they emit, power companies must either buy expensive low-sulfur coal or install special scrubbers to remove sulfur from their emissions. The more sulfur dioxide they are allowed to emit, the lower these extra costs. Suppose that we can calculate how much money the power industry would save if it were allowed to emit an additional ton of sulfur dioxide. That saving is the marginal benefit to society of emitting an extra ton of sulfur dioxide.

Using hypothetical numbers, Figure 19-1 shows how we can determine the **socially optimal quantity of pollution**—the quantity of pollution society would choose if all its costs and benefits were fully accounted for. The upward-sloping marginal social cost curve, *MSC*, shows how the marginal cost to society of an additional ton of pollution emissions varies with the quantity of emissions. (An upward slope is likely because nature can often safely handle low levels of pollution but is increasingly harmed as pollution reaches high levels.) The marginal social benefit curve, *MSB*, is downward sloping because it is progressively harder, and therefore more expensive, to achieve a further reduction in pollution as the total amount of pollution falls—increasingly more expensive technology must be used. As a result, as pollution falls, the cost savings to a polluter of being allowed to emit one more ton rises.

The socially optimal quantity of pollution in this example isn't zero. It's Q_{OPT}, the quantity corresponding to point O, where *MSB* crosses *MSC*. At Q_{OPT}, the marginal social benefit from an additional ton of emissions and its marginal social cost are equalized at $200.

But will a market economy, left to itself, arrive at the socially optimal quantity of pollution? No, it won't.

The **marginal social benefit of pollution** is the additional gain to society as a whole from an additional unit of pollution.

The **socially optimal quantity of pollution** is the quantity of pollution that society would choose if all the costs and benefits of pollution were fully accounted for.

PITFALLS

SO HOW DO YOU MEASURE THE MARGINAL SOCIAL BENEFIT OF POLLUTION?

Similar to the problem of measuring the marginal social cost of pollution, the concept of willingness to pay helps us understand the marginal social benefit of pollution in contrast to the marginal benefit to an individual or firm. The marginal social benefit of a unit of pollution is simply equal to the highest willingness to pay for the right to emit that unit across all polluters. But unlike the marginal social cost of pollution, the value of the marginal social benefit of pollution is a number likely to be known—to polluters, that is.

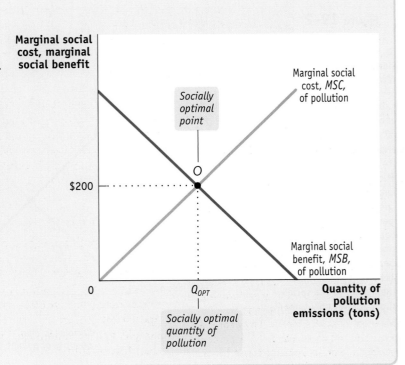

Figure 19-1

The Socially Optimal Quantity of Pollution

Pollution yields both costs and benefits. Here the curve *MSC* shows how the marginal cost to society as a whole from emitting one more ton of pollution emissions depends on the quantity of emissions. The curve *MSB* shows how the marginal benefit to society as a whole of emitting an additional ton of pollution emissions depends on the quantity of pollution emissions. The socially optimal quantity of pollution is Q_{OPT}; at that quantity, the marginal social benefit of pollution is equal to the marginal social cost, corresponding to $200.

Pollution: An External Cost

Pollution yields both benefits and costs to society. But in a market economy without government intervention, those who benefit from pollution—like the owners of power companies—decide how much pollution occurs. They have no incentive to take into account the costs of pollution that they impose on others.

To see why, remember the nature of the benefits and costs from pollution. For polluters, the benefits take the form of monetary savings: by emitting an extra ton of sulfur dioxide, any given polluter saves the cost of buying expensive, low-sulfur coal or installing pollution-control equipment. So the benefits of pollution accrue directly to the polluters.

The costs of pollution, though, fall on people who have no say in the decision about how much pollution takes place: people who fish in northeastern lakes do not control the decisions of power plants.

Figure 19-2 shows the result of this asymmetry between who reaps the benefits and who pays the costs. In a market economy without government intervention to protect the environment, only the benefits of pollution are taken into account in choosing the quantity of pollution. So the quantity of emissions won't be at the socially optimal quantity Q_{OPT}; it will be Q_{MKT}, the quantity at which the marginal social benefit of an additional ton of pollution is zero, but the marginal social cost of that additional ton is much larger—$400. The quantity of pollution in a market economy without government intervention will be higher than its socially optimal quantity. (The Pigouvian tax noted in Figure 19-2 will be explained shortly.)

The reason is that in the absence of government intervention, those who derive the benefits from pollution—in this case, the owners of power plants—don't have to compensate those who bear the costs. So the marginal cost of pollution to any given polluter is zero: polluters have no incentive to limit the amount of emissions. For example, before the Clean Air Act of 1970, midwestern power plants used the cheapest type of coal available, regardless of how much pollution it caused, and did nothing to scrub their emissions.

The environmental costs of pollution are the best-known and most important example of an **external cost**—an uncompensated cost that an individual or firm

An **external cost** is an uncompensated cost that an individual or firm imposes on others.

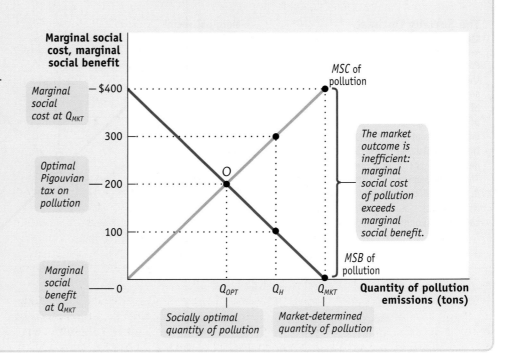

Figure 19-2

Why a Market Economy Produces Too Much Pollution

In the absence of government intervention, the quantity of pollution will be Q_{MKT}, the level at which the marginal social benefit of pollution to polluters is zero. This is an inefficiently high quantity of pollution: the marginal social cost, $400, greatly exceeds the marginal social benefit, $0. An optimal Pigouvian tax of $200, the value of the marginal social cost of pollution when it equals the marginal social benefit of pollution, can move the market to the socially optimal quantity of pollution, Q_{OPT}.
>web...

TALKING AND DRIVING

Why is that woman in the car in front of us driving so erratically? Is she drunk? No, she's talking on her cell phone.

Traffic safety experts take the risks posed by driving while talking very seriously. Using hands-free, voice-activated phones doesn't seem to help much because the main danger is distraction. As one traffic safety consultant put it, "It's not where your eyes are; it's where your head is." And we're not talking about a trivial problem. One estimate suggests that people who talk on their cell phones while driving may be responsible for 600 or more traffic deaths each year.

The National Safety Council urges people not to use phones while driving. But a growing

"It's not where your eyes are, it's where your head is."

number of people say that voluntary standards aren't enough; they want the use of cell phones while driving made illegal, as it already is in Japan, Israel, and several other countries.

Why not leave the decision up to the driver? Because the risk posed by driving while talking isn't just a risk to the driver; it's also a safety risk to others—especially people in other cars. Even if you decide that the benefit to you of taking that call is worth the cost, you aren't taking into account the cost to other people. Driving while talking, in other words, generates a serious—sometimes fatal—negative externality.

imposes on others. There are many other examples of external costs besides pollution. Another important, and certainly very familiar, external cost is traffic congestion—an individual who chooses to drive during rush hour increases congestion and so increases the travel time of other drivers.

We'll see later in this chapter that there are also important examples of **external benefits,** benefits that individuals or firms confer on others without receiving compensation. External costs and benefits are jointly known as **externalities,** with external costs called **negative externalities** and external benefits called **positive externalities.**

As we've already suggested, externalities can lead to individual decisions that are not optimal for society as a whole. Let's take a closer look at why, focusing on the case of pollution.

> An **external benefit** is a benefit that an individual or firm confers on others without receiving compensation.
>
> External costs and benefits are known as **externalities;** external costs are **negative externalities,** and external benefits are **positive externalities.**

The Inefficiency of Excess Pollution

We have just shown that in the absence of government action, the quantity of pollution will be *inefficient:* polluters will pollute up to the point at which the marginal social benefit of pollution is zero, as shown by the pollution quantity Q_{MKT} in Figure 19-2. Recall that an outcome is inefficient if some people could be made better off without making others worse off. In Chapter 6 we showed why the market equilibrium quantity in a perfectly competitive market is the efficient quantity of the good, the quantity that maximizes total surplus. Here, we can use a variation of that analysis to show how the presence of a negative externality upsets that result.

Because the marginal social benefit of pollution is zero at Q_{MKT}, reducing the quantity of pollution by one ton would subtract very little from the total social benefit from pollution. In other words, the benefit to polluters to that last unit of pollution is very low—virtually zero. Meanwhile, the marginal social cost imposed on the rest of society of that last ton of pollution at Q_{MKT} is quite high—$400. This means that by reducing the quantity of pollution at Q_{MKT} by one ton, the total social cost of pollution falls by $400, while total social benefits fall by virtually zero. So total surplus rises by approximately $400 if the quantity of pollution at Q_{MKT} is reduced by one ton.

If the quantity of pollution is reduced further, there will be more gains in total surplus, though they will be smaller. For example, if the quantity of pollution is Q_H in Figure 19-2, the marginal social benefit of a ton of pollution is $100, but the marginal social cost is still $300. This means that reducing the quantity of pollution by one ton leads to a net gain in total surplus of approximately $300 − $100 = $200. This tells us that Q_H is still an inefficiently high quantity of pollution. Only if the quantity of pollution is reduced to Q_{OPT}, where the marginal social cost and the marginal social benefit of an additional ton of pollution are both $200, is the outcome efficient.

Private Solutions to Externalities

Can the private sector solve the problem of externalities without government intervention? Bear in mind that when an outcome is inefficient, there is potentially a deal that makes people better off. Why don't individuals find a way to make that deal?

In an influential 1960 article, the economist and Nobel laureate Ronald Coase pointed out that in an ideal world the private sector could indeed deal with all externalities. According to the **Coase theorem,** even in the presence of externalities an economy can always reach an efficient solution provided that the costs of making a deal are sufficiently low. The costs of making a deal are known as **transaction costs.**

> According to the **Coase theorem,** even in the presence of externalities an economy can always reach an efficient solution as long as **transaction costs**—the costs to individuals of making a deal—are sufficiently low.

To get a sense of Coase's argument, imagine two neighbors, Mick and Britney, who both like to barbecue in their backyards on summer afternoons. Mick likes to play golden oldies on his boombox while barbecuing; but this annoys Britney, who can't stand that kind of music.

Who prevails? You might think that it depends on the legal rights involved in the case: if the law says that Mick has the right to play whatever music he wants, Britney just has to suffer; if the law says that Mick needs Britney's consent to play music in his backyard, Mick has to live without his favorite music while barbecuing.

But as Coase pointed out, the outcome need not be determined by legal rights, because Britney and Mick can make a private deal. Even if Mick has the right to play his music, Britney could pay him not to. Even if Mick can't play the music without an OK from Britney, he can offer to pay her to give that OK. These payments allow them to reach an efficient solution, regardless of who has the legal upper hand. If the benefit of the music to Mick exceeds its cost to Britney, the music will go on; if the benefit to Mick is less than the cost to Britney, there will be silence.

The implication of Coase's analysis is that externalities need not lead to inefficiency because individuals have an incentive to make mutually beneficial deals—deals that lead them to take externalities into account when making decisions. When individuals *do* take externalities into account when making decisions, economists say that they **internalize the externality.** If externalities are fully internalized, the outcome is efficient even without government intervention.

> When individuals take external costs or benefits into account, they **internalize the externality.**

Why can't individuals always internalize externalities? Our barbecue example implicitly assumes the transaction costs are low enough for Mick and Britney to be able to make a deal. In many situations involving externalities, however, transaction costs prevent individuals from making efficient deals. Examples of transaction costs include the following:

- The costs of communication among the interested parties—costs that may be very high if many people are involved
- The costs of making legally binding agreements—costs that may be high if the employment of expensive lawyers is required
- Costly delays involved in bargaining—even if there is a potentially beneficial deal, both sides may hold out in an effort to extract more favorable terms, leading to increased effort and forgone utility

In some cases, people do find ways to reduce transaction costs, allowing them to internalize externalities. For example, many people live in private communities that set rules for home maintenance and behavior, making bargaining between neighbors unnecessary. But in many other cases, transaction costs are too high to make it possible to deal with externalities through private action. For example, tens of millions of people are adversely affected by acid rain. It would be prohibitively expensive to try to make a deal among all those people and all those power companies.

When transaction costs prevent the private sector from dealing with externalities, it is time to look for government solutions. We turn to public policy in the next section.

economics in action

Thank You for Not Smoking

New Yorkers call them the "shiver-and-puff people"—the smokers who stand outside their workplaces, even in the depths of winter, to take a cigarette break. Over the past couple of decades, rules against smoking in spaces shared by others have become ever stricter. This is partly a matter of personal dislike—nonsmokers really don't like to smell other people's cigarette smoke—but it also reflects concerns over the health risks of second-hand smoke. As the Surgeon General's warning on many packs says, "Smoking causes lung cancer, heart disease, emphysema, and may complicate pregnancy." And there's no question that being in the same room as someone who smokes exposes you to at least some health risk.

Second-hand smoke, then, is clearly an example of a negative externality. But how important is it? Putting a dollar-and-cents value on it—that is, measuring the marginal social cost of cigarette smoke—requires not only estimating the health effects but putting a value on these effects. Despite the difficulty, economists have tried. A paper published in 1993 in the *Journal of Economic Perspectives* surveyed the research on the external costs of both cigarette smoking and alcohol consumption.

According to this paper, valuing the health costs of cigarettes depends on whether you count the costs imposed on members of smokers' families, including unborn children, in addition to costs borne by smokers. If you don't, the external costs of second-hand smoke have been estimated at about only $0.19 per pack smoked. (Using this method of calculation, $0.19 corresponds to the *average* social cost of smoking per pack at the current level of smoking in society.) If you include effects on smokers' families, the number rises considerably—family members who live with smokers are exposed to a lot more smoke. (They are also exposed to the risk of fires, which alone is estimated at $0.09 per pack.) If you include the effects of smoking by pregnant women on their unborn children's future health, the cost is immense—$4.80 per pack, which is more than twice the wholesale price charged by cigarette manufacturers. ■

(See source note on page xxii.)

> > > > > > > > > > > > > > > > > >

>>CHECK YOUR UNDERSTANDING 19-1

1. Waste water runoff from large poultry farms adversely affects their neighbors. Explain the following:
   a. The nature of the external cost imposed
   b. The outcome in the absence of government intervention or a private deal
   c. The socially optimal outcome

2. According to Yasmin, any student who borrows a book from the university library and fails to return it on time imposes a negative externality on other students. He claims that rather than charging a modest fine for late returns, the library should charge a huge fine, so that borrowers will never return a book late. Is Yasmin's economic reasoning correct?

Solutions appear at back of book.

Policies Toward Pollution

Before 1970, there were no rules governing the amount of sulfur dioxide power plants in the United States could emit—which is why acid rain got to be such a problem. After 1970, the Clean Air Act set rules about sulfur dioxide emissions—and the acidity of rainfall declined significantly. Economists argued, however, that a more flexible system of rules that exploited the effectiveness of markets could achieve lower pollution at less cost. In 1990 this theory was put into effect with a modified version of the Clean Air Act. And guess what? The economists were right!

In this section we'll look at the policies governments use to deal with pollution and at how economic analysis has been used to improve those policies.

Environmental Standards

The most serious external costs in the modern world are surely those associated with actions that damage the environment—air pollution, water pollution, habitat destruction, and so on. Protection of the environment has become a major role of government in all advanced nations. In the United States, the Environmental Protection Agency is the principal enforcer of environmental policies at the national level, supported by the actions of state and local governments.

How does a country protect its environment? At present the main policy tools are **environmental standards,** rules that protect the environment by specifying actions by producers and consumers. A familiar example is the law that requires almost all vehicles to have catalytic converters, which reduce the emission of chemicals that can cause smog and lead to health problems. Other rules require communities to treat their sewage, factories to avoid or limit certain kinds of pollution, and so on.

Environmental standards came into widespread use in the 1960s and 1970s, and they have had considerable success in reducing pollution. For example, since the United States passed the Clean Air Act in 1970, overall emission of pollutants into the air has fallen by more than a third, even though the population has grown by a third and the size of the economy has more than doubled. Even in Los Angeles, still famous for its smog, the air has improved dramatically: in 1988 ozone levels in the South Coast Air Basin exceeded federal standards on 178 days; in 2003, on only 68 days.

Despite these successes, economists believe that when regulators can control a polluter's emissions directly, there are more efficient ways than environmental standards to deal with pollution. By using methods grounded in economic analysis, society can achieve a cleaner environment at lower cost. Most current environmental standards are inflexible and don't allow reductions in pollution to be achieved at minimum cost. For example, Plant A and Plant B might be ordered to reduce pollution by the same percentage, even if their costs of achieving that objective are very different.

How does economic theory suggest that pollution should be directly controlled? There are actually two approaches: taxes and tradable permits. As we'll see, either approach can achieve the efficient outcome at the minimum feasible cost.

Emissions Taxes

One way to deal with pollution directly is to charge polluters an **emissions tax.** Emissions taxes are taxes that depend on the amount of pollution a firm produces. For example, power plants might be charged $200 for every ton of sulfur dioxide they emit.

Look again at Figure 19-2, which shows that the socially optimal quantity of pollution is Q_{OPT}. At that quantity of pollution, the marginal social benefit and marginal social cost of an additional ton of emissions are equal at $200. But in the absence of government intervention, power companies have no incentive to limit pollution to the socially optimal quantity Q_{OPT}; instead, they will push pollution up to the quantity Q_{MKT}, at which marginal social benefit is zero.

Environmental standards are rules that protect the environment by specifying actions by producers and consumers.

An **emissions tax** is a tax that depends on the amount of pollution a firm produces.

It's now easy to see how an emissions tax can solve the problem. If power companies are required to pay a tax of $200 per ton of emissions, they now face a marginal cost of $200 per ton and have an incentive to reduce emissions to Q_{OPT}, the socially optimal quantity. This illustrates a general result: an emissions tax equal to the marginal social cost at the socially optimal quantity of pollution induces polluters to internalize the externality—to take into account the true costs to society of their actions.

Why is an emissions tax an efficient way (that is, a cost-minimizing way) to reduce pollution but environmental standards are generally not? Because an emissions tax ensures that the marginal benefit of pollution is equal for all sources of pollution but an environmental standard does not. Figure 19-3 shows a hypothetical industry consisting of only two plants, Plant A and Plant B. We'll assume that Plant A uses newer technology than plant B and so has a lower cost of reducing pollution. Reflecting this difference in costs, Plant A's marginal benefit of pollution curve, MB_A, lies below Plant B's marginal benefit of pollution curve, MB_B. Because it is more costly for Plant B to reduce its pollution at any output quantity, an additional ton of pollution is worth more to Plant B than to Plant A.

In the absence of government action, we know that polluters will pollute until the marginal social benefit of an additional unit of emissions is equal to zero. Recall that

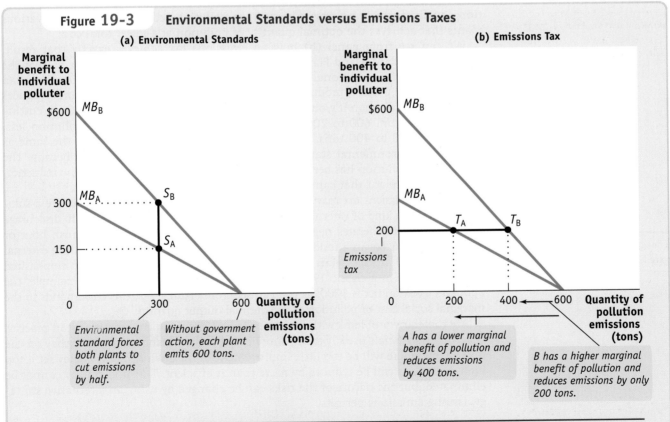

Figure 19-3   Environmental Standards versus Emissions Taxes

In both panels, MB_A shows the marginal benefit of pollution to Plant A and MB_B shows the marginal benefit of pollution to Plant B. In the absence of government intervention, each plant would emit 600 tons. However, the cost of reducing emissions is lower for Plant A, as shown by the fact that MB_A lies below MB_B. Panel (a) shows the result of an environmental standard that requires both plants to cut emissions in half; this is inefficient, because it leaves the marginal benefit of pollution higher for Plant B than for Plant A. Panel (b) shows that an emissions tax achieves the same quantity of overall pollution efficiently: faced with an emissions tax of $200 per ton, both plants reduce pollution to the point where its marginal benefit is $200. **>web...**

the marginal social benefit of pollution is the cost savings, at the margin, to polluters of an additional unit of pollution. This means that without government intervention each plant will pollute until its own marginal benefit of pollution is equal to zero. This corresponds to an emissions quantity of 600 tons each for Plants A and B—the quantity of pollution at which MB_A and MB_B are each equal to zero. So although Plant A and Plant B value a ton of emissions differently, without government action they will each choose to emit the same amount of pollution.

Now suppose that the government decides that overall pollution from this industry should be cut in half, from 1,200 tons to 600 tons. Panel (a) of Figure 19-3 shows how this might be achieved with an environmental standard that requires each plant to cut its emissions in half, from 600 to 300 tons. The standard has the desired effect of reducing overall emissions from 1,200 to 600 tons but accomplishes it in an inefficient way. As you can see from panel (a), the environmental standard leads Plant A to produce at point S_A, where its marginal benefit of pollution is $150, but Plant B produces at point S_B, where its marginal benefit of pollution is twice as high, $300.

This difference in marginal benefits between the two plants tells us that the same quantity of pollution can be achieved at lower total cost by allowing Plant B to pollute more than 300 tons but inducing Plant A to pollute less. In fact, the efficient way to reduce pollution is to ensure that at the industry-wide outcome, the marginal benefit of pollution is the same for all plants. When each plant values a unit of pollution equally, there is no way to re-arrange pollution reduction among the various plants that achieves the optimal quantity of pollution at a lower total cost.

We can see from panel (b) how an emissions tax achieves exactly that result. Suppose both Plant A and Plant B pay an emissions tax of $200 per ton, so that the marginal cost of an additional ton of emissions to each plant is now $200 rather than zero. As a result, Plant A produces at T_A and Plant B produces at T_B. So Plant A reduces its pollution more than it would under an inflexible environmental standard, cutting its emissions from 600 to 200 tons; meanwhile, Plant B reduces its pollution less, going from 600 to 400 tons. In the end, total pollution—600 tons—is the same as under the environmental standard, but total surplus is higher. That's because the reduction in pollution has been achieved efficiently, allocating most of the reduction to Plant A, the plant that can reduce emissions at lower cost.

The term *emissions tax* may convey the misleading impression that taxes are a solution to only one kind of external cost, pollution. In fact, taxes can be used to discourage any activity that generates negative externalities, such as driving during rush hour or operating a noisy bar in a residential area. In general, taxes designed to reduce external costs are known as **Pigouvian taxes,** after the economist A. C. Pigou, who emphasized their usefulness in a classic 1920 book, *The Economics of Welfare*. In our example, the optimal Pigouvian tax is $200; as you can see from Figure 19-2, this corresponds to the marginal social cost of pollution at the optimal output quantity, Q_{OPT}.

Are there any problems with emissions taxes? The main concern is that in practice government officials usually aren't sure how high the tax should be set. If they set the tax too low, there will be too little improvement in the environment; if they set it too high, emissions will be reduced by more than is efficient. This uncertainty cannot be eliminated, but the nature of the risks can be changed by using an alternative strategy, issuing emissions permits.

Tradable Emissions Permits

Tradable emissions permits are licenses to emit limited quantities of pollutants that can be bought and sold by polluters. They are usually issued to polluting firms according to some formula reflecting their history. For example, each power plant might be issued permits equal to 50 percent of its emissions before the system went into effect. The more important point, however, is that these permits are *tradable*. Firms with differing costs of reducing pollution can now engage in mutually beneficial transactions: those that find it easier to reduce pollution will sell

---

Taxes designed to reduce external costs are known as **Pigouvian taxes.**

Tradable emissions permits are licenses to emit limited quantities of pollutants that can be bought and sold by polluters.

some of their permits to those that find it more difficult. In other words, firms will use transactions in permits to re-allocate pollution reduction among themselves, so that in the end those with the lowest cost will reduce their pollution the most, while those with the highest cost will reduce their pollution the least. Using our original example, this means that Plant A will find it profitable to sell 100 of its 300 government-issued licenses to Plant B. The effect of a tradable permit system is to create a market in rights to pollute.

Just like emissions taxes, tradable permits provide polluters with an incentive to take the marginal social cost of pollution into account. To see why, suppose that the market price of a permit to emit one ton of sulfur dioxide is $200. Then every plant has an incentive to limit its emissions of sulfur dioxide to the point where the marginal benefit of emissions is $200. This is obvious for plants that buy rights to pollute: if a plant must pay $200 for the right to emit an additional ton of sulfur dioxide, it faces the same incentives as a plant facing an emissions tax of $200 per ton. But it's equally true for plants that have more permits than they plan to use: by *not* emitting a ton of sulfur dioxide, a plant frees up a permit that it can sell for $200, so the opportunity cost of a ton of emissions to the plant's owner is $200.

In short, tradable emissions permits have the same cost-minimizing advantage as emissions taxes over environmental standards: either system ensures that those who can reduce pollution most cheaply are the ones who do so. The socially optimal quantity of pollution shown in Figure 19-2 could be efficiently achieved either way: by imposing an emissions tax of $200 per ton of pollution or by issuing tradable permits to emit Q_{OPT} tons of pollution. If regulators choose to issue Q_{OPT} permits, where one permit allows the release of one ton of emissions, then the equilibrium market price of a permit among polluters will indeed be $200. Why? You can see from Figure 19-2 that at Q_{OPT}, only polluters with a marginal benefit of pollution of $200 or more will buy a permit. And the last polluter who buys—who has a marginal benefit of exactly $200—sets the market price.

It's important to realize that emissions taxes and tradable permits do more than induce polluting industries to reduce their output. They also provide incentives to create and use less-polluting technology. In fact, the main effect of the permit system for sulfur dioxide has been to change *how* electricity is produced rather than to reduce the nation's electricity output. For example, power companies have shifted to the use of alternative fuels such as low-sulfur coal and natural gas; they have also installed scrubbers that take much of the sulfur dioxide out of a power plant's emissions.

The main problem with tradable emissions permits is the flip-side of the problem with emissions taxes: because it is difficult to determine the optimal quantity of pollution, governments can find themselves either issuing too many permits—that is, they don't reduce pollution enough, or issuing too few—that is, they reduce pollution too much.

In practice, after first relying on rigid environmental standards, the U.S. government has turned to a system of tradable emissions permits to control acid rain, and current proposals would extend that system to other major sources of pollution. The Economics in Action that follows describes how the system has worked in practice.

economics in action

Controlling Acid Rain

The Clean Air Act of 1970 instituted what even the Environmental Protection Agency (EPA) calls a "command-and-control" regime, in which businesses and individuals were given detailed instructions about what to do to reduce air pollution. When the act was revised in 1990, however, the EPA made an effort to move in the direction of market-based remedies. The most notable of these is the program designed to reduce sulfur dioxide emissions from coal-burning electric power plants, the major source of acid rain.

The sulfur dioxide program issues "allowances" to power plants based on their historical consumption of coal. Each allowance is the right to emit one ton of sulfur dioxide during or after a specified year. Power companies are free to buy or sell allowances. However, they must present the EPA with enough allowances to cover their own emissions. So plants with extra allowances can sell them, but plants without enough allowances must buy the difference.

Since the program began in 1994, the price per allowance has fluctuated, sometimes going below $100 and sometimes above $200; in 2004 it was $260. This is well below the price most analysts expected, and some environmentalists have taken the low price as a sign that the government should seek further reductions in pollution levels.

Economists who have analyzed the system believe it has led to large savings compared with what would have been the costs of achieving the same quantity of pollution under a regulatory rule that did not allow the power companies to trade. ∎

< < < < < < < < < < < < < < < < < < <

>> CHECK YOUR UNDERSTANDING 19-2

1. Some opponents of tradable emissions permits object to them on the ground that polluters that sell their permits benefit monetarily from their contribution to polluting the environment. Assess this argument.

2. Explain the following:
   a. Why an emissions tax smaller than or greater than the marginal social cost at Q_{OPT} reduces total surplus
   b. Why a system of tradable emissions permits that sets the total quantity of allowable pollution higher or lower than Q_{OPT} reduces total surplus

Solutions appear at back of book.

Production, Consumption, and Externalities

Nobody imposes external costs like pollution out of malice. Pollution, traffic congestion, and other harmful externalities are side effects of activities, like electricity generation or driving, that are otherwise desirable. We've just learned how government regulators can move the market to the socially optimal quantity when the side effect can be directly controlled. But as we cautioned earlier, in some cases it's not possible to directly control the side effect; only the original activity can be influenced. As we'll see shortly, government policies in these situations must instead be geared to changing the quantity of the original activity, which in turn changes the quantity of the side effect produced.

This approach, although slightly more complicated, has several advantages. First, it gives us a clear understanding of how the quantity of the original, desirable activity is altered by policies designed to manage its side effects (which will, in fact, typically occur both when the side effect can be directly controlled and when it can't). Second, it lets us evaluate arguments against environmental policy—arguments that arise from the fact that desirable activities are unavoidably impeded by policies intended to control their negative side effects. Finally, it helps us think about a phenomenon that is different but related to the problem of external costs: what should be done when an activity generates external *benefits*.

Private versus Social Costs

Given current technology, there is no affordable way to breed and raise livestock on a commercial scale without hurting the environment. Whatever it is—cows, pigs, chicken, sheep, or salmon—livestock farming produces prodigious amounts of what is euphemistically known as "muck." But that's not all: scientists estimate that the amount of methane gas produced by livestock (the same gas produced when a person—heaven forbid!—belches) currently rivals the pollution caused by the burning of fossil fuels in the creation of greenhouses gases. From the point

Muck and methane gas: the costly side-effects of producing a side of bacon.

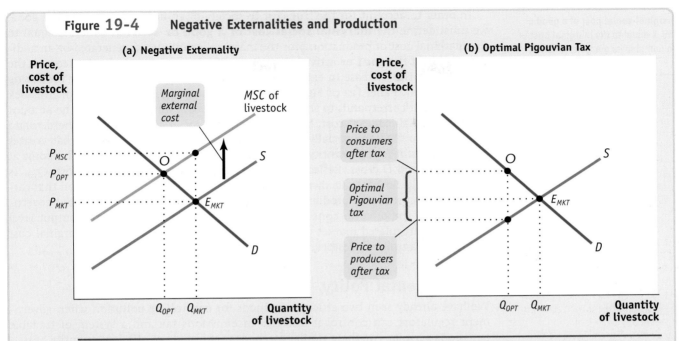

Figure 19-4   Negative Externalities and Production

Livestock production generates external costs, so the marginal social cost curve of livestock, *MSC*, corresponds to the supply curve, *S*, shifted upward by the marginal external cost. Panel (a) shows that without government action, the market produces the amount Q_{MKT}. It is greater than the socially optimal quantity of livestock production, Q_{OPT}, the quantity at which *MSC* crosses the demand curve, *D*. At Q_{MKT}, the market price, P_{MKT}, is less than P_{MSC}, the true marginal cost to society of livestock production. Panel (b) shows how an optimal Pigouvian tax on livestock production, equal to its marginal external cost, moves the production to Q_{OPT}, resulting in lower output and a higher price to consumers. **>web...**

of view of society as a whole, then, the cost of livestock farming includes both direct production costs to the farmer (payments for factors of production and inputs such as animal feed) and the external environmental costs imposed as a by-product. In the absence of government intervention, however, livestock farmers have no incentive to take into account the environmental costs of their production decisions. As a result, in the absence of government intervention, livestock farmers will produce too much output.

Panel (a) of Figure 19-4 illustrates this point. The market demand curve for livestock by consumers is represented by the curve *D*; the market, or industry, supply curve is given by the curve *S*. In the absence of government intervention, market equilibrium will be at point E_{MKT}, yielding the amount produced and consumed Q_{MKT} and the market price P_{MKT}. At that point, the marginal benefit to society of another unit of livestock (measured by the market price) is equal to the marginal cost *incurred by the industry* for producing that unit.

Let's look a little more closely at the supply curve. Assuming that the livestock industry is competitive, we know from Chapter 9 that the industry supply curve corresponds to the horizontal sum of all the individual supply curves of producers in the industry. In addition, we know that each individual producer's supply curve corresponds to its marginal cost curve. These two facts taken together imply that the industry supply curve is the horizontal sum of the individual producers' marginal cost curves: a given point on *S* corresponds to the total industry-wide marginal cost at the corresponding output level. But we also know from our earlier discussion that this estimation of marginal cost does not include the external cost that production imposes on others. In other words, when external costs are present, the industry supply curve does not reflect the true cost to society of production of the good.

The **marginal social cost of a good or activity** is equal to the marginal cost of production plus its marginal external cost.

In order to account for the true cost to society of an additional unit of the good, we must define the **marginal social cost of a good or activity,** which is equal to the marginal cost of production plus the marginal external cost generated by an additional unit of the good or activity. It captures the increase in production cost to the industry *and* the increase in external cost to the rest of society caused by producing one more unit. Panel (a) of Figure 19-4 shows the marginal social cost of livestock curve, *MSC*; it corresponds to the industry supply curve *shifted upward* by the amount of the marginal external cost. With the marginal social cost curve and the demand curve, we can find the socially optimal quantity of a good or activity that creates external costs: it is the quantity Q_{OPT}, the quantity corresponding to O, the point at which *MSC* and *D* cross. Reflecting the proper accounting for external cost, Q_{OPT} is less than Q_{MKT}. So left to its own, a market will result in too much of a good that carries external costs being produced and consumed. Correspondingly, without government action, the price to consumers of such a good is too low: at the output level Q_{MKT}, the unregulated market price P_{MKT} is lower than P_{MSC}, the true marginal cost to society of a unit of livestock.

Environmental Policy, Revisited

We have already seen two efficient methods for controlling pollution when government regulators can control it directly: an emissions tax and a system of tradable emissions permits. Are there similar methods that lead to an efficient quantity of pollution when regulators can target only the original activity or good, such as livestock production? Yes, there are—although they will take the form of a tax on livestock sales or a license to produce a unit of livestock rather than on the pollution created. These methods will move the market to the efficient quantity by compelling producers to internalize the externality caused by livestock production in their decisions.

Consider first the case of a Pigouvian tax on livestock transactions. Once such a tax is in effect, the cost to a livestock farmer of producing an additional unit of livestock includes both the marginal cost of production and the tax. If the tax is set at the right amount, it is exactly equal to the marginal external cost. As shown in panel (b) of Figure 19-4, the optimal Pigouvian tax will move the market outcome to the optimal point O.

A system of tradable production permits that restricts the industry-wide quantity of livestock produced to the optimal level has the same effect. Suppose that in order to produce an additional unit of livestock, a farmer must purchase a permit. The cost of this permit behaves like a Pigouvian tax, and once again external costs are completely internalized in the private decisions of producers. Even if the farmer already possesses the permit, its opportunity cost—the price it could command in the market for permits—acts like a Pigouvian tax.

So Q_{OPT}, the efficient quantity of livestock produced and consumed, corresponds to the efficient quantity of pollution generated by livestock production. You might ask yourself at this point how this analysis, in terms of the optimal amount of a good or activity that gives rise to an external cost, relates to our earlier analysis of the optimal amount of pollution. Except for the effect that emissions taxes and tradable emissions permits have on the creation and adoption of less-polluting production methods, the two approaches are equivalent: the difference between the two comes down to a matter of units. The first analysis was carried out in units of pollution and the second in units of a good or activity that yields pollution. But regardless of the framework we use, the underlying method is the same: to find the level at which society's marginal benefit from another unit equals society's marginal cost.

But our second analysis does create additional insights: we see how consumption choices are affected by policies designed to counteract external costs. Note that in panel (b) of Figure 19-4, consumers consume less livestock (in the form of meat purchased at supermarkets and restaurants) and pay a higher market price at the socially optimal quantity. (We know from Chapter 5 that exactly how the burden of the tax is allocated between producers and consumers depends on the price elasticities of demand and supply.) Moreover, this shows us that criticisms of environmental policies made exclusively on the basis that they "hurt consumers" are misguided.

Finally, you might ask which method a regulator would choose if a choice existed between policies that target pollution directly and policies that target production of the original good or activity. Generally, whenever feasible it is a good idea to target the pollution directly. The main reason, as we mentioned earlier, is that it gives incentives for the creation and adoption of less-polluting production methods. This, in turn, lessens the disincentive to produce the good (something, after all, that people want) when the good is targeted rather than when pollution is targeted.

As this book goes to press, an example of this phenomenon is being reported. A Florida-based company, Agcert, has developed technology whereby methane from pig-waste tanks can be drawn off and either burnt or used as "biofuel" to generate electricity. The company claims that this technology can achieve an average emissions reduction of one ton of methane gas per pig per year, a sizable savings in an industry where farms can have as many as 10,000 animals. Farmers could then be granted "credits" for their emissions reductions, which they could sell to producers in other industries who want to purchase a license to pollute. Such credits could be a lucrative source of income for farmers, given that the current market price for a one-ton credit for emissions is about $7 to $8. Agcert is currently valued at around $128 million. As some have commented, this invention has given new life to an old saying among plumbers and sewer workers: "Where there's muck, there's gold."

Private versus Social Benefits

Not all externalities are negative. In some important cases, an economic activity creates external benefits—that is, individual actions provide benefits to other people for which the producers are not compensated.

The most important source of external benefits in the modern economy probably involves creation of knowledge. In high-tech industries like semiconductors, innovations by one firm are quickly emulated and improved upon both by rival firms in the same industry and by firms in other industries. Such spreading of knowledge among individuals and firms is known as a **technology spillover.** Such spillovers often take place through face-to-face contact. As Economics in Action on page 471 explains, bars and restaurants in California's Silicon Valley are famed for their technical gossip, and the need to keep tabs on the latest innovations is a major reason so many high-tech firms are clustered near each other.

> A **technology spillover** is an external benefit that results when knowledge spreads among individuals and firms.

In Chapter 22 we'll discuss the economics of goods whose value lies principally in the knowledge or information they embody. For now, let's just look at the implications of external benefits in general for economic efficiency and economic policy. Suppose that the production of some good—say, semiconductor chips—yields positive externalities. How does this affect our analysis of the chip market, and does it create a justification for government intervention?

Just as external costs cause the marginal social *cost* of producing a good to exceed the industry's marginal cost, when there are external benefits from a good, the marginal social *benefit* exceeds consumers' marginal benefit. This is illustrated in panel (a) of Figure 19-5 on page 470, which shows the market for semiconductor chips. Since there are no external costs in this case, the industry supply curve, S, represents the true marginal social cost to society of production. The demand curve, D, represents the marginal benefit that accrues to *consumers of the good:* each point on the demand curve corresponds to the willingness to pay of the last consumer to purchase the good at the corresponding price. But it does not incorporate the benefits to society as a whole from production of the good—the technological spillover an additional unit provides to the economy as a whole.

To explore this phenomenon we need a new concept, the **marginal social benefit of a good or activity**—the marginal benefit that accrues to consumers from an additional unit of the good or activity, plus the marginal external benefit to society

> The **marginal social benefit of a good or activity** is equal to the marginal benefit that accrues to consumers plus its marginal external benefit.

Figure 19-5   Positive Externalities and Production

(a) Positive Externality

(b) Optimal Pigouvian Subsidy

Semiconductor chip production generates external benefits, so the marginal social benefit curve of chips, *MSB*, corresponds to the demand curve, *D*, shifted upward by the marginal external benefit. Panel (a) shows that without government action, the market produces Q_{MKT}. It is lower than the socially optimal quantity of production, Q_{OPT}, the quantity at which

MSB crosses the supply curve, *S*. At Q_{MKT}, the market price, P_{MKT}, is less than P_{MSB}, the true marginal benefit to society of semiconductor chip production. Panel (b) shows how an optimal Pigouvian subsidy to chip producers, equal to its marginal external benefit, moves the production to Q_{OPT}, resulting in higher output and a higher price to producers. **>web...**

from an additional unit. As you can see from panel (a) of Figure 19-5, the marginal social benefit curve, *MSB*, corresponds to the demand curve *D* *shifted upward* by the amount of the marginal external benefit.

The analysis in this case is very similar to that of external costs. Left to itself, the market will reach an equilibrium at E_{MKT}, the point at which the demand curve *D* crosses the supply curve *S* at a market price P_{MKT}. But the quantity of output at this equilibrium, Q_{MKT}, is inefficiently low: at that output level, the marginal social benefit of an additional unit, P_{MSB}, exceeds the industry's marginal cost of producing that unit, P_{MKT}. The optimal quantity of production and consumption is Q_{OPT}, the quantity at which marginal cost is equal to marginal social benefit.

How can the economy be induced to produce Q_{OPT} chips? The answer is a **Pigouvian subsidy:** a payment designed to encourage activities that yield external benefits. The optimal Pigouvian subsidy, shown in panel (b) of Figure 19-5, is equal to the marginal external benefit of producing an additional unit. Producers receive the price paid by consumers plus the per-unit subsidy, inducing them to produce more output. Such a subsidy is an example of an **industrial policy,** a general term for a policy of supporting industries believed to yield positive externalities.

Although the strict economic logic supporting such efforts is impeccable, economists are generally less enthusiastic about industrial policies to promote positive externalities than they are about fees and permit schemes to discourage negative externalities. This lack of enthusiasm reflects a mixture of practical and political judgments. First, positive externalities—which most often involve the creation of knowledge and new technologies—are typically much harder to identify and measure than negative externalities. (A simple sensor can keep track of how many tons of sulfur dioxide come out of a smokestack. But how do you tell whether and when a new product embodies a technology that will benefit other producers and consumers?) In

A **Pigouvian subsidy** is a payment designed to encourage activities that yield external benefits.

An **industrial policy** is a policy that supports industries believed to yield positive externalities.

2. The loud music coming from the sorority next to your dorm is a negative externality that can be directly quantified. The table below shows the marginal social benefit and the marginal social cost per decibel (dB, a measure of volume) of music.

Volume of music (dB)	Marginal social benefit of dB	Marginal social cost of dB
90		
	$36	$0
91		
	30	2
92		
	24	4
93		
	18	6
94		
	12	8
95		
	6	10
96		
	0	12
97		

a. Draw the marginal social benefit curve and the marginal social cost curve. Use your diagram to determine the socially optimal volume of music.

b. Only the members of the sorority benefit from the music and they bear none of the cost. Which volume of music will they choose?

c. The college imposes a Pigouvian tax of $3 per decibel of music played. From your diagram, determine the volume of music the sorority will now choose.

3. Many dairy farmers in California are adopting a new technology that allows them to produce their own electricity from methane gas captured from animal wastes. (One cow can produce up to 2 kilowatts a day.) This practice reduces the amount of methane gas released into the atmosphere. In addition to reducing their own utility bills, the farmers are allowed to sell any electricity they produce at favorable rates.

a. Explain how the ability to earn money from capturing and transforming methane gas behaves like a Pigouvian tax on methane gas pollution and can lead dairy farmers to emit the efficient amount of methane gas pollution.

b. Suppose some dairy farmers have lower costs of transforming methane into electricity than others. Explain how this system leads to an efficient allocation of emissions reduction among farmers.

4. The accompanying table shows the total social benefit from steel production and the total cost to steel producers of producing steel. Producing a ton of steel imposes a marginal external cost of $60 per ton.

Quantity of steel (tons)	Total social benefit	Total cost to producers
1	$115	$10
2	210	30
3	285	60
4	340	100
5	375	150

a. Calculate the marginal social benefit per ton of steel and the marginal cost per ton of steel to steel producers. Then calculate the marginal social cost per ton of steel.

b. What is the market equilibrium quantity of steel production?

c. What is the socially optimal quantity of steel production?

d. If you wanted to impose a Pigouvian tax to remedy the problem created by the negative externality, how high would the Pigouvian tax have to be per ton of steel?

5. Education is an example of a positive externality: acquiring more education benefits the individual student and having a more highly educated work force is good for the economy as a whole. The accompanying table illustrates the marginal benefit to Sian per year of education and the marginal cost per year of education. Each year of education has a marginal external benefit to society equal to $8,000. Assume that the marginal social cost is the same as the marginal cost paid by an individual student.

Quantity of education (years)	Sian's marginal benefit per year	Sian's marginal cost per year
9		
	$20,000	$15,000
10		
	19,000	16,000
11		
	18,000	17,000
12		
	17,000	18,000
13		
	16,000	19,000
14		
	15,000	20,000
15		
	14,000	21,000
16		
	13,000	22,000
17		

a. Find Sian's market equilibrium number of years of education.

b. Calculate the marginal social benefit schedule. What is the socially optimal number of years of education?

c. You are in charge of education funding. Would you use a Pigouvian tax or a Pigouvian subsidy to induce Sian to choose the socially optimal amount of education? How high would you set this tax or subsidy per year of education?

6. Getting a flu shot reduces not only your chance of getting the flu but also the chance that you will pass it on to someone else.

   a. Draw a diagram showing the supply and demand curves of inoculating different proportions of the population. Assume that the marginal cost of each flu shot is constant and is equal to the marginal social cost, and that the demand curve is downward sloping.

   b. Will the marginal social benefit curve be higher, lower, or the same as the demand curve? Why? Draw the marginal social benefit curve into your diagram.

   c. In your diagram, show the market equilibrium quantity and the socially optimal quantity of flu shots. Is the market equilibrium quantity of flu shots socially efficient? Why or why not?

   d. Many university health centers offer free flu shots to students and employees. Does this solution necessarily achieve efficiency? Explain, using your diagram.

7. Draw a diagram of the supply and demand curves for telephone service. The marginal cost of connecting another household to the telephone network is increasing, as it is more costly to connect another household as the size of the network grows larger. Assume that the demand curve is downward sloping.

   a. Label the market equilibrium in your diagram E_{MKT}.

   Telephone service is a positive externality (sometimes called a "network externality"). There is a marginal external benefit to connecting one more household to the telephone network, the benefit to everybody else of being able to call the newly connected household.

   b. Draw the marginal social benefit curve into your diagram, find the socially optimal point, and label it O.

   c. Explain why the market equilibrium E_{MKT} is inefficient.

   d. Governments subsidize phone service for rural households. Describe how such a Pigouvian subsidy eliminates the inefficiency.

8. According to a report from the U.S. Census "the average [lifetime] earnings of a full-time, year round worker with a high school education are about $1.2 million compared with $2.1 million for a college graduate." This indicates that there is a considerable benefit to a graduate from investing in his or her own education. Tuition at most state universities covers only about two-thirds to three-quarters of the cost, so the state applies a Pigouvian subsidy to college education.

   If a Pigouvian subsidy is appropriate, is the externality created by a college education a positive or a negative externality? What does this imply about the differences between the costs and benefits to students compared to social costs and benefits? What are some reasons for the differences?

9. Fishing for sablefish has been so intensive that sablefish were threatened with extinction. After several years of banning such fishing, the government is now proposing to introduce tradable vouchers, each of which entitles its holder to a catch of a certain size. Explain how fishing is a negative externality and how the voucher scheme may overcome the inefficiency created by this externality.

10. The two dry-cleaning companies in Collegetown, College Cleaners and Big Green Cleaners, are a major source of air pollution. Together they currently produce 350 units of air pollution, which the town wants to reduce to 200 units. The accompanying table shows the current pollution level produced by each company and each company's marginal cost of reducing its pollution. The marginal cost is constant.

Companies	Initial pollution level (units)	Marginal cost of reducing pollution (per unit)
College Cleaners	230	$5
Big Green Cleaners	120	$2

   a. Suppose that Collegetown were to pass an environmental standards law that limits each company to 100 units of pollution. What would be the total cost to the two companies of each reducing its pollution emissions to 100 units?

   Suppose instead that Collegetown issues 100 pollution vouchers to each company, each entitling the company to one unit of pollution, and that these vouchers can be traded.

   b. How much is each pollution voucher worth to College Cleaners? to Big Green Cleaners? (That is, how much would each company, at most, be willing to pay for one more voucher?)

   c. Who will sell vouchers and who will buy them? How many vouchers will be traded?

   d. What is the total cost to the two companies of the pollution controls under this voucher system?

11. Ronald owns a cattle farm at the source of a long river. His cattle's waste flows into the river, and down many miles to where Carla lives. Carla gets her drinking water from the river. By allowing his cattle's waste to flow into the river, Ronald imposes a negative externality on Carla. In each of the two following cases, do you think that through negotiation, Ronald and Carla can find an efficient solution? What might this solution look like?

   a. There are no telephones, and for Carla to talk to Ronald, she has to travel for two days on a rocky road.

   b. Carla and Ronald both have e-mail access, making it costless for them to communicate.

> **web...** To continue your study and review of concepts in this chapter, please visit the Krugman/Wells website for quizzes, animated graph tutorials, web links to helpful resources, and more.

www.worthpublishers.com/krugmanwells

>>Public Goods and Common Resources

THE GREAT STINK

BY THE MIDDLE OF THE NINETEENTH century, London had become the world's largest city, with close to 2.5 million inhabitants. Unfortunately, all those people produced a lot of waste—and there was no place for the stuff to go except the Thames, the river flowing through the city. Nobody with a working nose could ignore the results. And the river didn't just smell bad—it carried waterborne diseases like cholera and typhoid. London neighborhoods close to the Thames had death rates from cholera more than six times greater than the neighborhoods farthest away. And the great majority of Londoners drew their drinking water from the Thames.

What the city needed, said reformers, was a sewage system that would carry waste away from the river. Yet no private individual was willing to build such a system, and influential people were opposed to the idea that the government should take responsibility for the problem. For example, the magazine *The Economist* weighed in against proposals for a government-built sewage system, declaring that "suffering and evil are nature's admonitions—they cannot be got rid of."

But the hot summer of 1858 brought what came to be known as the Great Stink, which was so bad that one health journal reported "men struck down with the stench." Even the privileged and powerful suffered: Parliament met in a building next to the river. After unsuccessful efforts to stop the smell by covering the windows with chemical-soaked curtains, Parliament

What you will learn in this chapter:

➤ A way to classify goods that predicts whether a good can be efficiently provided by markets

➤ What **public goods** are, and why markets fail to supply them

➤ What **common resources** are, and why they are overused

➤ What **artificially scarce goods** are, and why they are underconsumed

➤ How government intervention in the production and consumption of these types of goods can make society better off

➤ Why finding the right level of government intervention is difficult

THE LONDON BATHING SEASON.
"COME, MY DEAR! COME TO ITS OLD THAMES, AND HAVE A NICE BATH."

London's River Thames then . . .

. . . and the same river now, thanks to government intervention.

finally approved a plan for an immense system of sewers and pumping stations to direct sewage away from the city. The system, opened in 1865, brought dramatic improvement in the city's quality of life; cholera and typhoid epidemics, which had been regular occurrences, completely disappeared. The Thames was turned from the filthiest to the cleanest metropolitan river in the world, and the sewage system's principal engineer, Sir Joseph Bazalgette, was lauded as having "saved more lives than any single Victorian public official." It was estimated at the time that Bazalgette's sewer system added 20 years to the life span of the average Londoner.

The story of the Great Stink and the policy response that followed illustrate two important reasons for government intervention in the economy. London's new sewage system was a clear example of a *public good*—a good that benefits many people, whether or not they have paid for it, and whose benefits to any one individual do not depend on how many others also benefit. As we will see shortly, public goods differ in important ways from the *private goods* we have studied so far—and these differences mean that public goods cannot be efficiently supplied by the market.

In addition, clean water in the Thames is an example of a *common resource*, a good that many people can consume whether or not they have paid for it but whose consumption by each person reduces the amount available to others. Such goods tend to be overused by individuals in a market system unless the government takes action.

In earlier chapters, we saw that markets sometimes fail to deliver efficient levels of production and consumption of a good or activity. We saw how inefficiency can arise from market power, which leads producers to charge prices that are higher than marginal cost, thereby preventing mutually beneficial transactions from occurring. We also saw how inefficiency can arise from externalities, which cause a divergence between the costs and benefits of an individual's or industry's actions and the costs and benefits of those actions borne by society as a whole, and from private information, which distorts incentives and leads to market failure.

In this chapter, we will take a somewhat different approach to the question of why markets sometimes fail. Here we focus on how the characteristics of goods often determine whether markets can deliver them efficiently. When goods have the "wrong" characteristics, the resulting market failures resemble those associated with externalities or market power. This alternative way of looking at sources of inefficiency deepens our understanding of why markets sometimes don't work well, and how government can serve a useful purpose.

Private Goods—and Others

What's the difference between installing a new bathroom in a house and building a municipal sewage system? What's the difference between growing wheat and fishing in the open ocean?

These aren't trick questions. In each case there is a basic difference in the characteristics of the goods involved. Bathroom appliances and wheat have the characteristics needed to allow markets to work efficiently. Sewage systems and fish in the sea do not.

Let's look at these crucial characteristics and why they matter.

Characteristics of Goods

Goods like bathroom fixtures or wheat have two characteristics that, as we'll soon see, are essential if a good is to be efficiently provided by a market economy.

- They are **excludable:** suppliers of the good can prevent people who don't pay from consuming it.
- They are **rival in consumption:** the same unit of the good cannot be consumed by more than one person at the same time.

When a good is both excludable and rival in consumption, it is called a **private good.** Wheat is an example of a private good. It is *excludable:* the farmer can sell a bushel to one consumer without having to provide wheat to everyone in the county. And it is *rival in consumption:* if I eat bread baked with a farmer's wheat, that bread can no longer be eaten by someone else.

But not all goods have these two characteristics. Some goods are **nonexcludable**—the supplier cannot prevent consumption of the good by people who do not pay for it. Fire protection is one example: a fire department that puts out fires before they spread protects the whole city, not just people who have made contributions to the Firemen's Benevolent Association. An improved environment is another: the city of London couldn't have ended the Great Stink for some residents while leaving the River Thames foul for others.

Nor are all goods rival in consumption. Goods are **nonrival in consumption** if more than one person can consume the same unit of the good at the same time. TV programs are nonrival in consumption: your decision to watch a show does not prevent other people from watching the same show.

Because goods can be either excludable or nonexcludable, rival or nonrival in consumption, there are four types of goods, illustrated by the matrix in Figure 20-1:

- *Private goods*, which are excludable and rival in consumption, like wheat
- *Public goods*, which are nonexcludable and nonrival in consumption, like a public sewer system
- *Common resources*, which are nonexcludable but rival in consumption, like clean water in a river
- *Artificially scarce goods*, which are excludable but nonrival in consumption, like pay-per-view movies on cable TV

There are, of course, many other characteristics that distinguish between types of goods—necessities versus luxuries, normal versus inferior, and so on. Why focus on whether goods are excludable and rival in consumption?

> A good is **excludable** if the supplier of that good can prevent people who do not pay from consuming it.
>
> A good is **rival in consumption** if the same unit of the good cannot be consumed by more than one person at the same time.

> A good that is both excludable and rival in consumption is a **private good.**
>
> When a good is **nonexcludable,** the supplier cannot prevent consumption by people who do not pay for it.

> A good is **nonrival in consumption** if more than one person can consume the same unit of the good at the same time.

Figure 20-1

Four Types of Goods

There are four types of goods. The type of a good depends on (1) whether or not it is excludable—whether a producer can prevent someone from consuming it; and (2) whether or not it is rival in consumption—whether it is impossible for the same unit of a good to be consumed by more than one person at the same time.

	Rival in consumption	Nonrival in consumption
Excludable	**Private goods** • Wheat • Bathroom fixtures	**Artificially scarce goods** • Pay-per-view movies • Computer software
Non-excludable	**Common resources** • Clean water • Biodiversity	**Public goods** • Public sanitation • National defense

Why Markets Can Supply Only Private Goods Efficiently

A market economy, as we learned in earlier chapters, is an amazing system for delivering goods and services. But it cannot supply goods and services efficiently unless they are private goods—excludable and rival in consumption.

To see why excludability is crucial, suppose that a farmer had only two choices: either produce no wheat or provide a bushel of wheat to every resident of the county who wants it, whether or not that resident pays for it. It seems unlikely that anyone would grow wheat under those conditions.

Yet the operator of a municipal sewage system faces pretty much the same problem as our hypothetical farmer. A sewage system makes the whole city cleaner and healthier—but that benefit accrues to all the city's residents, whether or not they pay the system operator. That's why no private entrepreneur came forward with a plan to end London's Great Stink.

The general point is that if a good is nonexcludable, rational consumers won't be willing to pay for it—they will take a "free ride" on anyone who *does* pay. So there is a **free-rider problem.** Examples of the free-rider problem are familiar from daily life. One example you may have encountered happens when students are required to do a group project. There is often a tendency of some members of the group to shirk, relying on others in the group to get the work done. The shirkers *free-ride* on someone else's effort.

Because of the free-rider problem, the forces of self-interest alone do not lead to an efficient level of production for a nonexcludable good. Even though consumers would benefit from increased production of the good, no one individual is willing to pay for more, and so no producer is willing to supply it. The result is that nonexcludable goods suffer from *inefficiently low production* in a market economy. In fact, in the face of the free-rider problem, self-interest may not ensure that any amount of the good—let alone the efficient quantity—is produced.

Goods that are excludable and nonrival in consumption, like pay-per-view movies, suffer from a different kind of inefficiency. As long as a good is excludable, it is possible to earn a profit by making the good available only to those who pay. But the marginal cost of letting an additional viewer watch a pay-per-view movie is zero because it is nonrival in consumption. So the efficient price to the consumer is also zero—or, to put it another way, individuals should watch TV movies up to the point where their marginal benefit is zero. But if the cable company actually charges viewers $4, viewers will consume the good only up to the point where their marginal benefit is $4. When consumers must pay a price greater than zero for a good that is nonrival in consumption, the price they pay is higher than the marginal cost of allowing them to consume that good, which is zero. So in a market economy goods that are nonrival in consumption suffer from *inefficiently low consumption.*

Now we can see why private goods are the only goods that can be efficiently produced and consumed in a competitive market. (That is, a private good will be efficiently produced and consumed in a market free of market power, externalities, or private information.) Because private goods are excludable, producers can charge for them and so have an incentive to produce them. And because they are also rival in consumption, it is efficient for consumers to pay a positive price—a price equal to the marginal cost of production. If one or both of these characteristics are lacking, a market economy will not lead to efficient production and consumption of the good.

Fortunately for the market system, most goods are private goods. Food, clothing, shelter, and most other desirable things in life are excludable and rival in consumption, so markets can provide us with most things. Yet there are crucial goods that don't meet these criteria—and in most cases, that means that the government must step in.

Goods that are nonexcludable suffer from the **free-rider problem**: individuals have no incentive to pay for their own consumption and instead will take a "free ride" on anyone who does pay.

PITFALLS

MARGINAL COST OF WHAT EXACTLY?

In the case of a good that is nonrival in consumption, it's easy to confuse the marginal cost of *producing* a unit of the good with the marginal cost of *allowing* a unit of the good *to be consumed.* For example, your local cable company incurs a marginal cost in making a movie available to its subscribers that is equal to the cost of the resources it uses to produce and broadcast that movie. However, *once that movie is being broadcast,* no marginal cost is incurred by letting an additional family watch it. In other words, no costly resources are "used up" when one more family consumes a movie that has already been produced and is being broadcast.

This complication does not arise, however, when a good is rival in consumption. In that case, the resources used to produce a unit of the good are "used up" by a person's consumption of it—they are no longer available to satisfy someone else's consumption. So when a good is rival in consumption the marginal cost to society of allowing an individual to consume a unit is equal to the resource cost of producing that unit—that is, equal to the marginal cost of producing it.

economics in action

A Policeman's Lot

We tend to think of crime prevention as a function of government, yet individuals take their own measures to prevent theft: homeowners put locks on their doors, and many businesses hire their own security guards.

Why, then, do we also have public police departments? Because law enforcement, as opposed to self-protection, is a public good. The benefits of keeping a potential thief off your own property are rival and excludable. But the benefits of tracking down criminals and bringing them to justice, and of policing public areas, accrue to all law-abiding citizens.

The beginning of modern police departments can be traced to two eighteenth-century institutions that concentrated on these clearly public-good aspects of crime prevention: the Bow Street Runners, an early detective agency that concentrated on finding and catching criminals, and the Thames River Police, who patrolled the dock areas. In 1829 Sir Robert Peel, building on the lessons from these institutions, oversaw the creation of a unified London police force, which served as a model for police forces throughout the world. To this day British police officers are known, after Sir Robert, as "bobbies." ■

> > > > > > > > > > > > > > > > > > > >

>>CHECK YOUR UNDERSTANDING 20-1

1. Classify each of the following goods according to whether they are excludable and whether they are rival in consumption. What kind of good is each?
   a. Use of a public space such as a park
   b. A cheese burrito
   c. Information from a website that is password-protected
   d. Publicly announced information on the path of an incoming hurricane
2. Which of the goods in Question 1 will be provided by a competitive market? Which will not be? Explain.

Solutions appear at back of book.

>>QUICK REVIEW

- Goods can be classified according to two attributes: whether they are *excludable* and whether they are *rival in consumption*.
- Goods that are both excludable and rival in consumption are *private goods*. Private goods can be efficiently produced and consumed in a competitive market.
- When goods are *nonexcludable*, there is a *free-rider problem*: consumers will not pay producers, leading to inefficiently low production.
- When goods are *nonrival in consumption*, the efficient price for consumption is zero. But if a positive price is charged to compensate producers for the cost of production, the result is inefficiently low consumption.

Public Goods

A **public good** is the exact opposite of a private good: it is a good that is both nonexcludable and nonrival in consumption. A sewage system is an example of a public good: you can't keep a river clean without making it clean for everyone who lives near its banks, and my protection from great stinks does not come at my neighbor's expense.

Here are some other examples of public goods:

- *Disease prevention.* When doctors act to stamp out the beginnings of an epidemic before it can spread, they protect people around the world.
- *National defense.* A strong military protects all citizens.
- *Scientific research.* More knowledge benefits everyone.

Because these goods are nonexcludable, they suffer from the free-rider problem, so no private firm would be willing to produce them. And because they are nonrival in consumption, it would be inefficient to charge people for consuming them. As a result, society must find nonmarket methods for providing these goods.

Providing Public Goods

Public goods are provided through a variety of means. The government doesn't always get involved—in many cases a nongovernmental solution has been found for the free-rider problem. But these solutions are usually imperfect in some way.

A **public good** is both nonexcludable and nonrival in consumption.

Some public goods are supplied through voluntary contributions. For example, private donations support a considerable amount of scientific research. But private donations are insufficient to finance huge, socially important projects like basic medical research.

Some public goods are supplied by self-interested individuals or firms because those who produce them are able to make money in an indirect way. The classic example is broadcast television, which in the United States is supported entirely by advertising. The downside of such indirect funding is that it skews the nature and quantity of the public goods that are supplied, as well as imposing additional costs on consumers. TV stations show the programs that yield the most advertising revenue (that is, programs best suited for selling antacids, hair-loss remedies, antihistamines, and the like to the segment of the population that buys them), which are not necessarily the programs people most want to see. And viewers must also endure many commercials.

On the prowl: a British TV detection van at work.

Some potentially public goods are deliberately made excludable and therefore subject to charge, like pay-per-view movies. In the U.K., where most television programming is paid for by a yearly license fee assessed on every television owner, television viewing is made artificially excludable by the use of "television detection vans": vans that roam neighborhoods in an attempt to detect televisions in nonlicensed households and fine them. However, as noted earlier, when suppliers charge a price greater than zero for a nonrival good, consumers will consume an inefficiently low quantity of that good.

In small communities, a high level of social encouragement or pressure can be brought to bear on people to contribute money or time to provide the efficient level of a public good. Volunteer fire departments, which depend both on the volunteered services of the firefighters themselves and on contributions from local residents, are a good example. But as communities grow larger and more anonymous, social pressure is increasingly difficult to apply, so that larger towns and cities must depend on salaried firefighters.

As this last example suggests, when these other solutions fail, it is up to the government to provide public goods. Indeed, the most important public goods—national defense, the legal system, disease control, fire protection in large cities, and so on—are provided by government and paid for by taxes. Economic theory tells us that the provision of public goods is one of the crucial roles of government.

How Much of a Public Good Should Be Provided?

In some cases, provision of a public good is an "either-or" decision: London would either have a sewage system—or not. But in most cases, governments must decide not only whether to provide a public good but also *how much* of that public good to provide. For example, street cleaning is a public good—but how often should the streets be cleaned? Once a month? Twice a month? Every other day?

Imagine a city in which there are only two residents, Ted and Alice. Assume that the public good in question is street cleaning and that Ted and Alice truthfully tell the government how much they value a unit of the public good, where a unit is equal to one street cleaning per month. Specifically, each of them tells the government *his or her willingness to pay for another unit of the public good supplied*—an amount that corresponds to that *individual's marginal benefit* of another unit of the public good.

Using this information plus information on the cost of providing the good, the government can use marginal analysis to find the efficient level of providing the public good: the level at which the *marginal social benefit* of the public good is equal to the marginal cost of producing it. Recall from Chapter 19 that the marginal social benefit of a good is the benefit that accrues to society as a whole from the consumption of one additional unit of the good.

But what is the marginal social benefit of another unit of a public good—a unit that generates utility for *all* consumers, not just one consumer, because it is nonexcludable and nonrival in consumption? This question leads us to an important principle: *in the special case of a public good, the marginal social benefit of a unit of the good is equal to the sum of the individual marginal benefits that are enjoyed by all consumers of that unit.* Or to consider it from a slightly different angle, if a consumer could be compelled to pay for a unit before consuming it (the good is made excludable), then the marginal social benefit of a unit is equal to the *sum* of each consumer's willingness to pay for that unit. Using this principle, the marginal social benefit of an additional street cleaning per month is equal to Ted's individual marginal benefit from that additional cleaning *plus* Alice's individual marginal benefit.

We all benefit when someone does the cleaning up.

Why? Because a public good is nonrival in consumption—Ted's benefit from a cleaner street does not diminish Alice's benefit from that same clean street, and vice versa. Because people can all simultaneously consume the same unit of a public good, the marginal social benefit of an additional unit of that good is the *sum* of the individual marginal benefits of all who enjoy the public good. And the efficient quantity of a public good is the quantity at which the marginal social benefit is equal to the marginal cost of providing it.

Figure 20-2 on page 482 illustrates the efficient provision of a public good, showing three marginal benefit curves. Panel (a) shows Ted's individual marginal benefit curve from street cleaning, MB_T: he would be willing to pay $25 for the city to clean its streets once per month, an additional $18 to have it done a second time, and so on. Panel (b) shows Alice's individual marginal benefit curve from street cleaning, MB_A. Panel (c) shows the marginal social benefit curve from street cleaning, MSB: it is the vertical sum of Ted's and Alice's individual marginal benefit curves, MB_T and MB_A.

To maximize society's welfare, the government should clean the street up to the level at which the marginal social benefit of an additional cleaning is no longer greater than the marginal cost. Suppose that the marginal cost of street cleaning is $6 per cleaning. Then the city should clean its streets 5 times per month, because the marginal social benefit of going from 4 to 5 cleanings is $8, but going from 5 to 6 cleanings would yield a marginal social benefit of only $2.

Figure 20-2 can help reinforce our understanding of why we cannot rely on individual self-interest to yield provision of an efficient quantity of public goods. Suppose that the city did one fewer street cleaning than the efficient quantity and that either Ted or Alice was asked to pay for the last cleaning. Neither one would be willing to pay for it! Ted would personally gain only the equivalent of $3 in utility from adding one more street cleaning—so he wouldn't be willing to pay the $6 marginal cost of another cleaning. Alice would personally gain the equivalent of $5 in utility—so she wouldn't be willing to pay either. The point is that the marginal social benefit of one more unit of a public good is always greater than the individual marginal benefit to any one individual. That is why no individual is willing to pay for the efficient quantity of the good.

Does this description of the public good problem, in which the marginal social benefit of an additional unit of the public good is greater than any individual's marginal benefit, sound a bit familiar? It should: we encountered a somewhat similar situation in our discussion of *positive externalities*. Remember that in the case of a positive externality, the marginal social benefit accruing to all consumers of another unit of the good is greater than the producer's marginal benefit of producing that unit and the market alone produces too little of the good. In the case of a public good, the individual marginal benefit of a consumer plays the same role that the producer's marginal benefit plays in the case of positive externalities. So the problem of providing public goods is very similar to the problem of dealing with positive externalities; in both cases there is a market failure that calls for government intervention. One basic rationale for the existence of government is that it provides a way for citizens to tax themselves in order to provide public goods—particularly a vital public good like national defense.

Of course, if society really consisted of only two individuals, they would probably manage to strike a deal to provide the good. But imagine a city with a million residents, each of whose individual marginal benefit from provision of the good is only a tiny fraction of the marginal social benefit. It would be impossible for people to reach a voluntary

Figure 20-2   A Public Good

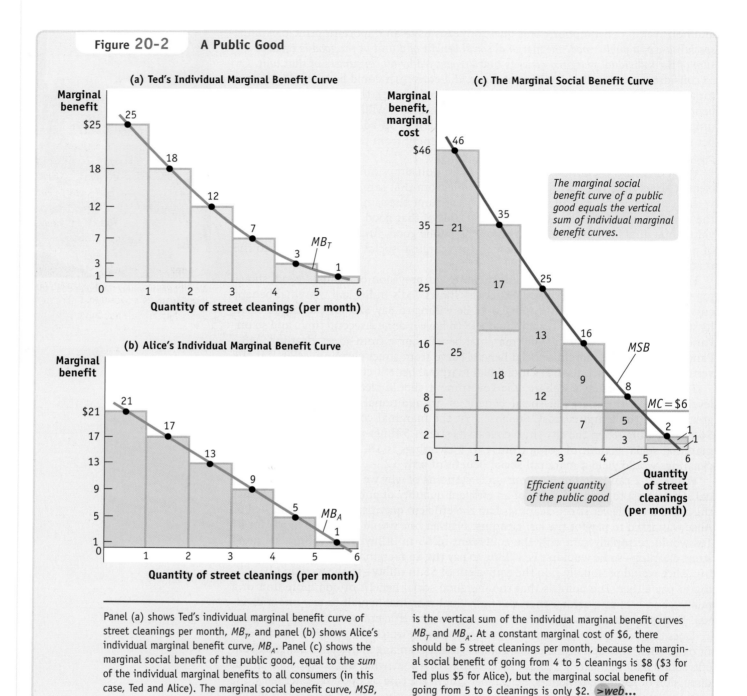

Panel (a) shows Ted's individual marginal benefit curve of street cleanings per month, MB_T, and panel (b) shows Alice's individual marginal benefit curve, MB_A. Panel (c) shows the marginal social benefit of the public good, equal to the *sum* of the individual marginal benefits to all consumers (in this case, Ted and Alice). The marginal social benefit curve, *MSB*, is the vertical sum of the individual marginal benefit curves MB_T and MB_A. At a constant marginal cost of $6, there should be 5 street cleanings per month, because the marginal social benefit of going from 4 to 5 cleanings is $8 ($3 for Ted plus $5 for Alice), but the marginal social benefit of going from 5 to 6 cleanings is only $2. **>web...**

agreement to pay for the efficient level of street cleaning—the potential for free-riding makes it too difficult to make and enforce an agreement among so many people. But they could and would vote to tax themselves to pay for a citywide sanitation department.

Cost-Benefit Analysis

Governments engage in **cost-benefit analysis** when they estimate the social costs and social benefits of providing a public good.

How do governments decide in practice how much of a public good to provide? Sometimes policy makers just guess—or do whatever they think will get them reelected. However, responsible governments try to estimate both the social benefits and the social costs of providing a public good, a process known as **cost-benefit analysis.**

It's a sad fact that many Americans who are eligible to vote don't bother to. As a result their interests tend to be ignored by politicians. But what's even sadder is that this self-defeating behavior may be completely rational.

As the economist Mancur Olson pointed out in a famous book titled *The Logic of Collective Action*, voting is a public good, one that suffers from severe free-rider problems.

Imagine that you are one of a million people who would stand to gain the equivalent of $100 each if some plan is passed in a statewide referendum—say, a plan to improve public schools. And sup-

pose that the opportunity cost of the time it would take you to vote is $10. Will you be sure to go to the polls and vote for the referendum? If you are rational, the answer is no! The reason is that it is very unlikely that your vote will decide the issue, either way. If the measure passes, you benefit, even if you don't bother to vote—the benefits are nonexcludable. If the measure doesn't pass, your vote would not have changed the outcome. Either way, by not voting—by free-riding on those who do vote—you save $10.

Of course, many people do vote out of a sense of civic duty. But because political action is a public good, in general people

devote too little effort to defending their own interests.

The result, Olson pointed out, is that when a large group of people share a common political interest, they are likely to exert too little effort promoting their cause and so will be ignored. Conversely, small, well-organized interest groups that act on issues narrowly targeted in their favor tend to have disproportionate power.

Is this a reason to distrust democracy? Winston Churchill said it best: "Democracy is the worst form of government, except for all the other forms that have been tried."

It's straightforward to estimate the cost of supplying a public good. Estimating the benefit is harder. In fact, it is a very difficult problem.

Now you might wonder why governments can't figure out the marginal social benefit of a public good just by asking people their willingness to pay for it (their individual marginal benefit). But it turns out that it's hard to get an honest answer.

This is not a problem with private goods: we can determine how much an individual is willing to pay for one more unit of a private good by looking at his or her actual choices. But because people don't actually pay for public goods, the question of willingness to pay is always hypothetical.

Worse yet, it's a question that people have an incentive not to answer truthfully. People naturally want more rather than less. Because they cannot be made to pay for whatever quantity of the public good they use, when asked how much they desire a public good people are apt to overstate their true feelings. For example, if street cleaning were scheduled according to the stated wishes of homeowners alone, the streets would be cleaned every day—an inefficient level of provision. So governments must be aware that they cannot simply rely on the public's statements when deciding how much of a public good to provide—if they do, they are likely to provide too much. In contrast, as the For Inquiring Minds explains above, relying on the public to indicate how much of the public good they want through voting has problems as well—and is likely to lead to too little of the public good being provided.

economics in action

Old Man River

It just keeps rolling along—but now and then it decides to roll in a different direction. In fact, the Mississippi River changes its course every few hundred years. Sediment carried downstream gradually clogs the river's route to the sea, and eventually the river breaches its banks and opens a new channel. Over the millennia the mouth of the Mississippi has swung back and forth along an arc some 200 miles wide.

So when is the Mississippi due to change course again? Oh, about 35 years ago.

The Mississippi currently runs to the sea past New Orleans; but by 1950 it was apparent that the river was about to shift course, taking a new route to the sea. If the Army Corps of Engineers hadn't gotten involved, the shift would probably have happened by 1970.

A shift in the Mississippi would have severely damaged the Louisiana economy. A major industrial area would have lost good access to the ocean, and salt water would have contaminated much of its water supply. So the Army Corps of Engineers has kept the Mississippi in its place with a huge complex of dams, walls, and gates known as the Old River Control Structure. At times the amount of water released by this control structure is five times the flow at Niagara Falls.

The Old River Control Structure is a dramatic example of a public good. No individual would have had an incentive to build it, yet it protects many billions of dollars' worth of private property. The history of the Army Corps of Engineers, which handles water-control projects across the United States, illustrates the problems with government provision of public goods. Everyone wants a project that benefits his or her own property—if other people are going to pay for it. So there is a systematic tendency for potential beneficiaries of Corps projects to overstate the benefits. And the Corps has become notorious for undertaking expensive projects that cannot be justified with any reasonable cost-benefit analysis.

In other countries the counterparts of the Army Corps of Engineers are even more prone to overspending. In Japan, almost every river now runs through a concrete channel, and an amazing 60 percent of the coastline is now "armored" with concrete barriers. ■

< < < < < < < < < < < < < < < < < <

>>CHECK YOUR UNDERSTANDING 20-2

1. The town of Centreville, population 16, has two types of residents, Homebodies and Revelers. Using the accompanying table, the town must decide how much to spend on its New Year's Eve party. No individual resident expects to directly bear the cost of the party.
   a. Suppose there are 10 Homebodies and 6 Revelers. Determine the marginal social benefit schedule of money spent on the party. What is the efficient level of spending?
   b. Suppose there are 6 Homebodies and 10 Revelers. How do your answers to part a change? Explain.
   c. Suppose that the individual marginal benefit schedules are known but no one knows the true numbers of Homebodies and Revelers. Individuals are asked their preferences. What is the likely outcome? Why is it likely to result in an inefficiently high level of spending? Explain.

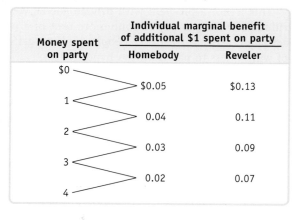

Money spent on party	Individual marginal benefit of additional $1 spent on party	
	Homebody	Reveler
$0		
	$0.05	$0.13
1		
	0.04	0.11
2		
	0.03	0.09
3		
	0.02	0.07
4		

Solutions appear at back of book.

Common Resources

A **common resource** is a good that is nonexcludable but is rival in consumption. An example is the stock of fish in a limited fishing area, like the fisheries off the coast of New England. Traditionally, anyone who had a boat could go out to sea and catch fish—fish in the sea were a nonexcludable good. Yet because the total number of fish is limited, the fish that one person catches are no longer available to be caught by someone else. So fish in the sea are rival in consumption.

A **common resource** is nonexcludable and rival in consumption: you can't stop me from consuming the good, and more consumption by me means less of the good available for you.

Other examples of common resources are clean air and water as well as the diversity of animal and plant species on the planet (biodiversity). In each of these cases the fact that the good, though rival in consumption, is nonexcludable poses a serious problem.

The Problem of Overuse

Because common resources are nonexcludable, individuals cannot be charged for their use. Yet, because they are rival in consumption, an individual who uses a unit depletes the resource by making that unit unavailable to others. As a result, a common resource is subject to **overuse**: an individual will continue to use it until his or her marginal benefit of its use is equal to zero, ignoring the cost that this action inflicts on society as a whole. As we will see shortly, the problem of overuse of a common resource is similar to a problem we studied in Chapter 19: the problem of a good that generates a negative externality, such as pollution-creating electricity generation or livestock farming.

Fishing is a classic example of a common resource. In heavily fished waters, my fishing imposes a cost on others by reducing the fish population and making it harder for others to catch fish. But I have no personal incentive to take this cost into account, since I cannot be charged for fishing. As a result, from society's point of view, I catch too many fish. Traffic congestion is another example of overuse of a common resource. A major highway during rush hour can accommodate only a certain number of vehicles per hour. If I decide to drive alone to work rather than carpool or work at home, I make the commute of many other people a bit longer; but I have no incentive to take these consequences into account.

In the case of a common resource, the *marginal social cost* of my use of that resource is higher than my *individual marginal cost*, the cost to me of using an additional unit of the good.

Figure 20-3 illustrates the point. It shows the demand curve for fish, which measures the marginal benefit of fish—the benefit to consumers when an additional unit of fish is caught and consumed. It also shows the supply curve for fish, which measures the marginal cost of production of the fishing industry. We know from Chapter 9 that the industry supply curve is the horizontal sum of each individual

> Common resources left to the market suffer from **overuse**: individuals ignore the fact that their use depletes the amount of the resource remaining for others.

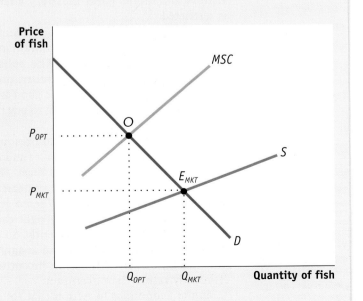

Figure 20-3

A Common Resource

The supply curve *S*, which shows the marginal cost of production of the entire fishing industry, is composed of the individual supply curves of the individual fishermen. But each fisherman's individual marginal cost does not include the cost that his or her actions impose on others: the depletion of the common resource. As a result, the marginal social cost curve, *MSC*, lies above the supply curve; in an unregulated market, the quantity of the common resource used, Q_{MKT}, exceeds the efficient quantity of use, Q_{OPT}.

fisherman's supply curve—equivalent to his or her individual marginal cost curve. The fishing industry supplies the quantity where its marginal cost is equal to the price, the quantity Q_{MKT}. But the efficient outcome is to catch the quantity Q_{OPT}, the quantity of output that equates the marginal benefit to the marginal social cost, not to the fishing industry's marginal cost of production. The market outcome results in overuse of the common resource.

As we noted, there is a close parallel between the problem of managing a common resource and the problem posed by negative externalities. In the case of an activity that generates a negative externality, the marginal social cost of production is greater than the industry's marginal cost of production, the difference being the marginal external cost imposed on society. Here, the loss to society arising from a fisherman's depletion of the common resource plays the same role as the external cost plays when there is a negative externality. In fact, many negative externalities (such as pollution) can be thought of as involving common resources (such as clean air).

The Efficient Use and Maintenance of a Common Resource

Because common resources pose problems similar to those created by negative externalities, the solutions are also similar. To ensure efficient use of a common resource, society must find a way of getting individual users of the resource to take into account the costs they impose on other users. This is basically the same principle as that of getting individuals to internalize a negative externality that arises from their actions.

There are three fundamental ways to induce people who use common resources to internalize the costs they impose on others.

- Tax or otherwise regulate the use of the common resource
- Create a system of tradable licenses for the right to use the common resource
- Make the common resource excludable and assign property rights to some individuals

Like activities that generate negative externalities, use of a common resource can be reduced to the efficient quantity by imposing a Pigouvian tax. For example, some countries have imposed "congestion charges" on those who drive during rush hour, in effect charging them for use of the common resource of highway space. Likewise, visitors to national parks must pay a fee and the number of visitors to any one park is restricted.

A second way to correct the problem of overuse is to create a system of tradable licenses for the use of the common resource much like the systems designed to address negative externalities. The policy maker issues the number of licenses that corresponds to the efficient level of use of the good. Making the licenses tradable assures that the right to use the good is allocated efficiently—that is, those who end up using the good (those willing to pay the most for a license) are those who gain the most from its use.

But when it comes to common resources, often the most natural solution is simply to assign property rights. At a fundamental level, common resources are subject to overuse because *nobody owns them*. The essence of ownership of a good—the *property right* over the good—is that you can limit who can and cannot use the good, and how much of it can be used. When a good is nonexcludable, in a very real sense no one owns it because a property right cannot be enforced—and consequently no one has an incentive to use it efficiently. So one way to correct the problem of overuse is to make the good excludable and assign property rights over it to someone. The good now has an owner who has an incentive to protect the value of the good—to use it efficiently rather than overuse it.

As the Economics in Action that follows shows, a system of tradable licenses has been a successful strategy in some fisheries.

economics in action

A Tale of Two Fisheries

On August 27, 2000, the *New York Times Magazine* carried a story titled "A Tale of Two Fisheries," which compared the lives of lobstermen in two places: Port Judith, Rhode Island, and Port Lincoln, Australia.

Port Judith used to call itself the "tuna capital of the world," but tuna—along with swordfish, cod, halibut, and other species that used to be plentiful offshore—are now hard to find anywhere in the vicinity. Fishermen in the United States have been free to catch as many fish as they like; as a result of overfishing, the once-great fisheries of New England have largely collapsed. This includes lobsters, except for some areas of Maine where "lobster gangs" have protected the common resource by sabotaging the boats of outsiders. As lobster stocks have plunged, life for the lobstermen of Port Judith has gotten increasingly difficult.

In Australia, however, a different system prevails. To set a lobster trap, you must have a license, and only a limited number of licenses have been issued. A license now sells for about $21,000. At first Australian lobstermen were skeptical of a system that limited their fishing. But they now support the system enthusiastically, because it sustains the value of their licenses—and also sustains their livelihood.

The system is popular because it works: an Australian lobster trap typically comes up with more and bigger lobsters than its American counterpart. As a result, the lobstermen of Port Lincoln, Australia, are far more prosperous than those of Port Judith, Rhode Island.

By the way, we don't want to give the impression that establishing property rights over common resources is un-American. The New Jersey clam fishery, which was in serious trouble in the late 1980s, now operates under a license system similar to that of the Australian lobster fishery. And both the clams and the New Jersey clam industry have staged a spectacular comeback. ■

> > > > > > > > > > > > > > > > > > >

>>CHECK YOUR UNDERSTANDING 20-3

1. Rocky Mountain Forest is a government-owned forest in which private citizens were allowed in the past to harvest as much timber as they wanted free of charge. State in economic terms why this is problematic from society's point of view.

2. You are the new Forest Service Commissioner and have been instructed to come up with ways to preserve the forest for the general public. Name three different methods you could use to maintain the efficient level of tree harvesting and explain how each would work. For each method, what information would you need to know in order to achieve an efficient outcome?

Solutions appear at back of book.

Artificially Scarce Goods

An **artificially scarce good** is a good that is excludable but nonrival in consumption. As we've already seen, pay-per-view movies are a familiar example. The marginal cost to society of allowing an individual to watch the movie is zero, because one person's viewing doesn't interfere with other people's viewing. Yet cable companies prevent an individual from seeing a movie if he or she hasn't paid. Many *information goods* like computer software are also artificially scarce; we will discuss the economics of information goods at greater length in Chapter 22.

As we've already seen, markets will supply artificially scarce goods: because they are excludable, the producers can charge people for consuming them.

But artificially scarce goods are nonrival in consumption, which means that the marginal cost of an individual's consumption is zero. So the price that the supplier of an artificially scarce good charges exceeds marginal cost. Because the efficient price

>> **QUICK REVIEW**

➤ A *common resource* is rival in consumption but nonexcludable.

➤ The problem with common resources is *overuse*: a user depletes the amount of the common resource available to others but does not take this cost into account when deciding how much to use the common resource.

➤ Like negative externalities, a common resource can be efficiently managed by Pigouvian taxes, by the creation of a system of tradable licenses for its use, or by making it excludable and assigning property rights.

An **artificially scarce good** is excludable but nonrival in consumption.

Figure 20-4

An Artificially Scarce Good

An artificially scarce good is excludable and nonrival in consumption. It is made artificially scarce because producers charge a positive price but the marginal cost of allowing one more person to consume the good is zero. In this example the market price of a pay-per-view movie is $4 and the quantity demanded at that price is Q_{MKT}. But the efficient level of consumption is Q_{OPT}, the quantity demanded when the price is zero. The efficient quantity, Q_{OPT}, exceeds the quantity demanded in an unregulated market, Q_{MKT}. The shaded area represents the loss in total surplus from charging a price of $4. **>web...**

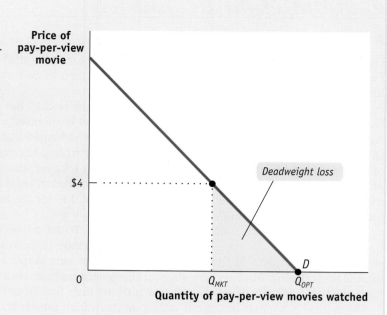

is equal to the marginal cost of zero, the good is "artificially scarce," and consumption of the good is inefficiently low. However, unless the producer can somehow earn revenue for producing and selling the good, he or she will be unwilling to produce at all—an outcome that leaves society even worse off than it would otherwise be with positive but inefficiently low consumption.

Figure 20-4 illustrates the loss in total surplus caused by artificial scarcity. The demand curve shows the quantity of pay-per-view movies watched at any given price. The marginal cost of allowing an additional person to watch the movie is zero; so the efficient quantity of movies viewed is Q_{OPT}. The cable company charges a positive price, in this case $4, to unscramble the signal, and as a result only Q_{MKT} pay-per-view movies will be watched. This leads to a deadweight loss equal to the area of the shaded triangle.

Does this look familiar? Like the problems that arise with public goods and common resources, the problem created by artificially scarce goods is similar to something we have already seen: in this case, it is the problem of *natural monopoly*. A natural monopoly, you will recall, is an industry in which average total cost is above marginal cost for the relevant output range. In order to be willing to produce output, the producer must charge a price at least as high as average total cost—that is, a price above marginal cost. But a price above marginal cost leads to inefficiently low consumption.

economics in action

Blacked-Out Games

It's the night of the big game for your local team—a game that is being nationally televised by one of the major networks. So you flip to the local channel that is an affiliate of that network—but the game isn't on. Instead, you get some other show with a message scrolling across the bottom of the screen that this game has been blacked out in your area. What the message probably doesn't say, though you understand quite well, is that this blackout is at the insistence of the team's owners, who don't want people who might have paid for tickets staying home and watching the game on TV instead.

So the good in question—watching the game on TV—has been made artificially scarce. Because the game is being broadcast anyway, no scarce resources would be used to make it available in its immediate locality as well. But it isn't available—which means a loss in welfare to those who would have watched the game on TV but are not willing to pay the price, in time and money, to go to the stadium. ∎

> > > > > > > > > > > > > > > > > > > >

>> CHECK YOUR UNDERSTANDING 20-4

1. Xena is a software program produced by Xenoid. Each year Xenoid produces an upgrade that costs $300,000 to produce. It costs nothing to allow customers to download it from the company's website. The demand schedule for the upgrade is shown in the accompanying table.

   a. What is the efficient price to a consumer of this upgrade? Explain.

   b. What is the lowest price at which Xenoid is willing to produce and sell the upgrade? Draw the demand curve and show the loss of total surplus that occurs when Xenoid charges this price compared to the efficient price.

Price of upgrade	Quantity of upgrades demanded
$180	1,700
150	2,000
120	2,300
90	2,600
0	3,500

Solutions appear at back of book.

• A LOOK AHEAD •

In 2003 the various levels of U.S. government—federal, state, and local—spent about $3 trillion. Where did the money go?

The answer, in large part, is that it went to provide public goods. National defense and homeland security took a big chunk; so did education, which is widely regarded as a public good. Then there was spending on highways, public health, fire prevention, and so on.

Not all government spending is on items that can easily be described as public goods. As we'll see in Chapter 21, much spending at the federal level goes for *social insurance*, programs intended to help individuals and families in trouble. But providing public goods is still a central feature of government budgets.

And that brings us to the next question: where does the money that pays for public goods come from? The answer, of course, is that it comes from tax revenue. But taxes, in turn, have economic effects, because they change incentives.

In the next chapter we'll take a deeper look at how taxes affect a market economy. We'll also look at the related effects of social insurance.

SUMMARY

1. Goods may be classified according to whether or not they are **excludable** and whether or not they are **rival in consumption.**

2. Free markets can deliver efficient levels of production and consumption for **private goods,** which are both excludable and rival in consumption. When goods are nonexcludable, nonrival in consumption, or both, free markets cannot achieve efficient outcomes.

3. When goods are **nonexcludable,** there is a **free-rider problem:** consumers will not pay for the good, leading to inefficiently low production. When goods are **non-**

rival in consumption, they should be free, and any positive price leads to inefficiently low consumption.

4. A **public good** is nonexcludable and nonrival in consumption. In most cases a public good must be supplied by the government. The marginal social benefit of a public good is equal to the sum of the individual marginal benefits to each consumer. The efficient quantity of a public good is the quantity at which marginal social benefit equals marginal cost. Like a positive externality, marginal social benefit is greater than any one individual's marginal benefit, so no individual is willing to provide the efficient quantity.

5. One rationale for the presence of government is that it allows citizens to tax themselves in order to provide public goods. Governments use **cost-benefit analysis** to determine the efficient provision of a public good. Such analysis is difficult, however, because individuals have an incentive to overstate the good's value to them.

6. A **common resource** is rival in consumption but nonexcludable. It is subject to **overuse,** because an individual does not take into account the fact that his or her use depletes the amount available for others. This is similar to the problem of a negative externality: the marginal social cost of use of an individual's common resource is always higher than his or her individual marginal cost. Pigouvian taxes, the creation of a system of tradable licenses, or the assignment of property rights are possible solutions.

7. **Artificially scarce goods** are excludable but nonrival in consumption. Because no marginal cost arises from allowing another individual to consume the good, the efficient price is zero. A positive price compensates the producer for the cost of production but leads to inefficiently low consumption. The problem of an artificially scarce good is similar to that of a natural monopoly.

KEY TERMS

Excludable, p. 477
Rival in consumption, p. 477
Private good, p. 477
Nonexcludable, p. 477

Nonrival in consumption, p. 477
Free-rider problem, p. 478
Public good, p. 479
Cost-benefit analysis, p. 482

Common resource, p. 484
Overuse, p. 485
Artificially scarce good, p. 487

PROBLEMS

1. The government is involved in providing many goods and services. For each of the goods or services listed, determine whether it is rival or nonrival in consumption and whether it is excludable or nonexcludable. What type of good is it? Without government involvement, would the quantity provided be efficient, inefficiently low, or inefficiently high?

   a. Street signs

   b. Amtrak rail service

   c. Regulations limiting pollution

   d. An interstate highway without tolls

   e. A lighthouse on the coast

2. An economist gives the following advice to a museum director: "You should introduce 'peak pricing': at times when the museum has few visitors, you should admit visitors for free. And at times when the museum has many visitors, you should charge a higher admission fee."

   a. When the museum is quiet, is it rival or nonrival in consumption? Is it excludable or nonexcludable? What type of good is the museum at those times? What would be the efficient price to charge visitors during that time, and why?

   b. When the museum is busy, is it rival or nonrival in consumption? Is it excludable or nonexcludable? What type of good is the museum at those times? What would be the efficient price to charge visitors during that time, and why?

3. In many planned communities, various aspects of community living are subject to regulation by a homeowners' association. These rules can regulate house architecture; require snow removal from sidewalks; excluded of outdoor equipment, such as backyard swimming pools; require appropriate conduct in shared spaces such as the community clubhouse; and so on. There has been some conflict, as some homeowners feel that some of the regulations are overly intrusive. You have been called in to mediate. Using economics, how would you decide what types of regulations are warranted and what types are not?

4. A residential community has 100 residents who are concerned about security. The accompanying table gives the total cost of hiring a 24-hour security service as well as each individual resident's total benefit.

Quantity of security guards	Total cost	Total individual benefit to each resident
0	$0	$0
1	150	10
2	300	16
3	450	18
4	600	19

   a. Explain why the security service is a public good for the residents of the community.

   b. Calculate the marginal cost, the individual marginal benefit for each resident, and the marginal social benefit.

   c. If an individual resident were to decide about hiring and paying for security guards on his or her own, how many guards would that resident hire?

d. If the residents act together, how many security guards will they hire?

5. The accompanying table shows Tanisha's and Ari's individual marginal benefit of different amounts of street cleanings per month. Suppose that the marginal cost of street cleanings is constant at $9 each.

Quantity of street cleanings per month	Tanisha's individual marginal benefit	Ari's individual marginal benefit
0		
	$10	$8
1		
	6	4
2		
	2	1
3		

a. If Tanisha had to pay for street cleaning on her own, how many street cleanings would there be?

b. Calculate the marginal social benefit of street cleaning. What is the optimal number of street cleanings?

c. Consider the optimal number of street cleanings. The last street cleaning of that number costs $9. Is Tanisha willing to pay for that last cleaning on her own? Is Ari willing to pay for that last cleaning on his own?

6. Anyone with a radio receiver can listen to public radio, which is funded largely by donations.

a. Is public radio excludable or nonexcludable? Is it rival in consumption or nonrival? What type of good is it?

b. Should the government support public radio? Explain your reasoning.

c. In order to finance itself, public radio decides to transmit only to satellite radios, for which users have to pay a fee. What type of good is public radio then? Will the quantity of radio listening be efficient? Why or why not?

7. The village of Upper Bigglesworth has a village "commons," a piece of land on which each villager, by law, is free to graze his or her cows. Use of the commons is measured in units of the number of cows grazing on it. Assume that each resident has a constant marginal cost of sending cows to graze (that is, the marginal cost is the same, whether 1 or 10 cows are grazing). But each additional cow grazed means less grass available for others, and the damage done by overgrazing of the commons increases as the number of cows grazing increases. Finally, assume that the benefit to the villagers of each additional cow grazing on the commons declines as more cows graze, since each additional cow has less grass to eat than the previous one.

a. Is the commons excludable or nonexcludable? Is it rival in consumption or nonrival? What kind of good is the commons?

b. Draw a diagram, with the quantity of cows that graze on the commons on the horizontal axis. How does the quantity of cows grazing in the absence of government intervention compare to the efficient quantity? Show both in your diagram.

c. The villagers hire you to tell them how to achieve an efficient use of the commons. You tell them that there are three possibilities: a Pigouvian tax, the assignment of property rights over the commons, and a system of tradable licenses for the right to graze a cow. Explain how each one of these options would lead to an efficient use of the commons. Draw a diagram that shows the Pigouvian tax.

8. The accompanying table shows six consumers' willingness to pay (his or her individual marginal benefit) for one MP3 file copy of a Dr. Dre album. The marginal cost of making the file accessible to one additional consumer is constant, at zero.

Consumer	Individual marginal benefit
Adriana	$2
Bhagesh	15
Chizuko	1
Denzel	10
Emma	5
Frank	4

a. What would be the efficient price to charge for a download of the file?

b. All six consumers are able to download the file for free from a file-sharing service, Pantster. Which consumers will download the file? What will be the total consumer surplus to those consumers?

c. Pantster is shut down for copyright law infringement. In order to download the file, consumers now have to pay $4.99 at a commercial music site. Which consumers will download the file? What will be the total consumer surplus to those consumers? How much producer surplus accrues to the commercial music site? What is the total surplus? What is the deadweight loss from the new pricing policy?

9. Butchart Gardens is a very large garden in Victoria, British Columbia, renowned for its beautiful plants. It is so large that it could hold many times more visitors than currently visit it. The garden charges an admission fee of $10. At this price, 1,000 visitors visit the garden each day. If admission were free, 2,000 visitors would visit the garden each day.

a. Are visits to Butchart Gardens excludable or nonexcludable? Are they rival in consumption or nonrival? What type of good is it?

b. In a diagram, illustrate the demand curve for visits to Butchart Gardens. Indicate the situation when Butchart Gardens charges an admission fee of $10. Also indicate the situation when Butchart Gardens charges no admission fee.

c. Illustrate the deadweight loss from charging a $10 admission fee. Explain why charging a $10 admission fee is inefficient.

10. In developing a vaccine for a new virus called SARS, a pharmaceutical company incurs a very high fixed cost. The marginal cost of delivering the vaccine to patients, however, is negligible (consider it to be equal to zero). The pharmaceutical company holds the exclusive patent to the vaccine. You are a regulator who must decide what price the pharmaceutical company is allowed to charge.

a. Draw a diagram that shows the price for the vaccine that would arise if the company is unregulated, and label it P_M.

What is the efficient price for the vaccine? Show the deadweight loss that arises from the price P_M.

b. On another diagram, show the lowest price that the regulator can enforce that would still induce the pharmaceutical company to develop the vaccine. Label it P^*. Show the deadweight loss that arises from this price. How does it compare to the deadweight loss that arises from the price P_M?

c. Suppose you have accurate information about the pharmaceutical company's fixed cost. How could you use price regulation of the pharmaceutical company, combined with a subsidy to the company, to have the efficient quantity of the vaccine provided at the lowest cost to the government?

>web... To continue your study and review of concepts in this chapter, please visit the Krugman/Wells website for quizzes, animated graph tutorials, web links to helpful resources, and more.

www.worthpublishers.com/krugmanwells

>> Taxes, Social Insurance, and Income Distribution

A TAX RIOT

ON MARCH 31, 1990, HUNDREDS OF thousands of British citizens marched across London, protesting a new tax that had been introduced by Prime Minister Margaret Thatcher. As some protesters clashed with police, the initially peaceful demonstration turned into a riot, with hundreds injured. The violence came as a surprise, but maybe it shouldn't have: the tax had aroused angry opposition throughout Britain. Later that year, Mrs. Thatcher was forced to resign, and many observers believed that the tax controversy was the prime cause of her fall.

The tax at issue was officially known as the "Community Charge" but was popularly known as the "poll tax." Until 1989 local public services like street cleaning and trash collection had been financed with "the rates," a tax that depended on the value of people's homes. (Most local services in the United States are financed with similar property-based taxes.) Mrs. Thatcher, however, replaced these property taxes with a payment from each individual over the age of 18. Although the amount of the poll tax varied from town to town, every adult in a given town owed the same amount, regardless of income or the value of his or her property.

Supporters of the poll tax argued that it was more efficient than the tax it replaced. Because the old tax depended on the value of property, it discouraged people both from buying more expensive homes and from improving the homes they had. Supporters also argued that the poll tax was fair, because the cost of providing local public services depended mainly on how many people lived in a town, not on how rich those people were.

But opponents argued that the poll tax was extremely unfair because it did not take into account differences in people's ability to pay— a single mother who worked as a waitress and

What you will learn in this chapter:

- ➤ Why designing a tax system involves a **trade-off between equity and efficiency**

- ➤ Two concepts of fairness in taxation: the **benefits principle** and **the ability-to-pay principle**

- ➤ The different kinds of taxes and their effects on people's economic behavior at different levels of income

- ➤ The major types of government spending and how they are justified

- ➤ What income inequality is and why there is a policy debate about it

Margaret Thatcher and these protesters differed sharply over the fairness of the poll tax.

493

a millionaire stockbroker owed the same amount if they lived in the same town.

One moral of the story is that making tax policy isn't easy—in fact, if you are a politician, it can be dangerous to your professional health. But the deeper moral is that making tax policy always involves striking a balance between the pursuit of efficiency and the pursuit of perceived fairness. Or, as economists say, there is a *trade-off between equity and efficiency*. In this chapter we will show why this trade-off exists and how attempts to make the best of the trade-off influence the design of actual tax systems.

Principles of Tax Policy

A tax system achieves **tax efficiency** when it minimizes the direct and indirect costs to the economy of tax collection.

A tax system achieves **tax fairness,** or **tax equity,** when the "right" people actually bear the burden of taxes.

Tax policy always has two goals. On the one hand, governments strive to achieve **tax efficiency:** they try to minimize the direct and indirect costs to the economy of tax collection. On the other hand, governments also seek **tax fairness,** or **tax equity:** they try to ensure that the "right" people actually bear the burden of taxes. The central dilemma in tax policy—the dilemma that led to London's poll tax riot—is that an efficient tax may not seem fair, and a seemingly fair tax may not be efficient. So there is a fundamental trade-off between equity and efficiency.

The Burden of Taxes: A Quick Review

We analyzed some of the basic economics of taxation in Chapter 6. Here we briefly revisit the results of that analysis. As in Chapter 6, we'll assume here that there are no market failures, such as negative externalities or common resources, that make a tax efficiency enhancing (that is, make it a Pigouvian tax) rather than efficiency diminishing. Figure 21-1 shows the effects of an excise tax—a tax on sales—imposed on some good, in this case automobiles. Excise taxes are only one part of the U.S. tax system, but the principles suggested by this analysis apply to all taxes.

In the absence of a tax, the equilibrium price of autos would be P_E and the quantity bought and sold would be Q_E. Once a tax is imposed on the purchase or sale of an automobile, it *drives a wedge* between the price paid by consumers and that received by pro-

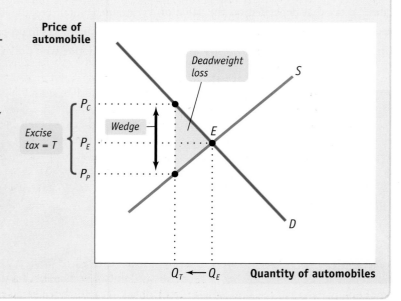

Figure 21-1

The Deadweight Loss of a Tax

Here an excise tax of the amount $T = P_C - P_P$ is imposed per auto sold. The quantity transacted falls from Q_E to Q_T, and there is a deadweight loss equal to the shaded area. The tax creates a wedge between the price paid by consumers, P_C, and the price received by producers, P_P. As a result, incentives are distorted and inefficiency arises: consumers consume less than is efficient and producers produce less than is efficient.
>web...

ducers. In this case, a tax of T per unit is imposed. In the new equilibrium the price paid by consumers rises to P_C and the price received by producers falls to P_P. The difference, $P_C - P_P$, is equal to the tax. As a result of the tax, the quantity bought and sold falls from Q_E to Q_T. So the tax changes people's behavior: less of the good is bought and sold.

Our analysis in Chapter 6 revealed three key results:

1. Consumers are hurt by the tax to the extent that the price they pay rises, and producers are hurt to the extent that the price they receive falls. But how much P_C rises and how much P_P falls does not depend on who pays the tax to the government—in fact, in Figure 21-1 we have not even specified whether this is a tax on producers or on consumers. So the incidence of a tax—who actually bears the burden—cannot be determined simply by looking at who pays the money to the government.

2. The price elasticities of supply and demand determine the incidence of the tax. The higher the price elasticity of supply, the more the price paid by consumers rises as a result of the tax and the greater the tax burden on consumers. The higher the price elasticity of demand, the more the price received by producers falls and the greater the tax burden on producers. The party with the lower price elasticity (producers or consumers) will bear the greater burden of the tax. If demand is relatively inelastic compared with supply, then consumers will bear a greater tax burden because quantity demanded is relatively insensitive to an increase in the price paid. If supply is relatively inelastic compared with demand, then producers will bear a greater share of the tax burden because quantity supplied is relatively insensitive to the decrease in the price received.

3. The tax causes a loss in efficiency—a deadweight loss—by creating a wedge between the price paid by consumers and the price received by producers. At Q_T in Figure 21-1, the marginal benefit of an additional unit of consumption is greater than the marginal cost of producing that additional unit. This means that the economy loses the potential gain from greater production and consumption of the good. The total deadweight loss from the tax can be measured by the area of the shaded triangle. This deadweight loss represents the *excess burden* of the tax—the cost to society over and above the tax revenue the government collects.

A tax system causes deadweight losses because taxes *distort incentives:* the incentives at the margin for producers to produce and consumers to consume are different from what they would have been without the tax, so people change their behavior. As a result, the tax that distorts incentives the least also minimizes any deadweight losses. So if the goal, in choosing whom to tax, is to minimize deadweight loss, then taxes should be imposed on those who have the most inelastic response—people who will change their behavior the least in response to the tax. (Unless they have a tendency to riot, of course.)

In considering the efficiency of a tax, we must also take into account something not shown in Figure 21-1: the resources actually used both to collect the tax and to pay it. These are called the **administrative costs** of the tax. The most familiar administrative cost of the U.S. tax system is the time individuals spend filling out their tax forms or the money they spend on accountants to do their taxes for them. (The costs of operating the Internal Revenue Service are actually quite small by comparison.)

The **administrative costs** of a tax are the resources used both to collect the tax and to pay it.

If maximizing efficiency is the only goal, a tax system should be designed to minimize the sum of its deadweight loss and its administrative costs. But tax policy is not driven by efficiency alone, because the voters who must approve a tax system also care about fairness, or equity. As we will see, fairness in a tax system usually comes at the expense of efficiency.

Tax Fairness

We have just seen how economic analysis can be used to determine who bears the burden of a tax. But who *should* bear the burden? Governments have wide discretion in choosing what to tax and how to tax it. How should they exercise this discretion?

One answer is that the tax system should be fair. But what exactly does fairness mean? We could say that fairness, like beauty, is often in the eyes of the beholder. However, most debates about taxes rely on one of two principles of tax fairness: the *benefits principle* and the *ability-to-pay principle*.

According to the **benefits principle** of tax fairness, those who benefit from public spending should bear the burden of the tax that pays for that spending. For example, those who benefit from a road should pay for that road's upkeep, those who fly on airplanes should pay for air traffic control, and so on. The benefits principle is the basis for some parts of the U.S. tax system. For example, revenue from the federal tax on gasoline is specifically reserved for the maintenance and improvement of federal roads, including the Interstate Highway System. In this way motorists, who benefit from the highway system, also pay for it.

The benefits principle is attractive from an economic point of view because it matches well with one of the major justifications for public spending—the theory of public goods. If government's role is to provide people with goods that could not otherwise be made available, it seems natural to charge each person in proportion to the benefits he or she gets from those goods.

Practical considerations, however, make it impossible to base the entire tax system on the benefits principle. It would be too cumbersome to have a specific tax for each of the many distinct programs that the government offers. Also, attempts to base taxes on the benefits principle often conflict with the other major principle of tax fairness: the **ability-to-pay principle,** according to which those with greater ability to pay a tax should pay more.

The ability-to-pay principle is usually interpreted to mean that high-income individuals should pay more in taxes than low-income individuals. Often the ability-to-pay principle is used to argue not just that high-income individuals should pay more taxes but that they should pay a higher *percentage* of their income in taxes. We'll consider the issue of how taxes vary as a percentage of income later.

The London protest described at the beginning of this chapter was basically a protest against the failure of the poll tax to take the ability-to-pay principle into account. In some parts of Britain, the poll tax was as high as £550 (equivalent to around $900) per adult per year. For highly paid executives or professionals, £550 was not a lot of money. But for struggling British families, £550 per year was a crushing burden. It's not surprising that many people were upset that the new tax completely disregarded the ability-to-pay principle.

Equity versus Efficiency

Margaret Thatcher's poll tax was an example of a **lump-sum tax,** a tax that is the same for everyone regardless of any actions people take. It was widely perceived as much less fair than the tax structure it replaced, in which local taxes were proportional to property values. Under the old system, the highest local taxes were paid by the people with the most expensive houses; because these people tended to be wealthy, they were also best able to bear the burden.

But the old system definitely distorted incentives. People who were considering home improvements knew that such improvements, by making their property more valuable, would increase their tax bills. The result, surely, was that some home improvements that would have taken place without the tax did not take place because of it.

In contrast, a lump-sum tax does not distort incentives. Because people have to pay the same tax regardless of their situation, it does not lead them to avoid doing things that would raise their taxes. So lump-sum taxes, although unfair, are better than other taxes at promoting economic efficiency.

The example of the poll tax debate illustrates a general point. Unless a tax system is badly designed, it can be made fairer only by sacrificing efficiency; conversely, it can be made more efficient only by making it less fair. So there is normally a **trade-off between equity and efficiency.**

According to the **benefits principle** of tax fairness, those who benefit from public spending should bear the burden of the tax that pays for that spending.

According to the **ability-to-pay principle** of tax fairness, those with greater ability to pay a tax should pay more tax.

A **lump-sum tax** is the same for everyone, regardless of any actions people take.

In a well-designed tax system, there is a **trade-off between equity and efficiency:** the system can be made more efficient only by making it less fair, and vice versa.

FOR INQUIRING MINDS

POLL TAXES AND REVOLTING PEASANTS

Perhaps Margaret Thatcher wouldn't have tried to impose a poll tax if she had remembered her English history. For it was the tripling of an existing poll tax that set off the great English peasant rebellion of 1381.

In that rebellion, peasants under the leadership of Wat Tyler marched on London to demand a repeal of the tax. One of their slogans was "The first thing to do is to kill all the lawyers." (Lawyers at that time were responsible for enforcing the tax.) The rebels did kill quite a few lawyers and tax collectors; they also burned part of London and

A lesson from history: in 1381, English peasants revolted over unfair taxes.

came close to taking King Richard II hostage. However, they dispersed after the king promised some concessions—a promise he promptly broke. After all, in 1381 royal promises to peasants didn't count: as the king declared before hanging Wat Tyler and the other rebel leaders, "Villeins ye are, and villeins ye shall remain." (*Villein* is a fourteenth-century English term for a peasant.)

Nonetheless, the fact that the rebellion came so close to success struck terror into the hearts of the nobility, and it remained a cautionary tale for centuries.

Economic analysis cannot say how much weight a tax system should give to equity and how much to efficiency. That choice is a value judgment, one we make through the political process.

economics in action

Federal Tax Philosophy

What is the principle underlying the federal tax system? (By federal, we mean taxes collected by the federal government, as opposed to the taxes collected by state and local governments.) The answer is that it depends on the tax.

The best-known federal tax, accounting for about half of all federal revenue, is the income tax. The structure of the income tax reflects the ability-to-pay principle: families with low incomes pay little or no income tax. In fact, some families pay negative income tax: a program known as the Earned Income Tax Credit "tops up" or adds to the earnings of workers who receive low wages. Meanwhile, those with high incomes not only pay a lot of income tax but must pay a larger share of their income in income taxes than the average family.

The second most important federal tax, however, is set up very differently. The payroll tax, a tax on an employee's paid earnings, was originally introduced in 1935 to pay for Social Security, a program that guarantees retirement income to qualifying older Americans and also provides benefits to workers who become disabled and to family members of workers who die. (Part of the payroll tax is now also used to pay for Medicare, a program that pays most medical bills of older Americans.) The Social Security system was set up to resemble a private insurance program: people pay into the system during their working years, then receive benefits based on their payments. And the tax more or less reflects the benefits principle: because the benefits of Social Security are mainly intended to assist lower- and middle-income people, and don't increase substantially for the rich, the Social Security tax is levied only on incomes up to a maximum level—$87,900 in 2004. (The Medicare portion of the payroll tax

TABLE **21-1**

Share of Income and Federal Income Taxes, by Quintile, 2001

Quintile of income group	Percent of total pre-tax income received	Percent of total federal income tax paid	Percent of total payroll tax paid
Lowest	4.2%	−2.3%	4.2%
Second	9.2	0.3	10.3
Third	14.2	5.2	16.0
Fourth	20.7	14.3	25.6
Top	52.4	82.5	43.9

Source: Congressional Budget Office, 1979–2001

continues to be levied on incomes over $87,900.) As a result, a high-income family doesn't pay much more in payroll taxes than a middle-income family.

Table 21-1 illustrates the difference in the two taxes, using data from a Congressional Budget Office study. The study divided American families into quintiles: the lowest quintile is the poorest 20% of families, the second quintile is the next poorest 20%, and so on. The second column shows the share of total U.S. pre-tax income received by each quintile. The third column shows the share of total federal income tax collected that is paid by each quintile. As you can see, low-income families actually paid negative income tax, and even middle-income families paid a substantially smaller share of total income taxes collected than their share of total income. In contrast, the top quintile, the richest 20% of families, pays a much higher share of total income taxes collected compared with their share of total income. The fourth column shows the share of total payroll tax collected that is paid by each quintile, and the results are very different: the share of total payroll taxes paid by the top quintile is substantially *less* than their share of total income. ■

< < < < < < < < < < < < < < < < < < <

>>CHECK YOUR UNDERSTANDING 21-1

1. Assess each of the following taxes in terms of the benefits principle versus the ability-to-pay principle. What, if any, actions are distorted by the tax? Assume for simplicity in each case that the purchaser of the good bears 100% of the burden of the tax.
   a. A federal tax of $500 for each new car purchased that finances highway safety programs
   b. A local tax of 20% on hotel rooms that finances local government expenditures
   c. A local tax of 1% of the assessed value of homes that finances local schools
   d. A 1% sales tax on food that pays for government food safety regulation and inspection programs

Solutions appear at back of book.

>>QUICK REVIEW

➤ Other things equal, government tax policy aims for *tax efficiency.* But it also tries to achieve *tax fairness,* or *tax equity.*
➤ In addition to deadweight loss, taxes typically incur *administrative costs.*
➤ There are two important principles of tax fairness: the *benefits principle* and the *ability-to-pay principle.*
➤ A *lump-sum tax* is efficient because it does not distort incentives, but it is generally considered unfair. In any well-designed tax system, there is a *trade-off between equity and efficiency* in devising tax policy.

Understanding the Tax System

An excise tax is the easiest tax to analyze, making it a good vehicle for understanding the general principles of tax analysis. However, in the United States today, excise taxes are actually a relatively minor source of government revenue. In this section, we develop a framework for understanding more general forms of taxation and look at some of the major taxes used in the United States.

Tax Bases and Tax Structure

Every tax consists of two pieces: a *base* and a *structure.* The **tax base** is the measure or value that determines how much tax an individual pays. It is usually a monetary measure, like income or property value. The **tax structure** specifies how the tax depends on the tax base. It is usually expressed in percentage terms; for example,

The **tax base** is the measure or value, such as income or property value, that determines how much tax an individual pays.

The **tax structure** specifies how the tax depends on the tax base.

homeowners in some areas might pay taxes equal to 2 percent of the value of their homes.

Some important taxes and their tax bases are as follows:

- **Income tax:** a tax that depends on the income of an individual or family from wages and investments
- **Payroll tax:** a tax that depends on the earnings an employer pays to an employee
- **Sales tax:** a tax that depends on the value of goods sold (also known as an excise tax)
- **Profits tax:** a tax that depends on a firm's profits
- **Property tax:** a tax that depends on the value of property, such as the value of a home
- **Wealth tax:** a tax that depends on an individual or family's wealth

Once the tax base has been defined, the next question is how the tax depends on the base. The simplest tax structure is a **proportional tax,** also sometimes called a *flat tax,* which is the same percentage of the base regardless of the taxpayer's income or wealth. For example, a property tax that is set at 2 percent of the value of the property, whether the property is worth $10,000 or $10,000,000, is a proportional tax. Many taxes, however, are not proportional. Instead, different people pay different percentages, usually because the tax law tries to take account either of the benefits principle or the ability-to-pay principle.

Because taxes are ultimately paid out of income, economists classify taxes according to how they vary with the income of individuals. A tax that rises *more* than in proportion to income, so that high-income taxpayers pay a larger percentage of their income than low-income taxpayers, is a **progressive tax.** A tax that rises *less* than in proportion to income, so that higher-income taxpayers pay a smaller percentage of their income than low-income taxpayers, is a **regressive tax.** A proportional tax on income would be neither progressive nor regressive.

Figure 21-2 illustrates the relationship between tax payment and income for proportional, progressive, and regressive taxes with three curves, one corresponding to each type of tax. In the case of a proportional tax, plotting the tax due against income yields a tax schedule that is a straight line from the origin. For a progressive tax, the curve gets steeper as income increases; for a regressive tax, the curve gets flatter as income increases.

The U.S. tax system contains a mixture of progressive and regressive taxes, though it is somewhat progressive overall.

An **income tax** is a tax on an individual's or family's income.

A **payroll tax** is a tax on the earnings an employer pays to an employee.

A **sales tax** is a tax on the value of goods sold.

A **profits tax** is a tax on a firm's profits.

A **property tax** is a tax on the value of property, such as the value of a home.

A **wealth tax** is a tax on an individual's wealth.

A **proportional tax** is the same percentage of the tax base regardless of the taxpayer's income or wealth.

A **progressive tax** takes a larger share of the income of high-income taxpayers than of low-income taxpayers.

A **regressive tax** takes a smaller share of the income of high-income taxpayers than of low-income taxpayers.

Figure 21-2

Proportional, Progressive, and Regressive Income Taxes

The curves show how tax payments vary as income changes. A proportional tax schedule is represented by a straight line because the percentage of income paid in taxes is constant. With a progressive tax, the percentage paid increases as income increases—high-income families pay a larger percentage of their income than low-income families. Hence, a progressive tax schedule becomes steeper as income increases. With a regressive tax, the percentage paid increases as income decreases—low-income families pay a larger percentage of their income than high-income families. Therefore, a regressive tax schedule becomes flatter as income increases. >web...

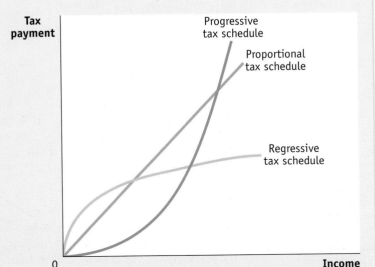

Equity, Efficiency, and Progressive Taxation

Most, though not all, people view a progressive tax system as fairer than a regressive system. The reason is the ability-to-pay principle: a high-income family that pays 35 percent of its income in taxes is still left with a lot more money than a low-income family that pays only 15 percent in taxes. But attempts to make taxes strongly progressive run up against the trade-off between equity and efficiency.

Figure 21-3 shows once again a progressive tax schedule on income. Consider a particular individual whose income is N; given that income, he will find himself at point A on the tax schedule and will pay taxes equal to T. His **average tax rate on income** is the ratio of tax payment to income, equal to T/N. As shown in Figure 21-3, it is equal to the slope of a line from the origin to point A.

But what effect does the tax have on his incentive to earn income—say, by working longer hours, or by investing? The answer depends on his **marginal tax rate on income,** the additional tax he pays if his income goes up by $1. It is the marginal tax rate, not the average tax rate, that affects an individual's incentives to earn another $1.

In Figure 21-3, the marginal tax rate of an individual with income N is the slope of a line tangent to the tax schedule at point A. Clearly, in this example the marginal tax rate is higher than the average tax rate. This is always true in the case of a progressive tax: *when a tax is progressive, the marginal tax rate is higher than the average tax rate at every income level.*

To deepen our understanding of this point, let's consider a simplified tax system. Imagine that income taxes work as follows: families pay no tax on the first $40,000 of income but pay a 50 percent tax rate on any income over $40,000. This system would be strongly progressive: families with less than $40,000 in income will pay no taxes, but families with high incomes will pay up to 50 percent of their income in taxes.

At the same time, this system will lead to a high marginal tax rate for many families, even if their *average* tax rates aren't very high. Consider a family with an income of $50,000. It will pay taxes only on the last $10,000 of that income, so its average tax rate will be $5,000/$50,000, or 10 percent. However, the family will pay $0.50 in taxes for each additional $1 it earns; its marginal tax rate is 50 percent.

In fact, the federal income tax works a lot like that. Family income below a certain amount (the amount depends on the size of the family and other criteria) isn't taxed. Income above that amount is taxed at a rate of 10 percent, up to another threshold

The **average tax rate on income** is the ratio of income taxes paid by an individual to his or her income.

The **marginal tax rate on income** is the additional tax an individual pays if his or her income goes up by $1.

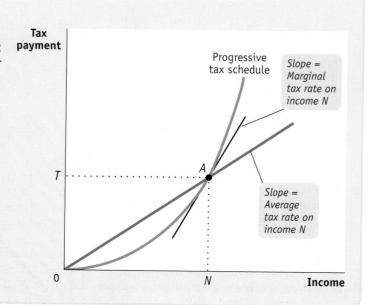

Figure 21-3

The Marginal Tax Rate versus the Average Tax Rate for a Progressive Tax

Under the progressive tax schedule shown here, a taxpayer with income N finds himself at point A on the tax schedule and pays taxes of T. His average tax rate at income N is the total tax paid divided by the total income, T/N, which is equal to the slope of the line connecting the origin to A. His marginal tax rate at income N is the tax rate paid on an additional $1 of income at point A. This is equal to the slope of the line tangent to the tax schedule at A. As shown, for a progressive tax the marginal tax rate is greater than the average tax rate. As a result, compared to a proportional or regressive tax, progressive taxes result in reduced incentives for higher-income people to work and invest. **>web...**

at which the tax rate rises to 15 percent, and so on. In 2003 the average federal income tax rate was about 11 percent, but taxpayers faced marginal rates as high as 35 percent. In the past, marginal rates in the United States have been as high as 94 percent, and the highest marginal rate stayed above 50 percent until the 1980s.

The excess burden of a tax comes from its effect on marginal incentives. Suppose that a highly progressive tax system implied a marginal tax rate of 70 percent on successful businesspeople. An entrepreneur might look at that rate and decide that the risk and effort of expanding her business just wasn't worth it. So high marginal tax rates distort incentives, reducing the incentive to earn more income by working more or investing money rather than spending it. In short, the ability-to-pay principle pushes governments toward a highly progressive tax system, but efficiency considerations push them the other way.

Taxes in the United States

Table 21-2 shows the revenue raised by some major taxes in the United States in fiscal year 2002. (For reasons not worth going into, fiscal years start on October 1 of the preceding calendar year.) Some of the taxes are collected by the federal government, the others by state and local governments.

TABLE **21-2**

Revenue from Major Taxes in the United States, Fiscal Year 2002 (billions of dollars)

Federal	State and local
Income tax: $858.3	Sales tax: $333.5
Payroll tax: 700.8	Income tax: 200.7
Profits tax: 148.0	Property tax: 267.8
	Profits tax: 33.5

Source: Statistical Abstract of the United States, 2004.

There is a major tax corresponding to five of the six tax bases we identified earlier. There are income taxes, profits taxes, payroll taxes, sales taxes, and property taxes, all playing an important role in the overall tax system. The only item missing is a wealth tax. In fact, the United States does have a wealth tax, the *estate tax,* which depends on the value of someone's estate after he or she dies. But at the time of writing, the current law phases out the estate tax over a few years, and in any case it raises much less money than the taxes shown in the table.

In addition to the taxes shown, state and local governments collect substantial revenue from other sources as varied as driver's license fees and sewer charges. These fees and charges are an important part of the burden of taxes but very difficult to summarize or analyze.

Are the taxes in Table 21-2 progressive or regressive? It depends on the tax. The personal income tax is strongly progressive. The payroll tax, which, except for the Medicare portion, is paid only on earnings up to $87,900, is somewhat regressive. Sales taxes are generally regressive, because higher-income families save more of their income and thus spend a smaller share of it on taxable goods than do lower-income families. In addition, there are other taxes principally levied at the state and local level that are typically quite regressive: it costs the same amount to get a new driver's license no matter what your income is.

Overall, the taxes collected by the federal government are quite progressive. Table 21-3 on page 502 shows estimates by the Congressional Budget Office of the average federal tax rate paid by families at different levels of income earned in 2001. These estimates don't just count the money families pay directly; they also attempt to estimate the incidence of

TABLE **21-3**

Quintile of income group	Average pre-tax family income	Average tax rate
Lowest	$14,900	5.4%
Second	34,200	11.6
Third	51,500	15.2
Fourth	75,600	19.3
Top	182,700	26.8

Federal Taxes Paid as a Percentage of Average Family Pre-tax Income, by Quintile, 2001

Source: Congressional Budget Office.

TABLE **21-4**

State and Local Taxes as a Percentage of Income, by Income Category, 2002

Lowest quintile	11.4%
Second quintile	10.4
Third quintile	9.9
Fourth quintile	9.4
Next 15 percent	8.9
Next 4 percent	8.1
Top 1 percent	7.3

Source: Institute for Taxation and Economic Policy.

taxes directly paid by business, like the tax on corporate profits, which ultimately falls on individual shareholders. The table shows that the federal tax system is indeed progressive, with low-income families paying a relatively small share of their income in federal taxes and high-income families paying a greater share of their income.

Since 2000, the federal government has cut taxes for most families. The largest cuts, both as a share of income and as a share of federal taxes collected have gone to families with high income. As a result, the federal system is less progressive (at the time of this writing) than it was in 2000, and it will become even less progressive over the next few years, as some delayed pieces of the post-2000 tax cut legislation take effect. However, even after those changes, the federal tax system will remain progressive.

As Table 21-4 shows, however, taxes at the state and local level are generally regressive. That's because the sales tax, the largest source of revenue for states, is somewhat regressive, and other items, such as vehicle licensing fees, are strongly regressive.

Different Taxes, Different Principles

Why are some taxes progressive but others regressive? Can't the government make up its mind?

There are two main reasons for the mixture of regressive and progressive taxes in the U.S. system: the difference between levels of government, and the fact that different taxes are based on different principles.

FOR INQUIRING MINDS

TAXING INCOME VERSUS TAXING CONSUMPTION

The federal government in the United States taxes people mainly on the money they *make*, not on the money they spend. Yet most tax experts argue that this distorts incentives. If someone earns income, and then invests that income for the future, she gets taxed twice: once when she earns the original sum, and again on any earnings she makes on her investment. So a system that taxes income discourages people from saving and investing and provides them with an incentive to spend their income today.

Moving from a system that taxes income to one that taxes consumption would solve this problem. In fact, the governments of many countries get much of their revenue from a value-added tax, or VAT, which acts like a national sales tax. In some countries VAT rates are very high; in Sweden, for example, the rate is 25 percent.

The United States does not have a value-added tax for two main reasons. One is that it is difficult, though not impossible, to make a consumption tax progressive. The other is that although VATs may not distort incentives as much as income taxes, they typically have quite high administrative costs.

State and especially local governments generally do not make much effort to apply the ability-to-pay principle. This is largely because they are subject to *tax competition*: a state or local government that tried to impose high taxes on people with high incomes might find those people moving to other locations where taxes are lower. This is much less of a concern at the national level, although a handful of very rich people have given up their U.S. citizenship to avoid paying U.S. taxes.

Although the federal government is in a better position than state or local governments to apply principles of fairness, it applies different principles to different taxes. We already saw this in Economics in Action on page 497. The most important tax, the income tax, is strongly progressive, reflecting the ability-to-pay principle. But the second most important tax, the payroll tax, is somewhat regressive, because most of it is linked to specific programs—Social Security and Medicare—and, reflecting the benefits principle, is levied more or less in proportion to the benefits received from these programs.

economics in action

Marginal Tax Rates in the United States

Congress keeps fiddling with the federal income tax. There were nine major revisions of the tax between 1980 and 2003. Tax rates on high-income families, for example, were cut during the 1980s, raised again in the 1990s, and cut again after 2000.

Although the politics of the income tax constantly seesaws, there has been a clear trend toward lower marginal tax rates on income. This trend is driven largely by economic arguments: many politicians have picked up on the idea that high marginal tax rates discourage productive activity.

In 1980 the highest-income families faced a marginal tax rate of no less than 70 percent. Tax cuts in the 1980s brought that down to 28 percent; tax increases in the 1990s pushed it back up again, but only to 39.6 percent. The rate is now 35 percent. Less affluent families never paid that high a marginal rate, but at almost all income levels marginal rates are considerably lower now than they were in 1980. Currently, families in the middle of the income distribution—about 60 percent of families, who earn $30,000 to $80,000 a year—typically pay a marginal rate of either 10 or 15 percent, depending on income and the number of deductions they can take.

The U.S. tax system still imposes a substantial wedge between the pre-tax earnings of families and their after-tax income. But the wedge is considerably smaller than it was a generation ago. ■

> > > > > > > > > > > > > > > > > > >

>>CHECK YOUR UNDERSTANDING 21-2

1. A wealth tax taxes 1% of the first $10,000 of wealth and 2% on all wealth above $10,000. Show that the average rate is smaller than the marginal rate for someone with wealth of $20,000.

2. When comparing households at different income levels, economists find that consumption spending grows more slowly than income. Assume that when income grows by 50%, from $10,000 to $15,000, consumption grows by 25%, from $8,000 to $10,000. Compare the percent of income paid in taxes by a family with $15,000 in income to that paid by a family with $10,000 in income under a 1% tax on consumption purchases. Is this tax a proportional, progressive, or regressive tax?

3. True or false? Explain your answers.
   a. Payroll taxes do not affect a person's incentive to take a job because they are paid by employers.
   b. A lump-sum tax is a proportional tax because it is the same amount for each person.

Solutions appear at back of book.

Understanding Government Spending

One way or another, governments in the United States collected 27 percent of total U.S. income in 2003. And that's actually low by international standards: Canada collects more than 35 percent total of Canadian income, and European countries on average collect more than 40 percent of national income. Where does all the money go?

It's easy to make fun of government spending; everyone has a favorite story of wasted money, and some of those stories are even true. But most government spending is done for reasons that seem sensible to a large fraction of the electorate. Let's take a look at the major types of spending in the United States.

Types of Spending

Broadly speaking, governments spend money for three reasons: to provide *public goods,* to provide *social insurance,* and to engage in *income redistribution.*

We defined public goods in Chapter 20. They are goods that are nonexcludable so that people cannot be forced to pay for consuming them, and nonrival in consumption so that people *should* not have to pay. As a result many public goods are provided by the government. One public good in particular—national defense—has traditionally been the largest component of spending by the federal government, (although this is no longer true).

Much modern government spending is not for public goods but for **social insurance:** programs intended to protect people against some of the financial risks in life. The clearest examples are government programs that pay for medical care. When someone needs expensive medical treatment, the cost can be a severe burden; indeed, sometimes people cannot afford the treatment at all. This is widely viewed as unfair—the ability-to-pay principle again. So many governments provide some kind of national health insurance that covers many medical bills. The United States offers extensive health insurance for people 65 and older, although not for younger people unless they are indigent. The concept of social insurance can be extended more broadly to include items like unemployment insurance, which provides temporary income to people who have lost their jobs, and programs that support people after retirement.

Finally, most governments also engage in **redistribution of income:** taking money via taxes from the relatively well-off and using it either to provide income for the poor or to provide the poor with benefits like housing and medical care. The case for redistribution can be made in a couple of different ways. One is to think of it as an extension of the ability-to-pay principle: the poor, you could argue, are not only less able to pay taxes than the affluent—they could actually use some help with other expenses.

Alternatively, you can think of poverty reduction as a sort of public good. Most of us prefer to live in a society where everyone has enough to eat, decent housing, and so on; these sentiments motivate us to give to charity. But each of us is tempted to free-ride on the positive effects of charitable giving by others. So just as most people agree that they should be taxed to provide for national defense, many agree that they should be taxed to provide aid to the poor.

This raises the question of what we mean by saying that people are "poor." How do we define poverty? We'll discuss that question in the next section, where we also look at poverty trends in the United States.

How do we draw the line between social insurance and redistribution? Both typically involve **transfer payments:** money that an individual receives from the government for which no good or service is produced for the government in exchange. A transfer payment is the opposite of a tax. And don't social insurance programs often help the poor? Aren't programs for the poor a sort of social insurance for those of us who might end up poor one day?

The answer is that the line between social insurance and income redistribution is a fuzzy one. However, one way economists often draw that line is by distinguishing between programs that are *means-tested* and those that are not. A **means-tested** program

---

Social insurance is government spending intended to protect people against financial risks.

Governments engage in **redistribution of income** when they tax the well-off and use the money to support those less well-off.

A **transfer payment** is money that an individual receives from the government but for which no good or service is produced for the government in exchange.

Means-tested government programs are available only to those with sufficiently low income.

is available only to an individual who can show that he or she has a sufficiently low income to qualify; such programs clearly redistribute income. Programs that aren't means-tested are more generally viewed as social insurance.

Spending in the United States

Figure 21-4 shows the composition of federal spending in fiscal year 2003. Let's consider how the categories shown here fit into the categories of spending we have just described.

National defense is, of course, the budget of the U.S. military. It is clearly a public good: the government can't defend some people without defending others, and my security doesn't come at your expense.

The category labeled "nondefense discretionary" consists of everything from running the court system and medical research to highway construction and education. Broadly speaking, it also fits the definition of public goods.

Social Security and Medicare are the two major social insurance programs. Both benefit older Americans: Medicare covers most of their medical bills, and Social Security provides retirement income. In 2003, Congress added a significant new benefit to Medicare, so that starting in 2006 the program will cover some of the cost of prescription drugs for older Americans. The category "other mandatory" includes unemployment insurance, pensions for federal workers, and a variety of other expenses; by and large they can be regarded as social insurance.

Finally, Medicaid is a means-tested program that provides health insurance for low-income families, and "other means-tested" spending includes such programs as food stamps and housing subsidies. These programs are best viewed as income redistribution.

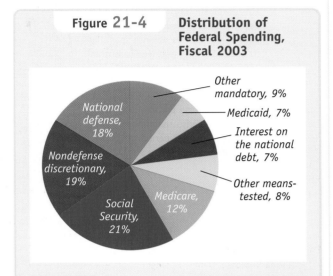

Figure 21-4   Distribution of Federal Spending, Fiscal 2003

This pie chart shows how the federal government spent money in fiscal year 2003. National defense and "nondefense discretionary" can be considered spending on public goods. Social Security, Medicare, and "other mandatory" (which includes unemployment insurance) are social insurance programs. Medicaid, which provides medical insurance for people with low incomes, and "other means-tested" (which includes food stamps) are best viewed as income redistribution. (Due to rounding error, percentages do not add up to 100%.)
Source: Congressional Budget Office

Comparisons Across Time and Space

Politicians invariably denounce "big government"—unless they are demanding more government spending on themselves or their constituents. Economic analysis cannot tell us whether the government spends too much or too little. But it is useful to have some sense both of how the level of government spending in the United States compares with its level in the past, and of how spending here compares with spending in other advanced nations.

Figure 21-5 on page 506 shows federal spending as a percentage of *gross domestic product* (GDP) over the past four decades. GDP is a measure of all the income generated in the economy in a year—the sum of payments to all factors of production like labor, land, and capital.

The basic message of Figure 21-5 is that the overall size of the federal government compared with the economy hasn't changed much for a long time. It has fluctuated, but the share of federal spending as a percentage of GDP was only slightly higher in 2003 than it was in the early 1960s. (State and local spending grew somewhat faster, from about 7% of GDP in the early 1960s to about 10% in 2003.)

Although federal spending has stayed roughly constant as a share of the economy, its composition has changed. Figure 21-5 also shows two components of federal spending. One curve shows defense spending as a percentage of GDP. In the 1960s defense spending, at 9% of GDP, accounted for about half of federal spending. After the collapse of the Soviet Union in 1991, the huge military forces that the United States maintained to guard against the Soviet threat were downsized, and defense spending fell to only 3% of GDP. Since the terrorist attacks on September 11, 2001,

Figure 21-5

Total U.S. Federal Government Spending, 1962–2003

This graph shows the percent of GDP devoted to total federal spending and the percent devoted to defense spending and to Social Security and Medicare from 1962 to 2003. Although the percent of GDP represented by total federal spending was roughly the same in 2003 as it was in the 1960s, the percent of GDP represented by defense spending has declined markedly over that period.

Source: Office of Management and Budget

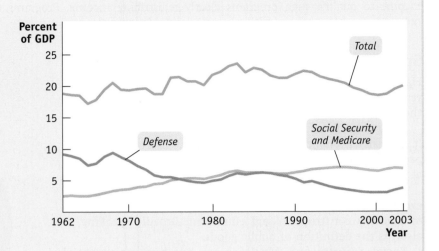

defense spending has risen rapidly, but it still plays a much smaller role in the federal budget than it did at the height of the Cold War.

Given the decline in defense spending, why hasn't the share of government spending in the economy decreased? The answer is growth in social insurance spending, mainly on Social Security (established in 1935) and Medicare (established in 1965). As the curve in Figure 21-5 shows, combined spending on Social Security and Medicare has risen steadily as a share of GDP. We have gone from a government that spent tax dollars mainly on public goods to one that now spends heavily on social insurance. In 2002 one senior official at the Treasury Department described the U.S. government as "a gigantic insurance company with a sideline business in national defense and homeland security."

However, the United States spends *less* on social insurance as a share of GDP than most other advanced nations. As a result, U.S. government spending actually makes up a smaller share of GDP than that of any other major economy. Figure 21-6 compares government spending (state and local as well as federal) as the share of GDP for the world's seven largest economies in 2002. The United States was at the bottom of the list.

Figure 21-6

Government Spending as a Percent of GDP in 2002

In 2002, France devoted the largest share of its GDP to government spending among the major industrial countries: 53.4%. The United States devoted the smallest share among these countries: 35.3%. Canada appears to have been around average, at about 40.6%.

Source: OECD Economic Outlook

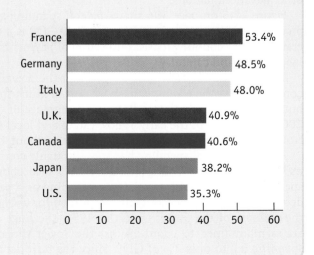

economics in action

Greedy Geezers?

In 1998 *The New Republic* startled many readers with a cover bearing the slogan "greedy geezers." Although the title was shocking, the story did draw attention to a substantive point: programs providing benefits to older Americans have become increasingly important as a share of both federal spending and the total economy. In 1970 Medicare and Social Security combined cost 3.6 percent of GDP, less than half as much as that year's defense budget. In 2003 the two programs combined cost 6.8 percent of GDP, almost twice the current defense budget.

Spending on older Americans has grown more rapidly than the economy or the overall budget. One of the main reasons is the rising cost of medical care.

Why has spending on older Americans grown more rapidly than the economy or the overall budget? One reason is demographics: the percentage of Americans age 65 and over has steadily risen for the past 30 years. This demographic trend will become dramatic after 2011, when members of the "baby-boom" generation become old enough to receive Social Security and Medicare benefits.

The other main reason for rising spending on the elderly is that medical care has become much more expensive. Experts in health economics say that this is not mainly because the costs of medical care have risen. Instead, it is because progress in medicine has made it possible to do much more for the elderly. Many treatments that are now common, such as heart bypass surgery, were experimental, rare, or not yet developed 30 years ago. So Medicare now spends more because there are more useful ways to spend money on health care than ever before.

So should rising spending on the elderly be viewed as a burden on the budget or as a sign of progress? Probably both. ∎

> > > > > > > > > > > > > > > > > > >

>> **QUICK REVIEW**

➤ There are three main types of government spending: spending on public goods, *social insurance,* and *redistribution of income.*

➤ Although the line between social insurance and redistribution is somewhat blurry, a program that is *means-tested* is usually considered redistribution and one that is not means-tested is considered social insurance.

➤ The U.S. government spends substantial sums on all three types of programs. Historically, spending on defense—a public good—was the largest component of federal spending. But today spending on social insurance, especially for older Americans, is considerably larger.

>> CHECK YOUR UNDERSTANDING 21-3

1. Unemployment insurance is financed by taxes on employed workers, who collect benefits if they become unemployed. Suppose that workers in Alaska are unemployed and workers in Florida are employed during even-numbered years, but the opposite is true during odd-numbered years. Explain why workers in these two states can benefit from an unemployment insurance program that covers both states.

2. Classify the following programs according to whether they redistribute income or provide social insurance.
   a. Natural disaster emergency relief
   b. Heating cost assistance for low-income families
   c. Health care for people over 65
   d. Aid grants to low income students

Solutions appear at back of book.

Poverty and Public Aid

Public aid—government spending that is means-tested and is intended to reduce poverty—is a relatively small part of government spending compared with social insurance. But it is the subject of intense debate, not only about how much public aid should be given but about the criteria for aid and its effect on society. Let's look at how poverty is defined, how it has changed over time, and how it is affected by public policy.

Defining Poverty

The **poverty line** is a minimum annual income that the government defines as adequate. Families whose income falls below the poverty line are considered poor.

What does it mean to be "poor"? Any definition is somewhat arbitrary. Since 1965, however, the U.S. government has maintained an official definition of the **poverty line:** a minimum annual income that is considered adequate. Families whose income falls below the poverty line are considered poor. The history of this official definition is described in For Inquiring Minds on page 509.

The poverty line depends on the size and composition of a family: in 2004 the poverty line for an adult living alone was $9,310, whereas the poverty line for a family of 4 was $18,850. Also, the official poverty line is adjusted each year to reflect changes in the cost of living. Contrary to some popular misconceptions, however, the poverty line has *not* been adjusted upwards over time to reflect the long-term rise in the average standard of living. This means that as the economy grows, and average incomes rise, you might expect the percentage of the population living below the poverty line to decline steadily. Has this actually happened?

Trends in Poverty

The **poverty rate** is the percentage of the population living below the poverty line.

Figure 21-7 shows the U.S. **poverty rate**—the percentage of the population living below the poverty line—from 1959 to 2003. As you can see, the poverty rate fell steeply during the 1960s and early 1970s. But since then progress has been much more questionable. The poverty rate rose from 1973 until 1993, then fell in the boom economy of the 1990s. But even at the end of that boom, in 2001, the poverty rate was no lower than it had been almost 30 years earlier.

The failure of the country to make clear progress against poverty has led to widespread debate both about the causes of poverty and about the nature and effectiveness of public aid. We turn first to the question of who is poor.

A Portrait of the Poor

Many Americans probably have in their minds a stereotyped image of poverty: an African-American or Hispanic family with no husband present, and the female head of household unemployed at least part of the time. This picture isn't completely off-base: poverty is disproportionately high among African-Americans and Hispanics as well as among female-headed households. But a majority of the poor don't fit the stereotype.

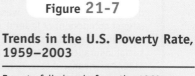

Trends in the U.S. Poverty Rate, 1959–2003

Poverty fell sharply from the 1960s to the early 1970s but has not shown a clear downward trend since then.
Source: U.S. Census Bureau

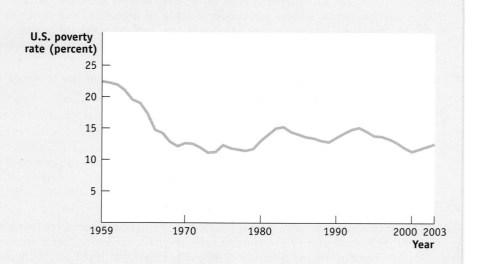

WHO DEFINED POVERTY?

Who decided how much income an American family needs to escape poverty? Mollie Orshansky! Orshansky, a research analyst at the Social Security Administration, developed initial estimates of the poverty line in 1963–1964.

Orshansky started by estimating the cost of buying an inexpensive but nutritionally adequate diet. She then observed that families with children spent about one-third of their income on food; so she argued that any family earning less than three times the cost of purchasing an adequate diet did not have adequate income.

Was this the right measure of poverty? When it was created, Orshansky's calculation made a

lot of sense, and it has been the basis for U.S. poverty statistics ever since. But many experts now think that this measure of poverty is badly outdated because the composition of spending by low-income families has changed significantly since the 1960s. On average, the share of income expended on food has fallen to less than 20%, while the share spent on things such as housing, health care, transportation, and child care has risen. Many state governments have recognized this trend and now use an income benchmark of 150% to 200% of the poverty line to determine a family's eligibility for assistance programs (and some states use a benchmark as high as 275% to 300% of the poverty line).

In 2003, about 35.9 million Americans were in poverty—12.5 percent of the population. About one-quarter of the poor were African-American and a roughly equal number Hispanic. Among these two groups, poverty rates were well above the national average: 24 percent among blacks, 22 percent among Hispanics. But there was also widespread poverty among non-Hispanic whites, who had a poverty rate of 8 percent.

Female-headed families with no husband present had a very high poverty rate: 28 percent. Married couples were much less likely to be poor, with a poverty rate of only 5.4 percent; still, about 41 percent of poor families were married couples.

What really stands out from the data, however, is the association between poverty and lack of adequate employment. Adults who work full time are very unlikely to be poor (only 2.6 percent in 2003). Adults who work part time or have no work at all during the course of a year make up the great majority of the adult poor. Many industries, particularly in the retail and service sectors, now rely primarily on part-time workers. In addition to lacking benefits such as health plans, paid vacation days, and retirement benefits, most part-time work pays a lower hourly wage than comparable full-time work. As a result, many of the poor are *working poor*: workers whose income falls at or below the poverty line.

The Origins and Consequences of Poverty

Educational attainment clearly has a strong effect on income level—those with more education earn, on average, higher incomes than those with less education. And those with less education have, as a group, seen their fortunes decline over time: the average young, male non-college-educated worker now earns 25 percent less than someone in a similar situation in 1973. For females, the comparable number is 13 percent.

Like lack of education, lack of proficiency in English can create a barrier to higher income. For example, Mexican-born workers in the United States—two-thirds of whom have not graduated from high school and many of whom have poor English skills—earn less than half of what native-born men earn.

Although discrimination is less pervasive today than it was 30 years ago, it still generates a formidable barrier to advancement for many Americans. Nonwhites with comparable levels of education earn less and are less likely to be employed than whites. Women with similar qualifications earn lower incomes than men. Studies find that African-American males suffer persistent discrimination by employers in favor of whites, African-American women, and Hispanic immigrants.

In addition, one important source of poverty that should not be overlooked is bad luck coupled with the lack of a safety net. Without adequate health care coverage or savings, many families find themselves impoverished when a wage-earner loses a job or a family member falls seriously ill.

The consequences of poverty are often severe, particularly for children. Nearly 17 percent of children in the United States live in poverty. For their families, health care is often erratic, leading to further health problems that erode the ability to work. Affordable housing is frequently a problem that leads poor families to move often, disrupting school and work schedules. Because parental income is the single most important factor influencing children's later socioeconomic attainment, children raised in poverty have a greater likelihood of living in poverty as adults than do those raised in nonpoor families. Low income is strongly correlated with a low level of pre-school ability, and low preschool ability often leads to lower test scores in elementary school and higher high school dropout rates. Low-income children are at higher risk of mental health problems and behavioral disorders than the children of parents with higher income. And lower-income children are less likely to be covered by health insurance, leading to higher rates of illness and hospitalization. Poverty, in short, is not good for children.

Antipoverty Programs

Aid to the poor takes three main forms: *welfare, in-kind transfers,* and *negative income tax.* **Welfare** refers to monetary aid to poor families. The main welfare program in the United States is Temporary Assistance for Needy Families. This program does not aid simply anyone who is poor; it is available only to poor families with children and only for a limited time.

Critics of welfare have long argued that it creates perverse incentives for the poor. First, they argue that it tends to encourage family breakup, because a family with both spouses present may not qualify for aid. Second, they argue that it encourages out-of-wedlock births, because a single woman alone will not qualify for aid. These claims are hotly disputed by other analysts.

In any case, welfare is a generally unpopular program, and this has been reflected in public policy changes over time. Because payments to welfare recipients have not kept up with inflation, in real terms benefits are considerably less generous today than they were a generation ago. Also, welfare programs now contain time limits, so that welfare recipients—even single parents—must eventually seek work.

In-kind transfers provide the poor not with cash but with specific goods and services. The most important in-kind transfers are *food stamps*, which can be used only to purchase food; *Medicaid*, which provides health insurance; and *housing subsidies*, which generally take the form of subsidies for rent.

Finally, economists use the term **negative income tax** for a program that supplements the earnings of low-income working families. The United States has a program known as the Earned Income Tax Credit (EITC), which provides additional income to millions of workers. Only workers who earn income are eligible for the EITC, and over a certain range of incomes the amount of EITC a worker receives increases with his or her earnings. That is, for low-wage workers the EITC acts as a negative income tax.

In 2003, married couples with two children earning less than $10,500 per year received payments from the government equal to 40 percent of their earnings. (Payments were slightly lower for single-parent families or workers without children.) At higher incomes the EITC is phased out, disappearing at an income of $34,692.

Taken together, these three programs provide substantial aid to poor families. This does not mean that there is a consensus about the size and nature of antipoverty

Welfare is monetary aid to poor families.

In-kind transfers provide poor families with specific goods and services.

A **negative income tax** is a program that supplements the earnings of low-income families.

programs. Some critics argue that the programs distort incentives and perpetuate poverty; we discuss this further in Economics in Action below. Others note that U.S. antipoverty programs are considerably less generous than comparable programs in other advanced countries.

economics in action

Old Poor, Young Poor

Over the past 30 years, the overall poverty rate has been roughly constant. But in some ways this stability is misleading: poverty has fallen for some groups but risen for others. The most striking difference involves age. Traditionally, poverty has been most common among two groups: the elderly, who often cannot work, and families with children, who often have difficulty making ends meet. As a result, poverty rates among the young and old have usually been higher than those for the population at large. As Table 21-5 shows, this traditional pattern was still true in 1973. Since then, however, the poverty rate for Americans age 65 and older has fallen sharply and is now below the average for the entire population. But the poverty rate for Americans under age 18 has risen.

Why this divergence? There are a number of reasons, but one important cause is the change in the nature of government spending over time. The items in the national budget that have experienced the most growth over time are Social Security and Medicare—programs that benefit older Americans and often help keep them above the poverty line. Public aid programs, which are more likely to benefit families with children, have received much less funding and have failed to keep pace with the rate of inflation. ■

TABLE 21-5

Poverty Rates in the United States

	1973	2003
All Americans	11.1%	12.5%
Americans under age 18	14.4	17.6
Americans age 65 and older	16.3	10.2

Source: Census Bureau

> >

>> CHECK YOUR UNDERSTANDING 21-4

1. Explain why the poverty rate has fallen for Americans over 65 since 1973 but has risen for Americans under 18.

2. Do you think that the introduction of a negative income tax makes it more or less likely that unemployed low-income adults will become employed? Explain.

3. The current U.S. poverty rate is no lower than it was in 1973 despite the fact that the poverty line has not been adjusted to take into account the long-term rise in the standard of living in the country since 1973. What does this imply about the change over time in the gap between the living standards of a family living at the poverty line and the living standards of the average family above the poverty line?

Solutions appear at back of book.

> **>> QUICK REVIEW**
>
> - Families are considered poor if their income falls below the *poverty line*. The overall *poverty rate* in the United States fell steadily until 1973, but since then it has moved up and down, with no clear trend.
> - The most important factors contributing to poverty are lack of education, discrimination, and adverse events. The consequences of poverty are often severe, particularly for children.
> - Families below the poverty line receive three main types of government aid: *welfare, in-kind transfers*, and *negative income taxes*.

The Big Debate: Taxes, Transfers, and Income Distribution

The great majority of Americans agree that the ability-to-pay principle should be given some weight in tax and spending policy—that high-income individuals should pay more in taxes than low-income individuals and that at least some public aid should be offered to the poor. But *how much* weight should ability to pay be given?

That is not a question of economic analysis; it is a political question, perhaps *the* political question. Roughly speaking, conservatives believe that at present the United States gives too much weight to the ability-to-pay principle, that taxes are excessively progressive, and that is too much redistribution of income. Liberals believe the opposite.

Although we can't resolve this debate, we can shed some light on it by clarifying the issues involved.

The Distribution of Income

A starting point for the big debate is to have a sense of how much families differ in their ability to pay—that is, of the distribution of income among families. Look back at Table 21-1: the second column summarizes the distribution of income among U.S. families in 2001. The numbers show a considerable amount of inequality: the poorest 20% of families received only 4.2% of the income, and the richest 20% received more than half of total U.S. income. Recent estimates suggest that the top 1% of families receive about 18% of total income. The average income among the top 1% is 18 times as high as the overall average income and 90 times as high as the average income of the poorest 20% of families.

Economists are in general agreement that these numbers overstate the true degree of inequality in America, for several reasons. One is that the incomes of individual families fluctuate over time: many of those near the bottom in any given year are having an unusually bad year and many of those at the top are having an unusually good one. Over time, their incomes will revert to a more normal level. So a table showing average incomes over, say, a 10-year period would not be quite as striking. Also, a family's income tends to vary over its life cycle: most people start off earning considerably less than they will later in life, then experience a considerable drop in income when they retire. The numbers in Table 21-1, which combine young workers, mature workers, and retirees all in the same pool, would therefore show considerable inequality even if all families had similar incomes at the same points in their lives.

Nonetheless, there is a considerable amount of genuine inequality in the United States. And for the last quarter-century the degree of inequality has been increasing. The causes of this increase in inequality are a subject of some controversy, but probably the most important cause is rapid technological change, which has increased the demand for highly skilled or talented workers more rapidly than the demand for other workers. Growing international trade may have contributed to inequality by allowing the United States to import labor-intensive products from low-wage countries rather than making them for itself. This depresses the wages of domestic workers employed in industries that compete with imports. Rising immigration may also be a source of growing inequality. On average, immigrants have lower education levels than native-born workers and increase the supply of low-skilled labor while depressing low-skilled wages.

Figure 21-8 shows one indicator of growing inequality: the percentage increase in average income within each quintile between 1979 and 2002. The average income of the poorest fifth of families rose 5.8%; that of families in the middle fifth rose 13.0%; that of families in the top fifth rose 45.7%. Not shown in the figure: the average income of families in the top 5% rose 70.3%. Clearly, the gap between the best-off and the worst-off families increased.

The fact that some people in the United States are extremely well-off—indeed, better off than ever before—but others remain quite poor leads advocates of income redistribution to argue for higher taxes on those with high incomes and greater aid to those with low incomes. Let's look briefly at their argument and then at the arguments that others make against redistribution.

The Case for Redistribution

Those who advocate more progressive taxation and redistribution of income to people in the lower part of the income distribution base their position on an extended version of the ability-to-pay principle. High-income families should pay high taxes, they argue, because they will still have after-tax income that is higher than average. Low-income families not only should not pay taxes, they should

Figure 21-8   **Percentage Increases in Household Income by Income Group, 1979–2002**

This graph shows that income inequality increased from 1979 to 2002: the incomes of higher-income families grew faster during this period than the incomes of lower-income families. The first quintile is the 20% of families with the lowest income, the second quintile the next poorest 20%, and so on. From 1979 to 2002, average income in the lowest quintile rose, but by only 5.8%. Meanwhile, average income in the top quintile rose by 45.7%.

Source: U.S. Census Bureau.

receive aid from the government, because even with that aid they will have incomes lower than average. So the redistribution is justified because the money transferred adds more to the welfare of the recipients than it subtracts from the welfare of the taxpayers.

Wouldn't the logical conclusion of this argument be that the government should tax away any income above the average and top up the income of anyone who makes less than the average? No, because even the most ardent advocates of progressive taxes and redistribution recognize that there is a trade-off between equity and efficiency—that the taxing and spending policies of the government must take care not to do too much damage to incentives. That brings us to the case, or rather cases, against income redistribution.

Arguments Against Income Redistribution

There are two different kinds of arguments against income redistribution. One is based on philosophical concerns about the proper role of government. Some political theorists believe that redistributing income is not a legitimate role of government— that government's role should be limited to maintaining the rule of law, providing public goods, and controlling externalities. We cannot go into this debate at length, but because it is an influential point of view, you should be aware that it exists.

The more conventional argument against taxing the rich and making transfers to the poor involves the trade-off between efficiency and equity. We've already seen part of this argument: a tax system that tries to put all of the burden on the very well off will have to be highly progressive. A highly progressive system implies high marginal tax rates, and high marginal tax rates reduce the incentive to work hard or otherwise increase a family's income. As a result, a highly progressive tax system makes society as a whole poorer, and may hurt even those who pay little or no tax. That's why even economists who strongly favor progressive taxation don't support a return to the extremely progressive system that prevailed in the 1950s, when the top marginal rate was more than 90 percent.

A similar trade-off between equity and efficiency occurs as a result of programs that aid people with low incomes. Consider the following example: suppose there is some means-tested benefit, worth $1,000 per year, that is available only to individuals with earnings of less than $10,000 per year. Now suppose that an individual is currently earning $9,800 per year and is deciding whether to take a new job that will raise his income to $10,200. He will actually make himself worse off by taking the job because he will lose the $1,000 government benefit.

This situation, in which earning more actually leaves an individual worse off, is known as a *notch*. It is a well-known problem with programs that aid the poor, and behaves much like a high marginal rate on income. Most programs are designed to avoid creating a notch. This is typically done by setting a sliding scale for benefits, so that they fall off gradually as the recipient's income rises rather than coming to an abrupt end. Even so, as Economics in Action on page 515 illustrates, means-tested programs have indeed led to high effective marginal tax rates for low-income workers.

The Politics of Equity and Efficiency

In the real world, however, decisions about how much efficiency to trade off for equity and vice versa aren't based on philosophical discussions. They're the result of elections in which political parties try to convince voters that their policies are in the voters' interests. But voters differ in their interests: a tax and spend policy that maximizes the welfare of a family earning $15,000 per year will look very different from a policy that maximizes the welfare of a family earning $1.5 million a year.

Generally speaking, voters toward the bottom of the income distribution favor highly progressive taxes and strong redistribution, with voters toward the top of the distribution favoring less progressive taxes and less generous redistribution. There are, of course, many exceptions—there are billionaires who, on principle, favor high taxes and generous poverty programs, and there are people with low income who strongly believe that redistribution undermines self-reliance. Still, there are clear differences in the interests of different voters. Whose interests prevail?

Let's suppose that voters can be lined up in order of the policy they prefer. In each panel of Figure 21-9, the horizontal axis shows the preferred share of government spending in national income; this share will be larger if the government engages in more redistribution and smaller if it engages in less redistribution. (We put higher government spending on the left of each panel, reflecting the long tradition under which politicians who favor redistribution are considered to the "left" of politicians who don't.) On the vertical axis are hypothetical percentages of voters who prefer a given level of government spending. For example, reading from left to right, 1% of voters are willing to sacrifice a lot of efficiency in order to increase equity and favor government spending equal to 50% of total income. Another 3% prefer spending of 45% of total income, and so on. (Such preferences typically reflect voters' own financial positions, but that's not necessary for the argument.) A famous result called the *median voter theorem* says that if voter preferences can be represented this way, and that if two parties compete for votes, actual policies will reflect the preferences of the *median voter*—the voter in the middle of our left-right lineup. In both panels of Figure 21-9, the median voter prefers government spending equal to 30% of total income.

The two panels of Figure 21-9 illustrate how the median voter argument works. In panel (a), we suppose that party D stakes out a position that is well to the left of the median voter's preferences, advocating spending equal to 45% of total income. If a rival party, R, advocates a position slightly to D's right, it can get the votes of all those

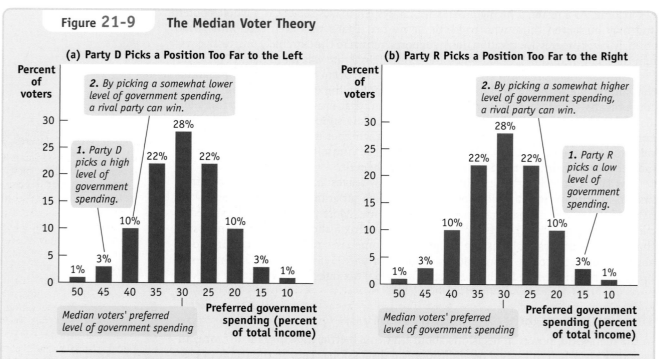

Figure 21-9   The Median Voter Theory

(a) Party D Picks a Position Too Far to the Left

2. By picking a somewhat lower level of government spending, a rival party can win.

1. Party D picks a high level of government spending.

(b) Party R Picks a Position Too Far to the Right

2. By picking a somewhat higher level of government spending, a rival party can win.

1. Party R picks a low level of government spending.

In this hypothetical example, voters have preferences about the level of government spending as a share of total income, measured from high levels on the left to low levels on the right. In both panels, the height of each bar represents the percent of voters who prefer a given level of spending. The median voter prefers spending equal to 30% of total income. In panel (a), party D picks a position—spending equal to 45% of total income—that is well to the left of the median voter's preferences. A rival party can easily win by picking a policy that is closer to the center, leaving D with only the voters represented by blue bars. In panel (b), party R picks a position that is well to the right of the median voter's preferences. Again, a rival party can win by picking a position closer to the center, leaving R with only the voters represented by red bars.

voters who prefer a smaller level of government spending. D will get only the voters indicated by the blue bars—4% of the electorate—and R will get the other 96%, indicated by the red bars. So party D, by choosing a position to the left of the median voter, makes it easy for R to win.

Panel (b) shows the opposite case: R stakes out a position well to the right of the median voter, advocating spending equal to only 15% of total income. By choosing a position slightly to R's left, D can ensure that R gets only the voters indicated by the red bars—and win. Clearly, then, the only way parties can avoid giving their opponents an easy way to win elections is to pick positions close to the middle—positions that reflect the preferences of the median voter. We can summarize the result as follows: in an election by majority rule where voters decide how much of a given policy action should be taken, the **median voter theorem** says that actual policies will most closely reflect the preferences of the median voter.

In practice, however, things are a bit more complicated. Politics isn't one-dimensional: parties can compete on other issues, such as foreign policy. Also, political activists and interest groups within each party tend to pull parties' political positions away from the center. In the United States, statistical studies by political scientists suggest that the two major parties held similar positions on economic issues a generation ago but have diverged since then: Republicans are currently well to the right of Democrats on economic policy. Still, the median voter theory is a useful model for understanding how democracies resolve the trade-off between equity and efficiency.

> In an election by majority rule where voters decide how much of a given policy action should be taken, the **median voter theorem** says that actual policies will most clearly reflect the preferences of the median voter.

economics in action

Effective Marginal Tax Rates on the Poor

Because means-tested programs are available only to families with sufficiently low incomes, families that manage to increase their earnings find that they lose benefits. So in effect they face a high marginal tax rate on their earnings, although the stated marginal tax rate is quite low.

The importance of this effect was emphasized in a 2002 study by Laurence Kotlikoff, an economist at Boston University, and two of his students. This study tried to calculate how much hypothetical couples with different levels of income get to keep of an additional dollar of income once the whole range of tax and benefits policies are taken into account.

They found that almost all couples in the United States face an effective marginal tax rate of more than 50 percent. The highest rates—up to 70 percent—aren't at the top of the income distribution; they're toward the lower end, where families find that higher income leads to reductions in means-tested benefits. ∎

> > > > > > > > > > > > > > > > > > > >

>>CHECK YOUR UNDERSTANDING 21-5

1. Suppose that the government offered free health care to families with incomes of less than $15,000 per year, but no health care assistance for families with incomes of $15,000 per year or more.
    a. What problem would this program create for incentives? Explain this problem in terms of a marginal tax rate.
    b. How would you restructure the program to make the problem less severe? Again, explain in terms of a marginal tax rate.
2. Describe the trade-off between equity and efficiency in the following programs:
    a. A program that supplements the income of farmers during poor crop years
    b. A program that pays rent for low-income families

>>QUICK REVIEW

- Income in the United States is quite unequally distributed among families, and this distribution has become more unequal in recent decades.
- The same reasoning that underlies the ability-to-pay principle on taxes can be used to argue for some redistribution of income, although not everyone agrees with this argument. Even those who favor redistribution recognize that, like progressive taxes, redistribution involves a trade-off between equity and efficiency.
- An implication of the *median voter theorem* is that parties that compete for votes on how much redistribution to undertake will choose positions close to the preferences of the median voter. But in practice, parties' positions have not obeyed that result.

Economists and the Tax System

As the opening story of Britain's poll tax suggested, tempers often run high when it comes to tax policy. The same is true when it comes to government spending for social insurance or income redistribution. What makes these disputes especially hard to resolve is that there is *no right answer:* there is always a trade-off between equity and efficiency, and two people who agree about that trade-off can disagree about what weight to give to each goal.

What role can economics play in this eternal debate? First, the economist can try to keep the debate honest. Politics being politics, those who advocate policy changes that will increase equity are always tempted to deny that their proposals will come at the expense of efficiency, and vice versa. It is the job of economists to point out when a proposed change in taxes or spending is being offered under false pretenses.

The other job of economists is to point out opportunities for clear improvement. An ideal tax system would offer no way to improve efficiency without reducing equity. Real tax systems probably can be made better, allowing progress toward both goals, and economic analysis should be used to show the way.

• A LOOK AHEAD •

We have now almost completed our study of microeconomics. We've learned a lot about how the economy works and about the role of government policy.

But do the models we have studied—models that reflect a couple of centuries of economic analysis and observation—still apply? In recent years there have been dramatic changes on the economic scene, as information technology has transformed the way we live and work. Some people talk of a "new economy" whose rules differ drastically from those of the past. In the next chapter, we'll look at how technology changes microeconomics—and how it doesn't.

SUMMARY

1. **Tax efficiency** is achieved when the costs of a tax—the sum of the deadweight loss or excess burden due to distorted incentives and the **administrative costs** of the tax—are minimized. However, **tax fairness,** or **tax equity,** ensuring that the right people pay taxes, is also a goal of tax policy.

2. There are two major principles of tax fairness, the **benefits principle** and the **ability-to-pay principle.** The most efficient tax, a **lump-sum tax,** does not distort incentives but performs badly in terms of fairness. The fairest taxes in terms of the ability-to-pay principle, however, distort incentives the most and perform badly on efficiency grounds. So in a well-designed tax system, there is a **trade-off between equity and efficiency.**

3. Every tax consists of a **tax base,** which defines what is taxed, and a **tax structure.** Different tax bases give rise to different taxes—the **income tax, payroll tax, sales tax, profits tax, property tax,** and **wealth tax.** A **proportional tax** is the same percentage of the tax base for all taxpayers.

4. A tax is **progressive** if higher-income people pay a higher percentage of their income in taxes than lower income people, and **regressive** if they pay a lower percentage. Progressive

taxes are often justified by the ability-to-pay principle. However, a progressive tax on income can distort incentives to work, save, and invest because the **marginal tax rate on income** is higher than the **average tax rate on income.**

5. Money raised in taxes is spent in three main ways: for **social insurance** and for **redistribution of income** (which are implemented through **transfer payments** to individuals) and for public goods. Defense spending, a public good, used to be the biggest item, but now social insurance, largely for older residents, is the largest item.

6. The **poverty line** is an estimate of the minimum annual income needed to achieve an acceptable standard of living. The **poverty rate** is the fraction of the population with incomes below the poverty line. Despite rising average incomes, the poverty rate in the United States has shown no clear trend over the past 30 years.

7. The most important causes of poverty are lack of education, discrimination, and adverse events. The effects of poverty are often severe, particularly for children.

8. Aid to the poor takes three main forms: **welfare,** cash payments to the poor; **in-kind transfers** such as food stamps, Medicaid, and housing subsidies; and **negative income taxes.**

9. Income redistribution is often justified by the inequality of income distribution. But a highly progressive tax system makes society as a whole poorer, a fact that limits the level of progressivity that supporters advocate. Like progressive taxation, redistribution forces a trade-off between equity and efficiency. An example of this is a **means-tested** program, which places high effective marginal tax rate on low-income families.

10. According to the **median voter theorem,** in an election by majority rule where voters decide how much of a given policy action to undertake, the outcome will most closely reflect the preferences of the median voter. Consequently, parties will choose positions close to the one preferred by the median voter. But for various reasons, this result has not happened in recent American politics.

KEY TERMS

Tax efficiency, p. 494
Tax fairness, p. 494
Tax equity, p. 494
Administrative costs, p. 495
Benefits principle, p. 496
Ability-to-pay principle, p. 496
Lump-sum tax, p. 496
Trade-off between equity and efficiency, p. 496
Tax base, p. 498
Tax structure, p. 498

Income tax, p. 499
Payroll tax, p. 499
Sales tax, p. 499
Profits tax, p. 499
Property tax, p. 499
Wealth tax, p. 499
Proportional tax, p. 499
Progressive tax, p. 499
Regressive tax, p. 499
Average tax rate on income, p. 500
Marginal tax rate on income, p. 500

Social insurance, p. 504
Redistribution of income, p. 504
Transfer payment, p. 504
Means-tested, p. 504
Poverty line, p. 508
Poverty rate, p. 508
Welfare, p. 510
In-kind transfers, p. 510
Negative income tax, p. 510
Median voter theorem, p. 515

PROBLEMS

1. Assume that the demand for gasoline is inelastic. The government imposes a sales tax on gasoline. The tax revenue is used to fund research into clean fuel alternatives to gasoline, which will improve the air we all breathe.

   a. Who bears more of the excess burden of this tax: consumers or producers? Show in a diagram who bears how much of the excess burden.

   b. Is this tax based on the benefits principle or the ability-to-pay principle? Explain.

2. Assess the following three taxes in terms of the benefits principle versus the ability-to-pay principle.

   a. A tax on gasoline that finances maintenance of state roads

   b. An 8% tax on imported goods valued in excess of $800 per household brought in on passenger flights

   c. Airline-flight landing fees that pay for air-traffic control

3. Consider the following deductions, which reduce the amount of income tax an individual must pay. Can they be justified on the basis of the ability-to-pay principle?

   a. Amount of charitable contributions

   b. Amount of interest paid on a mortgage

   c. Number of dependent children

4. You are advising the government on how to pay for national defense. There are two proposals for a tax system to fund national defense. Under both proposals, the tax base is an individual's income. Under proposal A, all citizens pay exactly the same lump-sum tax, regardless of income. Under pro-

posal B, individuals with higher income pay a greater proportion of their income in taxes.

   a. Is the tax in proposal A progressive, proportional, or regressive? What about the tax in proposal B?

   b. Is the tax in proposal A based on the ability-to-pay principle or on the benefits principle? What about the tax in proposal B?

   c. In terms of efficiency, which tax is better? Explain.

5. Each of the following tax proposals has income as the tax base. In a diagram with the tax base—income, ranging from $0 to $50,000—on the horizontal axis and the taxes paid on the vertical axis, draw the income tax for each of the following tax proposals. For an individual who earns $25,000, what is the marginal tax rate under each proposal? What is the average tax rate for that individual? Is the marginal tax rate higher than, lower than, or equal to the average tax rate? Accordingly, classify the tax as being proportional, progressive, or regressive.

   a. All income is taxed at 20%.

   b. All income up to $10,000 is tax-free. All income above $10,000 is taxed at a constant rate of 20%.

   c. All income between $0 and $10,000 is taxed at 10%. All income between $10,000 and $20,000 is taxed at 20%. All income higher than $20,000 is taxed at 30%.

   d. Each individual who earns more than $10,000 pays a lump-sum tax of $10,000. If the individual's income is less than $10,000, that individual pays in tax exactly what his or her income is.

6. In Transylvania the basic income tax system is fairly simple. The first 40,000 sylvers (the official currency of Transylvania) earned each year are free of income tax. Any additional income is taxed at a rate of 25%. In addition, every individual pays a social security tax, which is calculated as follows: all income up to 80,000 sylvers is taxed at an additional 20%, but there is no additional social security tax on income above 80,000 sylvers.

   a. Calculate the average and the marginal tax rates for Transylvanians with the following levels of income: 20,000 sylvers, 40,000 sylvers, 80,000 sylvers, and 120,000 sylvers.

   b. For each of the income levels in part (a), is the tax system progressive, regressive, or proportional?

7. You work for the Council of Economic Advisers, providing economic advice to the White House. The president wants to overhaul the income tax system and asks your advice. Suppose that the current income tax system consists of a proportional tax of 10% on all income and that there is one person in the country who earns $110 million; everyone else earns less than $100 million. The president proposes a tax cut targeted at the very rich so that the new tax system would consist of a proportional tax of 10% on all income up to $100 million and a marginal tax rate of 0% (no tax) on income above $100 million. You are asked to evaluate this tax proposal.

   a. For incomes of $100 million or less, is this tax system progressive, regressive, or proportional? For incomes of more than $100 million? Explain.

   b. Would this tax system create more or less tax revenue, other things equal? Is this tax system more or less efficient than the current tax system? Explain.

8. In the city of Metropolis, there are 100 residents, each of whom lives until age 75. Residents of Metropolis have the following incomes over their lifetime: Through age 14, they earn nothing. From age 15 until age 29, they earn 200 metros (the currency of Metropolis) per year. From age 30 to age 49, they earn 400 metros. From age 50 to age 64, they earn 300 metros. And finally at age 65 they retire and are paid a pension of 100 metros per year until they die at age 75. Everyone consumes each year whatever their income is that year (that is, there is no saving and no borrowing). Currently, 20 residents are 10 years old, 20 residents are 20 years old, 20 residents are 40 years old, 20 residents are 60 years old, and 20 residents are 70 years old.

   a. Study the income distribution among all residents of Metropolis. Split the population into quintiles according to their income. How much income does a resident in the first quintile have? in the second, third, fourth, and fifth

quintiles? Which share of total income of all residents goes to the residents in each quintile? Construct a table showing the share of total income that goes to each quintile. Does this income distribution show inequality?

   b. Now look only at the 20 residents of Metropolis who are currently 40 years old, and study the income distribution among only those residents. Split those 20 residents into quintiles according to their income. How much income does a resident in the first quintile have? in the second, third, fourth, and fifth quintiles? Which share of total income of all 40-year-olds goes to the residents in each quintile? Does this income distribution show inequality?

   c. What is the relevance of these examples for assessing data on the distribution of income in any country?

9. The country of Marxland has the following income tax and social insurance system. Each citizen's income is taxed at an average tax rate of 100%. A social insurance system then provides transfers to each citizen such that each citizen's after-tax income is exactly equal. That is, each citizen gets (through a government transfer payment) an equal share of the income tax revenue. What is the incentive for one individual citizen to work and earn income? What will the total tax revenue in Marxland be? What will be the after-tax income (including the transfer payment) for each citizen? Do you think such a tax system that creates perfect equality will work?

10. In the city of Notchingham, each worker is paid a wage rate of $10 per hour. Notchingham administers its own unemployment benefit, which is structured as follows: If you are unemployed (that is, if you do not work at all), you get unemployment benefits (a transfer from the government) of $50 per day. As soon as you work for only one hour, the unemployment benefit is completely withdrawn. That is, there is a "notch" in the benefit system.

   a. How much income does an unemployed person have per day? How much daily income does an individual have who works four hours per day? How many hours do you need to work to earn just the same as if you were unemployed?

   b. Will anyone ever accept a part-time job that requires working four hours per day, rather than being unemployed?

   c. Suppose that Notchingham now changes the way in which the unemployment benefit is withdrawn. For each additional dollar that an individual earns, $0.50 of the unemployment benefit is withdrawn. How much daily income does an individual now have who works four hours per day? Is there an incentive now to work four hours per day rather than being unemployed?

> **web...** To continue your study and review of concepts in this chapter, please visit the Krugman/Wells website for quizzes, animated graph tutorials, web links to helpful resources, and more.
>
> **www.worthpublishers.com/krugmanwells**

>> Technology, Information Goods, and Network Externalities

SUING CHILDREN

IN SEPTEMBER 2003, THE RECORDING Industry Association of America—a group representing big record labels—sued Brianna Lahara, a 12-year-old schoolgirl, for copyright infringement. Her mother settled the case for $2,000.

Was Brianna in the music piracy business? Not exactly. All she did was participate in Kazaa, a file-swapping network whose members use the Internet to download digitized music, among other things, from each others' computers. But recordings of musical performances are copyrighted—and by swapping files of these recordings with other Kazaa members, Brianna was indeed breaking the law. By the way, the reason the recording industry went after individuals like Brianna was that the company behind

Kazaa—chastened by the legal action brought against Napster, the company that made file-swapping famous—insisted that it bore no responsibility for what other people did with its software.

But what about the economics of the case? Are people who swap music files truly engaged in theft? File-swappers and the companies whose software facilitates their activities say no—they're not making off with physical goods, and they aren't doing anyone any harm. If I listen to a bootleg recording of my favorite band, I don't make the band's music any less available to you. Or do I?

The fight over file-swapping flared up just two years after another high-tech legal drama. In 2001 a federal judge ordered the

New technology has changed the way we access music, but it has also created new economic challenges. Brianna Lahara (shown at right) learned this the hard way.

What you will learn in this chapter:

➤ The growing importance of goods embodying new technology and the unique economic problems they pose

➤ How the economics of **information goods** differs from that of other goods

➤ The importance of **network externalities** and why they lead a consumer to prefer the good used by most other consumers

➤ Why information goods can lead to **critical mass** effects, in which a market suddenly explodes in size, or to **tipping**, in which the market swings to favor one good over another

➤ The special dilemmas information goods pose for antitrust policy breakup of Microsoft, the producer of the Windows software that runs most personal computers, only to have his ruling thrown out on appeal. Both cases vividly illustrate the extent to which changing technology—and in particular the growing importance of digital products—is changing the economic landscape and presenting new problems for economic policy.

Why does technology change the landscape? Because products like software and music files, unlike most of the goods and services traded in an economy, are *information goods:* their value comes not from their physical attributes but from the information they embody. They are also goods whose value to a consumer depends in large part on how many other consumers use the same good. As we'll see, the growing importance of information goods takes some issues we have discussed in earlier chapters—monopoly, positive externalities, and the dilemmas of antitrust policy—to a new and higher level.

The Economics of Information Goods

Even now most workers in the U.S. economy are employed in the production of conventional goods and services: cars, houses, haircuts, and so on. But considerable resources are now also devoted to producing **information goods**—products whose value comes not from their physical characteristics but from the information they embody.

There is no sharp line dividing information goods from other goods. A computer file is clearly an information good, but conventional goods also contain information. For example, the value of a piece of furniture is partly the result of the knowledge of the furniture-maker, embodied in its form. But although almost all recordings sold these days are in digital form and can be sent over the Internet, many consumers still prefer a physical CD to a downloadable file. By any definition, however, the importance of information goods in the economy has clearly been increasing. As we'll see next, this creates some new challenges for a market economy.

> An **information good** is a good whose value comes from the information it contains.

Producing and Selling Information Goods

The fight over file-swapping is widely seen as a landmark dispute, with significance that goes well beyond the music industry. Why? Because the dispute poses, in a very clear way, the question of how society should deal with the production, sale, and distribution of information goods.

To understand why this is an issue, let's start by examining the production costs for an information good. It seems clear that the marginal cost of producing an additional unit of an information good is very low. For example, once the master of a recording has been created, the cost of making an additional digital copy—or burning a copy onto a compact disc—is very small. Similarly, it costs Microsoft very little to produce and ship another copy of Windows. Indeed, many information goods have nearly zero marginal cost.

But that doesn't mean that an information good is costless to produce. A master recording requires many hours of work by songwriters, musicians, audio technicians, producers, and so on, many of them working with expensive equipment. Producing a large software program may require tens of thousands of hours of work by highly skilled and highly paid programmers. These costs are, however, *fixed*—they are the same regardless of how many copies of the product are sold. Whether a recording goes multiple platinum or is never released, the costs of making it are the same. So the characteristic cost structure of information goods involves *high fixed cost* and *very low marginal cost*. This means that information goods have the kind of cost structure we discussed in our analysis of natural monopolies in Chapter 14.

Figure 22-1 illustrates the typical cost structure of an information good and its consequences. Here we imagine that Def Ear Ventures, a record company, is considering producing a new recording by a group that has a large but not huge potential audience. If the recording is made, Def Ear will have a monopoly on its sales, since it owns the copyright. But the company must decide whether the recording is worth producing.

Def Ear's management believes that the demand curve for the new recording is shown by the demand schedule in Figure 22-1: at a price of $10, sales are zero, but if the recording were free, 1 million people would take it. The graph in Figure 22-1 shows the demand curve *D*, along with its associated marginal revenue curve *MR*. (Remember from Chapter 14 that a monopolist's marginal revenue curve is always below the demand curve.)

Figure 22-1

The Profit-Maximizing Quantity of an Information Good

An information good such as a musical recording has high fixed cost and low marginal cost, a situation similar to natural monopoly. Here, Def Ear's fixed cost is $1.5 million, and the marginal cost of manufacturing a single recording is zero. As a result, the average total cost curve, *ATC*, is downward sloping. Given the demand curve, *D*, with its associated marginal revenue curve, *MR*, the profit-maximizing quantity of output is 500,000 recordings, the quantity at which marginal revenue equals marginal cost, as indicated by the optimal point *M*. The profit-maximizing price, P_M, is $5, the average total cost, ATC_M, is $3, resulting in a per-unit profit of $2. **>web...**

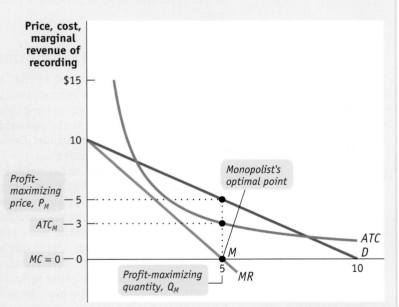

Demand for Recording		Production Cost of Recording		
Price of recording	Quantity of recordings demanded (hundreds of thousands)	Quantity of recordings produced (hundreds of thousands)	Fixed cost (millions)	Average total cost
$10	0	0	$1.5	—
9	1	1	1.5	$15.00
8	2	2	1.5	7.50
7	3	3	1.5	5.00
6	4	4	1.5	3.75
5	5	5	1.5	3.00
4	6	6	1.5	2.50
3	7	7	1.5	2.14
2	8	8	1.5	1.88
1	9	9	1.5	1.67
0	10	10	1.5	1.50

The company also believes that it will cost $1.5 million to produce the master recording, but that no additional costs will arise from distributing it. This cost structure is also shown in Figure 22-1. Average total cost is equal to $1.5 million divided by the number of recordings sold; so average total cost falls as the number of recordings sold increases, leading to the downward-sloping average total cost curve *ATC*. When only 100,000 recordings are sold, the average total cost per recording is $15, but the average total cost is $1.50 when 1,000,000 recordings are sold. Marginal cost, though, is always zero.

We can apply the *optimal output rule* from Chapters 9 and 14 to find Def Ear's profit-maximizing quantity. The company should produce the quantity at which marginal revenue equals marginal cost, as indicated by the optimal point *M*. Because marginal cost is zero, the profit-maximizing quantity, Q_M, is 500,000 recordings, the quantity at which marginal revenue is equal to zero.

The price at this profit-maximizing quantity, P_M, is $5 per recording and the average total cost, ATC_M, is $3 per recording. So the recording is profitable: Def Ear earns $2 per recording sold, generating a profit of $1 million on sales of 500,000 recordings.

Pricing Problems for Information Goods

The economic analysis we just applied to Def Ear's recording is standard monopoly theory. So what makes an information good different from any other good?

The answer is illustrated by the problem of file-swapping. Suppose that a music-copying technology, such as the one exploited by file-swappers, allows some potential buyers to download copies of Def Ear's new recording for free. Is this good or bad from an economic perspective?

It depends on whether the recording would still be produced. If Def Ear, knowing that some customers will make free copies, still produces the recording, free downloading increases total surplus. Remember, the marginal cost to the company of producing one more copy is zero. So inefficiency arises whenever anyone decides not to buy the recording because the price is greater than zero. If a person who wouldn't have bought the recording downloads a free copy, the music company doesn't lose anything, the listener gains something, and total surplus increases.

Figure 22-2 shows the gains to total surplus from free copying, compared with the original monopoly outcome: they are equal to the area of the triangle labeled *E*, the gain in consumer surplus from letting those who would not otherwise have bought the recording listen to the music for free. Q_O, 1 million copies, is the socially optimal quantity of output because at Q_O, the marginal benefit to the consumer of the last copy (the millionth copy) is equal to marginal cost—that is, zero. Those who defend file-swapping are in effect basing their argument on these potential gains to total surplus represented by the area *E*.

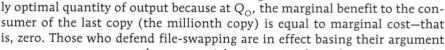

This analysis may look familiar: it is basically the same as the analysis of *artificially scarce goods* in Chapter 20. These are goods that are nonrival in consumption, so the marginal cost of allowing an additional individual to consume the good is zero. For such goods, efficiency is achieved when the price to consumers is zero.

But you may already have seen the problem: consumers can't download music that hasn't been produced. If Def Ear expects many listeners to download its recording for free—not just those who would not otherwise have bought the recording, but some or all of those who *would* have bought one—producing the master recording won't be profitable in the first place.

MOZART DIED PENNILESS.

BUMMER. WAS EVERYONE GETTIN' HIS TUNES FREE OFF 'NAPSTER'?

MIKE LUCKOVICH
ATLANTA CONSTITUTION

By permission of Mike Luckovich and Creators Syndicate, Inc.

Figure 22-2

The Problem of Achieving Efficiency with an Information Good

The profit-maximizing record company behaves like a monopolist and will produce 500,000 recordings, Q_M, leading to consumer surplus of area A and profit or producer surplus of area B. Area C represents the producer's total cost. But the efficient quantity is 1 million recordings, Q_O, the quantity at which price is equal to marginal cost. Offering the good for free leads to a gain in total surplus of area E. Knowing, however, that it will be forced to provide the good for free is likely to lead the music company to forgo producing the good altogether. **>web...**

And if the recording isn't produced, both Def Ear and its potential consumers are worse off than if the recording were produced, even if it is priced above marginal cost. In Figure 22-2, if Def Ear is able to charge the profit-maximizing monopoly price of $5, it earns enough to cover its total cost, measured by the area of the rectangle C, and earn profits equal to the area of the rectangle B. The profits represented by the area B are the producer surplus compared to a situation in which the good is not produced at all. In addition, consumers receive the consumer surplus measured by the area of the triangle A. So if the company is deterred from producing the recording, both producer and consumer surplus (the sum of areas A and B) are sacrificed.

Clearly, then, information goods create a special tension. Monopoly is a bad thing, other things equal: it is inefficient to charge a price that is above marginal cost. But the expectation of monopoly profits is necessary to induce the company to produce the good at all. Indeed, economists generally agree that when it comes to information goods, a *temporary* monopoly may be the necessary price of progress.

Why temporary? As we will now see, both law and natural forces tend to limit the duration of the monopolies associated with information goods.

Property Rights in Information

The conundrum we have just seen is not new; indeed, it has plagued inventors for centuries. Some, like Samuel Morse, who invented the telegraph in 1837, were criticized for allowing their inventions to become the source of monopoly power. Others, like Eli Whitney, who invented the cotton gin in 1793, couldn't make money from their inventions. (Whitney's design was easy to copy, and he was never able to enforce his patent.) But the growing importance of information goods has made the dilemma more critical today than ever before. How has it been dealt with?

To make it worthwhile for people to incur the cost of producing information goods, they must be given some kind of property rights to the information the goods embody that, in turn, allows them to earn revenue. Traditionally this has been done through

A **patent** gives an inventor a temporary monopoly in the use or sale of an invention; a **copyright** similarly gives the creator of a literary or artistic work sole rights to profit from that work.

two closely related legal instruments: **patents** and **copyrights.** Both instruments give creators of knowledge property rights to the knowledge. Patents give inventors the sole right to make, use, or sell their invention for a period that in most countries lasts between 16 and 20 years. Copyrights give the creators of literary or artistic works a similar monopoly for a longer period. One of the strange aspects of the digital revolution, by the way, is the blurring of the distinction between items subject to patent law and those subject to copyright law. Is a piece of software, which takes the form of thousands of lines of program code, an invention or a literary work? Because copyrights last much longer than patents, millions or even billions of dollars depend on how that question is answered.

The justification for patent and copyright law is clear from our earlier discussion. If inventors were not protected by patents, they would gain little reward from their efforts: as soon as a valuable invention was made public, other people would copy it and sell products based on it. And if inventors could not expect to profit from their inventions, they would not incur the costs of invention in the first place. So the law gives a temporary monopoly through the creation of temporary property rights to encourage invention. In effect, the law tries to ensure that the gains measured by the areas *A* and *B* in Figure 22-2 take place.

But why are patents temporary? Again, Figure 22-2 illustrates the logic that underlies the law. As long as production of an information good is assured, it is efficient to set its price at marginal cost. But granting a permanent monopoly means creating a permanent gap between price and marginal cost. As a result, the gains from making the invention freely available, measured by the area *E*, would be permanently forgone.

Patent and copyright laws try to strike a compromise. Inventors are granted a temporary monopoly, which, it is hoped, will compensate them for the cost of invention. Because the monopoly eventually ends, the gap between marginal cost and marginal benefit is ultimately eliminated.

Because the length of the temporary monopoly cannot be tailored to specific cases, this system is imperfect and leads to some missed opportunities. Although some potential inventions are not created because the property rights don't last long enough, some monopolies go on longer than necessary. So the length of patents involves a trade-off. Furthermore, it's not clear whether the actual duration of patents makes the best of this trade-off.

FOR INQUIRING MINDS

PROTECTING MICKEY MOUSE

Until 1998 copyright law in the United States gave individual authors the sole right to publish their works for their lives, plus 50 years. Works of corporate ownership received 75 years of protection. But the Sonny Bono Copyright Term Extension Act of 1998 (yes, that's its real name) extended copyrights to 70 years beyond the life of the author and 95 years for corporate creations.

As we've explained, setting the duration of patents and copyrights involves a trade-off: nobody knows whether the new, longer copyrights are better or worse for the economy. But economists and consumer advocates were outraged at the 1998 act because it made the copyright extension *retroactive:* existing copyrights, including many that would have expired in the near future, suddenly got a new lease on life.

This made no sense from an economic point of view. The fixed costs on a decades-old artistic creation had already been incurred, so extending the copyright wouldn't lead to more creation. The only effect was to prolong the inefficiency of monopoly—and, of course, to sustain the monopoly profits of the copyright's owner.

Not surprisingly, the act was passed in large part because of lobbying from big entertainment companies, especially Disney. You see, Mickey Mouse was introduced as a character in 1928; without the act, he would have entered the public domain in 2003; now he is scheduled to enter the public domain in 2023. Critics of the 1998 bill often refer to it as "the Mickey Mouse protection act."

In any case, the effectiveness of patents and copyrights varies, depending on the characteristics of the product and industry. In some industries, patents are a highly effective protection for innovators and are the principal incentive for invention. Economics in Action below describes one such industry, pharmaceuticals. In other industries, however, innovations are less easy to patent. For example, the innovation may not be a discrete, patentable invention as much as a combination of existing ideas. A case in point is Wal-Mart, which became the nation's number-one retailer by, among other things, building large stores away from traditional downtowns, and using information technology to manage inventories efficiently. Nothing in that system could be patented, yet the combination gave Wal-Mart a huge cost advantage over competitors. Or it may be possible for competitors to engage in what is known as "reverse engineering": taking a patented product apart, figuring out how it works and how it was made, then developing something similar that avoids violating the letter (but perhaps not the spirit) of the patent.

Even in cases where innovations cannot be patented, however, innovators often have "first-mover" advantages over potential rivals that allow them to establish temporary monopoly positions. The innovating firm's head start in production can give it a technological advantage. If reputation is important to consumers, the first firm into a market can establish brand-name recognition. And in an industry characterized by *network externalities,* which we describe later in this chapter, the first firm in an industry can have a powerful advantage. All of these first-mover advantages arise because reverse engineering and other forms of copying take time.

A good, relatively recent example of first-mover advantage is Amazon.com, the first large-scale online book retailer. Its leadership is based not on patents—other online booksellers offer similar services—but on the advantages of size and name recognition among book buyers.

Such first-mover created monopoly positions, unlike those created by patents, are real even though they have no legal standing. Despite the fact that companies don't have legal property rights to their innovation, they are able to use their head start to gain a privileged market position. Even so, the monopoly positions established by innovators tend to erode over time, much as if patents were expiring. There are two reasons for this. One is that eventually competitors manage to duplicate the innovation. The other is that newer innovators come up with products that make the original innovation obsolete. For example, in the late 1990s AOL dominated the residential market for Internet access, which at that time relied almost completely on dial-up connections. But its position has rapidly eroded in recent years as broadband access via DSL and cable has become widely available at home.

So temporary monopoly tends to be the norm for many kinds of innovation, including those that cannot be effectively protected by patents.

economics in action

Drugs on the Market

The trade-off between the good aspects of a monopoly (it encourages innovation) and the bad aspects (it discourages consumption) is vividly illustrated by the pharmaceutical industry.

It may not be apparent that prescription drugs are information goods. But once they have been developed, most drugs are relatively inexpensive to manufacture. Most of their cost comes from the resources required for research and development. In other words, the drug embodies the information created by researchers, which gives it a high fixed cost but a low marginal cost.

How high are these fixed costs? One study, conducted in 2001, found that developing a successful drug costs, on average, about $800 million. Another study, which included spending on failed drugs (for every successful drug, several unsuccessful ones are developed) and marketing campaigns, came up with an average cost of $1.7 billion per successful drug.

Drugs are protected by patents, which give the producer a temporary monopoly. As with other patents, this monopoly lasts 20 years. But in the case of drugs, a 20-year patent length is misleading. Pharmaceutical companies normally receive a patent after laboratory testing suggests that a drug might be medically useful. However, before a company can sell a drug it must go through a series of clinical tests on groups of human subjects to demonstrate that the drug is safe and effective. These tests often take more than a decade—and sometimes as much as 14 years. So the actual period during which a drug company can make use of its monopoly can be as short as 6 years. After that, it will face competition from other companies that produce versions of the drug. So some observers have wondered whether the 20-year patent life on drugs is too short because it does not give enough incentive for research and development.

Still, the monopoly position of a patent holder means that many patients end up paying high prices for medicine that is actually cheap to produce. In some cases, this means that people can't afford medicine that might be significant to their well-being, and even save their lives. ■

>>CHECK YOUR UNDERSTANDING 22-1

1. Which of the following are information goods? Which are not? Explain your answer.
    a. A premium cable show delivered to cable viewers
    b. A winter coat made from a newly developed high-tech fabric
    c. A newspaper
    d. A car that contains a new, highly fuel-efficient motor
2. It is often said that "bigger is better" in industries in which the good has the characteristics of an information good. Explain this statement.

Solutions appear at back of book.

Network Externalities

Suppose you owned the only fax machine in the world. What would it be worth to you?

The answer, of course, is nothing. A fax machine derives its value only from the fact that other people also possess fax machines so that you and they can exchange faxes. And in general the more people who have fax machines, the more valuable a fax machine is to you.

This phenomenon, in which a good's value to an individual is greater when many other people own or use the same good, is common in technology-driven sectors of the economy. This is called a **network externality** because the most obvious versions of the "fax machine effect" occur when the goods involved form some kind of communications or transportation network. But the phenomenon is considerably more widespread than that.

Network externalities play a key role both in the modern economy and in a number of policy controversies. Let's look at where and how network externalities occur and then at some of the issues they raise.

A good is subject to a **network externality** when the value of the good to an individual is greater when a large number of other people also use that good.

Types of Network Externality

The most obvious examples of network externalities involve communications. At different points in history the prime examples have been telegraphs, telephones, fax machines, and e-mail accounts. In each case the value of the good is derived entirely from its ability to link many people possessing the same good. As a result, the marginal benefit of the good to any one individual depends on the number of other individuals who use it.

However, network externalities can also arise in less dramatic ways. For example, network externalities can exist when other users are not strictly necessary for the use of a good, as long as they enhance its usefulness. In the early days of railroad development, a railroad from New York to Chicago would have had considerable value all by itself, as would a railroad from Kansas City to Chicago. However, each line was worth more given the existence of the other, because once both were in place, goods could be shipped via Chicago between New York and Kansas City. In the modern world, a scheduled flight between two airports becomes more valuable if one or both of those airports is a hub with connections to other places.

Even this kind of direct link need not be necessary to create important network externalities. Any way in which other people's consumption of a good increases your own marginal benefit from consumption of that good can give rise to network effects.

Perhaps the classic case of indirect network externalities is that of computer operating systems. The operating system of a computer is the underlying software that runs the machine's basic operations, underpinning and coordinating the various programs—word processors, spreadsheets, e-mail programs, and so on—that the user runs. Most personal computers around the world run on Windows, the system sold by Microsoft—although a significant minority of users own computers produced by Apple, which has its own operating system. And a growing number of computers run on Linux, a system designed by programmers who believe that operating systems should not be corporate property.

Why is Windows so dominant? Is a personal computer running Windows like a fax machine, which is useful only to the extent that other people possess the same good? Not in a direct sense: a computer can be used to type a term paper, do calculations on a spreadsheet, even send and receive e-mail regardless of how many other people have computers running the same operating system. So there isn't a literal network issue making Windows the preferred system.

Nonetheless, the dominance of Windows turns out to be self-reinforcing, for at least two indirect reasons. First, it is easier for a Windows user to get help and advice from other computer users than for someone using a less popular system. So it's a good idea, if possible, to use the same system that your colleague in the next office uses. Second, because Windows is used so widely, it attracts more attention from software developers. As a result, there are more programs that run on Windows than on any other operating system.

Network externalities in this broad sense occur for many goods. Even your choice of a car is influenced by a form of network externalities. Most people would be reluctant to switch to a car that does not run on ordinary gasoline—for example, a vehicle that runs on natural gas—if only because fueling the car would be difficult: very few gas stations offer alternative fuels. But the reason they do not offer alternative fuels is, of course, that few people drive anything other than gasoline-powered cars. Or to take a less drastic example, people who live in small towns are reluctant to drive an unusual imported vehicle: Where would they find a mechanic who knows how to fix it? So the circularity that makes one person choose Windows because everyone else uses Windows also applies to non-high-tech goods like cars.

Nonetheless, experience suggests that network externalities are more important for information goods than for other goods. And network externalities lead to two characteristic features of markets for information goods: *positive feedback* and *tipping*.

Positive Feedback

When a good is subject to a network externality, it is likely to be subject to **positive feedback.** If large numbers of people buy the good, other people become more likely to buy it. If people *don't* buy the good, others become less likely to buy it. So both success and failure tend to be self-reinforcing.

Because of positive feedback, certain "story lines" recur in the history of information good industries. One of these is the story of a small network that suddenly takes off when it reaches *critical mass*. Another is that of competition between two alternative technologies, neither obviously better than the other, that is resolved decisively through market *tipping*. Let's look at each story line in turn.

Goods subject to network externalities experience **positive feedback:** success breeds success, failure breeds failure.

Critical Mass and Industry Takeoffs Fax machines have existed for a remarkably long time. The basic technology was developed by the Scottish inventor Alexander Bain in 1843, and AT&T introduced a wire photo service using fax technology in 1925. Really widespread use of fax machines, however, began only in the 1980s. And the rise was sudden indeed. Sharp introduced the first low-priced fax machine in 1984 and sold 80,000 that first year. In 1987 a million fax machines were sold, and by 1989 they were everywhere.

E-mail and the Internet present a similar picture. The first e-mail message was sent in 1969, but at the beginning of the 1990s only a relative handful of people were online; by about 1996, e-mail had become essential to business, and tens of millions of people had access to the Internet.

What accounts for these sudden explosions? In each case the technology improved: low-priced high-quality fax machines like the one Sharp introduced in 1984 were made possible by the rapid progress of microelectronics. But the explosive growth of fax machine use wasn't just because the technology improved; it also resulted from the network externality in fax use.

To see why, let's consider a simplified description of the decision to acquire a fax machine. We assume that there are two types of potential buyers. First, there are "unconditional" fax users—people who will want a fax machine regardless of how many other people have them. (An example might be corporations, who use faxes to send documents between their own branches.) Second, there are "conditional" users, who will want a fax machine only if the network of fax machines is large enough—that is, if enough other people already have them. In addition, both the number of unconditional users and the level of fax machine ownership that would persuade the conditional users to buy machines depend on how much the machines cost and how well they work.

Suppose that there are 1 million potential fax machine users, the total number of conditional and unconditional users. Suppose also that given the current technology and price of fax machines, 100,000 of them are unconditional users. But the other 900,000 potential users will find it worthwhile to buy a machine only if the number of machines already out there exceeds a **threshold network size** of 300,000. That is, they will buy machines only if 300,000 other people (the unconditional users) have machines because they won't have enough occasions to send or receive faxes otherwise.

The initial situation of the demand for fax machines is shown in panel (a) of Figure 22-3. Here we assume for simplicity that all fax machines are produced with the same technology so that all consumers face the same price and quality. On the horizontal axis is the quantity of fax machines currently in use at the given price and quality. On the vertical axis is the quantity of fax machines demanded—the number of people who *want* fax machines. The two blue lines show what we have assumed about the demand for fax machines. The blue line on the left shows that there is an unconditional demand for 100,000 fax machines—100,000 people will acquire fax machines regardless of how many other people have them. The blue line on the right shows that if the number of fax machines in use reaches 300,000, the number of users suddenly increases to 1 million. (In this case we have assumed that all conditional users have the *same* threshold network size, but the story would stay the same as long as they have sufficiently similar thresholds.)

How many people will acquire fax machines in this situation? There are two possible equilibria, represented by points L_1 and H. The point labeled L_1, at which 100,000 people acquire fax machines is a possible equilibrium—each individual is making his or her best choice given what everyone else is doing. The point labeled H, with 1 million fax machines in use, is also a possible equilibrium. But if, as is typically the case, machines built with the original technology are relatively expensive given the quality, you would expect the number of unconditional users to be relatively small. So we can safely assume that L_1 is indeed the initial equilibrium in this market, and not H.

Now suppose that improved technology makes faxes cheaper and better. This will both increase the number of unconditional users and reduce the threshold network

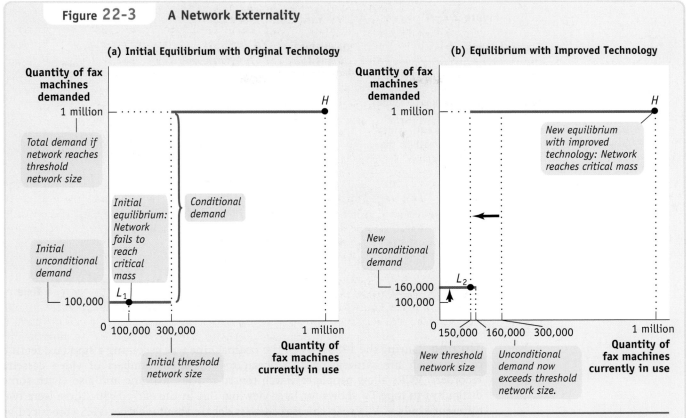

Figure 22-3   A Network Externality

(a) Initial Equilibrium with Original Technology

(b) Equilibrium with Improved Technology

With a network externality, small changes in the cost or quality of a good can lead the market to suddenly explode. Here, conditional users will not participate in the network unless the number of users (the unconditional demand) equals or exceeds the threshold network size. Panel (a) illustrates the network under the original technology, where the initial threshold network size is 300,000. The initial equilibrium is L_1. The network fails to reach critical mass because the unconditional demand, 100,000, is less than the threshold network size under the original technology, 300,000, and conditional users refuse to participate. Panel (b) illustrates the network when the technology has improved. Due to the better technology the threshold network size falls to 150,000, the unconditional demand rises to 160,000, and the new equilibrium is H. The network has now reached critical mass: conditional users participate in the network because unconditional demand exceeds the threshold network size.

size for conditional users. If the improvement in technology is substantial enough, the new number of unconditional users will equal or exceed the threshold network size and the fax machine industry will take off.

Panel (b) of Figure 22-3 shows how this might happen. Due to the cheaper and better machines, the number of unconditional users rises from 100,000 to 160,000, and the threshold network size drops from 300,000 to 150,000. The number of current users now exceeds the threshold network size, leading the 840,000 conditional users to jump in and buy fax machines. The network quickly expands and a new equilibrium is reached at H.

The moral of this story is that improvements in the technology of goods subject to network externalities may at first lead to only gradual increases in the size of the network. But when the network reaches a certain size—a **critical mass**—it suddenly explodes.

Because of the critical mass effect, industries subject to network externalities often exhibit the pattern of growth shown in Figure 22-4 on page 530: a long period of slow growth, followed by a sudden, rapid expansion, with growth leveling off again once the conditional buyers have been brought in.

The **critical mass** of a network is the size at which it suddenly begins to grow rapidly.

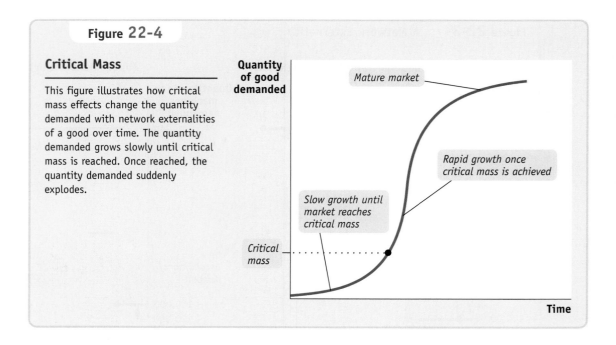

Figure 22-4

Critical Mass

This figure illustrates how critical mass effects change the quantity demanded with network externalities of a good over time. The quantity demanded grows slowly until critical mass is reached. Once reached, the quantity demanded suddenly explodes.

Quantity of good demanded

Mature market

Rapid growth once critical mass is achieved

Slow growth until market reaches critical mass

Critical mass

Time

Tipping During the 1980s, when the fax machine was becoming a standard feature of American life, Americans also began to buy large numbers of video cassette recorders. VCRs allow people to watch rented movies at home and also (with some difficulty) to tape TV shows for later viewing. But in the early 1980s there were two different kinds of VCRs. To this day there is debate about whether VHS (produced by several companies) or Betamax (produced only by Sony) was the better system. However, after a period in which both were in use, consumers swung decisively to VHS and Betamax eventually disappeared.

What made consumers choose VHS over Betamax? The key point was that VHS enjoyed an initial advantage. Most of the videos available for rental were VHS—and that was because most of the customers to whom rental stores catered had VHS players. So ultimately consumers chose VHS because other consumers had chosen VHS—a case of positive feedback at work.

The situation in which a small initial advantage for one of two competing goods or technologies proves self-reinforcing, eventually driving the other competitor out of the market, is known as **tipping.** Tipping is similar in its logic to the critical mass effect on sales of a single good. And it leads to somewhat similar patterns of change over time. Figure 22-5 shows the characteristic path of a market subject to tipping. On the horizontal axis is time; on the vertical axis is the quantity of a good demanded. A good that has a substantial but not dominant share of the market may stay in that range for an extended period. Then, quite suddenly, and often for no obvious reason, the market tips either for or against it, and the good either becomes dominant or fades away.

> **Tipping** occurs when positive feedback due to network externalities causes consumers to swing to one of two competing goods or technologies.

Competition in the Face of Network Externalities

Companies that produce information goods are aware of the importance of network externalities. But how do these effects change the behavior of firms? The general answer is that when companies believe that their products are subject to strong network externalities, they typically place a strong emphasis on building their sales network, even at the expense of short-term profits. This strategy is sometimes reflected by saying that in information industries you need to lose money to make money.

To see why, consider the case of a good subject to a critical mass effect—say, camera phones that also allow speakers to see each other. If only a few companies

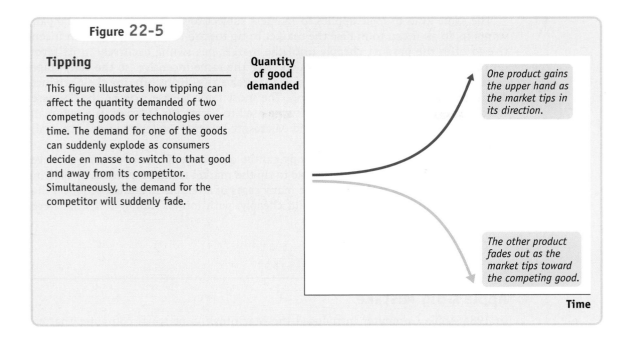

Figure 22-5

Tipping

This figure illustrates how tipping can affect the quantity demanded of two competing goods or technologies over time. The demand for one of the goods can suddenly explode as consumers decide en masse to switch to that good and away from its competitor. Simultaneously, the demand for the competitor will suddenly fade.

Quantity of good demanded

One product gains the upper hand as the market tips in its direction.

The other product fades out as the market tips toward the competing good.

Time

are supplying those phones, it is clearly in their interest to get the industry to critical mass—to get the explosion of sales that will occur when many people feel that they should have camera phones because so many other people have them. But how can these companies get the industry to critical mass? One way is to sell the product cheaply—perhaps at a loss—in order to increase the size of the network. So we often see companies introducing new high-technology products at a price well below production cost.

FOR INQUIRING MINDS

WHOSE NETWORK IS IT, ANYWAY?

Suppose that Sharp, when it introduced the first cheap fax machine, had engineered it so that it could send and receive faxes only from other Sharp machines. That would not have been good for the fax network—but it might have been very good for Sharp.

Sound implausible? Consider the case of America Online and instant messaging.

AOL is a sort of Internet within the Internet—subscribers can access all the usual web pages and also have special access to services only AOL offers. And at the end of the 1990s, AOL introduced a new service: instant messaging, e-mail that pops up immediately on the recipient's screen. This was supposed to be available only between AOL subscribers: the company viewed it as an additional selling point that would increase the number of subscribers. But AOL subscribers wanted to be able to send instant messages to

non-AOL subscribers, and vice versa. So a sort of arms race developed, as programmers wrote software that allowed non-AOL users to send instant messages and to receive them from AOL users, to which AOL responded by introducing countermeasures, to which the programmers responded with new software, and so on.

Who was serving the public interest? As in the case of file-sharing, the answer is ambiguous. Instant messaging is more useful if it's available to everyone; but companies like AOL won't make innovations unless they believe that they can profit from them. So although AOL eventually opened up their instant messaging service to non-AOL users after it became the subject of antitrust scrutiny, the original belief that sales would be increased by the threat of excluding non-AOL users made the innovation possible.

The same kind of logic applies in markets subject to tipping. Because a company wants to do all it can to induce the market to tip toward its product, it has an incentive to offer the product cheaply until the market has swung decisively in its favor. Of course, firms offering rival products have the same incentive, so the early stages of competition in information goods often involve rival firms offering their products for very little—in some cases nothing. The most famous case may be the "browser wars" of the 1990s. A browser is software used to access the Internet; the two main competitors—Netscape Navigator and Microsoft Internet Explorer—were both available for free.

In the real world, of course, nobody can be quite sure if a new product will ever achieve critical mass or if it is possible to tip the market toward a product by offering it cheaply. The result is that there are many cases of attempts to launch products that seem foolish in retrospect: goods sold cheaply, with lots of money lost, that never took off.

economics in action

Apple's Big Mistake

In 1984 Apple Computer introduced the Macintosh, a personal computer that co-founder Steve Jobs described as "insanely great." Many observers agreed. Before the Mac, personal computers were operated by typing in cumbersome commands or possibly by choosing a command from a menu. The Mac introduced the much more powerful graphical user interface, also known as point-and-click: you use a mouse to move an arrow to an image on the screen, then click a button. Graphical user interfaces have now become standard for all personal computers.

But sales of the Mac were never as good as Apple expected. And even though Apple's computers were clearly technologically superior to the alternatives well into the 1990s (devotees say they still are), they have remained a small part of the market.

What happened? At the time the Mac was introduced, most computer users had PCs that ran on DOS, an operating system created by Microsoft. Apple knew that its product was better and so charged a premium price. This kept Apple's customer base relatively small. Apple failed to recognize the strength of the network externality that caused many users to stick with an inferior product that was widely used, especially given the fact that the superior alternative was considerably more expensive.

Over time, Microsoft developed its own version of a graphical user interface, Windows. Windows, especially in its early versions, was still technologically inferior to Apple's system: it took a long time to boot, and it was notoriously vulnerable to crashes. (The joke went around that if Microsoft made cars, they would take five minutes to start and would occasionally stop suddenly for no apparent reason.) But again, the network externalities already achieved by DOS induced many people to stay with the technologically inferior Microsoft system.

In retrospect, it seems likely that if Apple had understood the force of network externalities and priced the Macintosh lower, it would have come to dominate the industry. ∎

< < < < < < < < < < < < < < < < <

>>CHECK YOUR UNDERSTANDING 22-2

1. For each of the following goods explain the nature of the network externality present.
   a. Appliances using a particular voltage, such as 110 volt versus 220 volt
   b. 8½-by-11-inch paper versus 8-by-12½-inch paper

2. Suppose there are two competing companies in an industry that has critical mass effects. Explain why the market is likely to tip to the company that can sustain the largest initial losses.

Solutions appear at back of book.

Policy Toward Information Goods

Does the growing importance of information goods require new kinds of economic policy? Most economists would answer with a qualified no. The principles of economics remain the same as ever, and the issues raised by information goods are not new. Still, the emphasis shifts: issues that may have seemed unimportant in the past become very important in this new world.

Let's look at two types of policy concerns raised by the growing importance of information goods: antitrust policy and standards.

Antitrust Policy

We saw in Chapters 14 and 15 that market power creates problems for economic efficiency. As a result, the government attempts both to limit the growth of monopolies and to keep oligopolies from behaving like monopolies. But how should antitrust policy be conducted in information goods industries?

As we saw earlier in this chapter, monopoly is a natural outcome in industries with high fixed costs but low marginal costs, which is the case for information goods. Furthermore, it is the hope of achieving a monopoly that leads potential producers to incur those high fixed costs in the first place.

However the antitrust laws do not, strictly speaking, forbid monopoly. Rather, they only prohibit "monopolization"—efforts to create a monopoly. If you just happen to end up ruling an industry, that's okay, but if you take actions designed to drive out competition, that's not okay. So we could argue that monopolies in information goods, because they occur naturally, should not pose legal problems.

Unfortunately, it isn't that simple. Firms investing in new technologies are clearly trying to establish monopoly positions. Furthermore, in the face of positive feedback, firms have an incentive to engage in aggressive strategies to push their goods to critical mass, or to tip the market in their direction. So what is the dividing line between legal and illegal actions?

At this point the rules are somewhat in flux. In the Microsoft antitrust case, described in the Economics in Action on pages 534–535, reasonable economists and legal experts disagreed sharply both about whether the company had broken the law by pursuing a monopoly position, and whether the company should be broken up to diminish its ability to tip new markets in its favor.

Setting Standards

The United States, though at the technological cutting edge in most respects, lags noticeably behind other advanced countries in one area: cell phones. As one Boston-based computer expert put it in 2003, "After two days of touring Wales, a country that apparently has yet to discover the mixing faucet [a single faucet combining hot and cold water], it has become apparent that there is better mobile phone coverage in the remotest sheep pasture or coastal outcrop than in downtown Boston." Why?

The answer has to do with the European decision, at the end of the 1980s, to adopt a common **standard** for digital cellular phones—a set of rules for operation that induced competing cell phone companies to form a common network—so that every cellular phone would work everywhere on the continent. A GSM (General Standard for Mobiles) phone works equally well anywhere in Europe; because of the common standard, supporting antennas are plentiful and there is good coverage almost everywhere. In the United States, by contrast, there is no common standard among competing cell phone companies: some use the GSM, but others use alternative standards. Even if there is a transmission tower near you, it may not carry a signal your phone can use. (At the time of writing, the authors had a GSM cell phone that worked fine even in remote European locations but received no signal in or near their New Jersey home.)

> A **standard** is a set of rules for operation that induces competing goods to operate as a single network.

Standards are by no means a new issue. In the nineteenth century the most important choice of standard was the gauge of railroads—how far apart the rails of a track were. The problems created when two railroads with different gauges met were obvious, yet in 1860 there were no fewer than seven different railroad gauges in use in the United States. (The two main versions were the 4-foot-8½-inch gauge used in most of the North and the 5-foot gauge used in most of the South.) The South finally switched to the "standard" 4-foot-8½-inch gauge in a coordinated move, taking place over two days in 1886.

Both the old railroad example and the modern cell phone example suggest that the need for common standards creates a justification for government intervention in the economy. Left to itself, the market may fail to converge on a common standard. And as in the case of early U.S. railroads or contemporary U.S. cell phones, an industry may suffer from avoidable inefficiency because of failure to converge. So the government can play a useful role by prodding the private sector into that convergence, as it did in the case of European cell phones.

An important point about standards is that getting *some* standard is often more important than *which* standard is chosen. For example, American railroads would have done equally well with a 5-foot gauge, as long as they had all coordinated on it. And it isn't always necessary for the government to enforce a standard. Sometimes industries do it voluntarily. A number of companies agreed on the standard for digital video discs (DVDs), which are rapidly replacing video cassettes. In other cases a standard simply evolves as firms try to match each other.

But do unplanned standards—standards that arise as a natural market outcome—get it right? In some cases, different standards will lead to different results: one standard may lead to lower costs or superior quality than another, and there is no guarantee that the market will choose the better standard. So could an industry get "stuck" with one standard when some other standard is clearly better?

Economists have long debated this issue, which has come to be known as the **QWERTY problem**. The name comes from the top row on a standard keyboard, which reads QWERTYUIOP. Why are keyboards laid out that way? Basically because they started out with that layout, which was chosen partly because it helped prevent keys on a mechanical typewriter from jamming—not a concern on a computer—and partly because it allowed salesmen to quickly pick out the letters "TYPEWRITER," which are all in the top row of the QWERTY keyboard. So that is what typists learn, and that is what typewriter manufacturers, and more recently computer keyboard manufacturers, provide—it's a self-reinforcing loop.

The question is whether QWERTY is the best keyboard layout. Might there be a better layout, one that would allow faster typing, that nobody uses because network externalities have locked us into the standard layout?

The evidence on keyboards is mixed. Other layouts seem to be somewhat better. But a computer can be easily reprogrammed to use a different keyboard layout, so if the gains from a switch were really large we would expect a widespread move away from the QWERTY layout; this hasn't happened. Nonetheless, in principle government intervention might be useful in moving an industry to a superior standard.

An industry that gets stuck using an inferior standard suffers from the **QWERTY problem**.

---

economics in action

The Microsoft Case

In 2000 the Justice Department took on Microsoft in one of the most watched antitrust cases in history. By that time, Microsoft had become the world's most valuable corporation, and its founder, Bill Gates, was the world's richest man. What the government sought was nothing less than the breakup of the company.

The case involved almost all of the issues raised by information goods. Microsoft was, by any reasonable definition, a monopoly: leaving aside the niches of Apple customers and Linux users, just about all personal computers ran the Windows operating system. The key fact sustaining the Windows system was the force of a network externality: people used Windows because other people used Windows.

The government did not, however, challenge the Windows monopoly itself (although some economists urged it to). Basically, everyone agreed that monopoly per se is a natural thing in such industries and should not be prevented. What the government claimed, however, was that Microsoft had used its monopoly position in operating systems to give its products an advantage over competitors in other markets. For example, by including Internet Explorer as part of the Windows system, it was alleged, Microsoft was giving itself an unfair advantage over its rival Netscape in the browser software market.

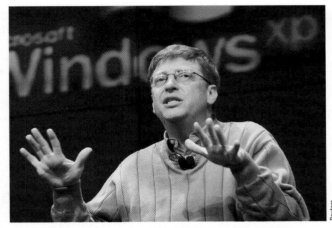

The Microsoft case involved almost all of the issues raised by information goods.

Why was this considered harmful? The government argued both that monopolies were being created unnecessarily and that Microsoft was discouraging innovation. Potential innovators in software, the government claimed, were unwilling to invest large sums out of fear that Microsoft would use its control of the operating system to take away any market they might win by producing a competing product that would then be sold as a bundle with the operating system. For its part, Microsoft argued that by setting the precedent that companies would be punished for success, the government was the real opponent of innovation.

At first the case went against Microsoft, when a judge ordered the company split in two—into an operating-system company and a company selling the firm's other products. But this judgment was overturned on appeal. In November 2001, the government reached a settlement with Microsoft in which the company agreed to provide other companies with the technology to develop products that interacted seamlessly with Microsoft's software, thus removing the company's special advantage acquired through bundling its products.

Competitors complained bitterly that this settlement had far too many loopholes, and that Microsoft's ability to exploit its monopoly position would remain. And by early 2004, the government agreed: antitrust lawyers from the Justice Department reported to the judge who negotiated the original settlement that they were increasingly uneasy about the plan's ability to spur competition. A particular concern was a rumored Microsoft move to take over the market in publishing software, in which Adobe Acrobat was the current leader. ■

>>QUICK REVIEW

➤ Information goods pose difficult problems for antitrust policy.
➤ Information goods also create a possible role for the government in setting *standards*. Left to themselves, industries may fail to arrive at a common standard or suffer from the *QWERTY problem*, getting stuck with an inferior standard.

>>CHECK YOUR UNDERSTANDING 22-3

1. As described in the For Inquiring Minds on page 531, America Online (AOL), the biggest Internet service provider in the United States, was at one time the subject of antitrust scrutiny of its instant messaging service. In the original form of the program, when an AOL customer sent a message to another AOL customer, the message instantly popped up on the receiver's screen. But AOL did not allow non-AOL senders to access the service when they sent messages to an AOL customer. Was this an antitrust violation on AOL's part? Give arguments pro and con.

Solution appears at back of book.

SUMMARY

1. **Information goods**—goods whose value derives mainly from the information they embody—are increasingly important in the economy.

2. Information goods typically have high fixed costs but low or zero marginal costs. This means that once an information good has been created, efficiency requires that it be free or almost free to consumers. But innovators must have some way to earn back their fixed costs if the good is to be produced at all.

3. To enhance efficiency, governments have created **patents** and **copyrights,** which give innovators a temporary monopoly. But these temporary monopolies often arise naturally due to first-mover advantages from innovation.

4. Many information goods are also characterized by **network externalities:** the value of the good to an individual is greater when a large number of people also use the good. Network externalities cause **positive feedback,** in which either initial success or initial failure is self-reinforcing.

5. Because consumers may have a **threshold network size** at which they are willing to purchase a good, information goods may have a **critical mass,** a market size at which growth explodes. Or they may experience **tipping,** in which a small advantage to one of two competing goods leads it to become dominant. These features often lead firms to price their goods or technologies very low in the hope of greatly increasing sales.

6. Information goods pose difficulties for antitrust policy because firms investing in new technologies may engage in aggressive tactics to establish monopolies, tactics that may or may not be legal.

7. To facilitate network externalities, industries must coordinate on **standards** that let competing goods work together. Government can play a useful role both in helping an industry establish a standard and in helping it avoid getting trapped in an inferior standard, known as the **QWERTY problem.**

KEY TERMS

Information goods, p. 520
Patents, p. 524
Copyrights, p. 524
Network externalities, p. 526

Positive feedback, p. 527
Threshold network size, p. 528
Critical mass, p. 529

Tipping, p. 530
Standard, p. 533
QWERTY problem, p. 534

PROBLEMS

1. Information goods are characterized by high fixed cost and very low or zero marginal cost. Suppose the government grants the producer of an information good a patent so that the producer is the only seller of that good.

   a. If the government forces the producer to charge a price equal to marginal cost, would the firm's profit be greater than, equal to, or less than zero?

   b. If the government forces the producer to charge a price equal to average total cost, would the firm's profit be greater than, equal to, or less than zero?

2. Werck, a pharmaceutical company, is developing a new AIDS drug. The demand schedule for the drug, once it has been developed, is shown in Table 2a. If Werck can act as a monopolist, its marginal revenue from selling the drug will be as given in Table 2b.

Table 2a

Price of dose	Quantity of doses demanded (thousands)
$100	0
90	20
80	40
70	60
60	80
50	100
40	120
30	140
20	160
10	180
0	200

Table 2b

Quantity of doses (thousands)	Marginal revenue (per dose)
0	
	$90
20	
	70
40	
	50
60	
	30
80	
	10
100	
	−10
120	

Werck's fixed cost in developing the drug is $4 million. The marginal cost of producing the drug is zero.

a. If Werck develops the drug and can act as a monopolist, which quantity of output will it choose to produce? What will its profit be? Does Werck therefore have an incentive to engage in the costly development of the drug?

b. Suppose now that the government announces that in order to make AIDS drugs more widely available, it will force the producer to sell the drug at marginal cost. If Werck develops the drug, what will the price be and how much of the drug will be sold? What will its profit be? Does Werck have an incentive to engage in the costly development of the drug?

3. British Biotech is developing a new cancer drug. The demand schedule for the drug, once the drug has been developed, is shown in Table 3a. If British Biotech can act as a monopolist, its marginal revenue from selling the drug will be as shown in Table 3b.

British Biotech's fixed cost of developing the drug is $750 million. Its marginal cost is zero.

a. If British Biotech is granted a monopoly for one year, what will its revenue be that year?

b. If British Biotech does not have a monopoly, other drug makers will copy its product without incurring any development cost and the price will fall to marginal cost. What will British Biotech's yearly revenue be in that case?

c. If the government sets the length of British Biotech's patent at four years so that British Biotech is a monopolist for four years and then other firms can imitate the product (and therefore after four years the price falls to marginal cost), what will British Biotech's revenue be over those four years? Is this enough to cover British Biotech's fixed cost of developing the drug? (Ignore the issue of discounting over time.)

d. How long would the patent have to be for British Biotech to cover its fixed cost and so want to invest in development of the drug?

4. Explain the following situations.

a. In Europe, many cell phone service providers give away for free what would otherwise be very expensive cell phones when a service contract is purchased. Why might a company want to do that?

b. In the United Kingdom, the country's antitrust authority banned one cell phone service provider (Vodaphone) from offering a plan that gave customers free calls to other customers of Vodaphone. Why might Vodaphone have wanted to offer these calls for free? Why might a government want to step in and ban this practice? Why might it not be a good idea for the government to interfere in this way?

Table 3a	
Price of dose	Quantity of doses demanded (millions)
$50	0
45	1
40	2
35	3
30	4
25	5
20	6
15	7
10	8
5	9
0	10

Table 3b

Quantity of doses (millions)	Marginal revenue (per dose)
0	
	$45
1	
	35
2	
	25
3	
	15
4	
	5
5	
	−5
6	

>web... To continue your study and review of concepts in this chapter, please visit the Krugman/Wells website for quizzes, animated graph tutorials, web links to helpful resources, and more.

www.worthpublishers.com/krugmanwells

>> Solutions to "Check Your Understanding" Questions

This section offers suggested answers to the "Check Your Understanding" questions found within chapters.

Chapter One

1-1

1. a. This illustrates the concept of opportunity cost. Given that a person can only eat so much at one sitting, having an additional slice of chocolate cake requires that you forgo eating something else, such as a slice of the coconut cream pie.

b. This illustrates the concept that resources are scarce. Even if there were more resources in the world, the total amount of those resources would be limited. As a result, scarcity would still arise. For there to be no scarcity, there would have to be unlimited amounts of everything (including unlimited time in a human life), which is clearly impossible.

c. This illustrates the concept that people usually exploit opportunities to make themselves better off. Students will seek to make themselves better off by signing up for the tutorials of teaching assistants with good reputations and avoiding those teaching assistants with poor reputations. It also illustrates the concept that resources are scarce. If there were unlimited spaces in tutorials with good teaching assistants, they would not fill up.

d. This illustrates the concept of marginal analysis. Your decision about allocating your time is a "how much" decision: how much time spent exercising versus how much time spent studying. You make your decision by comparing the benefit of an additional hour of exercising to its cost, the effect on your grades of one less hour spent studying.

2. a. Yes. The increased time spent commuting is a cost you will incur if you accept the new job. That additional time spent commuting—or equivalently, the benefit you would get from spending that time doing something else—is an opportunity cost of the new job.

b. Yes. One of the benefits of the new job is that you will be making $50,000. But if you take the new job, you will have to give up your current job; that is, you have to give up your current salary of $45,000. So $45,000 is one of the opportunity costs of taking the new job.

c. No. A more spacious office is an additional benefit of your new job and does not involve forgoing something else. So, it is not an opportunity cost.

1-2

1. a. This illustrates the concept that markets usually lead to efficiency. Any seller who wants to sell a book for at least $X does indeed sell to someone who is willing to buy a book for $X. As a result, there is no way to change how used textbooks are distributed among buyers and sellers in a way that would make one person better off without making someone else worse off.

b. This illustrates the concept that there are gains from trade. Students trade tutoring services based on their different abilities in academic subjects.

c. This illustrates the concept that when markets don't achieve efficiency, government intervention can improve society's welfare. In this case the market, left alone, will permit bars and nightclubs to impose costs on their neighbors in the form of loud music, costs that the bars and nightclubs have no incentive to take into account. This is an inefficient outcome because society as a whole can be made better off if bars and nightclubs are induced to reduce their noise.

d. This illustrates the concept that resources should be used as efficiently as possible to achieve society's goals. By closing neighborhood clinics and shifting funds to the main hospital, better health care can be provided at a lower cost.

e. This illustrates the concept that markets move toward equilibrium. Here, because books with the same amount of wear and tear sell for about the same price, no buyer or seller can be made better off by engaging in a different trade than he or she undertook. This means that the market for used textbooks has moved to an equilibrium.

2. a. This does not describe an equilibrium situation. Many students should want to change their behavior and switch to eating at the restaurants. Therefore, the situation described is not an equilibrium. An equilibrium will be established when students are equally as well off eating at the restaurants as eating at the dining hall—which would happen if, say, prices at the restaurants were higher than at the dining hall.

b. This does describe an equilibrium situation. By changing your behavior and riding the bus, you would not be made better off. Therefore, you have no incentive to change your behavior.

Chapter Two

Check Your Understanding
2-1

1. a. False. An increase in the resources available to Tom for use in producing coconuts and fish changes his production possibility frontier by shifting it outward. This is because he can now produce more fish and coconuts than before. In the accompanying figure, the line labeled Tom's original *PPF* represents Tom's original production possibility frontier, and the line labeled Tom's new *PPF* represents the new production possibility frontier that results from an increase in resources available to Tom.

b. True. A technological change that allows Tom to catch more fish for any amount of coconuts gathered results in a change in his production possibility frontier. This is illustrated in the accompanying figure: the new production possibility frontier is represented by the line labeled Tom's new *PPF,* and the original production frontier is represented by the line labeled Tom's original *PPF.* Since the maximum quantity of coconuts that Tom can gather is the same as before, the new production possibility frontier intersects the vertical axis at the same point as the old frontier. But since the maximum possible quantity of fish is now greater than before, the new frontier intersects the horizontal axis to the right of the old frontier.

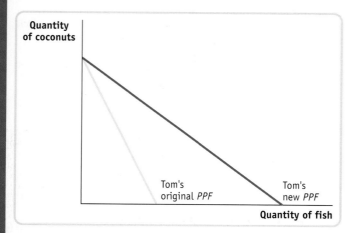

c. False. The production possibility frontier illustrates how much of one good an economy must give up to get more of another good only when resources are used efficiently. If an economy is producing inefficiently—that is, inside the frontier—then it does not have to give up a unit of one good in order to get another unit of the other good. Instead, by becoming more efficient, this economy can have more of both goods.

2. a. The United States has an absolute advantage in automobile production because it takes fewer Americans (6) to produce a car in one day than Italians (8). The United States also has an absolute advantage in washing machine production because it takes fewer Americans (2) to produce a washing machine in one day than Italians (3).

b. In Italy the opportunity cost of a washing machine in terms of an automobile is $\frac{3}{8}$: $\frac{3}{8}$ of a car can be produced with the same number of workers and in the same time it takes to produce 1 washing machine. In the United States the opportunity cost of a washing machine in terms of an automobile is $\frac{2}{6} = \frac{1}{3}$: $\frac{1}{3}$ of a car can be produced with the same number of workers and in the same time it takes to produce 1 washing machine. Since $\frac{1}{3} < \frac{3}{8}$, the United States has a comparative advantage in the production of washing machines: to produce a washing machine, only $\frac{1}{3}$ of a car must be given up in the United States but $\frac{3}{8}$ of a car must be given up in Italy. This means that Italy has a comparative advantage in automobiles. This can be checked as follows. The opportunity cost of an automobile in terms of a washing machine in Italy is $\frac{8}{3}$, equal to $2\frac{2}{3}$: $2\frac{2}{3}$ washing machines can be produced in the time it takes to produce 1 car in Italy. And the opportunity cost of an automobile in terms of a washing machine in the United States is $\frac{6}{2}$, equal to 3: 3 washing machines can be produced in the time it takes to produce 1 car in the United States.

c. The greatest gains are realized when each country specializes in producing the good for which it has a comparative advantage. Therefore the United States should specialize in washing machines and Italy should specialize in automobiles.

3. An increase in the amount of money spent by households results in an increase in the flow of goods to households. This, in turn, generates an increase in demand for factors of production by firms. Therefore there is an increase in the number of jobs in the economy.

Check Your Understanding
2-2

1. a. This is a normative statement because it stipulates what should be done. In addition, it may have no "right" answer. That is, should people be prevented from all dangerous personal behavior if they enjoy that behavior—like skydiving? Your answer will depend on your point of view.

b. This is a positive statement because it is a description of fact.

2. a. True. Economists often have different value judgments about the desirability of a particular social goal. But despite those differences in value judgments, they will tend to agree that society, once it has decided to pursue a given social goal, should adopt the most efficient policy to achieve that goal. Therefore economists are likely to agree on adopting policy choice B.

b. False. Disagreements between economists are more likely to arise because they base their conclusions on different models or because they have different value judgments about the desirability of the policy.

c. False. Deciding which goals a society should try to achieve is a matter of value judgments, not a question of economic analysis.

Chapter Three

Check Your Understanding 3-1

1. a. The quantity of umbrellas demanded is higher at any given price on a rainy day than on a dry day. This is a rightward *shift of* the demand curve, since at any given price the quantity demanded rises. This implies that any specific quantity can now be sold at a higher price.

b. The quantity of weekend calls demanded rises in response to a price reduction. This is a *movement along* the demand curve for weekend calls.

c. The demand for roses increases the week of Valentine's Day. This is a rightward *shift of* the demand curve.

d. The quantity of gasoline demanded falls in response to a rise in price. This is a *movement along* the demand curve.

Check Your Understanding 3-2

1. a. The quantity of houses supplied rises as a result of an increase in prices. This is a *movement along* the supply curve.

b. The quantity of strawberries supplied is higher at any given price. This is a rightward *shift of* the supply curve.

c. The quantity of labor supplied is lower at any given wage. This is a leftward *shift of* the supply curve compared to the supply curve during the school vacation. So, in order to attract workers, fast-food chains have to offer higher wages.

d. The quantity of labor supplied rises in response to a rise in wages. This is a *movement along* the supply curve.

e. The quantity of cabins supplied is higher at any given price. This is a rightward *shift of* the supply curve.

Check Your Understanding 3-3

1. a. The supply curve shifts rightward. At the original equilibrium price of the year before, the quantity of grapes supplied exceeds the quantity demanded. This is a case of surplus. The price of grapes will fall.

b. The demand curve shifts leftward. At the original equilibrium price, the quantity of hotel rooms supplied exceeds the quantity demanded. This is a case of surplus. The rates for hotel rooms will fall.

c. The demand curve for secondhand snowblowers shifts rightward. At the original equilibrium price, the quantity of secondhand snowblowers demanded exceeds the quantity supplied. This is a case of shortage. The equilibrium price of secondhand snowblowers will rise.

Check Your Understanding 3-4

1. a. The market for large cars: this is a rightward shift in demand caused by a decrease in the price of a complement, gasoline. As a result of the shift, the equilibrium price of large cars will rise and the equilibrium quantity of large cars bought and sold will also rise.

b. The market for fresh paper made from recycled stock: this is a rightward shift in supply due to a technological innovation. As a result of this shift, the equilibrium price of fresh paper made from recycled stock will fall and the equilibrium quantity bought and sold will rise.

c. The market for movies at a local movie theater: this is a leftward shift in demand caused by a fall in the price of a substitute, pay-per-view movies. As a result of this shift, the equilibrium price of movie tickets will fall and the equilibrium number of people who go to the movies will also fall.

2. Upon the announcement of the new chip, the demand curve for computers using the earlier chip shifts leftward, as demand decreases, and the supply curve for these computers shifts rightward, as supply increases.

a. If demand decreases relatively more than supply increases, then the equilibrium quantity falls, as shown here:

b. If supply increases relatively more than demand decreases, then the equilibrium quantity rises, as shown here:

In both cases, the equilibrium price falls.

Chapter Four

Check Your Understanding
4-1

1. a. Fewer homeowners are willing to rent out their driveways because the price ceiling has caused a decrease in the payment they receive. This reflects the concept that the quantity supplied decreases as the price decreases. It is shown in the following diagram by the movement from point E to point A along the supply curve, a reduction in quantity of 400 parking spaces.

b. The quantity demanded increases by 400 spaces as the price decreases. At a lower price, more fans are willing to drive and rent a parking space. It is shown in the diagram by the movement from point E to point B along the demand curve.

c. Under a price ceiling, the quantity demanded exceeds the quantity supplied; as a result, shortages arise. In this case, there will be a shortage of 800 parking spaces. It is shown by the horizontal distance between points A and B.

d. Price ceilings result in wasted resources. The additional time fans spend to guarantee a parking space is wasted time.

e. Price ceilings lead to inefficient allocation of a good—here, the parking spaces—to consumers.

f. Price ceilings lead to black markets.

2. a. False. By lowering the price that producers receive, price ceilings lead to a decrease in the quantity supplied.

b. True. Price ceilings lead to a lower quantity supplied than in a free market. As a result, some people who would have been willing to pay the market price, and therefore would have gotten the good in a free market, are unable to obtain it when a price ceiling is imposed.

c. True. Those producers who still sell the product now receive less for it and are therefore worse off. Other producers will no longer find it worthwhile to sell the product at all and therefore will also be made worse off.

Check Your Understanding
4-2

1. a. Some gas station owners will benefit from getting a higher price. Point A indicates the sales (0.7 million gallons) made by these owners. But some will lose; there are those who made sales at the market price of $2 but do not make sales at the regulated price of $4. These missed sales are indicated on the graph by the fall in the quantity demanded along the demand curve, from point E to point A. Overall, the effect on station owners is ambiguous.

b. Those who buy gas at the higher price of $4 probably will receive better service; this is an example of *inefficiently high quality* caused by a price floor as gas station owners compete on quality rather than price. But opponents are correct to claim that consumers are generally worse off—those who buy at $4 would have been happy to buy at $2, and many who were willing to buy at a price between $2 and $4 are now unwilling to buy. This is indicated on the graph by the fall in the quantity demanded along the demand curve, from point E to point A.

c. Proponents are wrong because consumers and some gas station owners are hurt by the price floor, which creates "missed opportunities"—desirable transactions between consumers and station owners that never take place. Moreover, the inefficiency of wasted resources arises as consumers spend time and money driving to other states. The price floor tempts people to engage in black market activity. With the price floor of $4, only 0.7 million gallons are sold. But at prices between $2 and $4, there are drivers who cumulatively want to buy more than 0.7 million gallons and owners who are willing to sell to them, a situation likely to lead to illegal activity.

Check Your Understanding
4-3

1. a. The price of a ride is $7 since the quantity demanded at this price is 6 million: $7 is the *demand price* of 6 million rides. This is represented by point A in the following figure.

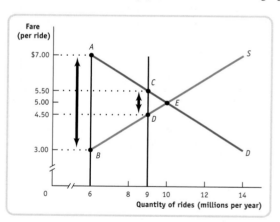

b. At 6 million rides, the supply price is $3, represented by point B in the figure. The wedge between the demand price of $7 and the supply price of $3 is the quota rent per ride, $4. This is represented in the figure above by the vertical distance between points A and B.

c. At 9 million rides, the demand price is $5.50, indicated by point C on the figure, and the supply price is $4.50, indicated by point D. The quota rent is the difference between the demand price and the supply price: $1.

2. The figure shows how a decrease in demand by 4 million rides, represented by a leftward shift of the demand curve from D_1 to D_2: at any given price, the quantity demanded falls by 4 million rides. This eliminates the effect of a quota limit of 8 million rides. At point E_2, the new market equilibrium, the equilibrium quantity is equal to the quota limit; as a result, the quota has no effect on the market.

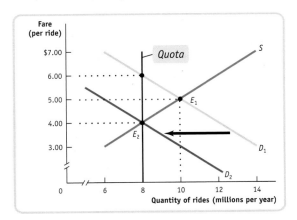

1. a. Under the quota, only 9 million pounds of butter are bought and sold. We can limit the amount of butter that dairies want to sell to 9 million pounds by setting the supply price to $0.90, as indicated by point D in the following figure, which is a replication of Figure 4-3. Similarly, we can limit the amount of butter consumers want to buy to 9 million pounds by setting the demand price to $1.20, as indicated by point C. The difference between these two prices, $0.30, is therefore equal to the tax that reduces sales to only 9 million pounds, indicated by the vertical distance between points C and D. Thus a tax of $0.30 per pound generates the same inefficiency as a quota of 9 million pounds.

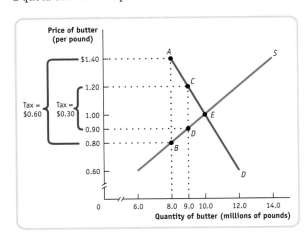

b. To answer this question, we must find a supply price and a demand price that generate the same quantity of butter but differ by $0.60. Examination of the supply and demand schedules shows that the supply price of $0.80 (indicated by point B) and the demand price of $1.40 (indicated by point A) satisfy these conditions: They give rise to the same quantity transacted, 8 million pounds, and they differ by $0.60. Therefore, a quota of 8 million pounds will generate the same level of inefficiency as a tax of $0.60. (Note that a supply price of $1.20 and a demand price of $0.60 also differ by $0.60 and give rise to the same quantity, 12 million pounds. Why is this choice not the right answer here? Because 12 million pounds is more than people want to buy in the free market, so it can't be a valid quota level.)

c. In part a, the unrestricted equilibrium price is $1 per pound. So consumers pay $0.20 ($1.20 − $1.00) of the $0.30 tax and producers pay $0.10 ($1.00 − $0.90).

Chapter Five

1. By the midpoint method, the percent change in the price of strawberries is

$$\frac{\$1.50 - \$1.00}{(\$1.50 + \$1.00)/2} \times 100 = \frac{\$0.50}{\$1.25} \times 100 = 40\%$$

Similarly, the percent change in the quantity of strawberries demanded is

$$\frac{200,000 - 100,000}{(100,000 + 200,000)/2} \times 100 = \frac{100,000}{150,000} \times 100 = 67\%$$

Therefore the price elasticity of demand using the midpoint method is 67%/40% = 1.7.

2. By the midpoint method, the percent change in the quantity of movie tickets demanded in going from 4,000 tickets to 5,000 tickets is

$$\frac{5,000 - 4,000}{(4,000 + 5,000)/2} \times 100 = \frac{1,000}{4,500} \times 100 = 22\%$$

Since the price elasticity of demand is 1 at the current consumption level, it will take a 22% drop in the price of movie tickets to generate a 22% increase in quantity demanded.

3. Since price rises, we know that quantity demanded must fall. Given the current price of $0.50, a $0.05 increase in price represents a 10% change, using the method in Equation 5-2. This implies that

$$\frac{\% \text{ change in quantity demanded}}{10\%} = 1.2$$

so that the percent change in quantity demanded is 12%. A 12% decrease in quantity demanded represents 100,000 × 0.12, or 12,000 sandwiches.

Check Your Understanding Question 5-2

1. **a.** Elastic demand. Consumers are highly responsive to changes in price. For a rise in price, the quantity effect (which tends to reduce total revenue) outweighs the price effect (which tends to increase total revenue). Overall, this leads to a fall in total revenue.
   b. Unit-elastic demand. Here the revenue lost to the fall in price is exactly equal to the revenue gained from higher sales. The quantity effect exactly offsets the price effect.
   c. Inelastic demand. Consumers are relatively unresponsive to changes in price. For consumers to purchase a given percent increase in output, the price must fall by an even greater percent. The price effect of a fall in price (which tends to reduce total revenue) outweighs the quantity effect (which tends to increase total revenue). As a result, total revenue decreases.
   d. Inelastic demand. Consumers are relatively unresponsive to price, so a given percent fall in output is accompanied by an even greater percent rise in price. The price effect of a rise in price (which tends to increase total revenue) outweighs the quantity effect (which tends to reduce total revenue). As a result, total revenue increases.

2. **a.** Once bitten by a venomous snake, the victim's demand for an antidote is very likely to be perfectly inelastic because there is no substitute and it is necessary for survival. The demand curve will be vertical, at a quantity equal to the needed dose.
   b. Students' demand for green erasers is likely to be perfectly elastic because there are easily available substitutes: non-green erasers. The demand curve will be horizontal, at a price equal to that of nongreen erasers.

Check Your Understanding Question 5-3

1. By the midpoint method, the percent increase in Chelsea's income is

$$\frac{\$18{,}000 - \$12{,}000}{(\$12{,}000 + \$18{,}000)/2} \times 100 = \frac{\$6{,}000}{\$15{,}000} \times 100 = 40\%$$

Similarly, the percent increase in her consumption of CDs is

$$\frac{40 - 10}{(10 + 40)/2} \times 100 = \frac{30}{25} \times 100 = 120\%$$

Chelsea's income elasticity of demand for CDs is therefore 120%/40% = 3.

2. Sanjay's consumption of expensive restaurant meals will fall more than 10% because a given percent change in income (10% here) induces a larger percent change in consumption of an income-elastic good.

3. The cross-price elasticity of demand is 5%/20% = 0.25. Since the cross-price elasticity of demand is positive, the two goods are substitutes.

Check Your Understanding Question 5-4

1. By the midpoint method, the percent change in the number of hours of web-design services contracted is

$$\frac{500{,}000 - 300{,}000}{(300{,}000 + 500{,}000)/2} \times 100 = \frac{200{,}000}{400{,}000} \times 100 = 50\%$$

Similarly, the percent change in the price of web-design services is:

$$\frac{\$150 - \$100}{(\$100 + \$150)/2} \times 100 = \frac{\$50}{\$125} \times 100 = 40\%$$

The price elasticity of supply is 50%/40% = 1.25; hence supply is elastic.

2. True. An increase in demand raises price. If the price elasticity of supply of milk is low, then relatively little additional supply will be forthcoming as the price rises. As a result, the price of milk will rise substantially to satisfy the increased demand for milk. If the price elasticity of supply is high, then a relatively large amount of additional supply will be produced as the price rises. As a result, the price of milk will rise only by a little to satisfy the higher demand for milk.

3. False. It is true that long-run price elasticities of supply are generally larger than short-run elasticities of supply. But this means that the short-run supply curves are generally steeper, not flatter, than the long-run supply curves.

4. True. When supply is perfectly elastic, the supply curve is a horizontal line. A change in demand therefore has no effect on price; it affects only the quantity bought and sold.

Check Your Understanding Question 5-5

1. The fact that demand is very inelastic means that consumers will reduce their demand for textbooks very little in response to an increase in the price caused by the tax. The fact that supply is somewhat elastic means that suppliers will respond to the fall in the price by reducing supply. As a result, the incidence of the tax will fall heavily on consumers of economics textbooks and very little on publishers as shown in the accompanying figure.

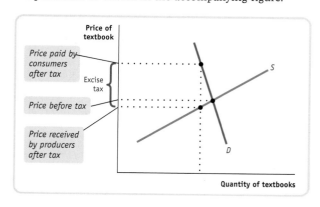

2. True. When a substitute is readily available, demand is elastic. This implies that producers cannot easily pass on the cost of the tax to consumers because consumers will respond to an increased price by switching to the substitute. Furthermore, when producers have difficulty adjusting the amount of the good produced, supply is inelastic. That is, producers cannot easily reduce output in response to a lower price net of the tax. So the tax burden will fall more heavily on producers than consumers.

3. The fact that supply is very inelastic means that producers will reduce their supply of bottled water very little in response to the fall in price caused by the tax. Demand, on the other hand, will fall in response to an increase in price because demand is somewhat elastic. As a result, the incidence of the tax will fall heavily on producers of bottled spring water and very little on consumers as shown in the accompanying figure.

4. True. The lower the elasticity of supply, the more the burden of a tax will fall on producers rather than consumers, other things equal.

Chapter Six

1. A consumer buys each pepper if the price is less than (or just equal to) the consumer's willingness to pay for that pepper. The demand schedule is constructed by asking how many peppers will be demanded at any price. The accompanying table illustrates the demand schedule.

Price of pepper	Quantity of peppers demanded	Quantity of peppers demanded by Casey	Quantity of peppers demanded by Josie
$0.90	1	1	0
0.80	2	1	1
0.70	3	2	1
0.60	4	2	2
0.50	5	3	2
0.40	6	3	3
0.30	8	4	4
0.20	8	4	4
0.10	8	4	4
0.00	8	4	4

When the price is $0.40, Casey's consumer surplus from the first pepper is $0.50, from his second pepper $0.30, from his third pepper $0.10, and he does not buy any more peppers. Casey's individual consumer surplus is therefore $0.90. Josie's consumer surplus from her first pepper is $0.40, from her second pepper $0.20, from her third pepper $0.00 (she is just indifferent between buying it and not buying it, so let's assume she does buy it), and she does not buy any more peppers. Josie's individual consumer surplus is therefore $0.60. Total consumer surplus at a price of $0.40 is therefore $0.90 + $0.60 = $1.50.

1. A producer supplies each pepper if the price is greater than (or just equal to) the producer's cost of producing that pepper. The supply schedule is constructed by asking how many peppers will be supplied at any price. The accompanying table illustrates the supply schedule.

Price of pepper	Quantity of peppers supplied	Quantity of peppers supplied by Cara	Quantity of peppers supplied by Jamie
$0.90	8	4	4
0.80	7	4	3
0.70	7	4	3
0.60	6	4	2
0.50	5	3	2
0.40	4	3	1
0.30	3	2	1
0.20	2	2	0
0.10	2	2	0
0.00	0	0	0

When the price is $0.70, Cara's producer surplus from the first pepper is $0.60, from her second pepper $0.60, from her third pepper $0.30, from her fourth pepper $0.10, and she does not supply any more peppers. Cara's individual producer surplus is therefore $1.60. Jamie's producer surplus from his first pepper is $0.40, from his second pepper $0.20, from his third pepper $0.00 (he is just indifferent between supplying it and not supplying it, so let's assume he does supply it), and he does not supply any more peppers. Jamie's individual producer surplus is therefore $0.60. Total producer surplus at a price of $0.70 is therefore $1.60 + $0.60 = $2.20.

1. The quantity demanded equals the quantity supplied at a price of $0.50, the equilibrium price. At that price, a total quantity of five peppers will be bought and sold. Casey will buy three peppers and receive consumer surplus of $0.40 on his first, $0.20 on his second, and $0.00 on his third pepper. Josie will buy two peppers and receive consumer surplus of $0.30 on her first and $0.10 on her second pepper. Total consumer surplus is therefore $1.00. Cara will supply three peppers and receive producer surplus of $0.40 on her first, $0.40 on her second, and

$0.10 on her third pepper. Jamie will supply two peppers and receive producer surplus of $0.20 on his first and $0.00 on his second pepper. Total producer surplus is therefore $1.10. Total surplus in this market is therefore $1.00 + $1.10 = $2.10.

2. a. If Josie consumes one less pepper, she loses $0.60 (her willingness to pay for her second pepper); if Casey consumes one more pepper, he gains $0.30 (his willingness to pay for his fourth pepper). This results in an overall loss of consumer surplus of $0.60 − $0.30 = $0.30.

b. Cara's cost of the last pepper she supplied (the third pepper) is $0.40, and Jamie's cost of producing one more (his third pepper) is $0.70. Total producer surplus therefore falls by $0.70 − $0.40 = $0.30.

c. Josie's willingness to pay for her second pepper is $0.60; this is what she would lose if she were to consume one less pepper. And Cara's cost of producing her third pepper is $0.40; this is what she would save if she were to produce one less pepper. If we therefore reduced quantity by one pepper, we would lose $0.60 − $0.40 = $0.20 of total surplus.

Check Your Understanding 6-4

1. a. At a price paid by consumers of $0.70, Casey's consumer surplus is $0.20 from his first pepper (he loses $0.20 compared to the market equilibrium), $0.00 from his second pepper (he loses $0.20), and he no longer buys the third pepper. Josie's consumer surplus is $0.10 from her first pepper (she loses $0.20), and she no longer buys the second pepper (she loses $0.10 of consumer surplus that she previously got from that second pepper). So the loss in consumer surplus is $0.70.

b. At a price received by producers of $0.30, Cara's producer surplus is $0.20 from her first pepper (she loses $0.20), $0.20 from her second pepper (she loses $0.20), and she no longer produces the third pepper (she loses $0.10 that she previously got from that third pepper). Jamie's producer surplus is $0.00 from his first pepper (he loses $0.20), and he no longer produces his second pepper. So the loss in producer surplus is $0.70.

c. Since three peppers are now sold and the tax on each is $0.40, the government tax revenue is 3 × $0.40 = $1.20.

d. Introduction of the tax resulted in a loss of total surplus of $0.70 + $0.70 = $1.40. Of that amount, $1.20 went to the government in the form of tax revenue. But $0.20 is lost: that is the amount of deadweight loss from this tax.

2. a. The demand for gasoline is inelastic because there is no close substitute for gasoline itself, and it is difficult for drivers to arrange substitutes for driving, such as taking public transportation. As a result, the deadweight loss from a tax on gasoline would be relatively small, as shown in the accompanying diagram.

b. The demand for milk chocolate bars is elastic because there are close substitutes: dark chocolate bars, milk chocolate kisses, and so on. As a result, the deadweight loss from a tax on milk chocolate bars would be relatively large, as shown in the accompanying diagram.

Chapter Seven

Check Your Understanding Question 7-1

1. a. Supplies are an explicit cost because they require an outlay of money.
 b. If the basement can be used in some other way that generates money, such as renting it to a student, then the implicit cost is that money forgone. Otherwise, the implicit cost is zero.
 c. Wages are an explicit cost.
 d. By using the van for their business, Karma and Don forgo the money they could have gained by selling it. So use of the van is an implicit cost.
 e. Karma's forgone wages from her job are an implicit cost.

Check Your Understanding 7-2

1. a. The marginal cost of doing your laundry is the opportunity cost of your time spent doing laundry today—that is, the value you would place on spending time today on your next best alternative activity, like seeing a movie. The marginal benefit is having more clean clothes today to choose from.
 b. The marginal cost of changing your oil is the opportunity cost of time spent changing your oil now as well as the explicit cost of the oil change. The marginal benefit is the improvement in your car's performance.
 c. The marginal benefit of another jalapeno on your nachos is the pleasant taste that you receive from it. The marginal cost is the unpleasant feeling of a burning mouth that you receive from it plus any explicit cost of the jalapeno.
 d. The marginal benefit of hiring another worker in your company is the value of the output that worker produces. The marginal cost is the wage you must pay that worker.
 e. The marginal benefit of another dose of the drug is the value of the reduction in the patient's disease. The marginal cost is the value of the increased side effects from this additional dose.
 f. The marginal benefit of assigning one more soldier to your invasion force is the increased probability of a successful invasion generated by that extra soldier. The marginal cost is the decreased probability of success in the alternative project for which you could use that soldier, such as defending your borders.

2. a. As can be seen from Table 7-6, the optimal quantity is 6 lawns when marginal cost is constant at $18.50. At the 6th lawn, Felix's marginal benefit is $19.00, exceeding marginal cost by $0.50. At the 7th lawn, however, marginal benefit is $18.00, implying a loss of $0.50 on the 7th lawn if he mows it. His total net gain is equal to ($35.00 − $18.50) + ($30.00 − $18.50) + ($26.00 − $18.50) + ($23.00 − $18.50) + ($21.00 − $18.50) + ($19.00 − $18.50) = $43.00.
 b. The lawn that generates the highest marginal benefit is the 1st lawn; it generates $35.00 in marginal benefit. So the optimal quantity is 0 when marginal cost is always greater than $35.00. In that case, it would never benefit Felix to do even the 1st lawn. In going from the 3rd to the 4th lawn, marginal benefit goes from $26.00 to $23.00. So any marginal cost less than or equal to $26.00 but higher than $23.00 implies an optimal quantity of 3.

Check Your Understanding 7-3

1. a. Your sunk cost is $8,000 because none of the $8,000 you spent on the truck is recoverable.
 b. Your sunk cost is $4,000 because 50 percent of the $8,000 spent on the truck is recoverable.

2. a. This is an invalid argument because the time and money already spent are a sunk cost at this point.
 b. This is also an invalid argument because what you should have done two years ago is irrelevant to what you should do now.
 c. This is a valid argument because it recognizes that sunk costs are irrelevant to what you should do now.
 d. This is a valid argument given that you are concerned about disappointing your parents. But your parents' views are irrational because they do not recognize that the time already spent is a sunk cost.

Check Your Understanding 7-4

1. a. The net present value of project A is unaffected by the interest rate since it is money received today; its present value is still $100. The net present value of project B is now $−10 + $115/1.02 = $102.75. The net present value of project C is now $119 − $20/1.02 = $99.39. Project B is now preferred.
 b. When the interest rate is lower, the cost of waiting for money that arrives in the future is lower. For example, at a 10% interest rate, $1 arriving 1 year from today is worth only 1/$1.10 = $0.91. But when the interest rate is 2%, $1 arriving 1 year from today is worth 1/$1.02 = $0.98, a sizable increase. As a result, project B, which has a benefit one year from today, becomes more attractive. And project C, which has a cost 1 year from today, becomes less attractive.

Chapter Eight

Check Your Understanding 8-1

1. a. The fixed input is the 10-ton machine, and the variable input is electricity.
 b. As you can see from the declining numbers in the third column of the accompanying table, electricity does indeed exhibit diminishing returns: the marginal product of each additional kilowatt of electricity is less than that of the previous kilowatt.

Quantity of electricity (kilowatts)	Quantity of ice (pounds)	Marginal product of electricity (pounds per kilowatt)
0	0	
		1,000
1	1,000	
		800
2	1,800	
		600
3	2,400	
		400
4	2,800	

c. A 50% increase in the size of the fixed input means that Bernie now has a 15-ton machine. So the fixed input is now the 15-ton machine. Since it generates a 100% increase in output for any given amount of electricity, the quantity of output and marginal product are now as shown in the accompanying table.

Quantity of electricity (kilowatts)	Quantity of ice (pounds)	Marginal product of electricity (pounds per kilowatt)
0	0	
		2,000
1	2,000	
		1,600
2	3,600	
		1,200
3	4,800	
		800
4	5,600	

Check Your Understanding 8-2

1. a. As shown in the accompanying table, the marginal cost for each pie is found by multiplying the marginal cost of the previous pie by 1.5. Variable cost for each output level is found by summing the marginal cost for all the pies produced to reach that output level. So, for example, the variable cost of three pies is $1.00 + $1.50 + $2.25 = $4.75. Average fixed cost for Q pies is calculated as $9.00/Q since fixed cost is $9.00. Average variable cost for Q pies is equal to variable cost for the Q pies divided by Q; for example, the average variable cost of five pies is $13.19/5, or approximately $2.64. Finally, average total cost can be calculated in two equivalent ways: as TC/Q or as $AVC + AFC$.

Quantity of pies	Marginal cost of pie	Variable cost	Average fixed cost of pie	Average variable cost of pie	Average total cost of pie
0		$0.00	—	—	—
	$1.00				
1		1.00	$9.00	$1.00	$10.00
	1.50				
2		2.50	4.50	1.25	5.75
	2.25				
3		4.75	3.00	1.58	4.58
	3.38				
4		8.13	2.25	2.03	4.28
	5.06				
5		13.19	1.80	2.64	4.44
	7.59				
6		20.78	1.50	3.46	4.96

b. The spreading effect dominates the diminishing returns effect when average total cost is falling: the fall in *AFC* dominates the rise in *AVC* for pies 1 to 4. The diminishing returns effect dominates when average total cost is rising: the rise in *AVC* dominates the fall in *AFC* for pies 5 and 6.

c. Alicia's minimum-cost output is 4 pies; this generates the lowest average total cost, $4.28. When output is less than 4, the marginal cost of a pie is less than the average total cost of the pies already produced. So making an additional pie lowers average total cost. For example, the marginal cost of pie 3 is $2.25, whereas the average total cost of pies 1 and 2 is $5.75. So making pie 3 lowers average total cost to $4.58, equal to (2 × $5.75 + $2.25)/3. When output is more than 4, the marginal cost of a pie is greater than the average total cost of the pies already produced. Consequently, making an additional pie raises average total cost. So, although the marginal cost of pie 6 is $7.59, the average total cost of pies 1 through 5 is $4.44. Making pie 6 raises average total cost to $4.96, equal to (5 × $4.44 + $7.59)/6.

Check Your Understanding 8-3

1. a. The accompanying table shows the average total cost of producing 12,000, 22,000, and 30,000 units for each of the three choices of fixed cost. For example, if the firm makes choice 1, the total cost of producing 12,000 units of output is $8,000 + 12,000 × $1.00 = $20,000. The average total cost of producing 12,000 units of output is therefore $20,000/12,000 = $1.67. The other average total costs are calculated similarly.

	12,000 units	22,000 units	30,000 units
Average total cost from choice 1	$1.67	$1.36	$1.27
Average total cost from choice 2	1.75	1.30	1.15
Average total cost from choice 3	2.25	1.34	1.05

Therefore, if the firm wanted to produce 12,000 units, it would make choice 1 because this gives it the lowest average total cost. If it wanted to produce 22,000 units, it would make choice 2. If it wanted to produce 30,000 units, it would make choice 3.

b. Having historically produced 12,000 units, the firm would have adopted choice 1. When producing 12,000 units, the firm would have had an average total cost of $1.67. When output jumps to 22,000 units, the firm cannot alter its choice of fixed cost in the short run, so its average total cost in the short run will be $1.36. In the long run, however, it will adopt choice 2, making its average total cost fall to $1.30.

c. If the firm believes that the increase in demand is temporary, it should not alter its fixed cost from choice 1 because choice 2 generates higher average total cost as soon as output falls back to its original quantity of 12,000 units: $1.75 versus $1.67.

2. a. This firm is likely to experience constant returns to scale. To increase output, the firm must hire more workers, purchase more computers, and pay additional telephone charges. Because these inputs are easily available, their long-run average total cost is unlikely to change as output increases.

b. This firm is likely to experience diseconomies of scale. As the firm takes on more projects, the costs of communication and coordination required to implement the expertise of the firm's owner are likely to increase.

c. This firm is likely to experience economies of scale. Because diamond mining requires a large initial set-up cost for excavation equipment, long-run average total cost will fall as output increases.

Chapter Nine

Check Your Understanding
9-1

1. a. With only two producers in the world, each producer will represent a sizable share of the market. So the industry will not be perfectly competitive.

b. Because each producer of gas from the North Sea has only a small market share of total world supply of natural gas, and since natural gas is a standardized product, the natural gas industry will be perfectly competitive.

c. Because each designer has a distinctive style, high-fashion clothes are not a standardized product. So the industry will not be perfectly competitive.

d. The market described here is the market in each city for tickets to baseball games. Since there are only one or two teams in each major city, each team will represent a sizable share of the market. So the industry will not be perfectly competitive.

Check Your Understanding
9-2

1. a. The firm should shut down immediately when price is less than minimum average variable cost, the shut-down price. In the accompanying diagram, this is optimal for prices in the range 0 to P_1.

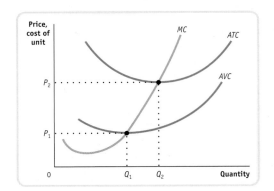

b. When price is greater than minimum average variable cost (the shut-down price) but less than minimum average total cost (the break-even price), the firm should continue to operate in the short run even though it is making a loss. This is optimal for prices in the range P_1 to P_2 and quantities Q_1 to Q_2.

c. When price exceeds minimum average total cost (the break-even price), the firm makes a profit. This happens for prices in excess of P_2 and results in quantities greater than Q_2.

2. This is an example of a temporary shut-down by a firm when the market price lies below the shut-down price, the minimum average variable cost. In this case, the market price is the price of a lobster meal and variable cost is the variable cost of serving such a meal, such as the cost of the lobster, employee wages, and so on. In this example, however, it is the average variable cost curve rather than the market price that shifts over time, due to seasonal changes in the cost of lobsters. Maine lobster shacks have relatively low average variable cost during the summer, when cheap Maine lobsters are available; during the rest of the year, their average variable cost is relatively high due to the high cost of imported lobsters. So the lobster shacks are open for business during the summer, when their minimum average variable cost lies below price; but they close during the rest of the year, when price lies below their minimum average variable cost.

Check Your Understanding
9-3

1. a. A fall in the fixed cost of production generates a fall in the average total cost of production and, in the short run, an increase in each firm's profit at the current output level. So in the long run new firms will enter the industry. The increase in supply drives down price and profits. Once profits are driven back to zero, entry will cease.

b. An increase in wages generates an increase in the average total cost of production at every output level. In the short run, firms incur losses at the current output level, and so in the long run some firms will exit the industry. As firms exit, supply decreases, price rises, and losses are reduced. Exit will cease once losses return to zero.

c. Price will rise as a result of the increased demand, leading to a short-run increase in profits at the current output level. In the long run, firms will enter the industry, generating an increase in supply, a fall in price, and a fall in profits. Once profits are driven back to zero, entry will cease.

d. The shortage of a key input causes that input's price to increase, resulting in an increase in average total costs for producers. Firms incur losses in the short run, and some firms will exit the industry in the long run. The fall in supply generates an increase in price and decreased losses. Exit will cease when losses have returned to zero.

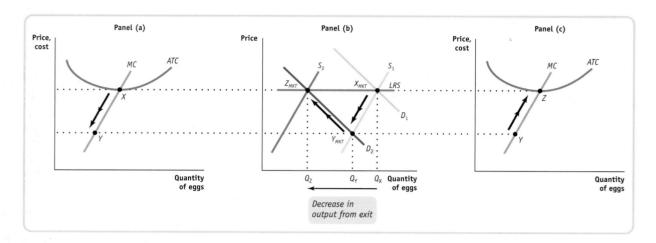

2. In the above diagram, point X_{MKT} in panel (b), the intersection of S_1 and D_1, represents the long-run industry equilibrium before the change in consumer tastes. When tastes change, demand falls and the industry moves in the short run to point Y_{MKT} in panel (b), at the intersection of the new demand curve D_2 and S_1, the short-run supply curve representing the same number of egg producers as in the original equilibrium at point X_{MKT}. As the market price falls, an individual firm reacts by producing less—as shown in panel (a)—as long as the market price remains above the minimum average variable cost. If market price falls below average variable cost, the firm would shut down immediately. At point Y_{MKT} the price of eggs is below minimum average total cost, creating losses for producers. This leads some firms to exit, which shifts the short-run industry supply curve leftward to S_2. A new long-run equilibrium is established at point Z_{MKT}. As this occurs, the market price rises again, and, as shown in panel (c), each remaining producer reacts by increasing output (here, from point Y to point Z). All remaining producers again make zero profits. The decrease in the quantity of eggs supplied in the industry comes entirely from the exit of some producers from the industry. The long-run industry supply curve is the curve labeled *LRS* in panel (b).

Chapter Ten

Check Your Understanding 10-1

1. Consuming a unit that generates negative marginal utility leaves the consumer with lower total utility than not consuming that unit at all. A rational consumer, a consumer who maximizes utility, would not do that. For example, from Figure 10-1 you can see that Cassie receives 64 utils if she consumes 8 clams; but if she consumes the 9th clam, she loses a util, netting her a total utility of only 63 utils. So whenever consuming a unit generates negative marginal utility, the consumer is made better off by not consuming that unit.

2. Since Marta has diminishing marginal utility, her first cup of coffee of the day generates the greatest increase in total utility. Her third and last cup of the day generates the least.

3. a. Mabel has increasing marginal utility since each additional unit consumed brings more additional enjoyment than the previous unit.
   b. Mei has constant marginal utility because each additional unit generates the same additional satisfaction as the previous unit.
   c. Dexter has diminishing marginal utility since the additional utility generated by a good restaurant meal is less when he consumes lots of them than when he consumed few of them.

Check Your Understanding 10-2

1. a. At a price of $5.00 for a movie ticket and income of $10.00, the maximum quantity of tickets that can be purchased is $10/\$5 = 2$ as shown in the accompanying diagram. This is the vertical intercept. At a price of $2.50 for a bucket of popcorn, the horizontal intercept—the maximum quantity of popcorn that can be purchased given the budget—is $\$10.00/\$2.50 = 4$. The slope of the budget line is equal to the rise over run: $-2/4 = -1/2$ (there is a negative sign because the line is downward sloping). The opportunity cost of a bucket of popcorn in terms of movie tickets is equal to minus the slope of the budget line, equal to $1/2$ in this case: 1 bucket of popcorn can be obtained if $1/2$ movie ticket is forgone.

b. At a price of $1.50 for a pair of socks and income of $12.00, the vertical intercept—the maximum quantity of pairs of socks that can be purchased—is $12.00/$1.50 = 8, shown in the accompanying diagram. The horizontal intercept—the maximum quantity of pairs of underwear that can be purchased—is $12.00/$4.00 = 3. The slope of the budget line is $-8/3 = -2\,2/3$. The opportunity cost of underwear in terms of socks is equal to minus the slope of the budget line, equal to $2\,2/3$ in this case: 1 pair of underwear can be obtained if $2\,2/3$ pairs of socks are forgone.

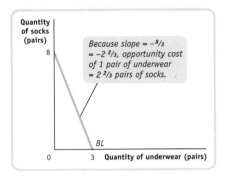

Check Your Understanding 10-3

1. From Figure 10-5 you can see that the marginal utility per dollar at 3 pounds of clams and the marginal utility per dollar at 8 pounds of potatoes are approximately the same, at a value of about 1. But it is not Sammy's optimal consumption bundle because it is not affordable given his income of $20; 3 pounds of clams and 8 pounds of potatoes costs $4 \times 3 + $2 \times 8 = $28, $8 more than Sammy's income. This can be illustrated with Sammy's budget line from Figure 10-4: a bundle of 3 pounds of clams and 8 pounds of potatoes is represented by point X in the accompanying diagram, a point that lies outside Sammy's budget line.

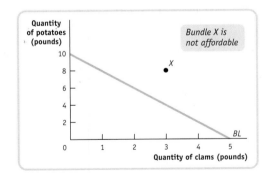

2. If Sammy chose the bundle that maximized his marginal utility per dollar for each good, he would choose to consume 1 pound of potatoes, where $MU_P/P_P = 5.75$, and 1 pound of clams, where $MU_C/P_C = 3.75$. But this bundle generates 26.5 utils for him. Instead, Sammy should choose the consumption bundle that satisfies his budget constraint and for which the marginal utility per dollar for both goods is equal.

Check Your Understanding 10-4

1. Since spending on orange juice is a small share of Clare's spending, the income effect from a rise in the price of orange juice is insignificant. Only the substitution effect, represented by the substitution of lemonade for orange juice, is significant.

2. Since rent is a large share of Delia's expenditures, the increase in rent generates an income effect, making Delia feel poorer. Since housing is a normal good for Delia, the income and substitution effects move in the same direction, leading her to reduce her consumption of housing by moving to a smaller apartment.

3. Since a meal ticket is a significant share of the students' living costs, an increase in its price will generate an income effect. Students respond to the price increase by eating more often in the cafeteria. So the substitution effect (which would induce them to eat in the cafeteria less often) and the income effect (which would induce them to eat in the cafeteria more often than at restaurants because they are poorer) move in opposite directions. This happens because cafeteria meals are an inferior good. In fact, since the income effect outweighs the substitution effect (students eat in the cafeteria more as the price of meal tickets increases), cafeteria meals are a Giffen good.

Chapter Eleven

Check Your Understanding 11-1

1. a. As you can see from the accompanying diagram, the four bundles are associated with three indifference curves: B on the 10-util indifference curve, A and C on the 6-util indifference curve, and D on the 4-util indifference curve.

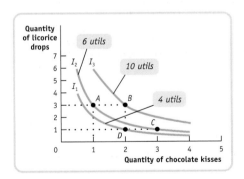

b. From comparing the quantities of chocolate kisses and licorice drops, you can predict that Samantha will prefer B to A because B gives her one more chocolate kiss and the same amount of licorice drops as A. Next, you can predict that she will prefer C to D because C gives her one more chocolate kiss and the same amount of licorice drops as D. You can also predict that she prefers B to D because B gives her two more licorice drops and the same amount of chocolate kisses as D. But without data about utils, you cannot predict how Samantha would rank A versus C or D because C and D have more chocolate kisses but fewer licorice drops than A. Neither can you rank B versus C, for the same reason.

2. Bundles A and B each generate 200 utils since they both lie on the 200 util indifference curve. Likewise, bundles A and C each generate 100 utils since they both lie on the 100 util indifference curve. But this implies that A generates 100 utils and also that A generates 200 utils. This is a contradiction and so cannot be true. It shows that indifference curves cannot cross.

Check Your Understanding 11-2

1. **a.** The marginal rate of substitution of books in place of games, MU_B/MU_G, is 2 for Lucinda and 5 for Kyle. This implies that Lucinda is willing to trade 1 more book for 2 fewer games and Kyle is willing to trade 1 more book for 5 fewer games. So starting from a bundle of 3 books and 6 games, Lucinda would be equally content with a bundle of 4 books and 4 games and Kyle would be equally content with a bundle of 4 books and 1 game. Lucinda finds it more difficult to trade games for books: she is willing to give up only 2 games for a book while Kyle is willing to give up 5 games for a book. If books are measured on the horizontal axis and games on the vertical axis, Kyle's indifference curve will be steeper than Lucinda's at the current consumption bundle.

   b. Lucinda's current consumption bundle is optimal if P_B/P_G, the relative price of books in terms of games, is 2. Kyle's current consumption bundle is not optimal at this relative price; his bundle would be optimal only if the relative price of books in terms of games is 5. Since, for Kyle, $MU_B/MU_G = 5$ but $P_B/P_G = 2$, Kyle should consume fewer games and more books, thereby lowering his MU_B/MU_G until it is equal to 2.

Check Your Understanding 11-3

1. Since Sanjay cares only about the number of jelly beans, not about whether they are banana- or pineapple-flavored, he is always willing to exchange one for the other at the same rate. This implies that his marginal rate of substitution of one flavor of jelly bean in place of another is constant. So they are perfect substitutes.

2. Cherry pie and vanilla ice cream are complements for Hillary since her marginal utility of cherry pie goes up as she has another scoop of vanilla ice cream. But they are ordinary goods, not perfect complements, because she gains some utility from having cherry pie without any vanilla ice cream.

3. Omnisoft's software programs and its operating system are perfect complements for its customers: they gain no utility from the software programs without the operating system. So their marginal rate of substitution of one good in place of the other is undefined, and their indifference curves have a right-angle shape.

4. Income and leisure are ordinary goods for Darnell: the more income he has made by working more hours, the less willing he is to earn yet more by giving up additional leisure time.

Check Your Understanding 11-4

1. **a.** Sammy's original budget line is illustrated in the accompanying diagram by BL_1. His original consumption is at point A. When the price of clams falls, his budget line rotates outward to BL_2, allowing him to achieve a higher level of utility. The pure substitution effect would involve the same change in the slope of his budget line, but without any increase in utility. So the pure substitution effect is illustrated by the movement from A to B. In fact, his utility does rise, so his consumption moves from A to C. The movement from B to C is the income effect.

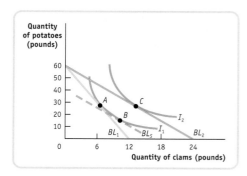

   b. Again, in the accompanying diagram Sammy's original budget line is BL_1, and his original consumption is at point A. The increase in the price of clams causes his budget line to rotate inward to BL_2. This reduces his total utility. The pure substitution effect is what would happen if the slope of the budget line changed but his total utility did not; it is shown as the movement from A to B. The full effect of the price change is the movement from A to C. The movement from B to C is the income effect.

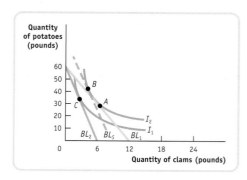

Chapter Twelve

Check Your Understanding 12-1

1. Many college professors will depart for other lines of work if the government imposes a wage that is lower than the market wage. Fewer professors will result in fewer courses taught and therefore fewer college degrees produced. It will adversely affect sectors of the economy that depend directly on colleges, such as the local shopkeepers who sell goods and services to students and facul-

ty, college textbook publishers, and so on. It will also adversely affect firms that use the "output" produced by colleges: new college graduates. Firms that need to hire new employees with college degrees will be hurt as a smaller supply results in a higher market wage for college graduates. Ultimately, the reduced supply of college-educated workers will result in a lower level of human capital in the entire economy relative to what it would have been without the policy. And this will hurt all sectors of the economy that depend on human capital. The sectors of the economy that might benefit are firms that compete with colleges in the hiring of would-be college professors. For example, accounting firms will find it easier to hire people who would otherwise have been professors of accounting, and publishers will find it easier to hire people who would otherwise have been professors of English (easier in the sense that the firms can recruit would-be professors with a lower wage than before). In addition, workers who already have college degrees will benefit; they will command higher wages as the supply of college-educated workers falls.

Check Your Understanding 12-2

1. **a.** As the demand for services increases, the price of services will rise. And as the price of the output produced by the industries increases, this shifts the *VMPL* curve upward—that is, the demand for labor rises. This results in an increase in both the equilibrium wage rate and the quantity of labor employed.

   b. The fall in the catch per day means that the marginal product of labor in the industry declines. The *VMPL* curve shifts downward, generating a fall in the equilibrium wage rate and the equilibrium quantity of labor employed.

2. When firms from different industries compete for the same workers, then each worker in the various industries will be paid the same equilibrium wage, *W*. And since, by the marginal productivity theory of income distribution, $VMPL = P \times MPL = W$ for the last worker hired in equilibrium, the last worker hired in each of these different industries will have the same value of the marginal product of labor.

Check Your Understanding 12-3

1. **a.** False. Income disparities associated with gender, race, or ethnicity can be explained by the marginal productivity theory of income distribution provided that differences in marginal productivity across people are correlated with gender, race, or ethnicity. One possible source for such correlation is past discrimination. Such discrimination can lower individuals' marginal productivity by, for example, preventing them from acquiring the human capital that would raise their productivity. Another possible source of the correlation is differences in work experience that are associated with gender, race, or ethnicity. For example, in jobs where work experience or length of tenure is important, women may earn lower wages because on average more women than men take child-care-related absences from work.

   b. True. Companies that discriminate when their competitors do not are likely to hire less able workers because they discriminate against more able workers who are considered of the wrong gender, race, or ethnicity. And with less able workers, such companies are likely to earn lower profits than their competitors who don't discriminate.

   c. Ambiguous. In general, workers who are paid less because they have less experience may or may not be the victims of discrimination. The answer depends on the reason for the lack of experience. If workers have less experience because they are young or have chosen to do something else rather than gain experience, then they are not victims of discrimination if they are paid less. But if workers lack experience because previous job discrimination prevented them from gaining experience, then they are indeed victims of discrimination when they are paid less.

Check Your Understanding 12-4

1. **a.** Clive is made worse off if, before the new law, he had preferred to work more than 35 hours per week. As a result of the law, he can no longer choose his preferred time allocation; he now consumes fewer goods and more leisure than he would like.

   b. Clive's utility is unaffected by the law if, before the law, he had preferred to work 35 or fewer hours per week. The law has not changed his preferred time allocation.

   c. Clive can never be made better off by a law that restricts the number of hours he can work. He can only be made worse off (case a) or equally as well off (case b).

2. The substitution effect would induce Clive to work fewer hours and consume more leisure after his wage falls—the fall in wage means the price of an hour of leisure falls, leading Clive to consume more leisure. But a fall in his wage also generates a fall in Clive's income. The income effect of this is to induce Clive to consume less leisure and therefore work more hours, since he is now poorer and leisure is a normal good. If the income effect dominates the substitution effect, Clive will in the end work more hours than before.

Chapter Thirteen

Check Your Understanding 13-1

1. **a.** eMarkets! will have to know the willingness to pay of every potential consumer—that is, the demand schedule. It will also have to know the seller's cost for each unit of output of every potential producer—that is, the supply schedule. (Equivalently, it must know the marginal cost curve of every potential producer.)

   b. Some producers who have a seller's cost greater than $99 will produce because they were mistakenly told that the price would be $299; some who have a seller's cost equal to or less than $199 will not produce because they were mistakenly told that the price would be $99. So producer surplus is lower because the market price cannot allocate production efficiently among producers. You cannot tell whether the output will be equal to, less than, or greater than the equilibrium output. Overproduction may occur if a relatively high number of producers think the price will be $299, and underproduction may occur if a relatively high number of producers think the price will be $99.

   c. Consumers with a willingness to pay of $299 who are told that the price is $399 will not purchase the good. For each of these consumers, consumer surplus of $299 − $199 = $100 is lost. Consumers with a willingness to pay of $199, who are allowed to buy the good at a price of $99 each, gain $119 − $99 = $20 in surplus. So this transfer of units from high-willingness-to-pay consumers to low-willingness-to-pay consumers results in a net loss of comsumer surplus of $100 − $20 = $80 per unit.

Check Your Understanding 13-2

1. a. Before the change in preferences, the Bountifullian labor market is in equilibrium, defined by the condition $VMPL_C$ = wage rate = $VMPL_S$. After preferences change, a greater demand for breakfast cereal will induce an increase in the price of cereal, P_C. $VMPL_C = P_C \times MPL_C$ will therefore rise, with the result that $VMPL_C$ > wage rate. A lower demand for sausage will induce a decrease in the price of sausage, P_S. $VMPL_S = P_S \times MPL_S$ will fall, with the result that $VMPL_S$ < wage rate. Sausage producers will let some of their workers go; these workers will move to cereal producers, who are hiring additional workers. As labor moves from the sausage to the cereal industry, MPL_C and $VMPL_C$ fall, but MPL_S and $VMPL_S$ rise.

   b. You will know that the economy has fully adjusted when the labor market has reattained equilibrium: when $VMPL_C$ = wage rate = $VMPL_S$ again. Because all consumers face the same price for cereal, P_C, and the same price for sausage, P_S, there will be *efficiency in consumption:* every consumer who consumes a good has a higher willingness to pay for it than someone who does not. Next, because cereal producers and sausage producers compete for workers in a perfectly competitive labor market, there will be no surplus of labor and all labor will be fully employed. So there will be *efficiency in production:* there is no way to produce more of one good without producing less of the other. Finally, there will be *efficiency in the output levels:* any other mix of cereal and sausage reduces welfare. Because $VMPL_C$ = wage rate = $VMPL_S$ in equilibrium, the allocation of labor to the two industries, and therefore the mix of outputs of the two goods, fully reflects consumers' valuations of the two goods.

Check Your Understanding 13-3

1. There is an objective way to determine whether an economy is efficient: determine whether there is another allocation of production and/or consumption that makes someone better off without making anyone else worse off. If not, it is efficient; if yes, it is inefficient. It is much harder to determine whether an economy is fair because there is no objective measure of determining this. What a person deems is fair typically depends upon his or her viewpoint.

2. a. The problem with this statement is that what one "should contribute" or "should receive" is subject to interpretation. Suppose one person has worked extremely hard to become wealthy but another is born wealthy and has never worked. Should each person be required to contribute the same to society? Some would say yes (those who think the amount of money a person has is the only criterion) but others would say no (those who think that people should be rewarded for working hard relative to those who don't)—it depends upon the person's viewpoint. Similarly, suppose one person needs an operation to be able to see, another person needs an operation to be able to walk, and society doesn't have the resources to perform both operations. Whose need is more important? Again, the answer is unclear because society has no way of measuring whether one person's needs are more compelling than another's.

   b. This statement is also subject to very different interpretations. First, how do we define "work hard"? Do people who spend years working on something they enjoy, such as writing a classical sonata, "work harder" than those who do less intense but very unappealing work? Also, this statement implies that people who cannot work hard for reasons outside their control—say, due to illness—should be rewarded less. Whether or not this is fair is again subject to a person's viewpoint.

Chapter Fourteen

Check Your Understanding 14-1

1. a. This does not support the conclusion. Texas Tea has a limited amount of oil, and the price has risen in order to equalize supply and demand.

   b. This supports the conclusion because the market for home heating oil has become monopolized, and a monopolist will reduce the quantity supplied and raise price to generate profit.

   c. This does not support the conclusion. Texas Tea has raised its price to consumers because the price of its input, home heating oil, has increased.

   d. This supports the conclusion. The fact that other firms have begun to supply heating oil at a lower price implies that Texas Tea must have earned profits—profits that attracted the other firms to Frigid.

   e. This supports the conclusion. It indicates that Texas Tea enjoys a barrier to entry because it controls access to the only Alaskan heating oil pipeline.

Check Your Understanding 14-2

1. a. The price at each output level is found by dividing the total revenue by the number of emeralds produced; for example, the price when 3 emeralds are produced is $252/3 = $84. The price at the various output levels is then used to construct the demand schedule.

   b. The marginal revenue schedule is found by calculating the change in total revenue as output increases by one unit. For example, the marginal revenue generated by increasing output from 2 to 3 emeralds is ($252 − $186) = $66.

   c. The quantity effect component of marginal revenue is the additional revenue generated by selling one more unit of the good at the market price. For example, as shown in the accompanying table, at 3 emeralds, the market price is $84; so, when going from 2 to 3 emeralds the quantity effect is equal to $84.

d. The price effect component of marginal revenue is the decline in total revenue caused by the fall in price when one more unit is sold. For example, as shown in the table, when only 2 emeralds are sold, each emerald sells at a price of $186/2 = $93. However, when Emerald, Inc. sells an additional emerald, the price must fall by $9 to $84. So the price effect component in going from 2 to 3 emeralds is (−$9) × 2 = −$18. That's because 2 emeralds can only be sold at a price of $84 when 3 emeralds in total are sold, although they could have been sold at a price of $93 when only 2 in total were sold.

Quantity of emerald demanded	Price of emerald	Marginal revenue	Quantity component	Price component
1	$100			
		$86	$93	−$7
2	93			
		66	84	−18
3	84			
		28	70	−42
4	70			
		−30	50	−80
5	50			

e. In order to determine Emerald, Inc.'s profit-maximizing output level, you must know its marginal cost at each output level. Its profit-maximizing output level is the one at which marginal revenue is equal to marginal cost.

2. As the accompanying diagram shows, the marginal cost curve shifts upward to $400. The profit-maximizing quantity falls, and so does profit, from $3,200 to $300 × 6 = $1,800. Competitive industry profits, though, are unchanged at zero.

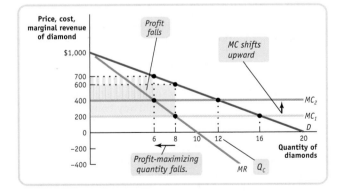

1. a. Cable Internet service is a natural monopoly. So the government should intervene only if it believes that price exceeds average total cost, where average total cost is based on the cost of laying the cable. In this case it should impose a price ceiling equal to average total cost. Otherwise, it should do nothing.

b. The government should approve the merger only if it fosters competition by transferring some of the company's landing slots to another, competing airline.

2. a. False. As can be see from Figure 14-8, panel (b), the inefficiency arises from the fact that some of the consumer surplus is transformed into deadweight loss (the orange area), not that it is transformed into profit (the green area).

b. True. If a monopolist sold to all customers who have a valuation greater than or equal to marginal cost, all mutually beneficial transactions would occur and there would be no deadweight loss.

3. As shown in the accompanying diagram, a monopolist produces Q_M, the output level at which $MR = MC$. A monopolist who mistakenly believes that $P = MR$ produces the output level at which $P = MC$ (when, in fact, $P > MR$, and at the true profit-maximizing level of output, $P > MR = MC$). This misguided monopolist will produce the output level Q_C, where the demand curve crosses the marginal cost curve—the same output level produced if the industry were perfectly competitive. It will charge the price P_C, which is equal to marginal cost, and make zero profit. The entire shaded area is equal to the consumer surplus, which is also equal to total surplus in this case (since the monopolist receives zero producer surplus). There is no deadweight loss since every consumer who is willing to pay as much as or more than marginal cost gets the good. A smart monopolist, however, will produce the output level Q_M, and charge the price P_M. Profit equals the green area, consumer surplus corresponds to the blue area, and total surplus is equal to the sum of the green and blue areas. The orange area is the deadweight loss generated by the monopolist.

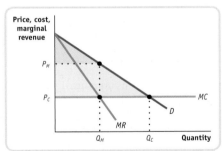

1. a. False. A price-discriminating monopolist will sell to some customers that a single-price monopolist will refuse to—namely, customers with a high price elasticity of demand who are willing to pay only a relatively low price for the good.

b. False. Although a price-discriminating monopolist does indeed capture more of the consumer surplus, inefficiency is lower: more mutually beneficial transactions occur because the monopolist makes more sales to customers with a low willingness to pay for the good.

c. True. Under price discrimination consumers are charged prices that depend on their price elasticity of demand. A consumer with highly elastic demand will pay a lower price than a consumer with inelastic demand.

2. a. This is not a case of price discrimination because all consumers, regardless of their price elasticities of demand, value the damaged merchandise less than undamaged merchandise. So the price must be lowered to sell the merchandise.

b. This is a case of price discrimination. Senior citizens have a higher price elasticity of demand for restaurant meals (their demand for restaurant meals is more responsive to price changes) than other patrons. Restaurants lower the price to high-elasticity consumers (senior citizens). Consumers with low price elasticity of demand will pay the full price.

c. This is a case of price discrimination. High-elasticity consumers will pay a lower price by collecting and using discount coupons. Low-elasticity consumers will not use coupons.

d. This is not a case of price discrimination; it is simply a case of supply and demand.

Chapter Fifteen

Check Your Understanding
15-1

1. a. The world oil industry is an oligopoly because a few countries control a necessary resource for production, oil reserves.

b. The microprocessor industry is an oligopoly because two firms possess superior technology and so dominate industry production.

c. The wide-bodied passenger jet industry is an oligopoly because there are economies of scale in production.

Check Your Understanding
15-2

1. a. The firm is likely to act noncooperatively and raise output, which will generate a negative price effect. But because the firm's current market share is small, the negative price effect will fall much more heavily on its rivals' revenues than on its own. At the same time the firm benefits from a positive quantity effect.

b. The firm is likely to act noncooperatively and raise output, which will generate a fall in price. Because its rivals have higher costs, they will lose money at the lower price while the firm continues to make profits. So the firm may be able to drive its rivals out of business by increasing its output.

c. The firm is likely to collude. Because it is costly for consumers to switch products, the firm would have to lower its price quite substantially (by increasing quantity a lot) to induce consumers to switch to its product. So increasing output is likely to be unprofitable given the large negative price effect.

d. The firm is likely to collude. It cannot increase sales because it is currently at maximum production capacity.

Check Your Understanding
15-3

1. When Margaret builds a missile, Nikita's payoff from building a missile as well is −10; it is −20 if he does not. The same set of payoffs holds for Margaret when Nikita builds a missile: her payoff is −10 if she builds one as well, −20 if she does not. So it is a Nash (or noncooperative) equilibrium for both Margaret and Nikita to build missiles, and their total payoff is (−10) + (−10) = −20. But their total payoff is greatest when neither builds a missile: their total payoff is 0 + 0 = 0. But this outcome—the cooperative outcome—is unlikely. If Margaret builds a missile but Nikita does not, Margaret gets a payoff of +8, rather than the 0 she gets if she doesn't build a missile. So Margaret is better off if she builds a missile but Nikita doesn't. Similarly, Nikita is better off if he builds a missile but Margaret does not: he gets a payoff of +8, rather than the 0 he gets if he doesn't build a missile. So both players have an incentive to build a missile. Both will build a missile, and each gets a payoff of −10. So unless Nikita and Margaret are able to communicate in some way to enforce cooperation, they will act in their own individual interests and each will build a missile.

2. a. Future entry by several new firms will increase competition and drive down industry profits. As a result, there is less future profit to protect by behaving cooperatively today. So each oligopolist is more likely to behave noncooperatively today.

b. When it is very difficult for a firm to detect if another firm has raised output, then it is very difficult to enforce cooperation by playing "tit for tat." So it is more likely that a firm will behave noncooperatively.

c. When firms have coexisted while maintaining high prices for a long time, each expects cooperation to continue. So the value of behaving cooperatively today is high and it is likely that firms will engage in tacit collusion.

Check Your Understanding
15-4

1. a. This is likely to be interpreted as evidence of tacit collusion. Firms in the industry are able to tacitly collude by setting their prices according to the published "suggested" price of the largest firm in the industry. This is a form of price leadership.

b. This is not likely to be interpreted as evidence of tacit collusion. Considerable variation in market share indicates that firms have been competing to capture each others' business.

c. This is not likely to be interpreted as evidence of tacit collusion. These features make it more unlikely that consumers will switch products in response to lower prices. So this is a way for firms to avoid any temptation to gain market share by lowering price. This is a form of product differentiation used to avoid direct competition.

d. This is likely to be interpreted as evidence of tacit collusion. In the guise of discussing sales targets, firms can create a cartel by designating quantities to be produced by each firm.

e. This is likely to be interpreted as evidence of tacit collusion. By raising prices together, each firm in the industry is refusing to undercut its rivals by leaving its price unchanged or lowering it. Because it could gain market share by doing so, refusing to do it is evidence of tacit collusion.

Chapter Sixteen

Check Your Understanding

16-1

1. **a.** Ladders are not differentiated as a result of monopolistic competition. A ladder producer makes different ladders (tall ladders versus short ladders) to satisfy different consumer needs, not to avoid competition with rivals. So two tall ladders made by two different producers will be indistinguishable by consumers.

    b. Soft drinks are an example of product differentiation as a result of monopolistic competition. For example, several producers make colas; each is differentiated in terms of taste, which fast-food chains sell it, and so on.

    c. Department stores are an example of product differentiation as a result of monopolistic competition. They serve different clienteles that have different price sensitivities and different tastes. They also offer different levels of customer service and are situated in different locations.

    d. Steel is not differentiated as a result of monopolistic competition. Different types of steel (beams versus sheets) are made for different purposes, not to distinguish one steel manufacturer's products from another's.

2. **a.** Perfectly competitive industries and monopolistically competitive industries both have many sellers. So it may be hard to distinguish between them solely in terms of number of firms. And in both market structures, there is free entry into and exit from the industry in the long run. But in a perfectly competitive industry, one standardized product is sold, while in a monopolistically competitive industry, products are differentiated. So you should ask whether products are differentiated in the industry.

    b. In a monopoly there is only one firm, but a monopolistically competitive industry contains many firms. So you should ask whether or not there is a single firm in the industry.

Check Your Understanding

16-2

1. **a.** An increase in fixed costs raises average total cost and shifts the average total cost curve upward. In the short run firms incur losses, and some will exit the industry. In the long run, this results in a rightward shift of the demand curves for those firms that remain in the industry, since each one now serves a larger share of the market. Long-run equilibrium is reestablished when the demand curve for each remaining firm has shifted rightward to the point where it is tangent to the firm's new, higher average total cost curve. At this point each firm's price just equals its average total cost, and each firm makes zero profit.

    b. A decrease in marginal cost lowers average total cost and shifts the average total cost curve and the marginal cost curve downward. Because firms make profits, in the long run new entrants are attracted into the industry. In the long run, this results in a leftward shift of each firm's demand curve since each firm now has a smaller share of the market. Long-run equilibrium is reestablished when each firm's demand curve has shifted leftward to the point where it is tangent to the new, lower average total

cost curve. At this point each firm's price just equals average total cost, and each firm makes zero profit.

2. If all the existing firms in the industry joined together to create a monopoly, they would achieve monopoly profits. But this would induce new firms to create new, differentiated products and then enter the industry and capture some of the monopoly profits. So in the long run it would be impossible to maintain a monopoly. The problem arises from the fact that because new firms can create new products, there is no barrier to entry that can maintain a monopoly.

Check Your Understanding

16-3

1. **a.** False. As can be seen from panel (b) of Figure 16-4, a monopolistically competitive firm produces at a point where price exceeds marginal cost—unlike a perfectly competitive firm, which produces where price equals marginal cost (at the point of minimum average total cost). A monopolistically competitive firm will refuse to sell at marginal cost. This would be below average total cost and the firm would incur a loss.

    b. True. Firms in a monopolistically competitive industry could achieve higher profits (monopoly profits) if they all joined together. In addition, since the industry possesses economies of scale, producing a larger quantity of output would lower the firm's cost. The effect on consumers, however, is ambiguous. They would experience less choice. But if consolidation substantially reduces industry-wide average total cost and therefore substantially increases industry-wide output, consumers may experience lower prices under monopoly.

    c. True. Fads and fashions are created and promulgated by advertising, which is found in oligopolies and monopolistically competitive industries but not in monopolies or perfectly competitive industries.

Check Your Understanding

16-4

1. **a.** This is economically useful because such advertisements are likely to focus on the medical benefits of aspirin.

    b. This is economically wasteful because such advertisements are likely to focus on promoting Bayer aspirin versus a rival's aspirin product. The two products are medically indistinguishable.

    c. This is economically useful because such advertisements are likely to focus on the health and enjoyment benefits of orange juice.

    d. This is economically wasteful because such advertisements are likely to focus on promoting Tropicana orange juice versus a rival's product. The two are likely to be indistinguishable by consumers.

    e. This is economically useful because the longevity of a business gives a potential customer information about its quality.

2. A successful brand name indicates a desirable attribute, such as quality, to a potential buyer. So, other things equal—such as price—a firm with a successful brand name will achieve higher sales than a rival with a comparable product but without a successful brand name. This is likely to deter new firms from entering an industry in which an existing firm has a successful brand name.

Chapter Seventeen

Check Your Understanding
17-1

1. a. To determine comparative advantage, we must compare the two countries' opportunity costs for a given good. Take the opportunity cost of 1 ton of corn in terms of bicycles. In China, the opportunity cost of 1 bicycle is 0.01 ton of corn; so the opportunity cost of 1 ton of corn is 1/0.01 bicycles = 100 bicycles. The United States has the comparative advantage in corn since its opportunity cost in terms of bicycles is 50, a smaller number. Similarly, the opportunity cost in the United States of 1 bicycle in terms of corn is 1/50 ton of corn = 0.02 ton of corn. This is greater than 0.01, the Chinese opportunity cost of 1 bicycle in terms of corn, implying that China has a comparative advantage in bicycles.

b. Given that the United States can produce 200,000 bicycles if no corn is produced, it can produce 200,000 bicycles × 0.02 ton of corn/bicycle = 4,000 tons of corn when no bicycles are produced. Likewise, if China can produce 3,000 tons of corn if no bicycles are produced, it can produce 3,000 tons of corn × 100 bicycles/ton of corn = 300,000 bicycles if no corn is produced. These points determine the vertical and horizontal intercepts of the U.S. and Chinese production possibility frontiers as shown in the accompanying diagram.

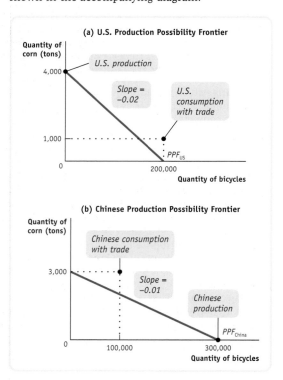

c. The figure shows the production and consumption points of the two countries. Each country is clearly better off with international trade because each now consumes a bundle of the two goods that lies outside its own production possibility frontier, indicating that these bundles were unattainable when each country was in autarky.

2. a. According to the Heckscher–Ohlin model, this pattern of trade occurs because the United States has a relatively larger endowment of factors of production, such as human capital and physical capital, that are suited to the production of movies, but France has a relatively larger endowment of factors of production suited to wine-making, such as vineyards and the human capital of vintners.

b. According to the Heckscher–Ohlin model, this pattern of trade occurs because the United States has a relatively larger endowment of factors of production, such as human and physical capital, that are suited to making machinery, but Brazil has a relatively larger endowment of factors of production suited to shoe-making, such as labor and leather.

Check Your Understanding
17-2

1. In the accompanying diagram, P_A is the price of U.S. grapes in autarky and P_W is the world price of grapes under international trade. With trade, U.S. consumers pay a price of P_W for grapes and consume quantity C_T, U.S. grape producers produce quantity Q_T, and the difference, $C_T - Q_T$, represents imports of Mexican grapes. As a consequence of the strike by truckers, imports are halted, the price paid by American consumers rises to the autarky price, P_A, and U.S. consumption falls to the autarky quantity Q_A.

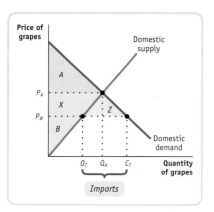

a. Before the strike, U.S. consumers enjoy consumer surplus equal to the area $W + X + Z$. After the strike, their consumer surplus shrinks to the area W. So consumers are worse off, losing consumer surplus represented by the area $X + Z$.

b. Before the strike, U.S. producers have producer surplus equal to the area Y. After the strike, their producer surplus increases to the area $Y + X$. So U.S. producers are better off, gaining producer surplus represented by the area X.

c. U.S. total surplus falls as a result of the strike by an amount represented by the area Z, the loss in consumer surplus that does not accrue to producers.

2. Mexican grape producers are worse off because they lose sales in the amount of $C_T - Q_T$, and Mexican grape pickers are worse off because they lose the wages that were associated with the lost sales. The lower demand for Mexican grapes caused by the strike implies that the price that Mexican consumers pay for grapes falls, making them better off. American grape pickers are better off because their wages increase as a result of the increase of $Q_A - Q_T$ in U.S. sales.

Check Your Understanding
17-3

1. a. If the tariff is $0.50, the price paid by domestic consumers for a pound of imported butter is $0.50 + $0.50 = $1.00, the same price as a pound of domestic butter. Imported butter will no longer have a price advantage over domestic butter, imports will cease, and domestic producers will capture all the feasible sales to domestic consumers, selling amount Q_A in the accompanying figure. But if the tariff is less than $0.50—say only $0.25—the price paid by domestic consumers for a pound of imported butter is $0.50 + $0.25 = $0.75, $0.25 cheaper than a pound of domestic butter. American butter producers will gain sales in the amount of $Q_2 - Q_1$ as a result of the $0.25 tariff. But this is smaller than the amount they would have gained under the $0.50 tariff, the amount $Q_A - Q_1$.

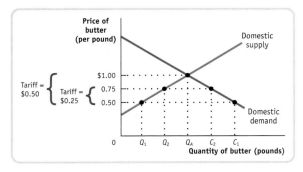

b. As long as the tariff is at least $0.50, increasing it more has no effect. At a tariff of $0.50, all imports are effectively blocked.

2. All imports are effectively blocked at a tariff of $0.50. So such a tariff corresponds to an import quota of 0.

Check Your Understanding
17-4

1. There are many fewer businesses that use steel as an input than there are consumers who buy sugar or clothing. So it will be easier for such businesses to communicate and coordinate among themselves to lobby against tariffs than it will be for consumers. In addition, each business will perceive that the cost of a steel tariff is quite costly to its profits, but an individual consumer is either unaware of or perceives little loss from tariffs on sugar or clothing.

2. Countries are often tempted to protect domestic industries by claiming that an import poses a quality, health, or environmental danger to domestic consumers. A WTO official should examine whether domestic producers are subject to the same stringency in the application of quality, health, or environmental regulations as foreign producers. If they are, then it is more likely that the regulations are for legitimate, non–trade protection purposes; if they are not, then it is more likely that the regulations are intended as trade protection measures.

Chapter Eighteen

Check Your Understanding
18-1

1. a. This will make it more likely that you will buy car insurance. Suppose you were uninsured. If a bad state of the world occurs and your car is damaged, you can no longer get to work. That is, in a bad state of the world, your income for consumption is reduced not only because you have to pay for car repairs but also because you no longer have income from work. This increases the risk to your income from damage to your car. If you are risk-averse, you are more likely to buy insurance.

b. This will make it less likely that you will buy car insurance. Suppose you were uninsured. If a bad state of the world occurs and your car is damaged, your parents can easily buy you another car. That is in a bad state of the world, your income is not reduced by as much as if you did not have wealthy parents. So the risk to your income from damage to your car is lower, making you less likely to buy insurance.

2. a. Karma's expected income is the weighted average of all possible values of her income, weighted by the probabilities with which she earns each possible value of her income. Since she makes $22,000 with a probability of 0.6 and $35,000 with a probability of 0.4, her expected income is (0.6 × $22,000) + (0.4 × $35,000) = $13,200 + $14,000 = $27,200. Her expected utility is simply the expected value of the utilities she will experience. Since with a probability of 0.6 she will experience a utility level of 850 utils (the utility to her from making $22,000), and with a probability of 0.4 she will experience a utility level of 1,260 utils (the utility to her from making $35,000), her expected total utility is (0.6 × 850 utils) + (0.4 × 1,260 utils) = 510 utils + 504 utils = 1,014 utils.

b. If Karma makes $25,000 for certain, she experiences a utility level of 1,014 utils. From the answer to part a, we know that this leaves her equally as well off as when she has a risky expected income of $27,200. Since Karma is indifferent between a risky expected income of $27,200 and a certain income of $25,000, you can conclude that she would prefer a certain income of $27,200 to a risky expected income of $27,200. That is, she would definitely be willing to reduce the risk she faces when this reduction in risk leaves her expected income unchanged. In other words, Karma is risk-averse.

c. Yes. Karma experiences a utility level of 1,056 utils when she has a certain income of $26,000. This is higher than the expected utility level of 1,014 utils generated by a risky expected income of $27,200. So Karma is willing to pay a premium to guarantee a certain income of $26,000.

Check Your Understanding
18-2

1. a. An increase in the number of ships implies an increase in the quantity of insurance demanded at any given premium. This is a rightward shift of the demand curve, resulting in a rise in both the equilibrium premium and the equilibrium quantity of insurance bought and sold.

b. An increase in the number of trading routes means that investors can diversify more. In other words, they can reduce risk further. At any given premium, there are now more investors willing to supply insurance. This is a rightward shift of the supply curve for insurance, leading to a fall in the equilibrium premium and a rise in the equilibrium quantity of insurance bought and sold.

c. If ship-owners in the market become even more risk-averse, they will be willing to pay even higher premiums for insurance. That is, at any given premium, there are now more people willing to buy insurance. This is a rightward shift of the demand curve for insurance, leading to a rise in both the equilibrium premium and the equilibrium quantity of insurance bought and sold.

d. If investors in the market become more risk-averse, they will be less willing to accept risk at any given premium. This is a leftward shift of the supply curve for insurance, leading to a rise in the equilibrium premium and a fall in the equilibrium quantity of insurance bought and sold.

e. As the overall level of risk increases, those willing to buy insurance will be more willing to buy insurance at any given premium; the demand curve for insurance shifts to the right. But since overall risk cannot be diversified away, those ordinarily willing to take on risk will be less willing to do so, leading to a leftward shift in the supply curve for insurance. As a result, the equilibrium premium will rise; the effect on the equilibrium quantity of insurance is uncertain.

f. If the wealth levels of investors fall, investors will become more risk-averse and so less willing to supply insurance at any given premium. This is a leftward shift of the supply curve for insurance, leading to a rise in the equilibrium premium and a fall in the equilibrium quantity of insurance bought and sold.

Check Your Understanding
18-3

1. The inefficiency caused by adverse selection is that an insurance policy with a premium based on the average risk of all drivers will attract only an adverse selection of bad drivers. Good (that is, safe) drivers will find this insurance premium too expensive and so will remain uninsured. This is inefficient. However, safe drivers are also those drivers who have had fewer moving violations for several years. Lowering premiums for only those drivers allows the insurance company to screen its customers and sell insurance to safe drivers, too. This means that at least some of the good drivers now are also insured, which decreases the inefficiency that arises from adverse selection. In a way, having no moving violations for several years is building a reputation for being a safe driver.

2. The moral hazard problem in home construction arises from private information about what the contractor does: whether she takes care to reduce the cost of construction or allows costs to increase. The homeowner cannot, or can only imperfectly, observe the cost-reduction effort of the contractor. If the contractor were fully reimbursed for all costs incurred during construction, she would have no incentive to reduce costs. Making the contractor responsible for any additional costs above the original estimate means that she now has an incentive to keep costs low.

However, this imposes risk on the contractor. For instance, if the weather is bad, home construction will take longer, and will be more costly, than if the weather had been good. Since the contractor pays for any additional costs (such as weather-induced delays) above the original estimate, she now faces risk that she cannot control.

3. a. True. Drivers with higher deductibles have more incentive to take care in their driving, to avoid paying the deductible. This is a moral hazard phenomenon.

b. True. Suppose you know that you are a safe driver. You have a choice of a policy with a high premium but a low deductible or one with a lower premium but a higher deductible. In this case, you would be more likely to choose the cheap policy with the high deductible because you know that you will be unlikely to have to pay the deductible. When there is adverse selection, insurance companies use screening devices such as this to make inferences about people's private information about how skillful they are as drivers.

c. True. The wealthier you are, the less risk-averse you are. If you are less risk-averse, you are more willing to bear risk yourself. Having an insurance policy with a high deductible means that you are exposed to more risk: you have to pay more of any insurance claim yourself. This is an implication of how risk aversion changes with a person's income or wealth.

Chapter Nineteen
Check Your Understanding
19-1

1. a. The external cost is the pollution caused by the wastewater runoff, an uncompensated cost imposed by the poultry farms on their neighbors.

b. Since poultry farmers do not take the external cost of their actions into account when making decisions about how much wastewater to generate, they will create more runoff than is socially optimal in the absence of government intervention or a private deal. They will produce runoff up to the point at which the marginal social benefit of an additional unit of runoff is zero; however, their neighbors experience a high, positive level of marginal social cost of runoff from this output level. So the quantity of wasterwater runoff is inefficient: reducing runoff by one unit would reduce total social benefit by less than it would reduce total social cost.

c. At the socially optimal quantity of wastewater runoff, the marginal social benefit is equal to the marginal social cost. This quantity is lower than the quantity of wastewater runoff that would be created in the absence of government intervention or a private deal.

2. Yasmin's reasoning is not correct: allowing some late returns of books is likely to be socially optimal. Although you impose a marginal social cost on others every day that you are late in returning a book, there is some positive marginal social benefit to you of returning a book late—for example, you get a longer period to use it in working on a term paper.

The socially optimal number of days that a book is returned late is the number at which the marginal social benefit equals the marginal social cost. A fine so stiff that it prevents any late returns is likely to result in a situation in which people return books although the marginal social benefit of keeping them another day is greater than the marginal social cost—an inefficient outcome. In that case, allowing an overdue patron another day would increase total social benefit more than it would increase total social cost. So charging a moderate fine that reduces the number of days that books are returned late to the socially optimal number of days is appropriate.

Check Your Understanding

19-2

1. This is a misguided argument. Allowing polluters to sell emissions permits makes polluters face a cost of polluting: the opportunity cost of the permit. If a polluter chooses not to reduce its emissions, it cannot sell its emissions permits. As a result, it forgoes the opportunity of making money from the sale of the permits. So despite the fact that the polluter receives a monetary benefit from selling the permits, the scheme has the desired effect: to make polluters internalize the externality of their actions.

2. **a.** If the emissions tax is smaller than the marginal social cost at Q_{OPT}, a polluter will face a marginal cost of polluting (equal to the amount of the tax) that is less than the marginal social cost at the socially optimal quantity of pollution. Since a polluter will produce emissions up to the point where the marginal social benefit is equal to its marginal cost, the resulting amount of pollution will be larger than the socially optimal quantity. As a result, there is inefficiency: if the amount of pollution is larger than the socially optimal quantity, the marginal social cost exceeds the marginal social benefit, and society could gain from a reduction in emissions levels.

   If the emissions tax is greater than the marginal social cost at Q_{OPT}, a polluter will face a marginal cost of polluting (equal to the amount of the tax) that is greater than the marginal social cost at the socially optimal quantity of pollution. This will lead the polluter to reduce emissions below the socially optimal quantity. This also is inefficient: whenever the marginal social benefit is greater than the marginal social cost, society could benefit from an increase in emissions levels.

   b. If the total amount of allowable pollution is set too high, the supply of emissions permits will be high and so the equilibrium price at which permits trade will be low. That is, polluters will face a marginal cost of polluting (the price of a permit) that is "too low"—lower than the marginal social cost at the socially optimal quantity of pollution. As a result, pollution will be greater than the socially optimal quantity. This is inefficient.

   If the total level of allowable pollution is set too low, the supply of emissions permits will be low and so the equilibrium price at which permits trade will be high. That is, polluters will face a marginal cost of polluting (the price of a permit) that is "too high"—higher than the marginal social cost at the socially optimal quantity of pollution. As a result, pollution will be lower than the socially optimal quantity. This also is inefficient.

Check Your Understanding

19-3

1. The London congestion charge acts like a Pigouvian tax on driving in central London. If the marginal external cost in terms of pollution and congestion of an additional car driven in central London is indeed £5, then the scheme is an optimal policy.

2. **a.** Planting trees imposes an external benefit: the marginal social benefit of planting trees is higher than the marginal benefit to individual tree planters, since many people (not just those who plant the trees) can benefit from the increased air quality and lower summer temperatures. The difference between the marginal social benefit and the marginal benefit to individual tree planters is the marginal external benefit. A Pigouvian subsidy could be placed on each tree planted in urban areas in order to increase the marginal benefit to individual tree planters to the same level as the marginal social benefit.

   b. Water-saving toilets impose an external benefit: the marginal benefit to individual homeowners from replacing a traditional toilet with a water-saving toilet is zero, since water is virtually costless. But the marginal social benefit is large, since fewer rivers and aquifers need to be pumped. The difference between the marginal social benefit and the marginal benefit to individual homeowners is the marginal external benefit. A Pigouvian subsidy on installing water-saving toilets could bring the marginal benefit to individual homeowners in line with the marginal social benefit.

   c. Disposing of old computer monitors imposes an external cost: the marginal cost to those disposing of old computer monitors is lower than the marginal social cost, since environmental pollution is borne by people other than the person disposing of the monitor. The difference between the marginal social cost and the marginal cost to those disposing of old computer monitors is the marginal external cost. A Pigouvian tax on disposing of computer monitors, or a system of tradable permits for their disposal, could raise the marginal cost to those disposing of old computer monitors sufficiently to make it equal to the marginal social cost.

Chapter Twenty

Check Your Understanding

20-1

1. **a.** Use of a public park is nonexcludable, but it may or may not be rival in consumption, depending on the circumstances. For example, if both you and I use the park for jogging, then your use will not prevent my use—use of the park is nonrival in consumption. In this case the public park is a public good. But use of the park is rival in consumption if there are many people trying to use the jogging path at the same time or when my use of the public tennis court prevents your use of the same court. In this case the public park is a common resource.

   b. A cheese burrito is both excludable and rival in consumption. Hence it is a private good.

   c. Information from a password-protected website is excludable but nonrival in consumption. So it is an artificially scarce good.

d. Publicly announced information on the path of an incoming hurricane is nonexcludable and nonrival in consumption. So it is a public good.

2. A private producer will supply only a good that is excludable; otherwise, the producer won't be able to charge a price for it that covers the costs of production. So a private producer would be willing to supply a cheese burrito and information from a password-protected website but unwilling to supply a public park or publicly announced information about an incoming hurricane.

Check Your Understanding

20-2

1. a. With 10 Homebodies and 6 Revelers, the marginal social benefit schedule of money spent on the party is as shown in the accompanying table.

Money spent on party	Marginal social benefit
$0	
1	(10 × $0.05) + (6 × $0.13) = $1.28
2	(10 × $0.04) + (6 × $0.11) = $1.06
3	(10 × $0.03) + (6 × $0.09) = $0.84
4	(10 × $0.02) + (6 × $0.07) = $0.62

The efficient spending level is $2, the highest level for which the marginal social benefit is greater than the marginal cost ($1).

b. With 6 Homebodies and 10 Revelers, the marginal social benefit schedule of money spent on the party is as shown in the accompanying table.

Money spent on party	Marginal social benefit
$0	
1	(6 × $0.05) + (10 × $0.13) = $1.60
2	(6 × $0.04) + (10 × $0.11) = $1.34
3	(6 × $0.03) + (10 × $0.09) = $1.08
4	(6 × $0.02) + (10 × $0.07) = $0.82

The efficient spending level is now $3, the highest level for which the marginal social benefit is greater than the marginal cost ($1). The efficient level of spending has increased from that in part a because with relatively more Revelers than Homebodies, an additional dollar spent on the party generates a higher level of social benefit compared to when there are relatively more Homebodies than Revelers.

c. When the numbers of Homebodies and Revelers are unknown but residents are asked their preferences, then Homebodies will pretend to be Revelers to induce a higher level of spending on the public party. That's because a

Homebody still receives a positive individual marginal benefit from an additional $1 spent, despite the fact that his or her individual marginal benefit is lower than that of a Reveler for every additional $1. In this case the "reported" marginal social benefit schedule of money spent on the party will be as shown in the accompanying table.

Money spent on party	Marginal social benefit
$0	
1	16 × $0.13 = $2.08
2	16 × $0.11 = $1.76
3	16 × $0.09 = $1.44
4	16 × $0.07 = $1.12

As a result, $4 will be spent on the party, the highest level for which the "reported" marginal social benefit is greater than the marginal cost ($1). Regardless of whether there are 10 Homebodies and 6 Revelers (part a) or 6 Homebodies and 10 Revelers (part b), spending $4 in total on the party is clearly inefficient because marginal cost exceeds marginal social benefit at this spending level.

As a further exercise, consider how much Homebodies gain by this misrepresentation. In part a, the efficient level of spending is $2. So by misrepresenting their preferences, the 10 Homebodies gain, in total, 10 × ($0.03 + $0.02) = $0.50—that is, they gain the marginal individual benefit in going from a spending level of $2 to $4. The 6 Revelers also gain from the misrepresentations of the Homebodies; they gain 6 × ($0.09 + $0.07) = $0.96 in total. This outcome is clearly inefficient—when $4 in total is spent, the marginal cost is $1 but the marginal social benefit is only $0.62, indicating that too much money is being spent on the party.

In part b, the efficient level of spending is actually $3. The misrepresentation by the 6 Homebodies gains them, in total, 6 × $0.02 = $0.12, but the 10 Revelers gain 10 × $0.07 = $0.70 in total. This outcome is also clearly inefficient—when $4 is spent, marginal social benefit is only $0.12 + $0.70 = $0.82 but marginal cost is $1.

Check Your Understanding

20-3

1. When individuals are allowed to harvest freely, the government-owned forest becomes a common resource, and individuals will overuse it—they will harvest an inefficiently excessive number of trees. In economic terms, the marginal social cost of harvesting a tree is greater than a private logger's individual marginal cost.

2. The three methods consistent with economic theory are (a) Pigouvian taxes, (b) a system of tradable licenses, and (c) allocation of property rights.

a. *Pigouvian taxes.* You would enforce a tax on loggers that equals the difference between the marginal social cost and the individual marginal cost of logging a tree at the socially efficient harvest amount. In order to do this, you

Check Your Understanding

22-3

1. ***Pro:*** It can be argued that AOL attempted to create a monopoly by creating artificial barriers to other Internet service providers. Because it is the largest Internet service provider, a potential customer would be more likely to use AOL than a rival company if AOL restricted its pop-up message service to its own customers. If you wanted to reach the largest number of people possible with pop-up messages, and most people were AOL users, and AOL restricted its pop-up messaging to its own customers, then you would have had to become an AOL user. So by pursuing this policy, AOL believed it could eventually achieve a monopoly position in the Internet service provider industry.

    Con: It can be argued that AOL was simply offering a superior product to its customers and that it has no obligation to offer it without charge to customers of competing firms. To put it another way, if AOL had been required to provide customers of other companies with the superior products it developed and provided to its own customers, then it could never charge its own customers a price large enough to recoup its investment in developing the product. So it had to restrict this product to its own customers in order to make it worthwhile to offer it. Using a term from Chapter 20, AOL must make the good "excludable" in order to earn revenue from it.

Glossary

Italicized terms within definitions are key terms that are defined elsewhere in this glossary.

ability-to-pay principle: the principle of *tax fairness* by which those with greater ability to pay a tax should pay more tax.

absolute advantage: the advantage conferred by the ability to produce a good more efficiently—at lower cost of *resources*—than other producers.

absolute value: the value of a number without regard to a plus or minus sign.

accounting profit: revenue minus *explicit costs* and depreciation.

administrative costs (of a tax): the *resources* used (which is a cost) both to collect the tax and to pay it.

adverse selection: occurs when an individual knows more about the way things are than other people do. Adverse selection problems can lead to market problems: private information leads buyers to expect hidden problems in items offered for sale, which leads to low prices, which leads to the best items being kept off the market.

antitrust policy: legislative and regulatory efforts of the government to prevent industries from becoming or behaving like *monopolies*.

artificially scarce good: a good that is *excludable* but *nonrival in consumption*.

autarky: occurs when a country cannot trade with other countries.

average cost: an alternative term for *average total cost;* the *total cost* divided by the total quantity of output.

average fixed cost: the *fixed cost* per unit of output.

average tax rate on income: the ratio of income taxes paid to income.

average total cost: *total cost* divided by the total quantity of output.

average variable cost: the *variable cost* per unit of output.

backward-bending individual labor supply curve: an *individual labor supply curve* that is upward sloping when the *substitution effect* predominates (usually at low to moderate wage rates) and downward sloping when the *income effect* predominates (at very high wage rates).

bar graph: a graph that uses bars of varying height or length to show the comparative sizes of different observations of a variable.

barrier to entry: something that prevents other firms from entering an industry. Crucial in protecting the profits of a *monopolist*. There are four types of barriers to entry: control over scarce resources or inputs, *economies of scale*, technological superiority, and government-created barriers such as *licenses*.

barter: the direct exchange of goods or services without the use of money.

benefits principle: the principle of *tax fairness* by which those who benefit from public spending should bear the burden of the tax that pays for that spending.

black market: a market in which goods or services are bought and sold illegally, either because it is illegal to sell them at all or because the prices charged are legally prohibited by a *price ceiling*.

brand name: a name owned by a particular firm that distinguishes its products from those of other firms.

break-even price: the market price at which a firm earns zero profits.

budget constraint: the cost of a consumer's *consumption bundle* cannot exceed the consumer's total income.

budget line: all the *consumption bundles* available to a consumer, assuming all income is spent.

capital: the combined value of assets; includes equipment, buildings, tools, inventory, and financial assets.

capital at risk: funds that an insurer places at risk when agreeing to provide insurance.

cartel: an agreement among several producers setting production quotas for each, thereby leading to oligopoly profits.

causal relationship: the relationship between two variables in which the value taken by one variable directly influences or determines the value taken by the other variable.

circular-flow diagram: a model that represents the transactions in an *economy* by two kinds of flows around a circle: a flow of physical things such as goods or labor and the flow of money to pay for these physical things.

Coase theorem: the proposition that even in the presence of *externalities* an *economy* can always reach an *efficient* solution as long as *transaction costs* are sufficiently low.

collusion: cooperation among producers to limit production and raise prices so as to raise one another's profits.

commodity: output of different producers regarded by consumers as all the same good; also referred to as a *standardized product*.

common resource: a *resource* that is *nonexcludable* and *rival in consumption*.

comparative advantage: the advantage conferred on an individual or nation if it can produce a good at a lower *opportunity cost* than another producer.

compensating differentials: wage differences across jobs that reflect the fact that some jobs are less pleasant or more dangerous than others.

competitive market: a market in which all market participants are price-takers.

competitive market economy: an *economy* in which all markets, for goods and for factors, are perfectly competitive. All market participants are price-takers.

complements: pairs of goods for which a fall in the price of one good results in greater demand for the other.

constant returns to scale: a range of production in which *long-run average total cost* is constant as output increases.

consumer surplus: a term often used to refer both to *individual consumer surplus* and to *total consumer surplus*.

consumption bundle (of an individual): the collection of all the goods and services consumed by a given individual.

consumption possibilities: the set of all *consumption bundles* available to a consumer, given that consumer's income and prevailing prices.

copyright: the exclusive legal right of the creator of a literary or artistic work to profit from that work; like a *patent*, it is a temporary monopoly.

cost (of potential seller): the lowest price at which a seller is willing to sell a good.

cost-benefit analysis: an estimate of the costs and benefits of providing a good. When governments use cost-benefit analysis, they estimate the social costs and social benefits of providing a public good.

critical mass: the size at which a network suddenly begins to grow rapidly.

cross-price elasticity of demand: the ratio of the percent change in the *quantity demanded* of one good to the percent change in the price of another good; a measure of the effect of the change in the price of one good on the quantity demanded of the other.

curve: a line on a graph, which may be curved or straight, that depicts a relationship between two variables.

deadweight loss (from a tax): the extra cost in the form of inefficiency that results because a tax discourages mutually beneficial transactions; also referred to as *excess burden.*

decreasing marginal benefit: *marginal benefit* that decreases with each additional unit of the activity.

deductible: a sum specified in an insurance policy that the insured must pay before being compensated for a loss; deductibles reduce *moral hazard.*

demand curve: a graphical representation of the *demand schedule,* showing how much of a good or service consumers would buy at a given price.

demand price: the price of a given quantity at which consumers will demand that quantity.

demand schedule: a list or table showing the relationship between price and the quantity of a good consumers would buy.

dependent variable: the determined variable in a causal relationship.

diminishing marginal rate of substitution: the principle that the more of one good that is consumed in proportion to another, the less of the second good the consumer is willing to substitute for another unit of the first good.

diminishing returns to an input: the effect observed when an increase in the quantity of an *input,* while holding the levels of all other inputs fixed, leads to a decline in the *marginal product* of that input.

diseconomies of scale: a range of production in which *long-run average total cost* increases as output increases.

diversification: reducing risk by investing in several different enterprises, so that the possible losses are *independent events.*

domestic demand curve: a *demand curve* for domestic consumers.

domestic supply curve: a *supply curve* for domestic producers.

dominant strategy: in *game theory,* an action that is a player's best action regardless of the action taken by the other player.

duopolist: one of the two firms in a *duopoly.*

duopoly: an *oligopoly* consisting of only two firms.

economic growth: a *long-run* trend toward the production of more goods and services.

economic profit: revenue minus the *opportunity cost* of *resources;* often less than *accounting profit.*

economic signal: any piece of information that helps people make better economic decisions.

economics: the study of *economies,* at the level of individuals and of society as a whole.

economies of scale: a range of production in which *long-run average total cost* declines as output increases.

economy: a system for coordinating a society's productive activities.

efficiency-wage model: a model in which some employers pay an above-equilibrium wage as an *incentive* to better performance.

efficient: description of a market or *economy* that uses its resources in such a way as to exploit all opportunities to make some individuals better off without making others worse off.

efficient allocation of resources: the case in which there is no way for an economy to reallocate *factors of production* among producers to produce more of some goods without producing less of others.

efficient allocation of risk: the case in which those most willing to bear *risk* are those who bear it.

efficient in consumption: description of an *economy* in which there is no way to redistribute goods that makes some consumers better off without making others worse off.

efficient in output levels: description of an *economy* in which no different mix of output would make some consumers better off without making others worse off.

efficient in production: description of an *economy* in which there is no way to produce more of some goods without producing less of others.

elastic demand: when the *price elasticity of demand* is greater than 1. A percentage increase in price will cause a correspondingly greater percentage decrease in quantity demanded, and vice versa.

emissions tax: a tax that depends on the amount of pollution a firm produces.

environmental standards: rules established by a government to protect the environment by specifying actions to be taken by producers and consumers.

equilibrium: an economic balance in which no individual would be better off doing something different; an equality of supply and demand.

equilibrium price: the price at which the market is in *equilibrium,* that is, the quantity of a good demanded equals the quantity supplied; also referred to as the *market-clearing price.*

equilibrium quantity: the quantity of a good bought and sold at the *equilibrium* (or *market-clearing) price.*

equilibrium value of the marginal product: the additional value produced by the last unit of a factor employed in the *factor market* as a whole.

equity: fairness; because individuals can disagree about what is "fair," equity is not as well defined a concept as efficiency.

excess burden (from a tax): the extra cost in the form of inefficiency that results because a tax discourages mutually beneficial transactions; also referred to as *deadweight loss.*

excess capacity: when firms produce less than the output at which *average total cost* is minimized; characteristic of *monopolistically competitive* firms.

excise tax: a tax on the consumption of a given good or service.

excludable: referring to a good, describes the case in which the supplier can prevent those who do not pay from consuming the good.

expected utility: the expected value of total *utility,* given uncertainty about outcomes.

expected value: in reference to a *random variable,* the weighted average of all possible variables; the weights on each possible value correspond to the probability of that value.

explicit cost: a cost that requires an outlay of money.

exporting industries: industries that produce goods or services for sale abroad.

exports: goods and services sold to other countries.

external benefit: an uncompensated benefit that an individual or firm confers on others; also known as *positive externalities.*

external cost: an uncompensated cost that an individual or firm imposes on others; also known as *negative externalities.*

externalities: *external benefits* and *external costs.*

factor distribution of income: the division of total income among labor, land, and *capital.*

factor intensity: the difference in the ratio of *factors* used to produce a good in various industries. For example, oil refining is capital-intensive compared to clothing manufacture because oil refiners use a higher ratio of capital to labor than do clothing producers.

factor markets: markets in which *firms* buy *factors of production.*

factors of production: the *resources* needed to produce goods or services. Labor and capital are examples of factors.

fair insurance policy: an insurance policy for which the *premium* is equal to the expected value of the claims.

financial risk: uncertainty about monetary outcomes.

firm: an organization that produces goods or services for sale.

fixed cost: a cost that does not depend on the quantity of output produced; the cost of a *fixed input.*

fixed input: an *input* whose quantity is fixed and cannot be varied (for example, land).

forecast: a simple prediction of the future under current assumptions.

free entry and exit: describes an industry that potential producers can easily enter or current producers can leave.

free trade: *trade* that is unregulated by government *tariffs* or other artificial barriers; the levels of *exports* and *imports* occur naturally, as a result of supply and demand.

free-rider problem: when individuals have no *incentive* to pay for their own consumption of a good, they will take a "free ride" on anyone who does pay; a problem with goods that are *nonexcludable.*

gains from trade: the benefit that each party receives from a trade, which, because of *specialization,* is greater than if each attempted to be self-sufficient.

game theory: the study of behavior in situations of *interdependence.* Used to explain the behavior of an *oligopoly.*

general equilibrium: an economic balance in which the *quantity supplied* is equal to the *quantity demanded* in all markets in an economy.

Hecksher–Olin model: a *model* of international trade that shows how a country's *comparative advantage* can be determined by its supply of *factors of production.*

horizontal axis: the horizontal number line of a graph along which values of the *x*-variable are measured; also referred to as the *x-axis.*

horizontal intercept: the point at which a curve intersects the horizontal axis, showing the value of the *x*-variable when the value of the *y*-variable is zero.

household: a group of people that share a dwelling and their income (a household may also consist of one person).

human capital: the improvement in labor created by education and knowledge.

imperfect competition: a market structure in which no firm is a *monopolist,* but producers nonetheless have *market power* they can use to affect market prices.

implicit cost: a cost that does not require the outlay of money; it is measured by the value, in dollar terms, of forgone benefits.

implicit cost of capital: the *opportunity cost* of the capital used; that is, the income that could have been realized had the capital been used in the next best alternative way.

import quota: a legal limit on the quantity of a good that can be imported.

import-competing industries: industries that produce goods or services that are also imported.

imports: goods and services purchased from other countries.

in-kind transfers: specific goods and services (such as food stamps) provided to poor families by government.

incentive: a reward offered to people who change their behavior.

incidence (of a tax): a measure of who actually bears the burden of a tax.

income effect: the change in the quantity of a good consumed that results from the change in a consumer's purchasing power due to the change in the price of the good.

income elasticity of demand: the ratio of the percentage change in *quantity demanded* of a good or service to the percentage change in a consumer's income.

income tax: a tax on the income of an individual or family.

income-elastic demand: when the *income elasticity of demand* is greater than 1. Occurs when the demand for certain goods (such as luxury goods) rises faster than the increase in income.

income-inelastic demand: when the *income elasticity of demand* is positive but less than 1. Occurs when the demand for certain goods (such as food and clothing) rises but more slowly than the increase in income.

increasing marginal cost: *marginal cost* that becomes greater with each additional unit of the activity.

independent events: events for which the occurrence of one does not affect the likelihood of occurrence of any of the others.

independent variable: the determining variable in a causal relationship.

indifference curve: a contour line showing all *consumption bundles* that yield the same amount of total *utility* for an individual.

indifference curve map: a collection of *indifference curves* for a given individual that represents the individual's total *utility function*; each curve corresponds to a different total utility level.

individual choice: the decision by an individual of what to do, which necessarily involves a decision of what not to do.

individual consumer surplus: the net gain to an individual buyer from the purchase of a good; equal to the difference between the buyer's *willingness to pay* and the price paid.

individual demand curve: a graphical representation of the relationship between *quantity demanded* and price for an individual consumer.

individual labor supply curve: a graphical representation of the relationship between the wage rate and the number of hours supplied by an individual worker.

individual producer surplus: the net gain to an individual seller from selling a good; equal to the difference between the price received and the seller's *cost*.

industrial policy: a policy that supports industries believed to yield *positive externalities*.

industry supply curve: a graphical representation that shows the relationship between the price of a good and the total output of the industry for that good.

inefficient: describes a market or *economy* in which there are missed opportunities for making some individuals better off without making others worse off.

inefficient allocation to consumers: a form of inefficiency in which consumers who are willing to pay a high price for a good do not get it, and those willing to pay only a low price do; often a result of a *price ceiling*.

inefficient allocation of sales among sellers: a form of inefficiency in which sellers who are willing to sell a good at a lower price are not always those who actually manage to sell it; often the result of a *price floor*.

inefficiently high quality: a form of inefficiency in which sellers offer high-quality goods at a high price even though buyers would prefer a lower quality at a lower price; often the result of a *price floor*.

inefficiently low quality: a form of inefficiency in which sellers offer low-quality goods at a low price even though buyers would prefer a higher quality at a higher price; often a result of a *price ceiling*.

inelastic demand: when the *price elasticity of demand* is less than 1. A percentage increase in price will cause a correspondingly lesser percentage decrease in quantity demanded, and vice versa.

inferior good: a good for which a rise in income decreases the demand for the good.

information good: a good whose value derives from the information it contains.

input: a good used to produce another good.

interaction (of choices)**:** the mutual influence of the choices of various parties (the results are often quite different from what was intended).

interdependence: the relationship among firms when their decisions significantly affect one another's profits; characteristic of oligopolies.

interest rate: the price, calculated as a percentage of the amount borrowed, charged by the lender.

internalize the externality: take into account *external costs* and *external benefits*.

international trade agreements: treaties by which countries agree to lower *trade protections* against one another.

invisible hand: a phrase used by Adam Smith to describe the way in which an individual's pursuit of self-interest can lead, without the individual intending it, to good results for society as a whole.

kinked demand curve: a model used to explain the stability of oligopoly pricing; a *demand curve* that kinks (bends) because the *oligopolist* will lose sales if price is increased but gain only momentarily if price is lowered (because the lower price will be matched at once by other oligopolists).

law of demand: a higher price charged for a good, other things equal, leads to a smaller quantity of the good demanded.

leisure: the time available for purposes other than earning money to buy marketed goods.

license: the right, conferred by the government or an owner, to supply some good or perform some activity, often in exchange for a fee.

linear relationship: the relationship between two variables in which the *slope* is constant and therefore is depicted on a graph by a *curve* that is a straight line.

long run: the time period in which all *inputs* can be varied.

long-run average total cost curve: a graphical representation showing the relationship between output and *average total cost* when *fixed cost* has been chosen to minimize *total cost* for each level of output.

long-run industry supply curve: a graphical representation that shows how *quantity supplied* responds to price once producers have had time to enter or exit the industry.

long-run market equilibrium: an economic balance in which, given sufficient time for producers to enter or exit an industry, the *quantity supplied* equals the *quantity demanded*.

lump-sum tax: a tax that is the same for everyone, regardless of any actions individuals take.

macroeconomics: the branch of *economics* concerned with the overall ups and downs in the *economy*.

marginal analysis: the study of *marginal decisions*, those resulting from small changes in an activity.

marginal benefit: the additional benefit derived by performing one more unit of an activity.

marginal benefit curve: a graphical representation showing how the benefit from undertaking one more unit of an activity depends on the quantity of that activity that has already been done.

marginal cost: the additional cost incurred by performing one more unit of an activity.

marginal cost curve: a graphical representation showing how the cost of undertaking one more unit of an activity depends on the quantity of that activity that has already been done.

marginal decision: a decision made at the "margin" of an activity to do a little more or a little less.

marginal product: the additional quantity of output produced by using one more unit of a given *input*.

marginal productivity theory of income distribution: the proposition that every *factor of production* is paid its *equilibrium value of the marginal product*.

marginal rate of substitution (MRS): the ratio of the *marginal utility* of one good to the marginal utility of another.

marginal revenue: the change in *total revenue* generated by an additional unit of output.

marginal revenue curve: a graphical representation showing how *marginal revenue* varies as output varies.

marginal social benefit of a good or activity: the *marginal benefit* that accrues to consumers plus the marginal *external benefit*.

marginal social benefit of pollution: the additional gain to society from an additional unit of pollution.

marginal social cost of a good or activity: the *marginal cost* of production plus the marginal *external cost* to society of that production.

marginal social cost of pollution: the additional cost imposed on society by an additional unit of pollution.

marginal tax rate on income: the additional income tax paid if income increases by $1.

marginal utility per dollar: the additional *utility* gained from spending an additional dollar on a good or service.

marginal utility: the change in total *utility* generated by consuming one additional unit of a good or service.

marginal utility curve: a graphical representation showing how *marginal utility* depends on the quantity of the good or service consumed.

market-clearing price: the price at which the market is in *equilibrium*, that is, the quantity of a good demanded equals the quantity supplied; also referred to as the *equilibrium price*.

market economy: an *economy* in which decisions about production and consumption are made by individual producers and consumers.

market failure: occurs when a market fails to be efficient.

market power: the ability of a firm to raise prices.

market share: the fraction of the total industry output represented by a given producer's output.

markets for goods and services: markets in which households buy goods and services from *firms*.

maximum: the highest point on a *nonlinear curve*, where the *slope* changes from positive to negative.

means-tested: having an income qualification, as certain government social programs.

median voter theorem: the proposition that in a majority-rule election concerning the extent of a given policy action, the actual policies will reflect the preference of the median voter—the one in the center of the left–right spectrum.

microeconomics: the branch of *economics* that studies how individuals make decisions and how those decisions interact.

midpoint method: a technique for calculating the percent change in which changes in a variable are compared with the average, or midpoint, of the starting and final values.

minimum-cost output: the quantity of output at which the *average total cost* is lowest—the bottom of the *U-shaped average total cost curve*.

minimum: the lowest point on a *nonlinear curve*, where the *slope* changes from negative to positive.

minimum wage: a legal floor on the wage rate. The wage rate is the market price of labor.

model: a simplified representation of a real-life situation that uses data and assumptions to make predictions about that situation and understand it better.

monopolist: a firm that is the only producer of a good that has no close substitutes.

monopolistic competition: a market structure in which there are many competing producers in an industry, each producer sells a differentiated product, and there is *free entry and exit* into and from the industry in the *long run*.

monopoly: an industry controlled by a *monopolist*.

moral hazard: the situation that can exist when an individual knows more about his or her own actions than other people do. This leads to a distortion of incentives to take care or to expend effort, especially when someone else bears the costs of the lack of care or effort.

movement along the demand curve: a change in the *quantity demanded* of a good that results from a change in the price of that good.

movement along the supply curve: a change in the *quantity supplied* of a good that results from a change in the price of that good.

Nash equilibrium: in *game theory*, the *equilibrium* that results when all players choose their optimal action given the actions of other players, ignoring the effect of that action on the *payoffs* of other players; also known as *noncooperative equilibrium*.

natural monopoly: a *monopoly* that arises because *economies of scale* over the range of output of an industry provide a large cost advantage to having all output produced by a single firm.

negative externalities: *external costs*.

negative income tax: a government program that supplements the earnings of low-income families.

negative relationship: a relationship between two variables in which an increase in the value of one variable is associated with a decrease in the value of the other variable. It is described by a *curve* that slopes downward from left to right.

net present value: the *present value* of current and future benefits minus the present value of current and future costs.

network externality: the increase in the value of a good to an individual is greater when a large number of others own or use the same good.

noncooperative behavior: actions by firms that ignore the effects of those actions on the profits of other firms.

noncooperative equilibrium: in *game theory*, the *equilibrium* that results when all players choose their optimal action given the actions of other players, ignoring the effect of that action on the *payoffs* of other players; also known as *Nash equilibrium*.

nonexcludable: referring to a good, describes the case in which the supplier cannot prevent those who do not pay from consuming the good.

nonlinear curve: a curve whose *slope* is not constant.

nonlinear relationship: the relationship between two variables in which the *slope* is not constant and therefore is depicted on a graph by a *curve* that is not a straight line.

nonprice competition: competition in areas other than price to increase sales, such as new product features and advertising; especially engaged in by firms that have a tacit understanding not to compete on price.

nonrival in consumption: referring to a good, describes the case in which the same unit can be consumed by more than one person at the same time.

normal good: a good for which a rise in income increases the demand for that good—the "normal" case.

normative economics: the branch of economic analysis that makes prescriptive statements about how the *economy* should work.

oligopolist: a firm in an industry with only a small number of producers.

oligopoly: an industry with only a small number of producers.

omitted variable: an unobserved *variable* that, through its influence on other variables, creates the erroneous appearance of a direct *causal relationship* among those variables.

opportunity cost: the real cost of an item, including what must be given up to obtain it.

optimal consumption bundle: the *consumption bundle* that maximizes a consumer's total *utility*, given that consumer's *budget constraint*.

optimal consumption rule: when a consumer maximizes *utility*, the *marginal utility per dollar* spent is the same for all goods and services in the *consumption bundle*.

optimal output rule: profit is maximized by producing the quantity of output at which the *marginal cost* of the last unit produced is equal to its *marginal revenue*.

optimal quantity: the level of activity that generates the maximum possible total net gain.

optimal time allocation rule: an individual should allocate time in such a way that the *marginal utility* of an hour spent working is equal to the marginal utility of an additional hour of *leisure*.

ordinary goods: in a consumer's *utility function*, those for which additional units of one good are required to compensate for fewer units of another, and for which the consumer experiences a *diminishing marginal rate of substitution* in substituting one good for another.

origin: the point where the axes of a two-variable graph meet.

other things equal assumption: in the development of a model, the assumption that all relevant factors except the one under study remain unchanged.

overuse: the depletion of a *common resource* that occurs when individuals ignore the effect their use has on the amount of the resource remaining for others.

patent: a temporary monopoly given by the government to an inventor for the use or sale of an invention.

payoff: in *game theory*, the reward received by a player (for example, the profit earned by an *oligopolist*).

payoff matrix: in *game theory*, a diagram that shows how the *payoffs* to each of the participants in a two-player game depend on the actions of both; a tool in analyzing *interdependence*.

payroll tax: a tax on the amount an employer pays to an employee.

perfect complements: goods a consumer wants to consume in a given ratio, regardless of their *relative price*.

perfect price discrimination: charging each consumer the maximum that consumer is willing to pay.

perfect substitutes: goods for which the *indifference curves* are straight lines; the *marginal rate of substitution* is constant, no matter how much of each is consumed.

perfectly competitive industry: an industry in which all producers are price-takers.

perfectly competitive market: a market in which all participants are price-takers.

perfectly elastic supply: the case in which even small changes in price lead to large changes in the *quantity supplied*, so the *price elasticity of supply* is infinite; the *supply curve* is a horizontal line.

perfectly elastic demand: the case in which any price increase causes the *quantity demanded* to fall to zero; the *demand curve* is a horizontal line.

perfectly inelastic supply: the case in which the *price elasticity of supply* is zero, so changes in price have no effect on the *quantity supplied*; the *supply curve* is a vertical line.

perfectly inelastic demand: the case in which the *quantity demanded* does not respond to price; the *demand curve* is a vertical line.

physical capital: manufactured resources, such as buildings and machines; often referred to simply as "capital."

pie chart: a circular graph that shows how some total is divided among its components; the proportions are indicated by the sizes of the "wedges."

Pigouvian subsidy: a payment designed to encourage activities that yield *external benefits*.

Pigouvian taxes: taxes designed to reduce *external costs*.

pooling: a strong form of *diversification*; the individual investor takes a small share in many *independent events*, so the *payoff* has very little uncertainty.

positive economics: the branch of economic analysis that describes the way the *economy* actually works.

positive externalities: *external benefits.*

positive feedback: put simply, success breeds success, failure breeds failure; the effect is seen with goods that are subject to *network externalities.*

positive relationship: a relationship between two variables in which an increase in the value of one variable is associated with an increase in the value of the other variable. It is described by a *curve* that slopes upward from left to right.

positively correlated: a relationship between events such that each event is more likely to occur if the other also occurs.

poverty line: a minimum income defined by the government as adequate; families whose income falls below the poverty line are considered poor.

poverty rate: the percentage of the population living below the *poverty line.*

premium: a payment to an insurance company in return for the promise to pay in certain circumstances.

present value: the amount of money needed at the present time to produce, at the prevailing *interest rate,* a given amount of money at a specified future time.

price ceiling: a government-set maximum price that sellers are allowed to charge for a good; a form of *price control.*

price controls: legal restrictions on how high or low a market price may go.

price discrimination: charging different prices to different consumers for the same good.

price elasticity of demand: the ratio of the percent change in the *quantity demanded* to the percent change in price at a given point on the *demand curve.*

price elasticity of supply: the ratio of the percent change in the *quantity supplied* to the percent change in price at a given point on the *supply curve.*

price floor: a government-set minimum price that buyers are required to pay for a good; a form of price control.

price leadership: a pattern of behavior in which one firm sets its price and other firms in the industry follow.

price regulation: a limitation by the government on the price a *monopolist* is allowed to charge.

price war: a collapse of prices when *tacit collusion* breaks down.

price-taking consumer: a consumer whose actions have no effect on the market price of the good bought.

price-taking firm's optimal output rule: the profit of a price-taking firm is maximized by producing the quantity of output at which the *marginal cost* of the last unit produced is equal to the market price.

price-taking producer: a producer whose actions have no effect on the market price of the good sold.

principle of diminishing marginal utility: the proposition that each successive unit of a good or service consumed adds less to total *utility* than did the previous unit.

principle of marginal analysis: the proposition that the *optimal quantity* of an activity is that at which *marginal benefit* is equal to *marginal cost.*

prisoner's dilemma: a game for two players in which the pursuit of self-interest rather than cooperation, if followed by both players, makes both worse off.

private good: a good that is both *excludable* and *rival in consumption.*

private information: information affecting all parties to a transaction or decision that only some parties have.

producer surplus: a term often used to refer both to *individual producer surplus* and to *total producer surplus.*

product differentiation: the effort by firms to convince buyers that their products are different from those of other firms in the industry. If firms can so convince buyers, they can charge a higher price.

production function: the relationship between the quantity of *inputs* used and the quantity of output produced.

production possibility frontier: illustrates the trade-offs facing an economy that produces only two goods. It shows the maximum quantity of one good that can be produced for any given production of the other.

profits tax: a tax on the profits of a firm.

progressive tax: a tax that takes a larger share of the income of high-income taxpayers than of low-income taxpayers.

property rights: the rights of owners of *resources* or goods to dispose of them as they choose.

property tax: a tax on the value of property, such as a home.

proportional tax: a tax that is the same percentage of the *tax base* regardless of the taxpayer's income or wealth.

protection: an alternative term for *trade protection;* policies that limit *imports.*

public good: a good that is both *nonexcludable* and *nonrival in consumption.*

public ownership: control of an industry by a public agency of the government to provide a good and protect the interests of the consumer; a response to *natural monopoly.*

quantity control: an upper limit, set by the government, on the quantity of some good that can be bought or sold; also referred to as a *quota.*

quantity demanded: the actual amount of a good or service consumers are willing to buy at some specific price.

quantity supplied: the actual amount of a good or service sellers are willing to sell at some specific price.

quota: an upper limit, set by the government, on the quantity of some good that can be bought or sold; also referred to as a *quantity control.*

quota limit: the total amount of a good under a *quota* or *quantity control* that can be legally transacted.

quota rent: the difference between the *demand price* and the *supply price* at the *quota limit;* this difference, the earnings that accrue to the license-holder, is equal to the market price of the *license* when the license is traded.

QWERTY problem: an inferior industry standard that has prevailed, possibly because of historical accident. Refers to the first six letters of a typewriter keyboard.

random variable: a *variable* with an uncertain future value.

recession: a downturn in the *economy.*

redistribution of income: a movement of income, such as revenue from taxes on the well-off, that is used to support those less well off.

regressive tax: a tax that takes a smaller share of the income of high-income taxpayers than of low-income taxpayers.

relative price: the ratio of the price of one good to the price of another.

relative price rule: at the *optimal consumption bundle*, the *marginal rate of substitution* between two goods is equal to their *relative price*.

rental rate: the cost, implicit or explicit, of using a unit of land or capital for a given period of time.

reputation: a long-term standing in the public regard that serves to reassure others that *private information* is not being concealed; a valuable asset in the face of *adverse selection*.

resource: anything, such as land, labor, and capital, that can be used to produce something else; includes natural resources (from the physical environment) and human resources (labor, skill, intelligence).

reverse causality: the error committed when the true direction between *variables* is reversed, and the *independent variable* and the *dependent variable* are incorrectly identified.

Ricardian model of international trade: a model that analyzes international *trade* under the assumption that *production possibility frontiers* are straight lines.

risk: uncertainty about outcomes.

risk-averse: describes individuals who choose to reduce *risk* when that reduction leaves the expected value of income or wealth unchanged.

rival in consumption: referring to a good, describes the case in which one unit cannot be consumed by more than one person at the same time.

sales tax: a tax on the value of goods sold.

scarce: in short supply; a *resource* is scarce when the quantity available is insufficient to satisfy all productive uses.

scatter diagram: a graph that displays points that correspond to actual observations of the *x*- and *y*-variables;

a curve is usually fitted to the scatter of points to indicate the trend in the data.

screening: using observable information to make inferences about *private information*; a way to reduce *adverse selection*.

share: a partial ownership of a company.

shift of the demand curve: a change in the *quantity demanded* at any given price, represented graphically by the movement of the original *demand curve* to a new position.

shift of the supply curve: a change in the *quantity supplied* at any given price, represented graphically by the movement of the original *supply curve* to a new position.

short run: the time period in which at least one *input* is fixed.

short-run individual supply curve: a graphical representation showing how an individual producer's optimal output quantity depends on the market price, taking *fixed cost* as given.

short-run industry supply curve: a graphical representation that shows how the quantity supplied by an industry depends on the market price, given a fixed number of producers.

short-run market equilibrium: an economic balance that results when the *quantity supplied* equals the *quantity demanded,* taking the number of producers as given.

shortage: the insufficiency of a good when the quantity supplied is less than the quantity demanded; shortages occur when the price is below the *equilibrium price*.

shut-down price: the price at which a firm ceases production in the short run because the market price has fallen below the minimum *average variable cost*.

signaling: taking some action to establish credibility despite possessing *private information*; a way to reduce *adverse selection*.

single-price monopolist: a *monopolist* that charges all consumers the same price.

slope: the ratio of the "rise" (the change between two points on the *y*-axis) to the "run" (the difference between the same two points on the

x-axis); a measure of the steepness of a curve.

social insurance: government programs intended to protect individuals against financial risk.

socially optimal quantity of pollution: the quantity of pollution that society would choose if all the costs and benefits of pollution were fully accounted for.

specialization: occurs when each person concentrates on the task that he or she is good at performing; generally leads to improved quality or to increase in output.

standardized product: output of different producers regarded by consumers as all the same good; also referred to as a *commodity*.

standard: a set of rules for operation that allows competing goods to operate as a single network.

state of the world: a possible future event.

strategic behavior: actions taken by a firm that attempt to influence the behavior of other firms.

substitutes: pairs of goods for which a fall in the price of one results in less demand for the other.

substitution effect: the change in the quantity consumed when a consumer substitutes a good that has become relatively cheaper for one that has become relatively more expensive.

sunk cost: a cost that has already been incurred and is not recoverable.

supply and demand model: a model that describes how a *competitive market* works.

supply curve: a graphical representation of the *supply schedule*, showing how much of a good or service would be supplied at a given price.

supply price: the price of a given quantity at which producers will supply that quantity.

supply schedule: a list or table showing the relationship between price and the quantity of a good or service that would be supplied to consumers.

surplus: the excess of a good that occurs when the quantity supplied is greater than the quantity demanded; surpluses occur when the price is above the *equilibrium price*.

tacit collusion: cooperation among producers, without a formal agreement, to limit production and raise prices so as to raise one anothers' profits.

tangency condition: on a graph of a consumer's *budget line* and available *indifference curves* of available *consumption bundles,* the point at which an indifference curve and the budget line touch. When the indifference curves have the typical convex shape, this point determines the *optimal consumption bundle.*

tangent line: a straight line that touches a *nonlinear curve* at a given point; the *slope* of the tangent line equals the slope of the nonlinear curve at that point.

tariff: a tax levied on *imports.*

tax base: the measure or value, such as income or property value, that determines how much tax an individual pays.

tax efficiency: the degree to which a tax system minimizes the cost to the *economy* of tax collection.

tax equity: the degree to which the "right" people bear the burden of taxes; also referred to as *tax fairness.*

tax fairness: the degree to which the "right" people bear the burden of taxes; also referred to as *tax equity.*

tax structure: specifies how a tax depends on the *tax base;* usually expressed in percentage terms.

technology spillover: an *external benefit* that is conferred when knowledge spreads among individuals and firms.

threshold network size: in a market subject to *network externalities,* the smallest number of current members of the network that leads a given individual to join.

time allocation: the decision about how many hours to expend on different activities, which leads to a decision about how much labor to supply.

time allocation budget line: an individual's possible trade-offs between consumption of *leisure* and the income that allows consumption of marketed goods.

time-series graph: a two-variable graph in which the values on the *hori-zontal axis* are dates and those on the *vertical axis* are values of a variable that occurred on those dates.

tipping: a sudden rapid increase in the network size that occurs when *positive feedback* due to *network externalities* causes consumers to swing to one of two competing goods or technologies.

tit for tat: in *game theory,* a strategy in which players begin cooperatively, then each repeats the other player's action in the previous round.

total consumer surplus: the sum of the *individual consumer surpluses* of all the buyers of a good.

total cost: the sum of the *fixed cost* and the *variable cost* of producing a given quantity of output.

total cost curve: a graphical representation of the *total cost,* showing how total cost depends on the quantity of output.

total producer surplus: the sum of the *individual producer surpluses* of all the sellers of a good.

total product curve: a graphical representation of the *production function,* showing how the quantity of output depends on the quantity of the *variable input* for a given amount of *fixed input.*

total revenue: the total value of sales of a good (the price of the good multiplied by the quantity sold).

total surplus: the total net gain to consumers and producers from trading in a market; the sum of the *consumer surplus* and the *producer surplus.*

tradable emissions permits: *licenses* to emit limited quantities of pollutants that can be bought and sold by polluters.

trade: the exchange of goods or services for other goods or services.

trade protection: policies that limit *imports.*

trade-off: a comparison of costs and benefits; the amount of a good that must be sacrificed to obtain another good.

trade-off between equity and efficiency: the dynamic whereby a well-designed tax system can be made more efficient only by making it less fair, and vice versa.

transaction costs: the costs of making a deal.

transfer payment: money received by an individual from the government for which no good or service is returned to the government.

truncated: cut; in a truncated axis, some of the range of values are omitted, usually to save space.

U-shaped average total cost curve: a distinctive graphical representation of the relationship between output and *average total cost;* the average total cost curve at first falls when output is low and then rises as output increases.

unions: organizations of workers that engage in collective bargaining to raise wages and improve working conditions for their members.

unit-elastic demand: the case in which the *price elasticity of demand* is 1. A specific percentage increase in price leads to an equal percentage decrease in quantity demanded, and vice versa.

util: a unit of *utility.*

utility (of a consumer): a measure of the satisfaction derived from consumption of goods and services.

utility function (of an individual): the relationship between an individual's *consumption bundle* and the total amount of *utility* it generates.

utility possibility frontier: on a graph plotting the total *utility* of two individuals or groups, the curve that shows how well off one individual or group could be for each given total utility level of the other.

value of the marginal product: the value of the additional output generated by employing one more unit of a given factor, such as labor.

value of the marginal product curve: a graphical representation showing how the *value of the marginal product* of a factor depends on the quantity of the factor employed.

variable: a quantity that can take on more than one value.

variable cost: a cost that depends on the quantity of output produced; the cost of a *variable input.*

variable input: an *input* whose quantity can be varied (for example, labor).

vertical axis: the vertical number line of a graph along which values of the *y*-variable are measured; also referred to as the *y-axis*.

vertical intercept: the point at which a curve intersects the vertical axis, showing the value of the *y*-variable when the value of the *x*-variable is zero.

wasted resources: a form of inefficiency; consumers waste resources when they must spend money and expend effort to deal with shortages caused by a *price ceiling*.

wealth tax: a tax on the wealth of an individual.

wedge: the difference between the *demand price* of the quantity transacted and the *supply price* of the quantity transacted for a good when the supply of the good is legally restricted. Often created by a quota or a tax.

welfare: government monetary aid to poor families.

willingness to pay: the maximum price a consumer is prepared to pay for a good.

world price: the price at which a good can be bought or sold abroad.

World Trade Organization: an international organization of member countries that oversees *international trade agreements* and rules on *trade* disputes.

x-axis: the horizontal number line of a graph along which values of the *x*-variable are measured; also referred to as the *horizontal axis*.

y-axis: the vertical number line of a graph along which values of the *y*-variable are measured; also referred to as the *vertical axis*.

zero-profit equilibrium: an economic balance in which each firm makes zero profit at its profit-maximizing output level.

Index

Key terms and the pages on which they are defined appear in **boldface** in this index.

Visit the Krugman/Wells website

econ X change

www.worthpublishers.com/krugmanwells

The companion Web site for Krugman/Wells *Microeconomics* offers valuable tools, including online simulations designed to help students master economic concepts. This completely customized Web site provides your students with a virtual study guide, twenty-four hours a day, seven days a week. The site provides your students with a pedagogically sound means of testing their understanding of text material. One of the features of ECon X-Change is the **Graphing Center**, developed by Cadre LLC in conjunction with Debbie Mullin (University of Colorado–Colorado Springs). Selected graphs from the textbook have been animated in a Flash format, allowing students to manipulate curves and plot data points when appropriate. Every interactive graph has accompanying questions that quiz students on key concepts from the textbook and provide feedback on student progress. Student responses and interactions are tracked and stored in an online database that can be accessed by the instructor. The following list indicates the graphs in *Microeconomics* that are available at the Graphing Center.

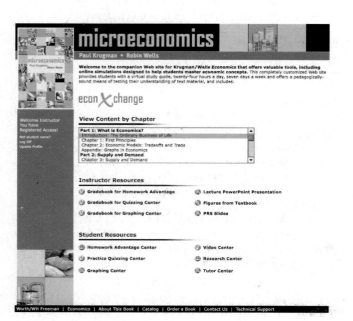

LIST OF ANIMATED FIGURES